Twentieth-Century
Literary Criticism

Guide to Gale Literary Criticism Series

When you need to review criticism of literary works, these are the Gale series to use:

If the author's death date is:	You should turn to:
After Dec. 31, 1959 (or author is still living)	**CONTEMPORARY LITERARY CRITICISM** for example: Jorge Luis Borges, Anthony Burgess, William Faulkner, Mary Gordon, Ernest Hemingway, Iris Murdoch
1900 through 1959	**TWENTIETH-CENTURY LITERARY CRITICISM** for example: Willa Cather, F. Scott Fitzgerald, Henry James, Mark Twain, Virginia Woolf
1800 through 1899	**NINETEENTH-CENTURY LITERATURE CRITICISM** for example: Fedor Dostoevski, Nathaniel Hawthorne, George Sand, William Wordsworth
1400 through 1799	**LITERATURE CRITICISM FROM 1400 TO 1800** *(excluding Shakespeare)* for example: Anne Bradstreet, Daniel Defoe, Alexander Pope, François Rabelais, Jonathan Swift, Phillis Wheatley **SHAKESPEAREAN CRITICISM** Shakespeare's plays and poetry
Antiquity through 1399	**CLASSICAL AND MEDIEVAL LITERATURE CRITICISM** for example: Dante, Homer, Plato, Sophocles, Vergil, the Beowulf poet *(Volume 1 forthcoming)*

Gale also publishes related criticism series:

CHILDREN'S LITERATURE REVIEW

This ongoing series covers authors of all eras. Presents criticism on authors and author/illustrators who write for the preschool to junior-high audience.

CONTEMPORARY ISSUES CRITICISM

This two volume set presents criticism on contemporary authors writing on current issues. Topics covered include the social sciences, philosophy, economics, natural science, law, and related areas.

ISSN 0276-8178

R

Volume 24

Twentieth-Century Literary Criticism

**Excerpts from Criticism of the
Works of Novelists, Poets, Playwrights,
Short Story Writers, and Other Creative Writers
Who Died between 1900 and 1960,
from the First Published Critical Appraisals
to Current Evaluations**

**Dennis Poupard
Editor**

**Marie Lazzari
Thomas Ligotti
Associate Editors**

**Gale Research Company
Book Tower
Detroit, Michigan 48226**

STAFF

Dennis Poupard, *Editor*

Marie Lazzari, Thomas Ligotti, *Associate Editors*

Paula Kepos, Serita Lanette Lockard, Joann Prosyniuk,
Laurie A. Sherman, *Senior Assistant Editors*

Faye Kuzma, Sandra Liddell, Keith E. Schooley, *Assistant Editors*

Denise Michlewicz Broderick, Melissa Reiff Hug, *Contributing Assistant Editors*

Jeanne A. Gough, *Permissions & Production Manager*
Lizbeth A. Purdy, *Production Supervisor*
Kathleen M. Cook, *Assistant Production Coordinator*
Suzanne Powers, Jani Prescott, Lee Ann Welsh, *Editorial Assistants*
Linda M. Pugliese, *Manuscript Coordinator*
Donna Craft, *Assistant Manuscript Coordinator*
Jennifer E. Gale, Maureen A. Puhl, Rosetta Irene Simms, *Manuscript Assistants*

Victoria B. Cariappa, *Research Supervisor*
Maureen R. Richards, *Research Coordinator*
Kent Graham, Filomena Sgambati,
Laura B. Standley, Mary D. Wise, *Research Assistants*

Janice M. Mach, *Text Permissions Supervisor*
Susan D. Battista, Kathy Grell, *Assistant Permissions Coordinators*
Mabel E. Gurney, Josephine M. Keene, Mary M. Matuz, *Senior Permissions Assistants*
H. Diane Cooper, *Permissions Assistant*
Eileen Baehr, Kimberly Smilay, Anita Lorraine Ransom, *Permissions Clerks*

Patricia A. Seefelt, *Picture Permissions Supervisor*
Margaret A. Chamberlain, *Assistant Permissions Coordinator*
Colleen M. Crane, *Permissions Assistant*
Lillian Tyus, *Permissions Clerk*

Frederick G. Ruffner, *Chairman*
J. Kevin Reger, *President*
Dedria Bryfonski, *Publisher*
Ellen T. Crowley, *Associate Editorial Director*
Laurie Lanzen Harris, *Director, Literary Criticism Division*
Dennis Poupard, *Senior Editor, Literary Criticism Series*

Library of Congress Catalog Card Number 76-46132
ISBN 0-8103-2406-7
ISSN 0276-8178

Computerized photocomposition by
Typographics, Incorporated
Kansas City, Missouri

Printed in the United States

Contents

Preface

It is impossible to overvalue the importance of literature in the intellectual, emotional, and spiritual evolution of humanity. Literature is that which both lifts us out of everyday life and helps us to better understand it. Through the fictive lives of such characters as Anna Karenina, Jay Gatsby, or Leopold Bloom, our perceptions of the human condition are enlarged, and we are enriched.

Literary criticism can also give us insight into the human condition, as well as into the specific moral and intellectual atmosphere of an era, for the criteria by which a work of art is judged reflects contemporary philosophical and social attitudes. Literary criticism takes many forms: the traditional essay, the book or play review, even the parodic poem. Criticism can also be of several types: normative, descriptive, interpretive, textual, appreciative, generic. Collectively, the range of critical response helps us to understand a work of art, an author, an era.

Scope of the Series

Twentieth-Century Literary Criticism (TCLC) is designed to serve as an introduction for the student of twentieth-century literature to the authors of the period 1900 to 1960 and to the most significant commentators on these authors. The great poets, novelists, short story writers, playwrights, and philosophers of this period are by far the most popular writers for study in high school and college literature courses. Since a vast amount of relevant critical material confronts the student, *TCLC* presents significant passages from the most important published criticism to aid students in the location and selection of commentaries on authors who died between 1900 and 1960.

The need for *TCLC* was suggested by the usefulness of the Gale series *Contemporary Literary Criticism (CLC),* which excerpts criticism on current writing. Because of the difference in time span under consideration *(CLC* considers authors who were still living after 1959), there is no duplication of material between *CLC* and *TCLC.* For further information about *CLC* and Gale's other criticism series, users should consult the Guide to Gale Literary Criticism Series preceding the title page in this volume.

Each volume of *TCLC* is carefully compiled to include authors who represent a variety of genres and nationalities and who are currently regarded as the most important writers of this era. In addition to major authors, *TCLC* also presents criticism on lesser-known writers whose significant contributions to literary history are important to the study of twentieth-century literature.

Each author entry in *TCLC* is intended to provide an overview of major criticism on an author. Therefore, the editors include fifteen to twenty authors in each 600-page volume (compared with approximately fifty authors in a *CLC* volume of similar size) so that more attention may be given to an author. Each author entry represents a historical survey of the critical response to that author's work: some early criticism is presented to indicate initial reactions, later criticism is selected to represent any rise or decline in the author's reputation, and current retrospective analyses provide students with a modern view. The length of an author entry is intended to reflect the amount of critical attention the author has received from critics writing in English, and from foreign criticism in translation. Critical articles and books that have not been translated into English are excluded. Every attempt has been made to identify and include excerpts from the seminal essays on each author's work.

An author may appear more than once in the series because of the great quantity of critical material available, or because of a resurgence of criticism generated by events such as an author's centennial or anniversary celebration, the republication or posthumous publication of an author's works, or the publication of a newly translated work. Generally, a few author entries in each volume of *TCLC* feature criticism on single works by major authors who have appeared previously in the series. Only those individual works that have been the subjects of vast amounts of criticism and are widely studied in literature classes are selected for this in-depth treatment. Sherwood Anderson's *Winesburg, Ohio* and Henry James's *The Turn of the Screw* are examples of such entries in *TCLC,* Volume 24.

Organization of the Book

An author entry consists of the following elements: author heading, biographical and critical introduction, principal works, excerpts of criticism (each followed by a bibliographical citation), and an additional bibliography for further reading.

- The *author heading* consists of the author's full name, followed by birth and death dates. The unbracketed portion of the name denotes the form under which the author most commonly wrote. If an author wrote consistently under a pseudonym, the pseudonym will be listed in the author heading and the real name given in parentheses on the first line of the biographical and critical introduction. Also located at the beginning of the introduction to the author entry are any name variations under which an author wrote, including transliterated forms for authors whose languages use nonroman alphabets. Uncertainty as to a birth or death date is indicated by a question mark.

- The *biographical and critical introduction* contains background information designed to introduce the reader to an author and to the critical debate surrounding his or her work. Parenthetical material following many of the introductions provides references to biographical and critical reference series published by Gale, including *Children's Literature Review, Contemporary Authors, Dictionary of Literary Biography, Something about the Author,* and past volumes of *TCLC.*

- Most *TCLC* entries include *portraits* of the author. Many entries also contain illustrations of materials pertinent to an author's career, including manuscript pages, title pages, dust jackets, letters, or representations of important people, places, and events in an author's life.

- The *list of principal works* is chronological by date of first book publication and identifies the genre of each work. In the case of foreign authors where there are both foreign language publications and English translations, the title and date of the first English-language edition are given in brackets. Unless otherwise indicated, dramas are dated by first performance, not first publication.

- *Criticism* is arranged chronologically in each author entry to provide a useful perspective on changes in critical evaluation over the years. All titles by the author featured in the critical entry are printed in boldface type to enable the user to ascertain without difficulty the works being discussed. Also for purposes of easier identification, the critic's name and the publication date of the essay are given at the beginning of each piece of criticism. Unsigned criticism is preceded by the title of the journal in which it appeared. When an anonymous essay is later attributed to a critic, the critic's name appears in brackets at the beginning of the excerpt and in the bibliographical citation. Many critical entries in *TCLC* also contain translated material to aid users. Unless otherwise noted, translations within brackets are by the editors; translations within parentheses are by the author of the excerpt.

- Critical essays are prefaced by *explanatory notes* as an additional aid to students using *TCLC.* The explanatory notes provide several types of useful information, including: the reputation of a critic; the importance of a work of criticism; the specific type of criticism (biographical, psychoanalytic, structuralist, etc.); a synopsis of the criticism; and the growth of critical controversy or changes in critical trends regarding an author's work. In many cases, these notes cross-reference the work of critics who agree or disagree with each other. Dates in parentheses within the explanatory notes refer to a book publication date when they follow a book title and to an essay date when they follow a critic's name.

- A complete *bibliographical citation* designed to facilitate location of the original essay or book by the interested reader follows each piece of criticism.

- The *additional bibliography* appearing at the end of each author entry suggests further reading on the author. In some cases it includes essays for which the editors could not obtain reprint rights.

An appendix lists the sources from which material in each volume has been reprinted. It does not, however, list every book or periodical consulted in the preparation of the volume.

Cumulative Indexes

Each volume of *TCLC* includes a cumulative index to authors listing all the authors who have appeared in *Contemporary Literary Criticism, Twentieth-Century Literary Criticism, Nineteenth-Century Literature Criticism,* and *Literature Criticism from 1400 to 1800,* along with cross-references to the Gale series *Children's Literature Review, Authors in the News, Contemporary Authors, Contemporary Authors Autobiography Series, Dictionary of Literary Biography, Concise Dictionary of American Literary Biography, Something about the Author, Something about the Author Autobiography Series,* and *Yesterday's Authors of Books for Children.* Readers will welcome this cumulated author index as a useful tool for locating an author within the various series. The index, which lists birth and death dates when available, will be particularly valuable for those authors who are identified with a certain period but whose death date causes them to be placed in another, or for those authors whose careers span two periods. For example, F. Scott Fitzgerald is found in *TCLC,* yet a writer often associated with him, Ernest Hemingway, is found in *CLC.*

Each volume of *TCLC* also includes a cumulative nationality index. Author names are arranged alphabetically under their respective nationalities and followed by the volume numbers in which they appear.

New Index

An important feature appearing for the first time in *TCLC,* Volume 24, is a cumulative index to titles, an alphabetical listing of the literary works discussed in the series since its inception. Each title listing includes the corresponding volume and page numbers where criticism may be located. Foreign language titles that have been translated are followed by the titles of the translations, for example: *Voina i mir (War and Peace).* Page numbers following these translated titles refer to all pages on which any form of the title, either foreign language or translated, appear. Titles of novels, dramas, nonfiction books, and poetry, short story, or essay collections are printed in italics, while all individual poems, short stories, and essays are printed in roman type within quotation marks. In cases where the same title is used by different authors, the author's surname is given in parentheses after the title, e.g., *Collected Poems* (Housman) and *Collected Poems* (Yeats).

Acknowledgments

No work of this scope can be accomplished without the cooperation of many people. The editors especially wish to thank the copyright holders of the excerpted criticism included in this volume, the permissions managers of many book and magazine publishing companies for assisting us in securing reprint rights, and Anthony Bogucki for assistance with copyright research. We are also grateful to the staffs of the Detroit Public Library, the Library of Congress, University of Detroit Library, University of Michigan Library, and Wayne State University Library for making their resources available to us. The editors also wish to acknowledge: Viking-Penguin, Inc. and The Newberry Library for the endpaper illustration of Winesburg, Ohio; Eva Reichmann for the endpaper caricature of Yeats and George Moore; and *Town & Country* mazagine for the endpaper caricature of Richard Harding Davis.

Suggestions Are Welcome

In response to various suggestions, several features have been added to *TCLC* since the series began, including: explanatory notes to excerpted criticism that provide important information regarding critics and their work; a cumulative author index listing authors in all Gale literary criticism series; entries devoted to criticism on a single work by a major author; and more extensive illustrations.

Readers who wish to suggest authors to appear in future volumes, or who have other suggestions, are cordially invited to write the editors.

Authors to Be Featured in *TCLC*, Volumes 25 and 27

Twentieth-Century Literary Criticism, Volume 26, will be an Archives volume devoted to criticism of various topics in twentieth-century literature, including the Surrealist and Harlem Renaissance movements, the literature of the Spanish Civil War and Russian Thaw, and the centennial of the first appearance of Sherlock Holmes.

Henri Bergson (French philosopher)—One of the most influential philosophers of the twentieth century, Bergson is renowned for his opposition to the dominant materialist thought of his time and for his creation of theories that emphasize the supremacy and independence of suprarational consciousness.

Chaim Bialik (Hebrew poet)—The most important Hebrew poet of the twentieth century, Bialik is often called "the national poet of Israel." His works—which reflect the personal sufferings of his childhood as well as the sufferings of the Diaspora—are considered instrumental in the twentieth-century renaissance of Hebrew literature and the modernization of the Hebrew language.

R. D. Blackmore (English novelist)—A minor historical novelist of the Victorian era, Blackmore is remembered as the author of *Lorna Doone.* This classic of historical fiction is often praised for its vivid evocation of the past and its entertaining melodrama.

Edgar Rice Burroughs (American novelist)—Burroughs was a science fiction writer who is best known as the creator of Tarzan. His *Tarzan of the Apes* and its numerous sequels have sold over thirty-five million copies in fifty-six languages, making Burroughs one of the most popular authors in the world.

Joseph Conrad (Polish-born English novelist)—Considered an innovator of novel structure as well as one of the finest stylists of modern English literature, Conrad is the author of complex novels that examine the ambiguity of good and evil. *TCLC* will devote an entry to critical discussion of his *Nostromo,* a novel exploring Conrad's conviction that failure is a fact of human existence and that every ideal contains the possibilities for its own corruption.

Francois Coppée (French poet and dramatist)—A popular French poet during the latter part of the nineteenth century, Coppee earned a reputation as the "poete des humbles" for his verses devoted to the lives of humble people whose colorless exteriors often concealed great happiness or misery.

Charles Doughty (English travel writer and poet)—Doughty is best remembered as the author of *Travels in Arabia Deserta,* one of the classics in the literature of travel and a celebrated model of epic prose.

F. Scott Fitzgerald (American novelist)—along with *The Great Gatsby, Tender is the Night* is one of Fitzgerald's most celebrated novels. In an entry devoted solely to this work, which was Fitzgerald's last completed novel, *TCLC* will present major critical essays examining its meaning and importance.

Joseph Furphy (Australian novelist)—Furphy's most famous work, *Such Is Life,* is a complex comic novel combining sketches, tales, literary parody, and philosophical speculation in the guise of a realistic chronicle by its fictional narrator, Tom Collins.

Edmund Gosse (English novelist and critic)—A prolific man of letters in late nineteenth-century England, Gosse is of primary importance for his autobiographical novel *Father and Son,* which is considered a seminal work for gaining insight into the major issues of the Victorian age, especially the conflict between science and religion inspired by Darwin's *Origin of the Species.* Gosse is also important for his introduction of Henrik Ibsen's "new drama" to English audiences and for his numerous critical studies of English and foreign authors.

Bret Harte (American short story writer and journalist)—Harte rose to fame in the latter half of the nineteenth century as the first local colorist of the American West. His most successful stories, including "The Luck of Roaring Camp" and "The Outcasts of Poker Flat," constitute a blend of humor and sentiment, and are often praised for their uncluttered style and fidelity to realistic detail.

Muhammad Iqbal (Indian poet and philosopher)—Considered one of the leading Muslim intellectual figures of the twentieth century, Iqbal was a political activist and the author of poetry calling for social and religious reform.

Franz Kafka (Austrian novelist and short story writer)—Kafka's novel *The Trial* is often considered the definitive expression of his alienated vision as well as one of the seminal works of modern literature. *TCLC* will devote an entire entry to critical discussion of this novel, which has been described by Alvin J. Seltzer as "one of the most unrelenting works of chaos created in the first half of this century."

Henry Lawson (Australian short story writer and poet)—Lawson's stories in such collections as *While the Billy Boils* and *Joe Wilson and His Mates* chronicle the hard lives of working people in the backcountry of Australia and are considered characteristic of Australian writing of the late nineteenth and early twentieth centuries.

Gaston Leroux (French novelist)—Although a prolific author of detective novels, Leroux is best known for his novel *The Phantom of the Opera.* The tragic title character of Leroux's most famous work has become an enduring figure in popular culture, and his bizarre story has been perpetuated through numerous film and dramatic adaptations.

Frederic Manning (Australian-born English novelist)—Manning is chiefly remembered as the author of *Her Privates We*, a classic of modern war literature that is considered one of the most important fictional accounts of daily life in the British infantry during World War I.

Edgar Lee Masters (American poet, novelist, and biographer)—Masters was a prolific writer who is remembered primarily for his *Spoon River Anthology*, a collection of epitaphs spoken by the dead in the Spoon River Cemetery. Controversial upon its publication for its free verse form, jaundiced view of small town life, and explicitly sexual considerations, the *Anthology* is considered important as one of the first works to view traditional small town America from an unsentimental perspective.

Dmitri Merezhkovsky (Russian novelist, philosopher, poet, and critic)—Although his poetry and criticism are credited with initiating the Symbolist movement in Russian literature, Merezhkovsky is best known as a religious philosopher who sought in numerous essays and historical novels to reconcile the values of pagan religions with the teachings of Christ.

S. E. K. Mqhayi (South African poet and novelist)—Mqhayi is recognized as a leading author in Xhosa-language literature and is especially celebrated for his *izibongo*, traditional African lyric poems that gained him the title *imbongi yesizwe*, equivalent to poet laureate of his poeple.

John Muir (American naturalist, essayist, and autobiographer)—In such works as *A Thousand Mile Walk to the Gulf* and *The Mountains of California*, Muir celebrated the North American wilderness. He was also a prominent conservationist who was instrumental in establishing the system of national parks in the United States.

Eugene O'Neill (American dramatist)—Generally considered America's foremost dramatist, O'Neill is the author of works examining the implacability of an indifferent universe, the materialistic greed of humanity, and the problems of individual identity. *TCLC* will devote an entry to O'Neill's *Long Day's Journey into Night*, a portrait of a tormented, self-destructive family that has been called one of the most powerful dramas in American theater.

Wilfred Owen (English poet)—Inspired by his experiences in World War I, Owen's poetry exposed the grim realities of war and its effect on the human spirit.

Benito Peréz Galdós (Spanish novelist and dramatist)—Considered the greatest Spanish novelist since Cervantes, Perez Galdos is known for two vast cycles of novels: the *Episodios nacionales*, a forty-six volume portrayal of nineteenth-century Spanish history; and the *Novelas espanolas contemporaneas*, explorations of social and ethical problems in contemporary Spain which have been favorably compared to the works of Charles Dickens and Honore de Balzac.

Mark Rutherford (English novelist)—Rutherford's semi-fictionalized accounts of his own life, published as *The Autobiography of Mark Rutherford, Dissenting Minister* and *Mark Rutherford's Deliverance*, are highly valued for the insights they provide into the crisis of religious faith experienced by many intellectuals of the late-Victorian era.

Pauline Smith (South African fiction writer)—In her fiction Smith provided one of the earliest and most artistic portrayals of Afrikaners, specifically those early Dutch settlers who lived in the region known as the Little Karoo.

Oswald Spengler (German philosopher)—Spengler rose to international celebrity in the 1920s on the basis of *The Decline of the West*, a controversial examination of the cyclical nature of history. Although frequently deprecated by professional historians, *The Decline of the West* became one of the most influential philosophical works of the twentieth century.

Gertrude Stein (American novelist and critic)—Stein is recognized as one of the principal figures of literary Modernism, both as a brilliant experimentalist in such works as *The Autobiography of Alice B. Toklas* and *Tender Buttons* and as an influence upon a generation of authors that included Ernest Hemingway and F. Scott Fitzgerald.

Leo Tolstoy (Russian novelist)—Along with *Anna Karenina*, *War and Peace* is considered Tolstoy's most important work and one of the greatest works in world literature. *TCLC* will devote an entire entry to the critical history of this epic novel.

Edith Wharton (American novelist and short story writer)—Wharton is best known as a novelist of manners whose fiction exposed the cruel excesses of aristocratic society at the turn of the century. Her subject matter, tone, and style have often been compared with those of her friend and mentor Henry James.

Thomas Wolfe (American novelist)—Wolfe is considered one of the foremost American novelists of the twentieth century. His most important works present intense and lyrical portraits of life in both rural and urban America while portraying the struggle of the lonely, sensitive, and artistic individual to find spiritual fulfillment.

Additional Authors to Appear
in Future Volumes

Abbey, Henry 1842-1911
Abercrombie, Lascelles 1881-1938
Adamic, Louis 1898-1951
Ade, George 1866-1944
Agustini, Delmira 1886-1914
Akers, Elizabeth Chase 1832-1911
Akiko, Yosano 1878-1942
Aldrich, Thomas Bailey 1836-1907
Aliyu, Dan Sidi 1902-1920
Allen, Hervey 1889-1949
Archer, William 1856-1924
Arlen, Michael 1895-1956
Arlt, Roberto 1900-1942
Austin, Alfred 1835-1913
Austin, Mary Hunter 1868-1934
Bahr, Hermann 1863-1934
Bailey, Philip James 1816-1902
Barbour, Ralph Henry 1870-1944
Benét, William Rose 1886-1950
Benjamin, Walter 1892-1940
Bennett, James Gordon, Jr. 1841-1918
Benson, E(dward) F(rederic) 1867-1940
Berdyaev, Nikolai Aleksandrovich
   1874-1948
Beresford, J(ohn) D(avys) 1873-1947
Binyon, Laurence 1869-1943
Bishop, John Peale 1892-1944
Blake, Lillie Devereux 1835-1913
Blest Gana, Alberto 1830-1920
Blum, Leon 1872-1950
Bodenheim, Maxwell 1892-1954
Bowen, Marjorie 1886-1952
Byrne, Donn 1889-1928
Caine, Hall 1853-1931
Cannan, Gilbert 1884-1955
Carducci, Giosue 1835-1907
Carswell, Catherine 1879-1946
Churchill, Winston 1871-1947
Corelli, Marie 1855-1924
Cotter, Joseph Seamon 1861-1949
Croce, Benedetto 1866-1952
Crofts, Freeman Wills 1879-1957
Cruze, James (Jens Cruz Bosen) 1884-
   1942
Curros, Enriquez Manuel 1851-1908
Dall, Caroline Wells (Healy) 1822-1912
Daudet, Leon 1867-1942
Day, Clarence 1874-1935
Delafield, E.M. (Edme Elizabeth Monica
   de la Pasture) 1890-1943
Deneson, Jacob 1836-1919
DeVoto, Bernard 1897-1955
Doughty, C(harles) M(ontague)
   1843-1926
Douglas, (George) Norman 1868-1952
Douglas, Lloyd C(assel) 1877-1951

Dovzhenko, Alexander 1894-1956
Drinkwater, John 1882-1937
Drummond, W.H. 1854-1907
Durkheim, Emile 1858-1917
Duun, Olav 1876-1939
Eaton, Walter Prichard 1878-1957
Eggleston, Edward 1837-1902
Erskine, John 1879-1951
Fadeyev, Alexander 1901-1956
Ferland, Albert 1872-1943
Field, Rachel 1894-1924
Flecker, James Elroy 1884-1915
Fletcher, John Gould 1886-1950
Fogazzaro, Antonio 1842-1911
Francos, Karl Emil 1848-1904
Frank, Bruno 1886-1945
Frazer, (Sir) George 1854-1941
Freud, Sigmund 1853-1939
Froding, Gustaf 1860-1911
Fuller, Henry Blake 1857-1929
Futabatei, Shimei 1864-1909
Gladkov, Fyodor Vasilyevich 1883-1958
Glaspell, Susan 1876-1948
Glyn, Elinor 1864-1943
Golding, Louis 1895-1958
Gould, Gerald 1885-1936
Guest, Edgar 1881-1959
Gumilyov, Nikolay 1886-1921
Gyulai, Pal 1826-1909
Hale, Edward Everett 1822-1909
Hawthorne, Julian 1846-1934
Hayashi, Famiko 1904-1951
Hernandez, Miguel 1910-1942
Hewlett, Maurice 1861-1923
Heyward, DuBose 1885-1940
Hope, Anthony 1863-1933
Hudson, W(illiam) H(enry) 1841-1922
Huidobro, Vincente 1893-1948
Ilyas, Abu Shabaka 1903-1947
Imbs, Bravig 1904-1946
Iqbal, Mahammad 1877-1938
Ivanov, Vyacheslav Ivanovich 1866-
   1949
James, Will 1892-1942
Jammes, Francis 1868-1938
Johnson, Fenton 1888-1958
Johnston, Mary 1870-1936
Jorgensen, Johannes 1866-1956
King, Grace 1851-1932
Kirby, William 1817-1906
Kline, Otis Albert 1891-1946
Kohut, Adolph 1848-1916
Kreve, Bincas 1882-1954
Kuzmin, Mikhail Alexseyevich 1875-
   1936
Lamm, Martin 1880-1950

Leipoldt, C. Louis 1880-1947
Lima, Jorge De 1895-1953
Locke, Alain 1886-1954
Long, Frank Belknap 1903-1959
Lopez Portillo y Rojas, Jose 1850-1903
Louys, Pierre 1870-1925
Lucas, E(dward) V(errall) 1868-1938
Lyall, Edna 1857-1903
Maghar, Josef Suatopluk 1864-1945
Maragall, Joan 1860-1911
Marais, Eugene 1871-1936
Masaryk, Tomas 1850-1939
Mayor, Flora Macdonald 1872-1932
McClellan, George Marion 1860-1934
McCoy, Horace 1897-1955
Mirbeau, Octave 1850-1917
Mistral, Frederic 1830-1914
Monro, Harold 1879-1932
Moore, Thomas Sturge 1870-1944
Morley, Christopher 1890-1957
Morley, S. Griswold 1883-1948
Murray, (George) Gilbert 1866-1957
Nansen, Peter 1861-1918
Nobre, Antonio 1867-1900
O'Dowd, Bernard 1866-1959
Ophuls, Max 1902-1957
Orczy, Baroness 1865-1947
Owen, Seaman 1861-1936
Page, Thomas Nelson 1853-1922
Parrington, Vernon L. 1871-1929
Peck, George W. 1840-1916
Pessao, Fernando 1887-1930
Phillips, Ulrich B. 1877-1934
Pinero, Arthur Wing 1855-1934
Pontoppidan, Henrik 1857-1943
Powys, T. F. 1875-1953
Prevost, Marcel 1862-1941
Quiller-Couch, Arthur 1863-1944
Radiguet, Raymond 1903-1923
Randall, James G. 1881-1953
Rappoport, Solomon 1863-1944
Read, Opie 1852-1939
Rebreanu, Liviu 1885-1944
Redcam, Tom 1870-1933
Reisen (Reizen), Abraham 1875-1953
Remington, Frederic 1861-1909
Remizov, Alexei M. 1877-1923
Riley, James Whitcomb 1849-1916
Rinehart, Mary Roberts 1876-1958
Ring, Max 1817-1901
Rivera, Jose Eustasio 1889-1928
Rohmer, Sax 1883-1959
Rozanov, Vasily Vasilyevich 1856-1919
Saar, Ferdinand von 1833-1906
Sabatini, Rafael 1875-1950
Saintsbury, George 1845-1933

Sakutaro, Hagiwara 1886-1942
Sanborn, Franklin Benjamin 1831-1917
Santayana, George 1863-1952
Sardou, Victorien 1831-1908
Schickele, René 1885-1940
Seabrook, William 1886-1945
Seton, Ernest Thompson 1860-1946
Shestov, Lev 1866-1938
Shiels, George 1886-1949
Skram, Bertha Amalie 1847-1905
Sodergran, Edith Irene 1892-1923
Solovyov, Vladimir 1853-1900
Sorel, Georges 1847-1922
Spector, Mordechai 1859-1922
Squire, J(ohn) C(ollings) 1884-1958

Stavenhagen, Fritz 1876-1906
Stockton, Frank R. 1834-1902
Subrahmanya Bharati, C. 1882-1921
Sully-Prudhomme, René 1839-1907
Sylva, Carmen 1843-1916
Thoma, Ludwig 1867-1927
Tomlinson, Henry Major 1873-1958
Totovents, Vahan 1889-1937
Tuchmann, Jules 1830-1901
Turner, W(alter) J(ames) R(edfern)
  1889-1946
Upward, Allen 1863-1926
Vachell, Horace Annesley 1861-1955
Van Dyke, Henry 1852-1933
Vazov, Ivan Minchov 1850-1921

Veblen, Thorstein 1857-1929
Villaespesa, Francisco 1877-1936
Wallace, Edgar 1874-1932
Wallace, Lewis 1827-1905
Walsh, Ernest 1895-1926
Webster, Jean 1876-1916
Whitlock, Brand 1869-1927
Wilson, Harry Leon 1867-1939
Wolf, Emma 1865-1932
Wood, Clement 1888-1950
Wren, P(ercival) C(hristopher) 1885-
  1941
Yonge, Charlotte Mary 1823-1901
Zecca, Ferdinand 1864-1947
Zeromski, Stefan 1864-1925

Readers are cordially invited to suggest additional authors to the editors.

Sherwood (Berton) Anderson

1876-1941

(Also wrote under pseudonym of Buck Fever) American short story writer, novelist, autobiographer, essayist, editor, poet, and dramatist.

The following entry presents criticism of Anderson's short story collection *Winesburg, Ohio*. For a complete discussion of Anderson's career, see *TCLC*, Volumes 1 and 10.

Anderson, one of the most original early twentieth-century writers, was among the first American authors to explore the influence of the unconscious upon human behavior. A writer of brooding, introspective works, his "hunger to see beneath the surface of lives" was best expressed in the bittersweet stories which form the classic *Winesburg, Ohio: A Group of Tales of Ohio Small Town Life*. This, his most important book, exhibits the author's characteristically simple prose style and his personal vision, which combines a sense of wonder at the potential beauty of life with despair over its tragic aspects. Anderson's style and outlook were influential in shaping the writings of Ernest Hemingway, William Faulkner, Thomas Wolfe, John Steinbeck, and many other American authors.

In 1913 at age thirty-seven Anderson left his family and a failing business in Elyria, Ohio, to settle in Chicago and work as an advertising copywriter. However, his ambition was to become a novelist, and as a copywriter he considered himself "a mere peddler of words" who trivialized his writing skill for money. During his free time he worked on his own manuscripts in a rooming house he shared with painters, musicians, and other writers; it was there that Anderson met Floyd Dell, who became his mentor and friend. Dell was an enthusiast of Freud's theory of the unconscious, and he included Anderson in gatherings at which participants psychoanalyzed one another and indulged in "games" of dream interpretation. Many commentators consider this exposure an instrumental influence on the explorations of the human unconscious which began to appear in Anderson's fiction with *Winesburg, Ohio*. It was also through Dell that Anderson met Carl Sandburg and other writers of the "Chicago renaissance." Comprising an informal coterie, these Midwestern poets, fiction writers, and editors advocated literary innovations in opposition to the genteel tradition in nineteenth century American literature, which inhibited the treatment of human sexuality, psychological aberration, or any unpleasant aspect of American life. Correspondingly, technical strictures such as the carefully manipulated plot, chronological action, and dramatic resolution were dispensed with to allow an unpatterned structure more closely imitative of human action and thought.

A new narrative form had already been suggested to Anderson by the paintings of such post-impressionist artists as Paul Cezanne, Vincent van Gogh, and Paul Gaugin: rather than attempting the faithful reproduction of an object on canvas, these artists painted images mirroring their impressions of an object at a given moment. Anderson paralleled these painters' techniques in prose narrative by following the flow of a character's thoughts and impressions. During this period Anderson discovered the highly experimental work of Gertrude Stein, whose immersion in the theories of avant-garde artists inspired her to

create a literary style that would reflect the abstract characteristics found in the paintings of Cezanne, Henri Matisse, and Pablo Picasso. Stein's influence is evident in *Winesburg, Ohio* in such elements as the repetition of words and phrases, the consistent use of characters' full names, and an almost exclusive interest in the inner lives of characters. A more direct influence on the Winesburg stories has been traced to the *Spoon River Anthology* of Edgar Lee Masters, published in 1915. Anderson read this poetry collection in that year and commentators have suggested that he may have unconsciously imbibed the jaundiced view of small town American life and concern with sexuality that informs Masters's work. Because Anderson was exposed to such a wide range of new creative ideas during this period, literary commentators regard these early years in Chicago as the most crucial period in Anderson's artistic development. Criticism of the early works Anderson wrote in Elyria confirms the view that little in these novels portend his achievement in *Winesburg, Ohio*.

Winesburg, Ohio constituted an original concept in American fiction which revolutionized the short story genre. Rejecting what he termed the "poison plot," Anderson focused on the psychological lives or "inner lives" of characters emotionally crippled by isolation, sexual repression, and lack of spiritual fulfillment. Anderson's frank yet tender depiction of these thwarted lives engages the imaginative participation of readers through techniques Burton Rascoe has described as "selective, indefinite, and provocative, instead of inclusive, precise, and explanatory." Although some of the stories have been the objects of individual analysis, critics cite several connective devices which impart a more profound significance to the work when it is considered as a whole. Among the most frequently identified unifying elements are the common setting of the stories; the character George Willard, whose maturation process is traced in the collection; the recurrence of characters and particular images; and a preoccupation with loneliness and repressed self-expression. Several of the stories in the collection were published as early as 1916 in the progressive magazines the *Masses*, the *Little Review*, and *Seven Arts*. Nevertheless, the editors of these journals—including Anderson's friends Dell and Waldo Frank—soon expressed reservations about publishing more stories of such an experimental nature. John Lane, publisher of Anderson's novels *Windy McPherson's Son* and *Marching Men*, rejected *Winesburg, Ohio* after Anderson's *Mid-American Chants* appeared in 1918 to uniformly negative reviews. However, Francis Hackett, literary editor of the *New Republic*, recommended Anderson's Winesburg stories to the small publishing house of Ben Heubsch, which had already issued controversial works by James Joyce and D. H. Lawrence. Heubsch's publication of *Winesburg, Ohio* brought Anderson international recognition as an important new voice in American literature. "Here is the goal that the *Spoon River Anthology* aimed at, and missed by half a mile," wrote H. L. Mencken. The "goal" that Anderson achieved was a fusion of simply-stated fiction and complex psychological analysis that revealed an essential loneliness and beauty in Midwestern town life. The results, in the case of *Winesburg, Ohio*, were disturbingly insightful yet compassionate studies of human life.

The innovative structure of *Winesburg, Ohio* was disconcerting to many of Anderson's contemporaries, who challenged the work's validity as fiction. Foremost among the aspects they found disturbing were the stories' plotlessness and Anderson's disregard for temporal sequence. Anderson, calling for a "new looseness of form," defended his method as an approximation of the chaotic, unselective movement of human thought and action, and noted that there are "no plot stories in life." Thus, rather than recount episodes, such stories as "Hands" and "Queer" capture the essence of lives isolated because of convention, insensitivity, circumstance, or personal weakness. "An Awakening," "The Untold Lie," and others disclose moments of spiritual epiphany or self-awareness. By limiting the use of dialogue, physical description, and dramatic action, these stories delineate in a concentrated form the psychology of their characters. This delineation is often achieved through the repetition of a carefully selected image or the accumulation of several images which elicit an associative emotional response from the reader. For example, in the story "Paper Pills," Dr. Reefy's knarled, twisted hands recall an earlier reference to apples that conceal an inner sweetness beneath twisted exteriors. Similarly, the central image of "Hands" becomes a leitmotif accumulating a variety of associations which illuminate Wing Biddlebaum's life as one that has been marked by affection, knowledge, and pride as well as brutality, confusion, and shame. In this brief, concise psychological portrait, glimpses of the present and of the near and distant past are revealed in almost imperceptible shifts between these periods in a continuum of overlapping time which many critics have compared to the temporal sequence of dreams.

Many of the stories in *Winesburg, Ohio* are set at twilight, which enhances an ethereal quality perceived by many critics.

The detailed description of the shabby town of Winesburg, which led some critics to classify the collection with other "revolt from the village" fiction, is now regarded as a mere backdrop of mundane reality to stories concerned with the dreams and subconscious impulses of the townspeople. The daytime behavior of such characters as Reverend Hartman, Kate Swift, and Alice Hindman conforms to town convention; however, as in dreams, subconscious impulses repressed in daylight are released at night. This repression is often of a sexual nature, although many modern critics argue that the characters, in their inarticulateness, express in physical terms their inexpressible desire for human communication and companionship, a desire best exemplified in the collection by the heightened, non-sexual relationship attained by George Willard and Helen White in "Sophistication." The sense of repression and despair captured in *Winesburg* is best summarized by the character Alice Hartman's observation that "many people must live and die alone"; however, this bitter vision is tempered by the poignant, lyrical quality of the stories, a lyricism enhanced by Anderson's prose style, which echoes biblical cadence and contributes an aura of dignity to even the most pathetic of the town's inhabitants.

Critics agree that it was in his short stories that Anderson was most successful in conveying his impressions of life. The stories "Hands," "The Untold Lie," and "Sophistication" from *Winesburg, Ohio*, and "The Egg," "I'm a Fool," and "I Want to Know Why" from later collections are considered to be among the best works of American short fiction. Utilizing Anderson's innovative form, which Mencken described as "half tale and half psychological anatomizing," these stories capture the essence of lives divided by insensitivity, convention, circumstance, and personal weakness, yet which are sometimes joined by love, sympathy, and shared moments of spiritual epiphany.

For his simple, impressionistic style and his frequent acknowledgement that he was puzzled by life's basic questions—an unfashionable admission to make during the intellectually self-assured Jazz Age and the politically opinionated climate of the Great Depression—Anderson has often been dismissed as a primitive minor talent who was of more value as a literary catalyst than as an artist in his own right. But the continued popularity of his works has led critics to reexamine them more closely, and Anderson has regained recognition as an important American author.

(See also *Contemporary Authors*, Vol. 104; *Dictionary of Literary Biography*, Vol. 4: *American Writers in Paris, 1920-1939*; Vol. 9: *American Novelists, 1910-1945*; and *Dictionary of Literary Biography Documentary Series*, Vol. 1.)

H. W. BOYNTON (essay date 1919)

[*Boynton was an American critic and the editor of texts on American and English literature. In the following excerpt, he discusses* Winesburg, Ohio *as a work which candidly treats the inner lives of typical small-town individuals.*]

Life gray and quiet is not the life of **Winesburg, Ohio**. A comparison between this book and the *Spoon River Anthology* is inevitable. Here, as there, the inner individual life of a typical American small town is laid bare, or let us say illuminated from within, so that we perceive its reality shining through the dull masks of convention and humdrum. It is a life of vivid feeling and ardent impulse doomed, for the most part, to be suppressed or misdirected, but still existent and potent as nothing is potent in the life of the community as a community. We must meet the fact at the outset that with this writer sex is wellnigh the mainspring of human action. At worst he seems in this book like a man who has too freely imbibed the doctrine of the psychoanalysts, and fares thereafter with eyes slightly "set" along the path of fiction. At best he seems without consciousness of self or of theory to be getting at the root of the matter—one root, at least—for all of us. His style is plain, staccato, perhaps a little deliberately unliterary:

> Wash Williams once had a wife. When he was still a young man he married a woman in Dayton, Ohio. The woman was tall and slender and had blue eyes and yellow hair. Wash was himself a comely youth. He loved the woman with a love as absorbing as the hatred he later felt for all women.

Wash Williams is the telegraph operator in Winesburg, the ugliest man in town. Our business with him is to hear how he became a woman-hater; and it is an unpleasant business, out of which shines the redeeming light of the man's battered yet not defeated idealism. And so it is with all these stories. Frank and momentarily disconcerting as their detail often is, we feel in them none of the spiritual grossness of the Russian naturalists and their imitators. Mr. Anderson is of the race of Stevenson; he also is "something of the shorter catechist." Always he seems to be after the true morality that so often governs men and women when they are at odds with, or merely conforming to, conventional morality. I do not know where in prose a tenser moral action is concentrated than in the dozen pages of **"The Strength of God,"** that amazing tale of the conversion of the Reverend Curtis Hartman, to whom, Peeping Tom that he is, God for the first time "manifests himself in the body of a woman." There are youth and hope and honest love in Winesburg, Ohio. Yet young George Willard, whose slim figure threads these pages, must go elsewhere to fulfil himself. . . . It may be suspected that most American readers will find themselves so busy recognizing Winesburg that they will have to be reminded to exercise their inherited prerogative of moral judgment upon it. (pp. 729-30)

> *H. W. Boynton, "All Over the Lot," in* The Bookman, *New York, Vol. XLIX, No. 6, August, 1919, pp. 728-34.*

FLOYD DELL   (essay date 1919)

[An American novelist and dramatist, Dell is best known today as the author of Moon-Calf *(1920), a novel which captures the disillusioned spirit of the Jazz Age. For several years he was a member, along with Carl Sandburg, Ben Hecht, Theodore Dreiser, and others, of the Chicago Renaissance, a group of writers who legitimized the American Midwest as a source of artistic material and achievement. A Marxist during his early career, Dell moved from Chicago to New York in 1914, and served as editor of the socialist periodical the* Masses *and its successor, the* Liberator, *for ten years. During the 1920s, Dell was associated with the bohemia of Greenwich Village and, with a series of novels and one-act plays, became known as a spokesman for society's rebels and nonconformists. His socialist sympathies softened over the years, although he remained an outspoken leftist throughout his career. Anderson regarded Dell as a mentor and literary father during his early years in Chicago; however, according to Anderson, Dell published only two of the Winesburg stories in the*

Masses *because he considered them fragmentary and morose. In the following excerpt from a review at variance with this view, Dell, on the basis of* Winesburgh, Ohio, *pronounces Anderson one of the most skilled and imaginative of American post-Naturalist writers.]*

The naturalistic movement was a reflex of Darwinian science, with its emphasis on "the struggle for existence": it was, as we see it now, an elaborate series of illustrations of the alleged fact that the strongest were the fittest to survive, and that beauty and idealism and soft-heartedness always got a raw deal. It is natural to expect that the literature of the present will be to some extent less a scientific and historical exposition of human nature than an emotional reflex of certain of the truisms of modern psychology—such as, for instance, the motivation of our lives by unconscious impulses, chiefly sexual. The lead has been taken in the neurotic rather than scientific illustration of such truisms by James Joyce, and there are writers in America who belong to the same school. Sherwood Anderson stands apart from them, not because of any scientific or historical method, but by virtue of greater power as a writer, a more thorough imaginative equipment, which makes his novels and stories pictures of American life that rank among the best yet produced. His new volume, **Winesburg, Ohio,** is a magnificent collection of tales, not free from neurotic compulsions of the same kind as those with which he deals, but vivid and in spite of some grotesqueries, beautiful, and in all but the finest sense true. If less faithful to fact than Mr. Dreiser [in the novel *Twelve Men*], he is more of an artist, and he has broadened the realm of American fiction to include aspects of life of the first importance.

> *Floyd Dell, in a review of "Winesburg, Ohio," in* The Liberator, *New York, Vol. 2, No. 9, September, 1919, p. 47.*

REBECCA WEST   (essay date 1922)

[West is considered one of the foremost English novelists and critics of the twentieth century. Born Cecily Isabel Fairfield, she began her career as an actress—taking the name Rebecca West from the emancipated heroine of Henrik Ibsen's drama Rosmersholm—*and as a book reviewer for the* Freewoman. *Her early criticism was noted for its militantly feminist stance and its reflection of West's Fabian socialist concerns. West's literary criticism is noted for its wit, its aversion to cant, and its perceptiveness. In the following excerpt, West contends that* Winesburg, Ohio *is best appreciated as poetry rather than fiction.]*

[**Winesburg, Ohio**] is not such a distinguished book as **The Triumph of the Egg** . . . ; but as that contains two of the half dozen most remarkable short stories written in this century that is not surprising. But it is an extraordinarily good book. Yet if one takes it as fiction, particularly if one has read and admired the class of fiction to which to judge from outward appearances it might be trying to belong—Booth Tarkington's provincial novels, Miss Jewett's and Miss Wilkins' and Miss Deland's short stories—one may be disappointed. But it is not fiction. It is poetry. It is unreasonable; it delights in places where those who are not poets could never find delight; it will not follow logic and find connections and trace "plots," but stands in front of things that are of no importance, infatuated with their quality, and hymns them with obstinate ecstasy; it seems persuaded there is beauty in anything, in absolutely anything. In such a spirit Mr. Anderson moves about his ugly little town and watches his dull ugly people. It lives, it glows, they exist as immortal souls. If we have listened truly to the sanctified old tunes we must know that this difficult new tune also is music. (pp. 443-44)

Rebecca West, in a review of ''Winesburg, Ohio,''
in New Statesman, *Vol. XIX, No. 484, July 22, 1922, pp. 443-44.*

SHERWOOD ANDERSON   (letter date 1932)

[*In the following excerpt from a letter to New York playwright Arthur Barton, with whom Anderson collaborated in adapting* Winesburg, Ohio *for the stage, Anderson discusses the central theme and main characters of* Winesburg.]

Now to me it seems that the theme of the **Winesburg** book, the thing that really makes it a book—curiously holding together from story to story as it does—is just that that there is a central theme. The theme is the making of a man out of the actual stuff of life.

An American boy as you see growing up in an American village. It is an ordinary American town. There are all sorts of influences playing over him and around him. These influences are presented in the form of characters, playing on his own character, forming it, warning him, educating him. I do not know whether or not you, Barton, were raised in a small town but that does not matter. The same sort of influences would be at work on any boy in American life whether he were raised in a small town or a city. In the midst of the confusion of life the boy is always accepting or rejecting the suggestions thrown out to him by other people, directly and indirectly. In this play we will have to get from the beginning a feeling of growth in the boy.

To go back again for a moment let me tell you something that may amuse you. These stories of the **Winesburg** book were really written in a Chicago tenement, not in a village, and the truth is that I got the substance of every character in the book not from an Ohio village but from other people living around me in the Chicago tenement. I simply transferred them to a small town and gave them small town surroundings. (p. 153)

Now let me go back a moment to the theme of **Winesburg**. There are these queer, interesting, sometimes essentially fine, often essentially vulgar figures of a town. Think, Barton, what a great percentage of American men and women who come into the theatre were raised either in small towns or on farms. They got their early impressions of life there. Just as our boy George Willard did and then they went away to live in the city as he did. You have heard the saying attributed to the Catholics—''Give me the child until he is ten and you may have him afterwards. I will not lose him.'' It seems to me that what is notable about **Winesburg** is that it does treat those American villagers, twisted as they may be—''queer hopping figures'' a critic once called them—it does treat their lives with respect. That also we will want to do. What the book says to people is this—''Here it is. It is like this. This is what the life in America out of which men and women come is like.''

''But out of this life does come real men and women.''

That it seems to me is the essence of the theme of the book and the thing we have to put across.

What your first synopsis has suggested to me is the possibilities that lie in four characters of the book. They are   .

the boy, George Willard
his mother
his father
the girl, Helen White.

These should be the dominant characters in the play because they will all affect most deeply the development of the boy George.

But before discussing them let me discuss also for a minute the young man Seth Richmond. This is what I think about Seth. There is nothing especially evil in him. He is simply a boy who sees life absolutely in terms of himself. He wants the girl Helen White for two reasons. She belongs to a respectable and well-to-do family—is you remember the only daughter of the town banker—and is also to Seth's mind beautiful.

But he will not be thinking of Helen's beauty as a thing worthwhile in itself—aside from himself. He wants to succeed in life, make money, be a big man, and he would like to have Helen to decorate his own successful life.

George Willard

George Willard is not like this. In the first place he is capable of even more brutality than Seth because he is essentially a dreamer. He does not figure out his own acts with the general scheme of his own life in mind. He dreams of becoming a writer but that is only because almost everything in his own life goes wrong and he has a vague feeling that in some novel or story he may write he may be able to build up an ordered fine life. George should be of the rather poetic brooding dreaming type. Always saying things he does not mean and yet in some queer way holding on to some idea of decent manhood and respect for other people and their lives.

The father is a man who began life as a hotel clerk in a shabby hotel in a little village. There was quite a remarkable and spirited girl there, the daughter of the hotel keeper. This could be one of the grand characters of the play and could give some actress a gorgeous opportunity. She is of the kind of girl and woman not so beautiful on the outside but having in her a lot of inner fire. As a young girl living in her father's little shabby hotel she meets all kinds of rather second-rate men, travelling men and others, and goes about with them. Several of them make love to her and she lets them but all the time there is something in her that is seeking a finer type of man who may give her real womanhood. This she never finds and she takes as husband the hotel clerk who becomes ostensibly George Willard's father. (pp. 153-55)

Now, Barton, in the book I made this woman a rather drab figure but we will have to be a little careful about her in the play. How about having her a prematurely grey woman of about thirty-five or forty, tall and slight, with tired eyes—rather pale, but still with the same spirit in her that attracted men when she was a girl, when excited or angry her form straightens and she becomes again a living thing capable still of attracting men. And then when the excitement is past swings again into this rather tired defeated woman. I believe there are actresses who could put this across.

I said a moment ago that this woman, when she was a young girl, had a dream of a certain kind of man who might be her lover that she never got. The dream transfers itself to the boy George and she is determined that he shall hang on to some sort of fine manliness she never succeeded in finding in the men who have been her lovers.

THE FATHER

The father, or at least the man who thinks he is George Willard's father, is the typical minded, small town man of the rather mean spirited sort. When he was young he would have been rather good looking. His ambition in life was to be a rich man. He is the boy Seth Richmond beginning to grow old.

Now he is a defeated man and knows he never will be a rich or a big man and like the mother he has transferred his dream of what he would have liked to be to his son but the dream is essentially a cheap dream.

The mother knows this and is afraid of his influence on the boy, thinking that if the boy became what the father wanted, or thought he wanted, he would be a cheap tricky man at bottom only out after some kind of showy success.

HELEN WHITE

I think we should take the girl Helen White as a figure very much like George's mother when she was a young girl.

There is this difference. Helen White belongs to one of the most prosperous families in the town. She is the only daughter. she is not exactly a beauty but is full of fire and spirit. Unlike the mother of George Willard when she was a young girl, Helen White is protected by all the forces of conservative society but like George's mother she is ready to break through conventions whenever she thinks she has found what she wants in a man.

I think of her, Barton, as a pretty shrewd girl really onto Seth Richmond and is in love with George Willard from the beginning but just the same she is not going to take George unless he can make a man of himself. (pp. 155-56)

What I think we want to do is to get away from the idea of making the small town ridiculous or too dreary or sentimental—in other words to make people feel that a cross-section taken thus from a life in a small town would not differ from a cross-section of life taken from anywhere and that the forces over this boy George Willard are the same kind of forces that play over all American boys. If we can do that we will have a real play. (p. 156)

Sherwood Anderson, in a letter to Arthur Barton on November 26, 1932, in his Sherwood Anderson: Selected Letters, *edited by Charles E. Modlin, The University of Tennessee Press, Knoxville, 1984, 152-156.*

WALDO FRANK (essay date 1941)

[*Frank was an American novelist and critic who was best known as an interpreter of contemporary civilization, particularly that of Latin America. A socialist and supporter of various radical groups in the United States, he was a founding editor of the* Seven Arts *(1916-17), a leftist, avant-garde magazine of literature and opinion. One of Frank's most significant works of criticism,* Our America *(1919), derides the "genteel tradition" in American letters and was an influential work in its support of realism in the nation's literature. In 1916 Frank's review of Anderson's novel* Windy McPherson's Son, *titled "Emerging Greatness," was published in* Seven Arts, *where some of the Winesburg stories later appeared. Frank and Anderson formed a friendship based on Frank's appreciation of Anderson's talent and Anderson's admiration of Frank's intellectual and artistic achievements. The friendship ended bitterly after several years. In the following excerpt, Frank dismisses Anderson's self-cultivated image as a talented but naive primitive, arguing that the quality and unity of aesthetic and technical elements in the work are the mark of a master.*]

Sherwood Anderson wrote his most famous book about a generation ago; and it reveals a Mid-American world that already then was a generation dead. A full half century therefore divides the mind that reads the book today from the life it portrays. Since, from this adequate perspective, the work stands firm in its form, true in its livingness, strong in its light upon our present, it is clear that *Winesburg, Ohio* is a classic.

I had not re-read the book since it was published. Many of its chapters were mailed to me in his own writing by Anderson himself, who then lived in Chicago and worked for an advertising house near Jackson Boulevard. I still see the long sprawling potent hand on the cheap paper, feel the luminous life that swelled miraculously from it. I recall sending him back one story which I wished to publish in *The Seven Arts,* because it was written down totally without commas; a few days later, it came back to me with commas sedulously spaced after each fourth or fifth word, irrespective of meaning. I had no doubt of the significance of this prose; otherwise, in 1916 I should not with such assurance have entitled my first essay on Anderson "Emerging Greatness"; but I know now that accidentals like the handwriting and the punctuation somewhat obscured for me, as the man's homespun did for many, the actual lineaments of this clear art. It is a dangerous hazard to re-read, after twenty-five years, a book involved in the dreams and fervors of one's youth; it is a blessing when that book stands forth from the test a rediscovery . . . indeed a prophecy and an illumination.

The first impressive realization that came to me with my re-reading was that *Winesburg* has form. The book as a whole has form; the work is an integral creation. The form is lyrical. It is not related, even remotely, to the aesthetic of Chekhov; nor to that of Balzac, Flaubert, Maupassant, Tolstoy, Melville. These masters of the short story used the narrative or dramatic art: a linear progression rising to a peak or an immediate complex of character-forces impinging upon each other in a certain action that fulfilled them and rounded the story. For an analogy to the aesthetic of the Winesburg tales, one must go to music, perhaps to the songs that Schubert neatly wove from old refrains; or to the lyric art of the Old Testament psalmists and prophets in whom the literary medium was so allied to music that their texts have always been sung in the synagogues. The *Winesburg* design is quite uniform: a theme-statement of a character with his mood, followed by a recounting of actions that are merely variations on the theme. These variations make incarnate what has already been revealed to the reader; they weave the theme into life by the always subordinate confrontation of other characters (usually one) and by an evocation of landscape and village. In some of the tales, there is a secondary theme-statement followed by other variations. In a few, straight narrative is attempted; and these are the least successful.

This lyric, musical form has significance, and the tales' contents make it clear. But it is important, first, to note that the cant judgment of Sherwood Anderson as a naïve, almost illiterate storyteller (a judgment which he himself encouraged with a good deal of nonsense about his literary innocence) is false. The substance of *Winesburg* is impressive, is alive, because it has been superbly *formed.* There are occasional superficial carelessnesses of language; on the whole, the prose is perfect in its selective economy and in its melodious flow; the choice of details is stript, strong, sure; the movement is an unswerving musical fulfillment of the already stated theme. Like Schubert, and like the Old Testament storytellers, the author of **Winesburg** comes at the end of a psychological process; is a man with an inherited culture and a deeply assimilated skill. He is a type of the achieved artist.

The theme of the tales taken as a whole follows the same pattern as the individual "chapters"—although less precisely. **"Hands,"** the first chapter, tells of Adolph Myers, alias Wing Biddlebaum, the unfortunate schoolteacher with sensitive, wandering, caressing hands, who gets into trouble because his loving touch upon his pupils is misinterpreted by a half-wit boy and the crude obscene men of the town. Because the tale is concretely, poetically realized, its symbolism is true; and because this symbolism is not intellectualized, not schematized, it would be false to tear it from its flesh and blood texture. Suffice it to say that the story suggests the tragic ambivalence of hands, which is the fate of all the characters of Winesburg. Hands, at the turn of the century, were making machines, making all sorts of things ("the thing is in the saddle"); making the world that was unmaking the tender, sensitive, intimate lives of the folk in their villages and farms. Hands are made for loving; but hands making mechanical things grow callous, preoccupied . . . fail at love. (pp. 29-30)

I have spoken of suggested symbols. Suggestion, if you will *indirection,* is the quality of this lyric form; and no more *direct* expression could have been devised for a book which so precisely portrays a world avid for the expression of eternal truths and forced, by the decay of its old cultural foundation, to seek truth anarchically, hopelessly, indirectly.

It has become a critical commonplace that Winesburg faithfully portrays the midwest village of two thousand souls during the post-civil war pre-motor age. Let us look. . . . No even bearably married couple is to be found in Winesburg; there are few marriages in the book, and these without exception are described as the harnessing together of strangers by the bondage of sex or a morality hostile to the spirit. There is no communion with children. There is no fulfilled sex life, sex being an obsession, a frustration and a trap. There is no normal sociability between men and women: souls lonely as carnivorae for once in their lives burst into melodic plaint to one another, and lapse into solipsistic silence. There is indeed more muttering than talk. There is no congregated worship, and no strength to organized religion except in the sense of a strong barrier; as in the piteous tales of the Reverend Hartman who sins by knocking a piece from his stained-glass church window (part of the figure of Christ) in order to gaze at the body of Belle Robinson in bed. There is almost no joy, beyond the momentary joy of contemplating nature. And the most mature of the characters, Doctor Reefy, Seth Richmond, Elizabeth Willard, the Rev. Hartman, et al., do not evolve beyond a sharp negation of the things that *are,* in favor of a nebulous dream of "life."

Now, these omissions are purposive; and as aesthetically true as they are factually false. The author's art, perhaps unconsciously to himself, traces the frontier of emotional and spiritual action which, in that deliquescence of an agrarian culture which was rotten long ere it was ripe, was a line of *decay,* a domain of deprivation. In those very institutions and traditions which had been the base of the world's health, Winesburg was found wanting.

The positive substance of the book is the solitariness and struggle of the soul which has lost its ancestral props: the energy of the book is the release from these old forms into a subliminal search for new ones. The farms of Robert Frost's "North of Boston" are also peopled by broken, lonely lives; but their despair is hard, heroic. The folk of Winesburg are soft in a tenderness, in a nebulous searchfulness, that have gone farther in decay than the still standing families and churches of Frost's New England. In all the book, only irony—the author's irony—is hard.

This trait of Sherwood Anderson has been too little recognized. Consider the acrid irony in **"Nobody Knows,"** where sex fulfillment ends in the boy's cowardly sigh of relief that "she hasn't got anything on me. Nobody knows"; in **"An Awakening,"** that turns a moment of mystical insight into a brutal, humiliating sexual frustration; in **"The Untold Lie"** (one of the great stories of the world); in the chapters of Jesse Bentley, "the man of God" who is transformed by the sling of his grandchild, David, into a clumsy, puny, ineffectual Goliath. This hardness of irony in the author points to his spiritual transcendence over his subjects. Anderson has inherited intact a strength long since vaporized in Winesburg—and yet the heritage of Winesburg. His sureness of vision and of grasp enable him to incarnate in a form very precise the inchoate emotions of his people. To portray the deliquescence of America's agrarian culture beneath the impact of the untamed machine age required a man spiritually advanced beyond that culture's death. This is a law of art (and of ethic) ignored by the hardboiled Hemingway school, who depict their gangsters *on the level of the gangsters.*

Sherwood Anderson liked to think of himself as a primitive or neo-primitive artist; as a naïve unlettered storyteller. The truth is, that he belonged at the end of a cultural process, and shares the technical perfection which, within the limits of the culture's forms, only the terminal man achieves. One book was the pabulum of these people: the Bible. And a Testamental accent and vision modulate every page of Sherwood Anderson's great story. Moreover, the nebulosity of these poor souls' search is an end, a chaos *after* a world. That world was already drooping when it crossed the ocean; it had been, in England, a world of revealed religion and sacramental marriage, of the May dance and the sense of each man's life as mystery and mission. It lives in the past of Winesburg; it has become a beat and a refrain in the blood. In the actual experience of these men and women, it is a recidivism, a lapse away into organic echoes. Thus, of revealed religion and sacramental marriage, of the structures of social and personal responsibilities, nothing remains on the record but the memory and the dynamic yearning. Life has become a Prompter with the text of the dialogue and even the stage missing.

In sum, Sherwood Anderson is a mature voice singing a culture at its close; singing it with the technical skill of literally, the *past master.* (pp. 31-2)

Waldo Frank, "'Winesburg, Ohio': After Twenty Years," in Story, *Vol. XIX, No. 91, September-October, 1941, pp. 29-33.*

ALWYN BERLAND   (essay date 1951)

[*In the following essay, Berland posits that characterization in* Winesburg, Ohio *avoids sentimentality despite the work's theme of frustrated dreams because of Anderson's balanced use of pathos, irony, and objectivity.*]

The interesting thing about **"The Book of the Grotesque,"** which introduces Sherwood Anderson's *Winesburg, Ohio,* is its implicit conception of life as pathetic, rather than as tragic. The sense of pathos is manifest throughout the preface:

> The carpenter had once been a prisoner in An-
> dersonville prison and had lost a brother. The
> brother had died of starvation, and whenever
> the carpenter got upon that subject he cried.

> The grotesques were not all horrible. Some were
> amusing, some almost beautiful, and one, a
> woman all drawn out of shape, hurt the old
> man by her grotesqueness. When she passed he
> made a noise like a small dog whimpering.

The danger of pathos, of course, is its affinity to sentimentality. But Anderson usually escapes sentimentalism by a careful juxtaposition of objective statement to pathetic insight. Thus, after telling how the carpenter cries, he adds:

> The weeping old man with the cigar in his mouth
> was ludicrous.

Following the simile of the whimpering small dog, comes:

> Had you come into the room you might have
> supposed the old man had unpleasant dreams
> or perhaps indigestion.

After telling us of the old writer's hopeful conviction that he knew people in a "peculiarly intimate way that was different from the way in which you and I know people," we are given this objective comment:

> At least that is what the writer thought and the
> thought pleased him. Why quarrel with an old
> man concerning his thoughts?

Throughout the stories in *Winesburg, Ohio* there is a similar guarding against sentimentality, while the same burden of pathos is elaborated.

Obviously his use of the pathetic is not designed simply to please the maudlin. What concerns us here is the nature of Anderson's pathos, and the assumptions about life on which it is based. This too is suggested in **"The Book of the Grotesque."** Here we are told that "in the beginning when the world was young there were a great many thoughts but no such thing as a truth." Man is supposed to have formed truths from these thoughts, all of them beautiful. But these truths in the hands of men render their believers grotesque. For "the moment one of the people took one of the truths to himself, called it his truth, and tried to live his life by it, he became a grotesque and the truth he embraced became a falsehood." Now such a conception can lead to pathos, but not to tragedy.

The source of falsehood, of grotesqueness, is not an improper manipulation of truths so much as the truths themselves, in their transition from ideal to concrete. There is no "flaw" or blindness in man which keeps him from realizing these truths, but the very nature of truth itself. More is fated to distortion and grotesqueness from the beginning. He has no real moral choice, except perhaps to choose the particular truths which must inevitably warp him. It is the determinism of naturalism; the only variation is Anderson's conception of "fate." For Dreiser it involves something like the uncontrollable chemistry of man's organization which determines his life. For Anderson, it is the ironic mutilation of the ideal become pragmatic.

Ideal truths are beautiful in Anderson's world, and provide human motivation. That is, despite the constant frustration which comes to his characters, they seem still to maintain some ideal image of life which is beautiful. Indeed, it is this ideal image which gives rise to the distortion of character. In the preface we are told of the writer that:

> The subject would become so big in his mind
> that he himself would be in danger of becoming
> a grotesque. He didn't, I suppose, for the same
> reason that he never published the book. It was
> the young thing inside him that saved the old
> man.

This young thing is glowingly described, but that it kept the writer from becoming a grotesque we may doubt, since the same "young thing" is present in Wing Biddlebaum, in Jesse and Louise Bentley, in Elizabeth Willard, and in Kate Swift—all "grotesques." Perhaps Anderson intends his irony, for he says that the writer "never published the book." But of course that book lies open before us.

The young thing which exists within the writer, described metaphorically as "a woman, young, and wearing a coat of mail like a knight," is echoed in the story, **"Hands,"** in the vision of Wing Biddlebaum:

> In the picture men lived again a kind of pastoral
> golden age. Across a green open country came
> clean-limbed young men, some afoot, some
> mounted on horses.

Wing Biddlebaum speaks "as one lost in a dream." His chief concern for George Willard, who evokes the dream, is that he will become as cloddish as the other people in Winesburg. "You want to be like others in town here." But being influenced by the others is evil. "'You are destroying yourself,' he cried, 'You have the inclination to be alone and to dream and you are afraid of dreams.'" Biddlebaum knows of a life whih is significant and beautiful, but this knowledge is available only through dreams. The *real*—the life around him—is a trap which destroys the dream. But when we come to inspect these others—the clods—more closely as we do in the succeeding stories, we discover that each of them has a dream, and that each fears this falling back to the mediocre, frustrate mass.

The Anderson protagonist is apt to think of himself as having an inner vitality that corresponds to the challenge of his dream. Jesse Bentley, in **"Godliness,"** is perhaps the best single example

> All over his body Jesse Bentley was alive....
> He had always been extraordinarily alive when
> he was a small boy.... As time passed and he
> grew to know people better, he began to think
> of himself as an extraordinary man, one set
> apart from his fellows. He wanted terribly to
> make his life a thing of great importance, and
> as he looked about at his fellow men and saw
> how like clods they lived it seemed to him that
> he could not bear to become also such a clod.

Or the character may feel the lack of this vitality, and despair of ever being able to realize his dream. In **"The Strength of God,"** Curtis Hartman

> was much in earnest and sometimes suffered
> prolonged periods of remorse because he could

not go crying the word of God in the highways and byways of the town. He wondered if the flame of the spirit really burned in him and dreamed of a day when a strong sweet new current of power would come like a great wind into his voice and his soul and the people would tremble before the spirit of God manifest in him.

The attempt to translate dream into action results in defeat. Jesse Bentley's eagerness to make something significant of his life drives him first to a relentless aggressiveness and then to a conflicting and fanatical religious mysticism. The stored-up passions in Curtis Hartman find release not through "the spirit of God," but through his uncontrollable desire for Kate Swift. And even when the individual wants only to communicate his dream to others, he is defeated. Wing Biddlebaum is beaten and run out of town because he tries to communicate his dream. The townsfolk are not completely wrong when they sense the sexual undercurrent of Biddlebaum's desire to communicate his Whitmanesque vision, but they are wrong in equating this with his idealism. Louise Bentley is taken by David Hardy as his mistress, when she wants (besides a lover) someone to whom she can express her dream. Elizabeth Willard had once found communication possible through sex. but it had seemed something more than physical desire. She is unable to communicate to her son, George, the dream that had once been hers and which she has projected as her ambition for him. "Always there was something she sought blindly, passionately, some hidden wonder in life." Kate Swift, **"The Teacher,"** is thought of by the people of the town simply as a "confirmed old maid," when actually "she was the most eagerly passionate soul among them. . . ." She tries to tell George that "you will have to know life. . . . Now it's time to be living," but she cannot really communicate her "passionate desire to have him understand the import of life, to learn to interpret it truly and honestly." She too is baffled and frustrated by her sexual desire, which she will not equate with her vision.

They are all grotesque because they all dream, but cannot live their dream; cannot, indeed, even articulate it. The dream is always the same, really. Life is beautiful, and the vitality of the individual must work toward and participate in this beauty. The vital individual must have real communion with others who are also striving. But this dream is *only* a dream—and it is significant that these characters realize life as beautiful only in dream, in vision, in fantasy. The dream is unrealizable; communion is impossible. The great truth concerns life itself, and is always the same. The many intermediate truths—passion and ambition, most frequently—are properly means for realizing the end, ideal life. But they are distorted into ends in themselves, and they cannot serve as ends. They are important, but in themselves they are meaningless.

Only Doctor Reefy is saved from the distortion of these mediate truths, and he is like a "gnarled apple that pickers have rejected." He does not try to live by his thoughts, and this is what saves him. "The moment one of the people took one of the truths to himself," Anderson has said, "called it his truth, and tried to live his life by it, he became a grotesque and the truth he embraced became a falsehood." Doctor Reefy writes his thoughts on scraps of paper which he then rolls into hard paper pills. Sometimes he throws them at his only friend, saying, "That is to confound you, you blithering old sentimentalist." He reads them to his wife, and "after he had read them he laughed and stuffed them away in his pockets to be-

come round hard balls." Elizabeth Willard comes to talk to him, and in her talk "a dream, half dead, flared suddenly into life." But he tells her, "You must not try to make love definite. It is the divine accident of life. If you try to be definite and sure about it . . . the long hot day of disappointment comes swiftly and the gritty dust from passing wagons gathers upon lips inflamed and made tender by kisses." But Elizabeth Willard is yet able to communicate to him, perhaps for the only time in her life, something of the passion which is her dream. She is almost transformed to the young girl she once was; she is almost taken by Doctor Reefy. But a casual, senseless interruption interferes. Later, she is taken, not by Doctor Reefy, but by death. And George Willard discovers her dead body to be "young and graceful. To the boy, held by some strange fancy, it was unspeakably lovely." And Anderson ends the story of her death speaking of "the release that after all came to her but twice in her life, in the moments when her lovers Death and Doctor Reefy held her in their arms."

Doctor Reefy, unlike all the others, has saved himself by rejecting the truths which the others must cling to in their desperate effort to realize life. He is a skeptic, but also a kind of grotesque, for life has rejected him, as the growers reject the gnarled apples. He is pathetic because life cannot be grasped except through the single truths, which themselves distort life. As for the others—Doctor Parcival tells George Willard that "everyone in the world is Christ and they are all crucified."

In Anderson's world they are all crucified because real life is a trap, from which none—not even Doctor Reefy—can escape to the dream life they desire. If it is pathos without sentiment, it is also pathos without tragedy. No one escapes. There are no alternatives; even death is pathetic because it reveals what ideal life might be if it were more than a dream.

When Stephen Daedalus, in *The Portrait of the Artist as a Young Man,* escapes Ireland, he can exclaim, "Welcome, O Life! I go to encounter for the millionth time the reality of experience and to forge in the smithy of my soul the uncreated conscience of my race." When George Willard escapes Winesburg, it is only to have Winesburg become "a background on which to paint the dreams of his manhood." He too is pathetic. He has seen the thwarting and the failure and the despair which in Winesburg is all of the real world. And "the young man's mind was carried away by his growing passion for dreams." (pp. 135-38)

Alwyn Berland, "Sherwood Anderson and the Pathetic Grotesque," in The Western Review, *Vol. 15, No. 2, Winter, 1951, pp. 135-38.*

IRVING HOWE   (essay date 1951)

[*A longtime editor of the leftist magazine* Dissent *and a regular contributor to* The New Republic, *Howe is one of America's most highly respected literary critics and social historians. He has been a socialist since the 1930s, and his criticism is frequently informed by a liberal social viewpoint. Howe is widely praised for what F. R. Dulles has termed his "knowledgeable understanding, critical acumen and forthright candor." Howe has written: "My work has fallen into two fields: social history and literary criticism. I have tried to strike a balance between the social and the literary; to fructify one with the other; yet not to confuse one with the other. Though I believe in the social approach to literature, it seems to me peculiarly open to misuse; it requires particular delicacy and care." In the following excerpt from his* Sherwood Anderson: A Biographical and Critical Study, *Howe contends that a complementary relationship between the characterization, im-*

Railroad depot, Clyde, Ohio—the town used as a model for Anderson's Winesburg. Used by permission of Viking Penguin Inc. and The Newberry Library, Chicago.

agery, symbolism, style, and themes in Winesburg, Ohio *contributes to the stifling aura of loss which permeates the work.*]

Winesburg is a book largely set in twilight and darkness, its backgrounds heavily shaded with gloomy blacks and marshy grays—as is proper for a world of withered men who, sheltered by night, reach out for that sentient life they dimly recall as the racial inheritance that has been squandered away. Like most fiction, **Winesburg** is a variation on the theme of reality and appearance, in which the deformations caused by day (public life) are intensified at night and, in their very extremity, become an entry to reality. From Anderson's instinctively right placement of the book's central actions at twilight and night comes some of its frequently noticed aura of "lostness"—as if the most sustaining and fruitful human activities can no longer be performed in public communion but must be grasped in secret. (p. 98)

Misogyny, inarticulateness, frigidity, God-infatuation, homosexuality, drunkenness—these are symptoms of their recoil from the regularities of human intercourse and sometimes of their substitute gratifications in inanimate objects, as with the unloved Alice Hindman who "because it was her own, could not bear to have anyone touch the furniture of her room." In their compulsive traits these figures find a kind of dulling peace, but as a consequence they are subject to rigid monomanias and are deprived of one of the great blessings of human health: the capacity for a variety of experience. That is why,

in a sense, "nothing happens" in **Winesburg.** For most of its figures it is too late for anything to happen, they can only muse over the traumas which have so harshly limited their spontaneity. Stripped of their animate wholeness and twisted into frozen postures of defense, they are indeed what Anderson has called them: grotesques.

The world of **Winesburg,** populated largely by these back-street grotesques, soon begins to seem like a buried ruin of a once vigorous society, an atrophied remnant of the egalitarian moment of 19th-century America. Though many of the book's sketches are placed in the out-of-doors, its atmosphere is as stifling as a tomb. And the reiteration of the term "grotesque" is felicitous in a way Anderson could hardly have been aware of; for it was first used by Renaissance artists to describe arabesques painted in the underground ruins, *grotte,* of Nero's "Golden House."

The conception of the grotesque, as actually developed in the stories, is not merely that it is an unwilled affliction but also that it is a mark of a once sentient striving. In his introductory fantasy, **"The Book of the Grotesque,"** Anderson writes: "It was the truths that made the people grotesques . . . the moment one of the people took one of the truths to himself, called it his truth, and tried to live his life by it, he became a grotesque and the truth he embraced a falsehood." There is a sense . . . in which these sentences are at variance with the book's meaning, but they do suggest the significant notion that the grotesques are those who *have* sought "the truths" that disfigure them. By contrast the banal creatures who dominate the town's official life, such as Will Henderson, publisher of the paper for which George Willard works, are not even grotesques: they are simply clods. The grotesques are those whose humanity has been outraged and who to survive in Winesburg have had to suppress their wish to love. Wash Williams becomes a misogynist because his mother-in-law, hoping to reconcile him to his faithless wife, thrusts her into his presence naked; Wing Biddlebaum becomes a recluse because his wish to blend learning with affection is fatally misunderstood. Grotesqueness, then, is not merely the shield of deformity; it is also a remnant of misshapen feeling, what Dr. Reefy in **"Paper Pills"** calls "the sweetness of the twisted apples." (pp. 99-101)

The grotesques rot because they are unused, their energies deprived of outlet, and their instincts curdled in isolation. As Waldo Frank has noticed in his fine study of **Winesburg,** the first three stories in the book suggest this view in a complete theme-statement [see excerpt dated 1941]. The story, **"Hands,"** through several symbolic referents, depicts the loss of creativity in the use of the human body. The second story, **"Paper Pills,"** directly pictures the progressive ineffectuality of human thought, pocketed in paper pellets that no one reads. And the third story, **"Mother,"** relates these two themes to a larger variant: the inability of Elizabeth Willard, **Winesburg**'s mother-figure, to communicate her love to her son. "The form of the mother, frustrate, lonely, at last desperate," Frank writes, "pervades the variations that make the rest of the book: a continuity of variation swelling, swirling into the corners and crannies of the village life; and at last closing in the mother's death, in the loss forever of the $800 which Elizabeth Willard had kept for twenty years to give her son his start away from Winesburg, and in the son's wistful departure." In the rupture of family love and the consequent loss of George Willard's heritage, the theme-statement of the book is completed.

The book's central strand of action, discernible in about half the stories, is the effort of the grotesques to establish intimate relations with George Willard, the young reporter. At night, when they need not fear the mockery of public detection, they hesitantly approach him, almost in supplication, to tell him of their afflictions and perhaps find health in his voice. Instinctively, they sense his moral freshness, finding hope in the fact that he has not yet been calloused by knowledge and time. To some of the grotesques, such as Dr. Reefy and Dr. Parcival, George Willard is the lost son returned, the Daedalus whose apparent innocence and capacity for feeling will redeem Winesburg. To others among the grotesques, such as Tom Foster and Elmer Cowley, he is a reporter-messenger, a small-town Hermes, bringing news of a dispensation which will allow them to re-enter the world of men. But perhaps most fundamentally and subsuming these two visions, he seems to the grotesques a young priest who will renew the forgotten communal rites by which they may again be bound together. To Louise Trunnion he will bring a love that is more than a filching of flesh; to Dr. Parcival the promise to "write the book that I may never get written" in which he will tell all men that "everyone in the world is Christ and they are all crucified"; to the Reverend Curtis Hartman the willingness to understand a vision of God as revealed in the flesh of a naked woman; to Wash Williams the peace that will ease his sense of violation; and to Enoch Robinson the "youthful sadness, young man's sadness, the sadness of a growing boy in a village at the year's end [which can open] the lips of the old man."

As they approach George Willard, the grotesques seek not merely the individual release of a sudden expressive outburst, but also a relation with each other that may restore them to collective harmony. They are distraught communicants in search of a ceremony, a social value, a manner of living, a lost ritual that may, by some means, re-establish a flow and exchange of emotion. Their estrangement is so extreme that they cannot turn to each other though it is each other they really need and secretly want; they turn instead to George Willard who will soon be out of the orbit of their life. (pp. 101-03)

The burden which the grotesques would impose on George Willard is beyond his strength. He is not yet himself a grotesque mainly because he has not yet experienced very deeply, but for the role to which they would assign him he is too absorbed in his own ambition and restlessness. The grotesques see in his difference from them the possibility of saving themselves, but actually it is the barrier to an ultimate companionship. George Willard's adolescent receptivity to the grotesques can only give him the momentary emotional illumination described in that lovely story, **"Sophistication."** . . . For George this illumination is enough, but it is not for the grotesques. They are a moment in his education, he a confirmation of their doom. (p. 104)

When Anderson first sent his **Winesburg** stories to the *Masses, Seven Arts,* and the *Little Review,* he intended each of them to be a self-contained unit, as in fact they may still be regarded. But there was clearly a unifying conception behind all the stories: they were set in the same locale, many of the characters appeared in several stories, and there was a remarkable consistency of mood that carried over from story to story. Consequently, when Anderson prepared them for book publication in 1919, he had only to make a few minor changes, mostly insertions of place and character names as connectives, in order to have a unified book. (p. 106)

Winesburg seems remarkably of a piece. The only stories that do not fit into its pattern are the four-part narrative of Jesse Bentley, a failure in any case, and possibly **"The Untold Lie,"** a beautiful story measuring the distance between middle-age and youth. Of the others only **"Tandy"** is so bad that its omission would help the book. On the other hand, few of the stories read as well in isolation as in the book's context. Except for **"Hands," "The Strength of God," "Paper Pills,"** and **"The Untold Lie,"** they individually lack the dramatic power which the book has as a whole.

Winesburg is an excellently formed piece of fiction, each of its stories following a parabola of movement which abstractly graphs the book's meaning. From a state of feeling rather than a dramatic conflict there develops in one of the grotesques a rising lyrical excitement, usually stimulated to intensity by the presence of George Willard. At the moment before reaching a climax, this excitement is frustrated by a fatal inability at communication and then it rapidly dissolves into its original diffuse base. This structural pattern is sometimes varied by an ironic turn, as in **"Nobody Knows"** and **"A Man of Ideas,"** but in only one story, **"Sophistication,"** is the emotional ascent allowed to move forward without interruption.

But the unity of the book depends on more than the congruous design of its parts. The first three stories of **Winesburg** develop its major theme, which, after several variations, reaches its most abstract version in **"Queer."** The stories following **"Queer"** seem somewhat of a thematic afterthought, though they are necessary for a full disposal of the characters. The one conspicuous disharmony in the book is that the introductory **"Book of the Grotesque"** suggests that the grotesques are victims of their wilful fanaticism, while in the stories themselves grotesqueness is the result of an essentially valid resistance to forces external to its victims.

Through a few simple but extremely effective symbols, the stories are both related to the book's larger meaning and defined in their uniqueness. For the former of these purposes, the most important symbol is that of the room, frequently used to suggest isolation and confinement. Kate Swift is alone in her bedroom, Dr. Reefy in his office, the Reverend Curtis Hartman in his church tower, Enoch Robinson in his fantasy-crowded room. Enoch Robinson's story "is in fact the story of a room almost more than it is the story of a man." The tactful use of this symbol lends *Winesburg* a claustrophobic aura appropriate to its theme.

Most of the stories are further defined by symbols related to their particular meanings. The story of the misogynist Wash Williams begins by rapidly thrusting before the reader an image of "a huge, grotesque kind of monkey, a creature with ugly sagging, hairless skin," which dominates its subsequent action. And more valid than any abstract statement of theme is the symbolic power of that moment in **"The Strength of God"** when the Reverend Curtis Hartman, in order to peek into Kate Swift's bedroom, breaks his church window at precisely the place where the figure of a boy stands "motionless and looking with rapt eyes into the face of Christ." (pp. 106-08)

> Irving Howe, *"The Book of the Grotesque," in his* Sherwood Anderson, *William Sloane Associates, 1951, pp. 91-109.*

SOPHUS KEITH WINTHER (essay date 1959)

[*Winther was a Danish novelist, critic, and educator. In the following excerpt, he discusses loneliness as a common quality of the characters and landscapes in Anderson's fiction.*]

There is a strange quality to the subject matter of all Anderson's stories. It is a quality that is developed by technique. It is easily recognized although not easily described, but technique is not all. The men, women, houses, roads, cornfields, the earth and all that is on it have a haunted quality that is as much a part of its being as the easily described and recognized outward form. It is very characteristic that George Willard should have thought of his mother and the hotel in the same terms "as things defeated and done for. . . . The hotel was a mere ghost of what a hotel should be." . . . His sense of a quality in things that is somehow related to the consciousness of man was always present in Anderson's mind. He describes it in his recollections of childhood; it beat in upon him with a furious and often maddening persistence in adolescence; sometimes it took on forms that soothed the disturbed mind and at other times it drove him near to madness. No matter how these forms presented themselves, the one quality they have in common is loneliness.

Most readers are aware of the way Anderson's characters struggle for recognition imprisoned behind walls, crying out against the unseen powers that have doomed them to loneliness. It is a quality of behavior that envelops the lives of men, and it is a characteristic of the physical world itself as Anderson sees it in most of his stories. It may very well be that loneliness more than any other aspect of life marks the quality that is Anderson.

There is a peculiar and unique atmosphere which clings to every great writer. It is often a quality difficult to define yet as recognizable as is the atmosphere of a landscape. One does not confuse the quality of an Arizona desert with that of the Everglades, nor does one confuse the character of Tolstoy's writing as expressed in Pierre Bezukhov with Dickens' David Copperfield. Each has an identifying aura that no reader can mistake. (pp. 145-46)

Anderson's world cannot be separated from the aura of loneliness that enfolds it. His characters, when they first appear in a story, may seem quite ordinary, even simple and clear. By the time their adventures are completed they have taken on a unifying quality of loneliness. It is their identifying mark, the one aspect of their lives, and their world that is distinctively Andersonian. (p. 146)

In *Winesburg* there is a story entitled **"Loneliness."** It is the story of Enoch Robinson, who could not cope with the world. It is a story that is perhaps most symbolic of the whole collection and the one that expresses best the idea which unites all the stories into a composite view of life. Exile is the price a man pays for imagination and insight into the meaning of life.

Enoch was a simple man, nervous, sensitive, a dreamer. His virtues made him eccentric and drove him away from other men. In his loneliness he achieved for a brief period of time a happiness with the people his imagination created. They were queer people. "There was a woman with a sword in her hand, an old man with a long white beard who went about followed by a dog, a young girl whose stockings were always coming down and hanging over her shoe tops." . . . There were a great many of these imagined people in his room, and they were his answer to the unbearable loneliness of his life. Then a woman came into his room and took possession of him. She drew him into the world until he could stand it no longer. He drove her away, but when she left, all the lovely people of the mind went with her. They went out the door and left him alone. For he had "dismissed the essence of things and played with realities" . . . and when he saw his error and drove her out, the "essence of things" followed her, leaving him only realities. Willard heard "the thin old voice whimpering and complaining. 'I'm alone, all alone here,' said the voice. 'It was warm and friendly in my room but now I'm all alone'." . . . (pp. 148-49)

The symbol of the wall as a barrier that forever imprisons man in the cell of his loneliness occurs so often in Anderson's stories that it may be accepted as typical. His characters are aware of their loneliness. They strive to escape from it, but there is an invisible wall between them and freedom. This wall is of their own making. Its origin, however, is buried so deeply in the past history of mankind that it is more like an inescapable force of nature, a part of God's plan for man, than a thing of his own creation.

There is something a man wants to do. He knows that if he could do it he would escape from the prison of loneliness in which he lives. He must do something to restore a balance between himself and other men. In his inactivity he stands on the brink of madness; yet there is nothing he can do, for the wall is between him and what he would be. (p. 149)

[The] wall as a symbol of loneliness rises everywhere across the paths and roads men follow in the world of Sherwood Anderson. They are barriers, but they are also mirrors that reveal the beautiful and the tortured spirit which is the true measure of man. It is difficult to recall an important character of the hundreds Anderson created who is not stopped in his progress toward some desired goal by a wall that in time reveals his true nature. . . . The typical characteristic of these men and women of Anderson's creation are like Elizabeth Willard. "There was something she sought blindly, passionately, some hidden wonder in life." It was for her a futile quest ending in a great hunger for death. "She personified the figure of death and made him, now a strong black-haired youth running over hills, now a stern quiet man marked and scarred by the business of living." She addressed Death. "'Be patient, lover,' she whispered. 'Keep yourself young and beautiful and be patient'." . . .

Strange symbols of her loneliness had appeared to her many years before her death. She had watched a furious mad contest between Abner Groff the baker and an alley cat.

> Sometimes Abner was so angry that, although the cat had disappeared he hurled sticks and bits of broken glass, and even some tools of his trade about. . . . Once when she was alone, and after watching a prolonged and ineffectual outburst on the part of the baker, Elizabeth Willard put her head down on her long white hands and wept. After that she did not look along the alley-way any more, but tried to forget the contest between the bearded man and the cat. It seemed like a rehearsal of her own life, terrible in its vividness. . . .
>
> (p. 151)

There was in Elizabeth Willard a great capacity for beauty, love and compassion—all the qualities that are a measure of man's humanity. Her harvest was a heartsick loneliness.

The symbols of loneliness in Anderson's stories are universal; they range from an October full moon rising over the yellow cornfields to a man-made road flanked by crooked fence-posts stretching westward into the sunset. The symbol of loneliness is a graveyard illuminated for an instant by a flash of lightning, firebugs like flint sparks along a swampy creek in summer, a man standing with sickness at his heart in the moon-made shadow of a barn, a woman watching a crazed baker throwing milk bottles at a cat, a cat seeking shelter in a printer's office, a man sitting on a patio on a summer night in the South, drinking to forget his pain, a man of God calling for proof, a boy lost in a storm, a woman running into the darkness out of nowhere into nothing, a man picking crumbs off the floor, a woman dying with only a pack of dogs circling in the snow as her companions, a labor leader walking to his death, a saleswoman creeping into a stranger's apartment, a little moron sitting in the midst of extreme poverty watching his aged wife who is tied to a chair, a rum-runner on a lonely road at night, moonlight, starlight, a meadow on a mid-summer afternoon, roads that curve over hills to the horizon, city streets at night, men seeking truth on the highways, in the darkness, in books, in music, in painting, love suddenly stripped of its pretense, the despairing cry of men and animals lost in the wilderness of reality—these and a hundred others are the symbols of the loneliness of men and in the stories of Sherwood Anderson. (pp. 151-52)

Sophus Keith Winther, "The Aura of Loneliness in Sherwood Anderson," in Modern Fiction Studies, *Vol. V, No. 2, Summer, 1959, pp. 145-52.*

MALCOLM COWLEY   (essay date 1960)

[*Cowley has made several valuable contributions to contemporary letters with his editions of important American authors (Nathaniel Hawthorne, Walt Whitman, Ernest Hemingway, William Faulkner, and F. Scott Fitzgerald), his writings as a literary critic for the* New Republic, *and, above all, with his chronicles and criticism of modern American literature. Cowley's literary criticism does not attempt a systematic philosophical view of life and art, nor is it representative of a neatly defined school of critical thought. Rather, Cowley focuses on works that he considers worthy of public appreciation and that he believes personal experience has qualified him to explicate, such as the works of the "lost generation" writers whom he knew. Cowley's undogmatic critical approach is characterized by a willingness to view a work from whatever perspective—social, historical, aesthetic—that the work itself seems to demand for its illumination. In the following excerpt, Cowley discusses the creative and mechanistic processes of Anderson's writing.*]

Anderson made a great noise . . . when he published **Winesburg, Ohio** in 1919. The older critics scolded him, the younger ones praised him, as a man of the changing hour, yet he managed in that early work and others to be relatively timeless. There are moments in American life to which he gave not only the first but the final expression.

He soon became a writer's writer, the only story teller of his generation who left his mark on the style and vision of the generation that followed. Hemingway, Faulkner, Wolfe, Steinbeck, Caldwell, Saroyan, Henry Miller . . . each of these owes an unmistakable debt to Anderson, and their names might stand for dozens of others. (p. 1)

After finding his proper voice at the age of forty, Anderson didn't change as much as other serious writers; perhaps his steadfastness should make us thankful, considering that most American writers change for the worse. He had achieved a quality of emotional rather than factual truth and he preserved it to the end of his career, while doing little to refine, transform, or even understand it. Some of his last stories—by no means all of them—are richer and subtler than the early ones, but they are otherwise not much different or much better.

He was a writer who depended on inspiration, which is to say that he depended on feelings so deeply embedded in his personality that he was unable to direct them. He couldn't say to himself, "I shall produce such and such an effect in a book of such and such a length"; the book had to write or rather speak itself while Anderson listened as if to an inner voice. In his business life he showed a surprising talent for planning and manipulation. "One thing I've known always, instinctively," he told Floyd Dell, "—that's how to handle people, make them do as I please, be what I wanted them to be. I was in business for a long time and the truth is I was a smooth son of a bitch." He never learned to handle words in that smooth fashion. Writing was an activity he assigned to a different level of himself, the one on which he was emotional and unpractical. To reach that level sometimes required a sustained effort of the will. He might start a story like a man running hard to catch a train, but once it was caught he could settle back and let himself be carried—often to the wrong destination.

He knew instinctively whether one of his stories was right or wrong, but he didn't always know why. He could do what writers call "pencil work" on his manuscript, changing a word here and there, but he couldn't tighten the plot, delete weak passages, sharpen the dialogue, give a twist to the ending; if he wanted to improve the story, he had to wait for a return of the mood that had produced it, then write it over from beginning to end. . . . Sometimes, in different books, he published two or three versions of the same story, so that we can see how it grew in his subconscious mind. One characteristic of the sub-conscious is a defective sense of time: in dreams the old man sees himself as a boy, and the events of thirty or forty years may be jumbled together. Time as a logical succession of events was Anderson's greatest difficulty in writing novels or even long stories. He got his tenses confused and carried his heroes ten years forward or back in a single paragraph. His instinct was to present everything together, as in a dream. (pp. 3-4)

His earliest and perhaps his principal teacher was his father, "Irve" Anderson, who used to entertain whole barrooms with tales of his impossible adventures in the Civil War. A great many of the son's best stories, too, were told first in saloons. Later he would become what he called "an almighty scribbler" and would travel about the country with dozens of pencils and reams of paper, the tools of his trade. "I am one," he said, "who loves, like a drunkard his drink, the smell of ink, and the sight of a great pile of white paper that may be scrawled upon always gladdens me"; but his earlier impulse had been to speak, not write, his stories. The best of them retain the language, the pace, and one might even say the gestures of a man talking unhurriedly to his friends.

Within the oral tradition, Anderson had his own picture of what a story should be. He was not interested in telling conventional folk tales, those in which events are more important than emotions. American folk tales usually end with a "snapper"—that is, after starting with the plausible, they progress through the barely possible to the flatly incredible, then wait for a laugh. Magazine fiction used to follow—and much of it still does—a pattern leading to a different sort of snapper, one that calls for a gasp of surprise or relief instead of a guffaw. Anderson broke the pattern by writing stories that not only lacked snap-pers, in most cases, but even had no plots in the usual sense. The tales he told in his Midwestern drawl were not incidents or episodes, they were *moments,* each complete in itself.

The best of the moments in *Winesburg, Ohio,* is called **"The Untold Lie."** The story, which I have to summarize at the risk of spoiling it, is about two farm hands husking corn in a field at dusk. Ray Pearson is small, serious, and middle-aged, the father of half a dozen thin-legged children; Hal Winters is big and young, with the reputation of being a bad one. Suddenly he says to the older man, "I've got Nell Gunther in trouble. I'm telling you, but keep your mouth shut." He puts his two hands on Ray's shoulders and looks down into his eyes. "Well, old daddy," he says, "come on, advise me. Perhaps you've been in the same fix yourself. I know what everyone would say is the right thing to do, but what do you say?" Then the author steps back to look at his characters. "There they stood," he tells us, "in the big empty field with the quiet corn shocks standing in rows behind them and the red and yellow hills in the distance, and from being just two indifferent workmen they had become all alive to each other."

That single moment of aliveness—that epiphany, as Joyce would have called it, that sudden reaching out of two characters through walls of inarticulateness and misunderstanding—is the effect that Anderson is trying to create for his readers or listeners. There is more to the story, of course, but it is chiefly designed to bring the moment into relief. Ray Pearson thinks of his own marriage, to a girl he got into trouble, and turns away from Hal without being able to say the expected words about duty. Later that evening he is seized by a sudden impulse to warn

the younger man against being tricked into bondage. He runs awkwardly across the fields, crying out that children are only the accidents of life. Then he meets Hal and stops, unable to repeat the words that he had shouted into the wind. It is Hal who breaks the silence. "I've already made up my mind," he says, taking Ray by the coat and shaking him. "Nell ain't no fool. . . . I want to marry her. I want to settle down and have kids." Both men laugh, as if they had forgotten what happened in the cornfield. Ray walks away into the darkness, thinking pleasantly now of his children and muttering to himself, "It's just as well. Whatever I told him would have been a lie." There has been a moment in the lives of two men. The moment has passed and the briefly established communion has been broken, yet we feel that each man has revealed his essential being. It is as if a gulf had opened in the level Ohio cornfield and as if, for one moment, a light had shone from the depths, illuminating everything that happened or would ever happen to both of them.

That moment of revelation was the story Anderson told over and over, but without exhausting its freshness, for the story had as many variations as there were faces in his dreams. Behind one face was a moment of defiance; behind another, a moment of resignation (as when Alice Hindman forces herself "to face bravely the fact that many people must live and die alone, even in Winesburg"); behind a third face was a moment of self-discovery; behind a fourth was a moment of deliberate self-delusion. This fourth might have been the face of the author's sister, as he describes her in a chapter of *Sherwood Anderson's Memoirs.* Unlike the other girls she had no beau, and so she went walking with her brother Sherwood, pretending that he was someone else. "It's beautiful, isn't it, James?" she said, looking at the wind ripples that passed in the moon-light over a field of ripening wheat. Then she kissed him and whispered, "Do you love me, James?"—and all her loneliness and flight from reality were summed up in those words. An-derson had that gift for summing up, for pouring a lifetime into a moment. (pp. 5-8)

Those moments at the center of Anderson's often marvelous stories were moments, in general, without a sequel; they existed separately and timelessly. That explains why he couldn't write novels and why, with a single exception, he never even wrote a book in the strict sense of the word. A book should have a structure and a development, whereas for Anderson there was chiefly the flash of lightning that revealed a life without chang-ing it.

The one exception, of course, is *Winesburg, Ohio,* and that became a true book for several reasons: because it was con-ceived as a whole, because Anderson had found a subject that released his buried emotions, and because most of the book was written in what was almost a single burst of inspiration, so that it gathered force as it went along. (p. 11)

All the stories were written rapidly, with little need for revision, each of them being, as Anderson said, "an idea grasped whole as one would pick an apple in an orchard." He was dealing with material that was both fresh and familiar. The town of Winesburg was based on his memories of Clyde, Ohio, where he had spent most of his boyhood and where his mother had died at the same age as the hero's mother. The hero, George Willard, was the author in his late adolescence, and the other characters were either remembered from Clyde or else, in many cases, suggested by faces glimpsed in the Chicago streets. Each face revealed a moment, a mood, or a secret that lay deep in

Anderson's life and for which he was finding the right words at last.

As the book went forward, more and more of the faces—as well as more streets, buildings, trades, and landscapes—were carried from one story to another, with the result that Winesburg itself acquired a physical and corporate life. Counting the four parts of **"Godliness,"** each complete in itself, there would be twenty-five stories or chapters in all. None of them taken separately—not even **"Hands"** or **"The Untold Lie"**—is as effective as the best of Anderson's later work, but each of them contributes to all the others, as the stories in later volumes are not expected to do. There was a delay of some months before the last three chapters—**"Death,"** **"Sophistication,"** and **"Departure"**—were written with the obvious intention of rounding out the book. First George Willard is released from Winesburg by the death of his mother; then, in **"Sophistication,"** he learns how it feels to be a grown man; then finally he leaves for the city on the early-morning train, and everything recedes as into a framed picture. "When he aroused himself and looked out of the car window," Anderson says, "the town of Winesburg had disappeared and his life there had become but a background on which to paint the dreams of his manhood."

In structure the book lies midway between the novel proper and the mere collection of stories. Like several famous books by more recent authors, all early readers of Anderson—like Faulkner's *The Unvanquished* and *Go Down, Moses*, like Steinbeck's *Tortilla Flat* and *The Pastures of Heaven*, like Caldwell's *Georgia Boy*—it is a cycle of stories with several unifying elements, including a single background, a prevailing tone, and a central character. These elements can be found in all the cycles, but the best of them also have an underlying plot that is advanced or enriched by each of the stories. In *Winesburg* the underlying plot or fable, though hard to recognize, is unmistakably present, and I think it might be summarized as follows:

George Willard is growing up in a friendly town full of solitary persons; the author calls them "grotesques." Their lives have been distorted not, as Anderson tells us in his prologue, by their each having seized upon a single truth, but rather by their inability to express themselves. Since they cannot truly communicate with others, they have all become emotional cripples. Most of the grotesques are attracted one by one to George Willard; they feel that he might be able to help them. In those moments of truth that Anderson loves to describe, they try to explain themselves to George, believing that he alone in Winesburg has an instinct for finding the right words and using them honestly. They urge him to preserve and develop his gift. "You must not become a mere peddler of words," Kate Swift the teacher insists, taking hold of his shoulders. "The thing to learn is to know what people are thinking about, not what they say." Dr. Parcival tells him, "If something happens perhaps you will be able to write the book I may never get written." All the grotesques hope that George Willard will some day speak what is in their hearts and thus re-establish their connection with mankind. George is too young to understand them at the time, but the book ends with what seems to be the promise that, after leaving Winesburg, he will become the voice of inarticulate men and women in all the forgotten towns.

If the promise is truly implied, and if Anderson felt he was keeping it when writing **"Hands"** and the stories that followed, then *Winesburg, Ohio* is far from the pessimistic or destructive or morbidly sexual work it was one attacked for being. Instead it is a work of love, an attempt to break down the walls that divide one person from another, and also, in its own fashion, a celebration of small-town life in the lost days of good will and innocence. (pp. 11-15)

Malcolm Cowley, in an introduction to Winesburg, Ohio *by Sherwood Anderson, revised edition, The Viking Press, 1960, pp. 1-15.*

REX BURBANK   (essay date 1964)

[*An American critic and scholar, Burbank has written studies of Thornton Wilder, Jane Austen, and early American literature. In the following excerpt from his* Sherwood Anderson, *Burbank discusses the significance of the unconventional narrative sequence used in* Winesburg, Ohio.]

In 1914, the famous exhibition of post-Impressionist paintings was held in the Chicago Armory, where Anderson went . . . on afternoons to see the works of Cezanne, Van Gogh, Gaugin, and others among the "French moderns." Like such "Impressionists" as Monet, Renoir, and Degas before them, these painters portrayed the impressions of experience upon the consciousness of the artist, or of an observer with whom the artist identified himself, rather than the external appearances of events and objects. But they went even beyond the Impressionists in attempting to convey not only the subjective experience of the artist or observer but the abstract structure beneath natural forms. (pp. 61-2)

Van Gogh deliberately distorted his figures, used violent splashes of color, and swirled his brush across his canvasses to signify his own tumultuous feelings. Gauguin, the one-time stockbroker who, like Anderson abandoned business for art, drew his Tahitian natives with bold colors restrained by simple but clear lines, thereby synthesizing complex and powerful inner feelings with external forms.

Anderson's interest in painting at this time was more than casual: he himself painted. . . . [The] techniques of composition in Impressionist and post-Impressionist art . . . offered possibilities in form and texture for fiction that were agreeable to his own views of life and art. More specifically, the new art suggested the shaping of a narrative sequence in accordance with the flow of feelings and thoughts, or impressions, of the narrator rather than according to time: according to psychological instead of chronological time. This meant that form would develop in two ways: first, from within the narrative (as Van Gogh saw nature's form as essentially an inner thing), which required that the traditional "plot" sequence of action (Anderson particularly despised the highly plotted stories of O. Henry) would be abandoned for a form that moves with the mind and feelings; and, second, because both mind and feelings operate in a continuum of time, following moods, attitudes, or ideas rather than a chronological order, form would grow by means of a series of disconnected images which are thematically and symbolically related and coalesce like the paintings of the French impressionists. (p. 62)

Though he deeply admired Dreiser (who himself had broken away from the neatly plotted story) for the uncompromising honesty with which he drew his characters, Anderson moved away from Dreiser's graceless journalistic style and from his brand of stark Naturalism and surface realism in favor of techniques that permitted him to penetrate the external forces of Naturalistic fiction, to bypass the ponderous collection of external social facts, and to get to the feelings and the irrational impulses of his characters, their innermost struggles.

The style and structural techniques of Impressionism and Symbolism lent themselves admirably to these aims, and so did the stylistic practices of Gertrude Stein, whose *Tender Buttons* and *Three Lives* Anderson read . . . in 1914. . . . In his **Memoirs** he declared that, through Stein, he adopted the conscious stylistic intention of capturing the color and cadence of his own Midwestern speech, to lay word against word "in just a certain way" in order to convey the feelings (as distinguished from the facts) of life by means of "a kind of word color, a march of simple words, simple sentence structure."

The influence of the post-Impressionists and of Gertrude Stein may best be demonstrated by perusal of **"Hands,"** one of the best tales in **Winesburg,** in which Anderson's technique of constructing the tales around epiphanies can be seen in the portrayal of Wing Biddlebaum, whose deeply creative nature has been thwarted and perverted, through a central image of hands whose restless, bird-like activities expend themselves in random and trivial actions. The incidents of the story are clustered about this image, intensifying it and in turn being unified by it. As the incidents charge the image with meaning, the narrative proceeds to a climactic epiphany which reveals Biddlebaum's defeat to be that of the innermost self.

The narrative opens with an objective, scenically rendered paragraph showing Biddlebaum's alienation from the town and suggesting a relationship between his alienation and his "nervous little hands." It then moves in succeeding paragraphs to a generalized exposition of his more intimate acquaintance with George Willard and Willard's curiosity about the hands. Another short-view scene follows, revealing the connection between Biddlebaum's thwarted, imaginative nature and his fear of his hands. Establishment of Biddlebaum's fear shifts the narrative to a review of the events that caused him to flee from Pennsylvania to become a recluse in Winesburg. In that review we see that his hands were his means of expressing love and that the nature of this love was creative, for it found its outlet in communicating to schoolboys, through his gentle caresses, his own tendency to dream. But his caresses were interpreted as homosexuality by stupid, insensitive townspeople, and he was driven from the town. In Winesburg, he has withdrawn from the lives of others; and, unable to find creative outlet for his imaginative life, he has become a human fragment, a grotesque. The hands change from image to symbol as the narrative progresses and the themes of alienation, fear, love, and shame become in turn associated with them; and as the symbol gathers its meanings the narrative builds toward the final symbolic act, the epiphany. The epiphany occurs after Willard leaves, and the full ironic meaning of Biddlebaum's life is felt in the discrepancy between his religious posture, as he kneels, and the meaningless drumming of his fingers as they pluck bread crumbs from the floor: Biddlebaum is a kind of defeated, strangely perverted priest of love.

The narrative structure thus follows the course of the omniscient author's mind as he explores various times in the past, probes into his characters' minds, relates bits of descriptive detail, and cites scraps of dialogue—all of which add up to the final symbolic scene in which Biddlebaum's defeat is seen in the fullness of its nature. As in the best stories of Chekhov and of Crane—Anderson's Impressionistic forebear—the final scene of **"Hands"** is anticlimactic, for nothing happens to Biddlebaum. If the story has a "climax," it comes at the point—about half way through—in which Biddlebaum urges Willard to leave Winesburg. By deliberately violating a straight time sequence, Anderson avoids the traditional, and often artificial, plot of clear-cut cause and effect actions culminating in a decisive action, and at the same time he gains an almost tragic irony. Nothing in Biddlebaum's life can be climactic any more. His life is characterized by disillusionment, futility, and defeat; and both the anticlimactic structure and the muted tone of reminiscence support the vision of an inner life quietly but desperately submerged, and of a static, imprisoned external life. The stasis of his life, the impasse between social repression and need for expression, can be seen in the following paragraph, in which the feeling of Biddlebaum's seething but frustrated passions is rendered by what Gertrude Stein approvingly termed "clear and passionate" sentences: sentences with simple diction and structure whose passion is conveyed by the contradictory effects of emotional balance and antithesis. We should notice how the terms *beat, action, desire, sought,* and *pounding* are subdued and counterpointed by *comfortable* and *ease:* "When he talked to George Willard, Wing Biddlebaum closed his fists and beat with them upon a table or on the walls of his house. The action made him more comfortable. If the desire to talk came to him when the two were walking in the fields, he sought out a stump or the top board of a fence and with his hands pounding busily talked with renewed ease."

Not all the tales in **Winesburg** are so felicitously constructed and executed as **"Hands,"** but the best of them, like the book as a whole, convey the feeling of isolation, loneliness, and defeat through grotesque characters. Though the tales are self-contained and complete in themselves and may be read individually with enjoyment, they gain an added and very important dimension when read consecutively as episodes in a single narrative; for **Winesburg** as a whole presents a unified portrayal of the growth to maturity and consciousness of young George Willard, who develops as the symbol of the "whole" man against whom the grotesques stand as fragments.

Like Dickens' *David Copperfield,* Meredith's *The Egoist,* and Joyce's *Portrait of the Artist as a Young Man,* **Winesburg** is—in addition to being a collection of tales—a *bildungsroman,* a story of a boy growing to manhood and becoming involved in the perplexing world of adults. Though he does not appear in all the tales, Willard shares importance in the narrative with the grotesques, to whom he is the symbolic counterpoint. (pp. 63-6)

In George Willard, Anderson presents the *making* of an artist of life. Willard wants to become a writer, but before he can do so he must serve his apprenticeship to life itself. In his development we see Anderson's implied belief that the solution to the "terrifying disorder" of life, the alternative to grotesqueness, is the kind of absorption of other lives that is seen in George and in the old man in the prologue. While the artist is the archetype of the psychologically and socially liberated person, liberation is not confined to the artist; for Willard achieves freedom before he becomes a writer, and the old writer never writes his book about the grotesques.

By contrast, the grotesques are so because for one reason or another they have (willfully or because of circumstances they cannot control) become isolated from others and thus closed off from the full range of human experience. Where the old writer has accepted isolation and opened his mind and imagination to the truth of all human experience, they have attempted to embrace a single truth to live by (often, because their alternatives are limited, they have *had* to), thereby closing off other possibilities of experience and compounding their loneliness and becoming enslaved by it. The writer himself is saved by the "young thing" inside him; his imaginative receptiveness to all human feelings. (pp. 67-8)

The structural form of the narrative from prologue to epilogue is psychological and episodic rather than linear; the tales are built about those moments of consciousness or revelation instead of following a simple sequence of time or causality. For Willard, those moments follow a pattern of progression toward increasing consciousness as he absorbs the experiences of the grotesques. On the other hand, these symbolic moments reveal the psychic limitations, confinement, or defeat of the grotesques whose lives are in a state of arrest. The narrator emphasizes in **"The Book of the Grotesque"** that the grotesques are not all horrible. Joe Welling in **"A Man of Ideas"** is comical; Dr. Reefy, in **"Paper Pills"** and in **"Death,"** is a man of insight and understanding; Louise Trunnion, in **"Nobody Knows,"** is simply pathetic.

All, however, are characterized by various types of psychic unfulfillment or limitation owing in part to the failure of their environment to provide them with opportunities for a rich variety of experience and in part to their own inability or reluctance to accept or understand the facts of isolation and loneliness. The nature of their psychic unfulfillment is revealed in the tales by epiphanies. Their development may roughly be compared to the action of a fountain which, fixed at its base and therefore moving toward nothing, suddenly overflows—as the pressure within builds up—and shows what has remained hidden from view. Just as a fountain retains the contents that have overflowed and returns them to their source, so the briefly revealed inner lives of the grotesques return unchanged to their imprisonment or defeat.

Like Joyce's Stephen Daedelus, Willard is the nascent artist serving his apprenticeship to life; but the important fact about him is that, while he is subject to the same environmental restrictions as the grotesques, he grows toward maturity and ultimately frees himself from Winesburg, while the grotesques do not. Like McPherson and McGregor of *Windy* and of *Marching Men*, Willard is a prototype of the man who is liberated from the confinement of a narrow and oppressive environment. But he differs from those earlier heroes in that he leaves at a point in his life when he has gained an intense love for the people of the town of his birth and youth, and his departure is prompted not by rejection of the town and hope for success but by a determination to broaden the range of his imaginative experience. (pp. 68-9)

Willard grows from passive observer of life to active partcipant, from aimlessly curious boy to intensely conscious adult. (p. 69)

At the death of Elizabeth Willard in **"Death,"** his adolescent resentment at the inconvenience caused by his mother's death in keeping him from seeing Helen White gives way to realization of the finality of death and to consciousness of the tragic beauty his mother represented. His full awareness of life's paradoxes comes in **"Sophistication,"** when he becomes conscious of the "limitations of life" and of "his own insignificance in the scheme of existence" while at the same time he "loves life so intensely that tears come into his eyes."

With this epiphany, which is also the climax of the book, Willard "crosses the line into manhood" as "voices outside of himself whisper a message concerning the limitations of life," and as consciousness of the condition of man's isolation and loneliness is followed by his beginning "to think of the people in the town where he had always lived with something like reverence." . . . He is now able to separate closely related

and confused, overlapping feelings; to distinguish passion from compassion, for instance. . . . (p. 71)

George Willard achieves maturity when he realizes and accepts loneliness as the essential human condition and understands the value of all human suffering. Understanding comes, paradoxically, only when he has emancipated himself from the Winesburg influence. . . . [He] can understand that all men are alone with their feelings and that only through sympathy and compassion toward others do those feelings have any meaning; or, to put it another way, those feelings are the only really meaningful things in life. The grotesques are people whose instinctive desires, aspirations, and deepest emotions have no meaning because they have no "other" who will impose a meaning upon them; thus they are drawn to the receptive, aspiring writer Willard, who accepts and will ultimately give meaningful expression to their feelings, or, in the case of Dr. Reefy and George's mother, to each other.

Those grotesques who are the most sensitive and articulate find their desires and aspirations thwarted by a repressive conventionalism that offers little opportunity for fruitful human relationships. (pp. 71-2)

In the portrayal of all these defeated people a vision of American small-town life emerges in which we see a society that has no cultural framework from which to draw common ex-

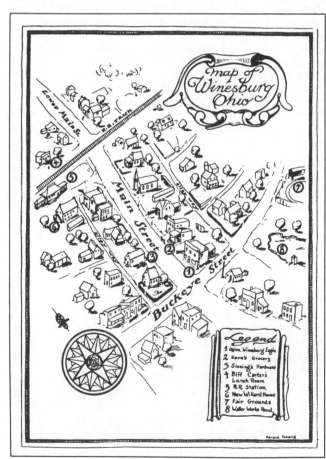

Map of Winesburg that appeared as the frontispiece of Winesburg, Ohio, *by Sherwood Anderson. Copyright 1919 by B. W. Huebsch. Copyright renewed 1947 by Eleanor Copehaver Anderson. Reprinted by permission of Viking Penguin Inc. and The Newberry Library, Chicago.*

periences; no code of manners by which to initiate, guide, and sustain meaningful relationships among individuals; no art to provide a communion of shared feeling and thought; and no established traditions by which to direct and balance their lives. They live in the midst of cultural failure.

The theme of cultural failure rises by suggestion from background images of decay and decomposition. The town is a wasteland ruled by dull, conventional people. Its religion has deteriorated into an empty moralism; its people have lost their contact with the soil. While Anderson uses his images sparingly, interweaving them subtly with narrative and dialogue, they evoke an atmosphere of desolation which impinges with crushing effect upon the lives of the grotesques; and, as the images recur, they become symbolic of a culture which, as Waldo Frank has said, has reached the final stages of deterioration. Rubbish and broken glass clutter the alleys and streets and of the village. . . . Dr. Reefy's office is located off a "dark hallway filled with rubbish"; Belle Carpenter lives in a "gloomy old house" in which the "rusty tin eaves-trough had slipped from its fastenings . . . and when the wind blew it beat against the roof of a small shed, making a dismal drumming noise that sometimes persisted all through the night"; and Wing Biddlebaum's small frame house offers a view of a "half decayed veranda." (pp. 73-4)

[Though] the characters who embody convention are shadowy or fragmentary, their power over the lives of the grotesques is felt as an intangible but decisive, sinister influence. They present a background of moral decay, calculation and artifice, of a rampant egoistic individualism. George Willard's father (**"Mother"**) and John Hardy (**"Surrender"**) embrace the religion of success; Wash Williams' mother-in-law and Helen White's mother (**"Sophistication"**) exploit sex with varying degrees of crudity and subtlety to draw men to their daughters. Collectively, the citizens of Winesburg torture Wing Biddlebaum with shouts of deprecation. The Hardy sisters crush the sensitive Louise Bentley with hypocritical and degrading conventional courtship rites characterized by crafty use of sex.

In such an atmosphere the grotesques typically isolate themselves in rooms as barren of joy as the town itself, emerging— often at night—to walk alone or with George Willard, in whom they confide. In the darkness or within their rooms, their secret inner lives "show forth" in an epiphany, an outburst of emotion, or in a casual, unguarded remark and reveal the full extent of their psychic defeat. (pp. 74-5)

The point of view of the omniscient author—of the mature George Willard, recalling tenderly but with detachment of time and place his small-town youth—softens the tone; it permits the town and the grotesques to emerge as objects of compassion rather than of attack, as they are in Master's' *Spoon River* and in Lewis' *Main Street*. Tone and point of view thus effectively and almost imperceptibly become thematic in themselves—in the manner of lyric poetry.

While Anderson later wrote individual tales that are superior to the stories in *Winesburg,* he never again wrote a long work that combines with such felicity the penetrating insights into the impoverished inner lives of broken, sensitive people; the sustained, pervasive mood of social degeneration; and the quiet, unforced portrayal of a hero liberating himself from the confines of his limited environment as *Winesburg* does. It is his most complete and authentic plea for freedom of expression of the inner life and for sympathetic receptivity to the needs of the human heart. Written at the dawn of an era of revolt against American provincialism and against the romanticized stories of idyllic and virtuous village life, it has outlasted both the nostalgic, sentimental romances and most of the iconoclastic satires about village life written before and since, precisely because it goes well beyond both of those oversimplified extremes to acknowledge both the worth and the tragic limitations of life in the small Midwestern towns and—by easy geographical extension—of all human life. (p. 77)

Rex Burbank, in his Sherwood Anderson, *Twayne Publishers, Inc., 1964, 159 p.*

TONY TANNER   (essay date 1965)

[*Tanner is an American critic and editor whose works include critical studies of the works of Saul Bellow and Joseph Conrad. In the following excerpt, he argues that Anderson's narrative style in* Winesburg, Ohio *reflects the fragmentary way in which reality is perceived.*]

Winesburg, Ohio, published in 1919, is undoubtedly Anderson's most important work and deserves special attention as it was also his most influential work. I want now to try and indicate the particular qualities in Anderson's writing. Perhaps the first thing that strikes one about Anderson's prose is the constant inclusion of seemingly gratuitous details. For instance in the story about Doctor Parcival we are told that he dines at Biff Carter's lunch room. The next sentence reads: "In the summer the lunch room was filled with flies and Biff Carter's white apron was more dirty than his floor." And then Biff Carter and his lunch room disappear out of the story for ever. Again, when George Willard takes out Louise Trunnion for a walk the account of his fumbling efforts with her is interrupted by this description of a brick sidewalk: "Some of the bricks were missing and the sidewalk was rough and irregular." Why tell us? They don't trip on the sidewalk or make love on its rough surface: it is just that as the author's eye goes over the scene it includes many of the surrounding facts. There is no apparent principle of selection and omission at work. Minor characters suddenly receive a moment of unrelated scrutiny. "When he laughed he scratched his left elbow with his right hand. The sleeve of his coat was almost worn through from the habit." That is Edward King who plays no part in the story at all. Such details would be capricious interruption if Anderson was working on a specific theme or up to a discernible dramatic crisis. But he is not. For him there aren't any. No one detail is more or less important than another: all merit attention. The eye is deliberately *not* informed by any selective modes of thinking. It sees without thinking, or perhaps we could fairly say, "it sees without looking."

The manner in which Anderson starts and ends a story is also significant:

> There were always three or four old people sitting on the front porch of the house or puttering about the garden of the Bentley farm. Three of the old people were women and sisters to Jesse. They were a colorless, soft-voiced lot. Then there was a silent old man with thin white hair who was Jesse's uncle.

> The farmhouse was built of wood, a board outercovering over a framework of logs.

Facts are suddenly thrust before us with no prior introduction. They present themselves to us insisting on their individual importance, an importance always left unexplained, or rather an importance which they are left to explain for themselves. They are never differentiated or appraised. Each fact—about the uncle, about the farmhouse—is separate and of equal importance: there are no connectives but rather a series of isolated impressions. We have the illusion not of Anderson bringing us the world, but of the world appearing to us in its own unpremeditated manner. Or put it this way: we are given the world seen in the simplest way and not filtered through any exegetical intelligence. The stories take us suddenly into an endless continuum. "Until she was seven years old she lived in an old unpainted house on an unused road that led off Trunnion Pike." That is how one story starts. Who is "she"? asks the reader who is used to the usual elaborate scene setting of the conventional novel. It doesn't matter, says Anderson. Wherever you turn your eye there are things going on: to try and make more out of the chaos of experience than that is to falsify it. Anderson does not bring us a life; he brings us a moment. It is a fragmentary view of life, and it is clear that Anderson's approach can only lead to fragmentation. His vision permits of no plot developments or notable dramatic crises: there are no gestures of summarizing significance, nor do the individual details accumulate to the point of revealing larger meanings. In **"The Philosopher"** we read, "the tales that Doctor Parcival told George Willard began nowhere and ended nowhere," and the same thing could be said of Anderson's tales. Things end, when they do, with a sort of dry abruptness: there is never a feeling of something consummated. "In the end she married a man who bought and sold real estate and was contented enough." There is almost a hard dead-pan irony of understatement in this manner of writing. Life tapers off as meaninglessly as this sentence: there are no true endings, only pointless cessations.

Often a paragraph containing or referring to a disaster will end with some comparatively minor and seemingly arbitrary detail of physical description. Unwilling to distribute emphases, intent on confronting only the facts, Anderson's prose has the effect of neutralizing experience: life's intensities come to us muted, potentially dramatic factors appear benumbed. Anderson's refusal to push big emotions and grand climaxes was a real achievement and his almost positivistic attempt to give us only perceived facts or verifiable factors reveals a commendable effort of honesty. At his best he does sometimes achieve that which Joyce said short stories should aim at—an epiphany. Sometimes his "day of facts" is a "day of diamonds," though where Emerson's diamonds sparkled of divinity, Anderson's are content to radiate some human significance. But all too often his material is rendered inert and inactive by the way it is assembled, the order in which it appears. Once again we see the problem of form confronting a writer who adopts the naive wondering vision in an effort to rediscover reality. As Anderson said, his form will be "broken," because life comes to the naive eye unarranged. His difficulty is to find some organizing principle of selection. The book has no insistent time sequence, no dramatic development, no increasing complexity, no knotting and unravelling. Things and people do not develop because they do not inter-mix. (The vague theme of George Willard growing up scarcely binds the book together.) What Anderson aims at is the moment, the mood; something glimpsed rather than something pursued; a fragment arrested rather than life's exfoliating growth. Hence the endlessly localized assembling of facts around separate and barely related nuclei, which produces that curiously stylized and stilted panorama which is the world of this book. It is indeed the world of all his books since his full length novels attempt but fail to transcend his short story method of sudden concentration on an all but static instant.

Consider for a moment the tone of [this passage:] . . .

> Once he killed a dog with a stick. The dog
> belonged to Win Pawsey, the shoe merchant,
> and stood on the sidewalk wagging its tail. Tom
> King killed it with one blow. He was arrested
> and paid a fine of ten dollars.

(pp. 208-10)

The silences between the clean staccato sentences seem at times to be as full of feeling as the silences in a Chekhov play. And yet no matter how welcome is the absence of an intrusive bullying authorial rhetoric, it must be said that it is dangerous for any writer to rely on the unsaid as much as Anderson seems to do in this book. Sometimes indeed, like Hemingway at his best, he avoids comment where comment would be superfluous: but at other times he avoids implying any sort of evaluation or reaction at all. If it is a prose which is very humane in its interest in ordinary human doings, it is also a prose which seems helpless to bring any significant light to bear on them. One sometimes has the feeling that Anderson never got over the staggering fact that there was a material visible world at all, and that he never took more than "the first step." And if that is true we should not forget that such an attitude and response would have earned Emerson's theoretic approval.

It is perhaps this refusal to comment on, to take any command of, his material that gives Anderson's prose its oddly stylized effect. (pp. 211-12)

Winesburg, Ohio is intended as a series of truths rather than a series of stories: there is no dramatic interweaving properly speaking, merely the careful annotation of incidents which reveals their "truth" without reference to any larger scheme of things and detached from any significant causal temporal sequence. From the clearly delineated and minutely observed detail Anderson will suddenly leap to the most vaporous mystical generalization about life, all life everywhere. And in between these two extremes there is nothing: no complex moral attitude towards life, no adjudicating subtleties, no finely drawn discriminations, no nuanced assessment of conduct, no embodied values. (pp. 213-14)

Anderson's writing seldom progresses beyond a deliberately naive reduction of experience to its simplest particulars, yet the stoical clippedness of utterance often conceals a vast amount of barely controlled emotionalism. It should not be necessary to add that this is not to say that these feelings are insincere. Anderson's compassion is a real and moving thing: the point is that he develops no satisfying method of injecting it into his style, of letting it tactfully inform and direct his prose. Anderson's compassion remains vague because it is divorced from perceptive judgement: as the great writers reveal, it is possible, indeed preferable, to keep the assessing faculties operative even when the sympathetic faculties are most engaged. Otherwise compassion precludes understanding, and we need to achieve understanding if our compassion is to develop into a valuable and enduring emotion. Anderson's compassion hovers over his material like a cloud, always threatening to burst and drench it in a lachrymose downpour. His failures are never failures of sympathy, but rather failures of insight and utterance. Certainly we should bear in mind the problem he set himself and which we noted at the start of the chapter: how to write about a certain sort of people in a certain sort of locale without having recourse to artistic schemata which will distort or devalue them. Yet is

Anderson's the only way in which an artist can do justice to crude, unsophisticated, inarticulate sections of the community? Think what Tolstoy could make of a farmer or peasant, to say nothing of what Cézanne could make of their faces. The short-comings of Anderson's writing are a function of his chosen strategy: he sees some things freshly, clearly honestly. But he sees only "little things," fragments of experience which catch the naive and wondering eye. Ironically enough it is finally his writing which undervalues the people and places he writes about, even though he addresses himself to them with such sympathy, because it is a kind of writing which, though it can make a new and welcome effort of attention, cannot make the necessary effort of penetration. (pp. 216-17)

> Tony Tanner, "Sherwood Anderson's Little Things,"
> in his The Reign of Wonder: Naivety and Reality in
> American Literature, *Cambridge at the University
> Press, 1965, pp. 205-27.*

JAMES M. MELLARD (essay date 1968)

[*Mellard is an American scholar and critic concerned with genre theory, theory of fictional modes, myth criticism, and history. In the following excerpt, he distinguishes four distinct narrative forms in the stories in* Winesburg, Ohio.]

Almost all its critics have assumed that the episodes of *Winesburg, Ohio,* reveal only one narrative form. For each critic, then, one episode can serve as a "model" for all the others. But a simple comparison will show that each episode is not identical with every other. Clearly, **"Hands"** does not have the same form as **"Mother,"** **"Mother"** that of **"Godliness,"** nor **"Godliness"** that of **"Nobody Knows,"** and it is thus as inaccurate to say that each tale has the same form as to say that the form of each is unique. Actually, *Winesburg* has four rather distinct narrative forms: a form (1) that focuses on a central symbol, (2) that portrays a character type, (3) that delineates a quality, state, or "truth," and (4) that depicts a simple plot development. Easily identified by their titles, these four narrative types may be conveniently and descriptively labeled symbolic, emblematic, and thematic stories and stories of incident.

The five symbolic stories are **"The Book of the Grotesque,"** **"Hands,"** **"Paper Pills,"** **"Tandy,"** and **"Drink."** Three characteristics distinguish these episodes from the other types: each focuses on a central symbol, each is essentially epiphanic, and each presents an *affirmative* value. Anderson's intention to develop a single dominant symbol is signaled, of course, in the titles. In the prologue, **"The Book of the Grotesque,"** the book is offered not only as the controlling image for the tale but also, perhaps, as a controlling image for the whole of *Winesburg, Ohio,* for Anderson originally intended to name the book *The Book of the Grotesque.* (p. 1304)

What it is exactly, or even approximately, that these symbols mean is not always so immediately obvious. Consequently, the movement of the narrative in each case is toward a concluding "epiphany," a "showing forth" for the reader through dialogue, exposition, or description. The epiphany in **"The Book of the Grotesque,"** truly important to *Winesburg, Ohio,* involves the term "grotesque": people who are "grotesques" are not necessarily "horrible," some being "amusing," "beautiful," and even, like the old carpenter, "understandable and lovable." In **"Hands,"** the significant revelation for the reader comes at the very end of the episode in Anderson's description of Wing Biddlebaum's picking up bread crumbs

from the floor: "In the dense blotch of light beneath the table, the kneeling figure looked like a priest engaged in some service of his church. The nervous expressive fingers, flashing in and out of the light, might well have been mistaken for the fingers of the devotee going swiftly through decade after decade of his rosary." . . . In this image we see clearly the nature of Wing's gift, the tragic irony of his situation, and the meaning of his hands in their divine expression of love and faith. The much less intense, but no less important epiphany for the reader in **"Paper Pills,"** the story of the tall dark girl and Doctor Reefy, occurs in the objective narration of its conclusion:

> In the fall after the beginning of her acquaint-
> anceship with him she married Doctor Reefy
> and in the following spring she died. During
> the winter he read to her all of the odds and
> ends of thoughts he had scribbled on the bits
> of paper. After he had read them he laughed
> and stuffed them away in his pockets to become
> round hard balls. . . .

Because the detail of the girl's untimely death is subordinated to the manifest happiness of the few months she and Doctor Reefy spent together, we realize that Reefy, like the old writer of the prologue, manages to avoid becoming a grotesque because he never allows the "thoughts," beautiful in themselves, to become distorting "truths." Consequently, for the tall dark girl, Doctor Reefy has the essential sweetness of the "twisted little apples," and her own life, brief as it is, achieves that same sweetness—a sweetness unattainable with the young men who have their "truths" of "passion," "virginity," and "lust." The meaning of **"Tandy"** is less difficult to perceive than that of either **"Hands"** or **"Paper Pills,"** for the stranger who bestows the name on the child also explain what it signifies: "It is the quality of being strong to be loved" . . . , he tells the little girl, who later insists, "I want to be Tandy. I want to be Tandy. I want to be Tandy Hard," and cries "as though her young strength were not enough to bear the vision the words of the drunkard had brought to her." . . . (pp. 1304-05)

Though it is seldom given much attention, **"Drink"** may offer the most complex epiphany among these stories, for it integrates elements from all the other four. In each of the other symbolic stories particular emphasis is given to "dreams"— dreams in sleep, of aspiration or vision, or of the creative imagination: the old writer "had a dream that was not a dream" and "figures began to appear before his yes" . . . ; Wing got into difficulty as a young man because he tried "to carry a dream into . . . young minds. . . . Under the caress of his hands doubt and disbelief went out of the minds of the boys and they began also to dream." . . . And he tells George Willard, "You have the inclination to be alone and to dream and you are afraid of dreams." . . . The tall dark girl in **"Paper Pills"** dreams three times before she becomes pregnant that one of her lovers "had bitten into her body and that his jaws were dripping." . . . And the drunken stranger in **"Tandy"** says, "I made up the name when I was a true dreamer and before my body became vile." . . . The dream usually has to do with a character's moment of insight and understanding. Thus in Tom Foster's story, "drink" becomes a means, along with nature itself, for Tom's achieving the kind of vision offered to others in more conventional dreams. In effect, getting drunk is equivalent to an initiatory loss of innocence and gaining of knowledge for Tom Foster, who had "never asserted himself" and who had always been "unmoved and strangely unaffected" by the pain and lust and squalor of the lives around him. After his experience with drink, however, Tom tries to convey his vision to George Willard:

> "It was like making love, that's what I mean," he explained. "Don't you see how it is? It hurt me to do what I did and made everything strange. That's why I did it. I'm glad, too. It taught me something, that's it, that's what I wanted. Don't you understand? I wanted to learn things, you see. That's why I did it." . . .

For the reader, the epiphany is not quite the same as for Tom, for we recognize that Tom Foster, simple as he is, represents as much as the old writer, Wing Biddlebaum, Doctor Reefy, or the drunken stranger Anderson's idea of the artistic consciousness. Thus we perceive that for Tom Foster, as for Anderson, the illumination of life is mystical and intuitive, stimulating and painful, so what better symbol for it than the dream or vision enhanced by *drink*?

These stories are also quite closely related to each other in ways besides their focus on a major symbol and their epiphanic moments. There are, for example, the interlocking motifs of "grotesques," "thoughts," "truths," and "dreams." But the most important feature, and one which emphatically distinguishes this particular narrative form from the others, is its development of *affirmative*, if not always triumphant, values. **"The Book of the Grotesque,"** a philosophic prolegomenon to the entire work, shows us Anderson's conception of the proper attitude toward "truth." . . . **"Paper Pills"** portrays a character, Doctor Reefy, who actually achieves the proper attitude toward thought and truth, and **"Hands"** develops Anderson's major symbol (hands) for effective communication, both verbal and non-verbal, and a theme of non-sexual love. That it requires strength both to love and be loved is the theme suggested in **"Tandy."** Finally, **"Drink"** brings together most of these themes in its showing that Tom Foster, who "plays" with "thoughts" and images like a poet, has finally gained an intelligible vision of life, experienced something like love in his inebriate's dream, and even attempted to get involved with another (George Willard) to whom he tries to communicate his revelation. Because these symbolic episodes present the positive side of Sherwood Anderson's vision of life, they are the real core of *Winesburg, Ohio*. That such is the case is borne out in the fact that these five episodes apparently fired Anderson's imagination enough to undertake the book, for not only were they the first five stories that Anderson wrote, he wrote them in the same order in which they appear in *Winesburg*.

The almost direct antithesis of the story of symbol in *Winesburg* is the story of incident. Including **"Nobody Knows," "Adventure," "An Awakening," "The Untold Lie,"** and **"Departure,"** this form of narrative is often identified by its titular focus upon action, event, or incident. . . . Because the narrative focus is on an event, these stories are also distinguished by their paucity of symbolism. Instead of symbolism, we get an almost mythic simplicity of narrative, for the central action, event, or incident itself seems to embody the meaning of the tale. Alice Hindman's "adventure" appears to represent the most dramatic, if not the most typical, behavior of the frustrated spinster, an impression all the more convincing because of the story's overtones of fertility ritual and myth; similarly, Ray Pearson's "untold lie," not the symbolism of *horses* (freedom) or *trains* (the contingencies of freedom), is the real "truth," Anderson implies, about mature marriage; and the three incidents of **"Nobody Knows," "An Awakening,"** and **"Depar-**

ture" represent three typical phases of the initiatory experiences of youth. The clue to the virtually mythic form, perhaps, resides in the rather archetypal titles of some: **"Adventure,"** Anderson's characteristic term for any incident of some significance, **"An Awakening,"** in which there are parody elements of the romantic quest, with its hero's battle, defeat, and "rebirth," and **"Departure,"** the generic term Joseph Campbell gives to the monomythic hero's leaving for the unfamiliar world. Also because narrative concerns the incident, rather than symbol, theme, or character, these stories are generally limited to present time, with past actions of a character given only to set the stage for the story's main event. **"Adventure"** seems to offer the greatest violation of this principle, and yet all the events of Alice Hindman's past are of a piece with the climactic adventure, for obviously her youthful affair, her long years of waiting, and her mother's remarriage all contribute to her running in the rain. Likewise, in **"The Untold Lie"** the seemingly extraneous tale about Windpeter Winters actually contributes to the characterization of Hal Winters and, therefore, to that of Ray Pearson, and details about Belle Carpenter in **"An Awakening"** lead up to the climactic encounter between George Willard and Ed Handby. Virtually nothing of a past time is included in **"Nobody Knows"** and **"Departure,"** except that which is fleetingly remembered in the present by Willard.

Along with the narrative focus on a central incident, the most important feature of these episodes is their movement toward a recognition for the protagonist himself. Unlike the epiphanic moment of the symbolic stories, the story of incident does not culminate in a dramatic "showing-forth," yet it does conclude with the central character's coming to a crucial understanding of himself, his life, or life in general. . . . **"Adventure"** and **"The Untold Lie"** offer two ironically complementary recognitions, for one shows the unwanted possibility of a life alone and the other the possibility that a life spent "harnessed" to an apparently loveless marriage might not be the worst thing that can happen to one. (pp. 1305-07)

The narrative forms designated "emblematic" and "thematic," like the symbolic episodes and the stories of incident, are also antipodal, for whereas the emblematic portrays a character, the thematic uses a character to expose an idea. The more complex of these, the thematic, includes **"Godliness"** (and its **"Surrender"** and **"Terror"**), **"Respectability," "The Strength of God," "Loneliness," "Death,"** and **"Sophistication."** As the titles indicate, these stories are the most nearly "thesis-ridden" of the four narrative types: each one subordinates character, event, and symbol to the exposition of the "truth," quality, or state of being signaled in the titles. Thus, this group of stories actually comes closest to fulfilling the prophecy of **"The Book of the Grotesque,"** for in these the protagonists almost invariably have seized upon a "thought," made it a "truth" or even "the truth," and consequently become a grotesque. Jesse Bentley, in **"Godliness,"** is so obsessed with the idea that he is important "in some divine plan" that Anderson describes him simply as a "fanatic." But Jesse is no more a fanatic than Wash Williams, of **"Respectability,"** whose physical grotesqueness manifests the spiritual warping caused by his misogyny and his contempt for "respectable" people. Nor than the Reverend Curtis Hartman, of **"The Strength of God,"** who "dreamed of a day when a strong sweet new current of power would come like a great wind into his voice and soul and the people would tremble before the spirit of God made manifest in him." . . . Nor than Enoch Robinson, who willfully drives from his life the woman who might have saved him from the fate of loneliness. Even Elizabeth Willard, who is essentially sympathetic, becomes obsessed with the idea of "death," which she personifies as "a strong black-haired youth running over hills" or as "a stern quiet man marked and scarred by the business of living." . . . Only George Willard escapes becoming a grotesque because of an obsession, and yet even he discovers not joy but "the sadness of sophistication," in which he sees that "he must live and die in uncertainty, a thing blown by the winds, a thing destined like corn to wilt in the sun." . . . (pp. 1307-08)

Each of the figures in these virtually allegorical tales finds his "truth" in one rather ritualistic scene or event. Because George Willard's discovery of "sophistication" is more necessary than willful, the formalized, even "choreographic" (to use Howe's term), scene in which George achieves his awareness is the only one among these tales that has positive overtones. (p. 1308)

The ironic form of these stories is pointed up in the nature of the ritualistic patterns as well as in the comment on life the stories attempt to make. Again, the pattern and the comment in **"Sophistication"** are essentially positive, and yet there is an inherent ironic paradox in Anderson's theme: "One shudders at the thought of the meaninglessness of life while at the same instant, and if the people of the town are his people, one loves life so intensely that tears come into the eyes." . . . The irony of this form is seen more clearly in the story which precedes **"Sophistication."** In **"Death,"** Elizabeth Willard, like her son, is seeking a truly meaningful human relationship, but for her it represents not a *discovery* of self but a *release* from self. The scene which epitomizes this release recurs several times in Elizabeth Willard's life. She remembers a lover of her youth "who in the moment of his passion" had originated the words that "expressed something she would have liked to have achieved in life"—"You dear! You dear! You lovely dear!" . . . Although she feels that for a middle-aged matron "adventure" is not "possible," she nevertheless achieves with Doctor Reefy what the younger lover had memorably expressed for her.

> When she came and knelt on the floor beside his chair he took her into his arms and began to kiss her passionately. . . . "You dear! You lovely dear! Oh you lovely dear!" he muttered and thought he held in his arms not the tired-out woman of forty-one but a lovely and innocent girl who had been able by some miracle to project herself out of the husk of the body of the tired-out woman. . . .

The full irony of these scenes is visible after Elizabeth Willard's death, for her son only then recognizes what the youthful lover and Doctor Reefy had seen in her:

> "My mother is dead," he said . . . he turned and stared at the door through which he had just come. "The dear, the dear, oh the lovely dear," the boy, urged by some impulse outside himself, muttered aloud. . . .

At the conclusion of this tale, Anderson tells us that Elizabeth Willard's "dream of release . . . came to her but twice in her life, in the moments when her lovers Death and Doctor Reefy held her in their arms." . . . Consequently, where George Willard achieves a meaningful release in **"Sophistication,"** Elizabeth Willard's release can only be ironic, for Anderson, as his epitaph attests, believes that "Life not death is the great adventure." (pp. 1308-09)

The final form of narrative in *Winesburg,* the emblematic, includes six episodes: **"Mother," "The Philosopher," "A Man of Ideas," "The Thinker," "The Teacher,"** and **"'Queer.'"** The most obvious distinction between these stories and those of the other three forms is their focus upon the character types indicated in their titles: each story creates a portrait, a sketch, an emblem, of a universal figure. In other words, Elizabeth Willard is "the mother," Doctor Parcival "the philosopher," Joe Welling "the man of ideas," Seth Richmond "the thinker," Kate Swift "the teacher," and Elmer Cowley "the 'queer'." Consequently, other distinguishing features of the emblematic form are related to the ways Anderson goes about etching the main figures in each story. In most of these Anderson devotes much of the narration to descriptions and expositions of character that suggest the unchanging, even archetypal natures of the protagonists. **"Mother,"** for example, begins with a long paragraph contrasting the appearances, actions, and attitudes of Elizabeth and Tom Willard, **"The Philosopher"** opens with a paragraph describing Doctor Parcival, and **"A Man of Ideas"** pictures Joe Welling in its opening paragraph.

Another distinguishing feature of these stories, in contrast to the stories of incident, is the way in which past events and actions are shown in order to *explain* a character rather than to lead up to an event. In **"Mother,"** Anderson shows the roots of Elizabeth Willard's attitudes toward her husband and son. . . . (pp. 1309-10)

Also related to the necessarily static characterization, yet another aspect of the emblematic episodes is their using present actions and attitudes to heighten the sense of *typical* behavior. Thus, where a character's past may show how he became what he is, his present simply reveals him being himself. Elizabeth Willard is shown being concerned about the welfare of her son. . . . Similarly, Doctor Parcival is often shown in his titular role: "Sometimes the doctor launched into long tales concerning himself. To the boy the tales were very real and full of meaning." . . .

Consequently, as the middles of these stories are filled with behavior patterns that exemplify the type, so the concluding passages show the central characters enacting typical, habitual concerns. At the end of **"The Thinker,"** Seth Richmond is shown *thinking* about his "adventure" with Helen White:

> "That's how things'll turn out. She'll be like the rest. I suppose she'll begin now to look at me in a funny way." He looked at the ground and pondered this thought. "She'll be embarrassed and feel strange when I'm around," he whispered to himself. "That's how it'll be. That's how everything'll turn out. When it comes to loving someone, it won't never be me. It'll be someone else—some fool—someone who talks a lot—someone like that George Willard." . . .
>
> (p. 1310)

The truth of the matter, of course, is that Helen White had been attracted to Seth until his penchant for thought had created a barrier between them. In the climactic episode of **"The Teacher,"** too, Kate Swift is shown counseling, teaching, George Willard with "passionate earnestness": "A great eagerness to open the door of life to the boy, who had been her pupil and who she thought might possess a talent for the understanding of life, had possession of her." . . . Although the tale ends with the pupil's, George Willard's, point of view, Kate Swift's role as teacher is nevertheless the central focus: "'I have missed something. I have missed something Kate Swift was trying to tell me,' he muttered sleepily." . . . And in "'**Queer**'" as well, the concluding incident simply solidifies the growing impression of Elmer Cowley's queerness. Resolving that he will prove to others that he is not peculiar, Elmer confronts George Willard, whom he sees as the representative of all of Winesburg, but when George asks him what he wants to say, Elmer freezes up, as he always does, and lapses into a phrase that joins him unquestionably with the half-witted Mook and "queer" old Ebenezer Cowley: "'Well, you see,' he began, and then lost control of his tongue. 'I'll be washed and ironed. I'll be washed and ironed and starched,' he muttered half incoherently." . . . (p. 1311)

It is well-known among Anderson's critics that his method of writing, though not artless, was extremely impressionistic. The impressionism of his method probably accounts for the general uniformity of each narrative type, for it is unlikely that Anderson was aware of the different patterns as he wrote. . . . Sherwood Anderson, like any other author, found himself developing in each story a symbol, an incident, a theme, or a character. The difference is that where another author would try to do things dramatically and objectively, anything Anderson does in *Winesburg* he does lyrically and emotionally. Therefore, the uniformity that critics have seen in narrative type is actually only a uniformity of the lyrical and associational technique and of tone and mood. The reason that critics have found only one narrative form is their concern to show that the book has an overall unity of structure, a unity about which there is little controversy today. However, an irony of the book's critical history is that attempts to answer charges of disunity have unwittingly laid it open to a more serious charge. Reading the critics, one wonders now whether it has enough variety to sustain prolonged interest. But the fact that readers over the years have shown little boredom with Anderson's masterpiece is perhaps our best argument that not only does *Winesburg, Ohio,* have the desired unity of effect, it also has a necessary diversity of form. (p. 1312)

> James M. Mellard, "Narrative Forms in Winesburg, Ohio," in PMLA, 83, Vol. 83, No. 5, October, 1968, pp. 1304-12.

FORREST L. INGRAM (essay date 1971)

[*Ingram is an American editor, critic, poet, and short story writer who has edited and contributed to critical anthologies concerned with the short story. In the following excerpt, he examines the ways in which the narrative voice in* Winesburg, Ohio *exerts control over the short story cycle and acts as one of several connective devices.*]

The unity of *Winesburg, Ohio* is the unity of a short story cycle, both in the sense of a connected series and in the sense of a recurring development in a set of narratives. The action of the book consists in the gradual emergence, from conception in "**The Book of the Grotesque**," to maturity in "**Departure**," of a fictive community in the distortive memory of the book's single narrator; and of a return, in "**Departure**" to the initial (now modified) situation—which had been presented in "**The Book of the Grotesque**."

Underlying all the stories and forming part of the weave, like threads in a carpet, run various connective devices. One of the most important is the consistent narrative voice which controls the tone and angle of vision in every story. (p. 147)

One need not read far into the Winesburg tales to discover that a single narrator is relating all the stories. But one must reread and reflect if he is to appreciate how the narrator maintains a delicate and consistent balance between sympathy and irony in his presentation of the characters of his fancy. No adequate understanding of the stories is possible without a firm grasp of the functions of this fictively realized narrator as he operates at the heart of each of the stories.

In the first place, as a *persona* who yet is the implied author, the narrator fuses the fictional world of the characters in the book with the real world of Anderson the author. He remarks, for instance, in "**The Book of the Grotesque**" (which is also a prologue to his own book of grotesques), that the old writer also had written a book which he had called "**The Book of the Grotesque**." "It was never published", the narrator says, "but I saw it once and it made an indelible impression on my mind." The book's central idea, he continues, "has always remained with me. By remembering it I have been able to understand many people and things that I was never able to understand before." . . . (p. 155)

The "I" of the above statements rarely comes to the surface as "I" in the stories that follow "**The Book of the Grotesque**." After being introduced in this "prologue" he usually calls attention to himself only as storyteller, as controller of the material of his fancy, and not as a participant—slight though his participation in this first episode may be—in the action of the book.

Anderson once wrote, "I have come to think that the true history of life, is but a history of moments." By "true history of life," however, he obviously meant "true history of fictional life." For in *The Modern Writer,* he wrote:

> Consider for a moment the material of the prose writer, the teller of tales. His materials are human lives. To him these figures of his fancy, these people who live in his fancy, should be as real as living people.

In *Winesburg, Ohio,* Anderson's narrator, though not the most impressive, may, for heuristic reasons, be the most important of his fictively realized characters. He assumes the role of "artist of life" like the old writer. Indeed, the old writer is his first creation.

From this point on, levels of reality and myth intermingle; the real is brother to the imaginary. The old carpenter who "became the nearest thing to what is understandable and lovable of all the grotesques in the writer's book" . . . may be a mere creation of the old writer as the old writer is of the narrator and the narrator is of Anderson. The people whose intimate lives are strung out across the pages of *Winesburg*—are they figures of the old writer's fancy, or of the narrator's fancy, or of Anderson's? Are they, perhaps, George Willard's people?

George himself, of course, is only a fictional character. He, too, however, intends to be a writer, a creator of fancied people. Some of the grotesques of Winesburg pour out their life stories to the young *Eagle* reporter, but most of them do not. If George were to write of them, the majority of his accounts would be invented, though he surely would base his stories on the impressions these people had made on him. George's future mimics the old writer's past. All of the men and women the old writer knew as a younger man have shrunk into a mild and mellow deformity as he aged. As he lies on his bed, the young thing in him drives "a long procession of figures before his eyes." . . .

He does not try to paint exact word portraits of the figures, but rather to describe the "deep impression on his mind" that the figures had made.

It is possible, then, that the old writer stands at the head of the work as a later George Willard, a prototype of the George Willard to come. It is possible, too, that the narrator, by summoning to fictional life the figures of the old writer and of George Willard, fictionalized his own initiation into, and projected culmination of his creative career. He stands midway between youth and old age and meditates through his creations both his past and his future as a writer. Finally, I think it probable that Anderson, through these three figures—his narrative *persona*, the old writer, and the young writer George Willard—discovered a suitable form for experimenting with his "new looseness" of structure, with lives flowing past each other, touching and not quite touching, connected and yet not really connected. The people in the stories of *Winesburg, Ohio,* are people many of whom George Willard surely would have known. The old writer knew only the old carpenter and figures of his fancy—probably not the grotesques of Winesburg. The narrator alone could have known all the grotesques of *Winesburg, Ohio,* with that intimacy with which they are revealed, for they all existed in his mind. They were "real" figures of his fancy.

Anderson's narrator often intrudes in the stories to comment on his own presentation of his materials. (pp. 155-57)

In **"Hands"** we find him judging his own formulation of Adolph Meyer's feeling for the boys he taught: "And yet that is but crudely stated. It needs the poet there." . . . And in **"The Untold Lie"** he asks pardon for the action of the narrative with the excuse that it will "be necessary to talk a little of young Hal so that you will get into the spirit of it." . . .

Throughout the stories, the narrator spins his tales within the traditions of oral storytelling. While treating the figures of his fancy as real people, he consciously addresses his audience: "You see," he tells them in **"The Book of the Grotesque,"** "the interest in all this lies in the figures that went before the eyes of the writer." . . . "You can see for yourself," he adds later, "how the old man . . . would write hundreds of pages concerning the matter." . . . (p. 157)

The intrusion of "you" and "I" into a narration which otherwise displays the characteristics primarily of a third person omniscient narrator consciously breaks the illusion of reality and so draws the reader away from over-involvement in the sorrows of the figure who happens for the moment to stand in the spotlight. The narrator also plays with his audience, seems to wink at them, smile at them with a knowing air. He tells them first that the old writer had known people in a peculiarly intimate way, but then adds: "At least that is what the writer thought and the thought pleased him. Why quarrel with an old man concerning his thoughts?" . . . A similar consortment with his audience plays a role in most of the stories. (pp. 157-58)

Other phrases which express a type of solidarity between the tale-teller and his audience recur throughout: (my italics) "Long before the time during which *we* will know him" . . . ; "In order to understand the man *we* will have to go back to an earlier day." . . . ; and "Of course something did happen. That is why he went back to live in Winesburg and why *we* know about him." . . . Obviously, the narrator would have known about Enoch Robinson even if Enoch had not gone back to Winesburg. But then he never would have told his story.

Occasionally, the narrator pauses to converse more at length with his audience in a homey, folksy way. . . . Sometimes he interrupts the flow of narrative to arouse his audience to pay attention to an important, usually symbolic fact. In **"Loneliness"** he is talking about Enoch's room:

> The room in which young Robinson lived in New York faced Washington Square and was long and narrow like a hallway. *It is important to get that fixed in your mind.* The story of Enoch is in fact the story of a room almost more than it is the story of a man. (. . . my italics)

Sometimes, too, he interjects comments on his storytelling that allow him to change his pace or to shift his perspective: "I go too fast" . . . ; or, "That is no part of this story." . . . (p. 158)

Even within the bounds of his customary stance as a third person narrator, the storyteller manages to maintain a delicate balance between a sympathetic presentation of suffering and a certain distance achieved through ironic comment on phraseology. In **"The Book of the Grotesque"** he describes the past sorrows of the old carpenter whose brother had died of starvation, but saves himself from sentimental involvement in the weeping man: "when he cried he puckered up his lips and the mustache bobbed up and down. The weeping old man with the cigar in his mouth was ludicrous." . . .

A similar kind of refusal to become emotionally enmeshed in his characters controls his presentation of the theatricality of Elizabeth Willard as she determines, at long last, to act—to save her son by driving her scissors, dagger-like, deep into the breast of her husband.

> The scene that was to take place in the office below began to grow in her mind. No ghostly worn-out figure should confront Tom Willard, but something quite unexpected and startling. Tall and with dusky cheeks and hair that fell in a mass from her shoulders, a figure should come striding down the stairway before the startled loungers in the hotel office. The figure would be silent—it would be swift and terrible. . . .

But in the next paragraph, all her imagined strength has flowed suddenly out of her and she stands "weak and trembling in the darkness . . . clutching at the back of the chair in which she had spent so many long days." . . . (p. 159)

"The Thinker," immediately after Seth Richmond says, with a smirk, that his mother expects him to "stay on here forever just being a boy," the narrator adds, "Seth's voice became charged with boyish earnestness." The narrator arranges word and action in ironic juxtaposition, so that Helen White thinks to herself, "This boy is not a boy at all, but a strong purposeful man;" but when she asks what Seth will do in Cleveland, he replies vaguely, "I'll do something, get into some kind of work where talk don't count. . . . I don't know. I guess I don't care much." . . . In **"'Queer'"** too, the narrator allows Elmer Cowley to bring judgment on himself by his deeds—he protests loudly that he will not be queer, but continues to act like a lunatic.

The narrator maintains his ironic distance, finally, by the use of *double-entendre*. He must be winking at his audience as he describes George Willard's walk with Belle Carpenter. George is filled with a new sense of masculine power; Belle is out to catch Ed Handby by one of the oldest of feminine tricks—arousal of jealousy. As she and George pause on a hill near the Fair Grounds, George presses Belle against his body, whispering into the night, incoherently, "lust and night and women."

> Belle Carpenter did not resist. When he kissed
> her upon the lips she leaned heavily against him
> and looked over his shoulder into the darkness.
> In her whole attitude there was a suggestion of
> waiting . . .

She does not have long to wait. In an instant George Willard is lying on his back in the bushes and Ed Handby is leading Belle away by the arm.

The narrator of *Winesburg* loves to generalize, universalize, and editorialize. Fortunately, the short story form does not allow the inclusion of extraneous materials to the same extent as does a novel. So *Winesburg* suffers less than Anderson's novels from passages in which Anderson allows his narrator to philosophize. Furthermore, the generalizations one finds in these stories normally have an immediate and close connection with the revelation of a central character or the meaning of a tale. In **"The Book of the Grotesque,"** for instance, we find: "The old writer, *like all of the people of the world,* had got, during his long life, a great many notions in his head" (. . . my italics). A similar unobstrusive comment occurs in **"Hands."** Adolph Meyers, the narrator says, "was meant by nature to be a teacher of youth. . . . In their feeling for the boys under their charge such men are not unlike the finer sort of women in their love of men." . . . (pp. 159-60)

In the first part of **"Godliness"** . . . the editorial comment expands itself to a distressing degree:

> In the last fifty years a vast change has taken
> place in the lives of our people. A revolution
> has in fact taken place. The coming of indus-
> trialism, attended by all the roar and rattle of
> affairs, the shrill cries of millions of new voices
> that have come among us from overseas, the
> going and coming of trains, the growth of cities,
> the building of the interurban car lines that weave
> in and out of towns and past farmhouses, and
> now in these later days the coming of the au-
> tomobiles has worked a tremendous change in
> the lives and in the habits of thought of our
> people of Mid-America. . . .

One would expect to find such a passage on the editorial page of a Cleveland newspaper, but not in a short story. (I have quoted only about a third of the passage as it appears in *Winesburg.*)

Two other incidences of editorializing must be mentioned. In **"Loneliness,"** Enoch Robinson inhabits a room to which a large number of artists come to talk of art. The narrator comments:

> Everyone knows of the talking artists. Through-
> out all of the known history of the world they
> have gathered in rooms and talked. They talk
> of art and are passionately, almost feverishly,
> in earnest about it. They think it matters much
> more than it does. . . .

Comments on art and artists in a work of art also serve the function of blending the levels of the imaginative and the real worlds.

At times the narrator's generalizing comments dive deep beneath the surface of lives into the core emotions of his people. While George and Helen stroll together in **"Sophistication,"** the narrator remarks, "In youth there are always two forces fighting in people. The warm unthinking little animal struggles against the thing that reflects and remembers." . . . While George and Helen pause on the hill above the fair grounds, the narrator continues:

> There is something memorable in the experi-
> ence to be had by going into a fair ground that
> stands at the edge of a Middle Western town
> on a night after the annual fair has been held.
> The sensation is one never to be forgotten. On
> all sides are ghosts, not of the dead, but of
> living people. . . . Farmers with their wives and
> children and all the people from the hundreds
> of little farm houses have gathered within these
> board walls. Young girls have laughed and men
> with beards have talked of the affairs of their
> lives. The place has been filled to overflowing
> with life. . . . One conceals oneself standing
> silently behind the trunk of a tree and what there
> is of a reflective tendency in his nature is in-
> tensified. One shudders at the thought of the
> meaninglessness of life while at the same in-
> stant, and if the people of the town are his
> people, one loves life so intensely that tears
> come into the eyes. . . .

(pp. 160-61)

An important function of the narrator is to "reach beneath the surface of lives," not only in his generalizations, but in the particular insights he offers about the figures of his fancy. Since the people in his story exist only in his imagination, he can penetrate the tissues of their feelings and come to the roots of their existence. But in the tradition of the breezy storyteller, he does not serve his insights in fancy phraseology, but in deceptively simple expressions, the most common of which are "————had a thought," or "an idea came to————," or the equivalent. (p. 161)

The narrator does not merely relate the abstract thoughts of his characters, but often expresses feeling patterns through imagery viewed from within the character. Before she married Dr. Reefy, the tall rich (unnamed) woman had many suitors, one of whom was a jeweler's son who spent long evenings talking earnestly to her of virginity.

> At times it seemed to her that as he talked he
> was holding her body in his hands. She imag-
> ined him turning it slowly about in the white
> hands and staring at it. At night she dreamed
> that he had bitten into her body and that his
> jaws were dripping. . . .

An entirely different inner conception of one's role in life is given in the case of Jesse Bentley who, in fancy, "saw himself living in old times and among old peoples. The land that lay stretched out before him became of vast significance, a place peopled by his fancy with a new race of men sprung from himself." . . . (p. 162)

Finally, the narrator directs his audience's responses by explicitly and implicitly judging the figures of his fancy. The old writer in **"The Book of the Grotesque"** got so full of his ideas about grotesques that he himself was in danger of becoming one. "He didn't, I suppose," the narrator remarks, "for the same reason he never published the book. It was the young thing inside him that saved the old man.'' . . . Similarly, the narrator counters with the weight of his privileged opinion the hasty judgments his readers might otherwise form about those grotesques who may be less likable than others on first meeting. One sees this especially in the case of Wash Williams, the misogynist. ''Wash Williams was a man of courage,'' we are told. ''A thing had happened that had made him hate life, and he hated it wholeheartedly, with the abandon of a poet.'' And later: ''There was something almost beautiful in the voice of Wash Williams, the hideous, telling his story of hate.'' . . . Even hatred had made ''a poet'' of him.

Critics have consistently misunderstood **''The Strength of God''** because they overlook the narrator's heavy, judgmental voice controlling the text. Curtis Hartman in no way represents the perversion of religion, as Schevill and others continue to suggest. True, he had had little experience with women—a rather common trait among clergymen. He was sexually aroused during one period of his life, by Kate Swift, and sexual awakening in inexperienced men is hardly a rare phenomenon. Like Wash Williams, Curtis Hartman is a brave man. He undergoes intense interior anguish because he has loved his ministry and yet he feels so deeply attracted toward sexual pleasures. The narrator stresses again and again the depth of his commitment: ''In reality he was much in earnest,'' he says. The minister has elected overt sin over what he considers hypocrisy. He is pre-pared to live openly in lust, to bear the brunt of public scorn, in order to be true to what he feels is deepest in himself at the moment—sexual passion. This passion, he feels, has replaced the passion to ''go crying the word of God in the highways and byways of the town.'' . . . The chip out of the picture window had ''just nipped off the bare heel of the boy standing motionless and looking with rapt eyes into the face of Christ.'' Since the minister symbolically fuses with the boy in the window, the boy's heel represents symbolically his own Achilles heel. Because of the hole in the boy's heel, the minister ceases to look into the face of Christ and begins to peer through the hole in the window at the bare neck and shoulders of Kate Swift. When the minister cries in triumph that ''God has manifested himself to me in the body of a woman'' he expresses, not a perverted sense of religion, but as deep an insight into incarnational spirituality as one may gather from poems of Donne or Herbert. For those who have experienced the vagaries of spiritual growth, Reverend Curtis Hartman's confusion is certainly comprehensible. When he says: ''What I took to be a trial of my soul was only a preparation for a new and more beautiful fervor of the spirit,'' he is not deluding himself but formulating an insight.

Reverend Curtis Hartman's smashing of the church window stands as one of the few violent acts in all the *Winesburg* stories. It is not the act of a hypocrite or a pervert, but of a sincere, zealous man. It is in some ways symbolic. For once a man has

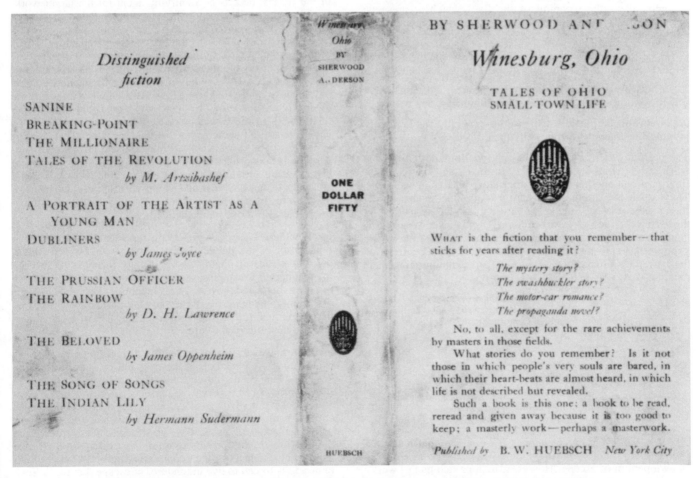

Dust jacket of the first edition of Winesburg, Ohio. *Used by permission of Viking Penguin Inc. and The Newberry Library, Chicago.*

experienced the force of sexual temptations, he can never again return to the days of unknowing innocence. The entire window will have to be replaced and a new, more mature relationship with Christ established. At the same time, hope for such a renewed relationship emerges through the imagery of the window, for the naked woman kneeling by her bed "looked like the figure of the boy in the presence of Christ on the leaded window." . . . Throughout this story, the narrator maintains a tone of serious involvement and respect toward Reverend Hartman. "What he wanted," the narrator stresses, "was to do the work of God quietly and earnestly." . . .

Throughout *Winesburg,* then, one narrative voice controls the tone, mood, direction, and presentation of all the stories. In his role as a fictionalized *persona,* the narrator

(1) draws together the real and the imaginary, fuses the fictional world with the real;

(2) presents in depth, from a privileged point of view and without restrictions of chronology or limitations of space, the psychologically related "figures of his fancy";

(3) comments on his own art of presentation;

(4) cultivates the oral storyteller's familiarity and solidarity with his audience;

(5) balances a sympathetic presentation with the objectivity of ironic distance;

(6) generalizes the meaning of the lives which he presents; philosophizes on youth and old age, on city and country life, and on other matters connected with his stories;

(7) so penetrates beneath the surface of lives that his audience may know what his protagonist thinks, feels, and imagines;

(8) brings his grotesques into such a peak of excitement that self-revelation floods from their trembling lips; and

(9) directs his audience's response by explicitly and implicitly judging his characters as he tells their stories.

The narrator, then, by controlling the feeling and form of his work, is the chief source of unity in the cycle. The lives that flow past one another in story after story all live in his fancy. They touch one another and hardly touch one another at all. In Winesburg itself, they seem hardly to know one another; in the narrator's mind they are brothers. As citizens of Winesburg, they mumble, jerk their arms, hide themselves from view, struggle to express themselves, and fail. Only as citizens of the narrator's fancy do they succeed in communicating their inner selves to his listeners. (pp. 164-65)

> *Forrest L. Ingram, "Sherwood Anderson: Winesburg, Ohio," in his* Representative Short Story Cycles of the Twentieth Century: Studies in a Literary Genre, *Mouton, 1971, pp. 143-99.*

SAM BLUEFARB   (essay date 1972)

[Bluefarb is an English-born American critic and fiction writer. In the following excerpt, he identifies a pattern of escape in Winesburg, Ohio.]

Like *Adventures of Huckleberry Finn* and *The Damnation of Theron Ware,* Sherwood Anderson's *Winesburg, Ohio* contains its own pattern of escape. However, in approaching this work, I have not blinked the fact that, by the strict application of techniques and criteria of the novel, *Winesburg, Ohio* is not a novel at all; it is—at least on the surface—a collection of tales, or episodes, strung together on intertwining threads of contiguous memories that involve a given time and place: a small town in Ohio in the late nineteenth century.

George Willard, in *Winesburg,* may be compared to Nick Adams in Hemingway's *In Our Time* (1925): the two young men grow to maturity by encountering a series of confrontations with life—sometimes "initiatory," sometimes in less traumatic "rituals of passage." But though Nick Adams is the central character of Hemingway's collection of stories, he does not serve as a focal point for the other characters. George Willard, on the other hand, is not only the most sustained character in Anderson's work, but also the reflecting agency by which the other characters in the town see themselves. In making Willard the repository for their problems, the characters in *Winesburg, Ohio* are able to gain some greater—if admittedly still small—insight into those problems. Further, by their confidences George Willard is able not only to gain some insight into the problems of his fellow townsmen but to learn something about himself.

Some of these stories may indeed be capable of standing alone and still make some sense. But fitted together into a larger work, as they are, they have been given a significance and a strength of meaning such as they otherwise could not have had. (p. 43)

Although it is true that George Willard is not the main character of the stories, he acts as a unifying agent for the larger work. If there were still some doubt as to the function of George Willard in *Winesburg, Ohio,* that doubt should be quickly dispelled when one comes to the last story, **"Departure."** It is in this story that George, in leaving Winesburg, will tie up the loose ends of his life there in order "to meet the adventure of life" in the big city. . . . Only if we see the town and George's past in it as the "background on which [he is] to paint the dreams of his manhood" . . . can we see this story in its proper relationship to those that precede it: the causes of George's departure are all there in the earlier chapters. That George leaves for parts unknown—the westbound train he takes suggests he is bound for Chicago—is of no great importance. But his departure certainly is, for he will be able to look back on the town of his boyhood and youth with greater detachment; he will thus be able to see it not only more clearly and objectively but also more sympathetically.

In *Winesburg* George Willard is a representative figure who typifies all of the buried yearnings of his fellow townsmen, but unlike most of them, George finally manages to succeed in escaping the town. His escape, however, signalizes the death of his boyhood and the birth of his manhood. Like the chrysalis of the emerging butterfly, Winesburg has nurtured and prepared the young man for the breakout from the shell of its dead past into the new life of the future.

Willard, however, cannot be seen as a representative type except against the backdrop of the past and the small town that has for so long been symbolic of it. The small town in American literature has been a pervasive presence, ever since that literature broke out of its own colonial chrysalis and became a collection of regional literatures that contributed to the larger national literature. Our writers, for the most part, approached the small town with mixed emotions, depending on their own experience either as young people growing up in small towns or as adults forced to live in, endure, or escape them. . . . Such once-obsessive themes as the fall from innocence, the initiation, and the escape itself have for a long time been subordinate to that of the small town and its impact on the emerging conscience. Anderson's Winesburg is, of course, one of the prime examples of that life.

Peeling off the outer layers of these lives in Winesburg, Anderson, in episode after episode, reveals what are essentially layers of respectability—or the appearance of it—to show us the core of reality that lies at the heart of the town. But if one cannot communicate, or find some degree of surcease from the loneliness in the consummation of a relationship with another, there is always of course, either in the first or last resort, the "out" of escape from those restrictions, an escape that Willard will eventually make. Insofar as he is more sensitive and articulate than the others in the town, George is also different. And it will be this difference that will eventually precipitate his escape from a place and a way of life where, though eccentricity and difference are not difficult to find, they still serve to arouse suspicion. Indeed, it is frequently by his contacts with the alienated souls in the town that George is permitted the partial insights that will lead to his maturity. (pp. 45-6)

Where many of his "grotesque" neighbors are self-centered, obsessed by their own personal problems to the point of psychosis, Willard, although he also has his problems, is never so absorbed by them that he cannot look at the world and his neighbors and take stock of both with relatively greater objectivity. He is a sensitive receiver, absorbing all of those impressions with which he will later come to "paint the dreams of his manhood" on the canvas of his small-town youth. George in being sensitive to the drift of things in the town, not only is articulate in his sensitivity but, through it, shows the makings of a poet. Yet it is not so much the poet or the man of articulation that draws the eccentrics, the freaks, and the "queers" to George; it is finally his sensitivity. To them Willard is a healer.

Further, whereas George is fairly articulate, his fellow townsmen find it difficult to express themselves other than through wild outbursts or inchoate gesticulations. It is only when he is on the verge of making his escape from the town that George can "think through" his own relationship with his neighbors and see them through that mixture of pity and scorn with which a young man of slightly superior talents may look upon those who are educationally inferior to him.

Perhaps more than anyone else in town, George's mother, Elizabeth, hopes to mold, or remold, her son closer to her heart's desire. Thus, she vicariously wishes to satisfy a yearning that had burned briefly in her young womanhood, and then had flickered out in the "airless" small-town existence that has destroyed the hopes and the lives of many of her neighbors. No longer able to nurture her own dreams—to escape Winesburg to join a company of itinerant actors—Elizabeth Willard has now superimposed something of her own unfulfilled ambitions onto George. She now thinks of him as that remnant of her own youthful self that has not died and that still seeks to find its way out of the buried life into the sunlit world "above the surface."

George's relationship with his father, Tom Willard, is not quite as close as his relationship with his mother. But Tom Willard has also been disappointed by life. He is the proprietor of the New Willard Hotel, which has seen better days and which symbolizes for Tom Willard all of the larger disappointments of his disappointed life. Instead of fulfilling the promise that it had once held for him, it is now a gnawing reminder of the promise that has been broken. (pp. 47-8)

For Tom Willard the hotel is a symbol not merely of the failure of his life generally but, more specifically, the failure of his domestic life. His recourse is to reach outward to that therapeutic panacea, or escape, of the American male who, defeated in the home, turns outward to those socially acceptable alternates of business or politics. For the most part Tom Willard's escape into local politics is virtually the only escape he is capable of. He still vaguely hopes that he will someday recoup his losses, i.e., his integrity as a man—he is "the leading Democrat in a strongly Republican community" . . .—perhaps getting himself elected to Congress, or even someday becoming Governor. Until then he will vest some of that hope in George.

Tom Willard hopes to justify his own faith in George by contributing the paternal influence toward George's success. But this ambition is not without its snags, for in Tom Willard's attempts to influence George, to capture some of the son's affection if not respect, the rivalry between Tom and his wife for George's love and respect comes to a head. Each wishes for the boy something that neither has had: fulfillment in some sort of success. The form which that success is to take is objectively irrelevant. The locus of irritation lies in the rivalry between the two parents for the possession of the boy's soul. It is a rivalry, of course, that is overwhelmingly reminiscent of another father-mother rivalry in the modern novel, that of Gertrude and Walter Morel in D. H. Lawrence's *Sons and Lovers*. The parallel between the two situations—both patently Oedipal—suggests, as some critics have noted, Anderson's debt to Lawrence in his use of the earlier writer's theme.

George's ambition to become a writer—as distinct from being a newspaper reporter—is obviously the manifestation of a far greater drive within him than even Elizabeth can control. Apart from literary ambitions, George feels the compulsion to make something of himself. As the boy develops into manhood, he finds that he must free himself for greater things than common expectations; and he must do so in his own way. Paradoxically, each of the parents wants for George what George wishes for himself. But he cannot be pressured into his encounter with the world; he must do it in his own way, at his own pace. It is significant that George's decision to leave Winesburg, to pursue his own course with a minimum of parental interference, is made early in the book, long before the death of his mother. Early in the book, perhaps to prepare her for the inevitable, George tells Elizabeth of his intentions:

> Sitting in a chair beside his mother he began to talk. "I'm going to get out of here," he said. "I don't know where I shall go or what I shall do but I am going away."
>
> The woman in the chair waited and trembled. An impulse came to her. "I suppose you had better wake up," she said. "You think that? You will go to the city and make money, eh? It will be better for you, you think, to be a business man, to be brisk and smart and alive?" She waited and trembled.
>
> The son shook his head. "I suppose I can't make you understand, but oh, I wish I could," he said earnestly. "I can't even talk to father about it. I don't try. There isn't any use. I don't know what I shall do. I just want to go away and look at people and think."
>
> .   .   .   .   .
>
> She wanted to cry out with joy because of the

words that had come from the lips of her son, but the expression of joy had become impossible to her. "I think you had better go out among the boys. You are too much indoors," she said. "I thought I would go for a little walk," replied the son. . . .

(pp. 48-50)

The dialogue sets the tone for the relationship between George and his mother and shows the kind of restlessness that George has inherited from her. As one can see from this exchange, Elizabeth's feelings are, to say the least, mixed. But her love for her son gives more than it takes (a giving symbolized by the $800 with which she unsuccessfully attempts to finance George's exodus from Winesburg); for in George's stated purpose, to "go away," Elizabeth seems to see some sort of vicarious resolution for her own girlhood restlessness; in George's escape, she too—like her husband—will enjoy a "reprieve" from the stagnation of their lives.

In spite of Elizabeth's concern for George's freedom of action, her concern for George is one expression of concern for herself, for the satisfaction of her own desires. Like those other townspeople who burden George with their problem and presences, there is something vampiric about Elizabeth's relationship with her son. Like any form of possessiveness, it must finally demand for its love object what it wishes for itself. Only in Elizabeth's death will George find complete release from whatever domination she has held over him. Like Elizabeth, Tom Willard the father is parasitical too, for like her, he also wishes for George what he had wished for himself—fame and glory. Both parents wish nothing more than to create, or re-create, in George the realization of their own image of what he ought to be.

As long as he remains in Winesburg, George Willard is the recipient of the confidence of the townspeople. Through these confidences he is slowly impressed with the private agonies that go on inside the hearts of even the most hardened types in the town. George, however, in playing the part of a Miss Lonelyhearts, will only go on playing that part to the extent that he is able to stand up under the constant assaults on his increasingly raw and hyperactive sensibilities. But he cannot go on like this indefinitely; when he reaches the point where he can no longer stand the town and the stunted souls who inhabit it, he will leave. Unlike Nathanael West's Miss Lonelyhearts, also a news reporter, George will not be—indeed, is incapable of making himself—the Christ figure for the burdens of others. For in fleeing the town George will save *himself* from the kind of Christlike immolation—another aspect of the "grotesque"—that West's character eventually submits to. In wishing to flee the "buried lives" of his fellow townsmen, George also wishes to flee those lives because they are constant irritants, constant reminders of his own buried life. He will occasionally bear the unburdening of these sick souls, and will even help them to alleviate their burdens. (Perhaps this is one way he can keep from becoming a "grotesque" himself.) But he can only continue to do so at the risk of dissipating his own energies, energies he will need for his own breakout from Winesburg and the struggle with the world beyond it.

There is at least one way in which George Willard expands his knowledge of the world—apart from his experience—and that is through books. This bookish knowledge may be seen as something that will permit him to impose some sort of pattern on his life and even, perhaps, on the lives of those around him. Some of these books tell of the Middle Ages—a flight back into the past. But this is only the reverse of his later escape, into the future. His interest in the Middle Ages at this stage suggests that the nature of George's escape is an inverted one—for the moment. Significantly enough, his interest in the Middle Ages suggests another facet of George's evolving personality—his romanticism. Yet the mooning romantic reading and dreaming about the Middle Ages must sooner or later break out into the world that he inhabits, the world that offers living experience. It must draw George out of the world of boyhood that he still, dreamlike, lives in, to thrust him into manhood.

In **"An Awakening"** we view a partial initiation of George from boyhood into manhood. In this episode one of these minor, or partial, initiations will start the machinery of George's escape mechanism moving and will prove to be the beginning of his explicit attempt to escape the town. This initiation comes about through the humiliation young Willard suffers at the hands of Ed Handby, the local bartender. It is this experience that brings George to one of the critical junctures of his "awakening"—the beginnings of true manhood—to the knowledge of his own limitations. In George's attempt to experience an adult sexual relationship with Belle Carpenter, a woman of the town, he is paradoxically made aware that he is still very much a boy. For Ed Handby, who unceremoniously breaks in upon that attempt, does not even deign to fight with George to assert his rights over Belle (who is only using the innocent young Willard as a pawn in her battle to bring back the jealous Handby to her). Handby not only will not dignify young Willard by challenging him to a fight, he thrusts George aside like a whipped puppy. . . . Ed Handby picks Belle Carpenter up off the grass and "marches" her away, having proven his own manhood in the face of young Willard's impotence. Thus, this incident, perhaps more than any other, paradoxically brings George to the beginning of manhood—by convincing him that he is still a boy with a boy's limitations. He finds neither physical nor romantic love in the Winesburg of his youth, for he is too puny to battle a full-grown man, and he is too timid to make love to a mature woman. As for Helen White, his sweetheart, she is still the object of Willard's boyish crush that may later develop into something more substantial but at this time is still in its idyllically romantic stage.

When George arrives back in town after the humiliating incident, he runs along a street of frame houses and begins to realize something he had not quite sensed before: for the first time he sees how squalid, miserable, and hopeless these streets and houses are. In this moment, through these "objective correlatives" of frame houses, the meanness and the futility of the town are crystalized for George. The houses now seem to bring out all of the meanings that heretofore had lain hidden from him. Not only do they crystalize the meaning of the town for George, but they appear as symbols of all the closed doors of his life.

This sprint along a street of squalid frame houses will be the beginning of something that will not cease until George has finally succeeded in running from the town itself. And when he does, his escape from Winesburg will be not merely a running away from, but a running toward, something—life, love, fame, adventure, anything, everything—that the town has (almost maliciously, it seems) denied him.

Elizabeth Willard dies of a paralytic stroke. Like her life, her death can only show itself as the paralysis so symbolic of all the paralyzed lives of this town. But if she has lived and died in one form of paralysis or another, her son George will at least act to break out of this grip on his life. Thus, with the death of his mother, George grows up in a hurry. For he is barely out of adolescence when Elizabeth dies, in the same month that George reaches his eighteenth birthday. But because there is still much of the boy in George, vestigial traces of innocence still cling to him. In spite of the experience he has undergone by this time, and in spite of Elizabeth Willard's death, George's innocence, though steadily diminishing, is still strong enough to act as a protective shield against the harsh facts of life and death. For though Willard is not exactly shocked by his mother's death, he finds it difficult to believe. Not only can he not seem to realize the fact of that death but, even more significantly, he cannot seem to realize the fact of death itself. This death in the family is still too unreal to register fully upon his consciousness. George may appear to be too callously detached, but that state of mind is induced by the unreal reality of the situation rather than by his lack of sensitivity.... Although he is much older than the Nick Adams of Hemingway's "Indian Camp," George, like Nick, is unable to face the reality of death, or to see any reference or suggestion that one human being's death is only part of a recurrent pattern that foreshadows one's own death. Like Nick, George is still young enough to feel "quite sure that he would never die"—though that feeling will not last much longer. Thus, as yet unable to consciously accept the fact of death, George turns aside to seek some other answer. He must look forward to tomorrow, signifying life and rebirth, rather than back into yesterday, signifying death, literally and figuratively.

In the episode **"Death,"** George decides to leave Winesburg; it is Elizabeth Willard's death that has impelled George to make that inevitable decision.... (pp. 50-5)

The last episode, **"Departure,"** in which George takes his leave of the town, places him on the borderline of manhood, but not completely across it into full maturity. At this time, there lies within George the potentiality for a full—or fuller—maturity. When it comes, his departure is both the precondition and the end result of a process of initiation and maturation for which all of his previous life in the town had merely been preparation.

George's departure from the town is not only a rebirth but a burial of the old self. Yet the death here is never really a complete death of that old self; for the mixture of memory and desire will keep George tied to the past, no matter how delicate or tenuous the attachment may be. Nostalgia dies hard; and it is not the big things but the small events of daily life, the seemingly unimportant minutiae, that hold George captive in a way to the past, a young man "on parole," so to speak, from that past. The small, carelessly overlooked details will stand out now that George must take his leave of them. (p. 56)

Significantly, George Willard, like Theron Ware before him but not necessarily for similar reasons, leaves Winesburg on a spring morning one month after Elizabeth Willard's death, an action that more than suggests the vernal quality of this ritual of passage; for Willard is at not only the season of spring in the world but in his life. He leaves town, one might say, at the instance, or *instant*, of his mother's death, the better that he may be reborn into the new life that awaits him; for it is as a young man scarcely out of boyhood—in his eighteenth year—that George leaves Winesburg. (p. 57)

Like so many escapers in the modern American novel, Willard is a type who both looks backward to the escapers who have preceded him and ahead to those who will follow. Like George, these escapers—the Huck Finns, Theron Wares, Frederic Hen-

rys, and John Andrewses—are generalized types, characteristic of so many escapers in American fiction. They are fleeing not merely a set of untenable circumstances (which all of them, in one way or another, do) but also something within their former selves that must be fled if they are to come to greater maturity. *En partant, nous mourons un peu*—in parting, we die a little; and the parting that George undertakes, like all such partings, indeed betokens a kind of death—not only of George's younger self but of the town he has left behind. Of course, in parting we also experience a rebirth of sorts too. Thus, his journey to the city is no simple geographical journey; it is a journey into life itself. Paradoxically, in spite of the suggestions of mutability and mortality in George's departure, the town begins to live again in his memories of it. (pp. 57-8)

> Sam Bluefarb, "George Willard: Death and Resurrection," in his The Escape Motif in the American Novel: Mark Twain to Richard Wright, *Ohio State University Press, 1972, pp. 42-58.*

DAVID STOUCK (essay date 1977)

[*In the following excerpt, Stouck discusses the "dance of death" as a leitmotif unifying the stories in* Winesburg, Ohio.]

Anyone familiar with Anderson's writing is aware of the frequency of the word death in his titles. In **Winesburg, Ohio** **"Death"** is the title of a key sequence concerning Elizabeth Willard. **"Death in the Woods"** is the title of one of Anderson's most accomplished short stories and was made the title of a collection of stories published in 1933. One of the best stories in that collection is titled **"Brother Death,"** a story of a boy who must die young but who, unlike his older brother, never has to part with his imagination. **"Death"** and **"A Dying Poet"** are two of the titles in *A New Testament* and "Death on a Winter Day" is a chapter title from *No Swank.* In the **Sherwood Anderson Reader** we find a magazine piece titled **"A Dead Dog"** and a sequence from the unedited memoirs published as **"The Death of Bill Graves."** The suggestion in these titles that Anderson was more than casually preoccupied with the theme of death is quickly borne out by an examination of his novels, stories, and memoirs.

In almost every book Anderson published, the death of a beloved character is of crucial significance and casts the protagonist's life in a wholly different perspective. And on a more philosophical level Anderson saw modern man, alienated from creativity by mechanized factory work and by a repressive Puritan ethic, caught up in a form of living death. These two forms of death—the death of an individual and the death of a society—correspond to the distinction in late medieval art between a dance of Death and the dance of the dead. Holbein's *Dance of Death,* artistically the most sophisticated expression of this theme, depicts Death claiming various individuals and leading them away singly from this life. The more popular representations, such as the relief on the cemetery at Basel, depicted the dead either in a procession or dancing with the living. One of the popular beliefs associated with the Dance of Death was that the dead appeared to warn the living of their fate. Such images and themes, as will be shown, were a part of Anderson's imagination throughout his career as a writer.

The death of Sherwood Anderson's mother when the author was eighteen likely determined, more than any other experience, the persistent preoccupation with death in his fiction. The mother's death is recorded several times in Anderson's writings, in both semi-autobiographical and fictional form. For some of Anderson's protagonists the death of the mother changes radically the course of their lives and initiates an unending quest to find a home and a place in the world. (pp. 526-27)

In more directly autobiographical writings the mother's death initiates the youth into the world of experience and awakens him to his own mortality. In *A Story-Teller's Story* it is an experience of profound alienation for the boy; Anderson writes "for us there could be no home now that mother was not there." Similarly in *Winesburg, Ohio* it occasions George Willard's departure from the town in which he has grown up. In *Tar: A Midwest Childhood* the mother's death spells the end of childhood and innocence. . . . In each instance the mother's death awakens the hero to the mortal view of existence and raises the difficult question of life's meaning and purpose. (pp. 528-29)

In *Dark Laughter,* Anderson's most Lawrentian novel, life is imaged as a dance. For the central character, Bruce Dudley, the image functions initially to suggest life's energy and potential rhythms ("Dance life . . . Pretty soon you'll be dead and then maybe there'll be no laughs"), but the image acquires a darker dimension when Dudley thinks of his dead mother as having been "part of the movement of the grotesque dance of life." . . .

As far as I know Anderson never referred to *Winesburg, Ohio* as incorporating the Dance of Death idea. The different images, however, fall together suggestively—life as a procession, life as a dance, life as a living form of death. (p. 529)

Winesburg, Ohio may not have taken shape directly around the Dance of Death idea, but it was most certainly influenced by a book, Edgar Lee Masters's *Spoon River Anthology,* of which the central theme is death. . . . Both *Winesburg* and *Spoon River* depict in episodic fashion a cross-section of life in a small midwestern town. In both books at the deepest level there is an intransigent sense of despair. The Spoon River poems are vignettes of lives lived at cross-purposes, with recognitions after death that life has been wasted and is now forever irrecoverable. Masters's poems incorporate the medieval idea of the dead appearing to warn the living of their inevitable end. The voices of the dead, each one telling a story from the tomb, was a formal design which must surely have influenced Anderson considerably, for we have seen him speak of his Winesburg characters as each walled in by fears and already dead or dying. Anderson's characters are not presented as spirits returned from the dead, and yet in a very important sense that is what they are, for the characters in *Winesburg, Ohio* are people from the narrator's memory of his home town, and many of them, most significantly the mother, are in fact long dead.

But what is particularly suggestive, given the fact that Anderson had seen Masters's book, is that several of Oliver Herford's illustrations for the first edition of *Spoon River Anthology* depicted the Dance of Death in various forms. Death swinging a lariat appears twice and, placed above the first of the poems, serves as a controlling visual motif throughout the collection. Death is also shown in the manner of Holbein leading away a child in one sketch and beckoning to a drunk in another. But two of the illustrations suggest actual situations in the Winesburg stories. One shows Death in bed as a lover and we are reminded of Elizabeth Willard's erotic personification of death in her last days. The other presents Death approaching an older man who has just taken a young wife, and we think of Doctor Reefy, whose young bride is snatched away from him by Death

only a few months after the couple are married. Anderson may not have consciously conceived of his stories being arranged like a medieval Dance of Death, but it is hard to believe that the Masters book with its death theme and design did not influence his imagination at some fundamental level.

In *Winesburg, Ohio* the idea of death does not signify only the grave, but more tragically it denotes the loneliness and frustration of the unlived life. As in *Poor White* we are aware in *Winesburg, Ohio* of movement as characteristic of American life, but here it is the restlessness of the individual who grows increasingly oppressed by his loneliness and his inability to express himself to others. In each story when the character reaches an ultimate point of insupportable frustration or recognizes that he can never escape his isolation, he reacts by waving his hands and arms about, talking excitedly, and finally running away. In a very stylized pattern almost every story brings its character to such a moment of frenzy where he breaks into something like a dance.

The introductory sketch, **"The Book of the Grotesque,"** is either ignored by critics or dismissed as a murky and confusing allegory. That Anderson intended it to carry significant weight in relation to the rest of the book is clear when we remember that "The Book of the Grotesque" was the publication title Anderson first gave to the whole collection of stories. In its oblique and terse fashion the sketch defines the relationship of the artist to his characters. The subject is an old man who is writing a book about all the people he has known. The first thing we notice is that the writer is preoccupied with fantasies about his failing health. When he goes to bed each night he thinks about his possible death, yet paradoxically that makes him feel more alive than at other times; thoughts of death heighten his awareness to things. In this state the old writer has a waking dream in which all the people he has known are being driven in a long procession before his eyes. They appear to the writer as "grotesques," for each of these characters has lived according to a personal truth which has cut him off from the others. These are the characters of Anderson's book. The procession they form is like a dance of the dead, for as mentioned above most of these people from Anderson's childhood are now dead. The youth in the coat of mail leading the people is the writer's imagination and also his death consciousness—his memory of the past and his awareness that loneliness and death are the essential "truths" of the human condition. We are told in this sketch that the old carpenter, who comes to adjust the height of the writer's bed and who instead weeps over a brother who died of starvation in the Civil War, is one of the most lovable of all the grotesques in the writer's book. Just such a character apparently befriended Anderson's lonely mother in Clyde, Ohio; this detail indicates both the personal and the elegiac nature of the book.

The first story, **"Hands,"** tells about Wing Biddlebaum whose unfulfilled life typifies the other life stories recounted in the book. From his little house on the edge of town Wing can watch life pass by:

> . . . he could see the public highway along which went a wagon filled with berry pickers returning from the fields. The berry pickers, youths and maidens, laughed and shouted boisterously. A boy clad in a blue shirt leaped from the wagon and attempted to drag after him one of the maidens, who screamed and protested shrilly. The feet of the boy in the road kicked

up a cloud of dust that floated across the face
   of the departing sun. . . .

With its archetypal images of the public highway, youths and
maidens, the berry harvest, and the cosmic image of the sun,
the scene Anderson has created is a tableau depicting the dance
of life. By contrast Wing Biddlebaum ventures only as far as
the edge of the road, then hurries back again to his little house.
He lives in the shadows of the town. Yet, like the berry pickers,
his figure is always in motion, walking nervously up and down
his half decayed verandah. His hands especially are always
moving and are compared to the beating wings of an imprisoned
bird. In *Tar* Anderson tells us that likely "the memory of his
mother's hands made him think so much about other people's
hands" . . . , again creating a link between his fictional characters and dead mother. Wing's story of being accused of
perverted love for the boys he teaches ends in his flight from
a small Ohio town. The newspaper reporter George Willard,
persona for the young Anderson, listens sympathetically to
Wing as he tries to describe his pastoral dream of living like
the classical teacher Socrates; but his hands, caressing George
Willard, betray him and he runs away to resume his endless
pacing in the shadows of his old house.

Several of the stories follow the basic pattern of "Hands": a
misfit in the town is telling George something of his story but
cannot express himself completely; he begins to wave his hands
about helplessly and breaks into a run. In **"Drink"** Tom Foster,
a gentle, passive boy, is described as living "in the shadow
of the wall of life." . . . He tries to tell George Willard that
he has made love to Helen White, but the reporter won't listen
because he too loves the banker's daughter. They take a long
walk in the dark. Tom raises his voice to an excited pitch to
explain that he wants to suffer because "everyone suffers,"
but George does not understand him.

In the story "**"Queer"**" George does not get an opportunity to
understand. Elmer Cowley, oppressed by his sense of being
different from everyone else, resolves that he will be like other
people. He goes on a long walk in the country where he encounters the half-wit named Mook. Walking up and down and
waving his arms about, he tells Mook that he won't be queer
any longer, and then goes on to tell of his resolution to George
Willard, whom he sees as typifying the town and representing
public opinion. They go on a walk together but Elmer cannot
explain himself to the reporter: "He tried to talk and his arms
began to pump up and down. His face worked spasmodically.
He seemed about to shout." . . . Having failed to communicate
to anyone, he decides to run away from the town, but as he is
leaving on the train he calls George Willard down to the station
to try once again to explain. Still speechless he breaks into a
grotesque dance: "Elmer Cowley danced with fury beside the
groaning train. . . . With a snarl of rage he turned and his long
arms began to flay the air. Like one struggling for release from
hands that held him he struck out, hitting George Willard blow
after blow on the breast, the neck, the mouth." . . . (pp. 530-34)

George is similarly struck at by the school teacher, Kate
Swift. . . . Like George's mother she wants him to be a serious
writer and to express something for the people of the town.
But confused by her love for the boy, she cannot express herself
adequately and winds up beating him on the face with her fists,
and then running out into the darkness. . . . Over and over
inarticulate characters in a moment of passion wave their hands
in the air and burst into a run.

Two of the stories present a macabre vision of life's "truth."
In **"The Philosopher"** Doctor Parcival tells George Willard

about his childhood, but when he reaches the point of telling
about his father's death in an insane asylum, he breaks off and
paces distractedly about the newspaper office. Doctor Parcival
is another of the book's failed artists; he is writing a book and
his sole vision is that life is a form of crucifixion, a long torture
and dying as it was for Christ on the cross. **"Respectability,"**
the story of the cuckold Wash Williams, also involves a vision
of living death. In reaction to his wife's faithlessness Williams
holds the idea that all women are corrupt and dead.

Wash Williams is perhaps most remarkable for his hideous
physical appearance. He is compared to "a huge, grotesque
kind of monkey, a creature with ugly, sagging, hairless skin
below his eyes and a bright purple underbody." . . . Everything
about Wash, including the whites of his eyes, looks unclean,
everything except his hands which in striking contrast are well
cared for. There is a medieval grotesqueness in the description
of several of the characters; as in medieval art, the twisted
inner nature of the people is manifested in imperfections and
distortions of the physical body. Doctor Reefy in **"Paper Pills"**
has a huge nose and hands; the knuckles of his hands are "like
clusters of unpainted wooden balls as large as walnuts fastened
together by steel rods." . . . This stylized image of the doctor's
physical body anticipates the description of his character as
being like the sweetness of the gnarled apples left on the trees
in autumn, and the image of the little balls of paper on which
he has written a number of truths. Some of the characters are
almost like gargoyles on medieval buildings. Doctor Parcival,
who believes all men are crucified, has a yellowed mustache,
black irregular teeth, and a left eye that twitches, snapping up
and down like a window shade. Elmer Cowley's father has a
large wen on his scrawny neck; he still wears his wedding coat
which is brown with age and covered with grease spots. Elmer
too is grotesque in appearance: extraordinarily tall, he has pale
blond almost white hair, eyebrows, and beard, teeth that pro-
trude, and eyes that are the colorless blue of marbles. Characteristically many of the physical portraits focus on hands.
The hands of Tom Willy, the saloon keeper, are streaked with
a flaming red birthmark, as if the hands had been dipped in
blood that dried and faded. Tom Foster's grandmother has
hands all twisted out of shape from hard work. When she holds
a mop or broom handle they look like "the dried stems of an
old creeping vine clinging to a tree." . . . There are two half-
wits in Winesburg as well: Turk Smollet, the old wood-chop-
per, who talks and laughs to himself as he passes regularly
through the village, and Mook, the farm hand, who holds long
involved conversations with the animals. Perhaps it is not accidental that George Willard thinks of the Middle Ages one
night when he is walking through the town, and that the first
word that comes to his lips when he looks up at the sky is
"Death." . . . (pp. 534-36)

In some of the stories George Willard does not appear except
of course as implied narrator; the characters nevertheless are
pictured as breaking into a run or dance at peak moments of
frustration or loneliness. Jesse Bentley in **"Godliness,"** who
has a vision of being a Biblical patriarch, runs through the
night imploring God to send him a son; years later when he
takes his grandson to sacrifice a lamb, hoping God will send
him a visible sign of His blessing, the scene ends with the
flight of the grandson from Winesburg. In **"Adventure"** Alice
Hindman, who has been waiting for years for the return of her
lover, one night runs out naked onto the lawn in the rain. . . .
Repeatedly the most vivid images in the book are those of
characters in grotesque or violent motion: Louise Bentley, the
estranged daughter of the Biblical patriarch, driving her horse

and carriage at breakneck speed through the streets of Winesburg; . . . Hal Winters' father, Windpeter Winters, drunk and
driving his team along the railroad tracks directly into the path
of an onrushing locomotive. Such images seem to have coalesced to form a grotesque procession in the writer's memory.

The procession becomes a Dance of Death when the writer
comes to recognize his own mortality. The death of his mother
awakens George Willard to both the brevity and the loneliness
of human existence. Elizabeth Willard, perhaps more than any
of the other characters, seeks some kind of release from her
perpetual loneliness. . . . After she married and still found no
communion with another human being, she drove her horse
and buggy at a terrible speed through the country until she met
with an accident. (The image of a woman hurt in an accident
or disfigured in some way recurs several times to the eyes of
the artist figures in the book: one of Enoch Robinson's paintings
depicts a woman who has been thrown from a horse and has
been hurt . . . , while the old writer in the introduction is crying
over "a woman all drawn out of shape" . . .). Eventually when
her long illness comes we are told that Elizabeth went along
the road seeking for death: "She personified the figure of death
and made him now a strong black-haired youth running over
hills, now a stern quiet man marked and scarred by the business
of living." . . . As a young woman she had taken several lovers
before she married; now her lover is Death.

"Sophistication," the penultimate chapter, is shaped around
George's growing awareness of life as a procession or dance
toward death. In the background is the Winesburg County Fair:
people are moving up and down the streets and fiddlers sweat
"to keep the feet of youth flying over a dance floor." But in
spite of the crowds George Willard feels lonely; he wants
someone to understand the feeling that has possessed him since
his mother's death. Significantly we are told that "memories
awoke in him" and that he is becoming conscious of life's
limitations. The narrator, reflecting on youth, generalizes: "There
is a time in the life of every boy when he for the first time
takes the backward view of life. . . . If he be an imaginative
boy a door is torn open and for the first time he looks out upon
the world, seeing, as though they marched in procession before
him, the countless figures of men who before his time have
come out of nothingness into the world, lived their lives and
again disappeared into nothingness." . . . At this point George
sees his own place "in the long march of humanity. Already
he hears death calling." . . . And in the last chapter he joins
the procession when he leaves on the train, and Winesburg
becomes a "background on which to paint the dreams of his
manhood." (pp. 536-38)

In a period of rapid economic growth and expansion, Anderson
was drawing attention to the tragedy of those people, like his
own parents, who did not succeed, and who were alienated
from each other by economic failure and by the repressive
American Puritan ethic. Seeing the lives of such people as a
form of living death underscores the social tragedy that the
book presents, and also suggests a continuity between Anderson's early writing and those later books and stories such as
Many Marriages and **"Out of Nowhere into Nothing"** where
he envisions America as a land of the dead. As a Dance of
Death *Winesburg, Ohio* functions as social satire to warn the
living of what is happening to their lives.

The Dance of Death idea is most closely associated with the
mother figure and directs us to a personal tragedy implicit in
the book—the narrator's sense of filial guilt. While she lived,
Elizabeth Willard and her son seldom spoke to each other;

before her death Elizabeth prayed that her son would some day
"express something" for them both. But the artist's central
insight in the book is that all truth is relative to the individual,
so that he cannot really express anything for his characters—
he can only hint at their secret, repressed lives. Ironically, in
attempting to give dignity to the lives of his people, the narrator
has made them grotesques. . . . At best the narrator, like the
author of the *Spoon River Anthology*, has erected out of love
a series of tombstones for the people he once knew. The Dance
of Death perspective functions then as a framework around the
book reminding us that these characters are now gone, and that
they were never released from the agony of their loneliness
while they lived. (pp. 540-541)

Anderson had dedicated the book as an expression of love to
his mother; we cannot help feeling that it has come too late.
But this of course does not mean that *Winesburg, Ohio* fails
as a work of art. On the contrary, seeing the book as a Dance
of Death further testifies to its richness of pattern and form.
The medieval Dance of Death was a highly ritualized art and
it is that quality of stylized repetition which is most striking
formally in Anderson's book. To see *Winesburg, Ohio* as a
Dance of Death is not only to underscore rightly its essentially
tragic nature, but also to recognize its considerable artistry.
(pp. 541-42)

> David Stouck, "'Winesburg, Ohio' as a Dance of
> Death," in American Literature, Vol. XLVIII, No.
> 4, January, 1977, pp. 525-42.

SAMUEL PICKERING   (essay date 1977)

[*Pickering is an American essayist, critic, and scholar whose
works are chiefly concerned with eighteenth- and nineteenth-century literature. In the following excerpt, he compares the literary
depictions of the growth of a young artist in* Winesburg, Ohio
and in George Moore's Confessions of a Young Man, *finding
both to be in the tradition of nineteenth-century romanticism.*]

Today Anderson is remembered primarily for *Winesburg, Ohio,*
a book which lends itself to creative criticism. In "Why Distant
Objects Please," William Hazlitt explained why far-off things
appealed to a viewer's imagination. Unable to distinguish an
object by sight alone, the observer relied on imagination to
complete his vision. The resulting artistic participation was
both creative and pleasurable. Similar to Hazlitt's distant object, *Winesburg, Ohio*'s short-story structure, partly-told tales,
and unclear thematic organization invite critical creativity and
make the book a sort of "unfinished masterpiece." Thus according to Anderson's best critics, *Winesburg* reflects a contemporary dilemma: the pathos brought about by isolation and
the inability of people to communicate. To some extent such
an interpretation is correct, and it is sounder than sociological
readings which find the novel to be an accurate picture of life
in an American small town. Nevertheless, the critical discovery
of contemporary preoccupations in *Winesburg* distorts Anderson's novel. The book is not primarily about isolation but
focuses instead on the artistic sensibility and the creative process. Anderson's portrait of the artist as a young man faces
backward rather than forward and reflects not modern man's
inability to communicate, but nineteenth-century romanticism.
Winesburg should not be viewed as an actual town ripe for
sociological analysis, but an artistic *milieu* through which the
artist in embryo, George Willard, passes.

Anderson's romanticism cannot be tied to a specific source.
Winesburg, Ohio is permeated by the romanticism that was "in

the air,'' and Anderson's picture of the young artist is conventionally romantic. To illustrate just how conventional Anderson's depiction is, one may compare *Winesburg* with George Moore's semi-autobiographical *Confessions of a Young Man.* Describing the artistic development of an aesthetic young man in Paris at *fin de siècle,* the *Confessions* at first seems literary poles apart from George Willard's growth in rural Ohio. Since romanticism plays so central a role in both books, however, the surface dissimilarity is deceiving; and Moore's and Anderson's views of the development of the artistic sensibility are strikingly alike. (pp. 27-8)

For the romantic, the artist was a rebel, out of step with his times, forever unsatisfied and pursuing the unobtainable. Like Childe Harold, he was not only the ''wandering outlaw of his own dark mind,'' but he was also the outlaw of society. Envisioning the artist in dynamic opposition to convention, romanticism postulated a dialectic in which the artist synthesized the tension produced by his conflict with society in his art. Thus Blake wrote that without contraries there was no progression. Attraction and repulsion, reason and energy, love and hate, he declared, were necessary to full human existence.

To remain a romantic one had to be an alien, that is, one had to avoid adopting a truth or a system. Such an adoption inevitably led, if not to corruption and heartlessness, to mental stagnation. Thus many of Dickens' novels were parables urging readers to adopt the spirit of Christianity and to reject doctrinaire religion. Accordingly *Barnaby Rudge* illustrated the danger of a mechanical acceptance of evangelical Protestantism, and *Hard Times* showed the human destruction brought about by Benthamite utilitarianism. Times became *hard* when one rejected the timeless ''once upon a time'' and adopted a truth. The true romantic was a wanderer able to change his identity. Going on a journey alone, Hazlitt wrote, enabled one to be romantic. ''Oh!'' he declared, ''it is great to shake off the trammels of the world and of public opinion—to lose our importunate, tormenting, everlasting personal identity in the elements of nature, and become the creature of the moment.'' In critical terms the refusal to be locked into an identity resembled Keats's ''poetical Character.'' For Keats the poetical character had no self, but being everything and nothing, it enjoyed light and shade and lived in gusto. This in turn depended, in Keats's words, on negative capability. Fact and reason were for Keats, as they were for Anderson and Moore, the enemies of negative capability. In *Lamia* for example, Keats stressed the danger of truth to the poetical character. Philosophy (truth), he said, would clip an angel's wings, conquer all the mysteries by rule and line, empty the haunted air, and unweave a rainbow. (pp. 29-30)

At the end of the nineteenth century, the devotion to vital imagination and belief in a creative dialectic caused by revolt against society led to despair. In the second edition of *The Renaissance* Walter Pater dropped the conclusion because he thought the effort of burning with a hard gem-like flame could lead to sterile, immoral posturing. Oscar Wilde became the classic illustration. Taking the letter of romanticism for the spirit, Wilde's attempts to demonstrate a vital imagination and a revolt against middle-class morality were postures of a man whose creative imagination was limited and who consciously adopted the trappings of a rebel. Like that of Milton's Satan, Wilde's freedom was specious; unlike the true romantic whose imagination ranged freely across all aspects of life, Wilde was in a sense the slave of convention, and his wit relied heavily on the conscious subversion of accepted aphorisms. Instead of

being the poetical creature of the moment, Wilde was the creation of middle-class conventions.

These romantic views of the imagination and creative dialectic—and the awareness that romanticism can enslave as well as free—pervade both Anderson's and Moore's portraits of the growing artist. To some extent both the *Confessions* and *Winesburg* are artistic self-help manuals, pointing out the dangers threatening the creative sensibility. Although Moore's persona swashbuckles his way to creativity and Anderson's hero remains detached from life, learning from the parable-like experiences of others, both main characters avoid similar pitfalls. Like the archetypical romantic hero of a fairy tale, both heroes leave home. For Moore, it is a matter of escaping from Irish provinciality into a world where he can enjoy a diversity of experiences. On the other hand, leaving Winesburg is a sign of George Willard's having escaped the ''truths'' which turn the town's inhabitants into grotesques. Physical separation from Winesburg enables him to attain artistic perspective on his past experiences. The ability to attain perspective is similarly important to Moore. The *Confessions* end with Moore alone in a Strand boarding house, having rejected the advances of his lascivious landlady, the pathos of Emma the maid, and the friendship of an actress at the Savoy. To reach the position of the lonely artist is not easy for Moore or George Willard. Not only do both young men leave home, but they escape family. On the death of his father, Moore springs ''like a loosened bough up in the light.'' . . . Similarly George Willard leaves Winesburg only after the death of his mother. In terms of romanticism, family ties limit the development of the poetical character. Specific responsibility restricts the free-play of the creative imagination; Disraeli's romantic Sidonia, for example, had to be ''a man without affections,'' riding in and out of people's lives on ''the Daughter of the Star.''

For both Moore and Anderson, religion threatens the artistic sensibility, for it justifies restricting imagination in the name of truth. For Moore Catholicism is more dangerous than Protestantism, which is not particularly good but which at least does not rob ''a man of the right of free will and private judgment.'' . . . In *Winesburg* Anderson provides **''The Strength of God''** as a parable illustrating the destruction of the imagination by Calvinist dogma. In passing it should be noted that Anderson's use of hands in the novel does not, as Walter B. Rideout suggests, symbolize ''the potential or actual communication of one personality with another.'' Instead, hands reveal the nature of Winesburg's frustrated artists, those people Anderson calls grotesques. For Anderson artistic creation does not involve the sense of touch but the ability to dream, and as people lose their poetical characters, they become things, most often hands. Thus Wing Biddlebaum becomes his ineffectual bird-like hands, Dr. Reefy his gnarled knuckles, and Curtis Hartman his bleeding hand. Similarly in *Hard Times,* Bounderby's factories slowly destroy his employees' imaginations, and they ultimately become ''Hands.''

Related to religion's threat to artistic development was respectability, or Arnold's philistinism. To be respectable one had to be in step with social convention, which destroyed the creative dialectic. Emphasizing his individuality, Moore celebrates his expulsion from a Roman Catholic school, scorns university education, and attacks Mudie's circulating library, the contemporary theatre, London clubs, and suburban villas. Such things, Moore writes, produce lethargy instead of promoting ''intensity of feeling'' and ''fervor of the mind.'' Aware of the seductive danger of comfort, he writes that ''art should

North Main Street, Clyde, Ohio, circa 1880.

be a practical protest against the so-called decencies of life.'' . . . Although more muted than the *Confessions, Winesburg*'s warning against respectability is just as strong. Near the end of the novel, wealthy, educated, attractive Helen White is George's for the asking. The epitome of self-satisfied respectability, she is the last and most dangerous threat to George's growth into an artist.

For Anderson lust or love threatened the development of the artist. Anderson uses the attempt to objectify love, moreover, as a metaphoric warning against an artist's forcing his imagination into a set form. Consequently *Winesburg* not only examines George's growing sexual awareness but also describes the destruction of artistic potential by love. In his memoirs Anderson simplifies Coleridge's belief that the imagination is vital while objects are dead, writing that men do not live in facts but in dreams.

In describing George's life, Anderson shows the artist's progression from a longing for the dead object to satisfaction with the vital imagination, or on another level from forcing his feelings into a set form to letting the form arise naturally out of the feelings. In particular George outgrows his hands; he progresses from thinking that to touch Louise Trunnion's gingham dress would be ''an exquisite pleasure'' . . . to being satisfied to walk with Helen White and to dream beyond the particular experience. Central to George's development and Anderson's examination of the vital imagination is **''An Awakening.''** In the story George wanders at night through Winesburg's dimly

lit slum. With the street lights throwing a gauze over reality and freeing George from the tyranny of sight, and with the missing portions of sidewalk breaking all straight lines, George's environment resembles an impressionistic painting. Moreover, the muffled sounds and smells of the slum combine with George's recent study of life in medieval towns to awaken his ''fancy,'' with the result that he feels ''oddly detached and apart from life.'' . . . (pp. 30-3)

For Anderson detachment from life, or stock literary convention, was necessary to artistic sensibility, and the ending of **''An Awakening''** stresses the importance of maintaining creative independence. Attempting to objectify his vague feelings, George tries to seduce Belle Carpenter, with the result that Belle's lover throttles him. No longer able to bear the sight of the slum which has so stimulated his imagination, George runs ''to get quickly out of the neighbourhood that now seemed to him utterly squalid and commonplace.'' . . . In Coleridgean terms the artist has been reduced to a sense of touch and a fixed object. As Philosophy in *Lamia* clips an angel's wings, so searching for an objective correlative to imaginative feelings destroys creativity. Several other of the Winesburg stories also warn against trying to objectify imaginative feelings, or impose conventional form upon inspiration. In **''Adventure''** Alice Hindman is an artistic dreamer until she attempts to find her dream in the objective world. Inevitably disappointed, she fails as an artist and metonymically becomes a thing, the dry goods in the store in which she works. Reversing the ''lived happily ever after'' view of the Pygmalion myth, **"Respectability"** shows the transformation of the artist into a beast.

First published in French in 1886, the *Confessions* does not stress the dangers of woman to creativity or use man's search for love to show that form should arise out of a work. Although he obliquely alludes to the dangers of marriage, Moore uses passion for books as Anderson uses passion for women. Despite likening himself to a wax tablet upon which impressions are continually being made, Moore's embryonic artist is more dynamic than Anderson's. For Anderson Keats's description of the poetical character as having no self meant that George had to be faceless. Living through the light and shade of *Winesburg*, George stores impressions for the time when he will write. Since George is the poetical character, Anderson tells little about George's thought processes and almost nothing about his actual appearance. For Moore, in contrast, having no self meant the aspiring artist prismatically changes personalities.

Actively searching for a form for his imaginative longings, Moore's growing artist enthusiastically reads "friends and books with the same passion." His youth, Moore writes, ran into manhood like a rivulet jumping from rock to rock and gathering strength at each leap. Instead of outgrowing Louise Trunnion, Belle Carpenter, and Helen White, Moore grows beyond Shelley, Gautier, Zola, Flaubert, and Goncourt. (pp. 33-4)

The *Confessions* and *Winesburg, Ohio* not only describe the growth of the artistic sensibility, but, by making form parallel content, the books invite readers' imaginative participation. In **"The Philosopher"** Dr. Parcival tells George tales that begin nowhere and end nowhere. Sometimes George thinks the stories are all invention; other times he is convinced they contain "the very essence of truth." Like the darkness and disorder in **"An Awakening,"** Dr. Parcival's stories appeal to George's imagination and force him to see beyond dead objects into an imaginative world. Likewise the structure of *Winesburg, Ohio* its irregular time continuum, and its mysterious characters like Dr. Parcival, force the reader's imagination to fill in narrative gaps. Correspondingly the semi-autobiographical *Confessions* challenges the reader to search for truth while the book's form, a compound of fiction, English and French poetry, critical essays, and drama thwart attempts to fit it into a conventional genre. (p. 35)

[Let] us examine the conclusion of the *Confessions*. Alone in his room, "haggard and overworn," the artist sits writing a novel. At first glance, he appears to have escaped the conforming pressures of the world. However, the artist's room is confining rather than expansive; instead of living in gusto amid the conflicting formative influences of Paris, he has retired to a garret suspiciously resembling a monk's cell. Having fled from a Catholic College as a youth, Moore has come full circle and embraced an ascetic life.

This view is reinforced by the catechism-like dialogue which he holds with his conscience. Of course Moore could have retreated from the world as George Willard left Winesburg because his varied experiences have gradually led to the maturity of artistic sensibility. This reasoning, however, seems doubtful, and if we interpret Moore's early creative efforts as foreshadowing what his novel will be, we should be pessimistic. Moore's poems, for example, were at best mere exercises; at worst they were dead, for like George Willard in **'An Awakening,"** he erred in trying to find an objective correlative for his vital imagination. As the lyric form he chose for his poems was inadequate, so we can conclude that the

form he will choose for his novel will be dead. Moreover, if we take the *Confessions* as the product of Moore's artistic sensibility, then we must conclude that he, like the Ancient Mariner, unconsciously makes his peace with the world and is no longer the romantic rebel. At best Moore is mocking, for the *Confessions*, like the Mariner's moral platitudes, are trite repetitions of romantic poetic theory. Instead of freeing his imagination, the artist chooses not only dead form but lifeless content. Like the Mariner, he is slavishly reduced to both histrionic living and writing.

Despair or reduction to a literary posture seems to be the inevitable lot of the romantic artist. Although *Winesburg* is structurally completed by George's departure, the novel is not thematically completed. Since the stories do not progress in temporal sequence, the novel invites the reader to search for a thematic, rather than a narrative, figure in the carpet. As a result *Winesburg*'s structure resembles that of *The Ring and the Book*. In the center is the truth, for Anderson a comprehensive view of the life of the artist; around the ring are various stories metaphorically describing the development of the creative sensibility, the dangers threatening the artist, and finally a picture of the inevitable fate of the artist.

Enoch Robinson's story foreshadows George's fate. Since Enoch is effectually George, **"Loneliness"** thematically concludes the novel. A native of Winesburg like George, Enoch leaves Ohio for New York when he is twenty-one. There he becomes the romantic artist that George will become. His impressionistic paintings "crude things, half-finished," Anderson stresses, embody the shadowed world of **"An Awakening."** Like George, Enoch is a dreamer, and when his New York friends, incapable of negative capability, discuss "line and values and composition," Enoch's incoherent stammering resembles George's muttering when he roams through Winesburg's slum. As Winesburg is the background on which George will paint the dreams of his manhood, so spots of light remind Enoch of the people he knew as a boy. After saying that one of his paintings shows a woman suffering, Enoch adds, "I didn't try to paint the woman, of course. She is too beautiful to be painted." . . . By refusing to restrict his painting to a dead object, Enoch keeps his imagination romantically vital.

Like Moore's developing artist, only Enoch's intense "passion for art" preserves his imagination. Unfortunately . . . , the world, in the form of "actualities" like money, marriage, children, taxes, and even streetcars, exerts an irresistible pressure to conform. Like Moore, Enoch resists the pressures by shutting himself away in artistic isolation. Even this, Anderson implies, was not enough to insure continued creativity. . . .

Enoch unconsciously lost his poetical character. Waking one morning to find his vital imagination gone, somehow worn away by living in the world, Enoch returns to Winesburg to spend the rest of his days . . . telling his story. . . . (pp. 37-8)

Both *Confessions* and *Winesburg* end on a despairing note. (p. 38)

Samuel Pickering, ''Winesburg, Ohio': A Portrait of the Artist as a Young Man," in* The Southern Quarterly, *Vol. XVI, No. 1, October, 1977, pp. 27-38.*

ROGER ASSELINEAU (essay date 1980)

[*Asselineau, a French poet, critic, and scholar, is considered an expert on the literature of the United States. Author of the study* Realisme, reve, et expressionnisme dans ''Winesburg, Ohio'' *(1957) and editor of* Configuration critique de Sherwood Anderson *(1963), Asselineau has also written and edited works on Walt Whitman, Mark Twain, and Edgar Allan Poe—all of whom Anderson admired—as well as on Ernest Hemingway, an early Anderson disciple. Characterizing his own work as a critic, Asselineau has stated that "I have chiefly written about poets—or about novelists or short story writers who were also poets, whether they were aware of it or not." In the following excerpt, Asselineau discusses Anderson's use of symbolism and expressionistic techniques in treating the mysterious life beyond appearances with which the stories in* Winesburg, Ohio *are concerned.]*

When *Winesburg, Ohio* appeared in 1919, people saw nothing but its realism or naturalism. It was hailed as a masterpiece of naturalism by reviewers who read it through Dreiser. Francis Hackett, for instance, called Sherwood Anderson "a naturalist with a skirl of music." It seemed to him and other critics that Anderson's main concern was an attempt to copy reality as faithfully and accurately as possible without shrinking from the coarser aspects of life. There is some truth in this, but it is not the whole truth. . . .

At first sight . . . the stories which make up *Winesburg, Ohio,* offer a satisfactory cross-section of village life in the Middle West in the author's time. Both the background and the characters are authentic. It has been proved that Sherwood Anderson used childhood memories, and Winesburg is the Clyde of his boyhood with hardly any change. He even preserved some of the original names of streets and tradespeople. There are indeed passages which read like descriptions in a guidebook. (pp. 124-25)

At times we have the impression of thumbing a collection of old picture postcards. The topographic and photographic realism is impeccable, and the observer remains as cold and detached as the lens of a camera. He shows no emotion and never smiles. He does not idealize, either, by smoothing over unpleasant details. As Sherwood Anderson himself said in *Tar:* "Being a realist in his writing and thinking, Tar (that is to say, himself) did not make the houses of his town very comfortable or the people particularly good or in any way exceptional."

The characters and their experiences are depicted in the same spirit of objectivity and complete neutrality:

> One afternoon a man of the town, Henry Bradford, who kept a saloon, came to the schoolhouse door. Calling Adolph Myers into the school yard he began to beat him with his fists. As his hard knuckles beat down into the frightened face of the school master, his wrath became more and more terrible. Screaming with dismay, the children ran here and there like disturbed insects. . . .

In such passages, Sherwood Anderson purposely confines himself to describing the behavior of the actors. True, it is not behaviorism properly speaking, since, to some extent, he interprets the gestures and screams which he describes and uses such words as "frightened" and "dismay" to help us understand what is taking place in the minds of the characters, but he passes no judgments and in appearance does not take sides.

However, despite this surface realism, it soon becomes obvious that his laconic descriptions are not truly realistic. A true realist is prolix and indulges in long and minute inventories of external reality based on careful observations methodically recorded in notebooks, for he always carries a notebook in his pocket to collect so-called true facts. Thus Arnold Bennett after walking along the Thames noted: "I passed 68 gulls sitting on the railings. . . ." The idea of counting gulls while taking a walk would have made Sherwood Anderson laugh. "The writer with a notebook in his hand," he noted in a letter, "is always a bad workman, a man who distrusts his imagination."

Anyway, though he described the surface of life with impartiality and candor, Sherwood Anderson wanted above all to go beyond it, as he said quite explicitly in dedicating *Winesburg, Ohio,* to his mother:

> To the memory of my mother, Emma Smith Anderson, whose keen observations on the life about her first awoke in me the hunger to see beneath the surface of lives, this book is dedicated.

He attributes the very same hunger to George Willard, the central hero of the book. . . . (pp. 125-26)

Realism merely provides Sherwood Anderson with a basis on which to build the almost fantastic stories of his grotesques. Lionel Trilling missed the point when he protested against the lack of reality of his fiction, against what he called "a pretty inadequate representation of reality." "In Anderson's world," he said, "there are many emotions, or rather many instances of a few emotions, but there are few sights, sounds, and smells, very little of the stuff of reality." Actuality was merely a springboard for Anderson's imagination. He was not interested in what realists rather naïvely call truth. At the very beginning of his foreword to *Tar,* he unequivocally declared: "I have a confession to make. I am a story teller telling a story and cannot be expected to tell the truth. Truth is impossible to me. . . ." And in his **"Note on Realism,"** he added: "No man can quite make himself a camera. Even the most realistic worker pays some tribute to what is called 'art.' Where does representation end and art begin? The location of the line is often as confusing to practicing artists as it is to the public." (p. 127)

[Sherwood Anderson] very clearly realized that art is not necessarily synonymous with artifice and must not therefore be avoided at all costs. He was fully aware that he was an artist himself whenever he let his imagination interfere with, and distort, reality—which happened most of the time when he was telling stories. He considered this an inevitable process and even a desirable one. For to his mind, realism, the mere reproduction of reality, must not be an end in itself, but only a means to an end. To what end?

By and large he was not particularly interested in banal everyday occurrences. He said himself in a *A Story Teller's Story:* "I have come to think that the true history of life is but a story of moments. It is only at rare moments that we live." Consequently, he felt he must select and give only a discontinuous image of life, throwing into relief those intense crucial moments when we cease to have standard reactions and fully become ourselves. He was therefore less interested in his characters' everyday gestures and daily experiences than in their dark and secret life, and that is why *Winesburg, Ohio,* is largely set in twilight or obscurity, as if the characters dared to become or express themselves only under cover of darkness, when sheltered by night. It is then that they can let out what they usually keep hidden or unexpressed for fear of being laughed at or even punished by the community in which they live. What is thus brought to the surface is often some neurosis of sexual origin, but, although some of them display abnormal tendencies—homosexuality in the case of Wing Biddlebaum, nymphomania in the case of Mrs. Willard before her marriage, exhibitionism in the case of Alice Hindman, who cannot resist the impulse to go out naked into the street, etc.—Sherwood Anderson was not interested in abnormal characters for their own sake. He was not a disciple of Freud. Though sex is a powerful urge in his characters' lives, it is never really an obsession. Their world is not ruled over by an all-pervasive *libido*. Moreover, Sherwood Anderson does not explore their minds in order to find out how they could best get readjusted to society, for he regards the individual as more precious than society and society as something dull and sterile.

He was not a sexual realist, either. Though frank about sexual matters, he remains very discreet on the whole. In **"Nobody Knows,"** we do not know, either, for he has censored the description of George Willard's intercourse with Louise Trunnion. All we get is a line of suspension points. But what his characters crave is less the satisfaction of a physical need than the fulfilment of a mysterious spiritual hunger, which psychoanalysts would no doubt interpret in terms of sexual love, but which he refuses for his part to consider in such a crude light. To him it is something ethereal and hardly expressible, and it is this hunger for love that he wants to express above all. What matters in his stories is not what he actually describes in a more or less realistic manner, but what he suggests and leaves unsaid. He has described his method himself in terms of painting in **"Loneliness":**

> When a picture he (Enoch Robinson, the hero of the story) had painted was under discussion, he wanted to burst out with something like this: "You don't get the point," he wanted to explain; "the picture you see doesn't consist of the things you see and say words about. There is something else, something you don't see at all, something you are not intended to see. Look at this one over here.... The dark spot by the road that you might not notice at all is, you see, the beginning of everything. There is a clump of elders there ... and in among the elders there is something hidden. It is a woman, that's what it is. She has been thrown from a horse and the horse has run away out of sight.... It's a woman you see, that's what it is! It's a woman and, oh, she is lovely! She is hurt and suffering but she makes no sound.... She lies quite still, white and still, and the beauty comes out from her and spreads over everything.... I didn't try to paint the woman, of course. She is too beautiful to be painted.

This passage gives us a key to Sherwood Anderson's aesthetics. What counts in *Winesburg, Ohio,* is not George Willard or the grotesques who people the village, but the love which they hide in their hearts, something *beyond* appearances. The grotesques in the book are not merely what they seem to be. Nothing in Winesburg really is what it seems to be. The hands of Wing Biddlebaum are not merely human hands, but "the piston-rods of his machinery of expression" or "the wings of an imprisoned bird." Further on, they are metamorphosed into "fluttering pennants of promise," closely akin to Whitman's "pennants of joy" in "Song of the Open Road" ... and "The Sleepers." ... (pp. 127-29)

Exterior resemblances do not count, but only the meaning, the secret life of things. Such images have very little plastic value.

They are not intended to describe the outside, but to suggest the inside of things. (p. 129)

Contrary to what contemporary reviewers thought, then, "realism" is not the term which must be applied to Sherwood Anderson's art. Two other words would be more appropriate, though he never used them himself: symbolism and expressionism.

There are indeed other symbolic hands in *Winesburg, Ohio,* besides the restless hands of Wing Biddlebaum—those of Dr. Reefy: "The knuckles of the Doctor's hands," Sherwood Anderson tells us, "were extraordinarily large. When the hands were closed, they looked like clusters of unpainted wooden balls as large as walnuts fastened together by steel rods." (As if they had been painted by Fernand Léger.) Later, Sherwood Anderson compares them to the gnarled, twisted apples left by the pickers in an orchard, and he adds: "Only the few know the sweetness of the twisted apples." This is obviously an elder bush, and we must look for the woman hidden in the middle of it.

Apparently hands had always obsessed Sherwood Anderson. The obsession dated back to his childhood, for in *Tar* he confessed: "People's hands, rooms in houses, the faces of fields were things the child did not forget: the old carpenter had short stumpy fingers. The nails were black and broken. The fingers of the doctor were, like his mother's, rather long." Once, during a serious illness, he had a nightmare: "Things that should be small became large, things that should remain large, became small. Often Tar's own hands, white and small, seemed to leave his arms and float away. They floated away over the tops of the trees seen through the window and almost disappeared into the sky." But young Tar-Anderson was especially impressed by his mother's hands: "The slender, long, work-roughened fingers of Tar's mother fascinated him. He remembered them clearly long afterward, when her figure began to grow dim in his mind. It may have been the memory of his mother's hands that made him think so much about other people's hands. With their hands, young lovers touched each other tenderly, painters spent a long lifetime training the hands to follow the dictates of their fancies, men in workshops grasped tools with their hands. Hands young and strong, boneless soft hands at the ends of arms of boneless soft men, hands of fighters—knocking other men down—the steady quiet hands of railroad engineers at the throttles of huge engines, soft hands creeping toward bodies in the night, hands beginning to age, to tremble, the hands of a mother that touch the babe, the hands of a mother remembered clearly, the hands of a father forgotten." (This list reads almost like one of Whitman's catalogues.)

Hands are thus charged with meaning for Sherwood Anderson, and he discloses what they mean to him incidentally, almost accidentally toward the end of *Winesburg, Ohio,* when, referring to George Willard's hands, he says: "With all his heart he wants to come close to some other human, touch someone with his hands, be touched by the hand of another." Hands thus mean communication and communion between men. It is through them that the love of one man for another can flow and that is why they loom so large in Sherwood Anderson's internal universe.

In the same way, many unobtrusive details in Sherwood Anderson's fiction have a meaning and are not mere inanimate stage properties. Bedrooms suggest the isolation of the individual who feels "choked and walled-in by life in (an) apartment." The church tower in which in the Reverend Hartman meditates and prays alone at night symbolizes a still greater degree of isolation. The repressed and unsatisfied craving for love of the inhabitants of Winesburg is again and again suggested by words like "hunger" or it corollary "to feed." All these words or images project us beyond appearances into a world where everything is different and mysterious. There are constant correspondences between the so-called real world and the spiritual world of love which it hides. Some of these images are quite transparent, but others are like thick clumps of elders on the roadside. They either fail to attract our attention because they seem so banal, or, if they somehow arrest us, we cannot pierce their mystery.

So, though we may not notice it, in **"The Strength of God,"** the Reverend Curtis Hartman's Bible is at first open on his desk and is the source from which he draws his inspiration for the sermon he is writing. Later, when he is assailed by temptation, the Bible is still there, but he does not even look at it. When he finally triumphs over temptation, it falls from his desk with a great clatter. All these are not mere realistic notations intended to give the reader a true picture of a minister's environment. They are much more than that. They are meant to illustrate the fact that "the strength of God," which originally emanated from the Bible, in the last scene, ironically enough, reaches the Reverend Hartman through the very temptations which very nearly destroyed him, and at that time the Bible is no longer of any use to him.

The same story contains more mysterious details. In the minister's study, at the top of the bell tower of his church, there is a stained glass window "showing the Christ laying his hand on the head of a child." When the Reverend Hartman discovers that from this window he can see a woman lying in bed and smoking in the upper room of the house across the street, he breaks one of the little leaded panes of the window the better to watch her without running the risk of being seen himself. Now, it happens that the broken piece of glass "just nipped off the bare heel of the boy standing motionless and looking with rapt eyes into the face of Christ." Why should it be the heel of the boy? Sherwood Anderson, of course, does not tell us. It is up to us to guess, up to us to remember Genesis III: 15, where the Lord curses the serpent in the following words: "And I will put enmity between thee and the woman, and between thy seed and her seed: it shall bruise thy head and thou shalt bruise his heel."

The heel thus stands for man's vulnerability to evil. It is our heel that the serpent stings and through our heel that evil invades us. It is natural therefore that evil thoughts should enter the minister's mind through the hole in the young boy's heel. But one night, just as the Reverend Hartman is about to yield to sinful thoughts, he catches sight of the woman kneeling on her bed and praying, looking exactly like the boy on the stained glass window. In short, he finds innocence where he expected to find sin. Purity is made whole again, and the minister, after smashing the window with his fist, goes out crying: "I have found the light. . . . God has manifested himself in the body of a woman."

Other episodes resist analysis. (pp. 129-32)

[We] do not always find the woman hidden away among the elders, but it does not matter, for what counts is not the precise meaning of this or that detail, but the light diffused through the sky over the clump of elders. (pp. 132-33)

Sherwood Anderson's tales are so many meditations on life in the form of images. They express, on the one hand, his conviction that life is absurd and, on the other hand, the love for all that lives, which he cannot help experiencing, as he says quite explicitly toward the end of **Winesburg, Ohio,** in **"Sophistication":** "One shudders at the thought of the meaninglessness of life, while at the same instant . . . one loves life so intensely that tears come into the eyes." Consequently, he is interested in his characters from a metaphysical or religious rather than a psychological or social point of view. In his eyes, they symbolized that baffling, impenetrable mystery of life which fascinated him. The spectacle of even the most humble life going on about him sometimes stirred intense emotions and nearly intoxicated him. (p. 133)

Like a true romantic artist he despised form: "You see, I have the belief that in this matter of form, it is largely a matter of depth of feeling. How deeply do you feel it? Feel it deeply enough and you will be torn inside and driven on until form comes." It is all a matter of inspiration. Nothing else really counts.

Actually, though "driven on" and "torn inside" to the point of abandoning his business and his family in order to devote himself wholly to his art, he was not at all indifferent to or unaware of the technical aspects of storytelling. For all his dash and passion, he was, in his own way, a conscious and conscientious artist. He did not write off his stories at one sitting, but often rewrote them several times. He thus gradually and gropingly evolved his own medium. When he started writing, it was the fashion to compose realistic stories, and so he wrote some like everyone else, but he soon developed his own form of realism by combining realistic descriptions with more or less elaborate symbolic images, and the result was sometimes quite close to expressionism.

*Ex*pressionism essentially consists in *ex*teriorizing subjective *im*pressions by *ex*aggerating certain aspects of *ex*ternal reality. Now this is precisely what Sherwood Anderson does in some of his stories where we can observe the abnormal predominance of some detail which obviously obsesses him. (p. 134)

Sherwood Anderson's ultimate aim was to communicate moods rather than tell stories. His subjects were "moments," as he said, "revelations," sudden intuitions provoked by some more or less banal incident. So he needed no plot and never had enough matter for a novel. Even in the story called **"Adventure,"** in fact, nothing really happens in spite of the promise of the title. His was a world of contemplation rather than action. And, in this connection, it must be noted that nobody, or hardly anybody, kills or gets killed in his stories. Even Wash Williams does not really kill his mother-in-law for all his passion: she rather anticlimactically dies of a fever one month after he has beaten her with a chair. How different from the worlds of Faulkner or Hemingway and all their successors! His stories, thus, are rather sketches than stories proper. Rather than fiction, they are lyric poetry in the form of fiction. Each of them is a poetic epiphany in the course of which we are suddenly brought into contact with the inexpressible mystery of life. At least Sherwood Anderson tries to make us feel it or get a glimpse of it. Unfortunately, he sometimes fails. The "new looseness" on which he counted so much and which was to free him from the shackles of convention occasionally proved to be a hindrance rather than a help. There are times when the clumps of elders are so thick and so dark that it becomes quite impossible to see the woman hidden among them or even suspect that there can be one there.

She is there just the same, unattainable, but almost within reach—like Emerson's oversoul. (p. 135)

Roger Asselineau, "Beyond Realism: Sherwood Anderson's Transcendentalist Aesthetics," in his The Transcendentalist Constant in American Literature, New York University Press, 1980, pp. 124-36.

FREDERICK W. SHILSTONE (essay date 1982)

[*In the following excerpt, Shilstone discusses the maturation of George Willard.*]

Sherwood Anderson's *Winesburg, Ohio* ... appeared in the same year as Irving Babbitt's scathing attack on early nineteenth-century literature, *Rousseau and Romanticism*. While history affords numerous examples of very different works appearing at the same time, many of Anderson's contemporaries would have seen logical harmony in this literary twin birth. Babbitt was joined by others like Paul Elmer More and even T. S. Eliot in accusing the Romantics of egocentric morbidity and isolation, flaccid imagery, and an improper sense of form; and overt hostility toward Shelley and others was natural in a forum soon to be dominated by the New Criticism, even if that school was to give the same begrudging nod to Keats's genius that Samuel Johnson had earlier extended to Shakespeare's. In that climate, to consider *Winesburg, Ohio* a Romantic work would have been virtually unthinkable, and, indeed, responses to the book, when not moralistic, tended to focus on its regional flavor and to appropriate the language of the relatively new and developing disciplines of sociology and psychology in interpreting it. ... To surmount the obvious limitations of a realistic appraisal of *Winesburg, Ohio,* it is necessary to look beyond its superficially regional qualities— its stylistic approximation of midwestern speech patterns, for instance—and to read the book in light of the tradition that so many of Anderson's contemporaries were attacking: the Romantic.

The image of Anderson as a chronicler of horses and men in the American Midwest has not completely diverted attention from the Romantic essence of *Winesburg, Ohio*. Both in the text of the book itself and in supporting documents one finds evidence that Anderson saw himself as a successor to those writers who preceded him by a century. His use of psychological rather than linear time in the arrangement of the narrative (or novelistic) element of *Winesburg*—an approximation of the dream sequence that passes before the aged writer's eyes in the introductory **"Book of the Grotesque"** ...—links the text with similar experiments in the writings of Coleridge, De Quincey, and others of their era. Further, Anderson's description of the writing process itself emphasizes the naturalness and spontaniety associated with the Romantic aesthetic: "The short story is the result of a sudden passion. ... All of my own short stories have been written at one sitting, many of them under strange circumstances." Echoes of Wordsworth's "spontaneous overflow," of Shelley's fading coal of inspiration, and of the denials of Coleridge and Poe that a long poem can be all poetry are clearly heard here. In response to these and similar hints, more recent approaches to *Winesburg* have admitted the Romantic tradition and have thus begun an important reappraisal of the book and its place in literary history.

Simply evoking Romanticism does not solve the riddle of *Winesburg,* however; radical disagreements existed among the writers of that era, and those disagreements have extended to students of the age ever since. Recent discussions of Anderson's work do concur that the key to its Romantic content is

the character George Willard, the young reporter for the *Winesburg Eagle* who actually or implicitly takes part in virtually all the stories told. In the most thorough analysis of Willard to date, Samuel Pickering places the young man in the Romantic tradition of the cursed, detached artist, a figure "in dynamic opposition to convention," one who must cast off all ties of religion, family, and love in his quest for artistic perfection [see excerpt dated 1977]. The title of Pickering's article alludes to Joyce's *Portrait of the Artist as a Young Man,* and the piece clearly sees George Willard and Stephen Dedalus as brothers in Romantic isolation. Willard's development does occur in Romantic terms, but not those that Pickering chooses. Rather, Willard moves from confused, immature adolescent to incipient poet, a process that involves not isolation but what the critic William Hazlitt called sympathetic imagination. For the specific tradition of Hazlitt and his disciple Keats clearly underlies the characterization of Anderson's protagonist. (pp. 105-06)

In the first *Winesburg* story after the introductory **"Book of the Grotesque,"** the narrator states that discussing Wing Biddlebaum "is a job for a poet." ... Significantly, Anderson is frequently described as a lyricist or prose poet, and I believe he was prone to see himself as occupying that highest place among writers (to use a Keatsian definition that has little to do with the peculiarities of the genre). To the extent, then, that George Willard's story embodies Anderson's view of his own development as a "poet," the stories in *Winesburg* chart the halting, error-ridden but nonetheless inexorable assumption of sympathetic imagination by the protagonist. (p. 107)

The ultimate coherence of the *Winesburg* stories lies in the way they reveal, gradually and subtly, the awakening of sympathetic imagination in George Willard's mind. George's progress as poet is not neat and linear, but his repeated exposure to the grotesques affects him in the same way Hazlitt's slaves will sway an imaginative (hence moral) individual. George tells his mother early on, "I just want to go away and look at people and think" ... , a sign that he has the potential to develop into a writer, since the listening he does early in *Winesburg* provides a necessary prelude to sympathy. The learning process involves his continuing and ever-intensifying curiosity about the very characters his townsmen continually shun. On viewing the "hideous, leering face" of Winesburg's filthy misogynist, Wash Williams, George is "consumed with curiosity." ... Whenever he sees the frustrated Elmer Cowley of the story **"Queer,"** he wishes "to make friends with the young merchant and find out what [is] in his mind." ... Such references pervade *Winesburg,* and the receptivity they chart occasionally has fruitful results, as in George's response to hearing Wash Williams' narrative: "The young reporter felt ill and weak. In imagination, he also became old and shapeless." ... But the breakthroughs in the early stories are few, while lapses in George's development of sympathetic imagination are many. In the story **"The Teacher"** (relatively late in the volume), Kate Swift perceives what George must do to become a writer, a profession whose real nature he does not at this stage understand: "You must not become a mere peddler of words. The thing to learn is to know exactly what people are thinking about, not what they say." ... In associating sympathetic imagination with the writer's trade, Kate hits precisely upon George's ideal and his struggle in achieving it.

"The Teacher" is one of the stories in which George finds himself baffled and unsure of himself in the presence of a woman, and George's relationships with the opposite sex are the most evident marks of his changing character. The lack of true communication between George and his mother—Anderson calls the "communion" between them "a formal thing without meaning" . . .—relates not only to the general theme of isolation in *Winesburg;* it also acts as only the first of many instances of a barrier that could well prevent George himself from escaping a form of "grotesqueness." (pp. 107-08)

George's egocentric treatment of females surfaces in tales scattered throughout most of *Winesburg.* Kate Swift's sobbing exit from the *Eagle* office after her seemingly tender overtures to the young reporter leaves George angry, then confused: "The resentment, natural to the baffled male, passed and he tried to understand what had happened. He could not make it out." . . . Even as late in the collection as the story **"An Awakening,"** one that charts further troubles with a woman, this time Belle Carpenter, George speaks the following nonsense: ". . . women should look out for themselves. . . . [T]he fellow who went out with a girl was not responsible for what happened." . . . But George's misapprehension of women is even more obvious in **"Nobody Knows,"** where Anderson draws the most unfavorable picture of the young reporter in the entire *Winesburg* collection. From the very outset of this tale, George acts in a sneaky, guilty, suspicious manner as he slinks to meet Louise Trunnion, who has reached out to him in another of the grotesques' futile attempts to communicate. George has taken the invitation as a sexual one, and Anderson makes clear that lust in George will have its day: "The whispered tales concerning [Louise] that had gone about town gave him confidence. He became wholly the male, bold and aggressive." . . . What reveals the link between George's behavior here and its role in hindering his development as "poet" appears in Anderson's summary of George's treatment of Louise: "In his heart there was no sympathy for her." . . . To the degree that George lacks true imaginative sympathy for women, he is, throughout most of *Winesburg,* unworthy to be a writer.

The main focus both of George's "affections" and of the theme of his apprehensions of women resides in his thoughts of and actions with Helen White, the banker's daughter, throughout *Winesburg.* Here, a pattern of improvement, by Hazlitt's standard, becomes clear. In the early stories, Helen White rarely appears in fact, but she certainly exists in George's thoughts— more properly, misapprehensions—of her. George's lack of sympathetic understanding for Helen surfaces in two distinct ways. First, Helen, as do so many other women in the adolescent reporter's mind, evokes his lustful fantasies. . . . The other side of George's misdirected "love" for Helen White forms an idealized dream, where this girl plays Sleeping Beauty to his Prince Charming. Throughout *Winesburg* we see George struggling to write a love story, and Anderson reveals in the tale **"The Thinker"** that it contains an idealized account of Willard's fantasies about Helen White. Here, the relationship between George's aspirations as a writer and his need to overcome his misapprehensions of women emerges as the dominant concern of this story and of the *Winesburg* collection as a whole. In the space of about two pages, George makes three absurd, but related, statements: that a writer's life is "the easiest of all lives to live," since it involves merely traveling around with "no one to boss you"; that George, in all of his ignorance of women, is "trying to write a love story"; and, finally, that he, through an arbitrary act of will, is "going to fall in love with" Helen White. . . . Clear in Anderson's presentation of this episode is his belief that George's true sense of the writer's craft will coincide with his breaking through his lack of sympathy for women, particularly Helen White.

The breakthrough for George does, fortunately, occur, and it forms the substance of the last two stories in *Winesburg,* **"Sophistication"** and **"Departure."** The first of these, subtitled "concerning Helen White," presents this character for the first time, for both George and the book's readers, as a realistically complex individual. And that presentation coincides with George's increasing maturity, the onset of which Anderson describes in terms that relate it to the young writer's development of sympathetic imagination. The **"Sophistication"** of this story's title begins with George's complete abandonment of the egotism that has marked his earlier treatment of Helen and other women: "To his mind his new sense of maturity set him apart, made of him a half-tragic figure." . . . This increasingly "imaginative boy" has been forced to accept the tragic vision of the writer's craft as he "looks out upon the world, seeing, as though they marched in procession before him, the countless figures of men who before his time have come out of nothingness into the world, lived their lives and again disappeared into nothingness." . . . With this realization, the grotesques' gift to Willard, the new sophisticate goes with Helen White to the deserted Winesburg fairgrounds, and there realizes the essence of his new vision. George thinks with embarrassment back on a summer evening when he walked with Helen and used her solely as a sounding board for his own ego, when he "boasted 'I'm going to be a big man, the biggest that ever lived here in Winesburg'" and "tried to say something impressive." . . . Now, on this "warm fall evening," George clearly has sympathy for Helen: "I have come to this lonely place and here is this other." . . . Anderson leaves no doubt about the source of that sympathy: "In youth there are always two forces fighting in people. The warm unthinking little animal struggles against the thing that reflects and remembers, and the older, the more sophisticated thing had possession of George Willard." . . . In overcoming the primary block to his developing the sympathetic imagination required of a writer, George, at least in Hazlitt's eyes, has arrived.

When George leaves Winesburg in **"Departure,"** he does so not with contempt or fear for the town and its effects on people, but rather with love. The images of the grotesques and, preeminently, of "Helen White standing by a window in the Winesburg post office" . . . pass through his memory and convince him of the lessons he has learned in this small Ohio town, "a background on which to paint the dreams of his manhood." . . . (pp. 109-10)

If the grotesques embody what Irving Howe sees as a primary concern of *Winesburg*—"the loss of love in the modern world"— George Willard reflects a theme equally as important: the poet's need sympathetically to portray the lives of his fellows in suffering. Anderson's *Memoirs* provide the final word on that theme, first in the "Preface," where this author describes the most admirable quality a person, and writer, can have: "that tenderness for others that can come only from freedom from the self-consciousness that plays such havoc with most of us." Later, in the "Forward," Anderson discusses how his *Memoirs* are an attempt to develop that admired quality in himself: "I would like to write a book of the mind and of the imagination. . . . I believe in the imaginative life, its importance and would like to write of that" [see *TCLC,* Vol. I]. In the story of George Willard's development in *Winesburg,* Anderson had long since realized this goal and, in so realizing it, had helped to preserve a vital facet of the Romantic vision in the modern world. (p. 111)

Frederick W. Shilstone, "Egotism, Sympathy, and George Willard's Development as Poet in 'Wines-

burg, Ohio'," in West Virginia University Philological Papers, *Vol. 28, 1982, pp. 105-13.*

ELLEN KIMBEL (essay date 1984)

[*In the following excerpt, Kimbel maintains that* Winesburg, Ohio *is a literary metaphor for the loneliness and fear experienced by the members of a culture in the midst of radical change.*]

That Sherwood Anderson . . . recognized and responded to the "modern" in Dreiser is not surprising. So altogether different in method, configuration, and effect from traditional modes are his own **Winesburg, Ohio** stories . . . that it is as though a new genre had been born. The influence of the work cannot be overstated: as a consequence of its publication, the American short story was never to look the same again.

Anderson's distinctiveness becomes most obvious when his techniques are contrasted to those of [Henry James, Edith Wharton, and Willa Cather], who, although nearly contemporaneous with him, were rooted in and shaped by literary modes and strategies very different from his own. The imaginative impulse of their stories is nearly always the same as that of their novels. It is abbreviated, of course, and modulated or intensified by the requirements of the shorter form, but it is essentially an outgrowth of related thematic ideas and is organized around conventional notions of fictional form: a verisimilitude of character and place; a fundamentally Aristotelian plot structure in which a situation is introduced, and conflicts emerge and are enlarged upon and, in one way or another, are resolved; and an orderly, which is to say linear, chronology. The narrative is shaped as a logical progression of events that inevitably leads either to a dramatic alteration of external circumstances or to a new condition of being for one or more characters . . . , and this, seen in the light of all that has gone before, reveals an identifiable moral nexus; that is, an implicit value judgment is made upon the character, the world with which he is in conflict, or both. Equally important is the degree to which all these authors assume, even as they despair its passing, an available code of conduct.

In Anderson, the representational mode, the tripartite structure, the assumption of verifiable patterns of behavior and the moral concomitant disappear. In their place is a form at once more allusive and epigrammatic, more mystical and poetic, and more psychologically suggestive than anything that had gone before it in American fiction. The effect is that of the Joycean epiphany in which a single gesture, a perception, or a bit of dialogue is caught, rendered permanent, and although never interpreted, dissolves into a myriad of implications for the reader. Fundamental to this form is that it shows a life, not in process, but revealed by a moment's flickering light in its quintessential meaning.

"I have come to think," Anderson was later to write, "that the true history of life is but a history of moments. It is only at rare moments that we live." The theory is not original. Walter Pater in the nineteenth century and Virginia Woolf early in the twentieth had both embraced this view, and Woolf's novels are the consummate expression in British fiction of the way in which life is composed of a series of "moments." But Anderson is the first writer to articulate this vision in the American short story, allowing the "moment" to reveal a hidden and not altogether flattering element in American experience.

This was a new kind of truth, one that gave the lie to the comfortable and cherished view of the health of the state.

Anderson was peculiarly qualified as spokesman for this darker perception. In a sense he had seen it all: as a laborer, soldier, and business executive; as a boy in a quiet, tradition-bound Ohio town; and as a man in the huge, complex metropolis of Chicago. Born and reaching adulthood in the nineteenth century, he lived for nearly half of the twentieth. Clearly, then, he was witness to the rapid and extraordinary shift in the American ethos and to the sudden displacement in sensibility it created. That which he saw was the deadening effect of urbanization and technocracy, the erosion of religious faith and its usurpation by the money-god, the separation of men and women from work that provided a sense of purpose, and a consequent drift toward bewilderment, malaise, and despair. To illuminate this other reality—the one beneath the smiling benignity of American progress—Anderson dramatized a single, often bizarre moment in the lives of his characters.

His perception of an all-pervasive cultural hypocrisy led to his candid treatment of sexual longing, a treatment that by today's standards is timid stuff, but in 1919 was, doubtless, regarded as shocking. His focus on sexuality ("the terrible importance of the flesh in human relations") is not sensationalist, but is part of a larger, clearly authentic, interest: the mysterious psychic history of modern men and women, who, thwarted by the increasing impersonality of the new age, became isolated, silent, and withdrawn, and thus could be rendered knowable only by way of a frozen moment in time that reveals the private, often sexually repressed self.

Through the decades, Anderson has frequently been disparaged as writer of intuition but no ideas. As is so often the case with sweeping generalizations, the crucial terms of the statement—intuition, ideas—remain undefined so that the concept is more a convenient tag for dealing with a new and unusual form than it is a valid assessment. It would be more accurate simply to acknowledge that in the introductory chapter to **Winesburg,** the author claims more philosophical content for his stories and characters than they demonstrate. He says that the people in Winesburg ("grotesques," he calls them) embody different kinds of truths, and in the moment that "one of the people took one of the truths to himself, called it his truth, and tried to live his life by it, he became a grotesque and the truth he embraced became a falsehood." His statement implies that, first, his characters define "truth"; then, that having established these truths as moral principles, they live by them; and last, that having done so, they find that they have been deluded. The theory does nothing to clarify the stories whose "truths" emerge without the aid of embellishment and whose characters are energized and defined not by their intellects but by their behavior.

There is, too, the matter of Anderson's style. None of the pellucid prose of Willa Cather appears here, nor the brilliant irony of Edith Wharton, and most assuredly, none of the modulations and refinements of language of Henry James. Instead, the narrative is composed of two seemingly irreconcilable, but as interwoven here, enormously effective patterns: the cadences of natural speech, approximating the beat and sense of immediacy of the oral tradition; and the highly stylized rhetoric of biblical prose—syntactical inversions, formal diction, controlled rhythms. There is a consequent tension in the prose, a quality at once native and oracular, recalling the character of Walt Whitman's poetry.

Anderson is said to have seen **Winesburg** as a novel, and, to be sure, there is a sense in which the Winesburg setting, the presence of the young newspaper reporter, George Willard, in many of the stories, the consistency of mood, and the cumulative power of the pieces give the work that continuity associated with the longer form. But the best of the stories are enormously effective as they stand alone; the least of them are not missed when they are omitted; and Anderson's method, as true of his novels as of the *Winesburg* stories, is by nature anecdotal and episodic, lacking that sustained momentum and integration of material essential to novelistic structure. Further, the focus on individual lives at a given moment in time—the very substance of these stories—is inappropriate to the longer narrative form with its requisite sequentiality and connectedness. The book is, in fact, a story cycle, the first of many in American fiction and the progenitor of the Nick Adams stories of Ernest Hemingway (a debt Hemingway later grudgingly conceded) and the Miranda stories of Katherine Anne Porter. But in Anderson, the emphasis is not on the growth to maturity and wisdom of the unifying character as in Hemingway and Porter, but rather on a succession of separate, isolated lives. Thus, while some of the stories can be seen as rites of passage for the young George Willard, their impact derives mainly from the odd creatures who shuffle awkwardly through the streets of Winesburg, Ohio, and whom George observes with sympathy and often with confusion. All are marginal types, those strange, unhappy beings who are increasingly to inhabit the American short story: men and women withering in the face of perplexing circumstances, unfulfilled capacities, atrophied emotions, and terrible loneliness.

The unrelieved isolation and repressed longings of the characters are expressed by way of an obsession, a physical defect,

Manuscript page from the story "Godliness." Reproduced by permission of Harold Ober Associates and The Newberry Library, Chicago.

or a sudden, quirky act so that they become, in an almost Dickensian way, identifiable by their peculiar traits or tics. But Anderson's interest is in penetrating beneath the visually discernible to a buried world that clarifies the surface one; and what he finds and illuminates there is an admixture of innocence, bewilderment, yearning, and pain. (pp. 62-5)

The midwestern rural setting of *Winesburg, Ohio* has led some commentators to read the work as Anderson's "revolt from the village," that too facile rubric attached to numberless fictions in the early decades of the century. But, taken together, the stories are clearly a great deal more than a statement of disillusionment at country freshness gone stale or pastoral innocence tattered and vulgarized. The frightened and lonely lives exposed by Anderson's method transcend time and place, expressing less a cynical than a tragic view, less a local or even national condition than a universal one. Settings and atmosphere work against the sense of a fallen agrarian world; indeed, it is most often in silent streets that characters are seen in their fugitive and puzzling encounters. The rare glimpses of a green world are on the outskirts of town in an open field or wooded area, settings not of pastoral serenity but of violent acts and terrible misunderstandings. Whatever the time of day, one has the sense of failing light, of the obscurely visualized, of a nighttime world whose gloom is wholly consistent with the mood of melancholy, inward-turning experience.

Nor are the creatures of Winesburg rustics. Rather, they form a procession of single souls, estranged from their environment and from one another, displaying a suspicious unease which at times erupts into lunacy. They do not live so much as they merely endure a joyless existence—joyless because devoid of love, companionship, sexuality, art, and faith, those timeless, unalterable, and absolutely essential sources of spiritual nourishment. And so they sit alone in the drab rooms of boardinghouses endlessly waiting; or they move woodenly through the nearly empty streets unremarkable but for the one convulsive moment in which Anderson catches and reveals them.

There are a number of characters whose frustration is of a specifically sexual nature. Such a character is Alice Hindman in **"Adventure."** (pp. 66-7)

Others in the town are thwarted by the absence of love, by the unfulfilled yearning for sexual experience. Kate Swift (**"The Teacher"**) is regarded by her students as cold, forbidding, unapproachable. The townspeople view her as a confirmed old maid who speaks sharply and lacks all human feeling. But "in reality, she was the most eagerly passionate among them," who often walks the streets of Winesburg at night, tormented by memory and desire. (p. 67)

The desperate need to make human contact, to move beyond the narrow limits of self, precipitate the abrupt, peculiar actions of each of the men and women in the *Winesburg* stories. In **"Godliness,"** Anderson states the case for all of them: "It seemed . . . that between [each of them] and all the other people in the world, a wall had been built up and that [each remained forever outside] the warm, inner circle of life." What Anderson catches and dramatizes with stunning economy in the stories is the profound paradox of human existence: while we live in a world crowded with others, we are, in fact, each of us, quite alone.

In his treatment of isolation as the defining characteristic of experience and in his recognition of the sexual impulse as an attempt to assuage it, Anderson is extraordinarily innovative and influential. No serious writer of the short story who followed him could fail to treat the twin issues of loneliness and sexuality. The writers before him had either avoided these subjects altogether, disguised them tactfully, or used them artfully in the service of some larger concern.

Of course, earlier writers had assumed a world, if not always moral, at least knowable, manageable, all of a piece. *Winesburg, Ohio* was published just at the ending of World War I. The agrarian dream had long since died; the humanist one was dying. Industrialism—the new reality—gave experience an odd shape: fragmentary, anonymous, nervous, unpredictable. It is just this quality that Anderson epitomizes in both vision and method in the *Winesburg* stories. In the best of them, he achieves nothing less than the literary metaphor by which the citizens of a radically changing culture could know themselves; in *Winesburg, Ohio,* the American short story was suddenly and resoundingly thrust into the twentieth century. (pp. 68-9)

Ellen Kimbel, "The American Short Story: 1900-1920," in The American Short Story: A Critical History, *1900-1945, edited by Philip Stevick, Twayne Publishers, 1984, pp. 33-69.*

A. CARL BREDAHL (essay date 1986)

[*In the following excerpt, Bredahl defines "the young thing within"—the quality that attracts the characters in* Winesburg, Ohio *to George Willard—as the complementary creative urges of art and sex, from which the dynamics and unity of the book grow.*]

When Sherwood Anderson rejected the novel form as not fitting an American writer, he rejected the values of continuity, direction, and completion implicit in the traditional form. To many late nineteenth-century writers, those values had already vanished from both life and art. Some responded by digging their heels in against change, some by committing a sort of literary suicide, and some—the most energetic—by exploring new possibilities. One of the latter responses was evidenced in the appearance of experimental art forms in general and a new narrative form, which I am calling "divided narrative," in particular. (p. 422)

In America, the literary ancestors of the divided narrative are works which include *Of Plymouth Plantation, Letters from an American Farmer, The Narrative of Arthur Gordon Pym,* and *The Education of Henry Adams,* works which struggle structurally to assert a traditional literary unity against the threatening shoals of an experiential world. Division results from the conflict between an assumed unity and encountered experience which denies that particular kind of unity. Many eighteenth- and nineteenth-century writers struggle with that denial, but twentieth-century writers find the American dream or Edenic myth just too difficult to reconcile with experience. Thus structural divisions that asserted themselves rather uncomfortably in Bradford or Crevecoeur become the norm for Anderson or Faulkner.

But the process is not one-sided. Nineteenth-century evolutionary and psychoanalytic thought rejected old unities while also establishing the possibility of new. Picasso's cubism, for example, decried as nihilistic, sought new relationships. Thus an age in which old values collapsed was simultaneously an age in search of new; in the twentieth century the existence of the divided narrative is part of that struggle. The structural divisions of *Winesburg, Ohio* are usually seen as solely indicative of collapsing traditional values. Less well-recognized is

the narrative effort in *Winesburg* to leap across those divisions. (pp. 423-24)

Most discussions of *Winesburg, Ohio,* in stressing division, fail to respond to "the young thing within," the creative and complementary urges of art and sexuality initially introduced in **"The Book of the Grotesque":**

> Perfectly still he (the old writer) lay and his body was old and not of much use any more, but something inside him was altogether young. He was like a pregnant woman, only that the thing inside him was not a baby but a youth. No, it wasn't a youth, it was a woman, young, and wearing a coat of mail like a knight. . . . The thing to get at is what the writer, or the young thing within the writer, was thinking about.
>
> The subject would become so big in his mind that he himself would be in danger of becoming a grotesque. He didn't, I suppose, for the same reason that he never published the book. It was the young thing inside him that saved the old man. . . .

The dynamics and unity of *Winesburg, Ohio* grow from this metaphoric pregnancy, new life trying to be born into a world that seeks to deny it. Though the breaks between the stories threaten any possibility of sustained development, a major narrative effort is being made to get that "young thing" to live.

An initial reading of *Winesburg, Ohio* focuses quite naturally on division, for it is the isolation of lives that is immediately striking and the focus of readings by David Stouck, Edwin Fussell, and Ralph Ciancio. The grotesques, as the narrator calls them, are people uncomfortable and unprepared for functioning in their environment. In **"Paper Pills"** Doc Reefy casually tosses rolled-up pieces of paper at a friend. That friend is a gardener, and the narrator tells us that "in Doctor Reefy there were the *seeds* of something very fine" . . . [italics are the critic's]. Images of fertility are frequent in **"Paper Pills,"** but it is finally a story of sterility, for the seeds are never planted. The last paragraphs even suggest that, though a doctor, Reefy is more a man of death than life. The tooth-pulling scene in which blood runs down the woman's white dress may initially suggest intercourse and pregnancy, but we are left finally with an abortion as Reefy extracts and discards a dead tooth. The next paragraphs support such implications when "the condition that had brought her [Reefy's future wife] to him passed in an illness." . . . The girl herself dies after six months of marriage to Reefy, during which time he reads to her from the crumpled bits of paper, those pills which do not restore health and seeds which do not germinate.

Frustrated by their inner urgings because of the continuing domination of older values, the grotesques become individuals who fear themselves, their own feelings. Wash Williams in **"Respectability,"** like **"Paper Pills"** a story lush with sexual images, is destroyed by such fear. In his youth, Wash had been the best telegraph operator in the state. An expert, therefore, at impersonal communication, Wash had used his talented hands like Doc Reefy to toss out messages from a safe distance. And like the earlier story, Wash's is concerned with seeds and fertility:

> He made for George Willard a picture of his life in the house at Columbus, Ohio, with the

young wife. "In the garden back of our house we planted vegetables," he said, "you know, peas and corn and such things. We went to Columbus in early March and as soon as the days became warm I went to work in the garden. With a spade I turned up the black ground while she ran about laughing and pretending to be afraid of the worms I uncovered. Late in April came the planting. In the little paths among the seed beds she stood holding a paper bag in her hand. The bag was filled with seeds. A few at a time she handed me the seeds that I might thrust them into the warm, soft ground." . . .

An attractive image is presented by Wash, but something is wrong with the sexual relationship, for Wash is seeding the land rather than impregnating his wife, a woman who only *pretends* fear of the uncovered worms. "There in the dusk in the spring evening I crawled along the black ground to her feet and groveled before her." . . . Wash does not respond to his wife as a living person. He sees her as a symbol and evidently is comfortable in that kind of worshipping relationship. His final explosion when his wife is thrust naked into the room with him indicates how unprepared he is to look at his world face-to-face. He would rather live with his illusions, continuing to grovel before the values he feels are represented by his wife.

Wash, of course, is not alone among the Winesburg grotesques in his inability to respond to naked flesh and blood. That condition torments even the book's central figure, George Willard. When Helen White and George come together at the book's end, we are apparently meant to see their relationship as one leading to healthy maturity: "For some reason they could not have explained they had both got from their silent evening together the thing needed. Man or boy, woman or girl, they had for a moment taken hold of the thing that makes the mature life of men and women in the modern world possible." . . . However, only a few paragraphs earlier George thinks of his relationship with Helen in a way that recalls Wash Williams's groveling: "He had reverence for Helen. He wanted to love and to be loved by her, but he did not want at the moment to be confused by her womanhood." . . .

Noting the continuing desire for reverence, even though individuals in Winesburg have been made grotesque by similar reverence, points to an ultimate timidity reflected in the narrative's structural divisions; but that timidity should not limit our recognition of the book's effort to assert new life. That effort is initiated in the opening paragraph of "Hands," *Winesburg, Ohio*'s first story. . . . [The] opening establishes a world of youth and energy; but, most importantly, that world is buried syntactically within a statement of decay and frustration. Laughing, shouting, kicking, screaming young pickers of ripe fruit are at the center of the paragraph—and at the center of the book, the town, and the grotesques. To get to them, one has to move past either the "decayed veranda" at the head of the paragraph or the "nervous little hands" and "tangled locks" at the conclusion. Like many of the grotesques in the first half of the book, Wing responds to his own internal energy, sensing the need for release. He pounds fence posts in an effort to relieve his tension; Doc Reefy tosses paper pills; Elizabeth Willard wants her son to break loose; and Louise Trunnion gives her body in the desperate desire to have someone want it. For each, the energy remains trapped inside, as it does in this opening paragraph; but for each, it is undeniably present.

The "young thing" appearing in many of these early stories is often associated with young people, in particular George Willard. **"Mother,"** for example, refers to the young thing within both Elizabeth Willard and her son. As a girl, Elizabeth sought to release the life within her. . . . She found, though, as presumably Louise Trunnion after her, that living demanded more than physical coupling. Life has been stifled in Elizabeth, but she now sees it moving in her son: "'Within him there is a secret something that is striving to grow. It is the thing I let be killed in myself.'" . . . (pp. 424-429)

Young people like Louise Trunnion, David Hardy, Louise Bentley, and Seth Richmond are all prominent in the early stories, and each is aware of an inner stirring. But most of the early stories describe failure and inability to give birth to new life. Contrasting structurally with this thematic failure is the story **"Tandy,"** the story of a little girl given a new name by a stranger, which appears almost at the center of the book. Two things are striking about **"Tandy's"** structural position. In the first place, the "young thing within" has been given tangible form, narratively as well as biologically, for a child is the subject of this "central" story, not a particular child so much as the quality of being childlike. Something has been brought forth where earlier grotesques like Wing Biddlebaum, Jesse Bentley, and Wash Williams found that inner strivings remained locked within. Secondly, at the same time that the child exists and suggestive of the divisions which dominate the book are the facts that the child is female (traditionally associated with home and church) and spoken of as the manifestation of God, worthy therefore of being reverenced—the debilitating attitude already noted in Wash Williams and George Willard.

Though existence of **"Tandy"** suggests that tangible form *can* be given to the "young thing within," that possibility immediately becomes the cause of anguish in the story which opens the second half of the book, **"The Strength of God,"** one of the most vivid examples of the tensions involved in emerging as a child of the new world. **"The Strength of God"** initiates a sequence of stories which focus on the nurturing of the "young thing." If indeed one can argue that the child has appeared at the center of *Winesburg, Ohio,* then it is suggestive and appropriate that new life move in the direction of adulthood. In **"The Strength of God,"** however, the Reverend Curtis Hartman is not a person of such possibility. Hartman's brief vision of a physical world is far more stimulating than he is prepared to accept; it becomes necessary, therefore, for him to call upon the strength of God to denounce his feelings. In contrast, in other words, to the characters in the first half of the book, Hartman undergoes a release of inner excitement but is so frightened by his experience that he must destroy it. Hartman has been pastor of the Presbyterian Church of Winesburg for ten years and neither stimulated by his work nor stimulating to his congregation. . . . All of this changes when by accident he sees Kate Swift not as the embodiment of femininity but as woman. . . . Previously, Hartman's experience with women was "a formal and prolonged courtship" with his wife. He "had never permitted himself to think of other women. What he wanted was to do the work of God quietly and earnestly." . . . But he cannot deny his fascination with "the bare shoulders and white throat of a woman"; he even experiences a mild transformation: "With his brain in a whirl he went down into the pulpit and preached a long sermon without once thinking of his gestures or his voice. The sermon attracted unusual attention because of its power and clearness," . . . power and clarity which are expressions of Hartman's visual contact with "bare" and "white" skin, the physical world he has always avoided but undeniably one to which he is capable of responding.

As with anyone divided against himself, a struggle immediately begins within the pastor. "He did not want to kiss the shoulders and the throat of Kate Swift and had not allowed his mind to dwell on such thoughts. He did not know what he wanted. 'I am God's child and he must save me from myself'" . . . is Hartman's cry that echoes the words of Melville's Father Mapple: "To obey God is to disobey yourself"; it is clearly the cry of an individual who has been trained to distrust the human body. . . . The struggle in Curtis Hartman is between belief in something beyond humanity and the urge to respond to the excitement of his world. . . . These powerful divisive drives bring Hartman to the verge of self-destruction until one night he sees "the woman of sin [begin] to pray." . . . At that point he rushes to George Willard and announces himself saved, for he no longer has to see her as a person. He can again imagine Kate Swift as "An instrument of God, bearing the message of truth," . . . a symbol rather than a human being.

The particular woman attractive to Hartman's eyes is the subject of the next story, **"The Teacher."** As a physical being who smokes and has travelled widely, Kate Swift's most important quality is the excitement she generates in the minds of young students like George Willard: "He took a pillow into his arms and embraced it thinking first of the school teacher, who by her words had stirred something within him." . . . On the particular night of her story, "it was as though the man and the boy [Hartman and Willard], by thinking of her, had driven her forth into the wintry streets," . . . her mind "ablaze with thoughts of George Willard." . . . The energy that puts Kate into motion excites the young thing within George. This is, in many ways, a sexual response, and what is being stimulated is a passion for life. . . . (pp. 429-32)

The young thing within, the growth of the individual, and the development of the artist finally come together in **"The Teacher,"** reinforcing the suggestions made in the introductory **"Book of the Grotesque,"** and point to the one story in *Winesburg, Ohio* which deals specifically with the life of an artist. That story, **"Loneliness,"** immediately follows **"The Teacher."** Enoch Robinson had the desire to be an artist, but he failed because "he was always a child and that was a handicap to his worldly development. He never grew up and of course he couldn't understand people and he couldn't make people understand him." . . . Apparently, it is not enough simply to give birth to the young thing; that child must be allowed to grow and mature if it is to flourish as a healthy adult. In other words, the existence of the story **"Tandy"** is important to the structure of *Winesburg, Ohio*, but childhood is only a step, not the final stance.

"The story of Enoch is in fact the story of a room almost more than it is the story of a man." . . . This could be said of everyone's story in *Winesburg, Ohio*, because all the grotesques live in boxes that they or others have constructed. . . . Enoch lives in a box, and there his art thrives. . . . When life intrudes upon the walled-in existence of Enoch, it shatters his illusions and leaves him lonely because all he has known is retreat. Like Curtis Hartman and Wash Williams, Enoch doesn't know how to begin looking at his world. (pp. 432-34)

Anderson suggests that the artist in the twentieth century must not be someone for whom words are little boxes into which abstractions of life can be fitted. He must desire instead to look at actualities like human skin and want to respond to the physical life swelling underneath. After Enoch's **"Loneliness"** comes George's **"Awakening,"** and in this story words seem to have a new pregnancy for George. "He felt unutterably big and remade by the simple experience through which he had been passing and in a kind of fervor of emotion put up his hands, thrusting them into the darkness above his head and muttering words. The desire to say words overcame him and he said words without meaning, rolling over on his tongue and saying them because they were brave words, full of meaning. 'Death,' he muttered, 'night, the sea, fear, loveliness'." . . . George has previously maneuvered these empty boxes on the pages of the Winesburg *Eagle,* but now he senses an excitement in the material that might allow him to tell stories of life rather than death. The physical beatings he takes in **"Awakening"** and in **"Queer"** awaken in George the sense of his own pomposity. He must learn the same thing with regard to language in order to use the power of the medium to express and develop the life within.

That life which will be George's subject is nowhere more evident than in one of the final scenes as George makes preparations for his departure from Winesburg:

> On all sides are ghosts, not of the dead, but of living people. Here, during the day just passed, have come the people pouring in from the town and the country around. Farmers with their wives and children and all the people from the hundreds of little frame houses have gathered within these board walls. Young girls have laughed and men with boards have talked of the affairs of their lives. The place has been filled to overflowing with life. It has itched and squirmed with life and now it is night and the life has all gone away. The silence is almost terrifying. . . . One shudders at the thought of the meaninglessness of life while at the same instant, and if the people of the town are his people, one loves life so intensely that tears come into the eyes. . . .

In spite of the frustrations that demand attention in the lives of the grotesques of Winesburg, the town and the people "squirm" with life. The structured divisions of the narrative do indeed isolate individual stories, but the book's narrative urge ultimately leaps across those divisions, grasping the relationships between the stories and vital impulses within the grotesques which drive them to seek out others and tell them their stories. Indeed the narrative act of establishing connections is so important in *Winesburg, Ohio* that one of the dominant characteristics of so many grotesques is their desire to narrate to George Willard their own inner squirmings. (pp. 434-36)

[The] grotesques of Winesburg are "impelled" individuals who seek to become "articulate," to give birth to the "young thing within" through the act of telling their stories. Though their impulsion is continually thwarted, that urge drives George forth from Winesburg to seek new life and a new story. (pp. 436-37)

A. Carl Bredahl, " 'The Young Thing Within': Divided Narrative and Sherwood Anderson's 'Winesberg, Ohio'," in The Midwest Quarterly, Vol. XXVII, No. 4, Summer, 1986, pp. 422-37.

ADDITIONAL BIBLIOGRAPHY

Anderson, David D., ed. *Critical Essays on Sherwood Anderson.* Boston: G. K. Hall & Co., 1981, 302 p.
> A collection of reviews and essays about Anderson and his work, as well as three previously unpublished items by Anderson. This collection includes essays about *Winesburg, Ohio* by Herbert Gold, Walter Rideout, Marilyn Judith Atals, Nancy Bunge, and others. An essay by David Stouck is included in the entry above.

Bunge, Nancy. "Women As Social Critics in *Sister Carrie, Winesburg, Ohio,* and *Main Street.*" In *Midamerica III*, edited by David D. Anderson, pp. 47-55. East Lansing, Mich.: Midwestern Press, 1976.
> Compares female characters in these works by Theodore Dreiser, Anderson, and Sinclair Lewis. Crediting them with "a healthy instinctual sense of absolute values," Bunge argues that these characters nonetheless "have difficulty preserving their broader perspective since they are continually influenced by a social structure which denies it."

Campbell, Hilbert H., and Modlin, Charles E., eds. *Sherwood Anderson: Centennial Studies.* Troy, N.Y.: Whitston Publishing Co., 1976, 275 p.
> Previously unpublished scholarly interpretations of Anderson's work, bibliographical information, previously unpublished letters by Anderson, information about the Newberry Library collection of Anderson papers, and an interview with Anderson's widow Eleanor Anderson. The volume includes the article "The Editions of *Winesburg, Ohio,*" by William L. Phillips.

Chase, Cleveland B. *Sherwood Anderson.* Folcroft, Pa.: The Folcroft Press, 1927, 84 p.
> Critical biography which concludes that *Winesburg, Ohio* is the only one of Anderson's books which will endure.

Crane, Hart. "Sherwood Anderson." *The Pagan* IV, No. 5 (September 1919): 60-1.
> An enthusiastic review of *Winesburg, Ohio.*

Fertig, Martin J. "'A Great Deal of Wonder in Me': Inspiration and Transformation in *Winesburg, Ohio.*" *The Markham Review* 6 (Summer 1977): 65-70.
> Argues that Anderson "repeatedly used the motif of romantic inspiration to resolve the conflict between the external and the internal states of his characters," and in *Winesburg*, "he objectified his own sense of inspiration by presenting actual transformation in the physical appearances of his characters."

Fussell, Edwin. "*Winesburg, Ohio*: Art and Isolation." *Modern Fiction Studies* VI, No. 2 (Summer 1960): 106-14.
> Considers *Winesburg, Ohio* an atypical bildungsroman that emphasizes a reciprocal relationship between the emerging artist and other members of society.

Gross, Barry. "The Revolt That Wasn't: The Legacies of Critical Myopia." *The CEA Critic* 39, No. 2 (January 1977): 4-8.
> Faults eastern and urban critics who knew "little about the village or the Middle West" for misinterpreting *Winesburg, Ohio*, Edgar Lee Masters's *Spoon River Anthology*, and Sinclair Lewis's *Main Street* as "revolt from the village" literature when in fact they were written "in revolt from the *myth* of the village as the great good place, as simple and innocent."

Hilfer, Anthony Channell. "Masters and Anderson." In his *The Revolt from the Village: 1915-1930*, pp. 137-57. Chapel Hill: University of North Carolina Press, 1969.
> Contends that *Spoon River Anthology* and *Winesburg, Ohio* are both books built "around isolated characters . . . unified by their reflection of the spiritual quality of the town, by the common theme of the buried life, and by the tone of naturalistic pathos qualified by irony," adding that "the major difference between the books is that while Masters' characters hide their feelings, Anderson's inarticulate characters hardly know what their feelings are."

Holladay, Sylvia A. "The 'New' Realism: A Study of the Structure of *Winesburg, Ohio.*" *The CEA Critic* XLI, No. 3 (March 1979): 9-12.
> Notes the influence of Freudian psychology and post-impressionist painting on *Winesburg, Ohio* and other literature of the period.

Kramer, Dale. *Chicago Renaissance: The Literary Life in the Midwest, 1900-1930.* New York: Appleton-Century, 1966, 369 p.
> Discusses Anderson, Floyd Dell, Theodore Dreiser, Carl Sandburg, and other influential writers of the era as personalities and writers. The writing and publication of *Winesburg, Ohio* are of central interest in the chapter "Chicago's 'Great Unpublished Author'."

Laughlin, Rosemary. "Godliness and the American Dream in *Winesburg, Ohio.*" *Twentieth Century Literature* 13, No. 2 (July 1967): 97-103.
> Examines the style, symbols, and characters in the story "Godliness" in *Winesburg, Ohio.*

Love, Glen A. "*Winesburg, Ohio* and the Rhetoric of Silence." *American Literature* XL, No. 1 (March 1968): 38-57.
> Attempts to show "how thoroughly Anderson explores the theme of human communication in *Winesburg*, how his treatment of that theme is linked to his attitude toward silence, words, and talk, and how these attitudes are in turn related to the strong, single idea which runs through all his work: the loss of human significance in America with the onset of urban, machine civilization."

Mahoney, John J. "An Analysis of *Winesburg, Ohio.*" *The Journal of Aesthetics & Art Criticism* XV, No. 2 (December 1956): 245-52.
> Seeks to determine "how Anderson in all of these tales achieves so strong and distinctive an aesthetic effect with means apparently so simple."

Mais, S. P. B. "Sherwood Anderson." In his *Some Modern Authors*, pp. 17-31. New York: Dodd, Mead and Co., 1923.
> Analysis and synopsis of individual stories from *Winesburg, Ohio.* Mais concludes that the work is "one of the most significant books of our generation. . . . It explains itself. Its artistry is perfect."

Maresca, Carol J. "Gestures As Meaning in Sherwood Anderson's *Winesburg, Ohio.*" *CLA Journal* IX, No. 3 (March 1966): 279-83.
> Notes the "conspicuously limited" use of dialogue in *Winesburg, Ohio*, and discusses the use of hands and eyes in the work to reveal meaning.

McAleer, John J. "Christ Symbolism in *Winesburg, Ohio.*" *Discourse* IV, No. 3 (Summer 1961): 168-81.
> Identifies "a pattern of Christ symbolism which appears throughout the book . . . reiterating Anderson's point—in the modern world suffering is the lot of every man."

McDonald, Walter R. "*Winesburg, Ohio*: Tales of Isolation." *The University Review* XXXV, No. 3 (Spring 1969): 237-40.
> Considers Anderson's characterizations in *Winesburg, Ohio* well suited to his theme of isolation and failed communication.

Murphy, George D. "The Theme of Sublimation in Anderson's *Winesburg, Ohio.*" *Modern Fiction Studies* XIII, No. 2 (Summer 1967): 237-46.
> Maintains that the stories in *Winesburg, Ohio* display "an extremely hesitant, almost puritanical attitude toward physical sexuality."

O'Neill, John. "Anderson Writ Large: 'Godliness' in *Winesburg, Ohio.*" *Twentieth Century Literature* 23, No. 1 (February 1977): 67-83.
> Credits the story "Godliness" with the integrative function of revealing the key psychological forces in *Winesburg, Ohio.*

Papinchak, Robert Allen. "Something in the Elders: The Recurrent Imagery in *Winesburg, Ohio.*" *The Winesburg Eagle* IX, No. 1 (November 1983): 1-7.
> Posits that Anderson abandoned the "pure novelistic form," achieving unity in *Winesburg, Ohio* through the use of recurrent imagery.

Phillips, William L. "How Sherwood Anderson Wrote *Winesburg, Ohio*." *American Literature* 23, No. 1 (March 1951): 7-30.
    Examines Anderson's letters, autobiographical works, and manuscripts to illuminate the methods he used to write *Winesburg, Ohio*.

Rigsbee, Sally Adair. "The Feminine in *Winesburg, Ohio*." *Studies in American Fiction* 9, No. 2 (Autumn 1981): 233-44.
    Discusses conventional male-female relationships in *Winesburg, Ohio* as hindrances to communication.

Rogers, Douglas G. *Sherwood Anderson: A Selective, Annotated Bibliography*. Metuchen, N.J.: Scarecrow Press, 1976, 157 p.
    Includes a brief biographical introduction and a bibiliography which focuses upon English and American criticism of works by and about Anderson.

San Juan, Epifanio, Jr. "Vision and Reality: A Reconsideration of Sherwood Anderson's *Winesburg, Ohio*." *American Literature* XXV, No. 2 (May 1963): 137-55.
    Strives to ascertain "to what in particular one may attribute [the] power and significance" of *Winesburg, Ohio*, examining Anderson's technique and the work's form and narrative style.

Schevill, James. *Sherwood Anderson: His Life and Work*. Colorado: University of Denver Press, 1961, 360 p.
    Critical biography. Schevill contends that the question lying at the center of almost all of Anderson's work is "What is it in our national life that had tended to inhibit the immense latent power of our artistic expression?"

Stewart, Maaja A. "Scepticism and Belief in Chekhov and Anderson." *Studies in Short Fiction* IX, No. 1 (Winter 1972): 29-40.
    Examines similarities in characterization and theme in the short stories of Anderson and Anton Chekhov.

Stouck, David. "*Winesburg, Ohio* and the Failure of Art." *Twentieth Century Literature* 15, No. 3 (October 1969): 145-51.
    Considers artistic failure a central theme of the book.

Sutton, William A. *The Road to Winesburg: A Mosaic of the Imaginative Life of Sherwood Anderson*. Metuchen, N.J.: Scarecrow Press, 1972, 645 p.
    Collection of biographical and critical essays and bibliographical information.

Thurston, Jarvis. "Anderson and *Winesburg:* Mysticism and Craft." *Accent* XVI, No. 2 (Spring 1956): 107-28.
    Argues that "*Winesburg* is particularly central to a critical definition of Anderson's art," because "for the first time in his literary career, Anderson found the way of closing the gap between his mystical impulses and the formal demands of art."

Walcutt, Charles Child. "Sherwood Anderson: Impressionism and the Buried Life." In his *American Literary Naturalism: A Divided Stream*, pp. 222-39. Minneapolis: University of Minnesota Press, 1956.
    Discusses Anderson's insights into repression and his utilization of naturalistic detail.

Way, Brian. "Sherwood Anderson." In *The American Novel and the Nineteen Twenties*, edited by Malcolm Bradbury and David Palmer, pp. 107-26. London: Edward Arnold, 1971.
    Considers Anderson a writer "caught at a moment of transition" in American cultural, social, and literary life" who "made the atmosphere of transition itself his subject and his concern." Way calls *Winesburg, Ohio* "a seminal influence on the new literature of the nineteen twenties."

White, Ray Lewis. "Of Time and *Winesburg, Ohio:* An Experiment in Chronology." *Modern Fiction Studies* 25, No. 4 (Winter 1979-1980): 658-66.
    Examines problems of chronologizing the events described in the *Winesburg* stories.

————, ed. *The Achievement of Sherwood Anderson: Essays in Criticism*. Chapel Hill: University of North Carolina Press, 1966, 270 p.
    Reviews, impressions, and critical studies, including discussions of *Winesburg, Ohio* by William L. Phillips, Irving Howe, Edwin Fussell, Waldo Frank, and others.

Zlotnick, Joan. "Of Dubliners and Ohioans: A Comparative Study of Two Works." *Ball State University Forum* XVII, No. 4 (Autumn 1976): 33-6.
    Compares and contrasts *Winesburg, Ohio* and James Joyce's *Dubliners*, concluding that they "bear testimony to the international nature of the oppressive middle-class life. . . . They attest to the enduring need for the artist to exorcise the ghosts of his past and to the perpetual paradox whereby the most barren of lives become, in the fecund imagination of the artist, the very seeds that germinate vital and inspiring art."

George Bacovia

1881-1957

(Pseudonym of Gheorghe Vasiliu) Rumanian poet.

Bacovia is regarded as one of Rumania's greatest poets. Although he is most closely identified with the French Symbolists, his work is both original and eclectic, and also displays affinities with Expressionism and Existentialist thought. Because Bacovia suffered from poverty, isolation, alcoholism, and emotional instability, many critics consider the depressed atmosphere of his writing to be an expression of his own misery. The poetry produced from such struggles brilliantly conveys the poet's personal anguish and nihilism.

The son of a shopkeeper and his wife, Bacovia was born in the town of Bacău, from which he derived his pen name. His first published writing appeared in 1898 in the journal *Literatorul,* and during the next five years he published work which attracted the attention of his contemporaries He also displayed talent in several nonliterary creative disciplines as an accomplished musician, composer, and painter. Although Bacovia studied law from 1903 to 1911 in Bucharest and Iaşi, he never entered the legal profession and instead worked as a copyist, bookkeeper, and art teacher while continuing to write. In 1916, Bacovia published his first volume of poetry, *Plumb* (*Lead*), which quickly achieved critical recognition. Although he subsequently published several volumes of poetry and prose poems, he was unable to support himself by his writings. His material deprivation and alcoholism contributed to the decline of his health and to a series of nervous breakdowns, as a result of which he spent much of his life in sanitariums. He continued to write up to his death in 1957, and during the last years of his life his critical stature increased due to the influence of Marxist critics who praised the poet's socialist perspective.

Bacovia was a literary disciple of such French Symbolist poets as Paul Verlaine and Arthur Rimbaud, and his early work, including the volumes *Lead* and *Scîntei galbene* (*Yellow Sparks*), reflects this influence, particularly as it attempts to express emotions and ideas by suggestion through the use of symbolic imagery. His poetry is somber and pessimistic, conveying a macabre atmosphere produced largely through the use of the colors white, black, and dark purple, the recurrence of images suggesting dampness, darkness, and coldness, and the obsessive repetition of key words and phrases. This oppressiveness also found expression in Bacovia's depiction of human relationships, for his protagonists are alienated from human society and eroticism is usually focused on sick or dying woman. As an intense expression of the poet's inner moods compressed into brief, powerful verse, Bacovia's poetry has also been compared to the works of such Expressionist authors as Georg Trakl and Gottfried Benn. While critics have also compared Bacovia's work to that of Franz Kafka and Samuel Beckett for its evocation of existential futility, helplessness, and suffering, the poet's later work, published in the volumes *Cu voi . . .* (*With You . . .*), *Comedii in fond* (*Comedies at Heart*), and *Stanţe burgheze* (*Bourgeois Stanzas*), encompasses wider social concerns and views life more ironically and with less anguish.

Bacovia is considered a limited but nonetheless powerful writer who has created a body of poetry remarkable both for its evo-

cation of despair and for its visionary qualities. Although underestimated during his lifetime, Bacovia is now recognized as one the greatest authors in Rumanian literature.

PRINCIPAL WORKS

Plumb (poetry) 1916
  [*Lead* (partial translation) published in *Lead,* 1980]
Bucăţi de noapte (prose poems) 1926
Scîntei galbene (poetry) 1926
  [*Yellow Sparks* (partial translation) published in *Lead,* 1980]
Cu voi . . . (poetry) 1930
  [*With You . . .* (partial translation) published in *Lead,* 1980]
Comedii în fond (poetry) 1936
  [*Comedies at Heart* (partial translation) published in *Lead,* 1980]
Stanţe burgheze (poetry) 1946
  [*Bourgeois Stanzas* (partial translation) published in *Lead,* 1980]
Poezii (poetry) 1956
  [*Poems* (partial translation) published in *Lead,* 1980]
Stanţe şi versete (poetry) 1970

Opere   (poetry and prose poems)   1978
Lead   (poetry)   1980

CEZAR BALTAG   (essay date 1972)

[*In the following essay, Baltag offers personal impressions of Bacovia and his work.*]

Never was I more impressed by someone's direct physical presence than in the case of poet Bacovia's person. I saw him but once; the memory's retina keeps, however, intact the image of a gentle and abstracted hermit, his strange and ardent figure of proletarian intellectual. He was embodying a world so wrapped up in itself that, catching sight of him I felt that the objects themselves kept silent, as if thrilled by a mild inner revelation. Bacovia's step was that of a lonely man. A peculiar reverie distinguished him, which was achieving almost automatically a strange correspondence between the light of a room and his state of mind. I then perceived, looking at George Bacovia, that privilege of the poet who, in any moment of his life, relates every gesture to his own spiritual destiny.

The poet's appearance somehow suggested a return in itself of the spirit. His thinking seems to be that of a large eye that sees outside its own content. Though, by its symbols, his poetry is deeply linked to the most intimate sensations—to what we might designate as consciousness' most intimate events—it makes us come into contact, at the same time, with what is much more than simply individual in man.

Alien and rejected, in the midst of a world which was strange and incomprehensible to him, launching on the cinder—or rather lead path, in brilliant and desperate counterpoints—his words and rhythms, Bacovia was conferring vast dimensions on the individual living. The whole world seemed to have been in the poet's nerves, so that invisibile links are joining up in a painful sensitive ensemble the images reflected in the ego's memory.

> For so many nights I hear the pouring rain
> I hear the matter crying . . .
> I am alone and thinking
> About the lacustrian dwellings.
>
> It seems as if I were sleeping on humid boards
> A wave is striking me from behind
> I give a start in my sleep, and it looks
> That I have not drawn the bridge from the bank.
>
> An historical void is stretching out—
> I find myself in times unchanged . . .
> And feel that because of so much rain
> The heavy piles are collapsing.

This poem—in which mist and rain are eternized, and turn from meteorological phenomena into a mode of the matter's existence—here represents a kind of inner cosmos, rustling to the rhythm of the diastoles of a heart wounded in its unknown depths.

Bacovia's art and fate are, as already said, an undefined refusal to be a certain thing, in an alienated world—that of bourgeois order. The sensation of his dual personality and of the multiplication in faded, weary mirrors, as well as the longing for that "crude green" of his childhood delaying excruciatingly its echo in the later conscience of the mature man—all these

convey the sadness of an irremediable antagonism between the ideal and the real; not despair, however, which would make communication itself impossible. One may detect here something which could be designated as the paradox of Bacovian lyricism: in Bacovia's poetry, hope is a gentle and nostalgic exasperation—a strange, spectral, even luminous one.

Bacovia—as I see him—is a poet belonging to a strange, phosphorescent species, fond of twilight and semi-darkness which were the mediums of his undefined refusal directed against the essential incoherence of a civilization alien to Man. I quite often experience, with rare emotion, when reading, the melancholy delight stirred up by the simple perception of a single Bacovian tone or colour, the perception of the commonplace—transformed through a sudden illumination of our secret ego into an artistic and spiritual peak. (pp. 39-40)

> *Cezar Baltag, "The Poet's Privilege," in* Romanian Review, *Vol. 26, No. 1, 1972, pp. 39-40.*

MIRCEA TOMUS   (essay date 1972)

[*In the following essay, Tomus emphasizes the sensitivity to social injustice expressed by Bacovia's poetry.*]

Last year we celebrated 90 years since the birth of George Bacovia, a poet whose discreet physical presence found a measure only in the contrast offered by his work, enriched by a load of life, suffering and visionary meditation, which contrast was brought to sometimes paradoxical form by the acute confrontation between the poetic ego and the most serious meanings of this existence. The incertitude of the real date of his birth (5th or 6th of September, 1881, in Bacău) that he himself tried to keep, or, at least, did not try to dissipate, expresses in the best way and acts as a prelude to a life whose enthusiasm lost not rarely its wings, whose revolts were smothered in an inner groan, whose generous constructive onsets were crumbled by the grounding of hostile times; there is nothing more anonymous and more common than the real biography of the one marked in civic papers with the name, also very common, Gheorghe Vasiliu, whom literary history remembers under the pen-name of Bacovia. The poet seems to have deliberately and programmatically withdrawn "saddened by the crimes of the bourgeoisie, without a word" from the concrete existence, for which he had no inclination, taking refuge in the universe of his work, where he seems to have lived his real life, as the main and most oppressed character of a devastating drama, tragic hero and accusing witness, multiplied by the hypostases of those

> Conquered and lost forever more
> In taverns or it attics hid,
> And those mad, wandering, silent, or
> Gesticulating in the street . . .

or, at other times, with a terrifying contour: . . .

> But the proletarian thinker
> In the book of times does spy:
> Only strikes and blood and madness
> And a universal cry. . . .

Bacovia's life appears now only through contrasts, like a negative film, out of the succession of its concrete events—the interrupted studies, the journalistic attempts, the experiences of an office-worker and those, much more often, of one in continual demand of work; its truth is outlined more pregnantly by the written work, witness to the cleanest soar towards the noble ideals of humanity, and also of a drama in which the hero is squashed under the rabble of a world whose ending he, himself had announced with an accusing gesture. But, before reaching this ending—a bright cogito, pulsing with life—poetry, as well as the entire existence of Bacovia went through and, implicitly expressed, sometimes with nuances, most times though diffusively, the reactions of an extremely sensitive creator to the demands of a social universe hostile to the affirmation of the human personality. For the most part, Bacovian poetry wears the insignia of this painful social reality, with acute reverberations in the creator's attitude before life, before injustice and suffering. That is the reason for a certain claustration in his own individuality, enstrangement in suffering, intimate secrecy of the sentiment of injustice—to which he was so sensitive—in the depth of his soul, the mute consummation of the revolts that troubled continuously his life as well as the lives of those around him, all these have created the image of the lonely poet taking refuge from the quakes and trials of an enemy society which he detested. Out of this fortuitous isolation was born that special flow of melancholy, of diffusive sadness, which reached the accents of agonic pessimism that traverse his poetry. Considered often enough as expressing the condition of one conquered, without the hope of ever finding out the answers to the great social problems that made vibrate the life of Romanian society between the wars, Bacovia's poetry, with its lyrical tonality seems, by contrast, to carry a protesting message, critical and expressed in a language full of a singular sensitivity. Incapable of making—in the order dominated by the concrete palpable event—the strong gesture of opposition, his work—through the most representative poems to be found successively in the volumes *Lead, Yellow Sparks, With You, Actually Comedies* and *Bourgeois Stanzas*—words one of the most moving and lucid condemnations of the bourgeois era, denouncing the apparent stability and forseeing the fiery sunset: "While the sunset barks out flames / On an ending heralded / On a millionaire backdrop," in the poems published in the review *Literary Life* of 1930. To the same meanings the poet dedicated the last part of his life, a new counterpoint, when he notes again, in 1956, the same habit of living for meaning and essence:

> I have fulfilled
> All my political
> Prophecies
> Happy I am
> Beautiful
> Is the sky
> Clear or angered.
> A well-known aphorism
> Makes one live . . .
> Not tomorrow
> Not today
> Not yesterday
> Is Time . . .

Having been recognized only in the poet's late years, by a movement that widened the circle of his audience from the few literary friends to a public that today admits and applauds the national audience of his poetry, Bacovia's work can not be understood with true meanings and values only with the help of the old phrases about the poet of "the rainy town" and of "the sad romances." No matter how deeply planted they be in Bacovian poetry, no matter how much suggestive material they might bring to the reader, guaranteeing for the most part its public success, now a reality, the two dominant notes through which it was explained—that is the specific musicality and the

visualizing quality of the verses—may keep today only auxiliary functions.

What is great, specific and even unequalled in the art of this poet, is the way in which his best work through the most humble details of the concrete, gives the final meanings of existence. In its most personal significance as in the most widely diffused ones, to the hypostases of such small, concrete annotations Bacovian poetry asks to be looked upon through a double effort of abstractization and concretization, within the concentric and superposed reality of the trajectories of the meaning. The verses of this poet never have one tone and one significant echo, no matter how simple and elementary his means of expression might be; his poetry reveals the great load of meditation, while it is socially active and even protesting, descriptive or evocative, lyrical or romantically sentimental. In order to be able to approximate the secret of its originality one is called upon not to forget that almost always these openings, or some of them, are achieved synchronically through a superposing of meanings, usually major ones upon minor, achieved with such natural spontaneity and artistical effect, that the interpretation knows not whether to choose the solution of pure intuition or the greatest artifice. Thus, if one can speak of a problematic nucleus of a tragical sort in Bacovia's work, this is done only at the price of the abstractizing stripping of the verses of their concrete dress and aromas.

In its social hypostasis, the Bacovian drama has a more concrete and individualized protagonist: the proletarian intellectual, growing directly from the militant writing of the socialist milieu at the end of the last century. If the social address of Bacovia's poetry has a double origin—one in the dynamic, anti-bourgeois poetry of A. Macedonski, the other in the literature of the review *Contemporanul* and the continuing group—his protesting hero goes only along the democratic line of the milieus directly influenced by the labour movement. Bacovia's verses, prolonging and amplifying the resounding words of poets like Stefan Petică and Tradem, keep unaltered the anti-bourgeois, Macedonskian attitude in its most violently sarcastic forms. Overwhelming through its force of expression and also through its unexplained form, of a problem in front of which commentary must calm down, is the close association, like a direct determination, between the clearest and categorical sentence of death passed upon the bourgeois world and the streams of distant and most general meaning that it holds and sets off at the same time. Romanian poetry of the first half of this century has from Bacovia a verse of direct and precise social protesting address:

> From the horizons opening
> The uncomprehended glaciers go
> Under a sky of song and flowers
> Rise, proletarians, in a row!

As it can be seen, it is a poetry able to spread the meaning of social problems towards the wider space of a generally human problem. A principle of major and total art invests the artistic experience of the poet with a great value and high dignity, justifying his great audience as well as the prestige he holds in front of literary history and criticism, a quality through which Bacovia's work recommends itself to the most representative fund of classics of our Romanian literary values. (pp. 46-8)

> *Mircea Tomus, "Artist of the Human Dignity," in*
> Romanian Review, *Vol. 26, No. 1, 1972, pp. 46-8.*

MIHAIL PETROVEANU   (essay date 1977)

[In the following essay, Petroveanu discusses existential meaninglessness, loneliness, and suffering in Bacovia's work, com-

paring the Rumanian poet to such authors as Franz Kafka, Fedor Dostoevski, Samuel Beckett, and Albert Camus.]

With Bacovia death does not crown life, it is not purely and simply the final moment of an existence which, in terms of a round harmonious development, experiences the exuberance of fulfilment, the plenitude of maturity and the majesty of decline. Granted to man on his birth, death is at the other end of life, in the sense in which the word *capăt* (end) designates in Romanian the end as well as the outset of all processes (A ajunge la *capăt* si a o lua la capăt—"To reach an end and to start again from the outset"). A permanent shadow, death has settled in the intimity of our being, where it acts as a corrupting, corrosive force, through a slow, insinuating siege, not leaving the victim a single illusion. Seen from this angle, life is a perpetual failure. So, to live means to suffer through no fault. In biblical mythology it was Job who suffered through no fault of his. Despite the arbitrary divine verdict, which was shockingly unfair, he continued to hope in salvation. Bacovia's modern hero was an agnostic and as such did not expect deliverance from sufferings by some merciful extrahuman instance. That is why he accepts his condition as a man alone in front of death, doomed to live under the burden of a useless consciousness, as it is helpless when faced by the inevitable. Job suffered his doom patiently with a stoicism transfigured by piety—the measure of the price paid by man to be forgiven for the sin of living. Bacovia, an atheistic spirit, could not believe existence had to be atoned for and that through the resources of beauty, intensity, euphoria it represents a value in itself. That is why he breaks the chain of apathy, struggles, denounces the injustice of life, tries to cling to some hope or another, or, as a passive form of his protest, he bemoans his destiny. The Romanian poet is a pathetic Job torn between the wish to accept his condition as captive of death without complaining, in a complete abolition of vitality, and the impulses to rebel against the jailer. Submissive or rebellious, accepting or rejecting a world controlled by the principle of the grief of the existing and, at the same time, oppressive society which defaces values, Bacovia speaks now on behalf of the collectivity, now in his own name. If, as a social rebel, he seems to be an interpreter of the crowd, of the proletariat, of the persecuted, when he clamours his existential suffering or records the symptoms of cosmic decomposition he is thinking of himself, careful, as it were, not to be suspected of setting himself up as an exponent of the feelings of others. Bacovia assumed exclusively the responsibility of his special destiny, that of a sick man. A poet of the tortured ego, and in this sphere a poet of an exceptional ego, was he not more attached to his own literary time than to the modern epoch which had driven away the ego from places where it seemed sacrosanct, from lyricism? Bacovia, remaining dependent on the symbolists through his language and the consciousness of the ego, flatly parted with them as they undermine the prestige of the intangible instance. It is not the crystallization, but the dissolution of the ego at the same time as that of the universe that forms the substance of his poetry, the obsession, the centre of the fears that consume him and against which he fights, now and then, successfully. The position is similar to Trakl's, it is expressionist; but Trakl and expressionism are the chosen heralds of contemporary sensitiveness. With Bacovia the terror when facing a convulsed world combines with the inclination to anonymity, with the annulment of the being, through a withdrawal from space and time, through taking refuge in the suburbs, in very small rooms, in cellars, on fields covered with snow or in forgotten prehistoric epochs. A saturnine poet, sombre and tortured, doubting his own self, Bacovia manifested himself through the impulses

peculiar to modern literature. The Kafkian hero adopted the defence reflexes of animals devoid of any offensive weapon, baffled by their own senses which ought to warn them of the presence of remote danger, hiding in dens, digging galleries for themselves as the mole does, identifying himself with an insect. In the *Metamorphosis*, Gregor Samsa does not feel *like* a beetle, but is a beetle. Beckett's freaks, in a similar involution, completely lose their human aspect through the atrophy of one of the organs of sense (hearing, sight, speech) or of the vital functions (locomotion, reproduction, the gradual complete or partial loss of lucidity). Bacovia, who could have uttered himself Baudelaire's invocation *"Ah, Seigneur! donnez-moi la force et le courage / De contempler mon coeur et mon corps sans dégoût"* ["O, Lord! give me the strength and the courage / To contemplate my heart and my body without disgust"], verified on the bodies of his fellow-creatures, on the face of his beloved, on his own body, the alteration of the face, the marks of consumption, the accelerated or slow advance in parallel with the moments of total numbness of his sensitiveness, the slips of lucidity, losses of memory—the fissures in the power of association of language included—harrowed by the feat and temptation of becoming vegetable or mineral. The poet always feels he is slipping, falling, attracted into the void of gravitation, a mere atom, some small object, some tiny toy. The comparison with the leaf snatched and dragged along by the wind, with the birds rustling like a cloth, does not represent only his moral condition, but the substratum of a physical analogy between man and inorganic or sensitive matter. Catalepsy, as an aspect of death, is one of the alternatives which lie in ambush; hence his contrary propensity to uninterrupted walking, considered an aspect of life. With Bacovia, the same as with Dostoevski, solitude—conceived as a part of lucidity, a serial unity and a vital action of the individual—undermines his personality instead of strengthening and enhancing it. In the iron circle of isolation in its own cell, the ego tends to be monopolized, "possessed" by its centrifugal dispersing forces which, rising from the "subterrane" of the being to "the level" of the mind become, with Dostoevski, the Christian name of the devil, and with Bacovia is mistaken for the various facets of the irrational: wakeful nightmares, the absurdity of relationships, madness, the spectres of death. Consciousness struggles with might and main against the presence of the inner daemon, making it resist the vertigo, first by seriously and consistently scanning the process. The same as the hero in *The Subterranean Voice*, the poet divides himself, splits into the two sides of his personality, and consciousness, neutral, now fascinated, now terrified, shares the progress of the "subterranean voice," the disintegrating effects of the monster's action. Thus the Bacovian soliloqui is a lyrical retort to the Dostoevskian self-analysis too. The analogy, emphasized by heart-rending accents, by the lamentations common to both of them, could be extended in another direction too. Like the Dostoevskian possessed, Bacovia's hero tries to run away from his own self, to escape. What else are the poet's continuous wanderings, his secret nocturnal roaming, cautious like a hunted creature, walking into public squares and venturing on the outskirts of the town? In the same way, the hero in *The Subterranean Voice* and those in other writings by Dostoevsky (*White Nights, The Humbled and the Offended*) strove to avoid the tyranny of existential darkness, the continually fiercer aggression of the evil residing in man. But Bacovia possesses a resource of his own, one unable to cure him once and for all, but able to maintain his hope, to keep up his obstinacy to live. I am referring to his confidence in the restoring future. But in this way we enter precisely the sphere of his relationships with the world, the domain of his vision of the universe and society. Here the contact points with Dostoevski become blurred in favour of a new contact with contemporary witnesses of the human inferno. Man suffers the contagious influence of the miraculous, provided it fits in with the ambience, it accepts the norms of cosmic alchemy.

In its representations of the world, modern literature submits to a figurative model, that of the closed space. The variants suggested can be more complicated or simpler, splendidly baroque or wretchedly naturalistic. The theatre of the Kafkian mythology substitutes the castle for the tribunal, the wall of China for the room, the den for the suspended box like a cage, the underground gallery purely and simply for a gate. The Kafkian space is squalid rather than spectacular, ridiculous, or banal at most. In *The Plague* by Camus, the action is set in a Mediterranean town in quarantine, a town which no one could enter or leave. The action in *With Closed Doors,* a play by Sartre, takes place between the walls of a hotel room, denuded of any monumental element. *The Labyrinth,* a novel by Alain Robbe-Grillet, mentions a town impracticable under the snow that covers it and whose architecture is not classifiable. Borges' favourite décor is one of labyrinthine type, in a gorgeous alarming version. He likes in general the palace-fortress which, with its enormous walls, inextricable passages, delapidated stairs, windows which will not open, is smothered under frenzied ornaments. The universe without any outlet of André Pieyre

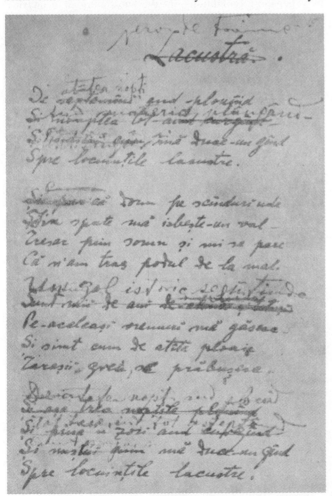

Manuscript of a poem in Plumb.

de Mandiargues is in a way similar but more directly fabulous owing to its delirious extravagance of surrealist extraction. When (as happens with Dino Buzzati (*The Tartars' Desert*) the space seems open, the impression is only a delusion, as the vast limits around the hypergeometrized fort are those of a boundless desert in which no one can leave the bastion in fact. So that, whatever the images, the motif of the closed space is identical with its essence, while the inhabitant, man, has to choose between being introduced into it, as an eternal prisoner, or remain outside it, excluded for all his life.

The Romanian poet's town has the configuration of the prototype of hermetic space. Rid of its geographical determinations, it becomes abstract, acquires such a general dimension that it can at most symbolize the "provincial" condition of the modern inferno. An inferno entirely similar to dull stagnant everyday life, slowly sinking into a wretchedness not only social and moral, but physiological and existential as well. Man thrown into it does not *exist;* he *is* only, as an object, an implement, a plant is: an anonymous part of matter, enjoying the vacant eternity of things, at any time substitutive for each other. This inferno has none of the awful greatness of the great classical models. Lacking dizzying tumults and diabolical tortures, Dantesque when it evokes the neutral limbo situated between hell and heaven, Bacovia's inferno is both mysterious and not mysterious. A transparent product of a double series of forces, on the one hand the oppressive mechanics of society, and, on the other, the mechanics of death, which in its insidious discharge corrupts passions, aspirations, the thirst to live, this inferno protects inexplicable initiatives, or the signs of upsetting practice. Whose are the stains of animal blood on the edge of the fortress? What dreadful murder must have been committed there? Why does death itself act so whimsically, striking unexpectedly or paralysing the will to resist before it has carried out its work and turning its victims into accomplices, resigned or voluptuous? Against this background of ambiguity and light, of brutality and obscure clandestine insinuation, we understand why lucidity throws off all restraint, is disjointed, to the benefit of the "subterraneous" creature, of the powers of disorder, nightmare and mild or historical insanity. Mystery, unless it appears rhythmically, periodically, could be borne and defied if need be. When its appearances obey no imperative, its tyranny becomes annoying and "turns one's head." Kafka's characters, in a complex of rebellion and submission, were struggling to grasp the sense. Bacovia can do without this effort. The Kafkian characters attempt to puzzle out the enigma of destiny in a roundabout way, by means of certain cunning tricks or by accepting the rules of the game. (Josef K. in *The Trial* does not contest the lawfulness of the tribunal.) Bacovia does not resort to such methods. He accuses the inferno, by calling it by its name to its face. It is a manner of denouncing it, of tearing away the halo of secondary occult reality. Whereas with Kafka the reasons of the suffering remain hidden, with Bacovia they are revealed.

The Bacovian province, hypostasized, having become a symbolic zone for man's complete exile (social, moral, existential), identifies itself with the modern vision of the town. Baudelaire, who had set up its myth, was still fascinated by its magic; his futurist dreams wove the image of a world living between the stone, glass and iron walls and, at the same time, was possessed by the idea that the town of the future shut up humanity as in a maze (the term appears in his works). The modern writers, taking over the myth, have abandoned the elements of seduction. The seat of human failure, with Kafka the town has turned into grey, squalid precincts, controlled by baleful crushing powers. Bacovia's town is in no way Daedalian, its streets are no intricate passages leading nowhere. But he is just as isolated from the rest of the universe and his humiliation is just as choking. The patriarchal element seems to add, by contrast, a note of grotesque irony to the ridiculous ensemble. Nature, whose intense presence in Bacovia's poetry might have belied its fundamental character of urban inferno, in fact supports the general conception. Its action fully collaborating to the corruption of the universe, to extending the realm of death over the individual, ratifies and even worsens his failure. The moments when vitality reacts, through a contact with the tonic powers of nature, are ephemeral. Spring is ''a delusion,'' as the infusion of fresh blood it brings along has no consequences. What is constant is the hostility which the nightmare displays through diluvial floods, the layers of polar snow, the aridity of summer and the devastating effects of autumn. With Bacovia, the sense of nature and hope in its restoring aptitudes was not atrophied (it always remains a model), the same as the prestige of lyrical descriptive poems never died away. That is why, without being entitled to state that in his poetry nature is an ''anti-nature,'' one may say that like the townscape which no matter how ''infernal'' is attractive in a way, the image of nature's elements appears ambivalent. In other words, Bacovia is attracted and rejected by nature. Compared to the Romanian poetry, however, in which the religious adoration of nature is prevalent, Bacovia's lyrical poetry represents an attempt at desecrating cosmic mythology. This is the spirit in which other aspects of Bacovia's contribution to the heritage of autochthonous poetry, to the multiplicity of the representations which constitute it, can be valorized. Bacovia is not the only Romanian poet to whom life appears an inferno. To Arghezi the world periodically appears, in accents of savage violence such as Bacovia never used, laid waste by the powers of evil, alias those of the devil. In his conception, strongly influenced by the religious vision, man can descend to the lowest stages of degradation, joining the loathsome condition of the impure matter, of a formless chaotic universe. The fall which lies in store for him at any moment is in the first place of spiritual and moral order. The perpetual process of human nature, Arghezi's literature in general (not his poetry only) belongs—as it has been repeatedly emphasized—to a moralist, a prophet, a relentless biblical spirit where sin is concerned. But due to the same prospects, salvation solutions are still possible. A sinner can rise above his own state of servitude, he reaches the restoring state of grace through everything the believer undertakes: prayer, penitence, humility, worship. The inferno was given to the human condition, so was paradise. In other words, the possibility of making a choice is ensured. Besides, as the universe avoids the dispute between good and evil, between God and Satan, it offers a perfect image of the creative power, a chain of perpetual miracles, an absolute guarantee. The cosmos testifies to the Creation and the Creator; both its planes, the celestial and the terrestrial, become support, a fixed landmark. With Bacovia, who is free from such views, life is infernal not as a consequence of some guilt in front of an instance superior to many which does not exist, but through life's own mortal essence, subjected to the influence of nothingness. Man, alone in the cosmos and alone in his own world, has no way out, or if there does exist one it depends exclusively on himself. Thus life is tragical, but of a specific tragicalness. It is the tragedy accompanying the endeavours of a weak creature, aware of the fragility of his own means to successfully withstand an opponent all the more discouraging as he seems duller, mean, more ridiculous. For that reason, man's tragicalness in the Bacovian inferno is, precisely, close to the modern anti-tragicalness, to the Sisyphean image of man in the Cosmos, to the hunted creature of Kafka's character, a blend of submission and rebellion and, *horribile dictu,* of Beckett's larval creatures. In this universe surrounded by nothingness all roads are barred. The protagonist of the tragedy goes on all the same, as we know, deciphering the liberating track. And as we know Bacovia also went about the whole town, along obscure streets, in the wretched muddy districts, on the outskirts of settlements, he entered the surrounding plain, where, for one moment, he thought he would come to the light. But sure of the invisible obstacles which stop him here too, he returns to the town, along the same streets or along others, it is of no consequence, because he returns to the same small square in the centre and there begins his wanderings over again, with his obstinate despair, after which he may have stopped at his beloved's house or will have tarried looking at the barred closed windows of the hostile houses where twin creatures are suffering agonies as he is. The wanderings which never reach their goal is one more favourite notion in modern literature, descending from the same ''closed space.'' Kafka's characters, on the way to the tribunal (*The Trial*) or to the castle (*The Castle*) are walking to no avail as the castle on the hill never opens its gates, while the tribunal supposedly to stand among the grey, indefinite offices along the Daedalian passages of the building where the petitioner enters, cannot be identified. With Kafka, it is not only the utility of the action, but the very reality of its object that are doubtful, for nothing assures us that the tribunal or the castle actually exist or, even if they do exist, we do not know whether they can meet the exigencies formulated: so a double symbol, regarding both the authenticity and the validity of human purposes, as well as the inadequacy and precariousness of the means resorted to, with a view to carrying them out. It is an ambiguity which is complete with Kafka and dissolves with Beckett. Life, an imprescriptible journey towards death, does not allow even of a hypothetic, or no matter how vague a chance of salvation. His characters are lamentable wayfarers, poor mollusks or worms crawling along a simple route towards a destiny they ignore, but which is the only one, without any resistance, in complete loneliness, making fewer and fewer mechanical gestures, exchanging with one another disconnected words, at long intervals, muttering, while others keep silent, or do not utter even one single scream of animal fear. An absurd procession, as the itinerary leads to no fixed goal, towards an abyss interrupted only by vain expectations. The road, a motif of an ambiguous destination with Kafka, fatal with Beckett, with Bacovia is an expression of the impossibility of eluding destiny. If we imagined it graphically, it would confirm the aspect of closed circle of the universe in which he pines away. This is a Kafka- and Beckett-like attitude, both due to the realistic data of his structure and to its artistic nature. With Bacovia, as with Beckett or Kafka, we keep within the limits of the familiar, everyday world. In their universe no factor extraneous to the common perception interferes, some factor belonging to other ''galaxies,'' respectively to the traditionally fantastic imagination. The new, strange character results from the overtaxing of the real, from the dilating, to the degree of hallucination, precisely of the traits peculiar to the most familiar, the most banal, most insignificant zones, if we think of Beckett. The common method is to reduce the universe to its elementary mechanisms and to reproduce them *ad infinitum.* Kafka's and Beckett's characters, Bacovia's lyrical hero repeat the same movements, travel over the same roads, utter the same replies. With Kafka and Beckett there happens, in parallel, an emptying of the world of all that might introduce variety, differentiation, animation. Beckett, more especially, drives away the slightest accent heralding change, be it only alternation. With Kafka too nature has disappeared. Not only nature is absent in the decor of Beckett's dramas, but civilization too, man's constitutive background of life. With Bacovia depressive nature still preserves islands of beauty, poetry. Its depressive realism has not succeeded in sterilizing all sources of beauty—be it even ephemeral, delusive, connected to the moment—of reverie, of inner dreams or mere aspirations towards a change of the real. Beckett, the prophet of the absolute pre-eminence of nothingness, denies art not only the claim of expressing, if not the real essence, at least the apparent beauty of life—for him a thing that goes without saying—but, consistent with a radical nihilism from an aesthetic angle too, he denies it the constitutive right to build up fictions, either in a humble way, as simple appearances, except the beautiful-ugly category, in other words the right to build up images. Beckett's theatre is not only an anti-theatre but an image of the anti-image. Kafka, whose ambiguous vision does not raise the problem of compulsory options in the life-nothingness relation, is inclined to admit the hegemony of the latter term, but without contesting the reality of the former. He believes we do not have the right to decide clearly in favour of any of these positions. That is why, as an artist, he believes in the comparative legitimacy of art as image, a neutral image, capable of suggesting, at the same time as non-beauty, the precariousness, the irreality of the real, as well as, however, doubt regarding the final triumph of nothingness. Bacovia is one of the artists who, if we are to resume a classification made by Gustav René Hocke "is delighted with appearances, because they can stand neither existence nor non-existence" (*Manierismus in der Literatur*). The only firm point such artists admit of is the image of their own art, the world of appearances it arouses. Only images can suggest the true nature of things, their essential duality, their hesitation between existence and nothingness, between reality and irreality, between near and remote, harmony and disharmony, stimulating beauty and paralyzing ugliness. A possible virtue due to the very structure of the image, that is to say to its ambiguous nature: "The nature of the image is inner ambiguity. . . . The ambiguity of the image (generally) corresponds to the ambiguity of the thing it represents" [G. R. Hocke, *Manierismus in der Literatur*]. From the stand of an absolute philosophic nihilism, Beckett refuses existence any reality. Bacovia's universe, though realist and "ugly," is at the same time chimerical and "beautiful." Thus its power of hallucination is double, attracting and rejecting, according to its double extraction. (pp. 128-32)

> *Mihail Petroveanu, "Bacovia," translated by Mary Lăzărescu, in* Romanian Review, *Vol. 31, No. 3, 1977, pp. 128-32.*

MARIAN POPA (essay date 1980)

[*In the following excerpt, Popa focuses on elements of Symbolism, Expressionism, and Existentialism in Bacovia's poetry.*]

It so happens that the formal criterion of alphabetical order provides the starting point for a grouping by value of modern Romanian poetry. It is currently believed that Romanian verse in this century is best represented by one A and three B's: Tudor Arghezi, Lucian Blaga, George Bacovia and Ion Barbu. The grouping is close in merit, but its order is not necessarily hierarchical: according to changing tastes and perspectives, one poet may appear to be more important than the others. It is certain, however, that each of them represents an essential trend in Romanian poetry and also reflects some more general areas

of poetic endeavour in Europe and in the West. George Bacovia holds a fundamental, irreplaceable and unequalled position of his own within that group.

A major peculiarity of Bacovia's work stems from its paradoxical freedom and from the development of its interpretation. During the period between the two world wars Bacovia was first considered strictly within the limits of Symbolism; he was subsequently detached from that movement, to the extent of having his Symbolist origins questioned, and he is now seen as a modern poet *par excellence*. Finally, it is interesting to note that, unlike other figures in twentieth century Romanian poetry, whose reputations have fluctuated, Bacovia is the only poet whose representative value has risen steadily and appears likely at the moment to continue growing. There are two possible explanations for this: first, Bacovia's work was initially underestimated, and second, because of its existential, nondoctrinaire character, it appears to be the best illustration of the condition of modern man.

Bacovia's work has elicited, next to Eminescu's, the greatest number of interpretations, and most critical viewpoints and approaches have used his oeuvre almost demonstratively in order to assert their own worth. If one claims that Bacovia's verse is the product of a neurotic state of mind, then psychoanalytical, clinical or pathological approaches may become possible and prove fruitful; if his work is regarded as the result of a conscious adherence to a definite literary credo, then one can pursue the significance of Symbolism as a starting-point for Bacovia's work, and particularly Bacovia's significance for Symbolism itself. A thorough consideration of his imagery and of the specific situations that he depicts might lead, and has led, to a discovery of the poet's Expressionism. And finally, his kind of vision might align him with Existentialism, while the pattern of behaviour of his poetic *persona* might warrant his being related to the literature of the absurd. Phenomenological analysis in the manner of Gaston Bachelard, and both semiotic and statistical analyses have been applied to Bacovia's work, perhaps more than to any other's. (pp. 25-6)

No doubt, Symbolism has a certain common stock of subjects, moods and images, which could be regarded as Bacovia's starting-point. One can therefore identify with Bacovia images that are similar to those of Paul Verlaine, Jules Laforgue, Rollinat, Georges Rodenbach, Tristan Corbière, Verhaeren. Common traits can also be traced to the Romanian Symbolists who had made a name for themselves in the early years of the century: Traian Demetrescu, Stefan Petică, Al. Stamatiad, Demostene Botez, D. Iacobescu. But Bacovia displayed such an emotional intensity in his presentation of lyrical motifs and concerns that he converted them into pure expressions of life. In many ways, without however stretching the comparison too far, the experience of his own time meant for Bacovia what Elizabethan theatre had meant for Shakespeare. For he also used a material so worn out as to have become a refuge for poetic competence in order to build a unique universe of his own, populated by a diminutive, though indisputably modern, lyrical personality.

This is one connection that may help the Western reader towards a general picture of the Romanian poet. Bacovia's lyrical personality is as fragile in its petty way as a character in Samuel Beckett's novels and plays. In a dull, depressing and frightening world, a sad, passive and sick buffoon acts his part: he talks, he sees things, he relates himself to the world, he mumbles, he puts on airs, and he is afraid. The world was once represented by the balance of the spiritual and the material between the king and the fool. From Shakespeare to Musset (in *Fantasio*) the world used to be bereft of its fool, who either had died or had been killed. In our own time, however, some believe that it is only the fool that has survived. Namely the Bacovian lyrical ego or the Beckett character. The world in which such characters come to be has another feature: the universe has no beginning and no end, it just exists, squalid and ridiculous, with no meaning left for either life or death. It is a world that lives on in tenacious agony. Ion Caraion, a distinguished Romanian poet, entitled with good reason one of his essays: *Bacovia, or the Continuous End.* Such an existence becomes the comic-sinister saga of pointless waiting filled with localized obsessions, of wandering in a space without time. To go on with the parallel, both the Beckett character and the Bacovian lyrical ego are engaged in a kind of continuous Brownian movement within a confined area, and so their Odyssey through space in the environment of a provincial town becomes a symbol of life seen as a journey toward a preordained end, which may sometimes be accepted, while at other times it is not even consciously perceived.

That existence is dominated by, or reduced to, a few concerns and basic existential demands: illness, fear, cold, love, elemental feeling and metaphysical paradox. And still the existential terms seem to be mutually determined: life seen as an affliction, illness and love, fear of living, a perception of life through life's sufferings. Bacovia's world does not necessarily become ugly because of that reduction; one can only say that it is not beautiful.

Bacovian man looks for a point of contact in a desolate universe only to discover its transient nature: in this empty space human encounters are sporadic and fleeting, they occur in a strange room, in a public house, in a street, in a vacant lot. People do not call out to each other, nor are they attracted to one another; they just meet by chance, they suffer each other's presence or they show their innate propensity to be mutual enemies, mere corpses that are still incomplete because of the residual life in them, sick passers-by. Beyond all that is the remote image of a regional or planetary community, which is perceived by the poet as something undifferentiated, defined by absurd behaviour and insanity; and that community is also reduced in order to depict the bourgeois, philistine spirit, a human reality which elicits his utter disdain, expressed either directly, from the standpoint of a metaphysical proletarian philosophy, or indirectly, through ironic observations.

The marginal and the provincial hold a special place in this kind of poetry. It is well-known that French Realism and Symbolism also attempted to explore new subjects and consequently paid greater attention to marginal and provincial life, which after Flaubert began to be seen in a grotesque light. Romanian Symbolist poetry developed marginal and provincial themes more than any others, converting the given realities into systems of generalized symbols. In such poems the marginal coalesced with the provincial into an image of the sordid and of boredom. Through Bacovia, who refined these themes exhaustively, the provincial and the marginal, failing to belong to a meaningful world centered on spiritual values, become general images of a world which is itself isolated and peripheral, as in Beckett's *Molloy* or *Murphy*, like the region of Macondo in Marquez's novel: a world that finds its meaning and purpose in an indeterminate futility.

It is to be noted that provincial life in Romania had little in common with that of the British countryside. It was neither colourful, nor relaxing, nor was it deemed to be a place to

escape to from civilization. It was mortifying, gloomy, dull, splenetic.

Finally, Bacovia used to associate his own time with primeval worlds, in which man was confronted only by the elements and by essential, ominous events. His poem **"Lacustrine"** is just one example of this.

Within such an existential periphery, unities of space and movement acquired precise significances. Bacovia's agoraphobia became dominant; a room was described as an uncertain space of love, while the burial vaults, graveyards, marketplaces or vacant lots were perceived as the standard environment of daily life, barren solitary places, where any human communication was impossible. Moreover, those places were afflicted by ambiguous weather conditions; snow, rain, drizzle, fog and smoke enhanced and substantiated the feeling that life was indefinite and transitory, images reminiscent of the paintings of Sisley or Pissarro. Another important feature is the feeling of emptiness, as represented by a destitute world, emphasized in a clear delineation of stylised space, either devoid of materiality or filled with stereotyped geometrical objects.

The spatial dynamics is correlated with the fiction of stylised space. Movements seem to lose their function, or at least to be oddly different from the usual ones: birds are falling or crawling, and human beings are wandering through indefinite spaces or swimming through the snow.

The determination of Bacovian poems in relation to time is also most peculiar. Autumn and winter are the prevalent seasons, displaying images of suffering and deterioration. Dusk and night, probably the most frequently used words in his poems, are also involved in that nexus of meanings; the hollow and irresolute mornings are mere extensions of the night, while the summers seem to be anticipations of the autumn or seasons of decay.

In terms of figurative rendering, a certain style of close-up and grimace, specific Expressionist features, deserves mention. The grotesque faces, bodies or movements are reminiscent of Munch, Nolde and Otto Dix. The scenery also appears to have come from the same source. Like the Expressionists, Bacovia does not resort to shades, but to solid colours, in general violently distributed: white, grey, black, red, yellow and violet monopolize his world and simplify it in the process, giving it the frenzied shapes, forceful quality and the precision of delirium. The sounds, or more exactly the noises, are of the same kind. A Symbolistic exaggeration fills Bacovia's poems with ludicrous brass bands, barbaric songs, and anachronistic instruments played by beggars. Both human beings and nature produce screams, howls, snarls, moans, roars, grindings, creaks or cracks in a way that recalls Expressionistic serial music.

The language is also made functional in order to emphasize Bacovia's own reality. It is a psychological law that a limited number of feelings evokes an impression of obsessive intensity, and Bacovia's verse does just that. It is an aesthetic law that in a universe furnished with a limited number of objects, such objects would acquire through reductive stylization both the character and the function of symbols. In Bacovia this, too, happens. Moreover, these two features are supplemented by a third: the use of a limited stock of words, in their main connotations, handled in a way that suggests a desire both to strip them to their essences and to exhaust the combinative possibilities of the chosen words. The immediate effect of such reductions is a feeling that the unity between the inner and the outer worlds is equally perceived as a stereotype and as an archetype. And that unity is accentuated by repetition. From the level of neurotic reactions to the level of phrasing and words, rhymes, rhythms and titles, lines and stanzas, repetition reigns supreme. On the other hand, Bacovia shows a certain tendency to free himself from the rules of prosody by breaks, lacunae, suspensions and syntactical compressions. Such poems can be considered as direct expressions of a neurotic state of mind or, in poetic terms, as a means of modernising lyrical discourse, which is reminiscent of Gottfried Benn.

Bacovia provides, therefore, the rare example of a poet whose originality lies in the fact that with him the feeling of art and the feeling of life become one, in a single, inexplicable and unfathomable sincerity which renders humanity less sublime and the universe less pleasant, but both more real. More artistic, in fact. (pp. 28-33)

> *Marian Popa, in a foreword, translated by Sergiu Celac, to* Lead *by George Bacovia, translated by Peter Jay, Minerva Publishing House, 1980, pp. 25-33.*

ION DODU BĂLAN (essay date 1981)

[*In the following excerpt, Bălan examines characteristics of style and theme in Bacovia's work.*]

George Bacovia . . . wrote symbolistic poetry expressing the typical Romanian soul and consciousness, and a native moral universe. In the melody and colours of his poetry one sees the author's effort to detach himself from the dull, grey, stifling everyday routine; he mocked with bitter irony the common-places and automatism in the life of provincial boroughs, and he sadly described the sufferings of poor people morally crip-pled by wrong and inhuman social conditions. Bacovia dis-played a perfect command of the language; he excelled in the art of using a limited number of carefully selected words, discovering new meanings in each of them, keying up our sensitiveness to them in an infinity of manners, uttering them at various pitches of spiritual tension, in various voices or tones. The musicality of his poetry rings beyond the meaning of words and the form of the verse. Over and above the common notions they denote, the words in Bacovia's poems create a new harmony and communicate a novel value; they convey new colours and images, irrespective of their logical or gram-matical relationships within the sentence:

> As the imprisoned soul
> For nothing'll yearn or pine—
> The leaves fall in the twilight
> Darling mine!
>
> The night is gloomy, low
> The star's a bitter line
> And soon it's sure to snow
> Darling mine!

Bacovia's typical borough is actually the embodiment of an entire society, a diseased century, a tragical world with a dis-tinct personality. His borough is benumbed by the frost or swamped in mud. The heavy lead of winter falls over his world. Thick fog covers everything like a funeral pall. Streams of griefs flood the old, ramshackle houses. The drizzle patters in an exasperating manner, as if causing the whole world to rot and instilling solitude, alienation, restlessness and cureless fear into every soul. All seasons pass over the borough and the poet as if tired and sick. The poet favours autumn which—for him as well as for Stefan George and Rollinat—is the time of death

and of heart-rending separations. It is the season of twilights, loaded with spleen and despair. Autumn utters sounds of agony, the flight of birds through a sullen sky carries along, like a shroud, the fear of death, the fright of life, worry and loneliness which are shared equally by human beings; Eminescu's mel-ancholy cowbell which used to be a source of magic and poetry, sounds sad and out of tune with Bacovia; the flowers in his verse are artificial, sometimes they are made of lead and have a funereal effect; squares and parks are desolate, the decor is reduced to the two fundamental colours: white and black. Those colours occasionally blend, however, in a strange kind of al-chemy, yielding a type of grey that suggests ashes, twilight, the approach of death:

DECOR

The trees are white, the trees are black,
All bare in parks which hummed of yore;
The décor mourns, the sets deplore . . .
The trees are white, the trees are black.

In parks regrets weep as before . . .

With feathers white and feathers black,
A bird whose voice sounds bitter, sore,
Rends parks of scores of years or more,
With feathers white and feathers black . . .

In parks the ghosts come to the fore . . .

The leaves are white, the leaves are black;
The trees are white, the trees are black;
And feathers white and feathers black,
The décor mourns, the sets deplore . . .

The snow is sparse, the park is hoar.

In that strange and frozen borough, the "deathly" sensation is conveyed by the horizon "like a wast mound," the land flooded by ceaseless rains that turn it into an immense tomb, the wailing of matter as tortured as are people, the leafless trees, the leaden or charred flowers, the phthysical maidens who play funeral marches, the poet who is also consumptive and ready to die, the metallic sounds played by trumpeters at the barracks, the lament of the street organ, the croaking of ravens, sleet, mud, the snow burning with the blood from the slaughter-house, the high school which is "the graveyard of our youth," the houses with "melancholy windows," with "old walls just about to crumble," defunct love affairs, the deep deserts in the streets and squares, in people's homes and souls. (pp. 54-6)

> *Ion Dodu Bălan, "George Bacovia," in his* A Concise History of Romanian Literature, *translated by Andrei Bantaş, Editura Ştiinţifică şi Enciclopedică, Social and Political Sciences, 1981, pp. 54-6.*

ADDITIONAL BIBLIOGRAPHY

Andreescu, Gabriel. "Classification of Poetic Items: The Volumes '*Plumb*' by Bacovia and '*Poemele Luminii*' by Blaga." *Revue Roumane de Linguistique* XXVI, No. 2 (March-April 1981): 181-88.
    A mathematical analysis of Bacovia's *Plumb* which concludes that "Bacovia's poetry relies on the accumulation of terms which

are endowed with power of suggestion as well as on the emphasizing by means of surprising semantic and emphatic constructions.''

Jay, Peter. Translator's foreword to *Lead,* by George Bacovia, translated by Peter Jay, pp. 35-7. Bucarest, Romania: Minerva Publishing House, 1980.

Discusses the translation of Bacovia's poetry.

''A Great Romanian Poet: George Bacovia (1881-1957).'' *Romanian Bulletin* VII, No. 9 (September 1978): 6.

A brief discussion of Bacovia's life and work. The critic comments: ''A modern poet, easy of access, but hostile to decadence, Bacovia is a unique figure and one of the most interesting in world poetry. This is due to the astounding simplicity of the means with which he created the symbols.''

W. N. P. Barbellion

1889-1919

(Pseudonym of Bruce Frederick Cummings) English diarist, essayist, and short story writer.

In literary history Barbellion figures among a relatively small group of authors whose reputations are based solely on private records of their daily lives. Published as *The Journal of a Disappointed Man* and *A Last Diary*, his journal has warranted the interest of readers for several reasons. A self-trained naturalist, Barbellion devoted many of its pages to detailed and expressive observations of nature as manifested in various forms of sea and land life. He was also determined to examine his own personality with similar scientific exactitude and detachment, producing a self-portrait which has been both condemned as indulgent egoism and praised for its illuminating candor. This process of self-examination was complicated when Barbellion discovered that he was dying from a degenerative disease. The reflections inspired by this painful situation represent his attempt to investigate and appraise the value of human life without the shield of conventional illusions, an ambition which has served to aggravate the controversy surrounding his journal. While some commentators find Barbellion's philosophical outlook unnecessarily cynical, others tend to emphasize the tragic heroism which gave dignity and purpose to his grim existence.

Barbellion was born in Barnstaple, North Devon, the youngest of six children. His father was a local journalist of some repute, and Barbellion grew up in a literate and cultured household. Stricken with pneumonia in infancy, he continued to suffer from poor health throughout childhood and remained at home, where he was tutored by one of his elder brothers. At the age of nine he entered a local private school and began to display the curiosity and intellectual acuity that are regarded as characteristic of his nature. He explored the local countryside, fascinated with the people he met and the natural life he observed. It was with the intention of keeping a record of his wildlife observations that Barbellion began his journal in early adolescence. By the time he was fourteen he had decided to pursue a career as a naturalist, an ambition that was seemingly realized in 1910 when he was offered an appointment at the Plymouth Marine Laboratory. Before Barbellion accepted the position, however, his father suffered a complete physical breakdown, and it became necessary for the family's survival that Barbellion assist as a reporter on his father's staff. The following year he was released from this responsibility and was able to compete for an opening at the Natural History Museum at South Kensington, London. Despite his lack of formal training he won the competition, although a physician's examination nearly disqualified him for the post. Thereafter, he increasingly suffered from various ailments, and ultimately his array of symptoms, which Barbellion described as "nervous derangements," conclusively indicated the terminal condition known today as multiple sclerosis. Although members of his family were informed of his illness, as was his future wife, Barbellion discovered the truth only inadvertently while examining a doctor's report that he was not meant to read.

Chronic ill health forced Barbellion to resign from the Museum in July 1917, and afterward he spent much of his time expanding and editing his journal for publication. *The Journal*

of a Disappointed Man was published in early 1919 and received mostly favorable reviews. A concluding note to the volume falsely reported that Barbellion had died on December 31st of 1917. Barbellion in fact lived long enough to see the reviews of *The Journal of a Disappointed Man,* and in his posthumously published *A Last Diary* he commented on the notices received by the earlier book: "As a whole, I am surprised and delighted with the extraordinary kindness and sympathy meted out to it, more than I deserve or it deserves, while one or two critics, with power that amazes, penetrate to the wretched Barbellion's core." Barbellion died on October 22, 1919, at the age of thirty.

In *A Last Diary,* which covers the period from July 1917 to October 1919, Barbellion wrote: "My life has certainly been an astonishing episode in human story. To me, it appears as a titanic struggle between consuming ambition and adverse fortune." While Barbellion's "adverse fortune" is readily identified from the superficial facts of his life, the nature of his ambition is something that emerges in its full range and intensity only in the pages of his journal. As critics unanimously observe, Barbellion possessed an overwhelming appetite for experience, for knowledge, and ultimately for conquest and distinction in some field of endeavor. Early in his life it seemed that achievement as a naturalist would provide him with some measure of what he sought from life, and indeed his exceptional scientific talent was recognized by a number of critics, beginning with H. G. Wells. The progressive crippling of his body, and intermittently of his emotions, turned his efforts in another direction, one that seemed inevitable for a temperament as reflective and eager for expression as Barbellion's. Barbellion's brother, Arthur J. Cummings, has noted that at one time Barbellion was planning an ambitious literary project on the scale of Honoré Balzac's *Comédie humaine*. Lacking the years, health, and perhaps creative resources necessary to such an undertaking, Barbellion made his journal the repository of frustrated aspirations that found only a partial outlet in science and literature, and that suggest a "consuming ambition" transcending both. In his essay "On Amiel and Some Others," Barbellion discusses what he terms the "sentiment for universality," and in a selection from his diary published under the heading "Infinities," he confesses: "I should like to be a god methinks. . . . To love merely one's own children or one's own parents, how ridiculous that seems, how puny, how stifling! To be interested only in one's own life or profession, to know and remain satisfied merely with one's own circumscribed experiences—how contemptible!" It is this overreaching search for experience that is often emphasized in critical discussions of Barbellion. Exemplary of what has been called his "hunger" for the extremes of feeling, as well as indicating his profound love of life, is a statement Barbellion made in a letter to his brother: "I have been to the top and to the bottom, very happy and very miserable. But don't think I am whining—I prefer a life which is a hunt, and an adventure rather than a study in still life. . . . If I were suddenly assured of wealth and health, long to live, I should have to walk about cutting other people's throats so as to reintroduce the element of excitement."

In comparisons with the great diarists of literature, such as Henri-Frédéric Amiel or Franz Kafka, Barbellion has not received the same attention or esteem. The quality of his thought and expression are often considered unequal to his expansive ambition, and he has been faulted for sustaining what some consider an exaggerated self-importance. In addition, his occasional pessimism regarding the value of human life, despite his more frequent celebrations of the joy of living, has been singled out for disapproval. Nonetheless, Barbellion has been widely admired for his heroic confrontation with disease and death and for the candid revelation of his experience in his journal. As Richmond H. Hellyar asserts in his study of Barbellion: "He embodies all that is finest and most valuable in human nature, displays pre-eminently the quality that has evolved man from subman—that everlasting, brave, persistent battle with the irrational play of Nature which has given us so supreme a power of self-assertion and adaptability in the face of difficulty."

PRINCIPAL WORKS

The Journal of a Disappointed Man (journal) 1919
Enjoying Life (essays, short stories, and journal) 1919
A Last Diary (journal) 1920

H. G. WELLS (essay date 1919)

[*Wells is best known today, along with Jules Verne, as the father of modern science fiction and as a utopian idealist who correctly foretold an era of chemical warfare, atomic weaponry, and world wars. Throughout much of his career, Wells wrote and lectured on the betterment of society through education and the advance of scientific innovation. A Fabian socialist and student of zoologist T. H. Huxley, Wells was, until his last bitter years, a believer in the gradual, inevitable moral and intellectual ascent of humanity. The following excerpt is from Wells's introduction to the original edition of* The Journal of a Disappointed Man.]

In this diary of an intensely egotistical young naturalist, tragically caught by the creeping approach of death, we have one of the most moving records of the youthful aspects of our universal struggle. We begin with one of those bright schoolboys that most of us like to fancy we once were, that many of us have come to love as sons or nephews or younger brothers, and this youngster is attracted by natural science, by the employments of the naturalist and by the thought of being himself some day a naturalist. From the very beginning we find in this diary the three qualities, from the narrowest to broadest. "Observe me," he says to himself, "I am observing nature." There is the self-conscious, self-centred boy. But he also says "I am observing nature!" And at moments comes the clear light. He forgets himself in the twilight cave with the bats or watching the starlings in the evening sky, he becomes just you and I and the mind of mankind gathering knowledge. And the diary, as the keen edge of untimely fate cuts down into the sensitive tissue, shows us presently, after outcries and sorrow and darkness of spirit, the habits of the observer rising to the occasion. Not for him, he realises, are the long life, the honours of science, the Croonian lecture, the listening Royal Society, one's memory embalmed in specific or generic names, the sure place in the temple of fame, that once filled his boyish dreams. But here is something close at hand to go on observing manfully to the end, in which self may be forgotten, and that is his own tormented self, with desire still great and power and hope receding. "I will go on with this diary," I read between the lines. "You shall have at least one specimen, carefully displayed and labelled. Here is a recorded unhappiness. When you talk about life and the rewards of life and the justice of life and its penalties, what you say must square with this." (p. viii)

> *H. G. Wells, in an introduction to* The Journal of a Disappointed Man *by W. N. P. Barbellion, Chatto & Windus, 1919, pp. vii-x.*

JOHN MIDDLETON MURRY (essay date 1919)

[*Murry is recognized as one of the most significant English critics and editors of the twentieth century. Anticipating later scholarly opinion, he championed the writings of Marcel Proust, James Joyce, Paul Valéry, D. H. Lawrence, and the poetry of Thomas Hardy through his positions as the editor of the* Athenaeum *and as a longtime contributor to the* Times Literary Supplement *and other periodicals. As with his magazine essays, Murry's book-length critical works are noted for their unusually impassioned tone and startling discoveries; such biographically centered critical studies as* Keats and Shakespeare: A Study of Keats' Poetic Life from 1816-1820 *(1925) and* Son of Woman: The Story of D. H. Lawrence *(1931) contain esoteric, controversial conclusions that have angered scholars who favor more traditional approaches. Nevertheless, Murry is cited for his perspicuity, clarity, and supportive argumentation. His early exposition on literary appreciation,* The Problem of Style *(1922), is widely revered as an informed guidebook for both critics and readers to employ when considering not only the style of a literary work, but its theme and viewpoint as well. In it Murry espouses a theoretical premise which underlies all his criticism: that in order to fully evaluate a writer's achievement the critic must search for crucial passages which effectively "crystallize" the writer's innermost impressions and convictions regarding life. In the following excerpt, Murry finds that Barbellion's confrontation with a severe physical and emotional ordeal, along with his dark view of human life, made him representative of the generation that came of age during the First World War.]*

By no determination can we make ourselves immune from illusion that different destinies are in store for ourselves. A tragedy remains a tragedy; we *cannot* see it as a commonplace. Something in us insists that it is grotesque, abnormal, all but impossible, a tyrannous irruption into human life; we cannot believe it is, what it is, part of life's very substance. The effort to desire life as it is leaves us exhausted, and we sink back on the lotus couch of the belief that life is as we desire it.

There we whisper to ourselves that the war was a nightmare, and persuade ourselves by the incantation of a word that it has faded like a nightmare. There we say that the life and death of W. N. P. Barbellion was a monstrosity, an aberration of our kindly Mother, who peradventure was sleeping while the body of one of her gifted children was being devoured by worms. Or, waking a little from our dream, we will say that he did indeed suffer undeservedly, but that his pains will be requited, like those of Keats, with the reward of immortality. The truth is that we will say anything on earth to preserve our faith in an immanent justice. Indeed, we have to say something. "One can hardly *live* in rebellion," said Ivan Karamozov most truly. Our business is somehow to live, and we have to suit our creed to our need.

Nevertheless it is salutary to try to square one's creed with the facts. Even though the attempt should fail for ever, we must make the attempt again and again. The secret voice says, Live! The mind says, Better to die. It is the secret voice that we obey. And since we obey, since we know in our depths that it is right that we should obey, somewhere, somehow, the mind must be wrong. We cannot see where or how. We stumble on blindly in the mist. (pp. 151-52)

What can we do? Believe? We will believe only what we know. It is not knowledge and faith that we long to reconcile. For faith we have no use, nor ever shall have. The reconciliation for which we long is the reconciliation of knowledge and instinct. Faith we do not, and never have possessed. But instinct we do. We cleave to life, we struggle on; blind Nature claims us for her children, and we acknowledge her claim. We are hers. Oh that her mind, her thoughts, were ours, and we at rest!

What can we do, but brood over the facts as we know them, and be thankful that they are sometimes revealed? Barbellion is a fact. He was also a man of scientific genius, and he showed his genius most clearly in this, that, knowing himself condemned to die, he set before himself the one scientific task he could achieve in the time allowed him. He presented the world with the fact of himself. (pp. 153-54)

It will be said, with some appearance of truth, that it was not a typical fact, that his was an isolated case. His case was isolated, indeed, but it was isolated in the experimental sense of the word rather than in the sentimental. His case was more closely observed and more faithfully recorded than others; but, with all its tragic particulars, it was one among many. In the last few years hundreds of thousands of men of Barbellion's age have had unwillingly to face the certainty of premature death; and many of these possessed as much genius as he. He was the child of his age, the representative of his generation.

His frustration was typical, his passionate desire to reveal the truth of himself not rare; his incapacity for life and his resentment against it were, characteristically, not balanced by any ecstatic assertion of the ideal. There have been no Shelleys among his contemporaries. It was not a quixotic orientation which made shipwreck of their lives; they had no orientation at all.

They were the desolate victims of a miasma, in whose mist their ineffectual lights flickered for a moment and went out. They were caught within the meshes of the greatest net that has, within human memory, been dragged through the shoal of mankind. They knew more than their forerunners, but they were less adequate to their knowledge; they had more cause for rebellion, but they were less rebellious; foreknowledge of failure haunted them. Truly Barbellion was not alone. One has but to look round upon the literary achievements of his contemporaries to see how thin and feeble has been the jet of their creative energy. What novel, for instance, of the generation which succeeded Mr. Wells, Mr. Conrad and Mr. Bennett can be compared for scope and veracity with this journal of Barbellion, or with Keeling's letters? Because we have no standards and are disinherited by the tradition, we can be gulled by sedulous impresarios into believing that ours is an epoch of creative activity. It is an epoch of impotence. We have now sham tradition and sham rebellion, sham society and sham social satire; if good or great work is being done, it is being done in secret, as Barbellion's *Journal* was written.

That is not, indeed, great work, like the *Journal* of Amiel; but it is good work. It puts us in possession of a fact, with which we have to square our creeds and our opinions of ourselves. Barbellion is a manifestation of the way of the universe with us and of our way with the universe. One of these two is a constant. The necessary adjustment must be made with the other. If we wish to build, we must build not on ourselves alone—that would be, at the best, to repeat Barbellion—but on our constant relation to the constant. If we could make that relation firm, we should at least have a landmark in the mist, from which we might safely set forth on that ordering of experience which is creation; and, before we had gone far in the quest, it is possible that we might find ourselves within hailing distance of the tradition we have lost. (pp. 160-62)

John Middleton Murry, "A Disappointed Man," in his The Evolution of an Intellectual, *1920. Reprint by Jonathan Cape, 1927, pp. 151-62.*

THE SATURDAY REVIEW, LONDON   (essay date 1919)

[In the following essay, the critic expresses a strongly unsympathetic judgment of The Journal of a Disappointed Man *and its author.]*

Whether Barbellion is a real man, or a fake (of which there have been so many of late years), we don't know; nor does it matter, except to excite our curiosity as to why Mr. Wells should have invented such a youth, if imaginary he be. [*The Journal of a Disappointed Man*] is in truth the dreariest book it has ever been our misfortune to handle, and in parts it is disgusting. The young man, the son of a provincial reporter, is a clever entomologist and gets a small post at the Natural History Museum. He is cursed with almost every ill that flesh is heir to, creeping paralysis, toothache, acute dyspepsia, with weak heart and lungs thrown in. He falls in love with a very nice girl, an artist, and the doctor lets him marry, and the girl is plainly told beforehand that he is a dying man, and they have a child, and he dies. So much for eugenics, as practised by one who prides himself on being a biologist. We ought to have added that neither husband nor wife has a shilling, and they see nothing wrong in putting disease and poverty together and bringing a child, a girl, into the world. The details of Barbellion's diseases and his remedies are sometimes dwelt on with an explicitness not often given to the reading public. The wretched man refuses to take the slightest interest in the war for the first two years, alluding to it briefly and contemptuously as "filthy lunacy," and towards the end he bleats in rather conventional fashion that his health keeps him at home. The thorough-paced egotist, whom Mr. Wells likens to "the solitary beasts," of course lives only for himself, and probably in most cases keeps a diary, in which he is his own audience. We do not say that there are no clever things in this diary: there are a good many; but not cleverer than we have heard from many young men, and much such as we should suppose every clever young person of the rising generation thinks and writes in diary or magazine or weekly journal. We cannot imagine why such a journal should be published, or why anybody should read it.

> *"A Dismal Diary," in* The Saturday Review, *London, Vol. 127, No. 3312, April 19, 1919, p. 381.*

THE NATION   (essay date 1919)

[*In the following excerpt, the critic praises the artistry and heroism displayed in Barbellion's journal.*]

The various London rumors concerning the authorship of *The Journal of a Disappointed Man* need trouble no reader of that remarkable document. All good fiction is, in the ultimate sense, autobiographical; all autobiography completes, by some creative process, the outlines that life leaves jagged and apparently meaningless. Hence it matters little whether we have here the actual journals of a young British naturalist who was born in 1889 and died in 1917, or whether we have a distinguished novelist's projection of certain phases of his spiritual past. The present reviewer inclines to the first supposition; the significance of the volume remains the same in either case.

That significance is very great, although it is far from obvious. The sensitive reader will observe almost at once, of course, that Barbellion possessed a high degree of literary power, although its expression is usually a little cramped and hard and always fragmentary. But his spirit was not, in any easy or easily approachable way, an attractive one. He was very bitter, inordinately egoistic, and, when his early death became a certainty, merely determined to "toss these pages in the faces of timid, furtive, respectable people." He was a creature of divided aims, regretting that he was "neither pure-bred science nor pure-bred art"; he held the unpopular belief that "life is pain" and refused to let "any sophistry win him over to any other view"; he had an ugly and disconcerting habit of breaking a good many fundamental silences and thus, by a vicarious absence of shame, dragging into the light the hidden things in the hearts of others. The war came, but it changed him in no respect. He went on with his journals and his researches, drawing assurance from the fact that Goethe had studied the geography of China while the nations were embattled at Leipzig, and that Hegel worked at his *Phenomenology of the Spirit* while Napoleon crushed his country at Jena. Conscription alone aroused him. He was, of course, physically unfit for military service. But that was only an accident in his eyes. "To send me a notice," he exclaims, "requesting me to prepare myself for killing men! Why I should feel no more astonished to receive

a War Office injunction, under dire penalties, to perform miracles, to move mountains, to raise from the dead. . . . I should sit still and watch the whole universe pass to its destruction rather than raise a hand to knife a fellow." What struck him in his environment was the "wild race for security," for "safe jobs" and "staff appointments," and the ugly rivalries and bitter recriminations that arose in this scramble. "Bereavement brought bitterness and immunity indifference." To most people, caught in the snares of the great tribal illusions, Barbellion must appear mean-spirited and unheroic at best.

Unheroic? That is precisely what he is not. Poor and ill and lonely, it never occurred to him that he could gain comfort through compromise either by yielding to the psychical forces about him or by relaxing the vigilance of his own mind. He permitted no collective mood, no popular passion, no uncritical assent to some easy consolation, to temper the bleakness of the spiritual weather in which he lived. He longed to be able to direct all his "energies to the great and difficult profession of life, of being man!" He was born late enough to have escaped all the traditional values of our civilization, and there is in his book no section, such as occurs in most autobiographies, that tells of his emancipation from any fixed religious or political faith. He started with a clean slate and knew at once and with an unfaltering certainty that it was the business of man to re-examine the sum of reality in nature and society and in his own mind, and to go on a quest for new values. His own quest was futile enough, if measured by the attainment of any visible goal. The warmth of a personal happiness did not come to him until he was doomed. His poverty and his appalling ill-health forced him into a continual preoccupation with sordid and meaningless things. But he was always bent upon his true business and gave in only to death itself. His book should be a bitter but a tonic document for all comfortable and healthy persons who drift with the easy currents of the collective life. (pp. 341-42)

> *"The Quest," in* The Nation, *New York, Vol. CIX, No. 2827, September 6, 1919, pp. 341-42.*

THE ATHENAEUM   (essay date 1919)

[*In the following essay, the critic favorably discusses Barbellion's writings in the posthumous collection* Enjoying Life.]

The readers of the *Journal of a Disappointed Man* will find that his second book [, *Enjoying Life,*] adds but little to their knowledge of Barbellion. It is not the less interesting on that account; certain aspects of Barbellion's character receive additional emphasis in this volume, and, apart from such considerations, much of the matter is interesting for its own sake. The extra pages from the *Journal* seem to have been chosen with the intent to show us that, after all, Barbellion was not a pessimist. They certainly bear witness to moods of almost fierce delight in the sheer multiplicity, bigness and rush of things in general. The millions of men in London, the millions of stars in the heavens, the microscopic infinities concealed in worms and beetles, induced in Barbellion that not unfamiliar feeling of limitless adventure and God-like power. "The world is a ship, on an unknown and dangerous commission. But I for my part, as a silly shipboy, will stand on the ratlines and cheer." In such a mood he can accept anything; he can exult in anything. But, of course, it fades. From seeing himself as an atom in the Universe he swings round to seeing himslf as the centre of it. Then the vastness frightens him; when he hears such formulas as "intrastellar space" or "secular time," he wants "to crawl away like a rat into a hole and die." As with all intelligent young men, the huge universe of science at once fascinates and terrifies him. How much his scientific training had become a part of him we see in this second volume. He was genuinely modern. Egotist as he was, his science enabled him to live in a wide world. His desire for knowledge was both courageous and passionate; he was scientific, and we think it is this fact which lends him his attraction. Without the courage and instant readiness to relate himself to wider things Barbellion could quite easily have been insupportable.

The essays are interesting enough, although they show less power and originality than the *Journal*. It is obvious that Barbellion was still at the stage when he badly wanted to write; these essays were written for the pleasure it gave their author to exercise his undoubted literary gift. An occasional remark, for its quaintness or its insight, will remind the reader that they are the literary exercises of an unusually able man. **"An Autumn Stroll,"** the earliest of these pieces, has some amazing writing for a boy of sixteen. His remarks on Amiel are good criticism, and, faced with these evidences of literary power, we wonder whether Barbellion would ever have been content with a purely scientific career. It is certain that the writing of scientific memoirs could afford no sufficient outlet for his desire to write. The popular scientific articles included in this volume show that this kind of writing could never have satisfied him. They are very good of their kind, but they lack the movement, the glancing lights, typical of Barbellion's genuine literary work. At the same time they show that his interest in science was passionate and likely to endure. It is impossible to say what compromise he would have effected; we do not think he would have been able to abandon either activity. Of the two short stories in the volume we can only say that their evidence is negative. They do not show that Barbellion was a story-writer, but they are not inconsistent with that supposition.

"A Young Modern," in The Athenaeum, *No. 4677, December 19, 1919, p. 1366.*

W. N. P. BARBELLION (essay date 1920)

[*In the following excerpt from* A Last Diary, *Barbellion comments on his journal and on the critical reception of* The Journal of a Disappointed Man.]

My diary is too unpleasant for popularity. It is my passion for taking folk by the nose and giving them a wigging, my fierce contempt for every kind of complacency. (p. 93)

February 13th, 1919.—I had a letter from H. G. Wells this morning. He says: "You will have seen my Preface by this time." (I haven't.) "Prefaces always devastate relationships. But I hope you didn't think it too horrible. I had to play up to your standard of frankness." I knew he would be rude. But I'm afire to see what he says. (pp. 96-7)

February 16th, 1919.—The publishers this morning sent me a proof of Mr. Wells' Introduction. It is excellent, and not rude at all. (p. 97)

Mr. Wells is sympathetic and almost too generous. Characteristically he concentrates on me as a biologist, whereas I like to look at myself posthumously as a writer.

He is a good fellow, and I am most grateful and most pleased. (p. 101)

February 28th, 1919.—I thirst, I thirst for a little music—to replenish my jaded spirit. It is difficult to keep one's soul alive in such an atmosphere.

ANALYSIS OF THE *JOURNAL OF A DISAPPOINTED MAN*

March 10th, 1919.

1. Ambition.
2. Reflections on Death.
3. Intellectual Curiosity.
4. Self Consciousness.
5. Self Introspection.
6. Zest of Living.

I wonder if any reviewer will bring out these points:

7. Humour.
8. Shamelessness.

My confessions are shameless. I confess, but do not repent. The fact is, my confessions are prompted, not by ethical motives, but intellectual. The confessions are to me the interesting records of a self-investigator.

If I live to read the review notices, I shall probably criticise them. I shall be criticising the criticisms of my life, putting the reviewers right, a long lean hand stretching out at them from the tomb. I shall play the part of boomerang, and "cop" them one unexpectedly. There will be a newspaper discussion: Is Barbellion dead? And I shall answer by a letter to the Editor:

Dear Sir,

Yes, I am dead. I killed myself off at the end of my book, because it was high time. Your reviewer is incorrect in saying I died of creeping paralysis. It was of another kindred but different disease.

P.S.—It may interest your readers to know that I am not yet buried.

Or,

Dear Sir,

There is an inaccuracy in your reviewer's statement. I was not in the Secret Service. It should have been the Civil Service, of which I was a member up to within eighteen months of my decease.

Or,

Dear Sir,

I should be glad if you would correct the impression generated by one of your correspondents that *Barbellion* is the name of an evil spirit appearing on Walpurgis night. As a matter of fact, my forbears were simple folk—tallow chandlers in B—. (pp. 114-16)

March 15th, 1919.—The first peep of the chick: among the publishers' announcements in *The Times*: "**The Journal of a Disappointed Man,** a genuine confession of thwarted ambition and disillusionment."

Am reading another of James Joyce's—*Ulysses*—running serially in that exotic periodical, *The Little Review*, which announces on its cover that it makes "no compromise with the public taste." *Ulysses* is an interesting development. Damn! it's all my idea, the technique I projected. According to the reviews, Dorothy Richardson's *Tunnel* is a novel in the same manner—intensive, netting in words the continuous flow of consciousness and semi-consciousness. Of course the novelists are behind the naturalists in the recording of minutiæ: Edmund Selous and Julian Huxley and others have set down the life of some species of bird in exhaustive detail—every flip of the tail, every peck preceding the grand drama of courtship and mating. But this queer comparison lies between these naturalists and novelists like William de Morgan rather than Joyce. (pp. 117-18)

March 30th, 1919.—Now that I have spurred my hippogriff to the journey's end, now that I have wreaked my will on that very obtuse gentleman, my Lord Destiny, who failed to take due measure of his man, now as soon as I have freed myself from the hard cocoon of my environment, and can sweeten and soothe my warped frame with a little of the delicious honey of kindly recognition, I can rest in the sun a while, soak up the warmth and sweetness into this tortured spirit and crave everyone's pardon before the end comes. For I know that the *Journal* will mean horror to some. I realise that a strong-minded man would by instinct keep his sufferings to himself—the Englishman above all—(but I doubt if I am an Englishman really. My true home I guess is further east). I have been recklessly self-willed and inconsiderate, and I have no sort of excuse except the most unprecedented provocation. I have been in the grip of more than one strong passion, and my moral strength has been insufficient to struggle with them and throw them off. I have been overcome, and the publication of my *Journal* is really the signal of my defeat.

Ah, but it takes a terrific lot of energy to set about putting one's moral house in order! It is too late, and I am too weakened. You must take me as I am and remember that with a longer life, just as I might have done better things intellectually, so also morally. Give me your love if you can. I love you all, and because I love you comfort my self-despondency with the thought that there *must* be some grain of goodness in me overlaid. (pp. 122-24)

April 29th, 1919.—Having cast my bread upon the waters, it amuses me to find it returning with the calculable exactitude of a tidal movement—*e.g.,* in my *Journal* I stroked *Public Opinion* and it now purrs to the tune of two and a half pages of review: the *Saturday Review* I cursed with bell, book, and candle and—*voilà!* they mangle me in their turn [see excerpt dated 1919].

For the most part the reviewers say what I have told them to say in the book. One writes that it is a remarkable book. I told him it was. Another says I am a conceited prig. I have said as much more than once. A third hints at the writer's inherent madness. I queried the same possibility. It is amusing to see the flat contradictions. There is no sort of unanimity of opinion about any part of my complex character. One says a genius, another not a genius; witty—dull; vivacious—dismal; intolerably sad—happy; lewd—finicky; "quiet humour"—"wild and vivacious wit." As a whole, I am surprised and delighted with the extraordinary kindness and sympathy meted out to it, more than I deserve or it deserves, while one or two critics, with power that amazes, penetrate to the wretched Barbellion's core. To Mr. Massingham I feel I can only murmur, "Too kind, too kind," like the aged Florence Nightingale when they came to present her with the O.M. But what sympathetic understanding! Compare one man who said I was a social climber; another that I was "finicky" on sexual matters (Ha! ha! ha! pardon my homeric laughter); another—or was it the same?—that I *shrank* from life—yes, shrank! Give me more life, to parody Goethe: I have shouted thus for years. Poor old reviewers! Friends and relatives say I have not drawn my real

self. But that's because I've taken my clothes off and they can't recognise me stark! The book is a self-portrait in the nude. (pp. 138-40)

May 18th, 1919.—In the *Journal* I can see now that I made myself out worse than I am, or was. I even took a morbid pleasure in intimating my depravity—self-mortification. If I had spoken out more plainly I should have escaped all this censure. The reviewers are only too ready to take me at my word, which is but natural. I don't think on the whole my portrait of myself does myself justice. (pp. 142-43)

> *W. N. P. Barbellion, in his* A Last Diary, *George H. Doran Company, 1920, 148 p.*

THE WEEKLY REVIEW (essay date 1920)

[*In the following excerpt, the critic disparages Barbellion's writings collected in the volume* Enjoying Life.]

Enjoying Life is about the most inappropriate title that the friends of the late W. N. P. Barbellion could have found for his literary remains.... The young zoölogist indulged a titanism that made for despair; his expression of the will to possess the world is generally hectic and occasionally vulgar. After bathing he loves his "cool pink skin." Meant to be Whitmanish, the emotion recalls rather Mary McLane. He would fain shatter himself upon adored mountains, drink up the beloved sea, be consumed by the sun. He cries, "I regret I was not alive in the days of ancient Rome. To have been nonexistent and unconsidered in such great affairs stings me sharply." Here is one of those flashes, quite Sir Thomas Brownish, which enliven the journal too seldom. The diarist in the next sentence proceeds to spoil matters, "I seem to be a sort of serious village idiot whose desire to help is viewed with smiles or friendly tolerance, or else is simply ignored—an energetic fly on a great wheel, puling out remonstrances because he isn't the engineer. I am piqued because I was not a witness of the gambolings of Dinosaurs and Pterodactyls." Naturally the aim of embracing all times, places, and persons ends in the conclusion, "To live is a continuous humiliation." Partly because we can not even realize our own emotions. "Should any experience, any emotion, whether grief or joy, of powerful voltage really establish a contact, death would be instantaneous from electrocution." While living in hope of electrocution we may at least fool ourselves into contentment. "It is impossible to circumvent the human soul—that precious quiddity that triumphs over all things, suffereth all things, is not easily provoked. But the psychological truth is that the so-called conquests of the soul are usually only strategic retreats dictated by the instinct for preservation of self." Our extracts may reveal at once the type of reflection and as well the odd blend of eloquence and sheer fustian in the style. To many readers it is ingratiating. For ourselves, a kind of cheapness and gush in Barbellion's titanism makes us wonder that his friends, after exploiting the vein most liberally in *The Journal of a Disappointed Man,* should feel constrained to make a second demonstration. Only the present indiscriminating appetite for human documents, however insignificant, can explain the matter.

> *"The Run of the Shelves," in* The Weekly Review, *Vol. 3, No. 79, November 17, 1920, p. 478.*

THE ATHENAEUM (essay date 1920)

[*In the following review of* A Last Diary, *the critic emphasizes Barbellion's abilities as a scientific writer.*]

[*A Last Diary*], unlike the two volumes which preceded it, is obviously the work of a diseased man. It is written in spurts, with a whipped-up energy; the entries are written by a man who comes alive for the occasion. There are but few places where we feel that Barbellion's mind is working freely, where the thoughts suggest a living and continuous context; more often it seems as if, his time terribly short, his little reserve of energy terribly low, Barbellion clutched at his idea. There is, therefore, some distortion. The Barbellion of the early diaries is still here, but we have to adjust the emphasis to see him properly. It is interesting to note that the one thing in him that remains perfectly steady and unforced is his genuine scientific quality. Barbellion was a student of natural history, a branch of science which seems, more than any other, to awaken a muddled emotionalism in its devotees. It seems to be a science which peculiarly attracts a host of camp-followers from amongst what William James might have called the "soft"-minded people. Barbellion, even when hysterical, has not a trace of this. As a scientific man he is clean right through. Barbellion was other things, but he was scientific: that was his birthright.

His literary quality we find more ambiguous. Certainly he could write; he could write very well, but when he says, of Wells' introduction to his book "Characteristically he concentrates on me as a biologist, whereas I like to look at myself posthumously as a writer," we are inclined to think that Mr. Wells had chosen the better part. We think it is not only a rarer, but a more valuable thing to have Barbellion's instinctive, scientific sense of veracity and proportion, than it is to have his literary ability. A sense for facts and the right kind of emotional hardness is a better thing than a sense for words and an agile fancy. A bigger man can be constructed from the first ingredients. Barbellion's writing, to our mind, is always at its best when he is being most scientific.

At these moments we feel that a true instinct takes control; we are then making contact with a mind which is mature, balanced, central. In the rest of his writing we sometimes feel free to attach as little importance as we please to what Barbellion says. We sometimes feel that he is saying something we know and have learned to neglect. This has no bearing, of course, on the value of the diaries as a revelation of a person; it merely has a bearing on the value of the person revealed. Regarded as a literary man, we find Barbellion less just, less precise, less really competent than, for instance, young Sorley, who died even younger than Barbellion. We insist that it is as the revelation of a young *scientific* man that the diaries are chiefly valuable, and that if Barbellion had turned to a predominantly literary career—as he very probably would have done—it is precisely his scientific quality which would have given his contribution its chief value.

In the present volume, written with an eye to publication, there are reminiscences, rather deliberately worked up, jottings on his day-to-day condition, a few notes on literary matters, and some disconnected comments on things in general. We find a true pathos in the whole effort, particularly in the little explosions of egotism, with their unconvincing bravado. It is easy to feel affection for the Barbellion who wrote these pages—as far from serenity as we are ourselves, and persuading himself that he is now reconciled to death, that the world is a painted show to him. And how eagerly he would have read this, or any other, criticism of his book!

J. W. N. S., *"Barbellion's Last Diary,"* in The Athenaeum, *No. 4727, December 3, 1920, p. 757.*

ARTHUR J. CUMMINGS (essay date 1920)

[*Cummings was Barbellion's elder brother. In the following excerpt from his essay "The Life and Character of Barbellion," Cummings comments on Barbellion's egoism and expresses admiration for the candor displayed in* The Journal of a Disappointed Man.]

It is not for me to try to do more than correct a few crude or glaringly false impressions of the kind of man Barbellion was. Others must judge of the quality of his genius and of his place in life and literature. But I can speak of Barbellion as the man I knew him to be. He was not the egotist, pure and simple, naked and complete, that he sometimes accused himself of being and is supposed by numerous critics and readers of the *Journal* to have been.

His portrait of himself was neither consummate nor, as Mr. Shanks well says, "immutable." "In the nude," declared Barbellion, more than once, with an air of blunt finality. Yes, but only as he imagined himself to look in the nude.

He was forever peering at himself from changing angles, and he was never quite sure that the point of view of the moment was the true one. Incontinently curious about himself, he was never certain about the real Barbellion. One day he was "so much specialised protoplasm"; another day he was Alexander with the world at his feet; and then he was a lonely boy pining for a few intimate friends. (pp. xxxv-xxxvi)

Mr. Wells has referred to him as "an egotistical young naturalist"; in the same allusion, however, he reiterated the fundamental truth that "we are all egotists within the limits of our power of expression" [see excerpt dated 1919]. Barbellion was intensely interested in himself, but he was also intensely interested in other people. He had not that egotistical imagination of the purely self-centred man which looks inward all the time because nothing outside the province of his own self-consciousness concerns him. He had an *objective* interest in himself, an outcome of the peculiar faculty which he divulged in the first of the two letters already quoted of looking at human beings, even his own mother, objectively. He described and explained himself so persistently and so thoroughly because he had an obviously better opportunity of studying himself with nice precision and attentive care than he had for the study of other people. He regarded himself quite openly and quite naturally as a human specimen to be examined, classified, and dissected, and he did his work with the detailed skill and the truthful approach of a scientific investigator. The "limits of his power of expression" being far beyond those of the average man, he was able to give a picture of himself that lives on account of its simple and daring candour. He is not afraid to be frank in giving expression to a thought merely because it may be an unpleasant or a selfish thought. If a shadowy doubt assails him, or an *outré* criticism presents itself about a beloved friend, he sets it down; if he feels a sensuous joy in bathing in the sea and loves to look upon his "pink skin," or derives a catlike satisfaction from rolling a cigarette between his fingers; if he thinks he sees a meanness in his own heart, or catches himself out in some questionable or unworthy piece of conduct, however trivial, the diary receives its faithful record. The dissimilarity between Barbellion and other persons is that, while those of us who have not been blessed or cursed with the temperament of an ox frequently experience these queer spontaneous promptings about common things and about ourselves and our fellow-creatures that come we know not how or why, so far from dragging the half-formed thought into the light of open confession and giving it definite shape, we avert our gaze as from an evil thing, or return to it in secret and stealth. It is scarcely possible, one imagines, to read Barbellion honestly without realising that he says in plain, forceful language what the rest of us often think but have not the nerve to say aloud either to others or to ourselves. (pp. xxxix-xli)

Nearly every writer who has tried to form an estimate of my brother's potentialities has discussed the question whether he would have deserted the science of zoology, his first consuming love, for the broader paths of literature. Now that he is dead it must appear to be a fruitless speculation. But it is not perhaps without interest. . . . He was that comparatively rare combination—a man of science, and a man of letters. He was in love with life as soon as he was in love with science, and the life of man inspired his imagination more than the lives of the animals it was his business to know about. His scientific zeal was aroused in "an extraordinary new form of bird parasite brought back by the New Guinea Expedition," as much because it was a new form of life as because it appealed to the enthusiasm of the trained zoologist. Years before he was filled with sickening disappointment by the drudgery of his labours and the narrow limitations imposed upon him in a department of Natural History that he cared for least, he was contemplating large literary schemes, some of which he unfolded to me with an infectious ardour of hope and determination. He planned in these years a novel that was to be of immense length, with something of the scope of the *Comédie Humaine,* and a series of logically developed treatises on the lines of his essay, **"The Passion for Perpetuation,"** which in his own words were to be his *magnum opus.* His hopes, high and unquenchable as they always appeared to be, were cut short by his lingering illness and his early death. There remain only a few documentary fragments that testify to the boldness of his intentions. His one published attempt at a short story, **"How Tom Snored,"** is in my opinion quite unworthy of his abilities. It is impossible to say in what direction his undoubted literary powers would have found their true outlet. It is certain that if he had lived in the full enjoyment of normal health the *Journal* in its present outward form or as a narrative of his career and an unreserved record of his personal reflections would never have been published. It is equally certain that . . . the bias of his mind was turning rapidly from the cause of biological science towards the humanities. His restless spirit demanded a wider range of expression, unhampered by the many exasperating futilities of his professional labours. But his published work is perhaps all the more valuable on account of his exertions in the laboratory, because even when he "meddles" in his fantastic and compelling way "with things that are too high for me, not as a recreation but as a result of intense intellectual discomfort"— even at these moments, when he plunges with impetuous gusto into the infinities of time and space and God, there is a certain sanity of statement, a suggestion of strength in reserve, a studied self-control in the handling of his theme that his scientific habit of mind makes possible and emphasises. This instinctive restraint can be discovered again and again in vehement passages that at a glance seem to bear the mark of reckless extravagance.

A Last Diary is the last of Barbellion as a writer. For those of us who knew and loved him as a boy and as a man the memory of his masterful personality—his courage, his wit, his magnetism, his pride of intellect and his modesty withal, his afflictions, his affectionate tenderness—will endure without ceasing. As the most modern of the journal-writers he addresses to the public a dauntless message, the value and significance of which time alone can measure. Like all men of abnormal

sensibility he suffered deeply; but if he suffered deeply he enjoyed also his moments of exquisite happiness. He lived fast. He was for ever bounding forward in an untameable effort to grasp the unknown and unknowable. Fate struck him blow upon blow, but though his head was often bloody it remained unbowed. Mr. Wells says the story of his life is a "recorded unhappiness." I prefer to think of it as a sovereign challenge. (pp. xliv-xlviii)

Arthur J. Cummings, "The Life and Character of Barbellion," in A Last Diary *by W. N. P. Barbellion,* George H. Doran Company, *1920, pp. v-xlviii.*

THE NEW REPUBLIC   (essay date 1921)

[*In the following excerpt, the critic compares* A Last Diary *to* The Journal of a Disappointed Man *and discusses Barbellion's character and accomplishments as a writer.*]

This **Last Diary,** which "Barbellion" planned should be published posthumously "under the sensational and catch-penny title" of the *Diary of a Dying Man,* differs in several respects from the earlier **Journal.** It was written evidently with definite thoughts of publication. The self-revelation is not obscured on that account; rather it becomes if possible more apparent. But there is a loss in artlessness; there is more concern for "effect." The rough edges are smoothed away; there is greater finish, a finer ease and limpidity. Not that any element of insincerity has crept in. The change is greater than that of literary form, and of that change the writer was himself conscious. In a touching entry he renounces the intellectual interests that had always held him and turns towards matters of ethical and spiritual concern. Especially after he has had the last satisfaction of reading his own book, of analyzing its qualities, and of commenting upon the comments of reviewers, does his thought take on an almost indescribable color of spiritual exaltation in the very face of death. If he thanks the gods for his unconquerable soul, it is with no blatancy; rather with a sweet serenity. The rare flashes of the old intellectual arrogance serve to make this spirit of calm acceptance the more marked. As death approaches his mind turns back to experiences of his youth and upon these he draws for some of the loveliest pages in this **Diary:** the ousel singing by the river at nightfall; the rabbits' golgotha; the bats in the deserted mine. The mysterious disease had now dragged on too far to permit of any further quests for out-of-the-way lore among the haunts of the feathered and furry creatures he loved. He records several scenes with his old nurse, an ignorant self-opinionated but kindly woman, which would move one to laughter but for the pathos behind "Barbellion's" quiet smile. He is constantly anxious lest he should die before he could see his book. There are depths of feeling happily unknown to most of us in his transcript of the lines—

O lente, lente, currite noctis equi!
The stars move still, time runs, the clock will strike,
The devil will come up, and Faustus must be damned.

One calls to mind other hapless souls in whom the instinct for expression struggled against physical infirmities: Leopardi; Phillip Marston; and especially the author of the *Sonnets of the Wingless Hours.* "Barbellion's" was a nature of sterner stuff than theirs. "No coward soul is mine," he cries with the gifted woman he admired and stood in awe of. In the presence of such a spirit one may suggest literary "parallels" but not trace them out.

The question of whether the literary or scientific talent was uppermost in "Barbellion's" temperament has occupied the critics. Mr. Wells thinks that he was primarily a scientist. "Barbellion" himself records his preference to be remembered as a man of letters. It may be suggested that the literary gift rose, after illness was upon him, out of that natural instinct for accurate and lucid exposition which is the endowment of many scientists. Had his health been normal he might have remained a biologist, one of the vast army of workers in the field of the natural sciences, perhaps forever unknown to "the public." As it was he learned in suffering what he taught in these self-revelations. He is more likely to be remembered than had he lived a normal life. Cold compensation for the wingless hours and wasted hopes! (pp. 268-69)

S. C. C., "Barbellion," in The New Republic, *Vol. XXVI, No. 334, April 27, 1921, pp. 268-69.*

JOSEPH WOOD KRUTCH (essay date 1921)

[*Krutch is widely regarded as one of America's most respected literary and drama critics. A conservative and idealistic thinker, he was a consistent proponent of human dignity and the preeminence of literary art. His literary criticism is characterized by such concerns: in* The Modern Temper *(1929) he argued that because scientific thought has denied human worth, tragedy had become obsolete, and in* The Measure of Man *(1954) he attacked modern culture for depriving humanity of the sense of individual responsibility necessary for making important decisions in an increasingly complex age. In the following excerpt, Krutch focuses on Barbellion's desire for knowledge and experience, his enforced detachment from life due to his progressive illness, and the value of his writings.*]

[Barbellion] was, it seems, a disappointed man and a failure. It is true that he wrote three fascinating books, and it is also true that if he was not a great scientist or a great writer, he was, nevertheless, a mind. All knowledge he took for his province, and if he conquered no larger part of it than those who desire world empire usually subjugate, he at least had a vivid sense of its extent. He loved nature with the ardor of a poet and studied her with the minuteness of a scientist. Fascinated by all books, from the poems of Villon to the *Encyclopaedia Britannica,* he loved life no less than he loved the printed page, and those gifts of mind and soul which had in no small measure been given him, he cultivated to the highest point which circumstances permitted. But he was not, as the world would say, "a success" and, as any reader of those helpful little books on self-development can tell us, not to be "a success" is manifestly to be a failure.

But surely his was not a failure either of aspiration or of appetite. His most obvious characteristic is a hunger for life. He realized that the world was indeed full of a number of things, and he desired them all. Science, literature, music, and all manner of adventures, physical and spiritual, beckoned to him, and his only despair arose from the realization that he could not have them all.

Robert Burton looked one day from the window of his library and sighed with momentary regret that he was not of the busy world, but in a moment he turned back to his books. Barbellion could achieve no such resignation, for to him at least two lives, one for study and one for action, seemed necessary. One imagines him as never thinking without feeling that he should be doing, and never doing without feeling that he should be thinking. To him a thousand lives were all too few, for he would have more loves than Semiramis and more knowledge than an

encyclopaedia. He echoes Amiel's disgust at the hopeless imprisonment of his soul in one body, and, like the fabled ass standing between two haystacks, he is in danger of starvation from an inability to choose amidst plenty.

One never gets time in his essays to grasp anything—a fleeting glimpse and it is gone. To read him is to rush past the world on an express train. A house set quietly upon a hill attracts our attention, but before we can realize it, it flashes by and gives place, perhaps, to a flooding river. Barbellion is drunk with life, for to him existence is not a vale of tears, not a school for discipline, and not a place where each has his duty to perform. Rather it is a debauch.

Even if one did not know, one would suspect that this was an appetite born of ill health, for there is something hectic in such eagerness. Barbellion's favorite allusions are to Amiel and Marie Bashkirtseff, and their expansiveness was, like his, partly the result of a bodily weakness which made them value life more because they felt themselves less able to grasp it. Just as *carpe diem* is proclaimed only by men who find themselves incapable of forgetting the morrow, so no man who felt existence completely happy would write an essay on *Enjoying Life.* His annals would be brief to the point of non-existence.

To himself, then, Barbellion was a failure because of his ill health. But one wonders how much literature owes to sickness. In spite of those who talk of the sanity of art, it is often, at its most delicate, a sign of ill health. Chaucer, Shakespeare, Fielding—they are robust and normal, but the quivering sensitiveness of Keats or Shelley is the result (in plain prose) of an unhealthful sensitiveness. Bodily infirmity drives even the active to study. Brântome fell from his horse; Montaigne was driven into studious seclusion as the result of high living; the roll of consumptives is long. In the case of Stevenson and Keats, fragility was the very essence of their genius. They were skinned all over. The self-protective callousness which, for our own comfort, we are compelled to grow over our souls as well as our bodies, has been in the case of them and of Barbellion stripped off, and they writhe under their emotions.

The psychologist, following the analogy of biology, tells us that intelligence is adaptation, and that that man is most intelligent who is most fit to adapt himself to life. By this standard the delicate artist is unintelligent. He is too delicate an instrument to stand the shock of the world. He is as unfit for the rough road as a horse with his hooves pared to the quick. His capacities for feeling, which should be sturdy horns to poke about in the stuff of experience, are like the delicate tentacles of a snail, which draw back shuddering at the slightest contact and feel the faintest touch like a blow. From the standpoint of evolution such natures are not fitted to survive. We have come to admire this supersensitiveness, but it has no place in nature, and she crushes it. "Culture" pronounces such souls noble, but culture is at war with nature.

Perhaps the more enlightened of our disciples of efficiency would admit (at this late date at least) that Keats achieved some success, but Barbellion failed for yet another reason. He refused to be a specialist. He stuck his greedy hand into the jar of nuts and could not draw it out because he had grasped too many. To have been merely a mathematician, or a writer, or a scientist would probably not have satisfied him. He desired rather to be a man—and that, as he conceived it, with all its implications of knowledge and development, is more than one can hope to be. He refused to confine himself so exclusively to one thing that most of his faculties would wither away. But achievement is theirs who will fix their eyes so intently upon their narrow way that they never look abroad. They chisel, often, so intently upon their own little block that they leave a monument without ever having lived. To be "useful" and "successful" one often finds it necessary to be content to be a cog, but Barbellion determined to contemplate, at least, the whole machine.

I would not be carried away by my theme and say too much for this young man. It is true that his was little more than aspiration, and that to the last he was pitifully young. Had he ended more happily there might be much material for comedy in the journal where his intense self-consciousness makes him always egoistic and sometimes pompous, and where he reveals the tendency of all bright youths to regard the universal experiences of adolescence as things peculiar to themselves. One might find excellent comedy in comedy in comparing the inside history of things as told in the *Journal* with the literary employment of the same experiences in the essays. The intimate and off-hand reference in the latter to Marie Bashkirtseff, for instance, as to one whom all his readers know and with whom he had been familiar from the cradle, contrasts very comically with the naive account in the *Journal* of the discovery of this, for him, completely unknown writer; and it is equally amusing to note that the young man who desired more loves than Semiramis was quite as ill at ease and quite as incompetent in managing such flirtations as fell to his lot as less ambitious young fellows are accustomed to be. But this is, after all, no more than the difference between the artist as known by his valet and the artist as he appears to his audience. The important fact is not that Burns celebrated a servant-girl, but that he saw in her the embodiment of the Eternal Woman, and if Barbellion's experiences were commonplace, his manner of looking at them was not. This is all that an artist can do.

It is, after all, not the man but the type for which I apologize. He is the eternal misfit who travels wide-eyed through a world for which his very excellences—his self-consciousness and his sensitiveness—render him unfit. It is well for most of us that we stop crying for the moon, but then, if one has ever really wanted the moon it is difficult to be content with anything else.

As to Barbellion, achievement was not his. He did not leave his mark. His writings will no doubt be forgotten, and he will have to be content to be as if he had not been. But his failure was not altogether a failure. As a citizen of this world he was not a success, but then he never pretended to be such a citizen. He was an acute and penetrating observer who could consider things most curiously. There are some who value being as well as doing, and to them he will seem something of a success; but, for the most part, detached observation must be content to be its own reward. The world passes such a soul by and continues to wear its path to the door of the man who can make a better mouse-trap than his neighbor. (pp. 478-80)

Joseph Wood Krutch, "Whom the Gods Love," in The Sewanee Review, Vol. XXIX, No. 4, October, 1921, pp. 477-82.

EDWARD SHANKS (essay date 1923)

[*An English poet, novelist, and critic, Shanks won honors for the poem* Queen of China *(1919), and reinforced his poetic reputation when* The Island of Youth *appeared in 1921. Editor of the* London Mercury *from 1919 to 1922, Shanks wrote notable critical essays on such authors as Bernard Shaw, Edgar Allan Poe, and Rudyard*

Kipling. *In the following excerpt, Shanks examines Barbellion's self-portrayal in his journal.*]

[Among references to his work which Barbellion makes in *A Last Diary*] there is none more illuminating than the last entry he ever made:—

> Friends and relatives say I have not drawn my true self. But that's because I have taken my clothes off and they can't recognise me stark! The Book is a self-portrait in the nude.
>
> (p. 24)

It is not difficult to understand the complaint made by his friends and relatives that he had drawn a misleading portrait of himself, any more than it is difficult to understand his own protest that he had drawn himself with the clothes off. Both points of view are exceedingly natural, and perhaps it is possible for a disinterested observer to see in the diary the whole truth which could not be immediately obvious either to himself or to those who were closely connected with him. We need not involve ourselves very deeply in the theories of psychoanalysis to make the point that a man who keeps a journal of this sort probably does so because there is something in him which ordinary life keeps under, which he desires to express and cannot, except thus in secret. Hence come apparent contradictions between the outward appearance and the confession. On one occasion Barbellion says:—

> I have no personal courage and all this pride boils up behind a timid exterior. I quail often before stupid but overbearing persons who consequently never realise my contempt of them. . . . Of course, to intimate friends (only about three persons in the wide, wide world), I can always give free vent to my feelings, and I do so in privacy with that violence in which a weak character usually finds some compensation for his intolerable self-imposed reserve and restraint in public. I can never marvel enough at the ineradicable turpitude of my existence, at my *double-facedness,* and the remarkable contrast between the face I turn to the outside world and the face my friends know. It's like leading a double existence or artificially constructing a puppet to dangle before the crowd while I fulminate behind the scenes. If only I had the moral courage to play my part in life—to take the stage and be myself, to enjoy the delightful sensation of making my presence felt, instead of this vapourish mumming—then this *Journal* would be quite unnecessary.

No man who is a hero to himself stands a very good chance of seeming a hero to other people. But in this passage Barbellion not only shows the difference between his appearance and his self-portraiture, but also directs attention to one of the factors which make his diary so interesting a document. He was aware of the contrast between what he allowed the world to see and the rest of his nature; but this contrast remained profoundly mysterious to himself. He understood himself enough to be able to describe himself, but not so thoroughly that the knowledge could remove all curiosity; and, in fact, while he knew much of his own character that no one else knew, there was something left over of which he was ignorant.

He once said:—

I am apparently a triple personality: (1) The respectable youth; (2) The foul-mouthed commentator and critic; (3) The real but unknown I. Curious that these three should live together amiably in the same tenement.

One might also say that the reader of the diary discovers another triple personality: (1) Barbellion as he must have seemed to others; (2) Barbellion as he thought he seemed to others; (3) The real Barbellion, not fully known even to himself, yet, between his appearance and his confessions, for ever unconsciously betraying himself. In actual fact, he was, it is agreed by all who knew him, a man of tremendous, almost daemonic, force of character. I have already alluded to the restless vigour with which he drove his failing body through all manner of tasks and difficulties, and this trait in him gives a fair idea of his spirit. From boyhood onward he was weakened by continual ill-health. The diary is full of medical observations and forebodings, but no one, not even his family, realised how constantly the fear of sickness and death attended him. He never mentioned his health save in a tone of cheerful cynicism: he never pampered himself or allowed himself to be pampered. In spite of his palpitating heart he exposed himself to fatigues and performed feats of endurance which a sound man might well have shirked. He worked furiously and unceasingly. He kept his balance and his courage under staggering blows of ill-fortune. Never was there so impossible an ambition as that of this sickly youth in a provincial town, who desired, without any help, without even any decent opportunities for self-instruction, to obtain a scientific appointment. Yet he overcame these obstacles and his ambition was fulfilled. And when this was taken from him, when nothing was left but a few painful months of life and his *Journal,* when it was infinite labour even to trace a few words on the page, he continued the self-portrait which had become his last ambition, as long as he could hold a pen at all. The straggling, irregularly-formed letters which sprawl across the paper are the last witnesses of his invincible courage.

And to others this timid and cowardly young man seemed strong, masterful, difficult to manage, frightening, sometimes savage and bitter in conversation, but always magnetic and fascinating. "I know," he says, "I am not prepossessing in appearance—my nose is crooked and my skin is blotched." In reality his height, his distinction of bearing and fine hair produced an immediate effect of good looks—which, with the emaciation of his final days, changed into an austere and painful beauty. He had particularly beautiful hands, and his photographs certainly represent him as being not only noticeable but also attractive. The disparity between what he says of himself and what others thought of him involves no real contradiction. He is writing of the hidden and secret personality which no one else knew, and the fact that no one else could know this personality, save by his own deliberate act of revelation, is another proof of his strength. He is describing the other side of the moon. (pp. 29-32)

In the introduction to [*The Journal of a Disappointed Man* (see excerpt dated 1919)], Mr. Wells very comprehensively lays stress on the circumstances of Barbellion's fate. He represents the diarist as saying, "You shall have at least one specimen carefully displayed and labelled. Here is a recorded unhappiness. When you talk about life and the rewards of life and the justice of life and its penalties, what you say must square with this." This is, of course, an aspect of the matter which no reader could manage to overlook, even if he desired (as he

might conceivably desire) to do so. It would be a pity, however, if we were to consider it to the exclusion of every other aspect. Barbellion was not essentially a *specimen* who by good luck had the ability to display and label himself. If his circumstances had been quite other than they were, he would still have been a remarkable man and would almost certainly have done remarkable work. His disease and death ought to play the same part in our conception of him that they do in our conception of Keats, with whom, besides, he had certain affinities which he half-consciously recognised. We do not know what part disease played in creating or forcing or conditioning Keats's genius; we only know that it infuses a poignancy and a colour into our picture of his life. He does not appear to us as the diseased poet, but as a poet who, as it happened, was stricken with disease. So with Barbellion: he had a personality and a gift for describing his experiences; and, since it fell out that his experiences were tragic, therefore the story he tells is a tragedy. But the tragedy is not interesting only as such. It is interesting because the principal figure in it is Barbellion. (pp. 34-5)

His *Journal* is a book of an enduring sort, not merely because it is an accurate and candid self-portrait, but also because of the inherent attractions of its subject. Barbellion was a poet, a humourist, an observer, a philosopher, as well as a truthful, passionate and amazingly courageous man. In drawing a picture of the last he also made a picture of the world as it seemed to the first four, and thus captured in it poetry, humour, observation, and philosophy. The subject is still too fresh, and, by the vividness of its presentment, too painful, for any attempt at a final valuation to be made. Not long ago, Barbellion was still alive, suffering and hoping; and, with the best will in the world, no critic can avoid being influenced by this fact. But his book is a fair topic for prophecy; and it is not very rash to predict that, as it loses the sharpness and painfulness of a record of fact, so its qualities as a work of literature will come more into prominence and we shall realise that Barbellion was not only a genius untimely overwhelmed by an evil fate, but a genius who, before he was overwhelmed, had opportunity to do some at least of his appointed work. Then, whatever may be the theoretical views we hold on the connection between disease and genius, we shall be able to think less of Barbellion as a "case" and more of him as a writer. We shall not, perhaps, think that we have a complete portrait of him in his *Journal* any more than that we have a complete portrait of Keats in the *Odes* or even in the *Letters*. The greatest of artists cannot entirely disclose himself in his work. Barbellion did so no more than others. But he was an artist, and, between what he wrote of himself and what was otherwise revealed, it is possible to form a picture of a remarkable personality. (pp. 44-5)

Edward Shanks, "W. N. P. Barbellion," in his First Essays on Literature, *1923. Reprint by Books for Libraries Press, 1968; distributed by Arno Press, Inc., pp. 23-45.*

RICHMOND H. HELLYAR   (essay date 1926)

[*In the following excerpt from his book-length study of Barbellion, Hellyar considers the impact and value of Barbellion's writings.*]

One of the most fascinating and least explored of bypaths in literary cause and effect, and one of the most delightful of idle occupations for the curious reader is the study of the particular influence of the individual writer on one's existence and way of life. . . . How interesting, for instance, it would be to know exactly how much one was changed by *The Return of the Native;* how much reality Bertrand Russell put into one's mind, and how much nimbleness and general literary "pep" was rammed down one's throat by Aldous Huxley's tours-de-force. (pp. 177-78)

One of the most immediate and smashing attacks on the weak points of one's personal armour, and certainly one of the most definite and lasting influences that have entered the minds of those who have read him with sufficient attention, was that of Barbellion.

Barbellion came to some of us like a gale out of the North East, sweeping away innumerable miasmas of youthful idiocies, half-baked conceptions, silly inconsistencies and cloudy generalizations; stiffening one's moral backbone, and bringing one into instant contact with new ways of living. There is no more admirable, more exhilarating introduction to the Art of Life, and the meaning and significance of the world, than *The Journal of a Disappointed Man*. This, together with the "Journal Essays" and the *Last Diary* forms one of the most personally valuable and directly profitable set of documents that have ever been written. It reveals a life lived fully, too fully, some may think; lived extravagantly and madly, say the poor-spirited and fainthearted. Nevertheless, there is no better stimulus, no keener spur to further effort, no finer example to live up to, than this man who paints his own portrait, and psycho-analyses himself for the benefit of mankind in general, and the generation to which he belonged in particular.

He is the challenge to classification. The critics made a bad mistake over Butler, despised Shaw as a quack, overlooked Hudson altogether. Barbellion is more indefinable and elusive than any. He is simply there. Like him or hate him; sympathize with his views or despise him as an unhealthy self-introspective cynic—one simply cannot deny him, cannot say he doesn't matter. He will not be merely tolerated either. Every page in fact asserts his independence of the lazy, thoughtless reader; he says over and over again in so many words "If you don't like me, you can do the other thing." It is his independence and vigour of expression indeed that make him so real a force, and his work so vivid and convincing. Bores, prigs, and hypocrites were his pet aversions; and his brother mentions that he "did not suffer them gladly." His books and his life are at any rate for none of them. Passionate interest and curiosity, a humble prostration in the face of the unknown (like Amiel "he came to his books as though to an altar"); and a ruthless, unceasing self-criticism—these are none of them qualities for those who are tired of life, or over-confident in their own beliefs, and own selves in general. His influence is essentially a purifying and healthy one. He not only helps to clean out our civilized Augean stables, however; there is a definite meaning in him and in his book. Barbellion's life, and conquests and defeats offer one a spectacle that is finer and more impressive, because truer and more actual than the greatest conception of Hardy, or the most searing and grimmest example of Greek Tragedy. His life seen simply as a piece of the Human Comedy is magnificent, is high art, touching the very summit in its splendid achievements, its fearful struggles, and terrible despairs.

Mr. Arthur Cummings says that he had conceived for the future that never came, a series of novels modelled on similar lines to Balzac's *Comédie Humaine*. He never lived to achieve it, but his own life is an amazing example of human destiny, and the courage and greatness that is latent in humanity. His own "Peau de Chagrin" shrunk to nothing in a pathetically short time, but his work was greater than Raphael's, because he, in great measure, made his own life, and certainly created his own opportunities, and reaped in his successes the fruits of his own mental strivings and agonies. Barbellion, crushed and restricted as he was, made a splendid thing of his life, had more to show at the end than a dozen others of less force and less determination. He made the very best of both worlds. He loved this world and its contents with an enthusiasm and a profound joy that puts healthy, vigorous-bodied youth into a very pale and colourless background; and he faced those things of the mind and of the Universe that are hidden from us, with a curiosity and a fierce wonder, so intense and so stirring that it could not but arouse the most sluggish and weakest imagination into a mild surprise at the discovery that Death is omnipresent, and the human mind a very strange and incomprehensible thing.

Barbellion is not only valuable in himself, in what he has done, what he has contributed to his fellows and mankind in general. He stands in addition to this for something more impalpable, something indefinite and abstract maybe, but none the less very significant and full of meaning. He was, seen from one point of view, a figure of supreme success. He stands for human achievement—with a serene, high courage and a clear definite reply to the cruel play of the illogical and abstract Being we call Nature. He was from this point of view as successful biologically as, say, a falcon, or any other animal which has asserted its independence and "right to live" over against the vagaries and adverse influence of its environment. He embodies all that is finest and most valuable in human nature, displays pre-eminently the quality that has evolved man from subman— that everlasting, brave, persistent battle with the irrational play of Nature which has given to us so supreme a power of self-assertion and adaptability in the face of difficulty. And his life from this standpoint is a complete triumph—a defeat of despair, a full and complete expression of personality. Humanly speaking, as an individual man, and as embodying the age-old tradition of Humanity, he lived for a purpose, lived an entirely, splendidly, useful life. Seen from another point of view, however, from above as it were, from the ideal position that man is ever trying to attain, Barbellion's life, in its pitiful shortness, its pain, and its misunderstanding, is an ugly, unnecessary, improvident waste. His contribution to the growth and fuller achievement of mankind was destroyed without any reason whatever; his life was cut short by the mere presence in his body of a number of very low and primitive organisms. He stands for the eternity of the human spirit, the insatiable curiosity of the human mind; but he also stands for the incompleteness of human evolution, the purely fragmentary and piecemeal control that man has over his surroundings, and especially over that most vital of environments, his own body, his own fleshly accoutrements. Barbellion was as completely and helplessly a victim of the meaningless mechanism of Nature as a woodlark struck by a sparrowhawk. He had as little control over the circumstances that were gradually hemming him in as the woodlark—less, for he could not even attempt to evade the disease that had him in its grip. His death makes one think along two distinct lines—the triumph of the individual and the failure of society.

It is in the *Last Diary* that one can see most clearly this conflict between the man and the fate that Nature meted out to him— in this brief record of the concluding two years of his life.

The *Last Diary* is magnificent, one of the most inspiring and most terrible of narratives—a "human document" in the very truest meaning of that much-abused phrase. It is a real tale of the terrors and awfulness that lie waiting in Nature for those unfortunate ones that chance chooses as victims: phantoms of pain that happily are only realized when experienced—and which, even when experienced, are soon forgotten unless, as here, their impress is permanent and progressive. It gives a thrilling and heartrending picture of man's clash with Nature—thrilling in the courage of the man, heartrending in the brutality of Nature. It is truly awful to watch him gradually going out of life, to see how paralysis gripped him more and more firmly; to see, too, the mental suffering he went through at the thought of leaving his wife and child to a world which, though he loved it only too well, had shown him in a vividly personal fashion what a bestial cruelty, what racking horrors—above all what blindness and irrationality there was in it.

A Last Diary carries one right into the very heart of life, wrings one's emotions by its exquisite, passionate pain, and lifts one to an altogether higher plane of existence by its brave patience, and perfect understanding. There is a beauty in it that stabs; that pierces the imagination and stamps itself on the mind in a way one can never forget. Its very living pain thrills one with the actual response that only Art can give; makes one believe with even greater certainty in the necessity of perfect sympathy, convinces yet again that human love is the greatest thing in life—the one really important thing—that gives life its meaning and its beauty.

It has rather surprised me that Barbellion is still, after five years, so comparatively little known, even among that class of reader we call "educated." His ideas are "unusual," and often involved; his outlook disturbing and his ambitions not of a popular kind. But when one considers what there is in him of fundamental truth and universal application, it is strange that one of the penny papers doesn't print a daily extract for the simple, human encouragement that his life and work everywhere exemplifies; or that some enterprizing correspondence college doesn't "take him up" and "boost" him to that multitude of feeble-spirited, greyminded individuals who would benefit by the electric contact of his personality. Perhaps, however, he is rather too electrifying, a little too real for comfort; and his hatred of platitudes, whether encouraging or not, would shock profoundly those readers of our "popular philosophers" who vaguely desire something "strengthening" or "uplifting," but most emphatically do not wish to see life as it really is. I am afraid that the first tap from Barbellion would so surprise them that they would close their ears in fear and resentment, and run away to avoid contamination with the ideas of so awful a fellow, and so frightful a revolutionary. He is brutally frank when he feels brutality is necessary. He leads off with his left at you straight away, and it is up to you to defend yourself and answer him back. His is no gentle pat on the back, a mild incentive to doing better next time. He hits straight and hard. And for those who can appreciate the vigour and reality of his ideas, that definite, uncompromising attitude is one of the best things about him. His message to this generation cannot be summed up in a few of the "helpful maxims" or "get-on-young-man" aphorisms that are daily instilled into the minds of hundreds of thousands of our fellow-countrymen—and immediately and unconsciously rejected by them. He must be read, and read again—not a very difficult or objectionable task—if one really wishes to understand what his life meant, and what he has to say on matters of immediate import, and on the affairs, both practical and philosophical, that continually crop up in the course of one's existence.

It is early yet to state what is his influence on his generation, or at least on those of it who have felt sufficiently interested in the man's way of life to read his work with the attention it deserves. One can, however, be certain that it is a great deal more than is apparent on the surface. Barbellion has been five years in his grave, but the force of his enthusiasm, the essence of his personality is as alive to-day as it was ten years ago in his own person. The keen energy and zest for life, and the intense intellectual curiosity that lay behind his success in life and the art of living has been made, by the genius with which he expressed it in his work, as transferable and general a piece of experience, as was the factual knowledge he himself obtained from the Tradition and store of wisdom that man has accumulated down the ages. The thrill of enjoyment, the passion for discovering meanings, the mental discomfort that forced him to investigate "things that were too high" for him—all these live in the pages of his *Journal* and all are as definitely and permanently contributions to human life, as his analyses of the homing instinct of newts, or the discovery of several new species of mallophaga are contributions to science. (pp. 178-88)

Richmond H. Hellyar, in his W. N. P. Barbellion, *George H. Doran Company, 1926, 191 p.*

E. W. MARTIN (essay date 1947)

[*In the following excerpt, the critic discusses Barbellion's nature as it is revealed in the published journals.*]

Almost twenty-seven years have elapsed since W. N. P. Barbellion's *The Journal of a Disappointed Man* made its challenging entry into the world of letters, demanding by its very sincerity and the tragedy it recorded a comparison with such journal-writers as Amiel and Marie Bashkirtseff. Now, however, it is an undeniable fact that Barbellion is forgotten; his three works [*The Journal of a Disappointed Man, Enjoying Life,* and *A Last Diary*], are known only to those who explore the by-ways of literature.

It is of interest to note that in 1919, when the *Journal* was published, it caused critics to speculate on the identity hidden behind a pseudonym. Barbellion was a mystery; and so evident were the artistry and passion of the book that one professor went so far as to give it as his considered opinion—in an article published in *History*—that certain literary artists had collaborated to make the diaries appear as the authentic record of one complex personality. As one critic later observed, some of these suggestions arose from an unconscious desire on the part of readers to escape from, and to deny, such final tragedy as the book records. The *Journal* was accorded special notice because it was a document of stark revelation; and because the late H. G. Wells contributed a kindly preface in which he made it clear that he believed Barbellion to be one of the most promising recruits to biological science. Here, indeed, was a tragedy of promise half-fulfilled, worthy of Hardy's inevitable and pessimistic pen. (p. 195)

The critic, Edward Shanks, who recognized Barbellion as a great artist, has commented on the fact that the real man, the diarist whose individuality gives to his book a colour and a permanence few such books can possess, was not the morbid person that one might suppose from reading some of his notes. In actual fact, Shanks states, it is agreed by all who knew him that he was a man of tremendous, almost demonic force of character [see excerpt dated 1923]. From the *Journal* alone we cannot know Barbellion as he was. (p. 196)

The second volume of Barbellion's work—*Enjoying Life and Other Essays*—shows him both as writer and scientist; it also bears a quotation from Amiel which applies equally to his fellow journal-writer: "I love everything, and detest one thing only—the hopeless imprisonment of my being within a single arbitrary form."

It is in *The Last Diary,* however, that Barbellion's courage in the face of pain and death is most marked. Though weak and helpless, he was able to write in 1919:

> You can search all history for an ambition more powerful than mine and not find it. No, not Napoleon, not Wilhelm II, nor Keats. No, I am not proud of it, not at all. The wonder is that I remain sane. I am sane or I could not make fun of it as I do.

The task of writing had become difficult with the spread of the disease, but Barbellion's determination to continue the struggle did not weaken. "I am not going to be beaten," he said, "if I develop all the diseases in the doctor's index. I mean to do what I set out to do if it has to be done in a bath-chair."

With increasing illness Barbellion had to surrender his post at the Museum, and he gave himself up to self-analysis. His thoughts now were visions lighting up his life. "During the past twelve months," he wrote in 1918, "I have undergone an upheaval, and the whole bias of my life has gone across from the intellectual to the ethical. I know that goodness is the chief thing."

It was a conclusion to which Coleridge arrived, and it is one that profoundly affects Barbellion's writing. *The Last Diary* is more of a fragment than the *Journal;* but in it we get glimpses of the real Barbellion; the whole personality is there and the war in the soul that disturbs the longer book is not so noticeable. H. G. Wells rightly called Barbellion an egotist; but it was an egotism which was balanced by a similar desire to know others. Barbellion was introspective, self-centred; but he was also equally other-centred. He wanted to know all about all things, the people he met, the things he saw, and the spiritual mysteries which he divined.

It seems as though Barbellion had the eyes of a seer, a nature divested of all but the highest of human passions, the passion for truth. As he lay in bed a World War was changing civilization, and it was on the nature of the change that Barbellion pondered:

> We are now entered on the kingless republican era. The next struggle, in some ways more bitter and more protracted than this, will be between capital and labour. After that, the millenium of Mr. Wells and the Spiritualistic age. After the aeroplane, the soul. Few yet realize what a transformation awaits the patient investigations of the psychical researchers. We know next to nothing about the mind force and spirit workings of man.

Strange words for a biologist; but words coming from one who was near to the things he thought about, to the solution of the mystery. In his *Journal,* Barbellion is often a cynical materialist, a sensitive introvert, an excited naturalist; in fact he is all things to all men in his thirst for experience and sensation. But in *The Last Diary,* if there is less tempestuous energy, there is a greater depth. There is no continuity of insight throughout the book because Barbellion was too weak for concentrated effort; but there is a settled sincerity surviving all changes of mood. The reason for this is made clear in the following passage:

> O all ye people! the crowning irony of my life—where is the sacred oil?—is my now cast-iron religious convictions shortly summarised as *Love and Unselfishness.* These, my moral code, have captured the approval not only of my ethical but my intellectual side as well. Undoubtedly, and dogmatically if you like, a man should be unselfish for good of the soul and also to the credit of his intellect. To be selfish is to imprison in a tiny cage the glorious ego capable of penetrating to the farthest corners of the universe. As for love it is an instinct and the earnest, like all beauty, physical as well as moral, of our future union into One.

Towards the end of his life Barbellion was also comforted by the way in which the critics and the public received his *Journal.* It was his child; and he was happy to have lived to witness its baptism. Barbellion died on 22 October 1919 in a tiny cottage at Gerrard's Cross, Buckinghamshire, at the age of thirty-one. From the direction in which his mind was moving it is probable that, had he lived, Barbellion would have given himself wholly to literature rather than to biology. He believed, with Sir Thomas Browne, that we carry within us all the wonders we seek without us, and thus the drama and the tragedy of his life was absorbing to him. Fate could not deny to him the triumph his courage had earned. From the struggle with ill health Barbellion wrested a calm and a contentment that nothing could disturb:

> Surely, I muse, a man cannot be accounted a failure who succeeds at last in calling in all his idle desires and wandering motives, and with utter restlessness concentrating his life on the benison of Death. I am happy to think that, like a pilot hard aport, Death is ready at a signal to conduct me over this moaning bar to still deep waters.

> (pp. 196-97)

E. W. Martin, "W. N. P. Barbellion (1889-1919),"
in English, *Vol. VI, No. 34, Spring, 1947, pp. 195-97.*

EDWARD SACKVILLE-WEST (essay date 1949)

[Sackville-West was an English novelist, biographer, musicologist, and critic. In the following excerpt, he focuses on Barbellion's reflections on his terminal illness.]

Few have had the courage to write a detailed study of physical disease from the patient's point of view. (p. 104)

A few important writers have touched upon it, usually as part of a larger context: one thinks of Montaigne, of Amiel, of Rilke (in *Malte Laurids Brigge*), of D. H. Lawrence (in his *Letters*)—especially perhaps of Virginia Woolf, whose essay "On Being Ill," says some new things and is extraordinarily accurate. This is a capital point. Objectivity is here neither possible nor really to be desired; but it is important to be very precise. Precision involves an intensity of concentration that is not always available; for concentration is very difficult, if not impossible, so long as the body insists on making its presence felt. (p. 105)

The problem is one of perpetual vigilance. What has to be charted is a graph of awareness: the patient is concerned to discover the point beyond which he knows he can no longer guarantee the minimum integration of thought and feeling; and it was, I believe, because she felt herself approaching the region (she had been there before) where such a guarantee becomes permanently impossible, that Virginia Woolf decided upon an abdication which was all the more courageous because she knew well that obtuse people would call it the reverse.

In a sense, then, a permanent watch upon the validity of this guarantee is the principal—often the only—activity of an invalid's existence; it is his ambition, his "moment of truth." Life, which once seemed a rocket-shower of enticing possibilities, is narrowed into a focus so tiny that the patient is obliged to develop some day-dream or other with which to counterbalance this exasperating stint. "W. N. P. Barbellion," whose real name was Bruce F. Cummings, who wrote the *Journal of a Disappointed Man*, who died before he was thirty of disseminated sclerosis, who despite this made a small but definite name for himself as a biologist, has described the battle with this particular angel so accurately and so comprehensively that what remains to be added to his account must take the form of comment and illustration. The *Journal* is a minor classic; it is also one of the most depressing books ever written, partly because Barbellion lost his battle, partly because there was something in him which wanted to lose it, as well as much more that wanted to win.

> The intense internal life I lead, worrying about my health, reading (eternally reading), reflecting, observing, feeling, loving and hating—with no outlet for superfluous steam, cramped and confined on every side, without any friends or influence of any sort, without even any acquaintances excepting my colleagues in journalism (whom I contemn)—all this will turn me into the most self-conscious, conceited, mawkish, gauche creature in existence.

His dread was not unfounded, although his self-pity bred a self-contempt which prevented him—except in rare moments of physical ease—from recognising his own unquestionable superiority of mind and spirit. The next entry, dated a month later, gives another turn to the screw.

> The facts are undeniable: Life is pain. No sophistry can win me over to any other view. And yet years ago I set out so hopefully and healthfully—what are birds' eggs to me *now*? My ambition is enormous but vague. I am too distributed in my abilities ever to achieve distinction.

That was in 1910. Barbellion was twenty, and had rather less than ten more years to live. In his long and deeply interesting Preface to the posthumous *Last Diary*, Barbellion's brother, Mr. Arthur J. Cummings, takes the critics of the *Journal* to task for describing its author as egotistical and self-pitying, and for their failure to discern the love of life which underlay the expressions of despair. I do not think he entirely succeeds in making his point. No one who did not know Barbellion personally would dream of denying the testimony of those who did, that in fact the joy of living was his salient characteristic, right up to the end. What can be objected is that, although both diaries are full of passages which bear witness to an almost inexhaustible courage, the aggregate effect of Barbellion's self-

revelation is depressing. No man has ever been able to put the whole of himself into his work—even when that work is an intimate diary; and it is even more difficult for the autobiographer to display the *balance* of his character as it appears to his friends. Nor is it desirable he should do so, for the truth is manifold, and only by collating disparate recensions can we arrive at it. As Barbellion himself remarked, in *A Last Diary:* "It is almost impossible to tell the truth. In this journal I have tried, but I have not succeeded." Perhaps he succeeded better than he knew; at all events he was conscious of the dilemma.

Meanwhile it is evident, even to one who had not the privilege of knowing Barbellion personally, that this man had a remarkable capacity for positive happiness. This was bound up—as in Englishmen it so often is—with the sense of adventure and the thrill of discovery. (pp. 106-08)

The sense of adventure is vividly present in the following passage, where the observation has a minuteness and a sensitiveness which recall the Notebooks of Gerard Manley Hopkins:

> I arrived only on the outside of the fringe in my study of the habits of the Greater Horseshoe Bat, but I got a lot of enjoyment out of the risky adventure of exploring the disused mines. The wooden struts were rotten, and the walls and roofs of the galleries had fallen in here and there. So we had sometimes to crawl on hands and knees to get past. All the borings were covered with a red slime, so we wore engineers' overalls, which by the time we had finished changed from blue to red, speckled with grease dropping from our candles. Occasionally, in turning a corner, a sudden draught would blow the candles out, and in one rather lofty boring we were stopped by deep water, and, boy-like, meditated the necessity of removing clothes and swimming on with candles fastened on our foreheads. One boring opened into the side of a hill by a small, insignificant, and almost invisible hole at the bottom of a steep slide. We slid down with a rope, and once inside the little hole at the bottom, found a big passage with a narrow-gauge line and abandoned truck—great excitement! Another entrance to the mines was by way of a shaft no bigger than an ordinary man-hole in a drain pipe, its mouth being overgrown with brambles. We fixed a rope round the trunk of a tree, and went down, hand over hand. We crawled along a narrow passage—three of us, leaving no one at the top to guard the rope—and at intervals espied our game, hanging to the roof by the hindlegs. We boxed three altogether, gently unfixing the hind legs, and laying the little creatures in a tin carefully lined with wool. The Horseshoe Bat is the strangest sight in the world to come upon in a dark cave hanging upside down from the roof like an enormous chrysalis in shape. For when roosting, this bat puts its two thin hind legs and feet very close together, making a single delicate pedicle, and wraps its body entirely in its wings, head and ears included. When disturbed, it gently draws itself up a little by bending its legs. When thoroughly awakened, it un-

folds its wings and becomes a picture of trembling animation: the head is raised, and it looks at you nervously with its little beady dark, glittering eyes, the large ears all the while vibrating as swiftly as a tuning-fork. These with the grotesque and mysterious leaf-like growth around its nose—not to mention the centrepiece that stands out like a door-knocker—make a remarkable vision by candle-light in a dark cave.

It is clear that such a man ought never to attempt to live in a town—above all, not in London, for many years Barbellion's exterior prison. But poverty nagged—as it had nagged George Gissing, another of those victims of whom the *Journal* irresistibly reminds us. There is about these unfortunate men a peculiar aura of ill-ventilated middle-class misery, so much more distressing to read about, because of its pathetic attachment to intangible values, than the cruder wretchedness of the very poor whose lives are more liable to be suddenly brimmed by some concrete satisfaction. The world of the genteel boarding-house, with its livid gaslight, shooting-gallery ornaments, bamboo furniture and hairy sofas, its smell of cabbage and stewed steak and Jeyes' Fluid; its grimy windows, creaking wardrobe and looking-glass which tips forward; its brown-leaved fern, its gamboge cake from the grocer's; a world where lovers hold timid hands over a plopping gasfire and where those whom love has ignored hug to their scrannel bosoms some political or religious quackery: this was the world, and this the atmosphere, in which the central movement of Barbellion's pathetic symphony reached an inconclusive end. It is a picture by Sickert, of the Camden Town period. The early volumes of Miss Dorothy Richardson's *Pilgrimage,* and Mr. William Plomer's *The Case is Altered,* are there for those who wish to document themselves still more fully in the evasions of this repellent milieu; but in Barbellion's case the surroundings do not loom so large because his illness, and its attendant self-absorption, burst the gimcrack framework of his life. His standard of happiness was not really low, in spite of references to ''dream pictures of a quiet studious life in the Cromwell Road,'' and a taste for the milk-and-soda ecstasies of Eugénie de Guérin: not low, because of his bright peculiar gift, his microscopic eye; because he so evidently loved the highest when he saw it—which was seldom, though that was hardly his fault. . . . (pp. 109-11)

When the *Journal* was first published, many readers were, as I have recalled, shocked by its egotism, to which, indeed, Barbellion himself draws constant attention. I wonder now what those readers expected, in the circumstances. Healthy people are judged by what they do, sick people by what they say; and surely the value of that resides in its honesty. But Barbellion is more than honest: his introspection has that supercharged quality, often found in German and Russian, but very seldom in English, literature—at all events since understatement became a national characteristic. It was not an accident that Barbellion saw himself reflected in Lermontov and Marie Bashkirtsev. Let me collate a few examples from the *Journal:*

Feel like a piece of drawn threadwork, or an undeveloped negative, or a jelly fish on stilts, or a sloppy tadpole, or a weevil in a nut, or a spitch-cocked eel. In other words and in short—ill.

Before now I have tried going off to bed. But that does not work—I don't sleep. Moreover,

I have been in the grip of a horrible mental unrest. To sit still in my chair, much less to lie in bed doing nothing seemed ghastly. I experienced all the cravings of a dissolute neurotic for a stimulus, but what stimulus I wanted I did not know. Had I known I should have gone and got it. The dipsomaniac was a man to be envied.

February 20.—Am feeling very unwell. My ill-health, my isolation, baulked ambitions, and daily bread-winning, all conspire to bring me down. The idea of a pistol and the end of it grows on me day by day.

February 21.—After four days of the most profound depression of spirits, bitterness, self-distrust, despair, I emerged from the cloud to-day quite suddenly (probably the arsenic and strychnine begin to take effect) and walk up to Exhibition Road with the intention of visiting the Science Museum Library so as to refer to Schaefer's *Essentials of Histology* (I have to watch myself carefully so that I may act *at once* as soon as the balance of mind is restored).

So many rubrics for an anthology of Discomfort. . . . The last of these is of especial interest, because it reveals the importance, for the chronic invalid, of acting *at once,* whenever the cloud happens to lift. Hence the feverish haste to accomplish the most trivial business of life, the anxiety to cram as much activity as possible into the precious hours of relief. . . . (pp. 112-13)

Unlike other writers on illness, who dance round the subject, or embroider it, Barbellion pierces to the inmost cell—that of nervous depression, which is the ultimate, featureless hell always liable to open and swallow up the sufferer. This prison is perfect. No warder is needed, because there is no door; there is no light, because no window, and printed words might be in Etruscan, for all the pleasure or instruction they communicate; no sound, except the lame Alexandrine of the blood; nothing but sensation—the body crammed with milling centipedes, from the roots of the hair to the soles of the feet. In such case nobility of nature can assert itself only in gestures of despair. The voice crying, ''This is not I!'' recedes beyond human earshot. But, because this horror must somehow be expressed, its results excused, the hand continues to write:

December 15.—I simply do not believe the conclusions I have drawn from my present condition, which has already lasted almost a year, my condition is too serious for that. Indeed, I do not even know whether I can say that it is not a new condition. My real opinion, however, is that this condition is new—I have had similar ones, but never one like this. It is as if I were made of stone, as if I were my own tombstone, there is no loophole for doubt or for faith, for love or repugnance, for courage or anxiety, in particular or in general, only a vague hope lives on, but no better than the inscriptions on tombstones. Almost every word I write jars against the next, I hear the consonants rub leadenly against each other and the vowels sing an accompaniment like Negroes in a minstrel show. My doubts stand in a circle around every word,

I see them before I see the word, but what then! I do not see the word at all, I invent it. Of course, that wouldn't be the greatest misfortune, only I ought to be able to invent words capable of blowing the odor of corpses in a direction other than straight into mine and the reader's face. When I sit down at the desk I feel no better than someone who falls and breaks both legs in the middle of the traffic of the Place de l'Opéra. All the carriages, despite their noise, press silently from all directions in all directions, but that man's pain keeps better order than the police, it closes his eyes and empties the Place and the streets without the carriages having to turn about. The great commotion hurts him, for he is really an obstruction to traffic, but the emptiness is no less sad, for it unshackles his real pain.

That quotation is . . . from Kafka's *Diaries*. If we turn now to Barbellion's *Journal*, we find the tone essentially the same.

> My sympathy with myself is so unfailing that I don't deserve anybody else's. In many respects, however, this Journal I believe gives the impression that I behave myself in the public gaze much worse than I actually do. You must remember that herein I let myself go at a stretch gallop: in life I rein in, I am almost another person. Here I stand revealed as a contemptuous arrogant malcontent. My life has embittered me *au fond*, I have the crabbed temper of the disappointed man insufficiently developed yet to be very plainly visible beneath my innate affable, unassuming, humble, diffident, cheerful characteristics.

To complain of the egotism of such passages is beside the point; even so, no reader can fail to be struck by the scarcity of references to the 1914-18 war, the course of which coincided with more than half of this *Journal*. But it is in the nature of illness to exclude what interests the healthy: "Nothing matters, provided the tongue is not furred" (March, 1915). There is the truth; to have stated it so baldly is perhaps shocking, but also courageous, since it is evident that Barbellion was acutely aware of the impression his *Journal* would create, as well as anxious that he should be given the benefit of the doubt. In the long run I believe he will be justified in his hopes, because fundamentally he was not disconnected either by illness or by temperament from love in any of its aspects.

> This morning how desirable everything seemed to me! The world intoxicated me. Moving again among so many human beings gave me the crowd fever, and started again all the pangs of the old familiar hunger for a fuller life, that centrifugal *élan* in which I feared for the disruption and scattering of my parts in all directions. Temporarily I lost the hegemony of my own soul. Every man and woman I met was my enemy, threatening me with the secession of some inward part. I was alarmed to discover how many women I could passionately love and with how many men I could form a lasting friendship. Within, all was anarchy and commotion, a cold fright seized me lest some extraordinary event was about to happen: some

> general histolysis of my body, some sudden disintegration of my personality, some madness, some strange death. . . . I wanted to crush out the life of all these men and women in a great Bear's hug, my God! this sea of human faces whom I can never recognise, all of us alive together beneath this yellow catafalque of fog on the morning of the announcement of world famine and world war! . . .

A passage like that throws all the windows wide open: the Cromwell Road, the stuffy lodging-house, disappear in a flash, and the free gift of humanity is revealed as the superpersonal spirit it is.

But our beginning is also our end. The child of thirteen who noted: "*Sept. 8:* Toothache. *Sept. 9:* Toothache. *Sept. 10:* Toothache. *Sept. 11:* Toothache."—was father to the man who closed his *Journal*, thirteen years later, with the entries: "*Oct. 14-21:* Miserable. *Oct. 21:* Self-disgust." It is the dates which horrify: six whole days given over to one ungovernable, destructive emotion. And then another. Then silence, for three months, of which we divine the dragging length.

The final entry in *A Last Diary*—"To-morrow I go to another nursing home"—can be taken in a hopeful sense. To my mind the phrase tolls like a bell, and would do so in any context. Between this statement (but it is also something more) and those I have quoted from the end of the *Journal*, Barbellion is far less laconic. As Death creeps nearer his spirit seems to widen out. Having learnt resignation to pain, if not to death, he could recollect in comparative tranquillity. (pp. 113-16)

But ultimately the word resignation does not apply to Barbellion; he was never more vividly himself than when his thoughts turned to the war which was approaching its end:

> Man made the war and we know his reasons. God made the world, but He keeps His own counsel. Yet if man, who aspires to goodness and truth, can sincerely justify the war, I am willing to believe—this is my faith—that God can justify the world, its pain and suffering and death.

And at the time of the Armistice he let fall a sentence—"After the aeroplane, the soul"—which shows how far his own spirit had voyaged in search of the desirable life. (p. 116)

> *Edward Sackville-West, "The Patient," in his* Inclinations, *Martin Secker & Warburg Ltd., 1949, pp. 104-16.*

H. PORTER ABBOTT (essay date 1973)

[*Abbott is an American educator and critic. In the following excerpt, he discusses Barbellion's accomplishments but ultimate failure as a diarist.*]

Great men who publish their diaries have little to fear but the tedium their readers may have to put up with. At worst they provide informative documents which will inevitably be treasured. The diarist of specialized interest also has nothing to fear. Neither is necessarily practicing an art. But for the unknown man who has the temerity to publish the record of his days, a diary must of necessity keep within certain formal requirements. *The Journal of A Disappointed Man* failed because its author misunderstood, or at least abused, his literary form. What is very sad about this is that Barbellion in other ways understood his form very well. He was a writer of considerable talent whose work deserves to remain in print. (pp. 45-6)

About a year after the publication of Barbellion's last volume an article appeared by the eminent historian A. F. Pollard which purported to be "a sort of historical exercise, the task of testing a diary" [see Additional Bibliography]. The subject was Barbellion's diaries, which were duly tested and as historical documentation found sadly wanting. Pollard found, for example, that Barbellion referred to the bringing down in flames of a Zeppelin over London a full month before the first Zeppelin was in fact brought down. In addition, Barbellion referred to the fall of Gorizia ten days before that event had occurred. He referred to Sundays when they were really Mondays or even Tuesdays, observed thunder and rainfall on days when the Greenwich Meteorological Observations said there could not possibly have been any, noted sunshine when there were only clouds, and observed the moon to rise and the sun to set when the moon could not possibly have risen, nor the sun set.

The historian's research prompted an angry response from Barbellion's brother H. R. Cummings. Cummings was most upset by Pollard's intimations not only of dishonesty but also of collusion: in particular Pollard's revival of the theory, attendant on the first publication of the *Journal*, that it had been the product of other hands, including that of H. G. Wells who had provided the Introduction. In the course of reply, Cummings managed to make the basic criticism that there are other kinds of truth than exact dates and that Professor Pollard, in what was a test of historical veracity, often implied that this was the only appropriate test for a diary. Unfortunately the point is muffled in Cummings' access of zeal on his brother's behalf. Undaunted, Pollard composed a rejoinder which was appended in brackets to Cummings' letter and which solemnly pointed out that "it is one of the merits of the historical method to show that honesty is the best policy":

> A man, who not only publishes a false statement of his death—apparently, like Brougham, in order to enjoy his obituary notices—but also . . . writes legible editorial comments on the illegibility of the author's handwriting, has only himself to thank if his readers attach some meaning to his self-description as "possessing the qualifications of an artistic liar," especially when both he and his editors advertise his book as a "self-portrait in the nude."

What constitutes nudity, of course, is the issue, and the case for the defense is that certain kinds of dress show more than the bare body: that "artistic lying" is a way of telling the truth.

It is easy to chide the professor of history for his determination to stick to the facts when dealing with a literary document; yet in so doing we may overlook just what kind of a literary document we are dealing with. The kind of defense which is being raised is essentially an apology for fiction. However, we are not dealing with ostensible fiction, nor fiction cast in the form of a diary, but with what purports to be an actual diary. And a diary has a rather different umbilicus to the real world than a novel. Our sense of the genuineness of its biographical particulars bears directly on the kind of emotional response we have to its subject. Cummings, despite his defense of Barbellion's casual attitude toward chronology, is obviously aware of this and takes pains to assure us of the "general" factual correctness of his brother's document: "The whole diary was genuine and was written up regularly from the very beginning.

We saw it in process, the manuscript proves conclusively that it was so written, and many living people know that the general facts of Barbellion's life as recorded in the diary are true."

The attempt to reassure us, unfortunately, is not enough. Pollard, for all his flatfootedness, has gone to the heart of an aesthetic flaw. The problem is that Barbellion's attitude toward his facts is not simply casual, but at times willful, and the willful distortion of historical fact has a very different effect in a diary than in a novel. Our distrust, of course, is not Pollard's; we do not fear being misled in our understanding of the facts, but we do fear being misled in our affections. Perceiving a distortion of fact calculated to mislead us in this way can have a disastrous effect. There is no suspending disbelief. One of the things which came out in Cummings' reply to Pollard was that before his death Barbellion composed a "detailed tabular scheme" for the careful re-arrangement of the entries in the *Last Diary*. His instructions were followed, and the *Last Diary* appeared according to the scheme. One result of this is that the published last entry is not the actual last entry. In the published version the last entry reads: "*June 3rd, 1919.*—To-morrow I go to another nursing home."

Once we know about this, I would contend, the diary has changed for us and changed for the worse. We perceive not simply a symbolic statement but a symbolic intention, and however acceptable the latter may be in fiction and even in a fictional diary, in what pretends to be a real diary it amounts to an abuse of the kind of trust which is necessary for the success of such a thing. One of the requirements of this art form, at least in this regard, is the appearance of a lack of art.

Yet Barbellion aspired to the status of fiction; it was crucial that his life not fail him. "It must be a hard thing to be commonplace and vulgar even in misfortune, to discover that the tragedy of your own precious life has been dramatically bad. . . . If only I could order my life by line and level." . . . Part of the problem was that his life itself was too seductive. It had all the seeds of high art. It offered an opportunity which was hard to pass up, and thus the quality of his denouement became an increasingly vital concern: "Pray God the curtain falls at the right moment lest the play drag on into some long and tedious anticlimax." . . . (pp. 49-52)

As a diarist, he had examples of dramatic endings, perhaps the most moving in English being that of B. R. Haydon:

> 18*th*—O God, bless me through the evils of this day. Great anxiety. My landlord, Newton, called. I said "I see a quarter's rent in thy face; but none from me." I appointed to-morrow night to see him, and lay before him every iota of my position. "Goodhearted Newton!" I said, "don't put in an execution." "Nothing of the sort," he replied, half hurt. . . .
>
> 20*th*—O God, bless us all through the evils of this day. Amen.
>
> 21*st*—Slept horribly. Prayed in sorrow, and got up in agitation.
>
> 22*nd*—God forgive me. Amen.

Haydon was found an hour later, dead of terrible self-inflicted wounds in his neck. Much more familiar to Barbellion was the record of Captain Scott's last expedition to the South Pole, a volume he treasured and continually referred to in his journal. In Scott's manuscript the last entry is barely legible:

We had fuel to make two cups of tea apiece and bare food for two days on the 20th. Every day we have been ready to start for our depot *11 miles* away, but outside the door of the tent it remains a scene of whirling drift. I do not think we can hope for any better things now. We shall stick it out to the end, but we are getting weaker, of course, and the end cannot be far.

It seems a pity, but I do not think I can write more.

R. Scott

Last entry.

For God's sake look after our people.

Scott was found eight months later, frozen with his diary under his shoulder.

It is surely possible that these and other dramatic conclusions were in Barbellion's mind as he approached the end of his own account. Yet the effect of his conclusion is very different indeed:

October 12
. . . You would pity me would you? I am lonely, penniless, paralysed, and just turned twenty-eight. But I snap my fingers in your face and with equal arrogance I pity you. I pity you your smooth-running good luck and the stagnant serenity of your mind. I prefer my own torment. I am dying, but you are already a corpse. You have never really lived. Your body has never been flayed into tingling life by hopeless desire to love, to know, to act, to achieve. I do not envy you your absorption in the petty cares of a commonplace existence.

Do you think I would exchange the communion with my own heart for the toy ballons of your silly conversation? Or my curiosity for your flickering interests? Or my despair for your comfortable Hope? Or my present tawdry life for yours as polished and neat as a new three-penny bit? I would not. I gather my mantle around me and I solemnly thank God that I am not as some other men are.

I am only twenty-eight, but I have telescoped into those few years a tolerably long life: I have loved and married, and have a family; I have wept and enjoyed; struggled and overcome, and when the hour comes I shall be content to die.

October 14 *to* 20.
Miserable.

October 21.
Self-disgust.

FINIS
[Barbellion died on December 31]

The missing corpse makes an extraordinary difference. Knowing the falseness of the editorial note augments the reader's sense that the prose itself is lifted from fiction (''I have wept and enjoyed; struggled and overcome . . .''), and gives the last two entries the appearance of a calculated frame to the gesture of defiance. Barbellion's enthusiasm for Dostoevsky becomes,

in this perspective, an embarrassing encumbrance: a manner (however genuine the original feeling that selected it) exploited for the purpose of drawing tears. Thus, the exposure of the false date brings an additional exposure of Barbellion as a writer.

Barbellion had considerable literary tact, and it was mainly the warping pressure of an immense ambition that made him punctuate his diary in the way he did; just as, in his prose, he was weakest at those moments when his sense of humor failed him and he became absorbed in his life as an affecting story. But Barbellion was probably half-aware that he had over-played his ending. One can see this, I think, in his choice of date of demise: December 31 (perhaps, too, in his conscious echo of the Pharisee). The coincidence is a give-away, a whimsical touch, which provides a kind of insurance. Once, in other words, the diary is exposed as unposthumous, it would begin to exist on another plane in which the trick ending is seen as an additional expression of the personality which is the diary's subject. Therefore, when Barbellion was criticized for his abuse of the public's confidence his response was to joke about it:

Dear Sir,

Yes, I am dead. I killed myself off at the end of my book, because it was high time. Your reviewer is incorrect in saying I died of creeping paralysis. It was of another kindred but different disease.

P.S. It may interest your readers to know that I am not yet buried. . . .

(pp. 52-3)

The same effect can often be observed within the *Journal*—the humorous, self-ridiculing, observer transcending the posturing melodramatist. (p. 54)

Barbellion's mishandling of his literary form becomes even stranger in the light of his extensive understanding of the form. His reading of diaries was prodigious and yielded two essays on the subject. In theory, at least, he should have been acutely aware of the kind of contract that must exist between the diarist and his reader. In addition, he appears to have increasingly favored a strain of journal-writing directly opposed to the conception which would have one give the story of a life in sharp tragic contours. This strain of journal-writing is a product of the encyclopedic motive which falls naturally on the diary as ''incondite miscellany.'' What appeals is the diary's digressive character, its fluidity and capacity for indefinite expansion, because ''for the diarist, the most commonplace things of daily life are of absorbing interest. Each day, the diarist finds himself born into a world as strange and beautiful as the dead world of the day before.'' . . . Thus Pepys, in the words of Edward Fitzgerald, was '' 'with child' to see every new thing.'' . . . In his essay on **''Amiel and Some Others,''** Barbellion described the continual claustrophobic self-scrutiny of Amiel as an example of the embittered frustration of this motive—a dark and abortive version of Walt Whitman or Sir Thomas Browne. ''All of them were powerful centrifugal forces rushing away from themselves in an incontinent desire for the whole universe.'' . . . It is the same itch that makes so many pages of most diaries achingly dull, for we must know that the writer ''Rose at 9:00. Had wind. Consumed every last gooseberry.''

It was as a writer of an incondite miscellany that Barbellion was admirably fitted, both by inclination and ability. Among his favorite reading was the encyclopedia (''I turn over the

pages and read everything of interest that catches the eye'' ...).
He could sit down in the public library and read in succession
"the *Gentlewoman,* the *Grocer,* the *Builder,* the *Horological
Journal,* the *Musical Times,* the *Bird Fancier,* the *Herald of
Health,* the *Bible Student.*'' ...

> I am a Magpie at a Bagdad bazaar, hopping
> about, useless, inquisitive, fascinated by a lot
> of astonishing things: e.g., a book on the quad-
> rature of the circle, the *gubbertushed fustilugs*
> passage in Burton's *Anatomy of Melancholy,*
> names like Mr. Portwine or Mr. Hogsflesh,
> Tweezer's Alley or Pickle Herring Street, the
> excellent, conceitful sonnets of Henry Con-
> stable or Petticoat Lane on a Sunday morn-
> ing. ...
>
> (pp. 56-7)

The self-description recurs time and again throughout the journals, and with it often recurs his sensation of the utter strangeness of things. "During a walk or in a book or in the middle
of an embrace, suddenly I awake to a stark amazement at
everything. The bare fact of existence paralyzes me.'' ...

Barbellion was too much of a skeptic ever to give way and
locate in these experiences proof of the deity. His language is
kept generally clean of mystical reverberations. The world is
not so much mysterious as bizarre, and much of the evocation
of strangeness depends on Barbellion's severe restraint, the
taut economy with which he simply presents. ... (p. 57)

[One] fashion of strangeness which Barbellion was particularly
well endowed both to perceive and express was the strangeness
of the *un*singular, the commonplace. It is a variety of the bizarre
which often evoked the best of his deceptively simple prose.
He had the power through which, according to Wordsworth's
precept, "ordinary things should be presented to the mind in
an unusual aspect'':

> Watched some men put a new pile in the pier.
> There was all the usual paraphernalia of chains,
> pulleys, cranes, and ropes, with a massive
> wooden pile swinging over the water at the end
> of a long wire hawser. Everything was in the
> massive style—even the men—very powerful
> men, slow, ruminative, silent men.
>
> Nothing very relevant could be gathered from
> casual remarks. The conversation was without
> exception monosyllabic: "Let go,'' or "Stand
> fast,'' But by close attention to certain obscure
> movements of the man on the ladder near the
> water's edge, it gradually came thro' to my
> consciousness that all these powerful, silent men
> were up against some bitter difficulty. I cannot
> say what it was. The burly monsters were silent
> about the matter. ... In fact they appeared al-
> most indifferent—and tired, oh! so very tired
> of the whole business. The attitude of the man
> nearest me was that for all he cared the pile
> could go on swinging in mid-air to the crack
> of Doom.
>
> They continued slow, laborious efforts to over-
> come the secret difficulty. But these gradually
> slackened and finally ceased. One massive man
> after another abandoned his post in order to lean
> over the rails and gaze like a mystic into the

> depths of the sea. No one spoke. No one saw
> anything not even in the depths of the sea. One
> spat, and with round, sad eyes contemplated
> the trajectory of his brown bolus (he had been
> chewing) in its descent into the water. ...
>
> (p. 59)

The youth who, according to his brother, could "stay for two
or three hours at a stretch in one tense position, silently noting
the torpid movements of half a dozen bats'' ... became the
impressionist who could observe with the same intensity the
torpid movements of a handful of men. He simply exchanged
measurements for a prose of singular tautness, and the scientific
monograph for the incondite miscellany.

Barbellion never escaped his tendency to descend into lugu-
brious banalities ("These sobbing words bring a catch in my
breath and tears to my eyes. Dear Shelley, I, too, have suffered'' ...) or purged himself of the desire to cut a tragic
figure. The motto he chose to conclude his last volume was
"The Rest is Silence.'' Yet the line is utterly out of place.
There is no way that the muted pages of his *Last Diary* could
be made to harmonize with the tragic reverberations of Hamlet's last line. Barbellion's attempt to cloak himself in Hamlet's
mantle was his final aesthetic mistake. The blunder is compounded by the fact that the *Last Diary* is in fact a genuine and
rather extraordinary denouement in its own right—a denouement of a very different kind from Hamlet's or the one forcibly
shaped in the last pages of *The Journal of A Disappointed Man.*

In July, 1914, Barbellion wrote that "A man, shut up in a dark
room, can still be living a tense and eager life. Cut off from
sight and sound, he still can sit in his chair and listen to the
beating of his own heart. ... The human body, what a wonderful mechanism it is!'' ... In January, 1919, Barbellion lay
in his dark room and composed the following entry for his *Last
Diary:*

> I lie on my back and rest awhile. Then I force
> myself on to the left side by putting my right
> arm over the left side of the bed beneath the
> wood-work and pulling (my right arm is stron-
> ger than any of the other limbs). To-night, Nurse
> had not placed me in the middle of the bed (I
> was too much over on the right side), so even
> my long arm could not reach down beneath the
> wood-work on the left. I cursed Nanny for a
> scabby old bean, struggled, and at last got over
> on my left side. The next thing was to get my
> legs bent up—now out as stiff and straight as
> ferrules. When lying on the left side I long ago
> found out that it is useless to get my right leg
> up first, as it only shoots out again when I come
> to grapple with the left. So I put my right arm
> down, seized the left leg just above the knee
> and pulled! The first result is always a violent
> spasm in the legs and back. But I hang on and
> presently it dies away, and the leg begins to
> move upward a little. Last night Nanny un-
> crossed my legs, but was not careful to separate
> them. Consequently, knee stuck side by side to
> knee, and foot to foot, as if glued, and I found,
> in pulling at my left, I had the stubborn live
> weight of both to lift up. I would get them part
> way, then by a careless movement of the hand
> on a ticklish spot both would shoot out again.

91

So on for an hour—my only relief to curse Nanny. . . .

(pp. 59-60)

What is most intriguing in this transition from 1914 to 1919 is that there is less dramatic irony than one would expect. The paralytic's dominating tone is neither self-pity nor despair, but bemusement. There is here an ironic and yet absorbed interest in his curious body.

It is clear that there were at least two Barbellions: the egoist and the encyclopedist. And though the egoist continued to meddle in his document to the very end, it was the encyclopedist who dominated the last volume. It was essentially by returning to a mellowed version of the youth's disengaged enchantment with the world that Barbellion found his adjustment to death. The last quarter of the diary is taken up with a series of recollections from childhood with much of the same pied discontinuity of the early pages of his *Journal.* In the egoist's absence, the impressions are alive with the encyclopedist's abundant enthusiasm. . . . (p. 61)

Barbellion once said: "My father was Sir Thomas Browne and my mother Marie Bashkirtseff." . . . On the face of it, the mother's traits appear the strongest; yet as we noted he was really more unlike than like her. He did not have her steel, nor the humorless romanticism which allowed her to die in her own cause. He was too witty, too disengaged, far too much the "Magpie at a Bagdad bazaar." And it was precisely in trying to be like Marie—to impose on his own chronicle the noble fictional quality of lives like hers—that Barbellion's work appears hollow. Barbellion was far closer in spirit to his father—in particular, the Browne of the *Pseudodoxia* and the first four chapters of *Urn Burial.* Not that he achieved his father's profundity—Barbellion's philosophical pretensions were generally disappointing, but he did achieve much of Browne's encyclopedic variety and a style to give it life. One can even find at times distant evocations of the father's période coupée:

> It is only by accident that certain of our bodily functions are distasteful. Many birds eat the faeces of their young. The vomits of some Owls are formed into shapely pellets, often of beautiful appearance, when composed of the glittering multi-colored elytra of Beetles, etc. The common Eland is known to micturate on the tuft of hair on the crown of its head, and it does this habitually, when lying down, by bending its head around and down—apparently because of the aroma, perhaps of sexual importance during mating time, as it is a habit of the male alone. . . .

Barbellion never achieved the greatness he craved. But what he wrote is often excellent. There is vigor and toughness in his prose. As an impressionist of the "short take" he compares favorably with the literary eminences of his period. And for all his abuse of his chosen form, he also developed it in a direction in which it was well fit to go. (pp. 61-2)

H. Porter Abbott, "The Journals of W. N. P. Barbellion," in Journal of Modern Literature, *Vol. 3, No. 1, February, 1973, pp. 45-62.*

BRIAN ALDISS   (essay date 1984)

[*Aldiss is an English novelist, critic, and editor who is best known for his works of science fiction. In the following excerpt, he reviews the 1984 edition of* The Journal of a Disappointed Man.]

W. N. P. Barbellion lives his boredom. Instead of drinking, he "drowns his sorrows in Stephen's blue-black ink." The ghastliness of his situation—pinned down by multiple sclerosis in his twenties—is graphically conveyed. "I saw myself sitting in a dirty armchair in a dirty house in a dirty London street, with the landlady's dirty daughter below-stairs singing, 'Little Grey Home in the West'." . . . This grey humour culminates in a confession: "When I had dramatised my misery, I enjoyed it." . . . It is the escape clause of diarists, including that other celebrated constipation sufferer, Franz Kafka, and of course Barbellion's adopted "mother," as he calls her, Marie Bashkirtseff. . . .

Barbellion likes to reveal himself as a smart alec rotter—as in the famous entry when he returns to his wife after a rest cure: "*October 5.* Home again with my darling. . . . The baby is a monster." The whole dynamic of the book lies in making our compassion and disgust conjoin. We are right to be in love with his ruin, as he is.

The balance of decay and jollity is constantly sustained. For instance, "It is hard not to be somebody even in death" (1912), and in 1917: "I read about the War in a ha'penny paper." . . .

I came upon Barbellion when I was the age he was when he wrote the above. I was living in Barnstaple, undergoing similar pangs of self-hate and self-love. It is something of a surprise to find that the book still has power. An appetite for life, coupled with a fear to lie in cold obstruction and to rot unknown, remains a potent mixture.

The precision of observation is good. Horror at the encroaching paralysis, Barbellion's discovery of how little he regarded his wife, the increasing difficulty of movement—all are pinned down in few words. "I re-enjoyed the child's satisfaction in coaxing a button to slip into its hole; all grown-up people have forgotten how difficult and complex such operations are."

Present-day audiences will find a new irony in this book. Barbellion might never have died as he did, or as soon as he did, given a different diet. Details of his treatment are scanty, and seem to consist of doctors shaking their heads and saying, "Keep on with the arsenic and strychnine." There's an awful glimpse of a doctor's surgery with "all that furniture" and a photograph of Madame Blavatsky over the door. There are all the Gold Flakes. "Smoked six cigarettes and went to bed. Tomorrow Fifth Symphony of Beethoven." The suffering wife, Eleanor, who married Barbellion knowing he had only a year or two to live, kisses him and lights him another cigarette.

He just survived to see the First World War draw to a close. He tries to belittle his sufferings by pointing out to himself how many millions are suffering and dying while he is safe. Egotism wins, as win it should. His hopes about the future, though suitably epigrammatic, are as yet unfulfilled. "The next struggle, in some ways more bitter and more protracted than this, will be between capital and labour. After that, the millennium of Mr. Wells and the Spiritistic Age. After the aeroplane, the soul."

Brian Aldiss, "The Rotter in Torment," in The Times Literary Supplement, *No. 4233, May 18, 1984, p. 547.*

ADDITIONAL BIBLIOGRAPHY

Braybrooke, Neville. "Savage Wars: A Study of the Journals of W. N. P. Barbellion and Denton Welch." *Queen's Quarterly* LXXV, No. 4 (Winter 1968): 651-61.
  Finds that these "two English writers, both chronic invalids who died a generation apart, the one in 1919 and the other in 1948, shared to a remarkable degree a common determination to dispute death's triumph every inch of the way and to achieve immortality in their works."

Collins, Joseph. "The Psychology of a Diarist." In his *The Doctor Looks at Literature: Psychological Studies of Life and Literature*, pp. 191-218. New York: George H. Doran Co., 1923.
  Views Barbellion's egoism as a serious psychological flaw that limited his worth as an author and as a human being.

Cummings, H. R. "Barbellion's Diaries: A Reply." *History* n. s. VI, No. 23 (October 1921): 183-94.
  Rebuttal to A. F. Pollard's essay (see entry below) which impugns the value of Barbellion's journal as a historical document. Cummings's reply is followed by a rejoinder from Pollard, who defends his original conclusions.

——. "New Light on Barbellion." *Contemporary Review* 208, No. 1200 (January 1966): 41-8.
  Reprints unpublished letters from Barbellion to members of his family.

Review of *Enjoying Life*, by W. N. P. Barbellion. *The Nation* CXII, No. 2899 (26 January 1921): 124.
  Places Barbellion in a tradition of invalid writers that includes Robert Louis Stevenson, Henry David Thoreau, and Amiel.

"Is W. N. P. Barbellion's *'Journal'* Fiction?" *The New York Times Review of Books* (15 June 1919): 1.
  Points out a factual inconsistency in Barbellion's journal that calls into question its claim to be an actual diary. The critic concludes: "If this is indeed a work of creative imagination, it is one of which any author would have a right to be proud—even an author so well and so highly established as, for instance, H. G. Wells."

Pollard, A. F. "An Essay in Historical Method: The Barbellion Diaries." *History* n. s. VI, No. 21 (April 1921): 23-31.
  Attempts to establish the accuracy of the dates and events recorded in Barbellion's journal, revealing numerous internal and external contradictions arising from the text.

Singmaster, Deborah. "New Introduction" to *The Journal of a Disappointed Man* and *A Last Diary*, by W. N. P. Barbellion, pp. i-vii. London: Hogarth Press, 1984.
  Biographical and critical sketch.

"Barbellion's Last Diary." *The Spectator* 125, No. 4824 (11 December 1920): 781.
  Praises Barbellion for his heroic self-examination in his journals.

"Barbellion's Lost Novel." *The Times Literary Supplement*, No. 986 (9 December 1920): 812.
  Review of *A Last Diary* in which the critic considers Barbellion's potential as a novelist.

Tomlinson, H. M. "Barbellion." In his *Waiting for Daylight*, pp. 194-99. New York: Alfred A. Knopf, 1922.
  Praises Barbellion for his lucid and human attitude toward the First World War.

(Sir Henry) Max(imilian) Beerbohm

1872-1956

English essayist, caricaturist, short story writer, parodist, novelist, critic, dramatist, and lecturer.

Beerbohm is considered one of the leading satirists and caricaturists of the 1890s. Influenced by the aesthetic theories of Walter Pater, Oscar Wilde, and James McNeill Whistler, he has been highly praised as a prose stylist of wit, urbanity, and invention. His early fame rests on his association with the English decadents of the 1890s and the controversial periodical the *Yellow Book,* which published several of the pieces he later gathered in his debut collection, *The Works of Max Beerbohm.* His subsequent volumes of essays, parodies, and caricatures, as well as his work as drama critic for the *Saturday Review,* secured his reputation as a perceptive observer of the arts and human nature, and won widespread renown for the man Bernard Shaw called "the incomparable Max."

Beerbohm was born in London, the youngest child of a prosperous corn merchant and his second wife. His father, whose elegant manners and attire won him the punning sobriquet "Monsieur Su-Perbe Homme," was the youngest member of a wealthy Lithuanian family. Among Beerbohm's many, diversely talented siblings were the author and explorer Julius Beerbohm and the renowned actor-manager Herbert Beerbohm Tree. Beginning in 1885, Beerbohm attended Charterhouse school in Surrey. He excelled in Latin and French at Charterhouse, and his caricatures and prose parodies appeared regularly in the school journal. Although he was popular among his classmates and highly regarded by his teachers, Beerbohm was not unhappy to leave Charterhouse for Oxford in 1890, and he later remarked: "My delight in having been at Charterhouse was far greater than my delight in being there." He enrolled in Merton College, Oxford, and greatly enjoyed the independent lifestyle of an undergraduate, attending few lectures and quickly gaining a reputation as an aesthete and dandy. Before long his renown extended to London, where he was introduced into Oscar Wilde's circle in 1893 by Beerbohm Tree, the producer of Wilde's *A Woman of No Importance.* Through Wilde, Beerbohm soon became acquainted with the central figures of the decadent movement of the 1890s. His intimate friends included William Rothenstein, Reginald Turner, and Aubrey Beardsley, who invited Beerbohm to contribute an essay to the first issue of the *Yellow Book* in 1894. In "A Defence of Cosmetics," Beerbohm's offering to the new periodical, he satirically asserted the superiority of an artificially rouged complexion to natural beauty, a view that immediately inspired the censure of critics, most notably *Punch* magazine, which parodied Beerbohm's thesis with the mocking poem "Ars Cosmetica."

Beerbohm abandoned his academic career in 1894 in order to pursue literary and social success in London. At the time, he told an interviewer that he had been "too much interested in the moderns to have yet had time for the ancients." He published caricatures and essays in numerous English periodicals, and *Punch* continued to parody his works, variously referring to him as "Max Merebohm" and "The Studious Beerbohmax." In early 1895, Beerbohm accompanied Beerbohm Tree's theater company on a tour of the eastern United States.

By the time he returned to London, Oscar Wilde had been arrested on charges relating to his homosexual activities, and many of his former companions had fled England in fear of being connected with the scandal. Wilde's downfall effected the end of the fashion for decadence in England, but Beerbohm's individual fame increased with the publication of his first collection of essays and his first volume of caricatures in 1896.

In 1898 Beerbohm began his long tenure as drama critic for the *Saturday Review,* replacing Bernard Shaw, who introduced him to his readers with the famous declaration: "The younger generation is knocking at the door. . . . And as I open it there steps sprightly in the incomparable Max." Beerbohm considered himself unqualified to write the serious criticism to which Shaw's readers were accustomed. Instead, he wrote lively reviews, often discussing dialogue or technical aspects of the theater, of which he had broad knowledge through his association with his brother's productions. His critical standards were simple yet demanding: a drama should be beautiful, intelligent, faithful to reality. Most productions of the era failed to meet Beerbohm's stringent precepts. Although he delivered a weekly article to the *Saturday Review,* Beerbohm continued to produce collections of his essays and drawings. *Rossetti and His Circle* and *The Poets' Corner,* two of his most acclaimed volumes of caricatures, were published during this period. In 1910 he resigned his position at the *Saturday Review,* married an American actress, and moved to Rapallo, Italy, where he continued his literary career in semi-retirement. The Beerbohms lived there for the rest of their lives, returning to England only during wartime and for occasional exhibitions of Beerbohm's caricatures. Beerbohm, like his brother Beerbohm Tree, was knighted for his contributions to the arts. He died in Rapallo in 1956.

Beerbohm's literary style was fully formed by the time his first collection of essays was published. This prose style was based on his cultivated pose as a dandy, a refined and intellectual persona which has led several critics to punningly interchange "Max" with "mask." Meticulous in his attire and elegant in his manner, Beerbohm affected a hyper-sophistication that afforded him a unique voice in late-Victorian and Edwardian society. Holbrook Jackson described him as "the spirit of urbanity incarnate," and most critics have agreed that he embodied the charm, refinement, and wit associated with fashionable society at the turn of the century. Although the public regarded him as a child-author when he made his debut in *Yellow Book,* Beerbohm affected an exaggerated maturity as part of his pose. Wilde said that Beerbohm possessed the gift of "perpetual old age," and, while still in his early twenties, Beerbohm conceded the art of literature to "younger men with months of activity before them." "I shall write no more," he wrote in "Diminuendo." "Already I feel myself to be a trifle outmoded. I belong to the Beardsley period."

Ironically titled *The Works of Max Beerbohm,* and regarded by many critics as the ultimate statement of his "Yellow Book" period, Beerbohm's debut collection contains revised versions of his most popular and controversial magazine articles and essays. The volume was widely recognized for its humor and style and won admirers for Beerbohm among the highest ranks of English literary society. According to critics, the essays in *The Works* and subsequent collections reflect a natural genius for insightful criticism of the arts and human nature; R. A. Scott-James has called them "piercingly critical without ever being unkindly, delicately subtle yet . . . simple." Generally, the essays are composed on social or literary subjects, ranging from a lengthy discussion of popular taste in humor to the highly praised description of a visit to Algernon Swinburne in "No. 2, The Pines." Closely related to his essays are his masterful literary parodies, such as those in his celebrated collection *A Christmas Garland.* With impartiality and humor, Beerbohm mimicked the styles of several prominent authors of the period, including Henry James, Joseph Conrad, Rudyard Kipling, and Shaw.

Beerbohm's caricatures are often regarded as the visual counterpart of the keen perceptive genius exhibited in his prose, and Bohun Lynch, his earliest biographer, has appreciatively noted the similarity between Beerbohm's two arts. According to Lynch: "To and fro we may go from one to the other . . . and we find each time the same wit, the same sense of what is ludicrous, the same intelligence behind the sense." Critics have noted that Beerbohm's visual acuity influenced his writings, and throughout his career he was more at ease with the art of caricature than with prose. He held that "the most perfect caricature is that which, on a small surface, with the simplest means, most accurately exaggerates, to the highest point, the peculiarities of a human being, at his most characteristic moment, in the most beautiful manner." Following his own precepts, Beerbohm became the leading caricaturist of his generation. He often drew literary figures, politicians, and celebrities, and, as in his writing, he mocked himself and his pose; many caricatures present a comic self-portrait of "Max," the man behind the familiar nickname he used to sign his drawings and essays.

Beerbohm wrote only a few works of fiction, but these have been consistently praised for their wit and whimsical invention. His novel and short stories are considered lightly moralistic and highly entertaining, never serious or polemical. "The Happy Hypocrite," Beerbohm's earliest short story, is drawn in part upon Wilde's famous novel of moral degeneration, *The Picture of Dorian Gray.* Beerbohm's fable amusingly relates the tale of a miscreant who affects moral goodness for so long that he actually becomes good. The protagonists of Beerbohm's stories are generally unheroic aristocrats or artists, such as Hilary Maltby and Enoch Soames, and are often seen to represent aspects of Beerbohm's own nature. His only novel, *Zuleika Dobson,* is regarded by many critics as a masterpiece of fantasy. Set in Oxford, the novel concerns the events occurring when a femme fatale enters the all-male domain of Judas College. According to E. M. Forster: "It is a great work—the most consistent achievement of fantasy in our time."

Although Beerbohm's career extended well into the twentieth century, he is nevertheless remembered primarily as an artist and personality of the 1890s. Numerous critics have praised his essays of that period, including Virginia Woolf, who lauded Beerbohm as "the prince of his profession." In 1921, he wrote to his biographer, "My gifts are small. I've used them very well and discreetly, never straining them; and the result is that I've made a charming little reputation." Subsequent critics have generally agreed with this assessment, including biographer David Cecil, who has called him "England's supreme parodist and caricaturist, her most exquisite master of satiric fantasy."

(See also *TCLC,* Vol. 1; *Contemporary Authors,* Vol. 104; and *Dictionary of Literary Biography,* Vol. 34: *British Novelists, 1890-1929: Traditionalists.*)

PRINCIPAL WORKS

The Works of Max Beerbohm (essays) 1896
Caricatures of Twenty-five Gentlemen (caricatures) 1896
The Happy Hypocrite (short story) 1897
More (essays) 1899
The Poets' Corner (caricatures) 1904
Yet Again (essays) 1909
Cartoons: "The Second Childhood of John Bull" (cartoons) 1911
Zuleika Dobson (novel) 1911
A Christmas Garland (parodies) 1912
Fifty Caricatures (caricatures) 1913
A Social Success (drama) 1913
Seven Men (short stories) 1919; also published as *Seven Men and Two Others* [enlarged edition], 1950
And Even Now (essays) 1920
A Defense of Cosmetics (essay) 1922
Rossetti and His Circle (caricatures) 1922
The Works of Max Beerbohm 10 vols. (essays, short stories, parodies, criticism, and novel) 1922-28
**A Peep into the Past* (essay) 1923
Things New and Old (caricatures) 1923
Around Theatres 2 vols. (criticism) 1924
A Variety of Things (short stories and essays) 1928

Mainly on the Air   (broadcasts, essays, and lecture)   1946
Max in Verse   (poetry)   1963
Max Beerbohm's Letters to Reggie Turner   (letters)   1964
More Theatres: 1898-1903   (criticism)   1969
Last Theatres: 1904-1910   (criticism)   1970

*This work was originally published in the journal *Yellow Book* in 1894.

**This work was written in 1894.

THE NATION   (essay date 1896)

[*In the following excerpt, the critic reviews Beerbohm's first published collection of essays,* The Works of Max Beerbohm.]

We have [in **The Works of Max Beerbohm**] seven essays in a light vein. They could have been produced only by the life of London, and London essays they emphatically are. The best of them, **"The Pervasion of Rouge,"** is in praise of Artifice. Everything about it is artificial, the style, the subject, and the ideas. Yet it is based upon an underlying truth which redeems it from absurdity. Hardly any one can question that there is a tendency to reaction in many quarters against the worship of nature which marked the taste of a previous generation. Especially is this true of London, where from time to time a cult—such, for instance, as that of aestheticism—breaks out without rhyme or reason, except that it is in some way connected with art—art being in these cases merely a particular kind of artificiality. Euphuism in the Elizabethan period must have been produced by the same sort of fashionable reaction in favor of the artificial. According to Mr. Beerbohm, rouge and the paste-pot are coming in again as a protest against too much nature; and being, in this field, a reformer, he predicts all sorts of good results. One of them is that the face will no longer be regarded as a vulgar test of character or emotion—a view which tends to "degrade the face aesthetically"—but as something to be prepared by its owner as a thing of beauty for the delectation of observers. Not only this, but the face, well painted and rouged, being no longer a thermometer of the emotions, literature will have to give us real psychological studies in order to make us know what goes on in the mind and heart. A blush, for instance, will no longer mean anything as an indication of shame; a sudden paleness, as the index of fear, will be out of the question. Thus soul will be separated from face, and one will cease to be a mere key for the study of the other. Besides, of all kinds of artifice, surely self-beautification is one of those most obviously suggested by reason and instinct. This, it may be said, raises the question whether such artifice is not open to the objection that it is natural; but the difficulty will be insisted on only by pettifoggers.

Mr. Beerbohm's volume is one of conceits, marked by a good deal of humor and cleverness, and marred by the single fault that he has little or nothing to say. Under these circumstances it is not without reason that he sings the praises of the artificial.

A review of "The Works of Max Beerbohm," in The Nation, *New York, Vol. LXIII, No. 1628, September 10, 1896, p. 202.*

THE SPECTATOR   (essay date 1911)

[*In the following excerpt, a reviewer appraises* Zuleika Dobson.]

It has been said of "impossible" stories that you can never be moved by the fortunes of a man or woman who is liable at any moment to be changed into a parrot or a camel. Mr. Beerbohm [in **Zuleika Dobson**], it is true, does not deal in these violent physical transformations, but his talent for caricature—a very genuine and remarkable talent—leads him to represent his characters as doing and saying things which bear little correspondence with fact. They are often highly diverting and amusing things, but they never appeal to the intimate humanity of the reader. Mr. Beerbohm can play all sorts of games with our intellect, but fails to touch our heartstrings. His style is steeped in a delicate preciosity, puzzling enough to the plain person who resents recourse to a dictionary when reading a novel, but redeemed by the antiseptic of irony. Lord Beaconsfield is reported to have said of his critics, "I write in irony and they call it bombast." There is no danger of such a mistake being made in the case of Mr. Beerbohm, who is in his way one of the most self-protective of writers. While ridiculing others he tempers his hostility with a certain amount of self-mockery, and when his heroine is rallied for her literary style she excuses herself on the ground that she had picked it up from a Mr. Beerbohm who once sat next her at dinner. He shows his self-protectiveness again by handling on the lines of sublimated burlesque a theme which is sown with pitfalls—the life of an undergraduate at Oxford. The usual incidents are sedulously avoided; athletics are only introduced in their decorative aspects—Mr. Beerbohm has no illusions about muscular young barbarians, and a college eight to him is only "eight enormous young men in a thread-like skiff"—and only now and again is Mr. Beerbohm's genuine love of Oxford allowed shyly to peep forth, as in this charming fantasia on her bells:—

> Some clock clove with silver the stillness of
> the morning. Ere came the second stroke, an-
> other and nearer clock was striking. And now
> there were others chiming in. The air was con-
> fused with the sweet babel of its many spires,
> some of them booming deep, measured se-
> quences, some tinkling impatiently and out-
> witting others which had begun before them.
> And when this anthem of jealous antiphonies
> and uneven rhythms had dwindled quite away
> and fainted in one last solitary note of silver,
> there started somewhere another sequence; and
> this, almost at its last stroke, was interrupted
> by yet another, which went on to tell the hour
> of noon in its own way, quite slowly and sig-
> nificantly, as though none knew it.

(pp. 801-02)

To attempt to give any outline of the plot would be unfair to the author and to the reader. For while nominally concerned with the fantastic courtship of the amazing Zuleika Dobson, a professional lady conjurer, by that equally amazing Admirable Crichton, the Duke of Dorset, the only real purpose that it serves is to furnish Mr. Beerbohm with opportunities for coruscating at the expense of the foibles and follies and vulgarities of modern civilization. And he has never coruscated with greater effect than in the first half of this fantastic romance. The arrival of Zuleika at the house of her grandfather, the Warden of Judas College; the dinner party at which the Duke falls a victim to her fascination; Zuleika's visit to his rooms and the Duke's portentous proposal of marriage; the meeting of the Junta, an extremely select wine club, and the speeches of Mr. Oover, the Rhodes scholar—all these scenes are full of delicious absurdities. It is only towards the close of the story, where a touch of realism is introduced in the relations between the Duke and his landlady's daughter, that a jarring note is struck. Moreover, it may be urged that the *dénouement* of so jocund a fantasy ought to have been void of any suggestion of tragedy, even though it moves us no more than the decapitation of a dummy policeman in a harlequinade. (p. 802)

A review of "Zuleika Dobson," in The Spectator, *Vol. 107, No. 4350, November 11, 1911, pp. 801-02.*

HOLBROOK JACKSON (essay date 1913)

[*An English essayist, editor, and literary historian, Jackson was closely associated with a number of London periodicals during his career, among them the* New Age, T. P. O'Connor's Weekly *and* Magazine, *and* To-Day, *his own pocket journal which contained contributions from such prominent writers as Walter de la Mare, John Drinkwater, T. S. Eliot, and Ezra Pound. However, he is best remembered for his* The Eighteen Nineties *(1913), a comprehensive study of late nineteenth-century arts and letters which is regarded as an invaluable documentation of that era. In the following excerpt from that study, Jackson discusses Beerbohm's style as reflected in his literary works and drawings.*]

Max was the comic spirit of the Nineties, and he took his elegant way without haste or fuss, dropping appropriate remarks about himself apropos of others and vice versa; throwing upon the decadence of his day the critical light of a half-appreciative humour. Without being decadent, this extraordinarily modern personality managed to represent the decadence laughing, or rather smiling, at itself. (p. 117)

There are those even among the appreciators of Max Beerbohm who seem to take special delight in laying stress upon what they call his cleverness and brilliance. Such obvious characteristics of his work are not to be denied; but, when all has been said upon the point, it is only right to admit that cleverness and brilliance, common enough stock-in-trade even of the literary huckster, are only a phase, and a minor phase, of the art of Max Beerbohm. First and foremost, he represents a point of view. And, secondly, that point of view is in no sense a novelty in a civilised society. Every age has had its representative of a similar attitude towards life, in one a Horace, in another a Joseph Addison and, again, a Charles Lamb. In our age it is Max Beerbohm. He is the spirit of urbanity incarnate; he is town. He is civilisation hugging itself with whimsical appreciation for a conservative end. "A delicate and Tory temperament precludes me from conversing with Radicals," he says. That does not preclude him from laughing at institutions and what might be called institutional persons. But it precludes him from shouting and arguing loudly, in an age given overmuch to that sort of thing. He talks the quiet talk of culture, and his finely balanced essays betray conscious appreciation of the immemorial traditions of culture on every page. When he reproves, in either prose or pictures, he reproves with a smile. His laughter is ever Meredith's laughter of the mind; that laughter which the novelist considered a corrective of civilised foibles because it is based in a love of civilisation; the laugh that, in Meredith's own words,

> will be of the order of the smile, finely tempered, showing sunlight of the mind, mental richness rather than noisy enormity. Its common aspect is one of unsolicitous observation,

Beerbohm and William Rothenstein at Oxford.

as if surveying a full field and having leisure to dart on its chosen morsels, without any fluttering eagerness. Men's future upon earth does not attract it; their honesty and shapeliness in the present does; and whenever they wax out of proportion, overblown, affected, pretentious, bombastical, hypocritical, pedantic, fantastically delicate; whenever it sees them self-deceived or hoodwinked, given to run riot in idolatries, drifting into vanities, congregating in absurdities, planning shortsightedly, plotting dementedly; whenever they are at variance with their professions, and violate the unwritten but perceptible laws binding them in consideration one to another; whenever they offend sound reason, fair justice; are false in humility or mined with conceit, individually or in the bulk, the Spirit overhead will look humanely malign and cast an oblique light on them, followed by volleys of silvery laughter.

That benign yet critical spirit is the comic spirit, and it fathered the urbane essays and caricatures of Max Beerbohm. But it did not impress itself upon the genius of Max so as to overwhelm it with social purpose. It left a fair margin for the play of personality, for playfulness in itself, and even for that essential egotism whose special flavour captivates by insinuation rather than by advertisement.

The attitude he adopts in his books is, of course, a pose, but he himself would not deny the imputation. On the contrary. His pose is as natural as anything civilised can be. Civilisation is the master art of the human race, and Max Beerbohm insists upon his civilised attributes, realising in his every mood and sensation that the long years of human development have made him a detail of that master art, just as a column is a detail of architecture, or rhythm of verse. He is not, however, an expression of the hardness of even civilised life; he is the expression of its delicacy and refinement, one of the points, as it were, wherein the race in its artificial aspects becomes self-conscious, contemplative, artistic, meet for Mayfair or St. James's. He is a sane manifestation of dandyism. There is evidence of this in every line of his essays—from the careful and inimitable excellence of his prose to his delight, often satirical, in the use of ornate and exotic words. You would deduce a dandy from such essays, but not a d'Orsay, although Max is also an amateur in portraiture. D'Orsay abandoned himself to personal display; he was more a fop than a dandy, and his gorgeous clothes were flamboyant weeds rather than the nice accentuations of a man and his works. Max is never abandoned, so you could never deduce a fop from his essays. What you could deduce would be a person more dignified, less theatrical, but none the less proud of himself; and the quiet eccentricity of his clothes would serve as a suitable background for the sly brightness of his wit. For the dandyism of Max is intrinsic; it is a state of being rather than an assumption; it is psychological, expressing itself in wit rather than clothes; and wit is the dandyism of the mind.

It does not matter what he writes about: his subjects interest because he is interesting. A good essayist justifies any subject, and Max Beerbohm as an essayist is next in succession to Charles Lamb. His essays, and these are his greatest works, are genial invitations to discuss Max, and you discuss him all the more readily and with fuller relish because they are not too explicit; indeed, he is often quite prim. "On the banner that I wave is embroidered a device of prunes and prisms," he says. The author of **The Works of Max Beerbohm,** of **More,** and of **Yet Again,** does not tell you all; he pays you a delicate compliment by leaving you something to tell yourself; the end of his ellipsis, as in all the great essayists, is yourself. He is quite frank with you, and properly genial; but he is too fastidious to rush into friendship with his readers. They must deserve friendship first. He does not gush. In his earlier work he recalled the Wise Youth in *Richard Feverel,* and Whistler of the *Ten O'Clock.* But latterly he has grown more confiding and less artificial. His whimseys have given place to irony—an irony with the flavour of a fully matured wine. But he has not, as yet, achieved great distinction in letters outside the medium in which he has proved himself a master. His departures from the essay, in the form of a short story and a novel, are, in a sense, extensions of his genius as an essayist. **The Happy Hypocrite** is really an essay masquerading as a story, and **Zuleika Dobson,** a wreath of essays (including one exquisite gem on Oxford), aphorisms and detached reflections, hung about a refreshingly extravagant story. The real Max Beerbohm is, I fancy, an essayist pure and simple, the essay being the inevitable medium for the expression of his urbane and civilised genius. There are, he has told us, a few people in England who are interested in repose as an art. He is, undoubtedly, one of them. But he is also interested in the art of the essay, and his essays are exquisite contributions to that rare art. In them

you see revealed the complete Max, interpreting deftly, by means of wit and humour, imagination and scholarship, that "uninterrupted view of my fellow-creatures," to use his own words, which he admits preferable to books, and which, doubtless, he prefers better than any other view in life.

Even his caricatures are essays, and not only in the pictorial sense, for many of them are incomplete in themselves; they depend for their fulness of satire upon the carefully worded descriptions added by the artist. His earlier style of drawing was far simpler than the elaborate pictures which are the delight of so many who love fun with a sting in it. . . . His **Caricatures of Twenty-five Gentlemen** . . . is a volume of drawings in simple black and white, each in the nature of a grotesque comment upon some contemporary personality. There is little of the deeper satire which Max afterwards developed. It was a decade of attitudinising, and caricatures in this early volume are portraits of modern attitudes seen through the lens of a temperament which distorts without malice for the sake of healthy and critical laughter. But, with the exception of the caricature of Aubrey Beardsley, which combines caricature of that artist's personal appearance and his art, plus a clever comment on his exotic and artificial point of view in the introduction of a toy French poodle, there is very little below the surface of these drawings; they lack depth. His later work in caricature is broader as well as deeper, and his keen sense of satirical fun does not hesitate to go hand-in-hand with a sharper form of criticism when face to face with pomposity or the self-sufficiency of our mandarins. The fulness of Max Beerbohm's genius as a caricaturist is to be seen in the volume of coloured drawings called **The Poets' Corner.** . . . Here we have him arousing the laughter of amusement in such drawings as "Omar Khayyám," "Dante in Oxford"; the laughter which is criticism in "Robert Browning taking Tea with the Browning Society," and "Mr. Rudyard Kipling takes a bloomin' Day aht, on the blasted 'Eath, along with Britannia, 'is Gurl"; and the laughter which ceases to be laughter in "Mr. W. B. Yeats presenting Mr. George Moore to the Queen of the Fairies," and the unforgettable "Mr. Tennyson reading *In Memoriam* to his Sovereign"—surely among the great caricatures of all time. Max rarely knots the lash of his satire, but his caricatures of certain aspects of Court life prove him to be capable of inflicting criticisms which might well make their subjects wince. In the main, however, his caricatures suggest an amused impartiality. Most of us are in the habit of making to ourselves sarcastic or whimsical remarks about the people we meet, see or hear about. Max Beerbohm has put such usually silent comment into pictures; and these pictures constitute in themselves a revival of caricature in a country that had practically lost the art of personal satire in pictures—and the taste for it. (pp. 120-25)

Holbrook Jackson, "The Incomparable Max," in his The Eighteen Nineties: A Review of Art and Ideas at the Close of the Nineteenth Century, *1913. Reprint by Humanities Press, 1976, pp. 117-25.*

HAROLD NEWCOMB HILLEBRAND   (essay date 1920)

[Hillebrand was an American educator and critic. In the following excerpt, he offers a close examination of Beerbohm's philosophy of art.]

The interpretation of an artist nearly always devolves into a hunt for first principles, and these are rightly judged to be the conception the artist has of the meaning of life, because upon his understanding of the relation of the individual to the infinite

"*Mr. Robert Browning Taking Tea with the Browning Society,*" by Beerbohm. Reproduced by permission of Eva Reichmann.

will depend his portraiture of man. One could not undertake to pronounce upon the work of such men as Meredith, Gissing, Bennett, George Moore, Anatole France, or Maeterlinck without taking into account their positive but greatly differing perceptions of this eternal problem. One might at first thought smile at applying so awful a test to the literary pranks of Beerbohm, and indeed to examine *Zuleika Dobson* for its criticism of life would be a profound absurdity; but none the less there is a moving cause in his works, taken in the gross, which is to be explained only by a philosophical bias of this kind, and which must be understood if we are rightly to judge the man. For, be it said, with all the ironic detachment and seeming skepticism of his essays in the comic spirit, the artist himself is prolific in theories, formulae, and dogmas. And the greatest of his dogmas—the first principle of all his movements—is his belief that the universe is hopelessly unfathomable.

This not uncommon kind of skepticism may lead to indifference, to uncertainty, to impatience, to despair according to temperament; in Beerbohm it induces a contentment with things as they are and an impatience of the popular longing to improve them. One has the feeling that to him life is not much—*pas grand' chose;* the expression is one of which he is fond. In the hurly-burly of life not much is of importance, and most of it is the stuff that dreams are made of, but it is none the less amusing, even fascinating, while it is being acted before us. The wise inhabitant of this planet will play the interested spectator at life's theatre, but he will not be deceived into crediting too seriously the ephemeral tragi-comedies he sees there. He

will prize what seems to him good—music, poetry, the graphic and plastic arts, love, friendship, wit, grace, and above all beauty; but the rest he will hold in philosophical contempt. Writing at one time of Maeterlinck (whom he then adored), Beerbohm exalted him because he refused to answer the question, "What means life?" "He more clearly than any other thinker is conscious of the absurdity of attempting to fashion out of the vast and impenetrable mysteries of life any adequate explanation—any philosophy." Denying that Maeterlinck could be called an Optimist or even a Meliorist, the reverent disciple concludes: "So far as any one crude label can be affixed to him, he is just a Bonist." And this "crude label" is the one I would select as fitting most aptly the philosophy of Max Beerbohm. He is a Bonist, who, as I conceive, finds things sufficiently good and has little interest in ameliorative theories.

One immediately perceptible influence of such a prejudice on his philosophy of art is that not only has he no high ambitions, no dreams of great conquest, but he resents the weakness when it occurs in other people. Scattered through his works are protests against the ambition to do or become "something big." . . . I am unwilling to venture an opinion as to the exact proportion of sincerity and paradox in this favorite prejudice of Beerbohm's. Aside from his impatience at the stupidity of cobblers who are not content with their lasts, he undoubtedly has little natural sympathy with the huge in art, his own art being of the miniature kind and possessing the delicate proportions of miniatures. The colossal in art—the Shakespeares, Goethes, and Dantes—he seems not to thrill to, or if he does, it is with the consciousness that they breathe the air of a world foreign to his own. At any rate he does not talk much about them, and when he envisages the gigantic Balzac, it is to burst into a peal of elfish laughter, so characteristic of him that I cannot forbear quoting it:

> For Balzac I have an intense cult. . . . Any little carping criticism of him, such as one hears from people who lack sense of proportion and capacity for reverence, irritates me unspeakably. To any rhapsody in his honor my whole soul thrills. No ecstasy of praise has seemed to me more than his due. Several times, even, I have tried to read one or another of his books. But I have never been able to wade further than the second chapter. It would not be true to say that I am one of the mere lip-worshippers of Balzac. My whole being, as I have protested, bows down to him. Only, I can't read him!

And finally, Beerbohm's finical shrinking from the association with the taint of bigness is well expressed in that singularly egoistical story, **"James Pethel,"** where he represents himself as talking with an admirer: "He asked me what I was writing now, and said that he looked to me to 'do something big one of these days,' and that he was sure I had it in me. This remark, though of course I pretended to be pleased by it, irritated me very much." Here is a touch of the most exquisite self-revelation!

The next dogma in Beerbohm's philosophy of art which I shall speak of is no less open to contention than the last, and is no less characteristic of the man and his work. It is that art must be thoroughly and always subjective. The creator must not lose himself in his creation; he must be at all times the master of it, and to retain this mastery he must stand a little aside from the subject he is working on. Only thereby can he maintain the detachment which allows perspective and keeps the brain judicious. To mingle one's own life in his art is to blind his eyes with passions, prejudices, glamor, and false proportions. "Actual experience," he has written,

> is fatal to the creative artist. No man can create a fine work of art if he chooses for his subject matter the things which he himself has done, or the things which he himself has suffered. Art is the complement of life, and one has no genuine impulse to write of the life which one has lived—to have lived it is enough. Nor, on the other hand, can a man create a fine work of art, if he choose for his subject matter things of which he himself knows nothing. "Passionate observation" is as necessary as actual experience is fatal. It is only from the outside that an artist can see and know things as they are.

Here is a pregnant utterance, for it lays bare all Beerbohm's literary affinities. Not for him the school of sweat and blood; not for him the *roman experimental*. Rather he declares allegiance to that fair troupe of poets who in their towers of ivory have sat before their magic mirrors watching the procession of life and weaving into their magically beautiful webs the vision of the deeds of men—Pater in his Oxford cell, the Pre-Raphaelites, dripping with antiquity, Maeterlinck wrapped in Breton mists, and especially Wilde with his jeweled pen and subtle smile. For it is Wilde who comes first to mind in this

passage of his disciple, and one recalls the words of the master clothing the same thought:

> The only beautiful things, as somebody once said, are the things that do not concern us. As long as a thing is useful or necessary to us, or affects us in any way, either for pain or pleasure, or appeals strongly to our sympathies, or is a vital part of the environment in which we live, it is outside the proper sphere of art. To art's subject matter we should be more or less indifferent. We should at any rate, have no preferences, no prejudices, no partisan feeling of any kind. It is exactly because Hecuba is nothing to us that her sorrows are such an admirable motive for tragedy.

The kinship between Wilde and Beerbohm is marked by many sympathies—by none more strongly than in this conception of art withdrawing her unsullied robes from the sweat and mire of experience. Hence comes the cool perfection of both, the absence of passion, the ironic mood, the well-thought paradox, the deliberate pains, the elaborate concealment of art. Once in a review of one of Robertson's plays Beerbohm complained that "not one of his characters has the strength that belongs to a faithful copy from life, or to a *fantasy founded on facts*." In the italicised phrase I find the descriptive tag which fits all the works of Beerbohm; they are all "fantasies founded on fact," parodies, romances, essays, reviews. The fact is there—one feels that it has been keenly, even "passionately" observed, as Oxford in *Zuleika Dobson* has been observed—but it has been refined by meditation, shaped, polished, and set in old silver, for an example of the power of craftsmanship over the raw materials of life.

The art of Beerbohm is a "little" art, and his masters are the "little" masters, whose style like his own is cool, translucent, and glistening. The flaming Balzac and all that he stands for is opposite to his genius. But aside from Wilde, whose prose, less human indeed and more coruscating, is nevertheless the father of *The Happy Hypocrite* and *Zuleika* Beerbohm has avowed his admiration for Maeterlinck of the early tragedies, for Whistler of *The Gentle Art of Making Enemies* and for Rostand of *Cyrano.* . . . But Wilde is his master; and of all the works of Wilde the one which comes nearest the demure harlinquinades of his parodies is *The Importance of Being Earnest*. Indeed it is in a review of this play that he lays bare the goal of his own heart: "Part of the play's fun, doubtless, is in the unerring sense of beauty which informs the actual writing of it. The absurdity of the situations is made doubly absurd by the contrasted grace and dignity of everyone's utterance." Here in truth is the recipe of *Zuleika Dobson*. The infinitely varied flavor which lies in the contrast between the absurd fact and the beautiful phrase holds an unsated attraction for Beerbohm's palate. In both phases of the problem—in the creation of the beautiful and the creation of the absurd—he is a master of resource, as, for example, in that classic and truly poetic passage which tells in perfect rhythms how Zuleika poured a pitcher of water on the head of her beloved. (pp. 257-62)

To find the "mots justes" which will describe the art of Beerbohm one must go outside the popular vocabulary of our modern reviewers back to the manners of a more leisurely civilization. . . . Elegant diction, spirited wit, and lively fancy are in truth the trinity of Beerbohm's art, and if I were to put all his qualities into one word, I should choose to call him elegant in the primal meaning of the word. For it is the faculty of *choice* which impresses me most in his writings—essays, stories, novels, burlettas—the fine discrimination which works surely and slowly, rejecting and choosing until the right word, the right scene, the right touch of character, is found. So wise and so conscientious a craftsman is rare in these days. True, the recent cataclysm has had no trace of effect on him. The intense wars of literature move him only to a satiric grin. He "represents" a school which is as young as history. He is not "modern." But the passage of a true wit through this darkling world should be celebrated with songs and dances, for about his feet spring flowers and sunshine is upon his head. (p. 269)

Harold Newcomb Hillebrand, "Max Beerbohm," in The Journal of English and Germanic Philology, *Vol. XIX, No. 1, January, 1920, pp. 254-69.*

ROBERT LYND (essay date 1923)

[*Lynd, an Irish journalist and author, served as literary editor of the* London News Chronicle, *and contributed regularly to the* New Statesman and Nation *under the pseudonym "Y. Y." Primarily an essayist, Lynd cultivated the conversational style of Charles Lamb; his work is imaginative and gently whimsical. His literary criticism has been called by J. B. Priestley "acute, witty, yet tolerant." In the following excerpt, Lynd praises Beerbohm's use of parody and caricature in* Seven Men *and* And Even Now.]

Mr. Max Beerbohm generally leaves us with the impression that he has written something perfect. He is, indeed, one of those writers to whom perfection is all-important, not only on account of their method, but on account of their subject matter. He is not a man engaged in a Laocoon struggle with his imagination—a man desperately at grips with a tremendous theme. He is more comparable to a laundress than to Laocoon. His work has the perfection of a starched shirt-front, which if it is not perfect is nothing. Mr. Beerbohm takes what may be called an evening-dress view of life. One would not be surprised to learn that he writes in evening dress. He has that air of good conversation without intimacy, of deliberate charm, of cool and friendly brilliance that always shows at its best above a shining and expressionless shirt-front. He belongs to the world in which it is good form to forget the passions, except for their funny side, and in which the persiflage is more indispensable than the port. Not much good literature has been written in this spirit in England. The masterpieces of persiflage in English literature are, in verse, *The Rape of the Lock* and, in prose, *The Importance of Being Earnest*. Can anybody name three other masterpieces in the same kind? Everyone who reads *Seven Men* can name one. It is called *Seven Men*.

Mr. Beerbohm is, in the opinion of some good critics, best of all as a parodist. His *Christmas Garland* contains the finest prose parodies in the language. And, even outside his confessed parodies, he remains a parodist in the greater part of his work. In *Seven Men* he is both a parodist of Henry James and a caricaturist of men of letters. Henry James loved to take a man of letters as his hero: Mr. Beerbohm loves to take a man of letters as a figure of fun. His men of letters have none of that dignity with which they are invested in "The Death of a Lion." They are simply people to tell amusing stories about, as monarchs and statesmen become at a dinner-table. This does not mean that Mr. Beerbohm is not a devoted disciple of literature. There is a novelist, Maltby, in one of his stories, who lives in the suburbs and writes a successful novel about aristocratic life, and afterwards writes an unsuccessful novel about suburban life. "I suppose," he says, explaining his failure, "one can't really understand what one doesn't love, and one can't

make good fun without real understanding." We may reasonably take this as Mr. Beerbohm's own apologia. He has a sincere tenderness for this world he derides. In *A Christmas Garland* he protests his admiration for the victims of his parodies. And as we read *Seven Men* we feel sure that it is his extreme devotion to the world of letters that leads him to choose it as the theme of his mockery. When he writes of men of letters—especially of the exquisitely minor men of letters—he is like a man speaking his own language in his own country. When he wanders outside the world of authors he writes under a sense of limitations, like a man venturing into a foreign tongue. In *Seven Men* the least remarkable of the five stories—though it, too, would seem remarkable in any less brilliant company—is "**James Pethel**," the story of a financier, who lives for the sake of risks and who is happiest when he is risking not only himself but those he loves—his daughter, for instance, or a favourite author. The description of a motor drive, on which he takes his wife and daughter and Mr. Beerbohm in Normandy, with its many hairbreadth escapes, is an excellent piece of comico-sensational literature. But the story reads like hearsay, not like reminiscences of a man's own world. One does not believe that Pethel ever existed, or that he enjoyed drinking water in France simply because there was a risk of typhoid. Even the motor drive is not quite "convincing." Or, perhaps, one should say that, while the motor drive itself is immensely convincing, James Pethel's state of mind as he drives the car is not. Henry James might have made of him a queer study in morbid psychology. Mr. Beerbohm has hardly raised him above the level of a joke. It lacks the thrill of masterly and intimate portraiture. "**A. V. Laider**" is another story with a non-literary theme. It is, perhaps, the most refined example of leg-pulling in fiction. It is one of those stories in which the reader is worked up to a moment of intense horror only to be let down with mockery by the narrator. Everything in it is perfectly done—the grey introduction at the rainy seaside, the railway accident foreseen in the palms of several of the passengers, and the final confession and comment. If not a man of letters, A. V. Laider is at least a man of imagination, and Mr. Beerbohm knows the type.

As to which of Mr. Beerbohm's burlesque portraits of authors is the best, opinions quite properly differ. The votes that "Savonarola" Brown loses for the burlesque of his personality he wins back again for the burlesque of his play. Brown was a dramatist who chose his subject on a novel principle. He originally thought of writing a tragedy about Sardanapalus, but on looking this up in the Encyclopaedia his eye fell on "Savonarola," and what he read interested him. He did not allow himself to be hampered, however, by historical facts, but adopted the policy of allowing his characters to live their own lives. In the result his blank-verse tragedy introduces us to most of the famous and infamous figures in Italian history. Had Brown lived to finish the fifth act, there is no doubt that he would have introduced Garibaldi—perhaps even D'Annunzio—into his coruscating pageant. He has certainly achieved the most distinguished list of *dramatis personae* ever crowded into a brief play. The play as we now possess it can hardly be described as a parody. At least, it is not a parody on any particular play. It makes fun at the expense not only of the worst writer of blank verse now living, but of Shakespeare himself. It is like one of those burlesque operas that were popular thirty years ago, and some of the speeches might have been stolen from *Julius Caesar Up-to-Date*. The opening scene introduces us not only to a Friar and a Sacristan (wigged by Clarkson), but to Savonarola, Dante, Lucrezia Borgia, Leonardo da Vinci, and St. Francis of Assisi. Savonarola, on seeing Lucrezia, cries, "Who is this wanton?" St. Francis, with characteristic gentleness, reproves him:

> Hush, Sir! 'tis my little sister
> The poisoner, right well-beloved by all
> Whom she as yet hath spared.

The central interest of the play is the swaying intensity of the love of the poisoner and Savonarola. In his passion Savonarola at one moment discards the monkish frock for the costume of a Renaissance nobleman. But the sight of his legs temporarily kills Lucrezia's feeling for him. She scornfully bids him:

> Go pad thy calves!
> Thus mightst thou just conceivably with luck
> Capture the fancy of some serving-wench.

This being too much for him, they part in the mood of revenge, and, after Lucrezia has made a desperate effort to force a poisoned ring on him, they both find themselves in gaol. When the curtain rises on Savonarola's cell, he has been in prison three hours. "Imprisonment," says the stage direction, "has left its mark on both of them. Savonarola's hair has turned white. His whole aspect is that of a very old, old man. Lucrezia looks no older than before, but has gone mad." How like nine-tenths of the prison scenes one has seen on the stage! But never on the stage has one heard a prison soliloquy half so fine as Savonarola's, from its opening sentence:

> Alas, how long ago this morning seems
> This evening!—

down to its close:

> What would my sire have said,
> And what my dam, had anybody told them
> The time would come when I should occupy
> A felon's cell? O the disgrace of it!—
> The scandal, the incredible come-down!
> It masters me. I see i' my mind's eye
> The public prints—"Sharp Sentence on a Monk!"
> What then? I thought I was of sterner stuff
> Than is affrighted by what people think.
> Yet thought I so because 'twas thought of me;
> And so 'twas thought of me because I had
> A hawk-like profile and a baleful eye.
> Lo! my soul's chin recedes, soft to the touch
> As half-churn'd butter. Seeming hawk is dove,
> And dove's a gaolbird now. Fie, out upon 't!

I do not think that anyone has produced a more unforgettable line of heroic decasyllabic verse than:

> The scandal, the incredible come-down!

Savonarola's fame will be increased as a result of that exquisitely inappropriate line. It is infinitely regrettable that Brown did not live to write the fifth act of his masterpiece. Mr. Beerbohm has attempted a scenario for a fifth act, and it contains many admirable things. But Mr. Beerbohm lacks Brown's "magnifical" touch, though he does his best to imitate it in the lines in which he makes Lucrezia say that she means:

> To start afresh in that uncharted land
> Which austers not from out the antipod,
> Australia!

Good as this is, it seems just to verge on parody. It is grotesque where Brown would have been moving. The play as a whole, however, will find a place among the minor classics. It is far,

far better than going to the pantomime. It is as good as the pantomime ought to be.

"Hilary Maltby and Stephen Braxton" is something new in literature—a comic ghost story. There are plenty of funny stories about ghosts that did not exist. This is a funny story about a ghost that did exist. It is a story of the jealousy of two novelists of the 'nineties, and tells how one of them was pursued by the ghost of his jealous rival to a week-end at a duchess's. It is a nightmare seen objectively—everybody's nightmare.

In **"Enoch Soames"**—which is the masterpiece of the book— Mr. Beerbohm fools, but he fools wisely. He never takes his eye off human nature. He draws not only a caricature, but a man. The minor poet—the utterly incompetent minor poet— has never before been drawn so brilliantly and with so much intelligence as in **"Enoch Soames."** The pretentiousness, the inclination to disparage, the egotism, the affected habits and beliefs—bad poets (and some less bad ones) have had them in all ages, but the type has not before been collected and pinned in a glass case. **"Enoch Soames"** is a perfect fable for egotists. It might be described as a sympathetic exposure. One feels almost sorry for Soames as Mr. Beerbohm subjects him to the terrible justice of the comic imagination. **"Enoch Soames"** is a moral tale into which the Devil himself enters as a character. Mr. Beerbohm made his reputation as an eccentric writer. In this story he suggests an attitude the reverse of eccentric. Perhaps it is that middle-age has descended on him. He has certainly added wisdom to playfulness, and in the result has painted an imaginary portrait which is as impressively serious as it is brilliantly entertaining. (pp. 171-79)

[In] his last book, *And Even Now,* we find once more a variegated human comedy in which all the principal characters are authors and artists or their works, and other human beings are only allowed to walk on as supers. First of all we have **"A Relic,"** in which Mr. Beerbohm sees a pretty lady in a temper, and a short, fat man waddling after her, and determines to write a story about them. He does not write it, but he writes a story about the story he did not write. Then comes **"How Shall I Word It?"**—a joke about a "complete letter-writer" bought at a railway bookstall. This is followed by **"Mobled King,"** describing a statue to King Humbert, which, though erected, has never been unveiled because the priests and the fishermen object, and concluding with a wise suggestion that "there would be no disrespect, and there would be no violence, if the bad statues familiar to London were ceremoniously veiled, and their inscribed pedestals left just as they are." Fourth comes **"Kolniyatch"**—a spoof account of the "very latest thing" in Continental authors. Few of us have read Kolniyatch in "the original Gibrisch," but Mr. Beerbohm's description of his work and personality makes it clear that he was an author compared with whom Dostoievsky and Strindberg were serene and saccharine:

> Of the man himself—for on several occasions
> I had the privilege and the permit to visit him—
> I have the pleasantest, most sacred memories.
> His was a wonderfully vivid and intense personality. The head was beautiful, perfectly conic
> in form. The eyes were like two revolving lamps,
> set very close together. The smile was haunting. There was a touch of old-world courtesy
> in the repression of the evident impulse to spring
> at one's throat.

After this comes **"No. 2, The Pines"**—yes, this is Mr. Beerbohm's masterpiece, too. Everybody writes well about Swinburne, but Mr. Beerbohm writes better than anybody else—better, if possible, even than Mr. Lucas. What other writer could drive respect and mockery tandem with the same delicate skill? Mr. Beerbohm sees the famous Putney household not only with the comic sense, but through the eyes of a literary youth introduced for the first time into the presence of immortals. The Pines may be a Lewis-Carroll Wonderland, but it is still a wonderland, as he recalls that first meal at the end of the long table—

> Watts-Dunton between us very low down over his plate, very cosy and hirsute, and rather like the Dormouse at that long tea-table which Alice found in Wonderland. I see myself sitting there wide-eyed, as Alice sat. And, had the Hare been a great poet, and the Hatter a great gentleman, and neither of them mad but each one only very odd and vivacious, I might see Swinburne as a glorified blend of those two.

"A Letter that Was Not Written," again, is a comedy of the arts, relating to the threatened destruction of the Adelphi. **"Books within Books"** is a charming speculation on books written by characters in fiction, not the least desirable of which, surely, was "Poments: Being Poems of the Mood and the Moment"—a work that made a character in a forgotten novel deservedly famous. The next essay, **"The Golden Drugget,"** may seem by its subject—the beam of light that falls from an open inn-door on a dark night—to be outside the literary-and-artistic formula, but is it not essentially an argument with artists that the old themes are best—that this "golden drugget" of light would somehow make a better picture than Smithkins' *Façade of the Waldorf Hotel by Night, in Peace Time?* Similarly, **"Hosts and Guests,"** though it take us perilously near the borderland of lay humanity, is essentially a literary causerie. Mr. Beerbohm may write on hosts and describe the pangs of an impoverished host in one of the "more distinguished restaurants" as he waits and wonders what the amount of the bill will be; but the principal hosts and hostesses of whom he writes are Jael and Circe and Macbeth and Old Wardle. **"A Point to be Remembered by Very Eminent Men,"** the essay that follows, contains advice to great authors as to how they should receive a worshipper who is to meet them for the first time. The author should not, Mr. Beerbohm thinks, be in the room to receive him, but should keep him waiting a little, though not so long as Leigh Hunt kept young Coventry Patmore, who had been kicking his heels for two hours when his host appeared "rubbing his hands and smiling ethereally, and saying, without a word of preface or notice of my having waited so long, "This is a beautiful world, Mr. Patmore!""

There is no need to make the proof of the literary origins of "Max" more detailed. The world that he sees in the mirror of literature means more to Mr. Beerbohm than the world itself that is mirrored. The only human figure that attracts him greatly is the man who holds the mirror up. He does not look in his heart and write. He looks in the glass and writes. The parts of nature and art, as Landor gave them, will have to be reversed for Mr. Beerbohm's epitaph. For him, indeed, nature seems hardly to exist. For him no birds sing, and he probably thinks that the scarlet pimpernel was invented by Baroness Orczy. His talent is urban and, in a good sense, prosaic. He has never ceased to be a dramatic critic, indeed, observing the men created by men (and the creators of those men) rather than the men created by God. He is a spectator, and a spectator inside four walls. He is, indeed, the last of the aesthetes. His aestheticism, however, is comic aestheticism. If he writes an unusual word, it is not to stir our imaginations with its beauty, but as a kind of dandyism, reminding us of the care with which he dresses his wit.

Within his own little world—so even the devil's advocate would have to end by admitting—Mr. Beerbohm is a master. He has done a small thing perfectly, and one perfect quip will outlive ten bad epics. It is not to be wondered at that people already see the first hint of wings sprouting from his supremely well-tailored shoulders. He is, indeed, as immortal as anybody alive. He will flit through eternity, not as an archangel, perhaps, but as a mischievous cherub in a silk hat. He is cherub enough already always to be on the side of the angels. Those who declared that he had a heart were not mistaken. There is at least one note of tenderness in the peal of his mockery. There is a spirit of courtesy and considerateness in his writing, noticeable alike in **"No. 2, The Pines,"** and in the essay on servants. Thus, though he writes mainly on the arts and artists, he sees in them, not mere figures of ornament, but figures of life, and expresses through them clearly enough—I was going to say his attitude to life. He is no parasite at the table of the arts, indeed, but a guest with perfect manners, at once shy and brilliant, one who never echoes an opinion dully, but is always amusingly himself. That accounts for his charm. Perfect manners in literature are rare nowadays. Many authors are either pretending or condescending, either malicious or suspicious. "Max" has all the virtues of egotism without any of its vices. (pp. 182-87)

> *Robert Lynd, "More or Less Modern: Mr. Max Beerbohm," in his* Books and Authors, *G. P. Putnam's Sons, 1923, pp. 171-87.*

WILBUR CROSS   (essay date 1924)

[*Cross was an American critic who wrote extensively on the English novel. In the following excerpt, he examines several types of humor employed by Beerbohm in his drawings and writings.*]

Beerbohm has the distinction of expressing himself, perhaps equally well, through two media. Humorists before him, Thackeray most conspicuously, have practised two arts, but one of them has always been secondary; whereas opinion is at variance on whether Beerbohm is better with words or with line and color. . . . In all his drawings, there is, he says, that "taint of exaggeration" which makes for caricature. The exaggeration may be slight as in his beautiful head of Tennyson (Mrs. Tennyson standing by and inquiring for the halo which, to her disappointment, is not there); or it may be exorbitant as in his George the Fourth with multiple chin tinged with red and an enormous abdomen. Whatever the exaggeration Beerbohm's caricatures rarely approach portraits; they are what one imagines the victims might have been had nature and circumstance dealt more harshly with them, in this or that feature, in this or that mental or moral bias or characteristic.

Beerbohm's original impulse, I should say, is towards caricature. Somewhere he protests that writing comes to him "with great difficulty"; whereas of his sketches he says: "I have seldom met anyone whom I did not, within a few hours of parting from him, try to portray with pen or pencil." In his *Seven Men* the drawings antedate by several years the tales woven about them. On the other hand, an essay on George the Fourth was published simultaneously with the caricature. Ev-

A self-caricature by Beerbohm (c. 1893).

erywhere Beerbohm's two arts interact. As Bohun Lynch has said before me: "There is hardly a turn of thought in his writings which does not find its counterpart in his caricatures. To and fro we may go from one to the other, backwards and forwards and back again, and we find each time the same wit, the same sense of what is ludicrous, the same intelligence behind the sense" [see Additional Bibliography]. If I were to put side by side the two things of Beerbohm's that give me most delight, I should take his twenty-three caricatures published as *Rossetti and His Circle* and his essay on Swinburne in *And Even Now.* In both there are not only those fine artistic qualities that Bohun Lynch observes, but a similar employment of contrast for the final humorous impression. Upon the ugly Victorian background, made uglier than it was, Beerbohm projects the Preraphaelite Brotherhood—Rossetti's wonderful portraits of women "with curled-up lips and amorous hair," and Swinburne with the lovely rhythms of "Atalanta in Calydon." And at the same time these men endowed with the Renaissance passion for beauty all accept as a matter of course their alien ambient—folding-doors, if it be a room, gas-brackets, and window sash bisecting the view of beautiful gardens. By that ambient from which they imagine themselves free, they, too, have been contaminated, as may be seen in their pose and manners, in what their faces say, and in their dress—crumpled frock-coats, with unnumbered wrinkles, and bags for trousers touching the floor. In the drawings the humor is conveyed

directly through visible images. In the essay on Swinburne the way of coming to it is longer and more complex, but it is as nearly the same as humor can be in another medium. The caricatures of Swinburne give him the legs and trunk of a pygmy, with a long full neck and a large head surmounted with a flaming aureole of hair. The essay can add that Swinburne had "the eyes of a god, and the smile of an elf," and can say of those delicate hands, seen in the drawing also, that they "fluttered helplessly, touchingly, unceasingly." Above all, we can hear Swinburne talk, "uttering a sound like the cooing of a dove." Each in its kind—essay and drawing—is high art. No one ought to say that one is superior to the other. And yet the insistence on physical peculiarities essential to caricature is less pleasing to many than the flexible humorous portraiture through a felicitous use of the written word. For me nothing elsewhere in Beerbohm quite equals his account of the "great moment" when he first saw Swinburne as he entered the dining-room at The Pines: "Here suddenly visible in the flesh, was the legendary being and divine singer."

Akin to caricature is parody, or burlesque (if we are to distinguish between them), which Beerbohm has refined to an art unequalled since Thackeray told the story of Ivanhoe's discomfort with Rowena and his escape to the arms of Rebecca and the quiet life of the synagogue. Parody, as I understand it, has to do outwardly with style, with imitation or mimicry of a writer's mannerisms; through style parody necessarily reaches ideas and sentiments. Burlesque has to do not so much directly with style as with ideas, sentiments, and characters; it admits of greater exaggeration than parody. Such a distinction, however, is theoretical rather than real. In practice the one passes into the other. Caricature hits the victim plumb in the face by magnifying a want of harmony detected there; and as are the features, the inference is, so is the mind. Parody and burlesque at once lay bare the weaker side of the victim's mental and artistic equipment as displayed in his writings. Like Lucian, Beerbohm usually begins with parody and ends in burlesque. Remembering a well-known passage where Stevenson says that, in learning to write, he "played the sedulous ape" to various writers dead centuries ago, Beerbohm remarks that he, too, in his youth, "acquired the habit of aping, now and again, quite sedulously, this or that live writer—sometimes, it must be admitted, in the hope of learning rather what to avoid." His books are strewn with comic apings of novelists, historians, essayists, poets, and "statesmen."

The cleverest of his parodies he collected some years ago in *A Christmas Garland,* where a number of popular authors are made to write essays or brief stories appropriate, from their point of view, to Christmas. Usually a just comparison between the authors of any age is difficult, for they do not write on precisely the same subject or take for their novels and plays precisely the same phases of life. And if they are poets they have their own metres. Hence the continuing dispute over the respective merits of Dickens and Thackeray. Beerbohm simplifies the problem for us by assigning to his authors an identical theme so that we may pass easily from style to style and at the same time gauge the mind of one writer by the side of another, comparatively. It was a shrewd device. Within the compass of a single small volume we have here before our eyes, as it were, the whole world of contemporary letters. Each story, each essay, so far as it goes, is complete in itself, and it is usually very interesting also. Quite easily a reader may imagine it to have been written by the assumed author, were the balance between his strength and his weakness so upset that the latter should tip the scales half way down. The burlesque, which is derivative from the parody, consists in the sober narrative of trivial incidents or the sober treatment of ideas utterly commonplace.

Henry James's little boy and girl lying in the bed clothes on Christmas morning cannot see their stockings hanging at the foot of their bed because of "the mote in the middle distance"; they see only the silhouettes of their stockings on the wall and begin to speculate on what Santa Claus has put into them. It does not occur to them to jump out of bed and look into the stockings. This same Santa Claus, as he came floating down from a roof to the pavement with a pack on his back, is arrested by Kipling's policeman (**"P.C., X, 36"**), and taken to the station as a burglar. A. C. Benson's Percy spends Christmas quietly alone in the country "out of harm's way," and when evening comes, lights the candles, and takes from the shelf "some old book that he knew and loved, or maybe some quite new book by that writer whose works were most dear to him because in them he seemed always to know so precisely what the author would say next, and because he found in their fine-spun repetitions a singular repose, a sense of security, an earnest of calm and continuity." H. G. Wells breaks away from a Christmas party in the country to devote himself to making over mankind—women as well as men—and fitting them into a new calendar with a twenty-hour day in accordance with "an ingenious scheme for accelerating the motion of this planet by four in every twenty-four hours, so that the alternations of light and darkness shall be re-adjusted to the new reckoning." To bring this about he feels that he has "got to do a lot of clear, steady, merciless thinking—now, to-night." Chesterton exposes "some damnable errors about Christmas," proving beyond question that Christmas comes, not as most people think, only once a year, but every day of the year. Likewise it is a fallacy to imagine that All Fool's Day is restricted to the first of April. Mankind seems to have lost "the glorious lesson" that we are all fools all the time.

Frank Harris, the Shakespearean critic (with whom silence is equivalent to a positive statement of fact), wonders why Shakespeare has no words worthy of his genius on Christmas, and concludes "through the logic of the heart" that the day was hateful to him because Anne Hathaway was born on that day. True, Shakespeare nowhere says that her birthday was Christmas. "But mark how carefully Shakespeare says never a word about the birthdays of the various shrews and sluts in whom, again and again, he gave us his wife." Emily Wrackgarth of Arnold Bennett's Five Towns gets a husband by filling the Christmas pudding with scruts which her lover crunches and swallows. John Galsworthy lets a robin starve and die in the snow on the window-sill because he has "no right to meddle in what ought to be done by the collective action of the State."

Edmund Gosse (who likes to tell of the conversations with the great men he has met) brings together, while in Venice during Christmas week, Browning and Ibsen, neither having heard of the other. The portraits of Browning and Ibsen are among the finest contrasts Beerbohm has ever drawn. "He [Ibsen] asked me whether Herr Browning had ever married. Receiving an emphatically affirmative reply, he inquired whether Fru Browning had been happy. Loth though I was to cast a blight on his interest in the matter, I conveyed to him with all possible directness the impression that Elizabeth Barrett had assuredly been one of those wives who do not dance tarantellas nor slam front-doors." In **"A Straight Talk"** by way of preface to **"Snt. George,"** Bernard Shaw, patronizing Shakespeare and Dickens, glories in the fact that he stole the plot of his play—its

"dramatic inventiveness, humor and pathos, eloquence, elfin glamour and the like"—stole everything—but stiffened it with "civistic conscience" which made a masterpiece out of a poor thing. George Moore, who has spent his life in kneeling to false gods, or scrubbing the wrong doorsteps, finally discovers the doorstep of Charles Dickens—the only doorstep worth scrubbing. His acquaintance with Dickens, as it turns out, is confined to one chapter of "Pickwick"—Mr. Wardle's Christmas party—from which he disengages for the reader "the erotic motive," which, he says, is all there is to literature, though there may be in real life "moments when one does not think of girls."

Burlesque like this is satire, but not in the old meaning. Pope and Byron pilloried their social and political enemies. Beerbohm cannot do that, for he has no enemies. No more is he of the genial satirists of the mid-Victorian era, who felt that society imposed a restraint upon their talents. It is well known that Thackeray suppressed a burlesque of Dickens, and among his contemporaries chose the lesser names. (His burlesque of Disraeli was never forgiven of him.) Likewise Dickens, whose novels are pervaded with incidental burlesque. They both concealed the individual in the humorous portrayal of the class or the institution. The main exception to the rule was the conspicuous political leader, who at all times has been regarded as fair game. Otherwise, it was held, personalities had better be confined to men and women who are dead. Beerbohm has sometimes gone to the dead. But always, both in his drawings and his essays, as in his recent cartoons, **"Tales of Three Nations"** in *Things New and Old,* he adjusts his past to the present. If he sometimes dips into history it is because, so he says, men of the moment, "numerous though they always are, are not numerous enough to satisfy my interest in mankind." They should not take an occasional lapse into the past as "a slight" upon them. He is the most modern of satirists since Fielding, who likewise kept close to his contemporaries. "Satire," he once remarked, "should be irresponsible, tilting at the strong and the established as well as at the momentary follies of the day." The satirist should have "the courage of his own levity," showing no favors. Of Beerbohm's levity there are just fears, but it rarely gives offense. His "sheer, delicious, damned cheek," as Bohun Lynch calls it, is neutralized by wit and humor in which no malice appears. Criticism he would disarm by quoting the old proverb: *On se moque de ce qu'on aime* ["One mocks what one loves"]. He had no dislike for the late William Watson, although he once referred to the poet's search "for adjectives long enough to express unqualified approval." He can admire "the wondrous works" of Meredith, "seething with wit, with poetry and philosophy," and yet legitimately have some sport with Meredith's cryptic style and "pagan young womanhood, six foot of it that spans eight miles before luncheon." (pp. 213-20)

Beerbohm's style is an echo out of the past. "I am cursed," he says, "with a literary conscience." Who is now cursed with a literary conscience? H. G. Wells? Arnold Bennett? Beerbohm began writing in the eighteen nineties, in the period of Whistler, *The Yellow Book,* and Aubrey Beardsley, when essays were built round sharp epigrams and brilliant phrases, when it was almost a virtue that words should have no meaning provided they had an exotic beauty. Among these writers Beerbohm first learned his art. For years he affected strange involutions of style, revived old words and coined new ones out of Latin and Greek. He was more interested, he once said, in the proper placing of a comma than in the political fortunes of the British Empire. Since then he has dealt with the 'nineties in light satire—with its "odd apparitions" like Enoch Soames and Savonarola Brown, with its verse which at some point was certain to deviate into nonsense. Beyond the old "elaborate ingenuities," to quote his phrase, he has now matured; but he still worships "the *mot juste, that Holy Grail of the period.*" This care for style may have its defects, but they are lost in its virtues. He is unable, he says, to begin a piece of writing before he knows just how it shall end. He pares, whittles, and polishes in a manner long "outmoded." Every sentence and phrase appears to have been examined after it was once written, for exactness, aim, color, cadence. The technique of his other medium, so far as it is available, is made use of here. Whatever he writes, he does not let go until it is as complete as one of his drawings. Artifice is made over into art. If, as Beerbohm wrote to Bohun Lynch, "my gifts are small," he has used them discreetly and well. His mind is not so capacious as was the mind of Dickens or Thackeray; but within the liberal bounds nature set for it, his art runs close to perfection. (p. 227)

Wilbur Cross, "The Humor of Max Beerbohm," in The Yale Review, *Vol. XIII, No. 2, January, 1924, pp. 209-27.*

VIRGINIA WOOLF (essay date 1925)

[*A British novelist, essayist, and short story writer, Woolf is considered one of the most prominent literary figures of twentieth-century English literature. Like her contemporary James Joyce, with whom she is often compared, Woolf is remembered as one of the most innovative of the stream of consciousness novelists. A discerning and influential critic and essayist as well as a novelist, Woolf began writing reviews for the* Times Literary Supplement *at an early age. Her critical essays, termed "creative, appreciative, and subjective" by Barbara Currier Bell and Carol Ohmann, cover almost the entire range of English literature and contain some of her finest prose. Along with Lytton Strachey, Roger Fry, Clive Bell, and others, Woolf and her husband Leonard formed the literary coterie known as the "Bloomsbury Group." In the following excerpt, Woolf discusses Beerbohm's achievement as an essayist.*]

[In Max Beerbohm] we have an essayist who has concentrated on the work and is without doubt the prince of his profession.

What Mr. Beerbohm gave [to the essay] was, of course, himself. This presence, which has haunted the essay fitfully from the time of Montaigne, had been in exile since the death of Charles Lamb. Matthew Arnold was never to his readers Matt, nor Walter Pater affectionately abbreviated in a thousand homes to Wat. They gave us much, but that they did not give. Thus, some time in the nineties, it must have surprised readers accustomed to exhortation, information, and denunciation to find themselves familiarly addressed by a voice which seemed to belong to a man no larger than themselves. He was affected by private joys and sorrows, and had no gospel to preach and no learning to impart. He was himself, simply and directly, and himself he has remained. Once again we have an essayist capable of using the essayist's most proper but most dangerous and delicate tool. He has brought personality into literature, not unconsciously and impurely, but so consciously and purely that we do not know whether there is any relation between Max the essayist and Mr. Beerbohm the man. We only know that the spirit of personality permeates every word that he writes. The triumph is the triumph of style. For it is only by knowing how to write that you can make use in literature of your self; that self which, while it is essential to literature, is also its most dangerous antagonist. Never to be yourself and

yet always—that is the problem. . . . [Some essayists] to be frank, have not altogether succeeded in solving it. We are nauseated by the sight of trivial personalities decomposing in the eternity of print. As talk, no doubt, it was charming, and certainly the writer is a good fellow to meet over a bottle of beer. But literature is stern; it is no use being charming, virtuous, or even learned and brilliant into the bargain, unless, she seems to reiterate, you fulfil her first condition—to know how to write.

This art is possessed to perfection by Mr. Beerbohm. But he has not searched the dictionary for polysyllables. He has not moulded firm periods or seduced our ears with intricate cadences and strange melodies. Some of his companions—Henley and Stevenson, for example—are momentarily more impressive. But *A Cloud of Pinafores* had in it that indescribable inequality, stir, and final expressiveness which belong to life and to life alone. You have not finished with it because you have read it, any more than friendship is ended because it is time to part. Life wells up and alters and adds. Even things in a book-case change if they are alive; we find ourselves wanting to meet them again; we find them altered. So we look back upon essay after essay by Mr. Beerbohm, knowing that, come September or May, we shall sit down with them and talk. Yet it is true that the essayist is the most sensitive of all writers to public opinion. The drawing-room is the place where a great deal of reading is done nowadays, and the essays of Mr. Beerbohm lie, with an exquisite appreciation of all that the position exacts, upon the drawing-room table. There is no gin about; no strong tobacco; no puns, drunkenness, or insanity. Ladies and gentlemen talk together, and some things, of course, are not said.

But if it would be foolish to attempt to confine Mr. Beerbohm to one room, it would be still more foolish, unhappily, to make him, the artist, the man who gives us only his best, the representative of our age. . . . His age seems already a little distant, and the drawing-room table, as it recedes, begins to look rather like an altar where, once upon a time, people deposited offerings—fruit from their own orchards, gifts carved with their own hands. (pp. 300-03)

Virginia Woolf, "The Modern Essay," in her The Common Reader, *Harcourt Brace Jovanovich, 1925, pp. 293-307.*

BERTRAND RUSSELL (essay date 1952)

[*A respected and prolific author, Russell was an English philosopher and mathematician known for his support of humanistic concerns. Two of his early works,* Principles of Mathematics *(1903) and* Principia Mathematica *(1910-13), written with Alfred North Whitehead, are considered classics of mathematical logic. His philosophical approach to all his endeavors discounts idealism or emotionalism and asserts a progressive application of his "logical atomism," a process whereby individual facts are logically analyzed. Russell's humanistic beliefs often centered around support of unorthodox social concerns, including free love, undisciplined education, and the eradication of nuclear weapons. In recognition of his contributions in a number of literary genres, Russell was awarded the Nobel Prize in literature in 1950. In the following excerpt, he praises Beerbohm's skillful wit and humor.*]

Both in writing and in pictures [Beerbohm] is, to my mind, the most faultless of my contemporaries. I do not mean by this that he is the greatest; but I do mean that he secures the effects at which he aims, and that these are wholly delightful. Not only do they show amazing penetration, but they express judgments which seem to me always just. (p. 18)

Max's skill in making wicked people look wicked, and absurd people look absurd, is positively devilish. He made a picture of d'Annunzio in which he managed to exhibit everything that was odious about that swashbuckling littérateur. As a penetrating comment on great events, I can hardly imagine anything better than his picture of "President Wilson's Peace." President Wilson is sitting alone in utter dejection. Lloyd George and Clemenceau are standing behind him at some distance. Lloyd George is chuckling with glee, nudging Clemenceau with his elbow and remarking, "Thought he was going to get the better of you and I." Another picture which gives me very great pleasure is the one of Lytton Strachey writing his *Queen Victoria,* which is called "Trying to see her with Lord Melbourne's eyes" in which process he is being assisted by a small bust of her as an old woman. The lackadaisical precision with which he is holding his pen is almost more like him than he was in the flesh. I rejoice in the picture of Bernard Shaw standing on his head with a broad grin, with Max looking on in astonished admiration, expressing, as he puts it, "mild surprise on revisiting England after long absence to find that the dear fellow has not moved."

I derive even more pleasure from his writings than from his pictures, not because I think them better, but because I am more at home with writing and better able to appreciate the fine shades. I remember the delight of the *Christmas Garland*—the Henry James children who on Christmas morning decide not to look into their Christmas stockings on the ground that actuality can never reach the heights reached by anticipation; Rudyard Kipling making friends with a policeman who arrests Santa Claus for illegally coming out of the chimney; Joseph Conrad on a remote island, who finds to his dismay that he is the Christmas dinner, but endures his fate with unsurpassable fortitude. The most devastating of all the satires in this volume is one on an author now forgotten, A. C. Benson, a master of platitude. I asked Max once whether people minded his caricatures, and he asserted that they did not.

"How about A. C. Benson?" I asked him. "Ah, well," he confessed, "He did say he would never write another line." This is the only case I can remember in which Max was unkind to a man for being merely silly, not wicked.

For my part, I prefer *Seven Men* to all his other books. And in this volume I prefer the story called "**Enoch Soames.**" Enoch Soames, a poet unrecognized in his own day, but convinced that he is destined for posthumous fame, says all the things that a poet of that day should say, such as: "Life is web, and therein nor warp nor woof is, but web only"; "Nor not strange forms and epicene"; "Lean near to life, lean very near, nearer." Soames has published a small volume, but the only praise that the publisher can find for the blurb is: "Strikes a note of modernity throughout. . . . These tripping numbers." This comes from "The Preston Telegraph," and it turns out that Soames is a product of Preston. He sells his soul to the Devil for an hour in the British Museum Reading Room, a hundred years hence, hoping to find that he had achieved immortality. But when he looks up "Soames, Enoch," in the catalogue he finds only "see Beerbohm, Max." The story ends with Max meeting the devil in one of the avenues that radiate from the Arc de Triomphe. Max means to cut the Fiend, but fails, and the Fiend cuts him.

Zuleika Dobson, though I read it with pleasure, is to my mind rather too long drawn out. But it represents, with immense

charm, the Oxford that the two World Wars have destroyed—absurd, perhaps, and to a social reformer preposterous, but with a charm that is not likely to be reproduced anywhere in the world for the next thousand years.

Max, like all the artistic young men of the Nineties, found his spiritual home in Paris. But in lieu of that paradise he could endure the limbo of the Café Royal. He seems, however, from his work to have been capable of tolerating the Pre-Raphaelites. Ruskin and Browning do not fare quite so well, and Sir Frederic Leighton comes in for a first class castigation. In his book devoted entirely to the Rossettis there is a charming picture in which Dante Gabriel is exhorting Christina to dress in Liberty fabrics, saying:

"What is the use, Christina, of having a heart like a singing bird and a water-shoot and all the rest of it, if you insist on getting yourself up like a pew-opener?"

To which she replies,

"Well, Gabriel, I don't know, I'm sure. You yourself always dress very quietly."

There is a charming picture in which John Morley brings John Stuart Mill to see Rossetti in order to learn from him both how to infuse warmth and color into his work and how to avoid the subjection of women.

Max had a keen nose for humbug, and I think that anybody who had attempted to take him in by fine sentiments would have exposed himself to merciless punishment. But although he can be pitiless to those who rouse his scorn, he is very far indeed from being unkind.

In spite of his loves and hates his view of the world is, in a sense, impartial, He does not love or hate by a formula or by a party label. His version is extraordinarily just and extraordinarily detached. He notices equally the self-deceptions of the pompous and the delusions of the idealistic. From each alike he extracts his fun.

It is customary to say that Max Beerbohm belongs to the Nineties and has never really grown beyond them. There is possibly some measure of truth in this, about as much as there would be if one said the same of Winston Churchill. Max Beerbohm's excellences, like Churchill's, are such as can only flourish in a man who has grown up with security and leisure. Our turbulent world gives little opportunity for the development of fine shades. A modern man must be a saint, a sinner, or a specialist. Civilized men in the past were none of these—except sinners, in moderation.

The younger people of our time, so far as I know them, would be ashamed of delicate artistic sensibilities, which they would think inappropriate to this rough world. The shrieks of Jews in Auschwitz and the tortures of slave-laborers in the Arctic have numbed men's capacity for delicate appreciations. Those who are not doing something about these horrors are consciously forgetting them and can forget them only by frivolity. Work such as that of Max Beerbohm is not frivolous but to the tortured nerves of modern men it may seem so. Such work can no longer be produced, and in this sense I fear it is only too true that he belongs to a past epoch. This is not to condemn him, but to condemn the present. (pp. 18, 41)

Bertrand Russell, '"The Faultless Max' at 80," in
The New York Times, *August 24, 1952, pp. 18, 41.*

ELLEN MOERS (essay date 1960)

[*An American educator and critic, Moers has been praised for her deft critical studies* The Dandy: Brummel to Beerbohm *(1960), and* Literary Women *(1976). In the following excerpt from the first-named work, Moers discusses Beerbohm's essays on dandies and dandyism.*]

From Bulwer to Wilde every writer on dandyism took the dandy seriously as a present ideal or pleasure or nuisance or threat. Beerbohm was the first to take him, possibly with greater seriousness, as a remnant of the past. When all about him in the 'nineties (Beerbohm included) pretended to become dandies in their own right, his was the voice that announced that an era had passed for good. He was, albeit loosely, the historical conscience of his period.

Beerbohm's first essay on dandyism appeared in an undergraduate magazine (edited by Lord Alfred Douglas) at Oxford in 1893. Entitled **"The Incomparable Beauty of Modern Dress,"** it was very much what was to be expected of a clever young man of twenty-one, at that time and place. Steeped in Wildesque aesthetics and Oscarian afflatus . . . the young Oxonian prated of "our artistic duty to the community." "As in Life our first duty is to realise the soul," he wrote, "so in Art it should be to idealise the body." So much for Oxford. . . . [In 1896] he wrote the essay **"Dandies and Dandies"** which was to open his first book. While it incorporated ideas and phrases from the Oxford piece, along with material from three articles printed in New York, Chicago and London periodicals, **"Dandies and Dandies"** was mature Beerbohm and something new and necessary for the 'nineties. Here was an approach to dandyism, long overdue, through the great original dandies; here was a snub to pretentious modernity through an ironic glorification of the Regency.

"How very delightful Grego's drawings are!" the essay begins. "For all their mad perspective and crude colour, they have indeed the sentiment of style, and they reveal, with surer delicacy than does any other record, the spirit of Mr. Brummell's day." As an opening sentence, this is an illuminating index to Beerbohm's concern with the Regency—in two ways. It shows the sort of reading and looking that, by 1896, had tied his interest in dandyism to the historical past. And it demonstrates that he was no historian. For the sentence is, of course, completely inaccurate. These were no "Grego drawings," but reengravings from authentic prints of "Mr. Brummell's day"; thus their crude perspective and sense of style. "I started off with a howler," Beerbohm said a few years ago, with the pained air of one who has not been allowed to forget. "It sounded like a very good way for a young man to start." (pp. 316-17)

Whatever Beerbohm may have known, at first hand, of Regency memoirs and Regency gossip, the legend of the *ur*-dandies came to him shaped by the intelligence and the wit of Barbey d'Aurevilly. **"Dandies and Dandies"** is first of all an irreverent answer to *Du Dandysme et de Georges Brummell,* and to all the intellectual posing that followed on Barbey. Beerbohm took it upon himself to provide a corrective to the Gallic intensity and Norman airs that Barbey had brought to the tradition. He looked at dandyism with the impudence and detachment and absence of melodrama proper to the native English dandy. The point of his essay is that the art of costume itself is the essence of Brummell's dandyism. Costume is not a mere outward show of some profound spiritual achievement. "Dandyism," Beerbohm writes, "is ever the outcome of a carefully cultivated temperament, not part of the temperament itself." The "oblique attitude toward life" that distinguished Brummell and attracted the aesthetes and the decadents after him, was not, in Beerbohm's view, an accomplishment peculiar to dandies; it was the sort of thing cultivated by *all delicate spirits*. . . . To Brummell's mastery of this attitude Beerbohm pays a full sentence of tribute:

> Like the single-minded artist that he was, he turned full and square towards his art and looked life straight in the face out of the corners of his eyes.

What set Brummell apart, however, was the cut of his clothes. "Those are true words," says Beerbohm of Carlyle's famous angry definition of the dandy as the clothes-wearing man; "they are, perhaps, the only true words in *Sartor Resartus.*"

Beerbohm laughs at Carlyle; he laughs at Barbey; and of course he has his laugh at Brummell, though all in the most polite manner. (Brummell is invariably "Mr. Brummell" in the essay; while Count D'Orsay, of whom Beerbohm thinks less, is D'Orsay). But the last laugh, somehow, is on Beerbohm's own contemporaries. By indirection, by sly comparisons, by careless asides and by irony, always irony . . . he rubs the sheen from the pretensions of the 'nineties. To all the *delicate spirits* of his day he opposes the cool dandies of the Regency, never troubling to say which group his reader shall find wanting. The aesthetic posing, the strenuous straining after Art with a capital letter he dismisses in a scornful reference to D'Orsay as a portraitist:

> It is the process of painting which is repellent; to force from little tubes of lead a glutinous flamboyance and to defile, with the hair of a camel therein steeped, taut canvas, is hardly the diversion for a gentleman. . . .

Here, after seventy years, is the quintessential Regency position (made as clear as it is made ridiculous): "The aesthetic vision of a dandy should be bounded by his own mirror."

Something had come over the young Max of Merton, who talked of Art and Life and the soul—something beside Gronow and Jesse, Regency prints and Barbey d'Aurevilly. He had learned to laugh at Oscar Wilde. There is amusing documentary proof of his growing detachment from the patron aesthete of the generation coming to maturity in the 'nineties. In 1894, two years before the **"Dandies and Dandies"** essay, one year after **"The Incomparable Beauty of Modern Dress"** (which had paid tribute to Wilde as a "poet" and the author of "that splendid, sinister work, *Dorian Gray*"), Beerbohm wrote a piece which would probably have annoyed Wilde more than anything else written about him, had it appeared during his lifetime. **"A Peep into the Past"** (what a title for a piece on Wilde!) was designed as Beerbohm's début in the first number of the *Yellow Book.* One can only imagine the circumstances of its rejection: the hearty laughter of Will Rothenstein, the malicious pleasure of Beardsley (both Beerbohm's friends at Oxford), the alarmed timidity of John Lane (to whom they had introduced Beerbohm). For this was no anonymous satire of Wilde transformed to Esme Amarinth, as in the *Green Carnation* of the same year, but a cool bit of open condescension from the younger generation to the older. And Wilde as homosexual was part of the fun.

"Oscar Wilde!" the essay opens. "I wonder to how many of my readers the jingle of this name suggests anything at all? Yet, at one time, it was familiar to many and if we search

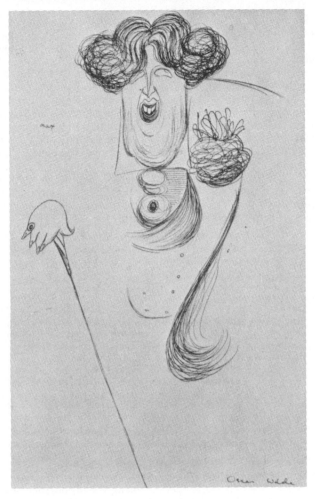

A caricature of Oscar Wilde drawn by Beerbohm. Reproduced by permission of Eva Reichmann.

back among the old volumes of *Punch,* we shall find many a quip and crank out at its owner's expense." Beerbohm presents himself as a student of Early Victoriana who ("knowing that Mr. Sala was out of town") hunts up the forgotten Mr. Wilde, now living in obscure retirement in Chelsea, as "the survivor of a bygone day." There he finds the old gentleman is a neighbourhood fixture, known for his old-fashioned clothes (though "evidently cut by a good tailor"), greeted on his daily walk up the King's Road ("the trades people . . . often waylay him as he attempts to pass on"), his well-ordered domestic life (which includes reading Ruskin to his children after an early dinner) and his insistence upon punctuality ("perhaps this accounts for the constant succession of page-boys, which so startles the neighbourhood . . ."). "As I was ushered into the little study, I fancied that I heard the quickly receding *frou-frou* of tweed trousers, but my host I found reclining, hale and hearty, though a little dishevelled upon the sofa."

Beerbohm makes fun of Wilde's sexual habits, his flashy Bohemianism, his peculiar family life, his Irish wit, his superficial scholarship and his imitative works (among them "a volume of essays, which Mr. Pater is often obliged blushingly to repudiate"). All this is stronger criticism than Wilde was used to from Philistia, yet the piece is not offensive. The young Max had already mastered an art which would serve him for the rest of his career: the art of satirizing, lambasting, insulting

with impeccable decorum; the art of getting away with it. Here the specific stings of the satire are overshadowed by the general conceit: that Wilde (then at the height of his career) belonged to the forgotten past. And the pose of the author, patronizing, maddeningly tolerant and excessively deferential on the grounds of age alone, never of talent, is so outrageous that the reader thinks of Max, not of his victim. (pp. 318-21)

In Beerbohm's individual perception, the old had a way of becoming the young, the young the old; and the *fin de siècle* seemed to change places with the Regency. As for himself, he was amused to think of his precocious career as ending before it had fairly begun. The public applauds me, he wrote in 1899, simply because "it knows me to be a child author, and likes to picture me at my desk, dressed in black velveteen, with legs dangling towards the floor." Three years before that, however, he had already declared himself dated and had said farewell, half-seriously, to an alien world. (p. 321)

For the budding essayist, drawn to that rare literary form as none had been since Thackeray, and as none has been since Beerbohm, the discovery of fresh subject matter was the essential luck; and the young-old Max could be most freshly original with material from the past. "To treat history as a means of showing one's own cleverness may be rather rough on history," he told Ada Leverson when she interviewed him in 1895, "but it has been done by the best historians, from Herodotus to Froude and myself."

Besides **"Dandies and Dandies,"** *The Works of Max Beerbohm* (Beerbohm's first book) contained a long essay entitled **"King George the Fourth."** It is a rambling, conversational, absolutely irresponsible reconstruction of the Regent's life story and the age he ornamented. Beerbohm takes as his thesis a statement that George was, "in the practical sense of the word, a fine king," and works out the argument as a reply to Thackeray, whose lecture on George IV he follows rather closely, with queries and quibbles. Thackeray, according to Beerbohm, had "applied to his subject the wrong method, in the wrong manner, and at the wrong time." Now that Victorian values themselves are in question, the moment has come for a sprig of the *fin de siècle* to redress old wrongs and admire in the last of the Georges the decorative virtues (intelligence, wit, sensitivity, taste and style, especially style) once again in fashion.

What was new, and essentially *Max* about the piece, was that the reader could never be sure exactly where Beerbohm stood: with the Regency, the medio-Victorians or the 'nineties. The mincing play of his irony made the footing slippery indeed. *Punch* was sure that the memory of its sacred Thackeray had been insulted and printed an angry parody ("A Phalse Note on George the Fourth") in Yellowplushese. "I meant all I said about George," was Beerbohm's answer; "but I did not choose to express myself quite seriously."

"A Good Prince," a little *tour de force* about the royal infant in his perambulator, appeared in the same volume and is generally considered a pendant to the essay on George IV. For here Beerbohm mocked the ideal of royal angelic imbecility erected by the Victorians in horrified reaction against the unmourned Regent. In "Dessein's," one of the *Roundabout Papers,* Thackeray had raised the ghost of Sterne to sentimentalize about his glimpse of a royal infant "in his cradle at St. James's, a lovely little babe; a gilt Chinese railing was before him, and I dropped the tear of sensibility as I gazed on the sleeping cherub." At the heart of Thackeray's irony was his knowledge that this prince had grown up to be George IV. Beerholm lived to relish the fact that *his* prince turned out to be the Duke of Windsor.

"Poor Romeo!", further on in *The Works,* was another step in Beerbohm's private Regency revival. A wistful tribute to the pseudo-dandy of Bath, Romeo Coates, it introduced a new satiric technique for the chastisement of the present by the past. Whimsy, fantasy and all the paraphernalia of the fairy tale were beloved of the literary 'nineties; Beerbohm spoofed the devices and, through them, the more grievous affectations of the age. On a larger scale, and in a work of fiction, he used the same technique to make fun of the pretension to wickedness, the presentation of evil shallowly understood which had made a book like *Dorian Gray* ridiculous. In *The Happy Hypocrite,* a long fairy tale written for the *Yellow Book* in the year that *The Works* appeared, Beerbohm clearly parodied Wilde's novel, and he used a Regency fantasy for his pleasant purpose.

"None, it is said, of all who revelled with the Regent," (the story begins) "was half so wicked as Lord George Hell." For the benefit of "my little readers" Beerbohm reveals that his hero-villain "often sat up at Carlton House until long after bed-time, playing at games, and that he generally ate and drank far more than was good for him. His fondness for fine clothes was such that he used to dress on weekdays quite as gorgeously as good people dress on Sundays . . .". (For the benefit of bigger readers, there are invented sources—like "Captain Tarleton's *Contemporary Bucks*"—which provide footnotes, and evoke a host of Regency memorialists.) The story of Lord George Hell owes something to the Regency legend of "Golden" Ball Hughes's elopement with a ballet girl. But the device of the saintly mask to cover an evil face and the dénouement of the mask's removal—to reveal a face grown saintly through the years of good behaviour—reverse the point and tone of Wilde's melodrama. Like Dorian, Lord George is "proud of being horrid," but Beerbohm destines him to play the *happy* hypocrite.

Zuleika Dobson, too, owes something to a novelist whose works were taken seriously in the *fin de siècle:* to Disraeli, who provided the 'nineties with a living tradition of dandy fiction. His early novels were little read, but his last two books, *Lothair* (1870) and *Endymion* (1880), had won him readers among the new literary generation. (pp. 323-26)

The dreamlike, all-is-gold-that-glitters quality of the late Disraeli novels is echoed in *Zuleika Dobson,* Beerbohm's famous full-length dandy novel. Its hero, John Albert Edward Claude Orde Angus Tankerton Tanville-Tankerton, fourteenth Duke of Dorset (and so on), is one more version of the nineteenth century's ideal young duke, caught as he steps across the fatal boundary of the past into the new era. (*Zuleika* was published in 1911.) Fabulously wealthy, miraculously gifted, consummately dandified, he is also—and this is the point which makes *Zuleika* the very last of the dandy novels—wholly insufferable. Like Disraeli, Beerbohm saw in the dandy hero a natural subject for romance; unlike Disraeli, whose lasting respect for the English aristocracy approached adoration, Beerbohm used the gilding of fantasy primarily to evoke laughter. *Zuleika Dobson* was written both as a devoted return to the tradition of full-fledged dandy fiction, and as an outrageous farce with a noodle of a dandy for its hero. "Better be vulgar with Byron than a noodle with Dorset!" reflects Beerbohm's dandy duke at the bitter crisis of his love affair. "Still, noodledom was nearer than vulgarity to dandyism."

Had Beerbohm ever been gravely presented with a choice between the old-fashioned gentleman, willing to die for his standards of class honour and personal dignity, and the New-fangled Woman, crass and overbearing in the freshness of her independence, he would unquestionably have opted for the dandy. He often expressed strong prejudices for the one and against the other. ("Women," he once said sourly, "are becoming nearly as rare as ladies.") But for Beerbohm the satirist there was no choice. Zuleika must triumph in all her vulgarity, and the Duke must sink to a watery grave, propelled to the final plunge by a few warning drops of rain. The dandy's last thoughts are for the fading magnificence of his finery. Thus the demands of caricature were satisfied, and the dandy was reduced in scale to fit a small, absurd, fantasy world where pearls turn pink or black to blush or mourn, and young men drown themselves, *en masse,* for love. (pp. 326-27)

Ellen Moers, "Epilogue: Sir Max Beerbohm," in her The Dandy: Brummell to Beerbohm, *The Viking Press, 1960, pp. 315-30.*

F. W. DUPEE (essay date 1966)

[*Dupee was an American editor, educator, and critic. An ardent Marxist, he served as editor of the left-wing journal* Partisan Review *from 1937 to 1941 and remained politically active throughout his subsequent teaching career. In the following excerpt, Dupee offers an examination of Beerbohm's fantasy works, focusing his discussion on stylistic elements in* Zuleika Dobson.]

Rereading Beerbohm one gets caught up in the intricate singularity of his mind, all of a piece yet full of surprises, as one does in Boswell's Johnson. In *Zuleika Dobson* his mind is in full flower, a kind of tropical bloom, lurid and elaborate, prickly but not poisonous, except to the foolish.

That his drawings and parodies should survive is no cause for wonder. One look at them, or into them, and his old reputation is immediately re-established: that whim of irony, that cleverness amounting to genius. What is odd is that his stories and essays should turn out to be equally durable. The mandarin of mandarins, Beerbohm wrote with a kind of conscious elegance that has since become generally suspect. This *nouveau riche* English has for us the fault of advertising to the world the abundance of its verbal resources. The plain declarative sentence is apt to be set off by a dazzle of rhetorical questions and apostrophes to the reader. Ostentatious connectives, from "indeed" to "however that may be," are *de rigueur.* No word is repeated if a synonym can possibly be found. (p. 12)

Beerbohm's mandarinism often tended to mock itself, subtly or bluntly. After starting a sentence with "indeed" he apologized in parentheses for the "otiose" word. He avoided not only the vaguely impressive but the crudely *ex*pressive. A friend wrote to him praising the sentence about the lightning in *Zuleika Dobson:* "A sudden white vertical streak slid down the sky." Beerbohm replied: "The word 'slid' was in the first draft 'slithered' which, though more accurate really, looked rather *cherché* and so was jettisoned." Thus he profited from the mandarin abundance while, on the whole, avoiding or deriding its excesses.

One now reads Beerbohm with recognitions beyond the powers of those of us who were literary neophytes in the Twenties. The elegant trifler contributed more than one had supposed to literary history. Beerbohm played an essential if deliberately minor role in the famous "revolution of taste" that took place between, roughly, 1910 and 1922, even though he was never a "modernist" in his own tastes, preferring the poetry of Swinburne and the novels of Trollope, Meredith, and James to *Ulysses* and *The Waste Land*. Nevertheless, he discovered before Pound and Eliot did the futility and pathos of the dandy and his lady. As a verbal caricature of the London literary life, **Seven Men** parallels at several points Pound's poem on the same subject, *Hugh Selwyn Mauberley*. *Mauberley* includes a verse portrait of Beerbohm under the name of Brennbaum. The portrait is, appropriately, a verse caricature of Beerbohm as dandy:

> The sky-like limpid eyes,
>   The circular infant's face,
> The stiffness from spats to collar
>   Never relaxing into grace. . . .

Naturally, the famous revolution in taste "went too far." In doing so, it has given work to critics and biographers ever since. Rehabilitating the major Victorians and in some cases the Edwardians has long been a reputable occupation. Tennyson, Kipling, and Queen Victoria herself have recovered from the clawings of Beerbohm's velvet glove.

Yet how exhilarating those clawings were at the time. I mean not only such celebrated caricatures as the one of Queen Victoria attending with majestic patience to a shrunken Tennyson reading *In Memoriam*. More devastating were the drawings that caricatured the political or the literary life in general. There was the bitter series called **Cartoons: "The Second Childhood of John Bull,"** chiefly inspired by Beerbohm's disgust with the Boer War. There was the series called **The Old Self and the Young Self**, in which eighteen well-known Edwardians were confronted in the fullness of their age and fame by the specters, gloating or reproachful, of their youthful selves. A real *terribilità* plays about the latter series. It could scarcely fail to impress the literary initiates of any period, from the Twenties to the Sixties.

With the foolish in mind, Max Beerbohm added to the 1946 edition of **Zuleika Dobson** a warning against interpretation. . . . It is only part of the "act," the very stagey act that **Zuleika Dobson** is throughout. If first-rate humorists are never to be taken too seriously, they are to be taken least seriously when they are most at pains to warn us against taking them seriously at all.

Beerbohm maintains that his book is "just a fantasy." No satirical or other serious comment is intended. But this is impossible in the nature of his genre as he names it here. "Fantasy" must have something which to fantasticate, and what can that something be except "reality" or some aspect of it? . . . The great fantasies embrace not only certain aspects of reality but just about all of it, even in some instances God and the gods. The authors make it their business to fantasticate the realities so thoroughly that, presto!, they come to look fantastic themselves. (pp. 12-13)

For some twelve years (1898-1910), Max Beerbohm wrote a weekly theater article for the *Saturday Review* of London. He was thus exposed to a good deal of trashy fantasy in dramatic as well as narrative form. Even the ballet came to bore him. Much of what he saw or read in this vein seems to have been delinquent in essentially the same way that much of what is today called "Black Humor" is delinquent. It broke the law of laws: it failed to take itself seriously enough. What he saw or read was not willfully wacky as the worst Black Humor is at present. For the Kafkan revolution in fantasy, of which Black Humor is the sometimes depressing offspring—depressing in

its mechanical frenzies—belonged to the far future. Thus the action of fantasy was not as yet generated in the disturbed psyche, where anything goes. Nor had history itself as yet reached the extremity of mad inventiveness which today leaves the average fantasist far behind and breathing hard.

It was simple waggishness that afflicted fantasy during Beerbohm's London years. An air of holiday high jinks, of forced festivity, hung about it. Preeminent of its kind and in its time was, of course, *Peter Pan, or the Boy Who Wouldn't Grow Up*. Barrie's play was beloved by many and derided by a few, doubtless for the same reason: It gave the frankest possible expression to the prevailing vogue for half-hearted escapism. Reviewing *Peter Pan* on its first appearance, in 1905, Beerbohm noted that Barrie had always incarnated the prevailing "child-worship" of the period but that in *Peter Pan* he had outdone himself. . . . Puck's doings were "credible and orderly" compared to "the riot of inconsequence and of exquisite futility" that made up Peter Pan's doings.

Nor was Beerbohm an infallible master of fantasy. An early example, **The Happy Hypocrite** . . . , has the interest for us of commemorating a significant moment in his development. As J. G. Riewald has shown, the youthful author of **The Happy Hypocrite** was imitating *The Picture of Dorian Gray* while at the same time trying to free himself from Wilde's influence. **The Happy Hypocrite**, in which a devilish dandy is transformed—not without irony on the author's part—into a loving husband, shows Beerbohm asserting his will to innocence and survival against Wilde's presumed will to the opposite fate. An amalgam of the parable and the fairy tale, **The Happy Hypocrite** is nevertheless a strained performance. So is a much later story, **"The Dreadful Dragon of Hay Hill"**. . . . This seems to have been written to order by "The Incomparable Max"—the title early bestowed, or perhaps foisted, on Beerbohm by a rival wit, Shaw—rather than by Beerbohm himself. By "Beerbohm himself" I mean the Beerbohm in whom the public and the private man, the insider and the outsider, the precocious child and the preternaturally youthful ancient oddly combined to form his intricate singularity of mind. (pp. 13-14)

In comedy, many a familiar jest, proverbial saying, or fashionable phrase comes literally true, and many a flower of poesy is born to blush for its presumption. One sometimes says of an unfortunate friend, or of oneself, that he, or one, is subhuman, a worm, an insect. In Kafka's well-known story, a certain self-despising salesman wakes up one morning to find that he *is* an insect, complete with many wiggly little legs. His family is appalled rather than gratified by his extraordinary act of self-realization, and the human insect presently dies of neglect and cruelty at their hands. The death of Kafka's salesman is paralleled, in a purely comic vein, by the fate of Enoch Soames, one of Beerbohm's creations in **Seven Men**. Soames is the harmless author of a small book of verse called *Fungoids* and a small book of essays called *Negations*. He is nevertheless an avowed poet of the Diabolist school, out of Baudelaire by way of Lionel Johnson, and has written such verses as

> Round and round the shuttered square
> I strolled with the Devil's arm in mine.

Eventually, and much to Soames's surprise, the Devil appears in person and makes off with Soames.

In that story, a single victim is claimed by the process I have been trying to describe—let us call it the process of comic literalization. In **Zuleika Dobson** the same mechanism is flagrantly at work and the victims are many. The casual wish is father to the deed on an unprecedented scale. The cliché bears watching lest it come true with a vengeance. Oxford dons, one learns, have often remarked that Oxford would be a splendid place if it were not for the undergraduates; Oxford undergraduates have expressed identical thoughts concerning the dons. The dons win in *Zuleika Dobson.* One evening, following the final race of Eights Week, they learn that the undergraduates have drowned themselves en masse in the Isis, as the stretch of the Thames at Oxford is known. "And always the patient river bears its awful burden towards Iffley," Beerbohm writes. This flower of poesy begins like a line from "Lycidas" and ends like something in small print in a guide to Oxfordshire. . . .

[Zuleika Dobson] is the woman, a conjurer by profession, for love of whom, ostensibly, the students have drowned themselves—all but the cad Noaks, who has chosen a belated and grimmer death. . . .

In Zuleika's career the literalizing principle is written large. She is a *femme fatale* whose brief stay at Oxford has been actually fatal to hundreds. Surely she has set a new high in the records of femme fatality, exceeding the combined tolls of Keats's La Belle Dame, Swinburne's Dolores, and Wilde's Salomé. One might expect her to be beaten to death with oars as Salomé is with soldiers' shields. She isn't, nor is she visited by any feeling except a resentful loneliness; like that of a popular actress who has made one curtain call too many and is suddenly confronted by an empty house. Whither Zuleika? Zuleika asks herself. After such triumphs, what expectations? True, she has had a gratifying talk with her grandfather. The stiff old Warden of Judas has confessed that he was in his youth an *homme fatal* with many female victims to his credit. What has occurred between the two is unmistakably a "recognition scene." It recalls—probably not accidentally—the scene in *Major Barbara* in which the Salvation Army commander and the ruthless old tycoon slyly discover that each is possessed by the Will to Power and that they are therefore father and daughter after all. Zuleika is somewhat cheered by her encounter with the Warden and presently she finds the answer to her Whither. Consulting her bejeweled copy of Bradshaw she orders a special train for Cambridge. Nothing can stop a fatal woman so long as she believes that somewhere there are more men eager to be fatalized.

Whether she found Cambridge as compliant as Oxford is not known. Beerbohm never composed sequels, except to other men's works (see his **"Sequelula to *The Dynasts*"** in *A Christmas Garland*). . . . Beerbohm did, nevertheless, reveal snatches of her later history by way of a letter signed Zuleika Kitchener and addressed to George Gershwin, who once thought of making a highbrow musical out of her book. In the letter she berated Beerbohm for misrepresenting her in the book and added a postscript saying: "I was married secretly to Lord Kitchener, early in 1915. Being so worried by his great responsibilities at that time, he no longer had the grit to cope with my importunities, poor fellow." (p. 14)

"In reading *Zuleika Dobson* as a description of life at Oxford we should be well-advised to allow for ironic intention," Northrop Frye observes in his *Anatomy of Criticism*. Not every reader has been able to make that allowance. The unreality of the story has made it a problem to some of its interpreters. To Edmund Wilson the part about the mass suicide of the undergraduates is "completely unreal." What parts of the book *does* Wilson find "real?" . . . Where fantasy is concerned, there really is no accounting for people's credulities.

But Wilson is not alone in his objection to *Zuleika Dobson,* and Beerbohm's dehumanizing of his characters does perhaps ask for a bit of explaining. For me, there is only one moment in the book when it is possible to "feel with" any of them. The Duke of Dorset is watching Zuleika's clumsy performance by moonlight and listening to her arch patter ("Well, this is rather queer"). He is so horribly embarrassed for her that he looks with rage on the other young men to whom his beloved is so recklessly exposing herself ("Damn them, they were sorry for her," he thinks). At this point, one guesses, Beerbohm could not help drawing heavily on his own intimate experience as a friend and lover of actresses, ultimately the husband of an indifferent one whose Pre-Raphaelite ecstasies and graces he found laughable, though lovable, even off-stage. For the rest, the author kept his distance from the goings-on in *Zuleika.* So much so that he was surprised when his oldest friend, Reginald Turner, wrote him that—to quote David Cecil's paraphrase of the letter—"he found the characters almost painfully real; he believed in Katie the serving maid too much . . . to take her sufferings in the spirit of comedy." To this Beerbohm replied that he "certainly hadn't realized that Katie and those others were at all real," adding that if "there were really dramatic scenes . . . without humanity," he "never would have admitted this in the *Saturday.*"

The reference to the *Saturday Review* seems conclusive. Much of the "ironic intention" of *Zuleika Dobson,* including the dehumanized characters, stemmed from Beerbohm's experiences as a theater reviewer for that periodical. *Zuleika* is not only about "life at Oxford"; it is about literature, above all the literature of the contemporary London stage, to which Beerbohm had been for so many years "enslaved" (his word) through his connection with the *Saturday.* His reviews show him to have been often sickened by the theater's hackneyed themes, stock characters, trumped-up motivations, transparent mechanics, and false diction. They violated his common sense, they told on his nerves. So did the conduct, professional and private, of certain leading performers: clumsy "conjurers" and would be *femmes* (or *hommes*) *fatales*. *Zuleika Dobson* is life at Oxford seen through the eyes of an inveterate "play-goer," some ideally demoralized veteran of the stalls. Beerbohm, it should be recalled, places the action of his story "in the middle of the Edwardian Age," a time when the theater, bad though much of it was, bulked larger as an institution than it ever has since in Anglo-American culture. (pp. 14-15)

A reading of *Around Theatres,* Beerbohm's collected reviews, is, then, more germane to an understanding of *Zuleika Dobson* than is a short history of Oxford, with maps. The Oxford setting creates itself, as one reads, especially the Oxford setting in its legendary or sentimental aspects. Here Matthew Arnold's too memorable paragraph about the "home of lost causes and impossible loyalties" does continual comic service. The parodying of Arnold starts with the first paragraph, where it is Oxford's railroad station and not her Gothic towers that "whisper to the tourist the last enchantments of the Middle Age." We soon learn that these enchantments still prevail elsewhere in the University. The Oxford of *Zuleika Dobson* remains "medieval" in its charm as well as in other, less lovable, ways; and it is still chivalrous, to the point of suicide. . . .

The Oxford Beerbohm knew as an undergraduate in the Nineties was, or seemed to him, lushly end-of-century. It made him, he later said, "insufferable," meaning idle, mocking, snobbish, an adherent of Oscar Wilde's cult and that of past dandies, D'Orsay and Disraeli. He claimed that he had read nothing at the University except Wilde's *Intentions* and Thackeray's *The Four Georges*. The eating clubs he frequented were exclusive, although not quite so exclusive as The Junta, of which it is said in *Zuleika Dobson* that the Duke of Dorset was for a while the sole member. To the young Beerbohm, abstaining from the more wholesome undergraduate pursuits was an agreeable duty. Once when he was out for a stroll he encountered a fellow student with an oar across his shoulder. "Bound for the river?" the student cheerily asked. "What river?" Beerbohm replied. What river indeed!

His reminiscences of his Oxford life are the caricature of a caricature, the original having been himself. (p. 15)

[At Oxford], as elsewhere later on, he was the outsider-insider, capable of mocking things he also cherished, including his own personality. So if he loved Oxford and mocked it only affectionately in *Zuleika Dobson,* as Oxonians tend to say, he loved it on his own terms. These involved much skepticism, enough to set flowing the tricky currents of satire in *Zuleika Dobson.* Here faddishness is seen to flourish in proportion as Oxford believes itself to be supremely privileged, proudly possessed of its own history and legality, grotesquely celibate (if that is the word), and capable of extending to its dons the privilege of indifferentism towards the undergraduates, towards everything but the dons' own studies and society.

From Christ Church meadow a mist is described as continually rising and permeating the whole place. A prime characteristic of Oxford, the mist is lovingly evoked by Beerbohm. The passage has become a famous set-piece, but unlike Arnold's set-piece it is full of *double-entendres*. The mist is seen to enclose Oxford in a circle of glamor, like a soft-focus photograph. It also shelters the place from "reality," like a smoke screen. Zuleika penetrates and scatters this mist—for the reader. Her presence at the University shows us that its precious faddishness, its cherished weakness for lost causes and impossible loyalties, exist plentifully in the world at large, where they are known, less flatteringly, as the "hard instinct" or "conformity." Zuleika's triumph at Oxford is only a specialized form of the triumphs she has enjoyed everywhere, from Paris to "final Frisco." The great dandy, Dorset, adores her, but so did George Abimilech Post, "the best-groomed man in New York." Self-destruction threatens the herd wherever it exists, although the herd may elect to die in more dignified ways than do the swine in the parable. This Beerbohm saw as early as 1911, with an instinct born of his own highly cultivated idiosyncracy.

It is not because she is "real" herself that Zuleika disperses the mist for us. On the contrary, it is because she is that most potent of forces, a figment of the mass mind. As a conjurer her skill is nil. Nor is she "strictly beautiful," Beerbohm states. . . . (pp. 15-16)

It is true that Zuleika has, or acts as if she had, a devouring passion. She wants to love—love, that is, a man self-sufficient enough to scorn her love. Naturally, the man eludes her. Nobody will let her play Patient Grizzel. The Duke of Dorset matches her in his own lovelessness and in the impossible demands he makes on women. But all these passions are as phantasmal as the two characters themselves are. The passions are "motivations" of the kind forcibly applied to the personages of inferior drama to make their actions plausible. Complaints against the arbitrariness in this respect of Pinero, who finds his motives in the stock room, or against Shaw, who sometimes supplies them from his intellectual laboratory, recur

in Beerbohm's theater reviews. So too with those reversals or, as Beerbohm with his mock pedantry calls them, "peripities," which keep the moral advantage shifting back and forth throughout the long scenes between Zuleika and Dorset. So tangible does this advantage become in its relentless to and fro that it almost materializes as a ball or a brick.

Dorset is more interesting than Zuleika. He is "motivated" by more than his need to love—by his obligations as a dandy and a great nobleman. The Duke is no fraud in these particulars as Zuleika is in her conjurer's role. He is just what he claims to be: the sum of all those titles, residences, servants, decorations, accomplishments, and clothes. Among his accouterments are the pair of owls that have always announced the coming deaths of Dukes of Dorset. The owls really appear on the battlements of Tankerton; they hoot *this* Duke of Dorset to his doom, even in the age of pre-paid telegrams. For the other undergraduates he sets the styles of dressing, of loving, and of dying. As a stage duke, Dorset is complete. The Noakses and the Batches are also complete, as stage plebians. Noaks is a "foil" to the over-privileged Duke. As such he may briefly arouse our democratic sympathies. But his sentiments are soon discovered to be as heavy as his boots and the iron ring he wears to charm away rheumatism. The plebian creations of Shaw, the great humanitarian, often surprise us by turning out to know their place; the clownish place reserved for members

Caricature of Zuleika Dobson from the manuscript of the novel. Reproduced by permission of Eva Reichmann.

of the lower orders, from Dogberry to Doolittle. Nor, one suspects, are Zuleika's French maid, Mélisande, and the American Rhodes scholar, Abimilech V. Oover, "strictly" caricatures; they are, again, caricatures of caricatures: the stage French maid and the stage American. . . .

Beerbohm's achievement in the art of fantasy is possibly *too* consistent. The lengthy speechifying, the tireless parodying of motivations and peripities, make certain scenes tedious. For the wary reader, however, the tedium is continually relieved by all sorts of "tricks" on the author's part—puns, *double-entendres,* dissonances, parodies within parodies, lyrical set-pieces in the descriptive or historical mode, intrusions of the supernatural, brief realistic "shots," so to speak, as of Zuleika applauding at the concert with her hands high above her head like the thorough professional she is. The ironic vision is, moreover, apt to shift its objects abruptly from one type of stage convention to another. Our playgoer gets his Maeterlinck mixed up with his Wycherley. Romance envelops the moonlight walk of Zuleika and Dorset to her quarters in Judas after the concert and her own impromptu performance, the latter a great scene. But crude farce breaks in when, from her bedroom window, she dumps on the Duke's waiting figure the contents of a water pitcher (read chamberpot).

Romance is a recurring attraction in *Zuleika.* The moonlight, the floating mist, the nodding lilacs and laburnums, the weedy bottom of the Isis—all are summoned on stage from the greenwood of English pastoral tradition. They remain lovely, though invariably touched with mockery—the mockery of the purple patch, of eloquence itself. Eloquence itself, high or low, is another motif. There are speaking parts for all: the flowers, the bells, the stony Emperors, together with the more or less human beings. And oh, the things people *say!* Nothing in *Zuleika Dobson,* I find, stays in the memory better than the things people say in it. "She doesn't *look* like an orphan" (the wife of the Oriel don referring to Zuleika). "By God, this college [Judas] is well-named" (Sir Harry Esson, betrayed by a former Warden, as he is stabbed and dies). "Death cancels all engagements" (The Duke of Dorset). "What harm has unrequited love ever done?" (Zuleika). "I say he was not a white man" (Oover of a lengendary Oxford libertine). "I don't know anything about music, but I know what I like" (Zuleika). *"Je me promets un beau plaisir en faisant la connaissance de ce jeune homme"* (George Sand's ghost). "For people who like that kind of thing, that is the kind of thing they like" (Pallas Athene, of *The Decline and Fall of the Roman Empire*). (p. 16)

The verbal tricks, the shifts of focus, the imagery of romance, the things people say—all these go to make up the marvelous surface of *Zuleika Dobson.* Indeed, one's pleasure in the book is largely in following the contours of this surface. *It* is real, however cunningly strewn with surprises. It assumes a reader who is capable of responding to it and who is therefore real, too. The author, above all, is real. He is never more so than when he writes, "You cannot make a man by standing a sheep on its hind-legs. But by standing a flock of sheep in that position you can make a crowd of men. If man were not a gregarious animal, the world might have achieved, by this time, some real progress towards civilization. Segregate him, and he is no fool. But let him loose among his fellows, and he is lost—he becomes just an unit in unreason."

Unlike its heroine, *Zuleika Dobson* is not an exacting mistress. It is not a book for everyone, the children included. One can enjoy it without claiming too much for it. Whether *Zuleika* is

Beerbohm's "masterpiece" is itself open to question. What is almost any writer's masterpiece except a token award for critics to quarrel about? *Seven Men* is as lively and pertinent as *Zuleika* is and has a less taxing consistency of ironic intention. In none of his writings is Beerbohm, the fantasist, in the same class with Swift or Gogol or Kafka. He was too reasonable to indulge, like the half-mad Swift, in prodigies of invention called forth in the name of Reason. *Zuleika Dobson* is a comic criticism not so much of passion itself as of the fashion for passion, the same phenomenon that Mario Praz was seriously to illustrate and analyze in *The Romantic Agony.* If we can judge by what we know of his love affairs, Beerbohm was not himself susceptible to the grand passions. His early history—to evoke that once more—probably predisposed him to feel affection rather than passion for others, possibly to feel affection more strongly because the exclusive ardors of sexual passion were foreign to him. It need hardly be said that popular Freudianism has perpetuated the romantic agony by putting it on "a scientific basis." To this glorification of sexual passion Beerbohm's entire life and work were opposed. "They were a tense and peculiar family, the Oedipuses, weren't they?" he once remarked.

His opposition arose chiefly from a quality of his mind rather than from a defect of his emotional nature. He had the rococco imagination—so much so that *Zuleika* is closer in spirit to *The Rape of the Lock* than it is to the work of fantasists today. Beerbohm saw things as small, discrete, sharply defined, existing in a world that was inexorably finite. From this here-and-now vision came, for one thing, those opinions of his which, often penetrating, sometimes fatuous, are frequently quoted. He objected, for example, that the modern theater lives always in its presumptive future rather than in its present. This opinion is still exemplary. He said of William Morris, "Of course he is a wonderful all-round man but the act of walking round him has always tired me." Amusing but not so exemplary. . . .

His opinions are one thing; the imaginary world projected by his rococco imagination and realized in his fiction and drawings is another. In his fiction, if ever in literature, style and substance live in wedded bliss, the perfect midget couple. The sentence is for him distinctly "an unit." He explores its possibilities as thoroughly as Pope did those of the heroic couplet. All known devices of rhetoric and syntax are set to performing for us with unobstrusive gaiety. Thus is bigness mocked by triumphant littleness—bigness and solemnity and the "tragic sense of life." Not that the *materials* of tragedy are lacking in his work. Misery is everywhere potential in it. Throughout *Zuleika Dobson* the strains of "Liebestod" can be heard swelling, only to dissolve into dissonance. The rococco ethos has been defined by Egon Friedell as a "last craving for illusion," illusion to assuage the painful mysteries of loving and dying. Max Beerbohm had no such craving. For him, loving and dying were mysteries too inscrutable to be encompassed by the word "tragedy." Assuagement lay in the contemplation of beauty and folly and in the act of laughter. (p. 17)

*F. W. Dupee, "Beerbohm: The Rigors of Fantasy,"
in* The New York Review of Books, *Vol. VI, No. 10, June 9, 1966, pp. 12-17.*

JOHN FELSTINER   (essay date 1972)

[*An American educator and critic, Felstiner is the author of* The Lies of Art: Max Beerbohm's Parody and Caricature *(1972). In the following excerpt from that work, he examines several of Beerbohm's works that illustrate his ideas on the nature of art.*]

Beerbohm had a superabundant literary milieu in which to realize himself as caricaturist, personal essayist, and critic. . . . His first books were published by the Bodley Head, the chief outlet for decadent writers, and Leonard Smithers—"known," Beerbohm later wrote, "to have been engaged in the sale of disreputable books"—brought out *Caricatures of Twenty-Five Gentlemen* in 1896. *Punch* had signed its second parody "Max Mereboom," but the implication of flash talent was not borne out. His notoriety allowed him to develop freely in various kinds of writing and to keep in touch with people not always in touch with each other, like Wilde, Yeats, Shaw, Beardsley. (p. 25)

In interviews and in personal essays, he had a habit of making up things about himself that reveal more than the truth would. He said, for example, that he had read only three books at Oxford: Thackeray's *Four Georges*, Wilde's *Intentions*, and Edward Lear's *Book of Nonsense*. Besides suggesting a matrix for some of Beerbohm's leading impulses—satire, paradox, and fantasy—his statement creates a guise of frivolity and idleness. The personal myths he establishes are always in some sense designed to lessen himself. "**Diminuendo**," a short essay he put at the end of the *Works*, concerns his choice at the age of eighteen to withdraw into contemplation. Beerbohm treats Walter Pater's doctrine of experience as if it were purely literal advice, as Symons and others did, walking the crowded streets in London. He says it may be well enough for the Prince of Wales to hunt and sail and dance and drink, to be (in Pater's words) "present always at the focus where the greatest number of forces unite in their purest energy." But Beerbohm cannot abandon himself to life, and decides instead for monotonous simplicity, a little villa in the suburbs where "no vital forces unite." (p. 26)

In announcing his retirement at the end of "**Diminuendo**," Beerbohm wrote that despite his precocious success, "the stress of creation soon overwhelmed me." His only specific self-parody, "**A Vain Child**," . . . appeared a few months after the *Works*, just as he began writing for the *Saturday Review*. It deprecates and promotes him at the same time:

> I write for a weekly paper, and call myself "We." But the stress of anonymity overwhelms me. I belong to the Beerbohm period. I have tumbled into the dark waters of current journalism, and am glad to sign my name.

The title and substance of the piece are based on Heinrich Hoffmann's *Struwwelpeter*—in particular, on Johnny Head-in-Air, who walks along watching birds in the sky and falls headlong into a river, losing his writing-book. "**A Vain Child**" borrows from the *Works* for an effect of superfluous literary flavor: Greek, Latin, and French tags, curious phrases ("it has indeed the sentiment of style") and diction ("furial," "fugient"), and precious intrusions ("for lo!"). Stylistically the parody is disappointing, an inferior version of the original, like *Punch*'s skits on Beerbohm. His early essays call more than enough attention to their own ingenuity, and "**A Vain Child**" reads like something he felt he ought to do. (p. 27)

In his essays and dramatic reviews, he also had the habit of breaking in with apologies for ignorance and mannerism. The opening, for instance, of "**Laughter**": "M. Bergson, in his well-known essay on this theme, says . . . well, he says many things; but none of these, though I have just read them, do I clearly remember." Confessions like this became part of Beerbohm's mask. They include their own reinstating power, for our response is to say, Maybe you're foolish or overliterary or unphilosophical, but we trust you more for telling us.

The kind of reflexive writing Beerbohm practiced was a source of poise, even of strength. Anthony Eden once asked him to address the Oxford Uffizi Society, but he wrote back declining to address them on any topic. "I am quite easy to dispense with. . . . I don't know of any subject on which I am *not* ignorant. My ignorance extends even so far as that!" (p. 28)

Conceiving himself was an ongoing job. It meant steady immunization against other people's intolerance and his own doubts, by doses of self-criticism. He had actual limitations; he could not, for example, comprehend Goethe or Whitman, who are trivially caricatured in *The Poets' Corner*. But self-irony gave him leverage. He says at the end of an impressionistic essay on the eighteen-eighties, in the *Works*: "To give an accurate and exhaustive account of that period would need a far less brilliant pen than mine." This mock of humility points ahead to the strong voice in his later stories and essays. As a gesture in the nineties, the pretense of insignificance mainly freed Beerbohm from being accurate and exhaustive—freed him, in effect, from responsibility, from unimaginativeness. (p. 32)

The critical impulse, the impulse to question artistic means and ends, runs all through Beerbohm's writing between 1897 and 1910, when he stopped reviewing theater, married, and left England. Earlier, in the *Works*, the strategy had been pretense, pure surmise—"Artifice is the strength of the world." His doctrine on cosmetics and his pieces on Whistler, Conan Doyle, and others created a flagrant posture for him. Life had to imitate art: at first, Beerbohm's skepticism about this claim was hard to recognize, a matter of taking his exaggerated arguments as parody. (p. 57)

Toward the turn of the century, he dropped the harlequinism of the *Yellow Book* period. Enoch Soames, the fin-de-siècle poet in a story from *Seven Men*, disappears from sight in 1897: he is presented as Max Beerbohm's alter ego, and that date can mark the end of Beerbohm's attentiveness to English decadent aesthetics. The job as a critic, and more simply, the fact that he was not so young a man, gradually altered his disposition. More of his subjects came from common experience, his style ran more evenly. He was no longer trying to juggle words and opinions faster than the eye could follow. Wilde had talked about the "shackles of verisimilitude": Beerbohm began examining them, looking directly at the play between art and actuality.

Criticism, understood as the vision of that play, took various forms. The essays in *More* . . . and *Yet Again* . . . expose deceptions, some deliberate and some in the nature of things, scattered throughout an urban existence. A series called *Words for Pictures* . . . relates literature and art, a painting and the characters within it, the characters and us, or explores patterns imposed by the artist on life and by the critic on a work of art. As a drama critic, Beerbohm looks for an illusion of reality, not for reality itself, and objects to Shaw's inartistically opinionated characters. In 1913, in *The Mirror of the Past*, he sets Pater's gospel of the "hard, gemlike flame" against his timid existence, and the caricatures in *Rossetti and His Circle* show a romantic artist at odds with circumstance. From this circle of instances, no one decision about adjusting art to life will emerge. Like a number of writers who follow him, Beerbohm in his criticism takes the flux between illusion and reality, or between literary means and ends, as a theme in itself rather than a problem to be solved.

The writing collected for *More,* his second book, almost always has to do with artifice or illusion. At times he wants to keep them in force, and will consider the "unintelligent realism" of photography. At other times he focuses on the false conventions of *Punch*'s cartoonists or asks for the fatuous old tunes of the music hall to come back in place of today's aesthetically demanding performances. The other subjects in *More* are such things as Madame Tussaud's, actors, and **"Pretending,"** while an essay on royalty suggests that wax robots would do much better. Most of the pieces in the book are slight compared to **"Dandies and Dandies"** and the **"Defence of Cosmetics,"** but they consistently expose what was hidden in the *Works*—namely, the traps of aestheticism. The rhetoric has changed from defending to explaining, from "Gracious goodness! why do not we have masks upon the stage?" to an 1897 formula: "The Actor's medium is himself." One piece in *More* resembles Wilde's argument for poisoning ugly people, but Beerbohm breaks down the aesthetic posture. He urges that fires are beautiful to behold, then says that he is organizing an Artists' Corps to go about slitting firemen's hoses and carrying its own filled with oil. Throughout *More* he alternately undercuts and asserts the influence of art in life, in order to rescue a comic question from what Pater treated solemnly and Wilde flamboyantly.

The essays in *Yet Again,* published mostly between 1900 and 1906, concern things likely to be met with by the average Londoner. On the subject of some waxen effigies shown to visitors in Westminster Abbey, Beerbohm argues carefully that lifelike art depends upon an illusion not a replica of life. He also urges the Dean to replace the Abbey's monotonous guides by parrots chained to each tomb and bust. Another essay describes a dejected nag he saw, and then reveals it to be a discarded rocking-horse. Or in civil courts he finds more of the excitement of the theater than in the theater itself. The key essay in *Yet Again,* **"Seeing People Off,"** also derives from Beerbohm's drama criticism. In Euston Station one day, after the emotionally awkward and unsuccessful business of seeing someone off, Beerbohm spots a man, an ex-actor whom he had known, in the midst of fervent good-byes with a woman. Both are in tears but it seems a rich experience. After she has left, Beerbohm learns that his friend is now working for a bureau that hires out people to see Americans off. The twist (recalling Hamlet's question about the tragedian: "What's Hecuba to him, or he to Hecuba, / that he should weep for her?'') is doubly funny and characteristic because it implicates Beerbohm: his friend offers to give him lessons, and though the fee is steep, he decides to accept.

While each of these essays has a point to make, their fundamental design is not to foster a choice between authentic and inauthentic events, any more than the parables of Jorge Luis Borges mean to say: this view of things is true, that untrue. Beerbohm's questions about the structure of consciousness turn into answers. In finding civil courts better than theater, he neither downgrades theater nor takes human trouble lightly, but discovers play at the heart of human behavior and belief.

"Madame Tussaud's," written in 1897, epitomizes all the essays of this period. It speculates on the waxworks as stiff, morbid, barren puppets, obscene images with tallowy faces, glass eyes, "smooth, nailless, little hands." The statues "were not life-like. They gave me no illusion. . . . Though these waxworks are made in so close an imitation of life, they have indeed, less verisimilitude than the outcome of any fine art."

Coleridge had illustrated his central principle by calling waxwork figures mere likenesses: genuine art, for him, displayed both likeness and unlikeness to nature. This distinction served Beerbohm as a critic, and it defines as well the exaggerating and thus life-giving technique of caricature. (pp. 57-60)

Beerbohm began by defending, in the person of his own style, the exclusive creative agency of art. In drama criticism and other writing around the turn of the century, such as *Words for Pictures,* his angle of vision shifted to what would directly expose the working of artistic illusion. Then a new form of expression, fusing those two impulses, emerged in *A Christmas Garland, Zuleika Dobson,* and *Seven Men.* Parody, the quintessence of that new form, is at once a creative and a critical act. It resolves, without quite deciding, the problem raised by Ibsen—whether art is worth it.

At the head of *A Christmas Garland,* Beerbohm placed his parody of Henry James. James's work stood for the whole of fiction, and Beerbohm imagined James rather than Wilde or Shaw as an example of the accomplished artist. His attention to James lasted throughout sixty years, in parodies, essays, reviews, letters, poems, caricatures, alterations, and a last reminiscence written in 1954. All together they present Beerbohm's fullest image of a writer, and a reflection of himself. (p. 141)

In December 1906 Beerbohm published **"The Mote in the Middle Distance,"** a fetish for anyone who either loves or disparages James.

The finely involved, central intelligence of the parody is Keith Tantalus, wondering with his sister Eva what the Christmas stockings at the foot of their beds contain, and whether to investigate them. What Beerbohm re-creates is the way every utterance, every human option in James is swaddled in layers of awareness. (p. 142)

Beerbohm's title and the rest of his parody develop the way of registering perceptions which James developed in his later novels. All the turns of style Beerbohm invents for Keith and Eva can be found in *The Wings of the Dove* and *The Golden Bowl.* They sometimes seem to be done better by Beerbohm, sometimes less well done: the broken sentences, roundabout simplicities, syntactical quibbles, colloquialisms made genteel by inverted commas, italics for delicate intonation, stunning double negatives, accumulated homely adjectives, abruptly placed, vague adverbs, banal metaphors worried and reworried, the narrator's unsettling glances into the future and his intimacy with "our friend" Keith, the exasperating, magnified scruples, and, at last, the vibrant moral renunciation by Keith and Eva— "One doesn't violate the shrine—pick the pearl from the shell!"

"The Mote in the Middle Distance," with its discriminations and qualifications, displays a perverse subtlety. One can compare Keith and Eva to the brother and sister in *The Turn of the Screw,* but really Beerbohm's children are a burlesque reduction of Merton Densher and Kate Croy in the final scene of *The Wings of the Dove.* Densher decides it would be better to return unopened an envelope containing his inheritance: Keith says finally, "One doesn't even peer" into the Christmas stockings. An undertone of frustration runs through the generally benign stylistic parody of James. For one thing, Beerbohm makes the children brother and sister, yet Keith thinks about Eva as nervously as one of James's lovers would: "his fear of what she was going to say was as nothing to his fear of what she might be going to leave unsaid." And the name Eva Tantalus clearly implies that some kind of sexual frustration lies behind James's imagining of his characters and their experiences. (pp. 142-43)

Beerbohm's ability to conceive **"The Mote in the Middle Distance,"** and his love for James, whom he came to know personally in the nineties, do not seem to have been affected by the clear contrasts between them: by James's passionate absorption in the art of fiction, and the great formal culmination, as against Beerbohm's versatility dwindling to a piece every few years; James's dense emotion and Beerbohm's lightness; James's massive aesthetic impersonality and Beerbohm's self-insinuations. Remaining aware of these disparities may even have been Beerbohm's way of accommodating himself as an artist. (p. 145)

During Beerbohm's active literary career—1893 to 1918—two phenomena became more and more significantly intermixed: the presentment of himself, and the displaying of aesthetic technique.... [We] have the image of a writer confessing inherent inadequacy by means of an adequate act of writing. Beerbohm could comprehend the language of *De Profundis*, if not the apocalyptic symbolism of *When We Dead Awaken*. In his own early prose, the rudimentary form of reflexive irony occurs when he excuses mannerisms by advertising them. He went on to change this coyness into a technique, a condition that alters the ends of literature by building in and questioning the means, including the writer himself.

"A Relic," written in 1918, illustrates this technique. Beerbohm deliberately placed the essay at the beginning of *And Even Now*, a collection otherwise arranged chronologically, 1910 to 1920. The "relic" is a broken-off butt from a cheap fan, dropped near him in a café at Dieppe in 1891 and left behind by a bitterly quarreling French couple, whose psychological drama led Beerbohm to begin his writing career with a *conte* modeled after Guy de Maupassant. He would be an "impersonal *je*" sitting at a table; "four or five short sentences would give the whole scene. One of these I had quite definitely composed.... 'Down below, the sea rustled to and fro over the shingle.'" But all he had was that one sentence, which was to recur quietly amidst emotional stress. He could get nowhere in trying to re-create their whole story. Perhaps the man kept a once-prosperous fan shop, now destitute because this woman always smashed his presents: "Ah, monsieur ... the fan she broke tonight was the last—the last, monsieur—of my stock.' Down below ...." The story failed to be written, yet **"A Relic"** paradoxically reaches what Maupassant was after. Between author and inadequate refrain, we glimpse an act of life that will not be made into something else.

With **"A Relic"** in mind, we can speak interchangeably, as Roland Barthes does, of the analysis and the creation of literature. Indeed, in more than half the essays of *And Even Now*, it is artists and works of art—of literature, above all—that activate Beerbohm's imagination: model letters, books within books, Swinburne, Slavic writers, a woman novelist's novel about a woman novelist, an unfinished painting, a veiled statue. The essay on laughter makes its points by means of Bergson, *Henry IV*, Tom Moore's life of Byron, and Boswell's *Johnson*. Limiting and secondhand as it seems, this recourse to literature, to Kolniyatsch's "broken rhythm," for instance, filters a richer consciousness of reality than some impartial viewpoint would. Parody is also an obvious filter, and the coincidence between Beerbohm's specific talent for parody and his habitual literary themes marks the true center of his inspiration.

A meditation on Boswell's biography of Johnson (the best book in the English language, Beerbohm thought), and a parody of Johnson's style, coexist in **"'A Clergyman'."** ... "A Clergyman" is merely Boswell's heading for the only remark made on April 7, 1778, at Thrale Hall by a man whose name he cannot remember. Beerbohm quotes the close of an exchange on the English preachers:

> BOSWELL. What I want to know is, what sermons afford the best specimen of English pulpit eloquence.
>
> JOHNSON. We have no sermons addressed to the passions, that are good for anything; if you mean that kind of eloquence.
>
> A CLERGYMAN. Were not Dodd's sermons addressed to the passions?
>
> JOHNSON. They were nothing, Sir, be they addressed to what they may.

This germinates into a beautiful surmise, a fiction, on the man who "solicits my weak imagination," as Beerbohm says. The conditional tense pervades this essay, along with constructions that emphasize how difficult it is to find the human truth behind the fact of events: "I suppose," "We may assume," "I think we can guess," "It is probable," "On no other hypothesis can we account," and so forth. Towards the end, Beerbohm shifts to constructions such as "I see him" and "I'm sure of it."

The dim, forgettable clergyman (pale face, receding chin, mouse-colored hair) must have come from the local church, felt himself a small actor among the great divines, and sat nervously waiting to make an impression on Doctor Johnson. Judging then from the cadence of his question, Beerbohm imagines that it was delivered in an irritatingly shrill voice, and that Johnson roared back deeply. "Boswell does not record that there was any further conversation.... Perhaps the whole company had been temporarily deafened." Toward the end of the essay, one sentence occurs as if by an act of primitive possession—"'Every man illustrious in his day, however much he may be gratified by his fame, looks with an eager eye to posterity'"—and goes on reproducing Johnson's diction and balance perfectly. Then Beerbohm finishes speculating on the fate of the clergyman:

> A robust man might have rallied under the blow. Not so our friend. Those who knew him in infancy had not expected that he would be reared. Better for him had they been right.... 'A Clergyman' never held up his head or smiled again after the brief encounter recorded for us by Boswell. He sank into a rapid decline. Before the next blossoming of Thrale Hall's almond trees he was no more. I like to think that he died forgiving Dr. Johnson.

The clergyman has, in effect, been killed, taken out of the minimal circumstances of Boswell's report and released into the freedom of an invented life so completely that he can die. It is the radical act of fictional creation and yet nothing but surmise.

The book that realizes the potential of **"A Relic"** and **"'A Clergyman,'"** indeed the potential of all Beerbohm's previous writing, is *Seven Men*.... *Seven Men* is a book of narratives about imaginary late-Victorian and Edwardian characters: a poet, a playwright, two novelists, a gambler, and a compulsive liar—six men in all. Beerbohm is the seventh, narrating the stories and participating as a ludicrously naïve version of himself.

He asked his publishers to give *Seven Men* (and *Zuleika Dobson* as well) an essaylike format. The reader should feel he has a book of actual memoirs in his hand, and these narratives do take that form. Their circumstances are autobiographical and depict Beerbohm's own sphere before his marriage: the Café Royal, a restaurant in Soho, the British Museum, a country estate, a seashore hotel, a casino in Dieppe. With narratives verging on the supernatural, he takes care to make the texture realistic. Arthur Balfour mingles with the guests in one story, and Beerbohm's early journalistic career forms part of another. To illustrate **"A. V. Laider"** for the American edition, he had special notepaper printed with the name of the hotel he and his character stayed at, and on it he made a rough sketch of Laider, done as if at the time of the story. Beerbohm had remarked hopefully to Reggie Turner that the realistic elements of *Zuleika Dobson* would make it "something to be worried about, something rather baffling." What marks *Seven Men* is again this desire to keep the reader's mind moving, reverberating, checking among alternatives. (pp. 190-91)

[**"Enoch Soames"**] develops the relationship between Soames, a nonvirulent follower of the English imitators of Verlaine and Baudelaire, and the young narrator, Beerbohm. Soames sips absinthe in the right cafés and says that Milton converted him to Catholic Diabolism. But he seems weak-minded. (pp. 199-200)

[Beerbohm], a novice writer, tries to find the *mot juste* for him. He settles on "dim," but Rothenstein calls Soames utterly nonexistent. Soames's first book, *Negations,* has a preface that begins, "Lean near to life. Lean very near—nearer. Life is web, and therein nor warp nor woof is, but web only." (p. 200)

Soames tells Beerbohm that the poems in his next book, *Fungoids,* will be . . . strange growths, wild, exquisite, full of poisons—though apparently the poet has a low opinion of Baudelaire, "a *bourgeois malgré lui.*" Beerbohm, pleased to be able to buy the book of a friend, buys *Fungoids* immediately and finds things that seem very good:

TO A YOUNG WOMAN

Thou art, who hast not been!
    Pale tunes irresolute
    And traceries of old sounds
    Blown from a rotted flute
Mingle with noise of cymbals rouged with rust,
Nor not strange forms and epicene
    Lie bleeding in the dust,
        Being wounded with wounds.

    For this it is
That in thy counterpart
    Of age-long mockeries
Thou hast not been nor art!

A certain inconsistency between the first and last lines may only indicate his failure, Beerbohm says, to see the depth of Soames's meaning. And "as for the craftsmanship, 'rouged with rust' seemed to me a fine stroke, and 'nor not' instead of 'and' had a curious felicity." Every irony that Beerbohm practices against himself rebounds onto Soames. Within the contorted, unmoving, semi-erotic, and falsely sinister verse, there is a parody of what Symons and others also imported from French Symbolism: a hermetic circularity and, in the pale tunes, traceries of sounds, and rouged cymbals, an infusion of literature with visual and musical experience. (pp. 200-01)

Fungoids gets only one review (from Soames's home town) and sells three copies; his third book goes unreviewed and Beerbohm cannot remember the name of it. One afternoon in June 1897, the two men lunch together. Soames anguishes over missing worldly recognition: if he could only be projected into the British Museum reading-room a hundred years hence—

"just for this one afternoon! I'd sell myself body and soul to the devil, for that! Think of the pages and pages in the catalogue: 'SOAMES, ENOCH' endlessly—endless editions, commentaries, prolegomena, biographies."

At that moment a stranger who has been sitting nearby during lunch, "a tall, flashy, rather Mephistophelian man," joins them. Against Beerbohm's desperate pleading, Soames makes his bargain.

The trip into the future, reversing a scheme Beerbohm was then working on for *The Mirror of the Past,* allows some anti-utopian satire. On returning from 1997, Soames reports that he made quite a stir in the reading-room. Everyone else was dressed in a Shavian wool uniform and wore a numbered metal disc on the left sleeve. Unfortunately the SN-SOF volume of the catalogue had only the three little slips he already knew. Soames could find nothing except one trivial mention of himself, in a late-twentieth-century literary history, which he copied out for Beerbohm. It is from T. K. Nupton's *Inglish Littracher 1892-1900,* "published bi th Stait" in 1992:

Fr egzarmpl, a riter ov th time, namd Max Beerbohm, hoo woz stil alive in th twentieth senchri, rote a stauri in wich e pautraid an immajnari karrakter kauld 'Enoch Soames'—a thurd-rait poit hoo beleevz imself a grate jeneus an maix a bargin with th Devvl in auder ter no wot posterriti thinx ov im! It iz a sumwot labud sattire but not without vallu as showing hou seriusli the yung men ov the aiteen-ninetiz took themselvz.

Soames is outraged, and Beerbohm insists desperately that it must be some idiotic mistake or coincidence. (pp. 202-03)

Soames accuses Beerbohm of not being a good enough artist: "so far from being able to imagine a thing and make it seem true, you're going to make even a true thing seem as if you'd made it up. You're a miserable bungler." Beerbohm protests that T. K. Nupton is the bungler, and besides, "I'm an essayist, an observer, a recorder." Finally Soames, with more dignity than Beerbohm had ever seen in him, says, "I see the whole thing. *Parlons d'autre chose.*" Beerbohm frantically suggests an escape to Calais, but the poet is soon called for and gone. "In the blinding glare of the near Jubilee" of Queen Victoria, no one notices his disappearance. (p. 204)

We are used to thinking about how the artist shapes his subject. **"Enoch Soames"** makes the most drastic case for that. Periit Soames: Beerbohm fecit. The irony is that the poet, like the clergyman, perishes when he attains most life, in the heroic, existential "I see the whole thing." Usually, in our imagination, fictional characters reach for more of the life that literature can give them. Here Soames is claiming actual life. He is a fiction struggling against fiction, and against the bungler, the man who stopped living for a while to write about him. We begin to feel a tension on the puppet strings and control being reversed. The story moves back to its own point of origin and on past.

Beerbohm urges that literature is no more and no less stylized than life. His writing institutes a primary world, something even he as character can appear in. If art survives in this century by the game of questioning itself, an essential part of this game finds its shape in Beerbohm's parody of literature.

With "**Enoch Soames**" Beerbohm had come a long way from the "**Defence of Cosmetics**," which he said perhaps should have been signed D. Cadent or Parrar Docks. In both works, he plays off against the reader's bafflement his own relation to decadent aesthetics. The change is from having to publish a corrective letter in the *Yellow Book* to inventing a "labud" story and the "curious felicity" of Soames's verse. He had come by way of Shaw, Ibsen, James, *Zuleika Dobson,* and *The Mirror of the Past,* enacting the contradictions he had to live with. (pp. 206-07)

[Beerbohm] is a pivotal figure historically. The major essays, criticism, parodies, and stories, *The Poets' Corner* and *Rossetti and His Circle,* taken together with private and uncollected sketches, notes, jokes—they all present images of art and the artist and, like a convex mirror, reflect modern literature from within. In questioning the value of the imagination and its constructions, Beerbohm belongs to the Romantic movement of thought. Whether deliberately or whimsically does not matter so much: he joined Arnold's and Pater's aesthetic idealism to the self-consciousness of James and Wilde in a generic parody of literature. As parody by its nature thoroughly pervades whatever form it takes, Beerbohm's writing is like an intake of breath or a shudder. It has all the signs of a literature breaking up and perhaps reconditioning itself. The writer ab-

Beerbohm in his later years. Reproduced by permission of Eva Reichmann.

negates himself, the process of composing essays and stories becomes a spectacle, and many of them express the precarious relation of form to content. Where ordinarily we neglect or take for granted the connections between an artist, a work of art, and ourselves, Beerbohm literalizes, energizes those connections—pretentiously, with "**A Defence of Cosmetics**," and in crucial ways later on. Paintings or characters come alive out of their frames; imitation and illusion take over as subjects, instead of remaining the means for conveying a subject. The author turns up in his own work, sometimes even a victim of it. Bits of actual life contend with invented things in narrative, and the reader is drawn in off balance. The mirror of art now generates light and images, and as in Lewis Carroll's books, language gets back something of its primordial life.

I do not mean that Beerbohm's writing is experimental in the sense that *Ulysses* forms a series of experiments. His comic vision works within structures of traditional symmetry and recurrence, and the skepticism in "**Enoch Soames**" or *A Christmas Garland* is of a different order from the gratuitous, subversive nonsense in Dada or the crumbling style of Samuel Beckett. Just as Beerbohm's taste for modern art stopped at the first stage of harmonious impressionism, he kept his preference for form and beauty in prose. He parodied facile realism and the Edwardian novel years before Joyce or Virginia Woolf began to break up conventional forms of narrative, yet his parody treats the methods of Bennett and Galsworthy as still negotiable. (pp. 216-17)

He was uncompelled to follow the winding path of modern consciousness, even though his writing under its own terms locates the otherness of events and people, the emptiness of culture and the self. A final, paralyzing awareness of these things did not seem to him the province or purpose of literature. As an instinctual parodist, Beerbohm says what Beckett's exhausted speaker says, "I can't go on, I'll go on," but with exuberance and a decided love for the order of language. He is still alive in the twentieth century because he wrote himself into a parody of literature that invents and conserves radical criticisms of itself, asking us not to stop the lies of art but to see through them and with them. (p. 218)

> *John Felstiner, in his* The Lies of Art: Max Beerbohm's Parody and Caricature, *Alfred A. Knopf, 1972, 283 p.*

MARSHALL LEDGER   (essay date 1976)

[*In the following excerpt, Ledger presents a close examination of* A Christmas Garland.]

Christmas 1912 must have been cheerier than usual, if only because of the publication of Max Beerbohm's *A Christmas Garland.* Seventeen of Beerbohm's contemporaries were amusingly parodied in this work; no one, I suppose, found difficulty in reading past the asterisks in J*m*s, K*pl*ng, W*lls, H*rdy, B*nn*tt, G*lsw*rthy, C*nr*d, M**re, M*r*d*th (among novelists); Ch*st*rt*n, H*rr*s, G*sse, B*ll*c, H*wl*tt, B*ns*n, and Str**t (among belletrists); and Sh*w. (p. 227)

A collection of parodies was not a new idea. In 1736, Isaac Hawkins Browne wrote *A Pipe of Tobacco,* praises put into the mouths of major authors of the day on what they put into their mouths; in 1784 a few cynical and disregarded poets gathered *Probationary Odes for the Laureateship;* in 1797-98 Canning, Ellis, and Frere parodied the politics of radical poets in the *Anti-jacobin,* and in 1812, James and Horace Smith wrote *Rejected Addresses,* supposed speeches celebrating the opening of the rebuilt Drury Lane Theatre. Collections of parodies such as Thackeray's *Novels by Eminent Hands* (1845) and Swinburne's *Heptalogia* (1880) appeared throughout the nineteenth century.

What distinguishes Beerbohm's collection from these others is a unique unifying agent: the use of the parodies to define the parodist's position as artist. All parodies can be read as being critical, fault-finding, or appreciative of their originals. All parodies bring up the question of dominance or control and suggest that the parodist is finding his place by taking this particular tack on the original. But only Beerbohm thought of himself as an artist who finds his identity exclusively through parodying others.

Beerbohm himself suggests this meaning in a prefatory "Note" to the book. He says that as a youth he parodied—"played the sedulous ape"—to find models for his own style, sometimes to discover what to avoid. This explanation is pat enough, common to many writers. But he caps his statements with revealing and typical wit: "The book itself may be taken as a sign that I think my own style is, at length, more or less formed." And of course there is nothing here that is not also someone else's. The laurel wreath, figured in the garland, belongs on Beerbohm's head. He is the hero, represented by no narrow set of literary devices describable as "Maxian" or less elegantly "Beerbohmian," but represented by the Jamesian and Shavian and Conradian devices all serialed together; nowhere pinned down and fixed by his own style, everywhere suggested by whosever style he chooses to present. (pp. 227-28)

For the space of this essay, let us treat parody as we would treat a work whose seriousness was beyond question. Let us assume that whatever in a work is separable from other elements and "can be thought of as distinct" is potentially grist for a parodist. So he will work not only with word choice, but also with larger elements like structure, situations, patterns. Let us look at the content of the parody as a serious choice of the parodist, not one forced on him by an author he has randomly chosen to parody. For a parodist, content is another element of style. Finally, since when a parodist chooses someone to parody, he commits himself to the original's entire bag of tricks, let us assume that each and every trick is one willingly taken on, not simply a requisite part of the original's paraphernalia, like the contents of a suit-case bought unopened at a post-office auction.

These requests are not outrageous. We grant them constantly, as far as they apply, to other kinds of literature. Here, they will permit me to make a case for the unity of *A Christmas Garland* as more than a string of parodies. My case is this: Beerbohm works himself up from the subservient position of parodist into the position of master over the original, overtaking the artist on his own grounds and, beyond the point of burlesque or ridicule, supplanting him; this is Beerbohm's way of laying claim to the title of artist. (pp. 228-29)

The Jamesian parody, **"The Mote in the Middle Distance,"** is the most famous and most often reprinted. It is the story of Keith Tantalus's moral awakening. He and his sister Eva wake up Christmas morning to find their stuffed stockings dangling at the foot of the bed. Keith wants to plunge right into them, but sensing something wrong with that act, tries to feel out Eva's attitude. She is a master of restraint—so much so that her sheer presence, rather than direct warning, wins Keith back from his unseemly impetuousness. They never do peek.

The parody includes what we usually term "style" and then extends out to subtler aspects which we also ought to call "style": "broken sentences, roundabout simplicities, syntactical quibbles, colloquialisms made genteel by inverted commas, italics for delicate intonation, stunning double negatives, accumulated homely adjectives, abruptly placed, vague adverbs, banal metaphors worried and reworried, the narrator's unsettling glances into the future and his intimacy with 'our friend' Keith, the exasperating, magnified scruples, and, at last, the vibrant moral renunciation" [John Felstiner, *The Lies of Art* (see excerpt dated 1972)]. To which let us add, terminology from painters, physical gestures and positions which seem like dynamic stills, the change wrought in the title through the development of the narrative; indefinite statements ("Oh, as to that!") and the assumption that the interpretation following such attenuation is correct; speculation about the other person, which seemingly could be put to rest by a direct question or two; indefiniteness of motive ("Perhaps it was to test this theory, or perhaps merely to gain time . . ."), raising doubts about how successfully one can penetrate the mind of another (Keith of Eva's mind, the narrator of Keith's); and the unknown line between fantasy and a good reading of another's intentions.

This list only begins to describe the parody's relation to the original. Distressingly it may not even approach the way Beerbohm actually apprehended James. Beerbohm pencilled on the rear cover of his copy of James's *The Finer Grain* what seems to be a few notes to himself:

> Never wrote verses—
> suppressed poet came
> out in letters—
> rhetoric
> alexandrines

The last word suggests that Beerbohm perceived in terms of rhythm, which he proceeded to parse in the vocabulary of his sound classical education. In **"The Mote,"** alexandrines abound:

> "They so very indubitably *are,* you know!" . . .
>
> It was with a certain sense of his rashness in
> the matter, therefore, that he now, with an air of
> feverishly "holding the line," said "Oh, as to
>   that!" . . .
>
> [The narrator won't ask if they peeked because of his
>   impression]
> —my sometimes all but throned and anointed
>   certainty—
> that the answer, if vouchsafed, would be in the
>   negative. . . .

Rhythm is doubtless a much deeper aspect of technique, one much less susceptible to cancellation or revision, than most of the preceding list, although all the items on the list tend, in James, to build to the rhythm Beerbohm heard.

Given all these elements, it is difficult to say exactly where burlesque or ridicule sets in. John Felstiner thinks of the parody as a "fetish for anyone who either loves or disparages James," expressing the delicate balance the parody maintains. The parody is so complete that it is difficult to ascertain Beerbohm's critical reaction to James; we see merely that his artistic reaction is reception in the highest degree. And no doubt we ought to take that felt balance as a way of looking at the parody. We might see Keith and Eva as a reduction of Merton Densher and Kate Croy in *The Wings of the Dove* (as Felstiner suggests), we can also see the toys in the stockings as a reduction of the beasts in Jamesian jungles. But reduction is not always belittlement; it can be a way of getting a handle on something. Beerbohm praised James' characters [in a review of *The High Bid*] for their "passion of conscience, a sort of lyrical conscience, conscience raised to the pitch of ecstasy, both in great matters and in small." If we think in these terms of technical accomplishment, rather than weight, we begin to think as Beerbohm did, with a mind tuned to psychology and art rather than to criticism.

To get at this parody, then, we must leave off measuring the critical stance, and treat it as a work with its own integrity. We don't look at it apart from the original—even though it does have a self-enclosed and complete story—but we ask what is in the parody that intrigued Beerbohm. To do this, we must examine the narrative as more than merely a peg on which Beerbohm hung Jamesian devices. (pp. 229-31)

What attracts Beerbohm to this story is more than its Jamesian origin. It is Beerbohm's own story of his relation to James. Eva and Keith are eidolons for James and Beerbohm. The awareness Keith grows into is analogous to the understanding a parodist has for his original. Although Eva may guess what is in the stockings, she restricts herself to the sure knowledge that they must not be pryed into. What is *in* the stockings represents the real nature of the children's desires and hopes and fatuities, but one doesn't get at them by ravage. The material thing, a reflection of the personality that wants it, must be approached gingerly, as one would deal with oneself, not grabbed. If one doesn't pick the pearl from the shell, it is not simply to play up to a mystery for mystery's sake, but to avoid missing the diaphonous personality by manhandling it. This is Jamesian. Analogously Beerbohm can get "at" James by showing that he understands the intricacies of the Jamesian mode of thought without flattening those intricacies by his own critical terms or by imposing his own interpretations. So he thinks in terms of "motes," which conceal, but to the perceiving eye reveal by suggestion, innuendo, implication, all the ways of Jamesian indirection. At the threshold of his realization, Keith says of the mote in the middle distance, "'Did you ever, my dear, know me to see anything else? I tell you it blocks out everything. It's a cathedral, it's a herd of elephants, it's the whole habitable globe. Oh, it's, believe me, of an obsessiveness!'" In Jamesian style, these words are *about* the Jamesian style, figured in the stockings. Keith swiftly comes to know that they sufficiently imply everything. In the course of his own reading and understanding, Beerbohm found himself in this relation to James.

The details in **"The Mote"** bear out the relation between original and parodist. The telephone is a device which lends aural closeness, but demands that the whole personality be inferred through voice alone. This is good enough for a parodist. When Keith falls into a momentary fit of disaffection and accuses Eva of his own failing, the lack of "propinquity," she (James) is perfectly right in turning his own phrase back on him. Keith calls propinquity a "trick," as we might label the tricks (not trickery) of a clever illusionist. Ultimately, propinquity becomes identification—Keith's with Eva's ways, Beerbohm's with James'. (pp. 232-33)

Like **"The Mote in the Middle Distance,"** Beerbohm's parody of Conrad, **"The Feast,"** is an excellent parody pertinent to Beerbohm's own interests. The narrative tells how Williams, a clerk for commerce stationed in Africa, has been led by his servant Mahamo to a place where he will exchange trinkets for valuable ivory. The time is Christmas Day, and Williams'

thoughts drift back to his fellow Englishmen celebrating the Christmas feast. Mahamo says that today is a feast-day for his own people, and Williams discovers that he has been brought to the feast—as the entree.

The parody is built on both little and large items associated with Conrad: postpositive adjectives, pairings, abstractions that lend themselves to philosophic statement (rivalling the concrete aspect of the narrative), foreshadowing, "exoticism," vegetation given the vigor of conscious beings, mystifying atmosphere, failure to read the landscape, misleading patterns in sensory things, ironies—of statement, of title, of situation, of job, the centrality of illusion, the "partnership" between black man and white, men seemingly getting along without feeling for one another, one's identification with one's office (at the sacrifice of the human and personal), the mocking of "human solidarity," the exploited outdoing the exploiter at his own game, the disaster befalling a lack of "imagination," and finally the fantasies represented by social institutions and "aims" in life, which prevent us—or protect us—from attending to the dark side of existence, the unknown and unintelligible. (p. 235)

Williams is an unknowing victim of the real world. He is human: he dreams of home, itches when bitten by mosquitoes, and resents the fate which he sees at last will be his. He has what he thinks is a responsible job of collecting ivory from natives, but in that office he has relinquished some human traits. He takes his own imperialistic work for granted, including his mastery over Mahamo. In Conrad, it is personally disastrous to be unaware of the implications of your work. Accordingly, although Williams doesn't intend to cheat the natives or sell Mahamo out, he ignores what it means for him to do what he is doing. He has rationalized his life—not in the sense of making the best of a bad situation, but in the basic sense of thinking thoughts and performing actions which conveniently protect him from questioning the status quo.

On this point, Beerbohm deeply understands Conrad; it happens to be a point of overlap with James. Beerbohm loves the rationalizations that one makes of one's situation. In James this typically human behavior is called "attenuation"; in Conrad, "illusion." The illusions Conrad writes of are those constructions of reality which prevent a person from ever shaming himself in front of his full consciousness (not to mention others). In the parody, Williams never lets go. Even in the moment of dawning that he shall not feast, but be feasted upon, he resorts to his structure of the world:

> As he turned in his flight he saw the goods so neatly arranged at his orders, and there flashed through him, even in the thick of the spears, the thought that he would be a grave loss to his employers. This—for Mr. Williams was, not less than the goods, of a kind easily replaced— was an illusion. It was the last of Mr. Williams' illusions. . . .

Even as this theme is Conrad's, so is it Beerbohm's. As a parodist and especially as a dandy, Beerbohm cautiously held himself in, playing up to ideas and styles that were already established in art.

Williams' mental shelter is paralleled by a series of physical ones: a mosquito net, a hut, the roofs of trees, the blue sky. All are ineffectual. The mosquito net was "itself illusory like everything else, only more so." This should have been an illusion Williams himself perceived! But even here he suppresses himself for his office; first he checks the goods, and only after seeing that they are safe does he relieve his agony by scratching. The other illusions are rendered as Conradian ironies. Williams stands in the "mouth" of the hut. Under the roofs of the trees takes place that "warfare implacable and daily" among all the insects of the jungle, even on this holy morning "newly roused to the task of killing and being killed." And the trees are silhouetted against the sky "like shapes cut out of black paper by a maniac who pushes them with his thumb this way and that, irritably, on a concave surface of blue steel"—a simile whose elements foreshadow the spear that finally imposes on Williams, "a young sapling tremulous, with a root of steel."

Ultimately there are no shelters, physical or mental. Williams is a man out in the open, exposed. In living up to his job, he closes out a sense of the world as it really is; he is "not imaginative." He lives in a dream-world as unreal as his nostalgic fantasy of lying in his bedroom in Marylebone, "late dozing, with great contentment." He is not so much punished for his faults as he is forced to succumb to the way of the predatory world.

"The Feast" does lack Conrad's moral seriousness. The eating of Williams is expected more as a psychological event than as a moral one. If Williams is a careless master, he is not brutish; if Mahamo is wily, he is not secretive and mysterious. There are no philosophic implications—no metaphysical skepticism, no parodic comment on Conradian pessimism; the cannibalism is not seen, as it is in "Heart of Darkness," as "unspeakable rites." In such words as "inexplicable" and "inilluminable," the parody has what Leavis has called in Conrad the "adjectival insistence upon inexpressible and incomprehensible mystery," but Beerbohm does not care about that mystery as Conrad does (or as Conrad, in purple passages, convinces himself he does).

Beerbohm chooses to ignore this rich aspect of Conrad because it does not suit his definition of self that is being made through Conrad. Only Conrad's sense of human relation is relevant, not the nature of man's mind and the fearful question of what man's mind is. The parody raises the question of who is in charge, a deep question to both Conrad and Beerbohm: the story is about how the servant is really the master. Talking about illusions and presenting them dominate the narrative because they are persistent Conrad motifs, and Beerbohm's major ones as well. For master or Williams, read Conrad; for servant or Mahamo, read Beerbohm. (pp. 236-37)

In two different writers, James and Conrad, Beerbohm found ways to insinuate his own place as artist; yet his parodies lose nothing for this extra interest. In fact, I would reverse the priorities: his own interests are not "extra" but entwined with the parodies. They doubtlessly conditioned the kinds of styles he could parody most fully. . . . As we read the parodies, we don't feel any lack of fulness, but we can readily suppose that, in defining himself through parody as an artist-scholar, Beerbohm selected with as careful an eye towards his own needs as towards adherence to his original authors. (p. 239)

Marshall Ledger, "Ring Around: 'A Christmas Garland'," in Aeolian Harps: Essays in Literature in Honor of Maurice Browning Cramer, *edited by Donna G. Fricke and Douglas C. Fricke, Bowling Green University Press, 1976, pp. 227-46.*

TERRY CAESAR (essay date 1986)

[*In the following excerpt, Caesar compares Beerbohm's parodies to those found in the works of such modern authors as James Joyce, Ezra Pound, and T. S. Eliot.*]

[The] kind of writing which Beerbohm evolved, though it was given the formal designation of parody, is not so different from that written by Eliot, Pound, or Joyce. Beerbohm's writing did not come into existence because of these writers, but he had to face, along with them, the common problem of inherited forms and "false orders." All of them had to shape fresh forms, new and vital strategies, of literary representation. Parody, for Beerbohm but also, I would argue, for the rest, was one of these strategies, one of the answers to the questions we have agreed to call "modern." It will not be to my purpose to present a detailed account of modernism. I will assume its questions to be those of origin and representation, rather than those attendant upon some crisis of belief or temporal and spatial reconfiguration of the external world. . . . My argument presumes that parody constituted one condition by which modern art made use of its own formal processes by, precisely, re-presenting them in order to explore its own origins. (pp. 23-4)

Though the integrity of the Victorian reading public was gone by 1912, and with it its exalted regard for poetry and the poet, Beerbohm could still count on a lingering sense of the spiritual authority of the literary enterprise. He could gain a purchase on its prestige, at the very least its topicality: his readers could well imagine Chesterton and Belloc actually writing essays at and on Christmas. Furthermore, Beerbohm is engaged in his parodies in the same sort of activity that the Victorian parodists were engaged in—reading through a style to a man; most of the subjects in *A Christmas Garland* overcame their yuletide themes with vigorous and aggressive displays of personality, or else use the occasion to decorate it with their own intellectual and temperamental tinsel. Beerbohm is still very much after the man in the manner, and this is one reason it is possible to read his G. S. Street with a great deal of amusement.

And yet Beerbohm's parodies do seem very different from anything which had come before. Even the parodists who were Beerbohm's contemporaries miss the heightened stylistic communion that he is capable of. (pp. 24-5)

[John Felstiner] writes in his excellent book on Beerbohm about the precise kind of parody Beerbohm produced: "Essentially, his parody was mimetic, not satiric, with the motive that literary representation itself has—to try out a form of expression." This is the reason for the eerie disquiet certain of Beerbohm's subjects—Bennett, James, George Moore, Maurice Baring—felt at reading themselves. . . . Felstiner goes on to speak of "the tendency of Beerbohm's parody to originate the very process of literary invention." Beerbohm, in other words, inverts the most venerable relationship between a parody and its model—that of parasite to host; rather than content himself with less energetic, subordinate energies, Beerbohm in his practice demonstrates a logic whereby the model or host itself gets transformed into another model or another host, potentially equal if not effectively overmastering aesthetically. Such a logic is, for example, the same logic as that of Pound's translations.

Beerbohm can be regarded as the last phase or the finest flower of Victorian parody, then, but from the perspective of either his or our own time he was in fact unique. He seems to have suffered little of the tyranny of the authority of poetry, from which the Victorians sought to distance themselves or otherwise come to terms with through parody. Felstiner notes that "the purely parricidal impulse was spent for Beerbohm when Wilde died." Though his roots are in aestheticism, where he developed, among other things, his keen and corrosive sense of prose sketches, *Words for Pictures,* which he wrote between

1898 and 1901, in which he contemplates Paterian and Wildean logic as a viewer of pictures by making his response part of what he sees and indeed co-equal with the creator of the painting himself. As parodist, Beerbohm presumed to be co-equal as well—a creator, whose creativity was expressed by recreating the words of others in himself.

But such a project is not without its own effaced tensions, and such presumption is established quite paradoxically. By definition, the motives that went into the writing of *A Christmas Garland* cannot speak openly of themselves in their own voice. The best place to examine the impulses which animated Beerbohm as a parodist is the group of essays he wrote between 1910 and 1920 and published in the collection *And Even Now*. One of them, **"No. 2, The Pines,"** his account of his visit to the aged Swinburne, is perhaps his most famous essay and certainly one of his finest. It is a study in heroism, or rather a comedy of hero-worship: Swinburne for his poets, Beerbohm for Swinburne. The comedy turns, specifically, upon the question of language: Swinburne is effusive and magisterial over his precious volumes, while Beerbohm can only feel hopelessly ill-read and ignorant. He has nothing to say. At one point, Beerbohm refers to Swinburne's "genius for self-abasement," . . . and we realize that what makes the essay so marvelous is Beerbohm's own considerable genius in presenting his own abasement during the course of the essay.

Then, perhaps, we realize that still another quiet paradox obtains: Beerbohm does have something to say—the very essay he himself has written. Indebted as he may be to his master, he has found words of his own: modest, circumspect, never contentious. They are not, certainly, the inflammatory words of Swinburne, whom he quotes at one point in the essay, concerning "the dotage of duncedom which cannot perceive, or the impudence of insignificance so presumptuous as to doubt, that the elements of life and literature are indivisibly mingled in one another, and that he to whom books are less real than life will assuredly find in men and women as little reality as in his accursed crassness he deserves to discover." . . . These are not Beerbohm's words, even though the burden of the essay is to affirm them, and affirm Swinburne for saying them. Indeed, this statement is the theme not only of the essay, but of virtually all the essays in *And Even Now*. Nothing is more characteristic of Beerbohm than the fact that he chooses to have another state it directly for him.

Life, the essays continually suggest, is one affair; literature (sometimes very broadly defined) is quite another. And yet there is a relationship, never fixed or static. One feels itself to be a version of the other. Beerbohm is content with the penetration, the indivisible mingling, and never anxious to inquire into the more mysterious matter of which sets the terms for the other. If there are rival claims to be mediated, Beerbohm disavows the role of mediator and retires from the conflict.

The peculiar way Beerbohm effaces the tension between literature and life can be traced in the short piece, **"A Letter That Was Not Written."** Beerbohm reads that Adam Street, Adelphi, is to be redone, and the Trivoli Music Hall abolished. Outraged, he sits down to write a letter to the *Times*. But the words do not come right. They lack restraint, and at last he resolves to revisit Adam Street for himself to freshen his inspiration. There he meets a friend and together they discover that they had never before realized the "hateful smugness of the frontage of the Trivoli." The proposed widening of the street will not be such a bad thing after all. The essay concludes:

"For I had not, after all, to resume my letter to the *Times*." . . . (pp. 27-9)

Like **"No. 2, The Pines,"** the essay's irony is fixed in terms of language. "Where before Beerbohm abided without any language of his own, here he *discovers* that he has none." The only truth the letter would have had would have been the truth of his own feelings, and even those he only thinks he knows, before they are rebuked by his own perception. The language he thought he had is exposed as fatuous—exposed, really, as literary; he thinks of Dr. Johnson, and transcribes a possible wording inscribed with heavyhanded, sonorous invocations of Empire. The fact that he suspects he is only being literary when he wants to be sincere is a prelude to the discovery he is wrong when he thought he was right.

So Beerbohm writes his essay instead of his letter. He recoups what he failed to do in what he succeeds in writing. It might even be possible to say what he failed to write amounted to a parody of what he did. Or should it be that what he did is a parody of what he failed to do? This sort of controversion is bound to sound too deliberate and rounded in analysis, but seems to have been remarkably easy for Beerbohm to produce or so his supple, fluid manner usually suggests. In the present instance, "literature" (i.e., the essay) was the product of "life," which was occasioned by "literature." If, in one sense, the result is the futility of saying anything at all, in another sense this result is converted into the very basis for saying something after all.

If we think of the words of any number of modern writers on, precisely, the limitations of words, on their inability to break through into existence—Eliot's "That was a way of putting it / Not very satisfactory," for example—then what distinguishes Beerbohm (setting aside the apparent triviality of his subject) is his satisfaction with what he has finally said, though only because he has inscribed within what he has not said.

This mode of statement not only is consonant with fundamental modernist themes. It is also the direct outgrowth of Beerbohm's parodic writing. There is the same interplay between presence and absence. There is the same equilibrium between what can be said and what cannot be said. Beerbohm impersonating Chesterton is no different from Beerbohm impersonating himself (in terms of the outrage he thought consistent with his own beliefs). The only difference is that in the parody Beerbohm gives himself over wholly to the illusion (the fact that it is a parody establishes it as such), while in the essay Beerbohm is pleased to expose it as such (he was not whom he thought he was).

Another beautiful little essay in the collection, **"Something Defeasible,"** reveals more raw and fierce emotions out of what I take to be the affective ground of Beerbohm as a parodist. On a Sussex shore he describes what we come to learn is a sand cottage built by a little boy. "But I surmised that to him, artist that he was, it seemed a poor thing beside his first flushed conception" . . .—and so Beerbohm goes over to the boy and tries to reassure him that the thing is "splendid," especially since his playmates are not impressed. But the artist is not very satisfied either, and eventually he lets the tide erode it. Beerbohm is horrified at first, but as the boy's playmates exult, and then the boy, he grows enthusiastic as well and realizes "as never before, how deep-rooted in the human breast the love of destruction, of mere destruction, is." . . . (pp. 29-31)

The theme of the essay is of course (again) destruction and creation, a relation which is actually an equivalence: to want to make is to want to unmake. What is interesting is not merely Beerbohm's sympathetic assent, but the way he hovers over the scene, expanding the budding creative drama with the gentlest irony. We have the feeling we are at, to use Felstiner's words, the very origin of the process of literary creation—which presumes the existence of something already creatable (if not created), as figured forth by the sand cottage. It is not Beerbohm's invention, but it is articulated, as it were, through him. He becomes a chorus, a kind of heightened conscience, for the created object: "The castle was shedding its sides, lapsing, dwindling, landslipping—gone. O Nineveh! And now another—O Memphis? Rome?—yielded to the cataclysm. I listened to the jubilant cries of the children. What rapture, what wantoning!'' (p. 31)

Such a meditation may seem far too portentous for such a small occasion, but its irony (for it is impossible to imagine Beerbohm was not conscious of any) is really a function of the fact that Beerbohm is entirely outside the scene. On the face of it, there is nothing but the castle that the boy has built, and then lets wash away. What Beerbohm is actually doing is taking imaginative possession of the scene, and embellishing it as an artistic *exemplum*. Or rather not the scene, but the castle, the work of art, which Beerbohm, in his meditation, "creates" in the process of its destruction.

It is the same stance, and the same psychology, which produces parody. Seemingly outside the work, the original, and at one remove from it, Beerbohm is actually inside it, and one with it. Indeed, it is even possible to say he is more at one with it than the artist himself (just as here, where the boy is too young to understand his dissatisfaction). The artist thinks he has created something, whereas he has in fact destroyed the purity of his original conception. Beerbohm, in parodying, or destroying the work, is more truly recreating that conception.

Another essay, **"The Crime,"** is a more personal, frank, and blunt account of destruction. It is another evocation of the paradoxes implicit in the created work—the very paradoxes so much modern literature is founded on. Beerbohm finds himself alone in a remote cottage. He decides to dissipate his gloom by reading a book, and he chooses one by a woman author, whose work he knows to be distinguished for its vitality. He reads a bit, before the fireplace, but grudgingly, and all of a sudden finds that he has thrown the volume into the fire. He is shocked intially at his "crime" but soon pleased and he stokes the fire until the book is thoroughly burnt. He makes out the letters, "hing. Tolstoi was right," but it is too late to know what Tolstoi had been right about. Regretful, even guilty, Beerbohm is still resigned to his action.

Throughout the essay, he makes the identity between the book and its author so complete (even mentioning he has met her) that it is hard to feel the murder is only symbolic. Beerbohm's idea of literature is, as always, a deeply humanized one, and, as I have suggested, it is one of the reasons he could write parody recognizably in the Victorian tradition. It is also one of the reasons he can feel the thrill of transgression—"the way of transgressors is hard," he thinks, somewhat wryly, at the end. . . . He might also have added, however, that the transgressor usually acts in the name of a still greater ideal, for in this essay there clearly is one and it is literature itself. Earlier after some ruminations on "the world's future," Beerbohm writes that he will concede a woman dabbling in the written word, "but that she should be an habitual, professional author, with a passion for her art . . . and a profound knowledge of human character, and an essentially sane outlook, is somehow

incongruous with my notions—my mistaken notions, if you will—of what she ought to be." . . . And so he destroys her, now utterly equivalent to her books, and thereby preserves the high calling to which she has presumed. It is not the calling as other modernist authors would have defined it—one cannot, say, readily imagine Yeats speaking of art's claim in terms of its sanity—but it is recognizably one with modernist claims that the artist provides a significant ordering of the world, and not the mere indulgence of individual sensibility. (pp. 31-2)

I find it impossible not to read this essay especially as anything other than a representation (re-presentation) of the parodic process. Beerbohm's "crime" here is not merely the crime of criticism, but specifically of parodic criticism, albeit one which has failed, and so the critic is left with the thrill of transgression, but none of its exultance. *That* emotion, presumably, is the task—and the triumph—of parody. Parody, furthermore, not only upholds the literary ideal but actually redeems it by representing another writer as but a tissue of mannerisms which the re-presentation that is the parody has seen through, by means of an "ideal" criterion that does not have to be made explicit in order to function. **"The Crime"** is flush with Beerbohm's sense of himself as an artist (here embarrassed as a mere reader), "the critic as artist" as fully co-eval and co-equal as Wilde could have imagined. To play on the title, the

"Mr. W. B. Yeats, Presenting Mr. George Moore to the Queen of the Fairies," by Beerbohm. Reproduced by permission of Eva Reichmann.

hidden crime is that in this instance critic and artist are not co-extensive.

"Books Within Books," another of the titles in *And Even Now* runs—and Beerbohm imagines what it would be like to have been able to read them, when only their imaginary existence was mentioned in certain novels. That *other* book he habitually sees struggling to emerge from the one at hand—this is the book he does not see (or does not choose to see) in the wretched volume he consigns to the flames in **"The Crime."**

Owen Seaman once claimed the following rationale for parody: "In its highest form, parody is a department of pure literary criticism. It is often the way that humor has of paying homage to serious achievement; of conferring its recognition of something beyond its own range, which it can honour but cannot hope to emulate." What is unique about Beerbohm's parody, and what I would claim enables it to participate in some of the central currents of modernist writing, is that it is not the product of any of the impulses Seaman asserts. It is not, or does not aim exclusively to be, humorous. It is not born out of a recognition that the original is aloof and inimitable.

It would be, I think, both foolish and fruitless to try to examine certain of Beerbohm's parodies and determine what personal emotions of his might be reflected there. (And what would be gained if it could be shown that his Belloc, say, was more deferential than his Kipling?) Nevertheless, it seems clear enough even without the psychology expressed in *And Even Now* that Beerbohm's parodies manifest a thoroughness and an aggressiveness quite different from the sort of respect Seaman is assuming. Such respect is the assumption of another, and previous, age.

Beerbohm's lovely little essay-fiction **"A Clergyman,"** collects itself around a moment when an insignificant clergyman, whom Boswell does not even bother to name, begs to differ with Dr. Johnson. He sits hushed before the Great Presence (as Beerbohm imagines Johnson) and, when he speaks, his words partake as much of the desire to blaspheme as to worship Johnson. So one must say of Beerbohm himself. He will have his own voice, and—if there was by 1912 any doubt—it will utter a sacralized language no more. Moreover, it presumes not only to emulate, but actually to rewrite. It is a literary criticism that is anything but "pure." In **"A Clergyman"** Beerbohm, who admired Boswell's biography more than any other book, even sports with Johnson's style.

What is what we have agreed to call "modernism" but such sport, played with any number of precursors? We remember, for example, with respect to the great number of poets referred to in "The Waste Land," that that poem was greeted by some as a parody when it was first published. We now know from the manuscript of "The Waste Land" that Eliot once considered an epitaph from *Our Mutual Friend*, "He Do the Police in Different Voices"—a rather exact description of what Beerbohm had already done in *A Christmas Garland*. We know that Pound originally criticized the opening of "The Fire Sermon," based on "The Rape of the Lock," because "you cannot parody Pope unless you can write better verse than Pope—and you can't." In effect, Pound was rebuking the undiluted parodistic energy expressed in Eliot's verse, and was urging him to be aware of it as such and to absolve himself of it. And indeed Pound is quite right: the parodist really does think he can write better than his original (though any parodist, certainly no Beerbohm, would like to admit it), whereas the poet ought to be content to think he can simply write, and not seek to address the power of his models in the direct and pre-emptive manner that only parody sanctions. The way of extinction was indeed better, which is to say more fruitful, "for it left the poet open to progress, more vulnerable to emotions which could endure as somehow original or otherwise fit for their own poetry."

Beerbohm's response to such a matter was not that of Eliot, or Pound, or Joyce. He was content to designate his writing as parody because he was comfortable within established conventions, impatient of such imponderables as history, and unconcerned about savage gods. Themes of self-consciousness and destruction are calmly, even blandly, impacted into his work. His was not a coercive temperament which has to edge out others from the imaginative space he must claim as his own. The subjective dimension in his writing is imperturbable, and Beerbohm does not trouble the world because it is not an aesthetic phenomenon. (pp. 33-6)

From our own vantage now we can see parody . . . as a discarded alternative, a path only minor writers and *belle lettirists* took, and Beerbohm but another instance, however exemplary, insofar as he took it himself. But parody was not a discarded alternative in the first decades of modernism, and, indeed, was one of the conditions for its emergence, . . . a way of blunting agonies (especially those of originality), sharpening irony, and perhaps even sustaining selfhood. Beerbohm's sense of himself was steady and unassuming, and therefore he was able to realize himself as a kind of absent presence in the parody of other writers. Eliot, Pound, and Joyce were each more exacerbated, more recondite and ambitious, and therefore too presumptive not to write parody without enlarging upon it to enhance their own originality; we might think of the Eliot, for example, who said that great poets steal while lesser talents merely betray an influence. Yet betrayal and theft are precisely what Beerbohm knew his own parody to be about, and the energies which lie so calmly submerged in *A Christmas Garland* competed with greater literature and were the same stuff out of which greater literature was made. (p. 36)

> Terry Caesar, *"Betrayal and Theft: Beerbohm, Parody, and Modernism,"* in Ariel, *(The University of Calgary), Vol. 17, No. 3, July, 1986, pp. 23-37.*

ROBERT VISCUSI (essay date 1986)

[*In the following excerpt from his study* Max Beerbohm; or, The Dandy Dante, *Viscusi considers the likenesses between Beerbohm and Dante Alighieri, proposing that Beerbohm's literary ambitions were not as modest as critics commonly assume.*]

Max Beerbohm has always held out to his readers the promise of agreeable surprises—the unlikely word, the memorable irony, the revealing vignette of some pompous hero in a moment of folly. One of Beerbohm's surprises lies still in store. He followed, both intently and secretly, the calling of the epic poet, and he concealed in his works of prose fantasy elaborate and profound allegories of the state of man's soul during the palmy days of the British Empire. . . .

Max called himself a "small" writer. He gained his reader's indulgence partly by self-deprecation and largely by fulfilling perfectly the demands of the minor arts he practiced—the elegant informal essay, the devastating economical caricature, the uncanny and unforgettable parody, the witty and pitiless critique. But this evident "smallness" of his should not mislead us: it was camouflage. Max Beerbohm was not an unassuming artist. Indeed, his real claims on posterity were precisely as large as they appeared to be tiny. (p. 3)

Beerbohm's writing is to other men's writing as are the dandy's clothes to other men's clothes: more correct, more carefully fitted, more perfectly arranged, and regarded by him as the sign of his ineffable and invulnerable superiority to everyone else. Other dandies, Beerbohm felt, had erred when they put their superiority to the test of vulgar acceptance. Brummel should not have bothered to insult the Regent, Disraeli had better not have bored himself in the House, Whistler and Wilde ought both to have avoided the courtroom. *Pas si bête* was the motto Beerbohm gave to his Duke of Dorset. The words summarized his own attitude. He never once stooped to elaborate upon his own pretensions anywhere in his long series of parodies and caricatures, even as he dismantled the pose of almost every significant figure in view, from Queen Victoria to Rudyard Kipling to Matthew Arnold's niece. (p. 4)

Though he chose not to lay his hand on his heart and confess to delusions of grandeur, Beerbohm had them and freely alluded to them—invariably, however, with so playful an irony that we are amused and do not suspect him of taking them seriously. "I have not lately been impersonating an English king," he remarks in the course of a review.... Or, "It distresses me," he writes in an essay, "this failure to keep pace with the leaders of thought as they pass into oblivion."... In an essay called **"Pretending,"** he lays down the general law that "all of us pretend," and he concludes with this coy revelation: "We are all of us, always, in everything, straining after contraries. Cicero plumed himself on his poor statesmanship, and Congreve was humiliated because Voltaire treated him as a writer rather than as a gentleman, and Gustave Doré, contemptuous of his true gifts, broke his heart in the vain ambition to be a painter. Philosophers make ghastly efforts to be frivolous, and—but I will leave the reader of this essay to complete my antithesis."... Leaving us to complete his antithesis—*his* antithesis, and without leaving much doubt as to what direction we ought to take—was an easy way to make claims without appearing to do so. The frivolous Max, here pontificating on the role of pretense in the lives of great men, was making one of many efforts at philosophy. And he was doing more. At the very time he wrote this essay, this "small" writer was, with a nice strategic feel for antithesis, planning to establish himself as "great."

"All of us pretend." The dandy's is an art of pretense, and Max Beerbohm, though he could rise to the demands of high company at noble tables, best concentrated his imaginings when he was alone in his study. Further, he knew that "there is in every fool's paradise an undergrowth of real brambles."... Thus, even in his study, where we often can detect him posing as king and emperor and even god, we never find him altogether ignoring the realities of the social world. In his essays, Beerbohm could make of these poses merely the fulcrum of a self-deprecation so persistent, so mannered, that we can do little more than wander in the circles of its infinite insincerity. Whatever he may seem to claim, and it is sometimes a great deal, Beerbohm does not leave us doubting his sanity. He may pose as anything, always reminding us that he knows the limits of a joke. But he had one arena where he might pretend as mightily as he liked, so long as he never made too great an issue of it. He was a writer. Why not pretend he was the greatest of writers?

This is precisely what he did. He would occasionally drop hints of what he was about. Indeed, in the very opening of his first

book's first essay, a tribute to Brummell, he said of Grego's etchings of the great dandy and his friends, "Grego guides me, as Virgil Dante, through all the mysteries of that other world."... But, like many another passing reference to Dante that we find in Beerbohm's prose, this one scarcely amounted to a clue, much less to a clear statement of intent. The real evidence of Beerbohm's secret ambition lies in two works of prose fiction that were its result.

The first of these, *The Happy Hypocrite: A Fairy Tale for Tired Men,* appeared in 1896, shortly after Beerbohm's twenty-fourth birthday. He kept his secret about this work very well. Though it has often been praised, no one has ever mentioned in print the meticulous parody of the *Commedia* that provides its real structure. Even Wilde, whose work gave Beerbohm the germ of the tale, seems not to have suspected what it contained. What it owes to Dante ... is more than the shape of its fable or some details of imagery, but a whole manner of expression, an economy of allegory that allows Beerbohm to say a great deal more than the surface of the tale would suggest. The Dantesque manner fulfilled in writing what Beerbohm saw as "that first aim of modern dandyism, the production of the supreme effect through means the least extravagant."... *The Happy Hypocrite* was one of those parodies that taught Beerbohm, as he said, both what to do and what to avoid. Two years after it appeared, he began the book that would show the full profit of those lessons.

Zuleika Dobson, or An Oxford Love Story, Beerbohm's one novel and his intended masterpiece, is a comic epic in prose. It is a very careful piece of work, having occupied his mind, on and off, for a full thirteen years before it saw the light of day. In this novel, Beerbohm imitated not so much Dante's poem as his pose, playing Homer in much the same way that Dante had played Virgil. Considered as epic allegory, this book will at first appear as "small" as everything else about Max. But the impression will be false. The real nature of this book is as little obvious as the real extent of Beerbohm's pretensions. Its prose glitters so brightly with the impeccable polish of Beerbohm's style that most readers are content to be carried along without questioning what depths may lie within. Nor does the book readily reply to such questioning. Beerbohm was content, here as elsewhere, to seem far more direct than he actually was.

He seemed, always, to employ with great skill the gifts of a born humorist, and he had the rewards that answered the appearance. He was praised, he was—despite his ticklish sarcastic temper—even loved. And the appearance had substance: Beerbohm was a born humorist, a great humorist, some say the greatest of his generation.... But he himself claimed, "Except in union with some form of high seriousness, humour does not exist for me."... What "high seriousness" can we expect in a humorist who is also a dandy? And how earnestly did Beerbohm play Dante?

To answer these questions, we must read Beerbohm's works with a sympathetic understanding they have not seemed to require. We must, as Pope advises, judge his work in the spirit that he wrote—even if the work has not often been read in this spirit. Such sympathy will not spring naturally from us. Our age makes no special place for dandies. But Beerbohm's did. Very much its child, Beerbohm could imagine himself the Dante of his time because he saw, or at least believed, that the dandy stood in it for something of permanently high value. He did not suppose the dandy merely a wit or an exquisite. He thought that the dandy, properly given to his art, might in his own fashion play the visionary, the philosopher, the prophet, even the epic poet. Such beliefs came naturally to him, for Beerbohm grew up in a family of dandies and went to a university of dandies on his way to a city where dandies had still a prominent part to play. It is a lost world. . . . We begin to understand how [Beerbohm's] works ask us to read: the dandy devoted himself to an occult perfection of art; so, to appraise his works at true value, we must learn to read the signals he uses. Beerbohm's prose epics are allusive and elusive works. They imply an informed and artful reader. We need not object to the implication: it amounts to nothing less than a faith in, a defense of, the impulse to intelligence. Beerbohm expected that *Zuleika Dobson* would forever have appeal as "a treasure for experts in fine literature." . . . Thus, in that work he plays us many an elegant compliment: he always entices our speculation to go just a little farther; he always suggests that we can find fresh secrets in a fresh reading; he invites us at every turn to practice a diplomatic ingenuity, though his own diplomacy never allows him the base pomposity of advertised obscurity. We read *Zuleika Dobson* best just as we read Dante best: again and again. (pp. 4-7)

Finding a way to make an honest coinage of words and images has preoccupied modern writers at least from Mallarmé to Joyce. Beerbohm's enterprise, which employs Dante as a kind of secret seal upon the artistic conscience, emeges from behind

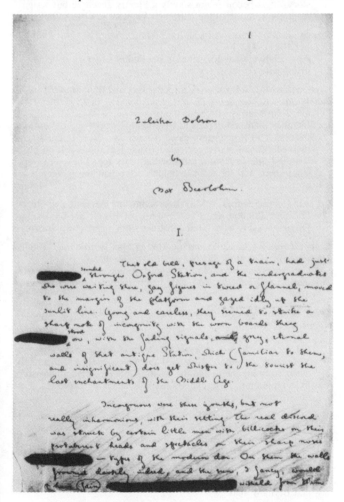

Title page of Beerbohm's manuscript of Zuleika Dobson. *Reproduced by permission of Eva Reichmann.*

the same ramparts as *The Waste Land* and *The Cantos.* For *Zuleika Dobson* presents itself as one of the modern *Commedias*—works that have made aesthetic capital of their inability to do what Dante could, making of the Florentine a sign of what a poet at his or her best might be and do—a sign, likewise, of what the present age has denied to such a poet, a comprehensive vision not only of the cosmos but of the human universe, a completely articulable philosophy that might find, as Dante's could, in any particular *virtù* the mark of the divine intaglio. Dante's presence in the *Four Quartets* and *Ash Wednesday* and *The Cantos* always carries with it the implication of shameful contrast: these fragments and incompletions offer their persistent, mute complaint against a moment that makes inconceivable the harmonious fulfillment Dante could achieve. . . . But *Zuleika Dobson* enacts fully for the first time both the attraction and the impossibility of the Dantean pose. Beerbohm learned this pose from Byron and Rossetti and Wilde; he made it his own in *The Happy Hypocrite;* and in *Zuleika Dobson,* he did with it all that he could, making of its impossibility the very secret of the drama.

Max Beerbohm never wearied of showing how the "great" might be less than they seemed. Concerning the "small," he would have liked us to complete his antithesis. "Smallness" allowed him to entertain, safely behind the Janus of a joke, hopes that would be implausible, impossible, ridiculous at full scale or out in the open air. And those hopes take on, in the fullness of consideration, something of the precious hidden quality of a sacrament, a symbol of the possible wholeness and health of human kind, a symbol, too, of its fugitive glimpse of divinity—what both Dante and Beerbohm could call, with whatever chasms of difference in the signified, Love. The differences are enormous: Love, for Dante, is not only the greatest of the virtues but equally the central theme in an exfloreate panoply of philosophy and drama and high epic verse that consummates a great moment of civilization; but for Beerbohm, Love can be no more than the great necessity, so battered and dismantled that it must be, as Rimbaud said, "reinvented." And he makes the attempt. This, more than anything else, joins him to the great Dante: that he defends and defines and works to recover what can be seen, through all the masks of self-deprecation and irony and even sarcasm, of what he can still call "a great catholic pattern." He cannot see it very clearly, and, as we shall discover, he can see it only in the dark. But is that not as it had to be? For was it not in the dark that he found himself?

The dark was the very isolation of pride which the dandies, echoing Descartes and Berkeley and foreshadowing Freud and Jacques Lacan, discovered as the human balcony that looked out into the universe and found there nothing but its own reflection. The dandies dramatized this lofty solitude, entertaining themselves with imperial ambitions that no authority but the mirror had sanctioned. Such a point of view encouraged a vision that was at the same time comprehensive and tiny. The dandy, alone before his mirror, might be, if the mirror could be made to agree, a king, a god, himself a *corpus mysticum;* in his gnostic closet, the dandy resurrected the *cosmos* in *cosmetic,* and could imagine the details of his toilette as symbols mysteriously efficacious of a universe. Wilde insisted that Life imitated Art. Beerbohm, Wilde's most gifted literary disciple, took him at his word. What became clear only after Wilde's arrest, however, was that the Art that Life imitated was tragedy. At this crucial point in his career, Beerbohm's vision of the dandy was transformed: no longer simply a sovereign, the dandy became a kind of Christ who must die to be king. This was the moment that Beerbohm "retired," and while some great ambition in him died then, another took shape: he would be, as it were, a dandy Christian—not precisely a Christian, to be sure, but a Christian whose Christ was a dandy. This was the sufficient germ of a "reinvented" love, and it implied a reinvented epic as well, a reinvented Dante to convey the vision it enabled.

Like so much that is important about dandies, this Dante of Beerbohm's lives in hiding. Just what he is must be something we can only decide after examining the treasures we have from this implausible deep dandy. They do not impose themselves. Rather, standing as they do where Beerbohm has, with an enterprising policy, slipped them in, along the shelves between the monuments of Homer and Cervantes, Dante and Virgil, they attract the hand with an engaging difference. They are written as beautifully as anything can be, but they *are* "small." We choose them, we read them, and we find their manner charming. They intrigue us, as we go, with the intricacy that fills with varied, gay and sometimes somber, hues their polished surfaces. We begin to read again. (pp. 8-10)

> *Robert Viscusi, in his* Max Beerbohm; or, The Dandy Dante: Rereading with Mirrors, *The Johns Hopkins University Press, 1986, 267 p.*

ADDITIONAL BIBLIOGRAPHY

Behrman, S. N. *Portrait of Max: An Intimate Memoir of Sir Max Beerbohm.* New York: Random House, 1960, 317 p.
  Illustrated biography of Beerbohm which includes personal reminiscences and discussion of his works.

Braybrooke, Patrick. "Peep Number Three: Max Beerbohm, Swinburne, and Other Things." In his *Peeps at the Mighty,* pp. 43-58. Freeport, N.Y.: Books for Libraries Press, 1966.
  Praises Beerbohm's essays, especially "No. 2, The Pines."

Bross, Addison C. "Beerbohm's 'The Feast' and Conrad's Early Fiction." *Nineteenth-Century Fiction* 26, No. 3 (December 1971): 329-36.
  Traces the sources for Beerbohm's successful parody of Joseph Conrad's fiction.

Cecil, David. *Max: A Biography.* Boston: Houghton Mifflin Co., 1965, 507 p.
  Narrative of Beerbohm's life and career quoting extensively from his works and letters. In his "Prefatory Note" Cecil concludes that "on his own chosen ground [Beerbohm] is unrivalled; England's supreme parodist and caricaturist, her most exquisite master of satiric fantasy."

Danson, Lawrence. "Max Beerbohm and *The Mirror of the Past.*" *The Princeton Library Chronicle* XLIII, No. 2 (Winter 1982): 77-153.
  Lengthy article including commentary on and plot reconstruction of Beerbohm's unfinished novel *The Mirror of the Past.*

Davies, W. H. "Artists All." In his *Later Days,* pp. 182-205. New York: George H. Doran Co., 1926.
  Reminiscences of Beerbohm. According to Davies: "Of all our living celebrities, his mind is the most subtle, and his knowledge of human nature is almost uncanny and diabolical."

Empson, William. "Chapter VI." In his *Seven Types of Ambiguity,* pp. 176-91. New York: New Directions, 1947.
  Quotes passages from *Zuleika Dobson* to demonstrate the "sixth type" of ambiguity, which occurs, according to Empson, when "a statement says nothing, by tautology, by contradiction, or by irrelevant statements, so that the reader is forced to invent statements of his own and they are liable to conflict with one another."

Felstiner, John. "Max Beerbohm and the Wings of Henry James." *The Kenyon Review* XXIX, No. 4 (September 1967): 449-71.
  Award-winning essay discussing Beerbohm's respect for and criticism of Henry James. According to Felstiner: "The caricatures, reviews, letters, poems, essays, and parodies suggest in themselves that Beerbohm's criticism of certain aims and inadequacies in James was indirect self-evaluation, a kind of literary transference."

Forster, E. M. "Fantasy." In his *Aspects of the Novel,* pp. 105-24. New York: Harcourt Brace & Co., 1927.
  Praises *Zuleika Dobson.* According to Forster: "It is a great work—the most consistent achievement of fantasy in our time."

Gorman, Herbert S. "The Incomparable Max." In his *The Procession of Masks,* pp. 57-74. Boston: B. J. Brimmer Co., 1923.
  Laudatory essay discussing Beerbohm's personality, reputation, and work. According to Gorman: "Max is more than a humorist—he is an ironist, almost a happy Voltaire, at times."

Graham, Kathleen. "The Good Dandy." *The Humanities Association Review* 29, No. 1 (Winter 1978): 37-60.
  Recounts Beerbohm's youthful romance with Ada Leverson, quoting extensively from his letters of 1893-1927.

Grushow, Ira. "The Chastened Dandy: Beerbohm's 'Hilary Maltby and Stephen Braxton'." *Papers on Language and Literature* VIII, Supplement (Fall 1972): 149-64.
  Extended analysis of Maltby and Braxton, concluding that the two characters in many ways suggest Max Beerbohm, and the story "thus becomes not simply a literary anecdote but a significant contribution to the narrator's knowledge of self."

Krutch, J. W. "Puck on Picadilly." *The Nation* 113, No. 2936 (12 October 1921): 413-14.
  Appreciative essay focusing on Beerbohm's literary style and satirical wit.

Lago, Mary M. and Beckson, Karl, eds. *Max and Will: Max Beerbohm and William Rothenstein, Their Friendship and Letters 1893-1945.* London: John Murray, 1975, 193 p.
  Includes many references to Beerbohm's works and exhibitions. In a letter to Rothenstein dated August 28, 1911, Beerbohm remarked: "I am really very glad I found it impossible to go on writing [*Zuleika Dobson*] in London years ago. I have developed since then; and the book wouldn't have had the quality it has now."

Layard, George Somes. "Max Beerbohm; or, Art and Semolina." *The Bookman* London XL, No. 239 (August 1911): 201-08.
  Discusses satire as exhibited in Beerbohm's caricature drawings.

Lewis, Roger. "The Child and the Man in Max Beerbohm." *English Literature in Transition* 27, No. 4 (1984): 296-303.
  Concludes that Beerbohm's "whole attitude evinces . . . a particularly late-Victorian and Edwardian trait: that of refusing to grow up."

Lynch, Bohun. *Max Beerbohm in Perspective.* New York: Alfred A. Knopf, 1922, 185 p.
  Appreciative biography that includes Beerbohm's famous letter to Lynch in which he assesses his career. According to Beerbohm: "My gifts are small. I've used them very well and discreetly, never straining them; and the result is that I've made a charming little reputation." He exhorts his biographer to "note that I am not incomparable. Compare me."

McElderry, Bruce R., Jr. *Max Beerbohm.* New York: Twayne Publishers, Inc., 1972, 185 p.
  Critical survey of Beerbohm's principal works.

Mix, Katherine Lyon. "Max on Shaw." *The Shaw Review* XI, No. 3 (September 1963): 100-04.
  Traces the personal and professional relationship of Beerbohm and Bernard Shaw.

———. *Max and the Americans.* Brattleboro, Vt.: Stephen Green Press, 1974, 210 p.

Biography focusing on Beerbohm's American connections, including his 1895 visit to the U.S., his long admiration of Henry James, and his marriage to Tennessean Florence Kahn.

Muggeridge, Malcolm. "A Survivor." *The New York Review of Books* V, No. 8 (25 November 1965): 31-3.
　　Personal reminiscences centering on Muggeridge's visits to Beerbohm at Rapallo.

Nadel, Ira B. "The Smallest Genius and 'the Wittiest Mind': Max Beerbohm and Lytton Strachey." *English Literature in Transition* 27, No. 4 (1984): 289-95.
　　Compares the literary styles and aesthetics of the two writers who "through their sense of each other's literary virtues, . . . were able to bisect a culture from two opposing angles."

Pritchett, V. S. "Max Beerbohm: A Dandy." In his *The Tale Bearers: Literary Essays*, pp. 9-17. New York: Random House, 1980.
　　Appreciative essay on Beerbohm, with a review of John Felstiner's *The Lies of Art*.

Raymond, E. T. "Henry James and Max Beerbohm." In his *Portraits of the New Century: The First Ten Years*, pp. 282-99. Garden City, New York: Doubleday, Doran & Co., 1928.
　　Comparative essay. According to Raymond: "In both was the idea that in the *beau monde*, as each knew it, lay the stronghold of civilization. Each saw the arts linked inevitably with the amenities of polite society. Only 'Max' knew far better than James that the stronghold was not strong, was indeed most ridiculously weak."

Riewald, J. G. *Sir Max Beerbohm: Man and Writer*. The Hague: Martinus Nijhoff, 1953, 369 p.
　　Detailed study including biography, criticism, and bibliography.

————, ed. *The Surprise of Excellence: Modern Essays on Max Beerbohm*. Hamden, Ct.: Archon Books, 1974, 265 p.
　　Compilation of biographical and critical essays by Louis Kronenberger, Edmund Wilson, Evelyn Waugh, John Updike, W. H. Auden, and others.

Roberts, Sir Sydney. "Max Beerbohm." *Essays by Divers Hands* XXX (1960): 115-29.
　　Introductory lecture delivered before the Royal Society of Literature 12 July 1957.

Scott-James, R. A. "Chesterton and Other Essayists." In his *Fifty Years of English Literature: 1900-1950*, pp. 47-53. London: Longmans, Green and Co., 1951.
　　Brief sketch on Beerbohm, concluding that "the same economy of line and character-sketching which distinguished his cartoons

reappeared in another form in his essays, which were piercingly critical without ever being unkindly, delicately subtle, yet as simple as the Bible."

Shand, John. "Max." *The Nineteenth Century and After* CXXXII, No. 786 (August 1942): 84-7.
　　Favorable discussion of Beerbohm's drama criticism.

Stevenson, Lionel. "Elegant Wits and Cynical Satirists." In his *The History of the English Novel: Volume XI—Yesterday and After*, pp. 155-98. New York: Barnes and Noble, Inc., 1967.
　　Brief praise of *Zuleika Dobson*. According to Stevenson: "On the surface, *Zuleika Dobson* is a neat parody of the sensational stories of scandals in high life that extended from Ouida to Elinor Glyn; but it grew into an epitome of the social atmosphere of the decade that started with Lily Langtry and ended with Rupert Brooke."

Swinnerton, Frank. "The Special Genius of Sir Max." *Saturday Review* XLI, No. 31 (2 August 1958): 13-14.
　　Appreciative review of *Mainly on the Air* and retrospective praise of Beerbohm as an ironist.

Viscusi, Robert. "Max And." *English Literature in Transition* 27, No. 4 (1984): 304-19.
　　Analysis of the importance of Beerbohm's caricatures and parodies to biographical and historical knowledge of the 1890s. According to Viscusi: "In Beerbohm we have one of those star-crossed cases where personal and historical endowments collaborate to create the perfect artist of a moment."

Ward, A. C. "Essayists and Critics." In his *Twentieth-Century Literature: 1901-1940*, pp. 202-21. New York: Longmans, Green and Co., 1940.
　　Introductory essay praising Beerbohm as "a creative critic of literature and life, with a generous streak of special genius."

Waugh, Evelyn. "The Max behind the Mask." *The Sunday Times* (London) No. 7382 (8 November 1964): 49.
　　A tribute to Beerbohm in a review of Cecil's *Max: A Biography* and *Letters to Reggie Turner*, edited by Rupert Hart-Davis.

Wilde, Oscar. *The Letters of Oscar Wilde*, edited by Rupert Hart-Davis, pp. 343ff. New York: Harcourt, Brace & World, Inc., 1962.
　　Numerous references to Beerbohm and brief comments on his works of the 1890s. Of particular interest is the letter to Beerbohm (circa) 28 May 1897 in which Wilde records his initial impressions of *The Happy Hypocrite*.

J(oseph) E(phraim) Casely-Hayford

1866-1930

Ghanian novelist and nonfiction writer.

Casely-Hayford was one of the most influential nationalists and a leading political thinker in Ghana in the early twentieth century. A pioneering scholar of African studies, he expounded cultural Pan-Africanism and political nationalism in his novel *Ethiopia Unbound* and other works. Recognized for its trenchant criticism of African colonial society and its farsighted recommendations for cultural advancement in the region, *Ethiopia Unbound* is generally regarded as one of the most significant contributions to African nationalist literature in the early twentieth century.

Casely-Hayford was the fourth son of a minister and his wife of the Anona Clan, Gold Coast (now Ghana). Educated at Wesleyan Boys' High School and Fourah Bay College, Freeport, he became a high school teacher in Accra. However, a nationalist-oriented press was flourishing in West Africa at the time, and he left education to pursue a career as a journalist. Working for his uncle, Prince Brew of Dunkwa, he advanced to the editorship of the *Western Echo* and later presided over several short-lived Gold Coast newspapers. In the 1890s he travelled to England, where he studied law at the Inner Temple, London, and Peterhouse College, Cambridge. Returning to Ghana, he combined his legal practice with a journalistic career, and his contributions to the weekly *Gold Coast Leader* brought him renown throughout the region for his articulate political commentary. In 1920 Casely-Hayford coordinated the meeting of the first National Congress of British West Africa, and his prominence in this organization gained him a wide reputation as a statesman. Later, he led delegations of African leaders to London to meet with representatives of the British government. In 1927 he was elected to the Ghana Legislative Council, and his support of the highly unpopular Native Administration Ordinance, which allowed the English government to retain a measure of control in Ghana, caused many of his followers to lose faith in him, believing that he had compromised his ideals. Casely-Hayford continued to work in journalism until his death in August, 1930.

Casely-Hayford's many nonfiction tracts reflect his fervent Pan-Africanism, which L. H. Ofosu-Appiah has defined as the aim to "[bring] together all black men in Africa and those of African descent." Calling for the political and cultural self-determination of African nations, Casely-Hayford wrote several works studying the effects of various laws and institutions on West Africa and West Africans. His only work of fiction, *Ethiopia Unbound,* has been praised by critics for its examination of African colonial society under British rule. Ostensibly the story of Kwamankra, a Ghanian lawyer whose background closely resembles Casely-Hayford's own, *Ethiopia Unbound* presents a synthesis of its author's religious and political ideas. In this novel and other works, Casely-Hayford urged his compatriots not to imitate Europeans but to take pride in their own heritage. One of his greatest concerns was the education of African youth, and in *Ethiopia Unbound* he envisioned the establishment of a Ghanian university. According to Casely-Hayford's proposal, the university would promote African studies, language, and dress and would save parents the great

sums of money that were being spent abroad to educate their children at British or American universities. He intended his novel to serve in the struggle to overcome racism, and in it he debated issues of morality, ideology, and social status. F. Nnabuenyi Ugonna has called *Ethiopia Unbound* "without a doubt the matrix of all the nationalist and cultural ideas of one of the ablest African political and intellectual leaders in West Africa."

While Casely-Hayford advocated internal self-government for Ghana, he maintained that the country should remain a part of the British Empire, and his popularity suffered late in his career because of that controversial view. After his death, many of his works went out of print, but Ghanian literary scholars began to reissue them in new editions in the late 1960s, reviving interest in his ideas. A beloved patriot and champion of African studies, Casely-Hayford is considered an instrumental figure in the development of African nationalism, and his novel *Ethiopia Unbound* is praised by modern critics as one of the most important works of West African literature in the early decades of the twentieth century.

PRINCIPAL WORKS

Gold Coast Native Institutions (nonfiction) 1903
Ethiopia Unbound (novel) 1911

Gold Coast Land Tenure and the Forest Bill   (nonfiction)
   1911
The Truth about the West African Land Question
   (nonfiction) 1913
*William Waddy Harris, the West African Reformer: The
   Man and His Message* (biography) 1915
United West Africa (nonfiction) 1919
*The Disabilities of Black Folk and Their Treatment, with an
   Appeal to the Labour Party* (nonfiction) 1929
Public Speeches of J. E. Casely-Hayford (lectures) 1970

UNITED EMPIRE (essay date 1911)

[*In the following review, the critic finds* Ethiopia Unbound *an important work to be read by Europeans seeking an understanding of colonial Africans.*]

[*Ethiopia Unbound*] is a book that must be read with patience and understanding. It is always difficult for the European to understand the point of view of the educated West African native, more especially when it is articulate. Mr. Hayford, a native of the Gold Coast, has written a book that is worth careful reading and sympathetic study. There is much in it that will jar upon the European reader, and much that may even cause the incautious and rash to throw the book down unread. But if the reader will persevere to the end he will be amply rewarded. However much he may dissent from some of the author's statements or resent some of his strictures, he cannot fail to appreciate Mr. Hayford's point of view or to understand better the forces that are working slowly but surely amongst the Ethiopian peoples. It is as easy to underestimate the influence of the educated native in West Africa as it is to overestimate it. In no case can it be regarded as more than the leaven that may affect the whole. But whether the African races assimilate European culture and thought or evolve a distinct Ethiopian civilisation of their own—as Mr. Hayford desires—it would be folly for the white man to close his eyes to the progress that is being made on all sides in Africa—a progress that is not merely material. There is much sterling commonsense in *Ethiopia Unbound*. Although it is quite impossible to follow the author to the heights of idealism to which he would lead us when he preaches the doctrine of an African nationality, taking what it will of Western thought but retaining its own inherent quality, yet there can be little doubt that Mr. Hayford advances upon eminently sane lines. Thus he disapproves of the aping of European dress which is so prevalent in the coastal districts, and desires a distinct national costume for the cultured African. He would found a national university for the Gold Coast and for Ashanti, not near the influence of the coast, but at Kumasi, away from the corroding effects of a spurious Western civilisation. This should be a national university in the fullest sense, with chairs for Fanti, Hausa, and Yoruba, and the teaching in one of these languages and not through the medium of English. He would sweep away what he regards as the mock Christianity that substitutes an unholy monogamy, in which there is more immorality than is possible under polygamy, for marriage customs and laws that are the result of centuries of ingrained habit and thought. Mohammedanism is wiser in this respect. It is easy to pick holes in all Mr. Hayford's arguments. It is easy to assert that the idea of Ethiopianism is a dream incapable of achievement on a continent where races are innumerable and nations, as we understand the term, do not exist. But the really important fact remains that there are those amongst the subject races of Africa who are thinking and working, not as hewers of wood and drawers of water, but upon lines that are at present foreign to European methods of thought. It is not upon the wrongs of oppressed peoples that Mr. Hayford writes but about the question of retaining all that is good in native institutions, and preserving fundamental laws and customs that are part and parcel of the national consciousness. In fact, he is striving for a national regeneration—but not upon a prosaic Western basis. (pp. 737-38)

> *A review of "Ethiopia Unbound: Studies in Race Emancipation," in* United Empire, *Vol. 11, No. 1, January, 1911, pp. 737-38.*

ROBERT W. JULY (essay date 1967)

[*An American educator and critic, July has written numerous articles and books examining African history, literature, and thought. In the following excerpt from his* Origins of Modern African Thought, *July offers a favorable appraisal of Casely-Hayford's style in* Ethiopia Unbound.]

In 1911 there appeared in London an unusual literary work entitled *Ethiopia Unbound*. The book was unusual primarily in its form and tone—a loosely constructed piece which appeared to be a novel but which included large portions of intellectual autobiography, of historical, philosophic and literary references, and which was spun out in such a shifting evanescent fashion as to create a dreamlike illusion of unreality. Characters drifted in and out of the loose and insubstantial narrative which was frequently interrupted by long treatises in which the author was able to set forth his ideas on matters which interested him or by dialogues conducted between idealized characters in a stilted language appropriate to their artificial aspect.

Cast as fiction, the work was in fact an attempt to rally the black people of the world in defence of their own culture, their own accomplishments, their own racial integrity. The African, it seemed to say, had to learn to be himself, not to be content with a role as counterfeit white. It was permissible for him to pursue his university study and professional training in Europe, but it was not satisfactory for him to turn into a black European. Aware of his own identity, he could take from Europe that which was useful and reject that which was inappropriate, employing the essential African soul as touchstone. Looking beyond the crudities of traditional African life he might probe the inner meaning and deeper purpose of the ancient social systems of Africa, clothing them with modern techniques and directing them towards newer contemporary objectives. In such a way could he best serve the cause of Negro independence and manhood.

The protagonist in *Ethiopia Unbound* was a Gold Coast man who had gone to London for a time to read law, and who had finally returned to his homeland only to discover heartache and ambiguity in what he saw there. One of his first visits was to the simple church of his boyhood, and when he arrived it was the hour of prayer. As he renewed acquaintance with the familiar but ageing faces, he was saddened by the inappropriateness of the scene. A Sankey hymn was being sung by the children in their Manchester homespun to the laboured accompaniment of a wheezy old harmonium. At the head of the choir stood the schoolmaster elegant in his cutaway coat, glazed cuffs, high collar and patent-leather shoes, but a bit of a fool in this costume so inappropriate to the people and the land. The minister was a white man preaching to a black congregation while outside the church a notice announced another service to be held later for Europeans only. The stranger returned home turned away in sadness and in anger. All at once he saw with a burst of insight what the mission of his life would have to be. He would dedicate himself to saving his people from the national and racial death which awaited them, practising these emasculated sentimentalities and shameless slanders proclaimed in the name of Christ. His people would have to be taught to recapture the virile religion of their past, to turn aside from a civilization which came with the Bible in one hand and the gin bottle in the other, which dismembered their tribes, alienated their lands, appropriated their goods, and drained the strength away from their time-tested authorities and institutions.

The book was to a considerable extent an exercise in autobiographical reminiscence as the vehicle for a personal profession of faith in the black race. Its author was a Cape Coast barrister and political figure, Joseph E. Casely Hayford who, like the protagonist in his story, had prepared himself in England for a legal career and returned to his home in the Gold Coast to lend his voice to the African protest against the inequities of British rule. His was to be a persistent voice over the years—intelligent and incisive in its criticism, resourceful and energetic in its proposals, sincere and courageous in its profession of patriotic faith; yet Casely Hayford, for all his insight and sensitivity, for all his liberalism and humanity, was no crusader and certainly no revolutionary. Poised against his contemporary, Attoh-Ahuma, who thundered forth his condemnation of the vagaries of British rule with bluff forthrightness, Casely Hayford was subtle, ironic, oblique. An accomplished legal practitioner and scholar like his colleague Mensah Sarbah, yet he was more at home in the political arena where his talents as writer and speaker joined with a natural flair for compromise to bring to life the master politician. A follower of the ideas of Edward Blyden, he lacked the old reformer's didactic persuasiveness, relying on indirection to achieve his objectives. *Ethiopia Unbound* was characteristic. A declaration on behalf of negritude as powerful as Blyden's best, it generated its argument through its subtleties and its sophisticated idealism, not through the purity and power of its logic. (pp. 433-35)

> Robert W. July, "The Metamorphosis of Casely Hayford," in his The Origins of Modern African Thought: Its Development in West Africa during the Nineteenth and Twentieth Centuries, *Frederick A. Praeger, 1967, pp. 433-57.*

F. NNABUENYI UGONNA (essay date 1969)

[*In the following excerpt from his introduction to* Ethiopia Unbound, *Ugonna examines Casely-Hayford's social and political philosophy.*]

Ethiopia Unbound is undoubtedly one of the most important contributions to the literature of African nationalism. Although it is primarily a work of fiction and so properly belongs to the field of African literature, it contains ideas that are indispensable to all those interested in African studies.... As a contribution to African literature, *Ethiopia Unbound* combines the literary and religious function of Bunyan's *Pilgrim's Progress* with the cultural significance of Arnold's *Culture and Anarchy.* Its importance to the Africanist can hardly be emphasised. (pp. xix-xx)

The ideas of Casely Hayford about African Nationalism, colonialism and racism are easily found in his numerous works.

Hayford's importance lies not only in his practical ability as a nationalist leader but in the fact that his political ideas have been immortalised in his literary works.... Between 1903 and 1929, he produced standard literary works on jurisprudence, African land tenure, indigenous institutions and Pan-Africanism or more precisely "West African Nationality." In 1903, Sweet and Maxwell of London published Casely Hayford's first work, *Gold Coast Native Institutions.* In this book Hayford discussed extensively the whole question of Native Administration, arguing that the authorities at Downing Street had better "confine themselves more to external administration, leaving the internal government of the people to develop upon the natural lines of their own institutions." (pp. xx-xxi)

In 1911 Hayford's second book *Ethiopia Unbound* was published by C. M. Phillips (London). Sub-titled "Studies in Race Emancipation" it is a veritable compendium of Casely Hayford's thoughts on politics, native institutions, race relations, African nationalism and allied subjects cast into a fictive and imaginative form. The book's literary structure will be discussed later. His two other books, *Gold Coast Land Tenure and the Forest Bill* . . . , and *The Truth About the West African Land Question* . . . , as their titles imply, try to explain the system of land tenure in West Africa. Although these books are of great sociological interest, they are primarily written from a legal angle, their main purpose being to argue against any scheme of land alienation in West Africa. The main theme of both books is an amplification of Mensah Sarbah's explication:

> According to native ideas there is no land without owners. What is now a forest or unused land will, as years go on, come under cultivation by subjects of the stool, or members of the village community or other members of the family . . .

Gold Coast Land Tenure and the Forest Bill in particular was published, we are told in the title page, at the instance of the kings and chiefs of the central and western provinces of Ghana in conference with the Aborigines Rights Protection Society. In 1919 *United West Africa,* a pamphlet appealing to the youths of West Africa to strive towards the attainment of West African nationhood, was published in London. Some of Hayford's most memorable public speeches were collected by Magnus J. Sampson and published under the title *West African Leadership,* in 1951. Hayford's other publications include **"The Progress of the Gold Coast Native"**, and *The Disabilities of the Black Folk.* . . . From these works one can glean the recurrent ideas of Casely Hayford.

Perhaps we can rightly say that Hayfordian philosophy is in essence based on the concept of "Ethiopianism." The idea of Ethiopianism itself is eclectic, being a crystallization of religious and political notions, associated with Ethiopia, then the only truly independent island in the sea of colonial Africa. Ethiopia thus became a symbol of African independence. He identified Africa with Ethiopia. In a slave or colonial era, Ethiopia, the only African state that had not been colonised, became a bastion of prestige and hope to thousands of Africans, especially those in America and the West Indies, who were taunted by the whites for the absence of any substantial collective achievement by their race and the inability of their people to rule themselves. (pp. xxii-xxiii)

Colonial Africa was to [Casely Hayford] Ethiopia chained. His political theory was that with Africans assuming control of their own affairs and developing their indigenous institutions, fettered Ethiopia would be unbound and eventually emerge as a giant among other nationalities. But how was this ideal to be effectively realised?

Casely Hayford believes religiously in the integrity of the African. He ridicules the idea of superior and inferior racial categories. The apparent difference between the African and the European stems from differential environmental influences and *Mutatis mutandis* the African stands on the same footing as the European. An educated man is an educated man whether he is white or black and a white nonentity is the same as a black one. To achieve greatness Africa must attain mature nationhood. Hayford advocated West African nationhood as a kind of *protasis* to African nationality. In effect he was the first African nationalist as distinct from Afro-American and Afro-West Indian nationalists, to stress so persistently the idea of what has become a pervasive theme in any discussion of African nationalism, the ideas of Pan-Africanism and African Personality. (p. xxvi)

The framework of Casely Hayford's Pan-Africanism is intrinsically cultural-nationalism. African cultural heritage, to him, is pre-eminently the index to African personality since it depicts what is unique about Africa. This emphasis on culture is not surprising. Confronted by white racists' propaganda to the effect that the African has no culture of his own, he had no choice but to prove them wrong. Unfortunately in the face of European sneers and sarcasm the contemporary African tended deliberately to suppress his culture. To combat this tendency and sustain the paramountcy of African traditional heritage, Casely Hayford ceaselessly fought for the preservation of native institutions even if in a modified form.

Advocates of African culture admit its obvious limitations and so they allow that useful western cultural patterns could be integrated into the African cultural scheme. This, from all indications, is Casely Hayford's postulate. The African should be himself. Casely Hayford deprecates all attempts to imitate closely the whites, for example, he dismisses as a "veritable fool" a school-master in his "elegantly cut-away black morning coat and beautifully-glazed cuffs and collar, not to speak of patent leather shoes." . . . In his writings he consistently advocated the wearing of native dress to the extent of suggesting that academic gowns should give way, in African Universities, to traditional garbs. He contends that the question of dress and habits matters because "it goes to the root of the Ethiopian's self-respect." Because of his earnest concern for the preservation of indigenous African culture, he tends to condemn any person who preaches any form of racial integration no matter how modified. On this score, he repudiated Booker T. Washington and W.E.B. DuBois, regarding both as provincial in their approach to racial questions while to him E. W. Blyden was universal in his approach. It is to be wondered whether Hayford was really justified in his criticism of Du Bois; for, without doubt, the problem of the Negro in American Society is far more complex. Du Bois was in fact ambivalent, for, although he insisted on integration he advocated also racial integrity—"the conservation of the races." Rightly or wrongly, however, Casely Hayford disparaged those Negroes who strive to be assimilated into American Society. He argued that "it is not so much Afro-Americans that we want as Africans" (*Ethiopia Unbound* . . .). What he warned against was close *imitation* which could be seized upon by white racists for disparaging the black race, thus:

How extraordinary is the spectacle of this huge race—millions of men without land or language of their own, without traditions of the country they came from, bearing the very names of the men that enslaved them.

In effect, Hayford was arguing that imitation robs the Ethiopian of self-respect because as Coleman has rightly observed, "any human relationship cast in the model imitator mould tends towards a superior-inferior stratification of attitudes. It is psychologically difficult for a model to regard an imitator as his equal." The way to project African personality is thus through the conservation of traditional cultural institutions.

African religions should be philosophically studied; this is Hayford's plea. In *Ethiopia Unbound* religious questions are broached. Christianity is constantly contrasted with indigenous religion to the disadvantage of the former. The Rev. Silas Whitely, the symbol of Christianity, is a time-serving clergyman who condones segregation and subordinates Christian principles to official policy in the West African colony. Before his ordination in England he entertained doubts about the divinity of Christ. As a clergyman in the Gold Coast he is supercilious, overbearing and vindictive. Mr. Kwaw Baidu, Whitely's African curate, is victimised and dismissed by him because Baidu dared to question the propriety of a graveyard segregation policy. In contrast, Kwamankra the so-called pagan is noble, bland, accommodating and understanding. According to his indigenous religious philosophy, he maintains, there is no reason why Christ's divinity should be doubted. From this point Hayford goes on to describe Fanti religious beliefs as an epitome of African traditional religion. (pp. xxviii-xxx)

Hayford's preoccupation with specified African institutions in his *Gold Coast Native Institutions* has been pointed out. His concern in this regard was to show that, first, Africa has a culture; second, that this culture is as rich and satisfying as any other; and third, that although there has been an inevitable diffusion of western culture in Africa, this should not be interpreted as signifying the desiccation of the cultures of Africa. In fact, the influence of western culture on African life and thought just as the effect of colonialism on the indigenous political systems, important as it may now appear, is only an historical phase in the over-all development of African culture.

In *Ethiopia Unbound,* one specific institution ubiquitously treated is marriage. In Hayford's view, the African marriage system has many advantages over the western monogamous system. The former has the advantage of fostering greater social cohesion than the latter. The African marriage system is also important for the resolution of personal and social tensions. Although Hayford does not condemn monogamy (the hero of *Ethiopia Unbound,* Kwamankra, had only one wife), he felt it was wrong for people to insist that it should supercede other forms of marriage. He observes that "any child of Eve who has deliberately become the mother of your child is worthy of your love, and to treat her as an outcast is to be unworthy of the name of a man." The reconciliation between Tandor-Kuma and Ekuba after years of separation and after Tandor-Kuma had legally married another woman and got children through this marriage, is a vindication of Casely Hayford's thesis.

A second aspect of African culture highlighted is the arts. Folksongs, the *Sankofu* (Fanti sea songs) for instance, are mentioned frequently and their deeper emotional effect as compared with Church hymns is posited. In this regard, Hayford certainly is one of the earliest African literary commentators to note the characteristic rhythm of African folk-poetry, a poetry of "drum and song," to use the expression of some contemporary critics.

Casely Hayford believed that education should be the cohesive force holding together all the strands of the great Ethiopian civilisation. Whole-sale imitation of the western form of education should be, as far as possible, eschewed. He therefore advocated in *Ethiopia Unbound* an Africanized Western University with Chairs for African History and African languages and literature. His envisaged university should primarily diffuse African culture. It is a felicitous commentary on the foresight of Casely Hayford that most African universities today are developing, though more conservatively, along his lines of thought. The distinct garb of students, male and female, Hayford tells us, amplifying his idealistic scheme for an African university, was national, with an adaptability suggestive of an advanced state of society." He stressed the need for a Faculty of Education in the university, an idea taken up seriously in West Africa only in the 1960's with the establishment of the University of Nigeria, Nsukka. G. N. Brown has remarked that "the university that is described in *Ethiopia Unbound* is astonishingly modern in conception.

Up till now, *Ethiopia Unbound* has hardly been appreciated as a work of art. This writer sees the book primarily as a fictional work comparable in certain respects to Swift's *Battle of the Books,* Johnson's *Rasselas* or even Mandeville's *Fable of the Bees.* It has the same ironic tone as these books and is as incisive of a West African colonial community as *Gulliver's Travels,* for example, is of the eighteenth century English society. That *Ethiopia Unbound* was not immediately recognised by Hayford's contemporaries, as basically a work of art, is not so surprising. Its author was a lawyer and a politician and his publications before and after *Ethiopia Unbound* cannot be described as literary works of art; they are either legal, political or propagandist treatises. The author himself probably helped to put off the literary scent by subtitling the book "Studies in Race Emancipation." In an age of black assertiveness fostered to a large extent by the outcome of World War I and the Japanese "revolution," it was almost inevitable for readers to cling to the ideas expressed in *Ethiopia Unbound* with avowed intentions, without caring seriously about the method of communication of these ideas. (pp.xxxi-xxxiv)

In recent years, there is an increasing awareness of the imaginative potential of *Ethiopia Unbound* and students of African Literature are trying to put the work into its apropos genre— the novel, in the context of the modern trend of *littérature engagée.* L. S. Senghor has remarked, "*La littérature Africaine est une littérature engagée.*" This is also true of *Ethiopia Unbound.* It is committed to a point of view. It is propagandist—a vehicle through which Hayford attempts to send his message of hope to the Ethiopians, his appeal for unity and the urgent necessity for a national regeneration.

Ethiopia Unbound is decidedly not a treatise. It is a fiction with fictive characters who live and act within a distinctly realistic social milieu, imaginatively conceived. Society is excoriated. Individuals, groups, institutions and systems are subjected to impartial criticism. The African, especially the ridiculous servile imitator of the English, is flayed alongside the vain and supercilious colonial administrator or drunken white miner who thinks he is superior to the African on grounds of colour alone. Analysing the work of destruction done by the colonialist, Hayford remarked:

> With the gin bottle in the one hand, and the
> Bible in the other, he urges moral excellence,

which in his heart of hearts he knows to be impossible of attainment by the African under the circumstance, and when the latter fails, his benevolent protector makes such a failure a cause for dismembering his tribe, alienating his lands, appropriating his goods, and sapping the foundations of his authority and institutions. (*Ethiopia Unbound . . .*).

The railway system is overdue for reform but there is no move to do so. It takes seven hours to cover thirty-nine miles! Other instances of satire abound throughout the book.

The language of the book is discursive, rhetorical, and allusive despite occasional quaintness and archaism. The influence of the Bible and *Pilgrims' Progress* is evident and there are many passages from Homer. It is evident that the author had been susceptible to epical influence during the time he wrote his only imaginative work.

Ethiopia Unbound is without doubt the matrix of all the nationalist and cultural ideas of one of the ablest African political and intellectual leaders in West Africa. (pp. xxxiv-xxxvi)

> *F. Nnabuenyi Ugonna, in an introduction to* Ethiopia Unbound: Studies in Race Emancipation *by J. E. Casely Hayford, second edition, Frank Cass & Co. Ltd., 1969, pp. v-xxxvi.*

WEST AFRICA   (essay date 1970)

[*In the following excerpt, the reviewer praises Casely-Hayford's nationalist ideas as reflected in* Gold Coast Native Institutions *and* Ethiopia Unbound.]

Outstanding among the early West African nationalists, both because of the length of his political career and because of the originality of his ideas, was Joseph Ephraim Casely Hayford. . . .

His books are now virtually unobtainable in the original, but they are slowly being reprinted. The first to be reprinted . . . , was *Ethiopia Unbound,* in which Hayford's views on a variety of questions are expressed through the conversation and experiences of a Ghanaian whom we first meet as a law student in London.

Hayford's main concern always was to assert the value of African tradition and culture. Although this was not then the view of all educated Africans, he was particularly critical of Africans who aped European dress (he urged a special dress for African students) and wanted the proposed university for the Gold Coast and Ashanti to be in Kumasi, away from the coast. 60 years ago he proposed establishment of schools of African studies in the United States—for the benefit mainly of Negro Americans. He particularly admired Japan which had become strong without losing its own character. Language, polygamy, temperance, music—all are discussed in *Ethiopia Unbound.* But his student is so unracial in outlook that he delights in his meeting with his future wife at a performance of Beerbohm Tree's Hamlet at the Haymarket Theatre.

Today little of this may seem very interesting. In 1911, when the book was published, it was very remarkable.

Now comes, in reprint, *Gold Coast Native Institutions* Hayford's first book, published in 1903. In this he urges "an intelligent and scientific study of Native Institutions," to help a British administration directed from Downing Street to avoid mistakes like the seizure of the Golden Stool. Hayford belonged to the generation of West African leaders who were sincerely loyal to the British Crown, and never hesitated to praise British officials (he saw the fairness of British judges as being the greatest support for British rule.) He wanted the country to develop in close co-operation with Britain. Yet while in *Ethiopia Unbound* he was concerned with the preservation of African customs and local culture, in *Gold Coast Native Institutions* he was concerned to show that the British had come to the Gold Coast as "honoured guests" and should not have interfered with the existing local administration. The ideal system would be for the British to look after external matters, leaving internal self-government to Africans.

To support this case he describes in great detail the actual operation of chieftaincy in the Gold Coast, the functions of the Linguists and Councillors, the "company" system, the traditional trade, the nature of local religion, etc. He also traces the way in which British rule had been established and asserts the significance of the "Bond of 1844" as an invitation to the British to co-operate but not to dominate.

For the most part his language is elegant and restrained; it is still hard-hitting. He complains, for example, that the Governor is allowed greater power than that exercised by the King-Emperor since he was not responsible to the local tax payers but to an "over-tasked official" some 3,000 miles away "who may or may not be a capable man" and who got all his information from the Governor himself.

This has been called a lawyer's book, but it is much more. For example, Hayford is anxious for Ashanti fully to share the political life of the Gold Coast and rejects the idea that there is an inevitable division between Ashanti and the South. He recalls with approval the way in which the early British administrators had understood and co-operated with the local people. He recalls Governor Pope Hennessy's comment (1872) on the Gold Coast: "My inquiries on the spot, and an examination of the archives of the Local Government convince me that the educated natives have contrasted favourably as a body with the European residents. I was certainly impressed favourably by their tone and manner in their several interviews with me."

Hayford ranges far; what is a good newspaper; what is the effect of the West African climate on Europeans; how useful are the local herbalists? Above all, as in *Ethiopia Unbound,* he shows himself to be a man proud of his country's past but in no sense racialist or reluctant to adapt customs and institutions.

> *"An Outstanding Nationalist," in* West Africa, *No. 2764, May 30, 1970, p. 585.*

O. R. DATHORNE (essay date 1974)

[*Dathorne is a Guyanese-born English novelist, short story writer, and critic whose fiction satirically examines the lives of expatriate black people in England and Africa. In the following excerpt from his study* The Black Mind: A History of African Literature, *he offers a review of* Ethiopia Unbound. *In an unexcerpted portion of the essay, Dathorne finds that while artistic intention in the novel is unfocused,* Ethiopia Unbound *nevertheless "pioneered the way for an important development in West African fiction."*]

Ethiopia Unbound, a work which takes the reader to London, West Africa, and even the underworld, is a literary expression of a wide variety of ideas. Kwamankra, the main character, is first seen in London conversing with Whiteley, a divinity student, on Christianity, a subject which is taken up time and again throughout the book. Kwamankra believes in a Black God and feels that Christ was "born of an Ethiopian woman." . . . He is next seen in West Africa where he is helping to establish a national university. Casely-Hayford devoted many pages to discussing the implications of such a university, arguing that "no people could despise its own language, customs and institutions and hope to avoid national death." . . . Kwamankra is then sent back to London to help translate books for the proposed university; he also becomes a law student and makes friends with another West African called "the Professor."

Education and Christianity, however, are not the only focal points of the book. Love also plays its part: one character, Tandor-Kuma, cannot marry the woman he loves because she is a maid; Kwamankra is more fortunate. After not having seen Mansa, his former girl friend, for many years, he finally meets her again. They marry and have a son, but Mansa dies when giving birth to their second child. Her death returns the author to the theme of Christianity; Kwamankra feels that through his love for Mansa "he had touched the depths of human happiness and the depths of human sorrow, and had come to know that the way to God led from one to the other." . . . (p. 144)

He visits her in the underworld, where she is a goddess. The style alters as the author smoothly blends a biblical prose with the rhythm of classical verse in his description of the underworld: "A number of peaceful avenues, wearing a beautiful green; like unto mass, which met in one grand broadway. Each avenue was edged with luxuriant shrubs and plants whose leaves showed the most delicate tints of the rainbow in beautiful blend." . . . Kwamankra's uncertainty about religious matters and his gesture toward Heaven are symbolized in a new structure which Mansa shows him and in which there is "unevenness in place where [there] should be uniformity." . . . His wife gives him advice on how he should live, and the visit concludes with a promise: "Say unto the mighty that the cry of the afflicted and the distressed among the sons of Ethiopia has come up to us, and we will visit the earth. . . . Lo! Nyiakrapon will establish in Ethiopia a kingdom which is different therein, and an angel of light, with a two-edged sword, shall guard the gate thereof." . . . (pp. 144-45)

When Kwamankra returns to the Gold Coast, he comes to the conclusion that he must restore the practice of indigenous religion to his people, instead of following "emasculated sentimentalities which men shamelessly and slanderously identify with the Holy one of God, His Son, Jesus Christ." . . . (p. 145)

Abruptly scene and character again switch; Kwamankra's old acquaintance Whiteley has decided to go to the Gold Coast as a missionary. In his mission work, he proves to be an ideal imperialist; he quarrels with his Black assistant chaplain and has him dismissed over the question of segregated cemeteries.

An attempt is now made to reintroduce Kwamankra into the story; Bilcox, a Gold Coaster, Whiteley, and Kwamankra meet at a party given by the chief magistrate. During the affair, Kwamankra describes his plan for segregating by ability, rather than by race: "If you took mankind in the aggregate, irrespective of race and shook them up together, as you would the slips of paper in a jury panel box, you would find after the exercise that the cultured would shake themselves free and come together, and so would the uncouth, the vulgar, and the ignorant; but, of course, you would ignore the law of nature, and, with a wave of the hand, confine the races in separate airtight compartments.'' . . . Kwamankra seems to be concerned solely with his own position, that of the privileged in an underprivileged community.

After a melodramatic meeting between Kwamankra and his son, Ekru Kwow, a meeting that has nothing to do with the development of the book, the Professor and Tandor unexpectedly re-enter the story. An amusing description is given of a train journey they take with Kwamankra in the Gold Coast. The Professor refuses to surrender his ticket, saying firmly to the ticket-collector, ''I have made it a rule never to give up my ticket on this line till I have landed safely at my destination, do you understand?'' . . . The bewildered ticket-collector does not know what to make of his passengers.

Another character is then introduced and dropped: Tony Palmer is of a Sierra Leonean family and with him Kwamankra talks about marriage, asserting that any woman who is worthy of his love is worthy to be his wife. Although no more is heard of Tony Palmer, this scene is juxtaposed with another, in which Tandor-Kuma, now married and ill, is nursed back to health by the mother of his child and the woman he had deserted.

Toward the end of the book, a meeting of the nations of the world on Mount Atlas is described. In this section the writer states his own opposition to colonialism and Christianity. Kwamankra is mentioned only tangentially, as giving a lecture at the African National University in America, where he puts forth his views on Edward Blyden, a pioneer African Pan-Africanist. Kwamankra is again dropped, and the author discusses the possibilities of the cultural unity of Africa, America, and the Caribbean. Kwamankra reappears as a delegate to the Pan-African Congress of 1905 where he again expounds Blyden's ideas for a unity of all Blacks. He criticizes ''the African who comes to his brethren with red-hot civilisation straight from Regent Circus or the Boulevards of Paris,'' . . . and identifies himself with those who ''walked the banks of the Nile in the days of yore.'' . . . At the end of the book, the author reinforces this idea of the equality of Africans and discusses Fanti belief and custom.

As has been seen, *Ethiopia Unbound* is a means by which Casely-Hayford attempted to express a hotchpotch of ideas. As far as action is concerned little happens, and the book vacillates between fantasy and detailed documentation. Kwamankra is allowed to disappear from the story for long periods, and either his place is taken by other characters or the author develops the ideas himself. Many of the ideas, however, lack clarity and consistency. For instance, Kwamankra goes to Britain to translate important books into his own language for the founding of the national university. Furthermore, when the author is not attacking the evils of westernization, he is advocating the study of the classics or giving his story a classical setting, as with Kwamankra's visit to the underworld and the meeting of the nations of the world on Mount Atlas.

The same vacillation is observed in his attitude toward class and Christianity. One character learns the lesson of social snobbery when he is nursed back to health by a woman he despises, but at the magistrate's party Kwamankra advocates a meritocracy. There is, however, cohesion between Kwamankra's ideas and the author's; although it is not satisfactory art when they interchange roles, it is nevertheless worth pointing out, in a book with so many deficiencies, that their ideological world is a mutual one.

If *Ethiopia Unbound* were intended as a novel, the conversations also seem unreal. Often they are stilted and in attempting to be always profound, they lack the ease which is associated with normal conversation. Pidgin English is only used once— in the train episode. This succeeds in maintaining balance, for so much of the book is serious and there are few light moments of relief.

Kwamankra has little private life. His thoughts are all concerned with the public issues of his day. One learns little about him as a person but a great deal about his attitude toward various matters. For example, in an unsuccessful scene he discusses colonialism and the ''yellow peril'' with his son. According to the author, ''he had a call to duty, and that in the service of his race.'' . . . But his race is identified with any that seems convenient at the moment—Egyptians, Greeks, Ethiopians, Chinese, Japanese, and West Indians. After a while Kwamankra's soul-searching inquiries about Christianity and his self-consciousness about race become a bore.

As the summary has indicated, the book abounds in sudden inexplicable shifts in time. But there seems to be no accompanying development in the characters. Kwamankra meets Whiteley at the beginning of the novel and then three years later, yet one is not aware of any change in Kwamankra. The marriage to Mansa is not treated in detail; it is as if Casely-Hayford feels that his book is one of ideas and that he must reserve the greater part for the expression of these ideas.

Archaisms predominate—''twain,'' ''the wind blowing where it listeth,'' ''he wot not the full meaning of what he had done''— although they are only appropriate in the description of the visit to the underworld. When Casely-Hayford aspires to a back-to-nature romanticism, the writing becomes absurd and trite. He has Mansa tell her husband: ''When we arrived in England the life of the people seemed to me artificial . . . Chance took me to Germany—there in the Black Forest, I got into direct touch with Nature; the song of the birds, the bleating of the lambs, the fragrance of the fields, all seemed so natural, and I said to myself; Here is my proper place; here the atmosphere wherein my nature may expand.'' . . . These seem strange sentiments coming from Kwamankra's wife, who, in the next breath, preaches world government by ''Ethiopians.''

Ethiopia Unbound is really a record of the author's own uncertainties and those of his generation. They were *évolués* who cherished their position, at the same time paying lip service to indigenous African beliefs. When Casely-Hayford therefore writes of a Fanti god, Nyiakrapon, he takes pains to show that he is like the Christian God. Without knowing it, Casely-Hayford was the earliest representative of a conflict—the man with irreconcilable cultural loyalties. (pp. 145-48)

> O. R. Dathorne, ''Beginnings in English,'' in his
> The Black Mind: A History of African Literature,
> *University of Minnesota Press, 1974, pp. 143-55.*

L. H. OFOSU-APPIAH (essay date 1975)

[*A Ghanian educator, critic, and translator, Ofosu-Appiah's works reflect his interest in African history, politics, and biography. In the following excerpt from his* Joseph Ephraim Casely Hayford: The Man of Vision and Faith, *he discusses the form and content of* Ethiopia Unbound.]

The most interesting of Casely Hayford's books is *Ethiopia Unbound.* It is a novel, but does not follow the pattern of a classical novel, since it is episodic, and in certain sections the author is merely writing speeches on politics and social injustices in Africa and America. But it appears to be a sort of autobiographical novel, and the author can be identified with the principal character, Kwamankra. The influence of John Bunyan is evident from the chapters on Love and Life and Love and Death. His wife's death affected him so much that he had to set down his feelings in those chapters. The book is also an attempt to interpret Akan Religion to a British theological student, Whitley, who eventually turns up in the Gold Coast to practise racial discrimination by insisting on separate cemeteries for blacks and whites! Apparently Whitley had not learned that there are only two things in which all men are equal by nature: All men are born naked, and all men die. The distinctions in civilisation arise after birth but end in death! Since Casely Hayford did not have much education in Fante, his Fante sentences cannot be understood without reference to his translations into English. His excursions into etymology are very odd. He claims that *Nyami* stands for *Nya oye me* or He who is I am! and *Nyiankropon* stands for *Nyia nuku ara oye pon*—He who alone is great! One can understand his desire to promote the study of African languages!

Ethiopia Unbound is also a criticism of the colonial system and the inefficiency which characterises some of its public services. The political agitator who is a lawyer appears in the person of Kwamankra, whom the white political officer dislikes; and we gather that white men who tend to sympathise with Africans have their careers cut short. His description of the 39-mile rail journey at the time sounds very much like rail travel in the 1970's. Apparently matches had to be borrowed to light the hurricane lamps in the train at night! No wonder Tandor-Kuma refused to surrender his ticket to the collector until the journey's end, for the 39 miles took seven hours to cover! He touches on the dilemma of a polygamous society and the evils of some Christian practices of the Europeans on the Coast. Racial discrimination is discussed by the mention of the yellow and black perils and the Black Man's burden. His interest in the Negro problem of the United States is evident from Chapter XVII, which deals with Race Emancipation. His aim in *Ethiopia Unbound* and in the *Gold Coast Native Institutions* is to impress upon Africans and Europeans that there is something good in the African way of life. But he does indulge in romanticism, for his Ethiopia which would raise its hands to God was not the ideal paradise of his dreams. It was a feudal slave-owning monarchy torn by strife and intrigues, and sunk in ignorance, poverty and illiteracy, in spite of the fact that Ethiopia has had its own script for centuries, and was known in Homeric times as the resting-place of the gods. The Ethiopians were called blameless by Homer. The romanticism was, however, meant to inculcate race consciousness, and here I think he met with some measure of success. In Africa one of the ways in which we get over our inferiority complex is to compare some features of our culture to those of the Ancient Greeks and Egyptians. Casely Hayford does that in *Ethiopia Unbound* where he makes Kwamankra discuss Nausikaa in Homer's Odyssey with his son Ekra-Ekow, and brings out the similarities between the two cultures. Perhaps if he had taken his Herodotus seriously, he could have saved himself all that trouble, since Herodotus regarded mankind as having several things in common, and most of what we now call African culture like drums and dances and the obsession with the dead have a long ancestry all over the world. (pp. 19-21)

L. H. Ofosu-Appiah, in his Joseph Ephraim Casely Hayford: The Man of Vision and Faith, *Academy of Arts and Sciences, 1975, 31 p.*

NNABUENYI UGONNA (essay date 1977)

[*In the following excerpt, Ugonna praises* Ethiopia Unbound *as an important contribution to the growth of African culture in the twentieth century.*]

Ethiopia Unbound is a remarkable story of ideas about race relations, a story whose main theme is the problem of universal human relationship. The relationship operates on two distinct but related levels: on the one hand it is the problem of human relationship between the colonizer and the colonized and on the other between white and black. The two trends imperceptibly fade into each other in so far as the colonizer is white and the colonized black. This is why invariably any attack on colonialism tends to be expressed in racial terms.

Ethiopia Unbound tells the life story of Kwamankra—his experiences, first, as a student in London, and then, as a legal practitioner in Ghana; his observations of social life both in London and in various Ghanaian towns—Kumasi, Cape Coast, Sekondi and Accra; his commentary on social institutions, on education, religion, economics; and his impartial criticism of the whole concept of colonial government as applied to the West African society—the corruption, callousness and exclusiveness of colonial missionaries and political officers, the neglect and dilapidation suffered by public utilities as railways, water supplies and electricity and the general absence of sound development schemes. To this extent, the work appears to be a social documentary. But then the book has another dimension which elevates it to the status of a classic: an epic quality, characterized by heroism and a sense of deep personal tragedy and stoical triumph.

The work is certainly an exercise in African cultural projection which is a subtle and positive way of protest. The ingenious device is to present characters, that is, African characters, in such light as to belie any suggestion of their inherent inferiority. Similarly, several aspects of indigenous African culture are rationalised. Their noble, useful, serene, elegant or remarkable qualities are highlighted while their grosser traits are either ignored or glossed over. Every creative artist, of course, follows this procedure. From chunks of life—battles, hatred, fear, birth, death, quarrels, eating, drinking, marriage, endearment, he selects those combinations that will answer to his own vision of life. (pp. 161-62)

Casely Hayford, in *Ethiopia Unbound,* has attempted to show that African culture is not synonymous with barbarism and cruelty, backwardness and crudity. As Mary Kinsley in a letter to the editor of the Liberian paper, *New Africa,* asked African nationalists who are conversant with their own indigenous culture to do, Hayford has indeed demonstrated that "African nationalism is a good thing, and that it is not a welter of barbarism, cannibalism and cruelty . . . that there is an African law and an African culture; that the African has institutions and a state form of his own."

This appeal has, as a matter of fact, been answered by other educated African nationalists in the form of treatises and newspaper articles but *Ethiopia Unbound* is clearly the first attempt to represent this idea in fiction. . . .

Throughout his public career, Casely Hayford endeavoured to preserve what is good and admirable in his culture. All his written works tend to be lucid expositions of different aspects of the African culture involving institutions, land tenure, communal life, justice, the arts, and so on. He knew it was important for Africans to come forward to project their culture themselves. (p. 162)

The problem was how best to demonstrate to the world that Africa has culture. Should revolutionary or violent methods be used? Casely Hayford rejected violence. Perhaps his legal education made him prefer constitutional and peaceful means. Yet he believed in action. "African manhood," he asserts, "demands that the Ethiopian should seek not his opportunity, or ask for elbow room from the white man, but that he should create the one or the other for himself." But he maintained that "the African's way to proper recognition lies not at present so much in the exhibition of material force and power, as in the gentler art of persuasion by the logic of facts and of achievements before which all reasonable men must bow." By using the words, "at present," Hayford shows that he was not after all totally against violence but that he was only being realistic and practical. Resorting to violence without adequate preparation, he surmised, would be disastrous. So his pacifism was only pragmatic. His policy was dictated by his own maxim, "Take what you get and get what you want." Rather than gain no immediate political ends, he would prefer to compromise on certain vital issues. This aspect of his character was responsible for the bitter criticism he received toward the end of his life, but he preferred a little measure of success to downright failure.

"The gentler art of persuasion"—this is the key to the general tone of *Ethiopia Unbound,* and it summarises the effect the work is designed to achieve, that is, to persuade all readers and especially whites and deracine Africans, that African culture developed independent of western culture. Hayford was aware that people are not persuaded by mere verbal protestations and unsubstantiated claims. He therefore stresses the need for resorting to "the logic of facts and of achievements." Consequently he makes his chief characters discuss different aspects of African cultural achievement with the aim of highlighting their important merits. The importance of African culture is dramatized by paralleling African cultural institutions with the corresponding western forms and then showing the advantages of the African patterns over the western.

This process begins in *Ethiopia Unbound* with the introduction in the first chapter, of two of the main characters in the book, Kwamankra and Whitely. Their personalities pervade the work but they hardly impress us as flesh and blood. They are more or less ideas personified and are used generally as mouth-pieces for expressing particular ideas. Kwamankra, in a sense, is like Samuel Johnson's Rasselas and just as *Rasselas* is a philosophical tale so is *Ethiopia Unbound* an ideological story. Kwamankra is conceived as symbolic of African personality: logical, dignified, rational, considerate, a negation of the typical western concept of the African. He believes in God, but this is after due consideration of the facts, not out of fear or superstition.

But his white foil, Whitely, a theology student, doubts the divinity of Christ. Whitely is torn between disbelief and a sense of obligation, not to God, but to his mother. To him (and he symbolizes white priesthood) belief or non-belief is not sufficiently disturbing, for, despite his doubts, he takes Holy Orders and later becomes a colonial chaplain in West Africa where he degenerates into a time-serving religious minister.

The story of *Ethiopia Unbound* opens, after a brief introduction by the narrator, with the hero Kwamankra and Whitely walking along Tottenham Court Road in London discussing ethics, religion and metaphysics. The philosophy of Marcus Aurelius, as expounded in his Meditations, is paralleled with the "teaching of the Holy Nazarene." The divinity of Jesus Christ is discussed, and Kwamankra, after contending that the Anglo-Saxon word from which God is derived does not in any way suggest the idea of *good,* argues that the Christian attributes of God—omnipresence, omniscience, omnipotence, are of course "borrowed from the Romans, who were pagans like ourselves, and who, indeed, had much to learn from the Ethiopians through the Greeks." Throughout the book preconceived ideas, familiar prejudices, and popular attitudes are subtly debunked by logical discussions and dialogue.

In Kwamankra's lodging the two friends continue to discuss religion. . . . The drift of Kwamankra's argument is that European philosophical, ethical and religious ideas were largely derived from Ethiopia, and Ethiopia ambiguously means Africa or Asia or both. By his logic Jesus Christ, Marcus Aurelius, Buddha, Confucius, Cleanthes and other stoics were Ethiopians since the idea of stoicism originated from Ethiopia.

Hayford has good reason for stressing the significance of African religious and philosophical ideas. The emphasis stems not merely from the fact that African social life is fundamentally religious but also from the feeling increasingly held at the turn of the century that Africa would have a tremendous moral influence on the rest of the world just as the West has had an unprecedented scientific impact on Africa. This is not to say that Africans envisioned a moral influence only. They also dreamt of a time when they would be (some would add, once more, implying that there was a time when Africa was) at the helm of all progress, scientific or moral. (pp. 163-64)

[Casely-Hayford's] attempt in *Ethiopia Unbound* is to bring home to the Africans the truth of his conviction that only by upholding her own distinctive culture could Africa win back her self-respect and dignity. Thus he makes his hero, Kwamankra, discuss at length not only African religion and philosophy but propound a theory of African education and advocate the African system of marriage. (p. 166)

The story of Tom Palmer, an ambitious youth, always dressed in "silk hat and patent leather boots" is illustrative of the cultural revolution *Ethiopia Unbound* is meant to bring about and therefore Hayford's concept of the ideal African personality. Tom Palmer is an African caught in an alien culture. At first he struts around as "leader of society" but later discovers, through the help of Kwamankra, the African sage, that love does not come only "when she is wooed in Parisian skirts and Regent Street high heels." Palmer ends up by marrying more than one wife and replacing his silk hat, etc., with sober African attire. Hayford's message here is unmistakable: return to African culture; develop it if necessary with what is edifying in the western culture. Africans should eschew a slavish imitation of the whites and should at all times maintain their cultural integrity. In this way a worthwhile, meaningful African personality would be created. (p. 168)

In *Ethiopia Unbound* Hayford has attempted to assert and define African personality. Through the character of Kwamankra he answers the question as to whether or not contemporary Africa has "collective achievement . . . like other nationalities." Kwamankra shows that Africa has a religion, a philosophy of life, music, art, law, etc.; that African culture though different from western culture is not inferior to it. He has also established that the African is a cultured man and is not inferior to the white man and that the only differences, psychological or mental, between a black man and a white man are "those which can be attributed solely to education and to cultural background." It is, in fact, the social heritage, the cultural tradition, the prevailing *zeitgeist,* which differentiates the black man from the white man and not any mystical gene or hormone or any transcendental power possessed by the one and lacked by the other. (pp. 168-69)

The need for the assertion of African personality arose as a result of either and denial of the existence of African culture or the misrepresentation of the African and his way of life. *Ethiopia Unbound* has thematically demonstrated both the deep-rooted existence of different aspects of the African culture and the cultural, intellectual and spiritual capabilities of the black man. Casely Hayford in this work has therefore made a tremendous contribution to the growth of the idea of Africanness. The importance of *Ethiopia Unbound* lies, indeed, in its being the earliest known work to give an aesthetic dimension to this otherwise philosophical concept of African personality. (p. 169)

> *Nnabuenyi Ugonna, "Casely Hayford: The Fictive Dimension of African Personality," in* UFAHAMU, *Vol. 7, No. 2, 1977, pp. 159-71.*

ADDITIONAL BIBLIOGRAPHY

Review of *Ethiopia Unbound. African Times and Orient Review* 1, No. 5 (November 1912): 7-8.
> Favorable appraisal of *Ethiopia Unbound* signed "W. F. H." According to the critic: "Through the whole story there rings the common cry of the African races who are waking. The cry of injustice from all, and the demand for equal opportunity from the educated, who claim a right to help in ruling and molding their native countries."

Eluwa, G. I. C. "Casely Hayford and African Emancipation." *Pan-African Journal* VII, No. 2 (Summer 1974): 111-18.
> Introductory essay discussing Casely-Hayford's life, works, and ideas.

Jones, Eldred Durosimi. "The Development of African Writing." *Journal of the Royal Society of Arts* 122, No. 5220 (November 1974): 837-45.
> Includes a brief discussion of *Ethiopia Unbound*, particularly the passage describing the meeting of the nations on Mount Atlas. According to Jones: "[*Ethiopia Unbound*], part autobiography, part allegory, part prophecy, is very modern in spirit and would certainly qualify as modern protest literature."

Hussain, Arif. "Iqbal and Casely-Hayford: A Phase in Afro-Asian Philosophy." *Ibadan* 29 (1971): 45-52.
> Discusses the similar philosophical beliefs of Casely-Hayford and Pakistani poet Muhammad Iqbal, his contemporary. According to Hussain: "The phase of Afro-Asian philosophy as represented by Casely-Hayford and Iqbal contains a philosophy which established the self-respect of the Afro-Asian world through faith and reason. It gave a justification for the freedom movements, a justification which is indigenous and original."

Sampson, Magnus J. "Joseph Ephraim Casely Hayford." In his *Gold Coast Men of Affairs*, pp. 160-73. London: Dawsons of Pall Mall, 1969.
> Details Casely-Hayford's political career. According to Sampson: "The career of Mr. Casely Hayford was a marvel of indefatigable application and industry, and . . . he had one of the most brilliant careers in the political history of the Gold Coast."

———. *West African Leadership.* London: Frank Cass & Co., 1969, 160 p.
> Summary of West African politics during Casely-Hayford's era. Sampson reprints several of Casely-Hayford's addresses and lectures.

Euclides (Rodrigues) da Cunha

1866-1909

(Also Euclydes; also wrote under pseudonym of Proudhon) Brazilian historian, journalist, essayist, and poet.

Cunha is remembered primarily as the author of *Os sertões (Rebellion in the Backlands),* which is considered by many critics to be one of the greatest works in Brazilian literature. An account of a rebellion led by the religious mystic Antonio Conselheiro against the Brazilian republic during the 1890s, *Os sertões* utilizes such diverse studies as geology, geography, anthropology, psychology, history, and religion as it examines the possible causes of the rebellion and the methods employed by the army to suppress the revolt. Although the subject of *Os sertões* is factual, the work is credited with exerting a strong influence on Brazilian fiction, primarily due to its lucid discussion of the complex populace of Brazil. The nationalism implicit in Cunha's search for a common Brazilian identity reflects Brazil's nationalistic self-discovery at the turn of the century, yet Cunha critically examines both positive and negative aspects of the Brazilian republic. The comprehensive scope of the work provides the basis for critics' estimation of *Os sertões* as a landmark in Brazilian letters.

Cunha was born in Santa Rita do Rio Negro, in the province of Rio de Janiero. After the death of his mother when he was three years old, Cunha was placed in a succession of relatives' homes and boarding schools for seven years until his father retired to Rio and gave his son a home and a formal education. Cunha received a liberal arts degree at the Colegio Aquino, where he assisted in founding *O democrata (The Democrat),* a periodical in which Cunha published his first literary work. During his years at the college, he was influenced by republican political ideas which advocated the overthrow of the Brazilian emperor and the establishment of a representative form of government. He was also influenced by the doctrines of scientific positivism, which is evident in the anthropological and philosophical bias of *Os sertões.* In 1886, after attending a polytechnic school for two years, Cunha entered the army and began officer's training at the Escola Militar da Praia Vermelha. However, his studies and his military career were ended two years later due to an act of insubordination, after which Cunha became a journalist, a career to which he had been attracted during his undergraduate years.

Following the creation of the Brazilian republic in 1889, Cunha was briefly reinstated in the army, only to resign after being demoted for protesting a death sentence given to two antirepublican arsonists. In 1896, while employed as a civil engineer, Cunha received an assignment from the *Estado de São Paulo* newspaper to accompany an army battalion which was embarking on a campaign to destroy a rebellion in the Brazilian backlands. There the mystic Antonio Conselheiro had assembled over a thousand followers who regarded him as a messiah who would usher in a millenial age of peace. Conselheiro had built Canudos, a communal city in which his word was the only recognized law, and had begun to preach against the republic, calling it the antichrist. His followers had begun to terrorize neighboring villages, and a threat by Conselheiro to take by force a shipment of lumber attracted the attention of the central government, which ordered the army to suppress

the revolt. Cunha assisted the army as an engineer, and during the year-long war he dispatched reports to the *Estado de São Paulo.* After the fall of Canudos, Cunha devoted five years, during which he was employed as an engineer, to the consolidation and expansion of his notes and newspaper articles on the rebellion. Cunha published the finished text of *Os sertões* in 1902. Although the book was highly successful, Cunha continued to work after its publication, serving as an engineer, a government surveyor of frontiers, and a professor of logic. He published several books during this period, but none of his later works are considered equal to the achievement of *Os sertões.*

In 1909, while Cunha was occupied with another book about the backlands, he was murdered by an army officer. Although it has been suggested that Cunha was murdered to prevent publication of this work, which may have exposed damaging facts concerning the army's conduct during the Canudos campaign as *Os sertões* had done, most critics believe that the motivation for the murder was purely personal. Since his death, Brazilians have retained a veneration for Cunha, and the site on which he wrote *Os sertões* is considered a national landmark.

Os sertões is divided into two sections. In the first part, "The Backlands," Cunha describes with scientific devotion to detail the geography, geology, and prehistory of Brazil, enumerates its native plants and animals, and discusses the climate and other aspects of the sparsely inhabited inland plateau of Brazil, after which the text turns to a discussion of the inhabitants of the backlands, or *sertanejos*. In this controversial chapter of the book, "Man," Cunha attempts to attribute the customs and superstitions of the *sertanejos* to their mixed origins in the three primary racial groups which populated Brazil at that time: Portuguese, Africans, and native Brazilians. While some critics consider Cunha's conclusions racist, others maintain that he merely echoed the pseudo-scientific theories of scientific determinism that were current among intellectuals during his lifetime. Moreover, his actual treatment of the backlands culture and people is highly sympathetic, and in his study of the rebellion Cunha shows great respect to the *sertanejos* while denouncing the barbarity of the supposedly civilized soldiers in the army. As Cunha's English translator, Samuel Putnam, states of the chapter on "Man": "It would . . . be a mistake to take it out of its larger context; all the rest of the book and all that we know of the author's life and of his mind as revealed in his work stand in contradiction to it." Although Cunha accepted deterministic racial theories, he was opposed to the prejudicial implications of such theories.

In the second section of *Os sertões*, "The Rebellion," Cunha relates the process by which the Canudos rebellion was crushed. During the siege of Canudos the Brazilian army discovered, through disastrous trial and error during four separate expeditions, the necessity of adapting to the backlands terrain in much the same manner as the *sertanejos* had done. However, during the assault upon the city, the army exceeded the level of barbarity which had been exhibited by the *sertanejos*. An example of cruelty common among many of the soldiers was the use of the belief held by the *sertanejos* that they could not attain salvation if killed by a steel knife, offering a prisoner death by bullet rather than by knife if he would give the soldiers information. Most of the prisoners refused, choosing to face eternal punishment rather than betray their comrades, and were stabbed and mutilated by the soldiers. Critics praise the power with which Cunha relates the final days of the struggle, in which the *sertanejos* continued to fight until the last man was killed. He maintains that the rebellion could have been prevented if the government had given more serious consideration to the fanaticism of Conselheiro's devotees and taken action earlier, and that the carnage could have been averted even in its final stages if the army had attempted to gain the trust of its prisoners through humane treatment, which would have induced the last survivors to surrender rather than fight to the death. Cunha skillfully conveys to the reader his horror of the enormity of such "crimes and acts of madness on the part of nations."

Although he is not widely known outside Brazil, Cunha has influenced a number of later Brazilian novelists, such as Jorge Amado and Mario Vargas Llossa, who have earned international recognition. Toward the end of his life, Cunha characterized *Os sertões* as "this barbarous book of my youth, this monstrous poem of brutality and force," but it is precisely the vividness of Cunha's depiction of such force and his attempt to discover its cause and any actions by which it could have been averted that provides the book's power. As Putnam observes: "In no other instance, probably, has there been such unanimity on the part of critics of all shades of opinion in acclaiming a book as the greatest and most distinctive which a people has produced, the most deeply expressive of that people's spirit."

PRINCIPAL WORKS

Os sertões (history) 1902
  [*Rebellion in the Backlands*, 1944]
Castro Alves e seu tempo (lecture) 1907
Contrastes e confrontos (essays) 1907
Perú versus Bolivia (history) 1907
A margem da história (essays) 1909
Canudos (essays) 1939
Obra completa (history, essays, and lectures) 1966

EUCLIDES DA CUNHA (essay date 1901)

[*In the following "Preliminary Note" to* Os sertões, *Cunha states his purposes for writing this work.*]

Written in the rare intervals of leisure afforded by an active and tiring life, [*Os sertões*], which originally set out to be a history of the Canudos Campaign, subsequently lost its timeliness when, for reasons which need not be mentioned here, its publication was deferred. We have accordingly given it another form, the theme which was the dominant one in the beginning and which inspired the work being now little more than a variation on the general subject here treated.

It is our purpose to sketch in, however inadequately, for the gaze of future historians, the most significant present-day characteristics of the subraces to be found in the backlands of Brazil. We do this for the reason that the instability of the multiple factors and diverse combinations that go to make up this ethnic complex, together with the vicissitudes of history and the lamentable lack of mental enlightenment which prevails among them, is likely to render these races short-lived, destined soon to disappear before the growing exigencies of civilization and the intensive material competition offered by the stream of immigrants that is already beginning to invade our land with profound effect. The fearless *jagunço*, the ingenuous *tabaréo*, and the stolid *caipira* are types that will soon be relegated to the realm of evanescent or extinct traditions.

The first effects of various ethnic crossings are, it may be, initially adapted to the formation of a great race; there is lacking, however, a state of rest and equilibrium, which the acquired velocity of the march of the peoples in this century no longer permits. Backward races today, tomorrow these types will be wholly extinguished. Civilization is destined to continue its advance in the backlands, impelled by that implacable "motive force of history" which Gumplowicz, better than Hobbes, with a stroke of genius, descried in the inevitable crushing of weak races by the strong.

The Canudos Campaign has, therefore, the undeniable significance of a first assault in a struggle that may be a long one. Nor is there any reason to modify this assertion in view of the fact that it was we, the sons of the same soil, who staged this campaign; inasmuch as, being ethnologically undefined, without uniform national traditions, living parasitically on the brink of the Atlantic in accordance with those principles of civilization which have been elaborated in Europe, and fitted out by German industry, we played in this action the singular role of unconscious mercenaries. What is more, these extraordinary native sons, living in a prevalent disunity upon a land that was in part unknown to them, are wholly separated from us by a co-ordinate of history—time.

The campaign in question marked a backward step, an ebb in the direction of the past. It was in the integral sense of the word a crime and, as such, to be denounced.

Hence, in so far as lies within our power, we propose to do justice to that admirable saying of Taine concerning the honest narrator who looks History in the face as she deserves: ". . . Il s'irrite contre les demi-vérités qui sont des demi-faussetés, contre les auteurs qui n'altèrent ni une date, ni une généalogie, mais dénaturent les sentiments et les moeurs, qui gardent le dessin des événements et en changent la couleur, qui copient les faits et défigurent l'âme: il veut sentir en barbare, parmi les barbares, et, parmi les anciens, en ancien" ["... He is angered by half-truths which are also half-lies, by authors who falsify neither a date nor a genealogy but who distort feelings and values, who preserve the outline of events and change their colors, who copy the facts and disfigure the soul: he wants to be a barbarian among barbarians, and, among the ancients, ancient"]. (pp. xxix-xxx)

> *Euclides da Cunha, "Preliminary Note," in his Re-bellion in the Backlands, translated by Samuel Putnam, University of Chicago Press, 1944, pp. xxix-xxx.*

ISAAC GOLDBERG (essay date 1922)

[*As a critic, Goldberg's principal interests were the theater and Latin-American literature. His* Studies in Spanish-American Literature *(1920) and* Brazilian Literature *(1922) are credited with introducing two neglected groups of writers to English-language readers. In the following excerpt, Goldberg discusses* Os sertões *and R. B. Cunninghame-Graham's* A Brazilian Mystic *(1920).*]

Os Sertões, which first appeared in 1902—a happy year for Brazilian letters, since it witnessed the publication of Graça Aranha's *Chanaan* as well—is one of the outstanding works of modern Portuguese literature. At once it gave to its ill-fated author a fame to which he never aspired. His name passed from tongue to tongue, like that of some new Columbus who with his investigation of the sertão had discovered Brazil to the Brazilians. His labour quickened interest in the interior, revealed a new source of legitimate national inspiration and presented to countrymen a strange work,—disturbing, illuminating, disordered, almost a fictional forest, written in nervous, heavily-freighted prose. Yet this is harsh truth itself, stranger than the fiction of Coelho Netto, wilder than the poetry of Graça Aranha, though instinct with the imagination of the one and the beauty of the other. The highly original work struck a deep echo in English letters and if Englishmen have neglected to read Richard Cunninghame-Graham's remarkable book called *A Brazilian Mystic: The Life and Miracles of Antonio Conselheiro*—a book that would never have been written had not Euclydes da Cunha toiled away in obscurity to produce *Os Sertões*—it is their loss rather than their fault. It is a hurried and a harried world. Who, today, has time for such beauty of thought and phrase as Richard the wandering Scots sets down almost carelessly in his books and then sends forth from the press with mildly mocking humour for his prospective, but none too surely anticipated readers? Yet it is not the least of Euclydes da Cunha's glories that he was the prime cause of Mr. Cunninghame-Graham's *A Brazilian Mystic.* Not a fault of English readers, surely; but none the less their loss. (pp. 210-11)

The plan of *Os Sertões* is that of a scientific spirit at the same time endowed with the many-faceted receptivity of the poet. Before approaching the campaign of Canudos itself, the author studies the land and the man produced by it; he is here, indeed, as [José] Verissimo early indicated, the man of science, the geographer, the geologist, the ethnographer; the man of thought, the philosopher, the sociologist, the historian; the man of feeling, the poet, the novelist, the artist who can see and describe. But nowhere the sentimentalist. From one standpoint, indeed, the book is a cold confirmation of the very law against whose operative details the author protests:—"the inevitable crushing of the weak races by the strong."

Though a sertanejo school of fiction had existed before *Os Sertões,* the book brought to Brazilians a nearer, more intimate conception of the inhabitants of those hinterlands. (p. 214)

Cunninghame-Graham, like Euclydes da Cunha, and like the better of the Brazilian's critics, feels a strong sympathy for the man [Antonio Conselheiro] in whom the new hopes of the sertanejos were centred. It is a sympathy, moreover, born of the understanding without which all knowledge is as fruit turned to ashes in the mouth. The Scot, like the Brazilian, is a psychologist. "Antonio Conselheiro himself did not so much rebel against authority as against life, perhaps expecting from it more than it had to give upon the spiritual side, not understanding that a fine day, with health to enjoy it, is the most spiritual of pleasures open to mankind," he writes, in his amiable, worldly-wise (and heavenly-wise) way. And later: "When all is said, it is impossible not to sympathize to some extent with the misguided sectaries, for all they wanted was to live the life they had been accustomed to and sing their litanies. Clearly Antonio Conselheiro had no views on any subject under heaven outside his own district. His dreams were fixed upon a better world, and his chief care was to fit his followers for the change that he believed was to take place soon."

It is Verissimo, who, with his almost unerring insight, extracts from his countryman's book its central significance. Here is a volume that is a remarkable commentary upon the formation of all religions,

> without excepting our own Christianity. In another milieu, under other conditions, Antonio Conselheiro is a Christ, a Mohammed, a Messiah, one of the many Mahdis, creators of religions in that fecund soil of human belief which is Asia. In the sertão, friends and enemies and even the constituted authorities, hold him (i.e., Antonio Maciel, the people's councillor) as a good, honest, upright man, despite the legend—and is it only a legend?—which attributes to a tragic matricide his transformation from a business man into a religious preacher, his life as a saint and a missionary of the sertão.

I find that I have spoken as much of Cunninghame-Graham as of the Brazilian in whom he found his most important source; that is because the Scotsman's book is the best possible revelation in English of the remarkable account given by Euclydes da Cunha.

Os Sertões stands alone in the nation's literature; we, in ours, have no book to parallel it in spirit, purport or accomplishment. Yet even today there are regions to which a similar method might be applied, for Verissimo's words about Asia seem to cover the United States as well,—in less degree, of course, but for our purpose with equal patness. More, a close reading of the government's application of force to a situation that might have yielded to less warlike methods,—or, at least, that might have been managed without the necessity of the final massacre—could teach something to all governmental departments that are brought into contact with alien or extra-social groups which must be incorporated into the national entity. *Os Sertões* is the best answer to the young Brazilian regionalists who have made the book a rallying-point. Here is a volume— and a thick, compact volume it is—dealing in quasi-reportorial spirit with a brief incident in the most hidden recesses of the national interior; it was not written with belles-lettres in mind; it is strewn with terms and processes of thought that baffle the ordinary reader. Yet the man who composed it was a vibrant personality, and whether knowingly or unwittingly, he made the book a symbol,—a symbol of uncomprehending persecution, of human fanaticism, of religious origins, of man's instinctive seeking after something higher. It is true that the persecution was in part necessary, that the aspect of fanaticism here revealed is most repugnant, that the spectacle of religious origins does not flatter our unctuous, supposedly civilized, superior souls. But it is true, likewise, that we must gaze into such depths as these to remind ourselves occasionally that we dwell in these inferiors. Such is the wisdom of Euclydes da Cunha, of Richard Cunninghame-Graham, of José Verissimo. (pp. 219-21)

Isaac Goldberg, "Euclydes da Cunha," in his Brazilian Literature, *Alfred A. Knopf, 1922, pp. 210-21.*

ALBERT R. LOPES   (essay date 1942)

[*In the following excerpt, Lopes discusses the importance of* Os sertões *in the development of the Brazilian novel.*]

Euclides da Cunha... laid the foundations for the modern Brazilian novel. Authors before him had manifested an interest in the Brazilian hinterland, but theirs was a fictional interest; da Cunha's, that of a man of science. In *Os Sertões* ..., the scientist is everywhere apparent—the sociologist, the ethnologist, and the geologist.

The *sertões,* the Brazilian hinterlands, together with their inhabitants, the *sertanejos,* are vividly portrayed. According to Euclides da Cunha, the *sertanejo* is a strong, graceless individual who is seemingly out of joint and crooked. His normally bad posture is made even more noticeable by his leaning against a door or wall when standing, or, if he is on horse, by his falling upon one of the stirrups, resting on the side of the saddle. Mysterious and silent as are the vast *sertões* that surround him, the *sertanejo* tends to be mistrustful and very superstitious.

This superstitious *sertanejo* and his religious fanaticism are faithfully depicted. At times, roused to a religious frenzy, the women vie with one another to see who will be the first to make the offering of a child in bloody sacrifice. The *sertanejo* hated the Brazilian government that took steps to halt these practices; his was the law of God; the government's, that of a dog. Thus it is that the *sertanejo* puts his faith in the Conselheiro (Councilor) who is to come to free him, and when their "king" comes, he who supports the government will regret it.

The importance of *Os Sertões* in the study of the Brazilian novel of today can not be exaggerated, for time and again novelists have found inspiration in these pages. Besides affording a wealth of material for plots, *Os Sertões* paved the way for the regional and social novel. And the modern Brazilian novel is basically regional and social! (pp. 18-19)

Albert R. Lopes, "The Modern Brazilian Novel," in The New Mexico Quarterly Review, *Vol. XII, No. 1, February, 1942, pp. 18-24.*

SAMUEL PUTNAM   (essay date 1943)

[*Putnam was a distinguished American biographer, editor, critic, and translator of works from French, Spanish, and Portuguese into English. Regarded among the most talented translators of his generation, he earned particular acclaim for his 1949 translation of Miguel de Cervantes's* Don Quixote. *He is also known for* Paris Was Our Mistress *(1947), a highly praised portrait of the colorful inhabitants of Montparnasse in the 1920s and 1930s and examination of the "Lost Generation" of expatriate American authors, and for* Marvelous Journey *(1948), a study of Brazilian literature. In the following excerpt, Putnam discusses Cunha's theories regarding the diverse races of Brazil, refuting the claim that the author was an advocate of racial prejudice.*]

To [Cunha], the entire episode of Canudos was a "crime" and an "act of madness" on the part of a nation. It was "the most brutal conflict of our age," the "major scandal in our history"; it marked "an ebb in the direction of the past." Cunha's book accordingly becomes a "cry of protest" against "those extraordinary representatives of civilization in our backlands who exhibited so lamentable a degree of barbarism toward semi-barbarians." For this was in reality a clash of two societies, a clash of cultures, between the society and culture of the seaboard and those of the interior; and it was the civilized men of the littoral whom the author of *Os Sertões* held to be the guilty ones. It was not that he defended the rebels; for the book was not one of defense but of attack. Once it had occurred, the rebellion of course had to be put down, and he helped to put it down; but it should never have occurred in the first place, that is his point. He was shocked by the fact that Brazilian soldiers were invading the interior of their own country as if it were "foreign territory" and sending to their own fellow-countrymen, whom they had left in darkness for centuries, "the legislator Comblain," that is, the Comblain rifle. In this respect, he saw the men of the seaboard, representing the Brazilian nation, as playing the rôle of "unconscious mercenaries." But let the author speak for himself; his thought is best summed up in a quotation:

What we had to face here was the unlooked-for resurrection of an old society, a dead society, galvanized into life by a madman. We were not acquainted with this society; it was not possible for us to have been acquainted with it. ... After having lived for four hundred years on a vast stretch of seaboard, where we enjoyed the reflections of civilized life, we suddenly came into an unexpected inheritance in the form of the Republic. Caught up in the swirl of modern ideas, we abruptly mounted the ladder, leaving behind in their centuries-old semi-darkness a third of our people, in the heart of our country. ... Shunning in our revolutionary zeal the slightest compromise with the exigencies of our nationalism, we merely succeeded in deepening the contrast between our own mode of life and that of our rude native sons, who were more alien to us in this land of ours than were the immigrants that come from Europe. For it was not an ocean which separated us from them, but three whole centuries. ...

And when, through our own undeniable lack of foresight, we permitted a nucleus of maniacs to form among them, we failed to see the deeper meaning of the event. Instead, we looked at it from the narrow-minded point of view of political factionalism. In the presence of these monstrous aberrations, we had a revealing fit of consternation; and with an intrepidity that was worthy of a better cause, we proceeded to put them down with bayonets. . . .

All this, in Cunha's eyes, constituted a "deplorable stumbling-block to national unity." As a modern literary historian puts it, what the author was revealing in his work was "the profound instability of our existence." Through it all, meanwhile, his deep and essential humaneness of spirit stands forth strongly. Gilberto Freyre has described him as "a social engineer animated by a political ideal," and adds that Cunha was "inspired by a cult of the human personality." This is unquestionably true. The pages of *Os Sertões* show a deep-seated abhorrence of violence and of any kind of aggression perpetrated by the strong upon the weak. Without being a pacifist, Cunha is a militant anti-militarist, and the latter portion of his work comes near to being a tract on the subject. He was horrified by the savage cruelty that was practiced on both sides in the Canudos campaign, but he particularly blamed the ones who were supposed to be "civilized." This, however, is merely the negative side of his humaneness, the positive aspect of which is to be seen in his obvious and passionate love of the native of the backlands, the *sertanejo,* and especially the *vaqueiro,* or cowboy. He may be said to have discovered for his countrymen the man of the *sertão,* and so in a manner to have enabled Brazil to discover itself; and herein lies the truly epic quality of his book. Lovingly he pictures for us the *mestizo* backwoodsman's way of life, his daily labors, his family life, his amusements, customs, superstitions, and religious observances. And in studying the *sertanejo,* his habits and habitat, in the course of this campaign, he finds himself squarely confronted with the question of race and nationality in Brazil.

What are his conclusions? The first one is that the existence of a Brazilian racial type is "highly doubtful if not absurd." He concludes that "we do not possess unity of race, and it is possible we shall never possess it." He then looks about him at the hinterland *mestizos* whom he admires and even loves, and endeavors to apply to them his baggage of positivistic science and pseudo-science, being influenced here especially by the views of Gumplowicz. That he himself is conscious of a disparity between life and that "rigid biologic determinism" which he derived from his sources, is evident from the title which he gives to this section of his chapter on "Man": "An Irritating Parenthesis." It is not merely an irritating parenthesis; it is a distressing one in the light of modern anthropological science and modern democratic ideals in a world that is engaged in a life-and-death struggle with Hitler and his "Aryans." If this passage were really representative of Cunha, he would not be worth reading and certainly not worth translating today. It would, however, be a mistake to take it out of its larger context; all the rest of the book and all that we know of the author's life and of his mind as revealed in his work stand in contradiction to it. In it he holds that the intermingling of highly diverse races leads to retrogression, to the development of a psychologically unstable type.

Cunha appears to be arguing with himself; for his "parenthesis" ends on a question: "If all this is true, how then account for the normality of an anthropological type which suddenly makes its appearance, combining tendencies which are so opposed?" And the very next section is entitled "A Strong Race"—referring to those same backland *mestizos* who have just been condemned to an inferior status! For the *sertanejo—mulatto,*

mameluco, cafuso, or a blend of these blends—does impress the chronicler of Canudos as a strong type. True, he finds in the *vaqueiro* a certain constant tendency to repose, when not directly engaged in the arduous labors of a cattleman's life, in riding the upland plains, or busying himself at the round-up or the cow-hunt in the *caatinga.* The backlands cowboy is "the man who is always tired," who will lean against the first doorpost, or loll back against his saddle when he pauses to chat with a friend, or drop to a squatting position and sit on his heels while lighting his pipe; and these are taken as signs of an inherited constitutional enervation and debilitation. Yet over against all this are the backwoodsman's many admirable qualities: his industry, his honesty, his devotion to his family and his herds; in brief, his moral strength of character. An explanation must be found, and Cunha's runs as follows:

> It was in this manner that our rude fellow-countrymen of the north were formed. The abandonment in which they were left by the rest of the country had a beneficent effect. It freed them from a highly painful adaptation to a superior social state, and at the same time prevented their slipping backward through the aberrations and vices of a more advanced milieu. The fusion that took place occurred under circumstances more compatible with the inferior elements. The predominant ethnic factor, while transmitting to them civilized tendencies, did not impose civilization upon them. This is the basic and distinguishing fact with regard to miscegenation in the back-lying regions of the littoral.

By this time the causes of our author's confusion on the subject of mixed races, and in particular the mixed race of the Brazilian backlands, should begin to be clear. Confronted with a retarded stage of cultural evolution, he endeavors to explain it largely on the basis of biology, physiology and heredity. It is true, he devotes considerable space to the effects of the physical milieu, the "variability of the physical environment," stressing especially the climatology, the droughts, the rugged terrain, and the like; but the economic factors as represented by the modes and forces of production and the property relationships in this primitive-seeming (in reality, semi-primitive) society apparently mean little or nothing to him in the determination and description of the culture of that society. He has read Buckle, Renan, and Gumplowicz, but gives no evidence of ever having heard of Marx.

Nevertheless, as has been stated, the conclusions at which he arrives in the end are progressive and democratic in character. While he is led to doubt the existence of a "Brazilian type," he finds that the backwoods *mestizo* is *"the very core of our nationality, the bedrock of our race";* and it was this core, this bedrock, which was being attacked by the rest of the nation at Canudos. The *sertanejo* is "a retrograde, not a degenerate type," and "the vicissitudes of history, by freeing him, in the most delicate period of his formation, from the exigencies of a borrowed culture, have fitted him for the conquest of that culture some day." Again: "Our biological evolution demands the guaranty of social evolution. We are condemned to civilization. Either we shall progress, or we shall perish. So much is certain and our choice is clear." Brazil may possibly develop "a historic race" in the future, depending upon "the autonomy of our national life." In the meantime, there is the lesson of Canudos:

This entire campaign would be a crime, a meaningless and a barbarous one, if we were not to take advantage of the paths opened by the artillery, by following up our cannon with a constant, stubborn, and persistent campaign of education, with the object of drawing these rude and backward fellow-countrymen of ours into the current of our times and our national life.

This, assuredly, is not the language of the modern exponent of "Aryanism"; yet Cunha has been accused both by native and by foreign critics of advocating doctrines of racial superiority. Muddled in his analysis of stages of cultural evolution and led astray by certain European writers of his time, he does speak of "superior" and "inferior," of "strong" and "weak" races; he fears, also, that the stronger races may be able to destroy the weaker ones, either through force of arms or through the vices of civilization; but nowhere does he once attempt to justify any act of aggression. In fact, the whole trend of his work and thinking is opposed to this. If he is guilty of what Freyre has expressively termed "ethnocentric exaggerations," this is because he was "the victim of scientific preconceptions with the appearance of anthropologic truths" such as were common at the turn of the century; but as Freyre further points out, he did not carry his racial theories to any mystical extreme. While passionately concerned for national unity, he was no narrow nationalist; and the author of *Casa grande e senzala* is rightly convinced that Cunha, had he lived today, would not have been a "totalitarian." The idea, indeed, is unthinkable. As a Spanish American critic has remarked, the man who wrote *Os Sertões* "believed with all his heart that a Negro, an Indian, were as much Brazilians as the president of the nation."

Addicted to an "intensely concentrated, tortured, and agrarian Brazilianism," and with a pronounced trait of the pathologic in his personality, Euclides da Cunha was none the less possessed of an honest, if a bitter and skeptical, genius-endowed, forward-looking mind. For one thing, he was not one of those who believed that the hinterland, with all its backwardness, benightedness, and fratricidal superstition, had been so decreed by heaven for all time. He believed in doing something about it; his biologic determinism did not stand in the way of this, did not lead to a fatalistic acceptance of the *status quo*. In this respect, he was socially in advance of his age, even though his thought shows many of its confusions. In any event, one thing that he undeniably did was to state the problem for his countrymen, putting into his statement all the emotional passion and anguish which they felt. A son of the smaller bourgeoisie, in a late nineteenth-century semi-colonial country practically without any industrial proletariat, he failed to take into account the powerful determining factor of the popular masses in the solving of questions of race and nationality. For a quarter of a century and more the problem which he posed was to be debated and threshed out, back and forth, with a life-and-death fervor which it is hard for us North Americans to understand, melting-pot nation though we may be. It was not until the 1930's, with the rise of the broad popular movement known as the National Liberation Alliance, under the leadership of the Brazilian working class, that modern sociologists and anthropologists like Gilberto Freyre, Arthur Ramos, Edison Carneiro, and others began working toward a solution that is in accord with the ideals of the democratic world of today. For in the end such problems can only be solved by the people, through a dialectical science of society that is based upon the needs, desires and aspirations of the masses and the "motive force of history" inherent in the common man of earth. Eu-

clides da Cunha was a man of his age, and even in advance of his age, but he had not made this great discovery. (pp. 330-37)

Samuel Putnam, "Race and Nation in Brazil," in Science and Society, *Vol. VII, No. 4, Fall, 1943, pp. 321-37.*

SAMUEL PUTNAM (essay date 1944)

[*In the following excerpt from Putnam's preface to his translation of* Os sertões, *he discusses the literary importance of this work.*]

There can be no doubt that Euclides da Cunha's *Os Sertões* is a work that is unique not only in Brazilian but in world literature as well. In no other instance, probably, has there been such unanimity on the part of critics of all shades of opinion in acclaiming a book as the greatest and most distinctive which a people has produced, the most deeply expressive of that people's spirit. On this the native and the foreign critic are in agreement. "*Nosso livro supremo*—our finest book," says Agrippino Grieco, in his study of "The Evolution of Brazilian Prose," and he adds that it is "the work which best reflects our land and our people." Stefan Zweig, Brazil's tragic guest, saw in *Os Sertões* a "great national epic . . . created purely by chance," one giving "a complete psychological picture of the Brazilian soil, the people, and the country, such as has never been achieved with equal insight and psychological comprehension. Comparable in world literature, perhaps, to *The Seven Pillars of Wisdom,* in which Lawrence describes the struggle in the desert, this great epic, little known in other countries, is destined to outlive countless books that are famous today by its dramatic magnificence, its spectacular wealth of spiritual wisdom, and the wonderful humanitarian touch which is characteristic of the whole work. Although Brazilian literature today has made enormous progress with the number of its writers and poets and its linguistic subtlety, no other book has reached such supremacy" [see Additional Bibliography].

"The Bible of Brazilian nationality," as it has been termed, *Os Sertões* has "enriched Brazil with a book laden with seed, filled with perspectives for our triumph in the world of culture." It is commonly looked upon as marking, in the year 1902, Brazil's intellectual coming-of-age. The site where it was composed has now become a national shrine, and the volume itself, heralding the "rediscovery of Brazil," is indubitably a historical landmark. Revealing "the profound instability of our existence," as one literary historian puts it, it was at the same time, in the author's own words, essentially based upon "the bold and inspiring conjecture that we are destined to national unity."

Both book and author, it is true, remained more or less of an enigma to their age. As one Spanish-American critic has observed, Cunha was in reality taking arms against an era. Skeptical, sincere, bitter, uncompromising, "almost brutal," displaying at times an "anomalous pessimism," particularly on the question of race, and endowed with an anguish-ridden personality that has in it more than a little of the pathologic, this "son of the soil, madly in love with it," nonetheless emerges, alongside the nineteenth-century novelist, Machado de Assis, as one of the two outstanding figures in all Brazilian letters. As Zweig remarks, these are "the two really representative personalities" with whom Brazil enters "the arena of world literature."

In the case of so exceptional a writer and a work so truly amazing as *Os Sertões,* it is perhaps not surprising that Euclides da Cunha's admirers should range far afield in quest of comparisons. Thus, this "Beethoven of our prose," this *"genio americano,"* or "Latin-American genius," as the venerable Monteiro Lobato describes him, has been likened to authors as diverse as Dickens, Carlyle, and the prophet Ezekiel! As a reporter he has been compared to Kipling recording the exploits of Lord Roberts in the desert; and a reporter of a most unusual kind he assuredly was, one who, writing amid the tumult of events and the emotional stress of the moment, succeeded in turning a journalistic account of a military campaign into an epic treatise on the geology, the geography, the climatology, the flora, the fauna, and the human life of the Brazilian backlands. *Os Sertões* is all this and a great deal more. Among other things, it is the definitive early-century statement of the national-racial question in Brazil, a problem that is a vital one today; and to his countrymen of the present its author remains "the representative genius *par excellence* of our land, of our people, and of our pure and lofty aspirations to heroism, beauty, and truth."

Above all, however, it is a thrilling, vividly told tale, a "great document, which, though not a novel, reads like fiction." Dealing with "one of the most virile episodes in our history," the incredibly heroic resistance of the backland natives at the siege of Canudos in 1896-97, it is a tale that should hold a special interest for this war-torn age of ours. Here is a campaign in which it required three months for a federal army of some six thousand men to advance one hundred yards against a handful of backwoodsmen! Here is guerrilla warfare in its pristine form, with the "scorched earth" and all the other accompaniments. And here, finally, after a months-long, house-to-house battle that recalls the contemporary epic of Stalingrad, are one old man, two other full-grown men, and a boy holding out against that same army until the last of them falls back dead in the grave which they themselves have dug!

"A cry of protest" the author calls his work, and it is indeed that. A protest against what he regards as a "crime" and an "act of madness" on the part of a newly formed republican government. For him, this "most brutal conflict of our age" was the "corpus delicti on the aberrations of a people," the "major scandal in our history." A clash between "two societies," between two cultures, that of the seaboard and that of the *sertão,* the Canudos Expedition appeared as a "deplorable stumbling-block to national unity." His book, accordingly, as he tells us, is not so much a defense of the *sertanejo,* or man of the backlands, as it is an attack on the barbarity of the "civilized" toward those whose stage of social evolution was that of semibarbarians. In this connection we North Americans well may think of our own Indian wars of the early days. The author's chapter on "Man" has been seen by Agrippino Grieco as "a precious lesson in things, given by a free man to the slaves of power, by a sociologist without a chair to the governors of the nation." Cunha, the same writer goes on to say, "told the truth in the land of lies and was original in the land of plagiarism." This honesty, set off by his originality and his boldness of attack, is perhaps his most prominent trait, the one on which all his commentators are agreed.

Whether or not his primary purpose was to defend the *sertanejo,* the author of *Os Sertões* certainly exhibits a passionate love of the mestizo backwoodsman and his way of life. The latter's customs, occupations, diversions, joys, and sorrows are all depicted with an affectionate wealth of detail. The "roundups," the merrymakings, the religious observances and superstitions of the region, are minutely chronicled, and the

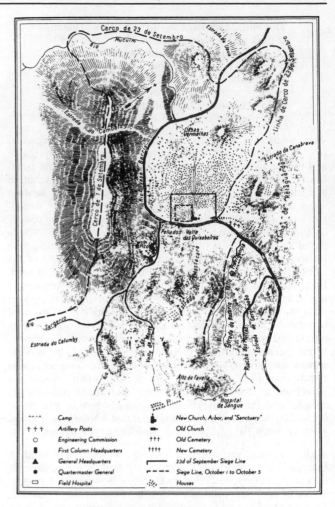

Map of Canudos and surrounding territory.

result is an authentic and unexcelled picture of the *vaqueiro,* or North Brazilian cowboy. Indeed, a Portuguese critic, none too friendly to Brazil, has said that this portion of the book contains the sixty-one finest pages ever written in the language. The description of the devastating backland droughts holds the tragedy of a people struggling with a blind fate as represented by the relentless forces of nature. How deeply Euclides da Cunha felt for this folk, how close to them he was, may be seen from any one of a number of vignettes that he gives us, each a small masterpiece in its kind: the cowboy's dead child and the *festa* that marks its funeral; the cattle dying of thirst and starvation on the edge of the pool where they were accustomed to drink; the *vaqueiro* and his lifelong vegetable friends, the umbú tree, the joaz tree, and the others; the homeward-bound herd and the herdsman's home-going song, the *aboiado;* the stampede; and then the hours of ease and relaxation, swaying in the hammock, sipping the savory *umbusada;* the festive gatherings and the "headstrong" *aguardente;* the poetic tourneys, or "challenges." It is the life of a race, the mestizo race of the backlands, that lives for us here.

Those who are strangers to Brazil hardly will be in a position to realize that the picture which the author paints for us is by no means an anachronistic one from the point of view of the present. As the country's latest sociological historian, Senhor Caio Prado Junior says, the contemporary Brazilian who visits the backlands may be a witness to his nation's past. The "angry land'' still lives on and is still a national problem of the first importance, one which the airplane may eventually do much to solve. Euclides da Cunha, meanwhile, is the greatest of those literary trail-blazers who, in the later 1890's, toward the end of the first decade of republican life, made their way into the *sertão,* to bring back its poetry, its tragedy, its myths, and the psychology of its inhabitants. His fellow-explorers, however, were interested chiefly in the picturesque features of the locale, its Indian heritage of animistic beliefs and superstitions, its haunting, morbid, hallucinatory, dreamlike aspects. Cunha was the first to reveal its basic social life and implications; for he was not of those who believed that the hinterland, with all its backwardness, benightedness, and fratricidal religious mania, had been decreed of heaven for all time. A military engineer by profession, or, in the words of Gilberto Freyre, ''a social engineer animated by a political ideal,'' he was at once reporter and scientist, man of letters and sociologist. To this day he is regarded as one of Brazil's greatest geographers.To quote a biobibliographical notice in the *Revista brasileira de geografia,* ''if there is one dominant aspect of the work of Euclides da Cunha, it is, certainly, the geographic. . . . He wrote and made geography,'' and *Os Sertões* is ''perhaps the most notable essay in human geography which a portion of our native soil has ever inspired in a writer.'' According to the well-known, present-day scientist, Roquette Pinto, Euclides was essentially an ecologist, being concerned with the relations between organisms and their environment. As a social scientist he is a forerunner of the brilliant group today which is represented by Gilberto Freyre, Arthur Ramos, Edison Carneiro, and others, even though these men frequently would disagree with his findings.

In literature, likewise, he was a pathfinder, being one of the two principal fountainheads of the modern Brazilian novel, the other being Machado de Assis. In the one case (Machado de Assis), the stress is on form; in the other, on context. *Os Sertões* may be said to have posed the problem which faces the twentieth-century novelist in Brazil: that of how to achieve an artistic synthesis of the rich social content which his country affords him. Because he grappled with this problem so valiantly and solved it in so extraordinary and individual a fashion, the author continues to be a symbol and an inspiration to creative writers. It is surely not without significance that there has grown up in this same general region, the Northeast, a school of novelists—Jorge Amado, Graciliano Ramos, José Lins do Rêgo, to mention but a few—who are at this moment bringing new life to Brazilian letters, and whose influence on the national literary scene has been so profound as to constitute something very like an ''invasion.''

It is not surprising, therefore, if *Os Sertões* is rapidly taking its place as a great South American classic. Even though there are those who assert that it is untranslatable or should be read only in the original, there can be no doubt that the recent Spanish-language rendering by Señor Benjamín de Garay of Argentina is a valuable contribution to the cause of cultural understanding in this hemisphere; and it is hoped that an English-language translation may serve the same end, by bringing to readers who may have enjoyed a book like R. B. Cunningham-Graham's *A Brazilian Mystic* the work which provided its inspiration.

In making the acquaintance of Euclides da Cunha, the North American has an experience awaiting him which is comparable in quality to that of the European of the last century listening for the first time to Walt Whitman's ''barbaric yawp.'' The comparison is a particularly valid one on the side of form and style. Just as Whitman had to shape a new form, just as he had to forge a new vocabulary and a new style for a content that was quite new and which could not be run through the time-honored molds, so Cunha, in portraying the newly discovered, or ''rediscovered,'' life of the Brazilian backlands, was compelled to hew out a literary implement that was suited to his needs. To his fellow-countrymen of the time, reared in a culture that was classic and prevailingly Gallic in character—to a Joaquim Nabuco, for example—his ''yawp'' sounded quite as barbaric as did that of Whitman to an Emerson. It was Nabuco, the great abolitionist intellectual, who said of Cunha that the latter wrote ''*com cipó*—with a liana stalk.'' This expression as applied to the author of *Os Sertões* has since become a famous one and is proudly quoted by Cunha admirers as the highest tribute that could be paid him; for the liana to a Brazilian is the symbol of the inhospitable *sertão.* Of himself Euclides said that his was ''the rude pen of a *caboclo*,'' that is, of an aborigine. His palette, he tells us, is composed of ''hues taken from the earth, from the black mud of the pits, with vermilion from the coagulated blood of the *jagunços*, and the sepia of bandit affrays in the hinterland.'' He does, in truth, paint the backlands, their suns and rains, their mountains, rivers, flora, with a barbaric brush, and this in a work which, starting out to be reportage, ends by being a blend of science, poetry, and color. It is easy to understand why this should have appeared as a ''barbarous art'' to another refined spirit of the age, José Verissimo, the historian of Brazilian literature. The colors at times are laid on with an exuberance that is truly tropical, accompanied by a certain primitive naïveté that puts one in mind of the Mexican canvases of a Douanier Rousseau. The style is then lush and sensuous in the extreme, marked by a verbal pomp that is almost purple-hued as ''the adjective reigns with the splendor of a satrap.'' This, however, is only in the author's more Amazonian moments, as they might be described. At other times—the greater part of the time—his prose is not tropical, but rugged, rugged as the *sertão* itself; it is nervous, dramatically intense, sculpturesque as the backland hills, and is characterized by a definite, brusque avoidance of lyricism and emphasis to the point of appearing overwrought and painful. Here is the ''liana stock.'' ''But this liana ensnares the reader, obliging him to remain and view the flowers and trunks of this magnificent wood.''

In his passion for landscape, the depth and warmth of human feeling that he puts into the description of a *paysage*, whether it be the stricken hinterland flora in the time of drought or a geological formation, Cunha has been compared to a poet-naturalist like Darwin; and he might also in this respect—in capturing the emotional drama of inanimate nature—be compared to a novelist like Thomas Hardy. He resembles Hardy, further, in the Latinizing tendency of his vocabulary, a quality that becomes a defect of which he is conscious, and which got him into trouble with his critics upon occasion. (pp. iii-x)

Toward the end of his forty-three years, Euclides would seem to have mellowed somewhat, if we are to judge from a letter to a friend which is published for the first time in the Spanish edition of *Os Sertões:*

> You ask me to send you a copy of *Os Sertões;* but I must tell you in advance that I do not do so spontaneously; for this barbarous book of my youth, this monstrous poem of brutality and force, is so strange to my present tranquil way of looking at life that it is sometimes all that I myself can do to understand it. In any case, it

is the first-born of my spirit, and there are audacious critics who assert that it is my one and only book. Can this be true, I wonder? It is hard to admit that with it I reached a culminating point and that I am to spend all the rest of my life coming down from this height. After you have read it, tell me, my distinguished friend, if I am to be condemned to so unenviable a fate as this. Your opinion will be most highly prized, and I should like to have it as soon as possible.

However this may be, *Os Sertões* remains a towering peak of Brazilian literature. (p. xviii)

> Samuel Putnam, "'Brazil's Greatest Book': A Translator's Introduction," in Rebellion in the Backlands *by Euclides da Cunha, translated by Samuel Putnam, University of Chicago Press, 1944, pp. iii-xviii.*

AFRÂNIO PEIXOTO (essay date 1944)

[*In the following essay, Peixoto discusses Cunha's scientific training and its effect on his writing.*]

Euclides da Cunha was a military engineer, one who came up from the ranks; later, he reported a military campaign for a large daily; and, finally, he was a builder of bridges and a surveyor of frontiers. This is as much as to say that his training as a writer had a scientific basis, with mathematics and geography as the vigilant handmaidens of his mind. In place of that bookish erudition which is common with those who set out to win fame in literature, he had a knowledge of nature gained through his previous studies which was to make of him an outstanding figure in our national letters.

This is reflected not alone in the content of his works but in the very style in which his thought is clothed. That freshness of imagery and of concepts which came to him from his exact and experimental knowledge of science stood in contrast to the artificial flowers of rhetoric to be found in other writers. With it, he cast a spell upon his contemporaries, a spell that endures to this day, after forty years; for the new generations which have since come upon the scene have not yet succeeded in emancipating themselves from the moldy images of the literary huckster's stock-in-trade, and Euclides da Cunha's directness and exactness in the matter of language only serve to throw into relief the general obsolescence of our writers, old and new, all of whom belong to the past in their way of thinking and their mode of speech. Euclides remains fresh and original. To employ the American word, he is *different!*

Meanwhile, the time has come to appraise him, not merely with regard to the external aspects of his style, but with regard, as well, to the contexture of ideas and tendencies discoverable in his writings. Euclides is our number-one geographer and sociologist, one who, in place of viewing his native land with patriotic emphasis as "my country, right or wrong," has, rather, seen it and studied it, and has drawn his deductions as to what this land really is and, as a consequence, what manner of man it is that springs from such a soil—how the land may be changed and man thereby may become a different being from the one he is. Sociology here is made dependent upon a historical moment in which human intercommunication, through miscegenation, is incapable of altering the population of a land— a population that remains a direct expression of the soil. The

truth is that the more rudimentary a civilization, the more it depends upon the physical environment; and civilization itself may be defined as the process of removing man from territorial contingencies. The prisoner of his native heath then becomes, through civilization, a man who has made his escape into the world.

Starting from the premise of the land, Euclides sketches in for us the rudimentary geography of the Brazilian backlands and the transitory, changing sociology of the backlands peoples. His masters were certain scholars, and it is a pleasure to state that they were North American scholars. From Orville Adelbert Derby he learned applied geography, and with John Caspar Bramer he delved into the mysteries of geology, having previously studied aboriginal archeology with Charles Frederick Hartt. And there were Maury and Milnor Roberts—how many others?—who were his able tutors, all of them. If as a reporter he was first of all impressed by the human panorama, as a scholar he looked beyond the apparent reality and from the earth proceeded to derive its people, explaining the human rebellion, half-religious, half-political, implicit in a civil war, by the backwoodsman's lack of culture and the primitive character of life in the hinterland.

Out of all this came his great book, *Os Sertões,* in which the shortsighted will find merely an account of a very ordinary military campaign in Brazil's uncivilized backlands; those of keener vision, on the other hand, looking beyond appearances, will find in it a scientific document dealing with a phase of human civilization in which man was governed by the earth and his destiny was determined by it. If it be true that natives alone are in a position to judge of the freshness, and I should go so far as to say the unexampled originality, of the style, yet even when translated into another language, leaving aside the reportorial leitmotiv of the military campaign, the better and greater part of the book, the definitive, the human part, remains, in the form of an always impressive document of man's struggle with the earth—an earth that bestows upon him its own direct imprint. In North America, where this sociological phase has long since passed, and in Brazil, where it still is to be seen here and there in all its virgin primitiveness, the geographer and the sociologist will ever welcome a work of science which is at the same time a work of art; for what this particular geographer and sociologist is giving us here are the history and the biography of our soil, nothing other than a slice of our Brazilian life and the life of our backlands.

If the Book of Genesis may be said to be, in the symbolism that it holds for the faithful, a biography of earth, Euclides da Cunha's *Os Sertões* is a Genesis which in epic accents tells of the meeting of civilization and barbarism; it is a saga of the first flaming days of the earth and of man and of primal man's first direct contact with other men known as civilized from other, supposedly cultured, lands that did not know how to bring civilization and, creating a slaughter-house of banditry, were able only to destroy. Like Genesis, *Os Sertões* has its moral.

Such is this book, worthy of appearing in a language that is broader, more universal in its appeal. It is a book that represents a moment in the history of humanity; and, thanks to its style, its art, and its science, that ephemeral moment is destined to be eternal. (pp. xix-xxi)

> *Afrânio Peixoto, in a preface to* Rebellion in the Backlands *by Euclides da Cunha, translated by Samuel Putnam, University of Chicago Press, 1944, pp. xix-xxi.*

ERICO VERISSIMO (essay date 1944)

[*Verissimo was a Brazilian novelist, short story writer, biographer, and critic. In the following excerpt, he discusses the writing style and subject matter of* Os sertões.]

If I had to choose just one book in Brazilian literature to be translated into other languages as a representative of my country and of my people, I would certainly pick up *Os Sertões*. It is really our greatest classic. Courageous, unbiased and dramatic, it tells you about an amazing racial melting pot. It shows you, with an almost photographic likeness, a tragic landscape, both geographic and human. It narrates an impressing story of violence, fanaticism, blood and misery—but a story, too, of courage and endurance. It is full of sympathy for the underdog. And it is a book surprisingly "new" and timely, because many of the problems it presents and discusses are still to be solved.

In conversation with Moisés Vellinho, one of the most distinguished Brazilian essayists, I remarked that the lack of psychological depth in our people and our life is rather a handicap for the novelist concerned with the novel of ideas and with psychological analysis. He agreed with me, and added: "But the most dramatic feature of our national life is the poor and neglected population of the backlands. That is why, notwithstanding its being a non-fiction book, *Os Sertões* is our greatest and most impressive novel."

Nowadays, statesmen and writers in Brazil are trying to solve the appalling problem of the backlands. No longer are they thinking in terms of armed expeditions, but rather in terms of human understanding, schools, hygiene, fair labor laws and social relief. Brazilian people are fundamentally anti-totalitarian, and they hate violent solutions. The keynote of their life is a delicious mixture of malice and kindness, blended with sentimentality and with a Bohemian touch. They have a wonderful sense of humor and don't care very much for a civilization expressed in terms of money and mechanical progress. And if they manage to defeat poverty, illiteracy and bad health—their most serious problems among the lower classes—I believe they can fulfill the hopes of Stefan Zweig—who saw in Brazil the land of the future.

It would be pretentious and futile to criticize or analyze here Euclides da Cunha's book. Studying it in the light of the most recent theories and discoveries, sociologists, geologists and anthropologists may find it guilty of some small mistakes or exaggerations, principally concerning race problems. But *Os Sertões* has endured the test of time. I had read it several times and I read it again this week in Samuel Putnam's admirable translation—in itself a literary landmark, for it is more difficult to translate da Cunha into English than to render into Portuguese, for example, the rich and untamed prose of Thomas Wolfe.

There is, by the way, a kind of similitude between both those writers. Both were passionately in love with their land and their people. Their prose has the same impetuousness, the same torrent-like quality, the same masculine touch. Both writers were solitary and unsatisfied men, full of brotherly dreams— and ferocious pride. Perhaps Wolfe was more of a poet than da Cunha. But, surprisingly enough, the streak of sentimentality was stronger in the American than in the Brazilian. (p. 20)

Erico Veríssimo, "Literary Milestone in Brazil," in The New York Times Book Review, February 6, 1944, pp. 1, 20.

RALPH BATES (essay date 1944)

[*Bates is an English novelist and critic. In the following excerpt, he comments on several stylistic and thematic aspects of* Os sertões.]

For the Anglo-Saxon, even if he reads Portuguese, perhaps only two Brazilian prose writers, Machado de Assis and Euclides da Cunha, walk out of the Amazonian forests of average and purely national goodness onto the upland plateau of universal excellence. And the latter carries to these heights only one book, *Os Sertões,* here translated into English for the first time. That the greatness of the book is accessible to everyone is certain, yet it is hard to give any sense of its uniqueness. It stands aside and above the foothills of Brazilian literature as say, *Don Quixote* dominates its own landscape; or as Jean-Richard Bloch's "*And Company*" stands firm as a granite axis above the sliding detritus of contemporary French literature. And to compare it with a book that sums up a mental process that is the polar opposite, Cunha's *Os Sertões* is as lonely above its Amazonian verdure as the Parnassian *Les Trophées* on its marble slopes.

It is a great and grand book, though its mental processes will tire many. The event which it records, the campaign of extermination which the newly established Republic waged against the insurgent mystic, Antonio Conselheiro, heretical builder of lovely churches, heroic defender of spiritual squalor, is set down with a projective force that is not only unflagging but almost physically sensible. It is a huge landslip of sensation that moves down upon one. Instinctively one compares its final chapters with the opening scene of Malraux's *La Condition Humaine*. But for Cunha the tragedy he records was more than an event. It was a judgment upon the past and the present and, doubtless, though nothing in the book says this clearly, a terrible prophecy for the future.

Every clause and epithet of this macabre rune must be commented upon, from the Counsellor's first appearance on the backlands tracks down to the freezing tragedy of Canudos, where his many thousand people were slaughtered to the last child. The death of this heroic moron of God is a Brazilian Pompilia's murder, calling from Cunha a historical and scientific *Ring and the Book*. As the thread of St. Catherine of Siena's life became, in Von Hügel's superb biography of that ecclesiastical reformer, a chain to hold together an entire philosophy of knowledge and being, so, for Cunha, the life and death of this religious rebel must organize a treatise on the entire social fabric of Brazil. (pp. 250, 252)

Two demerits of *Os Sertões* for the modern Anglo-Saxon reader, it seems to me, necessarily spring from its method, or from its intention. Though he wrote at the beginning of the present century, Cunha's sociological apparatus, together with much of his scientific grammar, is no longer current. And, like fashions in dress, nothing is stranger than the scientific vocabularies of a few decades back. Even to discuss *Os Sertões* in its own word-list reminds one of those conversations one enjoyed in minor Spanish university towns, where the future of Spain, then bleeding to death on the steps of a ruined church, was discussed in terms of the dead philosophy of the rationalistic Krauss, elsewhere forgotten by all save third-rate German pedants. And the second defect is this: one is dragged and incited, one is goaded into climbing the whole length of this mighty cordillera to its culminating precipice. And then one must either leap into the cold, cloud-filled space, as it were, or one must turn round and retrace all that immense, complicated journey, musing afresh over each tree and stone. For the last scene in *Os Sertões* is the digging up of the Counsellor's body, and the severance of the head with a knife. "That horrible face, sticky with scars and pus, once more appeared before the victors' gaze. . . . After that they took it to the seaboard, where it was greeted by delirious multitudes with carnival joy." Five lines only follow this, mentioning the name of a forgotten scientist and bluntly summing up that the event was crime and madness. But by this time the reader's mind has become athletic, and he demands more. That is the measure of the book's greatness, that at its close one feels that the tremendous journey is still unfinished and one longs to go on. It is possible that Cunha might some day have led one further. In 1907 it was rumored that he was preparing a new edition of *Os Sertões*. A soldier, to prevent fresh disclosures about the army, fired a bullet through the author's window and killed him at his work table.

But *Os Sertões* and its process is not a book to relinquish with summary remarks. Its method itself, apart from the cumulative organizational effect which all great disciplines have, is endlessly rewarding. There is the tedium of such sentences as this, from the outmoded and unsatisfactory delineation of Conselheiro's soul. "With an insane temperament marked by an obvious ideational retrogression, he was, certainly, a notable case of intellectual degenerescence." Against this are to be set countless brilliances of historical insight and allusion. The desert backlands of Brazil had maintained, in tattered form, something of the Messianism of the first Christian settlers. It was this which Antonio Conselheiro and his adjutant prophets inherited, Cunha insists. They were part and parcel "of the same people who in Lisbon, under the previous obsession of miracles and assaulted by sudden hallucinations, had beheld above the royal palace prophetic caskets, mysterious tongues of flame, throngs of white-hooded Moors passing in procession, and Paladin combats in the skies." The visibility of these glimpses and visions keeps one's imagination plastic throughout the book.

And irony, an attitude that is commonly expressed in urbane language, here reaches a tragic order. It is not so much that Cunha savagely mocks at the crime. He does not. He is quite free from sentiment. He never romanticizes about these impossibly brave rebels. Nor does he cheaply equate their opponents with them, and though he sees that this man's squalid faith inspires as great sacrifices as any other man's noblest ambitions, and despite the disillusions of his heart, he does not sneer that all faiths are equal. At its bitterest his mood is a contemptuous pity, or pitying contempt, for mankind. The irony does not lie in the style, as in Anatole France, but in the collision of facts and truths. Indeed, the whole ghastly God's-satire is embodied in Conselheiro himself, for the man's end, in its sublime squalor, gives as much sense of blasphemy as if we read that the last words from the cross were, "I am fed up with the world!" The man's life in those last months, when it cost six thousand troops three months to advance one hundred yards within his town of smashed hovels, was one long Via Crucis that ended, as it were, in a public convenience. The only loot at Canudos, indeed, was cheap rosaries and paper amulets and the like. The only victory on the government side was physical, while on the rebels' it was a tremendous and ghastly meaninglessness. The Counsellor's men believed that to be slaughtered by the knife was to go to hell, without hope of remission. The government troops, who took no prisoners, gave them the option of betraying secrets and dying by the bullet, or of honor and the knife. To die of calm purpose for one's faith is an act of courage. These men, for a few furtive superstitions, set their jaws and turned aside into hell, without

outward sigh. In this rather than in the terror of Canudos' end lies the savagery of this story.

Yet the telling of that end in Canudos is overwhelming. Four defenders were left alive in the last rifle pit to hold out. One old man, two able-bodied men and a child, still spitting death against five thousand, until the last of them slipped back into the blood and pus of putrescent bodies. And then the victors stood amid the blazing sunlight and the terrible silence. Silence, too, stands at the end of this book. It is why one cries out for one more word. But doubtless it was the silence of that last scene which over awed Cunha himself. (p. 252)

Ralph Bates, "A Brazilian Classic," in The New Republic, *Vol. 110, No. 8, February 21, 1944, pp. 250, 252.*

CLAUDE LEVI-STRAUSS (essay date 1944)

[*Considered one of the foremost French intellectuals of the twentieth century, Lévi-Strauss is noted both for his study of cultural anthropology and for the method with which he approached this study. The method, known as structuralism, avoids value judgments toward unfamiliar cultures or overt comparisons between such cultures and that of the anthropologist, seeking instead an objective identification of abstract structures found in all societies. Originating in such diverse fields of study as sociology, psychology, philosophy, linguistics, and mathematics, structuralism has as its aim the discovery of universal psychological patterns, located in the unconscious, which affect human behavior and communication. Although the validity of structuralism as a scientific method has been questioned because its very objectivity limits the researcher's ability to establish a relative basis for comparison between cultures, the concepts which Lévi-Strauss posited are widely recognized to have significantly affected the course of Western thought during the latter half of the twentieth century. In the following excerpt, Lévi-Strauss notes the influence of* Os sertões *on the development of Brazilian culture and on Brazil's political policy concerning the backlands.*]

Certainly [*Os Sertões*] is not a great literary work. But there are other reasons which make it worthy of its tremendous popularity in Brazil and abroad. At the time when it was written (1897-1902), Brazilian intelligentsia was under the influence of European scepticism and trying to imitate its disabused witticisms; attempting to escape from their national destiny, to forget its greatnesses together with its shortcomings, and to simulate the sophistication of Anatole France, Oscar Wilde, or Eiça de Queiroz. Quite different was Euclides da Cunha: this professional man (he was an engineer), a mixture of all the bloods which have made Brazil great, refused to be a schoolboy of the European masters; he turned back from the foreign inspiration, and by using the native words as tools, the native population as a theme, and the native landscape as an ever present background, he authentically started a Brazilian national literature. The primitiveness of his scientific ideas (which, after all, were only those of his time), the awkwardness of his style, the slowness of his pace, are of little importance when compared to the final result: his generous call, his vibrant indignation (which was to cost him his life), his ardent love for his land and its humblest inhabitants, partly succeeded in turning the Brazilian elite back to the Brazilian reality, symbolized by the unpleasant story of the slaughter, by the armies of the young Republic, of a handful of backward and mystic peasants. For Brazil to exist, its most primitive aspects, its ugliest spots were to be accepted; not to be ashamed of, but loved and cared for with utmost understanding and patience. Even now, *Os Sertões* stands to remind the Brazilian people that the achievements of the industrial civilization are not so great and indisputable that they should try to forget, instead of being proud of, those virgin sources of nature and humanity upon which, among all nations, they may rely for the building of a greater and better future. (pp. 395-96)

Claude Lévi-Strauss, "South America," in American Anthropologist, *n.s. Vol. 46, No. 3, 1944, pp. 394-96.*

GEORGE BARBAROW (essay date 1958)

[*In the following excerpt, Barbarow discusses Cunha's artistic methods of exploring the diverse topics treated in* Os sertões.]

There is consistency in the facts that Euclides da Cunha . . . was a creative writer and that at the close of his life he was a professor of logic; this extraordinary Brazilian was also adept at military and civil engineering, verse writing, and geodesy. Accustomed as we are to the notorious contemporary plethora of singly specialized experts, Cunha's versatility seems incredible. It is as if Leonardo had suddenly reappeared. We are sure that engineers can neither read nor write, and that writers need escort when crossing streets; we are therefore surprised to find an engineer creating an analogy with history as a base, surely one of the high forms of literary art.

Os Sertões . . . belongs in no section of a categorized library; it fits Philosophy as well as History, Sociology as well as Geography. In such a modern library, for example, there is no one shelf that will hold all the works of Thorstein Veblen, no comfortable spot for *Finnegans Wake* or for *Cybernetics*, yet the pressure to find such a place for *The Backlands* apparently led to the addition of "rebellion" to Cunha's title, thus modifying and weakening its significance. *Os Sertões* is not about rebellion, but about atavism, yet it would also be a mistake to call it "Atavism in the Backlands," because there is more than atavism in it, just as there is much more than rebellion. The book is no doubt properly to be regarded as History, although the author states in a Preliminary Note that, "It is our purpose to sketch in . . . the most significant present-day characteristics of the subraces to be found in the backlands of Brazil" [see excerpt dated 1901], (Anthropology!), and later called it ". . . this barbarous book of my youth, this monstrous poem of brutality and force . . .". It is history like no other, except that it has a tone of authenticity similar to that emanating from *The Peloponnesian War*, the sense of unhurried cultural description found in *The Conquest of Peru*, the feeling of spatial dimension in *War and Peace*, the shocking close views in *Sevastopol*. It is history that contains a biography of the rebel leader nowise surpassed by the personality-conscious Gibbon; that contains also an informed enthusiasm for fauna and flora and geology possessed by few persons, and here rivalling the *Beagle*-eyed Darwin in its attention to detail.

Os Sertões need not be read as history at all, if it is considered in the light of a general remark by Yvor Winters: ". . . it is worth noting that the historian is no longer allowed the privilege of shaping scenes in the interests of dramatic propriety, nor of analyzing the emotions of his characters. He must confine himself to the material in his documents, and if he wishes to go beyond what is given, he must speculate honestly as a bystander." (pp. 155-56)

Cunha was a participant, as a journalist, in the Fourth Expedition to Canudos, which exterminated a community of rebels there, and he deliberately analyzes not only the emotions of others, but also his own, and implicates in guilt for a "crime,"

not only the Brazilian government, but also the retrograde ("not degenerate") backlanders, the brave soldiers, and the reader himself. Thus the book is only nominally a history. The events described could have been invented (by a curious slip, one of our liberal weeklies listed it under Fiction among its summaries of the outstanding publications of 1944), because at this distance and at this time, the author's arrangement of established facts takes precedence over the facts themselves. Metaphors override literal subject matter (observed and recorded events) as they do in any work of art; as with *Hamlet* or *Oedipus*, it is of secondary importance whether the original actions really "happened." And Cunha is so little concerned with scholarly etiquette that he castigates,

> . . . we played in this action the singular role of unconscious mercenaries . . .

decries,

> The campaign in question marked a backward step, an ebb in the direction of the past. It was in the integral sense of the word a crime and, as such, to be denounced . . .

condemns,

> Canudos was appropriately enough surrounded by a girdle of mountains. It was a parenthesis, a hiatus. It was a vacuum. It did not exist. Once having crossed that cordon of mountains, no one sinned any more. An astounding miracle was accomplished, and time was turned backward for a number of centuries. As one came down the slopes and caught sight of the enormous bandit's den that was huddled there, he might well imagine that some obscure and bloody drama of the Stone Age was here taking place. The setting was sufficiently suggestive. The actors, on one side and the other, Negroes, caboclos, white and yellow skinned, bore on their countenances the indelible imprint of many races—races which could be united only upon the common plane of their lower and evil instincts. A primitive animality, slowly expunged by civilization, was here being resurrected intact. The knot was being undone at last. In place of the stone hatchet and the harpoon made of bone were the sword and the rifle; but the knife was still there to recall the cutting edge of the ancient flint, and man might flourish it with nothing to fear—not even the judgment of the remote future . . .

and ends in bitterness,

> The trouble is that we do not have today a Maudsley for acts of madness and crimes on the part of nations . . .

yet manages to sustain an extraordinary sense of objectivity throughout; Cunha is the Maudsley (an admired psychologist) whose absence he laments; his denunciation of the crime of Canudos is a denunciation of crimes of the future also, for his intuitive revelation of the fundamental motives of the "actors" of the "Stone Age drama" foreshadows more recent events, each made memorable by the name of a place: Guernica, Monte Cassino, Stalingrad, Buchenwald, Lidice, Hamburg, Malmédy, Berlin, Tokyo, Hiroshima, Budapest. It has taken the unamazed, accurate engineer's eye to discover the perilous proximity of the Paleolithic and Atomic ages, and the ultimate response is a cry of protest.

The engineer's eye is directed by an artist's temperament, and thus made capable of selecting among a staggering number of observed details, and of assembling them in significant order. The division of parts is deceptively simple: I—The Backlands, II—The Rebellion. The frantic actions at the end of Part II are the final evolutions of the nearly imperceptible geologic movements of the beginning, where the geographic description is used to reveal cataclysmic forces. The setting of the "Stone Age drama" is a product of both seismic and cosmic storms, a struggle between earth and sea, a constant battle between air and rocks. There follows in "Man" a pageant of types and races, in conflict among themselves and in conflict with their various environments, and at last one man, Antonio Vicente Mendes Maciel, Antonio Conselheiro, Anthony the Counselor, the distorted imitation of John the Baptist, who by 1896 was the head of a community of perhaps fifteen thousand recalcitrants—men, women, and children—bound for glory at the Millennium (presumably 1900). It was a miscellaneous jumble of human flotsam; bandits, refugees from religious and secular law, misfits, and failed farmers. Against them marched four fumbling military expeditions, the last powerful enough to transform the "mud-walled Troy" of the backlanders into a "crude slaughter pen."

Such a transformation could not have been accomplished, however, before the soldiers had unlearned their training in classic textbook warfare and learned to fight like the backlanders, animal fashion, with tooth and claw. It was this forced reversion that led Cunha into a chain of reflection culminating in his remarks about "primitive animality" uncovered in a place where "no one sinned any more." He had more than enough sensibilty to know that simple anathemas would not make his points for him; indeed, the parts quoted above represent nearly the sum of the direct personal expressions of anger and despair to be found in *Os Sertões*. This book has the character of a large parable, a compressed earth-history and culture-history at one time, gaining some of its strength because it deals with subject matter that "actually happened," yet attaining far more because of the author's genius for metaphor and simile. He who had observed a process in a remote place in another century could write a description of the building of a "city" that would fit the construction of most cities of the past and present:

> The settlement, accordingly, grew in dizzying fashion, sprawling out over the hills. The dwellings which were thrown up being extremely rude ones, the homeless multitude was able to erect as many as a dozen a day; and, as this colossal weed patch took shape, it appeared to reflect in its physical characteristics, as if by a stereographic process, the moral attributes of the social strata that had found refuge there. It was the objectivization of a tremendous insanity. A living document whose implications were not to be evaded, a piece of direct corpus delicti evidence on the aberrations of a populace. It was all done wholly at random, with the fervor of the mad.

And he could make plausible the inevitable action that is taken against adamant defense, by citing the hollow, but nevertheless always accepted reasoning:

> Obviously, other measures were imperatively called for in dealing with a foe who was so

impervious to all the forces of Nature, so schooled in havoc and destruction . . . and so, a certain lieutenant . . . now had them bring up from the camp dozens of dynamite bombs. This was fitting enough; it was absolutely the only thing to be done; for the sertanejos had inverted all the psychology of ordinary warfare; their resistance was stiffened by reverses, and they were strengthened by hunger, hardened by defeat.

The dynamite, symbol and symptom of frustration, is set off, with effects,

> And now, from the portion of the village beyond, there came an indescribable sound of weeping and wailing, screams and imprecations, reflective at once of terror and of pain, of anger and exasperation, on the part of the tortured multitude that was bellowing there. Amid the glow of the flames shadowy figures could be seen darting convulsively in and out: women fleeing their burning hovels, carrying their young ones in their arms or dragging them along as they ran down the lanes and disappeared in the maze of huts; figures fleeing wildly in every direction; floundering on the ground, their clothing in flames; bodies burned and writhing in agony, like human firebrands . . . .

and merely produces more of that "inverted psychology" it was supposed to destroy:

> And then it was that everywhere of a sudden, only a couple of paces distant from the line of fire, sinister physiognomies made their unexpected appearance, begrimed masklike faces, naked bosoms scarred and singed, as the jagunços once more, boldly, insanely, came back to the fray.

> These figures, these visages, had come to slay their adversary in his own trenches . . . .

Os Sertões is as much a tour of the backlands of mankind as of the backlands of Brazil. It could be such a great analogy only because it is the work of an artist. The Canudos Campaign was an insignificant event in world affairs, not only because of its small size, but also because of its purely local effects. So far as the rest of the world is concerned, the conflict existed only as the occasion for Cunha's book, and this may be the reason that his name is recognized only by the relatively few persons who have read *Os Sertões,* yet few who have read it can deny its emotional power and its amazing breadth of view. Here is a microcosm in 476 pages, compact, replete with overtones; it grows everywhere bigger than its original reason for being, and bigger still than the author's stated excuse for writing it. An apparent verbosity here frightens the casual bookstore browser, as it does in the work of Joyce; perhaps the publisher put "rebellion" into the title in order to sell a few more copies, and perhaps this expedient has helped to steer away more potential buyers than it has attracted. The trick does the book no good. Another "easy reading" strategy is the addition of hundreds of centered subheads, which were only marginal titles added to the 12th Brazilian edition (1933), being the effusions of the editor, one Nery. Inserted as subheads, the marginalia do further damage to the structure of the text, constituting a distortion of the author's arrangement, a constantly irritating series of stops that seem designed merely to excite the fading, failing attention of easily jaded readers. Long sentences, long paragraphs, and long chapters are characteristic of Cunha; and so the razzle-dazzle of the title change and the typographical breakup technique borrowed from *The Reader's Digest* are reprehensible, and indicate disrespect for the magnitude of Cunha's achievement.

As a measure of that magnitude, let it be said flatly that *Os Sertões* is one of the half-dozen best books of this century, and that an acquaintance of ten years has not diminished this estimate. (pp. 156-58, 160)

George Barbarow, "Cunha's Angry History," in The Hudson Review, *Vol. XI, No. 1, Spring, 1958, pp. 155-58, 160.*

JOHN VOGT, JR.   (essay date 1969)

[*In the following excerpt, Vogt discusses* Os sertões *as social criticism.*]

Euclides da Cunha belongs to that elite group of Brazilian scholars who, after the fall of the Empire, continued to question the philosophical path their nation was pursuing. For da Cunha, *Os Sertões* was more than simply a narrative of the gruesome events at Canudos; it was his challenge to the conscience of the nation for her actions there. It stimulated similar endeavors by other authors to examine their own land, particularly that vast portion of the nation removed from the urban centers of population along the eastern seaboard. The literary works of men like da Cunha and his contemporary Graça Aranha enlightened Brazilians about an area of their country of which most urban dwellers had very little knowledge. It also introduced the urban population to a new element in the Brazilian social structure. This was the *sertanejo,* or backlander, who inhabited the often hostile land of the *sertão* in the Brazilian interior.

One of the main criticisms leveled upon Brazilian society by da Cunha's *Os Sertões* was that, during the first decade of republican life, Brazil had been unable to emancipate herself from dominant European philosophical trends and European intellectual mentors. In the program of expansion undertaken by the military regimes of Deodoro da Fonseca and Floriano Peixoto, Brazil's leaders were following a path laid down by contemporary European nations, such as England and Germany, in their own expansionist policies. Brazilian military and governmental leaders, schooled in European tactics of warfare and diplomacy, looked to the imperial campaigns of these nations as models for their own frontier expansion. National spirit was high. The Republic was established, but social forces capable of toppling the new government still existed within the country. And any opposing forces, like the religious fanatics gathering at Canudos in 1895, were felt to threaten the security of the state. Therefore, the proved Bismarckian tactics of "Blood and Iron" seemed warranted for colonizing the frontier against the opposition of the *sertanejo.* These rebels could not be allowed to disregard government orders for fear that other groups of malcontents or monarchists would join them or follow their lead.

What da Cunha portrays in the cultural life of Brazil in this period is a "second-hand civilization." Brazilians had adopted many of the outward manifestations of European civilization and thought without fully comprehending the underlying principles. On their new national banner they had emblazoned the positivist principle of "Order and Progress." Yet in their republican revolutionary zeal, the radical Jacobins in the cities and the government only widened the gulf between the life of the Brazilian cities and the primitive society of Brazil's native sons of the *sertão.* So wide had the breach grown that by 1896 and the Canudos rebellion, the *sertanejos* were more alien to Brazilian urban society than were the immigrants fresh off the boats from Europe. As da Cunha himself states: "It was not an ocean that separated us from them, but three whole centuries." No one in Brazil at that time could conceive of these ragged backlanders as being capable of throwing back expedition after expedition of government troops with terrible losses. The only logical explanation seemed to be that the rebellion heralded an attempt by the dispossessed monarchists to regain power. A mass meeting of the citizenry of Rio in March, 1896, voiced its belief that the rebels at Canudos indeed were monarchist "gangsters," and the Cariocans pledged their active support to the government in suppressing the revolt.

So da Cunha recalled the Canudos campaign to the public, but he was not concerned with fictitious monarchical plots or military incompetency. Although filled with geological and topographical allusions, *Os Sertões* in 1902 was the first attempt to redefine the bases of Brazilian nationalism and to recognize the backlanders as forming a significant part of the Brazilian nation.

Before reviewing da Cunha's position regarding Brazilian nationalism, let us examine briefly just what is meant by nationalism as it affected Brazil. Since the eighteenth century, definitions of the word "nationalism" have multiplied, so that today it carries a number of connotations. In addition to chauvinism, it means national spirit, national consciousness, national thought, and even national policy. In the writing of history the word has generally been used since the 1920's to denote a theory as well. Hence, the term "age of nationalism." Thus the term is capable of evoking conflicting images, depending upon the context in which it is used. This does not mean that simpler, broader definitions of "nationalism" have not been attempted. The noted political scientist Hans Kohn, while writing on nationalism in the 1920's, defined the concept as "a state of mind, in which the supreme loyalty of the individual is felt to be due to the nation state." This definition, though acceptable as far as it goes, still does not enable the scholar to apply it to particular circumstances. A more useful approach to defining the term, used by many political scientists, is to divide nationalism into types, according to the most important meaning of the word for themselves and the particular set of conditions they are seeking to describe. Among historians, Carlton J. H. Hayes divides modern nationalism into five major categories. The Brazilian manifestation of nationalism in the 1890's seems best to fit one of the classifications laid down by Hayes: integral nationalism. As Hayes defines it, integral nationalism inherited the national and historical traditions of nationalism. However, it made the nation not a means to humanity but an end in itself. The spirit of integral nationalism was hostile to internationalism; it was jingoistic, militant, and inclined to imperialism. In domestic affairs integral nationalism was highly illiberal and sought to oblige all citizens to conform to a common standard of manners and morals. It subordinated all personal liberties to its own purpose. All this it would do "in the national interest." Hayes indicates that Auguste Comte and his positivist philosophy were major forerunners of integral nationalism.

Euclides da Cunha voices similar conclusions in *Os Sertões* when speaking of public opinion in the early years of the

Republic. He speaks of individuals who were devoid of any ideas or objectives, and who confined their thinking to preserving the new republic at any cost. Their exaggerated enthusiasm for Jacobinism made possible all sorts of excesses, one of which came to be the bloody Canudos campaign. Mob attacks on monarchist newspapers in Rio in March, 1896, were only outward manifestations of the forces of nationalism at work in Brazil. Euclides da Cunha calls the reaction of the masses to the defeats at Canudos "a common enough instance of collective psychology."

Da Cunha's *Os Sertões* is much more than an excellent report on the military events of the Canudos War in 1896-1897. The author is portraying in miniature the vivid details of friction and violence occurring all along the northeastern frontier in the late nineteenth century—the confrontation between two widely differing Brazilian cultures, those of the coast and the interior. The poor *sertanejo* native had been abandoned and forgotten for centuries. Economically, socially, and politically he did not exist in any of the statistical reports on the state of the Republic emanating from the capital at Rio. And then suddenly, in 1896, a small group of these same *sertanejos* were galvanized into action by a prophet, Antônio Maciel, and appeared to threaten the very existence of the nation. Antônio Maciel and his followers certainly represented an extreme manifestation of hatred toward the urban civilization of the coastal regions, but the same sort of distrust and resentment could be seen to a lesser degree over other areas of the *sertão*. The deeply religious and superstitious *sertanejos* could not comprehend the antireligious, positivist ideas that predominated in Rio, São Paulo, and other cities. The apocalyptic preachings of Antônio Maciel depicted the republican government as antichrist come to earth. Nor could the men in Brazil's capital understand the reluctance of the *sertanejos* to leave their traditional way of life and accept all the "progress" that civilization had to offer them. Thus the impasse persisted.

The problem of conflicting cultures in Latin America was not original with Brazil in the 1890's. The schoolmaster president Domingo Sarmiento had written his own version of the struggle in his native Argentina in the first part of the nineteenth century. Sarmiento's *Civilización y Barbarie* reflected the same basic conflict between the new European-oriented elements of Argentina and the reticent gauchos, who clung to their barbaric ways. To Sarmiento the gaucho was clearly the inferior element in the new Argentine society. Although he was physically superior, his stubborn reluctance to change was delaying Argentine progress. But his defeat was inevitable. When considering the ideal type of people upon which to build Argentine society, Sarmiento's contemporary Juan Alberdi chose not to educate the gaucho, but to eliminate him. Alberdi and Sarmiento both wanted European immigrants to come to people the land. They felt that these new groups would bring to Argentina agricultural skills and a tradition of self-sufficiency and national participation. In this way the outnumbered gauchos would be checked and pushed aside.

Da Cunha, in Brazil, also viewed the outcome of the struggle as inevitable: "We are condemned to civilization. Either we shall progress or we shall perish, and our choice is clear." But whereas Sarmiento looked upon the gaucho with contempt, da Cunha had discovered in the *sertão* a breed of men whom he admired. Physically strong, mentally alert, the *sertanejo* represented a group which had thrown off the veneer of European culture and had evolved its own rude native civilization. They desired only to be left alone. When the Republic exerted

pressure upon them to conform to its norm, they reacted by striking out at the "foreigners" who threatened their traditional society. *Os Sertões* clearly accuses the civilized European portion of Brazilian society of being intruders and aggressors. Since the outcome of the conflict was inevitable, da Cunha believed that the only way for the Republic to justify its military aggressions was to bring the *sertanejo* into civilization, but learning from him instead of simply imparting its own culture upon him at bayonet point. Otherwise, force would be required in innumerable new Canudoses. And force had already failed as an effective means of controlling the situation; it had been necessary to eliminate the heroic *sertanejos* at Canudos to the last man.

Da Cunha did not doubt that the task of achieving national unity for Brazil would be long and arduous. Nor did the general public immediately accept the ideas of nationalism reflected in his work. Yet da Cunha did lay the groundwork for a modernist school of Brazilians who were to continue searching for new meanings and new beauty in their own native soil of Brazil. These included Heitor Villa-Lobos in the field of music, Érico Veríssimo in the novel, Cândido Portinari in painting, Gilberto Freire in sociology, and numerous others. They, like da Cunha, felt that if Brazilians could free themselves from slavish imitation of European doctrines and make Brazil, rather than France or England, their spiritual home, national unity would be possible. As for the value to be placed on the *sertanejo* in twentieth-century Brazilian society, da Cunha was certain that this group would be vitally important in Brazil's achieving a unity of race, sometime in the future. His own evaluation of the *sertanejo* follows:

> I did encounter in the backlands type [*sertanejo*] an ethnic subcategory already formed and one which, as a result of historical conditions, had been freed of the exigencies of a borrowed civilization such as would have hindered its definitive evolution. This is equivalent to saying that in that indefinable compound—the Brazilian—I came upon something that was stable, a point of resistance, . . . And it was natural enough that, once having admitted the bold and inspiring conjecture that we are destined to national unity, I should have seen in those sturdy *caboclos* the hardy nucleus of our future, the bedrock of our race.

(pp. 43-9)

John Vogt, Jr., "Euclides da Cunha: Spokesman for the New Nationalism," in Artists and Writers in the Evolution of Latin America, *edited by Edward Davis Terry, University of Alabama Press, 1969, pp. 41-51.*

ELIZABETH HARDWICK (essay date 1983)

[*Hardwick is an American novelist and critic. In the following excerpt, she provides a recent evaluation of Cunha's work.*]

The pictorial in Brazil consumes the imagination; leaf and scrub, seaside and treacherous inlands long for their apotheosis as word. Otherwise it is as if a great part of the nation lay silent, unrealized. Your own sense of yourself is threatened here and speculative description seizes the mind. A landscape drenched in philosophical questions finds its masterpiece in the great Brazilian prose epic, *Os sertões,* translated into English by Samuel Putnam as *Rebellion in the Backlands.*

A Brazilian newspaper around the turn of the century noted: "There has appeared in the northern backlands an individual who goes by the name of Antonio Conselheiro, and who exerts a great influence over the minds of the lower orders, making use of his mysterious trappings and ascetic habits to impose upon their ignorance and simplicity. He lets his hair grow long, wears a cotton tunic, and eats sparingly, being almost a mummy in aspect."

The appearance of the deranged evangelist, "a crude gnostic," and his gathering about him a settlement of backlands people in the town of Canudos in the northeast was the occasion for military campaigns sent out from Bahia in 1896 and 1897 in order to subdue the supposed threat of the Conselheiro and his followers to the new Republic. Euclides da Cunha went on the campaigns as a journalist and what he returned with and published in 1902 is still unsurpassed in Latin American literature.

Cunha is a talent as grand, spacious, entangled with knowledge, curiosity, and bafflement as the country itself. The ragged, impenetrable Conselheiro is himself a novel, with his tortured beginnings as Antonio Maciel, his disastrous marriage, and his transformation as a wandering anchorite, solitary and violently ascetic in habit. His distorted Catholicism, his odd prophecies ("In 1898 there will be many hats and few heads"), and prediction of the return of the monarchy "with all his army from the waves of the sea," attracted ragged followers and he made his way north to Canudos.

The campaigns against the Conselheiro are the occasion for the book, the center from which Cunha engages Brazil itself and the nature of its people. Even to his great mind it is a mystery, a *mestizo* mystery of contradictions of blood, of north and south, backland and coast, soil, temperament, climate, destiny. (pp. 249-50)

Euclides da Cunha was a military engineer by profession and by curiosity and learning also a botanist, a geologist, geographer, a social historian and an inspired, inflamed observer. His mind is a thicket of interests and ideas and if some of them, such as "atavistic traits" as the result of racial mixture, come out of the science of the time, he transcends his own categories by humane, radical, obsessive genius. The extraordinary landscape of northern Brazil, the fantastical environment, and the people of the backlands who live in "unconscious servitude" to nature and isolation seem to appear to him as a demand, an intellectual and emotional challenge he must find his energetic art to give word to and to honor.

His "vaqueiros" and "jagunços" of the north are men of a different breed from the "gauchos" of the south, who live under the "friendly" natural abundance of the pampas. The gaucho "does not know the horrors of the drought and those cruel combats with the dry-parched earth . . . the grievous sight of calcined and absolutely impoverished soil, drained dry by the burning suns of the Equator."

This backland epic with its "philosophy" of environment and biologic predisposition is an unrolling landscape of collective psychology, of Brazilian temperament with its ebb of inertia and flow of primitive guerrilla and politically sanctioned violence and disorderly bravery. The book gives the sense of a summing up, a conclusion of a part of history that nevertheless stands amidst the unpredictability of Brazil, an astonishing country so peculiar that its inclusion in the phrase "Latin-American" never seems entirely appropriate. (pp. 252-53)

> Elizabeth Hardwick, "Sad Brazil," in her Bartleby in Manhattan and Other Essays, *Random House, 1983, pp. 244-59.*

ADDITIONAL BIBLIOGRAPHY

Amory, Frederick. "The Making of *Os sertões.*" *Romanische Forschungen* LXXVIII (1966): 126-41.
> Discusses the construction of *Os sertões* from the materials published in *Canudos.*

Binsse, Harry Lorin. "Latin American Pattern." *The Commonweal* XXXIX, No. 17 (11 February 1944): 422-24.
> Discusses the events and forces which preceeded and caused the rebellion.

Cunninghame Graham, R. B. *A Brazilian Mystic; Being the Life and Miracles of Antonio Conselheiro.* New York: Dodd, Mead and Co., 1920, 238 p.
> A fictionalized account of the rebellion, primarily based on *Os sertões.*

Frank, Waldo. "The Angry Land (The Sertão)." In his *South American Journey*, pp. 311-20. New York: Duell, Sloan and Pearce, 1943.
> Provides background information on the backlands and the Canudos rebellion.

Hambleton, Josephine. Review of *Rebellion in the Backlands*, by Euclides da Cunha. *The Canadian Forum* XXIII, No. 277 (February 1944): 262-63.
> A plot summary of *Rebellion in the Backlands* favoring the *sertanejos.*

Lynch, William. "They Died for Antonio Maciel." *The Saturday Review of Literature* XXVII, No. 5 (29 January 1944): 9-10.
> A short discussion of the origins, theme, and author of *Os sertões.*

Marchant, Alexander. Review of *Rebellion in the Backlands*, by Euclides da Cunha. *The American Historical Review* XLIX, No. 4 (July 1944): 773-74.
> Discusses Cunha and the creation of *Os sertões.*

Skidmore, Thomas E., and Holloway, Thomas H. "New Light on Euclides da Cunha: Letters to Oliveira Lima, 1903-1909." *Luso-Brazilian Review* VII, No. 1 (June 1971): 30-55.
> Letters written by Cunha, in Portuguese, with an English introduction discussing their worth for the study of Cunha.

Zweig, Stefan. "Culture." In his *Brazil: Land of the Future*, pp. 134-65. New York: Viking Press, 1943.
> Contains a short estimation of *Os sertões*, calling it Brazil's "greatest national epic."

John Davidson

1857-1909

Scottish poet, dramatist, novelist, short story writer, and essayist.

A controversial figure among the writers of the "Tragic Generation" of the 1890s, Davidson is primarily remembered for his poetry reflecting the changing social and philosophical attitudes of the late Victorian era. In his most successful works, the collections *Fleet Street Eclogues* and *Ballads and Songs*, he utilized traditional poetic forms while expressing a modern concern with the quality of urban life. He rejected Christianity and Christian morality for an atheistic philosophy based in part on prevalent scientific theories of the period, and his mature works advance a materialistic doctrine stressing the unity of all matter and the supremacy of the human will. Because of the proselytizing nature of his later works, Davidson fell out of favor with many critics of the time, though retrospective appraisals have recognized his poetry as instrumental in the transition from nineteenth- to twentieth-century poetics. According to Holbrook Jackson: "The Eighteen Nineties had no more remarkable mind and no more distinctive poet than John Davidson. From the beginning he was both an expression of and a protest against the decadent movement, and in his personality as well as in his tragic end he represented the struggle and defeat of his day in the cause of a bigger sense of life and a greater power over personality and destiny."

Born in Barrhead, Renfrewshire, in southwest Scotland, Davidson was the son of an Evangelical Union minister and his wife. A domineering personality, Alexander Davidson gained a considerable reputation as a forceful lecturer and persuasive temperance advocate. Although Davidson challenged his father's dogmatic Christian beliefs, most biographers have stressed that in his zealous adherence to scientific materialism Davidson remained as dogmatic as his father and resembled him in his desire to convert others to his creed. Davidson's literary interests were apparent even in childhood, when at age twelve he produced his first poem, which he later recalled as a "sturdy ballad on the Defeat of the Moors." He left school in the next year and, in an effort to supplement the family income, found employment as an assistant in the chemical laboratory of a local sugar company. In 1872 he became a pupil-teacher at the Highlander's Academy in Greenock, remaining there until 1876, when he briefly attended Edinburgh University. After leaving the university, Davidson held a number of teaching positions in towns throughout Scotland, including Glasgow, Perth, Paisley, and Crieff, and although he professed a distaste for the profession—describing it as a "hellish drudgery"—he has been portrayed as a sensitive and capable instructor. While employed as a teacher, Davidson published several dramas and a novel; he also made the acquaintance of Professor John Nichol of Glasgow University. Under the guidance of Nichol, he became familiar with the work of the Spasmodic poets—Scottish devotees of Lord Byron whose verses are characterized by formlessness and emotionalism. It was at Nichol's home in Glasgow that Davidson met Algernon Swinburne in 1878. Davidson already had extraordinary self-confidence in his abilities as a poet, and this conviction was fortified by his meeting with Swinburne, who greeted him, according to an account by Ed-

mund Gosse, by "laying his hand upon Davidson's head in a sort of benediction, and addressing him as 'Poet.'"

In 1890 Davidson moved to London, where he wrote literary reviews and articles to support his wife and two sons. A member of the Rhymers' Club, and familiar with most of the renowned authors and editors of the decade, Davidson enjoyed his greatest degree of critical and popular success in the early and mid-1890s. His success, however, did not bring financial security, and Davidson's already overburdened means were further strained by his responsibilities to his family in Scotland after his father's death in 1891. The ensuing difficulties culminated in Davidson's physical and emotional collapse in December 1896. His recuperation in Shoreham, Sussex, lasted until February 1898, when he returned to work in London. His financial decline continued, however, compounded by the critical and popular failure of several successive works and by his own ill health. In 1906, he was granted a Civil List pension of £100 annually, which he considered an insufficient award and one which in any case did little to improve his position. As a measure of economy and in hope of recovering his health, Davidson moved with his family to the coast of Cornwall in 1907, but the change proved of little benefit. At this time he informed his publisher that he had developed cancer and had "barely a year or two to live." He disappeared and was presumed drowned on March 23, 1909, when he failed to return from his daily walk along the coast. His body was recovered from the sea six months later, and his death was ruled a suicide. In *The Testament of John Davidson*, published in the previous year, Davidson had written:

> None should outlive his power. . . . Who kills
> Himself subdues the conqueror of kings:
> Exempt from death is he who takes his life:
> My time has come.

In Davidson's early writings critics have observed several themes that are exhibited again in his works of the 1890s and in his philosophical works composed after the turn of the century. The most important of these is the rejection of Christian dogma. Rebelling against the zealous Protestantism he had known in his youth, Davidson sought first to replace it with a creed of nature worship. In this spirit, he wrote several dramas and a novel which, unlike his later works, are considered light-hearted and romantic. Comedies such as *An Unhistorical Pastoral* and *A Romantic Farce* display a rejection of modern industrial and commercial society and focus on the Elizabethan age, which in Davidson's view was the last era in which drama had truly flourished. Consequently, his early "Shakesperean" dramas rely on Elizabethan settings and plot conventions and employ an archaic diction. In general, these works are considered derivative and immature, although many observers have praised the inventiveness of Davidson's blank verse and the relevance of these works to his evolving philosophical convictions. The representative of his new creed, the "Davidsonian hero," is identifiable even in the works Davidson produced in Scotland before 1890. Typically a poet or prophet, this figure is marked by a keen awareness of his own will and of the inviolability of love, and he emerges in subsequent volumes as an assertive, life-affirming man of action. The god Sarmion, for example, in *Scaramouch in Naxos*, an early drama attacking modern commercialism, chooses love as he sacrifices his immortality to remain on earth with his mortal lover, Ione. According to critic J. Benjamin Townsend, *Scaramouch in Naxos* is significant among Davidson's early works, for it indicates that although Davidson "still vacillated between revolt against the actual world and escape to one that matched his ideals, no work of the Scottish years anticipates as clearly his later ironic acceptance of all that life can offer, be it dark or bright so that it be real."

The decade of the 1890s forms the middle period of Davidson's career and was the decade in which he knew his greatest commercial successes. Publishing, among other volumes, the poetry collections *In a Music Hall, Fleet Street Eclogues*, and *Ballads and Songs*, Davidson was praised for his unique rendering of urban settings and situations. Acclaimed as "the poems of the hour," Davidson's verses of this period were recognized for their modernity and realism. In particular, "Thirty Bob a Week" is highly regarded for Davidson's masterful portrait of an urban worker and is often compared to the works of Rudyard Kipling and W. E. Henley for its use of idiomatic language and London slang. According to T. S. Eliot: "Davidson had a great theme, and also found an idiom which elicited the greatness of the theme, which endowed this thirty-bob-a-week clerk with a dignity that would not have appeared if a more conventional poetic diction had been employed. The personage that Davidson created in this poem has haunted me all my life, and the poem is to me a great poem for ever." In *Fleet Street Eclogues*, inspired in part by Edmund Spenser's *The Shepheardes Calendar* (1579), Davidson moved a tradi-

tionally pastoral dialogue form into the modern world of urban journalism. Exploring the values and beliefs of working literary journalists at the close of the nineteenth century, the *Eclogues* represent Davidson's own examination of various systems of thought, including nature worship, evolutionism, and materialism. Critics have suggested that by giving an equal voice to each through the speakers of the *Eclogues,* Davidson attempted to resolve his own unsettled beliefs. According to Carrol V. Peterson: "Though Davidson's eclogues are scarcely bucolic in tone, the generally low-keyed voices of the conversing shepherd-journalists . . . allowed Davidson to explore the important existential questions of his day without undue commitment to any side and with a happy absence of the revivalistic sermonizing which always seemed to be pressing its way to the fore in his work." His subsequent collection, *Ballads and Songs,* was well-received by contemporary critics, including the poet Lionel Johnson, who proclaimed the verses "rich in beauty and strength of a rare accomplishment." In his much-parodied "A Ballad of a Nun" from that collection, Davidson challenged conventional ideas of morality and divinity by rendering the tale of a cloistered nun who flees her isolated convent to find sexual fulfillment in the city. The nun's ballad is considered a paradigm of Davidsonian moral philosophy because it is a story of salvation achieved not through the nun's vow of celibacy but through her ultimate acceptance of the physical world.

During the 1890s Davidson also wrote or translated and adapted numerous dramas for the London stage, only one of which was successful, his English version of Francois Coppée's *Pour la couronne*. His unprofitable association with the theater, however, inspired him to write *The Theatrocrat: A Tragic Play of Church and Stage* in 1905. Never produced, *The Theatrocrat*, like Davidson's unfinished trilogy *God and Mammon*, was chiefly a vehicle through which he could propagate his creed. Davidson held that humanity represents matter in its highest form, the form to which all matter aspires. As a member of the highest species, an individual's reason for being is the realization and expression of his or her will. The greatest individual, then, is one who, like Davidson, comprehends his or her human greatness and expresses it accordingly. In Davidson's view individual self-expression is a moral duty. Like its predecessors, *The Theatrocrat* failed because, as critics observed, Davidson concentrated too narrowly on his message at the expense of his play. Several reviewers have emphasized the increasingly polemical nature of Davidson's later works and have also noted in them a growing sense of bitterness and desperation. *The Testament of a Vivisector*, published in 1901 and considered obscure by many contemporary critics, was the initial offering in a series of dramatic monologues designed to convert society to Davidsonian Materialism. Rooted in his youthful reading of Thomas Carlyle's works and in his adult study of the works of Friedrich Nietzsche, Davidson's creed developed over several decades. Comparisons have often been drawn between Davidson's doctrines and Nietzsche's, but many observers have demonstrated that Davidson consistently refuted Nietzsche's precepts concerning the evolution of the *Ubermensch* ("Overman"), believing that the *Ubermensch* already existed in the form of the modern Englishman. The *Testaments*, according to Peterson, suffer from the same fault as *The Theatrocrat*: "The message is a strange one indeed, but one might tolerate its strangeness if the message were not set forth with such battering-ram-like directness. The speakers, whether they be empire builders or prime ministers or John Davidson, all mount the soapbox and pound their message home in heavy, tortured, and humorless blank verse. . . . The message is un-relenting and unrelieved. Art is forgotten; the message is all.''

A popular success during the 1890s, especially for his collections of eclogues and ballads, Davidson lost favor with audiences and critics alike after the turn of the century. His materialistic credo, presented with ever-increasing dogmatism and bitterness, offended many contemporary reviewers and confused even more. Although many of his ideas have been eclipsed or discredited by subsequent intellectual trends, modern scholars see importance in Davidson's synthesis of the major currents in nineteenth-century Western thought, and they praise the power, integrity, and sincerity with which he expounded his philosophy. According to Peterson: ''Not only the ideas, but the forceful presentation of the ideas and their fervent expression is his strength.'' In addition, his works are considered significant because they have served as points of departure for many influential writers of the twentieth century, including T. S. Eliot, who enthusiastically concluded: ''In everything that Davidson wrote I recognize a real man, to be treated not only with respect but with homage.''

(See also *Contemporary Authors*, Vol. 118 and *Dictionary of Literary Biography*, Vol. 19: *British Poets, 1880-1914.*)

PRINCIPAL WORKS

Diabolus Amans [first publication] (drama) 1885
The North Wall (novel) 1885; also published as *A Practical Novelist*, 1891
Bruce [first publication] (drama) 1886
Smith [first publication] (drama) 1888
Plays [first publication] (dramas) 1889
Perfervid (novel) 1890
In a Music Hall, and Other Poems (poetry) 1891
Fleet Street Eclogues (poetry) 1893
Ballads and Songs (poetry) 1894
A Random Itinerary (essays) 1894
A Full and True Account of the Wonderful Mission of Earl Lavender (novel) 1895
St. George's Day: A Fleet Street Eclogue (poetry) 1895
A Second Series of Fleet Street Eclogues (poetry) 1895
New Ballads (poetry) 1897
Godfrida [first publication] (drama) 1898
The Last Ballad, and Other Poems (poetry) 1899
Self's the Man [first publication] (drama) 1901
The Testament of a Man Forbid (dramatic monologue) 1901
The Testament of a Vivisector (dramatic monologue) 1901
The Testament of an Empire-Builder (dramatic monologue) 1902
The Knight of the Maypole (drama) 1903
A Rosary (prose, poetry, and drama) 1903
The Testament of a Prime Minister (dramatic monologue) 1904
The Theatrocrat: A Tragic Play of Church and Stage (drama) 1905
Holiday and Other Poems, with a Note on Poetry (poetry and essay) 1906
**God and Mammon*. 2 vols. [first publication] (unfinished dramatic trilogy) 1907-08
The Testament of John Davidson (dramatic monologue) 1908
Fleet Street, and Other Poems (poetry) 1909
The Man Forbid, and Other Essays (essays) 1910

*This work includes the dramas *An Unhistorical Pastoral, A Romantic Farce,* and *Scaramouch in Naxos.*

**This work includes the dramas *The Triumph of Mammon* and *Mammon and His Message.*

THE ATHENAEUM (essay date 1886)

[*In the following excerpt, the critic offers an assessment of* Bruce: A Drama in Five Acts.]

Though Mr. Davidson's chronicle play [*Bruce*] has many faults, it is, on the whole, far superior to the dramatic productions of the day in general. Mr. Davidson falls at times into the error of developing his themes by elaborate reflections and ingenious similes which are fatal to its directness. Thus Bruce, in the moment of his repentance for having slain Comyn, is made to utter a speech so absolutely impossible as the following to a man under the torture of sudden remorse:—

> What have I done? A madman's dreadful deed!
> I was engulfed, and now I'm cast ashore.
> O, in our passionless, reflective hours
> We lock emotion in a glass-walled jail
> Of crisp philosophy; or give it scope
> As far as Will, the turnkey, may allow
> The chain of prudence to enlarge its steps!
> But to some sense a small distraction comes—
> Across the sight a butterfly, a flower—
> The fetters snap, the prison crumbles—off!—
> To clasp the air where shone our will-o'-wisp!
> For no gewgaw have I burst reason's bonds,
> But to avenge a gross iniquity
> That clamoured brazenly to heaven and earth.

How much nearer is the writer to true passion when Wallace, waiting for doom, on hearing the harrowing death of his wife recited, bursts forth:—

> Nay, hang me!—burn me!—I am sawn asunder!

The plot, too, wants concentration, and offers fine opportunities which have in some cases been neglected. But the author has skill in painting character. Bruce himself is boldly drawn. His wife, though a mere sketch, attracts by her devotion. Edward I., though shown as an ambitious tyrant, has justice done to him; he is allowed to describe his actions and his policy from his own point of view. The Countess of Buchan, too, must be mentioned as a very fresh and original study. Not seldom we meet with a fine thought forcibly expressed. Here is the musing of Bruce when he has been urged to struggle for the crown:

> I'm not a man
> Much given to meditate. When pending thoughts
> Hurtle each other in the intellect,
> Darkening that firmament like thunder-clouds,
> To let them lighten forth in utterance
> Clears up the sky, confused with swaying rack,
> My life begins a new department here;
> And like one dying all my time appears
> Even on the instant, in eternal light.

But the faculty most evident in the book is that of vivid description. This is shown in some of the details concerning

Wallace; above all in the relation, by an eye-witness, of the fight at Bannockburn while still in progress:—

> OLD MAN.I see them. But our spearmen! Do you see!
> This hill we stand on trembles with the shock:
> They budge not, planted, founded in the soil.
> And her charge! Now watch! Now see! Ugh! Ha!
> Did one spear flicker? One limb waver? No!
> These fellows there are fighting for their land!
> The English army through its cumbrous bulk
> Thrilled and astounded to the utmost rear,
> Twists like a snake, and folds into itself.
> Rank pushed through rank. Now are they hand to
>   hand! . . .

Mr. Davidson is more successful at present in dramatic description than in dramatic embodiment. But he has sympathy and fire enough to make us think the latter within his reach.

> *A review of "Bruce: A Drama in Five Acts," in* The Athenaeum, *No. 3071, September 4, 1886, p. 314.*

A. T. QUILLER-COUCH (essay date 1894)

[*Quiller-Couch was an English man of letters who is especially noted as the editor of* The Oxford Book of English Verse *(1900) and of several other distinguished anthologies. The author of many novels and short stories, his most famous work was* The Golden Spur *(1889), a novel which, like much of his fiction, is set in his native Cornwall. A contributor to various English periodicals, Quiller-Couch published many of his magazine essays under the pseudonym "Q." In the following excerpt from an essay originally published in* The Speaker, *7 April 1894, he discusses characteristic qualities of Davidson's work as exemplified by his* Plays *and other writings.*]

Now it would be easy and pleasant to express my great admiration of Mr. Davidson's Muse, and justify it by a score of extracts and so make an end: and nobody (except perhaps Mr. Davidson himself) would know my dishonesty. For indeed and out of doubt he is in some respects the most richly-endowed of all our younger poets. Of wit and of imagination he has almost a plethora: they crowd [his *Plays*], and all his books, from end to end. And his frequent felicity of phrase is hardly less remarkable. You may turn page after page, and with each page the truth of this will become more obvious. Let me add his quick eye for natural beauty, his penetrating instinct for the principles that lie beneath its phenomena, his sympathy with all men's more generous emotions—and still I have a store of satisfactory illustrations at hand for the mere trouble of turning the leaves. Consider, for instance, the imagery in his description of the fight by Bannockburn—

> Now are they hand to hand!
> How short a front! How close! *They're sewn together*
> *With steel cross-stitches, halbert over sword,*
> *Spear across lance, and death the purfled seam!* . . .

Or consider the fanciful melody of the Fairies' song in *An Unhistorical Pastoral*—

> "Weave the dance and sing the song;
> *Subterranean depths prolong*
> *The rainy patter of our feet;*
> Heights of air are rendered sweet
> By our singing. Let us sing,
>   Breathing softly, fairily,
>   Swelling sweetly, airily,
> Till earth and sky our echo ring.

> Rustling leaves chime with our song:
> Fairy bells its close prolong
>   Ding-dong, ding-dong."
>   (pp. 315-16)

I have opened the [*Plays*] at random for these quotations. Its pages are stuffed with scores as good. Nor will any but the least intelligent reviewer upbraid Mr. Davidson for deriving so much of his inspiration directly from Shakespeare. Mr. Davidson is still a young man; but the first of these plays, *An Unhistorical Pastoral*, was first printed so long ago as 1877; and the last, *Scaramouch in Naxos: a Pantomime*, in 1888. They are the work therefore of a very young man, who must use models while feeling his way to a style and method of his own.

But—there is a "but"; and I am coming at length to my difficulty with Mr. Davidson's work. Oddly enough, this difficulty may be referred to the circumstance that Mr. Davidson's poetry touches Shakespeare's great circle at a second point. Wordsworth, it will be remembered, once said that Shakespeare *could* not have written an Epic (Wordsworth, by the way, was rather fond of pointing out the things that Shakespeare could not have done). "Shakespeare *could* not have written an Epic; he would have died of plethora of thought." Substitute "wit" for "thought," and you have my difficulty with Mr. Davidson. It is given to few men to have great wit: it is given to fewer to carry a great wit lightly. In Mr. Davidson's case it luxuriates over the page and seems persistently to choke his sense of form. One image suggests another, one phrase springs under the very shadow of another until the fabric of his poem is completely hidden beneath luxuriant flowers of speech. Either they hide it from the author himself; or, conscious of his lack of architectonic skill, he deliberately trails these creepers over his ill-constructed walls. I think the former is the true explanation, but am not sure. (pp. 317-18)

Mr. Davidson has published much since these plays first appeared—works both in prose and verse—*Fleet Street Eclogues, Ninian Jamieson, A Practical Novelist, A Random Itinerary, Baptist Lake:* and because I have followed his writings (I think from his first coming to London) with the greatest interest, I may possibly be excused for speaking a word of warning. I am quite certain that Mr. Davidson will never bore me: but I wish I could be half so certain that he will in time produce something in true perspective; a fabric duly proportioned, each line of which from the beginning shall guide the reader to an end which the author has in view; something which

> *"Servetur ad imum*
> *Qualis ab incepto processerit, et sibi constet.*

> [See that it (a fresh character in a play) is kept to the end such as it starts at the beginning and is self-consistent. (Translation from *The Oxford Book of Quotations*.)]

Sibi constet, be it remarked. A work of art may stand very far from Nature, provided its own parts are consistent. Heaven forbid that a critic should decry an author for being fantastic, so long as he is true to his fantasy.

But Mr. Davidson's wit is so brilliant within the circles of its temporary coruscation as to leave the outline of his work in a constant penumbra. Indeed, when he wishes to unburden his mind of an idea, he seems to have less capacity than many men of half his ability to determine the form best suited for conveying it. If anything can be certain which has not been tried, it is that his story *A Practical Novelist* should have been cast in dramatic form. His vastly clever *Perfervid: Or, the Career of Ninian Jamieson* is cast in two parts which neither unite to make a whole, nor are sufficiently independent to stand complete in themselves. I find it characteristic that his *Random Itinerary*—that fresh and agreeable narrative of suburban travel—should conclude with a crashing poem, magnificent in itself, but utterly out of key with the rest of the book. (pp. 319-21)

With all this I have to repeat that Mr. Davidson is in some respects the most richly endowed of all the younger poets. The grand manner comes more easily to him than to any other: and if he can cultivate a sense of form and use this sense as a curb upon his wit, he has all the qualities that take a poet far. (p. 322)

> *A. T. Quiller-Couch, in an extract from "Mr. John Davidson," in his* Adventures in Criticism, *Charles Scribner's Sons, 1896, pp. 314-22.*

LIONEL JOHNSON (essay date 1895)

[*An English poet and critic, Johnson is considered one of the most important figures associated with the Decadent and Aesthetic movements of the 1890s. Like many of his contemporaries, he lived an eccentric life and died young, producing a small but distinguished body of works that reflects his deep interest in medieval literature and thought and demonstrates two major influences: Walter Pater's aestheticism and the poetry of the Celtic Revival. In the following excerpt, Johnson offers an appreciative review of* Ballads and Songs.]

"Lord! what a pleasure it is to come across a man that can *write!*" said Dickens of Tennyson. Certainly it is, and a rare pleasure, too; for the abhorrent amateur is always with us, but the true writers visit us like the angels. The most immediately felt charm of Mr. Davidson's verse is its goodly energy and force, its excellent vitality: there is life-blood in the strong and vehement lines. He has not a trace of waterish sentiment and prettiness: in the phrase of Coleridge, he does not seek to win us "with sonnets and with sympathy" of a miscellaneous sort. Each poem has lived in the poet's life, and issues from a living fire of passion, imagination, thought: there is no clever impersonality about it. And the defects of its qualities are not lacking: a certain feverishness at times, an unpruned wealth of words, a rapidity which makes the verse pant for want of breath. This poet's wine can be heady and rasping and crude. Even in his finest work there is just some lack of the *ultima manus*, with its perfecting and rounding touch: just that serenity and grace are sometimes absent, which mark the assured triumph of the masterpiece. "What verse he will be writing in ten years!" is the reader's conviction, rather than a complete confidence in the virtue of the verse before him. In short, *Sturm und Drang* are not wholly over yet: the elements of a perfect art are still in fusion and fermentation.

But [the poems in *Ballads and Songs*] are rich in beauty and strength of a rare accomplishment. For one thing, it is impossible not to see what the poet is at and about: the themes, intellectual and emotional, are extraordinarily vivid: they appeal, and arrest, and detain, with a dramatic intensity. As in the greatest preaching, all the ornate and wheeling periods come home from their imaginative flights, and close upon the text that gave them wings, so these poems have each their initial, central, culminating, consistency and unity of design. The "**Ballad of a Nun**," the "**Ballad of Heaven**," the "**Ballad in Blank Verse of the Making of a Poet**," with their refrains and repetitions, their returns upon their openings, their striking

of the same notes with an emphasis cunningly varied, have a singular lucidity and energy of imaginative thought. In each a situation, an emotion, has been faced and wrestled with and mastered: the solutions are triumphant and satisfying. Where Browning would have written psychological studies, with parry and fence, cut and thrust, of encountering emotions, Mr. Davidson chooses rather to throw his problem into a romantic ballad; applying, to subtle and spiritual themes, the direct narrative vigour, and pictorial charm of the ancient ballad story. He is happiest when using stanza and rhyme, especially the four-line octosyllabic stanza. It condenses and constrains his fervent rush of words, which in blank verse is not always under control. Thanks to the necessity of concentration, we have such splendours of phrase as these:

> For still night's starry scroll unfurled,
> And still the day came like a flood:
> It was the greatness of the world
> That made her long to use her blood:

or, again,

> I care not for my broken vow;
> Though God should come in thunder soon,
> I am sister to the mountains now,
> And sister to the sun and moon.
>
> (pp. 6-7)

One feels that, in a less coercing metre, Mr. Davidson might have let his imagination riot amid a wealth of imagery, far less impressive than the concise and chiselled beauty of these sudden phrases, left without amplification. All his lyrics have something of this excellent brevity and compression, which seem to bring dignity with them: elsewhere, he falls into phrases unennobled and without strength. Compare Mr. Davidson's

> with awe beheld
> A shaven pate mutter a Latin spell
> Over a biscuit;

with Browning's

> Hear the blessed mutter of the mass
> And see God made and eaten all day long.

Both are painful: but Browning's phrase has an imaginative irony and audacity in its realism, which lift it above mere crudity. Mr. Davidson's phrase has no such justifying power. The "**Ballad in Blank Verse**," where it occurs, abounds in resonant passages of beautiful writing, memorable and fine; but, as an whole, it has not the haunting and irresistible fascination of the lyrics. Yet, like all Mr. Davidson's poems, it betrays Mr. Davidson the novelist and essayist and dramatist, with a tenacious hold upon life, keenly sensitive and observant and imaginative, with humour at once human and fantastic. His "**Thirty Bob a Week**" and "**To the Street Piano**," like his earlier *Music Hall* poems, are written in a vein of curious intelligence, a comprehension of life in certain aspects, commonly treated by poets either with a lachrymose sentiment or a brutal bitterness. Mr. Davidson is content to interpret, with a moving sense of their tragi-comedy, human and divine, which stirs us strangely. His very rhythms and measures go with a sublime sort of "vulgarity," with a quaint pitifulness in the Cockney twang, half-jesting and half-despairing, yet defiant all the while. He renders with perfect precision the feeling which street sights and sounds, the pleasure and pain of the struggling crowd, can rouse in us, touching us to a sense of helpless pity, and useless tenderness, and an impulse of love for things "common and unclean." Mr. Davidson imports no

104 *105*

> But you never hear her do a growl or whine,
>   For she's made of flint and roses, very odd;
> And I've got to cut my meaning rather fine,
>   Or I'd blubber, for I'm made of greens and sod:
> So p'raps we are in Hell for all that I can tell,
>   And lost and damn'd and served up hot to God.
>
> I ain't blaspheming, Mr. Silvertongue;
>   I'm saying things a bit beyond your art:
> Of all the rummy starts you ever sprung,
>   Thirty bob a week's the rummiest start!
> With your science and your books and your theories about spooks,
>   Did you ever hear of looking in your heart?
>
> I didn't mean your pocket, Mr.; no:
>   I mean that, having children and a wife,
> With thirty bob on which to come and go,
>   Is n't dancing to the tabor and the fife:
> When it doesn't make you drink, by Heaven! it makes you think,
>   And notice curious items about life.
>
> I step into my heart and there I meet
>   A god-almighty devil singing small,
> Who would like to shout and whistle in the street,
>   And squelch the passers flat against the wall;
> If the whole world was a cake he had the power to take,
>   He would take it, ask for more, and eat it all.
>
> And I meet a sort of simpleton beside,
>   The kind that life is always giving beans;
> With thirty bob a week to keep a bride
>   He fell in love and married in his teens:
> At thirty bob he stuck, but he knows it isn't luck,
>   He knows the seas are deeper than tureens.

Manuscript page from Ballads and Songs *(c. 1894).*

pathos into these themes, he is unsparing and exact in his presentation; but the old *Homo sum* takes him to the heart of them. Indeed, there is a powerful humanity in all his work: the purely lonesome dream-world of many poets has not drawn him away from earth for long. His **"Autumn"** is full of the blessings of "mellow fruitfulness," bread for the hungry, the mirth of harvest.

> Let the wain roll home with laughter,
>   The piper pipe,
> And let the girls come dancing after,
>   For once again the earth is ripe.

And when he sings the spring, with its old memories of "merry" England and of mirth under the greenwood tree, of sylvan dance and gaiety, it is with a deeper meaning than meets the eye at first.

> Oh, foolish fancy, feebly strong!
>   To England shall we ever bring
> The old mirth back? Yes, yes; nor long
>   It shall be till that greater Spring;
> And some one yet may make a song
>   The birds would like to sing.

In his "Ballads" there is a curious kind of mystical folk-lore interwoven with the plain humanity of their motives. He reminds us here a little of Novalis, there a little of Richter; for all the sturdy and straightforward strength befitting a countryman of Scott, he is yet a poet who has not lived without undergoing its various influences in the age of Rossetti, of "aesthetic poetry," of a "romantic revival," of a "Celtic Renaissance." And he does not shrink from passing out of phantasies into grotesques with a sudden and daring power: power is in all his work, a singular effectiveness, even a sort of sporting with his own power. The **"Exodus from Hounsditch,"** like the **"Making of a Poet,"** is not without its freakishness, a not quite satisfactory caprice. "Be bold! be bold!" is excellent good advice: so is "Be not too bold!" Of most good younger poets just now we often wish that, in Mr. Saintsbury's phrase, "the sober blood in their decent veins" would "spurt in a splendid sally." They follow Rossetti or M. Verlaine, Arnold or Mr. Bridges, with a very chastened and unambitious pace. But Mr. Davidson is superbly ardent and alive, making adventures upon every side of literature: his perils come not from any over caution. But to compare this volume with its author's earlier *In a Music Hall* is to trace the "progress of poetry" from strength to strength. Few poems in that book, good as it was, had the assured perfection of some poems in this. There are stanzas which haunt the memory as only great art can:

> The adventurous sun took Heaven by storm;
>   Clouds scattered largesses of rain;
> The sounding cities, rich and warm,
>   Smouldered and glittered in the plain.
> Sometimes it was a wandering wind,
>   Sometimes the fragrance of the pine,
> Sometimes the thought how others sinned,
>   That turned her sweet blood into wine.

Indeed, only a poet of no mean order could have so felt and dramatised the "tragedy of the cloister," and the faith in Our

Lady, both together, as in this **"Ballad of a Nun,"** based upon a legend seven hundred years old, Mr. Davidson has done. And though in this volume, small as it is, there are two or three poems markedly beneath the rest, yet even the less excellent have distinction. Mr. Davidson's feeling for nature is strongly individual: each little lyric has its felicity of phrase and sentiment, no echo of Tennyson or of Arnold, but fresh from the imagination, deeply impressed, of one with eyes to see for himself, with ears to hear. And the prevailing "philosophy" is his own, with all its questionings, solutions, guesses, dreams, all valorous and fine, though not acceptable to all. In short, Mr. Davidson has given his critics that most welcome of gifts, a book which gives them occasion to experience "the noble pleasure of praising"; for, once more to quote Mr. Swinburne, it is a book rich beyond a doubt in "the imperishable excellence of sincerity and strength": rich also in graces, that do not always accompany and adorn those excellent virtues. (p. 7)

> *Lionel Johnson, in a review of "Ballads and Songs,"*
> in The Academy, *Vol. XLVII, No. 1183, January 5,*
> *1895, pp. 6-7.*

WILLIAM ARCHER   (essay date 1899)

[*A Scottish dramatist and critic, Archer is best known as one of the earliest and most important translators of Henrik Ibsen's plays and as a drama critic of the London stage during the late nineteenth and early twentieth centuries. Archer valued drama as an intellectual product and not as simple entertainment. For that reason he did a great deal to promote the "new drama" of the 1890s, including the work of Ibsen and Bernard Shaw. Throughout his career he protested critical overvaluation of ancient drama, claiming that modern works were in many respects equal to or better than Elizabethan or Restoration drama. Similar in prescience to his dramatic criticism is his* Poets of the Younger Generation *(1902), one of the first critical studies of many important modern English poets, including A. E. Housman, Arthur Symons, and W. B. Yeats. In the following excerpt from that study, Archer presents a survey of Davidson's early poetry collections.*]

Mr. Davidson's first book of non-dramatic verse, eentitled *In a Music-Hall,* was published in 1891, and contains poems ranging in date from 1872 to 1889. It need not detain us long. With the exception of its title-piece, consisting of half a dozen versified character-studies of music-hall "artistes," its contents show little originality and less accomplishment. The music-hall sketches are clever: no more. The sequence might have formed a modern counterpart to Burns's *Jolly Beggars,* but is very far from rivalling the vigour and spontaneity of that masterpiece. As for the remaining poems, their chief interest lies less in their promise than in their lack of it.... [He] would be a critic of unusual penetration who should with any confidence predict future eminence for the writer of these boyish lyrics and frigid ballads. (p. 137)

Inequality... is one of Mr. Davidson's abiding characteristics.... Take the very first [of the *Fleet Street Ecloques*], "New Year's Day." Here the moody Brian denounces the journalist's calling, while the gentle Basil interjects antiphons of nature-worship (a frequent and charming device of Mr. Davidson's) which fall like drops of oil on the troubled waters of Brian's rhetoric. For instance:

> From the muted tread of the feet,
> And the slackening wheels, I know
> The air is hung with snow,
> And carpeted the street.

One may not at first recognise this as an utterance of nature-worship; but it is not the least among Mr. Davidson's merits that Nature, for him, is not shut out by the four-mile circle. At the close of his lurid diatribe, comparing newspapers to "a covey of dragons, wide-vanned" who hide the sun and pollute the air, Brian sums up in this quatrain:

> Fed by us here and groomed
> In this pestilent reeking stye,
> These dragons I say have doomed
> Religion and poetry—

whereupon Sandy retorts with the following strophe, which I venture to call perfect in imagination and cadence:

> They may doom till the moon forsakes
> Her dark, star-daisied lawn;
> They may doom till doomsday breaks
> With angels to trumpet the dawn;
> While love enchants the young,
> And the old have sorrow and care,
> No song shall be unsung,
> Unprayed no prayer.

Nothing could be better than this little lyric. It has character, fervour, music and excellent form. Yet a page or two farther on we find the same poet, through the mouth of the same speaker, expressing himself thus:

> If people will go bare
> They may count on bloody backs;
> Cold are the hearts that care
> If a girl be blue-eyed or black-eyed;
> Only to souls of hacks
> Are phrases hackneyed.
> . . . . .
> Nor are we warriors giftless;
> Deep magic's in our stroke;
> Ours are the shoes of swiftness:
> And ours the darkling cloak.

It would be unfair to complain of the somewhat prosaic quality of the whole speech. In discursive poetry of this order, it is inevitable that there should be level, if not actually flat, passages. It would be too much to demand an unbroken sweep of lyric exaltation. But even in a professedly humorous passage it is going a little too far in the Hudibrastic direction to make such atrocious assonances pass for rhymes. (pp. 137-39)

To the critics, then, whose method is to prod at the weak points in a poet's armour, Mr. Davidson, in his *Eclogues* and elsewhere, offers ample opportunities for their favourite exercise. For my part, I do not envy the man who can read these *Fleet Street Eclogues* without recognizing in them an originality of thought, a freshness of vision, a wealth and vivacity of imagination, and in many cases a free and buoyant lyric movement, which far outweigh their worst defects of form.

"St. Valentine's Eve" presents a daring paradox of Love as the thrice-sufficient counter-weight to all the agonies of a tortured universe.... **"St. Swithin's Day"** declares the glory of the summer, touching its highest point, perhaps, in this quatrain:

> I would I lay beside a brook at morn,
> And watched the shepherd's clock declare the hours;
> And heard the husky whisper of the corn,
> Legions of bees in leagues of summer flowers.

"**Michaelmas**" is mainly given up to a dream, recounted by Basil, of which he himself remarks that it was "long, too long"—and one cannot but agree with him. Far more original is "**Queen Elizabeth's Day**" with its celebration of a London fog, its vision of man's secular quest of the Hesperides, and its assertion that

> God has no machine
> For punching perfect worlds from cakes of chaos.
> (pp. 140-51)

The blank-verse eclogue entitled "**Lammas**" is one of the most powerful things Mr. Davidson has ever done. It is vivid in description, penetrating in psychology, superb in imagination.... If this poem be not compact of pregnant thought and luminous imagery, I know not where to look for imagery and thought.

The eclogues of "**Midsummer Day**" and "**Mayday**" are pretty but comparatively unimportant pieces of nature-celebration; the latter embodying the pathetic story of a May-morn devotee, and Basil's spirited transcript of the nightingale's song. "**St. George's Day**" is, both in its strength and its occasional weakness, a typical example of Mr. Davidson's manner. But its strength far outweighs its weakness, and it is, in its general effect, a noble and spirit-stirring piece of work.

There remain to be considered Mr. Davidson's three books of miscellaneous poems: [*Ballads and Songs, New Ballads,* and *The Last Ballad and Other Poems*].... These may be treated as three volumes of one work; and I propose to survey and classify, rather than criticise, their contents, before attempting, in conclusion, to sum up the characteristics of Mr. Davidson's talent.

The ballad, or more precisely the parable in quatrains, is the poet's favourite form. But more notable to my thinking than any of the quatrain poems are three dramatic narratives in blank verse: "**The Making of a Poet**," "**A Woman and her Son**," and "**The Ordeal**." The first of these is absolutely masterly in its sustained vitality of feeling and utterance. It sets forth the rebellion of a pagan-hearted boy against the narrow Calvinism of his parents:

> His father, woman-hearted, great of soul,
> Wilful and proud, save for one little shrine
> That held a pinchbeck cross, had closed and barred
> The many mansions of his intellect.
> . . . . .
> His father's pleading done, his mother cried,
> With twitching forehead, scalding tears that broke
> The seal of wrinkled eyelids, mortised hands
> Where knuckles jutted white: "Almighty God!—
> Almighty God!—Oh, save my foolish boy!"

The vision of Aphrodite and Adonis that floats into the boy's mind in the midst of his parents' entreaties is very beautifully written; but lurid intensity rather than beauty is the note of the poem. His mother dead, his father "dying for his sake," the boy "yields tamely" and goes to "the table of the Lord . . . ghastly, with haunted eyes." . . . In the reaction from his hypocritical surrender, the son rushes to his father with a full confession of unfaith, and a doxology, not to God, but to man; whereupon, with "gaping horror" on his face, the old man

> Rose quaking; and "The unpardonable sin!—
> The unpardonable sin!" he whispered hoarse.

At first the father is fain to go with his son to hell:

> Boy, help me to blaspheme. I cannot face
> Without you her that nursed you at her breast.

But it is as impossible for him to disbelieve as for the son to believe; and his wonderfully dramatic and pathetic rhapsody ends thus:

> Beside the crystal river I shall walk
> For ever with the Lord. The city of gold,
> The jasper walls thereof, the gates of pearl,
> The bright foundation-stones of emerald,
> Of sapphires, chrysoprase, of every gem,
> And the high triumph of unending day
> Shall be but wildfire on a summer eve
> Beside the exceeding glory of delight,
> That shall entrance me with the constant thought
> Of how in Hell through all eternity
> My son performs the perfect will of God.
> (pp. 142, 145-147)

An outwardly similar, yet essentially different, situation is that treated in "**A Woman and her Son**." Here, in a graphically indicated environment of city squalor, we find an atheist-pessimist son beside the deathbed of his mother, who has unflinchingly borne a life of drudgery, privation and sorrow, in radiant and immovable faith that the life beyond would make all good to her. "Hard as the nether millstone" himself, her son would see her

> Harden with a hiss
> As life goes out in the cold bath of death.

She dies in the full confidence that she is going to heaven, where her husband and the seven children who have preceded her will welcome her with rapture. But after three days, her soul returns to her body, beside which her son is still watching; and she has nothing to report of the undiscovered country except a feeble dream which must have flickered through her mind in the moment of dissolution. Then she, in her turn, grows hard as the nether millstone, and, cursing the illusions of "love the cheat, And hope, the radiant devil pointing up," dies a second time in her son's arms. . . . (p. 148)

"**The Ordeal**," with its romantic setting, may stand as a sort of half-way house between these dramatic narratives and the ballads. It is longer than the other blank-verse poems, and somewhat laxer in style, but it belongs essentially to the same class inasmuch as it is an ironic indictment at once of the ordering of human life, and of the attitude of mankind towards the powers that so order it. (p. 149)

These three poems seem to me to rank with the "**Lammas**" Eclogue among the very strongest things Mr. Davidson has done.

His ballads run to a round dozen: all but one—the comparatively ineffective "**Vengeance of the Duchess**"—composed in rhymed quatrains. The measure sometimes becomes a little monotonous in Mr. Davidson's hands, mainly, I think, because of his fondness for what the Shakespearometrists call "end-stopped lines"; but he handles it with great force, if not with absolute freedom. They are all apologues, more or less distinctly water-marked with a moral; but they all embody a story, or at least a situation, and generally a very finely conceived one. "**A Ballad of the Exodus from Houndsditch**" is a fervid fantasy, suggested by Carlyle's often-quoted phrase. In "**A Ballad of a Nun**" and "**A New Ballad of Tannhäuser**" Mr.

Davidson makes use of mediaeval legends to help in "laying the ghost," as he puts it, "of an unwholesome idea that still haunts the world—the idea of the impurity of nature." The **"Ballad of a Nun"** is probably the most popular of all Mr. Davidson's writings, and has even become somewhat hackneyed; but it merits its popularity if only by reason of its magnificent opening:

> High on a hill the convent hung,
> Across a duchy looking down,
> Where everlasting mountains flung
> Their shadows over tower and town.
>
> The jewels of their lofty snows
> In constellations flashed at night;
> Above their crests the moon arose;
> The deep earth shuddered with delight.
>
> Long ere she left her cloudy bed,
> Still dreaming in the orient land,
> Om many a mountain's happy head
> Dawn lightly laid her rosy hand.
>
> The adventurous sun took Heaven by storm;
> Clouds scattered largesses of rain;
> The sounding cities, rich and warm,
> Smouldered and glittered in the plain.

The third stanza is slightly marred, to my thinking, by the recurrence of the dissyllabic epithets in "y"—"cloudy bed," "happy head," "rosy hand"; but the last stanza is magnificently pictorial, a Turner in four lines. **"The Last Ballad"** is a parable of the soul's decline into inert, Swiftian pessimism, and its recovery from that abyss. **"A Ballad of the Poet Born"** and **"A Ballad of Euthanasia"** celebrate the sweet compensations of life. **"A Ballad of a Workman"** seems, as I understand it, to commend a quietism, a lowly and reverent acceptance of that state of life to which it has pleased fate to call us, which can be regarded only as a transient eddy in the stream of Mr. Davidson's philosophy. The grandiose **"Ballad of Heaven"** and **"Ballad of an Artist's Wife"** sing the praises of strenuous idealism and humble duty respectively; while **"A Ballad of a Coward"** is a study of the soul-state its title suggests, and **"A Ballad of Hell"** sets forth the ultimate beatitude of "a soul that knew not fear." These ballads, certainly, are not all of equal merit. Two of them, the **"Ballad of Heaven"** and of **"Euthanasia,"** seem to me to fall notably below the level of the rest, while several of them contain inert and prosaic stanzas. But, taken as a whole, they show a wealth and variety of imagination, and a vivid energy of phrase, which would abundantly compensate for greater faults than can reasonably be laid to their charge.

Mr. Davidson's shorter poems may be roughly classified under five heads: poems of the Country, poems of the Town, Romantic, Political and Spiritual poems. (pp. 151-52)

The Country poems and Town poems are essentially of the same stuff of which the *Fleet Street Eclogues* are composed. They are lyrics which have not happened to fit into the quasi-dramatic eclogue setting. The most noteworthy of the Country poems are **"In Romney Marsh,"** **"A Cinque Port,"** the sequence on the four seasons, **"Spring Song,"** **"Sunset,"** **"A Highway Pimpernel,"** **"Winter Rain,"** **"Summer Rain,"** **"Afternoon,"** and **"The Last Rose."** Specialists have, I am told, thrown doubts on the correctness of Mr. Davidson's observation of birds, flowers, and trees. This is a matter on which I cannot pretend to arbitrate. All I can say is that Mr. Davidson,

at his best, or even at his second best, brings home to me the sound and colour, the atmosphere and aroma, the homeliness and the spaciousness, of English and Scottish scenery with a peculiar poignancy. His nature-painting is all open-air work; it never smells of the lamp; it is clear-toned, racy, or, as we should say in Scotland, "caller." (p. 153)

The admirable **"Song of a Train"** may stand as a sort of connecting link between the Country and the Town poems. In these Mr. Davidson's originality makes itself unmistakably felt. He tries to describe things, both animate and inanimate, not hitherto attempted, at any rate in classic verse; and, like all pioneers, he meets with an occasional misadventure. But the measure of success he achieves is, on the whole, remarkable; for instance, in **"A Northern Suburb,"** **"A Frosty Morning,"** **"In the Isle of Dogs,"** and that tragical lyric of labour, **"Piper, Play!"** quoted at the end of this article.

Of purely Romantic poems there are but two or three, for Mr. Davidson very seldom sings for the mere sake of singing. The most notable, I think, is **"The Prince of the Fairies,"** a set of "Stanzas for Music," as the poets of the early nineteenth century were wont to say. The mood in which they were composed—an idle mood of decorative fantasy—is not at all characteristic of Mr. Davidson. We owe to it, however, the poem entitled **"Serenade";** and that spirited piece of "gallows humour," **"The Stoop of Rhenish,"** may perhaps come under the same heading.

Among the group which I have designated Political poems, the **"War Song"** stands easily first, and next to it, perhaps, **"The Hymn of Abdul Hamid,"** powerful in conception, grimly prosaic in style. Other notable numbers in this group are **"Coming,"** **"Waiting,"** and **"The Aristocrat."**

Finally, we come to the Spiritual lyrics, among which, as is only natural, we find some of Mr. Davidson's best work. There are fine ideas in the verses **"To the New Women"** and **"To the New Men";** but they seem, on the whole, to have missed their perfect expression. (pp. 153-54)

I intend both compliment and criticism when I say that these two poems remind me of Emerson's excursions into metre. Less erratic in form, and certainly not less weighty in thought, are **"The Badge of Men,"** the impressive **"Earth to Earth,"** and that lyrical allegory of rare beauty and colour **"The Merchantman and the Market-haunters."** But, to my thinking, no other poem of this class can rival in intense and subtle significance the two stanzas entitled **"Insomnia."** (p. 155)

Mr. Davidson's talent is not one that can be readily focused in a phrase or even in a paragraph. His spirit is electrically fuliginous rather than radiant and serene. There is more of Aetna than of Olympus about it. He exemplifies the perfervid, not the "canny," side of the Scottish national genius. But he is beyond all doubt a personality, a temperament, a living spirit. There is thought as well as feeling in all he does—not systematic, close-knit reasoning, but that brave, translunary intuition, that swift penetration of the husks of sublunary things, in which lies the poet's true philosophy. He is an insistent, and for the most part an indignant, critic of life. He is not content to see and set down what he sees, to feel and take his feelings on trust. His mind is for ever occupied in weighing, comparing, analysing; contrasting the actual with the ideal; turning prejudice inside out, unmasking hypocrisy, impaling falsehood. Seeing vividly and feeling intensely, he throws his perceptions and emotions into a fiery furnace of passionate idealism, and then hammers them eagerly, impatiently, sometimes rudely enough, into weapons and missiles to be used in the battle of human progress. For at heart Mr. Davidson is an ardent me-liorist, though there be times when a blackness as of utter pessimism descends upon his mood. The theorists who would have art immutably serene and concilatory must naturally re-gard with horror Mr. Davidson's turbulent and disquieting on-slaughts upon many comfortable optimisms, euphemisms, and conspiracies of silence. Yet, though the tone of his thought is in the main gloomy, his temperamental vitality is throughout so high that the whole effect of his work is stimulant rather than depressing. He himself has given us a lightning-flash of insight into his nature in the lines prefixed to his *New Ballads"*:

> Some said, "He was strong." He was weak;
> For he never could sing or speak
> Of the things beneath or the things above,
> Till his soul was touched by death or love.
>
> Some said, "He was weak." They were wrong;
> For the soul must be strong
> That can break into song
> Of the things beneath and the things above,
> At the stroke of death, at the touch of love.

This is at once authentic poetry and true psychology. It goes far to account for what may be called the main positive and negative characteristics of Mr. Davidson's work: the presence of fire and the absence of finish. Poetry is not, to him, "emo-tion recollected in tranquillity." It is emotion at fever-heat, a rolling, glistering lava-stream; and when the lava has hardened it is too late to fine away the odds and ends of slag that have become embedded in the mass.

A cunning craftsman Mr. Davidson is not. It is evident that he has not given much thought ot metrical technique. He does not experiment in difficult measures, weave intricate ara-besques of rhyme, or build up his blank-verse periods with subtly-distributed pauses, accelerations and suspensions, over-laying the primary rhythm with numberless secondary move-ments, "cycle and epicycle, orb in orb." He is too much absorbed in what he has to say to consider thus curiously the manner of saying it. But his innate rhythmical faculty is very strong, and he achieves admirable effects in a large straight-forward style which, with all its simplicity, is anything but artless. His diction, again, is copious, colourful, vital. He has found multitudes of superb phrases, descriptive, contempla-tive, emotional, which we read with a thrill of satisfaction, thinking "This thing would not be better said." He now and then declines upon a commonplace, stereotyped epithet, now and then ventures a too daring colloquialism. For instance, we are scarcely prepared to encounter the term "pal," or the ex-pression "words they slung," in otherwise serious and dig-nified poems. But it must be remembered that it is part of his function as a realist, a poet of the living hour, to try to gain rights of poetic citizenship for racy-vernacular vocables and locutions; and we ought not to complain if his experiments are not uniformly happy. His taste in imagery is not irreproachable. (pp. 155-57)

Mr. Davidson has imagination, vision, thought, passion, el-oquence and melody. He is a humanist in the best sense. Nature he loves, but it is as an accessory to, not a refuge from, human passion. One may not always agree with his thought, one can-not always admire his workmanship. But he has the root of the matter in him; the world is alive to his eye, language is alive on his lips; and he is withal a strong, free spirit, untram-melled by cowardice, pedantry or cant. (p. 158)

William Archer, "John Davidson," in his Poets of the Younger Generation, *1902. Reprint by Scholarly Press, 1969, pp. 119-61.*

FRANCIS THOMPSON   (essay date 1901)

[*Thompson was one of the most important poets of the Catholic Revival in nineteenth-century English literature. Often compared to the seventeenth-century metaphysical poets, especially Richard Crashaw, he is best known for his poem "The Hound of Heaven" (1893), which displays Thompson's characteristic themes of spir-itual struggle, redemption, and transcendent love. Like other writ-ers of the fin-de-siècle period, Thompson wrote poetry and prose noted for rich verbal effects and a devotion to the values of aes-theticism. In the following excerpt, originally published in the* Daily Chronicle, *13 December 1901, he reviews* The Testament of a Man Forbid.]

[*The Testament of a Man Forbid*] is the second of those "Tes-taments" in which Mr. John Davidson—nothing if not "dar-ing" in the most modern sense, with all its coarser and violent accidents, no less than its desire of a certain kind of truth—has seemingly set out to show the age the form and body of itself, by means of chosen types. The full purpose of the series is still a thing obscure in Mr. Davidson's own mind. Will he sometimes deviate into the normal? Or is his marked preference for extreme types, which suit his own aggressive temperament, too definite for that? So far, at least, we are given types the most untypical, over-balanced minds which run all to one con-straining "humour," in Ben Jonson's sense of the word. The title of the series might, indeed, have been "Every Man in His Humour." One doubts Mr. Davidson's intention to give us anything else, because it so precisely accords with his own disposition. He has no half-tones in his outlook upon the world: he sees everything in primary colours; and red is not quite red enough, blue not quite blue enough for him, till he has dashed in a savage stroke of intensification from his most positive brush.

The *Testament of a Vivisector* was a study in morbidity, the analysis of a monomaniac ready to the hand of Nordau—him-self surely the chief of the monomaniacs he analyses. The "Man Forbid" is a type no less unpleasant and one-sided. Yet we think this is a more level poem than the *Vivisector*. In the *Vivisector* we had glimpses of Mr. Davidson's self. Here, if we may judge from his poems at large, we have a good deal of Mr. Davidson himself, and perhaps this accounts for the more equable display of power. Yet, in a series so dramatic, it is unsafe to assume anything but the dramatic standpoint; and as a dramatic presentment we view this *Man Forbid*.

Mr. Davidson's hirsute strength, disdainful and uncompre-hending of subtleties, is here, as we said, more sustained than in the previous poem. Your attention is seldom long uncaught by vigour, and imaginative vigour, of expression, which, after Mr. Davidson's manner, gives a pinion to what is least exalted in modern thought, poetises the anti-poetical, and wakens a sort of imagination in the earthiest actuality which it were profanation to call reality. It forces an amazed and sorrowful admiration to see the masterful persistence with which this poet claps Pegasus in the traces of a butcher's van; till Pegasus, feeling the authentic hand, bounds with his unwilling weight above the housetops, and we cry, despite ourselves, "Is it Phaeton?" Yes, Phaeton, but without the chariot of the sun. What Mr. Davidson might do did he cut the butcher's cart from its traces, we regretfuly surmise, from the brief glimpses he has given us. To yoke with poetry such matter as this, which becomes more and more his aim, requires no common power. The hero is one of those men who have deliberately forsworn and sent adrift the entire past of man—his religion, his art in the widest sense, his philosophy, his social ideas—and fiercely accepted the task of beginning all over again, with the firm belief in its possibility no less than its necessity:—

> Undo the past.
> The rainbow reaches Asgard now no more;
> Olympus stands untenanted; the dead
> Have their serene abode in earth itself,
> Our womb, our nurture, and our sepulchre.
> Expel the sweet imaginings, profound
> Humanities and golden legends, forms
> Heroic, beauties, tripping shades, embalmed
> Through hallowed ages in the fragrant hearts
> And generous blood of men; the climbing thoughts
> Whose roots ethereal grope among the stars,
> Whose passion-flowers perfume eternity,
> Weed out and tear, scatter and tread them down;
> Dismantle and dilapidate high heaven.
> It has been said: Ye must be born again.
> I say to you: Men must be that they are.

The sweeping denunciation preferred with such eloquent vehemence causes the orator to be shunned by his fellows—a result hardly wonderful. The request made to them is something sudden. He frames a solitude for himself, cheered by nature and the confidence of final success, for his principles if not himself. The poem ends with a landscape in Mr. Davidson's best manner:—

> Here in the Winter like a meshwork shroud
> The sifted snow reveals the perished land,
> And powders wisps of knotgrass dank and dead
> That trail like faded locks on mouldering skulls
> Unearthed from shallow burial. With the Spring
> The west wind thunders through the budding hedge
> That stems the furrowed steeps—a sound of drums,
> Of gongs and muted cymbals; yellow breasts
> And brown wings whirl in gusts, fly chaffering, drop,
> And surge in gusts again. . . .

In these beautiful lines Mr. Davidson gets his chance, and reaches his highest point. There is nothing quite so fine as the close of the *Vivisector;* but on the other hand the strength is more sustained throughout the poem. Here and there the strength passes beyond itself, and exceeds into violence, as is apt to be Mr. Davidson's way. But on the whole, if we cannot call this his best work, it is because he has handicapped himself too severely. What could be done with subject-matter so dark and dour he has probably done. Might we ask, however, whether it is not time to drop this weary and melodramatic convention of the thinker outlawed for his opinions? What was fact in the day of Byron and Shelley has become cant now. Mr. Davidson himself has struck blows almost as fierce as those of the *Man Forbid* at the traditions cherished by most of his countrymen; yet have they howled him across the seas? Do they not placably review—and many of them buy—the poems in which he swings his iconoclastic flail? Why keep the pose, when his slavish but good-natured countrymen will even invite the "man forbid" to dinner—and listen to his dreadful ideas between the courses? (pp. 102-05)

> *Francis Thompson, "Pegasus in Harness," in his*
> The Real Robert Louis Stevenson and Other Critical
> Essays, *edited by Rev. Terence L. Connolly, S.J.,*
> *University Publishers Incorporated, 1959, pp. 102-05.*

WALTER DE LA MARE   (essay date 1906)

[*An English poet, novelist, short story writer, dramatist, and critic, de la Mare is considered one of modern literature's chief exemplars of the romantic imagination. His complete works form a sustained treatment of romantic themes: dreams, death, rare states of mind and emotion, fantasy worlds of childhood, and the pursuit of the transcendent. Best remembered as a poet and writer of children's verse, de la Mare is also recognized for his novel* Memoirs of a Midget *(1921), a study of the social and spiritual outsider, a concern central to de la Mare's work. In the following excerpt, he condemns the didactic message of Davidson's drama* The Theatrocrat.]

"As a fresco in the series of my Testaments, and in order to bring home the matter contained in them by a closer application to life than is possible in dramatic monologue . . . I wrote in the autumn of 1904 *The Theatrocrat:* [*A*] *Tragic Play of Church and Stage.* "A closer application to life"—such, then, was one of Mr. Davidson's aims in writing *The Theatrocrat,* and none is more essential to a play of serious interest. There is but one difficulty—what is life? And to answer this question Mr. Davidson has devoted his energy, his enthusiasm, and his gifts throughout his book. It should follow then that on his answer to this enigma the reader must lay the burden, if dissent he must from the play as a play. And yet, so alien from life, as one conceives it, is the effect produced, that the author's conception does not seem to have influenced his tragedy more than superficially, and that only to its detriment. For the atmosphere of *The Theatrocrat* is that of a dream, dappled, as it were, by glimpses of broadest daylight. It suggests the atmosphere of the drama of the later Elizbethans. The sense of unreality and phantasy that steals over the reader is irresistible. And telephone, motor-car, and americanism serve only to prove that he is dreaming. This is due partly, perhaps, to the rare qualities of the verse, partly to the author's intense personality, but in a greater degree, we think, to the very motive that suggested drama for his medium. We feel that their creator delighted, not in his creatures themselves, moving across the silent stage of his imagination, but in the opinions he was prompting. They, at least, can never rise and accuse their maker of any tendency to anthropomorphosis. He is Fate, indifferent, unapproachable; brooding over the transitory scene. Their speeches made, the thesis expounded, annihilation is their goal.

But although none of the characters steps at any time once for all from dream into bright reality, there are many swift, dramatic touches in the play. In Warwick Groom's fine, heightened speeches, for instance. We stand face to face, too, a moment with Europa Troop; and with Boulder, the commissionaire:—

> "I hissed myself.
> I beg your pardon: I could no more keep
> From hissing than I could from crying out
> When once a dervish stabbed me at Khartoum.
> The gallery felt the same; I asked those near
> What set them on it, and they said they heard
> A hideous hiss that made them hiss like hell."

But the Bishop of St. James's; how willingly would we barter him with all his eloquence and his splendid imagery for another commissionaire—*and* another Testament! For "the play's the thing." Indeed, this very odd Bishop is the Dramatic Monologue that Mr. Davidson intended to supplant. How could he thus have ignored his own creatures' desperate appeal for life and consciousness had he not concentrated his energies elsewhere?

And that "elsewhere" is the poet's Introduction. It is an immense prologue where the theme is mainly the author, and the author's message "to the generation knocking at the door." It cries aloud for readers. It appeals to a public far beyond meek poetry's surmise. It is candid; and in the larger sense, that seems much too large for convenience, it is profoundly immoral. It comes about one's ears like a swarm of bees; and sometimes sweet of the hive. Were there ever so many aggressive, capricious, destructive assertions in so few pages? so many indiscriminate violences? Mr. Davidson's is a gospel of Intellect—beatified Materialism. But it seems rather a forlorn fire to warm one's bones at in this cold world.

> "Here we are left
> Unfriended on the surface, far from home;
> But that imagination which we are,
> Betrayed and lost on this outlandish earth,
> Believes itself to blame."

So says the Bishop, and offers a panacea—"Be matter pure as flame!"

One thing, at any rate, remains unassailable—Mr. Davidson's poetry. His theme allowing, all his mastery returns.

> "What call have I to go?"
>   "The call of night
> By sleepless fancies heard and souls set free.
> The forest calls you in your blood and brain:
> Like spell-bound tides the billowy woodlands sleep;
> Through labyrinthine thickets pencilled beams
> Explode in silvery silence; far withdrawn
> Behind the darknesses of clustered boles
> The emerald forest moonshine glances clear,
> Imprisoned wells of light. Come, Martha, come."

> "I mean to spend my fortune and my life
> In the high service of imagination
> For England's sake and man's."

Forgotten sinks all resentment against the Bishop of St. James's when his voice rings with echoes like that.

Then why must Mr. Davidson ventriloquise? "Message" and play had better have parted company. The benefit would have been mutual. Tragedy needs a prologue less than good wine a bush. (pp. 178-79)

> Walter de la Mare, "The Theatrocrat," in The Bookman, New York, Vol. XXIX, No. 172, January, 1906, pp. 178-79.

THE ACADEMY (essay date 1908)

[*In the following excerpt, the critic offers a condemnatory review of* The Testament of John Davidson. *For Davidson's reply and further discussion of the ensuing controversy, see the entry by Davidson in the Additional Bibliography.*]

The wonderful dulness of the "poetry" which is nowadays issued from the press cannot be denied. England may or may not be a nest of singing-birds, but it is certain that the birds who have managed to pipe publicly of late do not strike one as being in the least over competent. The fact is that with respect to poetry, as with respect to most of the other arts, the world would appear to be too much with us. There are fifty considerations and fifty distractions which our younger performers (not to mention their elders) find it more agreeable to encourage than an austere following of the muse. Of course they are not to be too severely condemned for this, inasmuch as they are constitutionally incapable of real achievement in their own art, and as they believe that they must live somehow it is natural that they should turn their hands to other matters than mere poetry. We have been moved to these remarks by the perusal of a new publication of Mr. John Davidson's which is called, very modestly, *The Testament of John Davidson*. . . . We do not think that Mr. Davidson has ever established any real claim to be considered a poet. On the other hand, he has written a great deal of verse, and a great deal of blank verse, and it is as poet that he wishes to figure before the world. So far as the poetry in the present volume is concerned we have no particular quarrel to pick with the author. He has no doubt done his best, though it is an ill best, and it is comforting to see a man striving, even though he fails. Our complaint about Mr. Davidson is that he cannot apparently be content to exercise the poetical function; he wishes us to take him for a seer and a prophet, and even for a god, and, consequently, he drops out of poetry into a sort of didactic blank verse, and out of didactic blank verse into common prose. . . . [One] is forced to the conclusion that Mr. Davidson writes both prose and verse, not because he has got anything to say, but because he feels it incumbent upon him to say something, and to say that something in a voice which will "attract attention." The dedicatory, or tract-like, portion of Mr. Davidson's dull volume takes the shape of an address to the "Peers Temporal of the United Kingdom of Great Britain and Ireland," and it contains matter which, not to put too fine a point upon it, is eminently unpoetical. The peers temporal are told, among other things that each of them has inherited or accepted a title which he "shares with the Creator of the Universe"—the common title of Lord. Mr. Davidson evidently imagines that this fetch is exceedingly smart, and that it will stamp him at once as an author of large perceptions and daring intellect. He works it in with his opening paragraph, and his pride in it is probably huge. But nobody but Mr. Davidson will be pleased with it. And we very much doubt, even, if it be new, for it seems to us more than likely that it must have occurred long ago to more than one of the zealous Atheistic orators who make Hyde Park and the other open spaces of London so hideous on a Sunday.

It is just this vulgar disposition to say the obviously outrageous and unnecessary thing that makes Mr. Davidson impossible. He is as full of brutal whimsies as an egg is full of meat, and when he has thrown them at you with a great air of genius you find yourself convinced that he is not a genius at all, but a despairing sort of posturer. As a sort of sample of what he can do in prose we may cite the following:

> There have been instances of men able to hold their own intellectually with women; and, indeed, man's rudimentary intellect is only a few marks lower in capacity than that of woman. . . .
> You are on the verge of reversion to a community of goods and women, a community of goods and men; some condition of things in which the old tribal system of polyandry and polygyny, never entirely superseded, will coalesce and become universal. . . . Thus I break the world out of the imaginary chrysalis, or cocoon, or Other World in which it has slumbered so long; and man beholds himself not now as that fabulous monster, half-god, half-devil, of the Christian era, but as Man, the very form and substance of the Universe, the material of eternity, eternity itself, becomes con-

scious and self-conscious. This is the greatest
thing told since the world began.

Mr. Davidson's sententious impudence will deceive nobody.
He is welcome to his own view about the superiority of the
feminine intellect, and we shall be quite willing to admit that
nine women out of ten are the intellectual superiors of Mr.
John Davidson. But we go no further. And when Mr. John
Davidson assures us that we are on the verge of a community
of goods and a community of women, or that he has told us
"the greatest thing since the world began," we know exactly
what manner of mountebank he is. According to the Socialists,
community of goods and community of women are to save the
world. Mr. Davidson is not by any means the discoverer of
this theory. Unfortunately, however, the world prefers to be
damned. And if Mr. Davidson imagines that the gospel of
materialism and the theory that man is God are new under the
sun—and we judge from his prattle about helping the world
out of cocoons that he does—he may take it from us that here
again he is vastly mistaken, and he can prove it for himself
by going round to the nearest free library and looking up the
subjects in an old encyclopaedia. Mr. Davidson is entirely
without a message for his time. It is no disgrace to him that
he should be so lacking. The pity of it is that he should waste
his energies in a vain endeavour to conjure up a sham and
spurious *Testament* which at the very best is an old testament,
and does not belong to John Davidson at all. And if in prose
Mr. Davidson makes himself ridiculous, what shall he not do
in blank verse? This is how he begins:

> When suddenly the world was closed to me,
> And every road against my passage barred,
> I found a door that opened into space;
> I built a lodge celestial for myself,
> An outcast's palace in the Milky Way;
> I banqueted my body and my soul
> On light and sound, the subtance of the stars,
> Ethereal tissue of eternity;
> And took my ease in heaven, the first of men
> To be and comprehend the Universe.

Despite his own view on the subject, Mr. Davidson is no more
the universe than is the next giraffe, and he has no more ultimate comprehension of the universe than the meanest man
that lives. There is nothing for any of us to comprehend which
we do not comprehend, and Mr. Davidson has found no way
out, nor will he or any other man ever find a way out of the
defined limits of human comprehension. It is not poetry to say
the thing which is not, even if you say it in blank-verse. Further
on Mr. Davidson grows very fierce and wild indeed. He gives
us such lines as:

> "Insanity!" the goddess cried; "a wild,
> A sacrilegious lie!"

> Quaternion of elements (vapours three,
> Azote and hydrogen, with oxygen,
> The great protagonist, and carbon, crowd
> And chorus, common tissue of the whole),
> Wherein the ether lightened into life
> Organical—amoebae, monera,
> Bacteria, diatoms, single cells
> That sped through differentiation, changed
> Environment and series manifold.
> By natural selection and sexual.

> *I come,* I said; and sang the body of man:—
> Mucus, the blood unlit; on fire as blood;
> In flesh, compact and baked like earthenware;

> In nerve as pith; as mineral in bone;
> Fibrous in muscle; and in the viscera,
> Vegetal; repeating, in the microcosm,
> Electron, atom, system, universe.

We suppose that this is some of the blank verse which the
Athenaeum describes as beautiful, and which has even ravished
the heart of *The Guardian,* and for ourselves we are free to
own that we do not like it, and that nothing could induce us
to like it. It is just vicious and undesirable metricism. And,
quite apart from considerations of verse, we are treated to
paraphrases of the *Freethinker* like the following:

> "I know of Him,"
> I said, eager to speak. "The sorcery
> Whereby he seemed to quell the other gods
> Was twofold. First and foremost, reiterant
> Assertion of supreme dominion, *I
> Am I; there is no God but Me,* assailed
> The Jewish mind for ages, and destroyed
> The sense of hearing for the voice of gods
> Less arrogant. To make Himself renowned
> Beyond all rivalry, in mythic times
> Jehovah had proclaimed Himself the world's
> Creator, never imagining that men
> Would wrest its secret from the Universe.
> Howbeit, long before we understood
> That all things of themselves evolved, His boast—
> He had pronounced the whole creation good!—
> Exposed Him to derision—great indeed,
> The world was and will always be, but good
> It never can become."

So that one way and another Mr. John Davidson evidently
imagines that he, at any rate, is not only superman but super-
god. We all know the tag as to the alliance of great wit and
madness. The relation of little wit to idiocy is strikingly borne
in upon us by this preposterous volume. (pp. 439-40)

> *"The Supergod," in* The Academy, *Vol. LXXV, No.
> 1905, November 7, 1908, pp. 439-40.*

HOLBROOK JACKSON (essay date 1913)

[*An English essayist, editor, and literary historian, Jackson was
closely associated with a number of London periodicals during
his career, among them* The New Age, T. P. O'Connor's Weekly
and Magazine, *and* To-Day, *his own pocket journal which contained contributions from prominent writers such as Walter de la
Mare, John Drinkwater, T. S. Eliot, and Ezra Pound. However,
he is best remembered for his* The Eighteen Nineties *(1913), a
comprehensive study of late nineteenth-century arts and letters
which is regarded as an invaluable documentation of that era. In
the following excerpt from that work, Jackson surveys prominent
characteristics of Davidson's works, placing them in the context
of the fin-de-siècle period in England.*]

The Eighteen Nineties had no more remarkable mind and no
more distinctive poet than John Davidson. From the beginning
he was both an expression of and a protest against the decadent
movement, and in his personality as well as in his tragic end
he represented the struggle and defeat of his day in the cause
of a bigger sense of life and a greater power over personality
and destiny. . . . [Curiously] enough, as in the case of so many
of those who gained distinction in art during the period, John
Davidson did not show any distinctive *fin de siècle* characteristics until he produced his novel, *Perfervid,* in 1890; and between that time and 1899 he remained an artist in the approved

Whistlerian sense, content in the main to express life in the traditional artistic manner, without any overweening desire to preach a particular doctrine. With the close of the decade his mental attitude seems to have undergone a revolution, which translated him from an artist pure and simple into a philosophic missioner using literature as a means of propaganda. (p. 177)

The poetry of John Davidson reveals on most pages a keen sense of life in its various manifestations struggling for power of one kind or another. His imagination is essentially dramatic, but his sense of conflict is often philosophic, his artistic sense always showing a tendency to give way to the imp of reflection which, through his imagination, was ever seeking to turn drama into philosophy and philosophy into science. Yet he was not immune from a certain whimsicality, particularly in his early prose works, in the fantastic novels, *Perfervid, Earl Lavender,* and *Baptist Lake,* and still more certainly, with a surer touch of genius, in his pantomime *Scaramouch in Naxos.* In the "Prologue" to this play, spoken by Silenus, Davidson goes far towards summing up his own peculiar attitude. The speaker alludes to a fondness for pantomimes, and proceeds to say:

> I don't know whether I like this one so well as those which I witnessed when I was a boy. It is too pretentious, I think; too anxious to be more than a Pantomime—this play in which I am about to perform. True *Pantomime* is a good-natured nightmare. Our sense of humour is titillated and strummed, and kicked and oiled, and fustigated and stroked, and exalted and bedevilled, and, on the whole, severely handled by this self-same harmless incubus; and our intellects are scoffed at. The audience, in fact, is, intellectually, a pantaloon, on whom the Harlequin-pantomime has no mercy. It is frivolity whipping its schoolmaster, commonsense; the drama on its apex; art, unsexed, and without a conscience; the reflection of the world in a green, knotted glass. Now, I talked to the author and showed him that there was a certain absence from his work of this kind of thing; but he put his thumbs in his arm-pits, and replied with some disdain, "Which of the various dramatic forms of the time may one conceive as likeliest to shoot up in the fabulous manner of the beanstalk, bearing on its branches things of earth and heaven undreamt of in philosophy? The sensational dramas? Perhaps from them some new development of tragic art; but Pantomime seems to be of best hope. It contains in crude forms, humour, poetry, and romance. It is childhood of a new poetical comedy." Then I saw where he was and said, "God be with you," and washed my hands of him.

Here we have Davidson, as early as 1888, concerned about something new in art, something elastic enough to contain a big expression of modernity, of that modernity which in the Eighteen Nineties, and in John Davidson more than in any other British writer of the time, was more than half reminiscent of the classical Greek idea of eternal conflict.

But with Davidson and the moderns, led philosophically by Nietzsche, Davidson's earliest master, the eternal conflict was not regarded with Greek resignation. It was looked upon as a thing which might be directed by the will of man. The modern idea was to make conflict a means of growth towards power:

the stone upon which man might sharpen the metal of his will until he could literally storm high heaven by his own might. Such an idea, often vague and chaotic enough, inspired the hour, making philosophers of artists and artists of philosophers, and seekers after a new elixir of life of all who were sufficiently alive to be modern. This idea, more than any other, informed the moods of the moment with restless curiosity and revolt. It filled the optimist with the conviction that he lived in a glorious period of transition which might at any moment end in Utopia, and the pessimist with the equally romantic notion that the times were so much out of joint that nothing short of their evacuation for the past or the future would avail. As Davidson sang:

> The Present is a dungeon dark
> Of social problems. Break the gaol!
> Get out into the splendid Past
> Or bid the splendid Future hail.

This resentment of the present was always Davidson's weakness despite an intellectual courage in which he had few equals in his time.

He could face with heroic fortitude the necessity of revaluing ideas, just as he could face the necessity of revaluing his own life by suicide. But he could not face the slings and arrows of outrageous fortune. He never realised that a man and his age were identical, or that tragedy was an essential of life to be courted even by the powerful. ("Deep tragedy," said Napoleon, "is the school of great men.") Instead of that he murmured against that which thwarted and checked him, regretting the absence of might to mould the world for his own convenience. That was his contribution to the decadence. The bigness of him, unknown to himself, was the fact that he did fight for the integrity of his own personality and ideas, and he did accomplish their conservation, even to rounding off his own life-work with a final "testament." But when one has said all one is forced to admit that the irregularities and incongruities of his genius were nothing less than the expression and mark of his time.

It is as a poet that Davidson must ultimately stand or fall, although the philosophy he expressed in his later volumes will doubtless attract far more attention than that which greeted its inception. (pp. 181-83)

Of his later intentions he declared, "I begin definitely in my Testaments and Tragedies to destroy this unfit world and make it over again in my own image." He was never weary of asserting the novelty of his aim and method, and although he admitted that there was no language for what he had to say, he was convinced that what he had said was both new in form and idea. "It is a new poetry I bring, a new poetry for the first time in a thousand years." He called this new poetry "an abiding-place for man as matter-of-fact," and his own purpose in writing it, "to say that which is, to speak for the universe." And the ultimate aim of such work was, again in his own words, "to change the mood of the world."

Nor was he less precise, nor less frank, in stating the new mood he would establish in the place of the old. In the *fin de siècle* search for reality few possessed his diligence, fewer his intellectual courage. The terrible and powerful poem, **"A Woman and Her Son,"** recalls something of his own unrelenting criticism of life; his own determination at all costs to face facts and re-value ideas:

> These are times
> When all must to the crucible—no thought,
> Practice, or use, or custom sacro-sanct
> But shall be violable now.

Early association with the ideas of Nietzsche had directed Davidson's innate pessimism into channels of creative inquisitiveness and speculation. He learnt more from Nietzsche than did any other poet of his time, but he never became a disciple. He learnt of that philosophical courage which Nietzsche called "hardness," and used it Nietzsche-wise in his continual questioning and re-valuing of accepted ideas. He was imbued also with the German philosopher's reverence for power. But he did not accept the Superman doctrine. This he repudiated equally with the Darwinian idea of sexual selection; both stood condemned by him because of their anthropomorphism—what in fact Nietzsche condemned in other directions as being "human-all-too-human." Against the idea of evolution by sexual selection, with the ultimates man and then superman, he set the idea of chemical selection, with the ultimate object of complete self-consciousness. Beyond self-consciousness he saw nothing; that in his view was the highest possible achievement of life. The essence of his teaching is based in the idea of Matter as the final manifestation of ether seeking, first, consciousness, which it has long since attained, and next, self-consciousness, which it has attained more recently in man. This last form of consciousness, according to Davidson, is capable of the highest ecstasy and all knowledge. He denies the inconceivability of eternity, the existence at any time of chaos, and the presence at any time of spirit. All is Matter, even the ether and the lightning are forms of Matter. And on this basis he works out a conception of sin as courage, heaven and hell as "memories of processes of evolution struggling into consciousness," and God as ether, from which man came and to which he will return. (pp. 189-90)

In announcing this theory of the universe he does not ask for scientific judgment or acceptance. He bases his claim for recognition on imaginative grounds and on the fact that he is a poet. "The world," he wrote, "is in danger of a new fanaticism, of a scientific instead of a religious tyranny. This is my protest. In the course of many ages the mind of man may be able to grasp the world scientifically: in the meantime we can know it only poetically; science is still a valley of dead bones till imagination breathes upon it." It was his desire as a poet to fill the conceptions of science, the world of atoms and electrons, of gases and electricity, of ether and matter, with the light of imagination, as a substitute for the dead rationalism of middle nineteenth-century culture.

> Art knows very well that the world comes to an end when it is purged of Imagination. Rationalism was only a stage in the process. For the old conception of a created Universe, with the fall of man, an atonement, and a heaven and hell, the form and substance of the imagination of Christendom, Rationalism had no substitute. Science was not ready, but how can poetry wait? Science is synonymous with patience; poetry is impatience incarnate. If you take away the symbol of the Universe in which, since the Christian era began, poetry and all great art lived and had their being, I, for one, decline to continue the eviscerated Life-in-Death of Rationalism. I devour, digest, and assimilate the Universe; make for myself in my Testaments and Tragedies a new form and substance of Imagination; and by poetic power certify the semi-certitudes of science.

In the Eighteen Nineties John Davidson strove always for the utterance of such feelings and ideas as absorbed his mind during his last years; but in the earlier period he was less conscious of definite aim, and his best work took the form of poetry and the place of great poetry. His ballads and eclogues, a few of his lyrics and passages in his poetic tragedies are already graven on the scroll of immortal verse. His "testaments" belonged to another realm as they belong also to another period. They lack the old fine flavour of the poetry of his less purposeful days, and they hardly fulfil his own promise of a new poetry. They are in the main arrested poetry. The strife of the poet for a new expression, a new poetic value, is too evident, and you lay these later works down baffled and unconvinced, but reverent before the courage and honesty of a mind valiantly beating itself to destruction against the locked and barred door of an unknown and perhaps non-existent reality. (pp. 191-92)

> Holbrook Jackson, "John Davidson," in his The Eighteen Nineties: A Review of Art and Ideas at the Close of the Nineteenth Century, *1913. Reprint by Humanities Press, 1976, pp. 177-92.*

HAYIM FINEMAN   (lecture date 1916)

[*In the following excerpt from his* John Davidson: A Study of the Relation of His Ideas to His Poetry, *Fineman closely examines Davidson's philosophy of scientific materialism.*]

Problems of cosmology, heaven, hell and sin loom large in all [Davidson's] poetry of the early nineties; for his upbringing in the environment of the kirk made these problems the very essence of life to him. When he lost his faith in God his serious Scotch mind could not live in mere negation or assume permanently the attitude of becoming a mere "thoroughfare for all the pageantry of time." His natural avenue of escape was a naïve materialism. That this materialism should have consisted largely in expounding modifications of Oswald Haeckel and others is incidental, and was probably due to his early training as a chemist and to the popularization of energistic monism at the close of the last century.

The relationship between Davidson's own mental proclivities and the Nietzschean ethics that he adopts is of the same character. The resemblance between Davidson's ethics and Nietzsche's immoral ideals are indeed many and striking. Davidson seemingly accepts practically all of Nietzsche's cardinal ideas, such as the will-to-power, class morality and *amor fati*. He is merely non-committal about the Eternal Recurrence and opposes definitely only one conception of Nietzsche—that of the Overman. The acceptance of Nietzsche's cardinal ethical tests is necessarily accompanied by an agreement with Nietzsche's corollaries on Socialism, government, woman, sin, asceticism, and Christianity. Even more close are the similarities between Nietzsche's views on art and Davidson's opinions on poetry. They both agree that poetry is essentially "the affirmation, the blessing, and deification of existence" and both oppose naked realism. . . . Both furthermore believed that poetic creation is the outcome of a tyrannical will which stamps its image on all things. . . . Yet these numerous likenesses notwithstanding, Davidson can hardly be called a disciple of Nietzsche. In his later work he passes the Nietzschean ideas through a materialistic crucible so that they practically become amplifications of his own point of view: Human beings should indeed, as Nietzsche says, be hard and not hesitate to cause pain, but this time for a new reason, namely, that matter demands this hardness is order to attain self-consciousness. Similarly man is to be a yea-sayer because all is matter and he should be proud of the fact that the entire universe is eager to become man. Finally man is to love the beauty and power of this world because there is no other world and such are the laws of matter. The chief reason why those ideas are adopted by Davidson is evidently because they harmonize with his own proclivities. As early as 1886, before he even heard of the name of Nietzsche, he already expressed a point of view approximating the Nietzschean in his play **Smith**. For Nietzsche's criticism of ethics is not so much a philosophy as a persistent emotional mood. Many of the attitudes, usually described as Nietzschean, were assumed, though with less poignancy and consistency, by many minds who preceded Nietzsche. Davidson felt some of those moods himself and formal Nietzschean thought merely intensified tendencies that already possessed him.

It is thus out of his own emotional moods that Davidson constructed his "new" poetry. If monism and certain ethical ideals did become with him a source of poetry it was only because they enriched his consciousness of life and thus served as an emotional cause. But such a condition could not be produced by a mere arbitrary superimposition of a foreign system of thought on one's feelings. Philosophy in a poet becomes a potent factor only when it augments preëxistent emotional states. Such at least was evidently the case with John Davidson. Certain ideas with which he started out kept on returning in his works with a steady recurrence of waves; each wave encroaching with greater volume of added thought a trifle further in the same direction. Those points of view gradually became conscious processes with him; they gathered to themselves sinews and flesh from various sources and at last became a systematic living whole; and as such they influenced intimately and determined the character of his most important work.

The significance of the realization that the primary origins of Davidson's ideas lie in a personal disposition of mind rather than in systems of thought offered by others becomes evident the moment one examines the relationship between his philosophy and his poetry. They both have a common origin and are practically inseparable. A healthy mind assimilates indeed a great deal of material; but it selects and rejects new ideas and experiences on a basis of like and dislike. It culls those suggestions that harmonize with its own tendencies and frequently constructs a system of thought that is really but an amplification of what it unconsciously felt before. Such at least seems to have been the process followed by Davidson in the development of his thought; whence its intimate relationship with his growth as a poet. There is thus a distinct continuity of ideas prevailing throughout all his work. Philosophic concepts were to him at all times a source of emotional strength and were usually presented as emotional attitudes. Even in his earlier work . . . the chief source of his strength was the search for the meaning of life. Since in his later poetry the greater keenness of thought in evidence was not a new current but an increase in the volume of a stream already flowing in his earlier work, there can be said to be no real change in the direction of thought or general characteristics of his poetry. His consciousness essentially metaphysical, invigorated by a thought that involved a general vision of the universe and a certain philosophic consistency, merely increased the intensity of his poetry. This increase of intensity is, however, very significant. Till Davidson created for himself his materialistic philosophy he was, his theory of art for life's sake notwithstanding, a minor poet struggling vaguely though passionately with a few modern situations and achieving a boat song in Scaramouch, a song or two in the eclogues, a few ballads suggestive of the turmoil of his age, and a few tender lyrics. In the main he was doing with slight variations, though with a sweetness and strength

that was his own, what Henley and Kipling had already accomplished. He was a poet of "empire" verse; of London poverty; of the turbulent elements of modern thought;—with an intense love of life, and a passionate delicacy. Now, under the inspiration of an intenser thought, his former concepts broaden out and he becomes a nature poet in the Lucretian sense. He does not try to describe semi-literary moods aroused within him by the presence of sea or sky nor does he attempt to construct an ideal nature out of bits of impressions of the real world. Instead he recreates in his Testaments objectively and philosophically the world and its processes. (pp. 30-3)

Attempts at putting modern scientific thought into verse were made in half-hearted fashion in English poetry before Davidson. Tennyson's "move eastward happy earth" and his exactitude of scientific knowledge in "Break thou deep vase of chilling tears That grief has shaken into frost" had already startled an earlier generation of readers. James Thomson, and even Robert Browning, likewise contribute their share in the poetic rendering of scientific ideas. But these touch the mere fringe. Davidson becomes *the* poet par excellence of natural creation. The creative processes of nature become the chief source of his inspiration. He dwells in a palace in the skies and sings of ether "eternal, stretching taut in bourneless space," "a sheer oblivous ecstacy"; of the wakening of the hungry lightning; of hydrogen's "first condensation of the infinite"; of passionate molecules swelling into "sumptuous nebulae"; of earth and neighboring worlds "shedding asteroids like a fiery sweat"; of "Earth delivered of its moon, And chilled without and tempered to endure Barbaric sculpture of the glacier." Then he proceeds to sing of the sifting of the elements that become warp and woof of life; of telluric history and of the deluge of fire,

> Compacture fierce and winnowing tides of air
> That forged and tempered and engraved the earth
> Enamelled it with sapphire seas and hung
> An emerald veil about its nakedness.

He traces in fervent glow the origin of species: "sex from ether strained as lightning," embodied in protoplasm; life organical speeding through differentiation "into the rose, the oak tree and the wine and unto men and women"; the brain, "the goal Unconscious lightning aimed at when it led The onset of eternity to man." Finally he reveals the very birth of the Gods and narrates their gradual destruction; the death of our earth that shall reel to its doom "orbit-slipped" or

> The weight of ice amassed at either pole
> Shall change our axis till a deluge wipe
> The citied world away.

As a poet of Nature Davidson is far indeed from being altogether successful. Though he places the entire world on his canvas and from a philosophic height judges everything that occurs within his ken, he cannot live long in the rare atmosphere of his heights. He fails to produce a single sustained effort in the manner of Lucretius. He expresses himself only fragmentarily in Testaments. Piecemeal he communicates that the world should rid itself of its past; that man is made of the same substance as the furthest stars and should therefore lustily enjoy the world and not be afraid of life or pain, "the growing labors of the universe"; and that the other world is at last to be destroyed. His visions of the processes of nature are presented in the Testaments and Tragedies only incidentally and spasmodically. He sees clearly only the outer causes of phenomena in their general outlines: but his vision of the details into which infinity disintegrates itself is often blurred. The precision that one does find in his work is frequently purchased at the expense of his becoming rhetorical or even through his producing mere prosaic cataloguing effects. His Hell is thus magnificently terrible in its general conception: he understands its suffering and interprets it with a tragic irony by making the "winnowing" space between Heaven and Hell mellow

> the shriek of women and the roar
> Of men into immortal harmony.

But when he comes to depict details, he offers an enumeration that is indeed impressive enough because of its sheer accumulative force, but yet resolves itself into mere rhetoric largely because the poet is perhaps in too great haste to deliver his message rather than sustain his imaginative powers by feeling intensely the details he visualizes. His poetry thus even in its highest moods frequently turns into violent rhapsody. This rhetorical quality is usually however the result of impatience rather than limitation of poetic powers and perturbs but slightly the general impression. In moments of calmer inspiration, Davidson's poetry has a grandeur of vision in the presence of which shrivels even Tennyson's "ambrosial air" that rolls "from the gorgeous gloom of evening" driving fancy "from belt to belt of crimson seas." Davidson's agonies of star dust fill the mind with a keener sense of everlastingness. His ability to view nature as a complete process disintegrating itself into mountains, oceans, flowers and men, works subtle magic into scenes conceived even on a smaller scale. The very declivities "that creep Unhonored to the ocean's shifting verge" communicate a feeling of suppressed energy due to a subconsciousness that the poet is aware that soon the willing earth will "leap to the bosom of the sun to be Pure flame once more in a new time begun." Purged by this pure flame, a dignity of mood and restrained melancholy of thought permeates his work. The very deformities of men and women that he describes with startling energy cease to be ugly sickening details: they are sublimated into processes of nature. In the height of his vision there is no room for meaningless details or mawkishness of sentiment. His images become gaunt, exact, intense, honest. His largeness of conception is, moreover, uttered in a rhythm of blank verse that rises to the occasion and contains a dignity and sweep that is Miltonic.

The same grandeur of the scale of vision makes possible the construction of his later tragedies that are attempts at producing world-dramas in which the significance of materialistic thought is the theme. The limitations of those plays are likewise evident enough. They are largely polemics in dramatic form; for Davidson does not start out with definite conceptions of characters or dramatic situations that are to be fitted into a general scheme but deliberately composes characters and situations in order to convey through them certain ideas. In *The Theatrocrat* the whole play thus resolves itself into message. Characters who hear the Davidsonian gospel are at once convinced; for the doctrine of materialism is "not to be apprehended but to be felt." Thus no serious attempt is made by Davidson in the play to reveal the process of character transformation or to trace rigorously the effects that this transformation produces on individual conduct. The most effective parts of the tragedy are those that contain an exposition of materialism and that attempt to appreciate the significance of religion as a cultural factor in the world's civilization. Davidson realizes clearly that all culture is based on some form of religion. He understands that the opposition to God will be fought by women "with babes at their breast" to the last drop of blood. All that have suf-

fered—those whose children and lovers are dead—will rise to defend the other world. It requires therefore great courage "to bid the dream avaunt once and forever." But though wars and convulsions will follow, the great truth must out; and the world will be thrilled with the splendor and terror of seeing itself without symbols. For in itself the universe is "a becoming, a passion and a pain, A rapt imagination." Davidson therefore hurls himself in passionate fury against the world, producing however as a result, not "a drama of church and state" but a rhetorical polemic containing here and there a few impressive rhapsodical visions. (pp. 34-7)

Similarly impressive are Davidson's attempts at expressing himself at the close of his poetic career in lyric poems, ballads, and dramatic monologues. These briefer poems are artistically more successful than his plays because in them he can make a passionate plea for his ideas without the need of entering into digressions. The entire poem becomes from beginning to end a means of conveying a single undivided mood. The very novelty of his philosophic point of view, moreover, gives an intensity to the moods and emotions that he elects to express. In *Holiday and Other Poems* and in *Fleet Street and Other Poems* Davidson is thus enabled to portray life effectively from the standpoint of the poet who enthroned himself above the galaxy and understands the entire universe from a cosmic rather than human morality. The dominating tone in back of the Holiday volume is thus that it is good to be alive, for life is the reason why we are here. . . . In the new eclogues ether and nebula seem to have lit his blood and he paints in the colors of the dawn. . . . His poems lack however the freshness that some of his earlier work contained; and the frequent use of Poe's repetend in his versification certainly does not lend them any youthfulness. The repetend has indeed something elemental about it; for like parallelism it carries one back to the very beginning of poetry; but it savors of the simplicity of age rather than of youth.

In *Fleet Street and Other Poems* poetry is written from the same heights but it deals with the work-a-day world. It describes satirically the stupid mob in the **"Crystal Palace"** enjoying its holiday; the insufferable bores one meets on **"Road and Rail";** the complacent forest folk; and the gutter merchants with their palsied souls and numbed affections. The drabness of the life of the railway stations seemingly enters his soul, and the hell of the unfit is lugged out for inspection. Davidson of the Fleet Street volume contemplates rather than feels the life that he sees. Accordingly he reasons, pleads, denounces, and expresses himself in parables that read like protestations of faith. This argumentative tone is seemingly partly the product of an apprehension that there be no one after him to feel intensely the full significance of the "message" that he wanted to deliver to his contemporaries. . . . He is therefore determined to do almost anything in his power in order to express himself unmistakably and he writes accordingly satires and parables in the *Fleet Street* volume and explanatory prefaces, dedications and notes in his other works in order to supplement and interpret the thoughts expressed in his testaments, plays and briefer poems.

This stupendous conception of his own value is with Davidson not so much an outgrowth of arrogance as of despair lest he may have lived his hard life in vain; a sentiment tempered by a dread that soon he will be compelled "to turn aside and attempt things for which people will pay." When he is more hopeful the arrogant tone is transformed into a courage that slays every dejection and "seeth the abyss but with the eagle's eye." He remembers that even the most repulsive flesh is great because it dares to live. . . . Similarly in his later eclogues the poet reflects that "harvests in winter's bosom sleep." This courageous tone is expressed most effectively in a poem like his epilogue to *The Testament of John Davidson:* . . .

> My feet are heavy now, but on I go,
> My head erect beneath the tragic years.
> The way is steep, but I would have it so;
> And dusty, but I lay the dust with tears,
> Though one can see me weep: alone I climb
> The rugged path that leads me out of time—
>   Out of time and out of all,
>   Singing yet in sun and rain,
>   "Heel and toe from dawn to dusk,
>   Round the world and home again."
>
> Farewell the hope that mocked, farewell despair
> That went before me still and made the pace.
> The earth is full of graves, and mine was there
> Before my life began, my resting place;
> And I shall find it out and with the dead
> Lie down for ever, all my saying said—
>   Deeds all done and songs all sung,
>   -While others chant in sun and rain,
>   "Heel and toe from dawn to dusk,
>   Round the world and home again."

In such a swan song he gave expression to the fullest compass of his emotions; to a manliness, an ecstacy of metaphysical vision and a subdued tragic feeling aroused by his sense of eternity. (pp. 41-4)

Imperfect as these later lyric poems, testaments and tragedies are, they represent not merely his maturest thought but also his most significant work. He personally considered these later productions as his greatest creations, and his opinion on the matter was unerring. That which he suggested unconsciously as a young man in his poetry in Scotland, and passionately strove to attain in the poetry of his growing manhood in the eighteen nineties, he definitely achieved in the full consciousness of his powers in his poems of the early twentieth century. In comparison with his more popular poems of the preceding decade his later work thus reveals a greater depth of vision, and intenser emotion and a greater hold on the understanding of the essentials of life. His technical skill displays a corresponding growth. He handles verse with more triumphant effectiveness. Blank verse is not only to Davidson "a supreme relief of nervous tension, the fullest discharge of emotion, the greatest deliverance of energy," but it communicates at its best to the reader a feeling of everlastingness and supreme contentment that one associates only with the most powerful and most permanent poetry. (p. 44)

Davidson had a mind that was essentially metaphysical; whence much of his poetry is full of a dignity that is sublime. Because the moods in most of his songs spring from a philosophic vision they not merely allure; they stimulate. His philosophy may be wrong but the emotion that it arouses is genuine and has a meaning to all who face things. If materialism is wrong, some other process is right; in either case the impending agonies of stars, the viewing of the world from an eternal aspect, cannot lose meaning. There may be another world; and the soul, in spite of Davidson, may be immortal; but Davidson's *amor fati*, his determination to live bravely, are bound to have meaning as long as courage means anything to the human mind.

It is a simple matter to enumerate Davidson's limitations; for he tried to create in his later works the well-nigh impossible: a poetry based on an ethics that was new and almost meaningless to his generation. Staggering under such stupendous attempt, his mind was evidently in a continuous state of tension and was impelled by a desire of propaganda that was unfortunately not relegated to prefaces and epilogues. Goaded on by a lust for dissemination of doctrine and by a passion for scientific detail he frequently became prosaic or rhapsodic. His very satiric powers, in spite of an intense moral passion, thus became impaired. He moreover lacked the power of sustained thought and naturally sought expression in forms that are loose. He did not elaborate his poetic ideas patiently but turbulently burst forth again and again with a passion that overpowered the mind and the imagination but failed to hold them altogether prisoner. He could interpret well perhaps only one human passion—the search for truth. Finally from the standpoint of thought value—the quality that to him was most significant—his poetry was largely a record of failure to solve the great problems that tortured him throughout life. In his "pleasures of youth" he thus insisted that love is the secret of the world—a thought that survived in a modified form to the very end. His attitude towards love was semi-metaphysical from the outset. Even in his early poems love was conceived not as a touch of finger tips nor as a wanton lust but as an ecstasy of creative desire. She later became his mate and joyously journeyed with him "Right into the heart of the sun On the morning or evening tide." But love failed to explain his universe; for the world's suffering gripped him—a ghost that he never laid. With pride he asserted in earlier days that a man is what he makes himself; yet the feeling that man can make himself only at the cost of suffering to others gnawed his conscience. Even after he had accepted in his later philosophy the seemingly inevitable by asserting that suffering—the whining of the rotting match girl— was the growing pains of the world that should not daunt, he still partly felt that he was evading an issue. Then the significance of sin, denial, and the glory of the world demanded solution; and he finally evolved through his own thinking and reading a system that served him as an explanation. This system of materialism was based on moods rather than on well-reasoned scientific or philosophic thought. It indeed satisfied, no matter whether right or wrong, his imagination and gave to his poetry consistency of thought, grandeur of vision and intensity of form. It did not however enable him to create a new poetry in the sense that he conceived it. He only talked of a new pathos; but he really did not create it. His poetry was new only in the sense that all original poetry is new. It did not offer a statement of the naked world freed of all symbols and of all traditions, but rather expressed Davidson's particular moods— lofty, passionate and philosophic. But though his poetry was not "a new poetry for the first time in a thousand years" yet Davidson's significance is none the less great. His very failures communicate a sense of power. As a thinker he helped to stem artistic pose and unimaginative naturalism and through the invigorating robustness of his poems gave direction to the new movements in English poetry. Though his own work is not free from the tangle of rhetorical verbiage, yet his insistence on the need of genuineness of thought and emotion helped to clear the air of a great deal of imitativeness. His attacks on matter-of-fact realism and his endeavors to create poetry on a basis that harmonized with what he thought was the most permanent in the temper of his own time were healthy seminal tendencies of a big mind. Finally he has created some of the most daring ballads and lyrical poems of the late nineteenth century full of a tenderness and earthiness and passionate thought that are peculiarly his own. His semi-dramatic poems contain an exaltation, a rush of power, and a largeness of utterance that thrill with their vastness. His poetry on cosmology, full of fervor and grandeur of vision, undoubtedly occupies a unique position in English literature. He falls indeed short of the greatest. He saw however visions of great things and his failures are due to his not resting satisfied with anything short of eternity. The contributions that he offered to English literature are therefore living poetry and his memory will remain significant to all to whom daring of thought and genuineness of poetic feeling are precious. (pp. 46-8)

Hayim Fineman in his John Davidson: A Study of the Relation of His Ideas to His Poetry, *University of Pennsylvania, 1916, 51 p.*

PADRAIC COLUM (essay date 1918)

[*An Irish poet, dramatist, editor, and critic, Colum was one of the major writers of the Irish Literary Renaissance. He was most noted for his efforts to make better-known the varied heritage of Irish literature through his writings and public lectures, but he is perhaps most important as a historical dramatist who established many precedents for the Irish national theater. Colum's poetry incorporated his knowledge of dramatic technique; in addition, his poems are admired because they do not display the nationalistic didacticism so prevalent in the poetry of his contemporaries. Because of his close and genuine links with the people and culture of Ireland, he is considered one of the few authentic national poets of Ireland. In the following excerpt, Colum discusses Davidson's philosophical views as presented in the "Testaments" and* Mammon and His Message.*]*

Is there in [Davidson's Testaments and his tragedy *Mammon and his Message*] anything of that which would justify his assumption of authority and the claim which he makes for the medium of his utterance? I, for one, think there is. If you are not repelled by a philosophy which has Zarathustra's destructiveness without Zarathustra's austerity you will find in his four Testaments and in *Mammon and his Message* astonishing eloquence, with imaginative fantasy and frequent passages of startling beauty.

We can best understand his thought if we begin by recognizing it as "theocentric." Like Francis Thompson, John Davidson is compelled to see everything as centering round God. With Thompson this makes for humility while with Davidson it makes for more and more violent self-assertion. John Davidson was a Calvinist through and through. Now you cannot take God from a man who is a Calvinist. Prove that the universality of matter leaves no place for God in the universe and you plant God in his own bosom. So it was with Davidson. He declares himself a materialist, but he is constantly asserting something about God. Finally, as matter in its highest self-consciousness, he himself is the end of all things, he himself is God. Then the world process is seen as a Calvinistic syllogism: there is still the elect and the reprobate, but the elect is now the beautiful, the strong, the assertive; while the reprobate is the ill-formed, the weak, the resigned.

Into his four Testaments and into his *Mammon and his Message* he has poured the full strength of a remarkable poetic power. Comparisons are a feeble help to judgment in such things, but one could compare Davidson's blank verse with Tennyson's or Browning's or Shelley's and say that it is as potent as theirs. One's response is the best test of poetry, and in a passage like this where Davidson's delight in vibrant life has full sweep, response becomes an ungrudging acknowledgment of the poet's

power. The man in *The Testament of an Empire-Builder* hears in a dream the beasts speak, and listens to the nag exult in its ancestry:

> Those valiant hearts
> Triumphant in the combat for the mares
> When the great miracle of grass begins,
> And simple emerald blades elaborate
> The soul of earth, the virtue of the sun,
> Replenishing the sexes—how might they,
> Those hearts of stallions eager for a heaven
> Of fragrant manes, wild glances, quivering flanks,
> Wherein to root their admirable race—
> How might they lose their courage, how admit
> The treacherous fear that undermines the will?

The poetry of the Testaments is constantly rising into such passages.

His four Testaments are the Evangels of Materialism. In the *Testament of a Vivisector,* we have the defense of a man who seeks through torture for pure knowledge—who in the end tortures for the sake of torturing. In *The Testament of a Man Forbid* we have the confession of one who cried to humanity to cast away their three thousand years of culture and to cease to balance libraries on their polls. In *The Testament of a Prime Minister* we have the statement of a politician who is led to renounce his career, because he has seen how crime and misery can make a man great by putting him beyond good and evil. In *The Testament of an Empire-Builder*—he might be Clive or he might be Cecil Rhodes—we have the gospel of exploitation and the announcement that the strong shall not only inherit the earth, but they shall have the heavens also, and that the weak shall not only be condemned in this life, but they shall be damned for all eternity.

The thesis that runs all through Davidson's poetry is that the soul is matter become self-conscious and that matter becomes more and more self-conscious through pain. The whole world process is towards the experience of more and more intensity of pain. This idea, fiercely expressed in his last, is present in his first poems:

> To reach the mood august in which we know we suffer pain—
> Napoleon! I am greater by this woe and by this chain.

The logical consequence of his idea is present in his last work. If there is nothing beyond the self-consciousness that matter attains to in us, why should we not experience at once all the pain and all the rapture there is in life? Why should we not live it all now? Davidson's characters attempt to make such a realization.—

> *We* have come after! *We* are posterity,
> And time it is we had another world
> Than this in which mankind excreted soul,
> Sexless and used and immaterial.
> Clear a space profane, that men at last
> May be themselves, the conscious universe!
> Who asks a higher task, a nobler game,
> A more heroic agony?

So speaks the King of Thule who has taken to himself the name of Mammon and who has begun a crusade against Christianity.

If we are repelled by the Testaments because of their alien and threatening psychology and their resolute attempt to transcend good and evil, what are we to say of the play that has for its hero one who is a parricide and a fratricide, a ravisher and a torturer, and the declared foe of the Christian idea? No point is made by saying that *Mammon and His Message* is immoral— it is intended to be immoral. We must read it as we read Marlowe's mad play. And it justifies itself by lifting the imagination by fervent rhetoric and by the spectacle it gives of unbridled power. It is the modern version of Tambourlaine. (pp. 311-12)

Padraic Colum, "The Poet of Armageddon: John Davidson," in The New Republic, *Vol. XIII, No. 167, January 12, 1918, pp. 310-12.*

CORNELIUS WEYGANDT (essay date 1937)

[*A historian and critic, Weygandt was one of the first American scholars to examine contemporary Irish drama, introducing its major practitioners to American readers in his* Irish Plays and Playwrights (1913). *In the following excerpt, Weygandt's discussion of Davidson's work indicates the poet's declining critical reputation.*]

John Davidson . . . has still his old magic for youth. I never put him on a reading list in my course in contemporary poetry but I get enthusiastic reviews of his ballads and eclogues, and even, sometimes, of his testaments. He is not to me now what he was when I was young. Yet I remember as if it were yesterday the time when he was wine to me. I was so weak from typhoid fever when Bert Brown brought me *Ballads and Songs* . . . in the late April or early May of 1895 that it took all my strength to sit up in bed. It was a Sunday afternoon that he came with the book, in those old days when Sunday afternoon was still a part of the Sabbath. He read bits of it to me, among others, bits of **"A Ballad of a Nun,"** which I recalled I had read in *The Yellowbook,* and some verses set to "Ta-ra-ra-boom-de-ay," which we all knew from the violent declamation of Lottie Collins. Davidson brought the music hall to me, and the *fin de siècle* magazine, but he brought, too, a glory of sun-swept countryside still drenched with rain:

> The adventurous sun took Heaven by storm;
>   Clouds scattered largesses of rain;
> The sounding cities, rich and warm,
>   Smouldered and glittered in the plain.

That seemed like a Turner to me, but I liked better than the poet's picture of so wide a landscape his pictures of smaller bits of landscape, a copse in spring, or an orchard in fall:

> Showers of sunlight splash and dapple
>   The orchard park;
> And there the plum hangs and the apple
>   Like smouldering gems and lanterns dark.

It all seemed rich in imagination; it was all prodigal of light and color; everything was dispensed with the free hand of youth. There was such a thrill of passion in it all, or so it seemed then, almost a sob of passion. There was such joy in the escape from the city to the country. In a word, it was all attuned to the eager boy who listened that day to it, and read and reread it all time and again. It helped to bring home to him the wonder of the world.

Yet the man who was so much to men who were young a generation ago, who is so much to young men even to-day, when attention is directed to him, has fallen almost wholly out of discussion. He is almost never mentioned when the talk turns to late Victorian poetry. Davidson is no more to most of those who read poetry than is Sir William Watson. No one

poem of Davidson, indeed, is as much alive as *Wordsworth's Grave* (1890) of Watson. Even the circumstances of Davidson's hard struggle in London and of his strange suicide in Cornwall are forgotten. He has passed, as James Thomson and Robert Buchanan, of that same dour stock of the Scottish Lowlands, have passed. (pp. 54-5)

The ballads of Davidson have, I think, been overpraised. Once I thought they could hardly be overpraised. There were special reasons, of course, why I should care very greatly for them and their maker. He wrote for newspapers, and so did I. He tried to fight in the newspapers for what was best in art and drama and letters, and so did I. He escaped, whenever he could, from the city to which the newspaper man is condemned for most of his time, and so did I. He knew his English out-of-doors, in all its details of bird and tree and flower, as I knew my Americ countryside. The greatest reason for my liking was, however, his youthfulness, the impetuosity of him, the power of feeling he had, the desire in him to make the old world over into something new and better. I liked too, the ease of his writing, its swing and reach, the vigor of his onset in ballads and songs, the intensity that carried through with a rush whatever he put his hand to.

Now I can see that true as are all these qualities of his verse, it is lacking in depth; that he discovers the obvious; that he mouths the issue of the hour. **"A New Ballad of Tannhäuser"** seemed to me once as rapturous as the Venusberg music of Wagner. It seems doctrinaire to me now, too insistent on its thesis, and crude.

There are certain poets who are for youth almost only, poets who give free rein to their passions, who are defiers of convention, who have a deep vein of satire in them, and that cleverness which is so beguiling to awakening wits. Byron is one such, I think, before the time of Davidson, and Rupert Brooke another since the time of Davidson. Though no other of the three ever made the appeal of Byron, it is just as well that the youth of to-day who glory in Brooke should know how quickly another apostle of youth has passed. The passion of all three men leaves middle years cold, as the passion of Marlowe does not, or of Keats, or of Yeats.

The best of all the ballads of Davidson is **"A Ballad in Blank Verse on the Making of a Poet."** It is obviously his own story that he tells here, though he has sensationalized it. "Sensationalize" is an ugly word, but it is needed to convey the meaning of what Davidson has in this instance, and in others, done with life. Overstatement, overemphasis, an overdecorative style mar much of his work. He relaxes, and he clarifies his writing, when he turns to blank verse. Rhyme, though he calls it "a property of decadence," he likes and writes. "The re-echoing rhyme" of Poe leads Davidson to call him "the most original genius in words the world has known."

Blank verse Davidson likes best of all forms of verse. He writes it best, too, witness the sea-piece in **"Lammas"** in *Fleet Street Ecologues.* "I know nothing," he writes in the note **"On Poetry"** in *Holiday,* "I know nothing so entertaining, so absorbing, so full of contentment, as the making of blank verse." He had, then, hours of happiness in his art, as well as in out-of-doors and with family and friends. He has written a good deal about his art, and somewhat contradictorily. Eventually, however, he had come to the opinion we find him expressing in **"On Poetry"**:

> Poetry is matter become vocal, a blind force
>   without judgment. Much there is a poet can

control; he acquires a vocabulary, sifts and sorts; he can select the theme of his poem, and the weight and convolutions of his brain determine the power and variety of his rhythm, but the purport of his poetry is not within his own control.

Such a belief was not acceptable to all his fellow-poets or to all the critics. It was, like almost everything else in his life, a something that had to be fought for, argued over, put into print, and sent out as propaganda. There was almost nothing in his life that led to real relaxation. That happiness he thought of as coming to him and his fellows in *Fleet Street Eclogues,* when he wrote:

> and now we'll think
> Of Eden silently a while,

was a rare happiness indeed. Even his escapes to the country were haunted by a realization that they must be turned into copy, "things for which people will pay."

Certain passages that I have quoted are good in themselves and intimations of the finer things he could have done had he been "divinely blessed by leisure hours." As it is there are only one or two lyrics in all of Davidson's twenty-odd books of verse that are perfectly done, **"In Romney Marsh"** in *Ballads and Songs* and **"Spring Song"** in *New Ballads.*

Those who admire Davidson most always fall back on his poetry descriptive of out-of-doors as his greatest asset. Poetry descriptive of out-of-doors, though, must be something more than poetry descriptive of out-of-doors to be cherished in the memory. It must be background to a human figure or figures, or have some association with the common experiences of life, with hunting, say, or nutting, or daisying, or sapping, or ploughing, or logging. It must be a part of what has been experienced before by man. If it is not, then it must be as surprising in its difference from all experienced before as a new planet swum into our ken.

Davidson realized these truths, I think, and believed that he had humanized his descriptions in his eclogues by the topical discussions of their protagonists. He did humanize them, partly, but not altogether. Often the descriptions seem dragged in. In a sense his failure was a failure in knowledge of life. He knew, neither at first hand nor in imagination, much life other than that which school-mastering in Scotland—he called it "mental bootblacking"—or journalism in England—he called it "sixpenny reviewing"—had brought his way.

Not only had Davidson too little time to write, but too little time to live, to get to know life. Nor had he had much time to think. He believed that he had had time to think, but he had thought few things out. He had not had enough experience, either, to test the truth of the thoughts which came to him, or enough reading to know the relation of his thinking to that of other men. The necessity of making a living for his wife and two boys was always present to his mind. His nose was always to the grindstone. His health, too, had been long undermined with asthma, and he believed, toward the end, that he had cancer. It was the fear of cancer that drove him to suicide. He had written all, I am sure, that he could have had any happiness in writing, and all that the world could have had any happiness in reading. Nor was the truth in him in his last years. The world had had of him, when he died, all he had to give, or all, perhaps I should say, that it had allowed him to give, or would ever have allowed him to give. (pp. 63-6)

Cornelius Weygandt, "The Beginnings of the New Order: Henley, Stevenson, and Davidson," in his The Time of Yeats: English Poetry of To-Day Against an American Background, *1937. Reprint by Russell & Russell, 1969, pp. 30-66.*

PAUL TURNER   (essay date 1952)

[*In the following excerpt, Turner contrasts Davidson's philosophy as conveyed in his novels of the 1890s to that conveyed in his post-1900 works as represented by* God and Mammon.]

[I suggest that Davidson's] novels and stories deserve more attention than either the poet or his public were willing to give them; first, because their unique blend of wit and fantasy gives them an intrinsic value; secondly, because they express a vital component of Davidson's personality, which was essential to the proper operation of his poetic faculty. The case of Byron is analogous. Byron's best poetry did not come until the humorous and unromantically human ingredients of his personality were allowed literary expression—first in *Beppo,* then supremely in *Don Juan.* Likewise Davidson's best poetry—and here I agree with his contemporaries—was composed in the 'nineties, at a time when his humorous and human sides were finding expression in prose fiction. When the novels and stories ceased to appear, the poetry soon degenerated; and it did so, I believe, because of a partial atrophy of his humour and his humanity—because he lost the power to ridicule his own tendency to megalomania.

This tendency is most pronounced in the unfinished trilogy, *God and Mammon,* which he planned as a final embodiment of his phiosophy; and it is by comparing the first two plays of this trilogy with passages from his prose fiction, that the antidotal effect of the latter can best be seen. Prince Mammon is the elder son of the King of Thule. He renounces Christianity, kills his father and brother, seduces his sister-in-law and then, by a system of military dictatorship less familiar, perhaps, in 1908 than it has since become, prepares to remould the Kingdom of Thule, and eventually the whole world, nearer to his heart's desire. In Davidson's words, "the great message which inspires Mammon enables him to transcend all dishonour, all crime, the utmost evil that he can do"; and much of the later play is concerned with testing the muscularity of Mammon's emancipated conscience. To this end, he puts a medieval torture-chamber once more into commission, and with the greatest deliberation, and the minimum of pretext, subjects an old man to the rack.

Now it is important to realize that Mammon is the hero, and that his "great message" is identical with Davidson's. He represents in a heightened dramatic form the general movement of the poet's mind during the last decade of his life. Ignoring the sadistic element, of which there are traces throughout Davidson's works, we may say that the two great failings of Mammon are a humourless literal-mindedness, and a grotesquely inflated egotism. I will explain what I mean by his literal-mindedness. Davidson's was a brain naturally fertile in paradoxes and fantastic theories, and on this fertility his novels and short stories flourished. His best characters are those whose action and conversation spring from the elaboration of some eccentric creed. Cosmo Mortimer, for instance, in the novel *Perfervid,* has, like Shandy *père,* a theory that proper names influence behaviour; accordingly, he proposes marriage to a lady named Thomsina, while assuring her that he does not, and will not, love her.

"Then why," asks the lady, "do you wish to marry me?" "I have told you, madam: to study the effect of my name on you. You see, you are a most suitable subject. You have lived for many years under an abominable name, by which your character has been reduced to zero, so that the slightest upward tendency will be visible at once."

Banderole, a similar character in one of the short stories, submits to Parliament an Aesthetic Bill, for the diminution of ugliness. It provides, among other things, "that railways should be bordered all their length by gardens, and so become, as it were, rivers of flowers flowing across and along the whole land. The lines themselves are to be made of steel, damascened with arabesques in brass and silver." There is paradox where it belongs, in the company of humour. But the paradoxes of Mammon are propounded in grim earnest. Here, in a tirade to an audience of beggars, is his solution of the aesthetic problem:

> I will decree
> That ugliness is criminal, and build
> A rich pavilion high upon a hill
> For folk to die at dawn and sunset in,
> With music, costly wines, and perfumed death
> In vapours of decay. In silence go.
> I bid you die at once. Go hence, and die.

The pavilion full of perfumed death is in fact a lethal chamber—one of Mammon's many anticipations of modern dictatorial method. Davidson was fond of referring to religion as "petrified metaphor"; much of Mammon's message is a sort of petrified wit—mental acrobatics bereft of their humour, and frozen into a practical programme of misgovernment. And yet the theme of the novel, *Baptist Lake,* is largely directed against this very misapplication. There John Inglis, after nearly succumbing to the perverse arguments of his witty friend, Baptist, and breaking up a marriage twenty-eight years old, says to his wife:

> Oh, damn all words, Mary! They have nearly driven me mad. They have nearly made me break your heart and my own—all for a pitiful paradox; because I thought myself cleverer than others.

But it is in his monstrous, unsmiling egotism that Mammon most exemplifies the worst aspect of Davidson's post-1900 mentality. Like his author, Mammon is convinced that he is the one and only human being in all history to comprehend the universe; and he is resolved, by an alternation of rhetoric and violence, to force his ideas upon the rest of mankind. Now it is precisely this attitude which is ridiculed in Davidson's best two novels, *Perfervid* . . . and *Earl Lavender.* . . . The subject of *Perfervid* is the campaign of Ninian Jamieson, provost of a small Scottish town, for obtaining the crown of Britain.

> "I feel in myself," he says, "the power to govern Britain as it has never been governed. I have the strength, if I can wrench from fate the opportunity, to weld together the English-speaking nations; to plant the cross in Constantinople; to people Africa; to open China; to dictate to the world. I fought with myself; I tried to learn Greek; I tried to paint; I read biographies in the hope of being attracted by some other career than that of a claimant to the throne of Britain. . . ."

In vain: the autobiography of Cellini inspired him, indeed, to work in metals; but all he produced in that line was a medal, bearing his own likeness, and incribed with the words: "NINIANUS PRIMUS, BRITANNIAE REX."

The last and best of the novels, *Earl Lavender,* describes the campaign of a brilliant young eccentric for converting London to the religion of Evolution. He is the perfect comic counterpart of Mammon. Here, first, is Mammon, seeing in himself the purpose of eternity fulfilled, and trying to share this view with Anselm, the Papal Legate:

> I'll carve the world
> In my own image, I the first of men
> To comprehend the greatness of mankind;
> I'll melt the earth and cast it in my mould,
> The form and beauty of the universe.
> Say after me. "Get thee behind me, God;
> I follow Mammon." Say it, say it!

Anselm refuses to say it, so Mammon takes him by the throat and kills him. And here is Earl Lavender explaining his unique position in evolutionary history:

> "I am thoroughly convinced that I am quite fit, and that I shall survive—why, there is no saying how long I shall survive, if, as I suspect, I am *the* fittest."
>
> "*The* fittest?" asked the middle-aged man.
>
> "Yes; not among the fittest only, but *the* very fittest human male at present breathing."
>
> 'What makes you think you are *the* fittest?"
>
> "It is not quite easy to tell; but the feeling of superiority to other people which is constant with me, and of equality with everything—with the universe, in fact—leads me to cherish this high opinion of myself."

He therefore sets out from a London hotel, as the apostle of Evolution. Like Mammon, he has a watchword, in which his own name figures strongly: "The fit shall survive, and Earl Lavender is the fittest." "This," he gravely assures a meeting of journalists, "you may use as a battle-cry. It is customary, I understand, on the promulgation of a new system, for the prophet or founder to prescribe rules of conduct. In this matter I propose to give my followers ample liberty, only exacting from journalists and authors constant allusion and reference to me and my mission."

The correspondence between the two heroes goes further. Mammon thinks it appropriate to be joined by a consort on the throne of the universe, and regards his seduction of Inga the Volsung, his best friend's fiancée, as the ultimate aim of evolution. . . . In the same spirit, Earl Lavender, as the Fittest Man, feels it his duty to mate with the Fittest Woman. Intuition tells him that he has found her in a veiled stranger who pays his bill at a restaurant; but this proves a mistake, and he decides to work more methodically.

> "It will be advisable," he says, "to have delegates from all peoples. Fifty Russian ladies, say; no French—an effete race; thirty Germans; a score of Norwegians; a hundred Chinese; a hundred Africans—assorted; and so on. The hotels about Charing Cross could be hired for their reception, and out of the mass I could

choose say a hundred of the best-favoured—the others being sent home—without prejudice. In two years, you see, I could live a week with each of these—if that were necessary; but in all likelihood it would not take me a half—a quarter of that time to find the fittest. Here it seems to me you have a very fair scheme of Natural Selection.''

His fiancée, to whom he has been outlining the scheme, disappoints him by her lack of enthusiasm.

Mammon orders the ancient Abbey of Christianstadt to be set on fire, and watches the flames with Neronian delight. ''The fiery cross?'' he says. ''The image pleases me,''—for it seems to symbolize the abolition of Christianity. Earl Lavender, likewise, has an eye for symbolic interpretations. In Epping Forest he comes upon a curious compound monster, clad partly in fur and partly in Rob Roy tartan, emitting a ceaseless combination of blood-curdling squeals and groans. At closer range, it proves analysable into an orangoutan seated upon a prostrate Scotchman, and trying to play his bag-pipes. But Earl Lavender clings nostalgically to his first impression, that here was the Missing Link; and persists in regarding the apt juxtaposition of a beast from Borneo and a man from Scotland as an evolutionary miracle designed to support the mission of The Fittest. ''If you cannot understand this actually,'' he tells the bystanders, ''then understand it symbolically.''

In their general approach to life, Earl Lavender and Prince Mammon are identical. But Earl Lavender has the distinction of being at last discredited. While trying to convert the president of a secret society of decadents, he collides unexpectedly with common sense.

> ''Let us arm ourselves,'' says the Earl. ''Let us sally forth in the middle of the night, and, crying 'The fittest shall survive, and Earl Lavender is the fittest,' seize London in the name of Evolution.''

''You are a caricature,'' says the Nameless One in a deep voice. With equal justice, the same might be said of Mammon; but of him it is never said, and he preserves to the end the dignity of a serious character. How on earth, one wonders, could the same mind create Earl Lavender and Mammon? It is a paradox at the centre of Davidson's personality. In the monster of Epping Forest, the Earl saw a type of the struggle between man and beast, with the ultimate triumph of man. Davidson himself was just such a bi-formed creature—a fanatic straddling a prostrate humorist. It is sad for English poetry that the harsh music of the fanatic finally silenced the voice of humour. (pp. 500-04)

Paul Turner, ''John Davidson: The Novels of a Poet,'' in The Cambridge Journal, *Vol. V, No. 8, May, 1952, pp. 499-504.*

T. S. ELIOT   (essay date 1961)

[*Perhaps the most influential poet and critic to write in the English language during the first half of the twentieth century, Eliot is closely identified with many of the qualities denoted by the term Modernism: experimentation, formal complexity, artistic and intellectual eclecticism, and a classicist's view of the artist working at an emotional distance from his or her creation. In general, he upheld values of traditionalism and discipline, and in 1928 he annexed Christian theology to his overall conservative world view.*

*In the following excerpt from his preface to a selection of Davidson's poems, Eliot praises Davidson's ''Thirty Bob a Week.'']

I feel a peculiar reverence, and acknowledge a particular debt, towards poets whose work impressed me deeply in my formative years between the ages of sixteen and twenty. Some were of an earlier age—the late sixteenth and early seventeenth centuries—some of another language; and of these, two were Scots: the author of *The City of Dreadful Night*, and the author of **''Thirty Bob a Week.''** It is because I am given an opportunity of expressing, once again, my gratitude to John Davidson, that I write this preface.

I have, indeed, no other excuse. . . . Modesty requires me to write briefly; but loyalty requires me to write.

What exactly is my debt to John Davidson I cannot tell, any more than I can describe the nature of my debt to James Thompson: I only know that the two debts differ from each other. Some may think, from what I have said on this subject before . . . , that the obligation to Davidson was merely for technical hints. Certainly, **''Thirty Bob a Week''** seems to me the only poem in which Davidson freed himself completely from the poetic diction of English verse of his time (just as ''Non sum Qualis Eram'' seems to me the one poem in which, by a slight shift of rhythm, Ernest Dowson freed himself). But I am sure that I found inspiration in the content of the poem, and in the complete fitness of content and idiom: for I also had a good many dingy urban images to reveal. Davidson had a great theme, and also found an idiom which elicited the greatness of the theme, which endowed this thirty-bob-a-week clerk with a dignity that would not have appeared if a more conventional poetic diction had been employed. The personage that Davidson created in this poem has haunted me all my life, and the poem is to me a great poem for ever.

I do not wish, however, to give the impression that for me Davidson is the author of one poem only. . . . **''The Runnable Stag''** has run in my head for a good many years now; and I have a fellow feeling with the poet who could look with a poet's eye on the Isle of Dogs and Millwall Dock. To me, Davidson's blank verse is rather hard going. I allow for the fact that, as in the case of Thomas Hardy, I find the philosophy uncongenial. No matter: in everything that Davidson wrote I recognize a real man, to be treated not only with respect but with homage. (pp. xi-xii)

T. S. Eliot, in a preface to John Davidson: A Selection of His Poems *by John Davidson, edited by Maurice Lindsay, Hutchinson of London, 1961, pp. xi-xii.*

HUGH MacDIARMID   (essay date 1961)

[*Hugh MacDiarmid, recognized as the most important Scottish poet of the twentieth century, is the pseudonym of Christopher Murray Grieve, an ardent nationalist and communist. Many of his best verses are written in Lowland Scots dialect and are often drawn on political and social themes. His lengthy, despairing poem* A Drunk Man Looks at the Thistle *(1926) has been favorably compared in scope and effect with T. S. Eliot's* The Wasteland *(1922). A founder of the Scottish Nationalist Party and the editor of* Voice of Scotland, *he has been called by Compton Mackenzie ''the most powerful intellectually and emotionally fertilizing force Scotland has known since the death of Burns.'' In the following excerpt, MacDiarmid discusses Davidson in the context of Scottish literature.*]

Davidson stood out head and shoulders above all the Scottish poets of his own time. He alone had anything to say that is, or should be, of interest to any adult mind. (p. 47)

Readers of my *Scottish Eccentrics* and other books will know that I have shown that in so far from being "kindly brither Scots," "canny" or anything of that sort, the majority of distinguished Scots have always conformed to the character the world long before ascribed to the Scot in the epithets *"fier comme un Ecossais"* and *"piper in naso,"* and also to the even earlier conclusions that the Scots were men of curious and restless learning, versatile, with little or no use for "watertight compartments," and likely to be found bestraddling several disciplines at once. Davidson was of this type. (pp. 48-9)

What Davidson, alone of Scottish poets, did was to enlarge the subject matter of poetry, assimilate and utilize a great deal of new scientific and other contemporary material, pioneer in poetic drama and other forms, and recognize thus early the exhaustion of English, writing as he did:

> Our language is too worn, too much abused,
> Jaded and overspurred, wind-broken, lame—
> The hackneyed roadster every bagman mounts,

and, above all, to write urban poetry (a development Scots like Alexander Smith and Thomas Hood had heralded, but which subsequent Scots poets failed to carry on . . .). (pp. 50-1)

The most powerful influences on Davidson himself were Ibsen and Nietzsche—both first translated into English by Scots—Nietzsche by Thomas Common and Ibsen by William Archer. Davidson was very well read in English literature, and also in French and German literatures, but like most modern Scots seems to have known little or nothing about Scottish literature nor suspected for a moment that he was posing himself against a hopelessly wrong background in English literature. When Dr. Gertrud von Petzold in her *John Davidson und sein geistiges Werden unter dem Einfluss Nietzsches* (Leipzig 1928), referring to one of Davidson's stories, expresses regret that he did not give us "more Jenny Macintoshes and fewer Earl Lavenders, more Scottish heart-notes of so full and deep a resonance, and fewer super-clever London extravaganzes," she was expressing what most discerning critics have felt about practically all modern Scottish writers . . . , but the pity was that, like most educated Scots of the time (and still) he was never put at school in possession of more than a few discrete fragments of his proper national heritage, and, above all, that he was unable to realize the far greater suitability of Scots for the expression of his ideas than English could ever afford. Social protest, espousal of the cause of the underdog, anti-religion, materialism, Rabelaisan wit, invective—all these find a place much more easily and prominently in the Scottish than in the English tradition. All these are salient features of Davidson's work. In short, like Byron, he was a Scottish, not an English, poet, although he used an alien language, and had apparently no knowledge of the independent Scottish tradition. Nor did he express much in the way of Scottish nationalist sentiment. (pp. 51-2)

In other directions, however, Davidson's work was a valuable corrective to two of the greatest curses that have affected, and still affect, modern Scottish literature—namely, the superfluity of minor versifiers and absence of poetic ambition, and, associated with that, the horrible humility of mediocrity which is willing enough, as Kierkegaard said, to admit any one to its ranks on an equal footing, but prompt to crucify any one who dares to lift his head above the ruck.

Statements of Davidson's with regard to these last two matters have stuck in my mind, and influenced me profoundly, for over forty years. For example, from *A Rosary:*

> A poet is always a man of inordinate ambition and of inordinate vanity. In his heart he says, "I want my poetry to be remembered when Homer and Dante and Shakespeare are forgotten."

Again, specially applicable to the Scottish scene, from *Sentences and Paragraphs:*

> The want of poetical power is the impelling force in the case of most versifiers. They would fain be poets, and imagine that the best way is to try to write poetry and to publish what they write. They will never see their mistake. *Equus asinus* still believes that the possession of an organ of noise is sufficient, with a little practice, to enable him to sing like a nightingale.

In another paragraph in the same book, Davidson hopes of those who were reconstructing Provencal poetry, that "the head, as of yore, and not the heart, will be the source of the poetical passion"—a view I share, and have frequently propounded, in a far wider context. I have always agreed with him, too, that "if one has a healthy mind it is wholesome to go from extreme to extreme, just as a hardy Russian plunges out of a boiling bath into the snow."

But the most important element in Davidson—and one to which attention should be directed most strongly if justice is to be done to him at last and his influence brought to bear effectively where it is most needed—is expressed in the following passage from *A Rosary.* It re-echoes for today what has been a main theme of Scottish poetry back through Burns to Henryson and Sir David Lyndesay:

> Poetry is not always an army on parade: sometimes it is an army coming back from the wars, epaulettes and pipeclay all gone, shoeless, ragged, wounded, starved, but with victory on its brows; for Poetry has been democratized. Nothing could prevent that. The songs are of the highways and the byways. The city slums and the deserted villages are haunted by sorrowful figures, men of power and endurance, feeding their melancholy not with heroic fable, the beauty of the moon, and the studious cloisters, but with the actual sight of the misery in which so many millions live. To this mood the vaunted sweetness and light of the ineffective apostle of culture are, like a faded rose in a charnel-house, a flash of moonshine on the Dead Sea. It is not now to the light that "the passionate heart of the poet" will turn. The poet is in the street, the hospital. He intends the world to know it is out of joint. He will not let it alone. . . . The offal of the world is being said in statistics, in prose fiction; it is besides going to be sung. There it is in the streets, the hospitals, the poorhouses, the prisons; it is a flood that surges about our feet, it rises breast-high, and it will be sung in all keys and voices. Poetry has other functions, other aims; but this also has become its province.

As J. Russell Lowell said, "Not failure, but low aim is crime." Davidson almost alone of the poets of his time cannot be convicted of this crime. This is his great significance. It is time that was fully realized. (pp. 52-4)

Hugh MacDiarmid, "John Davidson: Influences and Influence," in John Davidson: A Selection of His Poems *by John Davidson, edited by Maurice Lindsay, Hutchinson of London, 1961, pp. 47-54.*

J. BENJAMIN TOWNSEND   (essay date 1961)

[*An American educator, art historian and critic, Townsend is the author of the comprehensive critical study* John Davidson: Poet of Armageddon *(1961). In the following excerpt from that work, Townsend discusses the dramas* Godfrida, Self's the Man, *and* The Knight of the Maypole *and their place in the development of Davidson's work.*]

[*Godfrida, a Play in Four acts*] is set in the court of Provence around the middle of the fourteenth century. A study of passionate love, violent jealousy, and the conflict of strong wills, it has in ample measure all the faults of late nineteenth-century historic melodrama. The plot is artificial, relying on stale contrivance or arbitrary reversals of fortune to create suspense and achieve a denouement. While Isembert, the villain, may illustrate the author's philosophy of irony, his vacillation between satanic evil and selfless good strains credulity. Furthermore these quasi-allegorical figures who announce the author's ideas as if they wore sandwich boards are devoid of any originality. Siward and Godfrida, hero and heroine, are drawn partly after Chaucer's Troilus and Criseyde, partly after Othello and Desdemona; Jacobean drama affords numerous models for the antagonists, Isembert and Ermengarde. If the characters in *Godfrida* illustrated Davidson's message through consistent motivation and action rather than served as inconsistent mouthpieces for it, they might provide the excitement and violence of true romantic melodrama. Or if the conventions of the contemporary theater had permitted the playwright to invest his abstract principles with sufficient vitality, he might have written a powerful allegory. As it is, *Godfrida* flounders in some vague, unchartered morass between the two.

What militated against the new play's chances in its own day is the one thing that now recommends it for attention, its ideas. *Godfrida* seeks to prove that happiness and fulfillment can result only at the cost of an equal amount of suffering for someone. It further demonstrates that in the struggle of wills at the basis of all society, that will with requited and unselfish love on its side prevails, whatever the odds. Power and love when coupled are unassailable, irresistible forces in human affairs. In an imaginary prose colloquy between the Poet and the Interviewer which serves the play as prologue, Davidson states his purpose, with an eye to possible charges of obscurity by the critics. Its lesson, the Poet points out, is stated in the play itself:

> . . . no felicity
> Can spring in men, except from barbèd roots
> Of discontent and envy, deeply struck
> In some sore heart that hoped to have the flower.

Stung into defending the truth of these lines, Davidson later wrote to the editor of the *Daily Chronicle*, "They have perhaps no reference to lighter natures incapable of staking their lives in the game of fate, or to philosophers who only look on; but it seems to me true of those who *will* win or lose it all. There can be no triumph without defeat." This is "the order of the universe . . . victory and defeat are one—the flower and the root." *Godfrida,* a transitional work, attempts to present in dramatic terms the ironic vision which the poet had expressed through narrative and nature imagery in his lyrics of the nineties. More explicitly than in the lyrics, it also states in germinal form the morality of the later works, a morality reduced to strength of will, brains, and physical superiority. This morality finds its authority in nature, its driving and preserving force in sex, and its goal in power.

Still searching for a style in which to couch this message, the poet announces in the prologue to the play that he has cast his lot for romance rather than realism: "I mean by Romance the essence of reality. Romance does not give the bunches plucked from the stem: it offers the wine of life in chased goblets." The poet takes his characters from men and women as he knows them, "but that I myself may realise them, and make them more apparent and more engaging to an audience, I place them in an imaginary environment, and in the colour and vestments of another time." He has chosen the contemporary vogue for costume drama beause he seeks to entertain and to give delight: "to give delight is to impart strength most directly, most permanently." But how does the artist give delight? What in his work imparts strength? Truth; and truth soon comes to mean for him, like the irony in which he previously found the cohesive principle of the universe, matter. By a simple syllogism Davidson's aesthetics is inseparable from his metaphysics, just as his poetry gives way largely to philosophical assertion. (pp. 302-04)

The style of *Godfrida* and of his next work, *Self's the Man,* like their message, recall the early Spasmodic dramas, *Diabolus Amans* and *Smith*. They preach the same romantic lesson of unfettered action and self-realization, and they preach it in the same way, through rhetoric and melodrama. (p. 304)

[*Self's the Man, a Tragicomedy*] is a better play than *Godfrida* because it does not cater so laboriously to the tasteless fashions of the day. Still romantic and by present standards absurdly melodramatic, *Self's the Man* comes closer than its predecessor to the frank purposefulness of the poet's final works. For the first time since his Spasmodic dramas, Davidson does not permit the play's rhetoric to interfere with a forthright, unprettified delivery of his unpopular message. Although he certainly intended the drama for the stage, he also appealed to the reader's interest with extensive stage directions and "chapter headings" in the manner of Shaw. Whatever the author's intention, the work remains didactic closet drama along the lines of the later tragedies.

Set in the provincial court of Pavia during the middle ages, *Self's the Man* concerns the efforts of a dissident group of courtiers to depose Urban, an arrogant, autocratic, but humorous king who has been elected by popular acclaim. Like *Godfrida* it is a play of intrigue, treachery, and undying love. At the same time it is frankly a thesis play, and its thesis is boldly announced in the epigraph which the author has chosen from his own eclogue, **"Lammas"**:

> Be your own star, for strength is from within,
> And one against the world will always win!

The minor characters who serve as foils and agents are no more than stock figures, but the leading characters embody fixed principles of conduct from which they derive their vitality and interest. Of these Urban is the most important.

Urban, who combines the boyish charm and exuberance of Prince Hal with the ruthless ambition of Marlowe's Tambur-

Aubrey Beardsley's frontispiece to Davidson's Plays.

laine, is portrayed as a Renaissance Machiavellian politician. In actuality he is a nineteenth-century man of power. Davidson makes this clear in subsequent advertisements of the play:

> . . . it is a modern drama—a not altogether unsuitable sub-title might be ''new Wine in an Old Bottle,'' for some part of the comedy is a fermenting anachronism which bursts the wine-skin. Counterparts of Urban, the protagonist, may be found in Napoleon III, Dom Pedro, Amadeus of Spain, Alexander of Bulgaria, Milan of Servia, poets, students, or pleasure-seekers attempting or half-attempting to act, and to be masters of men. Urban embodies the prevailing mood of the nineteenth century, which was, like most centuries, an age of dreamers and unrealized ideals; and he represents also the net result of the intellectual effort of the nineteenth century, viz., the conscious egoism which inevitably exalts the mind above the soul and the senses, and destroys the natural harmony of man. . . . Fate, such as may be found within the covers of books, will not be detected anywhere in this play; only character, and the want of it, and the use or abuse the individual makes of the chances that occur.

Urban's philosophy is that of the Henleyan activist grafted to that of the Carlylean hero and the Nietzschean Overman. He is equally, however, the Spasmodic hero, motivated by self-love and exercising self-indulgence. When his friend rebukes him for his ambition, he replies that all men are consumed by their crowning passion:

> Oh, learn to love yourself!
> Consider how the silent sun is rapt
> In self-devotion! All things work for good
> To them that love themselves.

There is no room in his egoistic code for remorse, pity, or sentimental attachment to the past. ''Power is my chosen bride,'' he tells his discarded mistress, and he recognizes the will to power as the guiding instinct in man. But it is not enough for Urban to rule Lombardy. An imperialist of the Cecil Rhodes—Robert Clive—Warren Hastings school, he seeks to conquer the world:

> My lords, it is with nations as with men:
> One must be first.

In the paternalistic despot and the modern imperial state Davidson has found substitutes for the parent and deity in whom authority had traditionally been vested.

In willing his own destiny Urban has made one mistake. He has renounced his love for the pagan slave-girl, Saturnia, in order to please the people by marrying Osmunda, daughter of the leader of the opposition. Governed by intellectual principle and policy rather than by natural impulse, he is as yet only the precursor of the Overman. Great men should never compromise with their passions and must learn to defy custom:

> To laugh at policy, to over-ride
> Wisdom, authority, experience,
> To break with the ragged past, and be
> The demiurge of order and a time
> Stamped with my own image—is to chafe
> Mankind, and mark my power and daring . . .
> Is to read triumph in a storm of hate.

Because of his error Urban loses faith in his destiny, weakens, and repents. His downfall is followed Oedipus-fashion by prolonged exile and by death, but only after he has learned the last lesson of all, self-forgiveness and self-knowledge. ''Though you were Judas, learn to forgive yourself,'' he says to Saturnia with whom he is symbolically reunited in a final death scene. The dignity and nobility of the tragic hero are at last his, but his ultimate vision is that of the man of power's supremacy in a godless universe, not the humble recognition of a higher order which traditionally concludes a tragedy. The capacity for redemption like the capacity for error is solely within Urban's own grasp. Davidson refused to call his play a tragedy, preferring to label it a tragicomedy, although he felt that ''A farcical melodrama,'' ''A Serio-comic Play,'' anything indicating ''character'' would have done as well. By character he meant the role of paradox or irony in human destiny. In *Godfrida* Davidson had sitll compromised pretty much with the conventional dichotomy of good and evil by assigning each force to a single character, Siward the hero and Isembert the villain. The more complex Urban of *Self's the Man,* at once strong and weak, triumphant and defeated, like the later Mammon, embraces both roles. Ample precedent for this complexity of character exists in the protagonists of Kyd, Marlowe, and Shakespeare, whom Davidson certainly knew. But whereas the Elizabethan tragic hero reflects orthodox dualism and must ultimately resolve his divided nature by making a moral choice, Davidson's heroes recognize their ambivalence as part of the inevitable irony of the universe. Out of frailty, evil, and suffering, in oneself as well as in others, can come only good, the poet declares; and henceforth his amoral message will be:

> The complex heart of things
> Is never understood, till one is led
> To do wrong cheerfully that good may come.

Irony strengthened by suffering has led him at last to a bleak, pitiless code.

Self's the man has been commissioned by the actor-manager Beerbohm Tree who, Davidson remarked to Gosse, "with hardly a criticism, gave me carte-blanche to write it in my own way." . . . Quite understandably Tree regretted the carte blanche he had extended the author. Although an improvement over his previous plays and less sensational and strident than the later meldoramas, the play's almost pathological interest in torture, its occasional bloodthirstiness, its ideological nature, and its amoral message made it unsuitable for production. The poet preferred defeat to success on terms other than his own, and in time found grim satisfaction in predictable failure. (pp. 306-11)

Having failed to reconcile the requirements of the contemporary London theater and his discordant ideas, Davidson returned in *The Knight of the Maypole, a Comedy in Four Acts,* to the manner and themes of his early pastoral comedies. The imitation is a pallid one, without the conviction and liveliness of *An Unhistorical Pastoral* and *A Romantic Farce.* Its plot, a patchwork of situations from *Measure for Measure* and Restoration comedy, could not be more commonplace and belongs to the degeneration and provincialism of native English comedy before its resuscitation by Gilbert, Wilde, and Shaw. Laid in the dissolute days immediately following the return of Charles II to the throne, the play presents the rivalry of two cousins, Anthony and Gabriel Ashe, for the estate of their deceased uncle and the hand of Agnes Grey, the mistress of Richmond Court Palace. The setting may be musty and the plot creaky, but the characters illustrate Davidsonian weakness and strength. Like Urban of *Self's the Man,* Anthony is a prototype of the man of power and relentless will who, by allowing his reason and baser passions to dominate his natural impulses, destroys rather than fulfills himself. Gabriel, another nineteenth-century type, is the grandson of Childe Harold, noble, solitary, melancholy, indomitable. He is the victim of his own turbulent passions as much as of the vices and follies of others. Together the two cousins symbolize the conflict of rationalism and romantic idealism in the nineteenth century and the general failure of the century to recognize man's full, material being. Thus this play extends and applies to history an earlier, personal theme, the clash of generations in parent and child. In *The Knight of the Maypole* Davidson does not fuse his type of hero with his type of villain as he does in *Self's the Man* and the *Mammon* plays, because he is describing within the conventions of native comedy traditional man rather than the more fully integrated man. Even the apocalyptic *Mammon* plays depict the violence and brutality of a modern world caught between two warring dispensations. The borrowed convention of the rival cousins in *The Knight of the Maypole* may also symbolize, however unconsciously, the essential ambiguity which Davidson finds in all being and which he sought to subsume in his gospel of scientific monism. Just as the principal male characters in this play look back to those of the pastoral comedies, so Agnes is indistinguishable from Davidson's earlier heroines, who combine gentle domesticity and tender devotion with proud chastity; she does not share the sexual candor and freedom of the later heroines.

For a play that aims at being lighthearted, *The Knight of the Maypole* is solemn fare. It teaches with renewed doggedness that integrity of spirit, no matter how persecuted, will triumph over avarice and cynical indifference. Throughout Gabriel is the conscientious spokesman for self-reliance, the purity and imperishability of love, the cosmic order underlying terrestrial flux, and the privilege of suicide. There is much of the prig in him, as the author's pagan hedonism sours into an ascetic search for suffering and atonement. Ideological and dramatic inconsistencies make the play's message less than convincing. Although Davidson clearly regards the Restoration as an age of carefree hedonism close to his own youthful vision of a happy, natural world, he makes Anthony and King Charles reckless, unscrupulous libertines. At the same time, in order that Gabriel may have his sweetheart and property restored to him in a final scene, Charles implausibly abandons his pursuit of the heroine.

It is not its ideas which detract from *The Knight of the Maypole.* Amid the trite sentimentalizing, decrepit humor, contrived incidents and straining after quaintness, Davidson's nineteenth-century materialism strikes the reader as still vigorous. It is rather the gross incongruity and incompleteness, devoid of wit or persuasion, with which he joins these ideas to the archaisms of pastoral romance. Even Davidson came to recognize that somewhere along the way he had lost faith in ironic neutrality and had committed himself to arbitrary, final answers irreconcilable with the mirth in sadness of Elizabethan comedy. Henceforth he turned unswervingly to tragedy and melodrama as more fitting receptacles for his somber view of life. (pp. 316-18)

> *J. Benjamin Townsend, in his* John Davidson: Poet of Armageddon, *Yale University Press, 1961, 555 p.*

V. S. PRITCHETT (essay date 1961)

[*Pritchett is a highly esteemed English novelist, short story writer, and critic. Considered one of the modern masters of the short story, he is also one of the world's most respected and well-read literary critics. Pritchett writes in the conversational tone of the familiar essay, approaching literature from the viewpoint of an informed but not overly scholarly reader. In his criticism, Pritchett stresses his own experience, judgment, and sense of literary art, rather than following a codified critical doctrine derived from a school of psychological or philosophical theory. In the following excerpt, he assesses Davidson's career and philosophy.*]

Who reads the poems of John Davidson now? There is **"In Romney Marsh,"** a swift piece of descriptive elation, as true as the note of a tuning fork to the ear. There is **"Thirty Bob a Week."** There is **"The Runnable Stag"** which, as a ballad, is as good as any Assyrian coming down like a wolf on the fold. A poet of sound, more dramatic and spirited than furious—what does he signify? Is there anything? We know of him now as a *Yellow Book* poet, a tussler with Yeats, a protégé of Shaw's. There are echoes of Kipling and Housman. . . .

He is a sad prickly figure whom Gissing might have recorded, one of those penniless writers born at the wrong time in awkward circumstances and whose only hope is that justice will be done to them when it is too late. This perception angered him but, despite his truculence and eventual megalomania, he made his tragic decision "to rejoice unconscious matter" stoically and, one might guess, on principle.

His atheism was aggressive. Now he has his justice. A selection of his poems, prefaced surprisingly by T. S. Eliot and Hugh McDiarmid, has been done by another Lallan poet, Maurice Lindsay. Davidson is now reclaimed as one of the first Scots to write urban poetry; and T. S. Eliot [see excerpt dated 1961] says that the poet's **"Thirty Bob a Week"** showed him how to write poetry in a colloquial idiom. He is something of a London Bridge character from *The Waste Land:*

I ain't blaspheming Mr Silver Tongue
I'm saying things a bit beyond your art:
Of all the rummy starts you ever sprung
Thirty bob a week's the rummiest start!
With your science and your books and you the'ries
    about spooks,
Did you ever hear of looking in your heart?

I didn't mean your pocket, Mr, no:
I mean that having children and a wife,
With thirty bob on which to come and go,
Isn't dancing to the tabor and the fife;
When it doesn't make you drink, by Heaven! it makes
    you think,
And notice curious items about life.

That reads like Kipling; but at the back of it is something that Kipling did not have—the sense that "death had undone so many."

In Davidson's time romantic London was worn out. A bricked-in sadness, pathos, glumness and lethargy enter London literature. The city is claustrophobic, mean, even mingy. The newspapers say the future is nasty. The unemployed don't care for the present. Naturalism has come in but has lost Zola's obsessional force in the Channel crossing. . . .

Even when it is merry in this period, life is full of little ironies, not big ones; low comedy in Jacobs or Jerome has the shade of the social prison house. As for the natural sights—the Thames is preferred at low water when the mud prevails. A great deal of the realism seems to be the work of depressed immigrants who hanker for a Romney Marsh or an Innisfree, while they turn their scornful backs on the gaudy appeals for socialism, theism or salvation. The contrast between mid- or early-Victorian London and the London of the *fin de siècle* in literature is extraordinary; the heart has gone out of the later time. If they could have waited for a generation how much more fortunate in their material these writers would have been; two wars and a revolution would have digested it. If he could have waited two generations, Davidson would probably have been in the BBC! For by then, his mad and Victorian notion that one could live by writing poetry—he must have been one of the last to try—had been thoroughly knocked on the head. That is one thing the affluent society has settled in all the arts.

But there is another side to the little man of the mean London. If his life was grey, his mind was apt to be highly coloured; if he was forced to be timid, he raged with inner pugnacity; if his speech whined and his feet shuffled over his vowels, he had a bullfrog bursting with rhetoric inside. Villon was a fashion and the place was full, as Davidson himself saw, of "stylists." Being a Scot who had purged himself of evangelical religion, Davidson regarded London and all life, with a hard, foreign eye. He saw it through the eye of Nietzsche and, also,

Ibsen. The little man on thirty bob a week was a potential superman:

I step into my heart and there I meet
    A god-almighty devil singing small
Who would like to shout and whistle in the street,
    And squelch the passers flat against the wall;
If the whole world was a cake he had the power to take,
    He would take it, ask for more, and eat it all.

And not for personal reasons. He did not want to be the boss. On the contrary: his idea is that to "come it brave and meek" is heroically difficult:

Its walking on a string across a gulf
With millstones fore-and-aft about your neck.

To accept the superman is to accept the command of fate and Nature; and to see to it that one takes a stand against being part of Nature's enormous wastage, even if one has to accept that in the end. And so, as one reads Davidson's descriptions of **"The Isle of Dogs,"** or other reaches of the Thames, his account of the Clyde at Greenock or his various *Testaments,* his Fleet Street verses or that terrible poem in which an atheist boy fights to destroy his mother's belief in immortality at her deathbed, one sees a sort of intellectual battling, something cross-grained, inflating, rhetorical and strenuous in his writing. It is city stuff because it is heartening itself with opinions. There is the smell and swagger of newsprint. The evangelical becomes the atheistic Salvationist, at once filled with the Nietzschean pessimism and appeals on behalf of the message of the blood.

His final unfinished work is a monstrous drama of paradox: *The Triumph of Mammon.* Mammon has destroyed God and is reforming the Kingdom of Thule. He calls the factions together: socialists, neo-pagans, *i.e.* restorers of Roman mythology, the Inceptors of Teutonic Religion who wish to see a new God evolve. The Christian rebellion, under the Roman Catholics, is put down, the godless state created. Mammon is ruthless. Cruelty and horror entangle him. And there the epic breaks off. It is said that the final part was to show that Mammon could transcend every evil he could do, or that was done to him. This was not swank. Davidson did not grow up in the land of John Knox for nothing.

This poem is written in blank verse. It contains good lines, but it is grinding iron-grey stuff; the argument wrangles; the rhetoric tramps on and hardly gets off the ground. In the Thirties, it would have sounded like pure, little-man Fascism. When we say Davidson was born at the wrong time, we mean that the large forces about to be set loose on the world were only then forming themselves and that neither he nor anyone else could forsee how the human experience would go and what it would be like to pass through it. We think differently of the superman since Hitler, Mussolini and Stalin. The underdogs have not gone down the sewer at the command of nature; they have in fact risen everywhere. If he had lived through what we have lived through, Davidson would have been cured of the desire to project ethical epics; he lived in an impoverished time, when it was only too easy to turn hopefully from experience to expatiation, simply because the experience offered was poor. It was unlucky that all these "openings"—as an evangelical might say—should come to a minor lyrical poet; the sort of disaster that might happen today, if a man of genuine talent got caught up, say, in Moral Rearmament. For there was nothing of the mystic in Davidson; nothing to compare with the strange mind of Blake. Davidson's virtues are those of the literal descriptive writer. (p. 478)

V. S. Pritchett, "The Mean Time," in New States-man, Vol. LXI, No. 1567, March 24, 1961, pp. 478-79.

G. WILSON KNIGHT   (essay date 1962)

[*One of the most influential of modern Shakespearean critics, Knight helped shape the twentieth-century reaction against the biographical and character studies of the nineteenth-century Shakespeareans. Knight's analytic practice stresses what he calls, in his study* The Wheel of Fire *(1930), the "spatial" aspects of imagery, atmosphere, theme, and symbol in the plays. He thus parallels the New Critics with his emphasis on verbal texture; his discussions of symbolism are similar to Samuel Taylor Coleridge's notion of the symbolic as indefinite with multiple meanings. In the following excerpt, Knight examines Davidson's philosophy as presented in his dramas, particularly* The Triumph of Mammon.]

Davidson wrote various dramas, pastoral, historical and prophetic. *Smith,* subtitled "a tragic farce," . . . brings fervour and a straining ambition to bear on modern life; *Scaramouch in Naxos* . . . is a poetic fantasy critically dramatizing the relation of the modern theatre to the Greek god Dionysus; and *Self's the Man* . . . has a hero of power, vision and superlative abilities, with high designs above all normal categories of good and evil, a force of light refusing to use the death penalty, a believer in immortality. As he advances, Davidson's dramatic poetry becomes more and more powerful and his thoughts more dangerous. In *The Theatrocrat* . . . the decadence of modern drama is symbolized by an actor-manager in difficulties, a drunken leading actor and the failure of an attempted production of *Troilus and Cressida;* and new life is sought in a religious work by the actor-manager's friend, a bishop, whose prophetic message is directly opposed to Christianity and causes an uproar on the first night. The message is Davidson's; now he has his thoughts clear; the commercial theatre and orthodox religion are together attacked by a new, semi-Nietzschean, gospel of frightening power.

Davidson's mature teaching, as set out in the introduction to *The Theatrocrat* and the epilogue to *The Triumph of Mammon* . . . and the texts of both plays, rejects orthodox concepts of God and sin and all transcendent categories: the universe is quite unmoral (*The Theatrocrat* . . .). But the recognition is happy: we are urged to accept, and respond to, life's magic. The teaching has affinities to Wordsworth's, to which he refers, and to all poetry: "all convincing imagery is scientific truth" (*The Triumph of Mammon* . . .). Time is rejected and the eternal now—the "now" basic to dramatic art—alone real. . . . Davidson's metaphysic, relying on the omnipresent and invisible ether, the bisexual yet creative electricity (*The Theatrocrat* . . .) and matter, is in part derived from nineteenth-century physics, but it may also be related to occult and spiritualistic thought: light and colour are identified with sound and music, all together making "the ethereal warp and woof of the matter of which we ourselves are woven" (*The Triumph of Mammon* . . .). Similar statements are found in the accounts of other dimensions received through trance mediumship, and also in Gordon Craig's theories of dramatic art. We are urged to become newly conscious of life's elixir. Matter has become in turn "subconscious, conscious, and self-conscious" (*The Theatrocrat* . . .) and the language of the new self-consciousness is poetry: "It is a new poetry I begin, a new cosmogony, a new habitation for the imagination of men" (*The Triumph of Mammon* . . .).

Davidson is in line with Ibsen's prophecy of the man who "wills himself" in *Emperor and Galilean;* and with Nietzsche, though he rejects doctrines of a superman as too idealistic, . . . insisting instead on his own mystique of the actual and the now. All that is needed is a full consciousness of what we, which is the universe, are. Both Hardy and Davidson aim to break the opacity between man and nature, but whereas the one looks for a new consciousness in nature the other looks for it in man. Hardy wants the cosmos to respect human valuations; Davidson wants humanity to attune itself to the cosmos.

So much for philosophy; drama is a more severe test. Drama is as a laboratory for testing such theories. In *The Triumph of Mammon* and *Mammon and His Message,* the first two parts of a projected but uncompleted trilogy called *God and Mammon,* Davidson attempts a dramatic exposition.

The setting of *The Triumph of Mammon* is contemporary, in a Nordic country called "Thule." Battleships, flags, and colour enliven our first stage direction. We are in a modern world of State affairs and power. King Christian is opposed by his eldest son, called "Mammon" because of his atheistical and immoral beliefs:

MAMMON.	That which I am
	I am, and would be under any name,
	Immanuel, or Siddartha, or Herakles,
	A new force in the world. My title, Mammon,
	Delights me: I shall make this name renowned
	For things unprecedented through the earth.
KING CHRISTIAN.	What things?
MAMMON.	Things sifted from the stars in nights
	Of travail—exiled moons; things that shall change
	The thoughts of men and renovate the time.
	(II. iii)

"Mammon" was the god of riches, desire, war, adventure, discovery, power; his splendour has been degraded to a supposed "inferior devilry" by Christianity, which humbles pride, smirches sexual love, dilutes virility and tyrannizes over the intellect (II. iii). His blasphemies arouse wrath: the Abbot Gottlieb, symbolizing, as Mammon mockingly observes, the Christian tradition, suggests that, instead of being put to death, he be castrated. King Christian visits him in the Chapel Royal to perform the act.

Mammon (III. ii) is alone, tied to a pillar facing a crucifix on which he has been meditating. Though Christ may be honoured above all rivals hitherto, yet now the world "wearies of you"; economic theory and idealistic reforms cannot patch up a decaying order; new life is wanted. His father approaches, with a knife. After all, he says, God's elect are the virgins and celibates like Christ; life in Heaven will be a "single ecstasy" of "undesirous ravishment"; earthly sex "is sin, is Hell", and from this he will deliver his son (III. ii). Great issues are being dramatized. Is humanity to take sexual fulfilment or its denial as its highest aim? Both Christ and Nietzsche's Zarathustra were without it and it is once agreed in *The Theatrocrat* (I) that the artist is better celibate, like a priest. . . .

The scene develops. Mammon thinks of Gwendolen, his love:

> O father, sex is soul,
> The flower and fragrance of humanity,
> More beautiful than beauty, holier
> Than any sacrament, greater than God—
> I tell you, father, greater than all the gods,
> Being the infinite source of every thought
> Worth thinking, every symbol, myth, divine
> Delight of fancy.
>
> (III. ii)

The King says that thrones are falling, civilization disintegrating through irreligion and atheism; God is the only "keystone"; and God has ordained "this Christian surgery." Mammon in reply reasserts his own faith: "The Universe unveiled is there, there, there!" He "cannot speak such greatness." But he is terrified at the thought of being "a sapless thing." At the last moment he cries "God help me then! Christ save me!" The King stops. Mammon expresses repentance. The King cuts his bonds, whereupon Mammon "takes the knife and seizing King Christian by the throat stabs him." Then:

> Now, old, vain, foolish Christian man, who saw
> My terror—I, afraid!—go up to Heaven!
> Glare at me! Heart of Hell, what awful eyes!
>
> [*Stabs again*]
>
> I would you were the soul of Christendom!
>
> [*Stabs a third time*]
>
> I would you had been God!
>
> (III. ii)

We hear much of literary dramas not dramatic enough for production: here we have a scene too dramatic for production.

From now on Mammon's progress is rapid. Various parties solicit his approval (V. i). The Nietzschean Guild is repudiated on the grounds that Nietzsche's superman is really a Christology in disguise; the Teutonic god wanted by others is an artificial conception; reformers from "the Isles" (i.e. Britain) are rejected, theories of equality are denied. Most of what Mammon dislikes he regards as parasitic on the corpse of Christendom. What he looks for is an acceptance and intensification of the actual. He wills

> to make
> This mighty world a hundredfold itself.
> There shall be deeper depths of poverty,
> A more distressing toil, more warlike war,
> An agony of spirit deadlier
> Than that which drenched Gethsemane in blood . . .
>
> (V. i)

And yet, too, a "rapture," a "beauty," and a "glory" hitherto unknown, corresponding, we may suppose, to the state of being including, yet beyond, suffering announced in Shelley's *Prometheus Unbound*.

At a ceremonial gathering in St Olaf's Hall Mammon is denounced for his father's murder by the Abbot Gottlieb, and the Papal Legate excommunicates him. With the help of machine-guns he establishes himself, remarking that "secular change" inevitably demands a "crimson baptism." He crowns himself and announces his gospel. His philosophy has no room for the transcendent:

> No world but this, which is the Universe,
> The whole, great, everlasting Universe.
> And you are it—you, there, that sweep the streets,
> You that make music, you that make the laws,

> You that bear children, you that fade unloved.
> Oh, if there be one here despised and mean,
> Oppressed with self-contempt and cursed with fear,
> I say to him:—Not any where at all
> Is there a greater being than you—just you:
> You are the lustre of a million suns—
> The fuel of their fires, your flesh and blood;
> And all the orbs that strew ethereal space
> Are less than you, for you can feel, can know,
> Can think, can comprehend the sum of things:
> You are the infinite Universe itself
> Become intelligent and capable . . .
>
> (V. ii)

His words pour out, an amazing blend of precision and excess, in intoxicating torrents, concentrating on the "ether," "lightning," "electric lust for ever unconsumed," "twisexed fertility" and man

> The intellect, the passion and the dream,
> The flower and perfume of the Universe . . .
>
> (V. ii)

This Earth is Heaven and Hell; every moment is judgement day; time is a delusion; eternity is now. Since in man the whole universe has become self-conscious, labour for the future is nonsense: we ourselves are "posterity." It is all wonderful; its assertions, though not its denials, are mostly true; but the central thought is hard to hold for long and yet harder to translate into action.

In *Mammon and his Message* . . . we see Mammon at work. For beggars and criminals he plans a humane extermination; prostitutes, only needed under Christianity, are to change their ways; the capitalist system he intends to destroy. His conscience sometimes makes him see, like Macbeth, his past victims. However his recoveries are firm. He has Gottlieb tortured mainly in order to overcome his own inhibitions and master a full self-realization. . . . He naturally arouses opposition, which he meets with arms, emerging again victorious. There was to have been a third play but Davidson's suicide left the trilogy uncompleted. The last piece was presumably to have been tragic, since a note in his preface to the second indicates that it would have shown Mammon as strong in suffering as in power.

Under dramatic expansion Mammon's gospel of total acceptance and total living reveals its contradictions: if all men are so splendid, why tyrannize over them? Why disbelieve in social equality, if each man is the universe? So comprehensive an attempt to base a life-plan on tragic exultation inevitably forces paradox. Mammon certainly serves as a retrospective comment on three centuries of dark persons in drama and history, while also being prophetic of modern Europe. Davidson must not be supposed to subscribe to all Mammon's actions, and he is aware of objections to his philosophy, recognizing that the Catholic doctrine of the Real Presence is a profound symbol of the magic in matter he is announcing, and that his own system of "dynamic ether," material creation and atomic "force," "the polar tension couched and wed in every atom," is already covered by the Christian Trinity (II. ii). A Catholic might argue that what Davidson is telling us is both so true and so dangerous that it must for the present remain limited by dogma and locked in symbol. (pp. 312-17)

G. Wilson Knight, "Edwardian," in his The Golden Labyrinth: A Study of British Drama, *W. W. Norton & Company, Inc., 1962, pp. 308-41.*

ANDREW TURNBULL (essay date 1973)

[*In the following excerpt, Turnbull offers an examination of Davidson's thought as revealed through his works.*]

That Davidson has a place in the history of Victorian doubt is revealed by such early poems as **"The Voice"** and **"No Man's Land"** which exploit a vein of despair that recurs regularly in the poet's later work. A mood of gloomy questioning, an apprehension of the absurdity of life, is apparent in several of the eclogues: life comes to seem merely "a naked precipice / O'erhanging death's deep sea," and time "a dungeon vast / Where life lies rotting in the straw." Davidson's acute awareness of the predicament of the Victorian doubter is nowhere more clear than in the portrait of Ninian in **"Lammas,"** though his probing of this mood continues through **"Epilogue to Fleet Street Eclogues"** and **"Eclogue of the Downs"** where the images of the Sphinx and the "huddled city" on Truleigh Hill are powerfully expressive of the obscure, enigmatic, yet palpably inimical face presented by the universe to many men of the nineteenth century.

"Eclogue of the Downs" was based on prose pieces of 1898; early in the following year Davidson made public his own answer to "the cat-call of the universe" in a series of letters to *The Speaker*—the principle of "cosmic irony," a position that sees truth as emerging from conflict, paradox, and the tension between opposing forces, that, indeed, finds stability in the wholehearted acceptance of contradiction:

> Irony is centric, the adamantine axis of the universe. At its poles are the illusions we call matter and spirit, day and night, pleasure and pain, beauty and ugliness. By it our enterprises are whirled away from our most resolved intentions.... Irony is the enigma within the enigma, the open secret, the only answer vouchsafed the eternal riddle.

> Irony is not a creed. The makers of creeds have always miscalled, denied some part of the world. Irony affirms and delights in the whole. Consciously, it is the deep complacence which contemplates with unalloyed satisfaction Love and Hate, the tiger and the nightingale, the horse and the blow-fly, Messalina and Galahad, the village natural and Napoleon. Unconsciously, it is the soul of the Universe.

Though openly formulated only at a relatively late stage in the poet's career this position is, as we have seen, clearly adumbrated in much of his earliest work; opposition to "creeds," an important—one might say the most important—aspect of Davidsonian irony is certainly implied in his attitudes towards love, nature, and the "natural man," all of which imply a view of reality as diverse yet unified. The "ironic" approach is, indeed, discernible throughout the poet's pre-materialist phase, even as far back as the 1870s and '80s: what, for instance, are poems like **"The Male Coquette"** and **"The Rev. E. Kirk"** but "statements," as Davidson would put it, uncritical, dispassionate, of the characters almost as natural phenomena? The clearest example, however, of the existence in embryo of the ironic method in the poet's Scottish period is *Diabolus Amans*—Davidson's "spasmodic" drama—which airs a veritable plethora of attitudes towards God and the world, mediated by the positives of love, nature and the hero, ending, as J. B. Townsend remarks, "in a convenient compromise: Love . . . supersedes all faiths and resolves all differences."

It is to the work of the early 'nineties that we must look for the clearest statements of the position that Davidson was later to describe as "ironic"—to **"St. Valentine's Eve,"** for example, where pain and pleasure, love and hate, are seen as complementary, or to the anti-dogmatic **"Ballad in Blank Verse"**:

> No creed for me! I am a man apart:
> A mouthpiece for the creeds of all the world;
> A soulless life that angels may possess
> Or demons haunt, wherein the foulest things
> May loll at ease behind the loveliest;
> A martyr for all mundane moods to tear;
> The slave of every passion; and the slave
> Of heat and cold, of darkness and of light;
> A trembling lyre for every wind to sound.
> I am a man set by to overhear
> The inner harmony, the very tune
> Of Nature's heart . . .
>
>   Within my heart
> I'll gather all the universe, and sing
> As sweetly as the spheres; and I shall be
> The first of men to understand himself. . . .

It is his intuition of an "ironic" universe that is largely responsible for the puzzlingly varied quality of Davidson's poetry, its incongruity and apparent caprice. To a mind which accepts the validity of all experience, all modes of thought, and regards truth as "liker a diamond than a proposition: a brilliant, every facet and edge of which lightens with veracity," the contrast between, say, **"Coming"** and **"The Hymn of Abdul Hamid"** will not appear so incongruous. Hence, in Davidson's work we find what seems to be social criticism jostling the most blatantly élitist propaganda; seemingly sympathetic pictures of the underdog (as in **"A Northern Suburb"**) lie alongside poems, like **"The Aristocrat,"** which imply that strength is the only virtue; simple nature-poetry contrasts with the brash celebration of a steam-engine or city-life—poems which may themselves be followed by bleak pictures of slums or polluted rivers.

This "ironic" trend of thought is evident not only in the subject-matter of Davidson's verse but also in his style. A very noticeable feature of his diction, the rapid juxtaposition of grave and comic, colloquial and artificial, prosaic and lyrical elements is, in part, intended as a linguistic embodiment of the poet's "ironic" view of things and designed to communicate an impression of both multiplicity and inclusiveness. This is especially apparent in the eclogues—the first twenty lines of **"Michaelmas"** is a good example—but is also a prominent feature of his later verse. The example of Carlyle again seems to lurk in the background, and, as in Carlyle's style, the effect of these incongruities of diction, though frequently not ineffective, often seems merely mannered.

In some of his imagery, also, Davidson attempts to embody, rather more successfully, that "irony which is the soul of things." One of the better-known passages from the poet's work, the evocation of Greenock and the Firth of Clyde at the opening of **"A Ballad in Blank Verse,"** exploits a strain of imagery which not only underpins the vigorous mood of the passage but also supplies a new dimension of meaning. Basically, the metaphoric texture of the lines conflates or intermingles town and country: natural scenery is described in terms of man-made commodities, particularly textiles—the firth is "foam-embroidered," shores "fringe the velvet tides," and so on; while the actual products of human industry are described in terms of animals or plants—ships have "pinions" or, alternatively, "iron limbs," the town is likened to a bird, factory chimneys are "stalks," and the dead-metaphor in "cranes" is brought to life. (pp. xxi-xxii)

Finally, Davidson's use of form frequently mirrors his concept of "irony." This is apparent above all in the eclogues, where the dialogue—a favourite technique of Davidson's in his prose as well as his verse—enables him to present a wide variety of different opinions and aspects of a subject, to conflict with or complement each other, and occasionally to merge into a higher, more inclusive unity. The poet creates, in the talk of the individual journalists, each with clearly defined personality and opinions a clash of character and idea; while, at the most superficial level, the incongruity of the implied identification of Fleet Street journalists with Arcadian shepherds must have appealed to him. The form of the eclogues is an emblem of the contrasting, multitudinous variety that Davidson found in the world and in his own mind—we might, indeed, apply to these poems Davidson's own observation on the main characters in *The Theatrocrat:* that they "are made essentially out of the good and evil in myself."

The Davidsonian concept of irony does bear a certain resemblance to the prevailing Paterianism of the 'eighties and early 'nineties: we might compare the Scot's advice to the artist "to be open to all influences, to encounter the full stress of life" with Pater's dictum that we should be "forever testing new opinions and courting new impressions, never acquiescing in a facile orthodoxy," while the important passage in **"A Ballad in Blank Verse"** where the protagonist adopts an "ironic" standpoint echoes one of Oscar Wilde's early poems. However, Davidson's position owes more to the earlier Romantics; Goethe in particular, with his drive to unite apparent opposites, his acceptance of the mutual dependence of good and evil, truth and error, seems to lie behind many of Davidson's attitudes, although similar tendencies are present in much Romantic thought. (p. xxiii)

It is probably fair to say . . . that the germ of some kind of materialist system was inherent in Davidson's work from very early in his career. The general tendency of his views on man and nature towards a monistic synthesis of spirit and substance is obvious, while, like Goethe who, "because of the objective and sensuous character of his imagination," was also unable to accept a transcendentalist world-system and attempted his own synthesis of mind and matter, Davidson's intense apprehension of the physical world, his almost visceral response to nature, made it altogether likely that his ideas should evolve towards a vitalistic monism of substance. There is also, of course, the early contact with, and interest in, the world of science—an interest which must have deepened under the influence of Grant Allen, himself a scientific journalist of some note. At any rate, after its long gestation period Davidson's materialism quickly reached adulthood: born in *The Testament of a Vivisector* it is in all essentials complete with the appearance of *The Testament of a Prime Minister*—a poem begun in 1902 and completed by mid-1903. Although *The Theatrocrat,* the Mammon plays and *The Testament of John Davidson* state the doctrine in fuller terms, adding minor refinements, it is safe to say that with the *Prime Minister* Davidsonian materialism attained maturity.

Just as the foundations of his thought are constructed from not uncommon Romantic ideas, so the materialist edifice he raised upon them is built largely of no less common scientific theories—commonplaces of nineteenth-century physics. Particularly important in the poet's scheme was the theory of the ether, the extremely attenuated, imponderable substance filling the whole of space, which seemed a necessary postulate if the wave theory of light were not to founder on the problem of "action at a distance." The nebular hypothesis of Kant and Laplace, which put forward the view that planets condensed from a disc-shaped cloud of gas rotating about a solar nucleus, was the other main element of the poet's system. Both concepts, ironically enough, were already in the process of being discarded at the time of their wholehearted acceptance by the Scottish poet.

In the beginning then, according to Davidson, nothing existed but the eternal ether which, imbued with unconscious will and passion, its own "innate desire" for self-consciousness, evolved electricity. This "first analysable form of Matter" immediately reacted with the ether itself to produce hydrogen out of which the other elements were built up in the incandescent nebulae now filling the universe. In turn the nebulae condensed into stars and star-systems on the planets of which certain elements, notably carbon, hydrogen, oxygen and nitrogen, "sensitive" but as yet "unconscious," by means of "chemical selection" and the "intense and hungry chemical affinities," the vehicles of the inherent will of matter, evolved into conscious life. Finally, in man, the "primeval aim" of matter is realised, self-consciousness; not, however, by the Darwinian process of natural selection, but through the ceaseless experimentation of matter's unconscious will. As ponderable matter is continually evolving from the ether, so is it continually devolving back into its original state; systems collapse, stars collide, scattering and breaking down their elements to become the source of future stars and solar systems which, in turn, will repeat the process. Matter being indestructible, the process is never-ending.

Into this basic materialist framework Davidson incorporated most of his earlier beliefs and obsessions. His political views—imperialist and totalitarian—are given a materialist rationale in *The Testament of an Empire-Builder* and the **"Ode on the Coronation of Edward VII,"** while his views on poetry find a similar basis. As we have already seen, Davidson's view of the hero requires little modification in the last decade, although the poet's insistence upon the necessity for pain develops in importance: it is at the extremes of passion that we are most acutely conscious of our material being. Pain, then, the "medium of Matter's consciousness," and the sexual act are of equal importance in Davidson's later philosophy, the latter, indeed, being elevated to the status of a fundamental principle: it is seen as having its origin in the poles of the primeval lightning, creator of ponderable matter, and later as manifesting itself in the phenomenon of chemical affinity.

The principle of "irony," of course, remains an important feature of Davidson's thought, under a new name, however—"immorality":

> . . . there is no moral order of the Universe . . . everything is constantly changing and becoming and returning to its first condition in a perpetual round of evolution and devolution; and this eternal tide of Matter, this restless ebb and flow, I call immorality. . . . It may also be called by as many metaphysics as there are properties and qualities in Matter, and in Matter's accomplishment, man. . . . It is a profoundly satisfying thought that no serious pursuit of man, no cherished conception, however erroneous in itself, is ever based in error.

Perhaps the ether itself, "omnisolvent, omnicontinent, omnipresent, and omnipotent," was finally identified in the poet's mind with "worshipful irony," "the adamantine axis . . . the soul of the universe" that "affirms and delights in the whole":

> Steep irony in Chaos, and the universe will
> string itself about it like crystals on a thread . . .
> I perceive the universe as a golden bough of
> irony, flowering with suns and systems.

It was certainly the continuing power of his "ironic" view that led Davidson to explain the Christian myths as, in part, the mistaken interpretation of primeval material memories. The ideas of Heaven and Hell rise out of subconscious memories, present in every atom, of, respectively, the peace and stasis of the ether and the terrific force released in the nebula when ponderable matter was in the process of creation. The idea of God has a twofold origin in, again, primeval memories of ethereal peace, and partly in the stirrings of matter's unconscious will; while the notion of the Trinity is seen as deriving from a subconscious apprehension of the "triple form of the Universe"—ether, matter and energy. Sin, or rather consciousness of sin, Davidson explains as a result of an exhaustion, usually temporary in normal individuals but endemic in "worn out stock," of the "Material forces of Matter in man"; this is essentially a rationalisation, in materialist terms, of the mood expressed by Ninian in **"Lammas."** To Davidson, this discharge of material power, in "passion and imagination," is "the categoric imperative."

This, of course, is not the poet's only explanation for the fact of religious belief, but constant in his thought is the view that what are believed to be revelations of divinity are, in fact, the efforts of the imagination, the power by which we are able to apprehend ultimate reality, to body forth its most penetrating intuitions as to the nature of the universe. "The religious mood," he tells us, "is the highest mood of the imagination," and while there is truth in religious belief—as there is in all belief—it is symbolic truth; but man has failed to recognise the "metaphoric" nature of these intuitions, erecting them into actual dogma, fixed articles of belief, creeds which have distorted his view of reality and which he has used to hide from himself the real nature of things, propagating a false worship of weakness. Much of the immense body of religious imagery in Davidson's work may be interpreted as an attempt to restore religion to its metaphoric status, just as the ballads and certain of his other works refurbish, often with an "ironic" twist, traditional myths and legends.

The very commonness of the scientific ideas underlying Davidson's materialism makes it difficult, if not impossible, to ascribe the roots of his system to any particular source. . . . Sources, however, are relatively unimportant, since it will be evident that, though his system uses the materials and discoveries of modern science, Davidson's method is far removed from that of the scientist. (pp. xxvi-xxix)

[Davidson's] monism of substance is essentially little different from a monism of spirit—the idealism, for instance, of such Romantic egoists as Fichte and Max Stirner. Instead, however, of rejecting science, as many other Romantic irrationalists did, he poured science itself into a Romantic mould. It is significant how frequently references to alchemy and alchemical concepts crop up in the poet's work—both well before and long after 1900; the source of some of Davidson's most characteristic imagery, it casts indirect light on the peculiar quality of the "poetic scientism" he espoused: "science is still a valley of

dead bones till imagination breathes upon them." Proof lies, not in precise presentation and careful argument, but in unconscious, intuitive assent; science is advanced, conviction achieved, by something approaching a "leap of faith."

Given, then, that Davidson's views belong only superficially to the rational, scientific, empirical tradition it should not be altogether surprising that the philosopher whose thought seems to loom largest behind many of the poet's ideas is the idealist Arthur Schopenhauer. Even in their differences the two are related, many of Davidson's ideas being straightforward inversions of the pessimistic philosophy: for Schopenhauer, for instance, freedom is attained only through the renunciation of will, while, according to Davidson, it lies in wholehearted *identification* with the will of the universe. Again, while matter is to the German the purely phenomenal objectification of will, to Davidson matter is "the thing in itself," will being an inherent property of substance. Davidson, indeed, unwilling to let anything evade that desire for integration and inclusiveness which seems to have been the basic motivating force behind his thought, attempts to do for metaphysics in general what he had done for religion; an inveterate magpie with a habitually analogical turn of mind he incorporates all systems into his own:

> I perceive the identity of Spinoza's God, Hegel's Absolute, Fichte's Transcendental Ego, Schopenhauer's Will to Live, and Nietzsche's Will to Power. These all embracing categories are titles which Man in his madness has conferred on Matter.

This characteristic way of thinking—which lies behind the development not only of Davidson's "irony" but also of his concept of matter, the ultimate principle, capable of assuming innumerable forms, continually changing yet remaining essentially the same—is reflected in an important group of images which, while present in the work of Davidson's Scottish period, gradually increases in importance from the early 'nineties onward. Smelting and forging, moulding, distilling, dissolving, weaving, and the alchemical strain already mentioned are the main, though by no means the only, components of this group of images: elements diverse enough, but linked by a process common to them all—that of change or transformation, coupled with a sense of strenuous activity. Often, this notion of change involves less a sense of complete transformation than of the exploitation or realisation of certain inherent possibilities; thus, the process of smelting realises the potential inherent in crude ore, distilling produces an essence or concentrate of the original substance, while weaving, by a process of synthesis rather than analysis, has a similar effect of exploiting the potential of materials, this time in the creation of a new form which includes the old.

So much, then, for the main outlines of Davidson's ideas, and how these ideas relate to his poetic practice. What, however, of his position as poet and thinker? Certainly, if we wish to make any important claims for the poet we must concentrate our attention on the work of his materialist period. Despite the attractive qualities of the best of his atmospheric 'nineties lyrics, poems which at least equal in quality those of the most accomplished "decadent" poets, Davidson's work of this period, like that of Symons, Wilde, Johnson and the rest of their circle, remains essentially minor. The same might be said of the poet's experiments in "popular" verse, such as the early **"In a Music-Hall,"** **"Thirty Bob a Week,"** and **"To the Street Piano,"** which go no further than Kipling and Henley; while the ballads and eclogues, though interesting from the point of view of their formal procedures, are, in general, artistically unsatisfying. In the last ten years of his life, however, Davidson's work embodies two related developments which were not only highly individual and prophetic—much of the poet's earlier work had been all of that—but, it could be argued, give the poetry something approaching major status. These added factors are his incorporation into poetry of the discoveries of science and his development of a highly distinctive blank verse.

The occasional use of scientific language and ideas was, of course, nothing new in Davidson's work, nor was it a new departure in nineteenth-century poetry: both the Romantics—notably Shelley—and the Victorian poets had attempted to treat earlier aspects of scientific discovery in verse, while the admired Goethe had managed to combine poetic genius and a spirit of scientific inquiry, turning the results of his research into poetry; but Davidson, in his materialist phase, goes very much further than any poet of the period, or before, not only in his use of the esoteric language of chemistry, biology, geology and astro-physics, but in using specifically scientific concepts as the very basis of his world-view.

At times—perhaps too frequently in the "Testaments and Tragedies"—this can lead to a mere piling up of undigested scientific terminology in verse at once clotted and undisciplined, the impression being that Davidson regards the poetry as somehow inherent in the words and ideas themselves and not in any rigorous selection and arrangement effected by the poet; that Davidson felt that the words themselves had only to be written down in order to have the same profound effect on the reader that they evidently had on the poet himself is clear from his remarks in several prose works. For this reason his scientific verse, though locally successful in the **Testaments** (possibly entirely successful only in the *Vivisector*), is more consistently at its best in poems that he would probably have regarded as mere "interludes." These are works that explore themes similar to those of the "Testaments and Tragedies" but—unhampered by that missionary zeal in the delivery of his "message" which, while generating its own obsessive power, tends to flaw more "serious" poems—exploit a vein of humour or whimsy in a tone sometimes loosely conversational, sometimes deliberately artful. Such a poem is **"Snow,"** deceptively slight at first glance, yet embodying several of the poet's more important ideas in form and language admirably tailored to the subject. Moreover, the ideas—the presence of the life-principle in all matter, the ultimate importance of the will to self-fulfillment, the fundamental relationship of apparently disparate phenomena, good and evil, beauty and ugliness—are allowed to emerge from the subject without being unduly forced.

In admitting that much of the later work is less assured than the earlier lyrics we must remember, however, that not only was Davidson aiming much higher in his materialist period, the occasions when he hit the mark making the effort all the more worthwhile, but that he was breaking new ground. Clearly, he felt the frustration of having new things to say while lacking a fully mature medium in which to say them. As we have already seen, many of the distinctive stylistic features, both linguistic and structural, apparent in Davidson's work are the result of attempts to embody his "ironic" vision in verse; the poet's later blank verse is a similar attempt to embody that final view of the universe which combines the "ironic" position with scientific materialism. His aim was the development of a highly flexible form, capable of rapid modulation, varying in tone and rhythm to accommodate a wide range of moods

and themes—capable, in effect, of embodying in its own variety the variety of life itself.

Davidson, of course, was no stranger to blank verse, dramatic and non-dramatic; by the early 'nineties he had achieved a mature style, owing most, perhaps, to that of Alexander Smith, and already remarkably flexible. Already, also, most notably in parts of the eclogue **"Lammas"** and **"A Woman and her Son,"** the poet's verse had shown a tendency towards a less obviously "poetic" movement, corresponding more closely to the rhythms of everyday speech. Davidson himself suggests an analogy which, though prompted by the character of the work of the 'nineties, is even more closely applicable to the later blank verse:

> I use blank verse newly as Wagner did music.
> If you take a chromatic score of Wagner's and
> attempt to play it in common time in one key
> you will have a terrifying result. You can't
> sing-song my blank verse.

Though the comparison here is between the extreme chromaticism, the constant modulation of post-*Tristan* harmony and the subtle gradations of tone and stress that Davidson regards as distinctive features of his blank verse, an even more apt analogy might be the development of the Wagnerian vocal line which broke down and remodelled the conventional operatic distinctions betwen aria, recitative, ensemble and so on, modulating evenly from passages of great lyrical intensity to fairly dry declamation, always retaining its fluidity and feeling of continuous progression. We might extend the analogy: the freedom and flexibility of Davidson's later blank verse is due not only to its rhythmic freedom, being as much a matter of syntax, tone, verbal colour; just as Wagner, by sacrificing some local formal cohesion, changed opera from a sequence of self-contained dramatic structures to a form in which music and drama were welded into a larger, ultimately symphonic unity, so Davidson, in the interests of flexibility, tends to eliminate from his blank verse what might be called the more "operatic" features of the traditional form—the formal, periodic structuring of the verse paragraph.

Davidson's later blank verse owes much of its "roughness" to its deliberate lack of this kind of balance and periodicity. Clauses and sentences are piled up without a break, or with naturally occurring breaks that show little concern with traditional care in the placing of caesurae; furthermore, the distortions and compressions of syntax make for a quirky, knotted quality that contradicts our traditional expectations. Elsewhere, the verse, again with the aim of creating a more flexible, discursive medium, tends to accommodate itself more and more to the emphasis and cadence of ordinary speech; the opening lines of **"The Thames Embankment,"** for example, though technically quite regular blank verse, are not immediately experienced by the reader as such. In this general context we might point to the possible influence of Browning as well as to Davidson's practice of transforming passages from his prose journalism into verse.

The Scot's blank verse is probably at its best when he manages to combine these two developments, striking a balance between the informal and the mannered. In **"The Crystal Palace,"** for instance, the poet's finest individual achievement, much of the effect—particularly in the superb opening paragraph, described as "free verse" by A. E. Rodway [in the *Pelican Guide to English Literature: From Dickens to Hardy*]) but in fact, basically blank verse—springs from the tension between colloquial and artificial elements.

Finally, we must not ignore Davidson's influence on later writers. T. S. Eliot, for one, has admitted to a "debt" to the Scot [see excerpt dated 1961] though **"Thirty Bob a Week,"** the poem which Eliot singles out for specific mention as having "a very important place in the development of my own poetic technique," seems rather an odd choice since its exploitation of colloquial diction goes little further than that of Kipling, while Davidson's vein of "dingy urban" imagery comes to the fore rather more strongly in later work. Some of the later blank-verse, such as the opening lines of *The Testament of an Empire-Builder,* seems to foreshadow much more clearly the distinctive Eliotesque tone and movement. Again, **"The Crystal Palace,"** with its interesting exploitation of significant juxtaposition and allusion—we might note in particular the "sculpture" passages and the underlying religious imagery with its distinct allusions to Dante—anticipates the mature techniques of both Eliot and Pound, while the similarity of its thematic preoccupations to much of the work of these writers will be obvious.

Pond was, of course, acquainted with Davidson, as was D. H. Lawrence who, indeed, had read and admired some of the Scot's work. Other commentators, Priscilla Thouless in particular [see Additional Bibliography], have remarked on the similarity of many of Davidson's ideas to those of Lawrence; both, for example, regard sexuality as a fundamental principle of the universe, and share a belief in the ultimately physical nature of thought and feeling. Both, also, subscribe to a dynamic, power-based, high individualistic ethic. It is most unlikely, of course, that the Scot exerted any influence on the younger writer, but the similarity between the thought of Davidson and Lawrence is nonetheless interesting in that it serves to highlight the former's importance as a link between the earlier Romantic period and our own century. (pp. xxix-xxxii)

> *Andrew Turnbull, in an introduction to* The Poems of John Davidson, Vol. I *by John Davidson, edited by Andrew Turnbull, Rowman and Littlefield, 1973, pp. xiii-xxxiv.*

DEREK STANFORD (essay date 1974)

[*Stanford is an English critic, poet, and biographer known for his insightful studies of nineteenth and twentieth-century authors. His special area of critical interest is English art and literature of the 1890s. In the following excerpt, Stanford compares Davidson's poetry to that of fellow Rhymers' Club members Ernest Dowson and Lionel Johnson.*]

[Ernest Dowson, Lionel Johnson and John Davidson] were members of that loose *cénacle* of poets (a coterie or club without rules and officers) known as the Rhymers' Club which functioned between 1891 and 1894, exhibiting in the two anthologies it produced some of the finest poems of the decade. "Twelve very competent verse writers" is how the Rhymers have collectively been described and the phrase admirably defines most of its members. "Dainty" and "finicking" are terms that aptly describe the work of Victor Plarr, Herbert Horne, Ernest Rhys and others, but as well as W. B. Yeats, "the central figure of the gathering," Arthur Symons and the three poets included in this book belie this description. Such fellow Rhymers and associates as Plarr, Horne, Selwyn Image and G. A. Greene produced craftsmanlike verse which is sometimes exquisite, but they did not leave work stamped with its

author's life-style. Though the verse of Dowson, Davidson and Johnson is not confessional in the almost literal and continuous manner of D. H. Lawrence's poetry, the quintessence of the poets' lives is interpretably present in their poems.

Yeats in his *Autobiographies* named his fellow Rhymers "the tragic generation" and his father called them "the Hamlets of our age." Both phrases were apt ones for that Gallicized group of young men who were the British equivalent of Verlaine's *poètes maudits*. It is the older man's *mot*, however, which gets to the heart of the affair, implying, as it does, that these writers were up against dilemmas in their nature which they were unable to resolve.

> You had to face your ends when young—
> 'Twas wine or women, or some curse—

wrote W. B. Yeats afterwards of these

> Poets with whom I learned my trade,
> Companions of the Cheshire Cheese.

Yet all that Dowson, Davidson and Johnson may be thought to share as poets was an attempt at "writing lyrics technically perfect, their emotion pitched high." Even this is an overgeneralization since Davidson's **"Thirty Bob a Week,"** though flawed by certain intellectual "impurities," constitutes, along with Oscar Wilde's "Reading Gaol," a rare example of the deeply impressive "poem of some length" written in the nineties.

In a radio broadcast, T. S. Eliot once described Davidson as a poet "who had genius but the incapacity for perfection," and this statement helps to explain Davidson's attitude to the other members of the Rhymers' Club. Morley Roberts, a friend of his, reported Davidson's own conviction that "all of the Rhymers would not make one man of his worth." Pathological as his self-opinion later grew to be, his sense of the difference between his own work and that of his Rhymer colleagues was based on sure intuition. He had, remarked Max Beerbohm, "what I think the other poets had not: genius (and very robust genius)"; while another witness, Le Gallienne, adds his own critical evidence. "There is," he wrote in 1894, "a burliness of constitution underlying his most delicate fanciful work. . . . There is not another among them [the younger men] of whom it can be said . . . they suggest no such liberal strength as Mr. Davidson's least perfect work always suggests."

This secret (sometimes vocal) sense of superiority over the other members of the Rhymers' Club was strengthened by Davidson's contempt for what he took to be the littleness of their aims. Yeats reports that, "He saw in delicate, laborious, discriminating taste, an effeminate pedantry, and would, when the mood was on him, delight in all that seemed healthy, popular and bustling." With such feelings of separatist distinction, Davidson refused to contribute to the two anthologies of the Rhymers' Club or to become "an out-and-out member . . . saying that he did not care to be ranked as one of a coterie."

There is no real artistic distance between the verse of Ernest Dowson and Lionel Johnson, say, as that between Davidson and his fellow members of the Rhymers' Club. (pp. 26-7)

Davidson, the most imperfect of these three poets, had the most significant influence on the poetry which was to be written later. Although much of his work is flawed, he had a stronger imagination. But his impact lay not in the evolutionary ma-

THE LATE JOHN DAVIDSON.

20ᵗʰ septr — 1909 —

BODY RECOVERED FROM THE SEA

The Press Association's Penzance correspondent telegraphs:—"The greatly decomposed body of a man was on Saturday evening towed into the harbour of the fishing village of Mousehole, about three miles from Penzance, and there appears to be little doubt that the remains are those of Mr John Davidson, the well-known poet, who mysteriously disappeared from his Cornish home in March last. Upon the body were a pair of button boots and a long dark overcoat, which tally with the official description that was issued of John Davidson, while the build strongly resembles that of the missing poet. A gentleman who knew Mr Davidson is convinced the body is that of the author. In the pockets of the clothing were found a pipe, a packet of tobacco, a silver matchbox, a paper-knife, and some scraps of paper. Late on Saturday night one of Mr Davidson's sons identified these articles as his father's property. The body was seen by two men fishing near Mousehole.

It was on Tuesday, March 23, that Mr Davidson disappeared from his home at Penzance, after having posted to his publisher, Mr Grant Richards, the manuscript of a poem entitled "The Song of Empire." The alarm was raised, and during the week in which he disappeared reports were received from different places along the neighbouring coasts of a gentleman answering to Mr Davidson's description having been seen. These clues were diligently followed up by the poet's family, but without success, and inquiries in London yielded no more satisfactory results. Gradually the family began to give up hope, and on April 19 it was announced that "his family and friends have now reason to believe that his fate is no longer uncertain, and that in a moment of acute depression he has made an end of his life." At the same time they published a copy of his will made in the preceding August, and forwarded to Mr Grant Richards to be opened on Mr Davidson's death—"to-morrow or next day, or twenty years hence." In a parcel of documents was found a preface to a book in which the following passage occurred:—

The time has come to make an end. There are several motives. I find my pension is not enough. I have therefore still to turn aside and attempt things for which people will pay. My health also counts. Asthma and other annoyances I have tolerated for years, but I cannot put up with cancer!

At the same time a denial was given by the family to a statement published in the press that Mr Davidson met his death by drowning. "Nothing is known as to how Mr Davidson met his death." This information was really all that the future held for the family, and it has now been afforded by the finding of the body.

Davidson's obituary as it appeared in the Glasgow Herald *(20 September 1909).*

terialism of his thought which he himself so much esteemed, but in its trappings: the colloquial note and urban imagery.

T. S. Eliot has recorded how, when he was a young tyro at Harvard, it was "only the poets of the 'nineties . . . who at that period of history seemed to have anything to offer to me as a beginner," instancing three of them by name: Symons, Dowson and Davidson. "I got the idea," he continued, "that one could write poetry in an English such as one would speak oneself. A colloquial idiom. There was a spoken rhythm in some of their poems." Earlier, in a broadcast, he had paid specific respect to Davidson's **"Thirty Bob a Week"** ("his one great achievement . . . I know nothing quite like it"). Published in *Ballads and Songs,* . . . it may be thought of as giving a civilian voice to the military vernacular of Kipling's *Garrack Room Ballads* which had appeared two years earlier.

Nevertheless, this achieved colloquial note is to be found in Davidson only occasionally. His ballads feature much writing in dialogue and monologue; but, for the most part, employ the histrionic rhetoric of Elizabethan and Jacobean drama, as in **"A Ballad of a Workman"** and **"A Ballad in Blank Verse."** Only one other poem by him experiments in an interesting manner with the colloquial, namely **"Rail and Raid"**—an otherwise largely unsuccessful piece appearing in his posthumous volume *Fleet Street and Other Poems* . . .—whose middle passage seeks to convey the interminable chatter of a railway-compartment bore.

Too little attention has been accorded Davidson's other contribution to twentieth-century poetry—his metropolitan imagery. In his Preface to the edition of Davidson just quoted [see excerpt dated 1961], Eliot confessed that, like the nineties poets, "he had a good many dingy urban images to reveal," those not assuming the dress of Laforgue being nearer in manner to those of Symons (with their hinting at a Prufrockian bohemia) than to those of Davidson. Of the Rhymers themselves—Davidson excepted—it was Symons chiefly who had elaborated the metropolitan cartography in his poems. But Symons' London was largely a townscape of selected corners, choice spots and romantic vistas or prospects, for the most part imbued with a special atmosphere—Temple, the Embankment, Kensington Gardens, etc. It was also a somewhat demi-mondain terrain where the women were actresses, ballet-girls or whores, and where the men did not exist at all.

Davidson does not only describe certain representative men and women who make up the vast megapolis, but enters imaginatively into the pattern of their lives and fates (the poor clerk in **"Thirty Bob a Week,"** and the tramps, scavengers and kerb-sellers in **"Liverpool Street"**). In **"Holiday at Hampton Court"** (from *The Last Ballad and Other Poems* . . .) he paints the crowd in its Bank Holiday recreation, returning to the subject a decade later in **"The Crystal Palace"** (from *Fleet Street and Other Poems* . . .), the second attempt being verbally less finished but more realistic in incident and diction.

He also pushes back the boundaries of London on the poetic map in order to take in the house-and-garden suburbs and the pastoral fringes. **"November"** (from *Holiday and Other Poems* . . .) offers us a sequence of six vignettes: Regent's Park, the Enfield Road, Epping Forest, Box Hill, London, W., and the Chilterns. Living at Hornsey, as he did when he first came to London, Davidson would often take a north-bound direction when seeking release from the built-up area; **"A Northern Suburb"** records the town's continued encroachment on the land:

> In gaudy yellow brick and red,
>   With rooting pipes, like creepers rank,
> The shoddy terraces o'erspread
>   Meadow, and garth, and daisied bank.

With shelves for rooms the houses crowd,
Like draughty cupboards in a row—
Ice-chests when wintry winds are loud,
Ovens when summer breezes blow.

The advent of our new towns since the war only makes this poem more socially valid. One might hazard a guess—to instance but two names—that Edgell Rickword and Sir John Betjeman have read and digested such poems as this.

With the exception of the ungainly *Testaments*, it is, oddly, Davidson's later poems which are most "modernist" in subject and diction while being, at the same time, most technically and formally unfinished. Besides the pieces already cited in *Fleet Street and Other Poems*, . . . there are others which enshrine brief vignettes of the contemporary scene—swiftly passing images of *things clearly seen*—surrounded by a welter of verbose writing. **"The Thames Embankment"** and the title poem particularly repay study. Yet it cannot be claimed that Davidson wrote a single *entire* poem in the "modern " idiom; the nearest he came to it being **"In the Isle of Dogs"** from his last volume of verse published in the nineties, *The Last Ballad and Other Poems*. Its first twenty-four lines mix contemporaneity of reference with a fairly sparse diction; but from then on till its end some forty lines later, a literary-romantic language takes over. (pp. 28-30)

In their poetics of what is aesthetically quintessential, [Dowson, Johnson, and Davidson] are a bridge between Victorianism and the twentieth century as represented by the trad-modernism of Eliot, Pound and the mature Yeats. There is, for example, plenty of passionate moral contemplation in the latter's later work, but such a poem as "Easter 1916," say, would not have been written by him had he not learned his trade with those "Companions of the Cheshire Cheese." (p. 34)

> *Derek Stanford, in an introduction to* Three Poets of the Rhymers' Club *by Ernest Dowson, Lionel Johnson, and John Davidson, Carcanet Press, 1974, pp. 11-37.*

TOM HUBBARD   (essay date 1984)

[*In the following excerpt, Hubbard discusses Davidson's novels and short stories.*]

In a lecture given in 1860 Turgenev compared two characters from world literature, Hamlet and Don Quixote. He proposed that the former's passive scepticism and the latter's active idealism are the two forces of a dialectic that is fundamental to all existence. Hamlet is a cool intellectual, taking nothing on trust, always questioning; Don Quixote has all the passion and certainty of a fanatic. Hamlet's irony is the antithesis to Don Quixote's enthusiasm.

John Davidson was both a canny ironist and a reckless enthusiast. Towards the end of his life the enthusiast prevailed over the ironist and the result was tragic. Nobody took to the materialistic creed which he preached in his series of blank verse *Testaments* and tragedies. (p. 71)

I do not know if Davidson knew Turgenev's lecture; it is possible, for he took a keen interest in European literature and the 1894 translation would have been available to him. It would certainly have appealed to him, especially in view of his published comments on both the Danish prince and the Spanish knight. In Davidson's second novel, *Perfervid,* . . . the garrulous Cosmo Mortimer elaborates his theory of "greatness" to Ninian Jamieson, the character described by the novel's title. Cosmo protests that "greatness" is a very different quality from the quixotism of Ninian's attempts at diamond-making and claiming the British throne:

> "it doesn't follow that a great man must be a hero. Hamlet . . . was a great man, but he wasn't a hero. The difference between great men and heroes is that great men are wise and heroes are fools. . . . Heroes . . . are eccentric; heroism is eccentricity."

Although Davidson's own loyalties were divided he was able to entertain different points of view through the medium of the characters in his fiction and prose dialogues. This meant that for most of his working life he could avoid identification with one side to the exclusion of the other. Ninian Jamieson may be diminished when judged by Hamlet-like criteria, but these criteria can themselves come under scrutiny. In the dialogues, "the old doubter" Hamlet is assessed as

> the mediocrity, the man in the street; a loquacious person; a busybody, given to reading books after dinner and scribbling on the margins; one that kept a diary and wrote letters to the newspapers. A Parliament-man, a debater! He would have been a good bishop, a good under-secretary; and might have remained solvent as a stock-broker. . . . Hamlet, the middle-class man, stares out of all our middle-class literature. . . . Hamlet is a nobody. . . .

That would partly describe Cosmo Mortimer, and in that light Ninian would appear to greater advantage as a man of spirit blithely indifferent to tedious bourgeois common-sense. Yet Cosmo, for all his fussy pomposity, is not lacking in quixotic impulses; he has as many eccentricities as Ninian, and they are just as bizarre in their own way, if less impressive. Does Don Quixote, ultimately, get the last word? In another dialogue Davidson has the knight himself declare:

> Not Achilles, not Sigurd, not Orlando, not Faust,
> but I, Don Quixote de la Mancha, am he whose
> name the world would cherish should all others
> be forgotten.

Davidson ultimately took this to heart but in his fiction, published between 1885 and 1896, long before the testaments and tragedies, he offered artistic presentation of both sides of the dialectic. . . . One of Davidson's semi-autobiographical figures is Rorison, the Scottish journalist in *Earl Lavender,* who is described by a friend as "a very special blend of the *shrewdness,* simplicity and *fervour* which characterise his race. The title-hero of *Baptist Lake,* . . . a languid English decadent, tells his young Scottish friend that he and his compatriots are, paradoxically, both garrulous and reticent. As regards his principal characters, Davidson's irony requires that their lofty schemes will end in hilarious failure, but I hope to show that there is something in their ambition that both author and reader can find not just attractive, but exhilarating. Clearly we can expect Davidson to generate some powerful tensions.

Let us look more closely at what Davidson means by irony, for he means something quite specific, something that is at the heart of his philosophical concerns:

> [Irony] is centric, the adamantine axis of the universe. . . . By it our enterprises are whirled away from our most resolved intentions. A

playwright, wearing out his life in the abortive effort to found a county family, makes the literature of the world Shakespearian centuries after his death; the Pilgrim Fathers colonise America in the name of the Highest—that Tammany may flourish in New York; and out of the beautiful Shakespearianism may come evil; and out of Tammany, good. . . . Irony is not a creed. The makers of creeds have always miscalled, denied some part of the world. Irony affirms and delights in the whole. Consciously, it is the deep complacence which contemplates with unalloyed satisfaction Love and Hate, the tiger and the nightingale, the horse and the blowfly, Messalina and Galahad, the village natural and Napoleon.

Critical detachment, then, is to be preferred to single-minded commitment. He maintains that irony is not the same thing as mockery, but in practice he does not hesitate to make his protagonists as ludicrous as they are perfervid. Of paramount interest, however, is the strong evidence that Davidson's targets include himself. In his first novel *The North Wall,* . . . an "unsuccessful literary man," Maxwell Lee, maintains a lofty scorn for hackwork, preferring to produce dramas and philosophical romances which no publisher or editor will touch. Davidson himself had more success, but his attitude was much the same as Lee's. In 1909 he was to write: "Nine-tenths of my time, and that which is most precious, have been wasted in the endeavour to earn a livelihood. In a world of my own making I should have been writing only what should have been written. To the despair of his long-suffering wife, Lee decides to reject novel-writing in favour of novel-creation: instead of the "effete" practice of putting pen to paper he will direct the course of real life among a group of unsuspecting strangers. This he does, and his new art form proves to be a recipe for chaos. Unlike Lee, Davidson was always conscious of his family responsibilities, but in his last decade he made it clear that he wanted to go beyond literature and direct the course of real life. He considered himself to be the one who would usher in the new age. Twenty years earlier, Davidson seems to have been more cautious, and to have used fiction to warn himself. At that time his ambitions may not have been so grandiose but he seems to have recognised the need to keep a check on himself. In the even more autobiographical *Alison Hepburn's Exploit,* . . . Davidson challenges youthful illusions in a less fantastic, more realistic manner. This novella's nineteen-year-old heroine scorns the pious, petit-bourgeois milieu of her parents, who run a stationer's business off Leith Walk. At Waverley Station she boards the train for King's Cross, her pocket full of the manuscript of *A Godless Universe, and Other Poems,* her head full of the sensation which she expects these effusions will produce in the sophisticated metropolis. By the time the train reaches London, however, she has cold feet. She gets no further than the station exit, from where she looks out at the city with its fogs and fops. She turns on her heels, buys a ticket for home, and immediately makes use of it. Back in Edinburgh she submits to a life of provincial domesticity, married to the conventional, philistine son of one of her father's business associates. Davidson himself rebelled against his evangelical family and the more general narrowness of the Scottish scene; like Alison, he sought success in London with his ballads and blank verse; he too wanted to destroy established Christianity. But he had to struggle in order to achieve an all-too-brief literary acclaim, and in his more considered moments

he was unwilling to replace religious bigotry with atheistic bigotry—the "Theophobia" which is Alison's "disease."

Davidson's irony, then, whirls his characters away from their "most resolved intentions." But his more quixotic impulses could not accept their frustration by a Hamlet mode of "ripe judgment . . . all-comprehensive, but generally useless and condemned to inaction." (pp. 71-5)

An admirer of Balzac, Davidson seems to have been strongly attracted to the Frenchman's portrayal of people who are single-minded to the point of monomania. Balzac both criticises and celebrates that great nineteenth-century concept, aspiration; among his hopefuls are young provincials intent on conquering the big city, or something even bigger than that. Davidson works in this tradition when he presents us with the likes of Alison Hepburn, her namesake and fellow-writer the Rev. William Hepburn and the actor Alexander Murdoch in *Laura Ruthven's Widowhood,* . . . Ninian Jamieson in *Perfervid,* and Earl Lavender with his incautious evangelising for Evolution and the "new epoch."

For all their excesses, many of Davidson's protagonists seek what is genuinely liberating. They are subversive, upsetting the mindless conformity of respectable society. In fact they are rather like their creator at his best. They agree with Menzies in **"Michaelmas"** that "he who resists / His wanton moods for ever, ends / In being moodless." Davidson champions sexual love against social and religious codes. Victorianism is satirised in the pompous, repressed aunts of the spirited young heroines of *The North Wall* and *Perfervid.* Scottish Calvinism, in the person of a sadistic schoolmaster, blights for life the budding sexuality of a thirteen-year-old in **"The Schoolboy's Tragedy,"** arguably Davidson's best short story. An existential commitment to freedom informs his most important work; he is not entirely mocking when he gives us Earl Lavender's peroration on the Will to Happiness.

Davidson despised equally the dour philistinism of Scotland and the fashionable languor of London; he shared Earl Lavender's impatience at the vast majority of men and women:

"The average mind is a dirty sponge in a bathroom; it must be wrung out, washed clean, and kept in running water." The literary editor Meyrick Tunstall is his creator's mouthpiece in *Laura Ruthven's Widowhood;* indeed, Tunstall's polemic against Zolaesque naturalism can also be found, word for word, in Davidson's journalism. At a party largely attended by metropolitan literati and other supersophisticated twitterers, Laura Ruthven is impressed by Tunstall: "She had never before met anybody who had mastered, or so completely mastered, that dread of the cold indifference of society to all enthusiasm which puts a gag in more mouths than we imagine." In fact Tunstall is deeply troubled by his relationship with his milieu; he tells Laura:

> "I am a mere charlatan; and when I have imagined that I was leading opinion, I was only amusing and entertaining a public that had cheered me on as a high-class literary Merry-Andrew. . . . Oh, this psychological analysis! It is the curse of the age; it has made Hamlets of us all. We reason and argue, and examine our deeds, instead of going straight on doing, doing, and never doubting that what we do must be right just because we are able to do it."

In this crowd of Hamlets, then, Tunstall is a Quixote struggling to get out. He sums up his experience in the emphatic declaration that *"a passionless life is death."* In the advocacy of "passion" against the limitations of rationality we can discern a leading motif in existentialist writers such as Kierkegaard and Nietzsche: Davidson's name can certainly be linked with these, especially the latter. He denied that he was a *disciple* of Nietzsche but the undeniable *affinity* was to prove even stronger after the turn of the century.

We are still faced with the sturdily national origins of [Davidson's] work. Presiding over these novels and stories is Davidson the Scot, distrustful of the passionate exuberance in which he revels, eager for it to surge ahead even as he observes it with a wry grin. (pp. 75-6)

Davidson may have rejected Scottish Calvinism but he inherited its intense style. His theory of irony was opposed to creeds but he responded to the manner in which creeds were preached. He proved to be no mean preacher himself. Among the liveliest characters in his fiction are old Scots wives who suddenly burst into hard-line Calvinist flyting. Take **Baptist Lake**'s Mrs. Macalister, ill at ease in decadent England, answering the taunts of the barmaid Florrie. Florrie, who works for the unscrupulous Mrs. Tiplady, has just been mocking Mrs. Macalister's Scottishness with the image of "'kickin' up yer 'eels in short flounces an' tartan tights'." Mrs. Macalister lets rip:

> "Ye randy," she cried. "When that ill-scrapit tongue o' yours is danglin' oot o' the cracklin' o' yer rizzert mou like a coalie dug's, an' you an' Mrs Tippleleddy's sittin' on yer hunkers, groanin' for a drap watter, an' auld Niekie Ben pullin' awa' at the brimstane-tap, wi' nae 'mild or bitter' aboot it, but jist 'here, doon wi't,' pint efter pint, scaudin' het, it'll come intae yer mind when ye're se'rt wi' a spaecial drap that rives yer boesum an' gars yer 'een reel like a sicht o' green cheese, 'This is for lauchin' at a deacent Scotch bodie that only keepit a ta-baccy-shop an' me a barmaid!' Tartan tichts! Ye'll hae tartan tichts wi' a vengeance, when ye're skelpt an' scored frae tap tae tap wi' the de'il's cat-o-nine tails. It'll be casten up tae ye, that it will, ye ill-faured, towsy limmer! Awa' wi' ye! Get oot o' my sicht!"
>
> (p. 77)

If Davidson's predilection for prophecy reinforces the Nietzschean connection, it also suggests something of the Scottish minister who thunders from a text in Revelation. Increasingly zealous to "rehearse / Unheard of things," he seeks the destruction of old values and evangelises for a new epoch. *Fin de siècle* or *fin du globe*? As the century "totters tombwards" Davidson ceases to make fun of Earl Lavender and begins to take his rhetoric in deadly earnest. (Lavender is a corruption of 'l'avenir'—the future). But the novel's stylish eccentric is replaced, in the drama **The Triumph of Mammon**, . . . by a ruthless dictator. Mammon threatens poverty, toil and war more horrific than anything that has gone before. A Quixote's adventurism has metamorphosed into a megalomaniac's power. That is no laughing matter. (p. 78)

In two early short stories Davidson was prefiguring such apocalyptic frenzies with much greater detachment and even irony. In **"The Salvation of Nature,"** Sir Wenyeve Westaway and Professor Penpergwyn put into effect their scheme to turn an industrialised nation into the World's Pleasance. Scotland is accordingly destroyed by fire—is Davidson mocking the Calvinist hell?—and later reclaimed with the soil from a number of Polynesian islands. The whole enterprise appears to be a success and it catches on: other countries get the same treatment. Then everything goes wrong until there are only two people left in the world. Conveniently enough, however, they are Westaway's son and Penpergwyn's daughter. **"Eagle's Shadow,"** from [the collection **The Great Men and A Practical Novelist**], chronicles a future war involving Britain, Europe and the United States. Although peace is eventually established, no-one has reckoned on the potential threat from the Nihilists, who have set up a colony on the Central American isthmus. The Nihilists, it seems, have discovered how to control the weather. Consequently Britain is transformed into an iceberg: mankind is eventually destroyed except for—surprise, surprise—two people, "one, a little boy, who wakened up one morning at the North Pole, to find himself, as he thought, alone in the world; and the other, a little girl, who wakened up on the same morning at the South Pole with the same thought." The two stories vary on the same theme, taking different extremes of temperature as images of apocalypse; this tallies with Davidson's theory of irony and its contemplation of opposites. In each story human enthusiasm has resorted to one of these extremes—fire and brimstone or perpetual winter—and the result is near-oblivion. But there exists the opportunity for redemption and renewal.

Apocalyptic and Arctic imagery reappear in a late and uncollected story, **"The Realm of the Ultimate Pole."** The narrator is visiting the North Pole, where he witnesses the mass suicide of the Alanadoths, a race of heroic creatures whose blood is the temperature of molten metal. They appear to be the inhabitants of some unexplored Arctic region, but have been cast adrift on an iceberg. "Their sustenance being exhausted, and knowing no means whereby they might return to the only atmosphere and region at all tolerable to their extraordinary nature, they had, in the pride of their life and perfect possession of all their powers, stepped joyfully to their grave rather than be for one moment of their existence anything less than puissant and splendid Alanadoths." This is a much more serious tale than either **"The Salvation of Nature"** or **"Eagle's Shadow."** The dialectic of hot and cold is totally destroyed, with no hope of renewal.

Like the Alanadoths, Davidson drowned himself; his visionary energies had gone unheeded, and the world went on in its neglectful and negative way. The most tragic aspect of this life and work, however, was the split in his own sensibility. In most of his fiction, the ironic and the enthusiastic, the Hamlet and the Quixote, co-existed in a creative *discordia concors*. As with Stevenson's Jekyll and Hyde, however, when the one atrophied the other, the survival of either was no longer assured. (pp. 78-9)

Tom Hubbard, "Irony and Enthusiasm: The Fiction of John Davidson," in Scottish Literary Journal, *Vol. II, No. 2, December, 1984, pp. 71-82.*

ADDITIONAL BIBLIOGRAPHY

Bargainnier, Earl F. "Davidson and Hofmannsthal on Naxos." *Theatre Research International* V, No. 1 (Winter 1979-80): 70-82.

Compares and contrasts Davidson's *Scaramouch in Naxos* with Austrian Hugo von Hofmannsthal's opera *Ariadne auf Naxos* (1912). According to Bargainnier: "Davidson followed the nineteenth century English pantomime and Hofmannsthal followed the Baroque opera and the *commedia dell'arte*, each tradition providing a precedent for the wedding of Greek myth and harlequinade characters, and each providing a means for the dramatists to express their concepts of the mystical powers of love."

Chesterton, Gilbert K. "The Suicide of Thought." In his *Orthodoxy*, pp. 52-81. New York: John Lane Co., 1921.
Includes a discussion of the different concepts of "will" propounded by Shaw, H. G. Wells, and Davidson. According to Chesterton: "A brilliant anarchist like Mr. John Davidson feels an irritation against ordinary morality, and therefore he invokes will—will to anything. He only wants humanity to want something. It wants ordinary morality. He rebels against the law and tells us to will something or anything. But we have willed something. We have willed the law against which he rebels."

Crum, Ralph B. "In Conclusion: John Davidson." In his *Scientific Thought in Poetry*, pp. 228-38. New York: AMS Press, Inc., 1966.
Examines the influence of modern scientific thought on Davidson's poetry, noting that he fully accepted "the scientific point of view, along with the materialistic philosophy that accompanied it. . . . [Davidson] was not to attempt to escape from the consequences of this doctrine and its implications. These facts were not merely to be accepted but they were to be woven into the very texture of his poetry, and form the very framework of his imagination."

Davidson, John. "An Epistle of Davidson." *The Academy* LXXV, No. 1906 (14 November 1908): 461-63.
Davidson's response to the *Academy*'s November 7th condemnatory review of *The Testament of John Davidson* [see excerpt dated 1908]. According to Davidson: "Your eager abuse of my *Testament* and of myself does not concern me. It is the method of the abuse I wish to criticise. . . . It is the old method of false suggestion. You connote disconnected sentences, and upon your own rearrangement of his writing accuse the author of a meaning the reverse of his intention." The editor replies: "If Mr. Davidson wishes to clear himself of the charges which we bring against him it will be necessary for him to prove that he has written the whole of this *Testament* with his tongue in his cheek, and even then he will still lie under the shame of having perpetrated a disgusting and discreditable joke." (For further discussion of this controversy, see the *Academy* 21 November 1908, pp. 490-91; 5 December 1908, pp. 535-36; and 12 December 1908, p. 557.)

Review of *Ballads and Songs* and *Fleet Street Eclogues*. *The Edinburgh Review* 183, No. CCCLXXVI (April 1896): 488-515.
Concludes that in Davidson's works "the interest is more in the idea than in the treatment of it, and this is more emphatically the case with "Thirty Bob a Week," which might have been a fine and pathetic poem were it not defiled . . . by the futile realism involved in the use of slang."

Fletcher, Ian. "A Scots Poet." *Essays in Criticism* XII, No. 4 (October 1962): 435-41.
Presents a general assessment of Davidson's poetry, particularly praising "Thirty Bob a Week" and the ballad "A Woman and Her Son." According to Fletcher: "What irritates about [Davidson] is the richness of insight and the fussiness rather than poverty of technique. With the insights of our own century, he remains obstinately self-confined to the nineteenth."

Harris, Frank. "John Davidson: Ad Memoriam." In his *Contemporary Portraits*, pp. 127-58. New York: Bretano's Publishers, 1920.
A tribute composed chiefly of personal reminiscences of Davidson during the period from 1890 to 1909. Harris concludes: "Davidson will live with Burns, it seems to me; he is not so great a force: he has not Burns's pathos nor his tenderness nor his humor; but he is a master of pure English, and his best work touches extremes of beauty and tragic sadness."

Hind, C. Lewis. "John Davidson." In his *More Authors and I*, pp. 77-82. New York: Dodd, Mead and Co., 1922.
Biographical and critical sketch. According to Hind: "Davidson was a defiant poet and author. . . . In his writing he lacked charm; he lacked persuasiveness; he wanted to storm the heights of fame by a frontal attack; he did not realize that there is always a quieter and subtler way round."

Lester, John A., Jr. "Friedrich Nietzsche and John Davidson: A Study in Influence." *Journal of the History of Ideas* XVIII, No. 3 (June 1957): 411-29.
Traces themes and philosophical concepts common to both writers. Lester suggests that "to a large degree Davidson may have been a Nietzschean before he ever heard the name of Nietzsche," and maintains that "formal Nietzschean thought merely intensified tendencies that already possessed him."

———. *Journey Through Despair: 1880-1914*. Princeton: Princeton University Press, 1968, 211 p.
Places Davidson's works and philosophy in the context of late nineteenth and early twentieth-century literature and thought. Lester describes the era as one which "severely jarred and shifted the bearings of man's imaginative life and left him at times bewildered as to how to recover his lost meaning and purpose. . . . In literature it was a time of confusion and a nervous, often frenzied, search for new terms on which the imagination could live."

Moulton, Louise Chandler. "The Man Who Dares." *The Chapbook* II, No. 7 (15 February 1895): 291-301.
An appreciative review of *Ballads and Songs*. According to Moulton: "One closes Mr. Davidson's book with reluctance, and with a haunting sense of beauty, and power, and the promise of yet greater things to come."

Nelson, James G. *The Early Nineties: A View from the Bodley Head*. Cambridge, MA: Harvard University Press, 1971, 387 p.
History and brief criticism of works published by John Lane and Elkin Matthews between 1887 and 1894, including Davidson's *Plays, Fleet Street Eclogues*, and *A Random Itinerary*.

O'Connor, Mary. "Did Bernard Shaw Kill John Davidson? The 'Tragi-Comedy' of a Commissioned Play." *The Shaw Review* XXI, No. 3 (September 1978): 108-23.
An account of Shaw's commission and later rejection of Davidson's *The Game of Life*. O'Connor concludes that "despite the genius which Shaw recognized in Davidson, the affair of *The Game of Life* proved the poet to be inadequate. . . . Suicide was the unfortunate but conceivable outcome of the discouragement and despair Davidson must have felt in the face of Shaw's demands."

Parker, W. M. "A Princely Decadent: John Davidson." In his *Modern Scottish Writers*, pp. 223-44. Freeport, New York: Books for Libraries Press, 1968.
Praises Davidson's verse while noting that it is characterized by "three somewhat incompatible attitudes . . .—the attitudes of the pedagogue, the philosopher, and the decadent revolutionary."

Peterson, Carroll V. *John Davidson*. New York: Twayne Publishers, 1972, 163 p.
Biographical and critical study.

Richards, Grant. "His Publisher's Failure." In his *Housman: 1897-1937*, pp. 61-79. New York: Octagon Books, 1973.
Quotes Housman's letter to Richards of May 7, 1907, in which Housman remarks that Davidson's *The Triumph of Mammon* "is much more interesting to read than the *Theatrocrat;* but as for his knowledge which is going to change the world, it is just like the doctrine of the Trinity: probably false, and quite unimportant if true."

Stoddart, Jane T. "An Interview with Mr. John Davidson." *The Bookman: A Literary Journal* I, No. 1 (February 1895): 85-7.
Discusses the genesis of *Fleet Street Eclogues*, the influence of other authors on Davidson's work, and the choice of urban subjects

for his poetry. According to Davidson: "The later writers . . . whom I have read most are Tennyson, and, recently, Ibsen. I don't mean that you could trace Ibsen in my work, but he has certainly had a considerable influence on my thought."

Thouless, Priscilla. "John Davidson" and "Davidson's Later Dramas." In her *Modern Poetic Drama*, pp. 76-94, 95-114. Freeport, N.Y.: Books for Libraries Press, 1968.
A chronological survey of Davidson's dramatic works and an examination of his atheistic credo.

Watson, William. "The Tragedy of John Davidson." *The Times* (26 April 1909): 10.
Obituary tribute assailing the society that drove Davidson to suicide. According to Watson: "Davidson had exhausted himself long before his last volume saw the light. None the less, this was a man who, notwithstanding all the crudity of his later thinking, all the resentment against society and Fate which made much of his utterance so turbid, was yet a creature with something of the divine fire in him."

Yeats, W. B. "The Trembling of the Veil: The Tragic Generation." In his *Autobiographies*, pp. 277-350. London: MacMillan & Co., 1955.
Personal reminiscence tracing the acquaintance of Yeats with Davidson. Yeats observes: "With enough passion to make a great poet, through meeting no man of culture in early life, [Davidson] lacked intellectual receptivity, and, anarchic and indefinite, lacked pose and gesture, and now no verse of his clings to my memory."

Richard Harding Davis

1864-1916

American journalist, short story writer, novelist, essayist, and dramatist.

Davis, a celebrated travel writer and one of the most popular fiction writers of his day, is best remembered as an important early twentieth-century American war correspondent. From the 1890 Cuban war for independence until the beginning of World War I, Davis was responsible for many of the timeliest, most accurate, and most entertaining accounts of numerous national and international conflicts. He is generally considered a leading chronicler and an ideal representative of the era that Theodore Roosevelt termed "the Strenuous Age": a time when America was flourishing, boundaries were being expanded, and adventure was easily within reach of those with the courage to seek it out.

Davis was born in Philadelphia to newspaper editor Lemuel Clarke Davis and novelist Rebecca Harding Davis. Before her marriage, Rebecca had won fame in New England literary circles for her controversial and critically acclaimed novel *Life in the Iron Mills,* and she was by far the most important influence upon her son's life and career. Correspondence between the two reveals that she was a constant source of literary advice and encouragement. An indulged child, Davis was later an indifferent student whose poor grades forced his expulsion from both Lehigh and Johns Hopkins universities. Nevertheless, at both schools he was a fashion trendsetter, star athlete, and a regular contributor to student publications. After Davis left Johns Hopkins in 1886, his father arranged for him to work as a reporter for the Philadelphia *Record*. Fired within a few months, he found a position with the Philadelphia *Press* and applied himself more assiduously to this new job. Davis soon distinguished himself as a writer of human interest stories, achieving conspicuous success with a series of articles about the survivors of the 1889 Johnstown flood. After several years with a number of Philadelphia papers, Davis moved to New York in 1889 and was hired by the New York *Evening Sun*. He covered a variety of news beats, including sports and crime reporting, charity and society events, theater news, and horse shows. At this time he also began contributing short stories to such periodicals as *Scribner's* and *Harper's Weekly*. In these stories he created the socialite Courtlandt Van Bibber, described by one disparaging critic as "an office boy's idea of a gentleman" but a popular fictional creation with Davis's readers. Critics have said that the upper-class milieu of the Van Bibber stories served to assure wealthy readers that their world was a well-ordered place bounded by comforting rules, laws, and class distinctions, while less affluent consumers of magazine fiction believed the stories gave them a privileged glimpse into the lives of the rich. According to Davis biographer Gerald Langford, Van Bibber himself gave upwardly mobile Americans in search of culture "the lessons they needed in how to appear superciliously at ease in company." The popular illustrator Charles Dana Gibson, whose "Gibson girl" typified the ideal of American female beauty at the turn of the century, illustrated some of Davis's stories and appropriated Davis as a model. Davis's square-jawed, clean-shaven likeness, seen in proximity with many lovely women in Gibson's

sketches, is widely credited with contributing to the sudden unpopularity of beards and mustaches.

In 1890 Davis became magazine editor of *Harper's Weekly* and brought to its pages the short fiction of Henry James, Gertrude Atherton, and his friend Rudyard Kipling, among others. However, he was soon discontented with desk work and began to travel, recording his impressions of the American West, England, Central and South America, and Europe in essays that were first published in magazines and later gathered in the collections *The West from a Car-Window, Our English Cousins, The Rulers of the Mediterranean, About Paris,* and *Three Gringos in Venezuela and Central America*. While entertaining and informative, Davis's travel essays reveal a profound ethnocentricity: he judged everything from the unshakeable assumption that cultured Americans represented the height of civilized humanity, and he assessed all other cultures in comparison with his own. Trained as a journalist, he wrote quickly, relying on first impressions of exotic locales that he conveyed vividly to his readers.

In 1890 Davis went to Cuba to report directly on the Cuban war for independence. His articles from Cuba established his reputation as one of America's leading war correspondents, and he subsequently traveled the world to report on major and minor conflicts, becoming a celebrity in his own right for his various well-publicized exploits. For example, he joined Roosevelt's Rough Riders during the Spanish-American war and picked Africa for his honeymoon so that he could observe the Boer War, on one occasion nearly trapping his bride and himself in the crossfire of a battle. According to Scott Compton Osborn and Robert L. Phillips, Jr., Davis's extensive coverage of virtually every war between 1890 and 1914 resulted in his being "commonly regarded as the typical and perhaps most brilliant American war correspondent of his time." Among his volumes of collected war correspondence, *The Cuban and Porto Rican Campaigns* and *With Both Armies in South Africa* are two of the most highly regarded. Davis's flamboyant personality and penchant for showmanship annoyed some of his contemporaries and sometimes obscured his journalistic accomplishments. Nevertheless, he was respected within his profession for his scrupulous insistence on verifying all the facts in his stories, for his timely and accurate reporting, and for his disdain of "yellow journalism," the tendency toward sensationalistic reporting and scandalmongering that boosted the circulations of many late nineteenth- and early twentieth-century publications.

Although he is best remembered as a journalist, during his lifetime Davis was equally well known as a fiction writer. In the early part of his career he primarily wrote short stories which featured such characters as the amiable and wealthy clubman Van Bibber, resourceful newsmen involved in romance and adventure, and various other incarnations of the "gentleman adventurer." Davis utilized the haunts and homes of New York's wealthiest and most socially prominent individuals as background for his stories, earning him the epithet "the dress-suit snob of American fiction" from Frank Norris biographer Ernest Marchand. Norris himself, however, cited Davis as an early influence on his own career, as did many other early twentieth-century writers who began as reporters, including Jack London and Stephen Crane. Davis's successes with short fiction encouraged him to try writing novels, and his first, *The Princess Aline*, is generally considered his best. Utilizing romantic love, chivalry, international travel, and wholesome, energetic, moral young Americans as beau ideals, *The Princess Aline* is similar in theme and style to Davis's popular short stories. Well-liked by readers and critics, it signaled a promising career for Davis as a novelist, and his next novel, *Soldiers of Fortune*, seemed to confirm that promise. Davis's hero in *Soldiers of Fortune* is Robert Clay, an intrepid, courageous American civil engineer skilled at managing the assets of wealthy companies abroad. Clay reorganizes a failing iron works in the imaginary South American country of Olancho (insuring enormous profits for the company's United States owner), squelches a revolution, politely refuses the presidency of Olancho, and wins the heart and hand of an equally stalwart young American woman. The novel's nineteenth-century readers made it a best-seller and the most financially remunerative of Davis's books; however, in recent years the novel has been examined primarily as a product of the jingoism of its period. Clay is portrayed as an agent of American economic imperialism, paternalistically overseeing the resources of native South Americans who are depicted as either childlike or mendacious, thus making, according to Larzer Ziff, "an enormous contribution to the fantasy of the natural superiority of the American." *Soldiers of Fortune* clearly reflects the view, expressed in Davis's nonfiction writing, that the Central and South American "needs to have a protectorate established over him" and that "the Central American citizen is no more fit for a republican form of government than he is for an arctic expedition."

Soldiers of Fortune, however, was the last of Davis's novels to be well received. Beginning with his next novel, *The King's Jackal*, Davis's novels and short stories appeared to increasingly negative reviews and declining sales. He was particularly excoriated for depicting a character with questionable morals in a nonjudgmental way in the novel *Captain Macklin: His Memoirs*. Davis wrote plaintively to his mother that he had tried to tell the story of a cad who becomes a better person "not because of a woman—but because his finer qualities come out as he grows older in years and experience." Macklin's ungentlemanly aspect, however, offended longtime readers of Davis, while to a readership coming of age with the new century, this attempt at psychological realism seemed hopelessly old-fashioned when compared with the works of Stephen Crane and Theodore Dreiser. The strong disapproval that the book met with led Davis to contemplate abandoning fiction writing altogether. He was eventually prompted to continue writing both novels and short stories, primarily for the guaranteed income they brought him. However, reviewers of his post-1900 fiction and later commentators assessing his entire career are generally agreed that in these later works Davis was for the most part reworking old and familiar plots taken from his earlier successes. A reviewer of the 1908 novel *Vera the Medium*, for example, wrote that "the promise which the Van Bibber stories held years ago has never been fulfilled."

Davis was skilled at writing popular, if ephemeral, fiction—timely works that appealed to the readers of his era but that have not endured. Although some critics, notably John Solensten, have questioned the tendency to categorize Davis as a "superficial purveyor of journalized fiction," Davis's enduring place in American letters is generally held to be that of a preeminent journalist. "He was a reporter," according to Fred Lewis Pattee, "and the reporter must work always amid excitement, with rapidity and dash and brilliance." Summarizing Davis's career, Charles Lewis Hind has written that he "was an ideal magazine writer. . . . His interests were in the present, in people who are doing adventurous, odd, and amusing things. From the abundance his quick brain and moving eye selected the best magazine features, and he turned them into copy with confidence and brilliance, quite aware that Richard Harding Davis was doing it, and that in his opinion, what he did was the best of its kind."

(See also *Contemporary Authors*, Vol. 114 and *Dictionary of Literary Biography*, Vol. 12: *American Realists and Naturalists*, and Vol. 23: *American Newspaper Journalists, 1873-1900*.)

PRINCIPAL WORKS

Gallegher   (short stories)   1891
Stories for Boys   (short stories)   1891
Van Bibber and Others   (short stories)   1892
The West from a Car-Window   (travel essays)   1892
The Exiles   (short stories)   1894
Our English Cousins   (travel essays)   1894
The Rulers of the Mediterranean   (travel essays)   1894
About Paris   (travel essays)   1895
The Princess Aline   (novel)   1895
Cinderella   (short stories)   1896
Three Gringos in Venezuela and Central America   (travel essays)   1896
Cuba in War Time   (essays and journalism)   1897
Dr. Jameson's Raiders vs. the Johannesburg Reformers (essays and journalism)   1897
Soldiers of Fortune   (novel)   1897

THE BOOK BUYER   (essay date 1891)

[*In the following excerpt, the critic notes the "Dickens- or Zola-like" journalistic style of Davis's short story collection* Gallegher.]

In *Gallegher, and Other Stories,* Richard Harding Davis shows himself a born short story writer. He has, in unusual degree, the gift of rapid, easy and yet concentrated narrative, a quick eye for the picturesque in character and situation, and a native sense of the form in virtue of which a short story is not a novel cut down or condensed. These qualities alone, however, would not distinguish him as sharply as he is to be distinguished from the many successful writers of such stories that are now writing. The art of this kind of composition has been carried very far of late, and notably in this country; and, moreover, it seems particularly adapted to the American faculty of literary expression. Mr. Davis's distinguishing characteristics are perhaps rather his style and his sentiment than the bright cleverness he shares with so many. He has a particular leaning toward the human, the tender, the delicate, and gently pathetic; quite unalloyed with a weakness for the heroic and the tragic, but full of feeling, and thoroughly direct and simple. And his narratives have a manner at once marked enough and restrained enough to be called style—betraying care and attention on the one hand, and illustrating spontaneous felicities on the other in a very happy combination. [The stories in *Gallegher*] substantiate the genuineness of their author's recent vogue, and are as promising as they are unpretending. That which gives its title to the volume is the story of a newspaper office-boy whose pluck and intelligence win an important "beat" for his paper,

which is excitingly told, though the boy's own character is the centre of interest. **"A Walk up the Avenue"** and **"The Other Woman"** are, perhaps, the best, the most nearly literature, in being more penetrated with a sense of what life is, rather than by an appreciation of one of its spectacular and transitory aspects. **"There Were Ninety-and-Nine"** is very tenderly done; but Mr. Davis is not here—in England and at Monaco—as sure-footed as on his native heath. Here he is very sure-footed indeed, as the rest of the stories, which disclose a newspaper man's Dickens- or Zola-like acquaintance with the night and seamy, and picturesque and genuine sides of "the town," abundantly show. (pp. 163-64)

A review of "Gallegher, and Other Stories," in The Book Buyer, *Vol. VIII, No. 4, May, 1891, pp. 163-64.*

HARPER'S NEW MONTHLY MAGAZINE   (essay date 1891)

[*In the following excerpt, an anonymous critic offers a largely favorable review of* Gallegher.]

Such as the newspapers know them are many characters in Mr. R. H. Davis's rapid and graphic sketch of **"Gallegher,"** which lends its name to his volume of stories and studies. It is an excellent piece of work, in which the journalistic types are admirably ascertained, and the strong material is fitly subordinated to the interest of the treatment of persons and circumstances. He knows that the important thing is the character of the office-boy Gallegher, and not the incidents that develop it; and it is much in the writer's favor that with a pen so facile, and a public so cheaply amused as ours, he keeps himself well in hand, and remembers that the merit of a story is in the art of the telling. He does this, and respects himself even when his readers mostly would not care to have him respect them. We do not say that he has altogether freed himself from the bonds of romanticistic superstition, and does not sometimes portray the thing less as it is than as he thinks his reader would like it to be; but he gives abundant evidence of the artistic conscience which no gentleman should be without. Literature is still first with him; but he loves the look of life, and he cannot be patient to see it through print, or to seek in it those poses and expressions which literature has already appropriated. In some of his slighter sketches, such as those relating to the amiable swell Van Bibber, we find qualities that almost inspire us to prophesy, and which certainly enable us to congratulate a vivid talent upon its performance. This, perhaps, is better than to talk of its promise; and there is really so much substance of things done in Mr. Davis's book that we have no occasion to draw upon his future in praising him. At all times he suggests the presence of a fine humanity in his thought, without which there cannot be the finest art in our time. What we could desire this brilliant writer, if we had our wishing-cap on, would be a perfect unconsciousness of his reader's presence, and an entire willingness to trust others with his facts as simply as providence confided them to him. This is difficult, but it is the first thing to be desired.

A review of "Gallegher," in Harper's New Monthly Magazine, *Vol. LXXXIII, No. CCCCXCVI, September, 1891, p. 640.*

THE ATHENAEUM   (essay date 1892)

[*In the following excerpt, an English reviewer of* Van Bibber and Others *commends Davis's "art of telling an amusing story with effect."*]

Mr. Davis is said to be one of the most promising of the young writers in America, and he achieved some success with his first book, entitled **Gallegher.** In [**Van Bibber and Others**], without exhibiting any startling powers, he shows that he possesses the art of telling an amusing story with effect, and can describe the self-possessed and imperturbable young man of fashion with considerable humour. But what seems curious in a writer with these qualities, he displays a lack of humour when he tries to be pathetic, and his attempts at earnestness degenerate into the kind of maudlin sentiment associated with a tract or a Strand melodrama. The first story, in which Van Bibber takes up the high moral tone, is not convincing, and **"A Patron of Art"** smacks too much of the fairy godmother of our childhood, without the touch of romance and unreality which made her possible. But when the author sticks to the cynical cleverness which is evidently his forte, as in **"The Hungry Man Was Fed"** or **"An Experiment in Economy,"** the result is excellent reading; and stories of this description form the bulk of the volume. Now that we are being deluged with so much bad writing from America, it is a pleasure to be able to give praise to Mr. Davis's English style, which is pure and forcible throughout.

A review of "Van Bibber and Others," in The Athenaeum, *No. 3376, July 9, 1892, p. 60.*

THE CHAP-BOOK   (essay date 1894)

[*In the following verse, an anonymous poet satirizes Davis's journalistic prose style.*]

> "Good morning Mr. Davis." "Harding Davis, if you
>   please."
> "Oh! pardon! Mr. Harding Hyphen Davis, if you
>   please.
> I only called to say how much I like your journalese.
> A little more familiar and a little less at ease
> With the rules of English grammar than would suit a
>   Bostonese,
> 'T is yet a fitting instrument to render thoughts like
>   these,—
> The thoughts of Mr. Davis." "Harding Davis, if you
>   please."

(p. 172)

"Notes," in The Chap-Book, *Vol. 1, No. 7, August 15, 1894, pp. 172-74.*

Charles Dana Gibson illustration. The figure on the left is a likeness of Davis. © *J.B.R., Inc.*

THE BOOKMAN   (essay date 1895)

[*In the following excerpt,* The Princess Aline *is excoriated as inferior to the kind of fiction that Davis seemed likely at one time to produce.*]

Seriously we are sorry to see Mr. Davis write such namby-pamby stuff as **The Princess Aline,** when we know him to be capable of strong orginal work if only he would follow his own bent and nurse his gifts in solitude for a time, and eschew what artists contemptuously style the "pretty-pretty" in art. Mr. Davis promised when he first began writing to plunge into life with the zest and vitality of the diver who has his eye on the pearls, but he has only skirted the shores of experience so far, and played prettily with the pebbles on the beach. We want him to live deeply and richly, and to write some noble, beautiful thing that will confirm our faith in his latent power, and in a higher origin and destiny for mankind than is shown in **The Princess Aline.** (p. 191)

J. M., in a review of "The Princess Aline," in The Bookman, *New York, Vol. 1, No. 3, April, 1895, pp. 190-91.*

THE ATLANTIC MONTHLY   (essay date 1895)

[*In the following essay, Davis's career as a journalist and short story writer is discussed.*]

If one may take sequence of publication as indicative of sequence of production, Mr. Davis began his career as a story-teller before he set out on his travels; but both stories and sketches of travel thus far intimate that his dominant interest is in seeing the world and taking a *coup d'oeil* of people rather than in penetrating the mystery of the human mind. The order of his travel appears to have been, the Eastern city, the Western prairie and outpost, the shores of the Mediterranean, and England. He has shown himself a first-rate reporter, with a swift instinct for selection of points, and something more than a knack of hitting off telling incidents. That his first reports should have been of his friends and neighbors in an Eastern city is both a testimony to his artistic sense, and something of a prophecy of the final form of his art.

In summing up his record of a scamper in the West, Mr. Davis writes: "The West is a very wonderful, large, unfinished, and out-of-doors portion of our country, and a most delightful place to visit. I would advise every one in the East to visit it, and I hope to revisit it myself. Some of those who go will not only visit it, but will make their homes there, and the course of empire will eventually Westward take its way. But when it does, it will leave one individual behind it clinging closely to the Atlantic seaboard. Little old New York is good enough for him." This is the impulsive word of a man coming home, and fresh in the recollection of that sensation which witnesses to his strongest instinct, which is, after all, not for mere wandering, but for being at the centre of energy; and there is more than one passage in the same book which betrays the writer's half-unconscious comparison of life anywhere else with life in a great city which is native, if not accidentally the city of his birth.

But the two volumes of stories which introduced Mr. Davis to his readers are a more positive and a more interesting testimony to the nature of his regard of the world in which he found himself when he had served his apprenticeship. The neighborhood which is familiar to a story-teller is not that which he describes when he tells his stories; he assumes a knowledge of it; it exists as a background, and it is only when he comes back to it after a long absence, or desires to use it in connection with historic imagination, that he sets about a deliberate appraisal of its contents. The scene of the story which first brought Mr. Davis into marked notice—"**Gallegher**"— was laid, it is true, in Philadelphia, and he may be supposed to know best the city of his birth; but it is as true of New York as of Philadelphia that when Mr. Davis began to write, the novelty of mere externals could scarcely be reckoned as an element in his art, and he was free to occupy himself with modes of life, and not with scenery.

It is noticeable that Mr. Davis does not trouble himself to use the two cities, which stand to him for the East, as opportunities for the contrast of life. The adventure of "**Gallegher**" scarcely takes on any hue from locality; with change of names it might as well have been a New York adventure, and the stories which fill the two volumes, *Gallegher and Other Stories,* and *Van Bibber and Others,* though identified almost wholly with New York, belong there not so much by virtue of their close portraiture of the distinctive life of New York as because what depth of soil they spring from is New York soil. All this is to say that it is cheifly in his capacity as a traveler in his own city that Mr. Davis makes himself known in his early stories, and the kind of interest which he discloses in them intimates the kind of interest he takes in life.

Perhaps an experimental acquaintance with journalism accounts for the happy choice of Gallegher as a subject, but the stories generally in these two volumes hint at a sympathy with spectacular life, the existence which is on exhibition at clubs, in polite society, at races, among adventurers, at the theatre, at the police station, in the newspaper office, at Delmonico's or Sherry's; and the figures who make the most impression on his pages are either those who are lookers-on at the show, or those who conribute to the entertainment something which has a spice of deviltry about it. It is a young man's world into which we are invited, but it is an open world. The healthy ebullience of youth is in the stories, and also that delicious gravity of youth which is a world away from the vulgar element of knowingness, that air of the man of the world whose capacity for enjoyment is almost past the power of spice to revive. Mr. Davis recurs with a special fondness to an invention bearing the name Van Bibber, a most delightful creature, rich, addicted to club life, a cavalier in sentiment, with a happy-go-lucky mind that astounds him occasionally by its apparent astuteness, and a coolness of courage which the modern stage has accustomed us to associate with otherwise fatuous young club men. This innocent but perfectly well-informed youngster, this man who moves with calm assurance amongst the fragile specimens of humankind who constitute his ordinary companions, and never loses his self-possession when casually encountering burglars or reprobate men of the world, is the nearest to a type that can be found in Mr. Davis's pages. It is rather a variation than a distinct species. The modern drama has put a good many Van Bibbers on the stage, though Mr. Davis's gentleman has an ingenuity in his ingenuousness which is amusing and novel. Now and then an element is introduced which disturbs a little the consistency of the character, but on the whole Mr. Davis has brought away from his excursions into New York society a figure which unconsciously reflects a good deal of credit on his creator.

Alongside of Van Bibber, in these early stories, may be placed the paragon of the other extreme in the social scale, the Hefty Burke, for example, who is equally intrepid, and, according

to his lights, equally ingenuous. The gusto with which Mr. Davis enters into the adventures of the men whose club is the saloon gives an air of lifelikeness to the scenes, even when one is inclined to think that the principle of selection has been carried so far as to exclude tolerably natural accompaniments of the life of the tough. But the fun which rules in "**How Hefty Burke Got Even**" leaves one very indulgent toward a writer who can make high life below stairs so entertaining and so clean. Indeed, the restraint which is so marked an element in a writer possessed of such high spirits is one of the surest signs of true art, and a prophecy of growth.

One brings away from these two volumes of stories which stand for Mr. Davis's report of his incursions into the life about him an impression of spirited youth, ready for a lark, but really most interested in the behavior of the men and women who represent "good society;" the young men and the young women, that is, for there are very few persons in these stories over thirty, and the old gentlemen, so called, appear to be about fifty. The saving quality is to be found in the kind of interest taken, for it is always something more than mere superficiality which arrests the writer's attention. He explores motives now and then, and shows a desire to get, if he can, at the bottom of some perplexed human heart, but for the most part his stories are anecdotes, bright, often very amusing, and always indicative of an honest curiosity. The reader is likely to care least for those stories which have an air of subtlety about them. It is not subtlety, but frankness, which underlies the best of this writer's work.

We have said that these earlier stories are not so much inventions as reports of a young man's journey into the world about him, and they hint at a kind of faculty which is sometimes found in a first-rate journalist reporter. When he takes up reporting in earnest, Mr. Davis shows that he has this faculty in a high degree, but the work done displays a rapid increase in artistic power, and frequent suggestion that the story-telling gift is not an idle plaything, but likely to reassert itself finally as the dominant impulse. Perhaps this increase is due to the change of material. The first book of travel, *The West from a Car-Window,* is professedly nothing but a series of newspaper articles thrown off after a hasty run in Texas and Colorado, visits to mining-camps, to an Indian reservation, and at army posts. The sketches are drawn with a free hand; there is a slap-dash manner about them which gives them an ephemeral character, and occasionally the reader is disposed to resent a certain cocksureness in the author; but the most interesting notes are the personal ones, the vivid characterizations of typical lives, and now and then a report of specific adventures. Moreover, there is a wise forbearance in the matter of hearsay; the honesty of the reporter is seen in his determination to confine himself to the results of first-hand information. The dash and freedom of frontier life interest, but do not altogether fascinate him; courage, endurance, the fortitude of the soldier, the patient wisdom of an army officer, these arrest his attention; and though he comes back, as we have shown, to Eastern life with a sigh of relief, he impresses the reader as having executed a commission with fidelity and with considerable skill.

It is, however, in [*The Rulers of the Mediterranean*] that Mr. Davis is seen at his best on this side. There could scarcely be a greater contrast in material than that which lies between the Western frontier of the United States and the shores of the Mediterranean. In traveling over the great reaches of the West, Mr. Davis sought for a few characteristic scenes, and sketched them with directness, with some vividness even, but the selective art was shown chiefly in the simple choice of subject. In visiting Gibraltar, Tangier, Cairo, Athens, and Constantinople, he had a more difficult task of selection; he had to choose out of a prodigal range of new and striking scenes those which were best worth painting, and this calls for something more than the reporter's knack. What is observable in this book is the sense of color and form in the picturesque, the shrewd comment on contemporaneous affairs, and the quick perception of the artistic values in the several scenes which present themselves to the traveler. The advance over the art which depicted Western life is considerable, and it is chiefly seen in the compactness and solidity of the entire impression produced. A surer touch is everywhere evident. As in the earlier book, so here, the interest in persons is never very absent; yet it seems as if the scene, the setting, had a stronger power over the writer, and as if he were not quite ready to speak in confident tones of other nationalities than his own. Be this as it may, the book is clearly more given over to the record of impressions on the eye than to anything else, and the graphic force of Mr. Davis's mind is conspicuous.

If the reader readily pardons the absence of historic allusion in a narrative of travel among historic places, remembering how often he has been bored by travelers who are oppressed with their responsibility in such case, he is likely, all the same, to reflect that a writer almost inevitably discloses the furnishing of his mind when he falls to talking about historic cities, and he can scarcely escape the conclusion that Mr. Davis is very distinctly a contemporary, an observer rather than a student, a recorder and artist rather than a historian or a philosopher. He will feel this even more keenly upon looking to see what this writer has to say on so full a topic as *Our English Cousins.* Every man after his kind. There was a young American, of about Mr. Davis's age, who went to England two generations ago and took a survey of the people and the island. He too was a college-bred man, and he visited the universities of English make, and took some account of Englishmen as he found them. We do not wish to chide Mr. Davis for not being Mr. Emerson, but we do not wish to forget that one may be a young man, and still direct his attention, when he is travelling in a historic country, to other aspects of learning and politics than the social.

It is perhaps more to the point that in leaving the Mediterranean and taking up with England Mr. Davis returns more to the point of view where he took his first stand. That is to say, he assumes his background as in his New York stories, and engages directly in sketching the poeple whom he meets. It is the story-teller's mind that is at work, even though the form is not that of fiction. Here too the people who interest him are mainly the same sort that occupy his attention in his earlier stories, but of the English, and not the New York variety. Again the upper and the lower end of society entertain him, and persons, not problems, present themselves to him.

We said at the outset that Mr. Davis's writings so far intimate his dominant interest to be in seeing the world and taking a coup d'oeil of people, and we may reckon his travels as only an extension of the curiosity which first vented itself on New York. His latest collection, *The Exiles, and Other Stories,* gives an agreeable indication that the more exclusively dramatic faculty, certainly the story-telling faculty, is likely to assert itself more emphatically. These stories show how well he can use his experience of travel as a background from which to project his modeling of human figures in interesting relations. The title story is especially suggestive. Here is a character, fast bound

Davis and his first wife.

apparently in the swathes of convention, set free by being cast unexpectedly upon a society which has tacitly agreed to ignore conventions. Mr. Holcombe preserves his integrity in the midst of the loose fragments of Tangier life, but is impelled to strip himself of his clothes, as it were, and meet his antagonist as man to man. Despite a little forcing of the situation, the story is capitally conceived and executed. A similar motive is discoverable in the less successful, indeed rather artificial tale of "His Bad Angel"; but both stories show that Mr. Davis is not likely to be content with the merely dexterous arrangement of characters and scenes brightly taken from a limited and somewhat superficial survey of the nearest society. Yet the most entertaining, and we are inclined to think the most effective piece of work in the book is "The Right of Way," which has all the air of being but a slightly heightened narrative of actual experience. The aplomb of this tale, the humor of it, the nice reserves as well as the hearty abandon, make it almost seem as if Mr. Davis could never expect to show what he might do unless the European nations would be so obliging as to go to war that he might take the field as special correspondent.

It would be a pity, however, if his capacity for narrating adventure had such exceptional opportunities for expression as to arrest him midway in his development as a novelist. It is too soon to predict what he may do in this direction. His construction in *The Exiles* and in *The Princess Aline* rests on too slender a basis to make one wholly confident that he has at present the power to hold long a sustained motive in story-telling. At any rate, his earliest, splendid achievement, **"Gallegher,"** owed its charm to the swiftness with which a first-rate scheme was carried to a dramatic culmination, and his latest printed tale, *The Princess Aline,* is an amusing involution of a whim, the *dénouement* of which has been anticipated by the reader, who yet follows the turns with enjoyment for the humor of the successive situations. What confidence we have arises from the fact that a reading of Mr. Davis's books in their chronological sequence leaves us with the impression that a wider survey of the world has given a wider horizon to his mind; that his facility in transferring impressions has been confirmed; and that, not content with reporting the modes of men's minds, he has taken to exploring the recesses of human nature. Out of such a study comes a greater sense of the complexity of life, and out of this sense is born that conception of the dramatic meaning of life which underlies the successful construction of wholes in fiction. (pp. 654-58)

> *"Richard Harding Davis," in* The Atlantic Monthly, *Vol. LXXV, No. CCCCLI, May, 1895, pp. 654-58.*

ARTHUR BARTLETT MAURICE (essay date 1902)

[*Maurice, an American critic and historian, was an associate editor of the New York* Bookman *from 1899 until 1907 and editor of that journal from 1907 until 1916. In the following excerpt from a review of* Captain Macklin, *he calls for "alleged critics" to reevaluate Davis's fiction.*]

Among the considerable number of exceptional and adventurous men to whom Mr. Davis has introduced us in the last ten or twelve years there has been none who has made a better impression on first acquaintance than Captain Burke, the Promoter of Revolutions. In *Soldiers of Fortune* we did not see enough of him to be able to claim any degree of intimacy. He crossed the stage only once or twice in the course of the book, but we knew him at once to be possessed of the right kind of *insouciance,* philosophy and shrewdness. And then, his profession,—Promoter of Revolutions. What fine air castles it suggests! How it links the past and the present! Romance is not dead; and to-day, far from the lights and shop windows of Broadway and the tall tower of Madison Square, there are places on this globe where a man may carve out fame for himself and smell powder, and taste power and responsibility, and feel the lust of battle and the imminence of death. Now in the announcement of *Captain Macklin* we thought we saw the promise of a Burke. Macklin was to be a Soldier of Fortune, fighting under many flags and serving many causes. We had pictured him as a little unscrupulous, grown shrewd and cynical through much experience, and not over-particular as to the rights and wrongs of a war, so long as those at the head of the cause for which he worked kept faith and paid him well for his services. Some sentiment he would have had, and some enthusiasm and the tried valour which makes one brave enough to confess fear. As a matter of fact the Macklin of some future stories may be all this, but as yet he is very much unfledged. . . . Royal Macklin at the age of twenty-three has "sand" and loyalty; only, like most of Mr. Davis's heroes, he talks too much.

There are many ways in which *Captain Macklin* is unlike anything which Mr. Davis has written before. It is not in every respect an advance, but those who like to read between the lines will say the author has probably never written another book in which he has given so much of himself. One cannot help thinking of it as autobiographical; that is, autobiographical in moods and day dreams. In common with most men of any imagination, Mr. Davis has passed pleasantly many hours in the construction of fine air castles. These air castles have been the suggestion and inspiration of almost all of his tales of adventure. One of them was responsible for the story of **"The Reporter Who Made Himself King"**; another, or rather several others, showed him the way to the writing of *Soldiers of Fortune;* out of another grew the *Princess Aline.* In fact, this influence has been at work in everything that he has written, but in nothing quite so much as in *Captain Macklin.* (pp. 175-76)

Captain Macklin is not "a highly important contribution to the literature of to-day." It is an admirable story, clear-cut, brave, spirited. It shows Mr. Richard Harding Davis in his maturity. And it goes further to show that it is about time for alleged critics to cease writing about Mr. Davis as the rather clever chronicler of the poses of fresh young men, and to recognise him once for all as a serious and brilliant worker, and in his way very near the top among living American novelists. (p. 178)

> *Arthur Bartlett Maurice, "Richard Harding Davis's 'Captain Macklin'," in* The Bookman, *New York, Vol. XVI, October, 1902, pp. 175-78.*

THE NATION, LONDON (essay date 1908)

[*In the following excerpt, an anonymous reviewer of* Vera the Medium *assesses this novel and the general quality of Davis's fiction.*]

Mr. Davis is always easy to read. With his neat, tailor-made style, his aplomb, his skill at presenting a few types, he need never be at a loss for an audience. That he goes deep cannot be said. The promise which the Van Bibber stories held years ago, has never been fulfilled. He has not gone ahead; he still writes for the undergraduate, and still no doubt pleases him. *Vera the Medium* well illustrates his knack. The material is not of a durable kind, but it is well-tailored; it puts up a good Fifth Avenue front, and is perfectly at home on Broadway. In short, it is literature according to the *boulevardier* of the island of Manhattan, and may be hailed good-naturedly as such.

> *A review of "Vera the Medium," in* The Nation, *London, Vol. 86, No. 2243, June 25, 1908, p. 579.*

JOHN T. McCUTCHEON (essay date 1917)

[*McCutcheon was an American journalist and illustrator who is considered one of the leading cartoonists of his time. Working for the Chicago* Record *from 1889 to 1903, and for the Chicago* Tribune *from 1903 until his retirement in 1946, he became known for powerful political cartoons, one of which won a Pulitzer Prize in 1931. In the following excerpt, McCutcheon praises the title story of Davis's posthumously published volume of short stories,* The Deserter.]

When Mr. Davis wrote the story of **"The Deserter,"** he could not possibly have foreseen that it was to be his last story—the last of those short stories which gave him such eminence as a short-story writer.

He apparently was as rugged and as vigorous as ever.

And yet, had he sat down to write a story which he knew was to be his last, I do not think he could have written one more fittingly designed to be the capstone of his literary monument.

The theme is one in which he has unconsciously mirrored his own ideals of honorable obligation, as well as one which presents a wholesome lesson to young soldiers who have taken an oath to do faithful service to a nation.

It is a story with a moral so subtly expressed that every soldier or sailor who reads it will think seriously of it if the temptation to such disloyalty should enter his mind. This story of the young man who tried to desert at Salonika may well have a heartening influence upon all men in uniforms who waver in the path of duty—especially in these days of vast military operations when a whole world is in arms. It belongs in patriotic literature by the side of Edward Everett Hale's "The Man Without a Country." The motif is the same—that of obligation and service and loyalty to a pledge.

In "The Deserter," Mr. Davis does not reveal the young soldier's name, for obvious reasons, and the name of the hotel and ship in Salonika are likewise disguised. It is part of the art of the skilful story-writer to dress his narrative in such a way as to eliminate those matter-of-fact details which would be emphasized by one writing the story as a matter of news. (pp. v-vii)

But the essentials of the story are all true, and its value as a lasting influence for good is in no way impaired by the necessary fictions as to places and identities.

It was my privilege to see the dramatic incidents of the story of "The Deserter" as they unfolded during the time included in Mr. Davis's story. The setting was in the huge room—chamber, living-room, workroom, clubroom, and sometimes dining room that we occupied in the Olympos Palace Hotel in Salonika. (pp. vii-viii)

The city was seething with huge activities. We lived from day to day, not knowing what moment some disaster might result as a consequence of an incongruous military and political situation. (p. viii)

Into this atmosphere occasionally came the little human dramas that were a welcome novelty beside the big drama that dominated the picture, and it was thus that the drama of the young soldier who wished to desert came into our lives as a gripping, human document.

To Mr. Davis the drama was more than a "news" story; it was something big and fundamental, involving a young man's whole future, and as such it revealed to his quick instinct for dramatic situations the theme for a big story.

No sooner had "Hamlin" left our room, reclad in his dirty uniform and headed for certain punishment back at his camp, than Mr. Davis proclaimed his intention to write the story.

"The best war story I ever knew!" he exclaimed.

Of course the young solider did not see it as a drama in real life, and he certainly did not comprehend that he might be playing a part in what would be a tragedy in his own life. To him the incident had no dramatic possibilities. He was merely a young man who had been racked by exposure and suffering to a point where he longed to escape a continuance of such hardship, and the easiest way out of it seemed by way of deserting.

He was "fed up" on discomfort and dirt and cold, and harassed by the effects of an ill-healed wound received in Flanders some months before, and he wanted to go home.

The story, as Mr. Davis tells it, . . . is complete as it stands. (pp. ix-x)

> *John T. McCutcheon, in an introduction to* The Deserter *by Richard Harding Davis, Charles Scribner's Sons, 1917, pp. v-xvi.*

CHARLES LEWIS HIND   (essay date 1921)

[*In the following excerpt, after noting—and discounting—some of the more fulsome praise bestowed upon Davis, Hind commends the sense of the dramatic and the skilled descriptive writing that made Davis a popular writer of magazine fiction.*]

Richard Harding Davis was not a stylist, and he had little love or reverence for the tongue that Shakespeare spoke and Milton ennobled. He just used it as a vehicle for the expression of the interest that he, a Man of Action, took in life. He liked the kind of people and things that Kipling likes, but when a head-strong critic called him the American Kipling, and another said that his story called "Gallegher" is "as good as anything in Bret Harte," these gentlemen wrote nonsense. Kipling, like Davis, graduated from newspapers, but Kipling is a genius and nothing that Davis ever wrote approaches within sight of the wonder of Bred Harte's Californian tales.

But Richard Harding Davis was a very remarkable man, and few newspapers have ever had such a prize reporter and correspondent. One of the finest and most awesome stories written during the Great War was his account of the entry of the Germans into Brussels; and one of the best pieces of descriptive writing is his account of how he saved himself from being arrested by the Germans, and shot as a spy, through remembering, at the critical moment, that he was wearing a hat marked with the name of a well-known New York hatter, thus proving his identity, saving his life, and giving him a typical Davis newspaper story.

His sense of the dramatic was vivid; he saw himself as a person in the drama; and when he met something interesting and dramatic he could make a vivid story out of it, understandable of all men, without circumlocution, and without art.

He was an ideal magazine writer, and he had the sense of personal honour, of doing one's job, of playing the game, of seeing a trouble through and emerging victorious, that made him popular with every kind of reader. How well I remember the emotion and joy with which I first read his story called "The Bar Sinister," telling how a street dog, a mongrel, proved to be a champion with a perfect pedigree. It is beautifully told. I have given away copies of "The Bar Sinister" merely to watch the reader's heightened colour and air of gratification as this fine story unfolds. And "Gallegher," telling how the printer's devil made good, came through, "beat the town," how gay and full of gusto it is. "Gallegher" was enormously popular. Dickens would have liked it. Henry James, too. Every condition of man and woman likes "Gallegher" and "The Bar Sinister."

He was as well known in London as in New York. Indeed, he was known throughout the world, and he took good care not to let the world forget him. No war was complete without Richard Harding Davis. Correctly dressed, according to martial costume (he was no blue-serge suit and umbrella war correspondent), he acted as war correspondent in the Turkish-Greek, Spanish-American, South African, Russian-Japanese wars, and he went twice to the Great War. Cuba, the Congo, Egypt,

Greece, Central America—the efficient R. H. D. was every-where, and always in the limelight. (pp. 82-4)

His interests were in the present, in people who are doing adventurous, odd and amusing things. From the abundance his quick brain and moving eye selected the best magazine features, and he turned them into copy with confidence and brilliance, quite aware that Richard Harding Davis was doing it, and that in his opinion, what he did was the best of its kind. (pp. 84-5)

> *Charles Lewis Hind, "Richard Harding Davis," in his* Authors and I, *John Lane Company, 1921, pp. 80-5.*

FRED LEWIS PATTEE   (essay date 1923)

[*Pattee was an American literary critic and historian who, in such works as* A History of American Literature, with a View to the Fundamental Principles Underlying its Development *(1896) and* The First Century of American Literature *(1935), called for the recognition of American literature as distinct from English literature. In the following excerpt, from his* The Development of the American Short Story: An Historical Survey, *he condemns Davis's work as commercial and superficial.*]

As a genius [Davis] falls short. He was a clever workman with an eye always on the sales sheet. Literature to him was a thing for to-day's consumption: to-morrow it might be as old as yesterday's paper; he was not writing for to-morrow. There had been no ripening period in his life; no Hawthornelike study of life's meanings. He was a reporter, and the reporter must work always amid excitement, with rapidity and dash and brilliancy. To him the world existed to be recorded in news dispatches, in cabled correspondence sent hot from scenes of action, in moving stories of contemporary life dashed off for the monthly magazines. He was not a realist like Norris or an impressionist like Crane. There was a touch of the romantic in his nature verging upon the sensational; there was a touch, too, of the melodramatic and the theatric. He delighted in posing before the camera dressed faultlessly for the part he was playing. If he reported the English boat races he would be in boating costume, if it were the yacht-club races he would be faultless as a yachtsman.... These elements appear in his fiction. He is smart, cocksure, omniscient; he has been everywhere, in his ears have been whispered the secrets of five continents, the rituals of the whole world he knows by heart.

Gibson drawing that used Davis as a model. Copyright Collier's Weekly.

Superficial is the adjective that comes first to one's pen; artificial is the second. His stories have the perfection of Japanese paper flowers. One thinks of the stage with its painted scenery, its costumes and deftly managed lights, its clever illusions. It is not life: it is the simulacrum of life.

Davis was ... vain, theatric, brilliant, journalistic. His readers ... opened his pages because that through them they were to be admitted behind doors that were closed.... Davis could draw upon the whole world for his materials and motifs. His first story, **"Gallegher,"** admitted its reader to the reporter's quarters and the press rooms of a great city daily; his story, **"The Trailer for Room No. 8,"** transported him to the heart of the criminal area of New York City; **"Her First Appearance"** personally conducted him through the unknown world behind the asbestos curtain; **"The Exiles"** showed how defaulters fare in South American cities; **"In the Fog"** told of his own experience one memorable night in London, and one might go on with tales of Cairo or Cuba or Monte Carlo or Tangier, or the African mines, or the trenches of the World War.... [He] has been there; he is doubtless telling his own adventures; and he is doing it with gentility and vivacity, and with just enough of sentiment and spice and melodrama and movement. (pp. 345-46)

He had learned short-story art from his contemporaries and from his newspaper training. In the matter of form he was exquisite. His openings and his closings may be used as models; his dialogue is often distinctive and his climaxes are skillfully managed. He had learned his trade. But the short story is more than technique and more than vivacity and more than headlong movement.... [Davis] created no living character: Van Bibber is but a lay figure with opera hat and cane. There is no distinction of style, no depth of soil, no philosophy of life, nothing of the fundamental stuff of which all great literature has been made. It is journalism: a thing of the moment, to be thrown aside with the wood-pulp carrier that contained it. It may place its creator even at the head of the notable reporters of his generation, but it can do little more. (pp. 346-47)

> *Fred Lewis Pattee, "The Journalization of the Short Story," in his* The Development of the American Short Story: An Historical Survey, *Harper & Brothers Publishers, 1923, pp. 337-56.*

LARZER ZIFF   (essay date 1966)

[*Ziff is an American critic who has examined the combined effect of social and literary influences on American culture in the studies* The American 1890s: Life and Times of a Lost Generation *(1966),* Puritanism in America: New Culture in a New World *(1973), and* Literary Democracy: The Declaration of Cultural Independence *(1981). In the following excerpt, he contrasts the writing styles and literary approaches of Ambrose Bierce and Davis, both popular fiction writers who worked as journalists in the 1890s.*]

Ambrose Bierce's bitterness stood at one pole in the range of experience available to the writer coming of age in the nineties. His scorn for collective action, his dismissal of the realistic novel, his admiration for Poe and the role of the imagination in literature, and his immersion of the vernacular in a sea of latinate diction timed to the rhythms of formal syntax, all found followers, or, at the least, unconscious echoers.... Whenever life was seen as chaos by a writer who was committed to capturing some shred of that chaos as he condemned it, there Bierce stood as a model. His nearly brutal wrath might maim; but his imitators, lacking that wrath, were in danger of posing.

The society which cheerfully rippled on over and past the semi-submerged Bierces was not inarticulate, and the newspaper world which fostered the cynicism of the neo-Bierces also provided the adventures sought by clear-eyed young men who, born too late for the war and coming from comfortable homes, were determined to test their principles amidst danger. If those who dined at Delmonico's were ignorant or indifferent toward those who starved on Third Avenue, if those who gathered at studio teas would have been hard put to stay alive in a tropical forest, the master of life was he who had experienced stark problems of survival in a ravening wilderness and who could stride into the Waldorf, his weather-beaten face proclaiming his experience, and use the correct fork while reluctantly permitting the young ladies to draw from him the story of his most recent adventure. In the face of the postwar commercialization of life, the popular imagination began to construct for itself a hero who could have the best of both worlds; who would be accepted in the drawing rooms of the effete rich because his natural nobility gave him a place there; who could carry the principles of gentlemanliness into the most brutal situations and show that Americans, through birth and training, were adequate to them. That imagination received its hero in the person of Richard Harding Davis, whose adventurous achievements were proof against all the reservations the cynic could produce. He had been the confidant of criminals and he had been presented to the Queen; he had ridden with a man-hunting patrol in the wastes of the Mexican border and he had seen the coronation in Moscow. At the opposite pole from Bierce, he also attracted. (pp. 173-74)

[Davis first worked] at the Philadelphia *Press,* where a city editor who thought himself invulnerable to any new example of human folly gagged at the prospect of employing a cub reporter who went about his duties dressed like the Prince of Wales. But, the editor found, that dress was a costume signifying Richard Harding Davis, city reporter. The acolyte also had a slicker and straps to wear when he went out to report the Johnstown Flood and did a superb job, and a pea jacket and old sweater for his role as confidant of a gang of yeggman whom he betrayed to the police after planning a burglary with them.

Davis went about his job the way a twelve-year-old boy possessed of the Universal Jim Dandy Disguise Kit goes about his games, while a breathless city room waited for the inevitable fall, which never came. He did all the eager things that were good form in Sunday school and excruciatingly bad taste on the paper, but before the expectant eyes of his colleagues he soared from triumph to triumph. (pp. 176-77)

In Philadelphia, Davis began also to write stories for the magazines, tales of adventure about newspaper work, for the most part. The most celebrated of the early group was **"Gallegher,"** the story of a copy boy who helps capture the crook and then heroically delivers the news in time for a scoop. It was a romance about the invincibility of pluck, but it was nonetheless representative of the way real life was responding to Davis's humorless, clear-eyed pursuit of the virtuous man's duty, in the same way that Bierce's grotesqueries were representative of what he took the pattern of life to be. Davis continued his story-writing after joining the New York *Sun* in 1888, and as his golden luck held and he triumphed in one adventure after another, which he duly reported with all the boyish confidence with which he had intended to write up his freshman tennis match for the delectation of the readers of the Bethlehem *Times,* the popular imagination gratefully followed this living embod-

iment of the feasibility of principles that so many dissenters were crying down. Davis's perfection extended even to modesty, based on his appreciation of his father's charge that "a man entrusted with such talent should carry himself straighter than others to whom it is denied."

In 1890 *Harper's Weekly* appointed him editor; he was twenty-six years old. As his income increased and his stories about his adventures spread, his career exerted an attraction on all youngsters who dreamed of gaining fame before their youth was spent. (pp. 177-78)

During 1892 Davis visited the West and reported glowingly on hobnobbing with Mexican murderers, Texas Rangers, wizened prospectors, and women who smoked and drank in public; went off to England, where he mingled in Oxford undergraduate life and then London social life, throwing in a dash of Bohemia; returned to his summer home on Cape Cod, where Grover Cleveland, Joseph Jefferson, and Richard Watson Gilder were friends and neighbors; then, in the fall, went off to the dedication of the Columbian Exposition in Chicago. In 1893 he was having tea with official British society on Gibraltar, climbing a harem roof in Spain, handling a fakir's snakes in Morocco, and, in general, watching the way the English did things. . . . This was exciting enough until the papers arrived with news of trolley riots in Brooklyn, a crisis in France, war in the Balkans, and a revolution in Honolulu. Then Davis realized that that particular year he was not "in it," and he abused his luck.

For to be in it was everything, and the world provided a splendid variety of "it"'s. The normal flow of life and the inner workings of man, Davis believed, except when challenged by heightened incidents, are for nought. He may have appeared to his shrewder contemporaries to have been incredibly lucky though hopelessly naïve about virtuous living, and fantastically exhibitionist about everything, but they had not been through the events which obsessed Bierce and enervated the minds of his contemporaries, and they could not help admiring and envying him. Dick Davis was in it, and, from Crane to Hemingway, they wanted in too, in great part as a result of the attraction he exerted. He was in it, for instance, in 1896 and 1897 when he reported the coronation at Moscow, the Millennial Celebration at Budapest, the Spanish-Cuban War, the McKinley inauguration, the Greek-Turkish War, and the Queen's Jubilee. For the wars he had puttees and a pith helmet; for the royal events he had a velvet suit with steel buttoms, silk stockings, and pumps with buckles. He strapped on a pistol in Cuba; he strapped on a sword at the Court of St. James's. When, in 1898, Davis and his generation were finally provided with an American war, he could joyously write from Admiral Sampson's flagship, the *New York*: "The other night, we were heading off a steamer and firing six-pounders across her bows, the band was playing the 'star' song from Meistersinger." It was splendid fun; "Wagner and War struck me as the most fin de siècle idea of war that I had ever heard of."

Davis did not remain on the *New York*. He went into the rough country, pursuing adventure and placing himself in dangerous proximity to the fighting so that he could tell how it felt as well as what had happened. But success at this would have been pointless if he could not also have dined with the senior officers. Davis's ultimate appeal came not just from being in it, but from being able to move with ease from such adventures to lunch at the Waldorf. He demonstrated to those of his generation who would listen that their capacity for excitement was matched by the doings in the wide world. But he also demonstrated to an uneasy plutocracy, which was beginning to hear the clamor of protest from below, that their gospel of wealth coming to the virtuous and their public dedication to genteel manners and gentlemanly Christian behavior were indeed justified. Courage and the Sunday-school code, loyalty to chums, resistance to blackguards and their cronies, fair play to all—Dick Davis proved the practicality of these. He demonstrated that an Anglo-Saxon gentleman could face down a murderous half-breed because savagery and bad blood quailed naturally before civilization and breeding. Rudyard Kipling was telling Americans that the nation which won was the nation which knew enough to keep the dead out of the drinking water and which, knowing that, deserved to win. Richard Harding Davis showed that Americans were such a people.

Davis made an immense contribution to the fantasy of the natural superiority of the American, which halfway through the twentieth century still dominated Hollywood. For example, in *Soldiers of Fortune,* . . . which takes place in a Central American country where an American civil engineer is establishing a mining plant with the cooperation of the local authorities, who recognize the civilizing benefits that will be conferred on the natives as a result, the American hero is a bronzed young man who has fought as an officer with the British in the Sudan, been with the Foreign Legion, hacked his way through Brazil, and, as a result of such exploits, is the owner of countless foreign decorations carelessly thrown into his drawer. The novel also has a charming Irish-American gunrunner who contracts revolutions, a disgraced British officer hiding in exile but at the crucial moment redeeming his earlier shame by dying gallantly, and the girl of good blood, daughter of the mining company's president, who is a debutante but who can nevertheless appreciate engineering details, and who can drive a horse through a hailstorm of bullets. This team cannot lose to the discontented revolutionaries who would seize the mine, and it does not.

Davis knew more than this about such situations. In his reporting he had clearly shown that American interference in Central America was as bloody in its methods as was the practice of the native leaders who resented it, and that Wall Street had contracted for riots and executions. But he also carried in his reporting the assumptions of Social Darwinism, that the bare and poor houses in Venezuela were bare and poor not because the people were poor, but because they were indolent. "There is no more interesting question of the present day," he said, "than that of what is to be done with the world's land which is lying unimproved," and he set out to answer it. The natives of unimproved regions were like gangs of barbarians in beautifully furnished houses, and if they didn't live up to their surroundings they were to be turned out in favor of those who would.

Davis is also remembered for his stories of men about town, such as Van Bibber, or of international socialites, such as the Princess Aline. But his fiction's major attraction was its combination of high life and high adventure. The chief romantic impact of a Davis tale of heroism is not what happened to the hero so much as that what happened has been reported to those who count, that after he engineers the revolution, or builds the bridge, or rescues the heiress, he is there on Park Avenue among his equals to tell them about it. This hero represents the adequacy of the genteel principle to any possible crisis that can arise, and, with the aid of Gibson, the illustrator, Davis provided him with a mate: "A tall, fair girl with great bands and masses of hair, with a head rising like a lily from a firm,

Davis and Theodore Roosevelt in Cuba, 1898. The Granger Collection, New York.

white throat, set on broad shoulders above a straight back and sloping breast—a tall, beautiful creature, half-girl, half woman, who looked back at him shyly but steadily." As the Spanish-American War imposed a temporary unity on American life and de-emphasized the social conflicts which served as midwife at the birth of the nineties, so Richard Harding Davis counterbalanced the attraction that the commonplace and the discussion of social injustices might have had for the writers of his generation. He offered a vision of life in which the old ideals could still work, and his sun-bronzed man with his straight-backed mate walked hand in hand into a future which was totally under his control. (pp. 178-82)

Although he was only fifty-two when he died in 1916, Richard Harding Davis outlived the legend he helped to promulgate, and he recognized this. Reporting on the World War prior to American entrance, he met the young men who were to be, after the war, a lost generation, and he recognized that, just as his ideals had sent them off to chase after war and get into it before their country did, so being in this new kind of war would kill his ideals for them. As the kind of reporting he represented had kept Crane and Norris and Frederic from stifling under the influence of a view like Bierce's, so shortly before his death he offered a preview of the new man, such as Hemingway, who had found his legend attractive but who was to shed it.

In his story **"The Deserter"** Davis presents a young American who has served heroically as a volunteer in an English ambulance unit because his country is not yet at war. After fifteen months, however, the volunteer has had enough of slime and mutilation and visits a group of American correspondents to ask them to help in his plans to desert. He is ready now, he says, to go back to America and capitalize on his military experiences by writing about them. If he has been a hero, as they say, he wants now to return home and receive the hero's price in money and adulation rather than to remain and allow death to be the paymaster. The correspondents, men of Davis's generation, still hold to the principles of loyalty and bravery, and they attempt to argue the deserter back to the trenches on these grounds. He sneers at their arguments; he has been to war and knows that it is not like that. So they change their line of argument and appeal to his cynicism, explaining that if he tries to cash in on his heroism before the war is over somebody will discover that he has deserted and he will find all doors closed. This message hits home. The deserter accepts the horrible realization that he must see the war through to its end before he can profit from his part in it, and he leaves the reporters' hotel room to return. To their cheering remarks, he pauses at the door only long enough to reply before disappearing, "Go to hell." Richard Harding Davis died before American troops landed in France.

Ambrose Bierce, formed by armed conflict, saw in his America only a continuation of war without its cleanness and dignity and counseled contempt while privately searching for a vale of peace. Richard Harding Davis, born in Episcopal Philadelphia while Bierce was in battle, saw in his America a superior vitality which God would reward, and counseled confidence while publicly searching for areas of armed combat. They differed, yet their views intersected, and at the point of intersection they stood for the romantic above the commonplace, the violent as representative of rather than different from the deepest values in tranquility, and the writer as witness for the hero who might very often be himself. Davis experienced Wagner and war and found it *fin-de-siècle*. Bierce sneered at the twilight self-consciousness of the nineties but admitted it manifested itself in important ways. (pp. 183-84)

Bierce abused and Davis praised the newspaper office, but each took his place there to indicate where the writer was to hang his hat when he was ready for work. Neither offered a guide to style, to how to impress one's outlook on the material of his art. Both said, however, that that material, treat it as the writer would, was the violence of life, of which war was only the evident epidermis. (p. 184)

> Larzer Ziff, "The Poles of Violence: Ambrose Bierce and Richard Harding Davis," in his American 1890s: Life and Times of a Lost Generation, *The Viking Press, 1966, pp. 166-84.*

JOHN SOLENSTEN   (essay date 1971)

[*Solensten is an American educator and writer whose special field of study is the American Indian. In the following excerpt, he calls for a reassessment of Davis's place in American literature based upon an examination of both his journalism and fiction.*]

In approaching the work of Richard Harding Davis, whom both Jack London and Stephen Crane found approachable enough as a man in spite of marked differences in *modus vivendi*, one can become easily discouraged. The works themselves confront the reader with a disturbing array of short stories in volumes titled by most popular stories, problems in genre definition with oddities like **The Scarlet Car,** the lack of a thorough and

inclusive editing of the letters, a complex interweaving of themes and situations in the journalism and fiction, the absence of any central body of criticism by Davis himself, and, to this date at least, no major published studies devoted exclusively to either the journalism or the fiction. (p. 303)

In the process of using Davis for special purposes, biographers have tended to grab only vendible sensationalism and have done little to encourage the reader to enter Davis' house of fiction with serious intent or to consider that perhaps Davis, like Henry James, found more than one window.

This latter observation betrays, I suppose, my own personal frustration with Davis criticism and brings into focus the present status of Davis in American letters. With notable exceptions, Davis remains in a kind of literary limbo, his books (marked down for sale in Salvation Army stores) drifting toward popular culture libraries and the quaintness of "subliterature" while his house of fiction is nailed shut with pronouncements typified by the comment in *The Oxford Companion to American Literature* . . . (1965), that Davis' fiction showed "adept craftsmanship" but was "journalistic" and the product of a "facile" pen. Thus, Davis, who wrote over 80 short stories, has been generally classified as that most despicable of American writers—the superficial purveyor of journalized fiction. This latter trespass might not have been so serious if Davis had taken some less equivocal stand in the realism-romance controversy. He chose neither "poor, dear, real life," however, nor veritism nor [Frank] Norris' archetypal depths of romance.

But is that all for a man read and known so widely in his own time? One of my favorite teachers, after thumping Tennyson for three weeks, called on the class for "something more"— what he, in his Scandinavian wryness called a "Yah, but . . .' retort. Davis knew tags and caricatures in his own time. Like Cummings, Davis also had his own World War I identity crisis, barely avoiding being shot as a British spy. He cannot be tossed off so easily.

With a couple of exceptions, one gets the impression that hostile critics dismiss Davis without reading him or fail to recognize that if our generation of critics disregards Davis, few of the latter's contemporaries could afford to. In *The American 1890s: Life and Times of a Lost Generation,* . . . Larzer Ziff has rather neatly positioned Davis' derring-do opposite from Bierce's dark, bizarre violence [see excerpt dated 1966]. But no study has pointed out that both Bierce and Davis developed (primarily from journalism) a special kind of impressionism as fictionalists and that both, partly because of this technique, lined up against Norris' preference for the novel and his discounting of the short story. (pp. 304-05)

If Davis' fiction was a curious mixture of realism and romance, his self-defined "romance" ought to be compared not only with the definitions of Bierce and Norris but also with the Graustark and Ruritan formulae of George B. McCutcheon and Anthony Hope (Hawkins). If Davis was a "facile" writer of the formula short story, there seems to be some confusion as to what the formula was and whether or not O. Henry or N. P. Willis, for example, enters the picture as an influence. The travel literature of both Howells and James has been the subject of much study; but Davis saw more of the world than either, and his **Our English Cousins** and several other collections form a significant body of travel essays. Davis wrote enough plays . . . to be considered as at least a minor playwright prior to 1920.

Significantly, too, Davis had his own mystique of the city and an enduring fascination for New York. . . . (p. 306)

Students of American Studies and Popular Culture can hardly afford to dismiss a man whose works Theodore Roosevelt called "a textbook of Americanism." Anti-semitism, changing morals, violence, fascination with technology, ambivalent attitudes toward war and the Manifest Destiny, a kaleidescope of American Girl and Bitch Goddess, and the ever-present American version of the Anglo-Saxon hero are all there, as are darker elements and some moments of anguish when Davis *did* attempt to create a serious piece of fiction. Davis often dealt with Jamesian themes—especially innocence and experience and expatriotism, but Davis never really left "The Jolly Corner." If his works lack the psychological realism of James' and if his endings are less ambiguous or less convincing, they and the characters who shaped them were understandable to readers who could not quite get "the thing that supremely matters" in James.

Criticizing Davis for writing "smiling" romance or for adulterating realism is not quite the point. A complete reading of the fiction may reveal superficialities, but these are often surfacings of deep anxieties and aspirations of Americans Davis knew as journalist, writer, and man-about-town. Davis' composite picture of the aspects of American life he chose to write about has no more distortions than the work of some of his contemporaries. If Davis put an inherited set of values to the test and did not find them entirely useless, he did not have the monumental "scientific" obsessions of Henry Adams. Davis may not have been a writer who "dived," but when Davis' heroes are compared with Jack London's caricatures of Darwinism—heroes careering between Gotterdammerung and a Socialist Utopia—Davis' heroes seem less distorted even if they do not quite touch strange depths of naturalism converging with romanticism. (p. 307)

Davis' accomplishment as a man and a writer presents a vivid and readable record of Davis' own dominant role not only in recording the Strenuous Age and muscular American responses to the fin de siècle but also in creating the milieu while defining both its heroes and heroines. The letters exchanged between Davis and Theodore Roosevelt are not merely curious records of a friendship between notable personages; they are the voices of representative men. If Roosevelt, who labeled the Strenuous Age, was its toothy apotheosis as President and Rough Rider, Davis, more than Jack London or Stephen Crane, was the man of the hour in journalism and fiction. If a kind of "one-upmanship" in frenetic participation in the age is considered, Davis might well get the nod—except for politics and big-game hunting. And if Davis flirted with his own brand of respectable decadence through his Van Bibber, he astutely avoided the mauve and shared Roosevelt's contempt for pink-tea types.

Yet here is a typical temptation for biographer and critic: the temptation to throw "Richard-the-Lion-Harding" on his horse (after lunch at Delmonico's) and to watch him ride with jutting jaw and folding bathtub through Cuba and South America and all the jungles of jingo while the Gibson Girl waits smugly at home for her clean-cut, if somewhat quixotic Anglo-Saxon hero. The world of Swash and Buckle beckons to a boyish love of adventure, and in the process Davis becomes part-time Quixote and part-time Gibson Boy. (pp. 307-08)

The major accomplishments of Davis as hero and recorder of his own time with its fascination with both national and per-

sonal aggrandizement can be seen only through a total, careful reading of Davis' fiction *and* journalism. Davis' novel *The White Mice* can certainly be read as an adventure story, but under its swift pace and somewhat incredible series of adventures lie deeper questions. What role is the young American abroad to take in the internal affairs of South American countries evolving toward a new nationalism which threatens American business interests? What alliance between American business and the American military is necessary, and what are the personal as well as national effects of that alliance? These questions typify those issues moving beneath the surface of Davis' adventure stories.

Gringo? Davis knew what the term really meant. Democracy? Davis winced when he saw Spain, the antique and once-grand old empire, endure final indignities of battle when its ancient navy was defeated in the Spanish-American War. Perhaps this decline was disturbing to Davis because he, like Ambrose Bierce, nurtured certain anti-democratic feelings. *Van Bibber,* after all, is not merely a pleasant portrait of the adventures of an insouciant New York clubman; it is also a somewhat nostalgic portrait of decline. If Davis, who knew Edith Wharton, did not write a full history of the decline of the Knickerbocker aristocracy, he did not overlook that decline either. Both his fiction and his journalism reflect a longing for some American equivalent of European aristocracy. This from a writer consigned by many critics to writing facile stuff for the masses as he discretely avoided social issues.

Was Davis a writer "by gosh and by jingo?" I'm not sure I can answer that any more than I can define Davis' religion. . . . When Richard Outcault's "Yellow Kid" gave his name to an infamous chapter in American journalism and Randolph Hearst made Americans see red by reading yellow, Davis stood as a symbol of integrity while maintaining his rank as one of the most famous war-correspondents of his day.

Most importantly, Davis' integrity as a journalist involved no easy reliance on objective reporting. His concept of the journalist, and to a lesser extent the short-story writer, as impressionist made journalism more complex aesthetically, aligning it with important tendencies in French painting and American fiction. If Davis "journalized" the short story, was the journalizing only the transferring of "snappy" story formulae from news feature to fiction as Fred Lewis Pattee . . . insists? [see excerpt dated 1923]. Or did this journalizing demand that the writer, whether journalist or fictionalist, choose his moments carefully and thereby emphasize a more dynamic role for him as an artist? And this latter question raises another: how does Davis relate to Stephen Crane and Ambrose Bierce as impressionists?

The complete reading of Davis also demands a closer look at quieter moments in Davis' career—periods during which Davis took on routine work or completed assignments often de-emphasized by the biographers. The wonder is that Davis found time to write any fiction at all and that the fiction was readable and perceptive in its own way. Logically, then, it's unreasonable to expect that Davis would write any amount of literary criticism. Does that mean he never had to make discerning critical judgments? The relevance of this question is intensified by the general absence of any sophisticated critical vocabulary in his correspondence. The answer to the question may lie in an examination of one of the least swashbuckling periods in Davis' career, his work as managing editor for *Harper's Weekly* from February 1891 to October 1893. What kinds of stories did *Harper's* publish during that period? Was Davis an editor with both eyes on the counting-house? Is there any reflection of this brief career as an editor in Davis' subsequent fiction? I don't know.

I suppose that one might complain at this point that I've retreated completely to that despicable bastion of desperate apologists for obscure studies: the "my-author-was-a cultural-artifact position." . . . But Davis' voice becomes more significant as he is re-examined more carefully with an eye on those, including Sinclair Lewis, who followed him.

Ernest Hemingway's Lt. Frederic Henry and Erich Maria Remarque's Paul Baumer have become symbols of the sudden dislocation of values following traumatic experience in war. E. E. Cummings' *Enormous Room* presented to readers the awful realization that one need not be in battle to confront the Destructive Element in the twentieth century. Dislocation of traditional values, alienation, ex-patriotism, and the end of innocence have become dominant themes in modern American fiction.

Davis saw as many wars as any other American writer and certainly more than either Stephen Crane or Ernest Hemingway. As war-correspondent he covered the Cuban war, two Balkan wars, the Russo-Japanese war, the Boer War, the early phases of World War I, and several other minor disturbances in Mexico and South America. In some ways, I suppose, war was the culmination of the ideals of the Strenuous Age for Davis. Noble individual heroism was generally the most salient dramatized fact in Davis' fiction especially. But Davis, who recognized that nothing could quite match *The Red Badge of Courage* as a war novel, did not, except for the battle heroics of his soldiers of fortune, glorify either the Spanish-American or great World War in his fiction. (pp. 308-10)

As Larzer Ziff points out in *The American 1890s* (. . . 1966), the 1890's had been the "Life and Times of a Lost Generation." Whatever their degree of alienation and expatriotism, Americans abroad and specifically American artists in Paris were not overlooked by Davis—particularly in his magazine articles. I have not examined alienation as a theme in any detail in his fiction, but I believe that Davis reflects a generally sympathetic attitude toward the American artist abroad. Certainly he was not indignant that American artists were in Europe, though he did suggest some effects this expatriotism had on both artists and writers. Davis noted with gentlemanly reserve that Stephen Crane wasted more than time in Europe. (p. 311)

[Much] of what one reads in Davis' novels and short stories suggests a deep affinity between him and Fitzgerald. The perils of wealth and the obsession with it as a special state of grace, the role of the American girl in the Myth of Success, the sense of having been too much a part of an era to survive it, the romantic vision with its incredible belief in the second chance, the ambiguous treatment of idealism, and the fascination with the automobile—all are there. But none of Davis' works is included in listings of Fitzgerald's readings. An unacknowledged debt? Both admired Joseph Conrad. And can any scholar attempting to trace changing images of the woman in American fiction disregard either of these writers?

Davis was, after all, Charles Dana Gibson's model for the Gibson Boy. The latter suggests a handsome, but rather shallow and boyish figure, superciliously gallant and peering hopefully at the insolent eyebrows (but never breasts) of a Gibson Girl who looks strikingly like Alice Roosevelt. But a total and more careful consideration of Davis' work reveals a man—a man

Caricature of Davis as a war correspondent, by Vim, 1916. Courtesy of Town & Country.

who called "Stevie" Crane at a histrionic display of fatuous bullet-dodging in Cuba. Perhaps Davis can be allowed, as he allowed himself in the last phases of his career especially, to grow up and to be given more serious consideration in American letters. (p. 312)

John Solensten, "The Gibson Boy: A Reassessment," in American Literary Realism 1870-1910, *Vol. 4, No. 4, Fall, 1971, pp. 303-12.*

SCOTT COMPTON OSBORN AND ROBERT L. PHILLIPS, JR. (essay date 1978)

[*Osborn was an American educator and critic who wrote extensively on Davis. Phillips is an American educator and critic who has specialized in southern American authors. In the following excerpt, Osborn and Phillips provide an evaluation of Davis's career.*]

From first to last Davis was, as he himself always insisted, a journalist. He did his best work in the most ephemeral of literary modes because he chose to do so, not because he was commercially exploited by publishers. If he was exploited, he exploited himself. More than literary fame he desired the sense that he was a man of action and affairs, a participant in stirring historical events, a knight-errant adventurer. When the real world failed to supply him with color and adventure, he created in his own image a fictional world in which the adventures continued. But fiction was always secondary; life came first. As a reporter, traveler, and war correspondent, Davis was convinced that he was experiencing life at first hand, that he was closest to its vital pulse.

Temperament, not commercialism or "the times," can explain Davis. If he failed to "ripen" or to "develop" as a writer of fiction, the reason was inability. If he retained the simplicity, the ebullience, the philosophical passivity, the virginally fresh attitude of a permanent young man, he could not do otherwise. Preciousness in manners, gentlemanly code, individualism, theatricality, rosy optimism, hyperbolic style, vivacity, flippancy, rigid morality, hatred of the commonplace, strenuousness, "muscular Christianity," indignation at injustice, sentimentality—all these were properly and inseparably part of him. Their combination drove him into a pinwheel activity, a lifelong effort to disprove that the world was a dull and humdrum place, an attempt to remold it according to his vision of the right and the good. Admittedly an entertainer, Davis was also certainly a moralist; though he wrote for the sheer joy of writing, he also felt that he was doing good.

Within the limits imposed by his temperament, Davis did work of some merit. He can be justly charged with sentimentality, overwriting, inaccuracy, emotional midjudgment, oversimplification, idiosyncratic prejudice, excessive flourish, and overemphasis on ritualism and "good form." But he seldom failed to interest and move his reader, to transmit the thrill he himself felt, to reproduce the scene he had witnessed. Though not a professional humorist, he may be compared not unfairly with professionals like John Kendrick Bangs and George Ade. Contrary to all uninformed assumptions, he had a "social consciousness" and, according to his lights, vigorously attacked political, social, and economic evils and injustices. And no one can detract from the occasional brilliance of his visual imagery. His achievement was not of the highest order, but in his fiction, drama, and journalism he catches some of the spirit and tone of the 1890s and the Strenuous Age. (pp. 141-42)

> *Scott Compton Osborn and Robert L. Phillips, Jr., in their* Richard Harding Davis, *Twayne Publishers, 1978, 167 p.*

ADDITIONAL BIBLIOGRAPHY

Review of *The Lion and the Unicorn*, by Richard Harding Davis. *The Athenaeum*, No. 3765 (23 December 1899): 862.
    Assesses the short stories of the collection *The Lion and the Unicorn* as uninspired copies of Davis's earlier works, "only enough like those that have won him success to make one begin to analyze them and wonder if they were so good after all." The British reviewer also comments on Davis's "almost impudent" air of condescension toward the English.

Bierce, Ambrose. "Small Contributions." *Cosmopolitan* (July 1908): 220.
    Scathingly notes (with reference to *The Congo and Coast of Africa*) that Davis's failure to find any "atrocities" in the Congo did not prevent him from writing "a blood-addling book about them, all the same."

Boggs, W. Arthur. "Prologue to an Unpleasant Image (A Book Review Over Sixty Years Late)." *Phylon* XXIV, No. 2 (Summer 1963): 197-200.
    Blames the negative image of South Americans in the North American popular imagination on unfavorable portrayals in fiction, and specifically on Davis's *Soldiers of Fortune*, which Boggs describes as a jingoistic and imperialistic novel that perpetuates stereotypes of the indolent, dishonest South American and the intrepid North American.

Brooks, Van Wyck. "New York: Up-Town." In his *The Confident Years: 1885-1915*, pp. 103-17. New York: E. P. Dutton & Co., 1952.
    Evocative description of New York high society in the 1890s which calls Davis the symbol of this "young man's epoch."

Davis, Charles Belmont, ed. *Adventures and Letters of Richard Harding Davis*. New York: Charles Scribner's Sons, 1918, 417 p.
    Chronologically arranged letters to and from Davis and family members, interspersed with biographical and historical information by Davis's younger brother, who presents Davis in a uniformly flattering way.

Downey, Fairfax. *Richard Harding Davis: His Day*. New York: Charles Scribner's Sons, 1933, 321 p.
    Anecdotal, noncritical biography presenting Davis in favorable light.

Langford, Gerald. *The Richard Harding Davis Years: A Biography of a Mother and Son*. New York: Holt, Rinehart and Winston, 1961, 336 p.
    Extensively researched biography covering Rebecca Harding Davis's life to the time that Richard, her oldest child, began school, and focusing on Richard Harding Davis's eventful life thereafter.

Littell, Philip. "Richard the Lion-Harding." In his *Books and Things*, pp. 230-36. New York: Harcourt, Brace and Howe, 1919.
    Character sketch of Davis, containing the famous remark that "a perfect day, for Mr. Davis, would consist of a morning's danger, taken as a matter of course; in the afternoon a little chivalry, equally a matter-of-course to a well-bred man; then a motor dash from hardship to some great city, a bath, a perfect dinner nobly planned."

McNamara, John. "Beau Brummel of the Press." In his *Extra! U.S. War Correspondents in Action*, pp. 68-82. Boston: Houghton Mifflin Co., 1945.
    Anecdotal account of Davis's colorful and adventure-filled years as a war correspondent.

Miner, Lewis S. *Mightier than the Sword: The Story of Richard Harding Davis*. Chicago: Whitman, 1940, 225 p.
    Noncritical biography of Davis for young adult readers.

"Mr. Harding Davis Visits the Congo." *The New York Times Saturday Review of Books* (14 December 1907): 827.
    Review of *The Congo and Coast of Africa*, subtitled "Fails to Find 'Atrocities,' But That Doesn't Prevent His Writing Interesting Book About Them." The reviewer concludes that the content of the book is less important than the fact that "Mr. Davis takes an excellent photograph in a pith helmet."

Morris, Gouverneur, et. al. *R. H. D.: Appreciations of Richard Harding Davis*. New York: Charles Scribner's Sons, 1916, 112 p.
    Collection of reminiscences and encomiastic tributes to Davis published at his death. Included are essays by Booth Tarkington, Charles Dana Gibson, and Theodore Roosevelt, among others.

Osborn, Scott C. The 'Rivalry-Chivalry' of Richard Harding Davis and Stephen Crane." *American Literature* 28, No. 1 (March 1956): 50-61.
    Examines contemporary material pertaining to the theory that the character of Charles Channing in Davis's short story "A Derelict" was intended to represent Crane, with whom Davis at times competed for "scoops" as a war correspondent.

Pattee, Fred Lewis. "The New Journalism." In his *The New American Literature: 1890-1930*, pp. 49-63. New York: D. Appleton-Century Co., 1935.

Pronounces Davis "the leading type" of the roving war reporter and special correspondent journalist, noting also his successes in other literary fields.

Waldron, Robert. "Around the World with Swash and Buckle." *American Heritage* XVIII, No. 5 (August 1967): 56-9, 71-4.
Biographical essay exploiting the legends of Davis's adventurous life.

Williams, Blanche Colton. "Richard Harding Davis." In her *Our Short Story Writers*, pp. 105-28. New York: Moffat, Yard & Co., 1920.
Praises Davis as a short story writer, finding that he owes the fictional elements of "freshness and buoyancy," "spontaneity and enthusiasm" to his early journalistic training.

George Gissing

1857-1903

English novelist, short story writer, critic, and essayist.

Best remembered for the harsh realism of such novels as *New Grub Street* and *Born in Exile*, Gissing was a late nineteenth-century author whose works exemplify the changes which marked the transition from Victorian to modern literature. While his early works display a Dickensian concern for the plight of the poor and a belief in the effectiveness of social reform, later works manifest a distinctly modern sense of pessimism and moral uncertainty. Although Gissing's disillusionment is attributed to personal frustrations rather than to the failure of his Victorian ideology, critics note that his works nevertheless express the evolving philosophical awareness of his entire literary generation.

Born in Wakefield, Yorkshire, Gissing was the eldest son of a drugstore proprietor. The death of his father when Gissing was thirteen left the family destitute, so concerned friends and neighbors established a fund which enabled Gissing and his two brothers to attend a boarding school at Alderly Edge, in the nearby county of Cheshire. Gissing proved to be a brilliant student and thus earned a full scholarship to Owens College, an institution whose primary purpose was to prepare private school students for studies at the large universities. To his classmates and instructors at Owens, Gissing seemed destined for a distinguished academic career; he consistently took top honors and eventually earned a full scholarship to the University of London. In his final year at the college, however, an event occurred which ruined his plans and dramatically changed the course of his life.

During his first four terms at Owens, Gissing had continued to live at Alderly Edge, where lodging was inexpensive and his friends were numerous. However, in October of 1875 he moved to the industrial city of Manchester, where Owens was located, taking rooms in a rather shabby district. There he met and fell in love with a sixteen-year-old alcoholic prostitute named Nell Harrison. Believing Harrison to be a victim of circumstance who would gladly amend her behavior if given the opportunity, Gissing took it upon himself to support and educate her, in an attempt to effect her complete reform. His own financial means being extremely limited, he stole from his classmates in order to provide for Harrison, but the thefts did not go unnoticed. The college hired a private detective, and Gissing was apprehended in May of 1876, literally caught in the act. He was immediately dismissed from Owens, his prizes and honors were revoked, the offer of a scholarship was withdrawn, and he was sentenced to thirty days hard labor at the Manchester jail. His family decided upon his release that it would be best for him to go to America, where his disgrace would not be known and where he might have some kind of career despite his criminal record.

In America, Gissing did indeed begin a new career. Upon his arrival he settled in Boston, but he soon moved to Chicago, where he immediately began writing short stories for the local newspapers. Gissing's stories appeared in several Chicago publications during the early months of 1877, and, later that same year, he returned to England, planning to earn his living as a

writer. In London, Gissing began work on a novel which he left unfinished and about which little is known; his first completed novel, *Workers in the Dawn*, was written in 1879 and published in 1880. Although *Workers in the Dawn* was not a critical success, its sympathetic treatment of the poor did draw the attention of social critics, who applauded Gissing's frank disclosures of social and economic inequities.

Gissing continued to produce novels throughout the early 1880s despite the fact that his books sold poorly and brought almost no recompense. A further impediment to his work lay in his domestic situation, for he had resumed his relationship with Harrison upon his return from America, and her severe alcoholism made life extremely difficult. Gissing nevertheless wrote four novels between 1880 and 1885, the last of which brought him to the attention of a large number of readers. *Demos*, while not considered among Gissing's best novels, was a popular success because it dealt unsympathetically with organized labor and appeared at a time when violent workers' demonstrations had begun to alarm many in England. Its author, once regarded as a socialist, became the hero of English conservatives. Although Gissing returned to a sympathetic treatment of the poor in one subsequent novel, *The Nether World*, the remainder of his works written after *Demos* exhibit a similar disaffection from the lower classes, caused in part by his growing contempt for the incorrigible Harrison.

While *Demos* brought Gissing popular attention, it was the publication of *New Grub Street* five years later that earned him the admiration of critics and made him a widely respected author. The novels which followed, particularly *The Odd Women*, *Born in Exile*, and *In the Year of Jubilee*, proved equally successful, but this period of professional achievements coincided with a period of great personal unhappiness for the author. After Harrison's death from the complications of her alcoholism in 1888, Gissing actively sought a wife, but he felt that his past rendered him unfit to be the husband of a woman of his own class. In 1890, he married Edith Underwood, the daughter of a skilled tradesman. Within a few months, however, Gissing's new wife began to manifest signs of a severe emotional disorder, and her condition worsened steadily. By 1892 he was reporting in his correspondence that she had become prone to outbursts of extreme violence and that his life with her had become a source of great misery. Nevertheless, Gissing remained with her until 1897.

Gissing spent his final years in France, where, despite his rapidly failing health, he continued his habit of writing daily. It was during this last phase of his career that Gissing demonstrated his greatest versatility, producing a critical study of Charles Dickens, a travel memoir entitled *By the Ionian Sea*, and a fictionalized autobiography, *The Private Papers of Henry Ryecroft*. Although Gissing had never before attempted to work in these genres, his efforts were universally applauded, and *The Private Papers of Henry Ryecroft* is frequently considered one of his most enduring works. Stimulated by this positive reception, Gissing continued to plan new works throughout the final months of his life, but these were left unfinished when he died from a lung ailment in 1903.

One of the most outstanding characteristics of Gissing's fiction is its intensely autobiographical nature, and many critics assert that his works can only be fully understood when considered in the context of his life. As a result, the social, political, and philosophical attitudes implicit in his novels are commonly interpreted not simply as expressions of his intellectual position, but also as clear revelations of his personal response to the situations and people he encountered. The fact that his early novels display sympathy for the poor and outrage at the injustices they suffer is therefore viewed as a reflection of Gissing's perception of himself as a social outcast, unjustly censured for a minor youthful transgression, while the aristocratic tendencies of later works are attributed to his increasing success. Gissing's opinion of the effects of poverty, however, remained unchanged despite the shift in his sympathies: he consistently and adamantly maintained that poverty degrades and brutalizes human beings, and he vividly illustrated his point with graphic depictions of such existence.

This insistence upon the importance of environmental factors in the development of his characters has led Gissing's name to be linked with that of Emile Zola and other nineteenth-century Naturalists, although his work differs from theirs in the stronger sense of despair he conveyed. John Halperin has written: "It is interesting to note in Gissing's novels some of the most traditional motifs of nineteenth-century fiction side by side with the most prophetic modern themes," and it is this juxtaposition which most clearly distinguishes the transitional nature of Gissing's work. Traditional elements include plots complicated by secret marriages and undiscovered wills, a somewhat romanticized view of female characters, and a general concentration upon melodrama. Yet a distinctly modern sense of alienation and a strong note of pessimism are present in all the novels. Gissing's central characters, whether male or female, are typically unsuccessful in their careers and unhappy in their human relationships, with no hope for any amelioration of their condition. Critics note that Gissing's alienated protagonists presage the antihero figure that eventually came to dominate twentieth-century fiction.

The protagonists drawn most directly from Gissing's own life are those of *New Grub Street*, generally considered his best novel. In depicting the squalid existence of a group of struggling writers, Gissing drew heavily upon his own experiences and attitudes and confined his narration to the recreation of the London literary world with which he was intimately acquainted. As a result, critics consider verisimilitude and emotional authenticity the most outstanding features of *New Grub Street*. In addition, Gissing used aspects of his own tormented psyche in the creation of all central characters in the novel, thereby achieving a high degree of psychological realism.

When Gissing's novels first appeared, much of the critical response was extremely negative, focusing primarily on the pessimism of his tone and the baseness of his subject matter. When, in later novels, his denunciations gave way to what Halperin calls "a more urbane irony," his works became extremely popular, and at his death he was considered one of England's foremost authors. There followed, however, a long period of eclipse, during which even Gissing's finest works were ignored. It was not until the early 1960s that critics and readers rediscovered Gissing, and new editions of his works began to appear. Today, Gissing's works are frequently read and discussed, with much critical attention concentrating upon his treatment of female characters and his ambiguous position with regard to women's rights. Although his reputation rests primarily on a relatively small percentage of his total literary output—the novels *New Grub Street*, *Born in Exile*, *The Odd Women*, and *The Private Papers of Henry Ryecroft*—critical assessment of these works remains very positive.

(See also *TCLC*, Vol. 3; *Contemporary Authors*, Vol. 105; and *Dictionary of Literary Biography*, Vol. 18: *Victorian Novelists after 1885*.)

PRINCIPAL WORKS

Workers in the Dawn   (novel)   1880
The Unclassed   (novel)   1884
Demos   (novel)   1886
Isabel Clarendon   (novel)   1886
Thyrza   (novel)   1887
A Life's Morning   (novel)   1888
The Nether World   (novel)   1889
The Emancipated   (novel)   1890
New Grub Street   (novel)   1891
Born in Exile   (novel)   1892
Denzil Quarrier   (novel)   1892
The Odd Women   (novel)   1893
In the Year of Jubilee   (novel)   1894
Eve's Ransom   (novel)   1895
The Paying Guest   (novel)   1895
Sleeping Fires   (novel)   1895
The Whirlpool   (novel)   1897
Charles Dickens   (criticism)   1898
Human Odds and Ends   (short stories and sketches)   1898
The Town Traveller   (novel)   1898
The Crown of Life   (novel)   1899
By the Ionian Sea   (travel essays)   1901

GEORGE SAINTSBURY   (essay date 1880)

[*Saintsbury was an English literary historian and critic of the late nineteenth and early twentieth centuries. A prolific writer, he composed several histories of English and European literature as well as numerous critical works on individual authors, styles, and periods. In the following excerpt, Saintsbury discusses* Workers in the Dawn.]

Mr. Gissing is one of those persons for whom the heart of the sensitive reviewer feels a certain sorrow. His book [*Workers in the Dawn*] is in every sense an extravagant one. He has got into his head the very common notion that social order as at present established is the root of all evil, and he writes a long (a very long) novel to illustrate this notion. Nearly all his people of the upper class are foolish or wicked, and nearly all those of the lower are wretched and wronged. Yet, oddly enough, the bad ends to which nearly all, rich and poor, come are occasioned almost in every single instance by some personal error or folly which it is difficult to connect with the social system at all. Nor has Mr. Gissing been fortunate enough to make his portraits, at all events in the case of the upper classes, in the least life-like. Yet when the necessary and important deductions have been made for all these shortcomings, there remains something to be said for the author. He possesses sincerity, which is a great thing, and imagination, which is a greater. Although any reader of some little experience will know that his pictures are partly false and partly exaggerated, yet his book leaves on the mind a certain "obsession"—there is no word for it in English, though neither thing nor term is specially or properly French—which merely insignificant work never produces. It ought to be mentioned, perhaps, that *Workers in the Dawn* is not exactly intended for the well-known young ladies whose bread is cut in the equally well-known *tartines*. There is nothing in the least unclean in Mr. Gissing's handling of his subjects, but in his choice of them he is more adventurous than is usual with the English novelist. (pp. 76-7)

George Saintsbury, in a review of "Workers in the Dawn," in The Academy, *Vol. XVIII, No. 430, July 31, 1880, pp. 76-7.*

THE SATURDAY REVIEW, LONDON   (essay date 1886)

[*In the following excerpt, the critic praises* Demos.]

The average novel is such a poor, ill-favoured thing that, by comparison, a book like *Demos* appears to be almost a great work. It has many faults; but it has great merits. The author, who elects to remain anonymous, is, to begin with, remarkably well acquainted with his subject; he has, moreover, the judicial mind, and is incapable of misdirected enthusiasm; he knows his men and women by heart, but he handles them with an impartial sternness of purpose which, in these days of prejudice

and special pleading, is uncommon enough to have something of the charm of novelty. Another good point about him is that, unlike the run of modern novelists, French and English alike, he is sparing of commentary and elucidation; he loves to make his people explain themselves; out of their own mouths are they presented, and by their peculiar actions are they beatified or damned. Yet another quality of his work is sincerity; it is his aim to speak the truth, and to speak it of all and sundry; he is not afraid to convict his heroine of weakness, nor does he in any way incline to dissemble the good side of his wicked heroes. Last of all, it is to be noted that his sympathies are altogether with moral and intellectual beauty; he has given us a couple of heroines—one lovely, elegant, accomplished, well born; the other poor, lowly, plain, forsaken, disappointed—and if one be preferable to the other (which is doubtful), that one is not the fairer and the more obviously heroic. It is plain, indeed, that he is a writer to whom we may look for much, and not be disappointed. It seems unquestionable that *Demos* is a first book; it is certain that first books fuller of promise and performance are few.

The subject is Socialism, and Socialism as it exists in working London. From a cheap suburb do the personages proceed; and they have the characteristics of their circumstances. They have their good points, of course; but the impression they produce is eminently one of "underbredness" and vulgarity. They are true children of Demos, true scions of the mob, incapable of simple, single-minded devotion to an ideal; vain, jealous, egoistic, narrow; ambitious above all of personal pre-eminence; practising Socialism and the gospel of humanity, not for honour's sake or on the inspiration of faith, but, whether consciously or the reverse, simply as a form of the Struggle for Existence. Dick Mutimer, the Socialist hero, is a strong man in his way, and in his way by no means a bad fellow. But he is what his environment has made him; "vulgarity cleaves to him as an hereditary odour"; at his highest he is no better than a fireman in promotion; he is a type of subaltern humanity, and could never be anything stronger or better; as compared with his discarded sweetheart, Emma Vine, or even with his bitter, unrelenting, stanch old mother, he is almost abject. Beside the sweet and patient virtue of the one and the soured implacable honesty of the other his best qualities are seen to be contemptible. It is by the heart alone that social regeneration is possible; it is in the heart alone that its essential elements are generated. This the author of *Demos* has seen; and this he has discovered to his public with an intimacy of knowledge and a fulness of illustration that should secure his book the attention of every intelligent man and woman in the country.

A review of "Demos," in The Saturday Review, *London, Vol. 62, No. 1608, August 21, 1886, p. 261.*

WHITEHALL REVIEW   (essay date 1891)

[*In the following review, first published in the 18 April 1891, issue of the* Whitehall Review, *the critic praises* New Grub Street.]

Mr. Gissing's newest literary triumph is a singularly skilful piece of work, and proves how true a prophetic vision was ours when, on reading his first book a few years ago, we proclaimed him to be a man of no mean parts, with a great future, if he never deviated from the course he was commencing to hew for himself in the path of fame. Since then he has never disappointed us, and each fresh work he has published has been better and stronger than the one which preceded. In *New Grub*

Street we perceive the same masterly and original analysis of character, and the same truth of description, as in the other remarkable stories he has told us. He has a profound and intense sympathy with the lives and the sufferings of men and women, a wonderful insight into their hearts and souls, and an almost unparalleled directness of speech in expressing what most authors fail to convey—a sense of perfect reality. Critics and the public will grumble that the book is sad, morbid, gloomy; well, so is life, or at least that phase of life of which Mr. Gissing writes. The book is one long, desolate tragedy—the tragedy of helpless human nature in its struggle with the great forces of the universe. It is so sad because it is so real. Mr. Gissing points out with a truthful and realistic force what every sensible person cannot fail to recognise—that it is not the man who aims nobly who succeeds; that when punishment follows wrongdoing, it is not as retribution. The teaching of the whole book is that it is as well to follow duty, but on the clear understanding that no reward is the result. The motive-forces of the book are:—Life, which suffers so much, and has no respite until death steps in to help; faith, which dies hard, after an agonising struggle against circumstance; love, which gives all, and gains nothing in return. And to these motive-forces Mr. Gissing has given expression in a wonderful manner. The hard and painful literalness of poverty; the results of a combat with poverty on the varied natures of the characters: these are the trenchant themes on which he discourses so eloquently and ably. No matter how the world at large may judge this book, Mr. Gissing has made with **New Grub Street** an addition to contemporaneous "literature" which will be appreciated far and wide by readers of culture, refinement and taste. For those who cannot appreciate the genius which created, and the talent which perfected, such men and women as Amy and Edwin Reardon, Marian Yule and her father, and Jasper Milvain and his sisters, we have nothing but profound pity. There is a touch applied by the incidental reference in the third volume to an unsuccessful doctor, which the greatest writers of our, or any other, day might have envied. The man or woman who cannot appreciate, or who stoops to depreciate, such a book as **New Grub Street,** may surely be an object of pity to all who can enjoy this wonderfully clever, yet intensely sad, tragedy. (pp. 169-70)

> *A review of "New Grub Street," in* Gissing: The Critical Heritage, *edited by Pierre Coustillas and Colin Partridge, Routledge & Kegan Paul, 1972, pp. 169-70.*

WALTER BESANT   (essay date 1891)

[*Besant was a prolific English novelist, historian, and critic who used fiction to expose and denounce the social evils of late-Victorian England. In the following excerpt from a review originally published in* Author, *1 June 1891, Besant, who has been called "a low-powered Gissing," commends the verisimilitude of the characterizations in* New Grub Street.]

Mr George Gissing ought to be publicly thanked for introducing to the world a form of literary life which has long been known to all who have penetrated into the by-ways and slums of this many-sided calling. He presents to us [in **New Grub Street**] several well defined and by no means uncommon types. There is the young man of literary aspirations who rashly attempts to make of letters his livelihood, encouraged by the success of a single first novel. He has no education to speak of; he has no knowledge of society; he has no personal experiences; he has no travel. In fact, he is absolutely devoid of any equipment

except a true feeling for Art, and a burning desire to succeed. He cannot succeed. It is not possible for such a man to succeed. He fails dismally, and he dies. In real life such a man would not die. He would sink lower—lower—until he became the wretched drudge and hack of a penny novelette publisher, which is Malebolge itself. Next, there is the young man who looks about him, sees what will pay, and how men get on in the literary profession. He enters upon his work with the intention of succeeding, and he does succeed. In real life such a man might succeed in the way indicated, but not quite so easily. He becomes an Editor. Now, one of the chief requisites in a modern Editor is that he should know many men, and belong to certain social circles. This young man, with no social position, would certainly not be made an Editor quite so easily. On the other hand, his career illustrates the advantages to be derived from accepting the existing conditions, and trading upon them. But the truest, saddest figure in the book is that of the old *littérateur*, a critic of the former school, who hangs on to letters, getting more and more soured every day, having a paper accepted now and then, doing a stroke of work here and another there, living a life of absolute dependence upon publishers and Editors, whose work nobody wants, whose whole history has been one of humiliations, disgusts and disappointments, who waits humbly on publishers and hopes for their "generosity." Truly, as his daughter says, his is a loathsome profession. It is the utter degradation of letters; it is Grub Street with us still. But he degrades his profession still more for he meditates constantly upon the pride of being the Editor of a literary journal, and his only thought, in that capacity, is how he will tear and rend his brother writers. "I will show them," he says, "I will show them how to scarify." Yes, that is still the thought of certain authors. As it was in the days of Churchill, so it is now. Because a man follows the calling of letters, he must, by other followers of that profession, be slated, scarified, torn to pieces. Every other profession has its unwritten laws of decency and politeness. That of literature, none. I do not suppose that Mr Gissing's book can become popular, but from my own knowledge I can testify to its truth. I know them all, personally,—two or three of each—Mr Yule—Jasper—Edwin—and the fidelity of Mr Gissing's portraits makes me shudder. (pp. 181-82)

> *Walter Besant, in a review of "New Grub Street," in* Gissing: The Critical Heritage, *edited by Pierre Coustillas and Colin Partridge, Routledge & Kegan Paul, 1972, pp. 181-82.*

THE SPECTATOR   (essay date 1893)

[*In the following review of* The Odd Women, *the critic commends the intellectual depth of that work.*]

Mr. George Gissing is rather fond of choosing for survey the very ugliest facts, and gazing at them so intently that they disclose to his vision an unmitigated dolorousness of significance which, perhaps, may not really belong to them. Mr. Gissing's novels have never been exhilarating, but they have always been rich in a chilly kind of intellectual interest, and we do not think he has ever written a more interesting book than **The Odd Women.** The meaning of the title is made clear pretty early in the first volume during the conversation in which Rhoda Nunn informs Monica Madden that "there are half-a-million more women than men in this happy country of ours . . . so many *odd* women—no making a pair with them." What is the natural fate of these women under a system of *laisser faire?* and what possibility of escaping that fate may be provided by the action of intelligent leaders? are the two questions which Mr. Gissing sets himself to answer in such fashion as they can be answered in a fictitious narrative. That any one book, either didactic or imaginative, should solve the problem of the "odd women" is not a thing to be expected; indeed (though here we speak with hesitation), Mr. Gissing does not seem to offer more than a hint towards its solution; but an intelligent statement of a problem is, at any rate, something, and though Mr. Gissing's statement is coloured by his inveterate pessimism, he can hardly be charged with having set down aught in malice. It is true that of his odd women one dies of over-work, another commits suicide in despair, a third goes on to the streets, a fourth becomes a victim to drink, and a fifth, after contracting a loveless marriage for the sake of a home, is only saved from adultery and ruin by the contemptible cowardice of her lover,— and this is certainly a dreary catalogue; but it must be admitted that about the same number of the superfluous sisterhood manage to live useful, healthy, and, on the whole, happy lives. It may, we suppose, be presumed that the views of those sturdy pioneers, Miss Barfoot and Rhoda Nunn, represent Mr. Gissing's own opinions concerning the direction in which we are to look for a clue to the maze; but perhaps the wisest, and certainly the easiest course of procedure, is to regard *The Odd Women* as a novel pure and simple, rather than as a contribution to the discussion of one of the most difficult of social questions. The book is certainly remarkably clever, with a certain hard cleverness which is at once impressive and repellent. Every outline is sharp and firm, and, in a sense, true; but the entire absence of atmosphere gives a feeling of untruthfulness to the whole picture. It is perhaps unfair to make an accusation which cannot possibly be verified in the brief space that can be allotted to a newspaper review; but we believe that every reader of Mr. Gissing's novel, whether he agree or disagree with our verdict, will feel that it is not merely whimsical, but that it has reasons behind it. We feel it necessary to say this because such a book as *The Odd Women* may rightly claim a deliberate thoughtfulness of criticism which would be entirely wasted upon the ordinary circulating-library novel read to-day and forgotten tomorrow. Indeed, it seems to us that Mr. Gissing's eager intentness of vision, which is in itself admirable, does something to mar his sense of proportion and perspective. His details, his individual studies—such, for example, as his narrative of the courtship and married life of Widdowson and Monica— have a truthfulness of observation and rendering which is unassailable; but when the picture, of which these details are parts, is seen in its entirety, we have a vague feeling of dissatisfaction, and we say to ourselves: "This is not the world we know." One has the same feeling about all Mr. George Gissing's books; and it is given by his persistent preference for the lower levels of life. They are books which can be easily remembered even by a hard-worked reviewer of fiction; and the present writer can recall hardly a character in any one of them who lives on a really high plane of thought and feeling. A picture of a Dutch flat may be true to nature in Holland, but it is a very inadequate hint of the glory of the world's landscape; and Mr. Gissing's world is as a rule not merely a world of dull levels, but of ill-odorous swamps and morasses. *The Odd Women* is strong, it is thought-compelling, it is remarkably clever; and yet our predominant feeling is that it is a good novel to get away from. (pp. 707-08)

A review of "The Odd Women," in The Spectator, *Vol. 70, No. 3387, May 27, 1893, pp. 707-08.*

GEORGE GISSING (essay date 1895)

[*In the following essay, written in 1895 and later reprinted in* George Gissing on Fiction, *Gissing explains his personal approach to literary realism.*]

One could wish, to begin with, that the words *realism* and *realist* might never again be used, save in their proper sense by writers on scholastic philosophy. In relation to the work of novelists they never had a satisfactory meaning, and are now become mere slang. Not long ago I read in a London newspaper, concerning some report of a miserable state of things among a certain class of work-folk, that "this realistic description is absolutely truthful," where by *realistic* the writer simply meant painful or revolting, with never a thought of tautology. When a word has been so grievously mauled, it should be allowed to drop from the ranks.

Combative it was, of course, from the first. Realism, naturalism, and so on signified an attitude of revolt against insincerity in the art of fiction. Go to, let us picture things as they are. Let us have done with the conventional, that is to say, with mere tricks for pleasing the ignorant and the prejudiced. Let the novelist take himself as seriously as the man of science; be his work to depict with rigid faithfulness the course of life, to expose the secrets of the mind, to show humanity in its eternal combat with fate. No matter how hideous or heartrending the results; the artist has no responsibility save to his artistic conscience. The only question is, has he wrought truly, in matter and form? The leaders of this revolt emphasised their position by a choice of vulgar, base, or disgusting subjects; whence the popular understanding of the term *realist*. Others devoted themselves to a laborious picturing of the dullest phases of life; inoffensive, but depressing, they invested *realism* with another quite accidental significance. Yet further to complicate and darken the discussion, it is commonly supposed that novelists of this school propound a theory of life, by preference that known as "pessimism." There is but one way out of this imbroglio: to discard altogether the debated terms, and to inquire with regard to any work of fiction, first whether it is sincere, secondly, whether it is craftsmanlike.

Sincerity I regard as of chief importance. I am speaking of an art, and, therefore, take for granted that the worker has art at his command; but art, in the sense of craftsman's skill, without sincerity of vision will not suffice. This is applicable to both branches of fiction, to romance and to the novel; but with romance we are not here concerned. It seems to me that no novel can possess the slightest value which has not been conceived, fashioned, elaborated, with a view to depicting some portion of human life as candidly and vividly as is in the author's power. Other qualities may abound in the work; some others must needs be present. Tragic power, pathos, humour, sportiveness, tenderness: the novelist may have them one or all; constructive ability and the craft of words he cannot dispense with. But these gifts will not avail him as a novelist if he lack the spirit of truthfulness, which, be it added, is quite a different thing from saying that no novel can be of worth if it contain errors of observation, or fall short of the entire presentment of facts.

What do we mean by "reality"? Science concerns itself with facts demonstrable to every formal understanding; the world of science we call "real," having no choice but to accept it as such. In terms of art, reality has another signification. What the artist sees is to him only a part of the actual; its complement is an emotional effect. Thus it comes about that every novelist beholds a world of his own, and the supreme endeavour of his art must be to body forth that world as it exists for him. The novelist works, and must work, subjectively. A demand for objectivity in fiction is worse than meaningless, for apart from the personality of the workman no literary art can exist. The cry arose, of course, in protest against the imperfect method of certain novelists, who came forward in their own pages, and spoke as showmen; but what can be more absurd than to talk about the "objectivity" of such an author as Flaubert, who triumphs by his extraordinary power of presenting life as he, and no other man, beheld it? There is no science of fiction. However energetic and precise the novelist's preparation for his book, all is but dead material until breathed upon by the "shaping spirit of imagination," which is the soul of the individual artist. Process belongs to the workshop; the critic of the completed work has only to decide as to its truth—that is to say, to judge the spirit in which it was conceived, and the technical merit of its execution.

Realism, then, signifies nothing more than artistic sincerity in the portrayal of contemporary life; it merely contrasts with the habit of mind which assumes that a novel is written "to please people," that disagreeable facts must always be kept out of sight, that human nature must be systematically flattered, that the book must have a "plot," that the story should end on a cheerful note, and all the rest of it. Naturally the question arises: What limits does the independent novelist impose upon himself? Does he feel free to select *any* theme, from the sweetest to the most nauseating? Is it enough to declare that he has looked upon this or that aspect of life, has mirrored it in his imagination, and shows it forth candidly, vividly? For my own part, I believe that he must recognise limits in every direction; that he will constantly reject material as unsuitable to the purposes of art; and that many features of life are so completely beyond his province that he cannot dream of representing them. At the same time I joyfully compare the novelist's freedom in England of to-day with his bondage of only ten or twelve years ago. No doubt the new wine of liberty tempts to excess. Moreover, novels nowadays are not always written for the novel's sake, and fiction cries aloud as the mouthpiece of social reform. The great thing is, that public opinion no longer constrains a novelist to be false to himself. The world lies open before him, and it is purely a matter for his private decision whether he will write as the old law dictates or to show life its image as he beholds it. (pp. 83-6)

George Gissing, in an essay in his George Gissing on Fiction, *edited by Jacob Korg & Cynthia Korg, Enitharmon Press, 1978, pp. 82-6.*

THE TIMES LITERARY SUPPLEMENT (essay date 1903)

[*In the following excerpt, the critic praises the poetic quality of* The Private Papers of Henry Ryecroft.]

Mr. George Gissing is a realist, although he does not belong to that popular school of realists in fiction of whom it may be said that their books would be merely dull but for their truth—and it is their truth which makes them dreadful. Mr. Gissing's work is at once too sincere and too personal ever to be dull. The theory of life which he expresses is a sombre theory—it is reasonable, and painful, and hopeless. He is the champion, or rather he is the spokesman, of the dumb and the disinherited. His characters move in an atmosphere of care, and cruel effort, and perplexity. The lack of money, the lack of ease and security, the tragedy of sacrificed forces, the more sordid tragedy

of daily want forever dog the footsteps of these unoffending and doomed modern men and women. We see them born to undergo every cramping and degrading condition of those who work for their bread in the crowded loneliness of great cities. And if, for a little, Mr. Gissing's personages are allowed to escape from that mean Hell of mean houses which represents "London" to the very poor—if their author introduces us to suburban life, or even to the life of country towns, it is only to show us the members of a more educated class starving for a more intellectual form of nourishment and suffering from a keener sense of deprivation. Joylessness and Labour possess in turn the world of Mr. Gissing's imagination; but for all that it is a world which belongs to himself; which he grasps and understands and often sets before us with truly admirable and sober virility. Soberness, strength, and impeccable honesty; the unswerving, almost fatalistic, acceptance of the hardest facts; a deep, painful, vital sense of the brotherhood of our bewildered humanity; and the most masculine expression of pathos to be found in any contemporary English novelist—that brief, inexpressive, poignant pity for the individual, which can yet accept his pain as a necessary part of life—these are all characteristics of Mr. Gissing. His style is plain, and clear, and forcible—unillumined by any sense of plastic beauty or any liberating throb of romance. He is curiously undramatic. He never appears to see situations as a whole, or in a series of pictures. His climaxes are all reached—and they are reached—by the accumulation of scores upon scores of direct, patient, and honest observations. Mr. Gissing reminds us of Balzac in his methods of cumulative power; he is like Balzac in his disregard of the charm of words—the use of language as a fine art. Yet, take Mr. Gissing at his best, and Balzac, with a hundred times more vitality, a hundred thousand times more imagination and genius, has never built more solidly.

Mr. Gissing does not love London but he knows it. In a dozen volumes he has given us a picture of the great stony-hearted city of unremitting toil, which is neither splendid nor complete, but which presents the thwarted average life of the average thwarted man with a force and a precision which cannot fail to command recognition. For Mr. Gissing is never common, never glib, and never conventional. What is stranger than this, he writes of the most painful facts and he is never brutal. His very sobriety and plainness of speech save him from cynicism. Possibly his style is not brilliant enough to be cruel; but the serious, sober respect for the exact limits of the fact, carried to this degree, is a literary quality rare enough to atone for much missing brilliancy. Mr. Gissing may not amuse or excite his reader; he will always convince him. In this man's work we are never aware of that love of the phrase which underlines the hideous and dramatic side of life; we are not shown these men and women of the East-end silhouetted against a red background of savagery and horror, as in some of Mr. Morrison's books, and notably in Rudyard Kipling's "Badalia." Mr. Gissing's treatment of these themes is more like the work of some old Dutch painter; it is to conscientiousness, to effort, and to truth that he owes his sober successes.

But as Sainte Beuve has written (and Alfred de Musset has repeated it in a noble set of verses) there exists in each man's heart "un poète mort jeune et dont il se souvient" ["a poet who died young and whom he remembers"]. In Mr. Gissing's latest volume, *The Private Papers of Henry Ryecroft,* it would seem as if, at last, we had come upon traces of this dead and unforgotten poet. This book professes to be a collection of reflections and personal reminiscences, written in the Devonshire country, by a man of fifty-four. "Like other mortals he had lived and laboured; like other mortals he has entered into his rest,'' says Mr. Gissing in the preface which contains his biographical sketch of the man he prefers to describe as his dead friend. Ryecroft, we are told, began life under the sternest conditions. Miserably poor, in failing health, he earned an insufficient pittance by long and strenuous effort:—

> Naturally a man of independent and rather scornful outlook, he had suffered much from defeated ambition, from disillusions of many kinds, from subjection to grim necessity. . . . He did a great deal of mere hack work; he reviewed, he translated, he wrote articles; at long intervals a volume appeared under his name. There were times, I have no doubt, when bitterness took hold upon him . . . but on the whole he earned his living very much as other men do, taking the day's toil as a matter of course, rarely grumbling over it. . . . It was a bitter thought that after so long and hard a struggle with unkindly circumstance he might end his life as one of the defeated. . . .

But, in this instance, at least, Mr. Gissing did relent. After fifty years of London, Henry Ryecroft becomes the possessor of an unexpected life legacy of three hundred pounds a year. That he does not die in the very hour of this dazzling release from slavery, that Mr. Gissing allows him four more years in which to taste the exquisite peace of rest, and cessation from toil, and security, is indeed something to be grateful for.

For Ryecroft loves the country with the passionate, the minute, the allusive, the sophisticated love which is only possible in the exile, the weary dweller in great cities, the man whose jaded feet have known too long

> each chartered street,
> Near where the chartered Thames doth flow.

This little book is the record of the Emancipation of the Literary Slave. ''Every morning when I awake I thank heaven for silence. . . . Year after year this spot has known the same tranquillity . . . with ever so little of good fortune, I might have blessed my manhood with calm, might have made for myself in later life a long retrospect of bowered peace.'' ''The dead,'' he writes elsewhere, ''the dead amid this leafy silence, seem to whisper encouragement to him whose fate yet lingers.'' So incredible is the relief of weary sense, of jarred and aching nerve, that ''I could imagine a man who, by living alone and at peace, came to regard this everyday world (this world where men are fretting, raving, killing each other for matters so trivial) as not really existent, but a creation of his own fancy in unsound moments.'' In the midst of reflections on Democracy (and the man who writes has suffered in too intimate and personal ways to be a social democrat), or while discussing the disadvantages of a forced conscription in England, or the exact meaning of a passage in Homer, he breaks off again and again to note the dear and unfamiliar joy of watching an evening sky; the look of a flower in sunlight; ''the delight it is to me to see the bat flitting at dusk before my window or to hear the hoot of the owl when all the ways are dark.'' It is the emancipated slave, but the slave who has not forgotten. ''The surprise of budding branches covered in a night with green . . . meadows shining with buttercups . . . the sallow glistening with its cones of silvery fur and splendid with dust of gold . . . even the vision of that enchanted morning when the apple trees were in full bloom, and, as I stood gazing, the sun, which had all that day been

niggard of its beams, burst forth gloriously. For what I then saw I have no word; I can but dream of the still loveliness of that blossomed valley''—even sights of most natural joy, such as these, are powerless to exorcize the black remembrance of those grinding London years. ''I dare not think of those I have left behind me, there in the ink-stained world,'' cries Mr. Gissing—or, rather, Henry Ryecroft. He gives sixpence to a sobbing child and remembers when he could not have done it; when poverty paralysed his soul, and sixpence stood for a day's food and comfort.

> I once *found* sixpence in the street, and had an exultation which is vivid in me at this moment. . . . Would I live it over again—that life of the garret and the cellar? . . . With man's infinitely pathetic power of resignation one sees the thing on its better side, forgets all the worst of it. . . . Oh, but the waste of energy, of zeal, of youth! . . . I could shed tears over that spectacle of rare vitality condemned to sordid strife. The pity of it! . . . the bitter wrong!

This book, we have said, may well stand for Mr. Gissing's fullest expression of the poetry within him; the confessions of that mysterious poet who dies young and who is unforgotten. And how melancholy it all is!—how well written, how well felt, how well realized, and how infinitely joyless. Not even in Devon lanes and in high summer, can Henry Ryecroft forget that world where it is ever the man's bitter daily need—his poverty and not his will—that consents. The effect of this book upon any sympathetic reader holds the most vivid compliment to Mr. Gissing's careful art and skill. It is undoubtedly a book destined to command a small, but very ardent, following. In its way, Mr. Gissing has never written anything more remarkable. His cumulative method to which we alluded has never been used to better purpose. Yet, in the end, Henry Ryecroft is a character study rather than a character. Negation and self-suppression are undoubtedly necessary elements of life under modern conditions. But great art has never yet sprung from negation or suppression. Here we have the image of a man released from average and oppressive conditions, but we have not in Henry Ryecroft the final and authoritative type of such a man. Every detail carries conviction; the figure of Mr. Gissing's hero is *documenté;* it is solid; it is sincere; only never for one moment is it alive and independent of all documents. Compare this conception of a scholar, a philosopher, a calm and melancholy contemplator of other men's action to that other contemplator and scholar and philosopher, M. Émile Bergeret. It has become the fashion, within the last two or three years, to speak of Mr. Gissing as of a master; but this, which in many ways is his best work, strikes us as a *tour de force* of authenticity, never of revelation. (pp. 38-9)

''George Gissing,'' in The Times Literary Supplement, *No. 56, February 6, 1903, pp. 38-9.*

PAUL ELMER MORE (essay date 1907)

[*More was an American critic who, along with Irving Babbitt, formulated the doctrines of New Humanism in early twentieth-century American thought. The New Humanists were strict moralists who adhered to traditional conservative values in reaction to an age of scientific and artistic self-expression. In regard to literature, they believed a work's implicit reflection of support for the classic ethical norms to be of as much importance as its aesthetic qualities. More was particularly opposed to Naturalism, which he believed accentuated the animal nature of humans, and to any literature, such as Romanticism, that broke with established classical tradition. His importance as a critic derives from the rigid coherence of his ideology, which polarized American critics into hostile opponents (Van Wyck Brooks, Edmund Wilson, H. L. Mencken) or devoted supporters (Norman Foerster, Stuart Sherman, and, to a lesser degree, T. S. Eliot). He is especially esteemed for the philosophical and literary erudition of his multi-volume* Shelburne Essays *(1904-21). In the following excerpt, More discusses the evolution of Gissing's work.*]

When Gissing died at St. Jean de Luz, in 1903, broken down at the age of forty-six by years of toil and privation, he had begun to acquire in the world at large something of the reputation he had long possessed among a select circle. But it is to be feared that the irony of his later works, such as [*The House of Cobwebs, and Other Stories*], may create a wrong impression of his genius among these newly-won friends. For Gissing, more than most writers, underwent a change with the progress of time. His work, in fact, may be divided into three fairly distinct periods. Passing over the immature *Workers in the Dawn* . . . , we may mark off the first group of novels as beginning with *The Unclassed* . . . and ending with *Born in Exile* . . . ; between these two are *Isabel Clarendon, Demos, Thyrza, A Life's Morning, The Nether World, The Emancipated,* and *New Grub Street.* The second group, starting with *Denzil Quarrier* . . . , may be limited by *The Crown of Life* . . . , although the transition here to his final manner is more gradual than the earlier change. This second division embraces what are perhaps the best known of Gissing's novels—the *Year of Jubilee* and *The Whirlpool*—and here again there is danger of misunderstanding. These are books of undeniable power, comparable in some ways to Hardy's *Jude, the Obscure,* but pointed in the wrong direction, and not truly characteristic. One feels a troubling and uncertain note in all this intermediate work, done while the author, having passed beyond his first intense preoccupation with the savage warfare for existence, was still far from the fair serenity of his close. The greater Gissing is not to be found here, but in those tales which embody his own experiences in the cruel and primeval nether world of London— tales which together make what might be called the Epic of Poverty.

Poverty, the gaunt greedy struggle for bread, the naked keen reality of hunger that goads the world onward—how this grim power reigns in all Gissing's early novels, crushing the uninured dreamers and soiling the strong. It is the guiding power of *The Unclassed.* It casts its spume of misery and filth on the path of *Thyrza,* that fragile Madonna of the slums, yet finds even here its pathetic voice of song:

> A street organ began to play in front of a public house close by. Grail drew near; there were children forming a dance, and he stood to watch them.
>
> Do you know that music of the obscure ways, to which children dance? Not if you have only heard it ground to your ears' affliction beneath your windows in the square. To hear it aright, you must stand in the darkness of such a by-street as this, and for the moment be at one with those who dwell around, in the blear-eyed houses, in the dim burrows of poverty, in the unmapped haunts of the semi-human. Then you will know the significance of that vulgar clanging of melody; a pathos of which you did not dream will touch you, and therein the secret of hidden London will be half revealed. The life

of men who toil without hope, yet with the hunger of an unshaped desire; of women in whom the sweetness of their sex is perishing under labor and misery; the laugh, the song of the girl who strives to enjoy her year or two of youthful vigor, knowing the darkness of the years to come; the careless defiance of the youth who feels his blood and revolts against the plot which would tame it; all that is purely human in these darkened multitudes speaks to you as you listen.

A superb piece of imaginative prose, indeed, . . . and significant of the music which Gissing himself wrested from the misery of the London streets. The note rises in *Life's Morning* to tragic shrillness, making of it one of the most passionate stories in English of love striving against the degradation of destiny. Again, in *New Grub Street,* it sinks to the forlorn plea of genius baffled by unremunerative toil, and starved into despair. Those who care to know the full measure of agony through which the writer himself struggled, may find it portrayed here in the lives of the two unrecognized novelists. Only Gissing could tell how much of his own experience is portrayed in those "dwellers in the valley of the shadow of books"; how much of his fierce aspiration to paint the world as it really exists was expressed by the garret-haunting, hunger-driven Biffen; how often his breast, like Reardon's, swelled with envy of the prosperous commercialized man of letters. "He knew what poverty means. The chilling of brain and heart, the unnerving of the hands, the slow gathering about one of fear and shame and impotent wrath; the dread feeling of helplessness, of the world's base indifference. Poverty! Poverty!" I am not sure that it is good to know these things even by hearsay, but for those who are strong in pity and fortified by resolve they have been written out once for all, ruthlessly, without mitigation.

More general, gathering up all the suffering and foulness and crime of want, embracing too the clear-eyed, uncompromising charity of strength that asks for no reward, is that terrible story of *The Nether World.* Here, most of all, Gissing is conscious of his grave theme; and as a chorus through all the sounds of defeat and consternation he raises the clamorous cry of his "Mad Jack," like the prophesying of some Jeremiah of the slums:

> "Don't laugh! Don't any of you laugh; for as sure as I live it was an angel stood in the room and spoke to me. There was a light such as none of you ever saw, and the angel stood in the midst of it. And he said to me: 'Listen, while I reveal to you the truth, that you may know where you are and what you are; and this is done for a great purpose.' And I fell down on my knees, but never a word could I have spoken. Then the angel said: 'You are passing through a state of punishment. You, and all the poor among whom you live; all those who are in suffering of body and darkness of mind were once rich people, with every blessing the world can bestow, with every opportunity of happiness in yourselves and of making others happy. Because you made an ill use of your wealth, because you were selfish and hard-hearted and oppressive, and sinful in every kind of indulgence, therefore after death you received the

reward of wickedness. This life you are now leading is that of the damned; this place to which you are confined is hell! There is no escape for you. From poor you shall become poorer; the older you grow the lower shall you sink in want and misery; at the end there is waiting for you, one and all, a death in abandonment and despair. This is hell—hell—hell!'''. . .

Above the noise of the crowd rose a shrill, wild voice, chanting:

"All ye works of the Lord, bless ye the Lord; praise Him and magnify Him forever!"

It has seemed worth while to quote thus at length, because Gissing is one of the few English novelists whose trained and supple language makes itself felt in such extracts, and because they lead at once to the theory on which he worked. "Art, nowadays," Gissing declares boldly, "must be the mouthpiece of misery, for misery is the keynote of modern life." It is not entirely easy to reconcile such a theory with the judgment of Gissing's own riper years; for art, he came in the end to think, is "an expression, satisfying and abiding, of the zest of life." Certainly, it is this contrast between the misery and the zest of life, derived from the same materials, that makes a comparison between Dickens and Gissing so inevitable. Gissing felt it, and his [*Charles Dickens*] is one of the most ambiguous pieces of writing in the language. His intention is manifestly to praise, but he can never quite overcome his surprise and annoyance at the radical difference of Dickens's attitude toward poverty. And the same feeling crops out again and again in the earlier novels. Inextinguishable laughter were fittest, he says, musing on his own terrible nether world and thinking of the elder writer's gayety, but the heart grows heavy. In an essay last month, I tried to show how Dickens tended to portray his characters from the outside, without identifying himself with their real emotions. Here, on the contrary, we have a man whose ambition it was to strip off to the last rag those veils of melodrama and humor which prevented Dickens from becoming a realist, and which, it may be added, he himself by native right possessed in large measure. He would not be waylaid and turned from his purpose by the picturesque grimaces of poverty, but would lay bare the sullen ugliness at its core; he would, in a word, write from the inside. Only by taking account of the sordid realities of Gissing's life can we understand the mingled attraction and repulsion exercised on him by the large joyousness and exulting pathos of Dickens in dealing with the nether world. "The man who laughs," he said, reproachfully, "takes the side of a cruel omnipotence." The words are suggestive. Not "cruel," but *unimplicated*, let us say, and accept the phrase as a mark of the greater art. It is because Dickens stands with the powers above and is not finally implicated in his theme, that he could turn it into an expression, satisfying and abiding, of the zest of life. And it is, on the other hand, just because Gissing cannot entirely rise above the "misery" he describes, that all his marvellous understanding of the human heart and his chastened style do not save his art in the end.

And yet, if his theory and practice must from the highest standard be condemned, it would be unfair to overlook the reservations that should go with even so strict a judgment. For though the zest of life be lacking in these novels, there is something in them that strangely resembles it. "How," he exclaims in one of his latest works—"how, in the name of sense and mercy, is mankind content to live on in such a world

as this?" The question obtrudes itself upon the reader again and again, and slowly he becomes aware of the vast, dumb, tumultuous *will to live* that is struggling into consciousness through all these horrors and madnesses. The very magnitude of the obstacles, the unreason of endurance, is witness to the unconquerable energy of this blind will. What, after all, has been the substance of great literature, from the days when Sarpedon heartened Glaucus on the plains of Troy to the most modern singer of some soul divided against itself, but warfare, and again renewed war? And as one reads on in these novels of Gissing's, their plot begins to unfold itself as another and darker picture of the same battle. It is almost as if we were listening to the confused lamentation of a city besieged and captured by night, wherein the enemy is no invading army of Greece, but the more treacherous powers of hunger, and vice, and poverty. . . . (pp. 53-4)

And there is another element which helps to relieve the depressing nature of Gissing's theme. Literature of the slums is not lacking in these latter days. In each of our large cities you will find a college settlement where a band of prurient souls sit at type-writing machines glutting a morbid ambition on the sorrows of the poor. Now, Gissing did not learn the meaning of poverty in any such fashion; there is, at all events, nothing of the dilettante in his work. He wrote, not from callow sympathy or patronizing observation, but from his own deep experience; and, writing thus, he put into his acccount of the nether world the one thing commonly wanting to these pictures—the profound sense of morality. Through all these graphic, sometimes appalling, scenes one knows that the writer is still concerned primarily with the inner effects of poverty, and his problem is the ancient, insoluble antimony of the one and the many, the individual and the mass. Taken as a whole, the society he describes is the victim of circumstances. His philosophy is summed up in a gloomy determinism: "indigence is the death of the soul," and "misery is vice." Yet even here, as in that chorus of "Mad Jack" already quoted, the contradictory and less comprehensible law of morality makes itself heard at times; and when he touches the individual, the sure insight of the artist asserts itself and he orders his people not as automatons, but as characters moved by their own volition, and, though it may be in unaccountable ways, reaping as they have sown. The knot of fate and free-will is not always disentangled, there is no conventional apportioning of rewards and penalties such as Dickens indulged in at the end of his novels; but always, through all the workings of heredity and environment, he leaves the reader conscious of that last inviolable mystery of man's nature, the sense of personal responsibility. Had not he, George Gissing, been caught in the cruel network of circumstances, and had he not yet preserved intact the feeling that he was personally accountable? It is thus he attains by another road to something of the liberal enlargement of Dickens; the greatest art, it need scarcely be said, would combine both the free outlook of the older writer and the moral insight of the younger.

Those are the principles—the instinctive will to live and the law of moral responsibility—that saved the writer's tragic stage from insupportable dreariness; they furnished, also, the clue that in the end led the writer himself out of the labyrinth of doubtful questionings. But for a while it seemed as if they were to be lost, for it is not so much any lowering of literary skill as a change in these essential points that marks the transition from his first to his second period. The new spirit may be defined by a comparison of such novels as *The Nether World* from his first period and *The Whirlpool* from his second (the very names are significant), or as *Life's Morning* and *The Crown of Life*. In place of human nature battling with grim necessity, we now have a society of people contending against endless insinuations of tedium and vanity; in place of the will to live we meet a sex-consciousness, always strong in Gissing, but now grown to morbid intensity. And with this change comes a certain relaxing of moral fibre. The theme is no longer self-responsibility, or character in the strict meaning of the term, but a thousand vexatious questions of the day—anti-vivisection, anti-racing, anti-gambling, anti-hunting, anti-war, imperialism, the education of children, the emancipation of women, and, above all and more persistent than all, the thrice-dreary theories of marriage. It would be wrong to infer that the moral of his books is ever at bottom any other than sound. In the full swing of his middle period he could close a novel with the ejaculation of his hero: "Now I understand the necessity for social law!" But one is aware, nevertheless, that conventions have grown irksome to him, and that for a while his real interest is in the thronging, ambiguous problems of emancipation.

If the influence of modern Continental literature, especially of French and Russian, may be suspected of unsettling his inherited canons, his home-coming in the end was surely due in large measure to his devoted study of the classics. Strange as it may seem when one considers the topics he treated, there is scarcely a writer of the last century more thoroughly versed in Greek and Latin than Gissing, and throughout his struggle with poverty he commonly kept free of the pawnshop a few chosen books, Homer, Tibullus, Horace, Gibbon, Shakespeare. Writing the memoirs of his life, at ease, and with a library at his command, he recalls his difficulties:

> I see that alley hidden on the west side of Tottenham Court Road, where, after living in a back bedroom on the top floor, I had to exchange for the front cellar; there was a difference, if I remember rightly, of sixpence a week, and sixpence, in those days, was a very great consideration—why, it meant a couple of meals. (I once *found* sixpence in the street, and had an exultation which is vivid in me at this moment.) The front cellar was stone-floored; its furniture was a table, a chair, a washstand, and a bed; the window, which, of course, had never been cleaned since it was put in, received light through a flat grating in the alley above. Here I lived; here I *wrote*. Yes, "literary work" was done at that filthy deal table, on which, by the bye, lay my Homer, my Shakespeare, and the few other books I then possessed.

What a picture of the new Grub Street. One thinks of the deal table in Thoreau's hut at Walden on which a Homer lay, and one thinks, too, of Dickens in his comfortable study with his shelves of sham books. For most of his reading Gissing had to depend on public convenience:

> How many days have I spent at the British Museum, reading as disinterestedly as if I had been without a care! It astounds me to remember that, having breakfasted on dry bread, and carrying in my pocket another piece of bread to serve for dinner, I settled myself at a desk in the great Reading Room with books before me which by no possibility could be a source of immediate profit. At such a time I worked through German tomes on Ancient Philosophy.

> At such a time, I read Appuleius and Lucian, Petronius and the Greek Anthology, Diogenes Laertius and—Heaven knows what! My hunger was forgotten; the garret to which I must return to pass the night never perturbed my thoughts.

And Homer and Ancient Philosophy won the day. There was little occasion in the earlier novels to display this learning, yet here and there the author's longing for Rome and Italy breaks through, as in the passion of the apothecary's apprentice in *The Unclassed*. Then came the intellectual whirlpool. The release from that dizziness of brain shows itself first in a growing lightness of touch and aloofness from passion of all sorts. The novels and tales of the third period are chiefly distinguished by a tone of gentle and amused irony, in place of the satire of the middle group, and it is significant that the theme of *Will Warburton*, his last novel, is the same as that chosen by Biffen in the *New Grub Street* for his pronunciamento of rebellious realism—the life of a retail grocer. Only, in the actual novel there is no realism at all as Biffen would have understood it, but the witty and mock heroic story of a man of good birth who begins by selling groceries over the counter under an assumed name and ends by accepting his lot in all *gaieté de cœur*—so far had Gissing travelled from being at loggerheads with destiny. *Warburton* was written in Southern France when a moderate success had freed him from the hardest slavery of the pen, and when ill health had driven him from England. Here, too, he absolved himself from an ancient vow by composing with all the artistry he possessed, a story of classical life—his *Veranilda*—and here he wrote that restrained and every way beautiful piece of self-revelation, *The Private Papers of Henry Ryecroft*.

There is nothing in the language quite like this volume of half-veiled autobiography. In the imagined quiet of a home in Devon, the part of England Gissing so passionately loved, he writes out his memories of toil and the reflections that come to him as the sum of his experiences. Here is no bitterness, no complaining; all the lesser problems that harassed him have solved themselves by simply vanishing; he returns to his early convictions, with the added ripeness of long meditation. He had used the life of the poor for his greatest creative work, and the question of the growing democracy is the only one that still abides with him in his repose. Everywhere he sees the decay of that natural instinct on which the morality of the world at large must always depend, and in its place an ever-widening spirit of interrogation which only unsettles and sets adrift. "I am no friend of the people," he exclaims, and the words come with strange insistence from such a man. "As a force, by which the tenor of the time is conditioned, they inspire me with distrust, with fear. . . . Every instinct of my being is anti-democratic, and I dread to think of what our England may become when Demos rules irresistibly. . . . Nothing is more rooted in my mind than the vast distinction between the individual and the class." This doubt alone remained to annoy him, but with it he connected the other great movement of the day: "I hate and fear 'science' because of my conviction that, for long to come, if not for ever, it will be the remorseless enemy of mankind." To science he attributed the spread of that half-education which increases the powers of action while lessening the inhibitions of self-knowledge. It was from his close reading of the classics, I think, though he himself does not say so, came his notion of some salvation through the aristocratic idea—the essential idea of Greek literature:

> The task before us is no light one. Can we, whilst losing the class, retain the idea it em-

bodied? Can we English, ever so subject to the material, liberate ourselves from that old association, yet guard its meaning in the sphere of spiritual life? Can we, with eyes which have ceased to look reverently on worn-out symbols, learn to select from among the gray-coated multitude, and place in reverence even higher him who "holds his patent of nobility straight from Almighty God"? Upon that depends the future of England.

The business of the novelist is with the realities of life, and not with hypotheses; yet one cannot leave Gissing without wishing that he had found strength and occasion to express these fundamental ideas of his maturity in fiction. (pp. 54-5)

> *Paul Elmer More, "George Gissing," in* The Nation, *New York, Vol. LXXXIV, January 17, 1907, pp. 53-5.*

VIRGINIA WOOLF (essay date 1912)

[*A British novelist, essayist, and short story writer, Woolf is considered one of the most prominent literary figures of twentieth-century English literature. Like her contemporary James Joyce, with whom she is often compared, Woolf is remembered as one of the most innovative of the stream of consciousness novelists. Concerned primarily with depicting the life of the mind, she revolted against traditional narrative techniques and developed her own highly individualized style. Woolf's works, noted for their subjective explorations of characters' inner lives and for their delicate poetic quality, have had a lasting effect on the art of the novel. A discerning and influential critic and essayist as well as a novelist, Woolf began writing reviews for the* Times Literary Supplement *at an early age. Her critical essays, termed "creative, appreciative, and subjective" by Barbara Currier Bell and Carol Ohmann, cover almost the entire range of English literature and contain some of her finest prose. Along with Lytton Strachey, Roger Fry, Clive Bell, and others, Woolf and her husband Leonard formed the literary coterie known as the "Bloomsbury Group." In the following excerpt, Woolf considers Gissing's perception of life as it is exemplified in his novels.*]

Let any one who has spent his life in writing novels consider the day which has now arrived for George Gissing. The fruit of his life stands before us—a row of red volumes. If they were biographies, histories, books about books even, or speculations upon money or the course of the world there would be no need for the peculiar shudder. But they bear titles like these—*Denzil Quarrier, Born in Exile, New Grub Street;* places and people that have never existed save in one brain now cold. They are only novels. It seems that there is genuine cause for shuddering when one's work takes this form. Dead leaves cannot be more brittle or more worthless than things faintly imagined—and that the fruit of one's life should be twelve volumes of dead leaves! We have one moment of such panic before the novels of George Gissing, and then we rise again. Not in our time will they be found worthless.

An interesting letter to Mr. Clodd was printed the other day. In it Gissing wrote:—

> By the bye, Pinker has suggested to me that he should try to get all my works into the hands of some one publisher. I should like this, but I have a doubt whether the time has come yet. There is a curious blending of respect and contempt in the publishers' minds towards me, and I should like to see which sentiment will pre-

vail. If the contempt, one must relinquish ambitions proved to be idle, and so attain a certain tranquillity—even if it be that of the workhouse. I was always envious of workhouse folk; they are the most independent of all.

Respect has prevailed; Messrs. Sidgwick and Jackson reprint the eight later works both well and cheaply. One, ***Born in Exile,*** is to be bought upon railway bookstalls for sevenpence. Nevertheless it is his own word "respect" that seems to describe the attitude of the public towards him; he is certainly not popular; he is not really famous. If we may guess at the destiny of this new edition, we can imagine that it will find its way to houses where very few novels are kept. Ordinary cultivated people will buy them of course; but also governesses who scarcely ever read; mechanics; working men who despise novels; dons who place him high among writers of English prose; professional men; the daughters of farmers in the North. We can imagine that he is the favourite novelist of a great many middle-aged, sceptical, rather depressed men and women who when they read want thought and understanding of life as it is, not wit or romance. In saying this we are saying also that Gissing does not appeal to a great multitude; the phrase "life as it is" is always the phrase of people who try to see life honestly and find it hard and dreary. Other versions of life they reject. They are not, perhaps, in the majority, but they form a minority that is very respectable, and perhaps increasing.

If this is at all true of his readers, what shall we say of the writer himself? There is a great difference between writing and reading, and Gissing was a born writer. When a novelist has been dead for some years and his books are gathered together we want as far as possible to stand where he stood; not to be moved by one character or one idea, but to grasp his point of view. His books are very sad; that is the first thing that strikes the reader. The ordinary excitement of guessing the end is scarcely to be indulged in. Conceive the most gloomy, yet natural, conclusion to every complexity, and you are likely to be right. He had, as most novelists have, one great theme. It is the life of a man of fine character and intelligence who is absolutely penniless and is therefore the sport of all that is most sordid and brutal in modern life. He earns, perhaps, a pound a week. He has thrown up his job in an office because an editor has accepted one of his stories. He marries a woman of some refinement; they live in a couple of rooms somewhere off the Tottenham Court-road. In a short time they cannot pay the rent; they move; they sell pieces of furniture; they live off tea and bread and butter; then his books go; all day long, in spite of headache and sore throat, in bitter fog and clinging mist, the wretched man has to spin imaginary loves and imaginary jests from his exhausted brain. He has the additional agony of loving good writing; he can lose himself still in dreams of the Acropolis or in argument about Euripides. His wife leaves him, for the dirt repels her; at last his stuff has become too poor even to sell, and he dies knowing himself beaten on every hand.

Many readers, happily, rebound from their depression when the end is reached, exclaiming, "After all, this is only one side." There are quantities of people who have enough money to avoid these horrors; a few who can command luxury. But what Gissing proves is the terrible importance of money, and, if you slip, how you fall and fall and fall. With learning, sensitive feelings, a love of beauty both in art and in human nature—all the qualities that generally (one hopes) keep their possessor somehow afloat—he descended to the depths where men and women live in vast shoals without light or freedom. What a strange place it is—this Nether World! There are women as brutal as savages, men who are half animals, women still preserving some ghost of love and pity, men turning a stunted brain upon the problems of their lot. All the things that grow fine and large up here are starved and twisted down there; just as the squares and parks, and the houses standing separate with rooms measured off for different occupations, are shrivelled into black alleys, sooty patches of green, and sordid lodging-houses, where there is shelter, but only the shelter that pigs or cows have, not room for the soul. Without money you cannot have space or leisure; worse than that, the chances are very much against your having either love or intelligence.

Many writers before and after Gissing have written with both knowledge and sympathy of the poor. What, after all, is more stimulating to the imagination than the sight of great poverty or great wealth? There was Mrs. Gaskell, for instance, and Dickens; a score of writers in our own day have studied the conditions of their lives. But the impressive part about Gissing is that knowing them as he did he makes no secret of the fact that he hated them. That is the reason why his voice is so harsh, so penetrating, so little grateful to the ears. Can any one hate poverty with all their soul who does not hate the poor? "Some great and noble sorrow," he writes, "may have the effect of drawing hearts together, but to struggle against destitution, to be crushed by care about shillings and sixpences . . . that must always degrade." There is no sentimentalism about the fundamental equality of men in his works. Adela Mutimer in *Demos,* gazing at her husband's face opposite her, ponders thus; Gissing must often have thought the same:—

It was the face of a man by birth and breeding altogether beneath her.

> Never had she understood that as now; never had she conceived so forcibly the reason which made him and her husband and wife only in name. Suppose that apparent sleep of his to be the sleep of death; he would pass from her consciousness like a shadow from the field, leaving no trace behind. Their life of union was a mockery; their married intimacy was an unnatural horror. He was not of her class, not of her world; only by violent wrenching of the laws of nature had they come together. She had spent years in trying to convince herself that there were no such distinctions, that only an unworthy prejudice parted class from class. One moment of true insight was worth more than all her theorizing on abstract principles. To be her equal this man must be born again, of other parents, in other conditions of life. . . . She had no claims to aristocratic descent, but her parents were gentlefolk; that is to say, they were both born in a position which encouraged personal refinement rather than the contrary, which expected of them a certain education in excess of life's barest need, which authorized them to use the service of ruder men and women in order to secure to themselves a margin of life for life's sake. Perhaps for three generations her ancestors could claim so much gentility; it was more than enough to put a vast gulf between her and the Mutimers. Favourable circumstances of upbringing had endowed her with

delicacy of heart and mind not inferior to that of any woman living; mated with an equal husband, the children born of her might hope to take their place among the most beautiful and the most intelligent. And her husband was a man incapable of understanding her idlest thought.

It would have been so much easier to lessen the gulf; so much more graceful to waive the advantages of three generations of gentle birth. But to hate the vices of the poor is the way to incite the best kind of pity. The measure of his bitterness is the measure of his love of good.

But there is nothing surprising in the fact that Gissing was never popular. However harsh and censorious people are in their daily actions, they do it unofficially as it were; they shrink from any statement of the creed that makes them act thus. In fiction particularly, which is a relaxation, like golf, they detest anything severe. It is part of their enjoyment to see others looking rosy and thus to feel somewhat rosier themselves. Gissing had no sympathy whatever with this common weakness. "No, no," he makes Biffen say in **New Grub Street,** "let us copy life. When the man and woman are to meet for the great scene of passion, let it all be frustrated by one or other of them having a bad cold in the head, and so on. Let the pretty girl get a disfiguring pimple on her nose just before the ball at which she is going to shine. Show the numberless repulsive features of common decent life. Seriously, coldly; not a hint of facetiousness, or the thing becomes different." The novel that Biffen wrote on these lines is, of course, a failure, and eventually he takes his own life upon Putney Heath.

The reader, then, whose pleasure it is to identify himself with the hero or heroine, and to feel in some strange way that he shares their virtues, is completely baffled. His natural instinct is to find fault with the cynicism of the writer. But Gissing is no cynic; the real cynics are the writers who have a trivial merry view of life, and make people easily content and drugged with cheap happiness. What good Gissing finds in human beings is absolutely genuine, for it has stood such tests, and the pleasures he allows them, the pleasures of reading, companionship, and a few comfortable evenings, glow with a warmth as of redhot coals. His work has another quality that does not make for popularity either. His men and women think. When we seek the cause of his gloom is it not most truly to be found there? Each of the people who from one cause or another has to suffer the worst bruises in the Nether World is a thinking creature, capable not only of feeling, but of making that feeling part of a view of life. It is not gone when the pain is over, but persists in the form of melancholy questionings, What is to be said for a world in which there is so much suffering? By itself this peculiarity is enough to distinguish Gissing's characters from those of other novelists. There are characters who feel violently; characters who are true types; witty characters, bad ones, good ones, eccentric ones, buffoons; but the thinking man has seldom had justice done to him. The great advantage of making people think is that you can describe other relationships besides the great one between the lover and the beloved. There is friendship, for instance; the relationship that is founded on liking the same books, or sharing the same enthusiasms; there is a relationship between one man and men in general. All these, it seems to us, Gissing has described with extraordinary fineness. It is out of these relationships that he makes the texture of his works. Loves have exploded; tragedies have fired up and sunk to ashes; these quiet, undemonstrative feelings between one man and another, one woman and another, persist; they spin some kind of thread across the ravages; they are the noblest things he has found in the world.

Naturally Gissing practised what is generally called the English method of writing fiction. Instead of leaping from one high pinnacle of emotion to the next, he filled in all the adjoining parts most carefully. It is sometimes very dull. The general effect is very low in tone. You have to read from the first page to the last to get the full benefit of his art. But if you read steadily the low almost insignificant chapters gather weight and impetus; they accumulate upon the imagination; they are building up a world from which there seems to be no escape; violence would have the effect of an escape. But thus it comes about that it is difficult to point to any scene or passage and demand admiration. Do we even single out one character among all his men and women to be remembered? He has no Jane Eyres, no Uncle Tobys. But here is a passage that is characteristic of his terse workmanlike prose, glowing at the heart with a kind of flameless fire:—

> Manor Park Cemetery lies in the remote East-end, and gives sleeping places to the inhabitants of a vast district. . . . The regions around were then being built upon for the first time; the familiar streets of pale, damp brick were stretching here and there, continuing London, much like the spreading of a disease. Epping Forest is near at hand, and nearer the dreary expanse of Wanstead Flats.

> Not grief but chill desolation makes this cemetery its abode. A country churchyard touches the tenderest memories, and softens the heart with longing for the eternal rest. The cemeteries of wealthy London abound in dear and great associations, or at worst preach homilies which connect themselves with human dignity and pride. Here on the waste limits of that dread East, to wander among tombs is to go hand in hand with the stark and eyeless emblem of mortality; the spirit fails beneath the cold burden of ignoble destiny. Here lie those who were born for toil; who, when toil has worn them to the uttermost, have but to yield their useless breath and pass into oblivion. For them is no day, only the brief twilight of a winter sky between the former and the latter night. For them no aspiration; for them no hope of memory in the dust; their very children are wearied into forgetfulness. Indistinguishable units in the vast throng that labours but to support life, the name of each, father, mother, child, is as a dumb cry for the warmth and love of which Fate so stinted them. The wind wails above their narrow tenements; the sandy soil, soaking in the rain as soon as it has fallen, is a symbol of the great world which absorbs their toil and straightway blots their being.

We are in the habit of throwing faults upon the public as though it were a general rubbish heap, for it cannot bring an action for libel. But to be unpopular is a sign that there is something wrong, or how have the classics come to be the classics? Gissing's public we believe to be a very good public, but it leaves out much that is good in the great public. The reason is that he wrote his best only when he was describing struggles and

miseries and noble sufferings like those we have dwelt upon above. Directly he dealt with men and women living at ease he lost his grip; he did not see; directly he changed his sober prosaic prose for a loftier style he was without merit. He had a world of his own as real, as hard, as convincing as though it were made of earth and stone—nay, far more so—but it was a small world. There is no such place as "the" world; no such life as "life as it is." We need only consider the result of reading too much Gissing; we want another world; we take down *Evan Harrington*. Which is true—that misery, or this magnificence? They are both true; everything is true that can make us believe it to be true. Beauty beyond all other beauty, horror beyond all other horror still lie hidden about us, waiting for some one to see them. The thing that really matters, that makes a writer a true writer and his work permanent, is that he should really see. Then we believe, then there arise those passionate feelings that true books inspire. Is it possible to mistake books that have this life for books without it, hard though it is to explain where the difference lies? Two figures suggest themselves in default of reasons. You clasp a bird in your hands; it is so frightened that it lies perfectly still; yet somehow it is a living body, there is a heart in it and the breast is warm. You feel a fish on your line; the line hangs straight as before down into the sea, but there is a strain on it; it thrills and quivers. That is something like the feeling which live books give and dead ones cannot give; they strain and quiver. But satisfactory works of art have a quality that is no less important. It is that they are complete. A good novelist, it seems, goes about the world seeing squares and circles where the ordinary person sees mere storm-drift. The wildest extravagance of life in the moon can be complete, or the most shattered fragment. When a book has this quality it seems unsinkable. Here is a little world for us to walk in with all that a human being needs. Gissing's novels seem to us to possess both these essential qualities—life and completeness—and for these reasons we cannot imagine that they will perish. There will always be one or two people to exclaim, "This man understood!" (pp. 9-10)

Virginia Woolf, "The Novels of George Gissing," in The Times Literary Supplement, *No. 522, January 11, 1912, pp. 9-10.*

CONRAD AIKEN   (essay date 1927)

[*An American man of letters best known for his poetry, Aiken was deeply influenced by the psychological and literary theories of Sigmund Freud, Havelock Ellis, Edgar Allan Poe, and Henri Bergson, among others, and is considered a master of literary stream of consciousness. In reviews noted for their perceptiveness and barbed wit, Aiken exercised his theory that "criticism is really a branch of psychology." His critical position, according to Rufus A. Blanshard, "insists that the traditional notions of 'beauty' stand corrected by what we now know about the psychology of creation and consumption. Since a work of art is rooted in the personality, conscious and unconscious, of its creator, criticism should deal as much with those roots as with the finished flower." In the following excerpt, Aiken discusses Gissing's later works.*]

if, in his early work (**Demos,** for example) Gissing was occasionally tendentious, in his maturity he was first and last an artist. His purpose, in his descriptions of lower middle-class life, was not moral at all, but aesthetic: his problem was a problem of presentation. His novels and stories were his reports of life as he knew it; he was, in his narrower field, as honest an observer as Trollope; and if he was of far smaller stature as an artist than Chekhov, less poetically gifted, he shared with that great man a tendency to minimize "plot" and to make of his stories mere evocations of life.

In this regard, Gissing was very much ahead of his time. When one reflects that it is now almost a quarter of a century since he died, one reads this posthumous collection of his short stories with astonishment: for with only one or two exceptions these stories are strikingly, in tone and manner, like the sort of thing which, in the hands of such a writer as Katherine Mansfield, critics hailed as revolutionary. In most of these tales the "story" amounts to little or nothing. If one compares them with the contemporary work of Hardy or Meredith or Henry James, one finds a difference as deep as that which severed Chekhov from Turgenev. Here is little or nothing of Hardy's habitual use of tragic or poetic background, his intermittent reference to the backdrop of the Infinite; here is none of Meredith's brilliant, and brilliantly conscious, counterpoint of comment, with its inevitable heightening of distance between the reader and the story; none of the exquisite preparation and elaboration of James. Much more than he admitted, or realized, Gissing *was* interested in "human life"; it is above all for his uncompromising fidelity to his vision that we can still read him with pleasure and profit. He seldom shapes or heads his narrative as these others did, attached less importance than they to dramatic climax. He is content with a bare presentation of a scene or situation.

To say that Gissing would have been liked by Chekhov is to say that he is a "modern"—he is decidedly more modern than Hardy or James. James, of course, would have disapproved of him, as he disapproved of Mr Arnold Bennett, on the ground that he offered his reader a mere slice of life, the *donnée* without the working out. Whatever we may feel about that, and however much this sort of modernity may ultimately make Gissing appear old-fashioned, we must unquestionably accept him as an artist of the Chekhov generation, and a good one. He is not great—he lacks force, depth, range, subtlety; he has almost nothing of Chekhov's poetic profundity, only a tithe of his exquisite sensibility; by comparison with him, Gissing seems prosy, bread-and-butterish. But he is good. He can almost always be counted upon to tell his story with a clear eye and a fine gravity of spirit. There is no rhetorical nonsense about him, he is capable of no literary pyrotechnics, his style is level and undistinguished; but within his limits he is an honest and just creator of people and pictures, exaggerating nothing, never forcing a mood, and often using understatement with the most delicate skill. What could be better than the ending of his charming story, **"The Fate of Humphrey Snell?"** Humphrey was a queer stick—lazy, dreaming, impractical, not very strong; he had a passion for countryside; and eventually found a happy solution of his difficulties by becoming an itinerant herb-collector. He tramped the country, slept where he found himself, enjoyed this simple existence hugely. And then one day he fell in love with a girl who was no better than she should be; applied for a job as steward to a Workman's Club; and asked the girl to marry him. And this is how Gissing ends his story: "Annie, whose handwriting was decipherable only by a lover's eyes, answered his news by return of post: 'Send me money to come i shall want all i have for my things i cant tell you how delited I feal but its that sudin it taks my breth away with heepes of love and—'. . . . There followed a row of crosses, which Humphrey found it easy to interpret. A cross is frequently set upon a grave; but he did not think of that."

That is all—and it is all we need. And Gissing is just as good in his story of the two Cockney families who go to Brighton for their Bank Holidays, or in the story of the matrimonial failures of Miss Jewell. These tales are, in their kind, perfect. The Budges, the Rippingvilles, Miss Jewell, and the two splendid Cockney girls, Lou and Liz, are done from the life—they are as trenchantly recognizable as Mrs Laura Knight's etchings of Cockney folk on Hampstead Heath. And if the interior of an English middle-class boarding-house, with all its heavy smells and dreary sounds, its aspidistra plant and its scrubbed white step, has ever been better done, one doesn't know where to find it. (pp. 512-14)

Conrad Aiken, "George Gissing," in The Dial, *Vol. 83, December, 1927, pp. 512-14.*

Q. D. LEAVIS (essay date 1938)

[*Leavis was a twentieth-century English critic, essayist, and editor. Her professional alliance with her husband, F. R. Leavis, resulted in several literary collaborations, including the successful quarterly periodical,* Scrutiny, *in which she published many critical essays. Leavis's critical philosophy, as professed in her work for* Scrutiny, *stressed that "literary criticism is not a mystic rapture but a process of the intelligence." Furthermore, Leavis assigned to the critic the duty of remaining objective. She suggested that a responsible critic should ignore impressionistic responses to a work and, most importantly, asserted that a work should be judged on the basis of its moral value. In the following excerpt, Leavis discusses the biographical background to Gissing's works.*]

Gissing's life and temperament, with the problems that they raise, are the key to both his many failures and his single success as an artist. He made a false start in life, it is true (a blasted academic career, a spell in prison, a spell in America, an impossible marriage), but on the literary side his sending a copy of his first novel (**Workers of the Dawn** . . .) to Frederick Harrison resulted much like Crabbe's application to Burke. Harrison recommended Gissing to Lord Morley, then editor of *The Pall Mall Gazette,* and engaged Gissing as classical tutor to his two elder sons, also helping him to get other pupils. He was thus, with the *entrée* to the *P.M.G.* and as many pupils as he could teach, provided for congenially enough—that is, congenially enough for any other man of letters. But his unfortunate idea of what was suitable for the possessor of literary genius interfered with Harrison's benevolent arrangements. He refused to write more than one sketch for the *P.M.G.* on the grounds that journalism was degrading work for an artist, and though Mr. Austin Harrison says that from 1882 onwards Gissing had a living income from teaching which he could increase at will, he continued to live, if not actually in cellars and garrets on one meal a day as before, at least in near poverty, because, says Mr. H. G. Wells, "he grudged every moment taken by teaching from his literary purpose, and so taught as little as he could." The interesting point here is not Gissing's romantic conception of what is due to genius, but that he continued to describe himself as the starving and unrecognized martyr of letters; he was for long neither well-to-do nor famous, but Mr. Austin Harrison characterizes his accounts of his "continued struggles with abject poverty" as "fiction of fiction." Gissing apparently needed that fiction to support his self-esteem, his belief in his own genius, for actually he must have been well aware, like his wretched Edwin Reardon, that he had written mostly what was unworthy of his best abilities. He had to explain his failure by blaming material circumstances; and though his output was really enormous we find him in *Ryecroft,* in the year of his death, picturing himself as the writer obliged to earn his living uncongenially so that he could allow himself, ah but how rarely, the luxury of writing a novel at intervals of many years, and thus was his genius blighted. The facts, as we have seen, were otherwise.

It was not lack of time or means that hampered him, nor yet his unhappy temperament. The latter was perhaps his chief asset, since it produced an absolutely personal way of responding to life and his fellow-men, and when a measure of ultimate success came to (as they say) "mellow" him the results on his work, as seen in *Ryecroft,* were deplorable. It is instructive to compare the benevolent portrait in *Ryecroft* of the writer N., the successful author and good mixer, with the earlier study of the same type, Jasper Milvain, in *New Grub Street* (when any nineteenth-century novelist names a character Jasper I think we may safely conclude that that character is intended to be the villain). Apart from his temperament all the other qualities he brought to his novels—his scholarship, his bookishness, his enlightened interest in all the leading topics of his day (religious reform, politics, education, emancipation of woman, ethics, science, sociology . . .)—bear witness to his being an exceptionally cultivated man and exceptionally alive in his age, yet apart from *New Grub Street* how those novels date, how unreadable they now are! (It is thus that I seem to hear the literary critic of *Scrutiny,* Vol. L, describing the novels of Mr. Aldous Huxley, whom Gissing in some respects resembles). But there was no interaction between his subject-matter and his sensibility, so the exhibition of life he gives us seems arbitrarily blighted by a novelist always functioning below par as it were; Mr. Swinnerton, to account for his unpopularity, says "he was condemned by novel-readers as a writer who whimpered at life." But when he took as the subject of a novel his most vital interest—the problem of how to live as a man of letters, the literary world being what it is, without sacrificing your integrity of purpose—he produced his one permanent contribution to the English novel. I think it can be shown to be a major contribution. The subject was both inside and outside him. The best way to suggest his achievement is to say that put beside the other best treatments of the same subject—Maugham's *Cakes and Ale* and the many fine short stories on aspects of the literary life by Henry James which should be read as a whole—Gissing's *New Grub Street* is quite different, equally serious and equally successful as a piece of art.

The Gissing temperament suitably colours the book, which, like *Cakes and Ale,* is consistently written in one tone, here an irony weighted with disgust. This strikes one as being the right outlook on the literary world ("such things were enough to make all literature appear a morbid excrescence upon human life," the heroine reflects at one point), if less suited to life in general. However, life in general is here seen from the point of view of the slenderly talented Reardon who wants to support his family by his pen and yet at the same time write only novels and essays worthy of himself. We see him go under, weighed down by a wife who thinks social and material success the due of her beauty, by his lack of influential friends, most of all by his choosing to abide by the values of Dr. Johnson in an age where the policy of Alroy Kear had become requisite for success. We see his acquaintance Jasper Milvain deliberately choosing literature as a profitable field for his unliterary talents and ending up more successful than even he had dared expect, his marriage with Reardon's widow (become an heiress) symbolically ending the story. Delicacy and fineness, the strongly noble and the devotedly disinterested elements in human nature, are not ignored or denied, they are presented with complete success—this is a measure of Gissing's total success here—in the persons of Marian Yule, whom Milvain jilts and leaves

to wretchedness, and Reardon's friend Biffen who is driven to remove himself from a world that has no use for his devoted labours. Such are shown doomed to misery and failure. The old-style man of letters, part hack and part stiff-necked enthusiast, is skilfully contrasted (Alfred Yule) with the new-style man of straw (Whelpdale) successful because pliant in his complete lack of any literary conscience. There are many masterly studies of the emotions and conduct peculiar to those who live by literature and journalism, and in spite of a certain stiffness of style from which Gissing was never for long free the smallest touches are effective. The subject seems likely to remain of permanent interest and Gissing has raised crucial problems. The central problem, one ultimately of values, is put by Reardon to his wife thus:

> "A year after I have published my last book, I shall be practically forgotten. . . . And yet, of course it isn't only for the sake of reputation that one tries to do uncommon work. There's the shrinking from conscious insincerity of workmanship which most writers nowadays seem never to feel. 'It's good enough for the market'; that satisfies them. And perhaps they are justified. I can't pretend that I rule my life by absolute ideals; I admit that everything is relative. There is no such thing as goodness or badness, in the absolute sense, of course. Perhaps I am absurdly inconsistent when—though knowing my work can't be first-rate—I strive to make it as good as possible. I don't say this in irony, Amy; I really meant it. It may very well be that I am just as foolish as the people I ridicule for moral and religious superstition. This habit of mine is superstitious. How well I can imagine the answer of some popular novelist if he heard me speak scornfully of his books. 'My dear fellow,' he might say, 'do you suppose I am not aware that my books are rubbish? I know it just as well as you do. But my vocation is to live comfortably. I have a luxurious house, a wife and children who are happy and grateful to me for their happiness. If you choose to live in a garret, and, what's worse, make your wife and children share it with you, that's your concern'."

Whether Milvain could have existed at that or any time has, by way of objection, been doubted, but Seccombe, who was in a position to speak with authority, says "Jasper Milvain is, to my thinking, a perfectly fair portrait of an ambitious publicist or journalist of the day—destined by determination, skill, energy and social ambition to become an editor of a successful journal or review, and to lead the life of central London."

The original temper that the novel manifests is notable in every detail, *e.g.,*

> Alfred Yule had made a recognizable name among the critical writers of the day; seeing him in the title-lists of a periodical, most people knew what to expect, but not a few forebore the cutting open of the pages he occupied.

> They had had three children; all were happily buried.

> ". . . but I was never snobbish. I care very little about titles; what I look to is intellectual distinction."

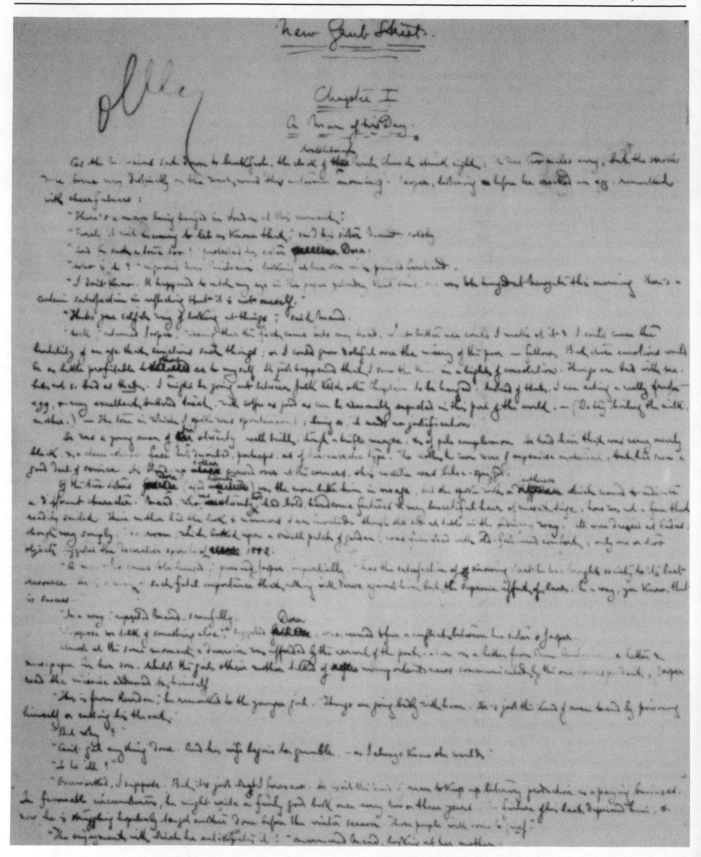

First page of the manuscript of New Grub Street.

"Combined with financial success."

"Why, that is what distinction means."

Amy now looked her years to the full, but her type of beauty, as you know, was independent of youthfulness. You saw that at forty, at fifty, she would be one of the stateliest of dames. When she bent her head towards the person with whom she spoke, it was an act of queenly favour. Her words were uttered with just enough deliberation to give them the value of an opinion; she smiled with a delicious shade of irony; her glance intimated that nothing could be too subtle for her understanding.

The last example is strikingly in the modern manner, and Gissing's best work, *New Grub Street* almost entirely, seems contemporary with us rather than with Meredith.

As a general thing, the same outlook characterizes Gissing's other novels, but elsewhere it seems merely depressed and therefore depressing. Poor Gissing was sliding down the hill which Dickens and his robust contemporaries had climbed in such high spirits. Seccombe explains it well:

> In the old race, of which Dickens and Thackeray were representative, a successful determination to rise upon the broad back of popularity coincided with a growing conviction that evil in the real world was steadily diminishing. . . . In Gissing the misery inherent in the sharp contrasts of modern life was a far more deeply ingrained conviction. He cared little for the remedial aspect of the question. His idea was to analyse this misery as an artist and to express it to the world. One of the most impressive elements in the resulting novels is the witness they bear to prolonged and intense suffering, the suffering of a proud, reserved and oversensitive mind brought into constant contact with the coarse and brutal facts of life. The creator of Mr. Biffen suffers all the torture of the fastidious, the delicately honourable, the scrupulously high-minded in daily contact with persons of blunt feelings, low ideals and base instincts.

Outside *New Grub Street* however you too often feel that the provocation is inadequate to the suffering. Gissing's susceptibilities are not all equally respectable and in some cases he seems only a querulous old maid, too easily provoked on such subjects as bad cooking, slovenly lodgings, ungenteel personal habits and lack of secondary school education. But in *New Grub Street,* just as what is elsewhere merely bookishness becomes transfused into a passionate concern for the state of literature, so his other minor feelings have turned into positive values, and he produced the one important novel in his long list. It occurs less than half-way down, so its unique success is not a matter of maturity or technical development.

The difference between its technical efficiency and the incompetence of the rest is startling too. It might have been written by a Frenchman rather than an Englishman of those days, and Gissing's interest in and admiration for the nineteenth-century Russian and French novelists is significant. He was never able to make use of them as consistently as did Henry James or Conrad, but he was conscious that the English novel tradition

he had inherited would not do and he was groping for help where it seemed to offer. (He later met Meredith and must have studied *The Egoist* with a certain degree of profit. Literary historians ought to inspect **Our Friend the Charlatan** . . . which obviously was conceived and treated in the spirit of *The Egoist* though without ceasing to be Gissing's). Gissing is an example of how disastrous it may be for a writer whose talent is not of the first order to be born into a bad tradition. A score and more of novels painfully sweated out of his system, the exceptional system of an exceptionally intelligent and well-educated and devoted writer, and only one that amounted to something. The absence of what now enables anyone in Bloomsbury to write a readable novel made Gissing's efforts mostly futile. Mr. Swinnerton justly talks of "the wreckage of the Victorian tradition by which it [Gissing's best work] is now encumbered." But in *New Grub Street* Gissing not only solved, if only temporarily, his own problems, he helped all later writers to solve theirs, and the recognition this novel at one time received from literary men is significant. It is probably an ancestor of the novel of our time. (pp. 73-9)

> Q. D. Leavis, "Gissing and the English Novel," in Scrutiny, *Vol. VII, No. 1, June, 1938, pp. 73-81.*

GEORGE ORWELL   (essay date 1948)

[*An English novelist and essayist, Orwell is significant for his unwavering commitment, both as a man and an artist, to personal freedom and social justice. His unpretentious self-examination and his ability to perceive the social effects of political theories inspired Irving Howe to call him "the greatest moral force in English letters during the last several decades." Throughout his career Orwell attacked exploitation of the weak by the powerful, whether in a modern democracy or a totalitarian state. He was particularly attuned to the confining effects of class and social standing in modern life. Foremost among Orwell's work is his novel* Nineteen Eighty-Four *(1949), one of the most influential books of the century. An attack on totalitarianism, it warns that absolute power in the hands of any government can deprive a people of all basic freedoms. Orwell's prose style, especially that of his essays, has become a model for its precision, clarity, and vividness. Many of his essays, which combine observation and reminiscence with literary and social criticism, are considered modern masterpieces. In the following excerpt, written in 1948 but not published until 1960, Orwell considers some socio-political implications of Gissing's novels.*]

In the shadow of the atomic bomb it is not easy to talk confidently about progress. However, if it can be assumed that we are *not* going to be blown to pieces in about ten years' time, there are many reasons, and George Gissing's novels are among them, for thinking that the present age is a good deal better than the last one. If Gissing were still alive he would be younger than Bernard Shaw, and yet already the London of which he wrote seems almost as distant as that of Dickens. It is the fog-bound, gas-lit London of the 'eighties, a city of drunken puritans, where clothes, architecture and furniture had reached their rock-bottom of ugliness, and where it was almost normal for a working-class family of ten persons to inhabit a single room. On the whole Gissing does not write of the worst depths of poverty, but one can hardly read his descriptions of lower-middle-class life, so obviously truthful in their dreariness, without feeling that we have improved perceptibly on that black-coated, money-ruled world of only sixty years ago.

Everything of Gissing's—except perhaps one or two books written towards the end of his life—contains memorable passages, and anyone who is making his acquaintance for the first time might do worse than start with *In the Year of the Jubilee.* It was rather a pity, however, to use up paper in reprinting two of his minor works [*In The Year of the Jubilee* and *The Whirlpool*] when the books by which he ought to be remembered are and have been for years completely unprocurable. *The Odd Women,* for instance, is about as thoroughly out of print as a book can be. I possess a copy myself, in one of those nasty little red-covered cheap editions that flourished before the 1914 war, but that is the only copy I have ever seen or heard of. *New Grub Street,* Gissing's masterpiece, I have never succeeded in buying. When I have read it, it has been in soup-stained copies borrowed from public lending libraries: so also with *Demos, The Nether World* and one or two others. So far as I know only *The Private Papers of Henry Ryecroft,* the book on Dickens, and *A Life's Morning,* have been in print at all recently. However, the two now reprinted are well worth reading, especially *In the Year of the Jubilee,* which is the more sordid and therefore the more characteristic.

In his introduction Mr William Plomer remarks that "generally speaking, Gissing's novels are about money and women," and Miss Myfanwy Evans says something very similar in introducing *The Whirlpool.* One might, I think, widen the definition and say that Gissing's novels are a protest against the form of self-torture that goes by the name of respectability. Gissing was a bookish, perhaps over-civilised man, in love with classical antiquity, who found himself trapped in a cold, smoky, Protestant country where it was impossible to be comfortable without a thick padding of money between yourself and the outer world. Behind his rage and querulousness there lay a perception that the horrors of life in late-Victorian England were largely unnecessary. The grime, the stupidity, the ugliness, the sex-starvation, the furtive debauchery, the vulgarity, the bad manners, the censoriousness—these things were unnecessary, since the puritanism of which they were a relic no longer upheld the structure of society. People who might, without becoming less efficient, have been reasonably happy chose instead to be miserable, inventing senseless taboos with which to terrify themselves. Money was a nuisance not merely because without it you starved; what was more important was that unless you had quite a lot of it—£300 a year, say—society would not allow you to live gracefully or even peacefully. Women were a nuisance because even more than men they were the believers in taboos, still enslaved to respectability even when they had offended against it. Money and women were therefore the two instruments through which society avenged itself on the courageous and the intelligent. Gissing would have liked a little more money for himself and some others, but he was not much interested in what we should now call social justice. He did not admire the working class as such, and he did not believe in democracy. He wanted to speak not for the multitude, but for the exceptional man, the sensitive man, isolated among barbarians.

In *The Odd Women* there is not a single major character whose life is not ruined either by having too little money, or by getting it too late in life, or by the pressure of social conventions which are obviously absurd but which cannot be questioned. An elderly spinster crowns a useless life by taking to drink; a pretty young girl marries a man old enough to be her father; a struggling schoolmaster puts off marrying his sweetheart until both of them are middle-aged and withered; a good-natured man is nagged to death by his wife; an exceptionally intelligent, spirited man misses his chance to make an adventurous marriage and relapses into futility; in each case the ultimate reason for the disaster lies in obeying the accepted social code, or in not

having enough money to circumvent it. In *A Life's Morning* an honest and gifted man meets with ruin and death because it is impossible to walk about a big town with no hat on. His hat is blown out of the window when he is travelling in the train, and as he has not enough money to buy another, he misappropriates some money belonging to his employer, which sets going a series of disasters. This is an interesting example of the changes in outlook that can suddenly make an all-powerful taboo seem ridiculous. Today, if you had somehow contrived to lose your trousers, you would probably embezzle money rather than walk about in your underpants. In the 'eighties the necessity would have seemed equally strong in the case of a hat. Even thirty or forty years ago, indeed, bare-headed men were booed at in the street. Then, for no very clear reason, hatlessness became respectable, and today the particular tragedy described by Gissing—entirely plausible in its context— would be quite impossible.

The most impressive of Gissing's books is *New Grub Street.* To a professional writer it is also an upsetting and demoralising book, because it deals among other things with that much-dreaded occupational disease, sterility. No doubt the number of writers who suddenly lose the power to write is not large, but it is a calamity that *might* happen to anybody at any moment, like sexual impotence. Gissing, of course, links it up with his habitual themes—money, the pressure of the social code, and the stupidity of women.

Edwin Reardon, a young novelist—he has just deserted a clerkship after having a fluky success with a single novel—marries a charming and apparently intelligent young woman, with a small income of her own. Here, and in one or two other places, Gissing makes what now seems the curious remark that it is difficult for an educated man who is not rich to get married. Reardon brings it off, but his less successful friend, who lives in an attic and supports himself by ill-paid tutoring jobs, has to accept celibacy as a matter of course. If he did succeed in finding himself a wife, we are told, it could only be an uneducated girl from the slums. Women of refinement and sensibility will not face poverty. And here one notices again the deep difference between that day and our own. Doubtless Gissing is right in implying all through his books that intelligent women are very rare animals, and if one wants to marry a woman who is intelligent *and* pretty, then the choice is still further restricted, according to a well-known arithmetical rule. It is like being allowed to choose only among albinos, and left-handed albinos at that. But what comes out in Gissing's treatment of his odious heroine, and of certain others among his women, is that at that date the idea of delicacy, refinement, even intelligence, in the case of a woman, was hardly separable from the idea of superior social status and expensive physical surroundings. The sort of woman whom a writer would want to marry was also the sort of woman who would shrink from living in an attic. When Gissing wrote *New Grub Street* that was probably true, and it could, I think, be justly claimed that it is not true today.

Almost as soon as Reardon is married it becomes apparent that his wife is merely a silly snob, the kind of woman in whom "artistic tastes" are no more than a cover for social competitiveness. In marrying a novelist she has thought to marry someone who will rapidly become famous and shed reflected glory upon herself. Reardon is a studious, retiring, ineffectual man, a typical Gissing hero. He has been caught up in an expensive, pretentious world in which he knows he will never be able to maintain himself, and his nerve fails almost immediately. His wife, of course, has not the faintest understanding of what is meant by literary creation. There is a terrible passage—terrible, at least, to anyone who earns his living by writing—in which she calculates the number of pages that it would be possible to write in a day, and hence the number of novels that her husband may be expected to produce in a year—with the reflection that really it is not a very laborious profession. Meanwhile Reardon has been stricken dumb. Day after day he sits at his desk; nothing happens, nothing comes. Finally, in panic, he manufactures a piece of rubbish; his publisher, because Reardon's previous book had been successful, dubiously accepts it. Thereafter he is unable to produce anything that even looks as if it might be printable. He is finished.

The desolating thing is that if only he could get back to his clerkship and his bachelorhood, he would be all right. The hard-boiled journalist who finally marries Reardon's widow sums him up accurately by saying that he is the kind of man who, if left to himself, would write a fairly good book every two years. But, of course, he is not left to himself. He cannot revert to his old profession, and he cannot simply settle down to live on his wife's money: public opinion, operating through his wife, harries him into impotence and finally into the grave. Most of the other literary characters in the book are not much more fortunate, and the troubles that beset them are still very much the same today. But at least it is unlikely that the book's central disaster would now happen in quite that way or for quite those reasons. The chances are that Reardon's wife would be less of a fool, and that he would have fewer scruples about walking out on her if she made life intolerable for him. A woman of rather similar type turns up in *The Whirlpool* in the person of Alma Frothingham. By contrast there are the three Miss Frenches in *The Year of the Jubilee,* who represent the emerging lower-middle class—a class which, according to Gissing, was getting hold of money and power which it was not fitted to use—and who are quite surprisingly coarse, rowdy, shrewish and unmoral. At first sight Gissing's ''ladylike'' and ''unladylike'' women seem to be different and even opposite kinds of animal, and this seems to invalidate his implied condemnation of the female sex in general. The connecting link between them, however, is that all of them are miserably limited in outlook. Even the clever and spirited ones, like Rhoda in *The Odd Women* (an interesting early specimen of the New Woman), cannot think in terms of generalities, and cannot get away from ready-made standards. In his heart Gissing seems to feel that women are natural inferiors. He wants them to be better educated, but on the other hand he does not want them to have freedom, which they are certain to misuse. On the whole the best women in his books are the self-effacing, homekeeping ones.

There are several of Gissing's books that I have never read, because I have never been able to get hold of them, and these unfortunately include *Born in Exile,* which is said by some people to be his best book. But merely on the strength of *New Grub Street, Demos* and *The Odd Women* I am ready to maintain that England has produced very few better novelists. This perhaps sounds like a rash statement until one stops to consider what is meant by a novel. The word ''novel'' is commonly used to cover almost any kind of story—*The Golden Asse, Anna Karenina, Don Quixote, The Improvisatore, Madame Bovary, King Solomon's Mines* or anything else you like—but it also has a narrower sense in which it means something hardly existing before the nineteenth century and flourishing chiefly in Russia and France. A novel, in this sense, is a story which attempts to describe credible human beings, and—without nec-

essarily using the technique of naturalism—to show them acting on everyday motives and not merely undergoing strings of improbable adventures. A true novel, sticking to this definition, will also contain at least two characters, probably more, who are described from the inside and on the same level of probability—which, in effect, rules out the novels written in the first person. If one accepts this definition, it becomes apparent that the novel is not an art-form in which England has excelled. The writers commonly paraded as ''great English novelists'' have a way of turning out either not to be true novelists, or not to be Englishmen. Gissing was not a writer of picaresque tales, or burlesques, or comedies, or political tracts: he was interested in individual human beings, and the fact that he can deal sympathetically with several different sets of motives, and makes a credible story out of the collision between them, makes him exceptional among English writers.

Certainly there is not much of what is usually called beauty, not much lyricism, in the situations and characters that he chooses to imagine, and still less in the texture of his writings. His prose, indeed, is often disgusting. Here are a couple of samples:

> Not with impunity could her thought accustom itself to stray in regions forbidden, how firm soever her resolve to hold bodily aloof. (*The Whirlpool.*)

> The ineptitude of uneducated English women in all that relates to their attire is a fact that it boots not to enlarge upon. (*In the Year of the Jubilee.*)

However, he does not commit the faults that really matter. It is always clear what he means, he never ''writes for effect,'' he knows how to keep the balance between *récit* and dialogue and how to make dialogue sound probable while not contrasting too sharply with the prose that surrounds it. A much more serious fault than his inelegant manner of writing is the smallness of his range of experience. He is only acquainted with a few strata of society, and, in spite of his vivid understanding of the pressure of circumstance on character, does not seem to have much grasp of political or economic forces. In a mild way his outlook is reactionary, from lack of foresight rather than from ill-will. Having been obliged to live among them, he regarded the working class as savages, and in saying so he was merely being intellectually honest; he did not see that they were capable of becoming civilised if given slightly better opportunities. But, after all, what one demands from a novelist is not prophecy, and part of the charm of Gissing is that he belongs so unmistakably to his own time, although his time treated him badly.

The English writer nearest to Gissing always seems to be his contemporary, or near-contemporary, Mark Rutherford. If one simply tabulates their outstanding qualities, the two men appear to be very different. Mark Rutherford was a less prolific writer than Gissing, he was less definitely a novelist, he wrote much better prose, his books belong less recognisably to any particular time, and he was in outlook a social reformer and, above all, a puritan. Yet there is a sort of haunting resemblance, probably explained by the fact that both men lack that curse of English writers, a ''sense of humour.'' A certain low-spiritedness, and air of loneliness, is common to both of them. There are, of course, funny passages in Gissing's books, but he is not chiefly concerned with getting a laugh—above all, he has no impulse towards burlesque. He treats all his major characters more or less seriously, and with at least an attempt at sympathy. Any novel will inevitably contain minor characters who are mere grotesques or who are observed in a purely hostile spirit, but there is such a thing as impartiality, and Gissing is more capable of it than the great majority of English writers. It is a point in his favour that he had no very strong moral purpose. He had, of course, a deep loathing of the ugliness, emptiness and cruelty of the society he lived in, but he was concerned to describe it rather than to change it. There is usually no one in his books who can be pointed to as the villain, and even when there is a villain he is not punished. In his treatment of sexual matters Gissing is surprisingly frank, considering the time at which he was writing. It is not that he writes pornography or expresses approval of sexual promiscuity, but simply that he is willing to face the facts. The unwritten law of English fiction, the law that the hero as well as the heroine of a novel should be virgin when married, is disregarded in his books, almost for the first time since Fielding.

Like most English writers subsequent to the mid-nineteenth century, Gissing could not imagine any desirable destiny other than being a writer or a gentleman of leisure. The dichotomy between the intellectual and the lowbrow already existed, and a person capable of writing a serious novel could no longer picture himself as fully satisfied with the life of a businessman, or a soldier, or a politician, or what not. Gissing did not, at least consciously, even want to be the kind of writer that he was. His ideal, a rather melancholy one, was to have a moderate private income and live in a small comfortable house in the country, preferably unmarried, where he could wallow in books, especially the Greek and Latin classics. He might perhaps have realised this ideal if he had not managed to get himself into prison immediately after winning an Oxford scholarship: as it was he spent his life in what appeared to him to be hack work, and when he had at last reached the point where he could stop writing against the clock, he died almost immediately, aged only about forty-five. His death, described by H. G. Wells in his *Experiment in Autobiography*, was of a piece with his life. The twenty novels, or thereabouts, that he produced between 1880 and 1900 were, so to speak, sweated out of him during his struggle towards a leisure which he never enjoyed and which he might not have used to good advantage if he had had it: for it is difficult to believe that his temperament really fitted him for a life of scholarly research. Perhaps the natural pull of his gifts would in any case have drawn him towards novel writing sooner or later. If not, we must be thankful for the piece of youthful folly which turned him aside from a comfortable middle-class career and forced him to become the chronicler of vulgarity, squalor and failure. (pp. 428-36)

> *George Orwell, ''George Gissing,'' in his* The Collected Essays, Journalism and Letters of George Orwell: In Front of Your Nose: 1945-1950, Vol. IV, *edited by Sonia Orwell and Ian Angus, Harcourt Brace Jovanovich, 1968, pp. 428-36.*

C. J. FRANCIS   (essay date 1962)

[*In the following excerpt from an essay originally published in the* Literary Half-Yearly *in 1962, Francis discusses characterization in Gissing's novels.*]

Discussion of Gissing's characterization is complicated by his frequent, though not total, lack of objectivity: his habit of including sympathetic semi-autobiographical characters, of idealising beautiful women and sensitive scholars, and conversely of expressing loathing of the ugly, vulgar and ignorant. Admittedly, no author, however objective his intention, is likely to see in character other than what he is predisposed to see; the objection to Gissing's subjective attitude is not that it involves a distortion of psychological truth, for that is merely relative, but rather that it leads to inconsistency in the study of motivation. In the same book, some characters may be supplied with the best motives, offered excuses for their conduct; others, less favoured, are presented in worse lights. The author's bias intrudes itself.

Nevertheless, if one attempts to penetrate below this visible bias and ask what Gissing thought constituted character, it appears that he held in common with other Realists a semiscientific view of psychology, which can be conveniently described under the three headings of heredity, environment and temperament.

He shared in the growing interest of the late nineteenth century novel in the complexity of man's consciousness, for its own sake, not only because it led to actions. Of one of his characters, Woodstock in *The Unclassed,* he says,

> I assure you the man is very lifelike; the only thing is that I have ventured to draw him more *faithfully* than any other English novelist would. Human nature is compact of strangely conflicting elements, and I have met men extremely brutal in one way who yet were capable of a good deal of genial feeling in other directions.

He was perfectly aware that character was not so simple a matter as the traditional classical or romantic novelist, and their Victorian descendants, might believe. In such novels, characters were neatly defined, and easily recognised as symbols. Their motives were directly related to their actions and consequently to schemes of virtue and vice, or social morality. But Stendhal in particular and other Realists made clear the new trend, the realisation that the majority of people were complex and did not act from a simple set of rules derived from their character. They realised that people might do the most unexpected and contradictory things; that they were likely to be influenced by their circumstances and surroundings; that they think about their own emotions, consciously attempting to analyse them—but not necessarily acting logically from their conclusions. Even as they came to understand that people were not neatly divided into good and bad, so they realised that they were not even divided into normal and abnormal; moreover, that people's thoughts were not exactly represented by their behaviour.

The psychological theory adduced in explanation was essentially deterministic, as the science and philosophy of the time would lead one to expect. They felt that there was no free will, and actions were wholly determined by motives; consequently, they thought, could all the motives be known, then the action could be accurately forecast. The basic idea was elevated into a thesis by Zola, who placed special emphasis on theories concerning heredity. This last concept, not in itself new (though previously men had thought more of inheritance of physical features than of character), enabled writers to think of men in terms of contemporary evolutionary theory, to see him as one of a species, related to his ancestors, his relatives and the rest of the human race in more than arbitrary ways. Due attention being given to its complications, i.e., that it was no simple rule, that a man was not the sum of the qualities of his parents but a selection of and also of more remote ancestors, it offered an explanation of things otherwise inexplicable: why men should be basically different from one another; why some should be given good characters and some bad, or indeed why they should be born with characters at all.

There is no evidence that Gissing made any close study of heredity, other than a brief mention of "Ribot's *Hérédité Psycologique*" as the reading matter of a "progressive" woman which appears to have no special significance. [In *The Private Life of Henry Maitland*] Morley Roberts says that he made no study of technical psychology at all which seems probable. Nevertheless, as May Yates points out [in *George Gissing, an Appreciation*], he was sufficiently concerned with it to take care over making his characters consistent with their parentage, when it is mentioned. She instances five characters. Thyrza, the girl of low social class who is yet refined, is provided by the author with a mother of some refinement as an explanation. (I would add that Arthur Golding, the artistic slum child in *Workers in the Dawn,* in similar fashion is made the son of a gentleman.)

Clara Hewett, in *The Nether World,* is as impatient of parental authority and poverty as her father is rebellious against social conditions. Godwin Peak's father, like his son, is of low birth but with strong impulses toward culture; he has a violent personal pride and perversity that recurs in his son's reasons for leaving the University and his awkwardness in accepting help (*Born in Exile*). Reardon's father betrayed the same lack of pertinacity as his son (*New Grub Street*).

Richard Dagworthy of *A Life's Morning* is an especially good example. He

> represented an intermediate stage of development between the hard-headed operative who conquers wealth, and his descendant who shall know what use to make of it.

His father had been a cunning, industrious and boorish business man; Richard "had doubtless advanced the character of the stock, and possessed many tastes of which the old man had no notion." The tragedy of his existence is the clash between ambitions towards gentility and refinement, aroused in him by the circumstance of inheriting wealth and consequently being brought up to what was materially at least the life of a gentleman; and the ruthlessness, independence and miserliness inherited from his father. Foreign travel was spoiled for him, for instance, because although he had an active curiosity he could not adapt himself to the unfamiliar conditions, presumably because he had not the necessary flexibility of mind; and also because he could not reconcile himself to the expense; "pursuit of money was in him an hereditary instinct."

The result of this clash is that Dagworthy, whose ambition is to marry a woman of refinement, because he feels that this will improve his own way of life, is driven to most ungentlemanly methods to attain his end.

> A mere uneducated Englishman, hitherto balancing always between the calls from above and from below . . . he could make no distinction between the objects which with vehemence he desired and the spiritual advantage which he felt the attainment would bring to him; and for the simple reason that in this case no such distinction existed. Even as the childhood of civilisation knows virtue only in the form of a concrete deity, so to Dagworthy the higher life of which he was capable took shape as a mortal woman.

The relation in Gissing's mind of hereditary character and the process of human evolution is clear.

Besides these examples given by Yates there are many more. In *The Nether World,* for instance, Jane Snowdon has the gentle nature of her grandfather, though her father is selfish. Sidney Kirkwood's father was, like his son, "an intelligent, warm-hearted man." Clem Peckover's cruelty and cunning is inherited from her mother.

> Who knows [asks Gissing] but this lust of hers for sanguinary domination was the natural enough issue of the brutalising serfdom of her predecessors in the family line of the Peckovers?

It is clear, in fact, that, although Gissing laid no special emphasis on the heredity theory, it lay at the back of his thinking about character. Nor was its importance limited to these studies of descent; it contributed to a special type of consistency in character drawing, typical of Gissing. Not for him are striking changes in character, radical conversions to good or evil such as may be fond in romantic novelists of the more facile kind. A slow development and alteration of attitudes can be seen in some characters, but it indicates no basic change; instead it is evidence of wisdom, of the growth in that character of wider and more balanced views of life. This is exactly according to the views of Schopenhauer, whose thinking matched that of the Realists in so many ways; he too believed that a man was born with a fixed inherited character, and that the only development of character was growth of knowledge. In Gissing, such changes are usually changes from bitterness and passion to calm and resignation—so, Gilbert Grail, for instance, who abandons his aspirations as impossible to realise (*Thyrza*). There is one striking change of character, that of Miriam Baske in *The Emancipated,* who from a religious bigot becomes a woman of calm and balanced mind; but this is the result of the growth of knowledge and experience, and the beginning of a study of art, developing potential qualities hitherto cramped by the narrow life of a religious community. The characteristics that were previously developed—sobriety and strength of will—undergo no alteration. Examples of consistency are plentiful. The dissipated Reuben Elgar, for instance, intends to reform himself and make use of his experience:

> All the disorder through which I have gone was a struggle towards self-knowledge and understanding of my time.

—but, perception or no, his basic weakness of will repeatedly prevents him from fulfilling this promise, and he falls again to dissipation.

Widdowson, in *The Odd Women,* has a possessive and jealous character that ruins his relations with his wife. Although he has himself brought about the disaster, he cannot reconcile himself even to believing that the child she bears him is his own, despite his wife's statement on her deathbed. His jealousy is still uncontrollable even when the cause is removed.

Godwin Peak is the opposite case to Elgar; he allows himself to be drawn into a course of deception, but when it is discovered, the strong and independent pride that he inherited from his father recurs; the exposure is almost a relief for him, and he bears it with such dignity as to seem a much better man than he was before.

Pride is the special characteristic also of Rhoda Nunn in *The Odd Women*. It lies behind her efforts towards individual independence of women. Although she does not believe in the forms of marriage, her pride of self in addition to her instinctive upbringing makes her insist that her suitor offer her legal marriage. On reconsideration of her position she decides to uphold the principle she has preached—this also from pride, and causing another clash with her suitor, who has now decided that legal marriage is preferable.

These are examples of situations that frequently occur in Gissing's stories. There is another example that is very convincing: it is the case of the elder Mrs. Mutimer in *Demos*, whose character is one of independence and self-sufficiency. When she is suddenly raised to affluence, she is distressed by the possession of a servant and greatly prefers to continue to do her own work and maintain her own home, to the extent that she does over again the work the servant has done.

This example introduces us to the second division of Realistic psychological theory, the influence of environment; and in doing so presents a problem that must be considered shortly. The interest in environment arises from the deterministic theory that actions follow necessarily on motives; a theory expressed in set terms by Waymark in *The Unclassed*, and more emotionally by Reuben Elgar, who wishes to decline responsibility for his actions:

> I tell you I am conscious of no sins. Of follies, of ignorances, of miseries—as many as you please. And to what account should they all go? Was I so admirably guided in childhood and boyhood that my subsequent life is not to be explained?

Of course determinism is divorced from ordinary morality, as it rejects free will; but we must not be led by Elgar's excusing the satisfaction of impulses, or by Zola and the Naturalistes' emphasis on *"le mécanisme humain,"* into thinking that this doctrine of necessity holds that men act only according to the influences of the moment. Clearly, under "motives" must be included the things of the mind, moral tendencies, prejudices, as well as purely material motives. The psychology of the Realists, I have pointed out, was a complication, not a simplification of character study. Consequently, one cannot illustrate the doctrine of necessity in itself from Gissing's analysis of motives, since those motives will be the same whether such things as moral instincts are regarded as being spiritually imparted or acquired through upbringing. Only, Gissing (while retaining a moral point of reference) tends not to condemn or approve, on the whole, which indicates a feeling that men are not really responsible for their actions.

However, if free choice is denied, it becomes obvious that not only must a preponderance of, for instance, reprehensible motives overcome a commendable motive in one instance, but also that a frequent repetition of the same situation will lead to the commendable motive losing power and significance in the mind of the man concerned. This brings us to the theory of the influence of environment: the circumstances in which a man lives will gradually influence his mental make-up, by constantly presenting to him motives in accord with the necessities of his life. Thus arises the antithesis between the romantic novelist, who believes, for instance, that virtue will always triumph over adversity, and the realist who believes that constant adversity will eventually diminish virtue.

The influence of circumstances is, of course, on the character's outlook; to use Schopenhauer's terms, on the knowing faculty: they do not affect his basic character, which has to do with the will. The examples of consistency of character which I have given are all variations of strength of will and the sense of self-importance.

The influence of environment is the particular aspect of the doctrine of necessity that the Realists set themselves to illustrate. They emphasize the effects of upbringing, as in the case of Reuben Elgar, and his sister Miriam Baske. Moral and religious adherence, it is implied, are not matters of character but only of knowledge, being acquired. So, Miriam becomes a strict religious observer, aided by her character trait of strength of will; in a different environment she loses this outlook, but retains the will. Reuben, in addition to his trait of weak-willed indolence, has strong passions, and the effect of this repressive upbringing is to make him rebel. There is of course no simplification here; the same motives do not produce the same effects, because the characters are different.

More noticeable a subject than the effect of education in Gissing, as in most Realists, is the special effect of poverty (though he showed himself always interested in educational problems). The effects of poverty are his major theme; there is hardly need to demonstrate his studies of ignorance and degradation amongst the lower classes. But it is worth while to observe the case of educated people.

His general theme was the depressing and disabling effect of poverty: of Reardon, he says.

> He was the kind of man who cannot struggle against adverse conditions, but whom prosperity warms to the exercise of his powers.

This situation in various forms arises again and again. Poverty not only cramps the abilities and distracts from concentration, but it develops in a man his less admirable qualities—avarice, cunning, ruthlessness—even though he may have been originally a man of integrity and altruism. This happens to most of the characters in *New Grub Street*. Amy Reardon is unwilling to face poverty; it constricts her love for her husband, and brings her to leave him to his own devices rather than to support him. It makes her think first of money, and only afterwards of artistic integrity and reputation. Her tendency to selfishness and to ungenerous instincts is developed. Reardon too suffers in becoming surly and querulous.

> A little money, and he could have rested secure in her love, for then he would have been able to keep ever before her the best qualities of his heart and brain. Upon him, too, penury had its debasing effect; as he now presentd himself he was not a man to be admired or loved.

Alfred Yule's bitterness and vindictiveness is the result of the defeats he has received in the struggle for existence:

> I am all but certain that, it he became rich, he would be a very much kinder man, a better man in every way. It is poverty that has made him worse than he naturally is; it has that effect on almost everybody. Money does harm, too, sometimes. . . .

Cunning and ruthlessness are more natural to the "villain" of the book, Milvain—but even in him they are emphasized by poverty, as he claims:

Selfishness—that's one of my faults. . . . If I were rich, I should be a generous and good man; I know I should. So would many another poor fellow whose worst features come out under hardship.

To all these people the same thing is happening: the constant presentation among their motives of the need to get money, at any cost, gradually blunts and renders impotent the motives of generosity, fairness, integrity and the like. It is worth noting that the aspirations of many characters become concentrated on some material object. Peak, like Dagworthy, lets his ambitions turn to acquiring a wife of refinement; Yule lowers his aims from literary success to the editorship of a magazine whence he can avenge himself on his critics.

"Money does harm, too, sometimes. . . ." Though most concerned with poverty, Gissing does not omit to give an example of damage done by wealth. Mutimer, the local leader and socialist speaker in *Demos,* has all the appearance of an honest and sincere man; and, by virtue of these qualities, bids fair to achieve the power and eminence he is led to desire by his character trait of ambition. When he comes into money, the character trait remains, but his behaviour alters in obedience to the change of motives. As he becomes aware of the possibilities that lie before him, he ceases to wish to be a representative of the people and to share their conditions. He retains enough of his social enthusiasm to wish to be a benefactor, and institutes an ideal manufacturing company; but in doing so he shows a growing tendency towards the autocratic methods of the employer. He sets out to acquire a gentlewomen for a wife, and acts unfeelingly towards his former friends.

When a will is discovered that takes away hs money, he shows actual dishonesty in attempting to conceal it. Although it is unlikely that he has analysed his own motives, he is betraying that the quest for power is his ruling passion; when success depended on integrity, he found it easy to be honest; now that it depends on the possession of wealth, he is dishonest. As soon as he has lost the money, he takes up again his former character of the honest man. This is a clear case of actions responding directly to motives, given the basic urge to power.

The problem raised by the case of Mrs. Mutimer, his mother, is this: if actions are decided by environment, why does not Mrs. Mutimer adapt herself to the conditions of wealth as her son does? We must begin by admitting that Gissing's irrational prejudice against the lower classes complicates his application of the theory of environment. He is ready enough to show them degraded by poverty; ready to show that such a man as Mutimer would be worse when in possession of wealth; but not to admit that a working-class person has possibilities of improvement. Lady Ogram in *Our Friend the Charlatan* is "an exception to the rule that low-born English girls cannot rise above their native condition." This prejudice has some part in the presentation of Mrs. Mutimer. Mutimer's brother and sister are depraved by wealth, as he is; Mrs. Mutimer is included as another aspect of the thesis that the lower classes cannot rise in the world. Nevertheless, she has the ring of truth; and I think she can reasonably be explained. Her children, whose strength of will, even in Richard, is not strongly developed in the direction of maintenance of principles, react rapidly to the change of circumstance. Mrs. Mutimer's integrity is strong, and her habits of life deeply ingrained with age, so that, within the period of the story during which she is possessed of wealth, she shows no change. It is not that the new circumstances have no effect upon her; they have the effect of making her cling more strongly

to her principles. Had Gissing a different purpose in mind, might one reasonably suppose he would have shown us Mrs. Mutimer slowly adapting to the new conditions. His study is usually of the gradual effect of environment; for example, Miriam Baske, equally strong-willed but much younger, does not break away from her narrow intellectual habits until she has for some time been exposed to a freer atmosphere.

Miriam Baske represents the good effects of an improved environment, and reminds us that Gissing does not deal entirely with adverse circumstances. Of course, his essential pessimism predisposed him to descriptions of misery; his own experience gave him special sympathy with the depressed intellectual, so common a figure in realistic novels of the age, and especially amongst Russian realists of the school of Gogol. The feeling of his books is the tortured suffering of Dostoievsky, whom he admired; his characters also were the oppressed and despairing, the "insulted and injured," those who suffered not only material but also social and spiritual harm from their circumstances. Yet he did not intend to convey that the effect of circumstances on character was invariably adverse. He gives full credit to the significance of inborn character (as when the same education has opposite results on Reuben Elgar and Miriam Baske). He does not over-simplify the theory of environmental influences, but he makes full allowance for it in his psychology.

Nor is his handling of the theory so mechanical as this discussion might suggest; he did not write an "experimental novel," but sees his characters as inseparable parts of their environments. The wish expressed by one of Gissing's readers, that he give his characters more money, emphasizes this point. We too sometimes wish that Gissing was a little less oppressively pessimistic; but we realise that not only does the struggle against circumstance form the subject and theme of most of his books, so that without it they would not exist, but also that the characters as they are presented would not exist if they were richer. They would be different men. They might be recognisably similar, but they would have changed in most respects. Gissing does create a few educated protagonists—Mallard (*The Emancipated*), Rolfe (*The Whirlpool*), Langley (*Sleeping Fires*)—who are not poverty-stricken; apart from their individual qualities, they are in general different men from the sufferers. In their personal relationships they are more capable, more balanced; all their faculties and interests are more harmoniously and soundly developed. (pp. 79-89)

C. J. Francis, "Gissing's Characterization: Heredity and Environment," in George Gissing: Critical Essays, edited by Jean-Pierre Michaux, Barnes & Noble, 1981, pp. 79-90.

P. J. KEATING   (essay date 1968)

[*In the following excerpt, Keating discusses* New Grub Street.]

New Grub Street was first published in 1891. It was Gissing's ninth of twenty-two novels, and is easily his most important and enduring work. It holds, however, an unenviable position in the history of the English novel. For although some critics, most notably Q. D. Leavis [see excerpt dated 1938] and Irving Howe, have had no hesitation in proclaiming it a work of art, its continuing interest for the twentieth-century reader lies in Gissing's astute and probing analysis of the "business of literature." First and foremost it is a sociological document; a sociological document of genius written in the form of a novel. Awareness of this point has led Irving Howe to conclude that:

"The book is not at all difficult, it is transparent, and to subject it to a 'close reading' in the current academic fashion would be tiresome. What *New Grub Street* asks from the reader is not some feat of analysis, but a considered fullness of response, a readiness to assent to, even if not agree with, its vision of defeat." It is true that an examination of *New Grub Street* for recurrent images and symbolic patterns would not enhance the reader's understanding in the same way as it would with a novel by, say, Dickens, Hardy or Eliot; and it is also true that Gissing's vision is one of defeat. But the "considered fullness of response" which is demanded from the reader can only be achieved by a complete awareness of the complexity of the issues being analysed, together with an appreciation of the way in which the author presents his case. Neither the argument nor the presentation of the argument is transparent.

Virginia Woolf pointed out that "Gissing is one of the extremely rare novelists who believes in the power of mind, who makes his people think," and in *New Grub Street* this quality is of particular importance. Not merely does each character represent certain cultural, social or economic forces, but he is continually made to argue the rights and wrongs of his position. It is as a great debate that *New Grub Street* should be viewed; a debate in which certain key words such as "success," "failure," "popular," "genius," "conscientious," "intellectual," and most of all "practical," recur, developing various shades of irony and ambiguous levels of meaning in such a way that virtually no statement in the book can be taken at face value. Its true meaning will depend on who is speaking, who is being addressed and what stage the debate has reached at that particular moment. The principal speakers fall into three distinct groups; the tradesmen (Milvain and Whelpdale), the artists (Reardon and Biffen) and the men of letters, represented by Alfred Yule. The theme of the debate is the role of literary culture in society, and the central conflict is clearly stated by Milvain in the first chapter:

> "But just understand the difference between a man like Reardon and a man like me. He is the old type of unpractical artist; I am the literary man of 1882. He won't make concessions, or rather, he can't make them; he can't supply the market. I—well, you may say that at present I do nothing; but that's a great mistake, I am learning my business. Literature nowadays is a trade."

This, however, is not really the definitive statement it sounds. The basic positions have been established; but the moral, social and cultural issues raised by such an attitude, become clear only when Milvain's bland assumptions are challenged. Is the artist necessarily "unpractical," and what exactly is meant by the word? Is Milvain stating facts, as he appears to be, or is he merely expressing opinions? Is it reasonable to take Reardon as the archetypal artist or would Biffen be a better example? When Milvain talks of supplying the market, does he mean he is satisfying a demand or creating one? These are just a few of the many questions posed by Gissing and to understand the conflicting answers that are given, and the moral crisis that gradually emerges, the allegorical significance of the major characters must be fully explored.

In terms of form there is little in *New Grub Street* to excite attention. Gissing adopted completely the traditional, though by this time fast disappearing, structure of the three-volume novel. The careers of Milvain and Reardon are shadowed by those of Whelpdale and Biffen, who in their minor roles serve both to adumbrate the major issues and to expand the application of those issues to society as a whole. The section dealing with the Yule family is employed as a conventional, though thematically relevant, sub-plot; while control of the action lies firmly in the hands of the omniscient author, who has no hesitation in addressing the reader in order to point the moral or underline a note of irony.

Yet in spite of the use of this unwieldy novel form ("a triple-headed monster, sucking the blood of English novelists," as Milvain describes it), *New Grub Street* attains a remarkable degree of unity. This is achieved by a concentration on the careers of a handful of characters, who in their relationships with each other provide a microcosmic view of society. Gissing's method relies heavily on a massive accumulation of detail (intellectual, social, and conversational) which, carefully organised and placed, is used to build up a complex ironic structure. By this means he creates an illusion of having presented to the reader a complete cross-section of the literary life of London. Yet the vicious Fadge, Markland the popular novelist, Jedwood the new type of publisher, the reviewers, the critics, and the society figures who wield such influence, none of the people who dictate the conditions within which the action takes place, ever actually appear in the novel. They exist in a world beyond Reardon's reach; a world to which Milvain goes and returns to report upon. Only in the final chapter do Milvain's influential friends appear, and then when Reardon is dead and Milvain himself is in a position to be both editor and host. The two worlds are completely incompatible. The success of one entails the annihilation of the other.

Where the two worlds do come together is in their role as guardians of the nation's taste, and they are united in the British Museum Reading-room, which is employed throughout the novel as a symbol of the accumulated knowledge of mankind. Milvain describes Alfred and Marian Yule as "obvious dwellers in the valley of the shadow of books," and his flowery remark anticipates the moment when Marian, gazing up at the Reading-room dome sees herself and the other researchers as "hapless flies caught in a huge web, its nucleus the great circle of the Catalogue." Reardon's response is totally different. He looks back upon his early days in London and remembers the Reading-room as "his true home," and when the drudgery of his three-volume novel is over he relaxes in the Museum, indulging his love of the classics by writing essays on esoteric literary themes. In Chapter VII the Reading-room is seen as a place of lost causes and sterile academic work. Mr. Hinks presents Marian with a copy of his "Essay on the Historical Drama" for her father; and Mr. Quarmby passes on his private information that Alfred Yule is at last to be offered the editorship he longs for—the gossip is as worthless as the book. The courtship between Marian and Milvain is conducted largely from the British Museum; he hurriedly consulting encyclopaedias and she dreaming of the day when a machine will be invented to take over her thankless task. Finally the Reading-room is the place where all illusions are shattered. Alfred Yule refuses to discuss his coming blindness with his daughter, dismissing her with: "You can read up the subject for yourself at the British Museum." And when Biffen plans to poison himself it is to the Reading-room he goes for the necessary knowledge.

This symbolic use of the British Museum is extremely successful but in the main Gissing did not feel at home with symbolism. Nothing could be more crude, for instance, than the moment in Chapter III when Milvain asks Marian to indulge him in a spot of "childishness" and go to watch the London express rush under a bridge. This experience is meant to symbolize both his driving ambition and the disconcerting sexual attraction Marian possesses for him; but the symbol is local and is not integrated into the novel. It is unnecessary and thus distracting. On the other hand, symbolic images, such as the hanged man or the worn-out horse, grow and develop as the novel progresses, heightening the moral uncertainty of a rapidly changing society. In this instance, as in all others, Gissing's craftsmanship is uneven, and his weaknesses should be acknowledged. His writing is at times ponderous and artificially literary and suffers from all of the faults he notes in Reardon's work and some of those in Alfred Yule's. Further, he often seriously underestimates the intelligence of the reader (a significant fault in the author of a book such as *New Grub Street*), and insists on too heavily underlining the motives and emotions of the characters. His sense of humour is best described in the same terms that Biffen uses to excuse Reardon's feeble riddle: "It'll pass. Distinctly professional though. The general public would fail to see the point."

He was a morbidly autobiographical novelist and this has, perhaps, prevented his best work from receiving the critical attention it deserves. Gissing's greatest admirers have often been so busy sifting the novels for biographical analogies that the work itself has been ignored. This is particularly true of *New Grub Street* and is a tendency which should be resisted. Sometimes, as in the portrait of Reardon, Gissing becomes too personally involved and this is a flaw which needs to be recognised, but, in this novel at least, Gissing usually succeeds in distancing himself from the action, and his own attitudes should be judged only when the total pattern of the work has been considered.

In terms of subject matter *New Grub Street* is virtually unique. Novels about novelists there have been in plenty but they tend either to concentrate on aspects of the novelist's life other than his writing; or they deal intimately with the growth of a single mind or sensibility. If one compares, for example, *David Copperfield* (1850) and *Pendennis* (1850) on the one hand, and *Portrait of the Artist as a Young Man* (1916) on the other, the change in treatment is astounding. Neither David Copperfield nor Arthur Pendennis seem to feel that being a writer is anything to make much of a fuss about. It is a profession which can bring both financial rewards and a place in society. It demands talent and a degree of worldly experience, but not creative agony. Such an attitude is meaningless to Stephen Dedalus. Society is something to escape from, and the very thought that one's work might bring public acclamation is enough to brand one as an inferior artist. The period of Gissing's life (1857-1903) coincides almost exactly with the most important phase of this complex revolution, and historically it is significant that the work nearest in tone to *New Grub Street* is the group of short stories on literary themes written by Henry James in the early 1890s.

The relevance of the title *New Grub Street* is primarily historical. There are several exact comparisons (principally with reference to the work of Reardon and Alfred Yule) but Gissing usually employs the phrase Grub Street in either a vaguely emotional or pejorative sense, or to establish an historical frame of reference. That he was fully aware of the various shades of meaning that surround the phrase is made clear in a letter he wrote to his German friend Eduard Bertz on the 26th April, 1891. He writes: "Grub Street actually existed in London some hundred and fifty years ago. In Pope and his contemporaries

the name has become synonymous for wretched-authordom. In Hogarth's 'Distressed Author' there is 'Grub Street' somewhere inscribed. Poverty and meanness of spirit being naturally associated, the street came to denote an abode, not merely of poor, but of in-insignificant, writers." He goes on to quote Dr. Johnson's famous definition: "Originally the name of a street near Moorfields in London, much inhabited by writers of small histories, dictionaries, and temporary poems; whence any mean production is called *grubstreet*." Later in the same letter Gissing says: "At present the word is used contemptuously. You know that I do not altogether mean that in the title of my book."

On one level Gissing is indicating that late Victorian England has created a Grub Street as pernicious as that which existed in the early eighteenth century. Many of the central issues such as the power of the publishers, the suffering and poverty of the authors, the hack-writing of the journalists, the virtual impossibility for anyone—save a genius—to rise out of Grub Street once he is there, the superabundance of mediocre work being churned out for an audience forever demanding more of the same—all this and more is relevant to both periods. But on another level Gissing is implying that *New* Grub Street is in many ways a logical development of the old. They are not two isolated periods, but both parts of a process of change (what Raymond Williams has called "The Long Revolution") which will lead ultimately to a culturally fragmented society. The chief historical fact Gissing has in mind when he refers back to the early eighteenth century is the rise of a large commercial middle class, together with the corresponding development of newspapers, the novel and the periodical. These are, of course, the very literary forms with which *New Grub Street* is concerned and each is shown to have suffered, in the process of time, fearful corruption. Jasper Milvain is the modern equivalent of Addison or Steele; Alfred Yule is surely Dr. Johnson; and a popular novelist such as Richardson has become Markland. Characters such as Whelpdale, Fadge and Jedwood are the eternal vampires feeding, consciously or unconsciously, on the blood of struggling writers. This last comparison pinpoints more exactly Gissing's personal attitude to Grub Street, for in some ways he is indulging in a spot of myth-making. It is believed by everyone in *New Grub Street* that genius, true, unadulterated genius, will either rise out of the mire and receive its just acclaim or will suffocate and die scornful of all material reward. Given the social conditions it is more natural that the latter will occur, but genius is *sui generis* and it could just as easily follow the former course. Whatever eventually happens, however, the possessor of genius will, at first, be forced to join the writers in Grub Street. He is not a hack himself but he must rise from the ranks of the hacks, or rather, dwell with them by necessity. Milvain expresses the accepted view: "I am speaking of men who wish to win reputation before they are toothless. Of course if your work is strong, and you can afford to wait, the probability is that half a dozen people will at last begin to shout that you have been monstrously neglected, as you have."

A further analogy being made between the two Grub Streets is the use made of literature to advance personal squabbles and vendettas. "To assail an author without increasing the number of his readers is the perfection of journalistic skill," writes Gissing, and everyone, whether tradesman, artist or man of letters, enjoys a good literary slanging match. When Fadge's periodical, *The Study*, publishes two conflicting reviews of the same novel, Alfred Yule is delighted because he hates Fadge, Milvain and Reardon roar with laughter because the error confirms their totally different views of the market, and even Biffen raises a chuckle.

The main issues examined by Gissing have all become commonplaces of twentieth-century critical thought and discussion. The alienation of the artist from society; the development of a new kind of popular press; an increasingly centralised society dominated by London; the new concept of the art of fiction; and the conscious acceptance by everyone involved of the intellectual, commercial and cultural division of English life. In Chapter XXIX Alfred Yule sums up the situation in a suitably pedantic manner:

> "How much better 'a man of letters' than 'a literary man'! And apropos of that, when was the word 'literature' first used in our modern sense to signify a body of writing? In Johnson's day it was pretty much the equivalent of our 'culture.' You remember his saying, 'It is surprising how little literature people have.' His dictionary, I believe, defines the word as 'learning, skill in letters'—nothing else."

It is the forces making for this change that Gissing sets out to analyse and in doing so brilliantly captures a crucial moment in a period of cultural crisis. (pp. 9-16)

> *P. J. Keating, in his* George Gissing: New Grub Street, *Edward Arnold (Publishers) Ltd., 1968, 62 p.*

LLOYD FERNANDO (essay date 1970)

[*Fernando is a Sri Lankan critic. In the following excerpt, he discusses anti-feminism in Gissing's novels.*]

In the present revival of interest in and sympathy for the Victorians there has been no discussion of the undeniably hostile cast of Gissing's novelistic practice in the portrayal of women and women's issues. Because his novels, especially those of the nineties, draw very fully upon the contemporary scene, it has even been assumed that he was umambiguously sympathetic to feminist claims. "On this subject at least," his most recent biographer, Jacob Korg, declares, "Gissing's opinions were clear, consistent, and uncompromising. An enemy of the Victorian myth of the inferiority of women, he believed firmly that women were the intellectual and spiritual equals of men." This essay argues that the opposite view is more tenable; it also examines the ways in which the novelist's art was adversely affected as a consequence. Certainly Gissing wished to see women given a wider general education, and he was concerned about their opportunities for employment. The fate of the large number of women doomed to a single life, as the population ratio of women to men clearly showed, engaged his sympathies. He is also on record as suggesting, more daringly, that "the only way" of effecting lasting improvements in the status of women was "to go through a period of what many people will call sexual anarchy." The letters, regrettably, do not elaborate this last point but his novels—*Denzil Quarrier* . . . , and *In the Year of Jubilee* . . . , notably—make it quite plain that he entertained the proposal only to dismiss it with a degree of shallow flippancy. Gissing is the only important novelist of the period whose approach to emancipation looks rather more like reasoned animosity to the movement. This claim gains considerable weight when examined in relation to his dismay at the growing vulgarity of the society around him. That was the novelist's wider concern, and it is fairest to see the issue in its light.

It is never easy to separate the person from the author in Gissing's novels. The works embody a broad scepticism towards society in general which George Orwell labelled as "close to being reactionary" [see excerpt dated 1948]. Gissing resented long and deeply his exclusion from the privileges of superior social status to which he felt he had a natural right by virtue of his education and intellectual qualities. Individual frustration taken together with his disgust at the dilution of social and moral values on the wider scene found a creative outlet in the impecunious intellectual hero who figures in almost every novel. These young men are the "unclassed," pacing restlessly on the outskirts of a society they have ceased to comprehend. They regard the woman problem from a superior vantage point as emblematic of social decay. Perhaps by association, Gissing's heroines, seeking to free themselves from traditional restraints, reflect some of this wider restlessness as well. Gissing wrote, after all, about a class of miscellaneous people bewildered by their social and cultural displacement in a rapidly expanding society. That is the underlying general aim in all his novels which gives us pause. But his error was to depend on "vulgarism," as he called it, as the principal lens for focusing his concerns in the nineties. As we shall see, it proved to be an inferior prism, lending itself to the idiosyncrasies of his vision rather than correcting it. In the latter phase of his long career as a novelist it effectively aborted any promise of full greatness in his art.

While he genuinely wanted the lot of the poor to be improved, years of enforced intimacy with them had only aggravated his personal repugnance for them. "Without wishing to be harsh to these people," he declared, "you must recognize how utterly impossible close relations with them become. . . . I fear they put me down for a prig, an upstart, an abominable aristocrat, but *que voulez-vous?*" The provision of fresh and more widely spread opportunities for education and employment meant little, if any, difference to the concept of a graded community. All classes will be elevated, but between higher and lower the distinction will remain." This exceptional caution about fundamentals of social improvements stemmed from a fear of dilution in the quality of life and society, an apprehension which Gissing found increasingly confirmed. Education brought only "extending and deepening Vulgarity," he told Bertz. Convinced that "the gulf between the really refined and the masses" had widened and would widen still more, he fell back on his rather wishful concept of an intellectual aristocracy. He called it "an Aristocracy of mind and manners" which would not demean itself by contact with a society of deteriorating values.

He regarded issues relating to the advancement of women in a similar light. He acknowledged feelingly—in a way that reminds us that he spoke from bitter personal experience—the effects upon woman of her depressed status. Comparing the average woman to "the average male idiot" he believed her condition could be redressed, in part at least, by education, not primarily to enable her to compete with men on equal terms, but for the greater well-being of society. Again, the distinctions between higher and lower would remain. Throughout his life he did not deviate much from the opinion he formed in 1880 that

> A girl's education should be of a very general and liberal character, adapted rather to expand the intelligence as a whole than to impart very thorough knowledge on any subject. General reading is what I should advise a girl to un-

dertake; and that reading should certainly *not* lie in the direction of the Higher Mathematics or Political Economy.

The letters to his sisters are full of fatherly advice, consistent with these principles, about the reading and other pursuits they should be undertaking to improve their minds. He believed that the proper adoption of his counsels—he often detailed approaches to particular authors somewhat like a schoolmaster— would in truth emancipate their minds. In his letters to them he is strangely silent, however, on other topics relating to feminine emancipation, notably women's relations with men. Arthur C. Young rightly points out that Gissing's prescriptions in fact aimed at producing the kind of refined woman he always had as an ideal, too far above him socially to be approached with love. Neither sister married.

References to reading, art and learning serve as significant pointers to the moral quality of the women characters in his fiction. The Peachey household (*In the Year of Jubilee*) is especially detestable for its evidence of half-education in the form of "cheap miscellanies, penny novelettes and the like" which lie scattered about. Gissing never once conceded, expressly or tacitly, that women are the full moral and intellectual equals of men. His heroes, with their author's approval, patronise their women, assuming a natural superiority in all important matters. Waymark, Quarrier, Barfoot, Tarrant, Hilliard, and Rolfe (in *The Unclassed, Denzil Quarrier, The Odd Women, In the Year of Jubilee, Eve's Ransom,* and *The Whirlpool,* respectively) all smugly accept the premise that, on the whole, women fall short of men in intellectual and, therefore, moral quality. Intellectual power and breadth of knowledge were the sole indicators of superior moral worth. These were male virtues rather than female. Only at the end of a life finally mellowed by his association with Gabrielle Fleury, did Gissing recognise the fallacy of equating intellectual capacity exclusively with moral fibre. "Foolishly arrogant as I was," he declared,

> I used to judge the worth of a person by his intellectual power and attainment. I could see no good where there was no logic, no charm where there was no learning. Now I think that one has to distinguish between two forms of intelligence, that of the brain, and that of the heart, and I have come to regard the second as by far the more important. I guard myself against saying that intelligence does not matter. . . . But assuredly the best people I have known were saved from folly not by the intellect but by the heart.

But by then—1903—his score or more of novels had already been written.

The real mark of Gissing's resistance to emancipation rests in the way he linked the discordant social reality around him with the feminist movement, and in the way he implied in his novels that emancipationist ideas gave direct rise to the social vulgarity he detested. His novels of the nineties—*Denzil Quarrier* . . . , *The Odd Women* . . . , and *In the Year of Jubilee* . . . , for example—reveal his gradually increasing skill, and the limits to which he succeeded, in embodying his views in valid artistic ways. *The Odd Women* and *In the Year of Jubilee,* projected simultaneously, resemble each other closely. Each was to be "a study in vulgarism—that all but triumphant force of our time." He wanted, as he acknowledged in a letter to Bertz,

"to deal with the great question of 'throwing pearls [i.e. education] before swine'," adding, pointedly, ". . . women will be the chief characters." His presentation of the Madden sisters in *The Odd Women* is not completely the unambiguous expression of his sympathy for single women which it may be taken to be; they were also to symbolise the growing vulgarity of society. In the event Gissing failed to achieve this second aim, but the attempt to associate vulgarity with the supposed intrinsic feebleness of female nature has undeniably left the spinsters, especially Alice and Virginia, more pitiably repellent than they need have been.

As for the career-feminists whom he knew, he could not resist distinguishing them from something called, at the time, "the womanly woman." In his novels they affect a mannishness of bearing, their countenances betray incipient masculinity. They are either guilty by innuendo like Mrs. Wade who is partly blamed for Lilian's death in *Denzil Quarrier;* or under the tutelage of a typical Gissing hero they rather unconvincingly acknowledge the folly of their ways, like Rhoda Nunn in *The Odd Women,* and Nancy Lord in *In the Year of Jubilee.* Particularly in the case of Rhoda Nunn's contest with Barfoot over their proposed marriage-experiment, an excellent opportunity was lost of illuminating love as a compulsive duel of the sexes, as Strindberg had done in his play, *The Father,* only six years previously. But Gissing was too close to the stuff of life he dealt with. Confronted by domestic and moral turmoil, he recoiled with loathing from the tawdriness of the "emancipated" women whom he saw as the cause of it. "Wherever you look nowadays there's a sham and rottenness; but the most worthless creature living is one of these trashy, flashy girls," old Mr. Lord says,

> "the kind of girl you see everywhere, high and low,—calling themselves 'ladies,'—thinking themselves too good for any honest, womanly work. Town and country it's all the same. They're educated; oh yes, they're educated. What sort of wives do they make, with their education? What sort of mothers are they? Before long there'll be no such thing as a home. They don't know what the word means."
> (*In the Year of Jubilee,* Pt. I Ch. V)

These novels are curious hybrids reproducing, virtually unchanged, contemporary views on feminist issues, but sustained on a literary level by Gissing's skill, discussed below, in older techniques of narrative and characterisation.

The marriage histories portrayed have a kind of seedy authenticity. Few could know better than Gissing the bitterness that could arise among maladjusted couples. One of his earliest successes with this theme was in *The Unclassed* . . . where he produced a chilling though abbreviated picture of a sensitive man's mortification in a bond which nullified every normal human feeling. Here Gissing was also at the heart of perhaps the most intractable moral problem of the age: the seeming unsuitability of the traditional conception of marriage in an era where ideals and duties were changing rapidly. He presented the impasse in marriage again in *The Odd Women* in the story of Widdowson and his wife Monica, the third of the Madden sisters; while in *In the Year of Jubilee* he showed how wide the gulf between husband and wife could be in his portrayal of the half-demented Ada Peachey and her husband Arthur. These marriages, forming important sub-plots, serve as the unamenable reality against which emancipationist theories were tested. No progressive theory could have much value which failed to alleviate this seemingly repetitive and harassing phenomenon. In his novels, Gissing brought these failed marriages into progressively closer contact with his feminist themes. His manner of doing it, however, reveals the limitations of his grasp of the issue of marital incompatibility. Largely influenced no doubt by his own harrowing experiences, he roundly blames the woman in each case for prejudicing the stability of the relationship. The men would be able to do the world's work, or pursue the ideal of secluded and cultured living, he seems to say, if only the women did not seek an exaggerated degree of independence in their lives. His partiality for the male point of view was offset, however, by the authenticity of his depressing histories, a quality which appreciably increased the literary merit of the novels. When in *The Whirlpool* . . . Gissing at least dealt centrally and at three-volume length with a foundering marriage-relationship, he had therefore devoted much thought to the problem and had the benefit of repeated preparation, as it were, for its literary presentation. *The Whirlpool* is Gissing's most skilful novel in every respect, but it has rarely been discussed. It embodies his mature vision with a technical assurance that must rank it very high among novels of the final decade of the nineteenth century. (pp. 43-7)

Gissing is the only novelist of stature to embody in his fiction the attitudes of reasoned opponents to female emancipation at the time when the movement had finally made its impact on

Drawing by Sir William Rothenstein.

the day to day living of ordinary young women. He is much more than the social historian William Plomer makes him out to be: his bitterness over the social changes he witnessed and the integrity of his attempts to understand them lend to even his limitations a harsh vividness which still communicates itself to us to-day. At the same time he is rather less than a major novelist because his focus is too close to his subject matter to permit a proportioned selection of detail or careful discrimination of essentials from ephemera. Strictly speaking his novels are problem-novels which, though far superior to the common run of examples in this sub-genre, still did not achieve full artistic stature in the way the problem-play did in the hands of Ibsen. It is not necessary to award Gissing bad marks for being anti-feminist *per se*. That, on balance, is what he was, and it would be patronising to think the fact needs to be glossed over especially since it was an integral part of his attitudes as a whole. There is no doubt that it gravely interfered with the novelist's selective process—even as uncritical partisanship of the opposite variety has now consigned numerous other novelists of the period to irretrievable anonymity. At least with Gissing, his perspective of wider social concern lifts him easily above the common rut. It is only when we examine the areas where this concern is attenuated by his residually *petit-bourgeois* presuppositions, including those relating to women, that we understand the peculiar place he occupies between major and minor novelists in the late nineteenth century. (pp. 50-1)

Lloyd Fernando, "Gissing's Studies in 'Vulgarism':
Aspects of His Anti-Feminism," in Southern Review,
Australia, Vol. IV, No. 1, 1970, pp. 43-52.

A. O. J. COCKSHUT   (essay date 1977)

[*Cockshut is an English critic who specializes in the study of Victorian thought and literature. In the following excerpt, he maintains that Gissing's fiction presents an inverted view of traditional sexual stereotypes.*]

The reader familiar with the work of the English novelists from Richardson to Hardy comes to Gissing with a shock of surprise. This man, surely not a profound or highly original writer, seems to be a denizen of a different world. We are well accustomed by now to differences of value and moral emphasis. Gissing seems to present us with a new world of facts, which implicitly denies what everyone else seems to have assumed as too obvious to need discussion.

To a large extent, and with the air of a man pointing out the obvious, and indifferent to the charms of paradox, Gissing ascribes to women the characteristics universally supposed to belong to men. In *The Nether World* . . . , we have the cruel, battling East End woman, Clem Peckover. Attacked by Pennyloaf, the wife of her lover:

> It was just what [she] desired. In an instant she
> had rent half Pennyloaf's garments off her back,
> and was tearing her face till the blood streamed.

Her domination over the weak husband is quite other than that ascribed by earlier novelists to strong-willed women, a function of determined will and moral influence. It is more like a proletarian version of the dominion exercised in other novels by fierce men over women, by Dickens's Murdstone, say, over David Copperfield's mother:

> his disposition now was one of hatred, and the
> kind of hatred which sooner or later breaks out
> in ferocity. Bob would not have come to this

pass . . . if he had been left to the dictates of
his own nature; he was infected by the savagery
of the woman who had taken possession of him.
His lust of cruelty crept upon him like a disease . . . .

Later we hear of Clem's attachment to Bob being "fierce,
animal."

Just as we have this female equivalent of the strong, brutal
male, so, in a different social setting, does Gissing present us
with a feminine version of the *idée reçue* of male superiority
in strength, intellect, education, sheer effectiveness in the world.
Gone is the old Dickensian and Ruskinian kind of feminine
superiority, the moral superiority of the angel in the house. In
books like ***Born in Exile*** . . . or ***The Crown of Life*** . . . , it is
the woman who is strong, who has an assured position in the
world, who can consider the question of marriage coolly on
its merits. The men are the fond, weak yearners, who are
unspeakably grateful for a smile or a glance. After proposing
marriage, Godwin Peake, in ***Born in Exile***, is characteristic of
a whole group of Gissing's male protagonists when he says:
"Such a piece of recklessness deserves no answer." Godwin
and others feel like despised and useless beggars aspiring to
implacable Queen Cophetuas. So the hero of ***The Crown of
Life*** reflects:

> Three years of laborious exile were trifling in
> the balance; had they been passed in sufferings
> ten times as great, her smile would have paid
> for all.

In the same book Miss Bonicastle discusses a young man's
wild oats in Paris with the easy worldliness previously reserved
for disreputable uncles like Jane Austen's Admirable Crawford,
and dismisses the ensuing qualms of conscience as absurd. And
after more than a generation in which novelists had meditated
on the problem of the "fallen woman," we have, perhaps for
the first time, the concept of the "fallen man." In saying this,
I naturally do not mean that all previous novelists treated male
chastity as a trivial question. That is plainly not true of Richardson, Jane Austen, Trollope and many others. But here we
have something other than moral disapproval; we have a man
experiencing a paralysing fear that his lapse from chastity has
devalued him for ever in the eyes of decent women. So Otway
cries, with an astonished triumph:

> She has mentioned me; that is enough. I am
> not utterly expelled from her thoughts, as a
> creature outlawed by all decent people.

and a moment later, after dreaming fondly of an interview:

> I cannot face her without shame—the shame of
> every man who stands before a pure-hearted
> girl.

One only has to think of the position in society held by Henry
Crawford in *Mansfield Park,* and held to the end despite all
misdemeanours, to see that we are dealing here with something
quite other than moral seriousness. No one would dream of
offering Gissing as a rival to Jane Austen in that quality. We
are dealing with a new vision of society, in which sexual roles
have been to an astonishing extent reversed. (pp. 131-32)

[Gissing's] ordinary reputation, as a patient observer of detail,
a kind of imitation urban Dickens without genius, poetry or
humour does not very greatly belie him. And he was, after his
early idealistic socialist novels, devoid of faith, impatient of

theory, an outspoken enemy of cant (a term under which he
included much that might seem to others simple moral decency.) He is tedious in his reiteration of the platitudes of
unenlightened common sense, that it is better to be rich than
poor, that the educated are more civilized than the uneducated,
that a mob is fickle and cruel. The unexpectedness of his
dominant women and shrinking men is due to a unique combination of detached observation and intense emotions. For a
variety of reasons, he felt the female sex to be dominant over
him. Both the violent, drunken shrew and the serene, unapproachable queen were constantly in his thoughts. His deep
personal sense of injury, of being denied his rights not just by
society, but by life itself, caused him to feel humiliated before
all women, both those he considered to be above him and those
he despised. Lacking much self-knowledge, he seems to have
projected his own feelings on to a variety of fictional characters
(some of them in other ways little like himself) without being
aware of it. This does not turn his picture of society into a
caricature; he is too careful an observer for that. It is more as
if a drawing, exact in every outline, had been made on paper
of some strange, unearthly colour. The likeness remains exact
enough, so long as one discounts the pervasive lurid gleam.

My account so far has been one-sided. A prolific writer, Gissing on other occasions follows a more conventional line, often
with an extra twist of sordidness startling to readers long familiar with the points he was making. Thus many of his predecessors had written of unscrupulous husband-hunting, realistically, like Trollope, or with gay fantasy, like Surtees. In
chapter XIII of ***The Unclassed*** . . . , characteristically headed
"A Man-Trap," Gissing makes the process more crude, and
the marital prospects more intensely gloomy. Harriet lures Julian into her bedroom to show him how she has hung an en-
graving. She lives in a boarding house, and she assures him
that the very fact that he has been in her bedroom in broad
daylight and fully-clothed for a few minutes will be death to
her reputation. Respectable conventions (suitably exaggerated
for the occasion) and the man's gentleness and credulity are
turned in a woman's hand into weapons of ruthless social destruction. It was typical of Gissing's negative cast of mind that
he saw the "old" tricky, husband-hunting woman as destructive, just as much as violent shrews and detached, superior
ladies. In the same way, he pours equal scorn on traditional
views and on progressive or revolutionary doctrines.

Gissing's cynicism and ruthlessness spring from oversensi-
tiveness about his marriage to a drunken prostitute. His supposed toughness is a façade and his stinging rebukes to idealists
read very much like lectures addressed to his dreamy, wayward
self. Occasionally, he allows this dreamy self to rhapsodize
undeterred by irony; when this happens the contrast with his
usual tone is both startling and revealing. Nor is it something
he outgrew; it is as likely to occur in his latest books as in
earlier. The following is from ***The Crown of Life*** . . . :

> Images of maddening beauty glowed upon him
> out of the darkness, glowed and gleamed by he
> knew not what creatᵢ e mandate; faces, forms
> such as may visit the delirium of a supreme
> artist. Of him they knew not; they were worlds
> away, though his own brain bodied them
> forth . . . . For the men capable of passionate
> love (and they are few) to miss love is to miss
> everything.

While in this mood, seldom but powerfully felt in his writings,
he is capable of regarding even an unrequited love as a blessing,

giving life purpose and meaning, and helping to save a man from mere slavery to the senses.

It is not easy to discern a central point of balance between Gissing's cynicism and his romanticism, between his angry denunciations and his tender musings. Massively unfortunate in domestic life himself, and lacking the highest creative powers to detach him from his own experience, it was hard for him to describe feelingly the ordinary decencies of marriage. Yet at times he does, with some hesitation, feel towards the idea that for many, domestic life, however much marred by circumstances, quarrels, disagreements and incompatibilities, is their strongest comfort in an unfriendly world. Perhaps the most touching example is to be found in what is on the whole his gloomiest book [*The Nether World*]:

> "Look Clara, you and I are going to do what we can for these children; we're not going to give up the work now we've begun it. . . . But I can't do without your help. I didn't feel very cheerful as I sat here a while ago, before you came down; I was almost afraid to go upstairs, lest the sight of what you might be suffering should be too much for me. Am I to ask a kindness of you and be refused, Clara?"
>
> It was not the first time she had experienced the constraining power of his words when he was moved with passionate earnestness.

The scene ends with a grudging promise on Clara's part to try again, and a shared resolve not to mar the peace and rest of the coming Sunday. The man, in this case the calmer and less selfish of the two, feels exhausted with the moral efforts of the dialogue, following upon his other worries and fatigues. But, "Never mind; the battle was gained once more."

This is not an attractive portrait of the married state. Yet the home is seen as the place of least unhappiness and greatest moral possibility in a grim social world. Classifications are arbitrary, however useful; and this scene is a salutary reminder that even Gissing was not quite the Platonic idea of the pessimist. Like a glimmering light seen in the distance in an underground passage, the high ideal of the family and joyful, innocent domestic life, is glimpsed by those who will never reach it. (pp. 133-35)

> *A. O. J. Cockshut, "The Pessimists: Gissing," in his* Man and Woman: A Study of Love and the Novel 1740-1940, *1977. Reprint by Oxford University Press, 1978, pp. 131-35.*

MICHAEL COLLIE (essay date 1979)

[*Collie is an English critic who has written extensively on Victorian authors. In the following excerpt, he examines Gissing's place in the development of modern fiction.*]

It was Gissing's achievement to have explored, in a series of remarkably interesting novels, sets of "modern" relationships between people in the class-structured but nonetheless essentially fragmented and dislocated urban societies of late nineteenth-century England. He was in fact the English master of dislocation, alienation, estrangement; fiction's foremost nihilist and the poet, one might almost say, of the rootless, displaced intellect. An important part of this was his perception that sexuality as often held people apart as united them (with which, of course, we need neither agree nor disagree here), that sexual

desires and needs undercut the type of rational behaviour associated "with being civilized," and that sexual jealousy was a powerful determinant of human behaviour. He understood that, in a godless world and in an urban society where the forces of an inhuman materialism always tended to overwhelm, or at least dwarf the individual, patterns of behaviour were bound to suffer, with the traditional giving way to the chaotic and unexpected. Evidently, in these circumstances, it was important for a novelist to know how people related to each other, just as it was important for a person who was not a novelist. This must be the very stuff of fiction. But while Gissing became adept at creating the breakdown of relationships, indeed was more adept at it than anyone else in England, the almost total denial of love in novel after novel gave his work as a whole a devastatingly negative quality. Nothing really withstands examination. Nothing is ultimately meaningful.

Of course, other writers, particularly existentialist writers at the beginning of the twentieth century, have been as negative. Where they differed from Gissing is chiefly in allowing their characters to suffer and agonize merely as a result of their failure to discover the Absolute. This *angst* Gissing would have regarded as a Romantic indulgence. If there is not a God, why agonize? If the forces of heredity and environment are always stronger than the individual will, why cry out? If sexual loneliness is a function of the need to perpetuate the species, why attach importance to marriage? If merely to think about the world leads to the conclusion that none of one's fundamental questions about its meaning will ever be satisfied, why suppose that two thinking people will ever find a basis for living with each other for the whole of their lives? What distinguishes Gissing from existentialist novelists, who allow their characters to agonize, is his ruthless or logically unremitting reluctance to resort to a panacea of any kind. Even limited and modest stratagems for living are regarded with the greatest scepticism, are always on the edge of the whirlpool, are invariably depicted within a larger environment characterized by breakdown and social dislocation.

It has been seen that Gissing's novels were part of the process by which established ideas about the author and society were challenged during the last two decades of the nineteenth century. In them the techniques of a more deliberately critical social realism that ever strained in the direction of an imported naturalism became, briefly, one of the means by which the novelist asserted his independence, his seriousness, his right to incorporate within his fiction the brainstuff of which Meredith talked and, in the case of Gissing, contained his most deeply felt insights, perceptions, and thoughts. Straight-forward advocacy of priniciples of social realism lasted only for a short period before the tide of public opinion turned against it. The Vizetelly case had brought the issues into the public domain. Zola by 1890 was familiar to English readers. Novelists like Hardy and Meredith had also begun to be more assertive, more free, and a new generation of novelists was already on the scene. The story of this process of liberation is familiar and a good number of critics have dated it precisely. G. T. Becker, for example, in the Introduction to *Documents of Modern Literary Realism*, wrote:

> The initial impact of realism had spent itself in France before the end of the century. "The Manifesto of Five against Zola" in 1887 and Jules Hûret's *Enquête* in 1891 indicate the turn of the tide. Huysmans broke away from the Médan group; Bourget's *Le Disciple* (1889) at-

tacked the moral premises and influences of realism. Actually 1893 is often taken as a terminal date: Maupassant and Taine died in that year; the Rougon-Macquart was completed; and Zola's arch-enemy Brunetière defeated him in a contest for a place in the French Academy.

This sort of comment raises, of course, as many issues as it resolves. The "initial impact of realism had spent itself" but the impact of the movement continued to be felt, in as far as the novel was regarded as a serious not an escapist mode, was taken more and more to be a legitimate artistic activity, not a second-rate citizen in the world of letters, was accepted as the vehicle for social commentary in fictions where the reader could understand the commentary was the characters' not necessarily the author's and was, in a more general sense, taken to be worthy of attention because no longer in its very nature committed to euphemism, evasion and the creation of fantasy worlds so utterly different from those in which the readers lived that no connection could be made between the two. Contemporary reviews . . . show that Gissing was understood to have played a major role in this process of liberation. But then so, of course, did the reader play a major role, by becoming more sophisticated, more capable of distinguishing between character and author, more appreciative of novels written from a variety of points of view, and more open minded about the doctrinal implications of books that did not directly satisfy his own moral sense. The reader had in part been put in this position by writers like Gissing, who in progressive stages tested what the reader would accept as they discovered what they themselves could do. It is important, historically, to see the extent to which Gissing developed as a craftsman—and at the centre of this book is the assertion that he did develop—because we happen to have here a writer whose career proceeds in step with public taste, as measured by what the public is prepared to accept, which is not to say that the novelist is the cause, certainly not the single cause, of the change. In England, the change was brought about by a combination of factors: the pragmatic judgements of publishers who realized, with their fingers on the public's pulse, that mid-Victorian restrictiveness was no longer wanted; the manufacturing processes that allowed the publication of cheaper, one-volume novels and so contributed to the demise of the circulating library; the changes in the American copyright law which made American agents travel to England to secure rights, thus introducing an element of competition which made the English novelist less dependent upon the judgement, or whim, of the English publisher; and the extension of the reading public itself, where rapid population growth, popular education and accelerated urbanization combined to produce new social circumstances and, literally, more people who wanted fiction to read. Gissing, as much as any other late nineteenth-century writer, was for two decades at the centre of all this. He perceived an opportunity, which he met by devising a type of social realism different in important respects from anything that had previously been published in England.

What Gissing might have done had he lived twenty more years is a matter of conjecture. His own work had brought him to the point at which he needed the breakthrough that was in fact achieved by D. H. Lawrence, the break-through involved in the perception that sexuality was not to be dismissed in Spenglerian terms as part of the "decay" of civilization, nor condemned as a destructive force in the whirlpool of modern life. Despite obvious differences, Gissing and Lawrence have much in common, not least their ability to make relationships between

characters develop by means of vivid, tersely written dialogue. If social realism, as it veered towards naturalism, were seen as a brief period of transition between high-Victorian fiction and the modern novel, then Gissing's work would fall completely within that period, so one would need to note that he was not only the principal, but perhaps the only major English novelist who did not span a different period at either end of his career. He never inhabited the world of George Eliot; he had only glimpses of the world of D. H. Lawrence. This being so, his fiction in all its strengths and weaknesses is inextricably mixed up with the process by which both the novel itself and the social role of the novelist altered radically. (pp. 164-69)

Looking back over Gissing's career as a novelist, one can see the strenuous, determined way in which he had . . . sought out his freedom and developed his craft, from the times in those early novels when the passionately concerned, moralistic narrator had to be Gissing himself, so unsubtle was the narrative technique, to the later novels which show, relatively speaking, his mastery of change of pace, change of perspective, change of narrative point of view. The new generation of novelists at the beginning of the twentieth century simply abandoned the conventions of the Victorian novel and started afresh; it was Gissing's special place to have been a profoundly committed novelist during the period of transition. (p. 170)

To sustain the notion that an author whose work was so varied and extensive failed to develop as a craftsman because preoccupied with his own early experiences is simply a mistake, as well as an injustice. Of course there is, there must be, a relation between a writer's life and his work and of course this relation can be studied in the case of Gissing just as well as in any other case. *The Unclassed* is a novel of his first marriage; *Demos, Thyrza* and *The Nether World* books written when he lived by himself in London; *New Grub Street* and *Born in Exile* reassessments of his own early work and his own turbulent existence written at the time of his second marriage; *In the Year of Jubilee* and *The Whirlpool* the novels of his stoutly professional years when he was an established writer; *The Crown of Life* a novel written during the full flood of Gissing's friendship with Gabrielle Fleury. And so on. Furthermore, when closer critical work has been done on Gissing's fiction, it will no doubt emerge that many characters in the novels are in fact portraits of people like Edith Sichel, Morley Roberts, Clara Collett and people Gissing knew in London and Wakefield. It will probably also emerge, not that the moralistic and pessimistic tone of the early books reflected his own early traumas, but that the repression of those traumas affected, maybe resulted in, his depiction of urban alienation later in his career. Whatever the merits of such lines of speculation, it would seem best, as a prudent first step, to extricate ourselves from the muddle of critical-cum-biographical talk about Gissing and avoid making simplistic connections between the man and his work. Gissing, the writer, quite obviously thought a great deal about how to write a modern novel. He experimented a lot. He revised his early work. He adopted new techniques at various stages of his career. He wrote a range of books that few others could emulate. It is on this level, as a writer, that it seems best to try to meet him.

As a powerful, resourceful and widely recognized contemporary writer, he clearly had limitations and some of them, like the avoidance of metaphor, were self-imposed. Realism denies metaphor. If the physical world in all its detail, down to its last detail, is to be described dispassionately just as the novelist sees it, novelist and character seeing it in a virtually identical way, it follows that the same details cannot participate, as it were, in metaphorical constructions which would tend to invalidate "phenomena" as *the* reality. A serious step for any writer to take. Throughout the manuscripts Gissing deleted passages that had the resonance of metaphor, which were in some way—perhaps unintentionally—symbolic. In doing so he was being entirely consistent. He was accepting one of his own "limits," to keep his own word (which does not mean "limitation"). Thus, in *In the Year of Jubilee,* Gissing deleted Tarrant's dream in which he had sighted Nancy Lord peering over a thick hedge luxuriant with flowers, had pursued her into the woods, feeling that if he could only reach her everything would be all right again, and had found, not her, but a baby lying by itself in a glade. There is no firm evidence of the reason for this particular deletion but one can see easily enough that its inclusion would have given the story a different dimension. This is only another way of saying that the unmetaphorical surface of a Gissing novel, which has the texture not of image but of brittle dialogue, was part, an essential and logically necessary part, of its overall design. A reader may crave for excitement, for metaphorical disturbances, for enigmas compatible with a sense of mystery and uncertainty, but there is no room in a realist novel for such indulgences. Gissing wrote a pure, disciplined English with great directness and economy, throughout his life admiring the same qualities in some Latin authors and avoiding rhetoric. His style was an efficient instrument that he adapted to his particular needs, learning in the end to balance crisply, economically written third-person narrative with vividly realized dialogue, in which characters realize themselves through their own words in dramatic situations that are so well conceived the intrusion of the novelist is no longer necessary. (pp. 170-72)

> *Michael Collie, in his* The Alien Art: A Critical Study of George Gissing's Novels, *Archon Books, Hamden, CT, 1979, 197 p.*

ROBERT L. SELIG (essay date 1983)

[*In the following excerpt, Selig discusses* New Grub Street *and* Born in Exile.]

New Grub Street . . . stands as Gissing's masterpiece and also one of the finest novels of the late-Victorian era. Part of its strength comes from his finally having restricted all his major characters in a novel to an occupation that he knew firsthand—the writer's profession. Every important male character writes for a living, as do many of the important females, and the other major women marry writers. As a result, *New Grub Street* avoids a common weakness of the novelist's lesser fiction: fabricated vocations stuck unconvincingly onto the characters' lives. In this most impressive example of Gissing's realism, work and domestic life form a seamless whole.

New Grub Street also draws strength from its ironic yet sympathetic exposure of illusory idealism—an idealism that fails to recognize that "everything is relative." Although Reardon, for example, resents his wife's failure to act like an "ideal" helpmate . . . , he ultimately admits that only a person with "shallow idealism" could blame either her or him for the chilling effects of poverty. . . . Then, too, his friend Harold Biffen dismisses Reardon's fantasy of a perfect marriage with a working-class wife as the dream of "a shameless idealist." . . . Later Biffen censures Reardon's "obstinate idealism" in remaining apart from Amy after she has inherited enough wealth to make them both comfortable. . . . Marian

Yule falls in love with all-too-"human" Jasper Milvain simply because "ideal personages do not descend to girls who have to labour at the British Museum." . . . The romantically susceptible literary man, Whelpdale, endures four jiltings by successive fiancées—the last a young woman who fulfills his absolute "ideal." . . . Believing in no "absolute ideals," Reardon concedes the absurdity of his moral distaste for writing potboilers. . . . And Milvain openly confesses that his own triumphs have sprung from a total lack of ideals: "It is men of my kind who succeed; the conscientious, and those who really have a high ideal, either perish or struggle on in neglect." . . .

Almost every page of the novel undercuts two aspects of life idealized in Gissing's earlier fiction: sexual love and art. A single tough-minded principle runs through *New Grub Street:* in a society that values only money, neither love nor art can flourish without sufficient cash. This one simple precept shapes the narrative pattern of intricate parallels, foreshadowings, repetitions, and disillusioned ironies. (pp. 53-4)

The novel emphasizes one basic paradox in the lives of late-Victorian writers: they work at a slow and ancient handicraft amid rapidly changing communication technology. Milvain notes that old Grub Street lacked telegraphy. . . . He also identifies his own journalistic zeal with a speeding railroad train ("it enspirits me" . . .)—a prime example of nineteenth-century mechanized efficiency. Yet although machines can speed up and expand the distribution of writing, Gissing's authors must still create in the ancient laborious way, word by word, sentence by sentence, page by page, with old-fashioned pen and paper. Books, in particular, take a long time to write, far longer than most other craft-produced goods. The conscientious novelist Reardon needs a full seven months to achieve his very best work. . . . The equally scrupulous Biffen takes just as long with his "Mr. Bailey, Grocer": "He worked very slowly. . . . Each sentence was as good as he could make it, harmonious to the ear, with words of precious meaning skillfully set. Before sitting down to a chapter he planned it minutely in his mind; then he wrote a rough draft of it; then he elaborated the thing phrase by phrase." . . . But when the need for money compels Reardon to hurry, he starts a book without adequate planning, keeps changing subjects, and commits "intolerable faults" of accidental rhyme and clumsy rhythm. . . . He contrasts his botched prose with the great poetry of *The Odyssey:* "*that* was not written at so many pages a day, with a workhouse clock clanging its admonition at the poet's ear." . . . (p. 59)

The struggle against time, the conflict between quality and speed, dominates the lives of *New Grub Street*'s writers. Marian Yule feels so oppressed by these occupational tensions that she ironically envisions a "Literary Machine," a mechanical author for adapting, reducing, and blending "old books" into marketable new ones. . . . Jasper, on the other hand, aims at human writing efficiency, although on a bad day he produces only a page. . . . But during one especially productive spurt, he dashes off a book review, a regular feature article, half of a short essay, and part of a longer piece in a mere thirteen hours and fifteen minutes. . . . Jasper, of course, concentrates on journalism, but he insists that, if he had the talent, he would grind out novels with the same commercial efficiency. . . . Yet his sister's question about "the value" of his high-speed writing raises a central issue of *New Grub Street.* When Jasper replies that his day's worth of work will bring in "ten to twelve guineas," she explains that she meant its "literary value," and the amused journalist revises his estimate: "equal to that of the contents of a mouldy nut." . . . (pp. 59-60)

Like humble nineteenth-century craftsmen such as carpenters, shoemakers, or tailors, Gissing's writers gain their living by selling what they make. And the quicker they make their works of prose, the more they will earn for each day of labor. But in their writing, Reardon and Biffen aim at a transcendental value beyond time and without a cash equivalent—a value called art. In contrast with, say, a maker of custom chairs who can raise his price for his painstaking work, Gissing's serious literary men get paid at the same rate as any slapdash journalist. In fact, they get paid rather less, because they strive for other effects than the current market demands. Apart from the isolation of these scrupulous writers amid capitalism's technological progress, they exemplify the survival of an almost religious reverence toward the written word—a reverence that harks back at least a thousand years to the age of theological faith. Although Reardon and Biffen do not believe in God, they worship great writing as though it contains the spirit of the Divine.

In spite of Reardon's and Biffen's veneration for the word, they experience inner conflict because they partially share their era's material values. Reardon feels obsessed by money's beneficent power, and even the tougher Biffen can write cadenced prose only about people who suffer from lack of cash and of ordinary middle-class comforts. "You," he tells Reardon, "are repelled by what has injured you; I am attracted by it." . . . In addition, neither writer achieves the unworldly goal of creating great art: at best, their careful work stands slightly above average. As a result, one can sympathize with Jasper's ironic complaint about these unsuccessful literary artists: "What the devil . . . is there in typography to make everything it deals with sacred?" . . . It seems a measure of Gissing's advance in objectivity that *New Grub Street* does not allow us to dismiss Jasper's question as mere shallow cynicism. Indeed, the question reverberates throughout the entire book.

In the following key passage, note the tough-minded eloquence, the psychological conviction, but also the sardonic humor of Marian Yule's despairing vision of the British Museum Reading Room, where she slaves at tasks assigned by her father:

> The fog drew thicker; she looked up at the windows beneath the dome and saw that they were a dusky yellow. Then her eye discerned an official walking along the upper gallery, and in pursuance of her grotesque humour, her mocking misery, she likened him to a black, lost soul, doomed to wander in an eternity of vain research along endless shelves. Or again, the readers who sat here at these radiating lines of desks, what were they but hapless flies caught in a huge web, its nucleus the great circle of the Catalogue? Darker, darker. From the towering wall of volumes seemed to emanate visible motes, intensifying the obscurity; in a moment the book-lined circumference of the room would be but a featureless prison-limit. . . .
>
> (pp. 60-1)

The ancient association of books and religion affects the entire paragraph, yet Marian's depression gives an ironic hue to ostensibly Christian imagery. The Reading Room's literary drudges resemble scribal monks, like those who produced the theological library described in Arnold's "Stanzas from the Grande Chartreuse" (1855):

> The library, where tract and tome
> Not to feed priestly pride are there,
> To hymn the conquering march of Rome,

> Nor yet to amuse, as ours are!
> They paint of souls the inner strife,
> Their drops of blood, their death in life.

But in far more famous words from the same poem, Gissing's literary hacks stand condemned to wander "between two worlds, one dead, / The other powerless to be born." These toilers among books have lost the divine afflatus yet cannot adjust to the mechanized ways of modern industrial factories. The Reading Room itself, however, serves as an old-fashioned factory for recycling printed words.

In Marian's caustic vision of the British Museum Reading Room, traditional religious symbols become merely bitter images for conveying literary futility. The fog that snuffs out sunlight suggests infernal as well as mental darkness. Marian compares the upper gallery's walker to a damned soul in Hell condemned forever to a fruitless reference hunt along infinite rows of books. This "black, lost" researcher may have literal difficulty in tracking down a scholarly citation, but, figuratively, he has lost the light of God. As Marian gazes at other readers extending along the spokes of the library's vast circle, she perceives these drudges in terms of Satanic torment: "flies" who have blundered into a spider web merely to be devoured. The Catalogue stands at the room's literal center but also functions like a predator: ensconced in the middle of its web, the spiderlike Catalogue deludes the swarm of readers with vain reference clues. The gloom deepens even more infernally, as "visible motes," or dark specks, appear to emerge from the Reading Room's many "volumes"; God's written word has become debased into an instrument of mental blindness. The final image of the Library as a circular prison reflects an historical and architectural oddity. Jeremy Bentham's 1790s design of a model penitentiary called the "panopticon"—"a circular . . . structure" with the guards' observation "rotunda" at the center—influenced the design of the British Museum Reading Room. Thus, Marian's initial vision of eternal damnation shrinks to a mere jail: a secular punishment imposed by society upon living men and women. In contrast with Gissing's idealizing novels, *New Grub Street* holds nothing sacred, not even the art of literature. Because of its hard-headed realism and its self-mocking balance, the work achieves a remarkable advance over Gissing's earlier books.

Born in Exile . . . contains Gissing's finest work as a psychological realist—a portrayer of a subtle mind's complex interaction with a convincing social milieu. The book centers around Godwin Peak, a brilliant yet self-tormenting agnostic from the lower middle classes who adopts the respectable camouflage of a candidate for the clergy because he aims at marrying a gentlewoman. The remarkable portrait of this troubled hero makes the novel one of Gissing's major achievements. The only slight flaw comes from perfunctory minor characters, such as Christian Moxey and Malkin, who inhabit weak little subplots. These seem designed to pad out the book to the three-volume length still expected by many late-Victorian publishers. The secondary elements seem especially disappointing compared with the Yules and Biffens of *New Grub Street*—a novel far more deft than *Born in Exile* at using many characters in counterpoint to a single overriding theme. Indeed, *Born in Exile*'s central motif—the fragile imbalance of human consciousness when it tries to break away from social conventionality—appears ill-suited to the old-fashioned multiplotted structure. Luckily, however, the Christian Moxey and Malkin episodes take up little space: they represent a small distraction in a generally masterful book.

In *Born in Exile* Gissing solves a basic problem of literary realism: how to imitate life's usually trivial flow and at the same time achieve coherent narrative form. In the past he had relied upon traditional plot devices, such as the sexual rivalry of two contrasting heroines or salvation by sudden inheritance. In Peak's story, however, the external events seem so basically unimportant that they avoid the appearance of contrivance. Yet meaning and form emerge from Peak's frantic effort to turn a commonplace meeting with former wealthy acquaintances into the social chance of a lifetime. Trifling occurrences derive both depth and point from Peak's grandiose aspirations and also his sense of shame. (pp. 61-3)

Born in Exile achieves particular impressiveness in those passages that analyze the hero's self-deception. The following remarkable description of Godwin Peak's shame occurs right after he has announced his intention of studying for the clergy:

> What had happened seemed to him incredible; it was as though he revived a mad dream, of ludicrous coherence. Since his display of rhetoric at luncheon all was downright somnambulism. What fatal power had subdued him? What extraordinary influence had guided his tongue, constrained his features? His conscious self had had no part in all this comedy; now for the first time was he taking count of the character he had played. . . .
>
> Yet such possibility had not been unforeseen. At the times of his profound gloom, when solitude and desire crushed his spirit, he had wished that fate would afford him such an opportunity of knavish success. His imagination had played with the idea that a man like himself might well be driven to this expedient, and might even use it with life-long result. . . .
>
> A cowardly instinct, this; having once acted upon it gave to his whole life a taint of craven meanness. Mere bluster, all his talk of mental dignity and uncompromising scorn of superstitions. A weak and idle man, whose best years were already wasted!
>
> He gazed deliberately at himself in the glass, at his red eyelids and unsightly lips. Darkness was best; perhaps he might forget his shame for an hour or two ere the dawn renewed it. He threw off his garments heedlessly, extinguished the lamp, and crept into the ready hiding-place. . . .
>
> (p. 69)

The first paragraph emphasizes the hero's attempt to dissociate himself from his own shameful conduct. He regards it as "what had happened" rather than what he had caused to happen. He remembers it as "a mad dream"—something that surged up from his unconscious mind rather than from his conscious will. But although this waking "dream" strikes him as "mad"—contrary to his usual rationality—it also has a "ludicrous coherence." Though he wishes to brush aside his contemptible masquerade as merely laughable, it makes all too much sense. His alternate explanation, "somnambulism," resembles yet differs from dreams: a somnambulist walks within the real world but without any perception of it. Yet Peak has hardly functioned as an unknowing sleepwalker, for he has told self-serving lies and worn fake expressions. He attempts to explain

his purposive behavior as the result of some "extraordinary influence," a mysterious force beyond his own control. In denying that "his conscious self had" performed any "part in" this disgraceful "comedy," Peak shifts his metaphors away from dreams to theatrical make-believe. "Taking count of the character he had played," he finds his role comic, yet he also insists that he acted it unawares. But this strange excuse raises an inevitable question: who, then, wrote the script?

The next paragraph gives a very odd answer. Peak himself wrote the script, but he did so long before he finally acted it out. During its enactment he forgot his own script yet also stuck faithfully to it. And when he first composed this farce, he did not think it comic, for it embodied his deepest frustrations. He saw his role then as despicable but not at all funny. He even toyed with the notion of assuming the role for life.

The concluding two paragraphs at last admit a connection between the man who wrote the script and the man who played it out. Here Peak judges himself in very harsh terms: "cowardly," "craven," mean, blustering, "weak," "idle." Yet the word "instinct" suggests a last feeble excuse: a powerful inborn impulse to cheat. Still, he need not have acted upon that impulse, so that he cannot, after all, escape the blame. In his final admission of disgrace, he derides even his own reflection in the mirror. He creeps to bed in order to hide his guilt in the dark oblivion of sleep—an ironic reminder of his first excuse that he had acted in a dream. In collapsing, however, into his psychic hiding place, the hero avoids the only course of honor still available to him: telling the Warricombes the truth. Here and throughout most of *Born in Exile,* Gissing achieves an intense yet subtle portrayal of corrosive bad conscience within a skeptical mind—a mind that doubts the validity of even its own shame. Although the book remains firmly grounded in external social details, it also probes the inward human reality of consciousness itself. (pp. 70-1)

> Robert L. Selig, in his George Gissing, *Twayne Publishers, 1983, 177 p.*

DAVID GRYLLS   (essay date 1984)

[*Grylls is an English critic. In the following excerpt, he demonstrates how apparently contradictory attitudes of hopeless pessimism and belief in the power of individual will complement each other in Gissing's works.*]

George Gissing was a pessimist who believed in will power. His fiction asserts the futility of hope while commending strenuous endeavor. Weighted with sorrow, frustration, and failure, it places an almost equal stress on the need for effort and determination. (p. 61)

That Gissing and his work are pessimistic might seem to require no laborious proof; but we need to take the measure of his pessimism to appreciate the scope, and the oddity, of his contrary impulses. First, then, Gissing was a pessimist by temperament; this was evident to all who knew him well. Ellen Gissing, the younger of his two sisters, recollected "that haunting depression which so often attacked my brother . . . that strange mental suffering so often his." His friend Morley Roberts insisted that Gissing "was truly hopeless, most truly pessimistic." His ex-pupil, Austin Harrison, reported, "I have never seen so sad and pathetic a face. In repose his features contracted into a look of ineffable dreariness, sorrow and affliction, of mute submissiveness and despair." The scars of Gissing's psychological torment are visible all over his journal and letters; expressions of acute misery punctuate their pages. (pp. 61-2)

But Gissing was not just a pessimist by temperament; he was also a pessimist by conviction: in his early twenties he was strongly impressed by the doctrines of Schopenhauer. The impact of Schopenhauer's central doctrine is traceable throughout Gissing's work, most explicitly in his article of 1882, **"The Hope of Pessimism."** Brutally abbreviated, Schopenhauer's argument is that the ultimate reality (Kant's "thing-in-itself") is the Immanent Will, which in organic beings manifests itself as the will-to-live. Will, for Schopenhauer, is an evil force, responsible for egotism, conflict, cruelty, and inevitable frustration. Misery is the result of the will being thwarted. Happiness, a negative quality, is merely the absence of obstacles to the will; as such it is closely akin to boredom, and indeed human life alternates between boredom and distress. The road to redemption is asceticism, renunciation of the will-to-live. In his article Gissing approves such denial; and he emphasizes Schopenhauer's conviction that acknowledgement of "the pathos of the human lot" is the only dependable basis of compassion, and hence of morality. In 1882, then, Gissing was a Schopenhauerian. How far he continued, while writing his fiction, to subscribe to Schopenhauer's beliefs is, as we shall see, disputable.

When we examine Gissing's fiction, we find it accords with his temperament and convictions in sentiment, tone, and structure. "All my work," he averred in 1887, "is profoundly pessimistic as far as mood goes." ... The truth of this is demonstrable on a number of levels. First, and most obviously, his fiction is strewn with pessimistic generalizations: "good things always come too late in this world," "misery is the key-note of modern life," "all mirth is unnatural to the reflective mind"—a threnody of sentiments such as these resounds through Gissing's work. Some are distinctly Schopenhauerian echoes: the notion, for instance, that nonexistence is preferable to even the happiest life, or that happiness itself, being merely "the exemption from painful shock," is appreciable only in retrospect. Secondly, both tone and characterization endorse the burden of such sentiments. Writing to Gabrielle, Gissing explained that his books lacked "that foolish optimism which is indispensable to popularity." ... Optimism, in Gissing's work, is almost invariably foolish. Set against the percipient pessimists—Sidney Kirkwood, for instance, with his "sad clearness of vision"—are shortsighted smilers like Whelpdale, Barmby, and Gammon. In *Will Warburton* there are two optimists, one "sturdy," one "disastrous," ... but both deficient in sympathetic imagination. Gissing was perfectly capable of mocking a pessimistic poseur—he does so in his short story **"The Pessimist of Plato Road"**— but in the main his wiser characters are those who expect the worst.

This brings us to the third and most basic point. Gissing's books are pessimistic in *structure*: pain, frustration, and disillusion are part of their architecture. Without doubt, Gissing's imagination was pulled toward the spectacle of decline and failure—in effect, to the medieval formula for tragedy, prosperity-to-wretchedness. A sketch for a story in the Pforzheimer Library displays the bare bones of this imaginative preference. "Two scenes," Gissing writes. "I. A father and mother with their little child. Happy for its future. Could not bear to think that it would suffer hardship for a day, all bright visions. II. Parents dead, and child, grown up, in some bitterly wretched position." ... In the novels such calamitous juxtapositions are

sometimes unleashed with almost comparable abruptness. *The Odd Women*, for example, opens serenely, with Dr. Madden's mellowed hopes for his children, but within a few pages he is thrown from a dogcart and his orphaned daughters are brought to grief; three are killed off in a couple of paragraphs, one, most appropriately, "by the overturning of a pleasure-boat." Grotesque misfortunes, in speeded-up sequence, are also on view in some of the short stories. Normally, however, Gissing was patient in depicting the slow erosion of hope—the entanglements of circumstance, the frailties of character, that conspire to ruin his protagonists' plans. For in Gissing virtually all plans fail: the philanthropic projects of Michael Snowdon and Walter Egremont, the self-serving schemes of Dyce Lashmar and Richard Mutimer, the artistic aspirations of Arthur Golding, the theatrical ambitions of Clara Hewett, the musical visions of Alma Rolfe, the complex designs of Godwin Peak— all end in unmistakable failure, leaving only a residue of bitterness and despair.

However, there is one preeminent area in which failure prevails in Gissing. A fact too easily overlooked is that *all* of Gissing's novels are basically romances: what they deal with most persistently is unsuccessful love affairs. These doomed relationships come in two kinds: either the lovers fail to unite, the result being loneliness and misery; or the lovers succeed in uniting, the result being company and misery. A Gissing lover is almost certain to be either thwarted or disenchanted. To list all examples would be tedious, but of Gissing's twenty-one completed novels, no fewer than twelve, in their sexual relationships, contain major failures of frustration, while at least nine have failures of attrition. Some of his best books contain both: the pattern begins with *Workers in the Dawn* and finds its subtlest expression in *New Grub Street*, where Jasper Milvain and Marian Yule fail to unite for the very same reasons, material and emotional, that undermine the union of Amy and Edwin Reardon. Here Gissing skillfully interweaves his two types of romantic collapse.

The two alternatives are neatly described by what Gissing said he intended to do in his unfinished novel "Will-o'-the-Wisps": to show "the failure of a number of people to gain ends they have set up for their lives, or, if they *do* gain them, their failure to find the enjoyment they expected." ... Put like that, it seems to be a Catch 22; and indeed the pervasive presence in Gissing of hopeless alternatives confirms the fact that his work is pessimistic in structure as well as in incident. Of many examples, two must suffice. In *New Grub Street* Amy's desertion of Reardon reveals the inability of a middle-class wife to endure the conditions of poverty. But when Reardon suggests that a man in his position ought instead to marry a work-girl, the suggestion is not only refuted by Harold Biffen, but also impugned by the story of Alfred Yule, whose marriage to a woman of the lower class is a miserable fiasco. In *The Odd Women* a traditional marriage, patriarchal and plainly benighted, is set against a more enlightened liaison. The retrograde relationship ends in disaster, but so does the seemingly progressive one—and for very similar reasons: jealousy, power, and insecurity.

The frequent appearance of this two-pronged trap is connected, of course, with Gissing's refusal to write reformist fiction. When Hardy was accused of pessimism, he would quote a line from his poem "In Tenebris": "If way to the Better there be, it exacts a full look at the Worst." But to Gissing, except in his earliest work, no such defense was open. As Morley Roberts observed in *The Private Life of Henry Maitland*, "It is perfectly possible, and even certainly true, that many of the most pessimistic writers are in reality optimists. They show us the grey in order that we may presently make it rose. But Maitland wrote absolutely without hope." . . . As I think should be apparent by now, a good deal of evidence could be adduced to corroborate this statement.

But—and here we come to the paradox—despite its pessimistic content, the general effect of Gissing's fiction is not dispiriting. Although his books are frequently grim, they cannot be said to be dreary. Extremely various, thoroughly readable, written with a kind of despondent verve, they sweep the reader into a world of minutely realized social detail, deftly handled psychological suspense, and unsparing moral analysis. The early books pulse with idealism; the later ones—such as *Jubilee*—crackle with an acrid energy. In his commentary on *The Nether World* Adrian Poole has noted the "discrepancy between the excessive passivity of the two central characters and the energy of the narrator." But across the range of Gissing's work it is not simply that the pessimistic themes are vitalized by a vigorous narration. The themes themselves are not purely pessimistic. Strangely for an author who believes that plans founder, that optimism usually correlates with crassness, that passion is most often a source of pain, Gissing believes in effort and endeavor, in striving, persistence, and determination. The commitment to pessimism coexists with belief in will power.

This belief is frequently implied by a scathing depiction of its opposite. Gissing's work is packed with warnings against weakness of will. The sketches and stories, in particular, are draped with drifters and spongers and idlers: Mr. Dent in **"The Medicine Man"** who "suffered from the common complaint of indolence: in conversation . . . he called it rheumatic gout"; Percy Dunn in **"Spellbound,"** lethargic, lazy, hypnotized in the public library; Marfleet in **"Our Learned Fellow-Townsman"** vaguely planning a continuation of Macaulay; or the spineless Isherwood in **"A Man of Leisure"** who loafs around, alcoholically cheerful, forever making resolutions and forever doing nothing.

Gissing concentrates especially on dawdling scholars like Egremont in *Thyrza*. But infirmity of will, in Gissing's fiction, is quite as much a moral as an intellectual scourge. Relevant here is the slippery, weirdly nonvolitional way that his characters fall into guilt. He is brilliant at describing slides, effected without any conscious decision, into compromising positions. One thinks of Osmond Waymark, Thyrza Trent, and James Hood, of Monica Madden, Eve Madeley, and Nancy Lord, of Marcian. Even where the lapse might seem abrupt—as with Peak's false profession in *Born in Exile* or Eustace Glazzard's treachery in *Denzil Quarrier*—it turns out on inspection to have been preceded by a hidden or subconscious slide. Discreditable lapses are related in Gissing to a temporary paralysis of will. So too are passionate impulses. His lovers are motivated by will in the sense of a blind and urgent compulsion (which is close to the Schopenhauerian meaning), but not in the sense of a conscious choice. Quite often they act like automata, as when Thyrza finds herself pulled toward Egremont (*Thyrza* . . .), or when Edmund Langley rides westward in *Sleeping Fires* . . . , or when Warburton crosses the whole of France in a febrile, infatuated dream (*Will Warburton* . . .). It seems at times like somnambulism—and indeed the very term is used of Peak (*Born in Exile* . . .), of Glazzard (*Denzil Quarrier* . . .), and of Piers Otway in *The Crown of Life,* when he courts Olga Hannaford. On awaking from their dreams, not a few of Gissing's characters discover that they are married or engaged. (pp. 64-9)

In Gissing's fiction a commitment to work is associated with virtue. Take Richard Mutimer in *Demos*. At first, while still uncorrupted, he is praised for his capacity and vigor. . . . He rises early and resists on principle any "temptations to personal ease." . . . He reproaches his brother as a shiftless shirker. . . . But as the book goes on, he becomes self-indulgent, and this leads to tyranny and cruelty. The message of the newly discovered will ("It is not my wish . . . to put the said Richard Mutimer above the need of supporting himself by honest work" . . . highlights the moral of the case with almost embarrassing clarity. (pp. 70-1)

Workers in the Dawn establishes a paradigm that helps to explain how pessimism and will power exist side by side in Gissing. The salient features of the pattern are these: a weakness of will in one of the protagonists that makes him or her excessively reliant on other people or on circumstances; a compensatory determination to resist the ensuing disadvantages; and a state of mind in which this resistance, taking the form of strenuous activity, is fueled by both a conscious acceptance of suffering and the persistence of an almost unconscious hope. Will power is exerted, then, to rectify adversity; the adversity has often been brought about by initial lack of will power. (pp. 77-8)

We have seen that [a] paradox exists in Gissing, and to some extent we have seen *how* it exists: the last question to ask is *why*. Two answers may be plausibly offered, one relating to Gissing's convictions, the other to his temperament. The first answer takes us back to Schopenhauer, whom we know to have influenced Gissing's thought. In the Schopenhauerian philosophy, pessimism is not always inconsistent with labor and endeavor. What Schopenhauer terms the will-to-live is not to be identified with what common sense calls will power. As it happens, Schopenhauer himself was notorious for his dogged application. There was no self-contradiction here, because what he was doing, in his own estimation, was exercising pure intellect—quite different from the force of will. Intellect was the origin not only of philosophy, but of literature and—in varying degrees—of all forms of art. Hence, from the inherent evil of the world, there is one other escape route apart from renunciation. As Gissing puts it in **"The Hope of Pessimism"**:

> There is, in truth, only one kind of worldly optimism which justifies itself in the light of reason, and that is the optimism of the artist. . . . In the mood of artistic contemplation the will is destroyed, self is eliminated, the world of phenomena resolves itself into pictures of absolute significance, and the heart rejoices itself before images of pure beauty. . . .
>
> (p. 80)

Does this explain the paradox? Certainly Gissing saw his own work as art and liked to imagine that his attitude to it was "that of the artist pure and simple." . . . As Waymark says in *The Unclassed:* "The artist is the only sane man. Life for its own sake?—no; I would drink a pint of laudanum to-night. But life as the source of splendid pictures, inexhaustible material for effects—*that* can reconcile me to existence, and that only." . . . The sentiments are similar to those of Flaubert. Regular, exhausting, artistic work is recommended as the only defense against the grimness of life. Perhaps, then, this is how Gissing managed to acclaim endeavor while facing despair. His fiction, after all, is by no means in favor of just any kind of work. Unlike Samuel Barmby, in *In the Year of Jubilee* . . . , Gissing did discriminate between Matthew Arnold and Samuel Smiles.

Frequently, he sets his weak-willed idealists against energetic, coarsely practical men: Egremont and James Dalmaine; Reardon and Milvain; Otway and Arnold Jacks. Where the stronger, more practical character is morally approved of by the author, he is usually an artist or an intellectual: consider Waymark, Gabriel, and Earwaker, contrasted with Julian Casti, Kingcote, and Peak. The vigorous Mallard, we remember, was an artist. If Gissing was indebted to Schopenhauer, he could certainly find sanction in this philosophy, within an acceptance of pessimism, for some kinds of strenuous effort.

But this, of course, is a rather large *if;* there is surely a difference between affinity of outlook and positive indebtedness. It seems as unlikely that Gissing needed Schopenhauer to license his belief in artistic work as that his encounter with the German philosopher was what caused his pessimism. In any case, Gissing did not, in his fiction, consistently endorse Schopenhaurian beliefs. He was deeply ambivalent about renunciation—the possibility or the desirability of "the calm of achieved indifference." . . . As a great deal of his fiction indicates, particularly *The Crown of Life,* Gissing, unlike Schopenhauer, continued to believe that sexual passion could find an ideal fulfillment.

The alternative explanation of the paradox invokes Gissing's own temperament—or, rather, the effects on his personality of his early experiences. Perhaps the answer, like so much in this author, goes back to the Manchester episode—the theft, the imprisonment, the disillusion, the killing of his scholarly career. Up to this point, his whole being was tuned to academic attainment. After it, his imagination was split. Part of his mind was, I suggest, burnt with a permanent disenchantment: what could be hoped for a world in which everything, one's entire edifice of aspiration, could be shattered by a single blow? But another part of him—understandably—could not so readily surrender hope. His single ambition had always been to gain distinction by work and study. Now he would have to work even harder; now he would have to make up for his error by superhuman toil. In this respect the pattern of *Workers* was the pattern of Gissing himself. "If it be true," he wrote in his Commonplace Book, "that the English national characteristic is to act without foresight, & then make up for the negligence by vigour and capability—what an Englishman I am!" Whether or not it were true of the English, it was certainly true of Gissing. He saw himself as one who was locked in a fight against almost impossible odds. Reviewing his life for Gabrielle, he addressed himself in just these terms: "Consider the story of your life. You began with nothing whatever but a good education. You were self-willed, passionate, foolish, and for years it seemed as if there could be no future for you. Nevertheless, by dint of hard work, you slowly, slowly, made your way in literature." . . . He was justly proud of his resolute strength. "Heavens, how I laboured in those days!" he recalled wistfully in *Henry Ryecroft.* . . . And surely, he thought, it demonstrated the power of his will: his sufferings, as he twice said to Gabrielle, "would have killed a weaker man." . . . And yet . . . the cause of his first great mistake, and of later mistakes like his devastating marriages—could that be called will power, or something else? Gissing was aware of the oddity here. "Dear," he wrote consolingly to Gabrielle, "whenever you are uneasy about my health, remember that I have a very strong *will*"— but he added, in parentheses, "in one way." . . . The point was, as everyone who knew him insisted, and as he himself was ready to admit, that Gissing's will was well developed only as a faculty of dogged perseverance. In terms of stability, of "rational self-guidance" . . . , he was, as he knew, disas-

trously weak. That is why his books extol application and dread indecisiveness.

There is no sound evidence that Gissing was a pessimist before the catastrophe at Owens College. After that explosion, his world was darkened; and though he looked for light in his powers of endurance, his gloom was thickened by a fear that his character was poisoned by some obscure weakness. He toiled on, to counteract his dark depression, but excessive toil only made him more depressed. He accepted suffering as inevitable, but continued silently to subsist on hope. He tried to believe in the human spirit; but no one ever had a sharper sense of the forces that conspire against it. Gissing, in short, believed simultaneously in determinism and determination. In *The Unclassed* Osmond Waymark expounds two allegories which, he says, define Pessimism and Optimism. The first, that of Adam and Christ, recommends pious "abnegation" and a total "denial" of life. The second, that of Prometheus, celebrates "prowess" and "aspiration," the triumph of man by "assertion" and "strength." Waymark seems clearly to favor the second, but a few lines later he becomes fatalistic: "I know that I could not have acted otherwise than I did in any juncture of my life; I know that the future is beyond my control." . . . The same split allegiance afflicted Gissing; it became a central paradox throughout his work. As readers, we have to decide for ourselves which aspect of the paradox we want to stress. We may see the work as a mournful monument to a man who, whatever his struggles and yearnings, was convinced that all effort was ultimately doomed. On the other hand, impressed by its advocacy of will power, we may prefer to dwell upon the courage of the author, to marvel at his battered but unquenchable vitality—to suspect, in fact, with Austin Harrison, that "Gissing, the sad man, had the zest of life." . . . (pp. 81-4)

David Grylls, "Determinism and Determination in Gissing," in Modern Language Quarterly, *Vol. 45, No. 1, March, 1984, pp. 61-84.*

ADDITIONAL BIBLIOGRAPHY

Auerbach, Nina. "Beyond the Self: The Spectacle of History and a New Religion." In her *Communities of Women,* pp. 115-57. Cambridge: Harvard University Press, 1978.
    Discusses *The Odd Women* and its portrayal of relations among women.

Buckley, Jerome H. "A World of Literature: Gissing's *New Grub Street.*" In *The Worlds of Victorian Fiction,* edited by Jerome H. Buckley, pp. 223-34. Cambridge: Harvard University Press, 1975.
    Discusses Gissing's recreation of the Victorian literary world in *New Grub Street.*

Burrell, Angus. "George Gissing: Release through Fiction?" In *Modern Fiction,* pp. 18-39. New York: Columbia University Press, 1934.
    Considers the relation between Gissing's life and his novels.

Chase, Karen. "The Literal Heroine: A Study of Gissing's *The Odd Women.*" *Criticism* XXVI, No. 3 (Summer 1984): 231-44.
    Suggests that while Gissing's personal attitude toward women is not discernible from his fiction, he "was situated in such a fashion, situated historically, economically, personally, that he was able to raise new possibilities for the Victorian heroine."

Collie, Michael. *George Gissing: A Biography.* Folkestone, England: William Dawson and Sons, 1977, 189 p.
    Biography which concentrates on the relationship between Gissing's life and his work.

———. *George Gissing: A Bibliographical Study*. Winchester, England: St. Paul's Bibliographies, 1985, 167 p.
Comprehensive information regarding the composition, sale, and publication of Gissing's works, including the locations of extant manuscripts.

Coustillas, Pierre, ed. *Collected Articles on George Gissing*. London: Frank Cass, 1968, 186 p.
Collection of significant essays by prominent critics and Gissing scholars.

Coustillas, Pierre and Partridge, Colin, eds. *Gissing: The Critical Heritage*. London: Routledge and Kegan Paul, 1972, 564 p.
Reprints criticism of Gissing's work from 1880 through 1912.

Davis, Oswald H. *George Gissing: A Study in Literary Leanings*. London: Johnson, 1966, 109 p.
A personal approach to Gissing's works.

Donnelly, Mabel Collins. *George Gissing: Grave Comedian*. Cambridge: Harvard University Press, 1954, 245 p.
Critical biography.

Frye, Lowell. "An Author at Grass: Ironic Intent in Gissing's *The Private Papers of Henry Ryecroft*." *English Literature in Transition* 24, No. 1 (1981): 41-51.
Considers purely fictional aspects of *Ryecroft*.

Gettmann, Royal A., ed. *George Gissing and H. G. Wells*. Urbana: University of Illinois Press, 1961, 285 p.
Includes a lengthy introductory essay by Gettmann, correspondence, and several critiques of Gissing's work written by Wells.

Goode, John. "Gissing, Morris, and English Socialism." *Victorian Studies* XII, No. 2 (December 1968): 201-26.
Discusses the ways in which *Demos* exemplifies nineteenth-century perceptions of socialism.

———. *George Gissing: Ideology and Fiction*. London: Vision, 1978, 205 p.
Thorough analysis of Gissing's work.

Grylls, David. *The Paradox of Gissing*. London: Allen and Unwin, 1986, 226 p.
Considers Gissing's *oeuvre* as a "persistently self-cancelling pattern," characterized by a continual repudiation of former values.

Halperin, John. *Gissing: A Life in Books*. Oxford: Oxford University Press, 1982, 426 p.
Comprehensive critical biography.

Harris, W. V. "An Approach to Gissing's Short Stories." *Studies in Short Fiction* II, No. 1 (Fall 1964): 137-44.
Maintains that Gissing's short stories are generally more optimistic in outlook than are his novels.

Hassam, Andrew. "The Oscillating Text: A Reading of *The Private Papers of Henry Ryecroft*." *English Literature in Transition* 28, No. 1 (1985): 30-40.
Maintains that "in *Ryecroft* the correspondences with Gissing's own 'private papers' (his diaries, the commonplace book, his letters) are so close and so extensive as to produce in the reader an uncertainty about the actual status of *Ryecroft* as fiction."

Jameson, Frederic. "Authentic *Ressentiment:* The 'Experimental' Novels of Gissing." *Nineteenth Century Fiction* 31, No. 2 (September 1977): 127-49.

Discusses the early novels in terms of Gissing's personal sociopolitical ideology.

Kennard, Jean E. "Her Transitory Self." In her *Victims of Convention*, pp. 136-57. Hamden, Conn.: Archon, 1978.
Discusses *The Odd Women* as a pro-feminist argument.

Korg, Jacob. *George Gissing: A Critical Biography*. Seattle: University of Washington Press, 1963, 305 p.
Critical biography which is considered definitive.

Lelchuk, Alan. "*Demos:* The Ordeal of the Two Gissings." *Victorian Studies* XII, No. 3 (March 1969): 357-74.
Analyzes political statements implicit in *Demos*.

Lesser, Wendy. "Even-Handed Oddness: George Gissing's *The Odd Women*." *The Hudson Review* XXXVII, No. 2 (Summer 1984): 209-20.
Maintains that *The Odd Women*, upon close examination, reveals neither a pro-feminist nor an anti-feminist sympathy.

Markow, Alice B. "George Gissing: Advocate or Provocateur of the Women's Movement?" *English Literature in Transition* 25, No. 2 (1982): 58-73.
Argues that in Gissing's fiction "where an apparent advocacy of women's rights is discernible, it will be discovered to be nominal only; and that he deliberately set up situations that would disclose the basic, often biological, inequality of women."

Poole, Adrian. *Gissing in Context*. Totowa, N.J.: Rowman and Littlefield, 1975, 231 p.
Comprehensive discussions of all Gissing's work in the context of late nineteenth- and early twentieth-century literature.

Roberts, Morley. *The Private Life of Henry Maitland*. London: Nash, 1912, 319 p.
An early, highly fictionalized biography written by a close friend.

Sichel, Edith. "Two Philanthropic Novelists: Mr. Walter Besant and Mr. George Gissing." *Murray's Magazine* III, No. XVI (April 1888): 506-18.
One of the earliest discussions of Gissing's work. Sichel concludes "It is a diseased truth which he gives us, devoid of sweetness and devoid of faith and hope."

Sloan, John. "The Worthy Seducer: A Motif under Stress in George Gissing's *In the Year of Jubilee*." *English Literature in Transition* 28, No. 4 (1985): 354-65.
Maintains that Gissing's treatment of sexual seduction in his novels reveals the literary and political conservatism to which he ultimately reverted.

Swinnerton, Frank. *George Gissing: A Critical Study*. 1923. Reprint. Port Washington, N.Y.: Kennikat Press, 1966, 200 p.
The first book-length critical study of Gissing's works.

Tindall, Gillian. *The Born Exile*. London: Temple Smith, 1974, 295 p.
Critical biography.

Ward, A. C. *Gissing*. London: Longman's, 1959, 43 p.
Brief monograph intended as an inroduction to Gissing.

Watt, George. "Ida Starr." In his *The Fallen Woman in the Nineteenth-Century English Novel*, pp. 119-46. London: Croom Helm, 1984.
Discusses biographical aspects of *The Unclassed*.

Waugh, Arthur. "George Gissing." *The Fortnightly Review* LXXV (February 1904): 244-56.
Biographical essay which provides a general assessment of Gissing's work.

Frank Harris

1856-1931

(Pseudonym of James Thomas Harris) Anglo-Irish novelist, short story writer, biographer, dramatist, journalist, and critic.

One of the most colorful figures in twentieth-century literature, Harris was a writer and editor whose career was distinguished by frequent and vigorous controversy. The accuracy of his biographical works, including his two-volume study of the life of Oscar Wilde, has been vehemently contested, while his lengthy autobiography, *My Life and Loves,* depicts sexual encounters so graphically that it has often been denounced as pornographic. Harris's fiction, written in a journalistic style which approximates that of literary realism, also portrays aspects of human existence in a forthright manner, but the focus of these works is primarily social rather than sexual. During the early years of this century, Harris exerted enormous influence in London literary society and was instrumental in launching the careers of many young writers, including H. G. Wells and Bernard Shaw. His power, however, was directly related to his affiliations with respected literary journals of the day, and when those connections were severed, his prestige waned dramatically.

In his 1959 biography of Harris, Vincent Brome wrote: "Frank Harris was born in two different countries on three different dates and his name was not Frank Harris," reflecting the fact that Harris's origins were for many years unclear. Recent biographers, however, have unearthed much information regarding his background and have thus been able to construct a reliable account to compare with Harris's own, which has long been suspect. Born in Galway, Ireland, Harris was the son of a Welsh coastguard steward assigned to patrol the Irish coast in search of smugglers. Harris's mother died when he was about three years old, and commentators believe that the early loss of maternal attention was a significant factor in Harris's morbidly insecure personality. Although it is known that he was sent away to school in the north of England when he was thirteen, allegedly in an attempt to subvert the Irish Republican sympathies he had developed, the events of the period which followed his departure from the school two years later remain somewhat obscure. Harris claimed that he won an academic prize and that he used the money to buy passage to America, where he worked as a hotel clerk, cowboy, cattle thief, and reporter, studied law, and became acquainted with Walt Whitman and Ralph Waldo Emerson, among others. Records show that he did in fact study at the University of Kansas in Lawrence, passing the bar examination in 1875, but that he spent much of his time in America working in the butcher shop he owned with his brother William. One point upon which Harris and his biographers do agree is the crucial role played by Professor Byron Caldwell Smith, a brilliant young classical scholar, in Harris's development: inspired by Smith's lectures, Harris decided to educate himself for a literary career, and he accordingly traveled to Europe, where he believed such knowledge was best acquired.

Harris enrolled at the University of Heidelberg in 1878, but his attendance was sporadic at best, and within a year he was ejected from the university for brawling. After touring Europe for three years he settled in London, where he hoped to secure

a position with one of the city's prestigious literary journals. Although Harris's first efforts were unsuccessful, he was able to obtain occasional writing assignments for the *Spectator* and the *Fortnightly Review,* and his persistence and talent soon earned for him an opportunity which determined the course of his career. Sometime in 1885 Harris was offered the editorship of the *Evening News,* a daily publication which had fallen into a precarious financial state, with the stipulation that he significantly and quickly improve the paper's economic situation. Through wise management and clever editorial policies, not excluding such ethically questionable practices as printing the intimate details of a current scandal, Harris was able to revitalize the *Evening News* and markedly increase its circulation. His reputation as a successful editor thus established, Harris left the *Evening News* after one year to assume editorship of the much more prestigious *Fortnightly.*

As head of a respected literary review, Harris automatically became one of the most influential figures in London society, with the power to arrange for or prevent the publication of literary works, and it is this fact that led to his claim to have discovered nearly every important writer of the period. The *Fortnightly* did publish the work of many of the decade's finest writers, but as time passed its pages were increasingly given over to articles on the social and political issues that most interested Harris, with the editorial content of the paper acquiring a socialist perspective that brought Harris into conflict with the paper's conservative directors. In addition, as Harris revelled more and more in his higher social position, entertaining artists and nobility in what one acquaintance called "baronial hall" fashion, he became less conscientious about his editorial duties, and these were eventually delegated to less competent subordinates. H. G. Wells, in his autobiography, describes the situation which ensued: "The directors of the *Fortnightly* became restive and interfering. [Harris] began to drink heavily and to shout louder as the penalties of loud shouting closed in on him." Finally, in September of 1894, Harris was dismissed from the paper.

However, he was not long unemployed. Having married an extremely wealthy woman, Harris now had a large income at his disposal, and he used this to purchase the important but ailing *Saturday Review* in October of that same year. In her biography of Harris, Phillipa Pullar explains that "his aim was to furnish the *Saturday* with as efficient and talented a staff as possible with a view to constructive rather than destructive criticism." Observers agree that Harris was quite successful in achieving this aim and that his direction of the *Saturday Review* represents the zenith of his long career. With Bernard Shaw as drama critic, John Runciman as music critic, and H. G. Wells as literary critic, Harris's review quickly became the most highly esteemed of London's many literary journals. Yet Harris's bombastic demeanor earned him enemies even as his influence was at its peak. An often repeated anecdote holds that Oscar Wilde replied to Harris's claim that he had been invited to every great house in London: "Yes, Frank, but only once." Wilde's implication that Harris was not well liked is echoed by others among Harris's contemporaries, and Bernard Shaw, in a letter to Harris, attempted to explain that his abrasive comportment had made him persona non grata in many circles.

Soon after he purchased the *Saturday Review,* Harris published his first work of fiction, *Elder Conklin, and Other Stories,* written between 1891 and 1894 during vacations in the south of France. Based upon his observations of America and set in the American West, the stories in this volume reflect Harris's journalistic background in their simple narrative style and their realistic treatment of subject matter. Realism, however, was not entirely accepted as a legitimate literary genre in 1895, and some critics were shocked by Harris's candid depictions of human existence. Nevertheless, many critics praised *Elder Conklin* and predicted a great future for its author. His time largely taken up with editorial duties, Harris did not publish another volume of stories until 1900, when *Montes the Matador, and Other Stories* appeared, although in 1899 he did write a play based on an idea sold to him by Wilde and entitled *Mr. and Mrs. Daventry.* While this play enjoyed a long and fairly successful run on the London stage, critics agree that drama was not the best vehicle for Harris's talents, and *Mr. and Mrs. Daventry* was the only one of Harris's three plays ever to be performed.

As with the *Fortnightly,* Harris eventually began to neglect the *Saturday Review* in favor of travel and entertainment, and his practices soon placed him in dire financial straits. In 1898, having left his wealthy wife, Harris was forced to sell the *Review* in order to resolve his debts, but the money from the sale was soon lost through unwise investment and uncontrolled spending. His subsequent editorship of several inferior journals brought him frequent libel suits, diminishing prestige, and little income. Harris therefore turned to fiction at the age of forty-

two not only as an outlet for his creativity, but also as his most promising source of income. Encouraged by the favorable reception accorded *Montes the Matador,* he produced several more volumes of short stories and four undistinguished novels. *The Bomb,* generally considered Harris's best novel, is a fictionalized account of the events surrounding the Haymarket Riot, which occurred in Chicago in 1886 when a bomb exploded during a labor protest, killing several protestors and policemen. While *The Bomb,* was largely well received, several critics pointed out that Harris had taken the concept of realism a step too far, using in his novel verbatim accounts from newspaper reports of the incident.

In 1909 Harris published *The Man Shakespeare and His Tragic Life Story,* a critical work in which he attempted to construct a more complete picture of the playwright's obscure private life. Through analysis of Shakespeare's central characters, Harris claimed to ascertain clear and recurrent statements of pessimism and sexual frustration, which he then correlated with the few known facts of Shakespeare's life. His conclusions pertained primarily to the playwright's relations with women and include the assertion that Shakespeare's wife was a disagreeable woman and that his statements of love were directed to his mistress. Reviews of *The Man Shakespeare* were mixed; while some critics applauded Harris for contributing to the world's appreciation of Shakespeare, others took great exception to his biographical hypotheses. Many agreed with Hugh Kingsmill's contention that "the faults of Harris's portrait of Shakespeare are due to two causes: a too complete identification of himself and Shakespeare up to a point, and, beyond that point, a too frequent anxiety to mark Shakespeare's inferiority to himself." Reviews of *The Women of Shakespeare,* published as a companion piece three years later, were almost entirely negative.

Harris is best known for his biographical and autobiographical works. The first of these, *Contemporary Portraits,* was published in 1915 and contains short biographical sketches and accounts of Harris's meetings with well-known artists, writers, and politicians. Yet critics note that while it is clear that Harris knew many renowned figures, he did not in fact know all of those he portrayed and did not know most of them as well as he claimed. Shaw called the accounts "very rapid impressionist sketches" and pronounced their author "the most impossible of biographers." The most controversial aspects of the *Contemporary Portraits* were not, however, the author's falsifications, but his frequent allegations regarding the sexual proclivities and abberations of his subjects. Nevertheless, many critics, unaware of or unconcerned with factual inaccuracies, praised this work as a brilliant and vivid piece of writing, and Harris subsequently published four more volumes of portraits. Harris's controversial biography of Oscar Wilde, with whom he was in fact well acquainted, contains similar inaccuracies, and these have been brought to light by Wilde's more recent biographers.

From the early days of their friendship, Shaw encouraged Harris to write an autobiography, believing that Harris was at his best when discussing himself, and in 1921 Harris decided to follow the dramatist's advice. Living in the south of France, Harris began work on what became an extremely lengthy and detailed account of his life. The result was dramatically different from what Shaw had envisioned, for Harris, in addition to repeating the now-infamous stories of his adventures, had also included explicit accounts of sexual experiences related in a highly colloquial manner. Shaw immediately denounced the work, while Harris, unable to find a British or American publisher willing to risk imprisonment, was forced to pay for its printing and to sell copies from his home. When copies of the work did become available, critics were shocked not only by the sexual content of the book, but also by what Oscar Cargill called its "elephantine seriousness." In a letter to Harris, Shaw wrote, "I told you what was missing in your life of Oscar Wilde was the figure of Frank Harris the buccaneer. A faint scrap of St. Francis of Assisi was perceptible, but nothing else. In a life of Frank Harris this defect is more serious. . . ."

Despite constant productivity, Harris was never quite able to earn sufficient income from his writings, and his final years were spent in a constant struggle for funds. Thinking that his long acquaintance with the highly-esteemed Shaw might provide a valuable literary commodity, Harris wrote to the dramatist in 1930 asking permission to write an authorized biograpy. Shaw, knowing Harris's penchant for scandalous manufactured revelations, refused, but later relented when the full extent of Harris's disastrous financial and physical conditions were made clear to him. Indeed, Frank Scully, hired as Harris's ghost writer for the project, claims that Harris was by this time much too ill to do any work, and that it was in fact Scully who wrote *Frank Harris on Bernard Shaw*. In any case, Harris died in 1931, before the book had been published, and Shaw himself edited, emended, and wrote an introduction for the finished manuscript.

Critical estimates of Harris's work vary widely and display a marked evolution. Early in his career Harris was generally esteemed as a talented writer, and it was only after the publication of his later, sexually-oriented works that critics began to question his motives and his work. During the decade following his death, as the full extent of Harris's biographical and autobiographical fabrications became apparent, his reputation reached its nadir. Writing in 1937, Robert Sherard maintained that "when one approaches Frank Harris, or his concerns, one becomes swathed in a miasma of mendacity and every single statement of his, one realizes, has to be regarded with suspicion." Later, when Harris's fiction was overshadowed by the work of other realistic writers and his subjective style of criticism was superseded by more modern methods, his censured works became the subject of renewed interest and the core of his critical importance. While Elmer Gertz today contends that Harris's short stories represent his finest work, many contemporary critics find his talents best revealed in precisely those works which had originally destroyed his reputation: *Contemporary Portraits,* the biography of Wilde, and *My Life and Loves*. Contending that the question of historical accuracy is irrelevant, such critics maintain that these works are important not because of what they purport to reveal about famous personalities, but because of what they unconsciously reveal about Harris himself. In addition, many point to the vivid prose style employed in his reminiscences but absent from his fiction. As a result, Harris is remembered today primarily as a talented if unreliable raconteur and as the creator of entertaining, anecdotal works which cleverly depict the artistic life of Edwardian London.

(See also *Contemporary Authors,* Vol. 109.)

PRINCIPAL WORKS

Elder Conklin, and Other Stories   (short stories)   1894
Mr. and Mrs. Daventry   (drama)   1899
How to Beat the Boer: A Conversation in Hades
   (nonfiction)   1900
Montes the Matador, and Other Stories   (short stories)
   1900
The Bomb   (novel)   1908
The Man Shakespeare and His Tragic Life Story   (criticism)
   1909
The Women of Shakespeare   (criticism)   1912
Unpath'd Waters   (short stories)   1913
Great Days   (novel)   1914
The Yellow Ticket, and Other Stories   (short stories)   1914
Contemporary Portraits. 4 vols.   (biographical sketches)
   1915-24
England or Germany?   (essays)   1915
Love in Youth   (novel)   1916
Oscar Wilde: His Life and Confessions. 2 vols.
   (biography)   1916
My Life and Loves. 4 vols.   (autobiography)   1922-29
Undream'd of Shores   (short stories)   1924
Latest Contemporary Portraits   (biographical sketches)
   1927
Confessional   (essays)   1930
On the Trail: Being My Reminiscences as a Cowboy
   (fictionalized autobiography)   1930
Pantopia   (novel)   1930
*Frank Harris on Bernard Shaw [with Frank Scully]
   (biography)   1931

*Authorship of this work remains a matter of dispute. Although Harris's name appears as author, Frank Scully claimed to have written the book without Harris's aid.

THE ATHENAEUM   (essay date 1894)

[*In the following review of* Elder Conklin, and Other Stories, *the critic discusses the strengths and weaknesses of Harris's prose, presenting a generally favorable assessment.*]

[*Elder Conklin, and Other Stories*] is a remarkable little book. To declare of it that it is the sort of book Guy de Maupassant might have written, had he been an Englishman, and had he spent the most impressionable years of his life in the Western States instead of in Brittany, unfortunately only takes us but a short way, for Maupassant was a Frenchman, and the distinction is vital. In France the tradition of a first-rate prose style is so vigorous that no writer of eminence can escape it. Sainte-Beuve praises, and praises justly, the prose of his nation as its supreme literary gift—"cette netteté remarquable d'exécution" ["this remarkable cleanness of execution"], as he says, whose strength lies in its lucidity and whose charm is beyond words. Mr. Frank Harris, who most obviously regards his work as a story-teller with extreme seriousness (the *limæ labor* is manifest again and again in this republished and selected collection), starts with the yet further disadvantage of a journalistic training in the handling of English prose. Of style as style he possesses little, and there is not the slightest apparent effort to attain to it. Whether from choice or necessity, he throws all purely literary uses aside, and stakes everything on the story and the characterization. His own personality counts for nothing, and it is difficult to tell from anything he has written what are his likes and dislikes, or how he looks upon this thing or on that. He covers a large portion of ground which has been covered (alas! too frequently and too effusively) by

Mr. Bret Harte, but the contrast is striking. Half of the pleasure to be found in the best and most characteristic work of the American lies in its charming subjectivity, in the constant play over the surface of the story of the delicate individual criticism of the writer. The same is true of Mr. Rudyard Kipling, who has done for Anglo-India a similar service. Yet so far as they concern Mr. Harris, whether in regard to similarity of subject or method of treatment, they might never have written at all. If we seek his conclusions on the life which he portrays, we must seek them in nothing less than the whole tendency of his work. Most of Mr. Bret Harte's Western Americans, in this respect evincing their unmistakable parentage, are somewhat too keenly aware of themselves. They know far too much about the point of view of Boston and New York, having even a vague intuition of that of London and Europe. Mr. Harris's Western Americans exist absolutely for and in themselves. They are devoid of the sense of cosmopolitan humour. They are ferocious in their provincialism, and quite blind to all social criteria but their own. Only once (in the title story) does a typical representative of the typical Eastern States intrude his dubious presence, and he brings no illumination with him. Mr. Harris would seem to wish to say his say concerning the land west of the Mississippi, and the people who inhabit that land, with the smallest possible foreign admixture, and even that only for the sake of contrast. The result is a picture as unlovely and barbaric as it is powerful and convincing. The sincerity of the work, its sombre insistence, its simplicity, give it an actuality which at times is painful. The men and women live and move and have their being with that sort of aching, overcharged emotionalism which we experience only for ourselves or others in moments of the keenest mental tension. Balzac, no doubt, could have drawn such a figure as Elder Conklin—so stonily pathetic, so hopelessly repellent in its tearless agony of bewildered frustration. To have put beside him such an incarnation of healthy, youthful, and lovely feminine animality as his daughter Loo is, indeed, a triumph in creative workmanship. The same sure hand presides over a little gallery of Western American girls, passing by grades of ascension into the two fair students who are rivals for the one really civilized and attractive male character who appears in all these stories. Of him, moreover (the Professor in **"Gulmore the Boss"**), "these States," in Whitman's claptrap phrase—or at any rate these Western States—very soon prove not only their desire but their capacity to promptly and finally get rid. The one other lovable character, Charlie Muirhead, the miner, is buried within a week of his arrival, though it is just to add that this was largely his own fault, since he had had full warning of the social usages of the place. As what the journalists love to call an indictment of the American civilization or sub-civilization, that social stage over the savage aspects of which Mr. Bret Harte has cast so illusive a glamour—the soullessly materialistic side of which Mr. Frank Harris is the first to present to our literature—this book is a stumbling-block for every believer in Transatlantic democracy. This, however, is Mr. Harris's first effort, at least as a story-teller, and is very unlikely to be his last; and in his next one we may perhaps hope to have work somewhat less remorselessly impartial, less scientifically realistic, less limited by what at heart seems the embitterment of disillusion. (pp. 785-86)

A review of "Elder Conklin, and Other Stories," in The Athenaeum, *No. 3502, December 8, 1894, pp. 785-86.*

THE NATION (essay date 1895)

[*In the following review of* Elder Conklin, and Other Stories, *the critic condemns both the style and content of most of the stories in the collection.*]

In Mr. Harris's volume of short stories entitled *Elder Conklin,* the sketch **"Gulmore the Boss"** is a very probable representation of the mischievous creature with the results of whose machinations we are painfully familiar. Still, he might have been drawn from hearsay or newspaper reports; there is no evidence that he was confronted in his den and studied from the life. The ingenuousness of Prof. Roberts, who undertakes to rout Gulmore and his gang, is surprising, but not unprecedented, and the characteristic means employed by Gulmore to teach the professor a lesson in practical politics, incidentally including points on human nature, suggest many actual parallels. Undoubtedly bad bosses could never be got rid of if the task were wholly relegated to gentlemen armed only with a knowledge of the classics and with good intentions.

The rest of Mr. Harris's stories conjure up horrid images of society in the State of Kansas. It is as if all the desperadoes of the West had been gathered together for a dance from which only one escaped to tell the tale. We fear that Mr. Harris lent too credulous an ear, sadly misunderstood the humor of that sole survivor of a Kansas holiday, and very grossly mistook his crude attempt to convey an impression of the unconventional fascinations of the prairie maiden. Mr. Harris has added to the probably natural rudeness and vulgarity of an Ida Gulmore or Loo Conklin an unblushing sensuality which no competent critic, however hostile, has ever before attributed to otherwise similar characters. Mrs. Hooper, in **"A Modern Idyll,"** is even more objectionable, and, in view of the conditions assumed, more absurd. So repulsive a pair as she and her lover, the Rev. John Letgood, rarely appear in print. The excuse which narrators of such modern idyls make to themselves is very well known, and it is always based on the conviction that they have perfectly performed an imperative duty to render in fiction the basest facts of life and the most revolting possibilities of character. Mr. Harris's strenuous effort to fulfil this duty fails ludicrously, and that is the reason why his story is not so bad as it might be.

A review of "Elder Conklin, and Other Stories," in The Nation, *New York, Vol. LX, No. 1541, January 10, 1895, p. 32.*

MAX BEERBOHM (essay date 1900)

[*Although he lived until 1956, Beerbohm is chiefly associated with the fin de siècle period in English literature, more specifically with its lighter phases of witty sophistication and mannered elegance. His temperament was urbane and satirical, and he excelled in both literary and artistic caricatures of his contemporaries. "Entertaining" in the most complimentary sense of the word, Beerbohm's criticism for the* Saturday Review—*where he was a long-time drama critic—everywhere indicates his scrupulously developed taste and unpretentious, fair-minded response to literature. Beerbohm was one of Harris's few lifelong friends, although he was occasionally outraged by his former editor's behavior. In the following excerpt, Beerbohm discusses Harris's dramatic technique and psychological portraiture in* Mr. and Mrs. Daventry.]

To what shall I liken this entry? I need a staggering metaphor. Mr. Meredith, only he, could find one for me—one of those monstrous blossoms which he uproots from gardens so remote.

His wit would fly off in quest, Puck-like, putting "a girdle round about the earth," and anon the far-fetched herb would be to hand. None but he could provide the necessary article. Inalienable is his genius for metaphors which, seeming, at first flash, merely far-fetched, are truly, as one sees a moment later, fitted with minute precision to their purposes. For ordinary occasions ordinary metaphors will serve. But now and again one envies Mr. Meredith his inspiration. Vainly I have quested, since the first night of *Mr. and Mrs. Daventry,* for a metaphor adequate. I return crestfallen. I can but offer to you the obvious old figure which I had rejected—the bull in the china-shop. This poor beast has been overworked so shamefully, for so many years, by so many drovers, that now, perhaps, he scarcely signifies a surprising and destructive energy. But he is all I can offer. Horns to the floor, hoofs in the air, tail a-whirl, the unkindly creature charges furiously hither and thither, and snap! crash! bang! into flying smithereens goes the crockery of dramatic laws and conventions, while the public lies quailing under the counter.

A noble, uncomfortable sight! Never did a dramatist play such havoc with what one is accustomed to hold sacred as does the author of what Mrs. Campbell has dared to produce at the Royalty Theatre. The first act of the play contains nothing relevant at all, except a few meagre hints of character to come. The curtain falls on a soliloquy in which these hints are recapitulated. A soliloquy is bad enough (to modern ears) even when it tells us something we did not know. But a soliloquy for the summing up of our knowledge! Mr. Harris revels in such soliloquies. At the end of the second act, Mrs. Campbell is again explaining to us what we perfectly understand. Can it be that Mr. Harris has a sentiment for the rococo? No, obviously, he does but wish, in his wantonness, to wound us. He stands there . . . , determined to have his horns through all our sacred prejudices, be they ancient or modern. We have a modern prejudice against irrelevant comic servants in serious plays? "Very well then," snorts Mr. Harris, with an ominous glare in his eyes. And forthwith he throws into his second act a comic English cook, into his third act a comic Irish valet, into his fourth act a comic German waiter. We expect the great excitement of a play to be kept till we are near the end of the third act? Accordingly, Mr. Harris drops his climax plump into the middle of his second act. When a good, unhappily-married lady is loved by a good man, we expect that he, not she, shall press for the elopement? Accordingly, Mrs. Daventry presses for the elopement, quite of her own accord. When the good lover is told by his valet that the bad husband has arrived unexpectedly, and asks the lady to retire to an inner room till her husband shall have taken his leave, we expect some variation on the "screen scene"? Nothing of the sort, accordingly, happens. The husband, in due course, takes his leave. The lady emerges and resumes the thread of her discourse. When the runaway pair is living in guilty comfort at Monte Carlo, and the bad husband wishes to put a bullet through the head of his supplanter, we do not expect him to put the bullet through his own head? Of course not. So he proceeds to do it.

You will observe that the prejudices gored by Mr. Harris are of two kinds; some are technical, others psychological. Some of our technical prejudices he ought, I think, to have spared. There is a real and sound objection to soliloquies, for example: they are unnatural, they spoil illusion. Sometimes it must be very difficult for a dramatist to avoid them; but he must learn to overcome the difficulty whenever it occurs. to do so is an essential point in dramaturgy. I am no over-rater of technique.

I would far rather see a play by an interesting man of letters who has not mastered the tricks of stage-craft than a play by a man who has done nothing else. I would willingly sacrifice the whole life-work of (say) Mr. Sydney Grundy for *Mr. and Mrs. Daventry*. I regret very much that the tricks of stage-craft are so many and so difficult that many interesting men of letters are by them frightened away from dramaturgy. If modern drama were a loose and fluid form, like the Elizabethan drama, we should have a far finer class of playwrights. But the fact remains that modern drama is a very close and precise form, and that modern plays cannot be well written except with closeness and precision. These qualities can be acquired, through patient practice, by any man who has a natural sense of drama. No one who knows Mr. Harris as a writer of short stories (or, for that matter, as an editor) will deny his natural sense of drama. No one who has read "**Elder Conklin**" and other little perfect works will deny that he is a master in the exigent art of the *conte*. The *conte* has its peculiar, necessary tricks, its artistic conventions, as Mr. Harris would admit—tricks that must be acquired, conventions that are binding. I suggest to him that dramaturgy has some similar tricks and conventions. Let him not despise them. Let him not, when he writes his next play, go in for—especially not go out of his way to go in for—soliloquies. Let him eschew comic servants, who do but impede the action and set our emotions out of tune. (Let him imagine what would have been the effect of comic servants in "**Elder Conklin**"!) Let him begin his play at the beginning of the first act, as strictly as he begins his every story at its first line. Let him postpone his great scene to the end of the third . . . no! my pen was running away with me. In putting his great scene into the middle of his second act, Mr. Harris has flouted a convention which is not essential to drama. He was quite right to flout it, and I applaud his courage. I do but regret that he did no go even further back, that it was not put into the middle of his first act that he put his great scene. I call it the "great scene" because it is undoubtedly the most exciting. Taken by itself, it has all the appearance of a *scène-à-faire*. But, taken in relation to the rest of the play, it is merely a preparation, a means to an end. It is a circumstantial crisis, easily "led-up to," necessary in the production of certain psychological crises. It puts the two chief characters to the test, reveals them to each other and to us, and from it their future relations are evolved. Mrs. Daventry is a witness to the misbehaviour of her husband, and subsequently leaves him on account of it. In the meantime, she shields him from a scandal, and he is won over to her by the pride which makes her shield him, and by the pluck and resource with which she does it. On this scene the whole play hinges. And that fact is, by the way, the scene's justification against the furious onslaughts on its decency. That so stalwart a vexillary of public prudery as the critic of the *Daily Telegraph* should cry out against it, was, of course, quite inevitable. To him all things are impure. With him one does not argue. But Mr. Walkley, whose gay banner bears "common-sense" for its legend, has professed himself terribly shocked, and I cannot help asking why. If nothing came of the scene, if it were dragged in without any relevance to character, then, no doubt, we might be shocked to our hearts' content. But, as the scene is an integral part of a serious drama, we ought not to call attention to such blushes as may mantle to our cheeks at sight of a married man in a darkened room kissing a lady who is not his wife and locking the door of the room into which they have stolen. Such blushes may be creditable to us as men; but surely we ought not, as serious critics of serious art, to be proud of them. Pressed to a logical conclusion, Mr. Walkley

A caricature by Max Beerbohm. The caption reads: "The Best Talker in London, with one of his best listeners." Reproduced by permission of Eva Reichmann.

would have to deny a dramatist's right to present, in any circumstances, or even to hint at, anything but the domestic virtues. That is a position from which he would certainly be averse. He must forgive me for calling attention to the momentary eclipse of his common-sense. Were not that orb so steadily radiant at other times, I should have said nothing.

The character of Mr. Daventry is admirably drawn. It sets Mr. Harris very far above the level of ordinary dramatists, and does much to atone for his faults in technique. I know no other stage-study of the apolaustic "barbarian" that can match it. The man is not heartless, but merely heavy and unimaginative. All his faults spring from his circumstances and his absolue lack of imagination. Having married a sensitive girl, he kills her ideals not because he would not respect them if he could understand them, but simply because they are unintelligible to him. She shrinks into herself, and he becomes bored. "You're looking a bit pasty, Hilda," he complains, "you ought to brisk about more." He turns with relief to an intelligible lady, one of his own type. His lips are eager for *"les verres épais du cabaret brutal,"* ["the heavy glasses of the seamy tavern"], some less brittle vessel. Under the shock of his wife's salvation of him from an unpleasant scene with the lady's husband, he veers heavily round. At first, he merely bursts out laughing. "By Jove, Hilda, how you scored! You scored all along the line!" But gradually the force of the incident penetrates his pachydermatous soul. His sluggish imagination is stirred at last. He conceives a canine admiration and adoration of his wife. Nothing can cure him of it. Her flight inflames it. He makes clumsy efforts to induce her to return to him. He cannot imagine how she can stand not being respectable. "You, of *all* women," he cries, unimaginative to the last. Told by her that she is quite happy with her lover and still hates the sight of her husband, and that she is going to have a child, he abandons his intention of shooting the lover. He shoots himself. The critics all exclaim that this is an unlikely action. It is not so. It is subtly right. He shoots himself because he cannot bear the idea that his wife should live with a man who is not her husband. By suicide he opens for her the way to matrimony. Stupid to the last, he regards that as her salvation. The good that has been aroused in him culminates in an act of blundering self-sacrifice. He dies from lack of imagination. His death is as characteristic of him as is his every other action. Mr. Harris is to be congratulated on a perfect essay in psychology. There are many other good things in the play. But the character of Daventry is the dominating feature of it, putting all the others into the shade. *Mr. Daventry* the play should have been called, simply. (pp. 551-52)

Max Beerbohm, "Enter Mr. Frank Harris," in The Saturday Review, *London, Vol. 90, No. 2349, November 3, 1900, pp. 551-52.*

BERNARD SHAW (letter date 1900)

[Shaw is generally considered the greatest and best-known dramatist to write in the English language since Shakespeare. Following the example of Henrik Ibsen, he succeeded in revolutionizing the English stage, disposing of the romantic conventions and devices of the "well-made play," and instituting the theater of ideas, grounded in realism. During the late nineteenth century, Shaw was also a prominent literary, art, and music critic, and his reviews were known for their biting wit and brilliance. During his three years at the Saturday Review, *Shaw determined that the theater was meant to be a "moral institution" and "elucidator of social conduct." The standards he applied to drama were quite simple: Is the play like real life? Does it convey sensible, socially progressive ideas? Because most of the drama produced during the 1890s failed to approach these ideals, Shaw usually assumed a severely critical and satirical attitude toward his subjects. Although he later wrote criticism of poetry and fiction—much of it collected in* Pen Portraits and Reviews *(1932)—Shaw was out of sympathy with both of these genres. He had little use for poetry, believing it poorly suited for the expression of ideas, and in his criticism of fiction he rarely got beyond the search for ideology. As Samuel Hynes has noted, Shaw was driven by a rage to better the world. A Fabian socialist, he wrote criticism that was often concerned with the humanitarian and political intent of the work under discussion. Shaw was frequently shocked by Harris's personal and literary frankness, and while he scrupulously avoided public comment on his former editor's writings, he often provided critical comments in his letters to Harris. In the following excerpt from one such letter, Shaw gives his opinion of* Mr. and Mrs. Daventry. *For Harris's response to Shaw's comments, see the excerpt dated 1900.]*

The play [**Mr. and Mrs. Daventry**] is good, and successful (which is not always the same thing) in exact proportion as it is Frank Harris. Before the curtain went up George Moore informed me that I should see at a glance that the whole play was by Oscar Wilde. What I did see was that this was George's honest opinion, because you have undoubtedly amused yourself by writing some imaginary conversations on Wilde's lines; and George, who has no sense of humor, cannot see the underlying difference. Here I think you should not encourage yourself, because it is not natural to you to play with an idea in Wilde's way, and make people laugh by showing *its* absurdity: your notion of gambolling is to unexpectedly fix your teeth in the calf of some sinner and hold on. And you cannot help yourself out by observation in this instance, because English society is not in the least witty, and always runs curiously to see a wit like Wilde's exactly as it sits down eagerly to *look* at a man playing the piano. The fact is, life does not *amuse* you as it amuses the humorist. You perceive its ironies with a mordant sensation about the corners of your mouth that may feel like laughter; but when your teeth snap, they close, not on the irony, not even on the unfortunate mortal who is the subject of it, but on the spectator whom you are getting at. Please observe that this is a perfectly legitimate comedic operation when it is done in your own manner. But when it is done by one of the impossible drawingroom epigrammatists of the Wilde theatre, one feels at once that the fun is not real fun—it hurts; and that the epigrammarian ladies are figments. Wilde was careful to provide an ideal husband to keep them in countenance; the whole force of your play comes from the reality of the husband. This is what sets Max Beerbohm trying to express his feeling by the bull in the china shop [see excerpt dated 1900]. The prattling ladies are very like china shepherdesses trying to play up to a real shepherd. I speak feelingly on this point because we all make the same mistake at first; the more connoisseurship we start with, the more certain we are to begin with a mixture of genres—of those which have struck our fancy with that which is our original own. In the first version of my play I introduced a lot of funny trifling of the Robertson-to-Pinero comic relief kind. The effect was perfectly frightful—like patching a suit of armor with a cheap chintz. Now Wilde's manner is immeasurably nearer akin to the new manner than the old comic relief was: consequently your drawingroom conversations produce no such disastrously hideous effect as my japes did; and you have saved the situation further by pure style; but still the incongruity is there, and it will come through and shew on the surface in a few years time, through the difference in wear between the two genres.

Fortunately for you, the play is a real beginning. You have hardly dug a foot into the vein as yet. The husband's suicide is all my eye. What you must do now is to begin a sequel to the play as follows:—

The shot does not kill Daventry (I have known a man recover and live for a long time after shooting himself straight between the eyes and lodging the bullet in the back of his skull). He sends a hurried note to the pair apologizing for the failure and warning them not to marry until he has divorced the lady, as he has, on reflection, become too curious to see how their marriage will turn out to reshoot himself more efficiently. His point is, that the lady's claim, carefully examined, is only a claim to a fool's paradise, and that her charge against him is simply that he has confronted her with a view of life which prevailed over her's, in spite of her prejudice against it, because the facts supported it and contradicted her's. Her feeling that the millionaire has restored her ideals means that she has met a young fool like herself, with money enough to make love's young dream seem for a moment like a real paradise even in such a sink as Monte Carlo. Therefore, says Daventry, I am going to wait until you are forty and see how a woman of your sort comes out when her imaginative illusions are gone. Already I have shattered—with my pistol—your fundamental illusion that the vileness of the world is only the vileness of my view of it. Further, I have shattered your notion that I am a mere animal because I am intelligent enough to keep the animal in me separate from the rudimentary poet and philosopher, and that you have attained a higher place than I because you scrupulously confuse your consciousness of the impulses which led you to hunt down and capture your millionaire. As you admit, I am a better man than you thought. It seems a simple thing to say *now*; but when you are my present age you will perceive that this is no mere sentimental-magnanimous admission, but a sinking away of the entire moral continent from under your feet into the depths of the sea, leaving you buffeting the waves for a moral foothold. Your millionaire has shewn himself so far the perfect dupe of the morality which can only justify itself by my proving a villain because I have kissed a coarser woman than my wife. The hole in my head goes straight through that morality; and whenever you return to it I shall point to the scar as the saints in the pictures point to their stigmata. And so on.

On this basis you get your drama, ending either in redivorce and remarriage (which would be *my* ending) or a *ménage à trois* like the Nelson-Hamilton one, but on a fleshless basis. Moral: the one woman who should be sacred to a man is his wife. That is the true reductio ad absurdum of marriage.

If you go and sit out the play again you will find that the husband is the interesting person in it, and that it is strong whilst he is on a positive basis and weak whilst he is on an apologetic basis. As a rascal redeemed by an act of self-sacrifice he is not worth halfprice at nine o'clock. As a moralist claiming a real basis for morals, he is worth all the money and more. It is his instructive clutches at the positive position that give the play its drive. It is the lapses from this that land it among epigrams and duels and reverence for the pretty lady's ideals and the like anachronisms. Only make good your footing on the new moral ground and you will spout enthralling plays as profusely as Calderon for the next twenty years. You have swallowed more life than a thousand ordinary playwrights: what you want is a new philosophic digestion that will make bone and muscle of the realities which the old drama excreted, and excrete the sentimentalities which the old drama assimilated. This could be more briefly expressed, but not more elegantly. (pp. 5-8)

> *Bernard Shaw, in a letter to Frank Harris on November 4, 1900, in* The Playwright and the Pirate: Bernard Shaw and Frank Harris, A Correspondence, *edited by Stanley Weintraub, The Pennsylvania State University Press, University Park, 1982, pp. 5-9.*

FRANK HARRIS (letter date 1900)

[*In the following excerpt from a letter written to Bernard Shaw, Harris defends* Mr. and Mrs. Daventry *and provides his own estimate of its quality. For Shaw's original comments, see the excerpt dated 1900.*]

All you say about the difference between Wilde's beautiful kindly humour and my sardonic bitterness is absolutely true—or at least seems so to me. You think I imitated him in the first act [of **Mr. and Mrs. Daventry**], and perhaps I did—at any rate it is certain that the first act is the weakest of the lot. The second act I think is spoiled by bad stage management; but then all we novices have to suffer at the hands of the actor or actress who knows that a part is greater than the whole.

You think the shooting of Daventry all wrong; you dismiss it as contemptuously as Archer does. Well, here is my idea of it.

The decay of Christianity and the belief in a future life has had for chief consequences 1st the demand on the part of the people for a better life on this earth—socialism—and 2nd the demand by the other oppressed class, woman, for a larger satisfaction of her instincts in this world. This new woman wants nothing but love, whatever form she may individually affect, affection or passion. I have taken her to demand affection in this case. But this new woman has been done before. Quite true; and it remains to be seen whether Mrs Daventry is 5% better or 5% worse than the new woman that other dramatists in our time have created. But I am the first to put opposite this new woman the old conventional view of sexual morality which is the husband's view and which I have here incorporated in the husband Mr Daventry.

Now I have been more than fair to this old convention. So far from making him brutal I have allowed him to repent on the stage, promise reformation &c. in order to win your sympathies. Now how should he end? I maintain the old convention dies of its own falseness, kills itself, in fact, and that is what Daventry does. If you tell me that the individual man of this sort, Daventry, would not kill himself, I say you are mistaken. He is a man of forty who has had all the best of life. Almost for the first time he has failed. He has got himself into an impasse. It is your disappointed realist who does blow out his brains—not your idealist whose soul is wide enough to have sympathy for others.

But there I could discuss the matter for ever. The truth is that naked intelligence is no good in judging a work of art. A verdict of the public is—I mean the best public; and the opinion of the half dozen who do count—is that Mrs Daventry is a creation and Daventry about as good.

I am glad to be able to tell you that this view of the matter is borne out by the box office. (pp. 9-10)

> *Frank Harris, in a letter to Bernard Shaw on November 27, 1900, in* The Playwright and the Pirate: Bernard Shaw and Frank Harris, A Correspondence, *edited by Stanley Weintraub, The Pennsylvania State University Press, University Park, 1982, pp. 9-10.*

THE SATURDAY REVIEW, LONDON (essay date 1908)

[*In the following essay, the critic commends the realism and narrative simplicity of* The Bomb.]

Mr. Frank Harris is not author of many books. His brilliant, invasive mind has expressed itself mainly through journalism for the public and through talk for his friends. Were he merely a born talker and a born journalist, we should not regret his devotion to these forms that endure not. But he is also a born writer of fiction; and we cannot but regret that, in an age in which so many hundreds of ladies and gentlemen are industriously cultivating for their livelihood an art for which they have no vocation whatsoever, and of whose rudiments they will never acquire a smattering, Mr. Frank Harris has been so grudging of his mastery. Those two books of his, **Elder Conklin** and **Montes the Matador,** contained the best short stories that have been written in the English language; at any rate none better have been written. In his perfect control of all that lies within the limits of the "conte" Mr. Harris stands apart, in the quaintly antithetical company of Mr. Henry James. There they stand: the extreme positive and the extreme negative, with no one in between them. And now Mr. Harris has given us a full-sized novel [**The Bomb**]. Mr. James, were he to choose the theme of it for one of his own novels, would leave us, at the last page, in a state of fascinating doubt whether the bomb had ever been thrown by the anarchist—perhaps whether it had ever been manufactured. That is not Mr. Harris' way. His book begins thus: "My name is Rudolph Schnaubelt. I threw the bomb which killed eight policemen and wounded sixty in Chicago in 1886"; and thenceforth Mr. Harris *is* Schnaubelt, with an amazing vividness, with an absolute translation of himself into the soul of this simple, emotional, painstaking, ordinary young German, who works his way out to America, and, after various embittering hardships in New York, drifts to Chicago, and falls under the spell of Louis Lingg, philosopher and anarchist. Mr. Harris—we had almost said Schnaubelt—uses his power of graphic presentment very finely in the early chapters in which he describes the hideous conditions of labour in the compressed air of the caissons, and the effects of phosphoric poisoning in match factories. He gives us a series of terribly living pictures, with no "word-painting" as of the indignant outsider, but with the simplicity of a man who had lived in the midst of the horrors. But these chapters are mere preliminaries to the actual drama of the book. Schnaubelt's express aim in writing is to give an impression of the greatness of Louis Lingg—his greatness in thought and in action. Hero-worship is always apt to be unconvincing—apt to rely on asseveration rather than on exposition, and leaving us sceptical and bored. Mr. Harris achieves, through Schnaubelt, the feat of making Lingg a really magnetic and impressive figure. His mistress,

Ida Miller, is drawn very vividly; and Elsie Lehman, a conventional but passionate young woman with whom Schnaubelt is in love, is realised through and through, in all the subtle contradictions of her. One of the most arresting scenes in the book is when Lingg, Ida Miller and Schnaubelt set forth to spend the day on the lake. It is Lingg who proposes the outing, "Why not let us go out and have a holiday? Take something to eat with us, German fashion, sausages, beer, bread, and a potato salad, *echt Deutsch*, eh?" Schnaubelt grows tired of rowing, and asks Lingg when they are going to stop and lunch. "When we can no longer see the city," says Lingg. In due course he reveals the reason of the holiday. He has come to test the power of a bomb that he has been making. "The eyes followed the black bullet in its long curve through the air. As it reached the water there was a tremendous report; the water went up in a sort of spout, and even at thirty or forty yards' distance the boat rocked and almost capsized." This is Schnaubelt's initiation into Lingg's policy; and thenceforth the drama of the book progresses steadily and swiftly to its climax. Mr. Harris touches a high level of tragic intensity in the scene between Schnaubelt, on the eve of his throwing the bomb, and Elsie, who is quite ignorant of his intention. And the scene of the actual throwing, and then the description of Schnaubelt's flight to New York in a state of mental and physical collapse, are marvels of tense narration. Altogether, the book is a thoroughly fine piece of work, worthy of the creator of Conklin. We hope it is the precursor of many other books from Mr. Harris.

> *"Mr. Frank Harris' New Story," in* The Saturday Review, London, *Vol. 106, No. 2770, November 28, 1908, p. 674.*

THE NEW YORK TIMES SATURDAY BOOK REVIEW (essay date 1909)

[*In the following essay, the critic explains why he considers* The Bomb *an unsuccessful work of literature.*]

As the tragedy of the Chicago Haymarket recedes more and more into the historical setting its mystery, its contradictory features, and its possibilities as an appalling climax seem to have an increasing fascination for writers of fiction. Already a number of novels have been published dealing with it from various points of view, each one offering a different solution of the mystery of the bomb. The latest to enter the field is Frank Harris, Anglicized American, long a resident of London. His novel **The Bomb** . . . purports to give, in the words of the man who threw the bomb, the inside history of the crime.

In a foreword to the American edition Mr. Harris says that in all the main incidents of his story he has kept to the facts as they were chronicled by the Chicago papers. During a visit to Chicago two years ago he made a study of the contemporary newspaper accounts and came to the conclusion that six out of the seven men who were punished were as innocent as he, and that four of these "had been murdered—according to law." This view of the men themselves and of their acts he has woven into his story. His hero, Ernest Schnaubelt, a young, well-educated German, tells the story of his coming to America, of his bitter experiences hunting work in New York, of his journey to Chicago, where he falls under the influence of Louis Lingg and develops for him an ardent admiration. When Lingg comes to the conviction that the only way to end the clubbing and maltreatment of laboring men by the police would be to strike one paralyzing blow, he volunteers to throw the bomb.

The theme is plausible, but in its fictional expression it breaks down in some places and moves clumsily in others, apparently because Mr. Harris has not the story-telling gift in the first place, and, in the second, writes fiction with a prentice hand. However, his narrative, his pictures of detached scenes, his character analysis, and his observations upon things American and upon men and women in general are very readable. But as a story it does not hold well together. His Ernest Schnaubelt, a youth in his early twenties, looks out upon the world with the eyes of a man of twice his age and experience and culture. His enthusiastic admiration for Louis Lingg is not given a convincing basis, nor is the reader made to feel that his self-immolation in the throwing of the bomb has its root in anything deeper than the necessities of the plot. The love story merely adheres to the main theme, is not a vital factor, and in itself is not attractive. True, all the world loves a lover, but it also loves to laugh at him if he gives it half a chance. And chapters upon chapters of mere lovemaking reduced to its primal elements become ridiculous when not offensive. Many of Mr. Harris's are both.

> *"The Haymarket Tragedy," in* The New York Times Saturday Book Review, *February 27, 1909, p. 118.*

T. E. PAGE (essay date 1910)

[*In the following excerpt, Page questions the conclusions reached by Harris in his first volume of biographical criticism of Shakespeare,* The Man Shakespeare.]

[The book **The Man Shakespeare**] is, in the judgment of its author, a great, or rather a unique one. He does not, he says, "wish to rail" at previous commentators on Shakespeare by talking, in the words of Carlyle, about "libraries of inanities . . . conceited dilettantism . . . and prurient stupidity," but in the next sentence he states, with a fine incoherence, that "he has found in them all this and worse." "Without a single exception," it seems, "the commentators have all missed the man and his story." Or rather there is "one exception," for Ben Jonson's view of Shakespeare is sound "as far as it goes," while Goethe and Coleridge saw him "by glimpses," though "alas, Coleridge, a Puritan born, was brought up in epicene hypocrisies . . . and mis-saw him far oftener than he saw him," and Mr. Harris now for the first time presents us with a true portrait of the man as he was. But as a "student-artist" of to-day, of "the twentieth-century with its X-rays that enable us to see through the flesh and skin of men, and to study the working of their organs and muscles and nerves," he is not content "with the outward presentment and form." His purpose is "to lay bare, as with a scalpel, the hidden motives and springs of action," and then, when the scalpel has done its work, "to re-create a man and make him live and love again for the reader, just as the biologist from a few scattered bones can reconstruct some prehistoric fish or mammal," and although the difference between "reconstructing" the skeleton of a mammal and "re-creating" the mind of Shakespeare may seem somewhat great, none the less, if Mr. Harris can only accomplish his task, no one, perhaps, should be critical about his analogies.

Almost superhuman, however, as that task is, his method of dealing with it is simplicity itself. He assumes as historic fact that Lord Herbert, to whom the earlier sonnets are addressed, was asked by Shakespeare to plead his love-suit with Mistress Mary Fitton, the "dark lady" of the later sonnets, that he betrayed his friend, and that this is the tragedy of the poet's life, who indeed "owes the greater part of his renown to Mary Fitton." He also assumes that from the beginning of his career Shakespeare's "chief aim" in writing plays was "to reveal and realise himself"—for one of his qualities was "inordinate vanity"—so that, by placing the plays in chronological order, we can see how Shakespeare "painted himself at full-length, not once, but twenty times, at as many different periods of his life." *Hamlet,* of course, is one of the finest of the series, and incidentally it may be noted that, as Hamlet was "fat," so Shakespeare was "probably podgy," though in an "aesthete-philosopher-poet" . . . this fact is to be regretted. But *Macbeth* is almost equally fine, for "the rugged Macbeth," as Hazlitt foolishly terms him, is really "our gentle, irresolute, humanist Hamlet masquerading in galligaskins as a Scottish thane." Then, too, the poet is Romeo, Jacques, the Duke in *Measure for Measure.* Posthumus, Biron, Valentine, Prospero, Othello, Antonio, "who is Shakespeare himself," and even Marcus Brutus, who is "an ideal portrait." Nor can it be denied that Mr. Harris shows with singular ability that all these characters frequently use language which seems to come from the poet's life rather than from their own, and is at times even inconsistent with their situation. It could indeed hardly be otherwise, for every dramatist must infuse something of his own mind into the creations of his fancy, and when Mr. Harris is content to illustrate certain moods of thought which recur again and again in the plays, he proves himself an interesting and instructive writer. We all love, as we read Shakespeare, to form as it were some image of him in our own minds, and we welcome any comment which makes that image more real and intelligible, but we recognise also that it must at best be only shadowy and indefinite. The inexhaustible variety of the poet's thought eludes all efforts at exact delineation. His characters we see and know, distinct in their marvellous diversity, but of "the man Shakespeare" we only catch fitful and uncertain glimpses, so that when Mr. Harris speaks of "fathoming the idiosyncrasies of his being" we start back with an instinctive and immediate recoil. Are then the depths of any man's being so easy to sound that Mr. Harris will "fathom" Shakespeare's? And who could trust him to take the measure even of a puddle when, as the result of his present researches, he reports that Shakespeare was "a neuropath" and "a snob"? One's very pen almost refuses to write the words in such a connection, but Mr. Harris has no timidity. "English snobbishness," "snobbishness heightened to flunkeyism," "inconceivable snobbishness," "obsequious flunkeyism," "ungovernable sensuality," "overpowering sensuality," and even "erotic mania"—these are the qualities assigned to William Shakespeare. Why he was "a snob" those who choose must inquire for themselves, but on the charge of "sensuality" a word at least must be spoken, for whatever other qualities Mr. Harris may possess, no healthy mind can accept his verdict on any question of morals, and a single proof will be conclusive. The passage beginning,

"Look here, upon this picture, and on this,"

in which Hamlet reproaches his mother, is known to every one. Its language is the language of honest human nature outraged beyond endurance in its holiest and best feelings. But to Mr. Harris it is nothing of the kind. Its "passionate intensity" is to him "wholly inexplicable," unless "Hamlet-Shakespeare" has identified the Queen with Miss Fitton and is inveighing against "Miss Fitton's faithlessness." For "why," we are asked, "did Hamlet hate his mother's treachery?" "Most men," we are assured, "would hardly have condemned it," and, our author adds, "if any one can imagine that this is the way a son thinks of a mother's slip, he is past my persuading." Such

is the new morality, the morality of "an age when conscience with its prohibitions is fading out of life," and it may well make us pause before we accept the new criticism of the "student-artist." Only when we have unlearned the Ten Commandments, and got rid of conscience, which is now . . . "evolving into a more profound consciousness of ourselves and others," shall we be able to welcome the criticism which declares that the "rarest spirit" which ever adorned humanity was housed in the body of a brute. (pp. 232-33)

> *T. E. Page, in a review of "The Man Shakespeare,"
> in* The Bookman, *London, Vol. XXXVII, No. 221,
> February, 1910, pp. 232-33.*

THE LITTLE REVIEW　(essay date 1915)

[*In the following excerpt, the critic objects to the preeminence of the figure of Harris himself in his portraits of others.*]

With what impatience I have awaited Frank Harris's **Contemporary Portraits!** Not that the name of the "painter" appeals to me tremendously. . . . But will you consider extravagant my expectation that any portraitist would reveal exciting things about such unique sitters as Whistler, Wilde, Verlaine, Swinburne, Maupassant, Maeterlinck, Rodin, France, or about such remote, semi-legendary personages as Carlyle, Renan, Burton, Browning?—The book gave me a slap in the face.

The very first chapter annoyed me. I could not make myself believe in the veracity of Mr. Harris's conversation with Carlyle, which took place some time in 1877 during a stroll. Mr. Harris is not a bad fiction writer, but as a hero of his own fiction he appears clumsy. The interview presents a study in black and white; the black is the crude, narrow, obstinate Scotchman, while the white is, of course, the brilliant, witty, condescending Mr. Harris. This is the leitmotif of the whole book. The "Portraits" are used to emphasize and accentuate the superior features of the "painter"; the "sitters" are familiarly patted on the shoulder, pulled by a string-like marionettes, and made to talk "nice" by whim of the ventriloquist. Defenceless dummies!

In one place Mr. Harris spontaneously exclaims—about the only time he gives the impression of spontaneity: "What a pity St. Paul did not write a 'Life of Jesus!'" Frank Harris would. He would surely not miss the opportunity of capitalizing such a "contemporary portrait." What a pity Mr. Harris has not met at a dinner given by Lady-and-So Mr. Socrates, or Mr. Moses, or Mr. Adam! What a loss of a good seller.

An editor of a brave magazine, which allows its contributors the free use of the first personal pronoun, has rebuked me for my too-subjective animosity towards Mr. Harris's book and for my failure to see its other, better, side. I find my justification in Mr. Harris's own words: "I put these portraits forth as works of art." In the same measure as the artist is allowed—or rather, expected—to present that which seems to his most intrinsic and striking in his subject, so am I, the appreciator, to have the liberty of criticising in a work of art those features that appear to me most salient and conspicuous. As a matter of fact I enjoyed reading Mr. Harris's characteristics of the persons he has met; he doubtless has an artistic touch in his pen-and-ink portraits; his criticisms on Mathew Arnold, John Davidson, Richard Middleton, are interesting. But it is the leitmotif of the book that gives you a general impression. The impression it made on me I have told in the preceding paragraphs. The pages on Whistler, Wilde, Verlaine, Renan, and

Cartoon of Harris surrounded by Jesus Christ, Shakespeare, Oscar Wilde, and Bernard Shaw.

others, are malodorous; the persons whom you admire or love appear blurred and maimed, for in front of them spins the annoying little figure of the portraitist, who preaches good behavior to Oscar, who is charitable to Jimmy, who tells silly anecdotes about Paul, who condescendingly smiles at old Renan, and journalistically interviews Anatole France and Maeterlinck. (pp. 43-4)

> K., "Egomania," in The Little Review, *Vol. II, No. 6, September, 1915, pp. 42-4.*

FRANCIS HACKETT   (essay date 1921)

[*Hackett was a respected Irish-American biographer, novelist, and literary critic during the first half of the twentieth century. His reviews appeared in the* New Republic, *the* Saturday Review of Literature, *and other prominent American periodicals. In the following excerpt, Hackett praises the imaginative vigor of volume three of Harris's* Contemporary Portraits.]

Frank Harris is a man of genius, one of the few men of genius living. By those swift and free movements which are possible only to the winged, by instant ascent to sweeping radiant vision, he is enabled to comprehend the pertinent realities toward which most of us plod, grub, and dig—usually in the wrong direction.

His genius, however, seems to me to be trammelled. With all his intuition, with superb muscle and will, Harris does not command his empire. He is, he says, a rebel. That is true. But what he most rebels against is not the external but the internal. He is not domesticated in his own soul. He talks mournfully of martyrs, with one eye on himself; he dreams Don Quixote. But the truth is that with all his sense of real quixotism and martyrdom and unpopularity, the division is in himself.

The source of this division I do not know, or fancy I know. I only feel that this man of genius transfers to the world a conflict which exists mainly in his bosom. And scarcely ever, for this reason, is his mind free of the problem in human domestication which is Frank Harris.

I could imagine him, with his flaming eyes, his fighter's moustache, his lion's voice, the leader of any renaissance crew. He should, perhaps, never have been a man of letters, but a tiger of adventure, framed with fearful symmetry—not, as he says, "dreadful" symmetry. But mysterious chance has made him a writing man. A real tiger, not the stuffed cat which is Clemenceau, he has all the same spent his life and subdued his nature in the sober harness of literary self-expression. In such harness he inevitably looks untamed, wild, disreputable. And no rebellion, no violence, no recklessness of statement, can ease such a man of action. He, like Cellini, should have had priceless jewels to play with and bombs to fling, to realize the rich, eager nature that came to him straight from the steaming earth.

Instead he wrote, significantly enough, "**Montes the Matador**" and *The Bomb.* He wrote that marvelous jewelled book, *The*

Man Shakespeare. And, in his uncommon and brave subordination of great gifts, he has produced sixty *Contemporary Portraits*.

This third series is as valuable as the earlier ones. Whatever the division in his nature, here he is sublimated and elicits from himself an amazing sweetness and tolerance. His intelligence is broad enough to hold men like Chesterton and Galsworthy whom his temperament alone could not accommodate. Many of his portraits flash with temperament. Some are deliberately gracious and in a few the reservations, especially as to sex, are plain. But you cannot read these sixteen sketches without feeling the warm romantic insight, the spiritual energy, the power to catch the soul in motion, the just perspective of fine taste. Take one line on John Morley, "The bleak face lighted up with a glint of wintry sunshine." Take one bit of the penetrating account of H. G. Wells: "Nothing arresting or peculiar in the face, save the eyes: eyes that grew on one. They were of ordinary size, a grayish blue in color, but intent, shadowed, suggesting depth like water in a half-covered spring; observant eyes, too, that asked questions, but reflection, meditation the note of them; eyes almost pathetic in the patience of their scrutiny."

With a flair of his own he sees Cunninghame Graham, Gaudier-Brzeska, Augustus John, Coventry Patmore. These he sees with an eye for differences, but with his constant love of gallantry. He is sympathetic to, rather than with, Arthur Symons, Upton Sinclair, Louis Wilkinson, W. L. George. He is no sweeter than a just witness should be. He is not cruel, even to Winston Churchill. And with glowing color he paints Huxley and Alfred Russel Wallace.

No one knows better than Frank Harris himself that in this book his wine is sometimes served in a chipped cup. It is a weary hand that writes: "Wilkinson has the heart of the matter in him I am persuaded and so I bid him gird up his loins and give us his very best." This is English without dignity. But the deeper laziness, laziness of perception, is not here. Frank Harris has not whittled, like Whistler, rather he has painted with full imagination, but his keen drawing, his ultimate fidelity to structure, is clear to the examining eye. When he comes to his Autobiography, which he now promises, we should have a masterpiece. Meanwhile the master's hand is to be seen in these Portraits. To read them is "to warm both hands before the fire of life."

Francis Hackett, in a review of "Contemporary Portraits," in The New Republic, *Vol. XXIX, No. 365, November 30, 1921, p. 21.*

H. L. MENCKEN   (essay date 1922)

[*From the era of World War I until the early years of the Great Depression, Mencken was one of the most influential figures in American letters. His strongly individualistic, irreverent outlook on life and his vigorous, invective-charged writing style helped establish the iconoclastic spirit of the Jazz Age and significantly shaped the direction of American literature. As a social and literary critic—the roles for which he is best known—Mencken was the scourge of evangelical Christianity, public service organizations, literary censorship, boosterism, provincialism, democracy, all advocates of personal or social improvement, and every other facet of American life that he perceived as humbug. In his literary criticism, Mencken encouraged American writers to shun the anglophilic, moralistic bent of the nineteenth century and to practice realism, an artistic call-to-arms that is most fully developed in his essay "Puritanism as a Literary Force," one of the*

seminal essays in modern literary criticism. A man who was widely renowned or feared during his lifetime as a would-be destroyer of established American values, Mencken once wrote: "All of my work, barring a few obvious burlesques, is based upon three fundamental ideas. 1. That knowledge is better than ignorance; 2. That it is better to tell the truth than to lie; and 3. That it is better to be free than to be a slave." In the following excerpt, Mencken assesses the quality of Harris's work.]

Though, so far as I know, this Harris is a perfectly reputable man, fearing God and obeying the laws, it is not to be gainsaid that a certain flavor of the sinister hangs about his aspect. (p. 182)

Well, what is in him? My belief, frequently expressed, is that there is a great deal. His *Oscar Wilde* is, by long odds, the best literary biography ever written by an American—an astonishingly frank, searching and vivid reconstruction of character—a piece of criticism that makes all ordinary criticism seem professorial and lifeless. The Comstocks, I need not say, tried to suppress it; a brilliant light is thrown upon Harris by the fact that they failed ignominiously. All the odds were in favor of the Comstocks; they had patriotism on their side and the help of all the swine who flourished in those days; nevertheless, Harris gave them a severe beating, and scared them half to death. In brief, a man of the most extreme bellicosity, enterprise and courage—a fellow whose ideas are expressed absolutely regardless of tender feelings, whether genuine or bogus. In *The Man Shakespeare* and *The Women of Shakespeare* he tackled the whole body of academic English critics *en masse*—and routed them *en masse*. The two books, marred perhaps by a too bombastic spirit, yet contain some of the soundest, shrewdest and most convincing criticism of Shakespeare that has ever been written. All the old hocus-pocus is thrown overboard. There is an entirely new examination of the materials, and to the business is brought a knowledge of the plays so ready and so vast that that of even the most learned don begins to seem a mere smattering. The same great grasp of facts and evidences is visible in the sketches which make up the three volumes of *Contemporary Portraits*. What one always gets out of them is a feeling that the man knows the men he is writing about—that he not only knows what he sets down, but a great deal more. There is here nothing of the cold correctness of the usual literary "estimate." Warts are not forgotten, whether of the nose or of the immortal soul. The subject, beginning as a political shibboleth or a row of books, gradually takes on all the colors of life, and then begins to move, naturally and freely. I know of no more brilliant evocations of personality in any literature—and most of them are personalities of sharp flavor, for Harris, in his day, seems to have known almost everybody worth knowing, and whoever he knew went into his laboratory for vivisection.

The man is thus a first critic of his time, and what he has written about his contemporaries is certain to condition the view of them held in the future. What gives him his value in this difficult field is, first of all and perhaps most important of all, his cynical detachment—his capacity for viewing men and ideas objectively. In his life, of course, there have been friendships and some of them have been strong and long-continued, but when he writes it is with a sort of surgical remoteness, as if the business in hand were vastly more important than the man. He was lately protesting violently that he was and is quite devoid of malice. Granted. But so is a surgeon. To write of George Moore as he has written may be writing devoid of malice, but nevertheless the effect is precisely that which would follow if some malicious enemy were to drag poor George out of his celibate couch in the dead of night, and chase him naked down Shaftsbury avenue. The thing is appallingly revelatory—and I believe that it is true. The Moore that he depicts may not be absolutely the real Moore, but he is unquestionably far nearer to the real Moore than the Moore of the Moore books. The method, of course, has its defects. Harris is far more interested, fundamentally, in men than in their ideas: the catholic sweep of his *Contemporary Portraits* proves it. In consequence his judgments of books are often colored by his opinions of their authors. He dislikes Mark Twain as his own antithesis: a trimmer and poltroon. *Ergo, A Connecticut Yankee* is drivel, which leads us, as Euclid hath it, to absurdity. He once had a row with Dreiser. *Ergo, The Titan* is nonsense, which is itself nonsense. But I know of no critic who is wholly free from that quite human weakness. In the academic bunkophagi it is everything; they are willing to swallow anything so long as the author is sound upon the League of Nations. It seems to me that such aberrations are rarer in Harris than in most. He may have violent prejudices, but it is seldom that they play upon a man who is honest.

I judge from his frequent discussions of himself—he is happily free from the vanity of modesty—that the pets of his secret heart are his ventures into fiction, and especially, *The Bomb* and "**Montes the Matador.**" The latter has been greatly praised by Arnold Bennett, who has also praised Leonard Merrick. I have read it four or five times, and always with enjoyment. It is a powerful and adept tale; well constructed and beautifully written; it recalls some of the best of the shorter stories of Thomas Hardy. Alongside it one might range half a dozen other Harris stories—all of them carefully put together, every one the work of a very skillful journeyman. But despite Harris, the authentic Harris is not the story-writer: he has talents, of course, but it would be absurd to put "**Montes the Matador**" beside *Heart of Darkness*. In "**Love in Youth**" he descends to unmistakable fluff and feebleness. The real Harris is the author of the Wilde volumes, of the two books about Shakespeare, of the three volumes of *Contemporary Portraits*. Here there is stuff that lifts itself clearly and brilliantly above the general—criticism that has a terrific vividness and plausibility, and all the gusto that the professors can never pump up. Harris makes his opinions not only interesting, but important. What he has to say always seems novel, ingenious, and true. Here is the chief lifework of an American who, when all values are reckoned up, will be found to have been a sound artist and an extremely intelligent, courageous and original man—and infinitely the superior of the poor dolts who once tried so childishly to dispose of him. (pp. 185-89)

> H. L. Mencken, "Five Men at Random: Frank Harris," in his Prejudices, third series, Alfred A. Knopf, 1922, pp. 182-89.

OSBERT BURDETT (essay date 1926)

[*In the following excerpt, Burdett discusses theme and style of several of Harris's principal works.*]

The vigour and robustness to be found in the writings of Mr. Frank Harris occur only in those uncommon authors who are primarily men of action. This characteristic quality of style is now explained on that page of his unfinished book, *My Life and Loves,* where he tells us that, at the age of fifteen, he used a sum of ten pounds won in a scholarship examination to pay his passage to America, a country at which he arrived unfriended and alone. Long before he turned author he had led

an active and adventurous life, and before the age of twenty had amassed more experiences in different parts of the world than fill the lives of many quiet and stay-at-home people. The effect of these adventures on his imagination is apparent in his subsequently written books. His style is as effective as a display of singlestick, but his experience of the world deepened also a temperamental tenderness, so that in his writings he responds principally to two appeals, the appeals of distinction and of pity. The two themes cross and recross each other in his work. Indeed they mingle, for distinction easily becomes tragic since it is exceptional, and misfortune may ennoble its victims. In both pity is not far at the moment when the distinction is felt.

When the temperament of the man of action is accompanied by a genuine literary gift, it always produces dramatic writing. Mr. Harris would have written more plays if his own personality did not step between his pen and his characters when he tries to create them through the medium of speech. Dialogue is not his strong point. He can display a character in set speeches or separate remarks better than he can allow it to issue continuously in its own words. His stories are all dramatic: his plays are like stories that have been dramatized. In the novels and tales he is content with the action itself for his effect. Consequently, even when he is moved to express his admiration or his pity, his pen moves a little roughly like a sword or a stick used to trace letters on the ground. If his style were as fine as his sympathies, he would be a great writer, but his work suffers because his material of beauty, coming fresh from the quarry of life, remains a little rough. In his own writings the raw material beguiles him more than workmanship upon it.

Perhaps, like Rodin or Philip Webb, he is careful never to efface the facettings of the tool marks. By this means he is able to render the illusion of fact and experience with a verisimilitude not easily to be surpassed, but sometimes at the price of suggesting the quality of journalism at its finest. There remains with the reader a (perhaps deceptive) sensation of haste, as if the author found his subject too pressing to admit of delay, and must treat it vigorously in time for the next edition. He admires genius beyond all else in the world, so much indeed that, though the ambitions and combativeness of the active man colour all his writings, no trace of envy is to be found in them. On the other hand, he seems unexpectedly sensitive to his own originality, and, for a spirit evidently generous in matters of literature, inclined to fancy that others may be plagiarizing his work, especially that part of which he is most proud, his studies of Shakespeare.

The enduring reflections enforced by his books are that nature and men combine to persecute all distinction, and that nature punishes men and women more severely for their slips than for their offences. From this he concludes that admiration and tolerance, the Hellenic worship of the noble and the Christian lesson of lovingkindness, are the two qualities of which the world stands most in need. These he would unite in a Pagan-Christian system of ethics: a very interesting idea. The absence of these virtues in average human beings and the blind indifference of Nature produce, according to Mr. Harris, the tragedies of life.

It is characteristic that the one story which Mr. Harris has translated from Hans Andersen is the tale of the ugly duckling who proved to be a swan. If he had written the fable himself, the cygnet might have been fatally maimed by his purblind neighbours and family. In the *Yellow Ticket,* the volume in which this rendering occurs, we have stories of an innocent girl who could not be admitted to Christian Moscow unless she enrolled herself as a prostitute, because her purse was empty though her head was full; of a youth whose diseased vision made the world so fantastically interesting that he became miserable when his eyesight was cured. In the end he was dissuaded from suicide by his observant, if cynical oculist, who told the boy that, if he cultivated the virtues, he and his fellows would seem as idiotic to each other as both had done before the oculist interfered.

Another favourite theme of the short stories is that of minorities, of exceptional or oppressed races and people. This has given to us several tales about the Jews. They are always treated sympathetically. In the tale of **"Isaac and Rebecca"** we are introduced to a young Jewess. She is eager for money; her father apparently is not, but at the critical moment the old man yields to the intuition of his race, and so beguiles the wealthy banker into proposing. In *Unpath'd Waters,* the best volume of his short stories, there is the admirable tale of the old Jew who explained the art of making money. He realized, almost at his mother's knee, that it is the middleman who makes the money, and most quickly when he sells things that have no fixed price. So he began with old clothes. He went on to curiosities. He passed to works of art and became a dealer in antiques. He ended as a banker, for by selling money he found a commodity the price of which varies every day. It is a capital story. As an artistic lesson in economics it should be compared with Mr. Belloc's *Mercy of Allah,* in particular with the tale therein about the merchant of camels. In time of war the Sultan offers him paper money for his herd. The merchant returns to the Sultan a sack of slips on each of which is written "this is a camel." How long shall we have to wait before such stories are included in the study of economics at our schools?

"A Daughter of Eve" is an admirable study of two sisters who are in love with the same man. It tells how the stronger, yielding to a momentary impulse of vanity, eventually sees in turn her sister and her brother-in-law attempt to drown themselves. It is, as the supposed narrator remarks, "just like life: no meaning it it; the punishment out of all proportion to the sin." Before she died the impulsive girl proved a devoted woman, loved in her own home and admired for her public spirit by the world. There is no reason to suppose that Daisy's true character was revealed in the momentary impulse to which she yielded, or modified by the tragic results that followed this. She was too strong to alter or to be crushed, but Nature chose to punish heavily a caprice without which Daisy would not have been entirely natural.

"Montes the Matador" is too well known to need analysis today. In **"Elder Conklin,"** the Sheriff and his Partner is a flash-light picture gone before we are aware of all that it means. It is nearly a perfect example of Wordsworth's dictum:

> Action is transitory—a step, a blow,
> The motion of a muscle this way or that—
> 'Tis done; and, in the after vacancy,
> We wonder at ourselves like men betray'd.

The story shows what Mr. Harris can do with incident, as Elder Conklin had shown how he could depict a character. Moreover, the other side of the author's imagination exemplifies Wordsworth's succeeding couplet:

> Suffering is permanent, obscure and dark,
> And shares the nature of infinity.

Portrait of Harris in 1895 by Sir William Rothenstein.

This brooding conviction has inspired many of Mr. Harris's tales.

More qualified praise must be given to his Shakespearean studies. His prime qualification is that he evidently knows most of the plays by heart. This intense familiarity led him to ask what type of personality had created them. His powers of memory and divination enabled him to evoke a portrait which is clear when he remembers that it is the personality, rather than the life-story, of the poet that the method reveals. The method breaks when employed to divine other real people, such as Shakespeare's mother, who have left no written record of themselves, and, unlike the Dark Lady, were not the constant subject of Shakespeare's verse: on the various studies of the Dark Lady Mr. Harris is plausible enough. Indeed, the method depends for its effectiveness precisely upon its limitations. It also assures us that nothing in the legends that have come down about the poet is out of character, for there is nothing surprising in the feats of a precocious youth, if he were Shakespeare. To such a poet a vagabond youth was a richer education than prolonged schooling, and his natural appetite for reading would be whetted by the extended instruction that he lacked. All his disadvantages, as they are called, would be advantages to a man of genius. It is therefore amusing to remember that only men of no genius have professed to find them insurmountable! (pp. 125-30)

Like much of Mr. Harris's characteristic work, *The Man Shakespeare,* is a vivid piece of portraiture. When he knows a character thoroughly, by intuition or in life, he is an admirable draughtsman. His life of Wilde is likely to be final, and is one of his vivid and courageous books.

Where his admiration or sympathy is aroused, Mr. Harris is a writer with a tender conscience. This is touched to the quick by nobility of thought or the persecution of weakness. The latter horrified him when the Chicago anarchists were the victims, and he so told their story in *The Bomb* as to immortalize its memory. If vividness were the whole of narrative, and candour all that men require in the presentation of passion, this novel would rank very high for it has both. The story could not be more vigorously told, but if the reader does not yield himself entirely to its movement and manfully preserves his critical sense, he lays the book down at last with the feeling that it is a masterpiece rather of reporting than of literature. If journalism were half as good as this, we should have excellent excuses for the time that we waste upon it. There is a distinction. Even the best journalism fails to touch the deepest springs. It suffers from an excess of excitement. It lacks the last achievement of repose, which is the moment when writing passes into literature. In *The Bomb* the events, the characters, their motives and feelings are set down in broad strokes with the effect of a superb poster.

A better novel is *Great Days,* its author's most artistic achievement in the longer forms of prose narrative. Against the background of the Napoleonic wars, a distant shadow that lends repose and dignity to the busy foreground of the story, we have a lively picture of the smugglers and merchant seamen on both the Channel coasts. These revolve round two centres of human interest, an English and a French family. They complement and contrast each other, and bring the characters of the two nations into relief. Every figure in each family we learn to know and understand, and event grows from event with unfaltering interest. It is odd that its author's most artistic creation seems not to have run into many editions. Perhaps his death, the last favour that fate confers upon an artist's reputation, will make known the merit of this book. The historical scene of *Great Days* is conveyed by a few deftly placed touches: the arrival of the napkin from France; the controversy over the right number of pommels on a side-saddle; the glimpses of Bonaparte and Fox.

On the subject of the Corsican, Fox says: "Successful men are never so great as they are made out to be. It's like judging a man by his shadow. . . . Great men are usually richer in temperament than Bonaparte appears to be, and richer in faults, too. . . . I did not wish to combat French ideas which seemed to me just and right. But now that Bonaparte is making himself a despot I should have no hesitation." On the idea of equality: "How would it be if there could be equality or a great approach to equality in necessaries, while keeping all the distinctions as honours. . . . Honours would be more esteemed if they could not be won by money." The opinions of the imaginary figures are equally in character, though they all tend to speak in the same vigorous way, and as a work of art *Great Days* is Mr. Harris's best novel.

His heroes are generally men of action, or imaginative people to whom action is made a martyrdom because they stir the world by their thoughts and words. To him particularly, words are the activity of thought; beauty and truth causes to be fought and died for. This energy of soul has occasioned one witty definition: "A gentleman, to me, is a thing of some parts but no magnitude: one should be a gentleman and much more." Louis Lingg in *The Bomb* makes a somewhat parallel statement, no less indicative of his creator's mind: "The writer tries to find a characteristic word; the painter some scene that will enable him to express himself. I always wanted a characteristic

deed." Mr. Harris's volumes are much like deeds. Each is meant to incite to action by the spell of its image or its idea, to imprint impressions that will last, like a thing seen, a thrilling experience, a personal revelation. Each book is intended to have on the reader "the tonic touch" of the experience itself.

The man of action is reputed to be dumb at moments of emotional crisis. Indeed, the author's most convincing example, Elder Conklin, is articulate only in his prayers. His silence is broken, so to speak, by his swift, unhesitating decisions. If this be true of such men, has Mr. Harris too much in common with the active temperament to find unforgettable phrases of beauty for the furthest reaches of his thought? It must be something of this kind that makes our reluctant qualifications necessary. The substance is often so good that we seem cheated of some quality in the treatment. Yet there is a tonic virtue in its denial. We do occasionally find actions that are like poems: the number of books with the quality of living tissue is hardly more numerous. Men of action can often write well. The rare thing is that such a temperament should devote itself to the practice of literature. When this happens (Florence Nightingale is a classic example) the writings have the gust of a sea-breeze.

In Mr. Harris's stories, the lovers are creatures of desire trying to rise into creatures of feeling. He gives to us the alphabet of passion, but the separate letters are always struggling to compose themselves into intelligible love. In **"Elder Conklin,"** Loo is a sketch compared with Ida in *The Bomb,* or Margaret Barron in *Great Days.* Mr. Harris has readier intuitions of his men, but the tender core beneath the rind of his temperament enables him to divine his heroines, of whom he writes with the fondness of a father for a favourite child. His heroines are those most likely to appeal to a thoughtful man of action, and they are depicted either passionately or with the tenderness that the proverbial soldier extends to children.

The volumes of *Contemporary Portraits* are very unequal, and more suggestive of hasty improvisation, possibly for the benefit of the American public, than any other of his works. Since his anecdotes are generally in character, their alleged invention does not much matter. They are, generally, dramatically right, and some licence is usually conceded to writers of reminiscences about famous, and therefore much debated, people. What may be written in haste is necessarily read with reservation.

Bernard Shaw has often suggested that Frank Harris should write his autobiography, but the first volume raised questions that cannot be discussed in a final paragraph. It is more like a bomb than any of his books, as if Casanova had timed his work to explode in the twentieth century. Only those capable of controlling their prejudices will be able to read it at all. Those incapable will not read far. Autobiographies fall into two classes: those of the adventurous and those of the introspective man. There is a middle category, filled by the reflective man of letters, a rank to which the introspective writer (being partly sterile) rarely wins. Cellini and Casanova are examples of the first; Rousseau and Gibbon of the middle order; Amiel, Barbellion, Marie Lénéru of the introspective type. Mr. Harris's life and confessions belong to the adventurous class. In deed and word he is wholly unashamed, but, as he is a man of intelligence, he gives us a series of reflections in support of this procedure. These are deeply felt, and not to be dismissed lightly.

The valid contention in his preface is that languages can die of euphemisms, and that nineteenth-century English suffered from them. The objection to his latest practice is that the vocabulary of corner-boys is no remedy. Some selection is the beginning of all literature; and, while a sincere man of letters must hold that there is no fact or fancy that literature cannot describe, yet he will add that the more physical you choose to be the less fit is the vocabulary of hooligans. With the world's literature before us, there is abundant proof that the coarsest of great writers never did write like corner-boys. The penalty of those who do is to be found unendurable by every one else. What a pity that a violent, if intelligible, reaction should destroy a perfectly valid plea for candour. Between euphemisms and the terms of the gutter the way of literature is perfectly clear. The masculine tongue of classic writers is as free from one as from the other.

At best, he has attempted in his old age that which he would have had done for himself by others in his youth, and that must be his condonation. When the man of action possesses also the power of communicating his experiences and their lessons, his writings have a way of surviving the criticisms that they arouse. In sum, Mr. Harris's works, from first to last, illustrate the maxim of Santayana, that "to turn events into ideas is the function of literature."

Looking back over his work, I recommend him as a stimulating author, a man with a wider than the average English view, a courageous man, a blunt man, whose vivid, rough, essentially dramatic, imagination gives to words the living quality of action. He has the faculty of the keen eyewitness, who is neglected to-day because he has excited strong distaste, wilfully, indeed, in part, but still more by his determination to make us see the other side of questions which we prefer to view through the darkened glasses of political or moral prejudices. Other authors go for the hearts, more rarely the heads, of their readers. Mr. Harris, like a boxer, goes straight for the epigastrium, and the luckless reader, when he has found his breath once more, has no choice but to run away or begin another bout. Neither alternative is without its humiliations, and, for the future, the reader usually resolves to leave this formidable person alone. Mr. Harris's pen is too devastating for the average English taste, which in political, biographical, and critical writings, much prefers authors who omit as many debatable issues as possible. The Englishman's castle is a dark old house, and he becomes indignant when anyone lets a ray of light enter one of its cherished gloomy corners. Yet the criticism, say of our educational ideals in the pamphlet entitled **How to Beat the Boer,** is still alive and worth having. (pp. 130-36)

> Osbert Burdett, "The Writings of Frank Harris," in
> his Critical Essays, Henry Holt and Company, 1926,
> pp. 125-36.

T. EARLE WELBY   (essay date 1932)

[*Welby was an English critic and journalist. In the following excerpt, he laments the fact that Harris's critical reputation stemmed largely from his biography of Shaw when he had written much better works which were often ignored.*]

The posthumously published book by Frank Harris on Mr. Bernard Shaw [**Frank Harris on Bernard Shaw**] has elicited in many quarters estimates not so much of its qualities as of the qualities of the two writers. There are thus brought to the bar of criticism two reputations, the one, as I think, considerably exaggerated, the other still not commensurate with the narrow, vivid, unpleasing genius of its possessor; and here is a case in which the typical jury will certainly prove incompetent.

For as to Frank Harris, we have a man against whose character and against many of whose journalistic and literary activities the public has long and justly been incensed. He was a braggart, he could be something of a bully, he had very few scruples, and his personality, when it came through his work, could not possibly excite affection or pity. Add that his claim to a permanent place in literature rests almost entirely on a few short stories repellent to the average reader by the brutality of their action or by an acrid flavour, or—and perhaps not least—by the writer's disconcerting refusal to interpose any mitigating charm of style between reader and subject. Not since Crabbe announced his programme, "nudity of description and poetry without an atmosphere", had there been uncompromisingly set up in English literature an ideal so repulsive to the plain man; and—a point particularly to be made—Frank Harris's ideal was set up in none of that feverish revolt against gracious things which is, after all, a tribute to them, but simply in obedience to the law of his own small, hard genius. The plain man, given time, has no great difficulty with what Tennyson called "wallowing in the troughs of Zolaism", and has come by now, poor soul! to a comprehension of the female fever for saying ineffable things defiantly: nothing can ever bring him to a comprehension of an art, in its own way austere, which seems to forego not only the luxuries of sentimental idealism, but the ignoble delights of the trough, the base rapture of release from all reticence. And even a subtler and more flexible type of reader may be somewhat taken aback by an art which seems to renounce so many of the privileges of art as defined (amusingly enough, by Zola!) as life seen through a temperament, and offers us only such a view of persons as we may have through a colourless pane of glass. There may well be moments when even the subtler and more flexible reader of my hypothesis supports the plain man by crying out over some page of Frank Harris's best stories, "This is not writing, this is only a way of making me an eye-witness!"

There shall be no question here, for all the little portraits inset in the popular reviews of the Harris-Shaw book, and for all the legends of Mr. Shaw and Frank Harris, of Hyperion and Satyr; but look at the other picture. And, while looking at it, call to mind what seems to me the capital truth about Irish writers born before the period in which Mr. Yeats and AE imposed complete artistic integrity on the literature of their nation: that Irish writers were much concerned to produce effects and extremely anxious to avoid giving opportunities for strictly aesthetic judgment of any part of their work. "Does the doctrine shock you? It was only my joke. Do you take that for a flippancy? It is part of my doctrine. And, anyhow, we are having a very enjoyable time, and at least we can agree in being, no one knows how seriously, agin' the Government in matters of literature, art and social conduct, no less than in matters of politics."

Between the loose responsiveness of this art—if that be art which spends the most of its energy in evading judgment as art—and the ferocious consistency of the art of Frank Harris in the few stories that matter there is a violent antithesis. Another antithesis presents itself when we observe the mode of the attack on the public made by these two writers. Frank Harris, in his most prosperous and useful period, tried to accommodate himself to English society, but only as a man, or perhaps rather as a chameleon which strives to its utmost and is the more infuriated by its eventual failure; as a writer he made no concessions whatsoever to English expectations. Bernard Shaw understood instinctively that a man who has not, so to speak, a ready-made place in English society is wise in flouting everything it values and in being not a definable but an incalculable rebel. Had Bernard Shaw remained and written in Ireland, where before the age of Mr. Yeats and AE cheeks suffered attrition from tongues, he would have been another of those very clever Irishmen who are always on the verge of delivering goods and not-so-goods to a public little exercised to distinguish things in one category from things in the other. His genius for a career brought him to England, where the public was probably more muddled than anywhere else in Europe, but, to its pitiful credit, unable to believe that anyone talking about the reconstruction of society could be mainly a buffoon. And having come to England he proceeded, after some years of doing nothing in particular, to create a public for himself; whereas Frank Harris did little but alienate successively every section of his potential public. Mr. Shaw had great talent for the conduct of his life; and Frank Harris, for all his resourcefulness in shady enterprises, had next to none.

So it comes about that to-day the man of genius is posthumously enjoying only a sort of success of disesteem, and even that only because his book happens to be about Mr. Bernard Shaw, whereas the man of many talents is universally applauded. No one is more adroit than Mr. Shaw in securing postponement of artistic judgment on his work; the cleverest lawyer in Chicago never got the evil day for his gunman client put off more ingeniously. But there is a limit to allowing a writer to evade judgment as he frisks about betwixt jest and earnest; would have us enjoy as economics what may not wholly delight us as drama, and applaud as drama what may seem perverse to us as economics; would have us tolerate the play for the brilliance of the preface, or find importance in the preface because it emanates from the author of the play. It has been a great game, played with immense skill and unflagging energy, but it is about time someone called "Stop!" to it.

It is about time, I say, because there has lately been a development far less to be suffered than any in the earlier history of Mr. Shaw's reputation. I mean, persons of great artistic endowment are now being made to appear of consequence only in the degree that they are or have been entangled with Mr. Shaw. The Ellen Terry of the moment is not the actress, but Mr. Shaw's correspondent; Ellen Terry's son is not a designer of genius, but somebody who has had some sort of row with Mr. Shaw; and Frank Harris is not the man who wrote *Montes, Elder Conklin, The Miracle of the Stigmata, Eating Crow,* but the ill-advised biographer of Mr. Shaw. (pp. 94-7)

Frank Harris's way of writing short stories was not the way that most appeals to me; and as I never knew the man, and as he affronted a scholar of my special admiration, and slandered a poet who is my friend, I can hardly be suspected of wishing to praise him for personal reasons. But when I find critics of repute implying that Frank Harris's only claim on our attention is that he has written a book, and, as it happens, rather a bad book, on Mr. Shaw, I am moved to protest on behalf of the man of narrow and sometimes repellent genius whose half-dozen best stories will abide the question of posterity, to protest against the prevalent belief that the planets become important in the degree in which they approach Mr. Shaw. (p. 98)

T. Earle Welby, "Frank Harris, Bernard Shaw: An Antithesis," in The Fortnightly Review, *n.s. Vol. CXXXI, January 1, 1932, pp. 94-100.*

JOHN MIDDLETON MURRY (essay date 1935)

[*Murry is recognized as one of the most significant English critics and editors of the twentieth century. Anticipating later scholarly opinion, he championed the writings of Marcel Proust, James Joyce, Paul Valéry, D. H. Lawrence, and the poetry of Thomas Hardy through his positions as the editor of the* Athenaeum *and as a longtime contributor to the* Times Literary Supplement *and other periodicals. As with his magazine essays, Murry's book-length critical works are noted for their unusually impassioned tone and startling discoveries; such biographically centered critical studies as* Keats and Shakespeare: A Study of Keats' Poetic Life from 1816-1820 *(1925) and* Son of Woman: The Story of D. H. Lawrence *(1931) contain esoteric, controversial conclusions that have angered scholars who favor more traditional approaches. Nevertheless, Murry is cited for his perspicuity, clarity, and supportive argumentation. His early exposition on literary appreciation,* The Problem of Style *(1922), is widely regarded as an informed guidebook for both critics and readers to employ when considering not only the style of a literary work, but its theme and viewpoint as well. In it Murry espouses a theoretical premise which underlies all his criticism: that in order to fully evaluate a writer's achievement the critic must search for crucial passages which effectively "crystallize" the writer's innermost impressions and convictions regarding life. Murry was one of a number of young intellectuals who gathered around Harris during his period of great influence only to later be repelled by the editor's eccentric behavior. In the following excerpt, Murry explains why his admiration for Harris waned.*]

For a short time [Frank] Harris was my hero. I cut adrift from him very soon; and, with more courage than I generally displayed, refused point-blank his peremptory invitation to become a director of *Hearth and Home.* I was not going to be mixed up in any way with his financial or journalistic enterprises. How quickly I came to that decision, I do not remember; but since Harris acquired *Hearth and Home* in the summer of 1912, and I had made up my mind to have nothing to do with it before the régime began, it cannot have taken very long. My defection was noticeable: for *Hearth and Home* was staffed from Dan Rider's shop, Dan himself being business manager, and Hugh Kingsmill and Enid Bagnold sub-editors. Lovat Fraser's father, who was a well-to-do solicitor, put up most of the money. And it had been so long a subject of enthusiastic anticipation among us what we would do "when Frankie got a paper" that I should be astonished by my own temerity in holding aloof, if I did not remember the cause of it.

The great topic, shortly after I entered the Harris circle, was the refusal of W. H. Smith to circulate a number of *The English Review* containing a short-story by Harris called **"An English Saint."** It went without saying that it was a masterpiece, and that its attempted suppression was a supreme iniquity. It was part of the creed. Unfortunately for my faith, I happened in those days to have become fascinated by Stendhal—rather at Harris's instigation—and to have begun a systematic reading of all his works. Suddenly, in a volume of his comparatively unknown stories I came upon the unmistakable original of **"An English Saint."** I kept my discovery to myself, but my attitude to Harris was changed in a moment. I did not trust him any more; for the shock of that discovery came at a fatal moment. I had just written and published in *Rhythm* a tremendous dithyramb about him. It is pathetic in its extravagance. Here are two paragraphs from it:

> I knew and loved the work of Frank Harris long before I knew and loved the man. To me, two years ago, the name Frank Harris meant a prince of artists too great for the people among which he wrote. (This was quite untrue.) But now the name means a prince among men, a prince of talkers and critics, a prince of the lovers of life as well. It means a man whose word of praise

can change the whole of life for me for months, and a word of condemnation make me cry till I think my heart would break. I cannot hope to write of such a man with the sober detachment of criticism. For Frank Harris is one of those great spirits whom I can but accept wholly, it may be even blindly, but with the security of knowledge that if I am mistaken, then life and art have no more meaning for me. . . .

It will always be the truth about Frank Harris which I shall endeavour to declare to the world. Moreover, in the next number I shall try to show exactly where and how Frank Harris is the greatest writer of short-stories England has ever possessed, and how **"Montes the Matador," "Sonia"** and **"The Stigmata"** will rank among the supreme creations of art; how, as the work of Frank Harris has progressed, he has touched higher and yet higher issues, while at every stage of his achievement his work has been of its kind supreme. I shall try to show where and how *The Bomb* is one of the greatest novels ever written in the English language. I shall try to show where and how Frank Harris is the greatest creative critic whom the world has known; how he has seen where his greatest predecessors in criticism, Coleridge and Goethe, have had but a half-vision. This is what I shall attempt to do. . . .

Frank Harris seems to have got more than his ten pounds' worth from me, after all. But it was a truly horrible position for me to be in to have discovered, within a few days of writing that, that one at least of his masterpieces was a masterpiece— of plagiarism. As my admiration and affection had been unbounded, so was my recoil. I could not write a word of the promised article on his work; nor could I offer a word of explanation why it did not appear, in the next number, or in any other. And the man who had thus let me down was the man of whom I had said in public, in complete sincerity, that he was one "whose word of praise can change the whole of life for me for months, and a word of condemnation make me cry till I think my heart would break." (pp. 178-81)

John Middleton Murry, "Ave, Imperator Amoris," in his Between Two Worlds: An Autobiography, *Jonathan Cape, 1935, pp. 174-83.*

E. M. FORSTER   (essay date 1938)

[*Forster was a prominent English novelist, critic, and essayist whose works reflect his liberal humanism. His most celebrated novel,* A Passage to India *(1924), is a complex examination of personal relationships amid the conflicts of the modern world. Although some of Forster's critical essays are considered naive in their literary assessments, his* Aspects of the Novel *(1927), a discussion of the techniques of novel writing, is regarded as a minor classic in literary criticism. In the following excerpt, Forster defends Harris's controversial biography of Oscar Wilde, despite its apparent deviations from the actual facts of Wilde's life.*]

"It should be our faith that everything in this world can be expressed in words," wrote Wilde. The gods heard his prayer, and ironically decreed that words should be his portion through life and after it. Words used not scientifically, but as implements of imprecision. He was a charming talker in the days

of his gaiety and happiness, then people began to talk about him and a trickle of gossip swelled into torrents of forensic eloquence, and swept him away. *"De Profundis!"* he cried in prison, but *"Ad te clamavi"* would have been the fitter title; it is an appeal, not a meditation. After prison, he resumed the old talk—less charmingly. And when he died the rest was by no means silence, for his friends began to quarrel and bring libel actions against one another, so that, nearly forty years later, words are still being bandied over his grave. He would not have disliked such an immortality, indeed he did what he could to forestall it. But it is time he took his place in English literature and English social history, apart from either scandal or *réclame,* and he is hindered by this slush of words.

Things are tightening up at last, and a few years ago Dr. [G. J.] Renier published an excellent and detached little monograph upon him [Oscar Wilde]. This "life" by Frank Harris [*Oscar Wilde: His Life and Confessions*] is also excellent, but it is far from detached. It vibrates from cover to cover with the very special voice of its author. It has a long forty-page polemical preface by Bernard Shaw, and it has no index. Nothing more typical of the subject, or less helpful to the student, can well be imagined. Written in 1910, when tempers were still high, it was published in America in 1918. Now it appears in England, with "a few emendations." We are not told what the emendations are, and if the truth about Wilde or about anything is of interest to us, we shall remain unsatisfied.

Harris was many things: liar, blackguard, swindler, blackmailer, renegade, snob, cad, editor of the *Evening News,* the *Fortnightly,* the *Saturday Review, Hearth and Home,* &c.; man of letters, novelist, composer of hotel-puffs, author of an anatomical autobiography; cowboy, company promoter, Tory-Anarchist candidate for Hackney; alternately rival to Bismarck, to Shakespeare, and to Christ; and friend to Oscar Wilde, and a most loyal, brave, generous and appreciative friend to him. He was all that, and one could extend the list. He had energy, intelligence, and insight, and could get at literature from the inside, but his temper was violent and judgements often extreme; on one occasion he referred to *The Spectator* itself as a "vile bubble." Possibly born in Ireland about 1855, probably Welsh by birth with a touch of Hebrew, fond of alluding to his school days at Rugby while wearing an Old Etonian tie, he first becomes clear to our astonished gaze at the University of Kansas, where he accuses one of the professors of sexual frigidity—a favourite form of snub. Returning to England, he took to journalism, and gained, he tells us, the intimate confidence of Thomas Carlyle, who once took off his hat when they were at Hyde Park Corner, and stood doing penance in the rain for Mrs. Carlyle's death. (Sceptics denied that he had ever met Carlyle; "I'm an artist, not a reporter," was his reply.) Then he made a good marriage, climbed into smart society, got to know Wilde about 1884, stuck to him through his misfortunes, and did his best to help him and make him work after he came out of prison. Later on he himself went to prison, for contempt of court, squealed for mercy, and then in a rage with all things English went to America and applauded Germany in the early years of the War. He died in 1931, in France.

These facts about Harris (they are taken from Mr. Hugh Kingsmill's study of him [see Additional Bibliography]) should be borne in mind while his life of Wilde is being read. They are not brought out in Mr. Shaw's introduction. Mr. Shaw is always generous to the bottom dog, even when the dog is Mussolini, and for Harris he has a chivalrous affection of long-

Harris being taken to prison, after his conviction on charges of libel. BBC Hulton Picture Library/The Bettmann Archive.

Wilde; to use a phrase which was dear to him and his set but now rings a little old-fashioned, he has created a masterpiece. (p. 194)

> E. M. Forster, "The Feast of Tongues," in The Spectator, *Vol. 161, No. 5744, July 29, 1938, pp. 194-95.*

VINCENT O'SULLIVAN (essay date 1939)

[*O'Sullivan was an American poet, novelist, and critic who was a close friend of Wilde. In the following excerpt, he condemns* The Life and Confessions of Oscar Wilde.]

[Frank Harris] will not survive as a writer. Already his **"Elder Conklin"** and his other stories are utterly forgotten. As to the play, *Mr. and Mrs. Daventry,* he protests in his book against those who saw in it the hand of Oscar Wilde. He was entirely right. The play is throughout by Harris, and it is worthless.

But he may survive as the author of one book. Bernard Shaw has said that Oscar Wilde must stand or fall by Harris' book. It is nearer the truth to say that Harris must stand or fall by his *Life of Wilde.* For it is certain that no other book of his will carry his name to the generations to come. And that because there will always be people wanting to know about Wilde. Wilde will carry Harris on his shoulders to posterity, little as Harris foresaw such an outcome.

That being the case, it behoves us to look a little closely at this production.

As a novel, it would not be a bad novel, with its brisk dialogues and interest sustained throughout—a sort of masculine *Manon Lescaut,* having Oscar as the capricious and extravagant Manon, the generous and much-enduring Harris as des Grieux, and Lord Alfred Douglas as the *spadassin* Lescaut. Or, if he had given it out as a "romanced life," a bastard form of art which had not come into being when he wrote it, it would be better than a whole crowd of such books we have seen of late years. But the awkward thing is that he is dealing with a real man and facts, and he travesties the man and distorts the facts. They say his book was written in 1910 or thereabout. It was published, or at any rate, put on sale in America while he was there during the war, under the title, *The Life and Confessions of Oscar Wilde*—a title copied from the Broad-sheets of the Eighteenth century which were sold to the mob that clamoured round the cart carrying some condemned man to Tyburn. The choice of such a title, with all its implications, gives the measure of Harris' good taste, and of the spirit in which the book was written.

Of all the books about Wilde, it is this which has done most harm to his memory. Shaw has no sympathy with the man or his work; but with Harris it was different. He professed immense admiration for Wilde and Wilde for him.

"Do you know Frank Harris?" Wilde asked me one day.

"Yes; he tries to imitate you."

"Frank?" cried Wilde indignantly. "He imitates nobody. He is originality itself."

I do not think that Harris realized what he was doing. On the last page he expresses some misgivings as to the accuracy of the portrait he has presented. He did not want to hurt the memory of Wilde, that I swear. When he spoke to me about Wilde nearly twenty-five years after his death, there were tears in his eyes. And yet his book has enabled Mr. Shaw, who had

standing, for they worked together in the old brilliant days of the *Saturday Review*. He cannot forgive the world for driving him into the wilderness, and he spends much time in proving that he was not a liar—employing the ingenious argument that if a man is called a liar by an untruthful person that man must be telling the truth. The *Life* is not a reliable document, and no amount of sidetracking will make it one. Its value is of another kind: it gives a convincing and touching picture of Wilde as a man, and its account of his misfortunes is terrific. The earlier chapters do not rise above good journalism, but the central part (Chapters 10 to 18) is tremendous in its cumulative effect, quietly written, superbly planned, and carrying the narrative over the smooth lip of the waterfall on to the complicated agonies below. Cruelty, cowardice, hypocrisy swirl round the victim, his very virtues suck him in, he is insulted and humiliated, yet he is recognisably a man. Harris, repelled by his temperament but alive in his genius and gentleness, is the perfect producer of his tragedy, falls into neither sentimentality nor cynicism, moves on from point to point till the whirlpool is passed and the draggled figure re-emerges. After prison, the book is less good. The action shifts to the Continent, and becomes slightly foolish and scabrous, and the boosting of the *Ballad of Reading Gaol* wakes the critic in some of us, and breaks the spell. Have we been listening to the truth? we wonder; were these words the right words?

The expert in Wildeana will certainly find much to query—facts amiss, reputations awry. Research of a sort has still to be done; there are diaries to be unlocked, toothless survivors to be cross-questioned; it has yet to be elicited who overheard whom saying exactly what to whom about whom in the Café Royal half a century back. Harris wrote from memory, as well as being a scamp. All the same, he has written *the* book on nothing else to go upon, for he never saw Wilde in his last years, to describe Wilde as an "unproductive drunkard and swindler."

There is much dialogue in the book. Some of the speeches—for they are quite that—Wilde no doubt pronounced, at least in substance; but many others have not Wilde's form of thought, and very few have the true ring. In one of them Wilde is made to say that he desires to have "the blue sea at my feet, the blue sky above, and God's sunlight about me." That "God's sunlight" came from Wisconsin, or somewhere like that; never from Wilde. And the whole phrase seems too commonplace for Wilde. On the other hand, the account of the relations between Wilde and Beardsley, their attitude towards each other, is very shrewd, very exact. Harris gets nearer to Beardsley, whom he saw much less, than he does to Wilde.

What is more serious is the general impression left by these talks between Harris and Wilde. It is that of a strong, wholesome man laying down jejune moral truths to a flabby impostor who wails and whines. Always Harris wins out; and readers having nothing else to go by must admire the virtue and apostolic fervour of that good Mr. Harris. As typical an example as any is the account given of a supper with Emilienne d'Alençon, a music-hall actress of the time. As Harris relates it, you would think that Mr. Mulberry of Zion chapel had been inveigled among the daughters of Babylon by the immoral Wilde. I can't imagine what public Harris thought he was writing for that he should unload all this popcock. His book was published in the United States, but at that date the Americans had long got beyond the camp-meeting view of life.

This tone recurs throughout. Always Harris has the noble part. He is the benefactor, generous and disinterested, who spares no trouble to lift up his fallen and sinful friend. He is Spartan; Wilde is self-indulgent. Wilde hated walking; Harris walked several miles a day. Wilde idles away the hours; Harris is a worker and a man of action. No; Harris did not mean to hurt Wilde's memory when he wrote his book, but he could not resist glorifying himself at the expense of Wilde, and that kind of thing has always fatal results.

Of the things remarkable in the book, one is the smarmy self-righteous cant, like a street-corner preacher. He is particularly scandalized by Wilde's so-called excesses in eating and drinking. That is almost comical coming from Harris, the man of lunches, and heavy dinners, and champagne. One has to have known him, one has to have seen his prowesses at the luncheon or dinner table, to appreciate to the full this severity displayed, this austerity. He does not quite snuffle about "Our Saviour," but you expect it every minute. This is the more odd because in his talk Harris did not seem to hold by the Christian religion as expounded in Churches and conventicles.

The book gives the effect of uninterrupted contact. As a fact, Harris did not see much of Wilde in his last years. When he came to Paris for a few days on his way to Monte Carlo, or somewhere else, and wanted to be amused, he would send for Wilde, and Wilde, for whom it meant a few days of excellent living, and perhaps some money, would come gladly and give forth his very best. But Harris' visits never lasted long, and there were long intervals between them.

"What is Frank Harris?" cried Smithers, the publisher, one day, seated among a group of his young poets. "What has he ever done but marry a rich woman?"

"Which of us could do that?" said Dowson. (pp. 15-18)

Vincent O'Sullivan, "Regarding Frank Harris," in The Dublin Magazine, *Vol. XIV, No. 1, January-March, 1939, pp. 7-18.*

OSCAR CARGILL (essay date 1941)

[*An American educator, historian, and literary critic, Cargill edited critical editions of the works of such major American authors as Henry James, Walt Whitman, Frank Norris, and Thomas Wolfe. In the following excerpt, Cargill denounces Harris's writings, maintaining that both their perversity and their literary quality have been overestimated.*]

[Oscar] Wilde was the source of Harris' first literary success, *The Man Shakespeare* . . . , which was originally published as separate essays, beginning with an article, **"The True Shakespeare,"** in the *Saturday Review* for March, 1898. Wilde had shocked England with his allegations of Shakespeare's immorality in "The Portrait of Mr. W. H."; taking his cue from Wilde, Harris sought a similar notoriety by dissecting the love life of the butcher's son of Avon. Of course, he could not agree with Wilde that Shakespeare was a pederast; instead he chose to represent him as a "frail sensuous singer," "a parasite," "a snob of the purest English water" who loathed his wife and became madly infatuated with a maid-of-honor named Mary Fitton. This hopeless passion Harris makes the spring of Shakespeare's work. The exposition of his thesis, however, is accompanied by a running fire of comment on those critics and professors who have made a "Puritan" out of Shakespeare. Even Coleridge, whom Harris admits has seen Shakespeare "by flashes," is not spared—

> . . . But, alas, Coleridge, a Puritan born, was brought up in epicene hypocrisies, and determined to see Shakespeare—that child of the Renaissance—as a Puritan, too, and consequently mis-saw him far oftener than he saw him. . . . There is a famous passage in Coleridge's "Essays on Shakespeare" which illustrates what I mean. It begins: "In Shakespeare all the elements of womanhood are holy"; and goes on to eulogize the instinct of chastity which all his women possess, and this in spite of Doll Tearsheet, Tamora, Cressida, Goneril, Regan, Cleopatra, the Dark Lady of the Sonnets, and many other frail and fascinating creatures. . . .

There is no point here in stressing how much Harris' book owes to some of the critics and professors, like Tyler, Brandes, Dowden, whom he condemns (Kingsmill in his two studies has brought this out adequately); the important thing to note is that *The Man Shakespeare* is one of the important documents on which the Intelligentsia pin their faith that one must be vicious or weak in order to write adequately about viciousness or weakness. We have little way of knowing what Shakespeare's character was, and we are probably as willing to accept the view of Harris as the view that the poet was the soul of virtue, but there is no compulsion to settle on either. There *are* both moral axioms and representations of virtue in the dramas, and it can plausibly be argued that it is as difficult to feign these things as it is to feign either viciousness or weakness without habit and experience. But to adopt either argument is to assume that Shakespeare was blind, dumb, and a blockhead. Five minutes on any street corner in the tumultuous London of his day would have acquainted his eager mind with sufficient specimens of both virtue and vice to fill a dozen plays, and there is no need of assuming that he ever preached at Paul's or lusted for the fickle Mary. As for the claim of the Intelligentsia, it does not follow that if lust produced some of Shakespeare's sonnets a comparable lust will produce anything like them. This theory was pretty much exploded in Greenwich Village in the early 'twenties. In passing, one is forced to remark that the swashbuckling vigor of *The Man Shakespeare* makes it a much more readable book than either the Dowden or Lee studies. Harris, like Whistler, who grappled with the Slade Professor of Art, and Wilde, who sneered at the morals of Oxford, has some consequence as a baiter and destroyer of the ponderous academicians.

Harris also wrote some short fiction in the early 'nineties, collected later in *Elder Conklin* and *Montes the Matador*. . . . These books received fulsome praise when Harris was a power in the critical journals of London, but almost any number of *Western Stories* contains yarns that are quite as good, and there are forgotten people in the early collections of O'Brien who did infinitely better work. In 1908, after a trip to America, Harris published his novel *The Bomb,* which is an account of the Haymarket affair from the point of view of one Rudolph Schnaubelt, who confesses that he threw the bomb which caused the death of eight policemen and for which the State of Illinois took the lives of Spies, Fischer, Engel, and Parsons. Schnaubelt is represented as a rather guileless, good young man, from Bavaria, who proves his goodness in the book by refusing to have relations with a girl, Elsie, despite her warmest entreaties. He comes under the influence of the stout-hearted anarchist, Louis Lingg (who reminds him of the Caesar of Mommsen), just at a time when his indignation at police brutality in Chicago, which he has witnessed as a reporter, makes him putty in Lingg's hands, and he agrees to throw the bomb. Lingg helps him to escape that he may give the world a true account of the affair. *The Bomb* is far from a distinguished piece of writing—indeed, when Harris quotes from "biased" newspaper accounts of the Haymarket affair (which he frequently does) or from current magazine articles on lead and phosgene poisoning among the workers, it is noticeable how the narrative "picks up" in interest. As a tract the book is ineffective because of its hash of doctrine—Socialism, Christianity, anarchy, and hero-worship. Yet *The Bomb* is a pretty good make-shift vehicle for some of Harris' favorite dogmas: the animalism of female passion, the stupidity of formal education ("books develop memories, not minds"), and the brutality of judges. To the 1920 edition is appended a characteristic "Afterword" in which Harris, after citing an alleged remark of Flaubert to the effect that he should have criticized *Madame Bovary* himself because no "fool-critic" could do it, proceeds to "dissect" *The Bomb.* He admits idealizing "Lingg beyond life size" but otherwise finds his own novel a very good job, particularly in view of "the problems" which confronted him—like rewriting the "police" pamphlet on the anarchists. We are not surprised to learn that he regards *The Bomb* as better than *Madame Bovary.*

Harris was proprietor and editor of *Vanity Fair* from 1907 to 1911; after selling this magazine, he began to write for the *English Review* in which were published in the first year of his connection as a contributor two very sensational articles from his pen—**"Thoughts on Morals"** and **"Carlyle,"** the first of his *Contemporary Portraits.* "Thoughts on Morals" contains in brief form the philosophy of abandon later set forth in *My Life and Loves;* the "Carlyle" portrait gave extraordinary offense because Harris alleged in it that Carlyle had confessed to him that his marriage with Jane Welsh had never been consummated. That Harris met Carlyle is conceded by D. A.

Wilson, Carlyle's biographer, but the latter believes that the whole story of the Scotch philosopher's confession is embroidered out of fancy and a "distorted recollection of what Mr. Froude had written. . . ." So, too, it may be doubted if Carlyle ever told Harris that "Heine was a dirty Jew pig." Despite all the assaults upon it, the Carlyle portrait was placed at the beginning of Harris' first volume of *Contemporary Portraits* in 1915. The five volumes . . . which Harris filled with more than ninety "portraits" of his contemporaries would be invaluable if it were possible to accept them for what Harris represents them to be—intimate conversations on vital topics with some of the most distinguished men of his time. The "portraits" have, however, little more factual basis, apparently, than the *Imaginary Conversations* of Landor—they are highly fanciful studies in the main of what Harris presumes he might have wheedled out of his subjects provided that they surrendered cheerfully to hypnotic suggestion. Harris appears to have had two objects in view: the promotion of his own stock (he always shows to advantage over the person whose portrait he draws) and the demeaning of his "sitter" by some revelation of sexual sterility, inhibition, bigotry, or meanness. When he knows nothing about the private life of his subject, or when it is obvious that his sexual life has been complete, Harris sneers at the moral fibre of his writing, as in the case of Upton Sinclair:

> . . . I have now read all of Sinclair's writings and I may as well confess it at once. There's a Puritanism in him that I can't stomach and that, I believe, injures all his work. . . .

There are rare exceptions in *Contemporary Portraits* where Harris praises his subjects, but these exceptions are generally in the case of persons, like Whistler, Shaw, and Mencken, whom Harris recognized to be of his own camp, the élite among the Intelligentsia. Before dismissing these *Portraits* we should note that they are one unsuspected source of Mr. Lytton Strachey's *Eminent Victorians . . .* , and *Queen Victoria. . . .* Strachey, of course, is subtle and erudite where Harris is preposterous and infantile, but he has merely refined the reasons of Harris for his supercilious scorn of Dr. Arnold and Gladstone. And doesn't every aphorism in *Eminent Victorians* proclaim, "What a witty fellow am I"?

Harris must have been at work on the two-volume *Oscar Wilde: His Life and Confessions . . .* when the first of the *Contemporary Portraits* was published, for he tells us that the manuscript had circulated among British publishers, who found it too sensational in its revelations, before he decided to bring it to America and issue it himself. His trip to America, incidentally, was hastened by a temporary unpopularity following a conviction for contempt of court and a short residence in Brixton Prison, after he had tried to shift the blame in his trial upon one of his subordinates. The Wilde biography perhaps should not be regarded as a biographical and critical study at all, but rather as an attempt to bait British Puritanism. Those who have found *Oscar Wilde: His Life and Confessions* prurient, however, should consult a good psychiatrist at their earliest opportunity. The book is vulgar but not obscene, and if one believes—as Harris does—that Oscar Wilde is "a tragic figure of imperishable renown" one is justified in discussing him with even greater frankness, and certainly with more accuracy, than Harris does in his book. One can fairly object, however, to the thesis that Wilde was punished for the envy he aroused in his inferiors— that "his fate in England is symbolic of the fate of all artists; in some degree they will all be punished as he was punished by a grossly materialised people who prefer to go in blinkers and accept idiotic conventions because they distrust the intellect and have no taste for mental virtues.'' The Harris biography is not a plea for a saner treatment of the sexual pervert (Harris denounces the degenerate Taylor who was convicted with Wilde) but a plea for the artist as a special and privileged person. Later (1925), when he accepts and prints the confession of Lord Alfred Douglas to the effect that Wilde was the chief mover in their crime, he attempts to exonerate Douglas also by finding very great merit in the latter's puerile poetry. (pp. 450-55)

My Life and Loves purports to be a candid account of the amorous adventures of a modern Casanova, with tested formulas for successful seduction and shirt-cuff memoranda of trial and error. In his introduction, Harris writes—

> There are two main traditions of English writing, the one of perfect liberty, that of Chaucer and Shakespeare, completely outspoken, with a certain liking for lascivious details and witty smut, a man's speech; the other emasculated by Puritanism, and since the French Revolution gelded to the tamest propriety; for that upheaval brought the middle-class to power and insured the domination of girl-readers. Under Victoria, English prose literature became half childish. . . . I am going back to the old English tradition.

Lascivious details jostle one another in the first volume of *My Life and Loves,* but there is a conspicuous absence of the ''witty smut'' our stalwart forebears are alleged to have relished and for which we ourselves have a taste. Instead, there are drooling dialogues between Harris and his loves which make one wish that he had for ever been confined to Brixton prison and forbidden the use of pen and ink. However glamorous his person, it is inconceivable that he ever seduced a woman worth seducing with his talk—if this is a sample. Instead of producing a rival for the *Confessions* of Rousseau, as he fancied he had done, Harris merely emitted a cheap, pornographic fiction convincing to small boys, to H. L. Mencken (before his marriage), and to Bernard Shaw. After feeling the social rebuke for his first volume (''everywhere I feel the unspoken condemnation and see the sneer or the foul sidelong grin''), Harris considerably ''toned down'' the subsequent volumes, to the probable disappointment of the aforementioned admirers.

The elephantine seriousness of *My Life and Loves,* the lumbering of behemoth in muck, is discarded in the ''unauthorized'' biography of *Bernard Shaw* . . . which Frank Harris completed a few months before his death on August 26, 1931. The success of this spirited book is in no small sense due to the fact that Harris had to match his wits against those of Shaw whose frequent letters to him he has interpolated throughout. It is easy to say that the book is lively solely because of these letters, but that is not altogether true. Harris' remarks that Shaw's father ''in spite of his abstinence'' lasted until 1885, that ''the naughty scenes'' in Shaw's plays are ''so spiceless they could hardly get into a benefit performance for the Girl Scouts,'' and that Shaw's letters to Ellen Terry read to him at times ''like Eugene Marchbanks on a busman's holiday'' give some intimation of the flavor of Harris' special contribution. Yet the critics are justified in preferring the interpolations of Shaw to the commentary of Harris, for they are without exception the better stuff. Frank Harris, lucky in life, was immeasurably lucky in death—he would have burst had he survived long enough to read the reviews of his last ''portrait.'' The universal opinion was that the sitter had outdone the can-

did-camera man. As it was, Harris died content that he was the cheekiest fellow of his generation. Devious are the ways to immortality. (pp. 456-57)

> *Oscar Cargill, ''The Intelligentsia,'' in his* Intellectual America: Ideas on the March, *The Macmillan Company, 1941, pp. 399-536.*

VINCENT BROME (essay date 1959)

[*Brome is an English biographer, novelist, and critic. In the following excerpt from his full-length biography of Harris, he assesses Harris's literary talents.*]

It is unfortunate that Frank Harris remains in the mind of the wider public as the author of a pornographic book and nothing else. Conceivably he would not have become a figure known throughout the world if he had not written *My Life and Loves;* but his reputation in those circles which appreciate great editing and very considerable powers of writing was not damaged by the pornography.

In the hey-day of the late nineteenth century, Frank Harris was not alone in living the life he did; it was, in one sense, his misfortune that economic necessity drove him to commercialize his private life, and expose it to the public eye. However, the motives which gave birth to *My Life and Loves* were complex and it would be absurd not to acknowledge very special twists in Harris' psychology which permitted him to write and publish such a book, where other people would have recoiled from it. Those twists were partly the result of early indoctrination, partly self induced and partly accidental.

As a critic he was perceptive in the sense of having an appreciation of great work which he could convey in the most stimulating way, but he was incapable of subtle analysis of acknowledged or unacknowledged masterpieces, and did not understand criticism in the academic sense of the word. As a novelist he did not amount to much on the evidence of *The Bomb* and *Great Days.* As an editor he was remarkable and brought those uneasy bed-fellows literature and journalism into a synthesis seldom realized since his day. As a short story writer his style, derivative from Maupassant, was admirably suited to his purpose and in two or three stories he employed his crisp evocative language to write narratives which still grip the attention and compare, in one or two cases, with some of Maupassant's work.

As a short story writer he matured comparatively late and he was advanced in years when his book *Undream'd of Shores* revealed his powers at work to write the savage little vignette **''A Fit of Madness,''** in which a husband goes mad, imagines his wife a stranger and makes love to her as he did when they were first married. Recovering from his madness he treats her coolly and carelessly again and his wife bursts out, ''My God! It's terrible to think you're cured so soon.'' A not unexpected blend of cynicism and sentimentality, brutality and tenderness marked these stories. On the surface, nothing could have been more Hemingway in its detachment than the cool representation of violence in **''A Chinese Story,''** but if one read carefully, echoes of a crudely concealed enjoyment came up to mar the detachment. Nothing could have been more sophisticated than the woman—loved by the narrator, in the story **''Central Africa''**—enjoying for dinner, part of the smoked thigh of a young girl of 13 killed in an accident, but once again, the narrator's revulsion rings false. Many kinds of horror are let loose in these stories, and several remain, underneath, sensual indulgences. It was Harris finding fresh ways of stirring his jaded appetites. He had always hoped that he would write a love story with the delicacy of Turgenev, or a piece of realism equal to Maupassant's *Bel-Ami*. It did not happen. But there were stories which at least bear some comparison with the lesser works of these masters—like the **"Miracle of the Stigmata."**

As a person . . . the inevitable concomitant of virility and toughness showed itself in his personality as a form of sentimentality. The roué had to romanticize the object of his appetites and Harris' apparent cynicism—especially with women—sometimes became sentimental. There was also the falsity of a man frequently acting the emotions he dare not, or could not, experience in reality, but his personality developed through many phases and it was only in young manhood that the unscrupulous opportunist showed the first seeds of what was to become a scoundrel. He did not desire to become a scoundrel because he enjoyed the experience of being one. He became a scoundrel because that was a short cut to the success he craved. Happier sides of his nature were frequently obscured by sheer gossip and notoriety.

He had known the experience called love, he had on occasion been generous, he did sometimes tell the truth devastatingly, and it needed great courage to face up to and survive the censure which his conduct inevitably brought down on his head. But, alas, nothing in the end could justify the life he led; not even the fact that he was a considerable writer, because in the end he wasted his talents on the tawdry, the sordid, and the second-rate.

So many of his talents were squandered. A man who could enthral Oscar Wilde, Bernard Shaw, Max Beerbohm and—sometimes—H. G. Wells with his talk, was no mean fellow. Developed and applied to different ends the combined abilities of Harris might have carried him to fame instead of notoriety in some very high places. Fate—and Frank Harris—decreed otherwise.

A biblical grandeur broke through his own last words:

> There is an end of time and an end of the evil thereof; when delight is gone out of thee and desire is dead, thy mourning shall not be for long . . . Yet the adventure of life was glorious and the magic of moments of love and pity and understanding beyond description or thanks.

In those words he had written the epitaph which he himself would have preferred. (pp. 231-33)

> Vincent Brome, in his Frank Harris, *Cassell and Company Limited, 1959, 246 p.*

STANLEY KAUFFMANN (essay date 1963)

[*Kauffmann is one of America's most well-known contemporary film and theater critics. A contributor of reviews to several magazines, he is currently the film critic of* The New Republic. *Although the theater and cinema are of primary concern to Kauffmann as a critic, he is also knowledgeable in the field of world literature. In the following excerpt, Kauffmann praises the courageous candor of* My Life and Loves.]

[Frank Harris's] most famous work . . . is his five-volume autobiography, *My Life and Loves*. . . . It was begun in New York in 1920 and was finished in France almost 10 years later. The serial appearance of the volumes, in France and Germany, had produced various scandals and police actions that had delayed

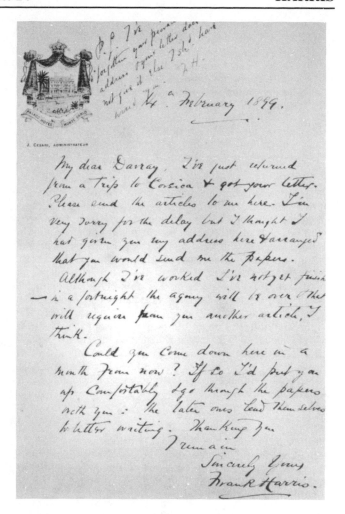

Holograph copy of a letter from Harris to his French publisher.

the aging and weakening man. This autobiography fulfills the prophecies of Shaw and George Moore. Shaw had written him in 1915: "Your most interesting book will be your autobiography." Moore had said, grandly but truly, "You have, in yourself, a subject that will carry your name down the ages, if you write it with the necessary sincerity: that of Jean-Jacques; and it will not surprise me if you do write it."

On every other score Harris is certainly a minor writer, largely a negligible one. *The Bomb*, a novel about the Haymarket murders in Chicago, is a wooden attempt at the then new naturalism, leagues below Frank Norris, not up to the level of Upton Sinclair's *The Jungle*. His stories are in the *fin-de-siècle* tradition that treated the short story as a minuscule melodrama, the dilution of de Maupassant aggravated by, among others, O. Henry. His work on Shakespeare, carefully analyzed by Shaw in the preface to *The Dark Lady of the Sonnets*, was, in its humanistic bent, an interesting departure in its day but is now of small value to scholars or general readers. His *Contemporary Portraits* are sporadically enlightening. His biography of Wilde must be used supplementally to a factually reliable and complete work but has many colorful memories and impressions. His Shaw biography, written in collaboration with Frank Scully, the American journalist, is factually dependable, as far as it goes, because of a possibly unique distinction: the subject himself corrected the proofs after the author's death. Shaw's postscript says:

> Frank knew very little of the facts of my life, and, having no patience for the very dull work of investigation . . . put in a good deal of guesswork. . . . I have got rid of the contradictions . . . by simply supplying or correcting the facts. . . . All the criticisms, jibes, explosions of passing ill humour, and condemnations have been piously preserved.

In sum, his other books assure Harris of little continuing readership. His autobiography, however, is a work of importance for three reasons. Firstly, the story—despite some inaccuracies, omissions, dilations—has narrative strength; and, unknown to its author, has an arch of pathos in his ebullient youth, rise, decline. Secondly, his meetings and friendships are fascinating: Whitman, Marx, Gladstone, Carlyle, Conrad, Taine, Bismarck, Wagner, Ruskin, Rhodes—this is a helter-skelter handful of some of the figures in the book. One can learn here about Prince Edward's German accent and taste in jokes, about an odd physical power of de Maupassant's, what Lady Randolph Churchill said about the terminal insanity of Winston's father. One can also learn that Harris thought that Henry James had a "Jewish-looking nose"—a remark that, ironically, was often made of Harris himself. In the fashion of the time, many people believed that Harris' *outré* behavior must be due to the fact that secretly he was a Jew—which gossip may explain the modish buzz of anti-Semitism that recurs in all his work. (pp. 24-5)

Third of the reasons for this book's importance is the factor that delayed its publication and gave it its *sub rosa* reputation: the account of the author's sex life, more fully detailed and frankly worded than any such factual account that I know, including those of Rousseau and Casanova.

What was the point of the sexual candor? Was it merely a 70-year-old man smacking his lips over his memories? Suspicion of this cannot be completely ruled out; but it is also clear, I think, that Harris thoroughly believed that a time had come in history to try to put a whole man on paper. Rousseau had said that his attempt was without precedent and would be without imitator. Harris eventually found the courage to disprove him. His fiction (see *The Bomb* and his long story, **"Sonia"**) strains to deal realistically with love and love-making while both his men and women wear literary corsets. When he came to write his memoirs, goaded by a frustrated impulse to truth that at last overwhelmed him and, to some extent, freed from restraint by the world's disregard, he fused the facts of life as he knew them with the world of literature that tried to distort them.

His sexual recollections begin with his peering up girls' dresses in his first school and continue through his explorations in a life-boat on his first sea voyage to various affairs of sorts that one might expect. But his life, and therefore his book, went further. He also describes, for instance, the procurement of girls at an Italian villa for the joint delight of his guests and himself; procurement of a 15-year-old on a ship, of a succession of 12-year-olds in Bombay. Harris does not merely recount sexual adventures of a kind known to many and at least tacitly approved by most; he dares to write details of what some men (Dostoevsky, Nabokov) have treated in fiction and countless others have secretly fantasied. He makes absolutely no moral judgments about any of it, nor does he pretend to such poetics as those of Genet's Divine. He writes of sensual experience

as such, as part of human existence. He does not hold himself up as exemplar but as example.

Shall the reader now transpose this completely amoral sexual biography into a moral context? In varying degrees, none of us can resist doing this. Few mature readers will be offended by the affairs with women, married or not. The sexual detail in them, as well as the language, is surprising to readers of 20th-Century fiction only because it is here used in autobiography. But it would be idle, fake modernism to pretend that the adventures with minors produce no slightest disquiet. It is not my intention to "excuse" them; if our society is to cohere and function, acts of that kind are sensibly taboo. But the preeminent point in the book is that Harris does not ask for our approval. He is telling us what he did—*everything* he did, from escapades that raise chuckles in mixed company to those that cause shock even in the smoking room. Because his sexual life encompassed a range that is fearful autism for most and because of his blazing, almost scornful honesty about it, the very amorality of this chronicle gives it a place in moral history.

The temple sculptures of Konarak, the murals and statuary of Pompeii are only two indexes of the regard in which sex was once held. These works are not Jiggs and Maggie cartoons, they are art by the best artists of the time, executed as public celebrations of esteemed activities in that society's life. These activities, in themselves, have of course not changed. (A gruff English colonel, in a room with me in Pompeii, inspected the wall paintings silently, then grunted: "Hmph. Nothing new under the sun.") What *has* changed is the social estimate of those activities. Despite the pendulum swings of Western conventions, from Cromwell to Restoration, from 18th Century to 19th, sex in our civilization had always been, at best, snigger. With the turn of our century and what can be called the Isadora Duncan age, sex became Beauty; with the emergence of Freud, it was named the chief motive in life, and our chief concern in our personal lives then became how to adjust that motive to the increasing constrictions of society. To Harris, sex was never either dirty or self-consciously Beautiful; nor was it a problem to be faced with deliberate, four-square sobriety nor a force that had to be reconciled to the demands of the times. It simply *was.* He lived, he ate and drank, he worked, he fornicated. (We still don't have a good printable word for it.) He thought as little of either defending or praising sex as he would have done with breathing.

Thus, on the sexual level, his book achieves something that even the great Joyce did not do. Joyce, as novelist, bared the last subconscious quivers of fantasy and wish, always in a context of social repression and disguise. Harris, as autobiographer, has no sexual morals, has (one may say) no subconscious, is not the least concerned with social context. It is not necessary to advocate voyeurism and the procurement of minors to recognize this achievement: that a man was able to record his life *sans* decorative cupids or evasive terminology. Is "Know Thyself" the poet's injunction? Harris has obeyed it in spades and in calling of spades. His sexual life may not be a paragon for the generations but it is certainly, as recorded here, sinless.

As with all his non-fiction, we next have to ask how much of it is true. Mr. Gallagher says in his introduction:

> There is the question of whether Harris invented sex episodes in the hope of increasing sales or heightening effect or whether his memory played him false in recalling details. It does not seem

likely that a man who could accurately quote at length, say, from Swinburne's *Anactoria* and from Macaulay's essay on history fifty years after reading them would find it difficult to remember the faces and anatomies of women.

It seems somewhat naïve to believe that Harris never consulted a text when he went into his occasional (and usually tiresome) bouts of quotation. But even if he did not, I find it easier to believe that he remembered Swinburne and Macaulay than that he remembered, not only most encounters with most women but every detail of most encounters. For example, a Kansas lady, during the act itself, apologized for her awkwardness. Harris says he replied: "Your awkwardness, however, excites me." To have remembered that line (commas and all) fifty-two years after such a moment—and only one among hundreds of such lines in dozens of encounters—beats *Anactoria* all hollow. Gallagher goes on to say: "Those persons still alive who knew him best deny there was any necessity for invention by him." That is conclusive enough; besides it is supported by the ambience, zest, and consistent tone of his sexual writing. The episodes themselves can be believed; it is the memory of minute detail that is in doubt and that is sometimes unwittingly funny. Harris had in general a deficient sense of humor. What other author would put a chapter on an Indian sexual device between a chapter on reminiscences of George Meredith and another on personal immortality?

His financial shadiness, his lies, his deceits, all flourished after he made the crucial mistake of his professional life, which was to give up serious editing for writing. He was a meteoric success as an editor; he was a writer without much success or distinction. His business failures (he died in relative poverty) drove him more and more to stratagems for money. He says that he was once considered for the editorship of *The* (London) *Times* but that his ideas frightened the directors. Both the consideration and the fright are credible. Nevertheless, in that post or a similar one, he would have been enabled to be honest, and might have magnificently redeemed his misdirected talents.

Even these memoirs have small distinction of writing as such. When Harris tries to "write," he gets stuffy. Most of this book is vivid because it seems to be eloquently *told*. One reason that the sexual monosyllables seem perfectly in place is that they are used by a man who seems quite accustomed to them in speech. (He once almost drove Browning up the wall by asking whether he got all the passion of *James Lee's Wife* from one woman, Elizabeth Barret.) Harris, a short man, was personally imposing by reason of his voice—thunderous and bass. Freudians can easily make out a case for his being an oral erotic. Certainly he thrived orally, and therefore this book—the one in which he seems to speak instead of writing and in which he insisted on speaking freely—is his best book. It even runs down with a gaffer's talkiness: the last volume is cranky and patchy and ends with an irrelevant attack on Woodrow Wilson.

Without *My Life and Loves,* Frank Harris was a literary footnote; with it, he now has a firm place in the main text. Surely a chief aim of literature is the deepening knowledge of man through significant communion of experience. The paradox of Harris' book is that, although he was a widely recognized rogue, his memoirs are grounded in a strong impulse to self-revelation, with what Moore called "the necessary sincerity." It is fittingly amusing that this famous liar should end up striking a blow for truth. For with all its shortcomings, in this book Harris has tried to tell the whole story *as far as he is capable of seeing it*. It is a high ambition and one not often genuinely undertaken. (pp. 25-7)

> Stanley Kauffmann, "The Importance of Being Frank," in The New Republic, *Vol. 29, No. 2, December 28, 1963, pp. 23-7.*

MALCOLM MUGGERIDGE   (essay date 1964)

[*An English man of letters, Muggeridge has long had a reputation as an iconoclast. A socialist and outspoken atheist during the 1930s, he later eschewed socialism and embraced Christianity during the 1960s. His conversion, however, did nothing to mitigate his stinging satire. Organized religion, public education, and egalitarianism have all been the objects of his wrath. In the following excerpt, Muggeridge discusses the entertaining braggadocio of Harris's autobiography.*]

It is a curious chance which has made Frank Harris's mendacious and lewd autobiography a valuable literary property some three decades after it was written. As far as he was concerned, it represented a last desperate effort to raise the wind. Like many another, then as now, he turned to pornography as the readiest means of collecting quick profits. The first volume was printed in Germany, and some photographs of nude women were included by way of illustrations to drum up sales. To evade legal troubles publication was ostensibily for private circulation only. Harris's friends (Hesketh Pearson, for instance) were expected to dispose of copies for him, just as they were expected when they visited him in Nice to bring out old Etonian ties and other upperclass regalia which he delighted to wear. . . .

The book's enduring literary reputation, such as it is, would have struck him as well-deserved and less than his due. Does he not characteristically describe it as "the best autobiography ever written"? He could not, however, have been expected to foresee the golden harvest, in both fame and cash, which was to accrue to subsequent purveyors of eroticism, particularly in the field of his own speciality—young girls, on whom he was ever ready to lavish attention, through predominantly, it would appear, with finger and tongue. In any case, through the years *My Life and Loves* had a steady sale under the counter, and embellished the auto-erotic fancies of classroom and bedroom alike. Only now does it take its place, along with other money-spinners in the genre, as a Public Prosecutor's Special on open display. (p. 886)

In his delightful life of Harris published shortly after Harris's death Hugh Kingsmill demonstrates conclusively that there just is no reliable information as to where and when Harris was born, how he spent his childhood, and what happened to him before he appeared in London as the up-and-coming editor of the *Evening News*. Least of all in *My Life and Loves.* Harris was such an inveterate and extravagant liar that even when he tells the truth (as Max Beerbohm remarked, even Harris's inventiveness about himself sometimes ran dry) he can scarcely be believed. The truly extraordinary thing is that nonetheless, with the passage of time, a guarded credulity has come to be extended to his preposterous accounts of conversations with figures like Carlyle, Maupassant, Tennyson and (a particular favourite of my own) General Skobelef at Plevna.

The ridiculous nature of such reminiscences (apart from difficulties over time and place) is well illustrated by what purports to be Jane Carlyle's description of the first night of her marriage, as allegedly retailed to Harris by Carlyle's physician, Sir Richard Quain, at a dinner in a private room at the Garrick

Club. One imagines the scene: the port circulating, the cigar smoking rising. Then Quain embarks on his anecdote, telling it in Jane's own words to him:

> "When we reached the house, we had supper and about 11 o'clock I said I would go to bed, being rather tired: he nodded and grunted something . . . A little later he came up, undressed and got into bed beside me. I expected him to take me in his arms and kiss and caress me. Nothing of the sort, he lay there jiggling like." ("I guessed what she meant," said Quain, "the poor devil in a blue funk was frigging himself . . .") "I thought for some time," Mrs Carlyle went on, "one moment I wanted to kiss and caress him; the next moment I felt indignant. Suddenly it occurred to me that in all my hopes and imaginings I had never got near the reality; silent the man lay there jiggling, jiggling."

In any collection of unconvincing club conversations this one must surely take its place with the hilarious exchange between Mellors and Lady Chatterley's father as recounted by D. H. Lawrence. It is not difficult to see that Harris has put his own inimitable gloss on Froude's suggestion that Carlyle was impotent, strengthening the authenticity by the use of direct speech. He would have made a great gossip-writer in our time. "The truth of Harris's assertions about Carlyle cannot be resolved here," Mr John F. Gallagher, the editor of the present edition of *My Life and Loves,* primly remarks in a footnote. "It is a question of whose word one is inclined to accept." I should say it was.

Another favourite episode of mine is Harris's account of a dinner given to the Lord Mayor of London, Sir Robert Fowler, by Sir William Marriott. Harris, naturally, was seated beside Lady Marriott. He was, he explains, an honoured guest at such gatherings, and "for years never missed the Lord Mayor's Banquet," being "given a good seat at the Lord Mayor's table, nearly opposite him and the chief speakers." At the Marriott dinner Harris

> had just taken a spoonful of clear soup when my nostrils were assailed by a pungent, unmistakable odour . . . I looked at Lady Marriott and saw a shrinking in her face corresponding to the digust I felt. I looked away again to spare her, when suddenly there came a loud unmistakable noise and then an overpowering odour . . . The atmosphere got worse and worse, the smells stronger and stronger, till I rejoiced each time a servant opened the door, whether to go out or come in.

After "another unmistakable explosion," Harris

> could not but look again at my hostess. She was as pale as death, and this time her eyes met mine in despairing appeal. "I'm not very well," she said in a low tone. "I don't think I can see it through!"

"Why should you?" Harris gallantly responded, and took the lady out on his arm, assuring her that, though the hostess, she would never be missed. Nor was she, he adds. Harris regarded himself as a specialist on polite behaviour, and was fond of boasting that his "table-manners were English of the best."

On one occasion he explained how, when put on to bowl in the Eton-Harrow match, he aimed the ball at a boy who deserved chastisement instead of at the stumps. Only those like himself brought up in the English upper classes, he went on, would fully understand the enormity of such an action.

These Harris fantasies, once their complete divorcement from reality is accepted, are not without their interest, and even charm. I like very much this exchange with Maupassant:

> "I suppose I am a little out of the common sexually," he resumed, "for I can make my instrument stand whenever I please."
>
> "Really?" I exclaimed, too astonished to think.
>
> "Look at my trousers," he remarked, laughing, and there on the road he showed me that he was telling the truth.

Or, again, his suggestion that Ruskin was allowed, in Rose Latouche's last illness, to hold her for one whole night in his arms before she died. One imagines the negotiations with the Latouche parents to get their consent to such an arrangement, Ruskin being at the time in his late fifties and completely crazy, and Rose in her early twenties. Harris, obviously, for once had doubts about his plausibility, for he adds that his "notes of all this scene are so fragmentary . . . I can only translate, so to speak, my vague impressions into words." Mr Gallagher, however, manages to provide one of his reassuring footnotes: "Nevertheless, what Harris says squares well with fact."

Harris's own sexual exploits are described with gusto. They began (one cannot but feel authentically) with dropping his pencil in class when a child of 10 with a view to staring up at the knickers of the little girls while searching for it: a spectacle which even then interested him more than the blackboard. Thenceforth, in the most literal sense, he never looked back. One notes an abiding concern not to squander his sexual resources, as, for instance, General Skobelef, that prodigious performer, had done. When retiring for the night Harris was accustomed to bind himself up to prevent nocturnal wastage. The only reliable indication I ever had of his own performance was from his amiable and gifted daughter, wife of an Anglican clergyman, who told me that a lady in a position to know (presumably her mother) had told her that there was nothing on earth which so scared the daylights out of poor old Frankie as a truly passionate woman. This judgment seems to me to be supported by Harris's own oddly inconclusive sexual disclosures.

Another side of him which remains inexhaustibly diverting is his valiant attempt to present himself to his readers as a kind of mystic: contemptuous of that which "wanted wings to lift it into the blue," dismissing whatever "had nothing for the soul." These high sentiments were propounded in his deep bass voice, and with a twirl of his moustache. Immediately after the stomach pump had done its work, he was inclined to reflect on the vanity of human wishes; when the girls the gardener has procured for him and his guests had finished their dance on the lawn ("You never saw a prettier sight!"), put on their clothes and gone home, his thoughts were liable to turn to Jesus and Gethsemane.

Kingsmill describes how when he was 22 he accompanied him to Paris, where they visited a brothel together. Some days later, walking along the Promenade des Anglais in Nice with Harris, Kingsmill became aware of an unfortunate consequence of his indulgence. Just at that moment he heard Harris observe: "Christ went deeper than I, but I have had a wider range of experience.'' I see the two of them: Kingsmill a good deal the larger, faltering a little in his step at the intimation of a disagreeable malady contrasted; Harris bounding energetically along; the fading evening light, the white Mediterranean waves and the yellow beach, the lights coming out along the coast. If Harris belonged anywhere, it was surely there. (pp. 886, 888)

> Malcolm Muggeridge, ''My Life and Lies,'' in New Statesman, *Vol. LXVIII, No. 1760, December 4, 1964, pp. 886, 888.*

SAMUEL HYNES (essay date 1964)

[*An American critic and educator, Hynes has written and edited numerous studies of English literature and literary figures. In the following excerpt, from an essay originally published in the* Times Literary Supplement, *12 November 1964, he considers egotism the defining factor in Harris's work.*]

Frank Harris belongs to a fascinating, if not very important, class of writers—the Literary Rascals. His peers are Doctor Johnson's friend Savage, and poor Chatterton, and Baron Corvo, all writers of small talent and large ambitions, all vain and resentful of the world's indifference, and all more appealing for what they were than for what they wrote. As a class the Literary Rascals are not likely to accumulate doctoral dissertations, or even examination questions; but for the curious reader they offer curious rewards, and none more than Harris. (p. 13)

In [his] picaresque, and on the whole unsuccessful, career Harris was sustained by the rascal's chief solace—a complete and unwavering vanity; he never ceased to believe in, and to proclaim, his own genius. He thought his stories were better than Maupassant's, his plays better than Shaw's; as a critic he placed himself with Ben Jonson, Goethe, and Coleridge—the four critics, he asserted, who had understood Shakespeare. And when an admirer dared to compare *My Life and Loves* to Casanova, Harris replied: ''Casanova! My dear man, Casanova is not worthy to untie my boot-strings!''

As his fortunes declined, his sense of his own greatness increased. In the books from *The Man Shakespeare* on, Harris-the-Prophet, or, as he was fond of describing himself, ''God's spy,'' becomes increasingly prominent. The Shakespeare book announced the approach of the ''Kingdom of Man on Earth,'' in which, it was clear, Harris would play the role of messiah, and the later writings show an increasing fondness for references to Christ, often as an implied analogy to Harris (in the *Life and Loves,* for example, he remarks ''I, too, had to be about my father's business,'' and refers to his ''disciples'' and his ''Beatific Vision''). Augustus John, after reading the first draft of Harris's *Oscar Wilde,* asked the author ''what the devil he meant by dragging in Jesus Christ on every other page?'' The answer is obvious: for Harris, Christ was a Harris-figure.

One's natural reaction to such egomania is to dismiss the author of it all as simply a crank; but Harris will not quite submit to such dismissal. Though his own estimates of his importance were wildly inflated, he was nevertheless a significant figure in the literary history of his time. It is not surprising that his real excellences were in those activities in which personal vanity is least freely expressible—in his editing, and in his journalistic reporting. His editing of the *Fortnightly* was able, but not distinguished, but the *Saturday Review* for the few years that he ran it was the best paper of its kind, and a glance at

the list of contributors—Shaw, Wells, Stephen Crane, Arthur Symons, Cunninghame Graham, and, of course, Max Beerbohm—shows that Harris had, for a time at least, an acute sense of literary promise.

Of Harris's nearly thirty books, only the biographical writings are readable today. Both the Wilde and the Shaw biographies are well done (though there is some evidence that the excellence of the Shaw owes more to Harris's ghost-writer, Frank Scully, and to Shaw himself than to Harris); and a clever editor could select one volume of very interesting sketches from the five volumes of *Contemporary Portraits*. Harris's biographies have been called impressionistic sketches, and this is a fairly accurate description, but one should add that in each frame there are always *two* faces at once, like a double-exposed negative: one is the ostensible subject, the other Harris's small-town-seducer's face, saying ''Look at me, I'm more interesting, more important, a better writer and a better lover than my subject ever was.'' Such portraiture can scarcely be called objective, but it is often extremely entertaining, in the way that indiscreet gossip is.

It is not surprising that Harris's best writing should have this gossipy quality, for many of his acquaintances—including Max Beerbohm in a caricature—have testified that he was ''the Best Talker in London.'' He was evidently a born teller of tales, and to this gift his years in America seem to have added skill in that characteristically American art form, the dirty joke (according to Harris he endeared himself to King Edward VII with such stories, though the examples he offers in *My Life and Loves* are not likely to make even a commoner laugh). But he did not write his stories as well as he told them, and when he turned from fiction to criticism and ideas he wrote very badly indeed. Harris did not have a mind equipped for fine discriminations, and his prose reflects his mind; his style is crude and aggressive, forceful at times, but full of hasty compromises with banality of phrase and triteness of idea. (Like most vain men Harris found even his own platitudes fascinating because they were his.) But his style reveals something more than vanity; it reveals his complete lack of sensitivity. He had, one feels, neither a sensitive ear, nor a sensitive eye, nor a sensitive heart (''On Harris,'' Shaw observed, ''delicacy was thrown away''). When he was aware of suffering, as in Wilde's case, he was capable of great loyalty and generosity; but he does not seem often to have been aware of other people, except as they reflected himself. There is a revealing confession of this fact in his ''portrait'' of Olive Schreiner. Harris had met her, and had found her attractive; he then introduced her to George Moore and to his astonishment saw that she was very much impressed, ''Curiously enough,'' he wrote, ''her admiration for Moore brought my interest in her to an untimely end. No one could be really important to me who admired Moore so intensely.'' The interesting thing is that he found such an obvious response to wounded vanity curious.

Harris's egotism is the defining characteristic of his mind. When circumstance or subject kept his ego at bay he was capable of good work: but when he made himself his subject his writing became preposterously inflated, uncontrolled, inaccurate, and at last simply dull. *My Life and Loves,* the work of his declining years, is a very revealing book, but not, one feels, in quite the way that Harris meant it to be. The best of it—the narrative of his early life and some of the portraits and anecdotes of the London years—is vigorously and vividly done. This is Harris the talker, and reading these pages one can believe Harris's boast that he had been invited to every great house in London. But reading the worst of the book—the crude, vulgar, vain worst—one can also believe Wilde's rejoinder to that boast: "Yes, Frank—*once.*" Unfortunately there is more of the worst than of the best in the book, and long before the end the Best Talker in London has become the Biggest Bore.

An account of Life and Loves would, one might expect, involve other people, but Harris had the egotist's instinct for treating people as aspects of himself, and his "portraits" became progressively more self-regarding and less distinct as he grew older. This instinct is also, of course, the instinct of the pornographer (who is merely the egotist at the keyhole) and it is not surprising that Harris, when he turned from his triumphs in society to his triumphs in bed, wrote about sex in the manner and style of the cheapest Soho trash. This is not to say that *My Life and Loves* is a pornographic book in any sense that the Director of Public Prosecutions would accept, but simply that its attitudes toward human sexual experience associate it with *What the Chambermaid Saw* rather than with *Lady Chatterley's Lover.* The faceless anonymity of the women involved, the emphasis on super-human sexual powers, the invariable success of the seducer—these are all characteristic of the pornographic attitude. Pornography dehumanizes sex by treating whole human beings as merely organs, and Harris's book is pornographic in this sense. The "truths" that he claims to reveal are not general truths about sex, but rather inadvertent exposures of his own emotional limitations. Psychologists may find the book a useful example of the Don Giovanni Complex (or perhaps rather the Leporello Complex, for, like most sexual braggarts, Harris would rather count than conquer); but seekers after the truth about sexual love will search in vain through these vain pages.

My Life and Loves is a poor thing, and an unworthy record of its author's life and character. During his best years Harris must have been an impressive man—certainly men of judgment freely testified to their admiration for him. Arnold Bennett called Harris "one of the most extraordinary men I ever met", Wilde dedicated *An Ideal Husband* (a most ironic choice) "To Frank Harris, a slight tribute to his power and distinctions as an artist, his chivalry and nobility as a friend"; and Shaw wrote his friend's epitaph: "Here lies a man of letters who hated cruelty and injustice and bad art, and never spared them in his own interest."

Though these are the praises of friendship, yet they point to real virtues. But it was Harris's flaw that he could not rest content with the praises of others; his vanity, as he once confessed, was as abnormally developed as his ambition, and no praises, not even his own, could satisfy it. *My Life and Loves* is a ponderous, gross book, a monument to that abnormal vanity, and not to the whole man; it would be a pity if such a complex and often entertaining literary rascal were to be remembered, not by his best writing, but by this, nearly his worst. (pp. 14-17)

Samuel Hynes, "Frank Harris: The Complete Literary Rascal," in his Edwardian Occasions: Essays on English Writing in the Early Twentieth Century, Oxford University Press, 1972, pp. 13-17.

RICHARD BOSTON (essay date 1971)

[*In the following excerpt, Boston contends that Harris's controversial autobiography displays admirable frankness and refreshing imagination.*]

Nowadays [Frank] Harris's fiction is largely forgotten, and even his books of Shakespeare and Wilde are hardly read. Max Beerbohm called him the best talker in London (in the London of Wilde and Shaw), but the spoken word is gone. He is portrayed memorably in *The Diary of a Nobody*, but how many readers know that Mr Hardfur Huttle is Frank Harris? Or care?

What does remain, and remains overwhelmingly, is *My Life and Loves,* the autobiography he wrote in five volumes at the end of his life. It is a more remarkable achievement than seems to be generally recognised. It is wrong to think of it simply as a dirty book. In the first place, the "loves" account for only a small proportion of the whole work, a tenth at most, and the least interesting part at that. Even so the erotic passages are by no means worthless and can't be dismissed as mere pornography.

Pornography takes place in what Steven Marcus calls "pornotopia," a utopia of sexual activity in which sexual organs that just happen to be attached to human bodies are juxtaposed in as many combinations as possible. With Harris, the penis never becomes more important than its owner (nothing could be more important than Frank Harris). Unlike writers of pornography, he describes a world in which such inconveniences as pregnancy, veneral disease, menstruation and jealousy are clear and present dangers. The girls are not, as in pornography, depersonalized objects but real people, and Harris usually treats them with consideration. It is not true to say, as Hugh Kingsmill does, that "It is frankly as his victims that Harris paints most of his early loves."

To have paved the way for Henry Miller may have been an achievement of questionable value, but Harris deserves credit for his courage in writing not only with such explicitness on subjects that were not at that time mentionable in polite society, but also for publishing it under his own name. Whether or not he was right in believing that the revolt against Mrs Grundy was "the most important social work of any writer today," it was a pardonable exaggeration and a sympathetic position. Apart from his own writing, Harris gave practical help to Vizetelly when prosecuted for publishing Zola, and shocked the "unco' guid," as he calls them, by refusing to dissociate himself from Oscar Wilde. Harris's anti-Grundyism brought him unpopularity, persecution and even prosecution, and amply refutes those who have interpreted his every action as motivated only by opportunism and self-interest.

The other attack made on *My Life and Loves* is that it is all a pack of lies. An early reply to the autobiography was called *The Lies and Libels of Frank Harris,* and Harris's biographers always gleefully point out that if we are to take his word for it he was born on three different dates in two different countries. Certainly Harris is frequently inaccurate, but his lies are usually in the good cause of making the truth more interesting. He refers to someone who died of hiccups in 1875: in fact the man died more boringly 37 years later of diabetes. Hugh Kingsmill remembers Harris late in life wearing an Eton tie and reminiscing about his schooldays at Rugby: needless to say he had been to neither school.

Obviously Harris is not a reliable witness, but he is a most entertaining one. He is like a latter-day Aubrey, presenting us with an incredibly rich, varied and vivid picture of the times and society he lived in on both sides of the Atlantic, in Africa and in Japan. There are anecdotes and portraits about everyone from Maupassant and Taine to Rhodes and Edward VII, and details (such as about Carlyle's impotence) which you find nowhere else.

What is remarkable is not the lies Harris told, but the truth. This is what really upset people. Harris says that if the mothers of England knew what goes on the dormitories of the boarding schools "they would all be closed, from Eton and Harrow upwards or downwards, in a day." That was (is) perfectly true, but when did anyone want to know the truth?

When Harris was prosecuted in Nice after the publication *My Life and Loves,* it seems to have been at the instigation of the British Foreign Office. Their objections were, apparently, to passages about Edward VII, Randolph Churchill, and an ex-Lord Mayor of London whose table manners, to use Kingsmill's phrase, were of the worst. From Kingsmill's pussy-footed account one might suppose that Harris had accused the City gent of using the wrong spoon. In fact what Harris did was to give an account (again, where else could one find it?) not simply of the gluttony that went on when the Victorian middle classes were at table, but also of the appalling stench of farting. It is typical of British hypocrisy that the opprobrium has been heaped not on the farters but on the man who asked for some fresh air.

My Life and Loves is fascinating not only as an unrivalled portrait of the times, not only for its wealth of social detail,

Harris shortly before his death. Arthur Leonard Ross.

not only for its anecdotes about literary and political personages, but above all for the character of Harris himself that comes so powerfully across. He is one of those writers who—like Svevo, like the Boswell of the London Journal, like Norman Mailer—have created comic masterpieces out of their own characters. Harris dominates the whole huge book, with his vanity and boasting, but above all by his tremendous vitality. He may have been a rascal, a rogue, a cad, but in the stifling, puritanical, repressed, hypocritical society he lived in, the bounder emerges as a distinctly attractive role. In his way Harris was the most honest of the lot of them. He was open and generous, and with his colossal energy seemed like a great force of nature. As Enid Bagnold says, "He *was* an extraordinary man. He had an appetite for great things and could transmit the sense of them."

Richard Boston, "Utterly Frank," in New Statesman, *Vol. 82, No. 2119, October 29, 1971, p. 596.*

ELMER GERTZ (essay date 1975)

[*Gertz is an American author and attorney who has been involved in many legal cases concerning literature and censorship. In the following excerpt, he discusses the liberating effect of Harris's moral iconoclasm.*]

[Frank] Harris had three great heroes—Shakespeare, Jesus, and himself, and not necessarily in that order. There can be no doubt that he read all of Shakespeare's plays and poems so often that they impressed themselves upon his memory, life, and style. He found himself differing almost violently with other students of Shakespeare, even when he borrowed from them. Inevitably, he wrote one major work on the subject, *The Man Shakespeare,* and other studies and a play as well. Just as the Wilde biographers have pecked at Harris, the Shakespeareans have been, if anything, more lividly bitter against him. They have accused Harris of making Shakespeare a man after the fashion of Harris himself—that is, a slave to passion. They have refused to believe that Shakespeare unlocked his heart, not alone in the sonnets, but in all that he wrote. They think of Shakespeare as being above his work. Harris sees him as a part of it. It is the great merit of Harris that his writings are like deeds—they stab, stimulate, anger, cajole. Everything bears his personal impress. It is a full-blooded man who has lived and written his stories, novels, essays, critiques. If you do not like the man, you may not like his writings.

The truculent Harris was devoted to the gentle Jesus, and fancied himself as following in His footsteps. He was conscious of no blasphemy. He could criticize Shakespeare for being a snob and weak in some of his ways. But he could not dissect Jesus in any such frank and brutal fashion, whether in his stories or elsewhere. He was persuaded that the world would have to adopt the ways of Jesus if it were to survive; and one cannot say, really, that he is wrong. We have Christians of the pew and pulpit, but few who understand His meaning.

His worshipper, Harris, scarcely emulated the gentle Jesus in his daily life. He sought out every sort of experience, noble and ignoble. He consorted with the money changers, and sought to shortchange them. He dealt with the politicians, the nobility, the generals, the gamblers, even the chefs and maître'd's. He served them for a price and was accused of blackmailing and defaming them. One result was his going to jail briefly, and into bankruptcy. Another was the enrichment of experience leading to his best stories, novels, contemporary portraits, journalism. He saw his punishment, not as flowing from his personal defects, but from the sins of England. He fled to America, at the outbreak of the First World War; wrote a book critical of England and somewhat sympathetic of Germany; gained control of a magazine, *Pearson's,* and made it a highly personal forum for a decade. Just as he had won the excessive devotion of gifted young men in his down-at-the-heels days in London, following his great *Saturday Review* period, he won the almost idolatrous support of other young people in America. Many of them felt that he was an authentic great man, suffering the wounds of neglect because of his qualities rather than his defects. There was, perhaps, some symbolism in his getting his clothes made at the shop run by Henry Miller's father. The young Henry helped Harris to take off and put on his pants for fittings. Miller recalls that Harris was the first great man he ever met. Harris encouraged him.

In this period of his life his great medium was the contemporary portrait—what might be called a psychograph of a celebrated person. There were five volumes of these portraits. The first and most controversial had been published in England; the others in the United States. Harris professed to know all of the poets, philosophers, painters and politicians of his day, and to depict them as they were, whether great or lesser or a mixture of qualities. It was difficult for ordinary critics who had not lived Harris's ample life to believe that the man could know so many of the highly placed persons of several continents. Ever some who knew the opportunities that had come to him questioned his portraits. Nobody, not even a parish priest, could be the recipient of so many confessions. His critics would have been better advised had they looked upon the portraits as the creative efforts of a born storyteller. His aim was to give verisimilitude, poetic truth, rather than factual accuracy in the fashion of census takers and statisticians. . . . Suffice it to say that the subjects of Harris's portraits at their best have a life that is more real than reality, and truer than the facts.

We see this in Harris's two superb novels, *The Bomb* and *Great Days.* The first mentioned is an account of the Haymarket tragedy in Chicago when some idealistic anarchists were unjustly hanged by a community more interested in repression than in curing social evils. The second, by way of contrast, deals with England and France in Napoleon's time. Both novels read like slices of the author's autobiography. It is as if Harris himself shared all of these historical experiences. He personalizes the impersonal; he makes what is outside one's ken as intimate as one's skin. He does this in his Shakespeare books, his Wilde biography, his *Contemporary Portraits,* his short stories, everything he writes. He is a part of everything he sees or imagines. The past becomes present. All become emanations of his spirit and drive.

Nobody knowing Harris would have imagined that he suffered from inhibition, the inability to express himself frankly. But he felt that he was prevented from speaking out with the utmost candor by the restraints imposed upon all creative writers by the Puritanical spirit of the Anglo-Saxon world. He believed that love, bodily love, was the greatest influence in life. Nobody could write of love if he were compelled to corset his women, conventionalize his language, pay undue tribute to the grim and glum Mrs. Grundy. He dreamed of a time when he would set an example for all creative spirits by writing a completely true, completely undraped, autobiography. So, as old age was upon him, when his memory was somewhat dimmed and his style less distinguished than it had been, he wrote his several volumes of autobiography, the first one called *My Life and Loves,* and went abroad to print and market them. We who are now accustomed to Henry Miller, Philip Roth, Norman Mailer, and their ilk, cannot grasp the incredulity with which the conventional world read Harris's narrative of sexual escapades. The police were set upon anyone who dared sell the books. Several young men went to prison for distributing the work. Harris was afraid to return to our shores for a visit until I received assurances from the renowned lawyer, Clarence Darrow, that he would defend Harris if he were arrested. Even in France, Harris was summoned by the police, and left undisturbed only when the great literary masters joined in a manifesto in his behalf.

This had been Harris's experience several times in his life. When he was editor of the *Fortnightly Review,* a popular clergyman, the Reverend Newman Hall, led the pack against him because of the candor with which he depicted a love affair in his story, **"A Modern Idyll."** And when he wrote that we would now regard as an innocuous essay, called **"Thoughts on Morals,"** the editor of the conventional journal, *The Spectator,* stormed against Harris for writing and *The English Review,* for publishing not wholly orthodox observations on life. Outstanding English writers, some of whom did not care for Harris personally, joined in a statement supporting freedom of utterance, which *The Spectator* found unimpressive. When, in his first *Contemporary Portraits,* Harris wrote of Carlyle's confession of impotency and its adverse effect upon his sexually unsatisfied wife, Scottish moralists and others were shrill in their attacks upon him, at least one writing a little book to dispute him. Ironically, this book proved that Harris, as a young man, did know Carlyle, a result certainly not intended by the critic.

By the time Harris died in August 1931, in Nice, France, one could not be sure of his ultimate place in the world's literature. He often expressed himself as confident that he would one day be accepted as a master. He would intone: "We are immortal only when we die." Harris had far greater influence than has generally been recognized. D. H. Lawrence's *Lady Chatterley's Lover,* perhaps James Joyce's *Ulysses,* are products, in some degree, of Harris's influence; even more so the writings of Henry Miller and a flock of good and bad imitators. It is recognized that our literature was retarded in its growth by the baneful power and narrow vision of Bowdler, Victoria, Comstock, Sumner, and a host of like-minded censors here and abroad and their unnamed imitators in numerous villages. Sex was, in Lawrence's phrase, a dirty little secret. Harris's great virtue was that he refused to be confined by the secret and those who guarded it. He spoke out, and he has had many followers, some of whom do not know his name, and others who have denigrated him.

His influences on literary portraiture and biography has been both unrecognized and considerable. We think of Lytton Strachey as being the father of the modern biographical realism and candor, but Harris has an equal claim. Wittingly or unwittingly, his *Contemporary Portraits* and his life of Wilde, of the same genre, have affected all who write of living or historical characters. Shakespearean criticism and biography will never be as they were before Harris. Harris has taught us that the true portrait must deal with blemishes as well as virtues, the inner person as well as the outer, the naked ape no less than the draped social creature. The secret loves are as much the man as the public papers and parades. (pp. 294-99)

I am still not sure whether Harris will live as a writing man, rather than a literary legend. At his best he has qualities that transcend his subjects, his style, and his words. In my time and in an earlier day he was able to inspire many young readers into an almost rapturous love of the great creative spirits and all high endeavor. He made us feel that great poetry, although surrounded by poverty, was nobler and spiritually more rewarding than the worldly successes of the Rockefellers and Astors and their bloated retainers and apologists. He inspired us to go forth boldly into a crass world and to change it by our tilting into a regal sphere fit for saints and seers and singers. Sometimes, later, when we settled into realism, we scolded him for not himself living up to the best that he asked of us. But is that not foolish? It is enough if one ennobles others; it is too much to expect the singer to be like his song. (p. 299)

> Elmer Gertz, "Afterword: The Legend of Frank Harris," in The Short Stories of Frank Harris: A Selection *by Frank Harris, edited by Elmer Gertz, Southern Illinois University Press, 1975, pp. 291-99.*

ADDITIONAL BIBLIOGRAPHY

Bain, Linda Morgan. *Evergreen Adventurer: The Real Frank Harris.* London: Research Publishing Co., 1975, 121 p.
   Brief biography concentrating on Harris's account of his adventures.

Baumann, A. A. "Frank Harris." In his *Personalities,* pp. 191-98. London: Macmillan & Co., 1936.
   Reminiscence revealing previously unknown facts regarding Harris's financial mismanagement of the *Saturday Review.*

Bennett, Arnold. Journal entries for 5 October 1909 and 6 October 1909. In his *The Journal of Arnold Bennett, 1896-1928,* pp. 335-37. New York: Viking Press, 1933.
   Calls *The Man Shakespeare* "masterful"; "the *only* book on Shakespeare."

Burnett, Whit. "Portrait of the Artist at 70-Odd." *Story* 36, No. 5 (1964): 43-51.
   Memoir of the critic's meeting with Harris in 1926.

Cumberland, Gerald. "Frank Harris." In his *Set Down in Malice: A Book of Reminiscences,* pp. 32-46. New York: Brentano's, 1919.
   Account of Cumberland's acquaintance with Harris.

Douglas, Lord Alfred. Chapter Eight. In his *Without Apology,* pp. 64-74. London: Martin Secker, 1938.
   Essay in which Douglas discusses the nature of his own relationship with Harris as well as Harris's relationship with Oscar Wilde.

Gilman, Lawrence. "An Author's Famous Friends." *North American Review* CCII, No. 721 (December 1915): 915-18.
   Takes exception to Harris's conclusions regarding notable authors in volume one of *Contemporary Portraits.*

Grendon, Felix. "Creative Portraiture." *The New Republic* IV, No. 46 (18 September 1915): 187.
   Laudatory review of the first volume of *Contemporary Portraits.*

Hamilton, Gerald. "Frank Harris." *Spectator* 196, No. 6654 (6 January 1956): 10-11.
   Biographical essay in which Hamilton concludes that it was as an editor that Harris excelled.

Hutchison, Percy. "Frank Harris Recalls His Bronco-Busting Days." *The New York Times Book Review* (2 March 1930): 5.
   Review of *On the Trail* in which Hutchinson states: "In [this book] Frank Harris spins a fine 'tall' tale."

Kingsmill, Hugh [pseudonym of Hugh Kingsmill Lunn]. *Frank Harris.* 1949. Reprint. New York: Haskell House, 1974, 176 p.
   Biography written by a former devotee who became disillusioned with Harris.

Krutch, Joseph Wood. "Harris versus Shaw." *The Nation* CXXXIII, No. 3468 (23 December 1931): 701-02.
   Review of *Frank Harris on Bernard Shaw* in which Krutch discusses the characters of the two.

Mencken, H. L. Review of *The Man Shakespeare and His Tragic Life Story,* by Frank Harris. *The Smart Set* XXX, No. 1 (January 1910): 158.
   Finds *The Man Shakespeare* to be entertaining and somewhat plausible, but not thoroughly convincing.

——. "In the Altogether." *The Smart Set* LXXI, No. 2 (June 1923): 139-40.
   Review of the first volume of *My Life and Loves* in which Mencken applauds the courageous honesty of the work.

——. "Frank Harris Again." *The Smart Set* VI, No. 22 (October 1925): 254-55.
   Review of volume two of the autobiography, which Mencken considers "a document in the case for chastity, a dramatic portrayal of [a] young man's struggle to free himself from his instincts and so get play for his ideas."

——. "Harris on Shaw." *The Smart Set* XXV, No. 98 (February 1932): 253-55.
   Review of the Shaw biography. Mencken considers the work "third-rate" compared to Harris's earlier works.

"Notes." *The Nation* 101, No. 2620 (16 September 1915): 361-62.
   Negative review of *Contemporary Portraits* in which the critic denounces Harris's condescending tone.

"Frank Harris Adds to His Portrait Gallery." *The New York Times Book Review* (2 October 1927): 2.
   Negative review of *Latest Contemporary Portraits.* The critic states that the book contains "scarcely a distinguished line, hardly one telling phrase, barely one arresting thought, and nothing to arouse emotion."

Newcomer, Alphonso Gerald. "*The Women of Shakespeare.*" *The Dial* LIV, No. 642 (16 March 1913): 237-39.
   Negative assessment of *The Women of Shakespeare* as wholly unconvincing.

Pearsall, Robert Brainard. *Frank Harris.* New York: Twayne Publishers, 1970, 196 p.
   Biographical and critical study.

Pearson, Hesketh. "Frank Harris." In his *Modern Men and Mummers,* pp. 95-124. New York: Harcourt, Brace and Co., 1922.
   Reminiscences and correspondence. Although this essay is laudatory, beginning "Frank Harris is the most dynamic writer alive," Pearson later revised his estimate of Harris significantly (see entry below).

——. "Rebel Artist." In his *Extraordinary People,* pp. 175-236. New York: Harper and Row, 1965.
   Biographical essay in which Pearson presents an essentially negative assessment of Harris's works and character.

Pugh, Edwin. "His Infinite Variety." *The Bookmen* XLVII, No. 281 (February 1915): 160-61.
   Review of *The Yellow Ticket, and Other Stories* in which Pugh states that Harris "just tells what he sees, and leaves comment to the shallowpates. And that is the crowning glory of his art."

Pullar, Phillipa. *Frank Harris.* London: Hamish Hamilton, 1975, 419 p.
   Recent and comprehensive noncritical biography.

Root, E. Merrill. *Frank Harris.* New York: Odyssey Press, 1947, 324 p.
   Sympathetic, noncritical biography which relies heavily on Harris's own statements regarding his life and adventures.

Roth, Edward. *The Private Life of Frank Harris.* New York: William Faro, 1931, 325 p.
   Noncritical biography based primarily on the stories Harris related to friends and acquaintances.

Scott, Temple. "*The Man Shakespeare.*" *The New York Times Saturday Review of Books* (6 November 1909): 685-86.

Laudatory review of *The Man Shakespeare*, which Scott considers a landmark in the field of Shakespearean criticism.

Scully, Frank. "Harris." In his *Rogue's Gallery*, pp. 210-238. Hollywood: Murray & Gee, 1943.

Memoir in which Scully claims to have written *Frank Harris on Bernard Shaw* entirely without aid from Harris.

Sherard, Robert Harbrough. *Bernard Shaw, Frank Harris, and Oscar Wilde*. New York: Greystone Press, 1937, 299 p.

Refutation of Harris's account of Wilde's life written by a close friend and admirer of Wilde.

Stephens, Kate. *Lies and Libels of Frank Harris*, edited by Gerritt and Mary Caldwell Smith. New York: Antigone Press, 1929, 197 p.

Reponse to Harris's allegations regarding Byron Caldwell Smith. In particular, Stephens denounces Harris's portrayal of his relationship to Smith as that of a "little husband," maintaining that Smith scarcely knew and did not like Harris, and presents evidence to refute Harris's claim that Smith died as a result of nocturnal emissions.

Stokes, Sewell. "Portrait of Frank Harris in Exile." *The Listener* LVIII, No. 1497 (5 December 1957): 919-20.

Account of the critic's encounter with Harris in Nice.

Tobin, A. I., and Gertz, Elmer. *Frank Harris: A Study in Black and White*. Chicago: Madelaine Mendelsohn, 1931, 393 p.

The only biography authorized by Harris.

Viereck, George Sylvester. "The Frankness of Frank Harris." In his *Glimpses of the Great*, pp. 286-93. London: Duckworth, 1930.

Description of an evening spent with Harris written by a young devotee and including extensive quotes from Harris himself.

Wells, H. G. *Experiment in Autobiography*, pp. 172ff. New York: Macmillan Co., 1934.

Numerous references to Harris as editor and literary figure.

Woollcott, Alexander. "The Last of Frank Harris." In his *The Portable Woollcott*, pp. 347-50. Edited by Joseph Hennessey. New York: Viking Press, 1946.

Brief biographical reminiscence.

Herman Heijermans

1864-1924

(Also wrote under pseudonyms of Samuel Falkland, Koos Habbema, Ivan Jelakowitch, and others) Dutch dramatist, journalist, essayist, short story writer, and novelist.

Heijermans is considered the most important Dutch playwright of the twentieth century and remains among the few Dutch writers to gain wide recognition outside of Holland. Often compared to Dutch genre painting for their attention to the details of daily life and the precise crafting of their stage settings, Heijermans's plays are meticulous studies of proletarian and middle-class life that emphasize the social inequities and suffering caused by class conflicts. To some extent these characteristics reflect the influence on Heijermans of the objective style and reformist aims of the Naturalist movement, especially as demonstrated in such dramatic works as Henrik Ibsen's *A Doll's House* (1879) and Gerhardt Hauptmann's *The Weavers* (1893). However, while he is credited with introducing Naturalism into modern Dutch theater, Heijermans did not subscribe to the deterministic philosophy on which Naturalism was founded, nor did he allow didactic intentions to obscure the individuality of the lives depicted in his dramas. Moreover, his best dramas, including *Op Hoop van Zegen (The Good Hope)*, *Ora et labora*, and *Eva Bonheur (The Devil to Pay)*, ultimately convey an optimism, compassion, and humor that are not restricted by the abstract program of any literary movement.

Heijermans was the oldest of eleven children born in Rotterdam to a poor Jewish couple. As a child he wrote skits that his siblings performed on special family occasions, and while still in his teens he wrote poems and short stories in Dutch, German, French, and English. Heijermans wanted to pursue advanced education and a writing career, but, unable to afford tuition to a university, he took a job at a local bank and later went into business for himself. He continued writing, however, and first attained critical and popular notice with the short story "n'Jodenstreek," which appeared in the periodical *De Gids*. Encouraged by the attention given this story, Heijermans moved to Amsterdam to pursue a literary career. There he came into contact with many musicians, artists, and writers, including the poet and critic Willem Kloos, the leader of de Berberging van tachtig (Movement of the Eighties), which promoted the doctrine of art for art's sake in Dutch literature. After a brief infatuation with this movement, Heijermans's growing awareness of economic and social injustices in Holland led him to reject the aestheticism of the "Eightiers." Shortly after his arrival in Amsterdam Heijermans became drama critic for the newly established periodical *De telegraaf*, writing harsh reviews of modern Dutch drama, which he regarded as frivolous because it did not address serious social concerns. During the 1892 theater season, however, the Paris *théâtre libre* introduced Naturalist drama to the Dutch stage, performing within three successive seasons works by Ibsen, Hauptmann, and August Strindberg. These performances had a profound effect on Heijermans, and in 1893 he produced his first play, *Dora Kremer*, a domestic drama inspired by Ibsen's *A Doll's House*.

Dora Kremer was not well received by audiences and was reviewed with hostility by most critics. To vindicate himself and to prove his contention that the only original works the Dutch appreciated were those by foreign dramatists, Heijermans produced the one-act play *Ahasverus* within weeks of the premier of *Dora Kremer*, clandestinely promoting it as the work of a Jewish playwright who had died in London after fleeing persecution in his native Russia. The play proved successful in Holland and was later produced in Paris, where Heijermans's authorship was revealed. He seized the opportunity to avenge himself by printing the details of the deception in his theater column, to the chagrin of the critics whom he had duped. Despite this dramatic coup, Heijermans did not produce another play until *Ghetto*, five years later. In the interim, he continued to publish drama criticism and began a weekly column of general interest that appeared for twenty years, first in *De telegraaf* then, after 1896, in the journal *Algemeen handelsblad*. That same year Heijermans moved with his wife to a small shore town in Holland where he founded the journal *De jonge gid*. Having become a member of the Socialist Democratic Worker's Party, Heijermans made frequent contributions to the Socialist magazine *De nieuwe tijd*; he also formulated an artistic credo around the ideal that art should serve life and determined to present socialist doctrine in subsequent dramas.

Heijermans reached the apex of his career in 1900 when his play *The Good Hope* earned him distinction as the first internationally acclaimed Dutch dramatist. The play's portrayal of life in a poor fishing community and the corrupt practices of the fishing industry was instrumental in bringing about the passage of the Dutch Schepenwet shipping act of 1909, which required strict inspection of fishing vessels. Heijermans's subsequent dramas were popular but not profitable: foreign producers, aware that Holland was not a member of the Berne Convention protecting works under international copyright law, pirated Heijermans's work without compensating him. He moved to a Berlin suburb in 1907, hoping to capitalize on his popularity in Germany, but had to resort to journalism to support his family. When he returned to Holland in 1912 he undertook the management of his own production company, which strained his financial resources and left him no time to write. It was only during his last years that he found time to resume writing. He died in 1924.

Heijermans's major themes were based on his Socialist convictions and were overtly didactic in purpose. Thus the dramas *The Good Hope* and *Ora et labora* are critical of the exploitation of workers, insufficient care of the aged, and other social issues, reflecting the author's belief that his primary role as a writer was to expose the injustices of his time and to promote Socialist solutions. Although Heijermans's most successful play, *The Good Hope*, was written specifically for this didactic purpose, it has received sustained critical attention as a well-constructed and skillfully written drama, rich in the naturalistic detail that has often led critics to classify Heijermans as a Naturalist writer. Heijermans, however, rejected Naturalist literary theory as false and "soulless," and his works are concerned with the personal tragedies of ordinary individuals involved in the mundane routine of daily living. *The Devil to Pay*, in particular, has received notice for its skilled character delineation. Despite the often tragic circumstances of the plays, their ultimate message remains essentially optimistic.

Although reformist aims inspired many of Heijermans's dramas, he did not neglect the aesthetic element of his work, and he is best remembered for the artistry with which he depicted his characters and their environment. Noting the optimistic attitude and the humor which distinguish Heijermans's realistic portrayals of human suffering, biographer Seymour L. Flaxman has called him "a unique phenomenon on the stage of his country," maintaining that "he put Dutch reality upon the stage. Not with photographic flatness, but with sincere emotion and poetic imagination."

PRINCIPAL WORKS

'n Jodenstreek (novella) 1892
Dora Kremer (drama) 1893
Ahasverus [as Ivan Jelakowitch] (drama) 1893
Schetsen. 18 vols. (short stories, sketches) 1897-1919
Ghetto (drama) 1898
   [*The Ghetto*, 1899]
Kamertjeszonde [as Koos Habbema] (novel) 1898;
   published in *Bibliotheek van "De Jonge Gids"*
Puntje (drama) 1898
De machien [first publication] (drama) 1899
Het zevende gebod (drama) 1899
Eén mei (drama) 1900
Op Hoop van Zegen (drama) 1900
   [*The Good Hope*, 1903]
Het pantser (drama) 1901

Ora et labora (drama) 1902
Het kamerschut (drama) 1903
Het kind (drama) 1903
In de jonge Jan (drama) 1903
   [*A Case of Arson*, 1905]
Sabbath (novella) 1903
Schakels (drama) 1903
   [*Links*, 1908]
Allerzielen (drama) 1904
Bloeimaand (drama) 1904
Diamantstad (novel) 1904
Uitkomst (drama) 1907
Feest (drama) 1908
   [*Jubilee*, 1923]
De meid (drama) 1908
   [*The Hired Girl*, 1917]
De opgaande zon (drama) 1908
   [*The Rising Sun*, 1926]
Glück auf! (drama) 1911
Eva Bonheur (drama) 1917
   [*The Devil to Pay*, 1925]
De wijze kater (drama) 1918
Van Ouds "De Morgenster" (drama) 1923
Keur wit de Beste Vertellingen van Samuel Falkland
   (sketches, short stories) 1934
Toneelwerken. 3 vols. (drama) 1965

MAX BEERBOHM (essay date 1903)

[*Although he lived until 1956, Beerbohm is chiefly associated with the fin de siècle period in English literature, more specifically with its lighter phases of witty sophistication and mannered elegance. His temperament was urbane and satirical, and he excelled in both literary and artistic caricatures of his contemporaries. "Entertaining" in the most complimentary sense of the word, Beerbohm's criticism for the* Saturday Review—*where he was a long-time drama critic—everywhere indicates his scrupulously developed taste and unpretentious, fair-minded response to literature. In the following excerpt from a review originally published in the* Saturday Review, *2 May 1903, Beerbohm favorably contrasts* The Good Hope *with trends in contemporary English drama, praising Heijermans's realistic presentation of humble characters and modern tragedy.*]

Ten years ago it was the fashion to call "unwholesome" any play which presented sincerely a not altogether jolly side of life. Well, the critics who encouraged such plays, and who were supposed to discourage any other kind of plays, have not drooped and died, one after another, to prove the aptness of the epithet. They are still among us, not apparently ailing. So another epithet has been hit on—"dreary," to wit. "Dreary" was much bandied last Monday afternoon, at the Imperial Theatre, in the entr'actes of *The Good Hope*. Ten years ago, the emergents into the foyer would have been angrily grimacing, gasping for what they would have called "a whiff of fresh air," and complaining of (a favourite phrase, then) "a nasty taste in the mouth." Last Monday, they merely looked glum. One of them, regarding me with a faint twinkle in an otherwise lacklustre eye, asked "Is this dreary enough for you?" I assured him that I was enjoying myself immensely. And so I was. Indeed, I had hardly ever felt so happy, so braced-up and buoyant, in a theatre. True, the play was a tragedy, and a very horrible one at that. But I do not see how it could produce a feeling of dreariness, and could fail to produce a definitely tonic effect, on any person capable of intelligent aesthetic pleasure. (p. 319)

I do not suppose that we have in England no man capable of writing as fine a tragedy as that which Hermann Heijermans has written. But I do know that such a play as *The Good Hope,* produced publicly, would be in England as signal a failure as it has been a success in Holland. And therefore (since, by the nature of his work, the dramatist, more than any other artist, needs encouragement) such a play is not written. Not from every kind of tragedy does our public flinch. It will tolerate Shakespearian tragedy, because it is not thereby reminded of realities. It will sometimes tolerate even a modern tragedy, for there is a way of writing modern tragedy without trenching on anything within our actual experience. A playwright can take a tragic theme from real life, and found a play on it, and yet make his characters and his atmosphere so unreal that no offence is given. No offence, did I say? Nay, very great pleasure. Our public loves to cry, to cry copiously, so long as its tears are not shed over something that is not a quite palpable figment. I can imagine a really popular British play made from the very same materials that Heijermans used for *The Good Hope.* The title itself is promising. Nor is the theme unfamiliar or unwelcome. Fisherfolk, living their lives in a constant tussle with the elements, are part and parcel of our national romance. (p. 320)

In the play, as it stands, there is practically no love-interest. Very little stress is laid on the fact that Greet and his cousin Jo are lovers, and the tragedy of his death at sea is marked for us quite as much through the bereavement of his mother as through that of his betrothed. Nor, indeed, are we called on to weep for him especially. The fate of his brother, and of the rest of the crew, seems not less lamentable than his. No one character predominates much over another. There is practically no story. The play simply represents a typical episode in a little fishing village. Most of the characters are fisherfolk, possessing much the same peculiarities of temperament as we may find in the fisherfolk in Cornwall or elsewhere, and possessing none of the peculiarities of fisherfolk as seen by us on the stage. There is nothing consciously heroic about them. They are ordinary creatures, with certain modifications and exaggerations produced by their peculiar life. And herein lies one of the sharpest differences between the work of Heijermans and the work of any English dramatist. Heijermans has deigned to take a respectful interest in humble life, and shows to us humble people as they are, not as every fool knows them not to be. An English dramatist, having to show a group of peasants, would be content to multiply the conventional stage-peasant. In the group of peasants shown to us by Heijermans every one is distinct from another, and all are human beings, and all, moreover, are normal human beings. Equally real and normal are the characters who do not happen to be peasants. I notice that some of my colleagues decry the shipowner, Clemens Bos, as a conventional villain. Are they themselves so saturated with convention that they failed to notice that his hinted desire for Jo in the first act was not succeeded by persecution of her in the later acts? As a matter of fact, the man takes no further notice of the girl. To pretend that he is a conventional villain merely because he speculates in unseaworthy ships is to deny the possible existence in Holland of what the late Mr. Plimsoll proved to exist in England. Perhaps it was some vague memory of Mr. Plimsoll's crusade that led these critics into the deeper absurdity of decrying the play as "a pamphlet". Certainly, it is a criticism of certain things in

life which the author holds to be horrible and unjust. In that sense it is a pamphlet. But it is also a very fine and scrupulous work of art. There is nothing incongruous in this duality. True, there is always the danger that an artist who is inspired by a moral purpose may distort life so as to make his moral the more striking. But he does not necessarily do so. Certainly, Heijermans has not done so. I wish that some of our so purely artistic dramatists could, through their coldly observant eyes, see life half as clearly and steadily as it is seen through the somewhat flashing eyes of Heijermans. (pp. 322-24)

Max Beerbohm, "A 'Dreary' Play," in his Around Theatres, *Vol. I, Alfred A. Knopf, 1930, pp. 319-24.*

THE NEW YORK TIMES   (essay date 1907)

[*In the following excerpt, the critic reviews* The Good Hope, *praising the power, strength, and interest of what is essentially a didactic work.*]

The man who wrote *The Good Hope* had a lesson to teach, and he was not squeamish about teaching it. He had a story to tell, and he proceeded to tell it without any great consideration for the people whose business might be hurt in the telling. And of this there can be no doubt—he felt the shame and the wrong and the injustice of the conditions he exposed.

Therein lies the power and the strength of this play of Heijermans about poor devils who go to the sea in ships and who never come back. . . .

[The] play strikes a human note from the start, and the note grows deeper and stronger and more appealing to the very end. There are scenes of laughter and of gayety, there are characters whose familiar, homely failings are sure to bring a smile, but one feels a sadness underneath it all.

Heijermans is a revolutionist and reformer, who does not hesitate to hand out in good round stinging phrases his ideas of abuses to which common sailors in the navy are subjected, but whose particular preachment in this play is against the men who grow rich and sleek on the profits of the herring fisheries, and who take no thought of the men who do their work. They may drown, their families may starve—what does it matter—so long as the underwriter sees to the insurance on the hulks?

Unlike most sermon plays, this one is interesting. Heijermans knows how to stir the pulse; he has the realist's sense of character and of incident, together with a force of cumulative detail. One gets intimately acquainted with the fisherfolk, with the petty affairs of their daily life, the routine duties of the household, the gossip of the family and the neighbors. But one gets, at the same time, a view of their lives in its more colorful sweeps. . . .

In the play one does not always get dramatic form in the sense of movement as it is generally regarded on the stage. The whole of the third act, for instance, is devoted to a scene in which Kniertje's neighbors drop in to gossip and enjoy a birthday cake. There is Saart, another widow, always in a hurry to go, but always finding time for a little gossip; there are two pensioners from the almshouse, honest folk, but useless now that their strength has gone. And the gossip goes on and the winds grow wilder, until Jo can stand the strain no longer, and tells her secret to Kniertje, who denounces her for the sin, then takes her in her arms.

Until the very end of the act there is no apparent effort at anything like dramatic effect, but it is absorbing and affecting. For it has the ring of truth.

The actors frequently get into a key higher, no doubt, than the author intended, and strong passages became too strong under melodramatic handling. It is the sort of tale that needs no particular underlining.

"Ellen Terry in Realistic Play," in The New York Times, *February 12, 1907, p. 9.*

ASHLEY DUKES (essay date 1911)

[*Dukes was an important English dramatist and drama critic during the first half of the twentieth century. He is most noted for his writings on modern European theater, particularly poetic drama. He had a broad knowledge of continental drama and, both as a translator and as the manager of his own theater, introduced English audiences to the work of several important French and German dramatists, including Ernst Toller, Georg Kaiser, and Lion Feuchtwanger. In the following excerpt, he proclaims Heijermans the last exemplar of Naturalism in drama.*]

There are playwrights who follow "movements" as street urchins march in step with a military band. Such a ragged group of imitators was attracted by the cry of "naturalism" in the European theatre of twenty years ago; and the more squalid and noisome the district traversed, the larger grew the following. The manufacture of slum drama, indeed, appealed irresistibly to the unemployed mind. The method was simple. Dirt, poverty and alcohol were the material ingredients. Ever-present dirt supplied the necessary sepia background. Poverty offered the motive for three hours of clutching speculation as to the fortunes of the characters. Alcohol, embracing psychological cause and effect with superb catholicity, assisted the play to stagger forward a few steps when the action threatened to halt; an immemorial stage device. At the same time, it added local colour. Lastly, an infusion of revolutionary thought, borrowed conveniently from a Social Democratic leaflet, provided the all-important "tendency," and enabled the author to flatter himself that he had joined the ranks of the moderns and was delivering a message to his age. (pp. 254-55)

I write, of course, only of the minor followers of the "movement." The leaders—dramatists like Hauptmann and Strindberg—were concerned with something more. . . . (p. 256)

There remain among the camp followers of modern realist drama some authors whose individuality saves them from becoming lost in the crowd, even though they break no new ground. One of them is the Dutch dramatist Heijermans, a master of the genre picture and (what is rarer among his school) an accomplished stage craftsman. His work has all the familiar characteristics of the older naturalism; dialect speech and a minutely detailed study of proletarian life; a certain intentional coarseness here and there, destined to startle the over-civilised audience of the city, and perhaps to challenge the censorship; a revolutionary bias, sentimental rather than virile, and much vehement denunciation of society, for the most part ill-expressed; lack of character in the figures eked out with naïve generalisations; but among all these false notes the truer ring of that home-bred philosophy which springs, like folk-song, from everyday action and observation of the common things of life, harvest and full nets of fish, wind and sky and sea, rather than from superimposed politics or opinions. The opinions, indeed, matter little. There are some few people to whom a revolutionary conception becomes real by experience, and

who are able at the same time to express their feeling clearly; but from most of the figures of realistic drama such expression comes unconvincingly, in the stilted language of an author who ceases to create in the effort to dictate. Hauptmann understood this dilemma when he wrote *The Weavers;* and although he took the side of the strikers throughout the play, he made the dramatic motive only a blind upheaval, meaningless to the cold-blooded observer, criminal in the eyes of the "moderate man," foolhardy to the experienced politician, but superb and wonderful as a symbol of an upward striving and a momentary realisation of the common desire.

Heijermans followed him in *Op Hoop van Zegen (The Good Hope),* and reduced the social conflict to banality, while he increased its theatrical force by a firmer technique of construction. The play is named "a sea-piece in four acts," and passes in a Dutch fishing village. A shipowner sends out a leaky trawler, *The Good Hope,* knowing her to be unseaworthy (and thereby becomes the villain of the piece). The ship is wrecked in a storm, and husbands, lovers and children are lost. That is all. From the social standpoint a fatal skirmish in the guerilla warfare of exploiters and exploited. The weapons are unfairly chosen, however, and here lies a weakness. The author goes out of his way to say that shipowners are unscrupulous scoundrels, and fishermen their unfortunate victims. The bias contributes nothing to drama, and makes the tragedy no more impressive. Good ships, as well as bad, may perish in a storm; and for the fisherman the sea itself is the symbol of fate. As one of the characters (forgetful for a moment of denunciation) says: "We take the fish, and God takes us." (The survival of the fittest?) Here is a conception more fruitful of great drama than a passing advantage upon one side or the other in the conflict of employers and employed; and the power of *The Good Hope* rests not in that conflict, one-sided as it is, but in the portrayal of the fishermen themselves at grips with life and death. A boy is dragged away to sea against his will, and is heard of no more except as "Barend Vermeer, aged 19," in the list of the drowned. His brother sinks in the same ship, and leaves a girl with an unborn child. The women and old men huddle together in a cottage fearful of the storm, and tales of the sea are told in the dark; of men overboard torn by sharks, of wrecks on the Dogger Bank, of ships long overdue and months of expectation ending in despair. A gale of wind and rain whistles through the play, sweeping the decks of life, tossing men out into the unknown. That is the power of Heijermans.

In *Ora et Labora* he turns to the peasantry, starving upon the banks of a frozen canal in winter—a genre picture again, dull grey as a December evening. "I ask," says Hiddes, the old bargee, "why the Lord made the winter. . . . The birds fly away and the beasts burrow . . . they're better off than men. That's queer. How comes it that the worms sleep and the swallows fly south, while we haven't even a warm room above ground? Why in thunder does the Lord make water and earth as hard as stone?" So the play runs on. There is no work, no warmth, no food. One figure after another comes from the hut or the frost-bound canal with the same lament. The last cow dies of disease in an outhouse, and its throat is cut so that it can be sold to the butcher. The father of the family sells it for a few shillings, and returns home drunk. His son Eelke enlists in the army as a last resort, and binds himself to colonial service in the West Indies for six years, leaving Sytske, the girl he was to marry. His first month's pay saves the family from the workhouse. Sytske refuses to forgive him, and the old peasants are left squabbling over the money he has brought. Again—that is all. A pitiful story, told as well as may be.

These two plays, with **Ghetto,** a tragedy of the Jewish quarter in a Dutch city, contain the best work that Heijermans has done. They reveal no very powerful personality; a kindly disposition but a commonplace intellect; sincere revolutionary conviction without enough creative force to translate it into terms of life; a fine sense of atmosphere, comparable with that of the Dutch masters, but lack of colour; stagecraft without inevitability. In a word, talent without genius. Such a playwright, straggling in the rear, marks the close of a period. He is the last of the naturalists. The main body of the movement he follows is long since dispersed. Tolstoy became a preacher, Strindberg a mystic; Hauptmann and Gorky are lost in byways. Heijermans still perseveres, but no matter how many leagues he may cover, he can go no further. The world is turning in the opposite direction. (pp. 257-63)

Ashley Dukes, "Belgium and Holland," in his Modern Dramatists, *Frank Palmer, 1911, pp. 242-63.*

DESMOND MacCARTHY (essay date 1917)

[*MacCarthy was one of the foremost English literary and dramatic critics of the twentieth century. He served for many years on the staff of the* New Statesman *and edited* Life and Letters. *A member of the Bloomsbury group, which also included Leonard and Virginia Woolf, John Maynard Keynes, E. M. Forster, and Lytton Strachey among its number, MacCarthy was guided by their primary tenet that "one's prime objects in life were love, the creation and enjoyment of aesthetic experience, and the pursuit of knowledge." According to his critics, MacCarthy brought to his work a wide range of reading, serious and sensitive judgment, an interest in the works of new writers, and high critical standards. In the following excerpt from a review of* The Hired Girl, *he considers the sympathetic portrayal of the maid Marie a triumph of impartiality.*]

The Hired Girl, by Herman Heijermans . . . is a remarkable play of its kind. Its kind is the excruciating naturalistic. . . . Appropriately enough, **The Hired Girl** is a study of a Dutch interior.

It is a sordid interior. No pearly indoor lights here; no doors opening on neat, sunny brick-paved yards or on speckless floors, reminding us that it may be true after all that man wants but little here below, and that order and quietness are very satisfying, very great and graceful boons. On the contrary, it is the desecrating spirit of blackmail that broods over the home of the unhappy little Fräu Grohman, left alone, while her husband is away on business. For she is in the power of Marie, her maid, who knows that one night she let a lover (her music-master) in. Marie uses that knowledge not only to extort money and every kind of "perk," linen, slippers, cigars, wines, omelettes, liqueurs—but also to humiliate and degrade her weak young mistress with a persistent virulence which makes the spectators squirm, and disguises from them (unless they happen to be people who can master even the impulse of pity) the underlying significance of the play. The author has hinted at it in his title: Marie is really the heroine of the piece. (p. 615)

I do not suppose there were many people in the audience on Sunday who looked at Marie as impartially as her creator did. They thought of her, I expect, as a mere monster, a sort of inhuman hydra, in whose slimy folds the life, the gaiety, the happiness of a helpless young wife were slowly sucked away. Marie *is* as hideous as an octopus; there is no getting over that.

But her ugliness . . . is after all in part the creation of the inhumanity of those she has served. It was so natural to be struck with her sour, pitiless insolence to the exclusion of everything else that the touches of humanity which her creator put into her might well have escaped notice. But they were there all the time. If I dwell on them a moment in preference to dilating upon the painful pity roused by the tortures of Lotti, it is in order that in retrospect those who saw the play may note that it was a profounder and a more impartial work of art than they perhaps thought, while they were shivering before the embodiment of the potential enemy of us all—the person who knows something about us which we would conceal, and uses the knowledge as a rod to drive and beat us. Marie drunk, entertaining her relations in the absence of her mistress, is a broken pane through which we can peep into her hidden nature; and, lo! there is, really is, at the bottom, even of this sordid harpy, some humanity. From her miserable soliloquies, interrupted by intoxicated giggles, we can piece together some explanation of her vindictiveness, and it has not such an inhuman cause after all. She went young into service with Lotti's family; Lotti the pretty, the petted. . . . Keeping the life of a household drudge in mind, we can understand something of the venomous, cynical satisfaction with which Marie, unlovely, thwarted, prematurely worn, miserable slavey that she is, smashes up the half-sham, roseate domesticity of Lotti's home, and the contemptuous relish with which she forces her spoilt mistress to clean the boots and light the fire herself. And we can admire the way in which the dramatist, in spite of making us sympathise almost intolerably with the victim, has still managed to hold the balance true, and thus be fair also to the sufferings of the vampire. She, too, is in a hell of her own—a hell not by any means entirely of her own making.

The curtain goes up on Marie lingering with lazy gulosity over a slovenly feast of sugar and omelette and wine. She is dirty in her person and the room is in nasty disorder. Her feet are on the table, and she is cooing over a little cur she has picked up in the streets, towards which she shows the silly tenderness of people whose human affections have been starved. The adoration of pets is a surer sign than mere shabbiness of failure in life. Where this animal is concerned Marie shows a tigerish devotion, and when it dies, her eyes . . . blaze with a light of a passion which has a pathos as real as that of pretty, pale Lotti, twittering and singing over her sweeping in order to deceive her husband into thinking she has a light heart and is doing it for fun—perhaps a deeper pathos, for it is the glare of the starving. Cruelty has never a sufficient excuse, but heart hunger is the best.

The drama consists of two situations, on which the changes are cunningly rung: Lotti's struggle to propitiate Marie and her efforts to disguise, first from her aunt, then from her husband when he returns, what she has to put up with from Marie. . . . The truth comes out. She cries and sobs: "Oh, at last you know. I'm glad you know. I'm glad you know," and he whimpers a little, and does not know what to say. He gets the only bit of permanent corroborative evidence out of Marie by letting her go off with her spoils, instead of in charge of the police. . . . We have taken our purge of pity and terror; the play is over.

But if we have swallowed it to the dregs, I think the imagination will also follow the departing figure of Marie with something like compassion. . . . She has been abominable; but if she had had a tithe of the happiness her miserable little victim was too heedless to guard, I do not think she would have ground her down with quite that rasping contempt which made the first gush of one's sympathy leap straight to Lotti. (pp. 615-16)

Desmond MacCarthy, in a review of "The Hired Girl," in New Statesman, Vol. VIII, No. 208, March 31, 1917, pp. 615-16.

A. J. BARNOUW (essay date 1925)

[*Barnouw was a Dutch scholar, historian, and journalist primarily interested in the literature and legends of various cultures. In the following excerpt, he argues that Heijermans's later dramas are his best because he does not subordinate sympathetic characterizations to propagandistic exposition.*]

Heijermans was a fighter all his life and the stage was his vantage ground of attack. As a socialist he despised the ideal of Art for Art's sake. Art to him had a purpose and a mission in fighting social evil and exposing the methods and the men that he held responsible for it. In *Ghetto* he exposed the unreasonable cruelty of Jewish orthodoxy, in *The Good Hope* the unscrupulous greed of shipowners who care more for the premiums from the insurance company than for the lives of the crews whom they send to sea on unseaworthy vessels, in *The Seventh Commandment* the bourgeois morality which is not based on conscience and principle but on hypocrisy and fear of scandal. It takes a consummate playwright to create drama out of matter that the preacher supplies, and even Heijermans' art was sometimes defeated by his missionary zeal. The hero in *Ghetto*, the rebellious son, bores the audience but does not convince it. If he had felt the pain of parting with inherited traditions which his reason taught him to despise, the conflict within him between domestic piety and the call of social duty might have made him a tragic figure. But the conflict that we see is one between a son entirely estranged from his antecedents and a father in whom these antecedents are embodied. The picture of that Jewish home is done with an artist's loving attention to picturesque detail, and it is that milieu, not the young hero's phrases, that we remember as the essential beauty of the play. In *The Good Hope*, on the other hand, the reformer's purpose does not mar the artist's picture. No play of Heijermans', nor of any other Dutch author, has held the stage so long, and more than twenty years after its first production it is still capable of keeping audiences spellbound by the truth of its characterization. The exposition of the merciless capitalist has nothing to do with this persistent success. The playgoer of today sees in the shipowner not the embodiment of a wicked system, but a wicked man as there are wicked men among his victims. And it is this triumph of the author's creation of a living character over the symbol that he intended his creature to be which lifts this play from the mass of timely propaganda literature into the realm of timeless art.

Hatred of the power for evil in society is the ground tone of this drama, but its correlative is the love for the weak and the downtrodden. As Heijermans' talent ripened with his years, this softer feeling became predominant in his plays. In *Uitkomst* he has given dramatic form to the dreams and fancies of a dying pauper child; in *All Souls* he has contrasted two different attitudes of the Roman Catholic priest towards life: the one for whom the prestige and the authority of the Church are his first and last consideration and the other who wants to practise the faith that it teaches by acts which obey not only the Church's authority but also the dictates of his own heart. In *The Maid* his indictment of the uncharitable social order has substituted for the picture of its hateful agent that of the no less hateful victim envenomed by harsh treatment, humiliation, and injustice. Having stolen the letter which contains the evidence of her mistress's sin, the maid acquires, with the power that the

knowledge of the secret gives her, a satanic pleasure in torturing her victim with the fear of its revelation. But even this loveless, revolting creature of the author's fancy has a craving for tenderness, and what little affection there is left in the dearth of her soul is spent on a waif from the street, an ugly mongrel of a dog. *Eva Bonheur* is a counterpart of this distorted human soul. Her bitterness is less convincingly accounted for, but its symptoms yield as effective material for dramatic characterization. And whereas in *The Maid* the woman's design is defeated by the husband's devotion to his wife, Eva Bonheur's evil nature is subdued by the kindness and lovableness of old Jasper, her landlord. In this character Heijermans has created his masterpiece: a serene philosopher who, having learned to view life *sub specie eternitatis*, accepts its joys and sorrows as the changing hues of a butterfly's wings in the sun. His gentle, playful irony disarms Eva's prickly temper, and awes the impudence of his daughter's betrayer into meekness and shame. His spirit prevails in the end, and in that spirit Heijermans himself, in his ripened years, had learned to view and interpret life, in spite of the fact that those years had dealt with his own life unmercifully. (pp. 110-12)

A. J. Barnouw, "Herman Heijermans," in Theatre Arts Monthly, Vol. IX, No. 2, February, 1925, pp. 109-12.

THE NEW YORK TIMES BOOK REVIEW (essay date 1925)

[*In the following excerpt from a review of* The Devil to Pay, *the critic considers the near-tragedy uplifting because of an underlying philosophy that reinforces positive human values.*]

Although Heijermans's play, *The Devil to Pay* . . . ends unhappily in many important details, and looks bravely, rather than ecstatically, into the future, still, with the promise of misery and pain, it cannot be considered tragedy. After the final curtain has dropped, one has the feeling that although this episode in Jasper's domestic life has not brought its full quota of joy, another episode is just beginning which may bring these Hollanders closer together than ever, and that they are the sort of people to whom personal relations are the dearest thing. Three acts of Heijermans's character study, hovering about this close-knit family, an interloping suitor and an acidulous lodger, are fraught with much delicate beauty of philosophy, portrayal and cosmic understanding. . . .

The Devil to Pay shares with *The Good Hope* the distinction of being his best and most popular drama. . . . [*The Good Hope*] is unrelieved tragedy. *The Devil to Pay,* however, sweetens the melancholy of its sombre fable with simple humors, sometimes quite naive, and with a pervasive tone of pity. In theme, in development and particularly in its dénouement, it is rich in human values. No doubt for the native people of Holland it has a significance that sometimes misses American understanding. Its only fault in the present production is a softness that sometimes verges upon the languorous. The emotions of the concluding act, however, rendered deeper by the gentleness of the playing, are fine—perhaps sublime.

Heijermans's composition blends story and character perfectly. In both those respects the play has three elements: the mother, father and daughter of the immediate family, quite happy among themselves; the lodger upstairs, "a pot of poison," who presses her advantage as a creditor unduly, and a young musician who makes love to the daughter, proves himself unworthy, and is accordingly dismissed in spite of the prospect of his becoming a father. Amid the flow of life in Jasper's pleasant livingroom, amid the garrulities and sentimentalities of a dreamy shop keeper to whom life is a constant mystery, these three elements come into play, resisting one another, recoiling and finally achieving a certain practical harmony.

What little story there is concerns Eva Bonheur, the lodger upstairs (whose apartment is revealed on a double-decked stage), and the advantage she takes of a small loan to her landlady below. In time she gets full possession of the house. This purely domestic secret is kept from Nanning Storm, a young musician, who is the accepted suitor for Marie's hand. When he begins to suspect it he leaves summarily, escaping at the same time, he believes, the pestilence of poverty that has ever dogged his heels. Three days later he returns to resume his former state, to make arrangements for his immediate marriage before a successful concert tour in America. But he comes too late. Marie and her family propose to get on without him.

In the meantime, the play unfolds many intimacies of folk-life, a festival birthday dinner with red and white wine and lobster as the symbols of high living, and the numerous unpleasantries concerning the tyrannical lodger.... And although Eva Bonheur is technically a subordinate character in the drama, Heijermans has invested it with the full substance of a being, and the truth of psychological accuracy. For behind the acerbidity of the Eva of the play is a lifetime of saving and penuriousness, of caution and planning, of oppression and insecurity.

Most of the philosophy is projected through the character of Jasper, dealer in stuffed animals and taxidermists' tools as a matter of trade, seeker after the eternal truths as a matter of fact. And the symbolism of *The Devil to Pay* is centred about Jasper's stiff leg. On the eve of his marriage these many years ago he met with an accident that crippled his leg. And at that time the prospective husband and wife both concluded that a crippled body did not matter—only a "crippled soul." Using this figure Heijermans shows that the young musician's unworthiness and Rosa's pretty reign of terror are wounds of the soul that are less easily mended.

"Dutch Character and Folk Life," in The New York Times Book Review, *December 4, 1925, p. 26.*

J. BROOKS ATKINSON (essay date 1927)

[*As drama critic for the* New York Times *from 1925 to 1960, Atkinson was one of the most influential reviewers in America. In the following excerpt, he praises the dramatic strength and realism of* The Good Hope.]

[*The Good Hope*] may seem a bit leisurely in the last two acts for our brisk modern manners. For all that, it is a rugged, noble drama, seething with humor, hatred and the black fate of the seaman; and the Civic Repertory company accords it a magnificent performance. Inevitably, *The Good Hope* takes rank with the best dramas in the Fourteenth Street coffers....

After three hours under the spell of the deeply bitten tragedy one can understand how enthralling it must have been to the Dutch who first saw it as a clean-cut image of their native life, and one sees why it ultimately resulted in reforming the Dutch shipping laws. For it is true in every detail of story, every line of dialogue, and particularly in every character of a fishing village where the church bell is constantly tolling the frightful news of death at sea. In substance *The Good Hope* merely chronicles the departure of the crew on a rotten schooner, and in the last act reports her loss at sea in a storm and reveals the

agony of those who are left husbandless, loverless and sonless ashore.

But in this play at least, Heijermans was no spinner of salty yarns; he was a master of character. And he tells his fable in terms of the men and women of the fishing village, high-spirited, brave, strong and honestly vulgar. Most of the action passes inside the cottage of a weathered old mother of two boys who put out to sea in the decayed schooner. There come the old mariners to drink and jest, the youngsters to dream of the future; and there on a wickedly stormy night came the women of the neighborhood—terrified by every blast—to chatter in hushed tones of what the sea has wrenched from their lives. Sometimes the talk is pot-house humor; sometimes it becomes rude poetry; sometimes it beats a snarling hatred of the fates that crowd their uncertain existence. For Heijermans matched their resilience with his own, and he wrote of them with loving understanding. Played quite as sympathetically they emerge on the stage as true portraits with the deep tonal values of a Dutch painting.

Since Heijermans was not merely a dramatist, but also a thinker with a sensitive social consciousness, *The Good Hope* passes beyond character portrayal to social distinctions. Part of the tragedy rises from the unequal working conditions by which the fishermen risk their lives, while Clemens Bos risks only the premium on his insurance. Especially in the last act Heijermans dwells relentlessly upon Bos's indifference to his responsibility for deaths in many local families. But not as crude propaganda. Even for this crucial point in the message of his drama Heijermans took pains to present his oppressor still in terms of character. Bos is hard and complacent. But he is no machine. A wailing sweetheart bruises him more than he dares to confess.

J. Brooks Atkinson, "The Play: Opening of the Civic Repertory," in The New York Times, *October 19, 1927, p. 24.*

JOSEPH WOOD KRUTCH (essay date 1927)

[*Krutch is widely regarded as one of America's most respected literary and drama critics. Noteworthy among his works are* The American Drama since 1918 *(1939), in which he analyzed the most important dramas of the 1920s and 1930s, and "Modernism" in* Modern Drama *(1953), in which he stressed the need for twentieth-century playwrights to infuse their works with traditional humanistic values. A conservative and idealistic thinker, he was a consistent proponent of human dignity and the preeminence of literary art. His literary criticism is characterized by such concerns: in* The Modern Temper *(1929) he argued that because scientific thought has denied human worth, tragedy had become obsolete, and in* The Measure of Man *(1954) he attacked modern culture for depriving humanity of the sense of individual responsibility necessary for making important decisions in an increasingly complex age. In the following excerpt, Krutch discusses the enduring realism of* The Good Hope.]

[*The Good Hope*] was first produced in 1900; ... and it belongs to one of the deadest of dead periods. Heijermans was a Dutch follower of Hauptmann who wrote at the time when the drama was just discovering the proletariat, when it was busy pointing a heavily accusatory finger at the sorrows of the humble, and when every social wrong was considered to constitute per se the materials of a drama; and yet he managed in this case to transcend the limitations of the mode. The play is said to have been written (God save the mark!) as a protest against the loose methods of Dutch companies in insuring unseaworthy vessels;

Scene from a production of The Good Hope. *Netherlands Information Service.*

I presume and hope that these methods have been since reformed; but whether they have or not the piece would be no more interesting on account of its purpose than *Hamlet* would be if our concern depended chiefly upon an active indignation against those things which were politically rotten in the state of Denmark toward the end of the ninth century. Fortunately, however, Heijermans built better than the theorist of naturalism thought necessary. His impulse toward social protest served only to supply him with an attitude and to sharpen his observation so that he might make the old story of the rotten ship and the wives at home real once more by giving it a local habitation and a name among particular people, in a particular place, at a particular time. He had the gift for indignation but he had much more conspicuously the gift for character drawing and for situation; so that he has painted the life of a fishing village with something of that realism, at once uncompromising and yet loving, which once served as the mark of his countrymen's graphic art; and he managed at the same time to rise to moments of almost painful tension like that in which the timid son is sent away to the ship by the mother who soon will mourn his death. One fancies that the play was written rather directly under the influence of Hauptmann's *The Weavers*, but it becomes, in spite of itself, much more than an imitation. There is a robustly cheerful good humor in the *genre* scenes which is most un-Hauptmannesque, and there is besides an individual vitality in the characters which makes them refuse to be merely either representatives of a class or straw men to serve as the subject of an argument. The play has life in it and it will not take its place quietly upon the shelf with the other documents for the study of an out-moded school. (p. 486)

Joseph Wood Krutch, "Dutch Interior," in The Nation, *New York, Vol. CXXV, No. 3252, November 2, 1927, pp. 485-86.*

DESMOND MacCARTHY   (essay date 1929)

[*In the following excerpt, MacCarthy examines some characteristics of* The Rising Sun, *noting points of acting and stage direction.*]

During the interval after the first act, a distinctly interestin one, with that much-more-to-come feeling running throug which every first act should possess, I fell to wondering wh *The Rising Sun* should not draw, and draw well, and this wa the only explanation I could hit upon: it is a drama of modes middle-class life. It is about a small shopkeeper's bankruptcy about a man with spirits disastrously above his business, who even had they not been, would have been inevitably crushe by the competition of a huge, cut-the-prices store in the sam street. (p. 84)

The theme of the dramatist in this case is that a girl, to save her father from ruin and falling into the hands of his enemy, burns down his premises for the sake of the insurance money. In the fire a young girl who is subject to fits and destined to idiocy is burnt to death upstairs. This is a tragedy which would ruin Sonia's life if she did not confess and face what punishment may befall. Her father guesses that the upsetting of the lamp in the shop was no accident, and brings her courage to the sticking point. This is the climax of the play, which gives both actors a magnificent opportunity. It is a moment difficult to stage.... The dialogue throughout the play is subtly and simply contrived to bring out and lead up to this moral situation. We believe in the ardent, natural affection and understanding between daughter and father; in the character of Strong himself, and the events which lead up to Sonia's reckless action. These were little and big things—her mother's cheerful tipsiness that night . . . is among the little ones. But the big one is her father's casual revelation of the fact that he had contemplated allowing a train to run over him at an unguarded level-crossing in order that his family should get the insurance money. It is at this moment (he is playing whist and drinking punch when he hints at it) that Sonia has an opportunity for a fine stroke of acting.... It is as important a moment in the play as Hedwig's silent transit across the stage just before she shoots herself in the Wild Duck's garret.... The moral sensitiveness of Sonia, and of her father, too—in spite of his casual handling of other people's money—is illustrated indirectly by the love-relation (subordinate to that between her father and herself) between Sonia and the young schoolmaster whose sister perishes in the fire, and by Strong's explanation of himself to Nathaniel. Nathaniel is a mild, shy, staunch, unimpressive youth—conspicuously unattractive. Sonia, in a charming little scene, leads him at last into saying he loves her. All this is necessary to leading up to the climax, which is of course an assertion of spiritual values, and one, to my mind, more immediately convincing than that at the end of *The Powers of Darkness*. (pp. 84-5)

Desmond MacCarthy, "The Rising Sun," in New Statesman, Vol. XXXIV, No. 861, October 26, 1929, pp. 84-5.

SEYMOUR L. FLAXMAN   (essay date 1954)

[In the following excerpt, Flaxman considers the influences of Naturalism and Socialism secondary in importance to Heijermans's work, citing Heijermans's own individualism as the chief shaping force of his drama.]

When Herman Heijermans began his career as a writer, he was filled with an enthusiasm for the new poetry of his day. After his arrival in Amsterdam, however, he found in the rising Socialist movement the promise of a new society. The spell of his early attraction to the Eightiers broke under the impact of Socialism, but not without leaving a permanent impression on his work. Even his appeal, *Workers of All Lands, Unite,* which is prefaced with a quotation from Shelley, betrays their influence.

It was with the drama, the art he adored, that he hoped to achieve his greatest victories in the battle for a new society, and the basis of this art would have to be reality.... The playwright should try "to approach reality, not the 'reality' of a *Théâtre libre* or of German 'moderns,' but *life in all its phenomena* as we perceive it, life stripped of its *pretense*, its *deceit*, its *surface*."

"I live in my time," he said, "in this country, next to Dutch proletarians. I am no naturalist, no realist, no idealist, no symbolist, and, indeed, I hate these classifications which are stuck fast to the bourgeois understanding of art." It might come as a surprise to find Heijermans pausing in his search for reality to deny any affinity for Naturalism, but it is true that, in spite of all he took from this movement, he can not be classed as one of its faithful followers. He was too full of enthusiasm for life to give ony a flat, black and white photograph of it. Naturalism was too narrow a doctrine to admit his belief in love, his pantheistic philosophy, and his idealistic theory of human progress and social evolution. Thus he rejected Zola and his idea of heredity as predestination because it was all based on a false scientific assumption. Besides, "Zola had no ideal, no horizon." For Heijermans there could be no great literature without an ideal, in his case, of course, the socialist ideal.

However much he may have abhorred the idea of art for art's sake, many of his plays contain the kind of fantasy and romantic imagination that is incompatible with consistent Naturalism. For him "every reality is reseated in a dream, and every dream lives in reality." Moreover, he had an overwhelming feeling for the theatre, and he was very much aware of the difference between literature and dramatic literature. He knew that his plays must contain living figures, who would bring action to the stage, for the dramatist must keep before him "the vision in the flesh of the *schwankende Gestalte*." How can this be reconciled with the Naturalist's view of life, which was supposed to be that of a scientist recording the details of the milieu in his notebook?

There was, indeed, something of the conscious artist in Heijermans, and for all his determination to present the socialist point of view, he was very sensitive to the word *tendenz*. He felt this word to be an accusation, and to the end of his life he denied any intention to propagandize. His plays flowed forth naturally out of the well of inner feelings and deep convictions, and thus they were innocent of *tendenz*, which "is laid on artificially from above."

Heijermans was not a profound philosophical thinker with a carefully developed dramatic theory, and there would be no point in attempting to reconcile his creative work with such principles as might be extracted from his critical articles. He did not always follow them, and they are not sufficient to explain his gifts as a dramatist. It is more profitable now, with what we know of his philosophy and his plays, to cast a brief glance over his work and observe the style and technique with which he created reality.

In the first place, although he refused to join the Naturalists, he had learned from them the valuable lesson in creating atmosphere. Heijermans never lost sight of the value of detail in providing a realistic setting for a play. Whether it was a secondhand shop in the Jewish quarter of Amsterdam, a fisherman's cottage, a Frisian peasant's hut, a kitchen in a wealthy home, the room behind a middle-class store, a tavern, or a shipowner's office, Heijermans put it on the stage as an essential part of his play, inseparable from the action and the characters. Sometimes he used these scenes for dramatic contrasts, and thus the scene of Gaaike and her mother setting the table in their comfortable home is followed in the second act by a view of Peter's room in de Pijp. Eva's lonely room upstairs is set off by the cosy atmosphere in which Jasper and his family live. Even the things that were put upon the tables, the coffee and cake in *Ghetto* and the "pigs in blankets" and punch in

The Rising Sun, brought life into the play. As Heijermans said in Eva's words, "I like Dutch culture and Dutch manners. . . ."

Heijermans sometimes failed to keep his command over the structure of his play as a whole and was unable to fuse a scene or even an act with the rest, for his passionate interest in the life of his time often ran away with him. But as an observer of the life about him he was without a peer, and he combined this talent with a highly developed sense of the theatre. He knew, as if by instinct, what would be effective on the stage, and even if his critics occasionally accused him of *"handigheid* (handiness)," none of his contemporaries could equal him in creating a striking scene. Heijermans was particularly careful with his curtain scenes, and he knew the importance of having the play end with a picture that would make a sharp impression on the spectator. It is only necessary to recall the final view of Kniertje in *The Good Hope,* of Eelke, Sytske, and her mother in *Pray and Work,* of Pancras in *Links,* or of Eva in *Eva Bonheur* to realize how skillful a craftsman he was.

When he was at his best, he would carefully prepare the way for his most dramatic scenes. In the first act of *The Good Hope* the fact that the *Anna* has arrived with a dead man aboard is introduced almost casually, and it is at this point that Geert enters, but at the end of the act, just as he expresses a longing to go to sea, the curtain descends on the dramatic revelation that the dead man is someone he knew well.

Heijermans was able to make effective use of sound, as with the carillon which forms the background for Larsen's decision to put his child to death, or with the clocks which all strike nine together as Mathijs' shop and home burn down. But he could make just as effective use of silence. Thus there is the pause as Mathijs, and the audience with him, takes in the scene of his family and his friends gathered around the table.

He could also employ a single remark or gesture to indicate the whole mood of a scene. At the beginning of *Ghetto* Esther complains that the room is hot and stuffy, thus indicating immediately the oppressive atmosphere of the ghetto. After the narrow-minded alderman has left in *All Souls,* there is a silence, and Nansen absent-mindedly breaks his pipe-stem into bits. This reveals the rage seething within him far more effectively than angry words.

In *The Way Out* Heijermans seizes the attention of the audience and creates suspense by having Jan casually reveal that he knows he is going to die. This remark precedes the dream sequence, so that interest in Jan's fate is maintained until the very last scene. Sometimes the playwright achieved suspense by using the analytic technique, as in *All Souls,* and then uncovering the details of his dramatic situation, one by one, but even without this he was able to maintain tension at a high level. In some plays he delayed the entrance of the hero or heroine until the first act had been well started and curiosity had been aroused, as in *Ghetto* and *All Souls.*

To relieve the tension and prevent it from becoming unbearable, Heijermans might inject a humorous remark or incident. But this was not his only use of humor, for he loved it for its own sake. Although this annoyed some very sober-minded critics, it brought life to the Dutch stage, and gave his work the warm, cheerful coloring that distinguishes it from Naturalism. Heijermans was angered by the suffering of the oppressed, but he knew that they had the courage to laugh at trouble, and he enjoyed laughing with them. Indeed, he was not above punning, and whether it was Pancras having fun with French, even though he did not know the language, or Robert and Bertram,

the playwright always managed to find an opportunity for a play on words. Heijermans often chose the names of his characters from the newspapers, but he also would give them names with a meaning that was applicable to the play. The meaning could be comical as well as serious, and it was with tongue in cheek that he used such names as Engel, Prosper Bien Aimé, and Eva Bonheur. If there is a certain irony in the names he gave his characters, it is even more apparent in the titles and subtitles of his plays: *The Seventh Commandment, Pray and Work, The Good Hope, Links,* a "happy play of the family fireside," *The Way Out, Good Luck!*

Heijermans employed his minor characters with great skill in creating the Dutch atmosphere in his plays. Engel and the tradesmen of de Pijp pull us into their world of harsh realities, while the servants in *Maytime* take us belowstairs. Then there are the magnificent tableaux. The sailors' wives and sweethearts gathered around the table during the storm in *The Good Hope,* the peasants singing their hymn in *Pray and Work,* and Mathijs and his family in *The Rising Sun.* In scenes like these Heijermans has really put a slice of Dutch life upon the stage.

The speech of his characters harmonizes with their background. Their language is the colloquial language of everyday, and Groeneveld, the actor, has praised his ability to reproduce the living speech of Holland. . . . He had too great a scorn for anything that smacked of literary estheticism to permit a worker or small business man to express himself in the winged words of poetry, although Karsten has said that his preference for succinctness in itself betrays a literary influence on his dialogue. . . . In *Ahasverus* and *Ghetto* Heijermans put Yiddish words into his dialogue, and in *Pray and Work* peasant sayings lend depth to the background of the play. It is only the evil characters, by the way, who speak French in any of the plays: Pancras' scheming children, Sylvia in *Good Luck!,* Funny in *Saltimbank,* Edi's mother in *Maytime.*

It is his stage pictures that have caused critics to compare Heijermans with the great genre painters of the seventeenth century, and in this respect he was the Jan Steen of the Dutch stage. But it would be wrong to compare him only with Jan Steen, for there is more to his art than that. He must be compared with Frans Hals, too, for his portraits of individuals show as much of the master as his paintings of groups. Dobbe, Sachel, Kniertje, Pancras, Mathijs, Jasper, and Eva have been created with the warmth and colors of life and the textures of reality. Those who have attempted to dismiss Heijermans' art as *Kleinmalerei* or *Armeleutemalerei* have ignored his contributions to the national gallery of full-length portraits.

His high regard for realistic detail might lead one to connect him with the Naturalistic movement, but the fact that he turned his back on Naturalism because it lacked ideals at once indicates the very distinguishing characteristic that sets him off from this group. Not only his socialist convictions, but his pantheistic and optimistic philosophy made it impossible for him to look down upon the workers with a gaze of glum objectivity. However difficult the struggle, paradise would ultimately be attained on this earth. Man must only learn to love his fellow men more than gold. By making the heroes of his early plays the combatants in this struggle, he seriously weakened them, and gave them a romantic cast which had an almost jarring effect in plays that gained their most powerful effects through realism. If he failed with Rafaël and Peter, in later years he learned to combine ideas with character, and succeeded with Mathijs and Jasper.

The individualism and symbolism of **Royal Dream** show that non-realistic elements were present in Heijermans' style even in his early years. In such plays as **All Souls, The Way Out, Sleeping Beauty,** and **Dawn,** romanticism, although firmly rooted in reality, becomes an important part of the style and atmosphere. Sometimes Heijermans' romantic tendencies would carry him so far that he would indulge in romantic irony, threatening to shatter the very illusion of the world he sought to create upon the stage. Thus Bart refers to himself as a *raisonneur* and Robert and Bertram address the audience from the stage. In **The Wise Tomcat** he dramatized a fairy tale, and in **Dawn,** although the verse is not very successful, his conscious effort to depart from the prosaic, in both senses of the word, is evidence of his romanticism.

In later years Heijermans was not inclined to devote his talent to the advancement of socialism with the same willingness he had shown at the beginning of his career. Yet, . . . there is really no definite line that can be traced in his development. The lines of romanticism and realism fade, deepen, and intertwine, crossing each other and then converging. At the same time, the playwright's determination to produce proletarian drama often yields to his talent for portraying the middle-class. But this is no misfortune, for his dramas of middle-class life belong among his best work.

Although he had no admiration for the Neo-Romanticism of his day, he knew the value of imagery and symbolism, and even in completely realistic plays, he used symbolism with dramatic effect. The senile, mumbling old woman in **Ahasverus,** and the grandfather puttering with his clocks in **The Rising Sun** are examples of this. Heijermans also combined sound and symbol, as with the whistle of the machinery in **The Machine** and the tapping of the shoemaker's hammer in **The Suit of Armor.**

Was Heijermans the Dutch Hauptmann? This question has often been asked by critics, and it has two possible meanings. If it means that Heijermans was a conscious, or even unconscious imitator of Hauptmann, a kind of Dutch version of the German playwright, the answer is No. Hauptmann was the representative of German Naturalism and Neo-Romanticism. Heijermans refused to become a convert to either of these movements, and he looked upon the latter with particular distaste. In the sense that Heijermans was the leading Dutch dramatist of his age and Holland's representative on the stages of the world, that he was to Holland what Hauptmann was to Germany, the answer to the question is yes.

But Heijermans was above all himself. In his genuine humor, his idealistic view of humanity, his warm-hearted imagination, his eye for Dutch life and Dutch character, he is a unique phenomenon on the stage of his country. It would really be a great injustice to think of Heijermans in terms of approximations to others, for he did achieve what he set out to do from the very beginning of his career. He put Dutch reality upon the stage. Not with photographic flatness, but with sincere emotion and poetic imagination. (pp. 228-35)

> *Seymour L. Flaxman, in his* Herman Heijermans and His Dramas, *Martinus Nijhoff, 1954, 266 p.*

HILDA VAN NECK YODER (essay date 1978)

[*Yoder is the author of* Dramatizations of Social Themes: Herman Heijermans' Plays as Compared with Selected Dramas by Ibsen, Hauptmann, and Chekhov. *In unexcerpted portions of the work,*

Yoder compares Heijermans's Ghetto, Op Hoop van Zegen, *and* Ora et Labora *with Henrik Ibsen's* Ghosts, *Gerhart Hauptmann's* Die Weber, *and Anton Chekhov's* The Cherry Orchard, *respectively. In the following excerpt, Yoder examines the effectiveness of the three dramas by Heijermans in addressing social problems in a rapidly changing society.*]

Ghetto, written in 1898, is Heijermans' second full-length play and his first real theatrical success. Set within the Jewish ghetto of Amsterdam, this play presented the Dutch audience with a powerful characterization of Sachel, the old Jewish rag-dealer, whose life is falling apart when his son Rafaël confronts him with severe criticism and rejection of the Jewish religion and of the business practices accepted in the ghetto. However, beside the strong and realistic portrait of Sachel, Rafaël and his girl friend Rose seem to be mere puppets. (p. 5)

In the play, Rafaël announces that he is no longer Jewish and is going to reject the obligation which he owes Sachel according to Jewish customs. He will not take over the business and assume the care of his blind father. Instead, he is leaving not only the ghetto but the whole stifling environment in which he was raised. At the end of Act II, he adds the shocking announcement that he considers himself married to Rose, the Christian servant who works for his father. Sachel tries hard to keep Rafaël from leaving by attempting to arrange a "good" marriage for him with Rebecca, the daughter of another merchant in secondhand clothing, Aaron. In Act III, Esther (Sachel's sister and housekeeper) and Aaron convince Rose that Rafaël has broken his promises to her and will marry Rebecca. Alone with Sachel, Rose begs him to tell her the truth about Rafaël and to swear by sacred relics, *mezoesos*. Sachel lies, swearing that Rafaël has promised to marry Rebecca, and Rose commits suicide by jumping into the canal in front of the shop. (pp. 5-6)

The action of **Ghetto** . . . is based on the relationship of Rose as wife and Sachel as father to Rafaël. Both have no existence other than through this relationship to a man who does not relate to them as husband and as son, because of his commitment to causes which reject the existing family structure. The basis of the motivation behind the characters is thus set within the melodramatic perspective, with Rafaël operating on a level totally different from that of Sachel and Rose. Because this dualistic perspective is an accepted structure of feeling, Heijermans considers it to be realistic, and actually made the gap between Rafaël and the other characters wider in the second version [of the play].

That Rafaël's arguments are expected to convince us is obvious from the way Heijermans reinforces the legitimacy of Rafaël's accusations of his father and the Rabbi; he never invites us to believe that Rafaël made the wrong decision in leaving these people. The center of the action is the falling apart of Sachel's world and the disclosure of his true humaneness, something Rafaël does not understand. Sachel is moved by the actions of his son who, in turn, is not affected by anyone.

There are two important factors relating to this struggle between father and son. First of all, Rafaël can only see his father and relate to him in his role as the merchant who cheats while counting on people's pity for his blindness. He is oblivious to any other aspect of his father's personality. . . . Although Rafaël's objections are part of a total rejection of the greed and religious intolerance of the ghetto, he expresses them in the action by rejecting his father. Secondly, Sachel cannot understand Rafaël's intellectual objections to his values and his profession, and can only see Rafaël's criticism as a personal rejection of himself as father. Although Sachel acts as if he did not care, his seeming indifference is a poor cover for the intensity of his feelings for his son. Thus, his feelings of fatherhood increase while Rafaël's arguments do not change his ethics. Their relationship is that of two opposing forces; one is based on the apparent pursuit of honesty, justice and a more humane life, while the other is based on an intense, but blinding, love. Neither character understands the other, but Sachel is the only one who suffers. The plot consists of Rafaël acting on the basis of a discovery made long ago. The result of watching Rafaël's rejection of his father evokes in us a feeling of sympathy with the father's suffering, rather than convincing us of the political philosophy which motivates his son.

What has happened is that Sachel, whose identity was based on the mores and business practices of the Jewish Ghetto, is suddenly confronted with the loss of his son, which calls forth a totally a-political, un-religious, and non-businesslike part of his nature. In his despair, religion and its laws have become meaningless to Sachel, and he is able to commit perjury by sacred Jewish relics. The urge to feel secure financially now yields to a more basic passion directed at keeping his son. The more Sachel tries to hold on to Rafaël, the more he loses him; and he develops from a greedy, dogmatic, Jewish merchant into a desperate, loving father whose overpowering passion requires no explanation. Ultimately, Sachel's fatherhood is the basis of his identity to which all other characteristics are subservient. Therefore, Rafaël's opponent gradually shows his real nature—that of fatherhood—while Rafaël continues to relate to him as the evil, crooked businessman. Our perception of Sachel no longer coincides with Rafaël's interpretation, and we reject the son and his actions. (pp. 8-9)

In the characterization of Sachel, Heijermans shows an ability to portray a tragic struggle but is too much concerned with making the message of Rafaël clear. He therefore moves the action back to the dualistic mode in which Sachel simply becomes the villain, the representative of the old, decrepit order—as opposed to Rafaël who is a messenger of a better future. While Heijermans wants to challenge the faith of the middle class in its own power to manage the world, he is dependent on nineteenth-century middle-class stereotypes to confront it.

In the suicide scene, Heijermans stresses how much Sachel and Rose have in common. They are conceived as finding their identities in the middle-class concept of the family. Rose's suicide finds its origin in the bourgeois stereotype of female faithfulness: once the beloved has left, death is preferred. Sachel's anger as the rejected father is very well handled in the play, building up and finding its climax and depth in the fact that it leads to some understanding in this suicide scene. Rose's actions are less well prepared, and the audience's acceptance of her suicide is based primarily on its acceptance of a stereotype. In the scenes in which Rose is without Rafaël, she is portrayed as a strong-willed, lovable woman who refuses to lie to Sachel and whom Esther admires as a servant. . . . In the third act, she is confronted with Esther and Aaron, who are attempting to get rid of her in a vicious manner, by offering her money, which she proudly refuses, and then lying to her by telling her that Rafaël has left to marry Rebecca. But they lose this battle. For Rose is intelligent and strong in her perseverance, acting upon what she knows to be right. She is far from being a submissive woman and seems to be able to look out for herself very well. In fact, she seems to have much more insight into other people than Rafaël. Therefore her despair and the consequent suicide are based on Heijermans' adherence

to stereotypes and on his inability to portray a woman who can find an identity separate from her lover. Why can Rafaël leave, almost unmoved by the loss of his beloved, while her life has to end in self-annihilation?

Neither Sachel's fatherhood nor Rose's unwillingness to go on living without her lover are based on particular character traits or on unique past experiences. Instead, both are based on stereotypes and are accepted unquestioningly by Heijermans as part of human nature. The generation gap here is explained not by a difference in values and ideas between father and son, but by a profound difference in "nature." Heijermans does confront his audience with radical ideas. But when we carefully look at them within the context of the play, it becomes clear that the values this play actually affirms are contrary to those ideas. Heijermans confronts us with disturbing situations and daring ideas, while in the action and characterization reaffirming the values of the middle class.

Rafaël questions the humaneness of the Jewish culture which he is supposed to uphold; he accepts Rose as his wife because of their love relationship rather than because of a legal document. But this apparent free-thinking is refuted by the action of the play. Sachel's insistence that Rafaël follow the Jewish customs is based on his feelings as a father, not on a belief in those customs. Ultimately, this points to Heijermans' belief that the Jewish tradition of a son taking care of his father and preserving the religious practices does indeed reflect human nature, and hence should not be questioned.

In this play, Heijermans comes full circle. First, through Rafaël the author attacks the Jewish customs which destroy human love and truly religious feeling. However, he then shows that those customs are not really important compared to the natural impulse of the parent to maintain a relationship with the child. This parental impulse is presented as absolute, universal, and beyond specific religious or social relationships. Rafaël's arguments for change are thus irrelevant and superficial, for the Jewish customs actually reflect human nature. What the play actually advocates is a preservation of the Jewish customs because they protect and channel the natural impulses into positive directions. Rafaël's agitation for a total uprooting of the existing social framework, his longing for a new society, is seen as the greatest threat to human happiness and fulfillment. This impulse to destroy is even more pronounced in the second version, because there Heijermans enhances Rafaël's unsympathetic nature.

The other controversial situation which *Ghetto* presents is that of Rose and Rafaël relating to each other as man and wife without being legally married, while belonging to different classes and religions. Here, too, the departure from convention leads to chaos, for the prejudice against interfaith relationships and free love is shown on stage to be justified. Rafaël and Rose scorn the reverence that the bourgeois society has toward legal documents and toward marrying a "proper" partner. However, except for the absence of a piece of paper, Heijermans has presented their relationship exactly like the bourgeois stereotype. Rafaël makes all the decisions and is intellectually superior to Rose. She represents the emotional aspect of their union and does so in a sacrificing manner. The absence of the marriage certificate adds a touch of the risqué; it implies no radical critique of traditional institutionalized relationships.

Heijermans seemed quite uncomfortable in the staging of an actual free-love, interfaith relationship. In the first version, the departure from conventions leads to a disastrous ending for

Rose (which could be taken as a suggestion of the "unnaturalness" of such a union), which hardly touches Rafaël, who can attain his goals just as well without her. Moreover, judging from the few moments that Rebecca is on stage, there seems to be little difference between her and Rose, making Rafaël's rebellion not very urgent.

In the same way as the second version increased the general destructiveness of Rafaël it also weakened the foundation of the love relationship, bringing out Heijermans' increasing fear of change via experimental solutions, which is also obvious in his later plays. In their last verbal exchange of this second version, Heijermans reveals the total mismatch of Rafaël and Rose and contradicts the very foundation on which their union was based—that, where people love each other, religious dogmas or laws are meaningless. (pp. 11-13)

Stripped of its rhetoric, *Ghetto* presents a conflict between those who love functioning within the framework of the family and those who egotistically destroy the family. There are not alternatives. After 1903 Heijermans clearly showed that he associated the future with this selfishness and materialism and the past with a golden age of love and family harmony. But in this early play, this outlook on life can already be distinguished underneath appearances which seem to point to the opposite. In his dramatic oeuvre, Heijermans showed that he had very little hope in a different future, and that the basis for a better life was to be found in the love relationships within the family. The conflict in *Ghetto* as well as in his later dramas is essentially based on a fear of the future and an alienation from his own generation, with its talk of change.

Sachel and Rose are created with the assumption that the audience would readily accept their stereotype. Rafaël, however, presents a new kind of person, needing a new basis for his behavior. Heijermans chose a "love" relationship to express Rafaël's attitudes and opinions. Rafaël's basic criticism is levelled at the emphasis on money which he sees in his father's life and in the Jewish community as a whole. [In his *Herman Heijermans and His Dramas* (1954), Seymour L.] Flaxman observes how well Heijermans has succeeded in showing how important a part of the Jewish community money has become. . . . Rafaël's separation from his father began when he saw his father cheat, and his refusal to marry the bride his father has chosen is based on the knowledge that that choice is based on money. (pp. 14-15)

Heijermans, therefore, had to eliminate all ties to money in his attempt to create a hero who opposes capitalist ethics. Rafaël is, therefore, totally "unpolluted" by money. This kind of character returns time after time in Heijermans' plays: a totally "innocent" hero, a man without any financial ties, is set in opposition to people who are obsessed by it.

But the lack of an economic basis in Rafaël's existence also brings with it a need to reveal his masculinity in some other way. For within the society as Heijermans knew it, to be able to provide financially was a masculine prerogative. Rafaël's identity, therefore, is expressed through the sexual relationship with Rose, for although Heijermans avoids presentation on the stage of the sexual aspect of their relationship, he stresses the physical link between the two rather than the emotional or intellectual one. Rose hardly shares Rafaël's new ideas, but within the action she serves to bring out his masculinity.

Apart from his behavior toward Rose, Rafaël plays a role usually assigned to women. When he first appears on the stage, he has flowers in his hand, having spent the day by his mother's grave. Indifferent toward financial success, he has forgotten all the messages he had to deliver for his father and is much better equipped to deal with morality than business. He has learned languages and reads widely—female occupations in a society in which masculinity is measured by the amount of money earned by the provider.

The masculinity asserted in Rafaël's sexual relationship to Rose is the only part of him which links him with the family-oriented society of his father. But instead of "normalizing" him, it emphasizes his extreme alienation from those who love him. The purely sexual nature of their relationship has increased in the second version, where Rose and Rafaël are even further apart intellectually. It is emphasized by Rose's pregnancy; in the end, the unborn child is all that unites them. The sexual role, which was so important to his father and to Rose, is only incidental to Rafaël's identity as intellectual and prophet.

The complete lack of a meaningful relationship between Rafaël and Sachel, and Rafaël and Rose, underlines the point essential to understanding Heijermans' vision. His perception of reality as expressed in *Ghetto* is dualistic. Sachel and Rose are both pushed to an extreme beyond the role which they play within the society presented on stage. At the point of crisis, Sachel is not the Jewish merchant but the archetypal parent, ready to destroy whoever comes between him and his son. Rose, too, moves from independent woman to the archetypal sacrificing maiden whose life is over once her lover has betrayed her. And Rafaël is drawn in the most extreme contrast to those around him by his total lack of attachment and involvement and, therefore, his total lack of guilt.

The inadequacy of the modality of dualism in dealing with contemporary problems can be seen within the action of *Ghetto*. Within the play Heijermans does not really know if he wishes to align himself with the status quo or with the young rebel. Intellectually, he sides with the critics of the status quo; emotionally, he sides with the middle class. By pushing both sides to the extreme, he refutes the argument of his play. For Sachel is excused because of his blinding parental love, but at the same time, he is the representative of a rotten society. Thus Rafaël can only be totally innocent by being totally heartless.

Ghetto is an attempt to use the theater to comment on social and economic inequality. However, this critical stance, which is based on a refusal to accept the nineteenth-century socioeconomic order as a reflection of nature, is expressed through conventions which are based on a static perception of life. On the level of the imagination, Heijermans expresses a fear for change and, at the same time, a desire for it; but he cannot deal with this ambivalence because he sees the world in terms of polar opposites. The clearest example of the author's tendency to believe in the impossibility of absolute goodness can be seen in his failure to keep Rafaël from becoming involved in evil, while Heijermans refuses to present Rafaël's involvement as problematic. When Rafaël and Rose discuss their future in the beginning of Act II, he informs her that he cannot tell his family about their relationship. . . . However, at the end of the same act, Rafaël confirms Sachel's suspicion [about his relationship with Rose]. . . . He leaves immediately and does not return until Rose's body is found. The author does not give us any clue as to where he went and why he did not make sure that he would protect Rose from the expected familial attacks. At one time, Esther wonders where he is, but nothing is made of her concern.

In fact, when Sachel realizes that Rose has committed suicide, he calls for help and knocks on a neighbor's door. Esther and

Aaron return from their walk, having heard him. That Heijermans did not quite know how to get Rafaël back immediately before the body of Rose is brought in, and how to convince us that he had not forgotten her, is clear. . . . Heijermans does not explain why he could not have heard Sachel's screams, nor why he was not waiting for Rose at home. That Heijermans does not present us with an alibi shows the author's awareness that Rafaël's absence could imply a failure on his part to protect Rose from the vicious attacks of his family. But Heijermans shies completely away from suggesting any responsibility on Rafaël's part for what has happened to Rose. This is directly related to Heijermans' avoidance of dealing with Sachel in terms of a tragic awareness. Within an analysis of reality in terms of black and white, one cannot deal with the proposition that the good may be just as guilty as the bad.

Related to Heijermans' belief in a static and absolute morality is his presentation of reality. What happens on stage never contradicts the interpretation which the characters give to it. What happened in the past is experienced and analyzed in much the same way by all of the characters involved. The audience sees Sachel's attempt to cheat in the very first scene, and is thus prepared to accept Rafaël's opinion of his father as the cheating merchant. Sachel does not give a different view of himself—he only attempts to shrug off the responsibility by saying that everyone cheats.

Heijermans presents the life of an old man who sees the values he has always believed in, and all the sacrifices he has made, being scorned by his son, who chooses a totally different direction for his own life. Sachel faces a future without the solid framework which the Jewish community has built around itself to protect its members from ideas which would reveal the contradictions. But at the moment Heijermans approaches an evaluation of human values and relationships in terms of a contemporary awareness, he relies not only on the archetypal impulse of parenthood to give Sachel an identity, but also presents reality within the play as totally stable, comprehensible, and as reaffirmation of everything that Rafaël questions.

While Heijermans expressed his conviction of the need for change in his essays and in his identification with the socialist cause, he did not express this conviction dramatically. There is a wide gap between the world of Rafaël and that of Sachel, and it is obvious from Heijermans' presentation of the destruction resulting from Rafaël's attempt to change the world that Heijermans was fearful of the period of change between the status quo and the utopia represented by Rafaël. In *Ghetto*, Heijermans presents the present as a destructive period where every good impulse leads to disaster. In the process of de-sanctifying the middle-class institutions of marriage and religion, he reaffirmed the very perception on which these institutions were based. Rather than finding modern problems to originate within the middle-class family, family relationships are depicted as reflecting human nature and therefore as being, in essence, good. (pp. 15-18)

In *Ghetto* it is already obvious that, even though Rafaël knows all the solutions to contemporary problems and has a vision of the future, he bases his answers on ideas found in the Old Testament. Moreover, his father's life is dominated by love for his son and the preservation of the family, while Rafaël's words only have a destructive effect on the people around him. Heijermans' early ambivalence about change, and about the generational conflict, is still apparent in his later plays. In *Ora et Labora* and in subsequent plays, Heijermans identifies the present and the future (i.e., the younger generation) with ma-

terialism and money, while the actions of the older generation are shown to be still based on harmony and love, values threatened by the modern world.

In *Op Hoop van Zegen*, Heijermans depicts the daily life of a poor fishing community. He concentrates on Kniertje, an old woman whose husband and whose two sons have drowned in the ocean some time ago and who will lose her last two sons before the play is over because the boat on which they work, the Op Hoop van Zegen, sinks. (p. 25)

While much of *Op Hoop van Zegen* may have been based on direct observations, the depiction of the life of the fishing people reflects Heijermans' sympathetic attitude toward poor workers—warm, loving and honest people who work extremely hard and are very courageous. Heijermans stresses the fact that their values are community-oriented rather than egocentric by presenting them as a group which celebrates birthdays, suffers anxieties, and finally shares alike in the grief about lost relatives.

The motivation behind all those actions is the struggle to maintain families. The first and the last scenes in which we see Kniertje dramatize a sense of responsibility for her own family and her community. When she first appears on stage, she scolds her youngest son, Barend, for not taking better care of their chickens—which are running on the neighbor's field. In the end, she does not only lament the deaths of Geert and Barend, but those of all the members of her family who were drowned long ago. . . . And rather than worrying about how she is going to feed and clothe herself, she is looking forward to the child which Geert's fiancée is expecting. . . . (p. 27)

The fishing people know each other well and get along with each other. Heijermans presents them as decent, family oriented, basically very obedient, and without evil. They do not drink, and the men and women are invariably faithful. In other words, Heijermans does not show any qualities in them which might affirm the bourgeois attitude toward poor people as lazy and shiftless.

Flaxman points to the courageous submissiveness of Kniertje and feels that "it is this patient bravery and this firm faith in the goodness of God and man that, in the end, make of Kniertje such a tragic figure." . . . But seen within their socio-economic setting, submissiveness toward authority and trusting faith in God become destructive qualities. For it is exactly Kniertje's submission which enables Bos (the shipowner) to carry on his business. (pp. 27-8)

Geert is the only character in the play who dares to stand up to Bos. He is Kniertje's son and has just returned from a Navy jail for striking a superior officer who had made a derogatory remark about Jo, his fiancée. Aware of the effects of the patriarchal relationship of Bos to the fishermen, he evokes Bos' rage by singing a socialist song in his mother's house. . . . And when Bos reminds him of all the risks he runs as ship owner, Geert tells him who really earns his money and runs those risks. . . . The only character who forms a threat to stability is, however, only talking and is killed before the play is over. Meanwhile, the women, represented by Kniertje, can only maintain the lives of their families by being submissive and enduring the exploitation.

Heijermans places the burden of doing something about these ills solidly on the shoulders of the middle-class audience. If we look at the way he has presented the poor, it becomes clear that he has very little faith in their ability to change their own

Scene from a 1930 production of Ghetto.

situation. Thus, although this is generally called a proletarian drama, it is written from the point of view of the bourgeoisie. For not only are we, the audience, the only ones who could change the wrongs presented on the stage, but Heijermans has only presented wrongs which can easily be changed by a middle class, without damage to its own socio-economic position.

On the one hand, Heijermans brings out the beauty and love of the fishing people, stressing those values which would be very attractive to a middle-class audience—hard work, honesty, family orientation and respect for authority. On the other hand, he shows that if Bos were a little less greedy, so that the old fishing people and the widows would get an adequate pension, and if there were laws which would protect the safety of the fishermen, the world of Kniertje and her family would be relatively happy and carefree. Heijermans accepts the authoritarian structure of society as being potentially ideal for people to work and to live in. Geert does not object to his relationship to Bos. He only asks that it be a professional relationship granting the fishermen independence of thought and action. Nowhere in the action of the play is there shown the potential of change from below, to be expected from a socialist writer. (pp. 28-9)

By portraying Kniertje as a symbol of the fishing people, rather than Geert or Jo, Heijermans has not made change (let alone revolution) but rather submission and endurance the moving,

convincing, positive qualities. It seems quite obvious that had Geert come back or had Barend been able to share his knowledge of the rotten boat with Geert's awareness of Bos' greed, the outcome of the play would have been very different. (pp. 29-30)

The wide gap between Kniertje and Bos is dramatized in Act IV. For while the first three acts were all set in Kniertje's one-room house and brought out the community spirit of the fishing people, the last scene is set in Bos' office in which the safe takes a central position. Here Bos quarrels viciously with his wife, accusing her of having stolen money from him, while she reminds him that if it were not for her he would not have any. Here, while Bos and his office clerk are taking inventory, Bos loses his temper when Kaps mistakenly gives the fund for widows and orphans one guilder too much. Kaps reminds Bos that when a mistake of a few zeroes in his favor was made, Bos did not think anything of it. In this scene, the true reason for the disasters of the fishing people becomes clear. Bos is not an evil man, but he has become enslaved by money. To the fishing people the lives of the men are most important; to Bos money has become the foundation of all his actions. In the confrontation with the angry, grieving Jo, Marietje, and Simon, Bos loses his patience. The real feeling towards them is expressed—showing the opposite side of the fatherly Bos of Act I. . . . (p. 32)

Heijermans has dramatized two enemies which threaten these people. On the one hand, they run terrifying risks on the ocean in order to support their families, while, on the other, they have no protection against exploitation by the shipowners. And it is the attitude with which they have managed to face and survive the dangers of the sea which makes them vulnerable to economic exploitation. They accept both enemies with the same submission and endurance. Heijermans has pointed out dramatically that these two enemies are very different. Economic exploitation is not a part of nature, but is man-made and can therefore be checked. But the attitude of rebellion, or standing up for one's own rights, is irrelevant to the struggle with the ocean and, therefore, alien to the mentality of these people. Geert is the only one who sees what is wrong and refuses to submit; he tells Bos that times are changing. But he is unrepresentative, for he has been away from the fishing community—in the Navy—and has been exposed to people who have begun to demand the right to make their own decisions.

Op Hoop van Zegen is a powerful play because of the twofold nature of the hardship of the fishing people. The author has made cause and effect very clear to the audience, underlining the fact that every facet of the evil which comes from Bos can be understood, explained, and changed. Moreover he has depicted the fishing people as totally helpless, innocent victims, whose love for each other elevates them high above the shipowner's greed.

Heijermans' own attitude toward exploitation and change emerges from the way he portrays the confrontation between the fishermen and Bos. He does not deal with it from a socialistic point of view—i.e. with a faith in the ability of the workers to change the economic relationships. Except for the short scene in Act II where Bos is confronted with Geert, Bos is invariably faced with weak people who really do not know the nature of the system which Bos represents. Heijermans makes Kniertje a heroine who lacks a rebellious or questioning mentality, symbolizing naiveté and innocence, totally incapable of changing her own fate. Heijermans writes for the middle class and presents them with a moving picture of a world in which evil is uncomplicated; and as far as it comes from people, it can be solved by that middle class, not by its victims. In *Op Hoop van Zegen,* Heijermans gives us a dramatization of the way he would like to see the evils of this world eradicated—by the goodness of the middle class who would protect the poor from the greed of their patrons so that both groups can continue to exist.

Heijermans is not ready to deal with a threat to the orderly existence of the middle-class world, as represented by Geert. For while supporting Geert's rhetoric, he does not allow it to be the basis of actions. Within the play, Geert's actions are in no way different from those of the other fishermen; his change so far is only verbal. Heijermans presents the fishing community as a beautiful institution which satisfies people's emotional needs and which can thrive under a *laissez-faire* system. His vision of change implies that if excessive greed can be modified and the lives and happiness of the workers can be recognized as having the same importance as money, more drastic changes are not mandatory.

Heijermans' fear of Geert, of people who want to make their own decisions, becomes apparent from the fact that when Geert spills out his ideas, the result of these very words is destructive; his mother loses her job. One is left to wonder what other hardships Kniertje would have to suffer from Geert should he have come back. Heijermans presents three threats to the happiness of Kniertje and her people in this play. He shows the harshness of nature, but maintains that these people have the capacities to withstand it. The second enemy is Bos, whose greed is extremely destructive; but the third enemy is Geert, who means well but whose ideas of change will indirectly hurt his own people who do not see the need for this change. Instead of equating Geert's rhetoric with Heijermans' faith in socialism, we should conclude that Geert's words and actions show the author's ambivalence about social change.

Heijermans chose to present a Geert who drowns rather than one who discovers Bos' scandalous greed before it would have been too late. He avoided a confrontation between Geert's socialistic ideals and the proof of actual scandal. In this play, the upheavals of his time are reduced to the conflict between innocent, brave fishing people and greedy capitalists. Heijermans expressed his faith that the middle class, rather than the proletariat, will do something about the injustices in society. Not exploring the potential of political action, this play, rather, implies Heijermans' fear of such actions. (pp. 33-5)

In *Ora et Labora,* Heijermans dramatizes the desperate attempts of three families to keep alive. Watze, his wife Maaike, their son Eelke and their daughter Froukje, and his neighbor Sytze with his seven children, were once able to make a comfortable living from the land they owned and worked. Before the play starts, Sytze has lost it all, and has resorted to begging to fill the mouths of his children; Watze has lost most of his land to a neighbor, Tjerk, and in the first act loses his last cow, while in Act III he faces the public sale of his remaining land and house because of debts. The third family consists of Hiddes, his wife Jeltje, and their daughter Sytske (the last surviving child out of twelve). They have a boat with which they transport peat from the farm to the city. But bad weather (frozen canals) has made trade impossible. While the author concentrates on the way in which Watze loses his last possessions, Hiddes' family is important because Sytske is in love with Watze's son Eelke. Sytze does not figure in the plot as such, but gives an impression of the general misery beyond the two main families.

The plot of *Ora et Labora* consists of two parts, both occupying about half of the play. The first part ends in the middle of Act II when Watze returns with twenty-eight guilders from selling the carcass of his last cow. Because he has incurred a court debt of 50 guilders, this money will not suffice to pay this debt off, let alone to support his family. The second part parallels the first, for Eelke sells his last possession, his body, to help his family out; he enlists in the army to fight in the Dutch colonies for six years, receiving two-hundred florins. He offers 150 guilders to his parents and fifty to the parents of his girl friend. But Watze and Maaike begrudge Hiddes and Jeltje the fifty guilders; after a vicious fight, Hiddes, Jeltje, and Sytske leave, insulted.

Much of the first part of *Ora et Labora* is occupied with establishing the intimate community feeling among the three families, their economic hardships and the beginnings of the destruction of this community feeling due to extreme poverty. Heijermans, at first, gives us a glimpse of how these people had learned to relate in "normal" times, when money was not a crucial issue. Maaike invites Hiddes into her house at the very beginning of the play when his boat gets stuck in the ice right in front of her hut. Although they have not seen each other for a long time, it is immediately clear that there is a strong bond between their families and that they sympathize with each other's hardships.

This warm feeling among members of the older generation is paralleled by a fond affection between their children, Eelke and Sytske. Just as Hiddes' boat happens to get stuck at this very place, Eelke happens to come back to see his parents. When he and Sytske see each other, they immediately pick up where they left off the last time they were together; they joke, burst into song, and laugh about their memories. Both their relationship and that between their parents is as it always has been—unaffected by the misery around them. But when Eelke tells Sytske of his plan to walk to Germany because he has no money and no work, their joy is clouded. The need for money makes it impossible for these two to relate to each other now as lovers, for Sytske takes Eelke's decision as a personal rejection. In the same way as their relationship is spoiled and eventually broken off because of money, so does the friendship between their parents turn into vicious hatred in the end.

Heijermans shows us different attitudes toward the terrible misery which these people suddenly face. He dramatizes options open to an individual dealing with a changing environment. On the one extreme, he shows us that Sytske, who openly resorts to begging, gives up all hope and merely tries to keep alive. Hiddes and Jeltje represent the other extreme, together with their daughter Sytske. For they refuse to change their ways, looking down on those that steal. . . . (pp. 45-7)

They have preserved the ethics on which their community was based before the depression started. Although they are very much aware of the extent of their own misery, they maintain a harmonious, loving marriage relationship. When Hiddes admits that he sees no way out and has contemplated suicide, Jeltje shares his feelings completely. . . . Their daughter is the only person who has preserved some kind of innocence and joy, and her reaction to the idea of suicide is typical of her initial carefree happiness. . . . Her ideas of life and the future are unaffected by the misery and the drastic changes around her, while her parents, rather than compromise their sense of ethics and goodness, think about committing suicide. Even when Maaike and Watze quarrel viciously with them over money,

Jeltje understands the cause of their changed behavior and forgives them. . . . (p. 47)

Between these two attitudes—that of giving up hope and depending on others to feed you, and that of proudly enduring, and refusing to act unethically—lie the responses of Maaike, Watze and Eelke, on whom the author concentrates. For none of them can patiently endure the hardships, like Jeltje and Hiddes, nor are they willing to resort to begging. Maaike shows the effects of the hunger and poverty by the way she snarls at her sick, dying mother-in-law and her retarded daughter, Froukje. Heijermans shows, through her, what happens when the old morality is invalidated through economic hardships and the person is left to struggle alone. It is most obvious in the many quarrels between her and her husband that the inability of the man to provide affects the structure of the family deeply. For when he comes home after the cow has died, and there is no hope for them to earn any money, Maaike cannot control her despair any more and blames him for their misery. They are just the opposite of Jeltje and Hiddes in the way they do change and compromise in order to stay alive. Through the greed of which Maaike and Watze eventually are capable, Heijermans makes these two families into symbols of the antithesis between money and the harmony within the family, between individuality and community.

In Watze, Heijermans dramatizes what happens to a man when all he believes in and lives for suddenly ceases to be of value, and he is forced to accept a different value system. While Maaike scorns Sytze for begging, she and her husband resort to stealing. That the new system of economy tolerates begging, but punishes stealing, becomes clear. Because Watze gets caught, he is about to lose his house and land, and if he is fortunate, he may end up in the poorhouse. It is interesting that Tjerk, the richer neighbor who caught him stealing, has tried twice (once in Act I and once in Act II) to settle with Watze out of court, a solution which would have been better for both parties. He offers Watze the dismissal of the court case and thirty guilders for his land. Watze stubbornly refuses and ends up having to sell both his home and land to cover the court costs. Heijermans shows why it is impossible for Watze to accept that offer and what is involved in this economic reshuffling. For to Tjerk, the land means money and a future income. To Watze, it is filled with sweat and memories—ties to the past which cannot be expressed in money. (pp. 47-8)

Eelke's attempts to come to terms with a changing world are contrasted with Sytske's refusal to do so. Eelke wants to work, and since there is no work in Friesland, he is willing to go to Germany. For him the most important thing in life is the ability to earn a living. For Sytske this is totally irrelevant, and she wants to be courted by Eelke the way men courted women in the past. In their relationship, Heijermans juxtaposes love with money, showing that Eelke loses both by his acceptance of the new order. When Sytske is faced with Eelke's decision, she still refuses to compromise her ideals; and in the same way that her parents prefer to commit suicide rather than change their mode of existence, she rejects Eelke and his money completely, preferring the termination of their relationship. . . . In their conversation in the last scene of Act II, their total inability to communicate contrasts clearly with the initial scene. Eelke explains that his family is going to lose its house and will starve, that her parents are thinking about suicide, and that therefore he wants to help. Her response seems completely irrelevant to these arguments; she tells him that he does not love her, and that she has never loved him, and that all is

finished between them. Heijermans shows here that communication, the basis for joy and love, cannot exist in a world of starvation and unemployment. (pp. 48-9)

Heijermans depicts a society which is changing so fundamentally that people are bewildered, losing all sense of ethics once the morality in which they were raised no longer applies. The desperate attempt to keep from starving overturns the communal values which were strongest in a peasant society. This destruction of unity and certainty is also expressed in the general conversations of the play. Everyone is fully aware that the order of the past is changing and that the present is experienced as chaos. There is much talk of the differences between the past and the present. . . . (p. 49)

Many times, characters in *Ora et Labora* ask why things have changed. But no one comes up with an explanation. These people functioned within a harmonious relationship with nature in the same way that the fishing people of *Op Hoop van Zegen* still had a vital relationship with the ocean. Suddenly, these peasants see that their environment has become hostile, and they wonder why. But they are not used to asking questions, let alone providing answers. . . . And in the same way as the peasants do not search for answers, neither does Heijermans try to find reasons for the change. He merely observes and laments.

Alienation from nature and from each other is expressed in the language and imagery of the play. Rituals can be seen as an attempt to superimpose human order at moments in which man is most aware of his dependency on a hostile nature. Through the ritualistic communal ceremonies, one establishes a sense of togetherness, creating an illusion of power over this wild and fierce nature. The use of proverbs and idioms has a similar function in the play, for they are attempts to fit frightening new experiences into the familiar, stable, framework of the cliché, which finds its origin in what seems to be an almost prehistoric past, and gives the feeling of a continuation of shared traditions at a moment when everything seems to fall apart. The fear of chaos and the bewilderment at new experiences express themselves in this play by the intense use of proverbs, especially by Maaike—who lacks the stability and the tools to handle her despair.

Maaike tries to stave off despair by fitting poverty into an old saying, thereby elevating it to a static and orderly concept of reality which transcends the chaotic present. . . . In *Ora et Labora,* Heijermans dramatizes people whose only remaining possession is their language. But because it is based on past truths, and the present needs a totally different set of values, even the strong idioms and proverbs have become powerless and dead.

In addition to the use of clichés and proverbs, the terror of the present is expressed within the framework of the Christian religion. All absolute religious *statements* immediately contrast with the reality of *actions* which are based on a survival instinct rather than on cultural traditions. (p. 50)

The attempt to understand and exercise power over the present by language rather than by behavior is the basis of the first half of the play. In the second part, Heijermans dramatizes through Eelke . . . an attempt to apply Christ's sacrifice to their present despair through actions. And in the same way as words had failed in the end of the first part, now the Christian foundation is shown to be totally inapplicable to the new times. Eelke discovers that his sacrifice only brings out the potential for viciousness in his parents. (p. 51)

It is especially in Heijermans' use of death that an interesting comparison can be made [between *Ora et Labora* and] *Op Hoop van Zegen*. Both plays show an unnatural situation in which the young die while the older generation lives. In *Op Hoop van Zegen*, the young men drown while their women live until they are old, broken with grief. The abnormality of this situation is caused by economic exploitation, while in *Ora et Labora* it is nature which rejects these people. While the problems depicted in *Op Hoop van Zegen* can be solved, the peasants in *Ora et Labora* live in a universe which is drastically changing and does not want them, no matter what they do. (p. 54)

It is clear that there are obvious points of comparison which point to a different intention behind *Op Hoop van Zegen* and *Ora et Labora*. The last scenes in both plays are easiest to compare and point to the basic differences between the two works. In the last part of Act IV, Kniertje hears that she has lost both her sons, and she stumbles into Bos' office to confirm the rumor. At this point, Kniertje is the symbol of motherhood. For in her grief over her two sons, she unites her whole family, those who have died, and those who will be born.... No matter what Bos does, the family as a unit is maintained; love is stronger than death. This has to be seen in contrast to the ending of *Ora et Labora,* where the opposite happens. Eelke sacrifices his own happiness for his parents, who in turn reject him.... While Kniertje's least concern was money ... in *Ora et Labora* Heijermans shows that money is capable of destroying the feeling of parenthood. While nature seemed to be out to destroy these people, money is still more virulent.

Both the community of Kniertje as dramatized and the community of Maaike as remembered are worlds in which the family is a central unit which lives for and is dependent on the larger unit, the community. Heijermans presents this peasant society, actually, as an ideal one where human love is the basic value. This ideal, because of the way in which history changes, then becomes threatened by money. In *Op Hoop van Zegen* the greed of Bos is set in sharp contrast to the love of Kniertje and her people, who can maintain their goodness because they are not tempted by money. But all those who are in a direct position to gain financially succumb to the power of money that destroys the communal values of peasant society. The actual downfall of the communal ideal and its values is dramatized in *Ora et Labora,* where Hiddes', Jeltje's and Sytske's refusal of money and the harmony of their family is contrasted with the way Watze, Maaike and Eelke sell themselves and all that was valuable in their life for money.

In *Ghetto* Heijermans' fear of change is already evident. Even in those plays which he wrote for the workers his ambivalent attitude toward change is visible. Now, in *Ora et Labora,* it comes clearly to the foreground. Heijermans here expresses a belief that the poor actually had it better in the past and are destroying themselves by joining a new value system in which money is seen as the answer to all the problems.

The importance of the rejection of contemporary history in the presentation of these farmers cannot be overestimated. For in the same way as it is strange for someone who identifies himself with the workers' struggle to present an agricultural depression which happened in his lifetime as some freakish event in nature, so does the portrayal of greedy peasants need an explanation. Instead of seeing the struggle toward a more humane society as being one in which particular injustices are eliminated (as Heijermans did in *Ghetto, Het Zevende Gebod* and *Op Hoop van Zegen*) he now analyzes the contemporary problems by blaming greed for all the evils in the world. In his later plays,

he shows how the individual can only combat this irrevocable direction of history by rebelling against it, not through action, but through the withdrawal into the purity of his own heart.

The author of *Op Hoop van Zegen* and *Ora et Labora* represents the poor as helpless people incapable of standing up for their own rights. And in *Ora et Labora,* the author sides completely with nature's intent to wipe out these people who are stupid, capable of viciousness and greed. By showing that they are not worth interceding for and that history gives them their deserved punishment, the author has rejected the dream of a different future which implied that one had to do something to make it happen.

In other words, *Ora et Labora* was not written to dramatize the hopelessness of the socio-economic situation of the peasants. Instead, Heijermans uses these people and their misery as a vehicle to express his own personal dilemma, which, because of the lack of political rhetoric, he shows here more clearly than in any other drama. It is the dilemma of the artist who understands and accepts the beauty and suffering of life, but who objects to the monetary values by which everything in his society is judged. Heijermans was an artist searching for beauty and purity in his personal life as well as in his plays. In his private life this meant joining the Socialist party early in his career, a link with a better future; in his plays this involved the creation of characters who search for a better society and who refuse to compromise their dreams. *Ora et Labora* is crucial to the development of Heijermans' dramas, for it shows that he no longer believed the utopia which he longed for would come in the future through socialism. Instead, he saw it as a golden age which definitely belonged to the past. This play is the only one in which Heijermans allows us to see his pessimism about the future. For in his play none of the peasants—only their wealthy neighbor—will participate in the future, will be able to enhance it with the humane past from which they come. Greed is significant in the end, for Heijermans saw the present as dominated by a selfish and dehumanizing hunger after money, while he longed for a past which was dominated by love and community feeling.

Heijermans' motivation to write and his untiring efforts to stage his plays in a certain way were based on the desire to dramatize a world which would reflect the drastic changes in values and social relationships at the turn of the century. He wanted a Dutch theater which would be part of the new theater movement that confronted audiences with contemporary problems and conflicts. (pp. 55-7)

> *Hilda Van Neck Yoder, in her* Dramatizations of Social Change: Herman Heijermans' Plays as Compared with Selected Dramas by Ibsen, Hauptmann, and Chekhov, *Martinus Nijhoff, 1978, 81 p.*

ADDITIONAL BIBLIOGRAPHY

Brown, Ivor. "The Theatre: Cup of Unkindness." *Saturday Review,* London 148, No. 3860 (19 October 1929): 446-47.
    Favorable review characterizing *The Rising Sun* as an admirable example of post-Ibsenite realism.

Brown, John Mason. "Sermons in Plays: Broadway in Review." *Theatre Arts Monthly* XI, No. 12 (December 1927): 893-909.
    Review of *The Good Hope,* in which Brown states that it is Heijermans's "sympathetic understanding of the tragedy of people . . . rather than his anger at any inhuman shipowner that

makes *The Good Hope* superlative as naturalistic drama and universal as tragedy."

Dukes, Ashley. "The Plays of Herman Heijermans." *The Drama* 2, No. 8 (November 1912): 3-15.
Plot synopses and critical discussion of Heijermans's principal dramatic works.

Flaxman, Seymour L. "Herman Heijermans on the New York Stage." *The Germanic Review* XXVII, No. 1 (February 1952): 131-37.
Examines performances of Heijermans's plays on the New York stage, including *Ghetto, At the Jonge Jan, The Good Hope, Eva Bonheur,* and others in order to assess their U.S. reception, which was overwhelmingly favorable.

Gassner, John. "Hauptmann's Fellow-Travelers and the Expressionist Eruption." In his *Masters of the Drama,* third edition, pp. 467-94. New York: Random House, 1954.
Discussion of characterization, setting, and theme in Heijermans's drama.

Nicoll, Allardyce. "Realism in Diverse Lands." In his *World Drama: From Aeschylus to Anouilh,* pp. 606-07. New York: Harcourt, Brace and Co., 1950.
Compares Heijermans to such dramatists as Henrik Ibsen, August Strindberg, and Gerhart Hauptmann, concluding that while they were "self-centered, Heijermans has a broadly humanitarian outlook upon the world: . . . even while we appreciate the qualities that animate his nature, we feel in his plays a lack of strength and a want of deeper intensity."

Rickert, Edith. "Herman Heijermans." *The Lamp* XXIX, No. 4 (November 1904): 318-23.
Assessment of Heijermans's success as a dramatist.

Sayler, Oliver M. "The Play of the Week: *The Good Hope.*" *The Saturday Review,* New York IV, No. 15 (5 November 1927): 275-76.
Calls *The Good Hope* "negligible today as a protest," yet valuable as oral literature because of its "vividness as a Dutch *genre* painting come to life, its distinctive atmosphere, its evocation of a series of moods."

Van Loon, Hendrik. "A Dutch Playwright: Concerning the Author of *The Good Hope* and His Background." *The New York Times* (23 October 1927): 2.
Discussion of Heijermans's life and the social and artistic impact of his drama.

Young, Stark. "Good Beginnings: *The Good Hope.*" *The New Republic* LII, No. 674 (2 November 1927): 285-86.
Calls *The Good Hope* "a classic for almost thirty years in the Dutch theater."

Eugenio María de Hostos (y Bonilla)

1839-1903

Puerto Rican nonfiction writer, essayist, critic, journalist, biographer, dramatist, poet, novelist, and short story writer.

A man of extraordinarily diverse accomplishments, Hostos was an important literary figure and social thinker in nineteenth-century Latin America whose works promoted human rights, specifically the rights of women and the political independence of Spanish colonies in the Caribbean. He aspired not to be a ''great man'' remembered long after his death, but rather to be a man useful to his time as a constructive force for human progress. An advocate of Pan-Americanism, he hoped for the unification of the nations of North and South America, although he feared that unity would only be achieved by imperialistic expansion of the United States. His complete works fill twenty volumes, of which his *Tratado de sociología,* a treatise on sociology, and his *Moral social,* a study of social morality and ethics, as well as his seminal essay on *Hamlet,* are the best known. Both for his writings and his lifelong activism on behalf of the emancipation of Cuba and Puerto Rico from Spain and the creation of a unified confederation of the Antilles islands, Hostos is highly respected by the people of Central America.

Born in Rio Canas, on the west coast of Puerto Rico, Hostos was educated in San Juan until the age of thirteen, when he was sent to Spain. He attended high school in Bilbao and at eighteen entered the Law School of the Universidad Central de Madrid. During his college years he began publishing articles advocating the liberation of the Spanish West Indies, and at twenty-four published a novel, *La peregrinación de Bayoán,* which addressed the same concern. Throughout his life he worked for the liberty and unification of a Federated Antillean Republic composed of Cuba, Haiti, Santo Domingo, and Puerto Rico. Convinced that the Spanish monarchy would never relinquish control over its colonies, Hostos joined the movement to establish a republican form of government in Spain. Although the leaders of the movement had promised to free Cuba and Puerto Rico from Spanish rule, Emelio Castelar, who became the first president of Spain upon the deposition of Queen Isabel II, refused to emancipate the islands. Bitterly disappointed, Hostos refused a position in the new government, denounced Castelar, and in 1869 emigrated to New York.

While in the United States, Hostos became involved in the Cuban Revolutionary Junta, a group committed to the liberation of Cuba from Spain, and he edited its official periodical, *La revolución.* Finding his efforts ineffectual, he began in 1870 a four-year tour of South America to engender public and material support for the revolutionary forces in Cuba, which had been waging war on the Spanish since 1867. Hostos earned his livelihood and publicized his cause by writing for newspapers, and he became a well-known, influential voice throughout Central America. On one occasion Hostos was offered $200,000 to endorse a Peruvian railway project which he had researched and found would in many ways be detrimental to the people of Peru; refusing the bribe, he denounced the harmful aspects of the project and saw them eliminated from the final plan for the railway.

Around 1875, Hostos moved to the Dominican Republic and subsequently to Venezuela, where he met and married the

daughter of a Cuban émigré. In 1878 the Spanish government suppressed the Cuban revolution, and Hostos, obligated to end his revolutionary activities, began a career in education which lasted over twenty years. During this time Hostos taught at universities in the Dominican Republic and Chile, founded a normal school, and advanced the public educational systems of both countries. His avowed goal was to ''teach the continent to think,'' and he asserted that the nations of South America were faced with a choice: ''Civilization or death!'' His hope for democracy was largely founded upon the example of the United States, which he admired, although he feared possible American expansion and subjugation of the Antilles. When the Spanish Civil War resulted in the independence of Cuba in 1898, Hostos travelled to the United States to work toward the liberation of Puerto Rico. His hopes were frustrated, however, by the annexation of Puerto Rico to the United States, and he returned to the Dominican Republic, where he died at the age of sixty-four, convinced of the uselessness of his political effort.

Hostos's writings are voluminous and diverse. Among his literary works are an early novel, *La peregrinación de Bayoán,* which championed the cause of Cuban independence by exposing the mismanagement of the island by Spain, and a critical study of *Hamlet,* which is considered to be the greatest piece of Spanish-language criticism ever written on the play. As a polemicist, Hostos wrote *La escuela normal y el instituto de señoritas,* in which he questioned the exclusion of women from educational opportunities enjoyed by men, thus becoming an early spokesperson for women's rights. Also comprising an important part of his output are his writings on constitutional law and sociology, which are highly regarded by experts in both fields.

Hostos's most famous work, *Moral social,* was written at the solicitation of his students in Santo Domingo and encapsulates the principles of his ethical thought. The book is predicated on his perception of industrial civilization as inherently opposed to moral values: he saw irreconcilable contradictions between the exercise of material or economic power and the practice of ethical responsibility. *Moral social* discusses various aspects of human relationships such as duty, law, necessity, and gratitude, and posits the family as the essential unit of civilization. The book follows this discussion with an examination of morality as it interacts with various social institutions such as education, religion, and art. The primary focus of Hostos's thought involved the duty of the individual toward humanity. "Man is above everything a human being," he wrote. "Whatever his birthplace, his racial tradition, the influence of his family, the character of his nation, the stamp of his civilization, he is indissolubly bound by his nature to every other man."

Although few of Hostos's hopes for political change were ever realized, the social importance of his work is widely recognized, and he is respected as a forerunner of the movements which later liberated Central American colonies and extended educational opportunities to women. He is also regarded as an expert in such diverse fields as literature, education, sociology, law, and politics. To many of his admirers, Hostos is a model of devotion to ideals which, even in the face of defeat, he refused to relinquish.

PRINCIPAL WORKS

La peregrinación de Bayoán   (novel)   1863
Romeo and Juliet   (criticism)   1867
Hamlet   (criticism)   1873
Inda   (novel)   1878
Cartas públicas acerca de Cuba   (travel essays)   1887
Derecho constitucional   (nonfiction)   1887
Moral social   (nonfiction)   1888
Tratado de sociología   (nonfiction)   1904
Lecciones de derecho constitucional   (lectures)   1908
Meditando   (criticism)   1909
La escuela normal y el instituto de señoritas   (lectures)   1933
Obras completas. 20 vols.   (novel, short stories, poetry, drama, autobiography, diaries, letters, criticism, lectures, essays, and nonfiction)   1939
España y América   (essays, letters, and criticism)   1954

JOSÉ A. FRANQUIZ   (essay date 1940)

[*In the following excerpt, Franquiz discusses the various works included in Hostos's* Obras completas.]

The Government of Puerto Rico has published the complete works of Eugenio Maria de Hostos, great Puerto Rican thinker and statesman. This is an event in American Scholarship. Up to this time there had prevailed an ignorance of Hostos' place in the world of thought, for aside from his *Moral social, Tratado de sociología, Derecho constitucional,* and his *Essais,* Hostos was unknown even in his native land. . . .

The first two volumes of his complete works include his *Diario*—a memoir of events, hopes and despairs, disillusions and expectations, feelings and extraordinary thoughts of this man of vision and action. The present reviewer would not find it strange that in the coming of time, a knowledge of Hostos' *Diario* may finally result in a Brownian resetting and understanding of the political checker-board of the Caribbean. The third volume *Paginas Intimas* contains the romance of his love and the stories and plays written for the entertainment of his children. Although of no special philosophical value, this volume gives the scholar interested in the ideology of Hostos, a glimpse into the inner life of this man of vision, who was as human and tender in the intimate experiences of his home affairs, as he was objective and scientifically analytic when dealing with the problems of society. The fourth volume, *Cartas,* contains the correspondence of Hostos with the Cuban and Puerto Rican Revolutionary Boards, and other letters which depict the moral tone of his daily life and his consciousness of prophetical mission. Hostos' writings in connections with the political freedom of Puerto Rico, the famous issue of the Puerto Rican Plebescite, and his profound studies of American Public Law as applied to Puerto Rico, are contained in his fifth volume *Madre Isla.* His sixth and seventh vols., *Mi viaje al sur* and *Temas Sudamericanos,* include his observations and studies made of Colombia, Panama, Peru, Chile, Argentina and Brazil between 1870 and 1874 during his campaign in favor of the freedom of Puerto Rico and Cuba. The fundamental character of these observations is mainly sociological, but is of paramount importance not only in the sense of these observations being the data upon which Hostos based his social theory of later years, but also in consideration of the fact that these sociological observations are rich in content of social philosophy and philosophy of history. *La peregrinación de Bayoán,* eighth volume of the complete works of Eugenio Maria de Hostos, is a memoir in form of a novel, with a political and social content of criticism against the Spanish ideals and institutions in the early sixties. The ninth volume, *Temas cubanos,* contains Hostos' writings about heroic Cuba during the Spanish dominion and the Cuban Revolution. *La Cuna de América,* the tenth volume, includes his scholarly works on history dealing with the discovery of America. It also contains his studies of men and events of importance in the historical evolution of the nation of Santo Domingo. It ends with his famous apostrophe to the nations of Latin America:—Civilization or Death!!—The eleventh volume *Critica,* deals with aesthetic criticism in general. Music, painting, sculpture, and literature, are among the subjects discussed. His famous criticism and analysis of Shakespeare's *Hamlet* is included. *Forjando el porvenir americano* is the title of the next two volumes, twelfth and thirteenth, which contain his philosophy of education. His campaign for the scientific education of women in 1873, his reformation of the school system and his emphasis on what he repeatedly calls "Concentric Education" on the basis of "organic philosophy," are among the interesting features of all the educational writings contained in these two volumes. Curricular justice to all facts of experience seems to be the key-note of his philosophy of education. Even such opposing extremes as military training and religious instruction find place in his system. The fourteenth volume, *Hombres e ideas,* comprises Hostos' writings about Belvis, Washington,

Johnson, Quinet, Mitchel, Matta, Betances, and others. It also includes numerous articles on miscellaneous subjects of literary interest. Volume fifteen, *Lecciones de derecho constitucional,* is one of the most important books Hostos ever wrote. In it he discusses his philosophy of law and applies it to the needs of the American nations. The State for Hostos is not an individual entity apart from the life of the individuals within the State. It derives its being from the actual existence and conditions of society. But the State is not an abstraction. It is a living organism, in which the individual, the municipality, the province, the nation, and the different institutions, cooperate. It is not made up of the group of public officials, but is society itself in its legal aspect. Apart from its component individuals, however, the State has no reason for existence. Hostos gives profound consideration to the problems of Democracy, and such issues as might and right, or power and law, sovereignty, jurisdiction, social and political regime, freedom and duty, notion and forms of government, legislation, church and state, are objects of penetrating insight in the legal system of Hostos, the underlining thought of which seems to be the value of personality, the dignity of man and the telic nature of all legal organization and enterprise. In the opinion of the present reviewer, Hostos' most important contribution to thought is his sixteenth volume, *Tratado de moral,* which includes his well known *Moral social* and the rest of his works on ethics. This volume begins with ten chapters of prolegomena to ethics, followed by the corresponding divisions of Natural Morality, Individual Morality, Social Morality, and Social Objective Morality. The volume is a monument of thought, a treasure of America, a Magna Charta of personalistic empiricism. Almost of equal importance to the *Tratado de moral,* is the seventeenth volume, *Tratado de sociología,* as solid and scholarly, as fair and coherent as any other system of social theory worth its name. Long before Giddings, Hostos had introduced Sociology into the curriculum of academic studies at the University of Santo Domingo, and in his *Tratado de sociología* had anticipated even Roscoe Pound and Cardozo in the postulates of the so called "Sociological Jurisprudence." . . . The last three volumes of Hostos' complete works, come all under a common heading, *Ensayos didacticos,* and include his writings on Science and History of Education, Penal Law, Constitutional Law, Logic, Grammar, History of the Spanish Language, History of the Semitic and Chinese Civilizations, Political Geography, Management of Globes and Maps, Evolutionary Geography, etc. The publication of Hostos' complete works will be welcomed by scholars interested to know this true American philosopher almost unknown until today, whose thought interpreting human experience in the light of all accessible facts during his time, consecrated itself to the defense of human rights and to the uplifting of human dignity. (pp. 35-6)

> *José A. Franquiz, in a review of "Obras completas,"
> in* Philosophic Abstracts, *No. 2, Spring, 1940, pp.
> 35-6.*

WILLIAM REX CRAWFORD   (essay date 1944)

[*In the following excerpt, Crawford discusses the diversity of Hostos's moral, political, and social thought.*]

Latin-American countries have a laudable custom of organizing commissions, sometimes with the excuse of an anniversary, and doing homage impressively to the great writers who are the glory of their people. The works of the great man are collected, rescued from the oblivion of being out of print that is so frequent in these countries, and given condign publication by decree of the government. Bibliographies, critical introductions, funeral orations, and a chronology of the events of the celebration complete the picture. To such proceedings we owe the many handsome volumes of our thinkers, the most recent of which are the sets of Hostos and of Martí, which facilitate the task of the student enormously. (pp. 236-37)

Rescue was needed for Eugenio María de Hostos. While there have been few men of his stature in Latin America, he has missed wide acclaim. A much more systematic thinker than [Argentine political writer Domingo] Sarmiento, more deserving of the title sociologist, he was also much more of an introvert, with less of the inborn talent for being his own publicity man. The consequence is that Hostos and his works have suffered a neglect that it is difficult to justify. Even on the ground of political activity, Hostos is notable; in time he learned to discipline the rebellion that was in him, but he continued to fight for freedom, and in its behalf made so great an Odyssey through Latin America that it was only natural that the first locomotive to cross the Andes should be given his name. (p. 237)

Uplift would seem to be the keynote of an early work, a kind of novel in the form of a diary, *The Pilgrimage of Bayoán.* Hostos introduced it with these words: "This book, more than a book, is a desire; more than a desire, an intention; more than an intention, a thirst. Thirst for justice and truth; intention to prove that there is another happiness greater than that men seek: desire that the example bear fruit." He addressed it only to "pilgrims"; let no others read it, he says, and let no one merely turn its pages, which is profanation. Pilgrims through life will find that it strengthens their courage and teaches that the very lack of happiness in their lives is something they would not willingly exchange for the "useless happiness of the happy." Dreaming and thinking of America, of "our islands," Cuba and Puerto Rico, is the ceaseless occupation of the characters, and the book ends with an embarkation for America.

Nine years later we find him explaining to the Chileans the simple facts of the geography of the West Indies, with Cuba and Puerto Rico "queens" among them, natural paradises converted by Spain into hells, their native sons treated as foreigners while Spaniards monopolized the best of everything. A new day, he insisted, was dawning; Cuba was poor, but heroic, ready to die if need be, but determined that the tyrants should go.

Once free, he explained to readers of Spanish in New York, the West Indies could do their part to carry out the four great positive progressive steps which modern history reveals. These began with the discovery of America, which "was the most resounding demonstration in the whole life of mankind of the superiority of science over ignorance," as well as the chief cause of that intellectual revolution which brought with it the growth of modern science. History will some day see a second great step in colonization, which marked a break in the age-long struggle of races for national superiority and substituted "the coöperation of all races in the work of civilization." Not all the colonizing nations, to be sure, recognized in the New World a new environment for something new in the moral and intellectual order; the contrast between North and South America is so striking that it will lead to an intellectual awakening, and out of it will come "a new moral and intellectual world which with the native virtues of the Latin race will perhaps combine those that make of the Anglo-Saxon the part of humanity that is most useful to civilization." The fourth step is also in the future: the transition from irrational to rational government of society. For any part of the New World to remain unfree is to handicap fatally the forward movement that Hostos finds so natural and desirable.

In spite of its desirability, Hostos recognized obstacles, chief among them the nature of society in Puerto Rico and Cuba, made up as it was of suffering Negro slaves, of white slaves who managed to make a good thing out of their slavery, of a greedy "dominant minority" that exploited them to retire satiated. Where were the right mental and moral conditions for directing the work of reconstruction to be found? He answered that the very struggle for freedom would create them, for struggle purifies and makes virile; but they would be produced even more by education, "educating reason in accordance with a system of education that is common, universal, and includes women and children, the freedman and the free, the rich and the poor, an education that will include enough acquaintance with scientific method to free the mind from fanaticism; an education of the conscience in the unlimited practice of all the liberties which affirm and strengthen human personality; an education of the spirit of nationalism through laws which will immediately prove favorable to economic reconstruction through work," through commerce and industry.

In 1874 he explained to the people of Buenos Aires that the Cuban revolution was not the work of a single class, and could not hope for success if it were. All Cubans were behind it. Moreover, it was not revolution looking toward annexation to the United States; nothing could make that annexation acceptable. "The United States has been almost as cruel and stupid with us as Spain," he says, and we detest the wrong when committed by the strong so much that "we are sure they can possess us only after destroying us, but with our will never."

Hostos continued to dream of more inclusive unions. "Federation was the goal of the ideals of the New World; the union of all nations." Certainly, however, imperialism is not the road to union. Imperialism it will be unless the peoples of his beloved islands rouse themselves from their dreams. Either "they organize themselves for civilization, or civilization will sweep them into its maw; the process of absorption has begun. . . . Civilization or death." And so we find him quoting with approval Alberdi's "To govern is to populate," calling for an immigration program that will bring selected *families* and establish them in agricultural colonies, and even condescending to argue about whether the streets are too narrow for street cars.

The mental grasp of Hostos, indeed, permitted him to comment enlighteningly on the most diverse topics; and without attempting to impose any unity on this diversity, we should like to offer a few samples.

The proof that peoples fit for democracy do exist is the history of the United States, of Switzerland, and off and on since 1863 of Colombia. These nations approach being true peoples, with clear common interests, well defined political and national aspirations. But elsewhere in Latin America he finds instead those "vicious social classifications which correspond to forms of government absolutely opposed to democracy," and diversity of education, of mentality, of hopes and aspirations.

"When you cannot be just through virtue, be so through pride," he says. "If you would know what justice is, let yourself be persecuted by injustice."

> There are complete men and incomplete men.
> If you would be a complete man, put all the
> strength of your soul into every act of your life.

> The better I know men, the more appalled I am
> at the difference between what they are and
> what they ought to be. Consider men to be
> children, so that your countenance may shine
> with benevolence. All men are good when they
> are not influenced by passion, interest or error.

> Fools are not free creatures because they are
> not reasonable creatures.

> Ignorance is as harmful as wickedness itself.

> Love is an instinct, a passion and a virtue. As
> instinct, it makes sick; as passion, it weakens;
> as virtue, it strengthens. Almost all rational
> beings love; almost none knows how to love.
> Almost all men love as animals; some love as
> wild beasts; only a few love as men.

> The most fruitful of words is the spoken word,
> for it is closest to action. The word is the action
> of a thought.

And surprisingly enough, in the philosopher of duty and work: "Why is dying sad? Because living is sad. And why is living sad? Because it is work." But he adds that work may be a delight, life may be harmonious, death may be serene.

There is something higher "than being a great man in the eyes of history, and that is to be a man useful to one's time. The thoughtless world and history itself have preferred the so-called great men to those who are useful: one of the innovations the New World is called upon to introduce is putting the second ahead of the first."

It was this "man useful to his time" that Hostos aspired to be and was. In time he became convinced that although war and revolution might be necessary, they were not for him, and that his usefulness lay in education. If we are to find a core to his teaching it is in such works as the treatises on Morals and on Sociology, which demand at least as much analysis as will send the reader to the originals.

Most of the former book is naturally devoted to social morality, but there is briefer consideration of those moral principles that Hostos calls natural and individual. Natural morality includes those duties that grow out of our recognition that we form a part of the physical world, that we owe nature gratitude and admiration, that we should respect ourselves as part of nature (and so refrain from homicide and suicide), that we should cultivate knowledge of nature, and recognize the limits beyond which our knowledge does not reach, spreading the scientific knowledge we have acquired but showing tolerance for those who differ from us with regard to the Unknowable, or as yet Unknown.

Man's relations to himself give rise to the duties that constitute individual morality. These duties he classifies as those toward the body, the will, the affective and rational sides of our nature. Self-preservation and self-development along physical lines, avoidance of agitation, education of the will to carry out necessary action energetically, and its training for a life which is certain to require abstentions and sacrifices, development of our rational factors and even more of conscience—all these are defined and defended as imperatives of the good life.

The thesis presented in the section on social morality is that duty is no austere, repulsive ideal, but is at the same time the purest source of morality and the natural mode of development for individual and society; that man is most a man when he does his duty, thus proving his rationality and worth; that to be civilized and to be moral is the same thing, and that morality and civilization are both attained by fulfilling one's duty in every relation of life.

Hostos develops at length the nature of our relation to the groups of which we form a part, and the debt of work and obedience that we owe them; thoroughly socially minded, he preaches the duty of being useful, of coöperating, of finding a way to reconcile what is useful to the we-group to what is useful to the they-group. As Royce is the philosopher of loyalty, so Hostos is the philosopher of duty—of the duty of being dutiful, not with the impulsiveness of heroism on grand occasions, but to the level of every day's most quiet need. For the solution of conflicts between duties, he proposes the primacy of the "most immediate, most extensive, most concrete."

In an extensive section that belongs to social science as much as to speculation, Hostos examines the relation of morals to other social institutions, such as the Church. In this instance, his emancipated conclusion is that Protestantism is more advanced than Catholicism, and that religious evolution is farther advanced in the United States than anywhere else, especially when religion takes the form of unitarianism and universalism. As a good positivist, he also holds that men of science live more conformably to the moral order than any others, and that their names are in general the purest and most honorable that humanity can point to. Of art he is more fearful, thinking of the vanity of the artist, his corruptibility by applause, and he can only hope that artists will be true to what they glimpse in their moments of contemplation, will find their mission within the larger framework of civilization, moralization, humanity.

It is not, however, only social institutions that Hostos analyzes in relation to morality, but individual men, for he concludes the volume with a series of case studies of virtue, taken in part from the history of Hispanic America but also including Franklin, Washington, and Peter Cooper. The Sunday-school tone is avoided, and an approach is made to a inductive ethics.

The *Treatise on Sociology* is also based on student notes, but while the [*Treatise on*] *Morals* dates from 1884, the lectures on sociology were given in 1901 and the book was first published posthumously.

There are critics who would say that there is something about sociology which ruins writing. At any rate, it seduces Hostos into a series of barbarous neologisms hard for a purist in things Hispanic to accept. Sociology is divided into socionomy, sociography, sociorganology, and sociopathy. Under the first heading fall the laws of society in general, which are seven: the law of sociability, without which there would be no society; the law of work, without which it could not function and survive; the law of progress, by which he seems to mean rather social continuity, for it includes death and decay as well as genesis and growth; the law of the ideal of the good, which ideal exists in direct proportion to the development of morality, inversely to the individual and social lack of capacity to comprehend religious and moral goals; the law of conservation, which points out that the continued life of societies depends on the vigorous functioning of their organs; and last, the law of means, according to which societal agents are modified by the means they use, the circumstances which surround their operation; this last is Hostos' curiously roundabout way of recognizing the importance of environment and culture.

Sociography for Hostos means a rather sketchy account of the State and other social institutions through history; sociorganology, a description of the organs of society and their role in the body social, for Hostos is in a loose sense a social organicist, who does not insist on the detailed comparisons of a Lilienfeld or Schäffle; his sociopathy makes the idea of sickness its point of departure, and diagnoses, especially in the countries of Latin America, pathological conditions of economic life, of the political system, those that he calls intellectual and moral, and deficiency or excess of attention to the immediate environment. Social hygiene, which has a more limited connotation with us in North America, is used to designate the whole application of our knowledge of healthy functioning to the prevention of these social ills. One must not expect to find in the skeletal twenty-five pages on social pathology that complete account of Latin-American social problems and the movements to combat them which to this day constitutes a glaring gap in our libraries. Hostos has written the sociology of his day, which is the day of Spencer and Ward, and it is a sociology without benefit of charts, tables, or photographs of housing conditions. Perhaps we can do without them and remain grateful for a life that was noble and devoted, for "truths that contained quite a lot of truth" as Blanco-Fombona remarks, and for two or three seminal books. (pp. 238-46)

> William Rex Crawford, "The Cubans and Hostos," in his A Century of Latin-American Thought, Cambridge, Mass.: Harvard University Press, 1944, pp. 218-46.

PEDRO HENRÍQUEZ-UREÑA   (essay date 1945)

[Henríquez-Ureña was a Dominican critic and man of letters. In the following excerpt, he discusses the importance of ethics and reason to Hostos's works.]

Both [Hostos's] political and his pedagogical campaigns were carried on with the help of a large amount of writing. His first book, *The Pilgrimage of Bayoán* . . . , is a political novel. His best, *Social Ethics* . . . , was planned as a school text. His most brilliant pages are probably contained in the addresses he read when the first groups of normal teachers received their degrees in Santo Domingo, the first group of men (1884) and the first group of women (1887). Antonio Caso, the Mexican philosopher, calls the 1884 address "the master work of ethical thought in Hispanic America."

As a thinker, Hostos is essentially ethical; at the same time, he is a rationalist, with a deep faith in the power of reason to ascertain truth. "Give me truth," he says, "and I shall give you the world. Without truth, you will destroy the world, while I, with truth, alone, shall rebuild the world as many times as you may have shattered it. And I should give you not only the world of matter, but also the world that the human mind perpetually builds above the natural world." He compels himself to believe that harmony (i.e., ethical conduct) and truth (mainly as knowledge) are the ultimate goals of human endeavor; he even thinks that the contemplation of the heavens impresses the law of order on our minds; but he ponders on "the eternity of efforts spent in the simple aim of making rational the only inhabitant of the earth who is endowed with reason," and the vast spectacle of conflict in individual and social life is for him a perpetual distress; only by a constant heroic effort does he maintain his metaphysical optimism, his mystic faith in reason and in "the constructive power of virtue." Despite his early and solid classical education (or because of it?), he developed a Platonic distrust of all literature that seemed to be in conflict with ethics. Fortunately, unlike Bernard Shaw, he discovered a moral lesson in Shakespeare and wrote a superb essay on *Hamlet* . . . , a psychological and moral analysis of all the characters in the play. In fact, whatever his distrust of literature, he was a born writer, with a powerful imagination— shown, for example, in the description of the peasant woman who mistakes his school for a church, kneels before it, prays, crosses herself, "and thus consecrates the temple." And another gift, the gift of eloquence, is shown on every page, even in letters jotted down in haste, in hardly legible script. (pp. 156-57)

> Pedro Henríquez-Ureña, "The Period of Organization: 1860-1890," in his Literary Currents in Hispanic America, *Cambridge, Mass.: Harvard University Press, 1945, pp. 137-60.*

EDGAR SHEFFIELD BRIGHTMAN (essay date 1954)

[*Brightman is an American educator, philosopher, and critic. In the following excerpt, he examines the primary features of Hostos's thought.*]

There are four outstanding traits of [Hostos]: love of liberty, devotion to reason, moral idealism, and educational leadership.

His love of liberty animated his whole career, and whether he was in Spain, in Santo Domingo, or in South America, he never forgot his patriotic love for the liberty of his native island. But he was no narrow patriot in the petty nationalistic sense. He did not love liberty for himself or his land and wish to deny it to others; his spirit was so large that he cared more for truth and justice than for any special political plan for the realization of liberty.

Indeed, it may be said that his love of liberty derived its grandeur from the fact that it was subordinate to his devotion to reason. This comes to classic expression in his famous address **"To the Masters of the Normal School"** before his first graduating class in Santo Domingo in 1884. "Give me the truth," said he, "and I shall give you a world. Without truth, you can destroy the world. I, with truth and nothing but truth shall reconstruct it as often as you destroy it." Such words are the foundation of culture and of civilized society everywhere in the world, and for them alone the name of Hostos is worthy of immortality. They were not a casual remark dropped in an oratorical moment; they expressed the passionate devotion to reason and rational truth which animated his whole thinking and conduct.

His devotion to reason was joined to an unfaltering moral idealism. History shows more than one man of acute powers of reason who has been devoid of moral sense; and even some men, who were possessed of reason to a high degree and who pursued liberty, have lacked conscience. But Hostos was distinguished, like Kant and Fichte, for his insight into the unity of the theoretical and the practical reason. In fact, he might almost be called the Fichte of Spanish-speaking America. For him, life meant fulfilment of duty, individual and social in an inseparable union. What was not right was not possible for him to consider. Few men have felt a purer loyalty to the moral ideal or have possessed a more fundamental insight into the importance of morality for social life, as well as for individual perfection.

His fourth great trait, that of educational leadership, is simply an application of the others. His moral idealism made it oblig-

atory on him to try to lead others to liberty and reason. In Santo Domingo and in various South American centers, he developed educational experiments, always with social aims, but yet allowing no compromise with social evils or abuses. He felt that it would be useless to continue teaching anywhere where he could not teach freely the principles of reason and goodness; but he continued long after others would have given up.

Looking on these traits and on his life work as a whole, one is inclined to describe Hostos as a philosopher of personality. The dignity of free personality; the authority of rational personality; the perfection of moral personality; and the remaking of personality, individual and social, by a sound educational method—such was the theme and the purpose of Hostos. He believed in free personality. Interest in purely natural science or in abstract studies was secondary and almost absent from his development. Knowledge about personality, its supreme value, its organic social cooperation, and its cosmic dignity,— this was the essence of the thought of Hostos. No one who is concerned with the interpretation of human values or with living a noble life can fail to learn much from this eminent American sage, truly a philosopher of personality. (pp. 16-18)

> Edgar Sheffield Brightman, "Eugenio Maria de Hostos: Philosopher of Personality," *in* Eugenio Maria de Hostos: Promoter of Pan Americanism, *edited by Eugenio Carlos de Hostos, Juan Bravo, 1954?, pp. 13-18.*

PEDRO DE ALBA (essay date 1954)

[*In the following excerpt, Alba discusses Hostos's ethical thought as advanced in* Moral social.]

It was fifty years ago that Eugenio Maria de Hostos warned his contemporaries. He foresaw the dangers involved in mechanical progress if it were not closely followed by spiritual and intellectual improvement.

He called attention to the increasing discrepancies that he observed between progress and morality, and made it plain that the civilization at the end of the 19th century, of which the men of that time were so proud, carried within itself irritating contradictions and the seeds of barbarism. That lack of accord between machine civilization and the world of moral values, which the distinguished philosopher Henri Bergson discussed not long ago in illuminating pages, was denounced by Hostos in the prologue to his **Moral social,** written in 1888.

Hostos was a classic thinker and a master of the best humanism. Ideas of apparent harmony and profound similarity guided his meditations; as a teacher he aspired to train the whole man. The incompatibility between the material and the spiritual; the contradictions between material power and the ethical sense; the antinomies between preaching and practice, he condemned in pages that are still fresh and applicable today.

The "complete man," he said, must be the fundamental unit of noble peoples and strong nations.

Impressed by the panorama of his times he wrote these notable words:

> Half men, half nations, partly civilized, partly savage, we men and nations of this flourishing age constitute societies outwardly as brilliant as the most powerful nations of ancient history and inwardly as benighted. Under the skin of

every society barbarism throbs. Thus, because of this contrast between material progress and moral development, Europe and America have again witnessed the shame of wars of conquest, the shamelessness of the supremacy of might over right, the humiliation of the idolatry of crime enthroned and omnipotent for twenty long years in the heart of Europe, and the indecency of the deification of brute force in the brain of the thinking continent. It is because of the immorality of our civilization that it has agreed to the renewal of the infamous and cowardly persecutions of the Middle Ages. . . .

If the Master of Mayagüez were living today he would have to make his jeremiad even more emphatic to scourge those who poison the air of our times and exalt over every moral standard of humanity their caprices, their hates, and their low appetites.

Perhaps he would feel bitter when he saw that all his preaching had been in vain, but as he was not a man who faltered in his task he would begin it anew. Hostos was not a mere rhetorician or an academic moralist, but a man of action, who fought for civilization. His essentially constructive mind set him apart from all theoretical doctrines, from all arbitrary empiricism. He was never satisfied merely with good intentions; ideas had to be set in motion, moral precepts had to be vitalized. Neither dogmatic nor magisterial, he maintained that morality must be founded on logical bases, on the principles of human sympathy, on the demands of social service.

Hostos had acquired a sound education and was familiar with the best in philosophical thought; at the same time he had creative intuition and the strength of those who are endowed with artistic temperament and apostolic fervor. By his life and work he showed that aesthetic education and philosophic feeling determine personality, and that moral disciplines are the basis of character.

A glowing and attractive personality, a firm and resolute character, belonged to this spirited champion; his artistic taste and his philosophic temperament were shown in his studies of *Hamlet,* his ethical views and his professorial temperament in the pages of his *Moral social.* These qualities were evident in his exemplary life. He could maintain his moral principles with authority because his theories were reinforced by his acts. When his students urged him to publish his lessons in ethics, he replied: "Ethics should be imprinted not in books but in deeds. Whoever leads an evil life, preaches evil, and whoever thinks evil and speaks evil leads an evil life." Since the students insisted, the professor agreed to publication on condition that the section chosen should be "that part of the book referring to the duties of society." He deliberately abstained from all dogmatism to take his stand in the realms of learning, natural law and human relations.

Eugenio María de Hostos is a brilliant proof that in Spanish America there can be orderly studies and methodical and sustained efforts. Many of our thinkers are excitable and volcanic; a passion for the fray makes them appear inconsistent and contradictory; the pressing demands of life do not permit them to put their ideas in order.

Hostos gives us an example of firm purpose and well-ordered industry. When he wrote his lessons in social morality, he emphasized scholarly and philosophical principles. Logical sequence, relationship between topics, correlation of the premises, a series of reasons supporting each other, raised the harmonious edifice that his intellect had devised. On this well-planned foundation his work was divided into two ample parts, containing invaluable material on the problems of the moral code and their solution. The first part is entitled "Relations and Duties," and the second "Morality and the Activities of Life." We shall comment on a few of the chapters that are the most interesting because of the author's originality in presenting his theme.

The two phases of Hostos' work that have long impressed us most, the aesthetic and the scholarly, we find reflected in many pages of the *Moral social.* The general headings on social relations are as follows: "Relation of Necessity," "Relation of Gratitude," "Relation of Utility," "Relation of Law," "Relation of Duty." We shall mention first the "Relation of Gratitude" because to us it is the most impressive title.

Hostos' discussions of social gratitude disclose his delicate sensibility and his profound human sympathy. These sentences ring with a noble conviction:

> A little reflection will show us that after our own necessities it is gratitude that binds us most closely to other men.

> Indeed, as members of a family we are so closely bound to it by gratitude that we recognize its effects from the cradle to the grave. If we are born we owe it to the family; if we grow up, it is through the protection of the family; if we are educated, it is the work of the family; when we are with the family we work for it; away from it we long for it; we are happy in the family and for its sake; if we are unfortunate, we regret it for the sake of the family; ill, we fear death for its sake, and dying we long for it.

Hostos considers the family the cornerstone of society, and in his discussion discloses the tenderness and unselfishness of his heart. He does not speak in terms of mere convenience, although he recognizes that relations of necessity come first; he leaves a place for the imponderables of sentiment.

This unselfishness and sentiment show that the moralist had an aesthetic temperament. It should not be believed that he confines the stimulus of gratitude only to the family, for it radiates therefrom in ever wider circles to the city, the province, the nation, humanity and nature. At the end of the chapter on gratitude Hostos writes: "As this relation of gratitude is extended to all men the power of human dignity becomes increasingly vigorous, so that the man who most deeply feels the gratitude that we owe to humanity for its unceasing benefits is the most human."

An optimistic declaration this, conceiving life as something good, considering as one of the prized things of life intercourse with one's fellow-beings, recognizing one's identification with the destiny of all humanity. The contemplation of natural beauty awakes in Hostos a sense of well-being in which his aesthetic emotions are nobly shown. . . .

Hostos had reason for complaint concerning his era and his contemporaries, but he rose above trifles and grudges to exalt his faith. Hostos' ideas were far removed from the Voltairian attitude of some present-day writers. His doctrine is the antithesis of the dictum of the well-known French novelist and poet, Henri de Montherlant, who takes an attitude of resigned negativism when he writes: "Men never do us all the evil that they could." ("Les hommes ne nous font jamais tout le mal qu'ils pourraient.")

Hostos, on the other hand, thought of man as representing a positive moral value and as being capable of gratitude for all the good things that life gives him.

If when he speaks of gratitude Hostos shows his aesthetic sensibility, when he discusses ideas of utility he displays his powers as a sociologist, sentimental only in so far as sentiment is not an antisocial menace; he believes that generous and romantic impulses should be at the service of a well-balanced mind and a firm will.

He never postulated absolute renunciation or absurd quietism, for he was well aware that the life of society is a struggle and that therefore it must be decided how best to be useful in that conflict for the general good.

The concepts of social utility upheld by the pragmatic philosophers and educators, James, Dewey and Henderson, had previously been expounded by Hostos in lessons to his classes in the normal school at Santo Domingo.

His logical mind insisted most strongly on defining the term *utility*. It was for this reason that he explained his ideas on this subject in the first section:

> If we consider useful only that which serves our use and redounds exclusively to our individual good, no duty would arise from utility except that of sacrificing everything to our individual good. But since utility is a natural property of physical and moral objects to serve the purposes of everyone, and since there is no individual purpose that can be fulfilled outside of society, it is clear that for a thing to be useful to us it is necessary that it should be naturally conducive to the achievement of our social purposes.

Later he added:

> To the common herd everything is useful from which selfishness derives from benefit; utility, therefore, is the property that things have of being utilized by man. It is easy to comprehend that, if what is beneficial is used for individual selfishness, the property of utility will be converted not into a source of duties, but into an inexhaustible spring of selfish instincts. But this does not arise from the fact that the concept of utility is inexact, or that the useful is bad in itself; it arises from the fact that the common concept of utility is incomplete and that the idea of the useful is exclusive.... According to economics, the most useful things are those that begin by benefiting society, in order thereby to benefit the individual; thus there is no true utility except in the intelligent combination of public interests with private, of general interests with individual ones....

If we consider carefully Hostos' exposition concerning utility and the useful we discover that Hostos had a deep-rooted conviction that the interest of society should have preference over the special interest of the individual. The idea that education should be useful to society, which American educators emphasize today, and the theories on the social functions of wealth found in books by economists and sociologists of various nationalities were analyzed in unequivocal and conclusive terms by Eugenio María de Hostos.

In vulgar minds the idea of utility carries with it such a desire for lucre and for rising profits that it is likely to constitute a danger to social justice and collective welfare.

Right-minded men believe that the idea of utility should be subordinated to moral precepts, to the principle that the citizen best trained for the life of society is he who can best serve others. Production, technical skill, wealth should derive from an equitable distribution of useful things so that public and private interests are intelligently combined, as Hostos believed they should be.

These ideas are not subversive, for in all ages and in all countries they have been maintained by men of different shades of philosophical belief, by priests of various religions. If we go back in history, we shall find them held by the Fathers of the Church; for example, St. Augustine said that the rich should be considered the administrators of the property of the poor.

Aristotle's saying that man is a political animal was echoed by Hostos. A politician, a component of the *polis*, the state or city, was an expression of the highest Greek culture, a social being first and foremost. However, the terms *politicians* and *political* have been deprived of their original meaning by being applied only to electoral candidates and contests. This is one of the common limitations that Hostos discussed in speaking of the concept of utility.

In the history of Spanish thought there are essayists of the highest intellectual standing, like Mariana, Saavedra Fajardo and Feijóo, who consider politics one of the noblest of human activities. Of this clan is Eugenio María de Hostos.

In the second part of his **Moral social,** which has as its subtitle *Morality and the Activities of Life,* our author considers ethics in relation to the most diverse factors in community life. There are, we find, such chapter headings as these: "Morality and the School," "Morality and the Philosophic Religions," "Morality and History," "Morality and Art," "Morality and Industry." We will comment briefly upon a few which are specially appropriate today and which are treated in a specially courageous and penetrating manner.

In Hostos' opinion, the practice of politics and of journalism should have the dignity of a priesthood; the bad practitioners of these professions should be treated as antisocial beings and as dangerous corrupters of society. Not only in respect to politics, but also as concerns journalism, Hostos revolts against the false concept that success is its own justification. To him success obtained outside the bounds of social morality, even though it be impressive and showy, is in reality despicable and ephemeral.

When all Europe thought Bismarck a political genius, Hostos attacked him, calling him "perniciously lucky," for he was one of those who see in politics nothing more than the art of employing power against law. If in the realm of international politics Hostos was implacable toward imperialists, in the field of domestic politics he raised his voice against those who trafficked in influence and against the grasping.

> Only absolute ignoramuses or consummate hypocrites could have the idea of separating what is by nature inseparable and of taking from the art of balancing power with law the dignity

conferred on it by its origin. . . . Politics without morality is unworthy; any game of chance, unworthy as gambling is, is more worthy than politics divorced from morality, because at least the only morality at stake in the repugnant episodes of a game is that of the gambler and his accomplices, but the immoral politician stakes by his example the public and private morality of his country.

For Hostos, the journalist who works for petty interests or the politician who sells his ideas are antisocial elements. He considers that the two poles of mercenary journalism are power and wealth.

> Journalism undertaken because of a thirst for power is a daily, weekly, or fortnightly example of intellectual immorality, continuous in its effects . . . and of lack of character, which is the worst kind of immorality. Since power, its objective, is subject to constant change, its judgment also becomes changeable. . . . Journalism inspired by desire for gain is also a constant example of immorality of feeling and will; it demoralizes public opinion, because it constantly exalts success and frequently jeers at all generous sentiments; it demoralizes the will of society, which is constantly being urged to further activities to secure physical benefits and to remain inert in the face of the moral evils of society. . . .

Hostos does, however, recognize the great good that journalism has accomplished by excoriating tyrannies, privilege, judicial malfeasance, and the abuse of capitalism, and also acknowledges its noble efforts to promote free competition and the recognition of real merit.

He urges journalists to be as dignified as if they were addressing not only their contemporaries but also posterity. He says that since journalism is essentially the continuous history of a part of humanity, it necessarily must expose unworthy deeds and wrong-doing, and that they should be exposed as they are, in continual conflict with uprightness and justice, and presented in such a way as to uphold the moral order as the goal of human dignity.

To Hostos democratic ideals, with their living expression of freedom of thought, freedom of the press, freedom of worship, and freedom of assembly, were not mere empty words or unattainable ideals. He believed, however, that if these powers were exercised without moral discipline and without envisioning the public-good, they might result in evil and that they should, therefore, be subjected to the requirements of individual responsibility and collective justice.

All campaigns for freedom of spoken or written thought should pay honor to the great sacrifices that humanity has made to obtain it. It would be an empty and foolish formula if it were not inspired in the highest principle of public good. Every political idea should be a noble aspiration of humanity; this in the last analysis means effective social justice and not mere words.

Like other men of analytical power and apostolic fervor, Hostos, because of his sympathetic comprehension of the problems of his fellowmen, was prophetic, although he did not set out to be.

The chapter of Hostos' book called "Morality and Time" contains much wise and foresighted comment, surprisingly applicable to the present day. The psychologist, the social reformer, and the teacher can there find the solution of many problems of our own time, the results of the study of a serious and profound student.

More than fifty years ago Hostos foresaw that industrial progress would give rise to many grave and disturbing problems. He remarked that progress proceeds in fitful waves, leaving many millions of men outside its benefits. He considered the pleasures of the intellect and of intellectual health as well as of the satisfaction of material needs. He also believed that work is one of the greatest blessings of the human race and that it must therefore be made attractive to the individual and profitable to the community. . . .

He thought of the people who lack culture, money, means of communication with their fellowmen, healthful recreation to help them raise their moral standards. He lamented the lack of opportunity for the masses in these words:

> The theatre, which is a good institution and a pastime more educational than any other since it reaches the mind and heart of the people most easily, is nowhere a national institution for the people. It is not for the people because it does not reach them systematically; it is not national because performances are given almost exclusively in great cities, very seldom in small ones and never in the country. . . . Lectures on literary, scientific, religious, political or economic subjects are also a privilege of large centers.

> Concerts for the people, which belie their name because the price of admission is almost never within the reach of the masses, should be a national institution in every country and extend their benefits to the village and rural population.

In answer to these requirements of Hostos the present age could present the radio as a source of popular culture and recreation. So powerful an instrument should be cherished as a treasure of humanity because of its possibilities; every country should promote education by means of broadcasts and free the air from the ineptitudes that now contaminate it.

Hostos would be pleased at the popularization of the motion picture and the radio, for he was tortured by the idea of the misuse of leisure time with all its possibilities of lurking vice. A proper use of free hours was to him one of the surest indices of culture.

> As long as a civilization does not know how to employ time left over from daily toil, it will not be a true civilization, for it will not be employing rightly its first and most important source of wealth.

> No one, no matter how toilsome his life, but has now and then a moment's idleness in which he may feel overwhelmed with boredom . . . in need of a social solace that he cannot find. . . . Most men have more than enough time to become bored with themselves and with others, to be forced to choose between boredom alone or vice in the company of others.

The great hope for the future of humanity is that as science advances work should be less hard and hours of labor shorter. The conquest of an eight-hour day is followed by the week of forty hours, and perhaps thirty or thirty-five hours. When this comes manual workers should be prepared to make good use of their free time. They should be ready to contradict effectively the charge that their leisure hours are spent in vicious pursuits of mere idleness. One of the divisions of the International Labor Office in Geneva is at present engaged in a campaign in favor of popular libraries, parks, casinos for workmen, evening schools, theatres for the people, country excursions, and community singing.

Even in our days we may look forward to the realization of the Utopian dream of Sir Thomas More that men should devote only six hours a day to labor and that the rest of their time should be used for enriching their minds and cultivating the finest human relations.

Contemporaneous technology can secure production sufficient for the necessities of everyone even with a thirty-hour week.

There are two factors hindering this; one is a desire for undue gain, and the other the hatred and uncertainty fostered by the nations of prey, aggressive, insolent and conquering. They have put other nations on the defensive and required more time to be spent in labor for war industries to meet the constant threats of those who have been "perniciously lucky," in Hostos' phrase, and are skilled in the evil arts of using power against law.

Antonio S. Pedreira, Hostos' excellent biographer, calls him "Citizen of America," a title well won by his cultural influence in all parts of our continent, by his long stays in the islands of the Caribbean as well as on the northern and southern continents. It is true that the civilizing apostleship of Hostos comprehended all the nations of the new World, but it did not stop there,—it embraced the intellectual scene of the whole world.

Of a noble line came those American thinkers who had a sense of the universality of culture, and were faithful to the belief that men must be nourished on the milk of human kindness.

The last chapter of the first part of the *Moral social* is entitled "Duties of Man towards Humanity." This was a subject on which the master constantly pondered. It appears in the introduction to the book, and in spite of the logical development of his work, Hostos feels himself so much under the necessity of emphasizing this topic that he even interpolates it in his discussion of other themes.

When he speaks of social responsibility and rights, his ideas are of broad scope. Before he came to the chapter cited, he had already said,

> Man is above everything a human being . . . whatever his birthplace, his racial tradition, the influence of his family, the character of his nation, the stamp of his civilization, he is indissolubly bound by his nature to every other man, because every other man is like him, the same living expression of the same biological and sociological necessities. . . .

The first sentences of the part we are now discussing have a familiar ring:

Social morality would be not only incomplete, but also limited in its scope and mean in its purpose, if it linked man only with the national society of which he is part. Far from excluding his relation to humanity, social morality should include it to such a degree that the first truth learned and the last truth practiced should be that man is part of humanity, for the natural place of every man is in the bosom of humanity.

This is not a rhetorical or empirical proposition, but a doctrine backed by a whole life of constant struggle for the ideal, a salutary idea and a tower of strength. Hostos relates it in a most admirable manner to the duties of patriotism and to the profoundest and broadest human sentiments.

In an admirable passage, Hostos says:

> One of the greatest efforts, or rather series of efforts, that the soul feels obliged to make is that of reconciling our duties as patriots with our duties as men. Therefrom arises the common incapacity of being at once a good son of one's country and a good son of humanity.

> But if it is recalled that the society of nations of which ours is a member is a true family of peoples in which, as in a family of individuals, each member is dependent on the prosperity of others; if this is borne in mind, it will be understood that patriotism is not incompatible with that logical and due subordination of the affection and duties that bind us to our country to the affection and duties that bind us to humanity. We should, therefore, subordinate the latter to the former, consider this subordination a duty, and carefully cultivate our duties of patriotism not towards our own country alone, for the deeper our patriotism, the more conscientious will be our subordination to the great cause of humanity.

America should be proud of this declaration of principles by a citizen of our continent, a declaration in harmony with the noble apothegm: America for Humanity. (pp. 107-21)

> *Pedro de Alba, "Eugenio Maria de Hostos and His Ideas of Social Morality," in* Eugenio Maria de Hostos: Promoter of Pan Americanism, *edited by Eugenio Carlos de Hostos, Juan Bravo, 1954?, pp. 101-24.*

ADDITIONAL BIBLIOGRAPHY

Coester, Alfred. "Santo Domingo, Puerto Rico, Central America." In his *The Literary History of Spanish America*, pp. 431-49. New York: Macmillan Co., 1919.
    Contains a biographical sketch of Hostos.

Garcia-Giron, Edmundo. "Hostos versus Beerbohm Tree: Plagiarism?" *Bulletin of Hispanic Studies* XXXIII (1956): 46-9.
    Discusses an accusation by Venezuelan writer Rufino Blanco-Fombina, based on textual evidence, that the British actor Sir

Herbert Beerbohm Tree plagiarized Hostos's essay on *Hamlet* in his book *Thoughts and After-Thoughts*.

Inman, Samuel Guy. "Assets of Latin America." In his *Problems in Pan Americanism*, pp. 15-44. New York: George H. Doran Co., 1921.
    Contains a discussion of the life of Hostos and the diverse fields of study and writing in which he was proficient.

Langley, Lester D. Review of *América: La lucha por la libertad* by Eugenio María de Hostos. *The Hispanic American Historical Review* LXI, No. 4 (November 1981): 762-63.
    Offers a number of biographical facts concerning Hostos.

Lee, Muna. "Eugenio Maria de Hostos: After One Hundred Years." *Books Abroad* XIV, No. 2 (Spring 1940): 124-28.
    A biographical essay listing Hostos's various political and educational accomplishments.

Henry James

1843-1916

American novelist, short story writer, essayist, critic, biographer, autobiographer, and dramatist.

The following entry presents criticism of James's novella *The Turn of the Screw*. For a complete discussion of James's career, see *TCLC*, Volumes 2 and 11.

One of the most controversial works in literature, *The Turn of the Screw* has inspired a variety of critical interpretations since its publication in 1898. Until 1934, the novella was generally regarded as a conventional though extremely horrifying ghost story. In that year, however, Edmund Wilson challenged this view with the contention that *The Turn of the Screw* is a psychological case study of the narrator, an emotionally unstable young woman whose visions of ghosts are merely hallucinations. Wilson's essay initiated a lengthy critical debate, which has continued for over fifty years, concerning the correct interpretation of the novella. Most critics now agree that James intended his work to remain ambiguous and allow several contradictory interpretations, though the purposes for and effects of such ambiguity, as well as the various possible interpretations that the text will support, are still widely debated.

The Turn of the Screw was written during James's "transitional period," the years immediately following his return to fiction after an unsuccessful attempt at writing for the theater and immediately preceeding his composition of the complex and imposing novels which would mark his "major" phase. During this period, James adapted to his fiction such dramatic technical devices as the presentation of action in scenic vignettes and the suppression of all information from an intrusive authorial voice. This suppression of objective information is the primary source of difficulty in critical interpretation of *The Turn of the Screw*. The story is narrated by a governess who is confronted by a pair of ghosts and who suspects them of corrupting the two young children in her charge. The ghosts are those of Peter Quint, a man formerly employed in the household, and Miss Jessel, the previous governess. As her suspicions deepen, the new governess confronts each of the children concerning their collusion with the ghosts; during each confrontation, one of the specters appears to the governess, greatly discomposing her and bringing the action to a crisis. The girl, Flora, denies having seen the apparitions and, apparently hysterical, is sent to her uncle in London. The boy, Miles, dies in the governess's arms at the culmination of a psychic battle between the governess and the ghost of Peter Quint.

Speculation concerning the objective truth of the events in *The Turn of the Screw* depends upon the reader's acceptance or rejection of the governess's reliability as a narrator. It is this question which, until the early 1960s, divided critical interpretation of the novella. Deriving from this critical polarity, the debate concerning *The Turn of the Screw* has focused on three main issues: the reality of the ghosts, the sanity of the governess, and the corruption of the children. According to the "apparitionist" reading, the ghosts are real, the governess is a sane and reliable narrator, and the children, according to the majority of apparitionist critics, are to some degree corrupted by the ghosts. The consensus among critics for twenty-

five years after the publication of *The Turn of the Screw* was to accept the novella as a literal ghost story or as an account of demonic possession of the children. Although a few critics expressed doubt concerning the governess's sanity and the ghosts' objective existence this possibility was considered subordinate as an issue of critical interest to the extraordinary horror of the tale. While accepting the novella on a literal level, the apparitionist view does not preclude alternate interpretations found beneath its narrative surface. Robert Heilman, one of the most noted apparitionist critics, offered an allegorical interpretation of *The Turn of the Screw* in which Bly, the country house which provides the setting for the story, represents a fallen Eden; the children, corrupted humanity; and the governess, a savior and priest. Heilman's interpretation gained wide critical acceptance, although detractors remarked that the religious imagery which provides the basis for Heilman's argument was not employed by an objective narrative voice but was rather a subjective depiction by the character of the governess. John Lydenberg, noting this objection, inverted Heilman's thesis in a presentation of the governess as an ironic savior whose inept attempts to save the children become the indirect cause of the breakdown of Flora and the death of Miles.

The "hallucinationist," or Freudian, interpretation opposes the apparitionist position in every significant detail: the ghosts are regarded as hallucinations of the governess, the governess as an unreliable narrator, either neurotic or actually insane, and the children as either uncorrupted or corrupted only by the treatment of the governess herself. Edna Kenton, who published the first hallucinationist reading of *The Turn of the Screw* in 1924, considered the narrative to be a complete hoax, with both the ghosts and the children imagined by the governess's diseased consciousness. Edmund Wilson expounded on Kenton's rather vague hypothesis and explicated the story with the aid of Freudian psychoanalytical principles. According to Wilson, the governess is a neurotic spinster whose repressed passion for her employer, the children's bachelor uncle, causes her to hallucinate. During her climactic scene with Flora, she terrifies the child by insisting that she admit to seeing the ghost of the girl's former governess, Miss Jessel; later, as the governess interrogates Miles, her questions and actions as the hallucinations recur frighten the boy to death. In the hallucinationist interpretation, as in that of Lydenberg and some other critics, the governess becomes to some degree responsible for the death of Miles. Certain passages remain difficult to explain by the hallucinationists, however, most notably one in which the housekeeper at Bly, Mrs. Grose, identifies the ghost of Peter Quint from the governess's description of him. Differing explanations of this scene have been offered by Harold C. Goddard and John Silver, but in the opinion of many critics, neither sufficiently resolves such difficulties.

The hallucinationists introduced several important thematic possibilities in their readings of *The Turn of the Screw*, most notably a discussion of the illicit sexuality which is suggested in the novella. Mrs. Grose hints of an affair between Quint and Miss Jessel before their deaths, a matter which would have been regarded at the first appearance of *The Turn of the Screw* to be particularly offensive due to Quint's inferior social status. Mrs. Grose also suggests that the children were aware of this liaison. A number of critics cite evidence to argue that the children's knowledge may have extended to complicity, and that James subtly suggests the existence of sexual relationships between the children and the two adults. Other critics dispute the extent to which the vague evidence in the text ought to be interpreted, citing the preface to the New York edition of James's works, in which James affirms that he purposely did not specify the nature of the horror in *The Turn of the Screw*, thus creating in the reader's imagination a greater sense of evil than any "weak specification" would support; nevertheless, James clearly allowed the hint of illicit sexuality to remain in the work and thus to suggest a possible facet of the evil which pervades Bly.

In 1962 Dorothea Krook proposed a solution to the debate between the divergent readings of James's text by maintaining that James intended his narrative to remain ambiguous; therefore, the full meaning of the tale is not to be found by proving either interpretation to be exclusively correct, but rather by examining the tension produced by two mutually exclusive readings, both of which are supported by the text. The majority of recent critics accept Krook's thesis, although many still implicitly incline toward one of the two interpretations. The acceptance of ambiguity in the novella has allowed critics to discuss other aspects of the tale, such as structural resemblances to mythology, as well as to indicate other ways in which the novella exhibits ambiguity, such as the possibility that the governess kills Miles through the violence of her actions in the final scene rather than merely through fear, or that Miles does not actually die and becomes the Douglas of the prologue, who possesses the governess's manuscript and admits to a past romantic attachment to her.

The Turn of the Screw is one of the most critically discussed works in twentieth-century American literature. Due to its relative accessibility compared to much of the author's work, the novella is often read as an introduction to James. In addition, this tale of mystery—a term James invested with new meaning—is among the classics of Victorian Gothic fiction and has inspired notable adaptations in other media, including opera and film. Considered among James's greatest achievements, *The Turn of the Screw* continues to be admired as one of the most artistic and enigmatic works in literature.

(See also *Contemporary Authors*, Vol. 104, and *Dictionary of Literary Biography*, Vol. 12: *American Realists and Naturalists*.)

THE NEW YORK TIMES SATURDAY REVIEW OF BOOKS AND ART (essay date 1898)

[*In the following excerpt, the critic discusses James's treatment of the subject of evil in* The Turn of the Screw.]

The Turn of the Screw is such a deliberate, powerful, and horribly successful study of the magic of evil, of the subtle influence over human hearts and minds of the sin with which this world is accursed, as our language has not produced since Stevenson wrote his "Jekyll and Hyde" tale, a work to which this is not akin in any other sense than the one here specified.

Mr. James's story is perhaps as allegorical as Stevenson's, but the allegory is not so clear. We have called it "horribly successful," and the phrase seems to still stand, on second thought, to express the awful, almost overpowering sense of the evil that human nature is subject to derived from it by the sensitive reader. We have no doubt that with such a reader Mr. James will invariably produce exactly the effect he aims at. But the work is not horrible in any grotesque or "realistic" sense. The strongest and most affecting argument against sin we have lately encountered in literature (without forcing any didactic purpose upon the reader) it is nevertheless free from the slightest hint of grossness. Of any precise form of evil Mr. James says very little, and on this head he is never explicit. Yet, while the substance of his story is free from all impurity and the manner is always graceful and scrupulously polite, the very breath of hell seems to pervade some of its chapters, and in the outcome goodness, though depicted as alert and militant, is scarcely triumphant. The most depraved "realist" (using that word in its most popular sense, for, correctly speaking, the artistic method of Mr. James is realism as opposed to idealism) could surely not be more powerful, though he might, in his explicitness, defeat his supposed purpose. Mr. James's present purpose, as we understand it, is amply fulfilled.

For some years past this man of remarkable gifts has suffered occasional lapses into sombre and not always explainable moods. **"The Middle Years,"** with its burden of a wail, and that queer tale of the private altar in an obscure London chapel, as well as some of his recent longer tales—*What Maisie Knew*, in particular, seems to have a clear relation to the work under notice—represent these moods. While they are upon him the writer may or may not be quite intelligible to his public, though his remarkable powers of expression surely never fail him, and to the elusive quality of his theme must any lack of clearness always be charged; but it is plain that he is then not the satirist, the man of the world, the subtle humorist of his earlier years, but quite another personage.

In this ***Turn of the Screw***—the title, used to express a stronger shade of horror and mental anguish than the ordinary ghost story represents, does not seem quite as apposite as some of Mr. James's titles—he is the seer and the moralist, whether designedly so or not. No eloquent outpouring of a Jeremy Collier or other avowed enemy of specified evils could produce a feeling of greater abhorrence for the object attacked. Yet Mr. James's method, as we have already intimated, is free from all superficial signs of a strongly didactic purpose. He simply tells, with no waste of words, as one who reads carefully soon learns, a story.

Just what that story is it would be unfair to divulge here, but a boy of ten years and a girl of eight figure in it prominently, and these are so lovely in their outward semblance of childlike innocence, so charming in their natural dispositions, and in many ways apart from the one way in which the reader presently comes to view them, so delightfully like the imaginative and inherently sagacious children of cultivated persons, that one recalls Kenneth Grahame's *Golden Age* and some of the other idylls of childhood as one reads of them. Yet these children are accursed, or all but damned, and are shown to have daily, almost hourly, communication with lost souls, the souls that formerly inhabited the bodies of a vicious governess and her paramour, who, in the flesh, began the degradation of their victims. The awful "imagination of evil" this fair boy and girl must possess, the oldness of the heart and soul in each young body, the terrible precocity which enables them to deceive their "pastors and masters" as to their knowledge of the presence of their ghostly mentors, these set forth with perfect clearness and the sobriety of a matter-of-fact narrative are what serve to produce the thrilling effect.

The allegory is plain or not, according to the reader's aptitude for discovering allegories. We do not insist upon that. But to the contention that this seemingly frail story—with a theme which would surely fail of effect, and might become simply ridiculous in the hands of almost any one of its author's contemporaries—is one of the most moving and, in its implied moral, most remarkable works of fiction published in many years, we steadfastly cling. No man could have undertaken to write it without feeling powerfully the importance of its subject, and no man could have carried the task through in whom interest in the theme did not grow as the story grew.

The introduction to this tale is sufficiently conventional, but one decides, in looking back, that it serves better than another would. A Christmas house party, with ghost stories told around the fireplace develops the ***Turn of the Screw*** in a tale of a ghost seen first by an innocent child, and this leads to the production of this ghost story read from the faded manuscript (supposedly) of a gentlewoman who had had experiences with these possessed children. The style of the manuscript, in spite of the insistence upon the woman's penmanship, is obviously the style of Mr. Henry James. But one appreciates not the less the characteristic touch in the statement that it was read "with a fine clearness that was like a rendering to the ear of the beauty of the author's hand." (pp. 681-82)

> "*Magic of Evil and Love,*" *in* The New York Times Saturday Review of Books and Art, *October 15, 1898, pp. 681-82.*

THE BOOKMAN, LONDON (essay date 1898)

> [*In the following excerpt, the critic praises technical aspects of* The Turn of the Screw *while regarding the narrative as a failure on the symbolic level.*]

Mr. James is in a queer mood. Nearly all his later stories have been tending to the horrible, have been stories of evil, beneath the surface mostly, and of corruption. His genius is essentially a healthy one, we have always felt, and he has had great respect in times past for the *convenances*. He does not outrage them now; his manners are perfect, even in his late studies of the putrescence of human existence. ***What Maisie Knew*** was one of these; but the story was a triumph of beauty in the end. Its theme was that purity and candour and joy could be strong enough in the heart of a young creature to counteract the miasma of the evil amid which she lived, not all unconscious either. His purpose was abundantly fufilled. The first of the two stories here—the other hardly counts, though it is a readable enough extravaganza—is another study of the same unpleasant kind of fact, but so much more horrible, that it surely marks the climax of this darker mood, out of which Mr. James may emerge with a profounder, or perhaps only a bitterer strain. The situation of Maisie is reversed. The circumstances, the conditions, in ***The Turn of the Screw,*** all make for purity, beauty, and joy; and on the surface these are resplendent. But underneath is a sink of corruption, never uncovered, but darkly, potently hinted. One's heart cries out against the picture of the terrible possiblity; for the corrupted are children of tender years. Every inch of the picture seems an outrage in our first heat. Even in colder moments, if we admit the fact of infant depravity, if we own that children are supreme actors, and can bar doors on their elders most effectually, we must deny the continuity and the extent of the corruption as suggested here. Mr. James has used symbolism to help him out with his theme; so, at least, we may speak of the two ghosts—one of a rascally valet, the other of an iniquitous governess—the origins of the evil in their lifetime, who haunt the children after their death. Their horrible invitations to evil are joyfully responded to. We have never read a more sickening, a more gratuitously melancholy tale. It has all Mr. James's cleverness, even his grace. The plottings of the good governess and the faithful Mrs. Grose to combat the evil, very gradually discovered, are marvellously real. You cannot help but assist at their interviews, and throb with their anxiety. You are amply convinced of the extraordinary charm of the children, of the fascination they exercise over all with whom they come in contact. The symbolism is clumsy; but only there in the story has Mr. James actually failed. It is not so much from a misunderstanding of child nature that he has plunged into the deep mistake of writing the story at all. Here, as elsewhere in his work, there are unmistakable signs of a close watchfulness and a loving admiration of children of the more distinguished order. A theory has run away with him. It is flimsily built on a few dark facts, so scattered and uncertain that they cannot support a theory at all. He has used his amiable knowledge of child life in its brighter phases to give a brilliant setting to this theory. His marvellous subtlety lends his examination of the situation an air of scientific precision. But the clever result is very cruel and untrue.

> "*Mr. James's New Book,*" *in* The Bookman, London, *Vol. XV, No. 86, November, 1898, p. 54.*

THE INDEPENDENT (essay date 1899)

> [*In the following excerpt, the critic expresses a strong aversion to James's tale of innocence corrupted.*]

The Turn of the Screw is the most hopelessly evil story that we have ever read in any literature, ancient or modern. How Mr. James could, or how any man or woman could, choose to make such a study of infernal human debauchery, for it is nothing else, is unaccountable. It is the story of two orphan children, mere infants, whose guardian leaves them in a lonely English country house. The little boy and little girl, at the toddling period of life, when they are but helpless babes, fall under the influence of a governess and her lover who poison the very core of their conscience and character and defile their souls in a way and by means darkly and subtly hinted rather than portrayed by Mr. James. The study, while it exhibits Mr. James's genius in a powerful light, affects the reader with a disgust that is not to be expressed. The feeling after perusal of the horrible story is that one has been assisting in an outrage upon the holiest and sweetest fountain of human innocence, and helping to debauch—at least by helplessly standing by—the pure and trusting nature of children. Human imagination can go no further into infamy, literary art could not be used with more refined subtlety of spiritual defilement.

A review of "The Two Magics," in The Independent, *Vol. LI, January 5, 1899, p. 73.*

HENRY JAMES (essay date 1908)

[*In the following excerpt from his 1908 preface to the volume of his collected works containing* The Turn of the Screw, *James discusses the inspiration for writing the novella and his artistic objectives in the work.*]

The Turn of the Screw . . . this perfectly independent and irresponsible little fiction rejoices, beyond any rival on a like ground, in a conscious provision of prompt retort to the sharpest question that may be addressed to it. For it has the small strength—if I shouldn't say rather the unattackable ease—of a perfect homogeneity, of being, to the very last grain of its virtue, all of a kind; the very kind, as happens, least apt to be baited by earnest criticism, the only sort of criticism of which account need be taken. To have handled again this so full-blown flower of high fancy is to be led back by it to easy and happy recognitions. Let the first of these be that of the starting-point itself—the sense, all charming again, of the circle, one winter afternoon, round the hall-fire of a grave old country-house where (for all the world as if to resolve itself promptly and obligingly into convertible, into "literary" stuff) the talk turned, on I forget what homely pretext, to apparitions and night-fears, to the marked and sad drop in the general supply, and still more in the general quality, of such commodities. The good, the really effective and heart-shaking ghost-stories (roughly so to term them) appeared all to have been told, and neither new crop nor new type in any quarter awaited us. The new type indeed, the mere modern "psychical" case, washed clean of all queerness as by exposure to a flowing laboratory tap, and equipped with credentials vouching for this—the new type clearly promised little, for the more it was respectably certified the less it seemed of a nature to rouse the dear old sacred terror. Thus it was, I remember, that amid our lament for a beautiful lost form, our distinguished host expressed the wish that he might but have recovered for us one of the scantest of fragments of this form at its best. He had never forgotten the impression made on him as a young man by the withheld glimpse, as it were, of a dreadful matter that had been reported years before, and with as few particulars, to a lady with whom he had youthfully talked. The story would have been thrilling could she but have found herself in better possession of it, dealing as it did

with a couple of small children in an out-of-the-way place, to whom the spirits of certain "bad" servants, dead in the employ of the house, were believed to have appeared with the design of "getting hold" of them. This was all, but there had been more, which my friend's old converser had lost the thread of: she could only assure him of the wonder of the allegations as she had anciently heard them made. He himself could give us but this shadow of a shadow—my own appreciation of which, I need scarcely say, was exactly wrapped up in that thinness. On the surface there wasn't much, but another grain, none the less, would have spoiled the precious pinch addressed to its end as neatly as some modicum extracted from an old silver snuffbox and held between finger and thumb. I was to remember the haunted children and the prowling servile spirits as a "value," of the disquieting sort, in all conscience sufficient; so that when, after an interval, I was asked for something seasonable by the promoters of a periodical dealing in the time-honoured Christmas-tide toy, I bethought myself at once of the vividest little note for sinister romance that I had ever jotted down.

Such was the private source of *The Turn of the Screw;* and I wondered, I confess, why so fine a germ, gleaming there in the wayside dust of life, had never been deftly picked up. The thing had for me the immense merit of allowing the imagination absolute freedom of hand, of inviting it to act on a perfectly clear field, with no "outside" control involved, no pattern of the usual or the true or the terrible "pleasant" (save always of course the high pleasantry of one's very form) to consort with. This makes in fact the charm of my second reference, that I find here a perfect example of an exercise of the imagination unassisted, unassociated—playing the game, making the score, in the phrase of our sporting day, off its own bat. To what degree the game was worth playing, I needn't attempt to say: the exercise I have noted strikes me now, I confess, as the interesting thing, the imaginative faculty acting with the *whole* of the case on its hands. The exhibition involved is in other words a fairy-tale pure and simple—save indeed as to its springing not from an artless and measureless, but from a conscious and cultivated credulity. Yet the fairy-tale belongs mainly to either of two classes, the short and sharp and single, charged more or less with the compactness of anecdote (as to which let the familiars of our childhood, Cinderella and Blue-Beard and Hop o' my Thumb and Little Red Riding Hood and many of the gems of the Brothers Grimm directly testify), or else the long and loose, the copious, the various, the endless, where, dramatically speaking, roundness is quite sacrificed—sacrificed to fulness, sacrificed to exuberance, if one will: witness at hazard almost any one of the Arabian Nights. The charm of all these things for the distracted modern mind is in the clear field of experience, as I call it, over which we are thus led to roam; an annexed but independent world in which nothing is right save as we rightly imagine it. We have to do *that,* and we do it happily for the short spurt and in the smaller piece, achieving so perhaps beauty and lucidity; we flounder, we lose breath, on the other hand—that is we fail, not of continuity, but of an agreeable unity, of the "roundness" in which beauty and lucidity largely reside—when we go in, as they say, for great lengths and breadths. And this, oddly enough, not because "keeping it up" isn't abundantly within the compass of the imagination appealed to in certain conditions, but because the finer interest depends just on *how* it is kept up.

Nothing is so easy as improvisation, the running on and on of invention; it is sadly compromised, however, from the moment its stream breaks bounds and gets into flood. Then the waters may spread indeed, gathering houses and herds and crops and cities into their arms and wrenching off, for our amusement, the whole face of the land—only violating by the same stroke our sense of the course and the channel, which is our sense of the uses of a stream and the virtue of a story. Improvisation, as in the Arabian Nights, may keep on terms with encountered objects by sweeping them in and floating them on its breast; but the great effect it so loses—that of keeping on terms with itself. This is ever, I intimate, the hard thing for the fairy-tale; but by just so much as it struck me as hard did it in *The Turn of the Screw* affect me as irresistibly prescribed. To improvise with extreme freedom and yet at the same time without the possibility of ravage, without the hint of flood; to keep the stream, in a word, on something like ideal terms with itself: that was here my definite business. The thing was to aim at absolute singleness, clearness and roundness, and yet to depend on an imagination working freely, working (call it) with extravagance; by which law it wouldn't be thinkable except as free and wouldn't be amusing except as controlled. The merit of the tale, as it stands, is accordingly, I judge, that it has struggled successfully with its dangers. It is an excursion into chaos while remaining, like Blue-Beard and Cinderella, but an anecdote—though an anecdote amplified and highly emphasised and returning upon itself; as, for that matter, Cinderella and Blue-Beard return. I need scarcely add after this that it is a piece of ingenuity pure and simple, of cold artistic calculation, an *amusette* to catch those not easily caught (the "fun" of the capture of the merely witless being ever but small), the jaded, the disillusioned, the fastidious. Otherwise expressed, the study is of a conceived "tone," the tone of suspected and felt trouble, of an inordinate and incalculable sort—the tone of tragic, yet of exquisite, mystification. To knead the subject of my young friend's, the supposititious narrator's, mystification thick, and yet strain the expression of it so clear and fine that beauty would result: no side of the matter so revives for me as that endeavour. Indeed if the artistic value of such an experiment be measured by the intellectual echoes it may again, long after, set in motion, the case would make in favour of this little firm fantasy—which I seem to see draw behind it to-day a train of associations. I ought doubtless to blush for thus confessing them so numerous that I can but pick among them for reference. I recall for instance a reproach made me by a reader capable evidently, for the time, of some attention, but not quite capable of enough, who complained that I hadn't sufficiently "characterised" my young woman engaged in her labyrinth; hadn't endowed her with signs and marks, features and humours, hadn't in a word invited her to deal with her own mystery as well as with that of Peter Quint, Miss Jessel and the hapless children. I remember well, whatever the absurdity of its now coming back to me, my reply to that criticism—under which one's artistic, one's ironic heart shook for the instant almost to breaking. "You indulge in that stricture at your ease, and I don't mind confiding to you that—strange as it may appear!—one has to choose ever so delicately among one's difficulties, attaching one's self to the greatest, bearing hard on those and intelligently neglecting the others. If one attempts to tackle them all one is certain to deal completely with none; whereas the effectual dealing with a few casts a blest golden haze under cover of which, like wanton mocking goddesses in clouds, the others find prudent to retire. It was 'déjà très-joli,' in *The Turn of the Screw,* please believe, the general proposition of our young woman's keeping crystalline her record of so many intense anomalies and obscurities—by which I don't of course mean her explanation of them, a different matter; and I saw no way, I feebly grant (fighting, at

the best too, periodically, for every grudged inch of my space) to exhibit her in relations other than those; one of which, precisely, would have been her relation to her own nature. We have surely as much of her own nature as we can swallow in watching it reflect her anxieties and inductions. It constitutes no little of a character indeed, in such conditions, for a young person, as she says, 'privately bred,' that she is able to make her particular credible statement of such strange matters. She has 'authority,' which is a good deal to have given her, and I couldn't have arrived at so much had I clumsily tried for more."

For which truth I claim part of the charm latent on occasion in the extracted reasons of beautiful things—putting for the beautiful always, in a work of art, the close, the curious, the deep. Let me place above all, however, under the protection of that presence the side by which this fiction appeals most to consideration: its choice of its way of meeting its gravest difficulty. There were difficulties not so grave: I had for instance simply to renounce all attempt to keep the kind and degree of impression I wished to produce on terms with the to-day so copious psychical record of cases of apparitions. Different signs and circumstances, in the reports, mark these cases; different things are done—though on the whole very little appears to be—by the persons appearing; the point is, however, that some things are never done at all: this negative quantity is large—certain reserves and properties and immobilities consistently impose themselves. Recorded and attested "ghosts" are in other words as little expressive, as little dramatic, above all as little continuous and conscious and responsive, as is consistent with their taking the trouble—and an immense trouble they find it, we gather—to appear at all. Wonderful and interesting therefore at a given moment, they are inconceivable figures in an *action*—and *The Turn of the Screw* was an action, desperately, or it was nothing. I had to decide in fine between having my apparitions correct and having my story "good"—that is producing my impression of the dreadful, my designed horror. Good ghosts, speaking by book, make poor subjects, and it was clear that from the first my hovering prowling blighting presences, my pair of abnormal agents, would have to depart altogether from the rules. They would be agents in fact; there would be laid on them the dire duty of causing the situation to reek with the air of Evil. Their desire and their ability to do so, visibly measuring meanwhile their effect, together with their observed and described success—this was exactly my central idea; so that, briefly, I cast my lot with pure romance, the appearances conforming to the true type being so little romantic.

This is to say, I recognise again, that Peter Quint and Miss Jessel are not "ghosts" at all, as we now know the ghost, but goblins, elves, imps, demons as loosely constructed as those of the old trials for witchcraft; if not, more pleasingly, fairies of the legendary order, wooing their victims forth to see them dance under the moon. Not indeed that I suggest their reducibility to any form of the pleasing pure and simple; they please at the best but through having helped me to express my subject all directly and intensely. Here it was—in the use made of them—that I felt a high degree of art really required; and here it is that, on reading the tale over, I find my precautions justified. The essence of the matter was the villainy of motive in the evoked predatory creatures; so that the result would be ignoble—by which I mean would be trivial—were this element of evil but feebly or inanely suggested. Thus arose on behalf of my idea the lively interest of a possible suggestion and process of *adumbration;* the question of how best to convey that sense of the depths of the sinister without which my fable would so woefully limp. Portentous evil—how was I to save that, as an intention on the part of my demon-spirits, from the drop, the comparative vulgarity inevitably attending, throughout the whole range of possible brief illustration, the offered example, the imputed vice, the cited act, the limited deplorable presentable instance? To bring the bad dead back to life for a second round of badness is to warrant them as indeed prodigious, and to become hence as shy of specifications as of a waiting anti-climax. One had seen, in fiction, some grand form of wrong-doing, or better still of wrong-being, imputed, seen it promised and announced as by the hot breath of the Pit— and then, all lamentably, shrink to the compass of some particular brutality, some particular immortality, some particular infamy portrayed: with the result, alas, of the demonstration's falling sadly short. If *my* bad things, for *The Turn of the Screw,* I felt, should succumb to this danger, if they shouldn't seem sufficiently bad, there would be nothing for me but to hang my artistic head lower than I had ever known occasion to do.

The view of that discomfort and the fear of that dishonour, it accordingly must have been, that struck the proper light for my right, though by no means easy, short cut. What, in the last analysis, had I to give the sense of? Of their being, the haunting pair, capable, as the phrase is, of everything—that is of exerting, in respect to the children, the very worst action small victims so conditioned might be conceived as subject to. What would *be* then, on reflection, this utmost conceivability?—a question to which the answer all admirably came. There is for such a case no eligible *absolute* of the wrong; it remains relative to fifty other elements, a matter of appreciation, speculation, imagination—these things moreover quite exactly in the light of the spectator's, the critic's, the reader's experience. Only make the reader's general vision of evil intense enough, I said to myself—and that already is a charming job—and his own experience, his own imagination, his own sympathy (with the children) and horror (of their false friends) will supply him quite sufficiently with all the particulars. Make him *think* the evil, make him think it for himself, and you are released from weak specifications. This ingenuity I took pains—as indeed great pains were required—to apply; and with a success apparently beyond my liveliest hope. Droll enough at the same time, I must add, some of the evidence—even when most convincing—of this success. How can I feel my calculation to have failed, my wrought suggestion not to have worked, that is, on my being assailed, as has befallen me, with the charge of a monstrous emphasis, the charge of all indecently expatiating? There is not only from beginning to end of the matter not an inch of expatiation, but my values are positively all blanks save so far as an excited horror, a promoted pity, a created expertness—on which punctual effects of strong causes no writer can ever fail to plume himself—proceed to read into them more or less fantastic figures. Of high interest to the author meanwhile—and by the same stroke a theme for the moralist—the artless resentful reaction of the entertained person who has abounded in the sense of the situation. He visits his abundance, morally, on the artist—who has but clung to an ideal of faultlessness. Such indeed, for this latter, are some of the observations by which the prolonged strain of that clinging may be enlivened! (pp. xiv-xxii)

Henry James, in a preface to his The Novels and Tales of Henry James: The Aspern Papers, The Turn of the Screw, The Liar, The Two Faces, *Vol. 12,* Charles Scribner's Sons, 1908, pp. v-xxiv.

HAROLD C. GODDARD (essay date 1920?)

[*Goddard was an American educator and critic. In the following excerpt from an article written no later than 1920 and published posthumously in 1957, he expounds for the first time the interpretation of* The Turn of the Screw *which regards the ghosts as hallucinations of the governess. The 1957 publication of this article renewed interest in the hallucination theory and offered explanations for certain difficulties in the psychological interpretation, primarily that of the identification of Peter Quint by Mrs. Grose.*]

A good many years ago I came upon *The Turn of the Screw* for the first time. I supposed I already knew what it was to be gripped by a powerful tale. But before I had read twenty pages I realized I had never encountered anything of this sort before. From the first, one of the things that chiefly struck me about James's tale was the way in which it united the thrills one is entitled to expect from a ghost story with the quality of being entirely credible, even by daylight. True, it evoked plenty of mystery, propounded plenty of enigmas, along the way. But the main idea of the thing was perfectly plain. So at any rate I thought. For it never occurred to me that there could be two opinions about that. What was my surprise, then, on taking it up with a group of students, to discover that not one of them interpreted it as I did. My faith in what seemed to me the obvious way of taking the story would have been shaken, had I not, on explaining it, found the majority of my fellow readers ready to prefer it to their own. And this experience was repeated with later groups. Yet, even after several years, it had not occurred to me that what seemed the natural interpretation of the narrative was not the generally accepted one among critics, however little it might be among students. And then one day I ran on a comment of Mr. Chesterton's on the story. He took it precisely as my students had. I began watching out in my reading for allusions to the story. I looked up several references to it. They all agreed. Evidently my view was utterly heretical. Naturally I asked myself more sharply than ever why I should take the tale as a matter of course in a way that did not seem to occur to other readers. Was it perversity on my part, or profundity? And then one day it dawned over me that perhaps it was neither. Perhaps it was the result rather of a remarkable parallelism between a strange passage in my own early experience (of which I will tell at the proper time) and what I conceived to be the situation in *The Turn of the Screw.* However that may be, at every rereading of the story I found myself adhering more firmly than ever to my original idea, and I continued to find that it met with hospitable reception among others. Not that there were no skeptics. Or now and then a strenuous objector.

It was not until long afterward that I happened to read James's own comment on *The Turn of the Screw* in the introduction to the collected edition of his works. A man with an hypothesis runs the risk of finding confirmation for it everywhere. Still, I set down for what it is worth the fact that in this introduction I thought I detected a very clear, but very covert, corroboration of the interpretation I favored, and later still, I got a similar impression, on the publication of James's letters, from passages referring to the story.

From the point of view of early critics of the tale . . . , the story may be summarized, in bare outline, as follows:

An English gentleman, by the death of his brother in India, becomes guardian of a small niece and nephew whom he places in charge of a governess at his country home, Bly. On his departure from Bly, he leaves behind him his valet, a certain

Peter Quint, with whom the governess, Miss Jessel, soon grows intimate. The valet is thus thrown in close contact with the children, with the boy in particular, who goes about with him as if he were his tutor. Quint and Miss Jessel are a depraved pair and the children do not escape exposure to their evil. As to the details of the contamination they suffer the author leaves us mercifully in the dark. But it is easy enough to guess its general nature. A point at any rate that is certain is the character of the language that the children pick up from their two protectors: language the use of which, later, was the cause of the boy's mysterious expulsion from school. Prior to this, however, Peter Quint, while drunk, slips on the ice and is killed, and Miss Jessel, whose reason for leaving Bly is broadly hinted, goes away—to die.

The world seems well rid of such a pair. But it turns out otherwise. For it is precisely at this point that the full horror of the situation develops and the infernal character of the tale emerges. Such, it transpires, was the passion of Quint and Miss Jessel to possess the souls of the innocent children that they return to their old haunts *after death,* appearing to their helpless victims and infecting them still further with their evil. Meanwhile, however, a new governess has been procured, who, fortunately for the children, is herself susceptible to visitation from the world beyond, and who, accordingly, does not long remain in the dark as to what is going on. Moved by a love for her little charges and a pity for them as deep as were the opposite emotions of their former companions, she attempts to throw herself as a screen between them and the discarnate fiends who pursue them, hoping that by accepting, as it were, the first shock of the impact she may shield and ultimately save the innocent children. In her protracted and lonely struggle with the agents of evil, she succeeds, but at a fearful price. The children are indeed dispossessed. But the little girl is driven in the process into a delirium which threatens the impairment of her intellect, while the boy expires at the very moment when he is snatched back from the brink of the abyss down which he is slipping.

So taken, the story is susceptible equally of two interpretations. It may be conceived, literally, as an embodiment of the author's belief in survival after death and in the power of spirits, in this case of evil spirits, to visit the living upon earth. Or, if one prefers, it may be taken as an allegory, in manner not unlike *Dr. Jekyll and Mr. Hyde:* the concrete representation of the truth that the evil that men do lives after them, infecting life long after they themselves are gone. Either way, except for the heroism of the second governess, the story is one of almost unmitigated horror. One can understand Mr. Chesterton's doubt as to whether the thing ought ever to have been published.

It is possible, however, to question the fidelity of either of these versions to the facts of the story and to ask whether another interpretation is not possible which will redeem the narrative from the charge of ugliness and render even its horror subordinate to its beauty.

Consider the second governess for a moment and the situation in which she finds herself. She is a young woman, only twenty, the daughter of a country parson, who, from his daughter's one allusion to him in her story, is of a psychically unbalanced nature; he may, indeed, even have been insane. We are given a number of oblique glimpses into the young woman's home and early environment. They all point to its stifling narrowness. From the confinement of her provincial home this young and inexperienced woman comes up to London to answer an advertisement for a governess. That in itself constitutes a suffi-cient crisis in the life of one who, after one glimpse, we do not need to be told is an excessively nervous and emotional person. But to add to the intensity of the situation the young woman falls instantly and passionately in love with the man who has inserted the advertisement. She scarcely admits it even to herself, for in her heart she knows that her love is hopeless, the object of her affection being one socially out of her sphere, a gentleman who can never regard her as anything other than a governess. But even this is not all. In her overwrought condition, the unexplained death of the former governess, her predecessor, was enough to suggest some mysterious danger connected with the position offered, especially in view of the master's strange stipulation: that the incumbent should assume *all* responsibility, even to the point of cutting off all communication with him—never writing, never reporting. Something extraordinary, she was convinced, lurked in the background. She would never have accepted the place if it had not been for her newborn passion: she could not bring herself to disappoint him when he seemed to beg compliance of her as a favor—to say nothing of severing her only link with the man who had so powerfully attracted her.

So she goes down to Bly, this slip of a girl, and finds herself no longer a poor parson's daughter but, quite literally, the head of a considerable country establishment. As if to impart the last ingredient to the witch's broth of her emotions, she is carried away almost to the point of ecstasy by the beauty of the two children, Miles and Flora, who have been confided to her care. All this could supply the material for a nervous breakdown in a girl of no worldly experience and of unstable psychical background. At any rate she instantly becomes the victim of insomnia. The very first night she fancies that she hears a light footstep outside her door and in the far distance the cry of a child. And more serious symptoms soon appear.

But before considering these, think what would be bound to happen even to a more normal mentality in such a situation. When a young person, especially a young woman, falls in love and circumstances forbid the normal growth and confession of the passion, the emotion, dammed up, overflows in a psychical experience, a daydream, or internal drama which the mind creates in lieu of the thwarted realization in the objective world. In romantic natures this takes the form of imagined deeds of extraordinary heroism or self-sacrifice done in behalf of the beloved object. The governess' is precisely such a nature and the fact that she knows her love is futile intensifies the tendency. Her whole being tingles with the craving to perform some act of unexampled courage. To carry out her duties as governess is not enough. They are too humdrum. If only the house would take fire by night, and both the children be in peril! Or if one of them would fall into the water! But no such crudely melodramatic opportunities occur. What does occur is something far more indefinite, far more provocative to the imaginative than to the active faculties: the boy, Miles, is dismissed from school for no assigned or assignable reason. Once more, the hint of something evil and extraordinary behind the scenes! It is just the touch of objectivity needed to set off the subconsciousness of the governess into an orgy of myth-making. Another woman of a more practical and common sense turn would have made inquiries, would have followed the thing up, would have been insistent. But it is precisely complication and not explanation that this woman wants—though of course she does not know it. The vague feeling of fear with which the place is invested for her is fertile soil for imaginative invention and an inadvertent hint about Peter Quint dropped by the housekeeper, Mrs. Grose, is just the seed that that soil requires. There is no more significant bit of dialogue in the story. Yet the reader, unless he is alert, is likely to pass it by unmarked. The governess and the housekeeper are exchanging confidences. The former asks:

"What was the lady who was here before?"

"The last governess? She was also young and pretty—almost as young and almost as pretty, Miss, even as you."

"Ah then I hope her youth and her beauty helped her!" I recollect throwing off. "He seems to like us young and pretty!"

"Oh he *did*," Mrs. Grose assented: "it was the way he liked everyone!" She had no sooner spoken indeed than she caught herself up. "I mean that's *his* way—the master's."

I was struck. "But of whom did you speak first?"

She looked blank, but she coloured. "Why, of *him*."

"Of the master?"

"Of who else?"

There was so obviously no one else that the next moment I had lost my impression of her having accidentally said more than she meant.

The consciousness of the governess may have lost its impression, but we do not need to be students of psychology to know that that inveterate playwright and stage manager, the subconscious, would never permit so valuable a hint to go unutilized.

Mrs. Grose, as her coloring shows and as the governess discerns, is thinking of some one other than the master. Of what man would she naturally think, on the mention of Miss Jessel, if not of Miss Jessel's running mate and partner in evil, Peter Quint? It is a momentary slip, but it is none the less fatal. It supplies the one character missing in the heroic drama that the governess' repressed desire is bent on staging: namely, the villain. The hero of that drama is behind the scenes: the master in Harley Street. The heroine, of course, is the governess herself. The villain, as we said, is this unknown man who "liked them young and pretty." The first complication in the plot is the mysterious dismissal of the boy from school, suggestive of some dim power of evil shadowing the child. The plot itself remains to be worked out, but it will inevitably turn on some act of heroism or self-sacrifice—both by preference—on the part of the heroine for the benefit of the hero and to the discomfiture of the villain. It is a foregone conclusion, too, that the villain will be in some way connected with the boy's predicament at school. (That he really was is a coincidence.) All this is not conjecture. It is elemental human psychology.

Such is the material and plan upon which the dreaming consciousness of the governess sets to work. But how dream when one is the victim of insomnia? Daydream, then? But ordinary daydreams are not enough for the passionate nature of the governess. So she proceeds to act her drama out, quite after the fashion of a highly imaginative child at play. And the first scene of her dramatic creation is compressed into the few moments when she sees the stranger on the tower of Bly by twilight.

Whence does that apparition come? *Out of the governess's unconfessed love and unformulated fear.* It is clearly her love that first evokes him, for, as she tells us, she was thinking, as she strolled about the grounds that afternoon, how charming it would be suddenly to meet "some one," to have "some one" appear at the turn of a path and stand before her and smile and approve, when suddenly, with the face she longed to see still vividly present to her mind, she stopped short. "What arrested me on the spot," she says, "—and with a shock much greater than any vision had allowed for—was the sense that my imagination had, in a flash, turned real. He did stand there!—but high up, beyond the lawn and at the very top of the tower. . . ." Instantly, however, she perceives her mistake. It is not he. In her heart she knows it cannot be. But if her love is too good to be true, her fears, unfortunately, are only too true. And forthwith those fears seize and transform this creation of her imagination. "It produced in me," the governess declares, "this figure, in the clear twilight, I remember, two distinct gasps of emotion, which were, sharply, the shock of my first and that of my second surprise. My second was a violent perception of the mistake of my first: the man who met my eyes was not the person I had precipitately supposed. There came to me thus a bewilderment of vision of which, after these years, there is no living view that I can hope to give." What has happened? The hint that the housekeeper dropped of an unnamed man in the neighborhood has done its work. Around that hint the imagination of the governess precipitates the specter who is to dominate the rest of the tale. And because he is an object of dread he is no sooner evoked than he becomes the raw material of heroism. It only remains to link him with the children and the "play" will be under way with a rush.

This linking takes place on the Sunday afternoon when the governess, just as she is about to go out to church, becomes suddenly aware of a man gazing in at the dining room window. Instantly there comes over her, as she puts it, the "shock of a certitude that it was not for me he had come. He had come for someone else." "The flash of this knowledge," she continues, "—for it was knowledge in the midst of dread—produced in me the most extraordinary effect, starting, as I stood there, a sudden vibration of duty and courage." The governess feels her sudden vibration of duty and courage as the effect of the apparition, but it would be closer to the truth to call it its cause. Why has the stranger come for the children rather than for her? Because she must not merely be brave; she must be brave for someone's sake. The hero must be brought into the drama. She must save the beings whom he has commissioned her to protect. And that she may have the opportunity to save them they must be menaced: they must have enemies. That is the creative logic of her hallucination.

"Hallucination!" a dozen objectors will cry, unable to hold in any longer. "Why! the very word shows that you have missed the whole point of the story. The creature at the window is no hallucination. It is he himself, Peter Quint, returned from the dead. If not, how was Mrs. Grose able to recognize him—and later Miss Jessel—from the governess's description?"

The objection seems well taken. The point, indeed, is a capital one with the governess herself, who clings to it as unshakable proof that she is not mad; for Mrs. Grose, it appears, though she seems to accept her companion's account of her strange experiences, has moments of backsliding, of toying with the hypothesis that the ghosts are mere creatures of the governess' fancy. Whereupon, says the latter, "I had only to ask her how, if I had 'made it up,' I came to be able to give, of each of the persons appearing to me, a picture disclosing, to the last detail, their special marks—a portrait on the exhibition of which she had instantly recognized and named them." This retort floors Mrs. Grose completely, and she wishes "to sink the whole subject."

But Mrs. Grose is a trustful soul, too easily floored perhaps. If we will look into the matter a bit further than she did, we will perceive that it simply is not true that the governess gave such detailed descriptions of Peter Quint and Miss Jessel that Mrs. Grose instantly recognized their portraits. In the case of Miss Jessel, indeed, such a statement is the very reverse of the truth. The "detailed" description consisted, beyond the colorless fact that the ghost was pale, precisely of the two items that the woman who appeared was extremely beautiful and was dressed in black. But Mrs. Grose had already told the governess explicitly, long before any ghost was thought of, that Miss Jessel was beautiful. Whether she had been accustomed to dress in black we never learn. But that makes little difference, for the fact is that it is *the governess herself and not Mrs. Grose at all who does the identifying:*

> "Was she someone you've never seen?" asked Mrs. Grose.
>
> "Never," the governess replies. "But some one the child has. Some one *you* have." Then to show how I had thought it all out: "My predecessor—the one who died."
>
> "Miss Jessel?"
>
> "Miss Jessel," the governess confirms. "You don't believe me?"

And the ensuing conversation makes it abundantly plain that Mrs. Grose is still far from convinced. This seems a trifle odd in view of the fact that Peter Quint is known to be haunting the place. After having believed in one ghost, it ought not to be hard for Mrs. Grose to believe in another, especially when the human counterparts of the two were as inseparable in life as were the valet and the former governess. Which makes it look as if the housekeeper were perhaps not so certain after all in the case of Quint. Why, then, we ask, did she "identify him"? To which the answer is that she identified him because the suggestion for the identification, just as in the case of Miss Jessel, though much more subtly, comes from the governess herself. The skill with which James manages to throw the reader off the scent in this scene is consummate.

In the *first* place, the housekeeper herself, as we have had several occasions to remark, has already dropped an unintentional hint of someone in the neighborhood who preys on young and pretty governesses. This man, to be sure, is dead, but the new governess, who did not pay strict enough attention to Mrs. Grose's tenses, does not know it. We have already noted the part that the fear of him played in creating the figure on the tower. When now that figure comes closer and appears at the window, it would be strange indeed if, in turning over in her head all the possibilities, the idea of the unknown man to whom the housekeeper had so vaguely referred did not cross at least the fringe of the governess' consciousness. That it actually did is indicated by her prompt assumption that Mrs. Grose can identify their extraordinary visitor. "But now that you've guessed," are her words.

"Ah I haven't guessed," Mrs. Grose replies. And we are quite willing to agree that at this point she hasn't. But notice what follows:

The governess has assured Mrs. Grose that the intruder is not a gentleman.

"But if he isn't a gentleman—" the housekeeper begins.

"What *is* he?" asks the governess, completing the question and supplying the answer:

> "He's a horror."
>
> "A horror?"
>
> "He's—God help me if I know *what* he is!"
>
> Mrs. Grose looked round once more; she fixed her eyes on the duskier distance and then, pulling herself together, turned to me with full inconsequence. "It's time we should be at church."

What was the thought which was seeking entrance to Mrs. Grose's mind as she gazed at the duskier distance and which was sufficiently unwelcome to make her throw it off with her gesture and quick digression? Was it something that the word "horror" had suggested, something vaguely hinted in the gov-

Photograph of James taken a year before publication of The Turn of the Screw.

erness's "He's—God help me if I know *what* he is!'"—as if
their visitant were a creature not altogether mortal? We cannot
be sure. But when, immediately afterward, the governess refuses to go to church on the ground that the stranger is a menace
to the *children,* there is no longer any question as to the thought
that dawns over the housekeeper. *A horror in human form that
is a menace to the children!* Is there anything, or anyone, in
Mrs. Grose's experience that answers that description? A thousand times yes! Peter Quint. Can there be a shadow of doubt
that it is Quint of whom she is thinking when, to use the author's
words, her

> large face showed me, at this, for the first time,
> the far-away faint glimmer of a consciousness
> more acute: I somehow made out in it the de-
> layed dawn of an idea I myself had not given
> her and that was as yet quite obscure to me. It
> comes back to me that I thought instantly of
> this as something I could get from her; and I
> felt it to be connected with the desire she pres-
> ently showed to know more.

So the governess' fears and repressed desires and the housekeeper's memories and anxieties unconsciously collaborate.

The conversation is resumed and the governess gives, in the
most vivid detail, a picture of the man she has seen at the
window. Following which, from the governess's challenge,
"You *do* know him?" the housekeeper holds back for a second,
only to admit, a moment later, that it is Peter Quint and to
stagger her companion, in the next breath, by her calm declaration that Quint is dead.

Now with regard to all this the critical question is: Granted
that Mrs. Grose's mind was already toying with the idea of
Quint, how could she have identified him unless the governess'
description tallied with the man? For, unlike Miss Jessel's, she
has received no advance hint with regard to Quint's personal
appearance, and the description, instead of being brief and
generalized, is lengthy and concrete. The objection seems fatal
to the view that the apparitions were mere creatures of the
governess' imagination. But upon exmaination this line of argument will be found, I think, to prove too much.

Suppose a missing criminal is described as follows: "A squat,
ruddy-cheeked man about thirty years old, weighing nearly two
hundred pounds; thick lips and pockmarked face; one front
tooth missing, two others with heavy gold fillings; big scar
above left cheek bone. Wears shell glasses; had on, when last
seen, brown suit, gray hat, pink shirt and tan shoes." Then
suppose a man, flushed with excitement, were to rush into
police headquarters exclaiming that he had found the murderer.
"How do you know?" the chief detective asks. "Why! I saw
a man about thirty years old with shell glasses and tan shoes!"

Well, it is only a slight exaggeration to say that Mrs. Grose's
"identification" of Peter Quint, in the face of the governess'
description, is of exactly this sort. The picture the latter draws
of the face at the window, with its red curling hair and peculiar
whiskers, is so vivid and striking that Mrs. Grose, if she was
listening and if it was indeed a description of Quint, ought not
to have hesitated a second. But she did hesitate. It may of
course be said that she hesitated not because the description
did not fit but because Quint was dead. But if so, why, when
she does identify him, does she pick out the least characteristic
points in the description? Why, when she does "piece it all
together" (what irony in that "all"!), does her identification
rest not at all on the red whiskers or the thin mouth, but, of

all things, on the two facts that the stranger wore no hat and
that his clothes looked as if they belonged to someone else?
As if good ghosts always wore hats and bad ones carried their
terrestrial pilferings into eternity! That touch about "the missing waistcoats" is precisely at Mrs. Grose's intellectual level,
the level, as anyone who has ever had the curiosity to attend
one knows, of a fifty-rate spiritualist seance.

The thing is really so absurd that we actually wonder whether
Mrs. Grose was listening. Recall the beginning of the dialogue:

> "What's he like?" [asks Mrs. Grose]
>
> "I've been dying to tell you. But he's like
> nobody."
>
> "Nobody?" she echoed.
>
> "He has no hat." Then seeing in her face that
> she already, in this, with a deeper dismay, found
> a touch of picture, I quickly added stroke to
> stroke.

We see what we expect to see. That Mrs. Grose should so
instantaneously find a touch of picture in the colorless item
that "he had no hat" is a measure of the high degree of her
suggestibility, as good proof as one could want that an image
is already hovering in the background of her mind waiting to
rush into the foreground at the faintest summons. That, as we
have seen, is exactly what the image of Peter Quint is doing.
And so, is it at all unlikely that in completing the picture of
which the mention of the hat has supplied the first touch, Mrs.
Grose pays scant attention to the other, verbal picture that the
governess is drawing? The point need not be urged, but at any
rate she gives no evidence of having heard, and at the governess' concluding sentence, "He gives me a sort of sense of
looking like an actor," her echoed "An actor!" sounds almost
as if it were at that point that her wandering attention were
called back. That of course is only conjecture. But what is not
conjecture, and significant enough, is the fact that the two
shaky pegs on which Mrs. Grose hangs her identification come,
one at the very beginning, the other at the very end, of a long
description the intervening portions of which would have supplied her, anyone of them, with solid support. When a man
crosses a stream on a rotten wooden bridge in spite of the fact
that there is a solid one of stone a rod or two away, you naturally
wonder whether he has noticed it.

"But why waste so much breath," it will be said, "over what
is after all such a purely preliminary part of the story and over
such an incidental character as Mrs. Grose. Come to the main
events, and to the central characters, the children. What *then*
becomes of your theory that Quint and Miss Jessel are just
hallucinations? How can they be that, when Miles and Flora
see them?"

Before coming to this certainly pertinent objection, I wonder
if I may interject the personal experience mentioned at the
beginning. It may be that this experience subconsciously accounts for my reading of *The Turn of the Screw.* If its influence
is justified, it is worth recounting. If it is unjustified, it should
be narrated that the reader may properly discount its effect on
my interpretation of the tale. It may be that for me this memory
turns into realism what for even the author was only romance.

When I was a boy of seven or eight, and my sister a few years
older, we had a servant in the family—a Canadian woman, I
think she was—who, I now see on looking back (though no
one then suspected it), was insane. Some years later her de-

lusions became marked, her insanity was generally recognized, and she was for a time at least confined in an asylum. Now it happened that this woman, who was of an affectionate nature and loved children, used to tell us stories. I do not know whether they were all of one kind, but I do know that the only ones my memory retained were of dead people who came to visit her in the night. I remember with extraordinary vividness her account of a woman in white who came and stood silent at the foot of her bed. I can still see the strange smile—the insane smile, as I now recognize it to have been—that came over the face of the narrator as she told of this visitant. This woman did not long remain a servant in our family. But suppose she had! Suppose our parents had died, or, for some other reason, we had been placed exclusively in her care. (She was a woman of unimpeachable character and kindliest impulses.) What might have happened to us? What might not! Especially if she had conceived the notion that some of her spiritual visitants were of an infernal character and had come to gain possession of us, the children for whom she was responsible. I tremble to think. And yet no greater alteration than this would have been called for in an instance within the range of my own experience to have duplicated essentially what I conceive to be the situation in *The Turn of the Screw.*

Now the unlikelihood of this situation's occurring is precisely the fact that in real life someone would recognize the insanity and interfere to save the children. This was the difficulty that confronted the author of *The Turn of the Screw,* if we may assume for the moment that I have stated his problem correctly. The extraordinary skill and thoroughness with which he has met it are themselves the proof, it seems to me, that he had that difficulty very consciously in his mind. He overcomes it by fashioning the characters of the master and the housekeeper expressly to fit the situation. The children's uncle, from the first, wishes to wash his hands entirely of their upbringing, to put them unreservedly in the hands of their governess, who is *never,* in any conceivable way, to put up her problems or questions to him in person or by letter. The insistence on this from beginning to end seems needlessly emphatic unless it serves some such purpose as the one indicated. The physical isolation of the little household in the big estate at Bly is also complete. The governess is in supreme authority; only she and the housekeeper have anything to do with the children—and Mrs. Grose's character is shaped to fit the plot. If she is the incarnation of practical household sense and homely affection, she is utterly devoid of worldly experience and imagination. And she is as superstitious as such a person is likely to be. She can neither read nor write, the latter fact, which is a capital one, being especially insisted on. She knows her place and has a correspondingly exalted opinion of persons of higher rank or education. Hence her willingness, even when she cannot understand, to accept as truth whatever the governess tells her. She loves the children deeply and has suffered terribly for them during the reign of Quint and Miss Jessel. (Her relief on the arrival of Miss Jessel's successor, which the latter notices and misinterprets, is natural.) Here is a character, then, a situation, ideally fitted to allow of the development of the governess' mania unnoticed. James speaks of the original suggestion for *The Turn of the Screw* as "the vividest little note for sinister romance that I had ever jotted down," expressing wonder at the same time "why so fine a germ, gleaming there in the wayside dust of life, had never been deftly picked up." His note, he says in one of his letters, was "of a most scrappy kind." The form which the idea assumed in his mind as it developed we can only conjecture. My own guess would be that it might, in content at least, have run something like this:

Two children, under circumstances where there is no one to realize the situation, are put, for bringing up, in the care of an insane governess. (pp. 3-19)

> Harold C. Goddard, "A Pre-Freudian Reading of 'The Turn of the Screw'," in Nineteenth-Century Fiction, *Vol. 12, No. 1, June, 1957, pp. 1-36.*

EDNA KENTON (essay date 1924)

[*In the following excerpt, Kenton asserts that James deluded his readers into believing in the ghosts of Quint and Jessel, while providing evidence that the ghosts were only hallucinations.*]

In the submerged and disregarded foreword to the tale, in which the young governess and the children's uncle are set brightly before us—few readers of *The Turn of the Screw* remember this at all—lies a little painted portrait of the exquisite young creature who undertook the portentous task at Bly. The children and the ghosts have crowded forward to hide the only light thrown on her except for the irrepressible unconscious lights she casts on herself. It is never to be forgotten that it is she—not Henry James—who tells the story of Bly and its inhabitants, bound within confines of understanding as narrowly drawn as the circle which limited and defined, for instance, *What Maisie Knew.* But her freedom to tell her story, with no omniscient author at her elbow, is the "long rope, for acting herself out," that her creator, so fondly participating in her reality, tied so lightly to his foreword and then played out to her. The foreword is the only light we have on her present or her past—her whole concern is with the children and the ghosts. But of these we have only her story, and we have got nowhere near the "story of the story" until, pressing resolutely through her irresistibly credible recounting of the horrors at Bly, we come into closer quarters with the secret causes of her admirable *flair* for the evil she finds there.

She was twenty, so the submerged foreword tells us, a clergyman's daughter seeking her first position when she came up to London to answer an advertisement of the children's uncle. She found him "such a figure as had never risen, save in a dream or an old novel, before a fluttered, anxious girl out of a Hampstead vicarage." He was handsome and bold and pleasant, offhand and gay and kind, gallant and splendid. It was a difficult situation offered her, and it was put to her fairly; the condition of her taking it was that she should assume full responsibility for house, children and servants and leave him free to live his life in peace. She hesitated, but she was under a spell. "She succumbed to it . . . she saw him only twice . . . but that was the beauty of her passion . . . she never saw him again."

But she went to Bly. The master had come into her house and had gone out of it; she had only the house. She found it at first full of brightness, greatness, beauty and dignity and she began to enjoy it almost with a sense of property. Days passed, filled with dreams and dreamings. But there came a change which broke the hush of the first beautiful week at Bly; and the change, "actually like the spring of a beast," came at the close of a beautiful afternoon, at the end of a lonely stroll in which she walked, wrapped in day dreams.

> One of the thoughts (wrote the little governess in her desperate diary), "that, as I don't in the least shrink from noting now, used to be with me in these wanderings was that it would be as charming as a charming story suddenly to

meet some one. Some one would appear there
at the turn of a path, and would stand before
me and smile and approve. I didn't ask more
than that—I only asked that he should know.

And that evening, as she came within sight of the house, "he
did stand there"—the figure that her dreamings had invoked.
(pp. 251-52)

This, no more, no less, is the first visitation of Peter Quint.
There came another, as unexpectedly as the first, on a rainy
Sunday afternoon.

He appeared thus again with I won't say greater
distinctness, for that was impossible, but with
a nearness that represented a foreward stride in
our intercourse and made me, as I met him,
catch my breath and turn cold. . . . On the spot
there came to me the added shock of a certitude
that it was not for me he had come there. He
had come for some one else.

So the little governess says, and upon it she acts—both so
convincingly as to sweep the reader, wary or unwary, headlong
with her into her nightmare of horrors. Her way of escape is
the reader's. And so subtlely does she build up the ring of fire
about her house of life—as frightened women, in pioneer forests with their men away, lighted circles of flames about their
homes to ward off the prowling beasts of night—that it is
desperately difficult to catch her in the act.

The children hounded by the prowling ghosts—this is the hard
and shining surface story of *The Turn of the Screw;* or, to put
it more accurately, it is the traditional and accepted interpretation of the story as it has come down through a quarter of a
century of readers' reactions resulting from "a cold, artistic
calculation" on the part of its highly entertained author. As a
tiny matter of literal fact, no reader has more to go on than
the young governess's word for this rather momentous and
sidetracking allegation. As a rather large matter of literal fact,
we may know, with but a modicum of attention paid to her
recital of these nerve-shattering affairs at Bly, that it is she—
always she herself—who sees the lurking shapes and heralds
them to her little world. Not to the charming little Flora, but,
behind Flora and facing the governess, the apparitional Miss
Jessel first appeared. There are traps and lures in plenty, but
just a little wariness will suffice to disprove, with a single
survey of the ground, the traditional, we might almost call it
lazy version of this tale. Not the children, but the little governess was hounded by the ghosts who, as James confides with
such suave frankness in his Preface, merely "helped me to
express my subject all directly and intensely." After her startling materializations of Peter Quint and Miss Jessel, Bly became a nest of lurking shapes, and she walked softly, in terror,
expectantly. She came to know the moods that brought them:

There were states of the air, conditions of sound
and stillness, unspeakable impressions of the
kind of ministering moment, that brought back
to me, long enough to catch it, the medium in
which, that June evening out of doors, I had
had my first sight of Quint. . . . I recognized
the signs, the portents—I recognized the moment, the spot.

So she made the shades of her recurring fevers dummy figures
for the delirious terrifying of others, pathetically trying to har-

monize her own disharmonies by creating discords outside herself.

"I meant to scare the whole world with that story," James has
been quoted as saying—seemingly with serious solemnity. And
indeed, in its exquisitely ironic Preface, he took up at length
with its readers the turning, precisely, of just this little trick
that has worked so well. He is more than confidential—he is
explicit as to just how the screw was tightened, revelatory as
to calculated causes of his calculated effects.

His problem here, he says gaily, was how *best* to convey that
sense of the depths of the sinister which was essential for
illusion. Portentous evil—how was that to be invoked; or,
invoked, how saved from the comparative vulgarity of "the
cited act, the limited, deplorable, presentable instance."

One had seen (he mused) in fiction, some grand
form of wrong-doing or, better still, of wrong
being, imputed, seen it promised and announced as by the hot breath of the Pit—and
then, all lamentably, shrink to the compass of
some particular brutality, some particular immorality, some particular infamy portrayed; with
the result, alas, of the demonstration's falling
sadly short.

So, from the heap of aesthetic failures lying along fiction's
path, he evolved, for the novel of evil, an aesthetic moral. Its
sinister agent, he concluded, be it man or ghost, must be, in
the last analysis, capable of *anything,* the very worst conceivable action. So far, very good; he had his sinister agent—his
pair of them—in his two "ghosts." But still the question remained, of how best to convey to the reader the sense of this
utmost capability without the author himself falling into the
deadly trap of the "cited act." And this is his answer:

Only make the reader's general vision of evil
intense enough, I said to myself—and that already is a charming job—and his own experience, his own imagination, his own sympathy
(with the children) and horror (of their false
friends) will supply him quite sufficiently with
all the particulars. Make him *think* the evil,
make him think it for himself, and you are
released from weak specifications. This ingenuity I took pains—as indeed great pains were
required—to apply; and with a success apparently beyond my liveliest hopes.

A success all the greater, incidentally, because he permitted
his innocent young governess to write herself his novel of evil.
She could not "specify," and readers of her tender, moving
tale have of necessity had to think the evil for themselves.
"Droll enough," adds James,

some of the evidence—even when most convincing—of this success. How can I feel my
calculation to have failed, my wrought suggestion not to have worked, that is, on my being
assailed, as has befallen me, with the charge
of a monstrous emphasis, the charge of all indecently expatiating. There is not only from
beginning to end of the matter not an inch of
expatiation, but my values are positively all
blanks save only so far as an excited horror, a
promoted pity, a created expertness—on which
punctual effects of strong causes no writer can

ever fail to plume himself—proceed to read into them more or less fantastic figures.

And the fantastic figures have been read into *The Turn of the Screw;* for once at least James succeeded in forcing his reader, however unconsciously, to do a share of the work left for him to do. Not all of it, however; the ironic beauty of his subtle device for best expressing the depths of evil is that it was at the same time the calculated trap of traps for the guarding of his heroine. The eager, thrilled, horrified reader, joined with her in her vivid hunt after hidden sins, has failed to think sufficiently of her; and has, all oddly, contrived to protect her quite as romantically as her creator permitted her to protect herself in her charming recital of the happenings at Bly. Her own story, so naively sympathetic, of the ghosts and children, has been her simple bulwark—even the cunning reader has been credulous.

So, on *The Turn of the Screw,* Henry James has won, hands down, all round; has won most of all when the reader, persistently baffled, but persistently wondering, comes face to face at last with the little governess, and realizes, with a conscious thrill greater than that of merely automatic nerve shudders before ''horror,'' that the guarding ghosts and children—what they are and what they do—are only exquisite dramatizations of her little personal mystery, figures for the ebb and flow of troubled thought within her mind, acting out her story. If the reader has won for himself a blest sense of an extension of experience and consciousness in the recognition that her case, so delicate, so complicated, so critical and yet so transparent, has never in its whole treatment been cheapened or betrayed; if he has had, in the high modern sense, all of his ''fun,'' he has none the less paid; he has worked for it all, and by that fruitful labor has verified James's earliest contention that there was a discoverable way to establish a relation of work shared between the writer and the reader sufficiently curious to follow through. (pp. 254-55)

Edna Kenton, ''Henry James to the Ruminant Reader: The Turn of the Screw,'' in The Arts, Vol. VI, No. 5, November 1924, pp. 245-55.

EDMUND WILSON (essay date 1934)

[*Wilson, considered America's foremost man of letters in the twentieth century, wrote widely on cultural, historical, and literary matters, authoring several seminal critical studies. He is often credited with bringing an international perspective to American letters through his widely read discussions of European literature. Wilson was allied to no critical school; however, several dominant concerns serve as guiding motifs throughout his work. He invariably examined the social and historical implications of a work of literature, particularly literature's significance as ''an attempt to give meaning to our experience'' and its value for the improvement of humanity. Although he was not a moralist, his criticism displays a deep concern with moral values. Another constant was his discussion of a work of literature as a revelation of its author's personality. In* Axel's Castle *(1931), a seminal study of literary symbolism, Wilson wrote: ''The real elements, of course, of any work of fiction are the elements of the author's personality: his imagination embodies in the images of characters, situations and scenes the fundamental conflicts of his nature.'' Related to this is Wilson's theory, formulated in* The Wound and the Bow *(1941), that artistic ability is a compensation for a psychological wound; thus, a literary work can only be fully understood if one undertakes an emotional profile of its author. Wilson utilized this approach in many essays, and it is the most-often attacked element of his thought. However, though Wilson examined the historical and psychological implications of a work*

of literature, he rarely did so at the expense of a discussion of its literary qualities. In the following excerpt from his essay ''The Ambiguity of Henry James,'' which was originally published in 1934, and revised in 1948, Wilson presents the first psychoanalytical interpretation of The Turn of the Screw.]

A discussion of Henry James's ambiguity may appropriately begin with *The Turn of the Screw.* This story, which seems to have proved more fascinating to the general reading public than anything else of James's except *Daisy Miller,* perhaps conceals another horror behind the ostensible one. I do not know who first suggested this idea; but I believe that Miss Edna Kenton, whose insight into James is profound, was the first to write about it [see excerpt dated 1924], and the water-colorist Charles Demuth did a set of illustrations for the tale that were evidently based on this interpretation.

The theory is, then, that the governess who is made to tell the story is a neurotic case of sex repression, and that the ghosts are not real ghosts but hallucinations of the governess.

Let us see how the narrative runs. This narrative is supposed to have been written by the governess herself, but it begins with an introduction in which we are told something about her by a man whose sister's governess she had been after the time of the story. The youngest daughter of a poor country parson, she struck him, he explains, as ''awfully clever and nice . . . the most agreeable woman I've ever known in her position'' and ''worthy of any whatever.'' (Now, it is a not infrequent trick of James's to introduce sinister characters with descriptions that at first sound flattering, so this need not throw us off.) Needing work, she had come up to London to answer an advertisement and had found someone who wanted a governess for an orphaned nephew and niece. ''This prospective patron proved a gentleman, a bachelor in the prime of life, such a figure as had never risen, save in a dream or an old novel, before a fluttered, anxious girl out of a Hampshire vicarage.'' It is made clear that the young woman has become thoroughly infatuated with her employer. He is charming to her and lets her have the job on condition that she will take all the responsibility and never bother him about the children; and she goes down to the house in the country where they have been left with a housekeeper and some other servants.

The boy, she finds, has been sent home from school for reasons into which she does not inquire but which she colors, on no evidence at all, with a significance somehow ominous. She learns that her predecessor left, and that the woman has since died, under circumstances which are not explained but which are made in the same way to seem queer. The new governess finds herself alone with the good but illiterate housekeeper and the children, who seem innocent and charming. As she wanders about the estate, she thinks often how delightful it would be if one should come suddenly round the corner and see the master just arrived from London: there he would stand, handsome, smiling, approving.

She is never to meet her employer again, but what she does meet are the apparitions. One day when his face has been vividly in her mind, she comes out in sight of the house and, looking up, sees the figure of a man on a tower, a figure which is not the master's. Not long afterwards, the figure appears again, toward the end of a rainy Sunday. She sees him at closer range and more clearly: he is wearing smart clothes but is obviously not a gentleman. The housekeeper, meeting the governess immediately afterwards, behaves as if the governess herself were a ghost: ''I wondered why she should be scared.'' The governess tells her about the apparition and learns that it answers the description of one of the master's valets, who had stayed down there and who had sometimes stolen his clothes. The valet had been a bad character, had used "to play with the boy . . . to spoil him," he had finally been found dead, having apparently slipped on the ice coming out of a public house—though one couldn't say he hadn't been murdered. The governess cannot help believing that he has come back to haunt the children.

Not long afterwards, she and the little girl are out on the shore of a lake, the child playing, the governess sewing. The latter becomes aware of a third person on the opposite side of the lake. But she looks first at little Flora, who is turning her back in that direction and who, she notes, has "picked up a small flat piece of wood, which happened to have in it a little hole that had evidently suggested to her the idea of sticking in another fragment that might figure as a mast and make the thing a boat. This second morsel, as I watched her, she was very markedly and intently attempting to tighten in its place." This somehow "sustains" the governess so that she is able to raise her eyes: she sees a woman "in black, pale and dreadful." She concludes that it is the former governess. The housekeeper, questioned, tells her that this woman, although a lady, had had an affair with the valet. The boy had used to go off with the valet and then lie about it afterwards. The governess concludes that the boy must have known about the valet and the woman— the boy and girl have been corrupted by them.

Observe that there is never any reason for supposing that any-body but the governess sees the ghosts. She believes that the children see them, but there is never any proof that they do. The housekeeper insists that she does not see them; it is ap-parently the governess who frightens her. The children, too, become hysterical; but this is evidently the governess' doing. Observe, also, from the Freudian point of view, the signifi-cance of the governess' interest in the little girl's pieces of wood and of the fact that the male apparition first takes shape on a tower and the female apparition on a lake. There seems here to be only a single circumstance which does not fit into the hypothesis that the ghosts are mere fancies of the governess: the fact that her description of the masculine ghost at a time when she knows nothing of the valet should be identifiable as the valet by the housekeeper. And when we look back, we see that even this has perhaps been left open to a double interpre-tation. The governess has never heard of the valet, but it has been suggested to her in a conversation with the housekeeper that there has been some other male about who "liked everyone young and pretty," and the idea of this other person has been ambiguously confused with the master and with the master's possible interest in her, the present governess. And may she not, in her subconscious imagination, taking her cue from this, have associated herself with her predecessor and conjured up an image who wears the master's clothes but who (the Freudian "censor" intervening) looks debased, "like an actor," she says (would he not have to stoop to love her?). The apparition had 'straight, good features' and his appearance is described in detail. When we look back, we find that the master's ap-pearance has never been described at all: we have merely been told that he was "handsome," and it comes out in the talk with the housekeeper that the valet was "remarkably hand-some." It is impossible for us to know how much the phantom resembles the master—the governess, certainly, would never tell.

The new apparitions now begin to be seen at night, and the governess becomes convinced that the children get up to meet them, though they are able to give plausible explanations of the behavior that has seemed suspicious. The housekeeper now says to the governess that, if she is seriously worried about all this, she ought to report it to the master. The governess, who has promised not to bother him, is afraid he would think her insane; and she imagines "his derision, his amusement, his contempt for the breakdown of my resignation at being left alone and for the fine machinery I had set in motion to attract his attention to my slighted charms." The housekeeper, hearing this, threatens to send for the master herself; the governess threatens to leave if she does. After this, for a considerable period, the visions no longer appear.

But the children become uneasy: they wonder when their uncle is coming, and they try to communicate with him—but the governess suppresses their letters. The boy finally asks her frankly when she is going to send him to school, intimates that if he had not been so fond of her, he would have complained to his uncle long ago, declares that he will do so at once.

This upsets her: she thinks for a moment of leaving, but decides that this would be deserting them. She is now, it seems, in love with the boy. Entering the schoolroom, after her conver-sation with him, she finds the ghost of the other governess sitting with her head in her hands, looking "dishonored and tragic," full of "unutterable woe." At this point the new governess feels—the morbid half of her split personality is now getting the upper hand of the other—that it is she who is intruding upon the ghost: "You terrible miserable woman!" she cries. The apparition disappears. She tells the housekeeper, who looks at her oddly, that the soul of the woman is damned and wants the little girl to share her damnation. She finally agrees to write to the master, but no sooner has she sat down to the paper than she gets up and goes to the boy's bedroom, where she finds him lying awake. When he demands to go back to school, she embraces him and begs him to tell her why he was sent away; appealing to him with what seems to her desperate tenderness but in a way that disquiets the child, she insists that all she wants is to save him. There is a sudden gust of wind—it is a stormy night outside—the casement rattles, the boy shrieks. She has been kneeling beside the bed: when she gets up, she finds the candle extinguished. "It was I who blew it, dear!" says the boy. For her, it is the evil spirit disputing her domination. She cannot imagine that the boy may really have blown out the candle in order not to have to tell her with the light on about his disgrace at school. (Here, how-ever, occurs a detail which is less easily susceptible of double explanation: the governess has *felt* a "gust of frozen air" and yet sees that the window is "tight." Are we to suppose she merely fancied that she felt it?)

The next day, the little girl disappears. They find her beside the lake. The young woman for the first time now speaks openly to one of the children about the ghosts. "Where, my pet, is Miss Jessel?" she demands—and immediately answers herself: "She's there, she's there!" she cries, pointing across the lake. The housekeeper looks with a "dazed blink" and asks where she sees anything; the little girl turns upon the governess "an expression of hard, still gravity, an expression absolutely new and unprecedented and that appeared to read and accuse and judge me." The governess feels her "situation horribly crum-ble" now. The little girl breaks down, becomes feverish, begs to be taken away from the governess; the housekeeper sides with the child and hints that the governess had better go. But the young woman forces her, instead, to take the little girl away; and she tries to make it impossible, before their depar-ture, for the children to see one another.

She is now left alone with the boy. A strange and dreadful scene ensues. "We continued silent while the maid was with us—as silent, it whimsically occurred to me, as some young couple who, on their wedding-journey, at the inn, feel shy in the presence of the waiter." When the maid has gone, and she presses him to tell her the reason for his expulsion from school, the boy seems suddenly afraid of her. He finally confesses that he "said things"—to "a few," to "those he liked." It all sounds sufficiently harmless: there comes to her out of her "very pity the appalling alarm of his being perhaps innocent. It was for the instant confounding and bottomless, for if he *were* innocent, when then on earth was I?" The valet appears at the window—it is "the white face of damnation." (But is it really the spirits who are damned or the governess who is slipping to damnation herself?) She is aware that the boy does not see it. "No more, no more, no more!" she shrieks to the apparition. "Is she *here*?" demands the boy in panic. (He has, in spite of the governess' efforts, succeeded in seeing his sister, and has heard from her of the incident at the lake.) No, she says, it is not the woman: "But it's at the window—straight before us. It's *there*!" . . . "It's *he*?" then. Whom does he mean by "he"? "'Peter Quint—you devil!' His face gave again, round the room, its convulsed supplication. 'Where?'" "What does he matter now, my own?" she cries. "What will he *ever* matter? I have you, but he has lost you forever!" Then she shows him that the figure has vanished: "There, *there*!" she says, pointing toward the window. He looks and gives a cry; she feels that he is dead in her arms. From the governess' point of view, the final disappearance of the spirit has proved too terrible a shock for the child and "his little heart, dispossessed, has stopped"; but if we study the dialogue from the other point of view, we see that he must have taken her "There, *there*!" as an answer to his own "Where?" Instead of persuading him that there is nothing to be frightened of, she has, on the contrary, finally convinced him either that he has actually seen or that he is just about to see some horror. He gives "the cry of a creature hurled over an abyss." She has literally frightened him to death.

When one has once got hold of the clue to this meaning of *The Turn of the Screw,* one wonders how one could ever have missed it. There is a very good reason, however, in the fact that nowhere does James unequivocally give the thing away: almost everything from beginning to end can be read equally in either of two senses. In the preface to the collected edition, however, as Miss Kenton has pointed out, James does seem to want to give a hint [see excerpt dated 1908]. He asserts that *The Turn of the Screw* is "a fairy-tale pure and simple"—but adds that the apparitions are of the order of those involved in witchcraft cases rather than of those in cases of psychic research. And he goes on to tell of his reply to one of his readers who objected that he had not characterized the governess sufficiently. At this criticism, he says, "One's artistic, one's ironic heart shook for the instant almost to breaking"; and he answered: "It was *'déjà trés-joli'* . . . please believe, the general proposition of our young woman's keeping crystalline her record of so many intense anomalies and obscurities—*by which I don't of course mean her explanation of them, a different matter* . . . She has 'authority,' which is a good deal to have given her . . ." The italics above are mine: these words seem impossible to explain except on the hypothesis of hallucination (though this is hardly consistent with the intention of writing "a fairy-tale pure and simple"). And note too, that in the collected edition James has not included *The Turn of the Screw* in the volume with his other ghost stories but with stories of another kind: between *The Aspern Papers* and *The Liar*—the

first a study of a curiosity which becomes a mania and menace . . . , the second a study of a pathological liar, whose wife protects his lies against the world, acting with very much the same sort of "authority" as the governess in *The Turn of the Screw.*

When we look back in the light of these hints, we are inclined to conclude from analogy that the story is primarily intended as a characterization of the governess: her somber and guilty visions and the way she behaves about them seem to present, from the moment we examine them from the obverse side of her narrative, an accurate and distressing picture of the poor country parson's daughter, with her English middle-class class-consciousness, her inability to admit to herself her natural sexual impulses and the relentless English "authority" which enables her to put over on inferiors even purposes which are totally deluded and not at all in the other people's best interests. Remember, also, in this connection, the peculiar psychology of governesses, who, by reason of their isolated position between the family and the servants, are likely to become ingrown and morbid. One has heard of actual cases of women who have frightened a household by opening doors or smashing mirrors and who have succeeded in torturing parents by mythical stories of kidnappers. The traditional "poltergeist" who breaks crockery and upsets furniture has been for centuries a recurring phenomenon. First a figure of demonology, he later became an object of psychic research, and is now a recognized neurotic type.

Once we arrive at this conception of *The Turn of the Screw,* we can see in it a new significance in its relation to Henry James's other work. We find now that it is a variation on one of his familiar themes: the thwarted Anglo-Saxon spinster. . . . (pp. 88-95)

Edmund Wilson, "The Ambiguity of Henry James," *in his* The Triple Thinkers: Twelve Essays on Literary Subjects, *revised edition, Oxford University Press, 1948, pp. 88-132.*

N. BRYLLION FAGIN   (essay date 1941)

[*In the following excerpt, Fagin proposes an allegorical interpretation, in opposition to the Freudian view, of James's novella.*]

The danger in the psychoanalytic method of criticism lies in its apparent plausibility. To Mr. Wilson, for instance, the young governess who narrates the story of *The Turn of the Screw* is "a neurotic case of sex repression" [see excerpt dated 1934]. And that, from a psychoanalytic point of view, is a plausible hypothesis. The daughter of a poor country parson, she has fallen in love with the children's guardian, "a bachelor in the prime of life," eligible and charming. Alone with her young charges, she wanders about the estate thinking of its master and thus comes upon the ghost of Quint, the valet, who is wearing the master's smart clothes. Quint, in Wilson's theory, "has been ambiguously confused"—in the governess's mind—"with the master and with the master's interest in her."

Mr. Wilson is less clear about the symbolism of Miss Jessel's ghost. The former governess had apparently had an affair with Quint and had been an accomplice in corrupting the children. "Observe," says Wilson, "from the Freudian point of view, the significance of the governess's interest in the little girl's pieces of wood and of the fact that the male apparition first appears on a tower and the female apparition on a lake." These hints, however, fail to explain Miss Jessel's symbolic necessity in James's Freudian pattern, and Wilson wisely drops her completely and devotes himself to Quint and his influence on little Miles.

The trouble with Wilson's interpretation—and Miss Edna Kenton's (to whose theory Mr. Wilson acknowledges indebtedness)—is that, although it may carry an air of plausibility, it clearly has no relation to James's intention. Mr. Wilson is, presumably, aware of the fact that Freudian psychology was something Henry James could not have been conscious of dealing with; he therefore places *The Turn of the Screw,* along with *Moby Dick* and the *Alice* books, among the "small group of fairy tales whose symbols exert a peculiar power by reason of the fact that they have behind them, *whether or not the authors are aware of it,* a profound grasp of subconscious processes." But by the same method it is possible to build up an excellent case for a Freudian interpretation of *Hamlet,* and surely that would not be reflective of Shakespeare's intention. Although it might be an interesting disclosure of the workings of the psychoanalyst's mind, it would tell us little or nothing about Shakespeare's. *The Turn of the Screw,* if read as Edmund Wilson reads it, becomes orthodox James Joyce or D. H. Lawrence; it ceases to be Henry James. Wilson fails to take advantage of much that we know of James's life, personality, and concepts and methods of art. In the light of this knowledge it is possible to read *The Turn of the Screw* more simply and, it seems to this writer, more convincingly. (pp. 197-98)

In simple terms, *The Turn of the Screw* is an allegory which dramatizes the conflict between Good and Evil. The apparitions are the personifications of evil; they are like Emerson's dead men's thoughts by which we permit ourselves to be guided, and like Ibsen's ghosts which come to haunt Mrs. Alving. The governess, the parson's daughter, is a sort of Guardian Angel, hovering protectingly over the two innocent children placed in her charge.

Read this way, the numerous hints throughout the story become significant and fall into the pattern. Perhaps even the names of the characters may have been selected with conscious aptness: Miles, the little show-off, who seizes every opportunity to flaunt the "badness" that is within him; Flora, part lovely flower and part wanton weed; Mrs. Grose, a simple, illiterate, undiscerning person. But it is not important to stress this point. The governess herself has no name: she's merely a point of view, that of a clergyman's daughter, for whom Evil would have strong and sinister power. Both children are outwardly angelically beautiful. How could they be corrupt? Yet Quint dominates the tower of their home, Quint who has red hair and red whiskers, the conventional guise of the Devil. The children want to get to the two horrors. "But for what?" asks the good and simple Mrs. Grose. "For the love of all the evil that . . . the pair put into them," says the governess. "And to ply them with that evil still, to keep up the work of demons, is what brings the others back."

All this is reminiscent of Hawthorne, of "Young Goodman Brown" and "Rappaccini's Daughter." And, indeed, these two stories were pronounced by James as "little masterpieces"; they were, in his opinion, representative of "the highest point that Hawthorne reached" in the field of fantasy and allegory. The purposes for which Quint seeks to meet little Miles are the same old purposes for which the Devil met young Goodman Brown in the woods near Salem. And little Flora is another Beatrice Rappaccini, outwardly marvelously beautiful, but inwardly corrupted by the poison of evil. Miss Jessel's rôle in the story is, of course, the same as that of Quint, although her

inclusion at all is probably due to James's sense of artistic balance. Miss Jessel is to Flora what Quint is to Miles; each is a corrupting influence: and each helps to complicate and thicken the texture of a capital story—which is what *The Turn of the Screw* set out primarily to be; it is an allegory only secondarily. The rôles of the uncle and Mrs. Grose have less significance; primarily they help the physical story; secondarily, they represent lack of vigilance, nay, indifference (especially the uncle) to the possibilities of evil.

It is logical for the governess to be tempted to run away from it all, but Duty keeps her on the spot, fighting for the souls of her charges. It is almost as if Hawthorne's Salem ancestors were writing about little Flora: "She was not at these times a child, but an old, old woman." Evil *is* old. After Mrs. Grose finally takes Flora away, the governess remains with Miles to extract his confession. "If he confesses," she says, "he's saved." But he doesn't confess—entirely. For just then Quint appears to make his last stand against the governess. As soon as Miles admits that he took the letter Quint disappears and "the air is clear again." Just as Miles is about to confess what things he had said at school Quint reappears, "as if to blight his [Miles's] confession and stay his answer." In the end the Agent of Good is almost successful, but little Miles is dead, like Beatrice Rappaccini, exhausted by the ordeal. "Frightened to death," says Edmund Wilson. More likely too corrupted to live without evil, like the beautiful wife in Hawthorne's "The Birthmark," whose husband, a surgeon, removed the one blemish to her perfect beauty, only to find that it was imbedded in her heart.

It is possible, of course, that we have read into this novelette more than its author intended it to convey. Perhaps it is really nothing but "a shameless pot-boiler" and our readings of it are merely fanciful? "I am only afraid," wrote James to Dr. Louis Waldstein, "that my conscious intention strikes you as having been larger than I deserve it should be thought." And yet, a little later, "*But,* of course, where there *is* life, there's truth, and the truth was at the back of my head." What was at the back of James's head is worth surmising, in the light of what we know of his ideas, his preoccupations, his methods, and, above all, the literary influences he acknowledged. This is not the same thing as surmising "subconscious processes" in the light of Freud. (pp. 200-02)

N. Bryllion Fagin, "Another Reading of 'The Turn of the Screw'," in MLN, Vol. LVI, No. 3, March, 1941, pp. 196-202.

KATHERINE ANNE PORTER, ALLEN TATE, AND MARK VAN DOREN (essay date 1942)

[*Porter, Tate, and Van Doren are regarded as three of the most prominent American literary figures in the first half of the twentieth century. Porter is widely acknowledged to be one of mid-century America's finest writers of short fiction. Tate, whose criticism is closely associated with two critical movements, the Agrarians and the New Critics, was a conservative thinker who attacked the tradition of Western philosophy which he felt has alienated persons from themselves, one another, and from nature by divorcing intellectual from natural functions in human life. Van Doren, whose work includes poetry, fiction, drama, criticism, and social commentary, examined in his criticism the inner, idealistic life of the individual. In the following excerpt from a radio symposium, Porter, Tate, and Van Doren discuss the supposed reality of the ghosts in* The Turn of the Screw, *as well as the character of the governess and the dominant themes of the novella. While they all reject the Freudian reading of the story, they also dispute some tenets of the apparitionist view, including the corruption of the children.*]

VAN DOREN: This great and famous story is told by a governess, who lets us know how she saw two children under her charge, a little boy and a little girl, in an English house of indeterminate antiquity and solitude, corrupted by the ghosts of two evil servants, recently dead. Now the first question we shall be expected to settle, if we can, is the question whether all that happens, all that is seen, is in the mind of the governess, or whether—or to what extent—there are objective existences here over which she has no control.

TATE: Mr. Van Doren, if you mean by "objective existences" only those existences which can be seen visually, I would say no, except in so far as the governess sees them; but I think there are objective existences which don't manifest themselves visually. Again, I think that these apparitions, in so far as they become agents in the action affecting human lives, are just as real as if they were people in the sense that we are people around a table. I don't want to quibble about it, but I think that a discussion along that line is the way to get at it.

VAN DOREN. Is that true for you, Miss Porter? Does it seem to you a false problem if I state it by asking whether everything happens in the mind of the governess or nothing does?

PORTER: When I first read this story, I accepted the governess's visions as real, that is, the ghosts were real in themselves, and not only the governess, perhaps, but others might have seen them; they had a life of their own. But as I went on reading the story and studying it through the years, and I read Henry James's notes on it, I decided that the ghosts were a projection of the governess's imagination and were part of her plot.

TATE: It is evident, Miss Porter, isn't it, that nobody actually sees these people but the governess?

PORTER: Nobody.

TATE: James is very adroit in convincing the readers that perhaps they can be seen by other people, or have been, but if you look closely it is perfectly evident that nobody sees them as physical existences but the governess. I don't say that that destroys their reality.

PORTER: Not at all.

VAN DOREN: And, of course, there's no possible doubt that she does see them. The statement "the governess sees the ghosts" is a true statement.

TATE: Oh, there's no question of that.

VAN DOREN: Not only does she have no doubt herself, but it never occurs to her that anyone else could question their presence.

TATE: She has a momentary doubt of a certain kind, Mr. Van Doren. Doesn't she say toward the end that if Flora goes out into the world and people come in from outside—for example, her employer, the uncle of the children—and look at the situation and find that the apparitions don't visually exist, then she will have to say: "Where am I?" Those are her exact words.

VAN DOREN: Yes, and there is one moment when Mrs. Grose, the housekeeper, the plain and simple woman of the story, fails to see Miss Jessel, the evil governess who has died.

TATE: That is one of the most interesting moments in the whole story.

VAN DOREN: The present governess even then, as you say, seems to understand that she may be lost if she can't make Mrs. Grose see this woman who is "as big as a blazing fire," for then she has no case. She does seem, at that moment, to think of herself as one having a case.

TATE: She has been so hard-pressed that she feels she must build the case herself even at the expense of the children. That is the sinister note which enters the second half of the story.

PORTER: In her attempt to vindicate herself she's doing the whole thing really at the expense of the children—I have always believed for the sake of destroying them, of putting them out of the way in some manner or other in order to clear a road to the master.

TATE: I agree with Miss Porter. But does the governess realize that consciously?

PORTER: No, never.

VAN DOREN: Well, this is the question then that frames itself in my mind: are we to take the story as a piece of psychology, as an exploration of a peculiar temperament, namely, the governess', suffering under illusions and hallucinations? I prefer not to take it that way. It seems to me that the story would shrink a great deal in power and significance if it were merely a story which psychoanalyzed an old maid.

TATE: I think we've got to take it that way and the other way, too—both at once—and perhaps if we take it both ways, we've got to take it in a third way which will explain the fact that the story is a unified thing, a single thing which is neither psychological wholly nor a mere naive attempt on the part of this governess to protect her children.

VAN DOREN: You see, I am interested in Miss Porter's statement that the first time she read the story she believed the governess. This is certainly true for me.

TATE: And for me, too.

VAN DOREN: And it still is. The first time Miss Porter read the story, it never occurred to her that the evil personified in these two persons—at least these two, because Miss Porter would add a third, or . . .

PORTER: Even a fourth, perhaps—

VAN DOREN: . . . all right, that the evil somehow was there. Now, I think we must take that as a fact. If the story were merely—I'm agreeing with you, Mr. Tate—if the story were merely a clever piece of psychology, no reader, even a child, would feel in it the powerful presence of evil.

TATE: That's absolutely right. It seems to me that given the time in which James lived and the growing interest then in the processes of the mind, we have to see James as taking that peculiar interest as a medium through which to set forth the reality of evil; because the reality of evil in this story is not destroyed, or made a false issue, by explaining it psychologically. In James's time the psychological basis was necessary. In the past, treatment of ghosts, the material projection of evil in earlier literature, didn't follow a psychological bent; it wasn't done psychologically; the evil creatures were presented in their full physical body and the public accepted them at their face value. We have become more sophisticated, and perhaps a little more decadent in our literature—certainly more critical. Don't we demand that all of these allegorical effects, all of these realities of evil, be set forth on some level that will also satisfy the critical point of view?

PORTER: Yes, that is important. James himself confessed that he wished to catch those not easily caught.

VAN DOREN: Exactly.

PORTER: And he made in effect booby-traps of a very high order, with a great deal of wit and a great deal of good humor. But I was thinking that one of the really interesting levels of analysis in this story is theological, admitting the existence of original sin, of the fact that we really are conceived in sin, brought forth in iniquity. I think that is a very interesting point in the study of this story.

TATE: Wasn't James always preoccupied with evil?

PORTER: Yes.

VAN DOREN: That is one reason we call him a great writer.

TATE: But wasn't his problem then to make that evil as dramatically convincing as possible?

VAN DOREN: Yes, but I think of him as suffering under the limitations which modern literature and the critical mind imposed upon him. He wasn't able to ask us to believe that anything like Furies or devils existed. Aeschylus could put the Furies on his stage, and even Shakespeare could put on a ghost. All James was able to do was to ask us to believe in the return—somehow—of two very evil individuals. They are not devils; they don't represent evil; they simply *are* evil. A very bad man, Peter Quint.

PORTER: Known to have been bad, yes. And the woman, known to have been bad.

VAN DOREN: A very tragic and dishonored woman, Miss Jessel.

TATE: Now, are they described as necessarily evil during their lives? My feeling is that they were merely "bad." Couldn't we make this distinction: that this story is not about good and bad, but about good and evil? The question of the way in which James makes evil dramatic and convincing has always fascinated me in this book. If you will remember, Quint first appears dressed in the master's clothes; it is the first thing the governess notices about him. Then she notices that he has red hair, and strange pointed eyebrows, and . . .

PORTER: All the physical attributes of the legendary devil.

TATE: Exactly.

PORTER: The evil eye.

TATE: Precisely. And I think James is playing with us a little there—bringing in an additional dimension of the imagination. But when she tells Mrs. Grose about Quint, it seems to me that James's dramatic powers, his powers as a writer of fiction, are at their very highest, because his job is to insert Quint into the scene and make him an actor in it, and that is very difficult. In order to do that, he must have the governess get some objective verification for her vision, and the way in which the governess makes the simple Mrs. Grose identify Quint establishes him in the scene. Well, that is—if you wish—a trick of fiction. It is the novelist's technique. Actually, at the same time, it doesn't invalidate Quint as an evil person. That's the ambivalent thing in the story.

VAN DOREN: And of course there are some wonderful strokes as Quint is painted. Remember, his first two appearances do

Lamb House, James's residence during the time he wrote The Turn of the Screw.

not reveal anything except the upper half of him. Once he is standing behind a sort of balustrade on top of the tower; another time he is merely looking in a window, but the lower half of him is not there—it is as if he were in some ghastly way truncated. I am also interested in the fact that he is pale—that he has a pale face with light hair. If he is the devil, at least he is a very special sort of devil; he's not swarthy or grimacing; his face is rigid. He has a thin face and light curly red hair.

TATE: He never changes his expression. I recall something that James says in his preface to this book about the presentation of supernatural creatures in fiction. We must remember that neither Quint nor Miss Jessel ever does much of anything; they just appear; they just stand there and look—and their mere appearance is enough to set all this machinery of horror into motion.

VAN DOREN: That's enough, incidentally.

TATE: Yes. He says supernatural creatures should do as little as possible, as little as is "consistent with their consenting to appear at all."

VAN DOREN: Exactly. The awful thing is that they should appear.

PORTER: The one thing we haven't talked about yet is the role of the children in this story. This, I think, is terribly important, because the governess persistently tries to fix upon the children evil motives and base actions, and takes seriously an accusation made against the little boy by the head-master of the school when he is sent home with a note saying that he had been an immoral influence. She was using this accusation as a weapon against the little boy—a kind of moral blackmail. The girl, who was in some ways a simpler nature, I think, and of a more positive mind than the little boy, was uncomplicated by the fact that she had had no sad experiences. Well, their simplest and most natural acts are interpreted by the governess as being of a suspicious nature, even when they got up in the night and went out to look at the moonlight, and that sort of thing. The governess constantly attempts to draw the children into her orbit of evil and force them to share it and prove them guilty. She transfers her guilty motives to them, making them accomplices to justify herself. But it seems to me that their conduct is perfectly simple and intuitive. They surmise the purpose and the enormous threat to them . . .

TATE: But the threat was real, wasn't it, Miss Porter?

PORTER: Very real. The children were frightened for good reasons, though they did not understand anything; they acted with the curious reserved defensiveness of children who don't know what is happening to them. They surmised evil, surmised the threat and were trying to escape. They even tried to get together to confide in each other, but the governess made constant efforts to keep them separate so that they would never be able to work up a common defense against her.

VAN DOREN: She assumes that when they are together they talk unspeakably evil things.

PORTER: Yes.

VAN DOREN: But I wonder if we're not a bit misleading about the governess. I quite agree that the children are in some sense innocent, beautiful and clear. But so is the governess. We are suggesting that she is more sinister than she ever, at any rate, knows herself as being.

TATE: She never knows herself as being sinister.

VAN DOREN: We almost have imputed to her a plot to corrupt the children herself. Now I'm willing to believe that it is she who corrupts the children and brings about the death of the little boy. Nevertheless, that is precisely my way of understanding how potent the evil in this story is. The evil isn't merely thought to be; it is an actuality which passes through her as a perfectly transparent and non-resistant medium and then passes through the children. The evil is somehow there.

PORTER: And finally it is projected to an immense distance.

VAN DOREN: Yes, for she has great power. If it were merely a story of what she thought, of what she could fool herself into seeing, she wouldn't have the power she has over us as readers; she wouldn't be able, as you say, to project Quint and Miss Jessel to great distances, across lakes; to the tops of towers, and so on.

TATE: Mr. Van Doren, couldn't we put it this way? The governess doesn't invent these apparitions; they merely use her as a medium. Because, obviously, the monstrous proportions of the evil are so great that they are beyond the power of any individual imagination to invent. There is something much stronger than the governess operating through her. She has her own innocent later existence, as is proved, I think, by the prologue of the story, where we learn that after this terrible incident had passed, she went on to other posts and nothing like it occurred again. It was some peculiar conjunction of forces which permitted this evil to merge through her here.

VAN DOREN: That is extremely interesting, Mr. Tate. You suggest to me another reason why James is a great writer. Living as he did in our time, which usually does not take stock in either good or evil, he was able to construct in the governess a creature almost like Cassandra, through whom evil tears its way without any instigation on her part at all—without, so to speak, her permission.

TATE: Don't you feel then that the governess, at the end of the story, in spite of the fact that you see what she's done, has a certain dignity of her own, that she is a person of great proportions? She is not in the least an insignificant creature.

VAN DOREN: She is no such creature as a story-teller makes his victim when he wants to deal in mere delusion. She is not ridiculous or trivial. As a matter of fact, she becomes tragic.

TATE: Exactly. It's her tragedy.

VAN DOREN: Of course, individual creatures can be the vehicles or channels of great good also. Just as Cassandra is a person through whom evil tears, so a saint may be a person through whom good pours in floods.

PORTER: An illuminant is not always an illuminant for good. The most dangerous people in the world are the illuminated ones through whom forces act when they themselves are unconscious of their own motives. And yet, no force has ever acted through either a saint or an evil person that wasn't somehow directed to further the ends and the ambitions and the hopes of that person, which makes me feel that the instrument is not altogether so innocent and so helpless as we have been saying. Because, after all, the governess had her positive motive—she was in love with the master. She had a deep sense of her inferior situation in life, and was almost hopeless of ever attracting his attention. And I do think that this love, which was quite hopeless, which was an ingrown thing, took this form; she herself, in her imagination—yes, unconscious of her motives—designed all this drama to make the desired situation possible—that she would arrive somewhere at a level with the man she loved and create some sort of communication with him.

TATE: I agree with you, Miss Porter, but it has always seemed to me that that level of the governess's experience—that is, her personal motivation, what she expected to get out of it and all that—has a perfectly naturalistic basis. Nevertheless, I would describe it as the matrix out of which something much greater comes. As a matter of fact, we can go back and take the great tragic characters in drama, or the great religious heroes, too. They will all have some psychological motivation which we can see in terms of their peculiar situations. At the same time, are we agreed that in the case of the true saints, of the great tragic heroes, possibly in the case of the governess here, the psychological basis doesn't explain it all?

PORTER: The popular psychological explanation is too superficial.

VAN DOREN: Otherwise we should be aware that an explanation is ready and easy as we read along, whereas the truth is—we all grant this—that as we read along we're not explaining anything to ourselves at all. We're not saying: Well, a dreadful, dreadful thing is happening, yet we know the reason. In a very important sense we don't know the reason. Something is loose here in the world, if only in the mind of a woman. Something is loose in the world which is very powerful and beyond the control of any human being.

PORTER: I would say quite beyond the Freudian explanation.

VAN DOREN: Oh, Decidedly.

PORTER: Here is one place where I find Freud completely defeated.

TATE: James knew substantially all that Freud knew before Freud came on the scene.

PORTER: All major artists do.

VAN DOREN: Any great story-teller has to, because a great story-teller has for his subject good and evil.

TATE: There is an aspect of this story which has always interested me very much. It is what we might call the technical aspects. I should think readers of the story would be very much interested in how James established the realities of these things which would otherwise be incredible. Consider the fact that the story is told by a governess and the fact that, as Mr. Van Doren said some time ago, in reading it we tend to forget that the governess is telling it; we think we are actually participating. That is due, I think, to the great art of James. Isn't it true that one trouble with the first-person narrative, the story told by somebody in the story, is that the authority of that person is usually not quite established? We say usually of such a person: she is participating in it, you can't expect her to give us an unbiased version of it; she's not sufficiently detached; she's not disinterested. But, while that's a liability in most first-person narratives, it seems to me that James's triumph consists in the fact that he has been able to take the defect of the method and use it for a positive purpose. The very fact that the governess is biased becomes a dramatic factor. The bias becomes a part of the story.

PORTER: Yes, and because she has no understanding at all of her real motive, she gives herself away completely and constantly.

TATE: Constantly. There are two levels: the level at which she sees the action and the level at which the reader can see it, and this creates an irony of which the governess is not aware.

VAN DOREN: She is not aware, for instance, of how much it is against her own nature and her own desire to plague the little boy at the end, to make him tell more and more and more about the bad things he had done. They turn out to be rather slight things, don't you think? No reader assumes that the little boy has done anything very bad.

TATE: Nothing bad at all.

PORTER: Some vague little offense against Victorian morality, no doubt.

VAN DOREN: Yet the governess all along has wanted to spare the children. Indeed, her declared intention was to protect, to shield them. Here she is forced by the irony of her character and fate to torture this little boy into confessions which he doesn't want to make, which he doesn't even know how to make because he has nothing to confess.

TATE: Isn't that a wonderful scene in Miles's room at night? The governess comes—it bears out just what you were saying, Mr. Van Doren—she comes to have a talk with him, as you will remember, and to try to get out of him what he did at school. It's a general stock-taking of Miles's situation. It is one of the most powerful pieces of irony I've ever read, because the governess is actually making love to the little boy and she doesn't know it. But he knows it in a curious instinctive way; he blows the candle out to get rid of her.

PORTER: And the scene is wonderfully written—his terror at this visit in the night, with what for him was ghost or devil, all evil in fact, everything he had reason to be terrified of, coming into his room with that unpardonable invasion of his privacy—this is all projected with such admirable simplicity and directness that the reader forgets the words and shares the impression.

VAN DOREN: His very childish understanding of the fact that she is in love with him comes out, it seems to me, in the conversation in which he suggests that he should be going back to school now, because, after all, he's just a "fellow," and has no right to spend all of his time with a lady.

TATE: He shows something perfectly wonderful there. It is so simple that the implications are sometimes lost on the reader. He is sitting with her and there's a silence. The governess says, "Well, here we are." And Miles says, "Yes, we're here." Just like that.

VAN DOREN: That's right. But again it seems to me that the fame of this story among all of James's stories is justified by the fact that the evil in it somehow remains pure and general, remains undefined. All of the attempts on the part of the governess to find out what it is, after all, are frustrated. There is never any danger that evil will shrink here into vice, into misdemeanor.

TATE: James says that evil is never credible in fiction if it is presented in "weak specifications."

VAN DOREN: We have all had the experience of reading a story about some villain whom we can believe to be unspeakable— we like to believe in unspeakable villains—and then of being shocked by the discovery that all he did was murder his grandmother. That never is enough.

PORTER: Yes, nearly always the specific act, the crime, does seem inadequate compared to the great force of evil which produces it.

VAN DOREN. I am reminded of Iago, whose evil is never explained by the specific motives he is said to have, and even himself thinks he has. Iago thinks that he is jealous of Othello, but it isn't jealousy, it isn't ambition, it isn't anything you can name at all. That is why Iago is a force. He is one of these figures who are being used.

TATE. But he's an evil figure, not merely a bad one. There's a fundamental difference between the evil and the bad.

VAN DOREN: Good and evil is the distinction. I wonder if everyone agrees with us that the great theme is good and evil. We keep saying so.

PORTER: Yes, or rather the conflict between them in the minds of men.

VAN DOREN: Do you suppose anyone doubts us?

TATE: Otherwise we get merely social literature, the literature of social problems, political and economic literature.

PORTER: I think that during the nineteenth century, when the perfectability of man was an accepted doctrine, James was one of the few who had this genuine knowledge of good and evil, and the courage to take it as his theme. (pp. 223-35)

> *Katherine Anne Porter, Allen Tate, and Mark Van Doren, in a radio symposium "James: 'The Turn of the Screw'," in* The New Invitation to Learning, *edited by Mark Van Doren, Random House, 1942, pp. 223-35.*

ROBERT B. HEILMAN   (essay date 1947)

[*Heilman is an American educator, poet, and critic. In the following excerpt, he disputes Freudian interpretations of* The Turn of the Screw.]

The Freudian reading of Henry James' *The Turn of the Screw*, which has had some currency in recent decades, does violence not only to the story but also to the Preface, which, like the story, demands scrupulous attention. The Freudian reading was first given public expression by Edna Kenton in 1924 [see excerpt above]; her view is that the ghosts and the attendant horrors are imagined by the neurotic governess, "trying to harmonize her own disharmonies by creating discords outside herself." Miss Kenton, however, adduces almost no evidence to sustain her interpretation, but simply enjoys a gracefully gleeful revel in the conviction that James, by permitting the ghosts to seem real, has utterly fooled all the other readers of the story. She is sure that this is so because of James's prefatory remark upon his intention "to catch those not easily caught"; but all James is doing in the passage quoted from is relishing—and deservedly, we may say—the success, with adult audiences, of what he modestly calls a "fairy-tale pure and simple"; he is talking about nothing more—as if this is not enough—than his having evoked the willing suspension of disbelief in those who by situation and experience might be supposed to be more than ordinarily skeptical. His tone is simply not that of one who has proudly hoaxed the credulous; it is that of one meditating upon an aesthetic problem. He points out, shrewdly, that the way to create belief in "portentous evil" is to present an undefined evil to the reader's imagination. Miss Kenton, most oddly, considers this choice of method a validation of her own definition of the evil. The dispassionate judge must conclude: *non sequitur*.

A decade or so later Edmund Wilson sets out to provide what we might call the scholarly foundation for the airy castle of Miss Kenton's intuitions: in an essay entitled "The Ambiguity of Henry James" he sets forth an astonishingly *unambiguous* exegesis of *The Turn of the Screw* [see excerpt dated 1934]. Wilson also misreads the preface—most conspicuously in the explanation, essential to his own case, that James, when he says he has given the governess "authority," means "the relentless English 'authority' which enables her to put over on inferiors even purposes which are totally deluded. . . ." It must be said unequivocally: James *means nothing of the kind*. In the context he is talking merely about technical problems of composition, and what he is saying is, to use the trite terms of the rhetoric book, that he is telling the story entirely from the governess's point of view. What is involved, too, is his general theory that the raw materials of the ghost story, to be effective, must be presented through a recording and interpreting consciousness; prodigies "keep all their character, . . . by looming through some other history—the indspensable history of somebody's *normal* [the italics are James's] relation to something." Once again, then, the word *authority* has brought about, in an unwary liberal, an emotional spasm which has resulted in a kind of hysterical blindness. James explains his inability to characterize the governess fully: it was enough of an aesthetic task to present the "young woman's keeping crystalline her record of so many intense anomalies and obscurities—by which I don't of course mean her explanation of them, a different matter; . . ." In the last clause James is merely, as a part of the statement of the technical problem, distinguishing two phases of the material presented through the governess—the phenomena she had observed, and her commentary upon them. Yet Wilson supposes that James is here giving it away that the governess has hallucinations! Wilson then continues with a general conclusion about the story that runs counter to a major statement of the preface—a statement which Wilson simply ignores. He insists that the story is "primarily intended as a characterization of the governess: . . ." James says flatly, ". . . I saw no way, . . . to exhibit her in relations other than those; one of which, precisely, would have been her relation to her own nature." Besides, James makes this statement even more unequivocally in a letter to H. G. Wells in 1898:

> Of course I had, about my young woman, to take a very sharp line. The grotesque business I had to make her picture and the childish psychology I had to make her trace and present, were for me at least, a very difficult job, in which absolute lucidity and logic, a singleness of effect, were imperative. Therefore I had to rule out subjective complications of her own—play of tone etc.; and keep her impersonal save for the most obvious and indispensable little note of neatness, firmness and courage—without which she wouldn't have had her data.

Here James not only explicitly states that the governess is not his subject but also gives his word for it that the phenomena to which she plays the part of recording consciousness are objective.

Wilson says he knew an actual case of a governess who frightened parents and children because of her psychological difficulties. But James writes, in both Preface and letter, of a story he heard about the ghosts of "bad" servants which appeared in an effort to "get hold of" young children. We must decide whether James is writing about what he heard about or what Wilson heard about. Indeed, the sly Freudian readers of the Preface—who ignore the letters entirely—seem to miss its whole tone and import: James speaks continually of the ghosts as if they are objective manifestations, and there is no sign whatever of a knowing wink to the rationalists. He is concerned almost entirely with defining his technical problems and with observing, almost gaily, how satisfactorily they have been met.

The Freudians misread the internal evidence almost as valiantly as they do the external. In the story, of course, there are passages that it is possible to read ambivalently; but the determining unambiguous passages from which the critic might work are so plentiful that it seems hardly good critical strategy to use the ambiguous ones as points of departure, to treat them as if they were *un*ambiguous, and to roughride over the immitigable difficulties that then arise. We cannot examine all the passages to which Wilson does violence, but a consideration of several of them will show how wobbly his case is.

Wilson supposes the governess to be seeing ghosts because she is in a psychopathic state originating in a repressed passion for the master. In view of the terrible outcome of the story, we should at best have to suspect the fallacy of insufficient cause. But the cause does not exist at all: the governess's feelings for the master are never repressed: they are wholly in the open and are joyously talked about: even in the opening section which precedes Chapter 1, we are told that she is in love with him. There is no faint trace of the initial situation necessary to produce the distortion of personality upon which Wilson's analysis depends. But Wilson does compel us to consider one point: why does James emphasize the governess's fascinated devotion to the master? For an important technical reason: it is the only way of motivating—although it is probably not quite successful—the governess's stubborn refusal to take the logical step of over-riding the master's irresponsible wish not to be bothered and of calling him in. The master's presence would change the situation and the focus and thus the whole story which James had planned. His absence is a datum: James wrote to Dr. Louis Waldstein in 1898, "But ah, the exposure indeed, the helpless plasticity of childhood that isn't dear or sacred to *some*body. That *was* my little tragedy—. . ." It is possible to argue that James's strategy is faulty; indeed, that he himself sensed the weakness of the governess's not calling the master is suggested by the retrospective irony with which he makes her comment upon her rash assumption of adequacy to the situation. But a technical procedure should not be mistaken for a psychopathological clue.

When the governess describes the ghost to Mrs. Grose, Mrs. Grose identifies it with Quint, the dead valet, whom the governess had never so much as heard of; and Mrs. Grose gives him—and later Miss Jessel—a character which is entirely consistent with what the governess has already inferred about the moral quality and intentions of the ghost. There can be no firmer dramatic evidence of the objectivity of the apparition, and Wilson acknowledges the difficulty: but in order to sustain his contention that the hallucination grows out of the repressed passion for the uncle, he advances the incredible hypothesis that the governess has got master and man confused—which is inconsistent with her obviously having a sharp eye for distinctions—and that Quint and the uncle may look alike. Even at his most unsubtle, James would hardly be found thus trafficking in coincidence. But if he were, it can hardly be supposed that Mrs. Grose, who in such matters is very observant, would

not at some time comment upon the strange resemblance of master and man.

Like Miss Kenton, Wilson infers the unreality of the ghosts from the fact that *only* the governess acknowledges seeing them; he does not stop to consider that this fact may be wholly explicable in aesthetic terms. Of course Mrs. Grose does not see the ghosts: she is the good but slow-witted woman who sees only the obvious in life—for instance, the sexual irregularity of Quint and Miss Jessel—but does not unassisted detect the subtler manifestations of evil. She is the plain domestic type who is the foil for the sensitive, acute governess—Cassandra-like in the insight which outspeeds the perceptions of those about her—whose ideal function is to penetrate and shape the soul. James's fondness for allegorical names is commonplace knowledge: Mrs. Grose is not called Mrs. *Grose* for nothing (just as the governess is not the governess for nothing: the narrator exhibits the ideal function of the tutorial type). But as, little by little, the tangible evidence, such as that of Flora's language, corroborates the racing intuitions of the governess, Mrs. Grose comes to grasp the main points of the issue as it is seen totally by the governess and to share her understanding of the moral atmosphere. The acceptance by Mrs. Grose is unimpeachable substantiation. We ought to observe here, also, how carefully the governess records all the initial doubts felt by Mrs. Grose in each new crisis—doubts which at times shake her belief in her own mental soundness. This is one of James's ways of establishing the reliability of the governess.

As for the children's appearing not to see the apparitions: this is one of the author's finest artistic strokes. James says that he wants to evoke a sense of evil: one of his basic ways of doing it is the suggestion, by means of the symbolic refusal to acknowledge the ghosts, of a sinisterly mature concealment of evil. But almost as if to guard against the mistaking of the denial of the ghosts for the non-existence of the ghosts, James takes care to buttress our sense of the reality of evil from another direction: he gives us the objective fact of the dismissal of Miles from school—a dismissal which is unexplained and which is absolutely final. This dismissal Wilson, in plain defence of the text, must attempt to put aside as of no consequence; of such a situation he says, indeed frivolously, that the governess "colors [it], on no evidence at all, with a significance somehow sinister." James invests the letter from the school with further significance by the fact that, despite her real shock, which is elaborated later, Mrs. Grose finds a private meaning in the dismissal—"She gave me a look that I remarked at the moment; then, visibly, with a quick blankness, seemed to try to take it back"; so, unless we are to repudiate the governess's testimony entirely, the letter gains dramatic value through what it intimates to Mrs. Grose. Further, Wilson cannot deal with the fact that at the end of the final scene Miles, without hearing them spoken by anyone else, speaks the names of Miss Jessel and Quint and indicates his belief that they may be present. Again in plain defiance of the text Wilson says that Miles has managed to see Flora before her departure and thus to find out what the governess is thinking about. Wilson says they met; James clearly indicates that they did not. But even if they had met, their meeting would not help Wilson especially. From Flora Miles might have learned the name "Miss Jessel"; but his spontaneous bursting forth with "Peter Quint" would still have to be explained.

Wilson admits that one point is inexplicable: the "gust of frozen air" felt by the governess when, at Miles's bedside, her effort to break down his moral resistance to her is interrupted by his shriek, a shaking of the room, and sudden darkness. Despite her feeling a strong blast, no window is open. Wilson takes literally Miles's statement that he turned out the light and suggests that the motive is shame at having to tell about his disgrace at school. But, for one thing, Miles *does not tell* about his disgrace, and, more important, his turning out the light of his own accord is absolutely incompatible with the theory that the governess is unbalanced. If she is unbalanced we must assume, at this stage of the story, that the children sense her disorder and are humoring her and treating her very carefully, not engaging in violent pranks that might be expected to be dangerously aggravating.

There are still other parts of the story that, on the Freudian hypothesis, are wholly inexplicable. First, as we have seen, is the fact that Mrs. Grose always comes into agreement with the governess—an agreement that is especially forceful because it usually follows upon doubt and hesitation. Further—and this is a very large point—the Freudian hypothesis fails completely to deal with the conduct of the children. In the first place, their night-time escapades are, for an eight- and a ten-year-old, virtually beyond the bounds of physical possibility. Wilson says blandly that the children "are able to give plausible explanations of their behavior"; but the fact is that children of that age simply are not wide awake, imaginatively alert, and capable of strategic maneuvering in the middle of the night. The fact that they are earnestly and imperturbably plotting in the middle of the night, and that they are sophisticatedly evasive in their gay response to questioning, is one of James's subtlest ways of suggesting moral disorder. What Wilson takes to be their "plausibility" is an index of their corruption. Second, the children's daytime conduct makes sense only in the light of the ostensible meaning of the story—the entertainment of the governess by one of them while the other escapes, Flora's difficult solitary trip on the final Sunday afternoon, her crossing the pond in a boat and hiding the boat apparently unaided ("All alone—that child?" exclaims Mrs. Grose), her majestically noncommittal manner when she is found strangely alone at a considerable distance from the house. Wilson simply ignores all these matters—ignores them as facts, and of course as the brilliant dramatic symbols they are of something unchildlike and inexplicably wrong. Third, there is the vulgarity of Flora's language after the governess has openly asked her about Miss Jessel—important evidence which can be intended only to show a temporarily concealed deterioration of character coming at last to the surface. Notably, too, it is Mrs. Grose who tells about this language and who, what is more, initiates the subject: "horrors," she calls what she has heard, showing no sign of suggestive pressure from the governess. Further, the whole manner of the children is incompatible with their being terrified and perverted by the "authority" of the governess. What is inescapable in them, despite the admirable subtlety with which all this is conveyed, is precisely their freedom, their skill in spending their time as they wish without open challenges, their marvelously disciplined catering to the governess—or appearing to do so—while doing exactly what they please. After Flora's departure what the governess especially feels is the slenderness of her personal, and the disappearance of her official, hold upon the boy. At no time do the children show any sign of unwillingness, compulsion, or fright—except in the final scene, in which Miles's fright, it seems logical to suppose, proceeds from the causes which the story says it does. In fact, James emphasizes strongly the falseness of Flora's apparent fear of the governess at the end by giving her a "grand manner about it" and having her ask "every three minutes" whether the governess is coming in and express a desire "never again to so much as look at you." These are signs of artifice, not fright; they indicate self-conscious acting, righteous indignation strategically adopted, the truculence of the guilty person who still seeks loopholes.

Such evidence suggests that a great deal of unnecessary mystery has been made of the apparent ambiguity of the story. Actually, most of it is a by-product of James's method: his indirection; his refusal, in his fear of anti-climax, to define the evil; his rigid adherence to point of view; his refusal—amused, perhaps?—to break that point of view for a reassuring comment on those uncomfortable characters, the apparitions. This theory seems to come very close to James's own view of the ambiguity, upon which, it conveniently happens, he commented in the year of the story's appearance. [To F.W.H. Myers, one of the founders of the Society for Psychical Research, James writes that he cannot give "any coherent account of my small inventions 'after the fact.' . . . The one thing and another that are questionable and ambiguous in them I mostly take to be conditions of their having got themselves pushed through at all."] The disturbing ghosts, of course, are to be taken as symbolic, a fact which the modern critic might easily grasp if he did not have to wrestle with another problem peculiarly uncongenial to modernity—the drama of salvation. The retreat into abnormal psychology is virtually predictable.

There is a final irony, however: if he does not break the chosen point of view, James at least does not adopt it until his main story is under way. At the start, then, we see behind the curtain and find important objective evidence for use in interpreting the governess's narrative. Now Miss Kenton, with considerable amusement at less observant readers, has discovered what she calls "the submerged and disregarded foreword," and what she has got from it is that the governess is in love with the master. Hence her whole interpretation. But had Miss Kenton herself read the foreword more observantly, she would have found the evidence that makes her interpretation untenable. For this initial section tells us what the governess was like some years later.

The governess, Wilson assures us, "has literally frightened him [Miles] to death": the neurotic approaches criminal insanity. For such an individual, only the gravest kind of prognosis could be made. We might expect progressive deterioriation, perhaps pathetic, perhaps horrible. We might barely conceive of a "cure," but we could hardly expect that it would obliterate all traces of the earlier disastrous tensions. What, then, does happen to the governess who at twenty is supposedly in so terrible a neurotic state? The prologue tells us explicitly: at the age of thirty or so she is still a spinster, still a governess, and therefore still heir, we may assume, to all psychic ills which Wilson imputes to her at the earlier stage. But at this age she seems, to a Cambridge undergradute whom, ten years her junior, we may expect to be thoroughly critical, a fine, gracious woman who can elicit liking and respect. She charms him so thoroughly that many years later he in no way repudiates, qualifies, or smiles at his youthful feeling. Many years later, in fact he can still say of her,

> She was a most charming person. . . . She was the most agreeable person I've ever known in her position; she would have been worthy of any whatever . . . she struck me as awfully clever and nice. . . . I liked her extremely and am glad to this day to think she liked me too.

To challenge this characterization of her one would have to challenge the testimony of a poised and graceful middle-aged gentleman; and, in addition to that, the testimony of the perceptive first-person narrator in the prologue, who is completely *en rapport* with the middle-aged gentleman. James's unqualified initial picture of the governess, then, is wholly irreconcilable with the Freudian interpretation of her. The conclusion is obvious: at twenty the governess was, aside from her unusual sensitiveness and charm, a perfectly normal person. (pp. 433-43)

Robert B. Heilman, "The Freudian Reading of 'The Turn of the Screw'," in MLN, Vol. LXII, No. 7, November, 1947, pp. 433-45.

ROBERT HEILMAN (essay date 1948)

[*In the following excerpt, Heilman interprets* The Turn of the Screw *as a Christian allegory which James constructed using various poetic devices. For a challenge to Heilman's reading of James's novella, see the essay by John Lyndenberg (1957).*]

It is probably safe to say that the Freudian interpretation of [*The Turn of the Screw*], of which the best known exponent is Edmund Wilson [see excerpt dated 1934], no longer enjoys wide critical acceptance. If, then, we cannot account for the evil by treating the governess as pathological, we must seek elsewhere an explanation of the story's hold. I am convinced that, at the level of action, the story means exactly what it says: that at Bly there are apparitions which the governess sees, which Mrs. Grose does not see but comes to believe in because they are consistent with her own independent experience, and of which the children have a knowledge which they endeavor to conceal. These dramatic circumstances have a symbolic import which seems not too difficult to get hold of: the ghosts are evil, evil which comes subtly, conquering before it is wholly seen; the governess, Cassandra-like in the intuitions which are inaccessible to others, is the guardian whose function it is to detect and attempt to ward off evil; Mrs. Grose—whose name, like the narrator's title, has virtually allegorical significance—is the commonplace mortal, well intentioned, but perceiving only the obvious; the children are the victims of evil, victims who, ironically, practice concealment—who doubtless must conceal—when not to conceal is essential to salvation. If this reading of the symbolism be tenable, we can understand in part the imaginative power of the story, for, beneath the strange and startling action-surface, we have the oldest of themes—the struggle of evil to possess the human soul. And if this struggle appears to resolve itself into a Christian form, that impulse, as it were, of the materials need not be surprising.

But the compelling theme and the extraordinarily vivid plot-form are not the entirety of *The Turn of the Screw;* there are other methods by which James extends and intensifies his meaning and strikes more deeply into the reader's consciousness. Chief of these is a highly suggestive and even symbolic language which permeates the entire story. After I had become aware of and begun to investigate this phenomenon, I found Mr. Matthiessen, in quite fortuitous corroboration of my own critical method, commenting on the same technical aspect of James's later works—his ability to "bind together his imaginative effects by subtly recurrent images of a thematic kind" and to "extend a metaphor into a symbol," and the fact that later in his career "realistic details had become merely the covering for a content that was far from realistic." In *The Turn* there is a great deal of recurrent imagery which powerfully influences the tone and the meaning of the story; the story

becomes, indeed, a dramatic poem, and to read it properly one must assess the role of the language precisely as one would if public form of the work were poetic. For by his iterative imagery and by the very unobtrusive management of symbols, which in the organic work co-function with the language, James has severely qualified the bare narrative; and, if he has not defined the evil which, as he specified, was to come to the reader as something monstrous and unidentified, he has at least set forth the mode and the terms of its operation with unrecognized fullness.

For a mature reader it is hardly necessary to insist that the center of horror is not the apparitions themselves, though their appearances are worked out with fine uniqueness, but is the children, and our sense of what is happening to them. What is happening to them is Quint and Jessel; the governess's awareness of the apparitions is her awareness of a change within the children; the shock of ghostly appearances is the shock of evil perceived unexpectedly, suddenly, after it has secretly made inroads. Mathiessen [in *Henry James: The Major Phase*] and R. P. Blackmur [in the introduction to James's *The Art of the Novel*] both refer, as a matter of course, to the corruption of the children; E.M.W. Tillyard, in a volume on Shakespeare, remarks incidentally that James "owes so much of the power with which evil is conveyed to showing it in the minds of children; where it should least be found." Perhaps two modern phenomena, the sentimentalizing of children and the disinclination to concede to evil any status more profound than the melodramatic, account for a frequent unwillingness to accept what the story says. James is not disposed to make things easier; he emphasizes that it is the incorruptible who have taken on corruption. He introduces no mere pathos of childhood catastrophe; his are not ordinary children. He is at pains to give them a special quality—by repetition which in so careful an artist can hardly have been a clumsy accident. As the repeated words achieve a cumulative tonal force, we can see the working of the poetic imagination.

Flora has "extraordinary charm," is "most beautiful." Miles is "incredibly beautiful." Both have "the bloom of health and happiness." Miles is "too fine and fair" for the world; he is a "beautiful little boy." The governess is "dazzled by their loveliness." They are "most loveable" in their "helplessness." Touching their "fragrant faces" one could believe only "their incapacity and their beauty." Miles is a "prodigy of delightful, loveable goodness." In midstory Flora still emerges from concealment "rosily," and one is caught by "the golden glow of her curls," by her "loveliest, eagerest simplicity," by "the excess of something beautiful that shone out of the blue" of her eyes, by "the lovely little lighted face." In both, "beauty and amiability, happiness and cleverness" are still paramount. Miles has still the "wonderful smile" and the "beautiful eye" of "a little fairy prince." Both write letters "too beautiful to be posted." On the final Sunday the governess sees still Miles's "beautiful face" and talks of him as "beautiful and perfect"; he smiles at her "with the same loveliness" and spars verbally with "serenity" and "unimpeachable gaiety." Even after Flora is gone, Miles is "the beautiful little presence" as yet with "neither stain nor shadow"; his expression is "the most beautiful" the governess has ever known.

James devotes an almost prodigal care to creating an impression of special beauty in the children, an impression upon which depends the extraordinary effectiveness of the change which takes place in them. In such children the appearance of any imperfection is a shock. The shock is emphasized when the

governess wonders whether she must "pronounce their loveliness a trick of premature cunning" and reflects upon the
possibility that "the immediate charm . . . was studied"; when
Miles's "sweet face" must be described as a "sweet ironic
face"; when his "happy laugh" goes off into "incoherent,
extravagant song"; and when, above all, the governess must
declare with conviction that their "more than earthly beauty,
their absolutely unnatural goodness [is] a game, . . . a policy
and a fraud."

Is James, then, laboriously overusing the principle of contrast,
clothing the children with an astonishing fascination merely to
accentuate the shock of their being stripped bare? Obviously
not. Beneath the superficial clash we can already sense a deeper
paradox. When James speaks of Miles's "beautiful fevered
face" and says that he "lives in a setting of beauty and misery," he puts into words what the reader has already come to
feel—that his real subject is the dual nature of man, who is a
little lower than the angels, and who yet can become a slave
in the realm of evil. The children's beauty, we have come to
feel, is a symbol of the spiritual perfection of which man is
capable. Thus the battle between the governess and the demons
becomes the old struggle of the morality play in new dress.

But that statement of the struggle is much more general and
abstract than the formulation of it made by the story itself.
When James speaks of "any clouding of their innocence," he
reminds us again of a special quality in their beauty which he
has quietly stressed with almost thematic fullness. The *clouding*
suggests a *change* in a characteristic brightness of theirs, a
brightness of which we are made aware by a recurrent imagery
of light. Flora, at the start, "brightly" faces the new governess;
hers is a "radiant" image; the children "dazzle" the governess;
Flora has "a lovely little lighted face," and she considers
"luminously"; in his "brightness" Miles "fairly glittered";
he speaks "radiantly"; at his "revolution" he speaks with
"extraordinary brightness." This light-giving quality of theirs
is more than a mere amplification of a charm shockingly to be
destroyed; it is difficult not to read it as a symbol of their being,
as it were, at the dawn of existence. For they are children, and
their radiance suggests the primal and the universal. This provisional interpretation is supported by another verbal pattern
which James uses to describe the children. Miles has a "great
glow of freshness," a "positive fragrance of purity," a
"sweetness of innocence"; the governess comments again on
the "rose-flush of his innocence"; in him she finds something
"extraordinarily happy, that, . . . struck me as beginning anew
each day"; he could draw upon "reserves of goodness." Then,
as things change, the governess remarks, on one occasion, that
"He couldn't play any longer at innocence," and mentions,
on another, his pathetic struggles to "play . . . a part of innocence." To the emphasis upon beauty, then, is added this
emphasis upon brightness and freshness and innocence. What
must come across to us, from such a context, is echoes of the
Garden of Eden; we have the morality play story, as we have
said, but altered, complemented, and given unique poignance
by being told of mankind at its first radical crisis, in consequence of which all other morality stories are; Miles and Flora
become the childhood of the race. They are symbolic children
as the ghosts are symbolic ghosts. Even the names themselves
have a representative quality as those of James's characters
often do: Miles—the soldier, the archetypal male; Flora—the
flower, the essential female. Man and woman are caught even
before the first hint of maturity, dissected, and shown to have
within them all the seeds—possible of full growth even now—
of their own destruction.

James's management of the setting and of other ingredients in
the drama deepens one's sense of a story at once primeval and
eternal, lurking beneath the surface of the action. Bly itself is
almost an Eden with its "lawn and bright flowers"; the governess comments, "The scene had a greatness . . ." Three times
James writes of the "golden" sky, and one unconsciously
recalls that Flora was a "rosy sprite" with "hair of gold."
Miss Jessel first appears "in the garden," where "the old trees,
the thick shrubbery, made a great and pleasant shade. . . ."
Here, for a time, the three "lived in a cloud of music and
love . . ."; the children are "extraordinarily at one" in "their
quality of sweetness." Now it is significant that James uses
even the seasons to heighten his drama: the pastoral idyl begins
in June, when spring is at the full, and then is gradually altered
until we reach the dark ending of a November whose coldness
and deadness are unobtrusively but unmistakably stressed: ". . .
the autumn had dropped . . . and blown out half our lights" (a
variation of the light-pattern); the governess now notices "grey
sky and withered garlands," "bared spaces and scattered dead
leaves." What might elsewhere be Gothic trimming is here
disciplined by the pattern. When, on the final Sunday night,
the governess tries hard to "reach" Miles, there is "a great
wind"; she hears "the lash of the rain and the batter of the
gusts"; at the climax there is "an extraordinary blast and chill,"
and then darkness. The next afternoon is "damp and grey."
After Flora's final escapade at the pond, James stresses the
governess's feelings at the end of the day; the evening is "portentous" without precedent; she blows out the candles and feels
a "mortal coldness." On the final day with Miles she notices
"the stupid shrubs," "the dull things of November," "the
dim day." So it is not merely the end of a year but the end of
a cycle: the spring of gay, bright human innocence has given
way to the dark autumn—or rather, as we might pun, to the
dark *fall*.

And in the darkness of the latter end of things we might note
the special development of the light which, to the sensitive
governess, the children seem actually to give off. It is, I think,
more than a coincidence that, when the governess mentions
Miss Jessel, Flora's face shows a "quick, smitten glare," and
that, in the final scene, Miles is twice said to be "glaring"—
the same verb which has been used to describe Quint's look.
All three characters, of course, look with malevolence; yet
glare must suggest, also, a hard, powerful, ugly light—an
especially effective transformation of the apparently benign
luminousness of the spring.

The same movement of human experience James portrays in
still another symbolic form. As the light changes and the season
changes and the children's beauty becomes ambiguous, another
alteration takes place in them. Their youth, of course, is the
prime datum of the story, and of it we are ever conscious; and
at the same time we are aware of a strange maturity in them—
in, for instance, their poise, their controlled utilization of their
unusual talents to give pleasure. Our sense of something that
transcends their youth is first defined overtly late in the story
when the governess speaks of her feeling that Miles is "accessible as an older person." Though she does not speak of
change, there is subtly called forth in us a conviction that years
have been added to Miles. So we are not surprised when the
governess assures Mrs. Grose, and goes out of her way, a little
later, to remind her of the assurance, that, at meetings with
Miss Jessel, Flora is "not a child" but "an old, old woman"—
an insight that receives a measure of authentication, perhaps,
by its reminiscence of the Duessa motif. The suggestion that
Flora has become older is skillfully conveyed, in the pond

scene, by her silence (and silence itself has an almost symbolic value throughout the story), by her quick recovery of her poised gaiety, and especially by the picture of her peeping at the governess over the shoulder of Mrs. Grose, who is embracing her—the first intimation of a cold adult calculatingness which appears in all her remaining actions. The governess says, ". . . her incomparable childish beauty had suddenly failed, had quite vanished . . . she was literally . . . hideously, hard; she had turned common and almost ugly." Mrs. Grose sums up, "It has made her, every inch of her, quite old." More effective, however, than any of this direct presentation of vital change is a delicate symbol which may pass almost unnoticed: when she is discovered at the pond, Flora picks up, and drops a moment later, "a big, ugly spray of withered fern"—a quiet commentary on the passage of symbolic spring, on the spiritual withering that is the story's center. When, at the end of the scene, the governess looks "at the grey pool and its blank, haunted edge," we automatically recall, "The sedge has withered from the lake"—the imagery used by Keats in his account of an ailing knight-at-arms in another bitter autumn.

Besides the drying of foliage and the coming of storms and darkness there is one other set of elements, loosely working together and heavy with implications, which suggest that this is a story of the decay of Eden. At Quint's first appearance Bly "had been stricken with death." After Miles's nocturnal exploit the governess utters a cliché that, under the influence of the context, becomes vigorously meaningful: ". . . you . . . caught your death in the night air!" There are, further, some arresting details in the description of Quint: "His eyes are sharp, strange—awfully; . . . rather small and very fixed. His mouth's wide, and his lips are thin, ..." These are unmistakably the characteristics of a snake. James is too fine an artist to allegorize the point, but, as he has shaped the story, the coming of Quint is the coming of the serpent into the little Eden that is Bly (both Miss Porter and Mr. Tate have noted other physical characteristics of Quint which traditionally belong to the devil). Quint's handsomeness and his borrowed finery, by which he apes the gentleman, suggest, perhaps, the specious plausibleness of the visitor in the Garden. As for the "fixed eyes": later we learn that Miss Jessel "only fixed the child" and that the apparition of Quint "fixed me exactly as it had fixed me from the tower and from the garden." Of Quint's position at Bly Mrs. Grose says, "The master believed in him and placed him here because he was supposed not to be well and the country air so good for him." The master, in other words, has nourished a viper in his bosom. The secret influence upon Miles the governess describes as "poison," and at the very end she says that the demonic presence "filled the room like the taste of poison." In the first passage the governess equates "poison" with "secret precocity"; toward the end she emphasizes Miles's freedom and sorrowfully gives up "the fiction that I had anything more to teach him." Why is it a fiction? Because he already knew too much, because he had eaten of the fruit of the tree of knowledge? We have already been told of the "dark prodigy" by which "the imagination of all evil *had* been opened up to him," and of his being "under some influence operating in his small intellectual life as a tremendous incitement."

We should not press such analogies too hard, or construct inflexible parables. Our business is rather to trace all the imaginative emanations that enrich the narrative, the associations and intimations by which it transcends the mere horror story and achieves its own kind of greatness. But by now it must be clear from the antipodal emphases of the story that James has

an almost religious sense of the duality of man, and, as if to manifest an intention, he makes that sense explicit in terms broadly religious and even Christian. The image of Flora's "angelic beauty" is "beatific"; she has "the deep, sweet serenity . . . of one of Raphael's holy infants"; she has "placid heavenly eyes." In Miles there is "something divine that I have never found to the same degree in any child." In a mildly humorous context the children are called "cherubs." Seeing no signs of suffering from his school experience, the governess regards Miles as an "angel." Mrs. Grose imputes to Flora a "blessed innocence," and the governess surrenders to the children's "extraordinary childish grace"—a noun which in this patterned structure can hardly help being ambivalent. In mid-story Flora has still a "divine smile"; both children remain "adorable." This verbal pattern, which is too consistent to be coincidental, irresistibly makes us think of the divine in man, of his capability of salvation. Now what is tragic and terrifying in man is that to be capable of salvation is to be capable also of damnation—an equivocal potentiality suggested early by the alternation of moods in the newly arrived governess, who senses immediately a kind of wavering, a waiting for determination, at Bly. And James, to present the spiritual decline of the children, finds terms which exactly balance those that connote their spiritual capabilities.

We are never permitted to see the apparitions except as moral realities. Miss Jessel is a figure of "unmistakeable horror and evil . . . in black, pale and dreadful." She is a "horror of horrors," with "awful eyes," "with a kind of fury of intention," and yet "with extraordinary beauty." Again she is described as "Dark as midnight in her black dress, her haggard beauty, and her unutterable woe. . . ." It is brilliant to give her beauty, which not only identifies her with Flora and thus underscores the dual possibilities that lie ahead of Flora, but also enriches the theme with its reminder of Milton's fallen angels who retain something of their original splendor—"the excess / Of glory obscured." So, with the repeated stress upon her woe, we almost expect the passage which tells us that she "suffers the torments . . . of the damned": she is both damned and an agent of damnation—another reminiscence of the Miltonic myth. She is called later a "pale and ravenous demon," not "an inch of whose evil . . . fell short"—which reminds us of James's prefatory insistence that the apparitions were to be thought of as demons. Again, she is "our infernal witness"; she and Quint are "those fiends"; "they were not angels," and they could be bringing "some yet more infernal message." "And to ply them with that evil still, to keep up the work of demons, is what brings the others back." They are "tempters," who work subtly by holding out fascinating "suggestions of danger." In the last scene Quint presents—the phrase is used twice—"his white face of damnation."

By this series of words, dispersed throughout the story yet combining in a general statement, James defines as diabolic the forces attacking the children of whose angelic part we are often reminded. Now these attacking forces, as often in Elizabethan drama, are seen in two aspects. Dr. Faustus has to meet an enemy which has an inner and an outer reality—his own thoughts, and Mephistopheles; James presents evil both as agent (the demons) and as effect (the transformation in the once fresh and beautiful and innocent children). The dualistic concept of reality appears most explicitly when Mrs. Grose asks, "And if he was so bad there as that comes to, how is he such an angel now?" and the governess replies, "Yes, indeed—and if he was a fiend at school!" By the *angel-fiend* antithesis James underscores what he sees as a central human contradiction, which he emphasizes throughout the book by his chosen verbal pattern. The governess speaks of the children's "love of evil" gained from Quint and Miss Jessel, of Miles's "wickedness" at school. In such a context the use of the word *revolution* to describe Miles's final taking matters up with the governess—a move by which, we should remember, he becomes completely "free"—cannot help calling to mind the Paradise and Eden revolutions of Judaeo-Christian mythology. The revolutionary change in character is nicely set forth by the verbal counterpoint in one passage. "He found the most divine little way," the governess says, "to keep me quiet while she went off." "'Divine'?" Mrs. Grose asks, and the governess replies, "Infernal then!" The divine has paradoxically passed into the infernal. Then we see rapidly the completed transition in Flora: she turns upon the governess an expression of "hard, fixed gravity" and ignores the "hideous plain presence" of Miss Jessel—"a stroke that somehow converted the little girl herself into the very presence that could make me quail." In Miles, by contrast, we see a protracted struggle, poignantly conveyed by a recurrent metaphor of illness. Early in the story Miles is in "the bloom of health and happiness," but near the end he seems like a "wistful patient in a children's hospital," "like a convalescent slightly fatigued." At the end he shows "bravery" while "flushing with pain"; he gives "a sick little headshake"; his is a "beautiful fevered face." But the beauty goes, the fever gains; Miles gives "a frantic little shake for air and light"; he is in a "white rage." The climax of his disease, the binding together of all the strands we have been tracing, is his malevolent cry to the governess—"you devil!" It is his final transvaluation of values: she who would be his savior has become for him a demon. His face gives a "convulsive supplication"—that is, actually, a prayer, for and to Quint, the demon who has become his total deity. But the god isn't there, and Miles despairs and dies. We need not labor the dependence of this brilliant climax upon the host of associations and evocations by which, as this outline endeavors to show, James prepares us for the ultimate resolution of the children's being.

There are glimmerings of other imaginative kinships, such as that already mentioned, the Faustian. Miles's "You devil" is in one way almost identical with Faustus's savage attack, in Marlowe's play, upon the Old Man who has been trying to save him; indeed James's story, in its central combat, is not unlike the Faustus story as it might be told by the Good Angel. But whereas Dr. Faustus is a late intellectualist version of Everyman, James, as we have said, weaves in persuasive hints, one after another, of mankind undergoing, in his Golden Age, an elemental conflict: thus we have the morality play, but in a complicated, enriched, and intensified version. When the governess first sees Quint, she is aware of "some challenge between us"; the next time it seems "as if I had been looking at him for years and had known him always"; near the end she says, "I *was* . . . face to face with the elements," and, of the final scene, "It was like fighting with a demon for a human soul."

What, then, does the story say about the role of the governess, and how does this contribute to the complex of the impressions built up in part by James's language? From the start the words used by the governess suggest that James is attaching to her the quality of savoir, not only in a general sense, but with certain Christian associations. She uses words like "atonement"; she speaks of herself as an "expiatory victim," of her "pure suffering," and at various times—twice in the final scene—of her "torment." Very early she plans to "shelter my

Daguerreotype of James as a child with his father.

pupils," to "absolutely save" them; she speaks variously of her "service," "to protect and defend the little creatures . . . bereaved . . . loveable." When she fears that she cannot "save or shield them" and that "they're lost," she is a "poor protectress." At another time she is a "sister of Charity" attempting to "cure" Miles. But by now what we cannot mistake is the relation of pastor and flock, a relationship which becomes overt when the governess tells Miles, "I just want you to help me to save you." It is in this sense that the governess "loves" Miles—a loving which must not be confused, as it is confused by some critics, with "making love to" or "being in love with" him. Without such pastoral love no guardian would consider his flock worth the sacrifice. The governess's priestly function is made still more explicit by the fact that she comes ultimately to act as confessor and to use every possible means to bring Miles to confession; the long final scene really takes place in the confessional, with the governess as priest endeavoring, by both word and gesture, to protect her charge against the evil force whose invasion has, with consummate irony, carried even there. In one sense the governess must elicit confession because, in her need for objective reassurance, she will not take the lead as accuser; but securing the confession is, more importantly, a mitigation of Miles's own pride, his self-will; it could soften him, make him accessible to grace. The experience has a clear sacramental quality: the governess says that Miles senses "the need of confession . . . he'll confess. If he confesses, he's saved." It is when he begins to break and confess that "the white face of damnation" becomes baffled and at a vital moment retreats; but it returns "as if to blight his confession," and it is in part through the ineptitude of the governess-confessor-savior, we are led to understand, that Miles is lost.

It is possible that there are even faint traces of theological speculation to give additional substance to the theme of salvation and damnation which finally achieves specific form in the sacramentalism of the closing scenes. Less than halfway through the story the governess refers to the children thus: "blameless and foredoomed as they were." By *blameless* she can only mean that she does not have direct, tangible evidence of voluntary evil-doing on their part; they still look charming and beautiful; she does not have grounds for a positive placing of blame. Why, then, "foredoomed"? May this not be a suggestion of original sin (which Miss Porter has already seen as an ingredient in the story), an interpretation consistent with the view of Bly as a kind of Eden? Three-quarters of the way through the story the governess again turns to speculation: ". . . I constantly both attacked and renounced the enigma of what such a little gentleman could have done that deserved a penalty." *Enigma* is perhaps just the word to be applied to a situation, of which one technical explication is the doctrine of original sin, by an inquiring lay mind with a religious sense but without precise theological tools. What is significant is that the governess does not revolt against the penalty as if it betokened a cosmic injustice. And original sin, whether it be natural depravity or a revolt in a heavenly or earthly paradise, fits exactly into the machinery of this story of two beautiful children who in a lovely springtime of existence already suffer, not unwillingly, hidden injuries which will eventually destroy them. (pp. 277-86)

Robert Heilman, " 'The Turn of the Screw' as Poem,"
in The University of Kansas City Review, Vol. XIV,
No. 4, Summer, 1948, pp. 277-89.

JOHN LYDENBERG (essay date 1957)

[*Lydenberg is an American educator and critic. In the following excerpt, he disputes Robert Heilman's interpretation of* The Turn of the Screw *as Christian allegory (see excerpt dated 1948). While not insisting that the ghosts are hallucinations, Lydenberg sees the governess as a false savior who becomes the agent of the very evil from which she tries to save the children.*]

[The governess in *The Turn of the Screw*] is of course the narrator, and as such she is never seen from the outside (except briefly in the prologue). Neither author nor other characters give us ready-made characterizations of the governess; she alone provides the information from which we can deduce the essential facts about her personality. Here it is certainly true that, as Spinoza said, "What Paul says about Peter tells us more about Paul than about Peter." The more we examine the governess' account, the more we feel that she is very much, and very tragically, a person with will and passion of her own. The richness—and the confusion and ambiguity of the tale—lie just here: we can know the children and the apparitions only through the governess, and we can know the governess only through her own words: her observations and actions and conclusions. To understand the events we must evaluate the governess' evaluations, and to do this we must evaluate the governess herself.

Heilman is fully aware of this [see excerpt dated 1948]. He sees that the governess is no blank automaton but an actor with characteristics that go beyond mere "firmness and courage." And he considers her central to the religious interpretation of the story. The words applied to her, he says, "suggest that

James is attaching to her the quality of savior, not only in a general sense, but with certain Christian associations." It is at this point that his otherwise admirable analysis slips a crucial notch. These words are not simply words that James attaches to her; they are words that James has *her* attach *to herself*. And the words suggesting that the children are angelic creatures corrupted by infernal agents are *her* words, words that give us her vision—or version—of the fall of the house of Bly. Heilman is quite right in holding that "the center of horror is not the apparitions themselves . . . but . . . the children, and our sense of what is happening to them." But when he says, "What is happening to them is Quint and Jessel," he oversimplifies. What is happening to the children is what the governess says is happening, and more than that, what is happening to them is, clearly and terribly, the governess herself.

Our sense of horror is indeed aroused by the plight of the children. But what exactly do we sense their plight to be? We feel an undertone of sexual perversity—but to build an interpretation of the whole story upon that, as in essence Wilson did [see excerpt dated 1934], is to give an explanation that is too rationalistic, too specific to accord with the full depth of the conveyed horror. We recognize that the children are symbols of the tortured state of mankind, and that the horror of their corruption is heightened by the fact that they are essentially such angelic children. But this Heilman interpretation is, if not too rationalistic, at least too abstract; it provides a symbolic interpretation that we can grasp intellectually but that we do not truly feel.

So it is for me, at least. Heilman's conception makes sense intellectually but not emotionally. I do not truly feel the corruption of the children or the horror of their putative relations with Quint and Jessel. What I feel is the governess ever tightening the screws. I respond—intensely as James wants us to respond—to the plight of two children, potentially angelic but human like all of us, harried to distraction and death by an overprotective governess. The character and outcome of the struggle, as I feel it, is determined not by the infernal ghosts but by the character of the protecting governess: she is anxious, fearful, possessive, domineering, hysterical and compulsive. The children are pawns which she must protect and can use, but for which she has no real concern; she is concerned primarily with herself. After seeing what she does with and to them I would say, paraphrasing Emerson, "if they are the Devil's children, let them live then with the Devil." Salvation by such as the governess doesn't save. And if it *had* saved the children for the governess' continued ministrations, that I fear would have been the greater of the two evils.

If then we are to see her as a would-be savior—and I agree with Heilman that we must—we see her as a false savior. And I rather think, though I certainly cannot be sure, that James unconsciously saw her so too. In theological terms, she embodies the sin of pride in daring to take upon herself, unaided, the task of saving the children. In other terms, she is a compulsive neurotic who with her martyr complex and her need to dominate finally drives to destruction the children she wishes to possess. Thus the Christian myth becomes twisted: the religious interpretation gives us a story which is, in some manner at least, antireligious. Or maybe, admitting as I do the essential ambiguity of almost everything in the story, I should more cautiously suggest that any religious significance we find here is necessarily double-edged. To me the governess is central; and although I grant that she puts up a heroic fight for the souls of her charges, I find myself basically suspicious of her, not of her good will and certainly not of her "firmness," but of her coolness, her judgment, her wisdom, and above all her ability to cope with human beings who as human beings are inevitably a mixture of good and evil.

Let us now listen to the governess in some detail. One particular paragraph merits careful reading.

> I scarce know how to put my story into words that shall be a credible picture of my state of mind; but I was in these days literally able to find a joy in the extraordinary flight of heroism the occasion demanded of me. I now saw that I had been asked for a service admirable and difficult; and there would be a greatness in letting it be seen—oh, in the right quarter!—that I could succeed where many another girl might have failed. It was an immense help to me—I confess I rather applaud myself as I look back!—that I saw my service to strongly and so simply. I was there to protect and defend the little creatures in the world the most bereaved and the most lovable, and appeal of whose helplessness had suddenly become only too explicit, a deep constant ache of one's own committed heart. We were cut off, really, together; we were united in our danger. They had nothing but me, and I—well, I had *them*. It was, in short, a magnificent chance. This chance presented itself to me in an image richly material. I was a screen— I was to stand before them. The more I saw, the less they would. I began to watch them in stifled suspense, a disguised excitement that might well, had it continued too long, have turned to something like madness. What saved me, as I now see, was that it turned to something else altogether. It didn't last as suspense—it was superseded by horrible proofs. Proofs, I say, yes—from the moment I really took hold.

I would almost be willing to rest my case on this one paragraph alone, which exhibits in concentrated form all the major traits of the governess, traits that go far beyond James's simple qualities of "firmness and courage." It is her "state of mind" that she, and thus we, are first of all concerned with, and she recognizes that her audience will not easily find it "credible." She sees herself as "committed" to a "service admirable and difficult" and is determined not to miss this "magnificent chance" to display her dedication so that it will be recognized "in the right quarter"—that of the master. She and the children are isolated, "cut off" and "united"; if she has lost herself in them, she has also found herself by *having them*, to "protect and defend" and indeed to possess. Thus, for her relations with the children, the servants are at the same time a threat and a necessity. Though she talks of stifling her suspense and disguising her excitement, she can in no wise do so, for she has worked herself into such a state of mind that, as she admits, it is essential to her sanity and salvation for proofs of the rightness of her imaginings to be forthcoming. So she eagerly offers herself as a screen. She will receive the images of the evil past, cut them off from the children—but the images will be there on that screen, and we might suggest that were the screen not there to bring them out, they would never become visible or effective.

Thus she "takes hold," with a compulsive "joy" in her heroism, a determination that the children shall submit not to the dark apparitions but to her. And she appears as an almost classic case of what Erich Fromm calls the authoritarian character: masochistic in that she delights in receiving the tortures as an "expiatory victim," a phrase she later applies to herself, and at the same time sadistic in her insistence on dominating the children and Mrs. Grose. (pp. 39-43)

I have attempted to demonstrate that the governess is an authoritarian character: hysterical, compulsive, sado-masochistic. Some readers may, however, prefer to use the terms *she* chooses in describing her actions: duty, service, expiatory victim, torment, atonement, savior. They may insist that the actions and attitudes I have characterized as authoritarian are simply those of the true Christian. They may hold that her incessant vigilance, unrelenting pressure, selfless submission, and refusal to compromise in any manner with evil are entirely proper and necessary in the unremitting struggle against the forces of evil. This would be to adopt what we loosely call the Puritan view of Christianity, and to say that the governess is essentially a Puritan. She would indeed have been worthy coadjutor of Paul or Augustine or Luther (though she is too blind to the possibilities of there being sin in *her* to have been wholly approved by them). If we accept this view of her, the important thing to note is that James pictured her battle as futile and fatal. If he approved her methods, he certainly did not deem them effective; if he approved her self-dedication as savior, he did not think that she could save.

Readers who do not have a predilection for this variant of Christianity will almost certainly see the governess differently, and believe that James saw her differently. Through her insistence on recognizing only the extreme whites of Edenlike innocence and the extreme blacks of Quint and Jessel, and her refusal to accept the shaded grays that are necessary for any true *human* understanding and sympathy, she alienates the children so completely that they have no alternative but to go to the devil. She looks upon them first as angelic then as infernal, never as something in between. Unable to offer them the positive, sympathetic love which might have helped them develop as humans and accommodate themselves to the evil with which all men must by their nature live, she can only strive to recast them in her rigid authoritarian mold. She turns the screws of Puritan discipline and suspicion until the children fatally crack under the strain. Whatever the multitude of ambiguities in this story, one thing is not ambiguous: once one fills the blanks with Christian values, one must see the story as a covert, if unconscious, attack on one strain of Christianity, a New England strain with which James was most familiar. (pp. 57-8)

> John Lydenberg, *"The Governess Turns the Screws,"* in Nineteenth-Century Fiction, *Vol. 12, No. 1, June, 1957, pp. 37-58.*

MANFRED MACKENZIE   (essay date 1962)

[*Mackenzie is an Anglo-Australian educator and critic. In the following excerpt, he discusses several elements that* The Turn of the Screw *has in common with literary Gothicism.*]

I want to examine here an interesting rhetorical effect of *The Turn of the Screw.* If such an analysis should make it seem too calculated one might answer that there was, on James's own admission, arch calculation. The consciousness of the story is extreme, which is as we should expect from this natural master of suggestion.

In the first place James cuts us off very deliberately from the present. He not only places the action in the depths of the country; he also pushes it far into the past. This is accomplished by a kind of introductory "patter" which throws a baffle over events to come. It is in part provoked by Douglas, the narrator whose attitude to telling the story is one of mingled reluctance and fascination. Douglas vouches for the governess (which is so important) but also impresses us that the story is very much a remembrance of things beyond our ken. At twenty he had been infatuated with the governess, who at that time was thirty. It now transpires that there is a further time lapse—one of ten years—as the governess had in fact been only twenty when engaged at Bly. Since one of the characters tells us that Douglas has hoarded his secret for forty years, we presume that he was about sixty at the time of the story's revelation. And the governess, Bly's chief witness, has died in the meantime.

There is yet another narrator, the "I" of the tale, who presumably has now published the manuscript which Douglas had originally read to the group by the fireside. But how has "I" received this manuscript? We learn that he had it from Douglas at the time of the latter's death; so that there has been still another time lapse, one of unknown length, before "I's" transmission of the story. In all, the events at Bly have been pushed back into the past at least fifty years. This unknown quantity in the retrospection would probably have been quite short, but as a blind spot it is perfectly in keeping with James's cultivating uncertainty throughout the tale. Further, thrown up like a fine silt in clear water, there are subtle postponements of the actual reading of the governess' manuscript. At first Douglas has to send to London for it, and only on the fourth night, after much anticipation, does it appear.

All this Jamesian huggermugger, or hooding of the action, is too complex not to have been deliberate. Why the slow, obscuring pace? There must be at least two reasons underlying this introductory section; and if we cannot ascribe them to James as intentional, the prologue nonetheless has the following effects. In the first place it put us at a remove in time and consequently helps James in his pursuit of the extraordinary: since by the time of publication the original and reliable witnesses, the governess and Mrs. Grose, are dead. Douglas, an indirect witness, has also died. As James does not allow any "verification" we can only trust in them entirely. We must submit to the governess' "authority" even though we may resist her account. James has thus managed to establish her complete authority while at the same time allowing himself extra latitude for his thrilling note. It may be an odd and tricksily managed feat, yet it is certainly brought off. And he rejoiced over his success in the Preface when he spoke of how the subject afforded him "a perfectly clear field, with no 'outside' control involved, no pattern of the usual or the true or the terrible 'pleasant' . . . to consort with." In this way, as an "excursion into chaos," *The Turn of the Screw* becomes more a finely controlled *tale* after Poe's fashion than a story of conventional type. Because of the initial touch of mystification, of Jamesian abracadabra, we have a credible combination of the fairy tale (the element of which is so stressed in the Preface) and the more ordinary ghost story. (pp. 34-5)

Then, too, the technique probably appealed to James's habitual inclination for the indirect and qualified. The involution serves as a sort of literary aperitif, setting above all the thrilled tone of wonder mingled with horror, which we should be expected to feel before such a vision of evil encroaching on innocence. Douglas in particular appears to feel a highly reluctant and even brooding necessity to reveal his manuscript; though it would be foolish to claim that this is on any deeply or urgently moral level. Rather we are at the level of exceptionally subtle sensation. James, for the sake of the thrill, is exploiting our natural reactions. He does no more than assume them. In this respect *The Turn of the Screw* is a modern Gothic tale—to give the term extended though not, I think, imprecise meaning— since the Gothicists were chiefly concerned with this area of experience. It is even probable that James had the Gothic novelists in mind and that he tried to catch their tone as he wrote: for what else are we to make of the governess' question, "Was there a 'secret' at Bly—a mystery of Udolpho or an insane, an unmentionable relative kept in unsuspected confinement?"

The prologue, which introduces this specially "conceived tone," is only a natural elaboration of the general narrative technique. The tale is told after the dialectic style described by Austin Warren, in which pairs or groups of characters gather and discuss, qualify, conjecture, comment on, scrutinize, and clairvoyantly debate the events and relationships in which they participate. (*Rage for Order*. . . .) This is the distinctive activity of James's later people, and in *The Turn of the Screw* we have a quite typical Jamesian collaboration between the governess and her *fidus Achates,* Mrs. Grose. These two, circling warily about the great Unsaid, establish the manuscript's "authority." They put the dialectic method which is found throughout a work like *The Golden Bowl* to a detective use.

Indeed James almost gave us both cause and effect of his method in the governess' report of a talk with Miles: "So we circled about with terrors and scruples, fighters not daring to close. But it was for each other we feared! That kept us a little longer suspended and unbruised." As so often elsewhere, James seems here to be taking two steps forward to one backward; not only to drive us on in our queer experience but also to be teasingly avoiding it. It is interesting that this kind of involution is a feature of certain other novels (such as *Wuthering Heights* and the remarkable *Absalom, Absalom!*) which exhibit traces of Gothicism. In these the technique renders the melodrama tolerable by helping to give it more serious meaning. The melodrama is transcended, and we have meaningful achievement as well as great excitement. It is as if the technique in both novels (particularly *Absalom, Absalom!*) symbolizes some difficult moral comprehension of the central action; and hence its apparent complexity. But *The Turn of the Screw* has a pseudo complexity, and James's elaborate way brings him deliberately close to self-parody.

It should be clear that the tale employs many devices of James's cunning atmospheric art. Of course, a great part of the tale's experience depends on the "ghosts," who are above all atmospheric. There is no need here to discuss the Freudian view which is, I think, sufficiently disproved. As Dr. Leavis has insisted they should be taken literally as the consistent bad ghosts of bad persons, and are therefore beyond our normal moral standards [see Additional Bibliography]. . . . They are there as in any ghost story as calculations, agents of "the dear old sacred terror," with the dire duty laid on them "of causing the situation to reek with the air of Evil." Nor has the Evil any particular significance, for it is diffuse to the point of abstraction. Even if James had wanted it to have moral substance—which on the evidence of letters, Notebooks and the Preface is unlikely—his procedure of evoking it wholly by atmospheric devices would have been self-defeating. In fact the overwhelming concern in the Preface was with the *hows* of suggestion: the *whys,* those limited deplorable presentable instances, were to be avoided with all cunning. (pp. 35-7)

The Turn of the Screw is James's superfine *Castle of Otranto*, "perfectly independent and irresponsible," in which atmosphere is being created in a way rather like self-spoofing. (James once regarded it as a "very mechanical matter . . . an inferior, a merely pictorial, subject, and rather a shameless pot-boiler." . . .) And if we do find figures in it, this is chiefly because the tale is a performance of such exceptional sophistication. In any case there should be no shock in ascribing the finer sensationalism to the James of those other more serious melodramas or part-melodramas, *The American, The Princess Casamassima* and *The Other House,* especially when the story itself was avowedly thrilling. James gives the artificial conditions, or dramatics of intense feeling without in any real way substantiating that feeling. He simply preys on our susceptibility to uncertainty or rumour. We do know we are being deeply implicated, but implicated in *what*? Perhaps in some portentous relation between appearance and reality? One could say that the story's sophistical power (for it is so wonderful) lies in its threatening at any moment to become, or to discover morality. Meanwhile it remains highly charged with what T. S. Eliot called in connection with Collins' *Armadale,* "the air of spurious fatality." (p. 38)

Manfred Mackenzie, " 'The Turn of the Screw': Jamesian Gothic," *in* Essays in Criticism, *Vol. XII, No. 1, January, 1962, pp. 34-8.*

DOROTHEA KROOK (essay date 1962)

[*In the following excerpt, Krook considers the governess as a flawed savior of the children and discusses the problem of ambiguity in the narrative of* The Turn of the Screw.]

[*The Turn of the Screw*] yields its full meaning when and only when it is read as a moral fable which powerfully dramatises certain fundamental facts of our spiritual experience—chiefly, the reality of evil ("evil as an absolute," in Mr Heilman's phrase), the reality of good, and the possibility of redemption ("salvation") for the victims of the evil by the power of human love.

The principal claim for this approach to *The Turn of the Screw* is that it is genuinely inclusive. It is consistent, to begin with, with James's explicit statement of his intention in his Preface and in his note on *The Turn of the Screw* in the *Notebooks.* It makes the most coherent sense of all the principal episodes and relationships in the story; it suggests an account of the governess's "guilt"—one of the most perplexing and elusive elements in the story—which is fully consistent with all the data; and it also attempts to explain, in the light of an hypothesis that aims to do justice to the level of James's treatment of it, that most perplexing and elusive element of all—the famous "ambiguity," which the attentive reader has rarely failed to respond to and yet has almost always found it difficult satisfactorily to account for. (p. 107)

The Turn of the Screw is . . . chiefly (though not exclusively) a fable about the redemptive power of human love: the power of love—here the governess's love for the children—to redeem the corrupt element in a human soul, and so to ensure the final triumph of good over evil; though (as so often in tragedy) at the cost of the mortal life of the redeemed soul.

To recognise this as the basic theme is not yet, however, to exhaust the meaning of the story. There is still a further . . . aspect to consider. . . . (pp. 121-22)

This . . . aspect has to do with the prevailing ambiguity and with the matter of the governess's guilt; and it is best approached by considering the problem of little Miles's death at the very end. For it *is* a problem: Why (one finds oneself impelled to ask) does Miles die? Why does he *have* to die? Why, if he has renounced the devil, as religious people would say; if he has embraced, or is about to embrace, God again; if he has thrown himself upon God's mercy through the agency of the good angel in the shape of the governess—why then must he die? Where is the moral necessity; where therefore the artistic inevitability?

The answer, I believe, is to be found by looking more closely at the second "movement," as one may call it, of the last scene. The first movement consists in the governess's effort to bring Miles to confess and repent that he may be saved. It reaches a climax with the appearance of Peter Quint in the moment that Miles is about to confess that he stole the letter; and comes to a triumphant resolution when it is evident that the child can no longer see his bad angel and Quint retires "baffled." This marks the triumph of the power of good over the power of evil; and here one might have expected the story to end.

But it does not end: there follows what is in effect a tragic reversal of the triumph we have witnessed in the first movement; and it is this tragic reversal that has to be accounted for. Why—that is now the question—does Peter Quint return? By what strength is the devil so suddenly revived and restored to power when it seemed that he had been totally vanquished? Or (to put the question in such a way as to bring us nearer to our answer): by what weakness, by what taint of evil or corruption, in the power of good itself was the devil revived and restored to power?

It is the governess who directs us to the answer in the important transition passages between the two "movements" of the scene. Peter Quint has vanished; little Miles has fallen back exhausted; and the governess exults in her victory:

> What was prodigious was that at last, *by my success*, his sense was sealed and his communication stopped. . . . The air was clear again and—*by my personal triumph*—the influence [was] quenched. . . . *I felt that the cause was mine* and that I should surely get *all.*

And so, determined to get all, she presses him. "And you found nothing?" (in the letter he stole, she means):

> He gave the most mournful, thoughtful little headshake. "Nothing."
>
> "Nothing, nothing!" I almost shouted in my joy.
>
> "Nothing, nothing!" he sadly repeated.
>
> I kissed his forehead; it was drenched. "So what have you done with it?" [with the letter].
>
> "I've burnt it."
>
> "Burnt it?" It was now or never. "Is that what you did at school?"
>
> Oh, what this brought up! "At school?"
>
> "Did you take letters?—or other things?"
>
> "Other things?" He appeared now to be thinking of something far off and that reached him

only through the pressure of his anxiety. Yet it did reach him. "Did I *steal?*"

It is evident that the child is in great anguish of spirit. He grows more and more vague as she continues to press him:

> He looked [she observes] *in vague pain* all round the top of the room and drew his breath, two or three times over, as if with difficulty. He might have been standing at the bottom of the sea and raising his eyes to some faint green twilight.

And yet she persists in her effort to wrest from him what it was that he had done at school. He tells her that he didn't "steal," but had only "said things." To whom (she asks) had he said whatever it was he had said. He tries to remember, but can't. "I don't know," he says. And then:

> He almost smiled at me in the desolation of his surrender, *which was indeed practically, by this time, so complete that I ought to have left it there. But I was infatuated—I was blind with victory,* though even then the very effect that was to have brought him so much nearer was already that of added separation.

She cannot stop, fatally cannot stop, though she can see that the child is receding from her. She can even feel that he is, in some way, turning back to the evil power that he has repudiated—perhaps appealing to it for help: "Once more, as he had done before, he looked up at the dim day as if, of what had hitherto sustained him, nothing was left but an unspeakable anxiety." But still she cannot stop: she must now *get all.* And she almost does:

> He turned to me again his little beautiful fevered face. "Yes, it was too bad."
>
> "Too bad?"
>
> "What I suppose I sometimes said. [Too bad] to write home."

If only she could have stopped there, even there. But she cannot:

> I can't name the exquisite pathos of the contradiction given to such a speech by such a speaker; I only know that the next instant I heard myself throw off with homely force: "Stuff and nonsense!" But the next after that I must have sounded stern enough. "What *were* these things?"

"My sternness," she adds, "was all for his judge, his executioner." But—"What were these things?," she demands, though she can see that the child is collapsing under the pressure. "What were these things?" And as she brings this out, Peter Quint reappears: "There again, against the glass, as if to blight his confession and stay his answer, was the hideous author of our woe—the white face of damnation." And from this point the scene proceeds to the tragic catastrophe.

What are we to understand by all this? It is plain, I think, that we are to understand that the governess herself is directly responsible for the return of Peter Quint; that she is therefore indirectly responsible for Miles's death; that she is, in short, guilty of some awful moral lapse which precipitates the final catastrophe. And this lapse (we come now to see) is only the last and most disastrous expression of something in the gov-

erness of which we have been uneasily conscious all the time: some flaw, some fatal weakness, in her moral constitution that has, in some elusive way, been present throughout in all her relations with the two children.

The nature of this "fatal flaw" is now not difficult to see. Its generic name is what Christians call spiritual pride; and the specific form it takes here is, first, the desire to know all—to "get all" (in the governess's own phrase) in the sense of putting herself in complete possession of the child's soul by a complete knowledge of all that he has done. This is the aspiration after complete and perfect knowledge which by Christian definition belongs only to God and not to man; and this, which in the traditional Faustus story is shown as the glorious and damnable sin of Faustus himself, the soul that had sold itself to the devil, is here transferred to God's own emissary, the "good angel" of the Faustus story. This is how James radically modifies the structure of the great traditional fable while retaining all its essential elements, and in doing so extends and deepens in a remarkable way its moral scope.

The governess's determination to "get all," however, also expresses another form of the Faustian pride. This may be called spiritual greed or possessiveness—the kind of greed which is an intrinsic constituent of spiritual pride if not actually coextensive with it, and as such suggests a significant connexion between two of the seven deadly sins in the Christian scheme, vanity ("pride") and greed. It is her determination to "get all" in this sense that makes her so desperately, so insanely, so pitilessly, insistent; and it is her insistence that kills little Miles—just this common, familiar, domestic form of the ruthlessness that can spring from spiritual greed. It is this that dispossesses the heart of the child—her compulsion to pursue him, to press him to a full confession of all his "crimes" at a point when the child has been harrowed already to the furthest limit of his small moral resources, when he has gone as far as he can in the way of confession and repentance.

She does it (this is the vital point) still for the sake of the good. "My sternness was all for his judge, his executioner," she says. She wants to purge his soul completely, to make him, as the Christian would say, a perfect vessel for God's grace; and in so far as this remains her principal motive to the end, she retains to the end her character of the good angel, the emissary of God.

But (as she herself comes to see afterwards but, fatally, does not see at the time)—this is not the sole spring of her action. She does it also out of that love of self which is inseparable from the Faustian pride, from the desire that *her* triumph, hers personally, may be complete. "By my personal triumph . . . the influence [was] quenched . . . ," she says; "I felt that the cause was mine and I should surely get all"; "I was infatuated—I was blind with victory"; and so on. What we are shown in the last scene of *The Turn of the Screw* is the disastrous, the heart-rending, consequence of this lapse from grace. For the moment the love that inspired the governess in her effort to save Miles ceases to be wholly disinterested, ceases to be directed solely to its object for the sake of the object, it turns to positive cruelty—the cruelty (as we have seen) of harrowing a poor little soul beyond its powers of endurance, of pressing it to a degree of self-exposure that cannot but destroy it. It is as if the eye which only a moment before was full of the light of love were suddenly stricken with a blind insensibility, so that it could no longer see or feel the suffering it was causing the beloved: this is the fearful transformation that love undergoes the moment it becomes tainted by the love of self that springs from spiritual pride. (pp. 122-27)

[What] neither Goddard nor Wilson on their side nor Heilman on his [see excerpts dated 1920, 1934, and 1947] appear to recognise is that the text [of *The Turn of the Screw*] in fact—not possibly or probably but actually—yields two meanings, both equally self-consistent and self-complete. This is what the term "ambiguous" *means* when applied to *The Turn of the Screw* (and *The Sacred Fount* and *The Golden Bowl*): it means that on one reading the children are—not *may be* but *are*—corrupt, the governess *is* their good angel, and the apparitions are in some sense real, while on the other reading the children *are* innocent, the governess *is* a monster, and the apparitions are in some sense unreal or hallucinatory. In respect to the ambiguity, therefore, the relevant critical question is not "Which is the 'true' meaning?" but "Why did James insist on making his text yield, with this ferocious consistency, both meanings, the 'innocent' and the 'guilty'?" The answer to this question is not to choose one meaning to the exclusion of the other—without, that is, taking the other fully into account—and declare the preferred meaning (on whatever grounds, Freudian or Christian or commonsensical) to the the true one. The critic here is not invited to choose or prefer; he is invited only to recognise the co-existence of the two meanings as equally self-complete and self-consistent, and then to explain it—to explain this very co-existence of the two meanings which defines the ambiguity. (pp. 388-89)

Dorothea Krook, in her The Ordeal of Consciousness in Henry James, *Cambridge at the University Press, 1962, 422 p.*

LOUIS D. RUBIN, JR.   (essay date 1963-64)

[*Rubin is an American critic and educator who has written and edited numerous studies of Southern literature. In the following excerpt, he proposes that Douglas, who reads the governess's manuscript in the prologue to* The Turn of the Screw, *is in fact Miles in the main story.*]

My notion about [*The Turn of the Screw*] . . . is based on the prologue. It requires that one take with the utmost seriousness certain things said and done in that prologue, and that one apply them to the narrative proper, as told by the governess. What I have to say is based on the supposition that when Henry James placed details and people in a story, he usually did so by deliberate intention. This I believe is a fair assumption to make about Henry James. I agree with T. S. Eliot's remark that, compared with James's fictional characters, those of most other novelists "seem to be only accidentally in the same book."

Very well. How does the prologue to *The Turn of the Screw* begin? In an old house in the country, a group of men and women have been telling ghost stories by the fireside. One of them, the authorial voice, is the narrator. Someone had been describing an apparition that had appeared to a child. The host, whose name is Douglas, is at length compelled to say that he knows a ghost story involving not one but two children. No one else, he declares, has ever heard the story, which is written out in a manuscript at his London apartments. He could, he suggests, send for the manuscript.

The narrator of the prologue notices at once that his host is peculiarly concerned about the story: "It was to me that he appeared to propound this—appeared almost to appeal for aid not to hesitate." The host "had broken a thickness of ice, the

formation of many a winter; he had his reasons for a long silence." . . . Whatever the story is about, it is obviously very important to the host.

The narrator thereupon asks the host whether it had happened to him. "Oh, thank God, no!" Douglas replies. . . . Then did Douglas transcribe it? "Nothing but the impression. I took that *here*"—he tapped his heart. "I've never lost it." . . . Douglas goes on to say that the manuscript is "in old, faded ink, and in the most beautiful hand." . . . He hesitates, then continues. "A woman's. She's been dead these twenty years. She sent me the pages in question before she died." . . . (p. 315)

At this point "there was someone to be arch," . . . to draw the inference that Douglas had once been in love with the woman. Douglas does not smile at the suggestion, but he does speak without irritation. "She was a most charming person, but she was ten years older than I. She was my sister's governess. . . . She was the most agreeable woman I've ever known in her position; she would have been worthy of any whatever. It was long ago, and this episode was long before. I was at Trinity, and I had found her at home on my coming down the second summer." . . . (pp. 315-16)

What has James said there? The syntax is ambiguous. He appears to be making Douglas say that the episode in question took place long before Douglas knew the governess. But grammatically at least there is also the possibility that "it was long ago" could refer to the time when the woman sent the manuscript to Douglas, or perhaps when she died, so that "this episode was long before" may be the time when the story itself took place.

The possibility may not at first seem either very likely or very important. But soon we learn some other details. We learn that the situation described in the governess's manuscript also involves the governess and a boy who was ten years younger than herself, that in both instances she had been sent to a country place to take charge of a young girl, that both times the girl's brother had come down from school for the summer. Thus in each case the situation is interestingly similar. (p. 316)

[What] I am suggesting, of course, is the distinct possibility, a possibility that I think James wishes us to entertain, that Douglas *is* Miles, and that the story Douglas reads, supposedly about another little boy and the governess, is in fact about *him*. If this were so, then the scarcely-disguised erotic implications of the narrative are of direct importance. They would mean that not only did Miles not die at the close, but that the whole basis for believing in the governess's narrative is seriously undercut. (p. 318)

[We] possess the following bits of information. Douglas was in love with a governess ten years older than himself. So was Miles. Douglas had a younger sister. So did Miles. The governess had been very fond of Douglas. The governess was very probably in love with Miles. Douglas kept the secret of his love for the governess for forty years. If the governess was in love with Miles, Douglas kept that story to himself for many years as well, revealing it only after "a long silence."

Could Douglas and Miles, then, have been one and the same person, so that the story that Douglas read to his guests, having "broken a thickness of ice, the formation of many a winter," . . . was the governess's account, revealed to him shortly before her death, of her love for him?

It all depends on how one interprets the facts. Leon Edel's explanation is that Douglas's acquaintance with the governess dates from a period of from eight to ten years after the events described in the narrative, and that James carefully worked this out to give the governess more time to learn the ways of the world, so that her narrative could reflect this greater wisdom [see Additional Bibliography]. He bases this on the reasonable assumption that Douglas must have been eighteen or twenty years old, since he was down for his second summer after beginning Trinity College. Since the governess was ten years his senior, and was thus twenty-eight or thirty, Douglas's visit must have taken place eight or ten years after the events at Bly, at which time the governess was only twenty years old herself. This is I think a plausible explanation, but it does not sufficiently account for the obvious, as I think, truth that Henry James went out of his way to draw striking parallels between Douglas's relationship with the governess and that of Miles. Why did he do it? Why was it necessary to have Douglas also home from school, to give him a younger sister, to dwell so archly on the possibility of his having been in love with the governess, and she with him? We can usually assume that when Henry James does something in a novel, he has a reason for doing so.

The only explanation that I can see for James's having done this, and I think it a very logical explanation, is that he very much wanted us to consider the possibility that Douglas was Miles, and therefore that Miles did not die at the end of the narrative, because the impact of this possibility would render still further suspect the reliability of the governess as objective narrator of the uncanny events she chronicles in her manuscript. For if, to repeat, the governess had been in love with Miles, and if Miles had not died in her arms at the end, then not only the final scene of *The Turn of the Screw* but the entire narrative takes on another level of meaning, and, for the purposes of fiction, of ambiguity.

The possibility is then much greater that the governess's narrative is not a truthful rendition of events at all, but a story which an unmarried, middle-aged woman sent to a man shortly before her death, a man with whom she had once been in love when he was still a boy, in order to tell him about that love. It would then be, in short, an allegory of love, as it were, the application of which the governess intended for her now-grown lover to guess. This would indeed go far toward accounting for Douglas's extreme concern over the whole thing in the prologue.

As Gerald Willen, who has also noticed the odd resemblance between the circumstances of Douglas and Miles, notes in the Introduction to *A Casebook on Henry James's "The Turn of the Screw,"* "the essential fact remains that the story told by the governess needs to be read at varying levels. This is all the more true if we say that her story is, in effect, a fiction."

Mr. Willen's observation, I believe, gets directly at the matter. Whether Douglas was indeed Miles, or whether he was not and learned the story at a later date, the fact remains that the possibility exists, and that the import of its existence is to remind us of the need at all times to examine very closely what the governess is saying throughout the story. She is *not* an unbiased observer. An observation made by Leon Edel in 1955 still essentially holds true, I believe, even though at least a half-dozen interpretations of James's novel have been published since he said it: "The governess's account of her stay at Bly is riddled with inconsistencies which the many critics who have discussed the story have never sufficiently perceived." In their zeal to "prove" that *The Turn of the Screw* is this or that kind of novel, whether Christian, Freudian, hal-

lucinatory, old-fashioned supernatural, social commentary, and so on, James's critics have again and again seized upon certain statements made by the governess in the course of relating her story, without always remembering that *almost every remark* that the woman makes is subject to suspicion. (pp. 318-20)

[If] the suggestions that James seemed to be making about Douglas's identity in the prologue are true, Miles did *not* die in the governess's arms after uttering the name of the dead valet. And if that is the case, then the whole story is to be doubted, and we can be certain of nothing. What do we have then?

I suggest that what we have is a fascinating ghost story by Henry James, who with consummate mastery has led us along first one trail and then another, until finally we have doubled back upon ourselves and we are just where we started. In short, true to his announced intention of tricking "those not easily caught," Henry James tells his tale of a governess and her two charges so very convincingly that he first makes us believe that we have read a true ghost story, in the traditional vein. Then when we begin thinking back on the events of the story, he makes us see that the whole narrative has been significantly qualified, so that there is every reason to doubt the existence of the ghosts at all. And the consequence of that is that we look closely at the dcescription of the circumstances in which the story has been told, only to have it hinted that it isn't a factual account at all. (p. 326)

Louis D. Rubin, Jr., "One More Turn of the Screw," in Modern Fiction Studies, *Vol. IX, No. 4, Winter, 1963-64, pp. 314-28.*

ERIC SOLOMON   (essay date 1964)

[*In the following excerpt, Solomon analyzes* The Turn of the Screw *from the viewpoint that Mrs. Grose is responsible for the deaths of Quint and Miss Jessel, and that she drives the governess insane to regain control of the children. In his unexcerpted introduction to this analysis, Solomon states that his essay "is unique for two reasons. There is no opening paragraph that includes a rich cluster of footnotes referring to the classic controversies over the short novel" and that his essay "is definitive and provides the one, incontrovertible explanation for the strange happenings at Bly. Never again need there be another explication of* The Turn of the Screw.*"]*

If only the governess had realized that the "dreadfulness" at Bly called for expert attention, she would have turned, as many of her compatriots did at this time, to the services of a master-detective. Sherlock Holmes, for example, would have cleared up the horrible crimes at Bly—for crimes they were—in an instant. He would simply have asked three questions familiar to all readers of mysteries: "Who is the least obvious suspect? What is the motive? What is the nature of the crime, and how did it take place?" Lacking the Holmesian advantage of on-the-spot investigation (for he would have rushed Watson onto the first train from Paddington), we must apply our investigative powers to the governess' manuscript. A careful reading of this deposition can leave no doubt. The least obvious suspect, and the criminal, is the housekeeper, Mrs. Grose; the motive is greed; the crime is murder, more than one murder! Let us read the governess' story with the care we would apply to, say, *The Hound of the Baskervilles* and watch the incredible become elementary.

Our first introduction to Mrs. Grose, presented with typical Jamesian irony, provides the key. The master had "placed at the head of the little establishment—*but below stairs only*—an excellent woman, Mrs. Grose, whom he was sure his visitor would like and who had formerly been maid to his mother. She was now housekeeper and *was also acting for the time as superintendent to the little girl,* of whom, without children of her own, she was by good luck, *extremely fond."* (My italics.) Motive? Love and ambition. Mrs. Grose has already risen from maid to housekeeper—why not to governess? Her obstacle is this young lady "who should go down as governess [and] would be in supreme authority." Thus the governess, who has the proper credentials for her role, replaces the housekeeper who, despite her lack of education, has had Flora for her own *since the death of the previous governess.* When the new governess' ordeal has ended, there will have been another death, and Mrs. Grose will again have control of Flora. How easily Holmes could have prevented this second tragedy!

Flora, of course, "the most beautiful child I had ever seen," would have tempted one less evil than Mrs. Grose. At the start, the governess herself is disturbed about the housekeeper whose position is being usurped. The governess has the sense to brood in the coach over the forthcoming relationship with the woman she is going to replace, but Mrs. Grose's decent curtsy, her appearance as a "stout, simple, plain, clean, wholesome woman," allay the governess' suspicions. Yet the curtsy is ironic, "as if I had been the mistress or a distinguished visitor"; Mrs. Grose seems "positively on her guard" against showing how glad she is to see the new governess. If only the governess had sustained her original misgivings, all might have been well. The evidence is there for the reader, however. "I wondered even then a little why she should wish not to show it, and that, with reflection, with suspicion, might of course have made me uneasy."

Once alerted to the possibility of duplicity in Mrs. Grose's actions, we see it in her every word and deed. She is supposed to be gratified that Flora will now sleep with the new governess instead of with her old friend. And the simple young girl is completely taken in. "Oh, she was glad I was there!" Glad, when every move of the new governess brings pain to Mrs. Grose: first the loss of Flora; then having it thrown in her face that she cannot read ("I winced at my mistake") and that she is stupid ("'To contaminate?'—my big word left her at a loss"). But even at this stage Mrs. Grose gets a little revenge. She raises a curiosity in the governess about Miles that "was to deepen almost to pain. Mrs. Grose was aware, I could judge, of what she had produced in me. . . ." The naive governess continues to push Mrs. Grose, only "fancying" that "she rather sought to avoid me."

The tone of **The Turn of the Screw** becomes more sinister. Mrs. Grose's reply to a question about the previous governess is virtually a threat. "'The last governess? She was also young and pretty—*almost as young and almost as pretty, Miss, even as you.*'" (My italics.) The mystery thickens as the two women misunderstand each other. When the governess says, "'He seems to like us young and pretty,'" referring to the Harley Street master, Mrs. Grose's mind turns on Peter Quint, the previous butler. "'Oh, he *did* . . . it was the way he liked everyone.' She had no sooner spoken indeed than she caught herself up."

Soon she blushes and becomes silent. Clearly she resented Quint's way with young and pretty women. Why? What was Quint to her? Why is Quint uppermost in her mind? Why is the "open" Mrs. Grose suddenly careful? "'Did she die here?' 'No—she went off.' I don't know what there was in this brevity

of Mrs. Grose's that struck me as ambiguous." But Mrs. Grose will not give herself away. "'. . . please, Miss,' said Mrs. Grose, 'I must get to my work.'" And we shall see just what is the nature of Mrs. Grose's work.

Although she may not be able to read, Mrs. Grose is extremely acute. The governess has only to make a vague statement and "She promptly understood me." With understanding, the governess thinks, must come affection, and the women embrace like sisters. Mrs. Grose's "work," then, is to gain the governess' confidence, and this the housekeeper does perfectly. For when the governess sees the figure on the battlements and at the window and, supposedly, describes Peter Quint, Mrs. Grose controls the whole episode. This crux of the story has given even Edmund Wilson pause, yet, when properly understood, it is not in the least confusing.

How can the governess describe Peter Quint unless he really exists? Only if Mrs. Grose, cleverly working on her victim's imagination, tells her that what she has seen is Peter Quint. After seeing the figure, the governess rushes to her friend, is convinced Mrs. Grose knows nothing, but, "Scarce anything in the whole history seems to me so odd as this fact that my real beginning of fear was one, as I may say, with the instinct of sparing my companion." Although some instinct warns her about Mrs. Grose, the young lady misinterprets the warning. Henry James, however, gives the perceptive reader the only clue necessary. Someone, the governess thinks, is practising upon her. But who? She does not know. "There was but one sane inference: someone had taken a liberty rather *gross*." (My italics.) Even Dr. Watson would catch the clue.

The governess has her second vision, and once again Mrs. Grose is immediately on the scene. This time, however, she appears frightened. "I wondered why *she* should be scared." Perhaps she thinks that the governess is on to her game, but after seeing the younger woman's face, she regains her confidence and returns to her work—of driving the governess mad. "'You're white as a sheet. You look awful.'" The ensuing dialogue between Mrs. Grose and the governess is a prime example of what the modern psychologist would call non-directive:

> "It's time we should be at church."
>
> "Oh, I'm not fit for church!"
>
> "Won't it do you good?"
>
> "It won't do *them*—!" I nodded at the house.
>
> "The children?"
>
> "I can't leave them now."
>
> "You're afraid—?"

Pushing the governess more deeply into her fears, Mrs. Grose manipulates her victim—who only vaguely suspects with whom she is dealing. "Mrs. Grose's large face showed me, at this, for the first time, the far-away faint glimmer of a consciousness more acute. . . ." The dialogue is a masterpiece of dramatic irony: "'I have my duty.' 'So have I mine,' she replied." Now the governess describes the man she has seen, partly like the devil, partly like the master. What is as important as a dog barking in the night, what a detective should grasp at once, is the fact that the governess—and the reader—*has only Mrs. Grose's word for it that the apparition is Peter Quint!* The governess might have been frightened into describing a club-footed midget, and Mrs. Grose could *still* have cried, "Quint!"

James with his sister Alice.

She presses her advantage; Quint was alone in charge of Bly last year (as the governess is this year), "'alone with *us*.'" (Mrs. Grose's italics.) And what happened? "'He died.' 'Died?' I almost shrieked." Mrs. Grose's work is off to a good start.

Henry James makes abundantly clear that the housekeeper dominates the situation. The governess realizes "my dreadful liability to impressions of the order so vividly exemplified, and my companion's knowledge . . . of that liability." James' irony is manifest. Mrs. Grose, the "honest ally," accepts what the governess says "without directly impugning my sanity." Not directly, but surely non-directly.

The reader-detective may wonder at this point why Mrs. Grose is intent on driving the governess mad. The answer clearly lies in the description of Mrs. Grose's relations with the late Peter Quint. "'Quint was much too free.'" Too free with Miles? wonders the governess. "'Too free with everyone!'" exclaims Mrs. Grose, dropping her mask for the moment. The innocent governess assumes that Quint was too free perhaps with the maids or with Miss Jessel—but the reader wonders how free a younger Quint had been with a younger Mrs. Grose.

Added to this possibility is the certainty that Mrs. Grose was bitterly jealous of Quint because he was in charge of "her" children. "'So he had everything to say . . . even about *them*.'" James' ironic stance plainly shows through the remainder of

this essential dialogue. "'Them—that creature?' I had to smother a kind of howl. 'And you could bear it!' 'No. I couldn't—*and I can't now!*'" (My italics.) Meaning not only that she couldn't stand Quint's control of the children, particularly Flora, *and* Mrs. Grose can't stand the present situation either. The governess is too obtuse to take warning—even though she faintly suspects the worst, she cannot face the truth.

The truth is, obviously, that despite Mrs. Grose's regained "rigid control" the next day, she has revealed herself as a passionate, jealous woman. And the governess, as well as the aware reader, is "still haunted with the shadow of something she had not told me." How did Peter Quint die?

> Peter Quint was found, by a labourer going to early work, stone dead on the road from the village: a catastrophe explained—superficially at least—by a visible wound to his head; such a wound as might have been produced—and as, on the final evidence, *had* been—by a fatal slip, in the dark and after leaving the public house, on the steepish icy slope, a wrong path, altogether, at the bottom of which he lay. The icy slope, the turn mistaken at night and in liquor, accounted for much—practically, in the end and after the inquest and boundless chatter, for everything; but there had been matters in his life—strange passages and perils, secret disorders, vices more than suspected—that would have accounted for a great deal more.

"Superficially"; "might have"; "accounted for much"; the missing link is obvious. Peter Quint was murdered, murdered by a Mrs. Grose who would stick at nothing to regain control of Flora. Whether the ghosts exist or not is unimportant. If they don't exist, Mrs. Grose is using the illusion to destroy the governess; if they do exist, they have come to see Mrs. Grose, but that hard case is still capable of handling them, in death as in life, and in using them for her own supreme purpose—to retain little Flora.

Mrs. Grose merely has to keep digging at the governess' apprehensions, which are doubled after Mrs. Grose has implanted the idea of Miss Jessel. Once more the mask slips, and we see Mrs. Grose's envy of Miss Jessel. Practically mesmerizing the governess—"She once more took my hand in both her own, holding it as tight as if to fortify me against the increase in alarm . . ."—she tells of Miss Jessel's beauty, infamy. For her part, the governess angers Mrs. Grose for the same reasons Miss Jessel had. The governess wonders at the relationship between Quint and her predecessor, "'In spite of the difference . . . she was a lady.' 'And he so dreadfully below,' said Mrs. Grose," completing the governess' implied insult to the housekeeper. Although she lost Quint to a "lady," although she must always lose Flora to a lady, Mrs. Grose will never give in. Miss Jessel, the housekeeper remarks, "'paid for it!'" by her death. The governess, as we learn from Douglas' introduction to the story, pays for it by a shattered life, post-Bly.

The two women continue their talks. And just in case the reader has missed James' first hint as to how the governess was able to describe the ghost, he reiterates: the governess gives a picture of the two—"a portrait on the exhibition of which she (Mrs. Grose) had instantly recognized and named them." That Mrs. Grose is the villain should be obvious from her very omnipresence, an element of the case rarely noticed. She is always at the governess, digging, probing, hinting. "She had told me, bit by bit, under pressure, a great deal; but a small shifty spot on the wrong side of it all still sometimes brushed my brow like the wing of a bat . . . 'I don't believe anything so horrible. . . .'" But she will. Mrs. Grose will see to that by perpetually adding to the horror.

The governess continually adds fuel to Mrs. Grose's anger. "'You remind him that Quint was only a *base menial*?' 'As *you* might say!'" (My italics.) Her naïveté is remarkable; this timid, inexperienced girl can say to her elder, "'. . . you haven't my dreadful boldness of mind, and you keep back, out of timidity and modesty and delicacy. . . .'" These words applied to Mrs. Grose! If the governess does not understand, the author, behind the narrative, certainly does. ". . . if my pupils practised upon me, it was surely with the minimum of grossness. It was all in the other quarter that after a lull, the grossness broke out."

The governess continues to see the ghosts; Mrs. Grose obstinately refuses to see them. "At that moment, in the state of my nerves, I absolutely believed she lied. . . ." Everything that she tells Mrs. Grose, by now her confidant and mentor, is received with that lady's "smooth aspect." Ironically, the governess thinks Mrs. Grose lacks imagination because of the "serenity in all her look," serenity because her plans are moving well. She assents to all the governess' changes of mood and shifting interpretations of the spirits' motives. And she plants the next seed in the governess' mind: she must write to the master. The governess assumes that Mrs. Grose misses the point: such a letter would mean either that the master might consider the governess mad, or she would feel it necessary to "'leave, on the spot. . . .'" A conclusion devoutly to be wished for, on Mrs. Grose's part.

The strain of Bly, the governess' shaky heredity, her inexperience—all make her an easy mark. She is tempted to run away, but she remains, despite her growing uneasiness about "Mrs. Grose's odd face." "So I see her still, so I see her best," remembers the governess when writing her report, "facing the flame from her straight chair in the dusky, shining room. . . ." A sinister figure, surely. And a pathetic one withal, at times tempted to confess ("'The fault's mine!' She had turned quite pale . . .") and then having her resolution stiffened by the constant reminders of her place, her illiteracy that must keep Flora in the hands of such as Miss Jessel and her successor—"My question [as to why Mrs. Grose does not write the master] had a sarcastic force that I had not fully intended."

The climax comes almost without Mrs. Grose's active participation, so well has she prepared the way. The frantic governess continues to put pressure on the children; Mrs. Grose continues to get "possession of my hand" and to insist upon the letter being sent, when matters work out even better than Mrs. Grose has hoped. She accompanies the governess to the lake where the latter avers that Flora will meet the ghost of Miss Jessel. Note that this excursion is described as one of the rare moments when Flora has been out of the governess' sight. How deprived Mrs. Grose must have felt! Once at the lake, Mrs. Grose forgets the governess: "She threw herself on her knees and, drawing the child to her breast, clasped in a long embrace the little, tender yielding body." Confident that Flora is hers, that the governess has gone too far and sent the letter, Mrs. Grose "kept the child's hand."

Indeed, the governess goes farther than Mrs. Grose expected. Insisting on Miss Jessel's visibility, the governess terrifies Flora,

and Mrs. Grose turns on her superior "very formidably," with "her loud, shocked protest, a burst of high disapproval." Ghost or no ghost, Mrs. Grose is holding on to Flora and looking at the governess with "negation, repulsion." Quick to grasp her victory, to settle the governess for good, Mrs. Grose unites with Flora "in pained opposition." We hear the note of triumph. "'She isn't there, little lady, and nobody's there—and you never see nothing, my sweet! How can poor Miss Jessel? when poor Miss Jessel's dead and buried? We know, don't we, love? . . . It's all a mere mistake and a worry and a joke—and we'll go home as fast as we can!'" And, the reader might add, we'll get away from this governess who threatened us as much as the others, but who was easier to handle. Flora is convinced; she begs Mrs. Grose to keep the governess away. Mrs. Grose's victory is complete. She is "mutely possessed of the little girl," and Flora spends the night in Mrs. Grose's bedroom—"the happiest of arrangements" for her.

The next morning, Mrs. Grose confidently solidifies her position. Having "girded her loins to meet me once more," the vindictive housekeeper really turns the screw on the governess. Flora now fears only her present governess and will never speak to her again, reports Mrs. Grose, cruelly—"with a frankness, which, I made sure, had more behind it." When the governess wails that Flora will give a bad report to the master, Mrs. Grose gleefully agrees, "'And him who thinks so well of you!'" Flora wants "'Never again to so much as look at you.'" And although matters do not work out exactly according to Mrs. Grose's plans—the governess sends her and Flora away to London instead of leaving herself—Mrs. Grose is satisfied. She has Flora. "'I'll go—I'll go. I'll go this morning.'" When the governess falters, "'If you *should* wish to wait . . .'" Mrs. Grose thinks quickly and throws the governess a sop: Flora does speak horrors, there must have been a ghost, the governess is justified—anything to assure the housekeeper's escape with Flora. The governess still tries to hold Mrs. Grose; there is no need to go, the letter will have given the alarm. Mrs. Grose is equal to this final obstacle. The letter, she says, never went; Miles must have stolen it. This desperate lie would be patent to anyone except the shattered governess who scarcely notices that "it was Mrs. Grose who first brought up the plumb with an almost elate 'You see!'" in order to make her departure.

The climax to Mrs. Grose's villainy comes when she and Flora roll out of the gates, reunited. The anticlimax, and a very serious one it is, would surely have been avoided if only Sherlock Holmes—or even Lestrade or Gregson—had been called in. The governess has been maddened by her experiences, which she believes to be the result of either Miles' and Flora's sins or to be supernatural effects. She frightens Miles to death by her fears of the ghosts. She never realizes, as the thoughtful reader must, that she, and Miles, and, indeed, Miss Jessel and Peter Quint, have all been the victims of that most clever and desperate of Victorian villainesses, the evil Mrs. Grose. (pp. 205-11)

*Eric Solomon, "The Return of the Screw," in Uni-
versity Review, Vol. XXX, No. 3, March, 1964, pp.
205-11.*

MURIEL WEST (essay date 1964)

[West was an American poet and critic. In the following excerpt, she maintains that the death of Miles occurred due to the governess's violent clutching of him in the final scene, rather than to simple fright at either the ghost or the governess's questioning.]

Critics have always been struck by the death scene that concludes *The Turn of the Screw* and, being struck, have given us a variety of interpretations—psychological, religious, poetic; but they have never accounted for the improbability that Miles—whose good health and sound heart are never quentioned in the tale—should die of heart failure. In James's other stories concluding with the death of a young boy (**"The Pupil"** and **"The Author of Beltraffio"**) we are prepared by earlier accounts of the boy's health to accept his final death. Not so with Miles. We are not even prepared to find him bewildered and demoralized by the series of embarrassing questions put to him by his governess: Miles is presented as remarkably well-poised for a ten-year-old.

Yet, critics continue to assume an implausible cause-and-effect relationship between (for instance) the governess' questioning and Miles's responses—including his death. For example, the governess is thought (by a recent critic) to be "indirectly responsible"; she is "in some sense, guilty" because of her sin of "Faustian pride": it is "her insistence that kills little Miles, . . . that dispossesses the heart of the child": she makes up her mind to "get all"—to force him to "a full confession of all his 'crimes' at a point when the child has been harrowed already to the furthest limit of his small resources, when he has gone as far as he can in the way of confession and repentance"; she is guilty of "harrowing a poor little soul beyond its powers of endurance, of pressing it to a degree of self-exposure that cannot but destroy it" [see Dorothea Krook excerpt dated 1962].

"A degree of self-exposure that *cannot* but destroy . . ."? The disproportion between the supposed cause and effect suggests that we follow James's advice to read *The Turn of the Screw* with more than "some attention." By a sober and careful reading or rereading we may be able to illuminate some of the ambiguities in the governess' "crystalline . . . record of so many intense anomalies and obscurities"; we may even see our way around her "explanation of them"—explanation that James says is "a different matter" . . .—and so be in a position to suggest a more satisfactory hypothesis in accounting for Miles's death than hitherto has been offered.

In the interest of clearer reading we may first observe that the subject matter of the last section of the tale may be roughly divided into what the governess and Miles *say* and what they *do*. For the most part the conversation is simple, perfectly clear and dignified. She asks him if he took from the hall table her letter to his uncle; he admits he did; she asks him why, and he answers simply: "To see what you said about me." . . . And so it goes. The so-called "harrowing of a poor little soul," the alleged "pressing [of] it to a degree of self-exposure that cannot but destroy it," is as easy to read as a child's primer. On the other hand, the governess' account of what she does, what Miles does, what Miles and the ghost of Peter Quint feel and think (as though she were in a position to know!) form an intricate, far from lucid, accompaniment to what may be called a simple—but curiosity-provoking—theme song. In other words, James presents at the same time (through the governess' confused hypersensitivity) the front and the back of the "tapestry"—but leaves it entirely up to the reader to determine how the governess' considerable physical and mental activity should be understood and how much her observations and her explanations should be accepted as fact. It is this part of her narrative that deserves our closest attention.

By examining a few of the long paragraphs that intervene between a simple question and a simple answer we may discover a good bit more about what happens in the finale of *The

Turn of the Screw* than comes to light if we merely satisfy our curiosity about what Miles will say in answer to the governess' persistent probing into his "crimes." (p. 283)

[In] the last chapter, when [the governess] follows her shaking (motivated by "pure tenderness") with the question, "What then did you do?" we may tamely follow her implication that her *question* makes [Miles] look "in vague pain all round the top of the room" and draw "his breath, two or three times over, as if with difficulty." . . . Or we may believe that her shaking is vigorous enough to make him short of breath and suffer from "pain" that is physical rather than mental. As we shall see, he continues to have difficulty in getting his breath and in making his answers. He appears "to weigh" a question, "but in a manner quite detached and helpless"; he tries to remember, but fails. For a brief interval the "desolation of his surrender" makes her question the rightness of what she is doing, for, as she says, it "was practically, by this time, so complete that I ought to have left it there." But she is "blind with victory," "infatuated," . . . and even when she asks herself the astounding question: "if he *were* the innocent what then on earth was I?"—she brushes the question aside; but before she does she is momentarily "paralysed," and "let[s] him go a little," with the result that he, "with a deep-drawn sigh" turns away, and is "soon at some distance" from her, "still breathing hard and again with the air, though now without anger for it, of being confined against his will." Once again he looks up "at the dim day as if, of what had hitherto sustained him," nothing is left "but an unspeakable anxiety." . . . (pp. 285-86)

Although he is at "some distance" from her, his freedom lasts only until he says he "suppose[s]" that what he "sometimes said" was "too bad . . . to write home." . . . She yields to a fleeting leniency ("Stuff and nonsense!"), but then immediately asks him, with a sternness that she claims is not for him but for "his judge, his executioner" (apparently meaning the master who expelled him): "What *were* these things?" . . . Her sternness, she says, makes him "avert himself again," and "that movement" makes *her*, "with a single bound and an irrepressible cry, spring straight upon him." She then attempts to cover up her admission (that his *movement* causes her gymnastic exuberance) by putting the blame on the reappearance at the window of "the white face of damnation." She bewails the "drop" of her "victory" and the return of her "battle"—adding that the "wildness" of her "veritable leap" only served as a "great betrayal." She lets the "impulse flame up to convert the climax of his dismay into the very proof of his liberation." . . . implying that his "dismay" is caused by his inability to see what she thinks she sees. For our part we may believe, rather, that his dismay is caused by the wildness of her veritable leap—by her springing straight upon him. Like a cat playing with a mouse, she has recaptured the small creature that she "let . . . go a little."

Before pushing on to a conclusion we may pause to remind ourselves that James says her explanations are "a different matter"—not to be confused with facts. And to remember also that James wrote Paul Bourget—directly after taking him to task for explaining too much in his novels, insisting that to do so is "an injury to the patches of ambiguity and the abysses of shadow which really are the clothing—or much of it—of the *effects* that constitute the material of our trade"—that *The Turn of the Screw* is "an exercise in the art of not appearing to one's self to fail." The governess as governess has certainly failed: Flora is gone and Miles has defied her. We may take her vivid but confused and often contradictory account of her actions and feelings as *her* exercise in the "art of not appearing to one's self to fail." And we may be sure that James, as the guiding hand behind her "exercise," has taken care not to let her explain away the "patches of ambiguity and the abysses of shadow" in which her tale abounds.

Some of these patches try to the utmost our efforts at explanation. For instance, after talking about Miles's "dismay," she excitedly goes on: "'No more, no more, no more!' I shrieked to my visitant as I tried to press him against me." . . . What does she mean by "him"—Miles or her "visitant"? Does she know which is which? From this point on her speeches lose a good measure of their earlier composure and clarity. Forgetting the whole purpose of her inspired "act" (to keep Miles "unaware"), she actually tells him where to look for the ghost: "But it's at the window—straight before us. It's *there*—the coward horror, there for the last time!" Next she tries to convince us (or herself?) that Miles's distress is caused by his inability to "see." But his continued struggle for air and, particularly, his being "at" her "in a white rage" . . . forcibly suggest that the earlier "desolation of his surrender" has left him. We can picture him fighting her now, struggling to free himself from her clutches—whatever they might be subsequent to her "veritable leap." The abyss of shadow is too deep for us to make out an armlock, a scissors hold, a side chancery, or a full- or half-Nelson. Whatever she is doing (most probably her action shifts from moment to moment), she presents us with a strangely confused description of Miles's response: "His face gave again, round the room, its convulsed supplication." . . . Is his "supplication" convulsed? Or his *face*?

As she continues, the ambiguities become even more complex—well-nigh indecipherable. She uses the word "launched" in a way that could be construed as a speech-label meaning "said vigorously," or as an action-word meaning "threw myself"; also, her wording is such that we cannot tell if she is speaking *to* Miles or to the "beast"—who is now, fantastically, diffused throughout the room "like the taste of poison." As a supreme example of James's "amusement" in creating reader wonder with ambiguity, the passage deserves exact quotation: "'What does he matter now, my own?—what will he *ever* matter? *I* have you,' I launched at the beast, 'but he has lost you for ever!' Then for the demonstration of my work, 'There, *there!*' I said to Miles." . . . If she is speaking to the "beast," then she is saying that *she* "has" him; that is, she now is "possessed," and Miles at last is free of a supposed "possession" by an evil spirit. Oddly enough (or rather, we might say, with a curious consistency) her last words echo the possession-theme: "his little heart, dispossessed, had stopped." On the other hand, if she is speaking throughout to Miles, she says she has *him* (at the same time she gives the "beast" a kick or a push) and she consequently is the "possessing" agent—an end-result she has long desired. When he earlier rebuffed her (on the occasion of her visit to his bedroom), saying (though "ever so gently") that he wants her to "let" him "alone," she continues to "linger beside him" and question him. When she senses "a small faint quaver of consenting consciousness," she says: "it made me drop on my knees beside the bed and seize once more the chance of possessing him." . . . (pp. 286-87)

In any case, just before his death Miles manages to jerk free enough to utter "the cry of a creature hurled over an abyss." Even then she will not let him go, but holds him at last with a "passion": "the grasp with which I recovered him might have been that of catching him in his fall. I caught him, yes, I held him—it may be imagined with what a passion; but at the end of a minute I began to feel what it truly was that I held." . . . It seems inescapable that we reject the opinion that Miles dies because his little soul has been pressed to "a degree of self-exposure that cannot but destroy it." It is the violent behavior of his governess that brings about his death—whether directly or indirectly is scarcely possible to determine without more investigation than our present close reading brings to light. Everywhere we are prevented by ambiguities and abysses of shadow from reaching a position that permits flat-footed statements. We may suspect that she kills him with "psychopathic compulsive violence"; or that (in effect) he kills himself because he fights back and the exertion is too much for him; or that he simply dies from the strain and the fright; or that all of these contribute to the final "dispossession" of his little heart. (p. 287)

[Our] present purpose . . . has been, simply, to read *The Turn of the Screw* with more than "some" attention and so reveal the absurdity of the contention that Miles dies because his little soul is made to confess beyond its powers of endurance—pressed "to a degree of self-exposure that cannot but destroy it"; and to point out, on the contrary, that the physical violence of the governess—generally overlooked by critics—may much more reasonably be said to cause his death. . . . Let it suffice, then, to conclude by saying: In the final section of *The Turn of the Screw* the governess indulges in an exuberant debauch of violence that contributes to the sudden death of the little Miles. . . . (p. 288)

> Muriel West, "The Death of Miles in 'The Turn of the Screw'," in PMLA, 79, Vol. LXXIX, No. 3, June, 1964, pp. 283-88.

THOMAS MABRY CRANFILL AND ROBERT LANIER CLARK, JR. (essay date 1965)

[*In the following excerpt, Cranfill and Clark examine James's revisions of* The Turn of the Screw *for the 1908 edition of his collected works.*]

Few critics except Leon Edel have had anything to say about the two texts of *The Turn of the Screw*. Nowadays the study of textual niceties is not popular in many circles. The usual practice seems to be to leave such drudgery as collation to the pedant who may be good for little else and thus free one's self to engage the energies, critical faculties, and imagination in pursuing images, allegories, paradoxes, symbols, ironies, ambiguities, theological implications—what not. But is it safe to overlook the considerable revisions the tale underwent before reappearing in the definitive New York edition of 1908—in the form in which James intended finally to leave it?

Those whom Ezra Pound accused of talking pettiness about James's style might have their eyes opened by the scores of conscientious, ingenious, and imaginative changes that James made in the original text of 1898 as he readied it for the New York edition. Practically without exception his alterations are improvements, stylistically and semantically. In perusing them, one should recall again James's pained rejoinder to the accusation of indecently expatiating: *The Turn of the Screw* contains "not an inch of expatiation," James insisted; as he composed it he fought for every grudged inch of space. He carried on the fight in his revisions, rendering dozens of passages more concise.

Clarity as well as conciseness concerned him greatly. He replaced pronouns whose antecedents were not clear, deleted words that verged on the archaic, relieved the text of superfluous punctuation, rendered metaphors consistent, italicized words to make immediately apparent an emphasis he sought, rearranged sentences and simplified word order, and thus clarified his drift. For the elaborate he everywhere substituted simpler words and expressions. He replaced "interlocutor" with "converser," "interlocutress" with "informant," "had beheld" with "had seen," "mounted afresh" with "revived," and "dreadfully austere inquiry" with "straight question enough."

He took pains to introduce strong words in place of the less effective, precise words and phrases in place of the vague, changing "sense" to "grasp," "Yes" to "Never," "see" to "trace," "done" to "administered," "the only thing" to "the one appearance," "thing" to "resource," "most strange manner," to "very high manner," "the business" to "the strain." He was careful to avoid needless verbal and phrasal repetitions, some of them already in the original text, others introduced by his revisions. As he read through his earlier text he apparently noticed that he had overworked "on the spot"; the phrase accordingly several times became something else or disappeared completely. To the extravagant repetition of sounds—to matters of euphony—he was also sensitive, so that he removed such phrases as "weary with watching" and "so terribly suddenly" and put "weary with vigils" and "so terribly all at once" in their place.

That he saw multifarious opportunities to improve the text of 1898 will not surprise those who recall that James dictated it. Not that there is anything weak or careless about the earlier version, stylistically or otherwise. On the contrary, it is a monument to James's powers of concentration and a magnificently effective story. James simply rendered finer an already finely wrought piece of prose. Both versions inspire admiration for James the craftsman, the stylist, the artist. The final version inspires admiration for James the editor as well. He clearly wanted his collected fiction to include *The Turn of the Screw* in as highly polished a state as adroit and painstaking revision could yield. The pains he lavished on the polishing should provide with food for thought critics who persist in accepting his dismissal of the tale as an irresponsible little fiction, an inferior subject.

The revisions illuminate much in addition to his lively artistic conscience. They tell us something about his intentions regarding, first, the governess' reactions to her experiences and, second, the general tone of the story. Though the governess impresses one as sufficiently effusive and nerve-wracked in the text of 1898, James set about to intensify her expressions of horror and suffering. Her "grief" of 1898 became her "anguish" of 1908. Similarly, James substituted "the unspeakable minute" for "the minute," "tension" for "excitement," "bolt" for "retreat," "turmoil" for "predicament," "wailed" for "sobbed," "ordeal" for "predicament," "my horrid plunge" for "my plunge," "my dreadful way" for "my way," and "his dreadful little mind," for "his little mind."

In his preface to *The Turn of the Screw* James asserted that "the study is of a conceived 'tone,' the tone of suspected and felt trouble." Analyzing James's revisions, Leon Edel noticed in his edition of *The Ghostly Tales* that the changes betrayed James's determination "to alter the nature of the governess' testimony from that of a report of things observed, perceived, recalled, to things *felt*." Edel arrived at the conclusion that the

tale is primarily a record of feeling. We could not agree more heartily. Our own study of the text validates Edel's findings, gives us a wholesome respect for James's prefatory remark, and leads us to believe that the master meant precisely what he said when he spoke of "felt" trouble.

Here are a few illustrations of how James reinforced this already conspicuous tone. He changed "I perceived" to "I felt" (twice), "I now reflect" to "I now feel," and "Mrs. Grose appeared to me" to "Mrs. Grose affected me." These in addition to the scores of passages in which the governess had already confided her feelings in the 1898 version. The result is unmistakable.

In the course of the novel the governess insists that she sees the ghost of the late valet, Peter Quint, four times. In Chapter IX, at the third encounter, in 1898, she writes, "I saw that there was someone on the stair." James amended the sentence to read, "I knew that there was a figure on the stair," the governess' feeling by now having grown sufficiently intense to constitute, for her, knowledge.

In the more than seven printed pages of the prologue in *The Turn of the Screw*, 1908, the word "feel" occurs not once, in any of its forms. But on the very first page of the governess' narrative she begins to use it, in her second sentence, and she continues to use some variant or derivative of it ("feel," "felt," "feeling," "feelings") until her very last page, where it occurs in her penultimate sentence. In all, it appears in her record eighty-two times.

Impressive though these statistics are, they do not tell the whole story. Keeping company with "feel" throughout are other words, repeated over and over, to show that the governess is recording, not what is provable, but what she senses or fancies or feels, how things appear or seem to her. Note the recurrences of some form of the following: "fancy" (used thirteen times), "appear" (eighteen times), "sense" (twenty-one times), "seem" (twenty-three times). Really, her manuscript puts one in mind of the last line of the saucy old limerick,

> There was a Faith Healer of Deal
> Who said, "Although pain isn't real,
> When I sit on a pin, and it punctures my skin,
> I dislike what I fancy I feel."

James wasted no time in giving his reader the clue, as these extracts from Chapter I of the governess' manuscript will show. The chapter encompasses about four and a half pages.

> I . . . felt indeed sure I had made a mistake.
> The little girl . . . affected me on the spot . . .
> . . . as I almost felt it . . .
> I felt within half an hour . . .
> . . . a sound or two . . . that I had fancied I heard.
> But these fancies were not marked enough . . .
> I felt quite sure she would presently . . .
> I remember feeling the impulse . . .
> What I felt the next day . . .
> I had the fancy of being . . .

Nor do the clues cease after the first chapter. They abound literally from first to last. These excerpts come from the final chapter.

> I felt how voluntarily . . . I *might*.
> I could feel in the sudden fever . . .
> I felt that the cause was mine . . .

I felt myself . . .
The only thing he felt was . . .
I seemed to float not into clearness . . .
. . . which . . . I suffered, feeling . . .
I felt a sick swim . . .
. . . it now, to my sense, filled the room . . .
at the end of a minute I began to feel . . .

So there we have it. We trust that none will argue that the repetitions are fortuitous or careless. The admirers of James's artistry as a prose stylist would find such an argument hard to bear. On the contrary, we fancy or feel—nay, are convinced—that James sounded these recurring notes purposefully and artfully to establish the tone of *"felt"* trouble for which he was striving. (pp. 16-20)

> *Thomas Mabry Cranfill and Robert Lanier Clark, Jr., in their* An Anatomy of "The Turn of the Screw," *University of Texas Press, 1965, 195 p.*

THOMAS J. BONTLY (essay date 1969)

[*Bontly is an American fiction writer and critic. In the following excerpt, he asserts that* The Turn of the Screw *sustains both the apparitionist and the hallucinationist theories regarding the ghosts, and does so in order to allow the narrative to remain credible while using ghosts to symbolize evil and sexual guilt.*]

Both the apparitionists and the psychoanalysts have, it seems to me, exceeded the boundaries of legitimate textual evidence in developing their theories, and their refutations of one another seem too well established to need recapitulation here. James's practice in fiction, it should be noted however, was never to let his reader take pertinent information for granted (a form of rhetorical anarchy he is sometimes credited with inventing, but which his criticism shows he would not have understood), but rather to allow the *established* facts to speak for themselves, and to indicate ironic alternatives and shades of meaning with great precision. Furthermore, neither the apparitionists nor the psychoanalysts have, it seems to me, adequately described James's vision of evil in *The Turn of the Screw* in a way that corresponds to his characteristic approach to this problem in the rest of his fiction. The purpose of this study, then, is to reassess the evidence of the tale itself, and to define as closely as possible the nature of evil and human sexuality as James presents them in dramatic terms.

Considering first of all the rival interpretations of what actually happens at Bly, I think the controversey can be set aside easily enough by a slight refocusing on the method and avowed purpose of the tale. As a ghost story, *The Turn of the Screw* attempts to evoke the thrill of the unknown and the unknowable, and to render the invasion of the unknown perfectly credible. James accomplishes this feat by sustaining two mutually exclusive interpretations of the events—a natural one and a supernatural one. By thus simulating an "actual" case of ghostly visitation, in which a natural explanation arises to challenge the supernatural one, and almost—but of course not entirely—dispels it, *The Turn of the Screw* achieves its hold on the imagination of those "not easily caught."

It is hard to see how any reader at all accustomed or sensitive to Jamesian irony can read *The Turn of the Screw* without forming his suspicions of the governess's sanity; yet the dramatic effect of these suspicions—if we read the story without recourse to Freudian theories—is *not* to discredit her story; it is rather to render her account more credible by keeping the natural explanation of her madness constantly before us. This, I assume, is what James meant in his preface by claiming that he had given the governess "authority" . . .—authority, that is, as a plausible narrator of implausible events. It is precisely because we are allowed to suspect for a while that the ghosts may not be real that—modern sceptics that we are—we believe in the story enough to be frightened by it, and our final acknowledgment of the supernatural is made possible. To write the last of "the good, the really effective and heart-shaking ghost stories" . . . in an age that, as a general rule, does not believe in ghosts—this was just the sort of technical challenge James loved and to which he was capable of devoting a seemingly inexhaustible ingenuity.

Yet even ghost stories, in their recourse to the psychology of fear and wonderment, may be vehicles of artistic truth. In a comparatively recent and persuasive analysis of *The Turn of the Screw,* Mark Spilka offers a *new* "Freudian" reading which turns not upon the neurosis of the governess herself but upon her symbolic role as a representative of the Victorian conscience, with all its sexual self-consciousness and anxieties and repressions [see Additional Bibliography]. Spilka's interpretation may require too rigid a social and Freudian scheme of reference for most readers, yet it is highly valuable in that it indicates an alternative to the bootless controversy over the reality of the ghosts. Following Spilka's example, we may examine the story as a parable in which the fantasy of one level of meaning ironically reveals the moral and psychological reality of another level of meaning. We can thus accept the events of the tale as they are given to us. We need not quibble about what the governess has suppressed, or what James has consciously or unconsciously suppressed about her. We may assume that she is telling the truth without assuming that her view of the universe is necessarily James's own. In other words, we may follow James's own contention that, while the governess has kept "crystalline her record of so many intense anomalies and obscurities," the philosophical conclusions we can draw from them may be altogether "a different matter." . . . (pp. 722-24)

The story which the governess tells us indicates, I think, a pattern of events which is perfectly compatible with the action she describes but of which she is nevertheless unaware. A young woman of twenty, the daughter of a country parson, with little experience of the world, she becomes the guardian of two orphans. The children's uncle has informed her in no uncertain terms that he does not wish to be bothered with them, and that their welfare is her sole responsibility. She is only too willing to assume this responsibility, since she has an intense desire to prove herself a capable and responsible woman. Whether or not the uncle has aroused her romantic interest, her primary motivation seems clear and completely natural. A young governess in her first position, she is anxious to prove her competence to herself.

The domestic circle at Bly is thus marked by the conspicuous absence of any adult masculine authority. It is a feminine world, presided over by a young, eager, naive governess and an ignorant and aging housekeeper. Miles, a young man of ten, feels keenly this lack of masculine companionship and guidance. As he tells the governess, "I want my own sort. . . . I want to see more life." . . . He exhibits increasing signs of restiveness as he is kept from returning to school by the governess's inability to cope with the complications of his expulsion from his last school, but she rationalizes her first significant failure by telling herself that "he was too clever for a bad governess, a parson's daughter, to spoil.'' . . . The governess betrays a notable lack of insight into the psychology of adolescent males when she tells herself further that Miles is "too fine and fair for the little horrid, unclean school-world" with its "stupid, sordid headmasters" and "vindictive" majority of common boys. . . . The governess here reveals both the maternal protectiveness and sexual self-consciousness which will distinguish her throughout the tale.

When the tranquility of their life at Bly is threatened by the apparitions, the governess feels keenly how much the welfare of the children depends upon her courage, her devotion, and her good judgment. Certainly, this young woman is a model of courage and devotion, but her judgment is open to question. Instead of sending for aid, or removing herself and the children from Bly, the governess sets out in a rather naive and melodramatic way to protect the children by exposing herself:

> I had an absolute certainty that I should see
> again what I had already seen, but something
> within me said that by offering myself bravely
> as the sole subject of such experience, by ac-
> cepting, by inviting, by surmounting it all, I
> should serve as an expiatory victim and guard
> the tranquility of the rest of the household. . . .
> I was a screen—I was to stand before them.
> The more I saw the less they would. . . .

This is the governess's first mistake in judgment, for by determining—with a lack of logic almost comic, were it not so frighteningly typical of all self-appointed censors—that the children, at all cost to herself, shall know nothing of the ghosts, she has made their knowledge, rather than their physical or moral welfare, the crucial issue. She has equated innocence with ignorance and knowledge with corruption, and she has assumed, in the greatest *non sequitur* of all, that her exposure to corruption will in some manner make it impossible for the ghosts to corrupt the children. The obvious and more logical alternative, which she seems never to consider, is that the ghosts will corrupt the children *through her*. We may just invert her proposition: the more she sees, the more, ultimately, will they be forced to see.

Her determination to shield the children causes the governess to watch them with a "stifled suspense, a disguised excitement that might well, had it continued too long, have turned to something like madness.'' . . . Here we cannot fail to be aware of the possibility which James explicitly places before us, yet the particular madness which begins to afflict the governess seems not that of imagining ghosts which do not exist, but rather the more common madness of imagining sophisticated depths in the children which the resources of eight and ten year olds render highly unlikely. She finds in their "portentous little activities" and their "greater intensity of play" and "invitation to romp" a sure indication that they are aware of the ghostly presences. . . . And before long she is convinced not only that the children are "talking of *them*—they're talking horrors!" but also that their "more than earthly beauty, their absolutely unnatural goodness" is all a "policy and a fraud.''. . . Ultimately, she sees herself and the children engaged in a fierce contest of wills:

> There were times of being together when I would
> have been ready to swear that, literally, in my
> presence, but with my direct sense of it closed,
> they had visitors who were known and were
> welcome. Then it was that . . . my exaltation

would have broken out. "They're here, you little wretches," I would have cried, "and you can't deny it now!'' . . .

Thus a very odd relationship develops between the governess and the children, for the more she loves them and pities them and desires to save them, the more she begins to suspect them of treachery, until at last she is convinced that they, in league with the ghosts, are ingeniously tormenting her.

The animosity and sense of persecution which an adult—especially one inexperienced and insecure in a position of authority—may feel toward her young charges seems indeed too common and natural an experience to be called madness. Yet we should recall that the governess's hostility toward the children is the direct consequence of her desire to shield them from knowledge rather than harm. All she really suspects them of, it seems, is of somehow *knowing* about the ghosts in spite of all her efforts. And *if* they know, she automatically concludes they must be corrupt.

Few critics have asked why the governess makes such an issue of the children's knowledge—fewer still why, before we have advanced very far into the novel, we, the governess, Mrs. Grose, and apparently even James himself, have associated that knowledge with some kind of sexual taboo which, in some vague and unspecified way, must result in the violation of the children's innocence. Although the ghosts may well be objective presences and although they may constitute a real threat to the children, it is the governess herself who, with an assist from Mrs. Grose, invests the ghosts with their sexual significance. It is she who instinctively identifies sex with the powers of darkness and evil, and who conjures up the murky atmosphere of sexual perversity which infests Bly. The ghosts themselves remain, as it were, asexual. They appear; they glare at the governess; they look around, apparently for the children; they go away. And no matter how promiscuous and vile Peter Quint and Miss Jessel may have been in life, it is never clearly explained why the vices of the living should appeal so very much to the dead, for whom it is surely difficult to postulate sexual offenses. "The grave's a fine and private place, but. . . .''

Perhaps with this anomaly in mind, James qualified the nature of his apparitions in the preface:

> Peter Quint and Miss Jessel are not "ghosts"
> at all, as we now know the ghost, but goblins,
> elves, imps, demons as loosely constructed as
> those of the old trials of witchcraft; if not, more
> pleasingly, fairies of the legendary order, wooing
> their victims forth to see them dance under the
> moon. . . .

This may help us to clarify the erotic quality of the ghosts, and it suggests further—since James refers Quint and Miss Jessel to both Puritan and pagan mythologies—that their sexual connotations somehow involve us in a more or less universal tendency to associate the horrific and the erotic, an association which the psychologist would doubtless explain through the origins of fear in the individual's sense of sexual guilt. Modern fiction, from Hawthorne to Faulkner, has investigated this association in depth, and it is not necessary to impute any special, technical knowledge of Freudian theories to James in order to see that he has drawn upon this residue of unconscious guilt not only in his characterization of the governess, but in his direction of the reader's response to the ghosts. "Only make the reader's general vision of evil intense enough," James claims to have taken for his working rationale, ". . . and you are released from weak specifications.'' . . . Yet it is surely the governess herself, not the ghosts or the children, who introduces us to this ''general vision'': we follow the implications of her tone throughout when we associate the ghosts with nameless sexual perversities and aggressions.

The range of possibilities as to the relationship of the ghosts and the children is in fact very wide. They may not be aware of the ghosts at all—at least, not at first. Or they may be, as the governess believes, wickedly in league with them from the start. Or, as an alternative which strangely never occurs to the governess, they may be aware of the ghosts' presence but untroubled and uncorrupted by it—immune, in their very innocence, to fear and guilt. The ghosts are there; perhaps the children see them, perhaps they don't. There is no way for us to be sure, but in either case their apparent innocence may still be innocence. Untroubled by sexual guilt, they are unaware of evil and unafraid. It is, however, otherwise with the governess. Her horror must be seen as a result of her own intense vision of sexual evil.

This view gains credence, it seems to me, from the many symbolic relationships between the governess and the ghosts. James has so contrived the tale that the governess frequently finds herself occupying the same position in which she has seen one of the ghosts, or recreating their movements and actions. She appears, both to the housekeeper and the children, with the same fierce and frightening aspect with which the ghosts have appeared to her. During a crucial exchange with Miles on the subject of his returning to school, the governess sinks down upon a tombstone; and twice, after encountering the ghosts, she refuses to go to church. Surely, these are not all accidental relationships, and James's efforts to call attention to the many resemblances between the governess and the ghosts cannot be ignored. Their implication, since the thesis that the governess is simply hallucinating has proved ultimately untenable, is that the ghosts are haunting her, and not the children. They are *her* ghosts, seen only by her, meaningful only to her, and hostile only to her—at least in so far as the events of the tale give us definite and concrete evidence. What then—since ghosts are generally supposed to want something when they appear to mortals—do Peter Quint and Miss Jessel want with the governess? Let us review some of their encounters.

Quint first appears to the governess from the tower which, in addition to its critically famous phallic symbolism, suggests also the dominance and power of the male set in station above the female. She sees him a second time peering in through the dining room window, and this reinforces her first impression of him as a hostile aggressor in the domestic circle—an interloper challenging her authority in the home. Their third encounter takes place on the stairway, and although she assumes he is seeking the children, the stairway leads to her bedroom as well as to theirs, and it is this circumstance which accounts, perhaps, for her peculiar description of a supernatural visitation: it was ''as human and hideous as a real interview: hideous just because it *was* human, as human as to have met alone, in the small hours, in a sleeping house, some enemy, some adventurer, some criminal.'' . . . Peter Quint characteristically appears to the governess, then, as a masculine invader of the feminized domestic circle, and his handsome brutality, his fixed stare, and his aggressive aspect all reinforce our sense that the animosity between them is inherently sexual. The governess's fear and hatred of Quint seems based not so much on his ghostliness as on his masculinity.

Her attitude to Miss Jessel, on the other hand, betrays an instinctive identification with this ''vile predecessor'' who has dishonored herself, her profession and her sex, by submitting to the dominance of a man—and a mere valet at that—and who furthermore violated her trust as the feminine protector of the home by allowing Quint to associate freely with Miles. The governess shows less hostility to this ghost, and less fear, but reveals instead an almost fascinated disapproval. When she meets her in the schoolroom, seated at her desk and writing with her implements, the governess responds to Miss Jessel's ''indescribable grand melancholy of indifference and detachment.'' She thinks of her as ''dishonored and tragic,'' and feels compelled to pronounce a moral judgment which is more than slightly defensive:

> Dark as midnight in her black dress, her haggard beauty and her unutterable woe, she had looked at me long enough to appear to say that her right to sit at my table was as good as mine to sit at hers. . . . I had the extraordinary chill of feeling that it was I who was the intruder. It was as a wild protest against it that, actually addressing her—''You terrible, miserable woman!''—I heard myself break into a sound that, by the open door, rang through the long passage and the empty house. . . .

I think we can safely say that, whatever the ghosts hope to accomplish by haunting the governess, she feels their presence as a personal challenge to her chosen role as a defender of innocence and the domestic hearth; they prey upon her insecurity in that role and upon her sexual fears, hostility, and sense of guilt.

There is one further and supremely important connection between the governess and the ghosts. While it is her greatest fear that the ghosts will in some unspecified way participate in intimacies with the children, it is she herself who fawns over them, kisses them and caresses them and seeks to possess them both emotionally and physically. Flora and Miles are ''extravagantly and preternaturally fond'' of her—which, she reflects, ''was no more than a graceful response in children perpetually bowed over and hugged.'' . . . Her maternal affection for them, quite natural in itself, is perverted by her sense of jealous rivalry with the ghosts and turns gradually to hostility and self-doubt—a nagging sense of her own hypocrisy and uncertain motives: ''There were moments when, by an irresistible impulse, I found myself catching them up and pressing them to my heart. As soon as I had done so I used to say to myself: 'What will they think of that? Doesn't it betray too much?''' . . . As usual, the governess is highly suggestive in her vagueness: betray too much of *what*?

With Miles, in particular, the governess's affection and possessiveness partakes of a sexual ambiguity which becomes more explicit and fearsome as the ghosts work upon her imagination. She has such an ''absolute conviction of his precocity'' that he appears to her ''as accessible as an older person . . . as an intelligent equal.'' . . . Thus her treatment of the boy paradoxically combines her desire to keep him sexually ignorant and innocent, and her impulse to act as if he were a mature and knowledgeable adult. Miles himself shows a tendency, quite natural and harmless in itself, to flirt with his governess, to attempt to act older than his years, but the governess's response, in its intensity and anguish, seems inevitably confusing and disturbing to the boy. Visiting him in his bedroom at night, she catches ''for the very first time a small faint quiver of consenting consciousness'' and drops on her knees beside the bed to ''seize once more the chance of possessing him.'' . . . Here, as elsewhere, the language the governess uses to describe her moral ardor is heavily laden with sexual connotations, and these connotations intensify as the tale nears its conclusion. Dining alone with Miles after Flora's departure, the two of them seem to the governess ''as silent . . . as some young couple who, on their wedding-journey, at the inn, feel shy in the presence of the waiter.'' . . . And when at last she thinks she has achieved a greater influence over Miles than that of Peter Quint, she cries out: ''What does he matter now, my own?—what will he *ever* matter? *I* have you . . . but he has lost you for ever!'' . . . (pp. 724-31)

The horror of this final, climactic scene arises, I think, from the reader's awareness that the governess indeed does have Miles, and that it is her jealous grasp which is strangling him. Yet it is not necessary to convict the governess of paranoia or schizophrenic delusions in order to see that the ghosts have preyed upon her own sexual fears and guilt, and have thereby used her as the medium through which to haunt the children. The governess's final and fatal error in judgment is her assumption that, in order to be saved from the apparitions, the children must be brought to feel her own sense of guilt and horror—must see the ghosts as she sees them. It is this *adult* awareness of evil that she labors to produce in them, and which she finally succeeds in inflicting upon them. Caught up in her

A caricature by Max Beerbohm, suggesting James's depiction of implicit sexuality. Reproduced by permission of Eva Reichmann.

effort to force some acknowledgment of her own vision from the children, she loses all sense of restraint and screams at Flora: ''She's there, you little unhappy thing—there, there, *there,* and you know it as well as you know me!'' . . . And again, with Miles, in a similar moment of evangelical frenzy: ''but it's at the window—straight before us. It's *there*—the coward horror, there for the last time!'' And then she forces from Miles's terrified breast the ''supreme surrender'' of the unutterable name: ''Peter Quint—you devil!'' . . . (pp. 731-32)

And just who, we might ask, has been playing the devil's game? Before her zeal has gotten the better of her, the governess herself has a sudden ''perverse horror'' of the confession she feels she must wring out of Miles:

> To do it in any way was an act of violence, for what did it consist of but the obtrusion of the idea of grossness and guilt on a small helpless creature who had been for me a revelation of the possibilities of beautiful intercourse? Wasn't it base to create for a being so exquisite a mere alien awkwardness? . . .

And again, when she is well along with her interrogation, there comes to her ''out of my very pity the appalling alarm of his being perhaps innocent. It was for the instant confounding and bottomless, for if he *were* innocent what then on earth was I?'' . . . (p. 732)

James's point in these rather pointed passages, it seems to me, is not that the governess somehow induces the children to see ghosts which do not exist, but simply that it is she who interprets the apparitions for them according to her own fears and guilt, who invests them with her own sense of sexual horror. Thus the ghosts—whatever they were to the children before—become, through the governess's prodding, definite, frightening, corrupting realities. It is their awakened sense of guilt which enables them to feel fear, anger, hatred—which destroys their innocence and introduces them at last to evil.

Yet neither the governess's errors of judgment nor the sexual associations which she habitually makes seem, upon review, psychologically abnormal or uncommon for a young woman in her circumstances at the turn of the century. If we define madness as a significant departure from normative human behavior, then the governess is *not* mad. If we define it as a temporary warp in one's rationality and self-control, then perhaps she is—but in that case it is a madness which is shared by most of the adults in her culture. For it is this very normality of the governess and the inevitability of her reactions which account for our deep sense of horror and tragedy in the tale. The governess truly loves the children and courageously strives to save them from a real evil, yet because her love is imperfect—because it is haunted by feelings of sexual guilt—it becomes an implement of evil, a destructive force more potent than the ghosts themselves.

What then are we finally to make of the ghosts and their metaphysical significance? Although they may represent a principle of evil in the universal order of things, we must assume—since they are incapable of destroying the children's innocence without the governess's intervention—that it is an evil which is, in itself, impotent, obliged to act through *human* agents. *The Turn of the Screw* does not commit, in other words, the Manichean heresy; its evil spirits are not to be construed as a positive force dualistically opposed to the powers of good. James's approach is firmly within the traditions of Christian Humanism, and evil appears in this tale as a negative principle (in this sense quite appropriately symbolized by the incorporeal figure of the ghost), an absence of good, a failure of human love and understanding. Evil is neither a prime (that is, causeless) nor an eternal principle of being, but rather an inevitable byproduct of the human condition, limited and temporal for all its tragic consequences.

Nor is evil to be intrinsically tied, in this story, to the flesh and human sexuality. That is the governess's aberration, not James's. We should recall that a basic element of the human family is missing at Bly, and it is this absence of masculine authority and strength which accentuates the governess's weaknesses and makes it possible for the ghosts to haunt her and to distort her relationship with the children. *The Turn of the Screw* may be seen as both a social commentary and as a statement on the requirements of the human soul, for it is precisely the incompleteness of the sexual basis of the family which is the ultimate cause of the tragedy. The ghosts are there because the conjugal love of a mother and father—strong, natural, life-giving—is not, and the irresponsibility of the children's uncle may thus stand as symbolic of a far-reaching disorientation of the family and its abandonment of the basic human needs it was formed to serve. As a parable of the loss of innocence, *The Turn of the Screw* tells us that everything human is essentially innocent and remains innocent until contaminated by fear and guilt. And such contamination can be explained only by failures in the individual's social and personal life—failures which, like original sin, are self-perpetuating as they pass from generation to generation. (pp. 732-34)

> Thomas J. Bontly, "Henry James's 'General Vision of Evil' in 'The Turn of the Screw'," in Studies in English Literature, 1500-1900, Vol. IX, No. 4, Autumn, 1969, pp. 721-35.

ERNEST TUVESON (essay date 1972)

[*Tuveson's work examines the role of philosophy in literature, often discussing the work of a writer in the context of the general history of ideas. In the following excerpt, Tuveson defends the reality of the ghosts, appealing to the original reaction to the story when it was first published and to the investigations of the Society for Psychical Research, of which James's brother William was at one time the president.*]

Although stories of supernormal and paranormal experiences form a considerable part of Henry James's whole work, few of them have gained much recognition. The most notable exception is, of course, *The Turn of the Screw*, which has been a storm center of criticism for many years, and which has entered the general culture. My purpose here is to attempt to unravel its mystery by placing it against the matrix of thought, the beliefs and interests which James assumed in his readers, rather than against the atmosphere of the later twentieth century. To do so, I believe, raises much of the obscurity which has surrounded it and which has hampered criticism.

Behind this, his most famous novella, is a movement for investigation of human psychology which interested many important thinkers towards the end of the century; and his own interest evoked memories of his own childhood and of the earliest ideas he must have acquired about the human spirit. He became, in short, involved in this story in a way that his imagination required, and to that fact, perhaps, may be ascribed the fact that he created a masterpiece.

It was recognized, some time ago, that the Society for Psychical Research must have been of some interest and importance to

Henry James. The full significance of this fact, however, has been missed, largely because the full scope and meaning of the productions of the Society have been misunderstood. There is a popular misconception that it consisted entirely of ghost-hunters, that its whole purpose lay in attempts to show by careful investigations whether such phenomena as spiritist séances were honest or bogus. These were indeed part of the work of its investigators. But by no means all; the whole body of the publications of the SPR—which extend to our own time—produced a theory of the human psyche which was in effect an alternative to the whole structure of post-Lockean, mechanistic psychology which has for so long dominated Western thought about man's mental processes. In many respects, furthermore, the productions of this group anticipated various forms of modern psychiatry and the contemporary study of extrasensory perception. (p. 783-84)

The great modern controversy about *The Turn of the Screw* has been about what James himself called the "authority" of the narrator, the governess. Is she, as F. L. Pattee suggested in 1923 [in *The Development of the American Short Story*], suffering from delusions resulting from her own frustrations and conflicts? Are the children really innocent, are the "ghosts" merely hysterical hallucinations, and does Miles die of fright? It seems that none of these questions occurred to James himself, or to the first readers of the work. The first impressions are well summarized by Rebecca West in her book *Henry James* (1916):

> The best ghost story in the world, *The Turn of the Screw,* is the more ghostly because the apparitions of the valet and the governess, appearing at the dangerous place, the top of the tower on the other side of the lake, that they may tempt the children they corrupted in their lives to join them in their eternal torment, are seen by the clear eyes of the honourable and fearless lady who tells the tale.

Two issues must be resolved if we are to accept this impression of the writer. Were the children, in fact, corrupted by the valet and the first governess? And are the hallucinations of the second governess what the SPR would call "veridical"—that is, caused by some force, whatever its nature, outside herself?

As to the first. That Quint and Miss Jessel were evil, and that they did educate the children in some form of evil, original readers seem to have taken for granted. The story appeared in 1898, just after the immense scandal of the Wilde trials, and only the most sheltered could have failed to see the significance of the fact. Victorians were afflicted with an obsessive fear of the bad influence servants might have on youth; William Lyon Phelps, testifying to the chilling effect of the work, says however that it is "profoundly ethical, and making to all those who are interested in the moral welfare of boys and girls an appeal simply terrific in its intensity" [see Additional Bibliography]. He claims that he informed James of his response, and that James answered, "'you had precisely the emotion that I hoped to arouse in everybody,'" and added the famous account of the phlegmatic Scottish stenographer, who to James's indignation was not moved at all by the account of the apparitions. The unnaturally angelic behavior of the children, especially, of Miles, gradually appears to be ambiguous: his hints at blackmail, for example, of how he could expose the governess, are not quite what one would expect from the pure child. But most substantial of all in the evidence is the fact of his having been sent down for good by the headmaster of his school, for mysterious misconduct that is evasively but unmistakably implied to have been of a "moral" nature. No responsible school has even in the prudish Victorian days taken such a drastic action lightly. The governess wonders, justifiably, what will become of Miles. He has in childhood been isolated from his world by the most effective kind of ostracism. Will he become a frustrated exile, despite his fortune and the obvious potentialities of his intellect? Has he the makings of a William Beckford?

And, I think it is not unreasonable to conclude, there is something wrong even about little Flora. She is, to be sure, younger and less responsible than Miles, so she escapes the clutches of the spectres. Yet Mrs. Grose's testimony has weight. She says she has heard "from that child—horrors!" . . . It is true that Mrs. Grose has the ironclad respectability of the superior servant of her time, but she is a servant after all, and a veteran one; surely she has heard "coarse" language in her time, and it is hard to believe that Flora's using a few expressions picked up from servants at random would be enough to shock her so intensely; and she, moreover, hints strongly that she knows the origin of the "horrors" Flora utters—"since I've heard some of it before!" In James's allusive, indirect context this statement clearly applies to Quint and Miss Jessel. (Incidentally, James's allusions in this story are, for him, remarkably straightforward; if one compares, say, *The Sacred Fount,* the fact is obvious.)

But we still have to ask whether there is any verification of the objective nature of the hallucinations. The corruption of the children could have occurred, but the governess might have projected her intuitive awareness into a vision of persons who might have been responsible. All the signs, however, point to the veridical nature of the apparitions. Most important, the governess does not learn of Quint's existence until *after* she describes the second apparition, in elaborate and fully identifying detail, to Mrs. Grose. The figure of Quint is strikingly different—how disappointingly different!—from that of the master, whom the governess has sentimentally hoped to see again. It seems to me, allowing for James's habitual indirection and coyness about direct statement, that Mrs. Grose's recognition of Quint from the governess's detailed description is conclusive. This *is* Quint. The verification is the more impressive because Mrs. Grose, unlike the run of servants in the popular ghost story, is emphatically not superstitious and not a vulgar body who yearns for sensastional experiences. Her stolidity, her reluctance to admit the very possibility of a "haunting," is unmistakable; it is, in fact, an important part of the difficulties the governess encounters. Mrs. Grose, by every indication is intended as a reliable witness for verification. Finally, the general impression given by the governess, her clear marshalling of facts, the general air of common sense about her—for example, her understanding of children, derived from her own vicarage days—seem to make us trust her account; she is, as Rebecca West says, "clear" of eye.

James's own intentions, for what they are worth, seem to be certain. "It constitutes no little of a character indeed, in such conditions, for a young person, as she says, 'privately bred,' that she is able to make her particular credible statement of such strange matters. She has 'authority,' which is a good deal to have given her. . . ." He says, as if answering Freudian critics in advance, that he has avoided giving her any definite, detailed "characterization." This statement is significant. The center of the story, he implies, is not the governess, her inner life, her history, etc., but the children and their relationship to the dead. She is a Jamesian observer, and any effort to turn the story into a clinical case history of her turns the whole structure topsy-turvy.

James, in fact, includes in the story just the kind of verification the SPR would require for such anecdotes. In response to Mrs. Grose's persistent doubts about whether the governess had "made it up," "I found that to keep her thoroughly in the grip of this I had only to ask her how, if I had 'made it up,' I came to be able to give, of each of the persons appearing to me, a picture disclosing, to the last detail, their special marks—a portrait on the exhibition of which she had instantly recognized and named them." . . . Certainly an artist could paint a portrait of Quint from her description. Then there are other, objective, indicators. There is the gust of air and chill and shaking of the room when the spectres are balked—for example, when the governess appeals to Miles to "help her save" him. This kind of phenomenon accompanied several séances, notably, those of the renowned medium, D. D. Home, and, needless to say, it is a stock accompaniment of supernatural appearances in all folklore. The narrator has the native wit to mark things that an investigator would want to know: how long the hallucinations lasted, how realistic the apparitions were, whether they gave the impression of being external persons, and the like. Even granting that these tests are passed—and James means us to think they are—there could, of course, be more than one explanation. [Frank Podmore, one of the founders of the SPR,] would theorize that the governess, a born "sensitive" who can receive telepathic communications, has gotten the images of the dead servants from the minds of Mrs. Grose and the children. Their memories have, in effect, been transmitted to the governess's inner vision. She has *impressions* about Quint—e.g., that he had been an actor—that would give some color of possibility to this explanation. However, partly for reasons that I shall suggest later, I think James's own intention is not to suggest this kind of phenomenon.

All this is not to imply the work has no real ambiguity. There is, to begin with, the all-pervading mystery of the occult itself, as I have pointed out. But, as becomes more and more clear, the central question is not the reality of the apparitions, but whether the children are merely feigning not to see them. The governess is in the familiar situation of the medium who sees apparitions where no one else can, like Hamlet, for instance, during his interview with the Queen. The problem arises frequently in the accounts submitted to the SPR. An ironical fact is that a sensitive may see a dead person of no special interest to him but dear to another individual who is with him—to whom, nevertheless, the figure is invisible. In fact, the whole function of the "medium" is to enter into communication with individuals mostly strange to him or her, but known to others in the "circle." The medium, it has generally been agreed, may be visited by apparitions without any action or indeed desire on his or her part. The mission of a medium may be a very burdensome one. The dilemma of the governess as the only "seeing" one in a group who all, for one reason or another, are deeply interested in the apparitions of persons wholly unknown to her, is, in the light of the vast amount of tradition on the subject, by no means unusual. Like all persons subject to hallucinations, she thinks others *must* see what she very clearly sees. Like such persons, she is persecuted for her doubtful privilege. And the likelihood that the apparitions must have returned to communicate with the children increases the anxiety—why else would they have come? Henry James said, of the accounts of the psychic research society, that one wonders why the dead should have taken the trouble to return. *The Turn of the Screw* might be taken as his answer.

Gradually, the governess (evidently not a reader of SPR material) begins to see what the situation must be. Even though it seems the children ought to see what she has perceived so vividly, still their vision "was not yet definitely proved." . . . What she does not realize is the full horrendous irony of her situation. She is, in fact, all unwittingly and certainly unwillingly, the medium who has made it possible at last for the dead servants to become known at all; and eventually it is she who makes it possible for the dead valet to reach Miles directly. How this can be is the supreme "turn of the screw"; and, properly understood, the cryptic last sentence is the key to the great irony of the whole.

The governess at length comes to the most frightful suspicion of all: the children do *not* see, although they have come to suspect something is going on, involving the dead valet and governess; and they *want* to see, to be with their dead friends. "'I want my own sort'" Miles exclaims. . . . What does this passionate exclamation really mean? The difficulty of approaching the children directly about such a delicate matter (particularly for the young lady product of a Victorian vicarage) is present with great narrative skill. The governess, however, mistakenly takes it for a "splendid sign" when she comes to suspect that Miles is looking through the window for something he cannot see. Is he not, then, innocent of contact with the ghosts? Can he—and his sister—not be saved from this visitation? But first, as the governess no doubt had learned from her clergyman father, there must be honest and voluntary confession. Miles must tell exactly what he has done, or at least make a sufficiently explicit admission of guilt.

When Peter Quint comes into view for the last time, with his "white face of damnation," the governess feels "like fighting with a demon for a human soul." Her feeling, the events show, is no delusion. She determines to approach the central issue as directly as a delicately nurtured young lady could. She elicits from Miles halting, vague admissions which she regards, wrongly, as confession. But her robust common sense wins out: this is not believable. "I only know that the next instant I heard myself throw off with homely force: 'Stuff and nonsense!'" Yet there is one last chance. Quint, "as if to blight his confession and stay his answer," has come into her view—but not of Miles. "The window was still to his own eyes free." Her impulsive move to save him, by the supreme irony, has the opposite effect: it reveals to the boy that something, obviously one of the apparitions, is there. Then comes the first verification. He thinks it is Miss Jessel. "'It's not Miss Jessel! But it's at the window—straight before us. It's *there*—the coward horror, there for the last time.'"

What this revelation does is to evoke the crucial statement, for which, we discover, the spirit of Quint has waited. Miles is in a fever of frustration, "glaring vainly over the place and missing wholly, though it now, to my sense, filled the room like the taste of poison, the wide, overwhelming presence. 'It is *he*?'" This is the fateful moment. When Miles says, "'Peter Quint—you devil!'" he has given the necessary sign. The last two words, in the context, seem to refer to the governess; it is hard to make any other interpretation. Miles's desire for Quint is an overt repudiation of her appeal. Thus the governess first has made it known that Quint is present; then she has made it possible for Miles to intimate the desire to be with "his own sort." It is a commonplace of folklore that supernatural beings must obtain the consent of mortals before the latter can be kidnapped. For example, in Irish stories, the little people must get a human being to speak to them and somehow

trick him into going with them voluntarily, before they can carry him off.

The climactic word, to which the whole story has been moving, is in the great final sentence: "We were alone with the quiet day, and his little heart, dispossessed, had stopped." It has been suggested that "dispossessed" means that Miles has been frightened to death; but surely this is a very odd and evasive way, even for James, of putting it. There is an intimation of doom; but why? What is it the apparitions really want? The governess, quite naturally, assumes it is to be with the children, to resume in some spectral way their relationship in life; but it is really to bring the children to them, in death. In his notebook entry of 12 January 1895, James says about the subject which apparently developed into this story: "the children may destroy themselves, lose themselves, by responding" to the dead, depraved servants. The means by which this is accomplished is "possession."

The most controversial theory of F.W.H. Myers [, a co-founder of the SPR,] was one which he first advanced in a long note to *Phantasms of the Living*. In a later book, he summarized his idea thus: "I still believe—and more confidently than in 1886—that a 'psychical invasion' does take place; that a 'phantasmogenetic centre' is actually established in the percipient's surroundings; and some presence is transferred, and may or may not be discerned by the invaded person." He explains that thus the invading spirit, or consciousness, literally ousts the mentality of the victim and uses the latter's organism in the same fashion as its owner is accustomed to use it (rather like a virus in a cell). Another consciousness may take over the direction of a body—automatic writing, that phenomenon which so much interested Yeats and others would be an example—and, presumably, if the control were strong enough, could cause the body of the victim to cease functioning. But, as Myers and some famous mediums agreed, such "spirit infections" could take root "only in congenial soil. The healthy spirit can repel their attack." Henry James, in the Notebook entry from which I have quoted, after proposing that the children "lose themselves" continues that "it is a question of the children 'coming over to where they are.'" We are to assume that the beckoning from dangerous places is a device to tempt them to go up there and to kill themselves; but, it would seem, James found a more ingenious method. The result in any event is that pure innocence is not arbitrarily destroyed; the story does sustain the moral order; the powers of darkness cannot violate innocence and purity at will. (pp. 789-96)

> *Ernest Tuveson, "'The Turn of the Screw': A Palimpsest," in* Studies in English Literature, 1500-1900, *Vol. XII, No. 4, Autumn, 1972, pp. 783-800.*

MARY Y. HALLAB (essay date 1977)

[*In the following excerpt, Hallab discusses elements of* The Turn of the Screw *which follow patterns occurring in fairy tales and myths.*]

James's comment [on *The Turn of the Screw* (see excerpt dated 1908)] has been taken by many critics—primarily those who oppose Edmund Wilson's Freudian interpretation—to indicate that the story means simply and plainly what it seems to mean. But if we read the complete preface, we see that James himself takes great pains to suggest the opposite. In the first place, he refers to the story as a fairy tale to indicate what he especially likes about it—that it is "short and sharp and single, charged more or less with the compactness of anecdote," as opposed to the fuller class of fairy tale represented by the Arabian Nights—the difference being in *form* rather than in subject, tone, or plausibility. Moreover, he values the simplicity and compactness of the anecdote for the very reason that it allows free exercise of the imagination, so we are led to enter "an annexed but independent world in which nothing is right save as we rightly imagine it." His tale, he says, actually combines the two kinds of fairy tales—the loose, various, endless tale represented by the Arabian Nights and the more compact tale, such as Cinderella, Bluebeard, Hop o' my thumb, and Little Red Riding Hood, and, James continues, "many of the gems of the Brothers Grimm." That is: "It is an excursion into chaos while remaining . . . but an anecdote—though an anecdote amplified and highly emphasized and returning upon itself; as, for that matter, Cinderella and Blue-Beard return."

His comments on the ghosts in *The Turn of the Screw* continue the analogy with the fairy tale. Quint and Jessel are ghosts, he says, not of the "recorded and attested" kind, but "goblins, elves, imps, demons as loosely constructed as those of the old trials for witchcraft; if not, more pleasingly, fairies of the legendary order, wooing their victims forth to see them dance under the moon." They are "demon-spirits," whose function in the story is to cause "the situation to reek with the air of Evil" while freeing the author from having to make weak specifications as to the exact nature of this Evil. In these statements James himself indicates that the ghosts are of the kind familiar to us, not from the reports of psychical research but from our childhood reading of fairy tales and folklore. Indeed, in folklore, the behavior of ghosts is often identical to that of the fantastical figures of Fairy or Elfland. In his study *The Science of Fairy Tales: An Inquiry into Fairy Mythology* (1891), Edwin Sidney Hartland says, ". . . we need not be surprised if the same incidents of story or fibres of superstition attach at one time to ghosts and at another to the non-human creatures of imagination, or if Hades and Fairyland are often confounded." The beliefs, dangers, prohibitions attached to Fairyland apply also, he says, to the classical Hades, and in seeking to explain them, "we must not be satisfied without an explanation that will fit both."

The Turn of the Screw is both ghost story and fairy tale, placed in a frame which sets it off from everyday experience. It begins with an elaborate introduction and preparation involving *two* narrators: Douglas, the original possessor of the manuscript, and an unidentified *I* who transcribes the tale for the reader. This introduction begins with the telling of another tale supposed by the narrator to be unusual—of a ghost appearing to a boy and his mother. The governess' tale is then introduced by Douglas as a similar story, but one having occurred (as so many ghost stories do) to someone the teller actually knew. The governess makes the link between the story and the real world, so that she functions in two capacities—both as storyteller and, more important, as a figure in the pattern of the tale.

Toward the beginning of her account, the governess, in fact, places herself within the fairy tale when she describes her first tour of Bly: "But as my little conductress, with her hair of gold and her frock of blue, danced before me round corners and pattered down passages, I had the view of a castle of romance inhabited by a rosy sprite, such a place as would somehow, for diversion of the young idea, take all colour out of storybooks and fairy-tales. Wasn't it just a storybook over which I had fallen a-doze and a-dream?"

When we examine it, we find that the tale does, in fact, follow the pattern of hundreds of folktales . . . in which fairies, elves, witches, or revenants steal or try to steal children and carry them off to their homes. In many cases, the children are of royal birth. Similar tales are familiar to everyone: the Snow Queen, Hansel and Gretel, Jorinda and Joringel, the Yellow Dwarf, the Nixie. In all of these, as in *The Turn of the Screw,* two children or young people, a boy and a girl, are involved. In *The Fairies in English Tradition and Literature* (1967), K. M. Briggs says: "The thing that everyone knows about the fairies is that they covet human children and steal them whenever they can." Although "mortals of all ages and both sexes are enticed into Fairyland," the stealing of unbaptized children is the most common, because they are regarded as still "little pagans." In her study *The Witch-Cult in Western Europe* (1921), Margaret Alice Murray makes the same point in regard to the stealing of children by witches, often for the purpose of sacrificing them. She mentions the tendency in folklore to confuse witches and fairies, thus supporting the connection between the two suggested by James in his preface. In *The Turn of the Screw,* the governess sees the children, Miles and Flora, as "a pair of little grandees, of princes of the blood." And although the children are not infants and certainly, in fact, have been baptized, they are described nevertheless in terms which suggest that they are, in spirit at least, pagan. From the beginning, they are associated with the charming pastoral setting at Bly. Early in the tale the governess remarks on their naturalness, their innocence, their apparent unawareness of good and evil. They both have a "glow of freshness," a "positive fragrance of purity."

Still other elements of the fairy tale appear in *The Turn of the Screw,* especially with regard to the ghosts; for example, like the elfin kidnappers of Fairyland, they lurk in and around the house, especially directly outside the windows, to attract the children, and Miss Jessel appears on a lake, a well-known entrance to fairyland as well as to the land of the dead. Like fairies, James's ghosts have the ability to appear and disappear at will, to cast spells over mortals, and to stop or speed up the passage of time; when they are present, the governess notes "a stillness, a pause of all life," which makes her wonder if she herself is alive. The governess seeks to thwart the ghosts by continual kissing or embracing of the children, a traditional method of effecting the disenchantment of an enchanted person. And her frantic clutching of Miles in the final scene of the tale can be explained, by reference to folklore, as among the ways to prevent a person from being snatched by fairies.

In spite of the governess' efforts, the children come more and more under the influence of the ghosts, gradually taking on sinister characteristics which associate them, in the governess' eyes, with the demons themselves. This development in their characters suggests the changeling tradition, according to which fairies or elves steal mortal children and substitute their own less desirable offspring. Like changeling children, Miles and Flora appear preternaturally precocious, especially at the times when the ghosts are present. Like fairies, they play tricks and sometimes, we are told, become foul-mouthed. They love music and under the influence of the ghosts use it to "enchant" the governess just as fairies use music to enchant and entice mortals to follow them into their realm.

Still another folklore motif, found also in primitive religion, is the *taboo.* According to Sir James G. Frazer in *The Golden Bough: A Study in Magic and Religion,* taboos against naming supernatural figures—fairies, ghosts, or gods—are common in folklore as well as in primitive religion, possibly because of the primitive belief that having the name of a spirit or god gave the namer a certain power to call it up or destroy it. One has only to think of the story of Rumpelstiltskin, in which the naming of the troll gives the queen power over him and allows her to save her child. The governess operates under two taboos: she must not call the uncle or bother him (this is a condition of her duty, which we will discuss later), and she must avoid mentioning the names of her predecessors. For a good part of the story the governess carefully avoids naming the ghosts, regarding such an act as a dangerous step in her relations with the children. When she finally does name them, she succeeds in exorcising the ghosts, but she loses the children as well. This again is a common characteristic of fairy tales: the bewitched do not survive the breaking of the enchantment.

The story line parallels that of the traditional ghost or fairy tale of the mortal enticed by fairies, witches, or revenants. The motifs which make up this pattern are those familiar to anyone who, as a child, has read fairly extensively in imaginative literature. On this level, Miles and Flora are the fairy-tale prince and princess, threatened or seduced by demons from another world. The uncle and Mrs. Grose fill the role of the helpless king and queen. The governess is the hero, or heroine in this case, who must do battle with the forces of evil to save them.

Yet a dismissal of the story as, in James's words, "a fairy-tale pure and simple" would be a mistake, if only because, as anthropological studies show, fairy tales are seldom as simple as they appear on the surface. Scholars writing about fairy tales seldom fail to note their similarity to pagan ritual and belief, and many speculate that fairy-tale figures are archaic or degenerated versions of pagan heroes, gods, or goddesses. In *The Fairy Mythology of Shakespeare* (1900), Alfred Nutt suggests that fairy lore preserves the memory of ancient vegetation cults, such as that devoted to Dionysus, and that the belief that fairies carry off children has its roots in rituals of sacrifice to the vegetation god. Margaret Murray makes a similar suggestion with regard to the witch cults of the Middle Ages. Briggs mentions various scholarly opinions that fairies are devils or witches, that they are spirits of the dead and that the fairy faith grew from the cult of the dead, or even that they are, as she says, "dwindled gods or nature spirits." The horror associated with them, including the strong sexual element and the degeneration of their characters—all this seen by the governess in the ghosts of Quint and Jessel—recalls the horror and dread with which Christianity has traditionally regarded the gods of the pagan religions which it supplanted.

Whatever the relationship between fairy tales and primitive myths, there is no doubt that we find in fairy tales the same themes and archetypes that we find in much mythology. Hartland sees a parallel between the changeling superstition and "the classic stories of children and adults beloved by gods of high and low degree. . . ." And as Quint and Jessel are ghosts, parallels which immediately suggest themselves are those myths in which a youthful vegetation god or goddess dies and is carried off to the underworld. Quint and Jessel are, in this view, archetypes of the god and goddess of the underworld. Quint is clearly a devil figure with his flaming red hair and burning eyes. Miss Jessel is a suitable consort with her pale face, her black dress, her tragic air of "unutterable woe." The boat in which Flora crosses the lake recalls the boats which in the myths and tales of many nations carry the souls to the underworld. The air of "timelessness" which surrounds the ghosts suggests an affinity with the gods.

The desire of the ghosts for the children parallels such myths as that of the kidnapping of Persephone by Pluto and the death of youthful gods such as Adonis, Osiris, and Dionysus. Flora, as her name indicates, corresponds to the maiden, daughter to the Earth Mother, Demeter, and the Sky-God, Zeus, who is abducted by the god of the dead while picking flowers. Miss Jessel is Persephone in her aspect of goddess of the underworld—dark, terrible, tragic. Miles, who has "something divine" about him, and Quint are their masculine counterparts. Mrs. Grose and the uncle also occupy archetypal roles. She is the Earth Mother, warm, protective, accepting. He is a kind of Sky-God, remote, idealized, demanding. They are the "good" or "ideal" counterparts of the "low" and evil Quint and Jessel. Quint's appearance on a height, the tower, and Miss Jessel's appearance on a lake suggest their affinity with the deities of earth and sky. Thus the figures in the tale form a kind of double, male-female, triangle or trinity. Miles and Quint are opposing aspects—child and devil, innocence and evil—of the abstract male deity represented by the uncle. The same is true for Flora, Miss Jessel, and Mrs. Grose. (pp. 493-98)

I do not intend to identify *The Turn of the Screw* with any single folktale or myth, but only to demonstrate that it follows the familiar pattern of one type of myth. Within this pattern, the children fill the role of those youthful gods whose death was mourned in rituals which suggest the cycle of the seasons, the yearly death and renewal of the vegetation. Their story begins in June and ends with the death of Miles in November. The children themselves gradually lose their innocent and child-like quality, becoming older in nature if not in actual appearance, until their destruction at the hands of the ghosts and the governess. At this point the story abruptly ends.

The governess bridges the gap between the tale and the reader, functioning on one level as the "real" person involved with the Other World. Yet on another level, she is one with the other figures, part of the pattern. She is the initiate who participates in the death of the vegetation god (even helping it along) in order to experience a rebirth, at the same time resisting the event, mourning the loss. Indeed, she seems to regard herself as a kind of female version of the Hero. She believes she has a task to fulfill, given to her by the children's uncle, to whom she devotes herself with something like religious zeal. It is she who must confront the evil, the demon, in the form of the ghosts, in order to fulfill her role.

In his *Rites and Symbols of Initiation: The Mysteries of Birth and Rebirth* (1958), Mircea Eliade says: "Whatever side one may take on this controversy on the origin and meaning of fairy tales, it is impossible to deny that the ordeals and adventures of their heroes and heroines are almost always translatable into initiatory terms." He points out that a typical feature of initiation ceremonies, and of myths and fairy tales containing elements of these ceremonies, is the initiate's confrontation with the spirits of the dead or with the gods of the Other World, often involving a kind of combat with them in order to capture a significant object. He notes this element, for example, in the Grail Legend, in which Percival must spend the night in a chapel with a dead body. One interesting allusion in James's tale which suggests a parallel interpretation occurs right before the governess takes the significant step of naming Miss Jessel to Flora. Her sudden awareness that it is the time to take action is expressed in these terms: "a flash like the glitter of a drawn blade, the jostle of the cup that my hand, for weeks and weeks, had held high and full to the brim and that now . . . I felt overflow in a deluge." This reference to the traditional sacred objects sought in the Quest myth of the Grail Legend reinforces the sense that, at this moment, for her, the quest has reached a climax—she is about to speak. In the Grail Legend, the success of Percival in restoring life to the land of the Fisher King hinges on Percival's speaking to the king, asking him, in essence, "What is the matter?" That is, he must, as the governess does, openly acknowledge the mystery in order to effect the desired result. In *The Turn of the Screw,* as in fairy tales, the expulsion of the evil spirits depends on gaining control over the spirits by naming them. The governess directly confronts the mystery for the first time by asking, "Where, my pet, is Miss Jessel?" And later by forcing Miles to name Peter Quint. (pp. 498-99)

> Mary Y. Hallab, " 'The Turn of the Screw' Squared,"
> in Southern Review, *Australia, Vol. XIII, No. 3,*
> *July, 1977, pp. 492-504.*

DAVID S. MIALL   (essay date 1984)

[*In the following excerpt, Miall offers a reading of* The Turn of the Screw *based on Sigmund Freud's essay* "The Uncanny" *(1919).*]

> Only make the reader's general vision of evil intense enough, I said to myself—and that already is a charming job—and his own experience, his own imagination, his own sympathy (with the children) and horror (of their false friends) will supply him quite sufficiently with all the particulars. Make him *think* the evil, make him think it for himself, and you are released from weak specifications.

The understanding of the evil that [*The Turn of the Screw*] presents is, according to this well-known statement of James, sufficiently available to the reader without the specific instance. In some way, James seems to be saying, the grasp of evil is already within the reader; the purpose of the story, which appears to have been realized most successfully, is to make the reader conscious of that potential vision, to make him conscious of what may exist unconsciously. The resources of language would not seem to be directly available for this task . . . but to require the tapping of realms of symbolic expression, structures of feeling that make present the source of the evil to the reader as an operative power without the limitations contingent upon naming it. In this work the simultaneous senses of death and familiarity provide a significant clue.

Freud begins his essay "The 'Uncanny' " with this point: "the uncanny," he says, "is that class of the frightening which leads back to what is known of old and long familiar." Freud's explanation for this . . . is that the uncanny represents a residue of the primitive childhood belief in animistic powers. This in itself might be thought frightening enough to account for the ghosts at Bly: as Freud goes on to say, in a comment apposite to James's story, a part of our fear of apparitions would seem to imply "the old belief that the dead man becomes the enemy of his survivor and seeks to carry him off to share his new life with him." This, of course, is just what the governess comes to believe of Quint and Jessel. Of Miss Jessel, for example, she describes to Mrs. Grose the "fury of intention" with which she looks at Flora at her first appearance by the lake, her intention being "to get hold of her." . . . This, if it were all, would make the governess a psychological curiosity, but it explains little of the power of the story. Freud has another more interesting explanation.

The sense of the uncanny, according to Freud, is also conveyed by coincidences and repetitions. Supposing a man comes across the figure 62 several times in one day—on the door of a hotel room, the number in an address, the compartment of a railway train. He may begin to feel a superstitious fear that the number 62 has some special meaning for him: perhaps it indicates the limit of his lifespan. The source of this fear actually lies in certain primitive instinctual impulses, the "compulsion to repeat," a compulsion which is "powerful enough to overrule the pleasure principle, lending to certain aspects of the mind their daemonic character." To be reminded in whatever way of this "compulsion to repeat" is to sense the uncanny. Freud's main account of the instincts behind this aspect of the uncanny (left somewhat obscure in this essay) is set out in *Beyond the Pleasure Principle.* Here he first elaborated his conception of the death instinct, whose aim is to restore the organism to the inanimate state from which (at the earliest time) it came. Such an impulse is discerned by Freud behind the "compulsion to repeat." Freud's concept of the death instinct is a forbidding and little-explored aspect of his later psychoanalytic theory. As J. C. Flugel remarks, in one of the few examinations of it in the literature, "it has a certain awe-inspiring quality" whose "profound implications . . . can be dimly felt though its precise significance as yet escapes clear consciousness." For present purposes two aspects of Freud's complex discussion will suffice.

Freud claims that the compulsion to repeat seems to be something "more primitive, more elementary, more instinctual than the pleasure principle which it over-rides." It is manifested, for example, in dreams which repeat a traumatic experience, which Freud concedes fall outside his earlier principle that all dreams originate in impulses of wish fulfillment. Here the impulse is described by Freud as the attempted mastery of a stimulus (that is, the original trauma) which proved too strong for the system. The dream has the purpose of "developing the anxiety whose omission was the cause of the traumatic neurosis." The attempt to master a stimulus by the induction of anxiety may thus be a major purpose of the uncanny, although Freud does not say so specifically in his essay on the topic.

The anxiety that is induced in the reader of *The Turn of the Screw* arises specifically from the recurrence of the ghosts, whose appearances are attended by images of silence, death, and immobility. Such a *repetition* of an apparition is, of course, a feature of many recorded hauntings. . . . It is this particular feature that is responsible for the ghosts' disturbing power: the image of stasis, of imprisoned consciousness, the doomlike repetition of the same routine over the apparition's territory. Where James's story departs most distinctly from the standard case is simply in its conversion of a passive to an active threat. His ghosts, like the vampires of traditional legend, are endowed with the will to draw others to follow their fate. Now the governess has not, so far as we know, been subject to a trauma before her arrival at Bly; the ghosts that she sees represent nothing directly relevant to her personal history. Their threat, if Freud is correct, cannot relate to her repression of sexuality: rather, they arouse a fear of something that is prior to the establishment of the pleasure principle itself, the primeval urge of the instincts to "restore an earlier state of things." Such instincts, Freud says, are "the expression of the inertia inherent in organic life." He continues:

> This view of instincts strikes us as strange because we have become used to see in them a factor impelling towards change and develop-

ment, whereas we are now asked to recognize in them the precise contrary—an expression of the *conservative* nature of living substance.

It is this inertia that seems to lie at the root of the uncanny, the death instinct (normally latent or repressed) in its untrammeled operation. Freud also notes that people's fear of analysis may have the same source, "a dread of rousing something that, so they feel, is better left sleeping," so that "what they are afraid of at bottom is the emergence of this compulsion with its hint of possession by some 'daemonic' power."

The appeal of the uncanny, it could be argued, thus lies in its address to the most primitive aspect of all instincts, the compulsion to repeat and, in this respect, the expression of the tendency to death. The readers' pleasure in the uncanny represents a type of effort at mastery—it is not he, after all, but the governess who has to deal with the irruption of ghosts. In the reading of *The Turn of the Screw* we can rehearse in safety our anxiety in the face of the final enemy, whose source turns out to be rooted in our own unconscious (hence the sense of familiarity).

The evil that James leaves unspecified is the stasis of death, but this death is not the inorganic inertia of Freud's account; it is the inertia of the prison inmate or the vampire's life-in-death, a state of immobility or paralysis. Death itself is perhaps inconceivable, as Freud observed elsewhere, so that another of the animistic survivals tapped by the uncanny is likely to be the buried belief in the immortality of consciousness. What the uncanny brings into question, particularly in the case of James's tale, is the *state* in which that consciousness survives. To be suspended like the Sibyl at Cumae, or fixed in ice like the figures at the bottom of Dante's "Inferno," in a state of perpetual, unmoving consciousness—this seems to be the final, the "designed horror" which lies in wait for the reader of *The Turn of the Screw.*

Other features of the story, if this is correct, fall into place in support of this account. The poignancy of the story, the extra turn of the screw, is given by the fact that ostensibly the chief victims of the predatory ghosts are children. Not only does the possible premature knowingness of Miles and Flora disturb, but even more unsettling is the presence of children, prime symbols of growth and development (suggested by the name "Flora"). Their lack of a personal history, apart from Miles's enigmatic behavior at school, intensifies the sense that they are dislocated from normal childhood processes. In this respect, also, they succeed in overturning the authority of the governess, becoming instead the governors of events until the final episodes of the story. The stasis threatened by Peter Quint and Miss Jessel is carefully suggested by their placement in the scenery of Bly. That Quint first appears on top of the house shows, as I have mentioned, that his authority is to supersede that of the governess. Appearing again (and at the end) framed in a window implants the notion of a blocked perspective, windows elsewhere (as, for example, in James's own image of the house of fiction) symbolizing rather some view of the future or a realizable potential. The staircase is another and more specific image related to the progressive in human potential: Quint is encountered and outstared on the staircase at Bly, a key moment of fixity that cancels the usual symbolic meaning of stairs. So with Miss Jessel: she is seen for the first and last time standing at the end of the view, blocking the farther reach of the path that has just been followed, whether on this or the other side of the lake. The setting itself, finally, turns out to represent a prison rather than the promised Garden

of Eden of the governess's first sight, a *hortus conclusus* from which there is no escape (even letters somehow cannot make their exit). This rigidly enforced isolation of the governess offers the ideal conditions within which the challenge of the ghosts can develop.

This is the unspecified evil which James's story, according to his preface, was intended to arouse in the reader. It was left unspecific because it supersedes all particular occasions or instances of it, and is the more powerful for that reason. The ghosts are the dramatic and highly effective agents of that evil, but their existence is not in the end the main point of the story; Quint and Jessel are the givens, the premises of something much more serious. The ghosts are only agents. The real source of the designed horror lies, since she is susceptible to it, in the governess; but by implication it lies much more significantly in ourselves. (pp. 322-27)

> *David S. Miall, "Designed Horror: James's Vision of Evil in 'The Turn of the Screw'," in* Nineteenth-Century Fiction, *Vol. 39, No. 3, December, 1984, pp. 305-27.*

ADDITIONAL BIBLIOGRAPHY

Aldrich, C. Knight. "Another Twist to *The Turn of the Screw*." *Modern Fiction Studies* XIII, No. 2 (Summer 1967): 167-78.

> Maintains that Mrs. Grose is jealous of the governess's authority over the house and the children, and so encourages the governess's impending madness.

Bangs, John Kendrick. "The Involvular Club: or, The Return of the Screw." In *The Antic Muse: American Writers in Parody*, pp. 136-41. New York: Grove Press, 1955.

> A parody of James's literary style as epitomized in *The Turn of the Screw.*

Bewley, Marius. "Appearance and Reality in Henry James." In his *The Complex Fate: Hawthorne, Henry James and Some Other American Writers*, pp. 79-113. New York: Grove Press, 1954.

> Discusses the treatment of Miles and Flora by the governess and supports Edmund Wilson's interpretation of her actions (see excerpt dated 1934).

Brooke-Rose, Christine. "*The Turn of the Screw* and Its Critics: An Essay in Non-Methodology," "*The Turn of the Screw*: Mirror Structures as Basic Structures," and "The Surface Structures in *The Turn of the Screw*." In her *A Rhetoric of the Unreal: Studies in Narrative and Structure, Especially of the Fantastic*, pp. 128-57, pp. 158-87, pp. 188-230. Cambridge: Cambridge University Press, 1981.

> An analysis of the criticism of *The Turn of the Screw*, demonstrating fallacious reasoning and misrepresentation of facts by several critics, and a structuralist analysis of the text. Brooke-Rose states that "a text which can generate, not only different interpretations but so many erroneous readings can indeed be regarded, on the one hand as an author's 'intended' test of his reader's inattention, a text composed on the very principle of ambiguity; but on the other, also as a text structured (intentionally or not) on the same principle that a neurosis is structured. . . . And the structure of a neurosis involves the attempt (often irresistible) to drag the 'other' down into itself, into the neurosis, the other being here the reader."

Cargill, Oscar. "*The Turn of the Screw* and Alice James." *PMLA* LXXVIII, No. 3 (June 1963): 238-49.

> Asserts that *The Turn of the Screw* is based on Sigmund Freud's "The Case of Miss Lucy R." and James's sister Alice's attacks of hysteria. Cargill explains: "The tenderest of men, Henry James could hardly have used the illness of his sister Alice as the basis for a story while she lived, or later, without elaborately disguising

it. . . . The product is one of the greatest horror stories of all time.''

Chase, Dennis. ''The Ambiguity of Innocence: *The Turn of the Screw*.'' *Extrapolation* XXVII, No. 3 (Fall 1986): 197-202.
Suggests a mutual sexual desire between Miles and the governess. The confusion arising from the innocence of both characters provides the complexity of their relationship.

Clair, John A. ''*The Turn of the Screw*.'' In his *The Ironic Dimension in the Fiction of Henry James*, pp. 37-58. Pittsburgh: Duquesne University Press, 1965.
Asserts that the ''ghosts'' of Miss Jessel and Quint are in fact living persons—an insane mute woman hidden in the house and a man who takes care of her—and that Mrs. Grose lies to the governess in order to keep the children from knowing.

Cohen, Paula Marantz. ''Freud's *Dora* and James's *The Turn of the Screw*: Two Treatments of the Female 'Case'.'' *Criticism* XXVIII, No. 1 (Winter 1986): 73-87.
Compares the *Turn* with one of Sigmund Freud's studies in psychopathology. Cohen observes: ''Freud writes a clinical case history; James, a ghost story. Yet a comparative reading of the two works not only calls into question their authors' use of these genres but also the basic assumptions about truth and fiction which we normally attach to the genres themselves.''

Collins, Carvel. ''James's *The Turn of the Screw*.'' *The Explicator* XIII, No. 8 (June 1955): Item 49.
Proposes that Douglas, the owner of the governess's manuscript, was in fact the Miles of the story as a child.

Cook, David A., and Corrigan, Timothy J. ''Narrative Structure in *The Turn of the Screw*: A New Approach to Meaning.'' *Studies in Short Fiction* XVII, No. 1 (Winter 1980): 55-65.
Discusses the meaning of *The Turn of the Screw* as a product of the tension between the apparitionist and nonapparitionist interpretations.

Costello, Donald P. ''The Structure of *The Turn of the Screw*.'' *Modern Language Notes* LXXV, No. 4 (April 1960): 312-21.
Analyzes the pattern of incidents and their interpretation by the governess. Costello states: ''I believe that a close examination of the structure of *The Turn of the Screw* will indicate that James so built his tale as to make it both puzzle the reader and to horrify him, that both these elements are planted in the very structure of the story. Any interpretation which takes away the ghosts weakens the story's ability to horrify; any interpretation which takes away the reader's uncertainty weakens the story's ability to mystify.''

Cranfill, Thomas Mabry, and Clark, Robert Lanier, Jr. *An Anatomy of ''The Turn of the Screw''*. Austin: University of Texas Press, 1965, 195 p.
Presents a detailed study of the novel from a non-apparitionist viewpoint.

Crowl, Susan. ''Aesthetic Allegory in *The Turn of the Screw*.'' *Novel: A Forum on Fiction* IV, No. 2 (Winter 1971): 107-22.
An analysis of *The Turn of the Screw* and the critical debate surrounding it. Crowl states that ''*The Turn of the Screw* is not primarily a psychoanalytic case history of an authoritarian character, a documentary of the egocentric predicament, nor, on the other hand, a pre-Freudian study of infantile sexuality. It is a brilliantly self-conscious piece of fiction, assigning its own criteria and defining its terms, and incidentally, distinguishing them from those of other disciplines.''

Dove, George N. ''The 'Haunted Personality' in Henry James.'' *Tennessee Studies in Literature* III (1958): 99-106.
Compares the governess to James's other characters who are confronted by ghosts.

Dyson, A. E. ''Murderous Innocence: James's *The Turn of the Screw*.'' In his *Between Two Worlds: Aspects of Literary Form*, pp. 53-80. London: Macmillan Press, 1972.

A Freudian analysis which attempts to provide additional evidence for the hallucinationist position and to refute apparitionist arguments.

Edel, Leon. ''The Point of View.'' In his *The Psychological Novel: 1900-1950*, pp. 35-52. London: Rupert Hart-Davis, 1961.
Discusses James's employment of the governess as narrator, attempting to demonstrate that her testimony is unreliable. Edel concludes that ''the governess's account of her stay at Bly is riddled with inconsistencies which the many critics who have discussed the story have never perceived. . . . She speculates and she assumes—and what she first states as fancy she later states as fact.''

Evans, Oliver. ''James's Air of Evil: *The Turn of the Screw*.'' *Partisan Review* XVI, No. 2 (February 1949): 175-87.
Rejects the hallucinationist theory of *The Turn of the Screw* and posits the conflict between appearance and reality as the central theme of the story.

Felman, Shoshana. ''Turning the Screw of Interpretation.'' *Yale French Studies*, No. 55/56 (1977): 94-207.
A discussion of criticism on *The Turn of the Screw* and of the story itself using psychoanalytical elements derived from Jacques Lacan's interpretation of Sigmund Freud.

Firebaugh, Joseph J. ''Inadequacy in Eden: Knowledge and *The Turn of the Screw*.'' *Modern Fiction Studies* III, No. 1 (Spring 1957): 57-63.
Discusses the corruption of the children as a form of knowledge and the governess as an ignorant protector who would shield them from that knowledge.

Ford, Ford Madox. ''Methods.'' In his *Henry James: A Critical Study*, pp. 149-75. London: Martin Secker, 1913.
Contains a discussion of James's method of producing horror in *The Turn of the Screw*.

Fraser, John. ''*The Turn of the Screw* Again.'' *The Midwest Quarterly* VII, No. 4 (Summer, 1966): 327-36.
Stresses the American, puritanical nature of the governess in *The Turn of the Screw*.

Fussell, Edwin. ''The Ontology of *The Turn of the Screw*.'' *Journal of Modern Literature* VIII, No. 1 (1980): 118-28.
Asserts that the governess's text is a novel of her own creation, not an autobiographical account of what actually took place at Bly.

Grunes, Dennis. ''The Demonic Child in *The Turn of the Screw*.'' *Psychocultural Review* II, No. 4 (Fall 1978): 221-39.
Discusses both psychological and religious elements in *The Turn of the Screw*.

Hoffman, Charles G. ''Innocence and Evil in James' *The Turn of the Screw*.'' *University of Kansas City Review* XX, No. 1 (Autumn 1953): 97-105.
Discusses the corruption of the children.

Jones, Alexander E. ''Point of View in *The Turn of the Screw*.'' *PMLA* LXXIV, No. 1 (March 1959): 112-22.
A summary discussion of criticism pertaining to the authenticity of the ghosts. Jones finds the hallucination theories of the novella untenable and views the governess as a reliable observer and a sympathetic character.

Lang, Hans-Joachim. ''The Turns in *The Turn of the Screw*.'' *Jahrbuch fur amerikastudien* IX (1964): 110-28.
A summary of previous criticism of *The Turn of the Screw* and an analysis of the imagery of turning in the novella.

Leavis, F. R. ''*What Maisie Knew*: A Disagreement by F. R. Leavis.'' In *The Complex Fate: Hawthorne, Henry James and Some Other American Writers* by Marius Bewley, pp. 114-31. New York: Grove Press, 1954.
A reaction to Bewley's essay (see Additional Bibliography entry above). Leavis attempts to place the focus of evil on the ghosts, rather than on the governess.

Levy, Leo B. *"The Turn of the Screw* as Retaliation." *College English* XVII, No. 5 (February 1956): 286-88.
Views the ambiguity in *The Turn of the Screw* as a hoax by which James made fools of his readers in order to repay his audience for their scorn of his play *Guy Domville.*

McElroy, John Harmon. "The Mysteries at Bly." *Arizona Quarterly* XXXVII, No. 3 (Autumn 1981): 214-36.
Examines the governess's character, actions, and culpability for the death of Miles, concluding that "when James's plot in this novella is laid out for inspection, his governess appears as neither criminally insane nor morally monstrous, but only as a neurasthenic and unfortunate young woman who made fatuous and fatally consequential decisions on her first job as governess."

Miner, Earl Roy. "Henry James's Metaphysical Romances." *Nineteenth-Century Fiction* IX, No. 1 (June 1954): 1-21.
Classifies James's supernatural tales as "metaphysical romances" and examines the critical controversy surrounding *The Turn of the Screw.* Miner defines James's "metaphysical romances" as works exhibiting "marked qualities of moral intensity and psychological insight in the context of supernaturalism."

Phelps, William Lyon. "Henry James." In his *Howells, James, Bryant and Other Essays,* pp. 123-55. New York: Macmillan Co., 1924.
A personal appreciation of *The Turn of the Screw.* Phelps states: *"The Turn of the Screw* . . . is the most nerve-shattering ghost story I have ever read, and I have read a great many."

Pound, Ezra. "Henry James." In his *Literary Essays of Ezra Pound,* edited by T. S. Eliot, pp. 295-338.
Briefly mentions *The Turn of the Screw* as being a "Freudian affair which seems to have attracted undue interest . . . because of its subject matter. The obscenity of *The Turn of the Screw* has given it undue prominence."

Rahv, Philip, ed. Introduction to *The Turn of the Screw,* by Henry James. In *The Great Short Novels of Henry James,* edited by Philip Rahv, pp. 623-25. New York: Dial Press, 1944.
Denies that the ghosts are hallucinations while affirming the theme of sexuality in the work.

Reed, Glenn A. "Another Turn on James's *The Turn of the Screw.*" *American Literature* XX, No. 4 (January 1949): 413-23.
Examines and refutes the hallucinationist reading of *The Turn of the Screw.*

Schleifer, Ronald. "The Trap of the Imagination: The Gothic Tradition, Fiction, and *The Turn of the Screw.*" *Criticism* XXII, No. 4 (Fall 1980): 297-319.
Compares *The Turn of the Screw* to Bram Stoker's *Dracula,* noting Gothic conventions in the novella which are epitomized by Stoker's novel.

Sheppard, E. A. *Henry James and "The Turn of the Screw."* New Zealand: Auckland University Press, 1974, 292 p.
Discusses several aspects of the creation of and reactions to *The Turn of the Screw,* including critical opinions, influences on James and possible sources for elements of the story, its artistic structure, and James's revisions of the novella.

Silver, John. "A Note on the Freudian Reading of *The Turn of the Screw.*" *American Literature* XXIX, No. 2 (May 1957): 207-11.
Explains the governess's description of Peter Quint by attempting to demonstrate that the governess had learned of Quint's existence, as well as the manner of his death, by inquiring in a nearby village.

Slabey, Robert M. *"The Turn of the Screw:* Grammar and Optics." *CLA Journal* IX, No. 1 (September 1965): 68-72.
A discussion of ambiguous pronouns in the text of *The Turn of the Screw* and the extraordinary eyesight of the governess.

Spilka, Mark. "Turning the Freudian Screw: How Not to Do It." *Literature and Psychology* XIII, No. 4 (Fall 1963): 105-11.
Repudiates the Freudian analysis of the story while acknowledging the truths such analysis does bring to light.

Stone, Albert E. "Henry James and Childhood: *The Turn of the Screw.*" In *American Character and Culture in a Changing World: Some Twentieth-Century Perspectives,* edited by John A. Hague, pp. 279-92. Westport, Conn.: Greenwood Press, 1979.
Studies the theme of childhood in *The Turn of the Screw.*

Thomson, A. W. *"The Turn of the Screw:* Some Points on the Hallucination Theory." *A Review of English Literature* VI, No. 4 (October 1965): 26-36.
A defense of the hallucination theory.

Tinter, Adeline R. "An Illustrator's Literary Interpretations." *A B Bookman's Weekly* LXIII, No. 13 (26 March 1979): 2275, 2278, 2280, 2282.
Discusses the illustration which appeared with *The Turn of the Screw* at its original publication in *Collier's Weekly.* Tinter maintains that the illustration suggests a psychoanalytical interpretation of the work.

Trachtenberg, Stanley. "The Return of the Screw." *Modern Fiction Studies* XI, No. 2 (Summer 1965): 180-82.
Enlarges on Louis D. Rubin's thesis that Douglas is Miles (see excerpt dated 1963) by proposing that Douglas's reading of the manuscript is a form of confession.

Voeglin, Eric. "A Letter to Robert B. Heilman" and "Postscript: On Paradise and Revolution." *The Southern Review* VII, No. 1 (January 1971): 9-24, 25-48.
Enlarges upon the religious themes which Heilman introduced in his essay *"The Turn of the Screw* as Poem" (see excerpt dated 1948). Voeglin's "Postscript" is a theological study of the novella.

Waldock, A.J.A. "Mr. Edmund Wilson and *The Turn of the Screw.*" *Modern Language Notes* LXII, No. 5 (May 1947): 331-34.
An early refutation of Wilson's Freudian interpretation.

West, Muriel. *A Stormy Night with "The Turn of the Screw."* Phoenix: Frye & Smith, 1964, 75 p.
A whimsical, fictionalized study which successively offers several different interpretations of *The Turn of the Screw.*

Wolff, Robert Lee. "The Genesis of *The Turn of the Screw.*" *American Literature* XIII, No. 1 (March 1941): 1-8.
Questions the anecdote by Archbishop Benson as the sole inspiration for *The Turn of the Screw* and suggests a picture entitled "The Haunted House," which had been published in a magazine issue that included James's ghost story "Sir Edmund Orme," as another possible source for the story.

Wright, Walter F. "The World of Inference." In his *The Madness of Art: A Study of Henry James,* pp. 173-88. Lincoln: University of Nebraska, 1962.
An examination of three major perspectives on the novel: those which regard it as religious allegory, ironic religious allegory, and case study of a sexually repressed spinster.

Eino Leino

1878-1926

(Born Armas Eino Leopold Lonnbohm) Finnish poet, dramatist, novelist, short story writer, journalist, memoirist, and critic.

The most important Finnish poet of his generation, Leino effectively combined the mysticism and allegorical style of the French Symbolists with the meters and subjects of traditional folk poetry. In his popular masterwork *Helkavirsiä*, an adaptation of several texts drawn from the Finnish epic *Kalevala*, Leino employed legendary characters and plots while reflecting modern social and political issues. He was closely associated with the neoromantic cultural movement Young Finland, whose members contributed significantly to the rising national consciousness of Finns in the 1890s. Leino's achievement was summarized by Cid Erik Tallqvist, who called the poet a "god-gifted singer, in whose art a highly decorative yet sensitive form expresses both passionate emotion and vigorous intellect."

Born in Paltamo in South Kainuu, Leino was the youngest of eleven children born to a surveyor and his wife. Leino attended schools in Oulu and Hämeenlinna before enrolling at the University of Helsinki in 1895. In Helsinki, his elder brother Kasimir introduced him into the literary and cultural society surrounding the Young Finland movement in the arts. Blending nationalism and neoromanticism, the creative artists of Young Finland found inspiration largely in the *Kalevala*, the Finnish national epic, which had been compiled in the mid-nineteenth century by folklorist Elias Lönnrot. Applying its themes, subjects, and motifs to their respective arts, the composer Jean Sibelius, the painter Akseli Gallen-Kallela, and Leino became the most influential spokesmen of their generation in Finland. Leino abandoned his studies without completing a degree, pursuing instead a career in journalism and editing an arts review with his brother. He published several collections of poetry in the late 1890s and quickly won recognition as Finland's preeminent poet and a leading political journalist. However, plagued by a fear of hereditary madness and the sorrow connected with the dissolution of his first marriage in 1908, Leino began to decline as a poet and his influence waned. In the years immediately preceding his death his heavy drinking and well-publicized love affairs focused interest more on his bohemian lifestyle than on his writings.

Fluent in several languages, Leino had considerable familiarity with the works of major European literary figures of the late nineteenth century. His early lyrics, influenced by Heinrich Heine and the nineteenth-century Finnish patriot-poet Johan Ludvig Runeberg, are considered conventionally romantic, optimistic, and musical. In addition, scholars have noted the influence of the Symbolist movement on Leino's works, praising the rich and varied use of allegory in his disciplined, often mystic verses. As he matured, however, he gradually assumed a more pessimistic tone and increasingly drew on Finnish history and folk poetry for his subjects. In his most important collection, the first volume of *Helkavirsiä*, he boldly transformed the ancient legends of the *Kalevala*, illustrating personal concerns as well as contemporary social problems. While utilizing enjambment, extensive rhyme, and alliteration in the

tradition of oral poetry, Leino presented ballads that expressed a distinctly modern view and blended tragedy with optimism. *Helkavirsiä*, published at the height of Leino's mature period, has been cited by many critics as the foremost achievement in Finnish lyric poetry.

A passionate advocate of Finnish political and cultural independence, Leino sought through his works to contribute to the growth of a Finnish national identity in literature. He accomplished this most notably in his verses which, according to Jaakko Ahokas, also typified "the mood of the times, the yearning for something higher and more beautiful than reality . . . , as well as a general feeling of vanity and the doubts in all human effort." His fiction and drama, however, are considered less accomplished. Of the nineteen dramas included in his six-volume *Naamioita*, only *Sota valosta*, based on a Kalevalan motif, was successfully produced. Nevertheless, Leino adapted the *Kalevala* itself for the stage and, in 1912, he proposed and sponsored the establishment of the Helka-theater, an outdoor venue to be used exclusively for productions of Kalevalan drama. While he sought expression in several genres, Leino's poetry continued to be his most important work. The second volume of *Helkavirsiä*, although not considered equal in achievement to the first, is nevertheless regarded by many critics as a valuable collection and the finest of Leino's later works.

Following a brief increase in critical attention after his death, Leino's reputation and influence declined. While centenary editions of his works, including English and French translations of *Helkavirsiä,* have brought new readers to his verses, Leino remains little read outside his homeland. Scholars of Scandinavian literature, however, generally consider him the leading lyric poet of modern Finland. According to Aleksis Rubulis, Leino was "the most gifted literary figure of the Young Finland movement and the greatest prodigy among Finnish poets of all time."

PRINCIPAL WORKS

Maaliskuun lauluja (poetry) 1896
Tuonelan joutsen [first publication] (drama) 1898
Johan Wilhelm [first publication] (drama) 1900
Sota valosta [first publication] (drama) 1900
Kangastuksia (poetry) 1902
Helkavirsiä. 2 vols. (poetry) 1903-16
     [*Whitsongs* (partial translation), 1978]
Simo Hurtta. 2 vols. (poetry) 1904-19
Talvi-yö (poetry) 1905
Naamioita. 6 vols. [first publication] (dramas) 1905-11
Tuomas Vitikka (novel) 1906
Jaana Rönty (novel) 1907
Halla (poetry) 1908
Olli Suurpää (novel) 1908
Tähtitarha (poetry) 1912
Elämän koreus (poetry) 1915
Musti (novel) 1916
Karjalan kuningas [first publication] (drama) 1917
Bellerophon (poetry) 1919
Juhana herttuan ja Catharina Jagellonican lauluja (poetry) 1919
Syreenien Kukkiessa (poetry) 1920
Elämäni kuvakirja (memoirs) 1925
Kootut teokset. 16 vols. (poetry, dramas, and novels) 1926-30

CID ERIK TALLQVIST (essay date 1947)

[*Tallqvist is a Finnish educator, translator, and critic whose works reflect his interest in English literature. In the following excerpt, he praises Leino's poetry.*]

Eino Leino . . . is a prodigy in Finnish literature even if we think only of the large quantity of work that he produced during a comparatively short life.

Naturally all that he wrote cannot be of the highest quality, but his best work represents the highest achievement in Finnish lyrical poetry. (p. 23)

As a poet he was at first under the influence of Heine, and of the national poet of Finland, Johan Ludvig Runeberg, and others, but he rapidly developed his own individual style, which was the natural expression of an independent and mature poetic personality. In it, he shows how rich and melodiously splendid Finnish verse may sound when written by a genius who has mastered the art of verse-writing, and is thoroughly familiar with, and capable of improving on, the subtlety and wealth of the old *Kalevala* metre and language.

In his best work he appears as a god-gifted singer, in whose art a highly decorative yet sensitive form expresses both passionate emotion and vigorous intellect. In it he has interpreted the thought and feelings of his nation, its anguish and pain, but also its unquenchable will to live, and its firm faith in life, and this he has done by expressing through the national symbols, his own inspired soul and inner vision. His mind, in doing this, was illuminated by the best European thought of his time, and so he achieved, in addition to the expression of his own thoughts and feelings and those of his nation, a universality such as has been achieved in modern times only by a few other artists inspired in the first instance by national idealisms—one thinks above all of Sibelius and of Yeats.

The work by which he will, above all, be remembered and through which Finnish critics are convinced he would have won European fame if he had written in one of the great European languages, is in Finnish, called **Helkavirsiä** (literally, "Songs sung at the Whitsuntide fires"), a name that might be rendered simply **Whitsun Fires**. In this collection, the poems have ballad form and treat of popular national and legendary themes. They are a kind of strongly lyrical short epic. They are written in the metre adopted by Longfellow in *Hiawatha,* of the Finnish national epic *Kalevala,* which our poet developed into a still more concentrated and forceful artistic medium, of great subtlety in its apparent metrical strictness, in this respect comparable with English blank-verse; it is in Leino also marked by a quality which might be described as pregnant stylization.

In these poems, then, Leino shows himself a representative of the national romantic school which flourished in literature at the end of the nineteenth and the beginning of the twentieth century.

As an artist he was, however, by no means restricted to a narrow nationalism. His thought and feelings moved among, and were inspired by, the general trend of European philosophy at the time when he lived.

As he is at the same time, the most national and the most universal of Finnish poets, so, in his personal poetry, to his indomitable faith in life is joined a curious fatalism and stoicism. But all this is expressed . . . in a form in which every line seems a diamond, fascinating and suggestive, and the whole a flaming diadem. (pp. 23-5)

> *Cid Erik Tallqvist, "Poems from a Finnish Anthology," in* Life and Letters and the London Mercury, *Vol. 52, No. 113, January, 1947, pp. 21-36.*

JAAKKO AHOKAS (essay date 1973)

[*Ahokas is a Finnish educator, translator, and critic. In the following excerpt from his* History of Finnish Literature, *he surveys Leino's poetry, dramas, and novels.*]

The first ten or fifteen years of this century can be called the period of national romanticism in Finnish literature, or even the period of Eino Leino. . . . Although many other writers began their careers approximately when he did, none equaled him as a poet, and the great novelists of his generation wrote their major works later. He typified in his poems, short stories, novels, plays, criticism, and newspaper articles the mood of the times, the yearning for something higher and more beautiful than reality, for heroic deeds, and for outbursts of burning passion, as well as a general feeling of vanity and the doubts in all human effort. Such feelings degenerate easily into theatrical attitudes and rhetoric, neither of which is lacking in Leino or his contemporaries. (p. 147)

Despite Leino's description of himself as a healthy country boy, there were but few gay, careless, and happy songs among his works, and his first poems which did not reflect his personal conflicts were in the rhetorical and ornately patriotic tradition initiated by Ahlqvist-Oksanen and Genetz-Jännes. He was able, however, to create good poetry about his own problems, and only after 1910 did the first signs of his coming breakdown appear in his art and his life. The great problems recurring in his works can be classified as the relationship between dream and fulfillment, the opposition between life and death, and the opposition between good and evil. Leino's poems, however, are about characters, not abstractions, except in a few cases, as in the section **"Ajan kirja"** (**"The Book of Time"**) of the collection *Talvi-yö (The Winter Night* . . .). His heroes are self-defeating; they either meet destruction in a struggle against superhuman enemies or receive ambiguous oracles which leave them unsatisfied. Artistically this description of man's eternal struggle for truth is more rewarding than a presentation of cut-and-dried answers to human problems. . . .

[Subjects] from old poetry and from Karelia recur in his poetry. Occasionally these subjects seem little more than pretexts for writing colorful, romantic descriptions of the past, as in the legends **"Luojan leipä"** (**"The Bread of God,"** in *Helkavirsiä* I . . .) **"Sininen risti"** (**"The Blue Cross"**), and **"Impi ja pajarin poika"** (**"The Maid and the Son of the Boyar,"** both in *Helkavirsiä* I . . .). Some build a metaphysical conception of life **"Väinämöisen laulu"** (**"Väinämöinen's Song,"** in *Kangastuksia*), **"Aika"** (**"Time"** . . .), and *Kouta* (name, in *Helkavirsiä* I). Some gave the poet the opportunity to analyze his own soul, **"Tumma"** (name, in *Helkavirsiä* I), **"Tuuri"** (name, same collection) **"Iku-Turso"** (name, in *Talvi-yö*), and **"Turjan loihtu"** (**"Turja's Spell,"** in the collection *Halla, The Frost* . . .).

Despite Leino's precociousness as a poet and facility for writing, recognition was not immediately given to his works, in which many critics saw only faults and oddities. (p. 148)

During these first years as an artist, Leino had met another poet, Otto Manninen, quite different from himself, with whom he established a lasting friendship after a few brushes due to Manninen's severe but just criticism of Leino's youthful works. After noting the weaknesses in, e.g., *Sata ja yksi laulua* and *Kivesjärveläiset*, Manninen fully recognized *Kangastuksia*, in which he believed Leino had reached a mastery of expression which, he hoped, would make possible the attainment of a higher level of perfection in Finnish poetry, not only for Leino, but also for poets who followed his example. Critics, somewhat bewildered by *Helkavirsiä* I, tended to view the collection negatively until Manninen, in a long article published in *Valvoja*, gave a penetrating analysis and placed it in the context of Finnish poetry. According to Manninen, until then there had been a rift in Finnish poetry, literature, and art between the followers of the old Finnish tradition and those who took their models from Western Europe, but Leino had combined both into a harmonious whole. Manninen maintained that the meters of old Finnish and new European poetry must remain separated, but that in Leino's works, especially *Helkavirsiä*, a Finnish and European way of seeing the world and expressing feelings were happily united. Other poets used the old folk meter before Leino, but almost no one used it after him, and the subjects from Finnish mythology or the legendary past were also discarded, both as reconstructions of a lost world and as expres-

sions of modern thoughts. Thus, Leino's work did not mark the beginning of a new era; it was more the culmination of an old one, if not an era in itself. National romanticism, the resurrection of the Finnish past and the creation of a new civilization from its elements and the modern world . . . was at best a dream of intellectuals and artists. (p. 149)

There is considerable difference in the treatment of the subjects from Finnish mythology and past in Leino's earliest collections and *Helkavirsiä* I. In **"Laulu suuresta tammesta"** the myth about a gigantic oak which overshadowed the whole world until an unknown, small, weak-looking man felled it, is treated superficially. . . . Väinämöinen is no longer spiritual leader of the nation; only an unknown old man sings of the great deeds of the past and predicts a better future, when a hero will fell the gigantic Swedish oak. The poem is really only an argument in the quarrels between the two linguistic groups in Finland. In *Tuonelan joutsen* the mythical motif already expresses something deeper. The *Kalevala* episode tells the story of Lemminkäinen, who, to win the hand of a maid, must perform seemingly impossible deeds, the last consisting of killing the swan of the underworld; he perishes in the attempt, but is revived by his mother. In his effort to represent allegorically the quest of man for the ultimate truth, the mystery of life and death, Leino followed this outline rather closely. He did not state all of the metaphysical implications in the poem, but, in a letter to Maila Talvio, he indicated that Lemminkäinen's defeat and death were due to the fact that he was a mere sinful human being. Only Christ, Leino concluded, can bring hope and solve the mystery of death for mankind, who lives and suffers in fear of it.

The collections that followed, *Yökehrääjä, Sata ja yksi laulua, Ajan aalloilla, Hiihtäjän virsiä*, and *Pyhä kevät*, were not remarkable. *Ajan aalloilla* is directly inspired by the Russian oppression, and the others, though some have remained popular as songs, show mainly that Leino had a great facility for writing light, melodious verse; he was duly criticized for these compositions. Although they contain a few poems based on subjects from the Finnish past, only the play *Sota valosta* is based on an episode in the *Kalevala*. Again, Leino was attracted by an episode largely composed for the epic by Lönnrot, in which original materials did not have a great part: the sun and the moon were kept in a mountain by the enemy of the *Kalevala*'s major heroes, who then set them free. In Leino's poem each of the heroes represents a human type: Väinämöinen is the leader of the nation, bringing it light and knowledge, Ilmarinen the artist, Lemminkäinen the warrior; but Pohjola, the enemy country, is a pure symbol of the negative side in human nature:

> Pohjola on siellä täällä
> vesissä ja vetten päällä
> maassa, puussa, kuolleen luussa,
> itse ihmisen lihassa.

> Pohjola is here and there
> On the waters, under them,
> In the earth and in the wood
> In the bones of all the dead,
> Even in the flesh of Man.

Leino alluded again to the political situation in Väinämöinen's proclamation of faith in the power of light and the human spirit, which will remain even after the Swedish conquerors and Christianity rob the heroes of the *Kalevala* of their strength. Leino's admiration for Nietzsche is often seen in the manner in which he describes his characters, reminiscent of the German writer's superman. Neither Leino nor his contemporaries considered this work of much value, but Bergbom, who died in 1906, produced it at the National Theater.

Leino's next collection, *Kangastuksia,* is introductory to *Helkavirsiä* I, so much so that Leino included two of its poems in the later collection. It still contains "some of everything," including an epic poem in twelve cantos, **"Perman taru"** (**"The Saga of Perma"**), in a meter typical of modern Finnish folksongs which he had also used in the earlier *Kivesjärveläiset.* As this meter is closely connected for Finnish readers with folk motifs and melodies, the difficulties of writing other poetry with it have kept its use infrequent; Leino progressively discarded it in his later poems. Seemingly exotic subjects in some of the compositions in *Kangastuksia* were used by Leino to express views on questions of general interest, for example. **"Tahtoisin nähdä mä Kartagon naisen"** (**"I Wish I Could See a Woman of Carthago"**), **"Imatran tarina"** (**"The Tale of Imatra"**), or **"Temppeliherra"** (**"The Templar"**), which exalt freedom and the fight for it. In **"Temppeliherra"** the concept of freedom includes any high ideal, expressed as "the man who lived for an ideal / is but sleeping, he cannot die / his sword is striking from beneath the ground." This philosophical vein is further pursued in some poems inspired by Finnish mythology, such as **"Väinämöisen laulu,"** in which the bard and hero is presented as an ideal for mankind with the warning that even the hero is not eternal—what endures is the ideal, the spirit, man himself. A complex pattern of interwoven motifs and ideas, reflected in Leino's life, appears in **"Aika."** Time, which Leino identifies with death, is an evil against which all heroes are called to fight, but the fight is purely spiritual. These heroes, "the stepping stones of their own ideals," are victorious only when doing "deeds of the spirit, which shall not disappear, even if all nations vanish." Here is Leino's basic fear of death, which reappears throughout his works though he tried to overcome it by philosophic and metaphysic considerations, the most common being that mankind does not disappear even though the individual is destroyed, and that great spiritual deeds live forever. The problem of good and evil, stated more clearly in *Helkavirsiä,* is here apparent insofar as Leino insists that it is not by warlike deeds and violence but by spiritual struggle that ultimate victory can be achieved. His hidden fear of the opposite sex is expressed in the personification of time as a Gorgon, a hideous monster, "half a lizard, huge and scaly, half a woman with lips burning red like flames," which devours its victims. (pp. 149-52)

In *Helkavirsä* I there are but few compositions on mythical and metaphysical problems, and no transpositions of motifs from the *Kalevala,* like *Sota valosta* or *Tuonelan joutsen.* Leino seems not to have been inspired by myths to treat them in verse, but to have been inclined to use them as metaphors for his own problems. The poems include ballads and legends, and it is in the first ones that his problems, or those of man as an individual, are presented by means of historical or mythical motifs. The main character of **"Ylermi"** is vaguely defined a medieval nobleman, a proud knight who defies God and is punished. Ylermi is a kind of Byronic hero, a Don Juan, and a Nietzschean superman, but he directs his rebellion not against God or a specific religion as much as against the slavish spirit of men who fear death; the hero hopes for a later generation, sterner than his, that will not bow to death or crawl on its way to the underworld. . . . There is little Finnish mythology in **"Kouta,"** although its subject seems to be taken from it; Leino admitted that he had thought of describing the main character, Kouta, as a shaman, but that he eventually gave him more

individuality and a yearning for the highest truth. He possesses all the knowledge of the gods and men, but not the ultimate wisdom, described as "binding the blue fire / opening the treasure troves." (According to Finnish beliefs mysterious blue flames burn over hidden treasures, which can be found if the flame is "bound.") Later the ultimate wisdom consists in the unveiling of the secrets of Death, held by the goddess of Time, Ajatar; the motifs of *Tuonelan joutsen* and **"Aika"** again appear here. Kouta eventually descends to the underworld and meets the goddess, who announces that he must be ready to sacrifice his own life to be allowed to partake of the deepest mystery; he declares his readiness and learns the words of wisdom. It is obviously dangerous for a poet to declare that he knows the ultimate secret of the universe, and Leino made his statement oracular enough to allow speculation on its meaning among Finnish scholars: *Elon huoli huomisesta / Mana mennyttä manaapi* ("Life's sorrow is about tomorrow / Death is conjuring the past"). Hardly mysterious, they seem to be a warning by Leino to himself not to brood about death, but to turn to life and the future.

The heroes of some of the other ballads, which are neither so metaphysical nor solemn as these two, though still tragic, are more ordinary human beings, caught in forces larger than their immediate experiences. (pp. 152-53)

Some of the poems classified as ballads in *Helkavirsiä* I are not at all supernatural or mythological and give only stirring, tragic, or violent descriptions from the past without implication of a deeper meaning. **"Räikkö Räähkä,"** named for the main character, gives a few essential facts from the story of a traitor. "He showed the road to the enemy on a dark autumn night between two cliffs, he did it because his life was threatened," but his neighbors do not retaliate directly; they only reject him, and he hangs himself. Although it was written during the Russian oppression, when some Finns were traitors and others, who thought they could prevent the worst by collaborating with the Russians, were branded as such, Leino was probably not using these facts in his poem, whose events could happen anywhere. **"Mantsin laulu"** (**"The Song of Mantsi"**), another story of old wars, is set in Finnish Karelia and tells of young men taking arms in vengeance upon their enemies, who have abducted a maid; **"Orjan poika"** (**"The Son of a Slave"**) is set in Lapland. Leino did not consciously imitate, but he recreated closely the atmosphere of old folk poems about border wars, feuds, and plundering expeditions, familiar in every country with a violent past. In **"Orjan poika"** the leader of a Finnish plundering expedition in Lapland carries away a Lapp boy and later kills him, fearing his evil eye—Lapps have always been considered great magicians and sorcerers. The murder is accomplished while the victim sleeps; a vision of his home country, experienced at the moment of death, closes the poem:

> Puikoivat punaiset pulkat
> punaisilla kukkuloilla,
> siukoivat siniset petrat
> sinisillä virran-suilla,
> jolui joutsenet hopeiset,
> käet kukkui kultahiset,
> käet kukkui, linnut lauloi,
> vihannoivat viidat kaikki
> Lapin suuressa suvessa,
> yössä päivän paistamassa.

> Red sleighs were sliding
> On high red hills,
> Blue reindeers were running

On the banks of blue brooks,
Silvery swans were swimming,
Golden cuckoos were calling
Cuckoos calling, birds warbling,
Blooming the green groves
In the sweet summer of Lapland
In the night of sun and light.

This vision, in the style of folk poetry, marks a slight break with the beginning of the poem. It is more the voice of Leino than that of an anonymous ballad singer by whom, we imagine, the first part of the story was told. The same break occurs in **"Räikkö Räähkä."** It begins—*Tuo turilas, Räikkö Räähkä / Neuvoi tien viholliselle* ("That varmint, Räikkö Räähkä / Showed the road to the enemy")—in an almost popular or familiar tone, but ends with a highly poetic vision, supposedly of the main character, about to hang himself, but actually of Leino: *Elo kaunis kangastihe / askar autuas inehmon / maan kovalla kannikalla* ("He saw as in a sight / life so light and fair / the blessed burden of Man / on the hard crust of Earth").

The quotation from **"Orjan poika"** is typical of the ornate verse written in imitation of old folk poetry. In descriptions of the wealthy and sumptuous or wonderful and supernatural, the old folk poems employed a set of colors, mainly blue, red, gold, and silver, the latter also metals; this device was conventionally applied, colors being assigned to objects for the alliterate effect common in Finnish folk poetry. (pp. 154-55)

The poems classified as legends in *Helkavirsiä* I deal with Christian subjects, also treated in old Finnish folk poems. Leino often set the action in orthodox Karelia, giving himself the opportunity to describe colorful, magnificent churches and monasteries topped by gilt cupolas, where priests in glittering chasubles performed the divine service under icons encased in precious metals midst clouds of incense, and holy men and hermits performed miracles.... Although Leino does not express deep emotional or religious involvement, he found more in the orthodox creed than mere outer pomp: the simple, child-like faith with which its believers accepted miracles, the direct intervention of the supernatural in everyday life, and the spirit of almost cheerful mysticism with which they approached their God, all banned by the more rational Protestant church and alien to the practical spirit of Finland proper. **"Sininen risti"** (**"The Blue Cross"**), typical of Leino's poems in this respect, tells of a young girl called by God to preach Christianity to the heathen Karelians; she proves her supernatural calling by walking through the closed gates of a monastery forbidden to women, is blessed by the monks, and sets out on her mission. When a man attempts to rape her, God changes her into a blue cross. (p. 156)

Often an author's best-known work is misleading in its representation of his art and personality.... Eino Leino, known in Finland as the author of *Helkavirsiä* I, does not suffer that misconception. *Helkavirsiä* I is so rich and complex in content and so perfect in form that it alone gives a not inadequate picture of its author and his art.

The years between the publication of *Helkavirsiä* I and the end of his first marriage in 1908 were the most stable in Leino's life; during that time he wrote some of his best poems, contained in the collections *Talvi-yö* and *Halla*. As the titles suggest, they are neither cheerful nor optimistic. The title **"Eyan kirja"** (**"Eya's Book"**), a section of *Talvi-yö*, is an allusion to his wife, Freya. Many of its erotic and sensuous poems have sumptuous and fantastic oriental settings indicated by the titles:

"The Children of Nineveh," "The Song of the Caravan," "The Bayaderes," in keeping with the current fashion, both abroad and in Finland. Not particularly personal, they are shadowed by insecurity and sadness behind the pictures of inebriating pleasure, and Leino's handling of the various verse forms is masterful. In **"Atlantica,"** in which Eya appears, the fabled continent Atlantis is presented as a land of bliss and happiness, doomed in a world for which it was too perfect; the poet himself did not trust his luck, and future events soon proved these premonitions true.

The other poems are meditations on the destiny of man, more specifically, the poet. They contain little mythology, although many are written in the old folk meter as used by Leino. **"Talvi-yö,"** the title poem, is basically pessimistic. It opens with an impressive description of a winter night: everything is dead, frozen, and snow-covered except a waterfall, roaring, free and alive amidst silence, under which an icy swan swims. Here we have, as in *Tuonelan joutsen* and other poems by Leino, this poetic bird par excellence, dear to so many symbolic artists and writers, whose role in Leino's art is the subject of a special study in Finland. The power of the spirit is like the waterfall which is free and alive in the dead landscape, but Leino's faith in the power of the spirit was obviously wavering. The lines in which the ephemeral character of all human efforts is described seem confused, as do other parts of the poem, because the author appears to have been unable to coordinate his thoughts and feelings.... (p. 157)

In **"Tuulikannel"** (**"The Eolian Harp,"** or "kantele," also "kannel") a poet's fate is described with the assertion that he must create, compose, sing like a harp played by the winds, even against his will. In **"Iku-Turso"** (a mythological sea monster) the monster raises its head from the waves and stares at a star shining on the heaven, a not unusual representation of the Beauty and the Beast, a yearning for an unattainable beloved or ideal, but then the monster "defeats" the star, which falls so that he can "drink" it "like a swan." The shifting moods are easier to follow if we consider the monster female, like the monster "half a lizard, huge and scaly, half a woman" who personifies time in **"Aika"** and "attracts her lover in her horrible embrace." Woman is the representative of the earth-bound, sensuous nature of mankind, the seductress who attracts man from the heights of ideals, absorbs, and destroys him. The poet (the narrator) also appears as a falling star in another poem in the collection *Halla*, **"Yksilön murhe"** (**"The Sorrow of the Individual"**): *Ma sammua tahdon / kuin tähdenlento / tien viitaten erämaan lampeen* ("I want to be extinguished / like a falling star / showing the way to a mere in the forests").

The publication of *Halla*, which reflects, even more than *Talvi-yö*, his depression, coincided with the end of Leino's first marriage. He felt that his ideals were shared by few, if any, and, although he was careful to say that this fact made him feel neither sad nor proud, it did not encourage him. However, his spirit was not yet broken (even later he almost never admitted that); his poems contain much of the Nietzschean superman, who proclaims that I, the ego, the poet's self, is the highest being; transposing the words of the Gospel, he stated in one of the four short poems commonly titled **"Minä"** (**"I"**):

Minä oli alussa
Minä
kasvoi luona Kaikkivallan
ja kaikki oli se minä
Itseys on ihanin mahti,
minkä sait sa syntymässä:
älä anna pois ikinä!

At the beginning was I
I
grew close to the Almighty
and that I was all

Your Self is the most wonderful power
which you received at your birth:
Never give it away!

In "Yksilön murhe," previously quoted, as in "Tuulikannel," Leino insists that the poet's fate cannot be avoided, though others are free to choose, but in "Keskiyön kuoro" ("The Midnight Song" or "Choir") the fulfillment of all dreams is defined as the doom of mankind: "The doom of Man will be there when the maddest fancies come true, when life is more beautiful than dreams, and nature fairer than the white snow of songs." "The white snow of songs" gave Leino an easy rhyme (*unta-lunta* "dream-snow"), but he probably felt that at that time his art was cold and dead, like snow.

Leino's next collection of poems, *Tähitarha* (best translated perhaps *The Starry Meadow*), was published in 1912. . . . It is in *Tähitarha* that he gives the best expression to his love, but even there it is not pure happiness. In "Loukatut" ("The Wounded" or "Hurt") he speaks of himself and his beloved as "two slaves, fettered together with the irons of love." In "Runokirje" ("A Rhymed Letter") he says that she may be merciless, cruel, and even unfaithful; he will accept all although he once felt that he should die when hearing of these things.

Other types of poems appear in the collection, including patriotic verse, such as the famous "Karjalan kannas" ("The Isthmus of Karelia"), which remained a standard feature at patriotic functions until 1944, when the Soviet Union took the whole region and a new era of better relations between Finland and Russia began. There are signs of an artistic breakdown in some of the poems, which are incoherent, not because of the poet's contrasting emotions, but because they are sloppily written, for example "Vaeltaja" ("The Wanderer"), in which many verbs are strung together without other connection than rhyme, or "Nuori Nietzsche" ("The Young Nietzsche"), in which "children" are called to raise against "the hordes of darkness, against the lion of human night." The following two collections, *Painuva päivä* (*The Setting Sun* . . .) and *Elämän koreus* (*Gaudy Life* . . .), are hardly better, although they still bear the mark of a great poet.

In 1916 Leino published the second collection of *Helkavirsiä*, which, like the first, contains some of his best poems and is much better than all else written near the end of his life. At that time, although he did not strictly adhere to that creed or apply it to his art, he was influenced by theosophical thinking, which was popular in Finland at the beginning of this century. . . . These metaphysical preoccupations appear in Leino's poetry in the form of vast cosmic visions, not always among his best writings. In *Helkavirsiä* I the legends with Karelian setting are simple, naive, and colorful, whereas in "Marjatan poika" ("Mary's Son"; Marjatta is a popular form of Maria applied to the Virgin in old poems), for example, included in *Helkavirsiä* II, the coming of Christ is announced by cosmic cataclysms, comets, "the blue flames of electricity," and a multitude of noises produced by the Savior's chariot and by heaven itself: the horses neigh, the axletree squeals, the air roars, the vaults of the sky echo. His material representation of heaven is not peculiar to him and could have been based on classical examples. The poem "Bellerophon," published a few

years later, shows his interest in classical mythology. The mention of a chariot is reminiscent of the myth of Phaethon and its treatment by, e.g., Ovid, a comparison rather disadvantageous for Leino. These cosmic poems are more turgid than majestic although, or perhaps because, the sun, the moon, and the stars are introduced as characters in a setting of timeless astral space. A somewhat morbid eroticism appears for the first time in Leino's poetry in the description of a female demon, a temptress, and her lover in "Ukon lintu ja virvaliekki" ("The Bird of God and the Ignis Fatuus"); note the Finnish word used for the Latin in English): they are twined around each other "like blue snakes," "burn against each other like two coals," and bring death to each other "like a poison in their veins." In "Auringon hyvästijatto" ("The Farewell of the Sun") the Sun takes farewell of the Earth, his mistress, another instance of eroticism in cosmic scope; the "sparks of electricity" appear again. (pp. 158-60)

Among Leino's last collections two stand distinctly above the others: *Bellerophon* and *Juhana herttuan in Catharina Jagellonican lauluja* (*Songs of Duke John and Catharina Jagellonica*), both published in 1919. . . . By that time V. A. Koskenniemi, quite unlike Leino, was beginning his wide, lasting popularity; Leino reportedly felt challenged to write on classical and historical subjects as well as his colleague could and produced these two volumes. Readers tended to notice the extraordinary virtuosity with which rhyme and rhythm were wielded rather than the content of *Bellerophon,* a very complex work. Leino used the framework of the classical myth and filled it in with his own materials; he was successful in creating a well-balanced whole which is reminiscent of the great romantic, metaphysical-philosophical poems such as Goethe's *Faust* and Byron's *Cain*. Bellerophon, a typical Leino hero, is related to the characters in the early poems, Lemminkäinen in *Tuonelan joutsen,* for example; he is the man in quest of the ultimate truth who is taken through heaven, hell and earth, and eventually reaches a state beyond human joys and sorrows when the Moirai announce to him that he will be changed into a star. (p. 161)

Leino's best nonpoetic works are his dramatic ones, some in verse. *Johan Wilhelm* . . . , one of the first, is unremarkable although superficially original. . . . The main character, who is insane, does not appear on stage, but his existence influences the action, for his brother is in love with his wife and her sister. These erotic, somewhat incestuous complications never lead anywhere; at the end of the play, Johan Wilhelm dies, still offstage, and his wife dies from the shock of the news of his demise.

After 1905 Leino published his plays in six collections called *Naamioita (Masks* . . .). In the preface to the fifth volume, he revealed his theory of drama, not unlike those of Gordon Craig, Appia, Reinhardt, Copeau, Meyerhold, or Evreinov, who were beginning to lead European theater away from realism and naturalism. Leino's aim was to stylize drama, carry the simplification of artistic means to extreme, render the theater beautiful to the eye and pleasant to the ear, and make the stage again a home for poetry, not only bourgeois taste and literary handicraft. Of Leino's plays, we might say that good intentions do not make good art, but some are still performed in Finland, especially those dealing with Finnish history. (pp. 161-62)

Characters from Finnish history appearing in Leino's plays are usually proud, violent, cruel, and perhaps ultimately defeated because of weaknesses within themselves. *Lalli* (second collection) is about the half-legendary pagan Finn who, according to a medieval chronicle and folk poems, killed the first Christian missionary in Finland, but was justly and miraculously avenged by God. . . . *Simo Hurtta* tells of an eighteenth-century nobleman, Simo Affleck, nicknamed *Hurtta* ("The Bloodhound") by the inhabitants of the district he was sent to govern because of his conduct there; he admits that a weakness in himself brought about his downfall. Leino also wrote two poems (1904 and 1919) about this character, who lived near Leino's birthplace. The most-performed of Leino's plays is *Maunu Tavast* (third collection), a peaceful play whose disturbances are in the memories of the main character, a great churchman of Catholic Finland who sinned in his youth but had a happy, successful life afterwards.

The dramas on classical subjects also deal with men who are reminiscent of the Nietzschean superman but ultimately fail, such as *Tarquinius Superbus* (fifth collection) and *Alkibiades* (fourth collection). *Alkibiades,* one of his most interesting and personal plays, was written in 1908 during a long journey abroad. Alkibiades lives in exile, speaks contemptuously of his home country, and declares himself a citizen of the world who feels most happy wherever he can fulfill his dream of individuality and enjoy the highest sensuous pleasures, but he also speaks of a mysterious world spirit with which man will one day be reunited. . . . In *Alkibiades* . . . Leino expressed his belief in the right of the individual to taste all pleasures and in the superior interest of the decadent and sick over the healthy. However, his sense of the precarious nature of such a philosophy is indicated in the play by a secondary character speaking to Alkibiades: "Truly, Alkibiades: you may drain the cup to the dregs, but never . . . fill it again."

Some plays with contemporary setting are more symbolic than realistic, e.g., *Melankolia* (*Melancholy,* second collection), a mere conversation between characters designated as the Man, the Woman, and the Friend, and *Ilotulitus* (*The Fireworks,* sixth collection), in which a pyromaniac is pushed to new crimes by a (real) character appropriately named Lucifer. In *Shakkipeli* (*A Game of Chess,* fifth collection), set in medieval surroundings, only one player is present; the other makes his moves but is away, dying. Others have more conventional plots, but often show that traditional moral values do not consistently resist the impact of contemporary life; whether he intended to criticize these values seriously or to satirize their supporters, the conservatives and the church, with whom he feuded all his life, is not clear. . . . In *Kirkon vihollinen* (*An Enemy of the Church,* sixth collection) a man with a technical education (representative of a modern civilization, already called American) clashes with a clergyman over his desire to marry the clergyman's daughter; the minister unexpectedly ends the argument by giving in, saying that he must not oppose the general evolution of the world. *Maan parhaat* (*The Country's Best,* same collection) is a light, satirical comedy on political and literary life containing easily recognizable caricatures of well-known contemporary personalities.

Leino's novels reflect his activities as a journalist rather than his poetic gifts. They are breezy, lively descriptions of contemporary life in Helsinki, but they are written in the fashion of the period, the "impressionistic" technique that Leino carried to extreme, often using an unnatural word order. (pp. 162-64)

[*Tuomas Vitikka* and *Olli Suurpää*] are the most superficial novels and are hardly more than Leino's observations on political life in Finland, the struggles between parties and linguistic groups, the Russian oppression, and so forth. *Jaana Rönty* is more concerned with the characters; Jaana is a poor country girl who comes to Helsinki, where she is debased and eventually attracted into the company of revolutionary socialists. At the end of her story, a description of the armed riots in Helsinki of 1906 in which socialist and nonsocialist vigilantes, the Red and White Guards, clashed for the first time, she appears as Fury, dressed in red and dancing among the dead. (p. 164)

Nuori nainen (*A Young Woman* . . .) which suffers least from his twisted sytle, is considered [Leino's] best prose work. It is spicy and even reminiscent of *Decamerone* as four gentlemen from Helsinki tell stories to each other in a restaurant, but its observations on love and the nature of men and women are penetrating:

> A loving woman always wants to be absolutely
> honest, share the joys and sorrows, the pains
> and sufferings, preferably just the latter, for
> only then she will feel a necessary being in the
> universe. But it is just this which, before long,
> will make her love so irritating to a man. . . .
> But women will never learn to stand on their
> own feet or to pay just casual visits to a man's
> heart. They want to snuggle up in a cozy place
> near the fire like cats, and they want to make
> a home in every smallest nook in their hearts. . . .
> But a man's true home is only that part of his
> soul in which he is alone and will remain alone
> forever.

Pankkiherroja (*Bankers* or *Financiers,* . . .) is the most typical period piece in Leino's production—a description of high life in Helsinki, big business, love, marriage, divorce, and parties, now taking on the romantic shimmer of a past era. *Paavo Kontio, lakitieteen tohtori* (*Paavo Kontio, LL. D.*) . . . verges on the detective story, but there is more emphasis on the character relations than the whodunit, and the crime remains unsolved. *Mesikämmen* (*Honey-Paw,* a popular name for a bear . . .), *Musti* (*Blackie,* a common name for a dog . . .), and *Ahven ja kultakalat* (*The Perch and the Goldfishes* . . .) are loosely allegorical stories without depth but attractive in their simplicity.

In 1917 Leino published *Alla kasvon Kaikkivallan* (*Before the Face of the Almighty*) and the tragedy *Karjalan kuningas* (*The King of Karelia*), his last great works, greater perhaps in conception than in execution, however. The subtitle of the first indicates that it consists of "thoughts, confessions, and distant visions." . . . In the book Leino sought answers to vast philosophical and metaphysical problems (or pseudoproblems), which he was not equipped to cope with. As a picture of his own personality and philosophy, however, it is not without interest. Unfortunately, he chose an artificial, pseudonarchaic style imitative of the *Kalevala* and folk poetry, for there was no tradition of artistic prose in Finnish folklore. *Karjalan kuningas,* a somewhat confused tragedy in verse, is set in a vague, half-mythological past with human, not divine or semidivine, characters. The young hero Lemmes, destined to become king of Karelia, falls in battle against the enemies of the country; Helka, his betrothed, drowns herself, and a man of peace, the old sage Turo; becomes ruler. As in Leino's earlier poems, a man reaches his highest goals only through self-sacrifice. Obviously, the poet was reflecting, as were more and more Finns, that the country should one day secure independence from Russia; but when thinking of an armed conflict with the ruling power, the poet was torn between his instinctive abhorrence for violence and his natural desire to see his country free. (pp. 164-65)

Jaakko Ahokas, "Literature in Finnish in the Twentieth Century from 1901 to the Independence," in his A History of Finnish Literature, *Indiana University, 1973, pp. 146-81.*

JOHN I. KOLEHMAINEN   (essay date 1973)

[*In the following excerpt, Kolehmainen discusses Leino's poetry based on the* Kalevala *and Kalevalan tradition.*]

[Eino Leino] made his debut with an assortment of poems, *Maaliskuun lauluja* (*Songs of March*). Not only did some of them show promise, but several, like **"Pyhät on pihlajat pihalla"** (**"Sacred Are the Mountain Ashes in the Yard"**), rested on Kalevalan foundations, as the three-line stanzas below indicate:

> Pyhät on pihlajat pihalla,
> pyhä on kukka pihlajassa,
> marjaset sitai pyhemmät.

> Pyhät on immen huulten marjat,
> pyhät on ruusut neien posken,
> pyhin puhtaus sydämen.

> Sacred are the mountain ashes in the yard.
> Sacred the rowan's flower.
> More sacred yet the berry.

> Sacred the berries of a maid's lips.
> Sacred the rose-blush of her cheek.
> Most sacred is her heart.

When Leino's fantastic career ended thirty years later, in 1926, he had won universal acclaim, not only as Finland's greatest lyricist, but as the *Kalevala's* poet laureate. "More passionately than any other neo-romantic writer," *The Finlandia Pictorial* said, "he embraced the spiritual values of the *Kalevala*. In fact so profoundly did he identify himself with the national epic that he has been sometimes called the 'last of the great Kalevalan bards.' In modern literature he represents the same relationship with the *Kalevala* as Gallen-Kallela does in painting and Sibelius in music." (p. 244)

In no Finnish writer have the sacred Pierian waters welled so profusely as in Eino Leino. His maiden *Songs of March* signalled not a vagrant springlet but the commencement of a lifelong torrent of verse, drama, satire, criticism, essays, history, translations, and newspaper articles. In the irrepressible surge, there were words old and new, prosaic and lovely, subdued and color-laden; born both of a far-ranging intellect and intense passion, they were sometimes open and soothing like a lullaby, then again wild and enigmatic; arranged in diverse patterns, echoing to differing tempos, they appealed to ear and eye, to heart and mind. Color especially fascinated Leino. Once as he and the artist Gallen-Kallela lamented its passing from Finnish art, he said it would be born again, "more mythically, stylistically, imaginatively, no longer objectively or concretely, but artistically more polished, idealistically more elevated and humane." This Leino helped bring about.

To Leino the gift of the gods was often more torment than joy. He deplored the birthright he could not cast aside, saying

> Muut sydämen saivat, ma kantelen
> muut murehti, nautti, ma en, ma en,
> en kurja ma elää, en kuolla voi,
> kun sykä ei syömeni, soi, vaan soi!

> Mun syömeni tuulikannel on,
> sen kielissä laulu on lakkaamaton,
> se yössä, päivässä, yksinään
> soi ilmahan ijäti väräjävään.

> Others, a heart received, I, a kantele,
> Others sorrow, rejoice, not I, not I,
> A wretch who cannot live nor die,
> Whose heart beats not, but sings, only sings!

> My heart is an Aeolian harp,
> In its strings a ceaseless song,
> At night, in daytime, by itself,
> It eternally reverberates in the air.
>
>   (pp. 246-47)

His aspiration, in the words of his biographer, was "to smooth over the duality that up to this time had prevailed between the European, or more particularly the Germanic, poetic meter and the Kalevalan, to build a bridge between the ancient Finnish cultural spirit and the contemporary, strongly-individualized world outlook, in a word, to create a broadly humane Finnish art-poetry on ancient, folk, and national foundations."

The outcome, *Helkavirsiä* I [*Whitsongs*], was incomparable, although considerable time elapsed before its full worth was recognized. It was, writes Professor Tarkiainen, "a cluster of lovely ballads and legends, in which the ancient Finnish mythological spirit is joined wondrously to the modern world's more personalized one. It was a thirty-five-year old poet's display of genius, and a crowning achievement in Finnish poetry, which is as rich and profound in meaning as it is masterful in structure."

Although *Helkavirsiä* I was "born during several blissful summer months" at Otto Manninen's Kangasniemi retreat, it was, in truth, the product of long maturation: "the ancient mythological themes had dwelled in him for years, and finally burst forth almost effortlessly." (pp. 250-51)

In July, 1903, Leino wrote to his wife: "I am writing better and more polished poetry; during the past days I have composed several legends and ballads that are without doubt the best I have ever done. Wild poetry in the ancient Finnish style, in which there is all the color of the middle ages, the sweet as well as coarse voices of past centuries—it will be something new. I have never felt so independent, never been in this emotional condition, never stood so clearly on my own ground. Manninen is much enthused and predicts thundering success." The following August he reported, "I am planning to publish for Christmas a small collection of poems, all in the Kalevalan meter, stylized 'legends and ballads'. Thank God, it will be the best work I have published." (pp. 251-52)

Leino's handling of the Kalevalan elements can best be seen in such *Helkavirsiä* poems as **"Ylermi"** and **"Kouta,"** whose opening lines are:

> Ylermi ylpeä isäntä
> ajoin temppelin ovesta,
> lausui kirkon laivan alta:
> 'Täss on mies tämän sukuinen,
> kadu ei tehtyä tekoa
> eikä taivasta tavota.'
> Paasiseinässä pakisi,
> puhui Neitsyt puusta tehty:
> 'Äsken sie sitä katunet,
> kun on tuhkana tupasi.'

Ylermi the haughty master
Drove through the temple door,
Shouted from the church's nave:
"Here stands a man who
Does not regret his deeds
Nor yearns for eternal bliss."
The stone walls, chattered,
Spoke the wooden virgin:
"A moment ago you did not rue
That your dwelling burned to ashes."

Lapin Kouta, kolkko miesi,
tuo on suurin tietäjistä
Turjan tunturin takana.
Kyyt viherti katsehesta,
suusta lenti yölepakot,
jalan alta ahmat nousi,
käden päällä kärpät juoksi,
haaskalinnut hartioilla.

Lapland's Kouta, frightening man,
Greatest of magicians
Beyond Turja's mountain.
Snakes shone from the countenance,
Bats flew from out the mouth,
Wolverines rose from under the feet,
Weasels ran over the hands,
Carrion birds across the shoulders.

Leino has clearly made the traditional meter do his bidding: "He determined its direction, manipulated it to his purpose." Trochaics, despite his original intention perhaps, do not appear throughout *Helkavirsiä* I, but manifest themselves sharply diminished, almost laconic. The poet frequently deviates from conventional practice as he strives for rhythmic variety. The meter neither drags nor pounds; it moves easily from "frightful horror and eloquent pathos to tranquil reverie and quiet narration." It is, indeed, the ancient meter raised to a new level of sophistication. Some fifteen years after *Helkavirsiä* I, Leino discussed poetics with Professor Tarkiainen, and said:

> Many believe that the structure of Kalevalan poetry is simple. But in reality, it is the most difficult of all. It demands very much in life's experiences in order to bring out a personal touch with all its nuances. But it best suits the Finnish language and the temperament of the Finnish people. The Kalevalan four-foot poetic line is the refined end-product of centuries of growth and experimentation. It is just as capable of interpreting the sensitive quivering impressions of the moment as the hidden mental impetuosity dwelling in the deepest layers of the Finnish character, which has erupted, for example, in Finnish magic with such shamanistic fury that to my knowledge it has no parallel in the poetry of any other country.

Other folk poetry features are found in *Helkavirsiä* I. Parallelism or reiteration is introduced, somewhat sparingly and deliberately, chiefly in purely descriptive passages or in reinforcing epithets. The traditional three-line division appears occasionally, but with telling effect. Leino's weaving of Kalevalan vocabulary into the text was magnificent: they were like "highly-colored yarns in a variegated ryijy of an archaic ballad. Radiantly they serve an esthetic purpose exclusively; there is no feeling of ethnography." Ancient and modern poesy are fused into a wholeness, to which is coupled a successfully conjured belief system in which, as Leino emphasized, shamanism was an important element. *Helkavirsiä* I, concluded *The Finlandia Pictorial*, "linked past and present with mighty arches of spirit and intellect and something of the innermost emotions of the folk soul."

Thirteen difficult and disheartening years, 1903-16, passed between the first and second volumes of *Helkavirsiä*. . . . In 1908 Leino revealed in a letter: "The songs of Lapland's spirit sometimes sing in my ears such wild, awful arctic songs that I am frightened from the depths of my heart." But his creative impulses could not be stilled, even though he asserted, "I have to repress, to constrain, the new ideas striving to be liberated into the air, for they do not want to be born into a circus atmosphere." So as he worked on the new *Helkavirsiä*, he said: "I know that a new challenge waits me, and I promise, if sufficient days of life remain, I shall again work at creating eternal values. The Finnish nation's spirit, which has already given birth to many great Kalevalan heroes, distinguished men of science and arts, beckons me." Late in August, 1915, he wrote: "Now at last I really know what poetry is . . . and it is not the same as writing. . . . Something new confronts me . . . every second I feel myself being born anew."

Helkavirsiä II came out in 1916, but it was not as good as its predecessor. It was abstract and obscurant, more intimately related to the poet's own unsteady and baffling experiences. The Kalevalan elements had given way to a more cosmic mythology, with a greater preponderance of new vocabulary and concepts. Some of the poetic visions, nonetheless, retained their virility, and Leino's thoughts on life, death, and destiny, were worth pondering. (pp. 252-55)

As Professor Tarkiainen pointed out, "No other Finnish poet has probed so deeply into the soul of our ancient folk poetry and brought forth from it so unspoiled, an archaic, yet at the same time so modern a feeling as Eino Leino. Ages-old legends are transformed into his personal experiences, nature myths take on new color and content in his hands. Enchanting visions flash against the indistinct mythical background: at times in the form of legends, then again as ballads, wild heroic spirits, delicate, trembling virgins of youth's morning dreams, sentiments of destiny, the beings of nature, and cosmic divinations."

Of course, not all of Leino's myriad lines of poetry, not excluding the Kalevalan, have withstood the test of time. Words came too easily to him, as he himself admitted: "Believe it or not, but the truth is that I have written frightful quantities of Finnish forests into the wastepaper basket, although my critics have generally insisted that I have become accustomed from earliest youth on to use the printing press as my waste receptacle. And it is possible that this might on occasion have happened." His technical facility responded to the slightest urging. There was at times verbal flamboyance without substance, brilliance without conviction, much that was ephemeral or obscure. These mercifully have been forgotten or will be. When *Helkavirsiä* I appeared, Otto Manninen observed: "It may well be that this collection's most powerful poems will endure longest to testify to Leino's poetic genius." He was right. (pp. 257-58)

John I. Kolehmainen, "Finnish Language, Literature, and the 'Kalevala'," in his Epic of the North: The Story of Finland's Kalevala, *The Northwestern Publishing Company, 1973, pp. 218-62.*

MICHAEL BRANCH (essay date 1978)

[*In the following excerpt, Branch discusses* Whitsongs *and places Leino's poetry in the context of Finnish literary tradition.*]

Curiously, both Leino and Yeats spoke of themselves as "the last Romantics": while in England, France and Germany Romanticism had developed into such movements as Symbolism and Realism, in smaller countries like Finland in the east and Ireland in the west Romanticism was predominantly the voice of national aspiration, even when these cultures were touched by the more sophisticated influences. But this is not to say that Finnish Neo-Romanticism, with its trolls and folklore, was conservative or parochial: Sibelius was exploring his own ideas of organic form, and Saarinen and his colleagues were employing techniques they had acquired through extensive travel. In literature too, and especially in the work of Leino, we see a national tradition which succeeds in being both modern and universal while remaining uniquely itself.

Leino and his contemporaries were heirs to two very distinct cultural traditions: to borrow Robert Redfield's terminology, a "little" tradition of the ordinary people—folk songs and folk tales, the popular culture of the non-learned and unlettered, best known to the outside world through the songs of the *Kalevala*—and a "great" tradition, which was handed down by education and which in terms of its genres and movements followed closely, even if a short step behind, what was happening elsewhere in Europe. These two components are familiar enough. It is the proportions and balance of the mix inherited by Leino's generation that deserve closer attention, for in Finland the two traditions were not interdependent in the way they were in most of Europe. (pp. 7-8)

In the early 1890s, Symbolism offered the Finns a form of expression that had a remarkable affinity with some of the poetry of little tradition. The form of Symbolism that found the most ready response in Finland had been argued by the Dane, Johannes Jørgensen, in 1893. Jørgensen reflects the ideas of the French Symbolists, but he develops them in the direction of pantheist mysticism, "a secret world in which the artist's or poet's soul is one with the soul of nature." This, which Leino later termed "metaphysical mysticism," rather than the French school of Symbolism as such, proved to be a catalyst to Finnish artists and musicians, especially in the 1890s. (p. 11)

Leino's writing, up to the turn of the century, is very much in the Finnish 19th-century great tradition, with the influence of Heine and Runeberg particularly evident; yet at the same time he also shows a familiarity with the *Kalevala* and the poetry of J. H. Erkko (1849-1906), one of the more important Finnish poets to write in the style of little tradition. Towards the end of the century a change comes over his writing. It becomes more personal, sometimes revealing his fear of the insanity that ran in certain branches of his family. His work contains grim hints of the forebodings Leino felt about the threatened position of the individual and especially of the poet in society; he wrote powerful allegories characterising his dismay at the introduction of Russification measures and the indifference with which many fellow Finns responded. At the same time he began to draw increasingly on *Kalevala* themes.

This was the prelude to his most mature period, lasting until 1908, of which the high point is the 1903 edition of the first collection of *Helkavirsiä (Whitsongs)*. . . . This period is dominated by images of winter, ice and frost, and darkness, Leino's symbols for death, desolation and loneliness, a time when he was pre-occupied with questions of creativity and the role of the poet. (p. 13)

The first volume of *Whitsongs* is generally held to be Leino's masterpiece. All the poems are composed in the style of little tradition using the Kalevala form. This type of poetry, which has been the main prosodic form in Finnish oral tradition for at least two thousand years, is known throughout the Baltic-Finnic area and is cast in unrhymed, non-strophic trochaic tetrameters. Complex rules govern both the stress patterns and the word-order of each line. Within these tight limitations the poet-singer, for traditionally these poems were sung, strove to alliterate. In certain genres of Finnish poetry, alliteration was regarded as more important than content, and even where this was not so, the tendency to alliterate often influenced imagery as the assonantal quality of a keyword, noun or verb, conditioned the choice of other items in the line.

Leino's use of the most sophisticated verse form of Finnish little tradition is a remarkable example of the influence of little tradition on great tradition. Leino's approach is neither condescending nor consciously imitative. He works within the tradition yet, following the example of the most gifted singers and his closest predecessor, Erkko, he does not hesitate to stretch or even break the rules (or create new rules) for a particular effect. Leino has been called "the last great Kalevala singer," for like his predecessors he knew how to revise the formal conventions of little tradition to allow it to meet new requirements and survive. Leino's contribution to the two-thousand-year history of Kalevala poetry was to transform an elegant oral tradition into an elegant literary tradition.

Leino has written a little about the genesis of *Whitsongs*. While he was working on the collection, he published an article criticising the state of poetry in Finland. He pointed to Finnish music, known throughout Europe, and to the painting and sculpture of the day, claiming that their strength and vigour derived from the inspiration, themes, and idiom of little tradition. Poets, he added, were working towards a "national style of poetry. . . . trying to achieve what has already been achieved in music and the visual arts." In a letter written about the same time, he described with great excitement his confidence that he had at last found the right idiom for his poetry and that he was working on something entirely new, "heady poetry in an ancient Finnish style, with the rich colours of the Middle Ages and the voices, delicate and brutal, of bygone centuries." Many years later he threw more light on the evolution of *Whitsongs* when he outlined how his original idea had been to write about the spirit powers that in ancient times were thought to determine all natural phenomena, but that in the course of writing this idea became secondary and more personal experiences became the substance of the poems.

Hence one way of attempting to understand the collection as a whole is to see it as a statement on the new Finnish poetry Leino was striving to create, and the role, character and sufferings of the poet. In some ways the sequence of the poems seems almost to reflect, indeed characterise the vacillation in Leino's personality, for it is possible to see each poem in some way as the reverse image of its predecessor. The basic ingredients of each poem can be rationalised as neat geological seams: from top to bottom, form, theme, symbolism and the transformation into a new national poetry, the poet's role, Leino's conscious problems, his fears, his guilt-ridden psyche. Perhaps more seams could be added and the pattern of layering rearranged. However, to see these characteristics in a way that tells us something about the collection, the seams must be violently disturbed so that some dip down and penetrate the lower levels, while others rise sharply; there must be gullies and fissures.

The suggestion that for Leino poetry was a healing ritual finds some support in the title of the poems, which hints strongly at ritual. Customs performed at Whitsun, *helka,* go back to ancient times and were once associated with rites to ensure fertility. Christian priests attempted to stop what they saw as debauchery yet were never wholly successful. Their solution was to invest these rites with Christian significance. In one instance, where the Christian form of the rites survived right up to the early 19th century (and was known to Leino), young girls walked the sign of the cross through a village singing old ballads. Despite the Christian twist to the songs, the texts still hint at activities symbolising fertility—their original function being to induce by example fertility in fields and livestock. Hence the title of Leino's collection performs two functions: at one level it is a familiar allusion to an aspect of little tradition directly associated with ballads and legends, but at a deeper level it hints at specific ritual associated with the act of creation.

The theme of ritual is also happily echoed in two of the most important poems of *Whitsongs*, "Kouta" and "The Dark One." Both are about journeys to the Otherworld. In ancient beliefs such a journey was undertaken by the shaman's soul in order to acquire knowledge, i.e. spells, with which to heal or to perform other tasks essential to the well-being of the shaman's community. The ritual act of communication, in which the shaman fell into a trance—regarded as a form of death—was mentally and physically demanding, and could sometimes be fatal. Hence the shaman occupied a special position in the community and was often its natural leader. Significantly, in later versions of folk poems about visiting the Otherworld, the purpose of the shaman's journey is to acquire the missing lines of a poem. The association of the shaman and shamanist ritual with the poet provides Leino with a powerful symbol to express his concern about the role and position of the poet.

Whitsongs comprises eleven poems in the style of the traditional Finnish ballad and six legends. Each poem is a miniature drama in two main parts: the setting out of a problem, culminating in an emotional or personal crisis, followed by a tightly controlled account of the consequences of the actions taken in the first part of the poem. Leino usually heightens the tension by incorporating various ballad devices in the first part of the poem, particularly incremental repetition and dialogue, leading some critics to divide these small dramas into several acts. The dénouement generally begins about the middle of the poem and is always characterised by a sense of finality: there is no reversing the process once it has started.

The first poem, "Ihalempi," develops a theme familiar in oral tradition and which has parallels in many parts of the world. Symbolising the fear of the unknown, it tells how a child is carried away by a natural force and is sought by a series of relatives until it is finally found in heaven. In Leino's poem, the girl is carried off by Demon Jack, symbolising death; she is found by the Creator in another world where she has witnessed the plunging of a star into a bubbling spring (a fertilisation symbol). For this reason and because she has experienced other miraculous phenomena the Creator makes her the bearer of a star, a hero, a great man. If we consider this poem in the context outlined above, it would seem that Leino is opening the collection with a fanfare of clear, strong notes: a fantasy of how he would wish the poet's creative process and his position in society to be.

This fantasy compares strikingly with the weary tone of resignation in the final poem, "The Dark One." The fifteen poems separating the opening fanfare and the quiet chords at the end of the collection seem to explore fifteen facets of the role of poetry, the creation of a Finnish national poetry, and Leino's own struggles. In "Tuuri" Leino uses the theme of time standing still to symbolise the act of creation that frees the poet from his *Angst,* even though everything else is lost. "The Song of Mantsi" and "The Serf's Son" stand out for two reasons: they are the only two poems set in the context of specific historical events and also incorporate an internal poet-singer apart from the anonymous narrator. In them Leino appears to be considering whether the poet should involve himself in acts of historic importance. The conclusion is that poetry has the capacity to inspire men to action, but the death that abruptly follows the series of paradise symbols in "The Serf's Son," seemingly questions the wisdom of this.

"Kimmo's Revenge," "Kaleva" and "The Blue Cross" can be seen at one level as the poet's analysis of different kinds of temptation: erotic adventures which call for revenge and end in murder, or require an act of atonement. But at another level these poems can be interpreted as symbolising the evolution of a new Finnish poetry: rejection of the foreign, a journey to the Otherworld in search of inspiration, reluctance to leave the Otherworld's siren-like delights, atonement and purification, travels in Karelia to gather strength and to spread the new word—the names *Kaleva* and *Blue Cross* have close and immediate associations with matters relating to Finland and its poetry.

"Ylermi" and "Räikkö the Wretch" are two poems in which the main characters defy conventions and are punished by death. Ylermi is a medieval knight, almost Quixotic in his determination: he defies the power of the Church, sees his wife and family perish rather than submit to a greater will, and defiant to the last is swallowed up by hell-fires, a spectacular though somewhat impersonal end. The associations with the Superman idea are clear, but the touches of humour in the poem leave the reader wondering whether Leino is caricaturing the posturing in which he sometimes indulged. Räikkö defies convention in a very different way, betraying his companions to the enemy in order to save his property and his family. When his wife makes the horror of his deed clear to him, he quietly goes off to the forest and hangs himself: the theme of the previous poem is curiously reversed and the man with base motives behaves nobly and with dignity.

"Tyyri's Girl" and "The Lord's Bread" both describe an encounter with Jesus in disguise and the winning of peace through the acceptance of one's lot. These two poems contrast sharply with "Oterma and Katerma" which probes very different emotions: suspicion, jealousy, passion and adultery leading to fratricide.

In "Kouta" Leino describes a shaman who goes to the Otherworld in search of ultimate knowledge, the secret of death. He acquires it only through his own death. While at one level the theme is suggestive of a Faust-like thirst for knowledge, there is no limit to the base deeds Kouta will do to achieve his end, at another level the poem is a fine illustration of Leino's use of the Otherworld concept to symbolise the poet's exploration of his own depths.

The death of a mortal who involves himself with things immortal also occurs in "The Bathing Maids." In this poem death is associated with the erotic, the theme and imagery of which are reversed in the following poem **"The Maid and the Boyar's Son."** The girl and the boy love each other but are condemned to part for ever when the boy kills his brother in battle and must purge his sin by living the rest of his life in a monastery. The account of the girl's life with a man she does not love is suggestive of **"The Dark One."** It is as if through the ritual of telling the poem, Leino is willing things to happen—yet another association with the ancient ritual function of Finnish poetry.

St. George provides a link between **"The Maid and the Boyar's Son"** and **"The Dark One."** It is a curious rendering of the legend of St. George. In Finnish little tradition the dragon is often inclined to eat the saint rather than the girl. Leino gives the legend another twist. When St. George finds that the girl and her captor are happy together—indeed their relationship is described in the most sensuous terms—he kills the girl. The poem is pervaded by a sense of bewilderment, against a background of swamps and swirling mists, as if the poet feels himself frustrated at every turn: what began as a chivalrous attempt to save the girl, ends with the dealing of death.

In **"The Dark One"** Leino's *Angst* manifests itself in a series of fantasies, reminiscent, as one critic has remarked, of the nature motifs used by architects at the beginning of the century. The main character is a boy "affrighted at birth," who struggles in vain to find his place in the community. Finally he goes to his father's grave and seeks to join him in the Otherworld. The image is a familiar one in Finnish tradition; shamans frequently went to the graveside of another shaman to seek knowledge; sometimes it was the place from which the journey to the Otherworld began. But the boy's dead father dissuades him from coming to the world of the dead and tells him to live the way his fathers did before. The boy returns to his community no longer fearful and able to accept the burdens of life "not rejoicing nor grieving, / piling up the days, as much / those coming as those passing, / the better much as the worse; / but the better ones on top." It is as if Leino is completing the process of ritual, concluding as Nietzsche in his *Geburt der Tragödie* that the poet is destined to take upon himself the tragedy of his own time. (pp. 13-20)

> *Michael Branch, in an introduction to* Whitsongs *by Eino Leino, translated by Keith Bosley, The Menard Press, 1978, pp. 7-20.*

ANNAMARI SARAJAS (essay date 1978)

[*Sarajas is a Finnish educator, journalist, and critic whose works reflect her interest in Finnish folklore and literary history. In the following excerpt from an essay commemorating the centenary of Leino's birth, Sarajas discusses his enduring importance in Finnish literature.*]

Helkavirsiä I [*Whit Songs*] was first published . . . when Eino Leino was 25. It was the first major collection of Leino's work and reveals the mature development of his genius. (p. 41)

It is interesting to analyse *Whit Songs* in its contemporary context. Leino was influenced not only by his native Finnish traditions but also by ideas from several important European sources. He closely followed the Swedish poetry of the day, but his most important source of outside inspiration was French symbolism.

When Leino entered the University of Helsinki in 1894 he immediately came into contact, through his elder brother Kasimir (a journalist and writer), with the major painters of the period, several of whom had been profoundly influenced by French symbolism. . . . We know that by 1897 Leino must have been familiar with symbolism, for in that year he wrote a review of Tolstoy's *What is Art?*, a work which contains a large and representative selection of French symbolist poetry (which Tolstoy presented as evidence of an art form that had degenerated and should therefore be condemned).

Leino, however, never regarded himself as a symbolist. He belonged rather to the Finnish neo-romantic tradition, and his work is an important part of the development of the Finnish voice in poetry, from the ideological and nationalistic movement rooted in oral tradition at the start of the nineteenth century, to the more sophisticated neo-romanticism at the end of the century. He differs from the symbolists like Mallarmé in certain obvious ways: the French poet will stop at a state of mind, man staring into the distance, trying to distinguish the eternal enduring pure idea. Leino goes a step further, to something more dynamic. He had an early interest in drama, especially the Shakespearean myth-making imagination, as we see it in *The Tempest*: Caliban, for instance, is a favourite symbol, often used by Leino, even in his letters, to indicate the misery always rumbling beneath the surface of every human being.

The connections between *Whit Songs* and Finnish oral tradition are strong. Leino took the style of Elias Lönnrot's *Kalevala*—itself rooted in native tradition—adapted and improved it, strengthened it, cut out the dull refrains, and boldly used enjambment as he saw fit. He perceived that the poetic forms, preserved and developed for centuries, were quintessentially and indubitably Finnish. The influence of folk poetry was immense. At the same time it gave his work a quality that makes it very difficult to translate into another language. [Keith Bosley, the English translator of *Whit Songs*] has successfully resolved the problem by using an analogous archaic English metre. The trochaic tetrameter of Finnish folk poetry is a melodic and complex poetic form only to Finnish ears. After mastering the traditional metre and form of Finnish folk poetry, Leino also began to adapt the forms of other European languages, including even the *ottava rima*.

At the same time it must be emphasized that Eino Leino never wrote pastiches of folk poetry. The message of **"Ylermi,"** for example, is a modern one in the spirit of Nietzsche: God is dead. The poem ends with a simple but undecisive line: "The mitten's on the stone still." A grim ending holding out hope for the future. The young Leino's Nietzschean traits were not just a fashion; the self-awareness of the gifted, creative individual is brilliantly depicted, bringing out the sense of his elevated and incomparable uniqueness. Leino still spoke of this in 1910, referring to Henrik Ibsen, whom he saw as a hero, a paragon who greatly enriched for him "the dream of the spiritual aristocrats, supermen of the day for whom thought would not be the enemy of the deed, who would desire and act greatly, instantaneously, with their whole beings, confidently."

"The Dark One" another poem from *Whit Songs,* throws more light on Leino's scale of values in 1903. The picture of deep resignation is disturbing, in sharp contrast to the atmosphere of **"Ylermi"** Leino uses the same contradictory juxtapositions in **"Jumalien keinu. . . ."** It is perhaps unwise to attach too much biographical significance to lines like "affrighted at birth," although we do know that throughout his life Leino carried the burden of a hereditary threat to his sanity. Perhaps it is merely the question of a man for whom the cares of life were unusually great. Or perhaps Leino suffered from the melancholy popularly attributed to the Finno-Ugrian peoples. When Tumma, "the dark one," in accordance with ancient ritual, goes "to the thicket of the dead," he receives a stern answer to his frightened questions about the role of man: "Your fathers took fright before / and yet they lived out their time."

"The Dark One" is an antichristian—or in its stylistic content—a pagan poem. Like **"Ylermi"** although it is not so violent, it offers no hope of life. But this was not Leino's final solution to the problem of life beyond the grave. In his short lifetime he experienced many national, political and personal disappointments; further strains were caused by the many facets of his intellectual life: he was a novelist, a political columnist, a devotee of the theatre, a dramatist—in other words, a man who, as one of his fellow writers remarked: "knew everything, knew everyone, had read everything."

The outbreak and continuation of the First World War was to him, as to many of his contemporaries, a devastating blow. This can be seen best in his second collection of *Whit Songs*, . . . not yet translated into English. All the progressive optimism of the previous century had been crushed: where man had assumed that his world was spontaneously and naturally progressing towards an ever more perfect happiness and harmony, the opposite was now true. The message of this volume is not just modern, it is prophetic and apocalyptic. When the reader who has experienced the Second World War hears of the violent destroyer, the leader Ukri, who "threw himself into the sea of nations, the nations fell on both sides" he does not assume that the references are to the time of Genghis Khan or Attila the Hun—he has terrifyingly closer and more familiar associations. Even more recently the space age reader will find it natural that the *dramatis personae* in that intense triangular love poem **"Auringon hyvästijättö"** (**"The Sun's Farewell"**) are "You, poor Earth Mother, I, poor Daystar, the third, the dead Moon Goddess, gone from us first."

It was at this time that Leino also became intensely interested in metaphysical questions. Undoubtedly his thinking was also stimulated by his experience of translating Dante's *Divina Commedia* into Finnish. The Finnish poet, L. Onerva, who knew this side of Leino better than anyone else, draws comparisons with Albert Einstein's thoughts on the different stages of faith: primitive religion of fear, civilized society's religion of morality, and the higher cosmic sense of faith. These ideas have a familiar ring—we have heard them from Einstein and many other modern geniuses in the field of physics. Einstein further described religious attitudes which Onerva says were characteristic of the mature Leino: "it is only exceptional individuals who ascend higher than the lower species. This I wish to call a cosmic sense of belief. It is difficult to explain to anyone who has not experienced it." . . . (pp. 41-6)

The English-speaker can more easily approach Eino Leino through W. B. Yeats. T. S. Eliot's observation of the latter could have applied equally to Leino: "He was one of those few whose [work] is the history of their time, who are a part of the consciousness of an age which cannot be understood without them." (p. 46)

Annamari Sarajas, translated by Mary Lomas, "Eino Leino: 1878-1926," in Books from Finland, *Vol. XII, No. 2, 1978, pp. 40-6.*

ADDITIONAL BIBLIOGRAPHY

Havu, I., ed. "Eino Leino." In *An Introduction to Finnish Literature*, translated by Paul Sjoblom, pp. 64-70. Helsinki: Otava, 1952.
    An introductory sketch accompanied by English translations of "Väinämöinen's Song" and "Ylermi." According to Havu: "Above all, Eino Leino is the spokesman of humanity, justice, and personal liberty in Finnish lyric poetry."

Rantavaara, Irma. "Symbolism and Finnish Literature." In *The Symbolist Movement in the Literature of European Languages*, edited by Anna Balakian, pp. 595-601. Budapest: Akadémiai Kiadó, 1982.
    Appreciative discussion of Leino's principal works and poetic theory.

Rubulis, Aleksis. "Finnish Literature." In his *Baltic Literature*, pp. 3-53. Notre Dame, Ind.: University of Notre Dame Press, 1970.
    Includes a discussion of the late nineteenth-century Young Finland cultural movement, whose participants included Leino, composer Jean Sibelius, and the painter Akseli Gallen-Kallela. According to Rubulis, Leino was "the most gifted literary figure of the Young Finland movement and the greatest prodigy among Finnish poets of all time."

Schoolfield, George C. Review of *Whitsongs*, by Eino Leino, translated by Keith Bosley. *Scandinavian Studies* 52, No. 3 (Summer 1980): 341-44.
    Discusses Leino's limited reputation outside Finland and assesses Bosley's English translation of *Helkavirsiä* I, a work that, according to Schoolfield, "deserves to be included—must be included—in any consideration of the Nordic literatures around the turn of the century."

Tarkka, Pekka. "The Death of a Poet." Translated by Hildi Hawkins. *Books from Finland* XVII, No. 4 (1983): 129-30, 132.
    Briefly compares the lives of Leino and Pennti Saarikoski (1937-83) in an obituary tribute to the younger poet. According to Tarkka: "Conservatives loathed both men for their polemic arrogance, and academic poets shunned them because of the way in which they radically revised the poetic tradition; all in all, they were anathema in a land in which, according to Leino, 'infants are born old men'."

Roger Martin du Gard

1881-1958

French novelist and dramatist.

Martin du Gard is best known as the author of the highly acclaimed multi-volume novel *Les Thibault (The World of the Thibaults),* for which he received a Nobel Prize in 1937. Led by his training as an historian to consider phenomena primarily in terms of context, he sought to create in his work a comprehensive, transcendent vision of human existence through the presentation of characters whose lives are determined by the interaction of innate qualities and purely environmental factors. In a study of his works, Catherine Savage has written that "Martin du Gard's fictional world is at the junction of nineteenth-century naturalism and psychological realism on the one hand, and the contemporary social and political novel on the other." This essential modernity has allowed Martin du Gard's work to survive the vicissitudes of popular and critical opinion despite the fact that the lengthy *roman-fleuve* form, of which *The World of the Thibaults* is considered a particularly fine example, has generally fallen into disfavor.

The son of a wealthy Parisian attorney and his wife, Martin du Gard attended several of the most prestigious schools in Paris. Influenced by his reading of the works of Leo Tolstoy, he decided to become a fiction writer while still in his teens, but studied historiography and paleography at the University of Paris, receiving his diploma in 1905. A few months after graduation, he traveled to North Africa, and it was there that he began work on his first novel. Soon, however, he judged the quality of his work to be unacceptable and destroyed the manuscript. Returning to Paris, Martin du Gard enrolled once again at the university, now taking courses in psychology but still hoping to make writing his career. In the spring of 1908, during a vacation in the countryside, he wrote a second novel entitled *Devenir!* and this work was published later that same year. Critical response was predominantly, though mildly, favorable, and provided encouragement to the aspiring author, who began planning a longer, more comprehensive work. A social scientist by training, Martin du Gard had soon created an extensive outline of the proposed novel, which he envisioned as the story of a woman's life from birth through death told in a realistic and historically accurate manner. However, when he realized that it would be impossible for him to fully comprehend a female character's perspective, he abandoned the project. Retreating to his country home in the province of Berry from 1910 through 1913, Martin du Gard finally composed his first major work, *Jean Barois,* the story of a young intellectual loosely based on the life of poet Charles Péguy and written entirely in dialogue form. Still unsure of his own talents, Martin du Gard considered destroying the manuscript of *Jean Barois,* but his friend and publisher, Gaston Gallimard, offered to send it to André Gide and to ask his advice in the matter. Gide advised Gallimard to publish the novel "without hesitation," and, as a result, Gide and Martin du Gard became close friends and remained so until Gide's death in 1951.

In the years that followed, Martin du Gard was occupied primarily with the creation of the massive *World of the Thibaults,* the first volume of which appeared in 1922. An extremely

reclusive man, he worked in seclusion at his various country homes, traveling to Paris only to transact essential business or to meet with Gide. By 1931, he had published seven volumes of the *Thibault* series and had outlined material for several more, but he had also begun to question the direction the novel had taken. Realizing that the work as originally conceived would require at least twelve additional volumes for completion and that it had become more psychologically oriented than seemed desirable, Martin du Gard abandoned his outline and destroyed a completed but unpublished manuscript, *L'appareillage.* Then, between 1931 and 1936, he composed *L'été 1914 (Summer 1914),* which recounts the Thibault family's involvement in the First World War, and it was the appearance of this section of the novel which secured for Martin du Gard the 1937 Nobel Prize.

Despite the worldwide recognition which came as a result of the prize, Martin du Gard remained an enigmatic figure. Although he did deliver an address at the Nobel award ceremony in Stockholm, he never again appeared in public, and he spent the final decades of his life primarily at his home in Nice, refusing all requests for interviews. During this period, he attempted to compose one final novel which would encapsulate his mature vision, but he was hampered by his own impeccable literary standards and by an increasing lack of confidence in the future of the human species. The novel was left unfinished at his death in 1958.

Martin du Gard's first published work, the short novel *Devenir!*, is considered significant only insofar as it reveals the origins of the author's thought, and critical discussion of his works has thus centered upon *Jean Barois* and *The World of the Thibaults*. Described by its author as a stylistic experiment, *Jean Barois* concerns a young man's involvement in the Dreyfus Affair, a scandal which surfaced in 1894 when a Jewish officer was erroneously convicted of espionage despite sound evidence to the contrary, leading to charges of anti-Semitism in the French government. The Dreyfus Affair divided the French people along clearly discernible ideological lines, with leftist intellectuals rallying to Dreyfus's cause while conservatives staunchly affirmed his guilt. Martin du Gard's account, told from the point of view of a young leftist, graphically illustrates the enormous impact of the scandal upon French society through a historically meticulous revelation of the events combined with a depiction of the personal experience of one who was intimately involved. Critic G. E. Kaiser has observed that the narrative style of the work, which is composed exclusively of dialogue, further enhances the reader's sense of participation. *Jean Barois* is not, however, an exclusively political novel, since it is also the story of an intellectual's inner struggle to free himself from the archaic beliefs of his predecessors.

In creating *The World of the Thibaults*, Martin du Gard sought to expand upon the theme of intellectual revolt presented in *Jean Barois* and to present a comprehensive statement of his personal world view, synthesized from the Naturalistic theories of social and biological determinism maintained by Emile Zola, humanist philosophy, and his own studies of the social sciences. Ostensibly the story of two families and their experiences during the opening decades of the twentieth century, *The World of the Thibaults* is in fact primarily concerned with tracing the intellectual development of two brothers, Antoine and Jacques Thibault, with the large cast of characters serving generally as catalysts to that process. The social and familial structures which surround the brothers are fully presented not only to provide an encompassing view of the society of the period, but also in order to illustrate the impact of biological and environmental factors upon the individual. Moreover, the contrasting natures of Antoine and Jacques, one committed to progress and science, the other in a state of revolt, allowed Martin du Gard to explore in a limited fashion the varying effects of such influences. Several critics, including Albert Camus, have thus found in *The World of the Thibaults* elements of Existential philosophy, since Martin du Gard was obviously concerned with the possibility of a uniquely personal and essentially positive response to the largely predetermined conditions of human existence.

Standing in marked contrast to Martin du Gard's two major works are his bucolic novel, *Vieille France (The Postman)*, and his two comedies, *Le testament du Père Leleu* and *Un taciturne*. During the composition of the *Thibault* series, it was Martin du Gard's habit to occasionally take time out to create a short, light piece as a means of recreation, and these three works were the result. Both *The Postman* and *Le testament du Père Leleu* deal with comic aspects of rural existence, and while the latter enjoyed only modest success when it was performed in 1918, *The Postman* is considered a fine example of Rabelaisian humor. *Un taciturne*, however, was poorly received as a result of its somewhat flippant treatment of homosexuality.

When Martin du Gard was designated the winner of the 1937 Nobel Prize for literature, very few readers outside of France even knew his name. Reporters who rushed to Paris in search of the author mistakenly interviewed his cousin Maurice, who was a journalist. Within a few years, however, Martin du Gard's work had become internationally renowned, and critical assessments began to appear. Generally favorable, critical response has traditionally focused on the sophistication of his philosophical and political ideas rather than on purely literary concerns, leading critic Albert Guérard to comment that "even in France, Martin du Gard is respected rather than popular." In addition, the extreme length of Martin du Gard's major work has limited the size of his audience; unlike the novel series of Honoré Balzac and Zola, in which the individual volumes stand as independent novels, *The World of the Thibaults* was intended as a single novel and should properly be read as such. Nevertheless, Martin du Gard's work continues to draw much critical and scholarly attention, since it so clearly manifests quintessential elements of nineteenth-century thought even as it presages much that is unique to modern philosophy.

(See also *Contemporary Authors*, Vol. 118.)

PRINCIPAL WORKS

Devinir! (novel) 1908
Jean Barois (novel) 1913
  [*Jean Barois*, 1949]
Le testament du Père Leleu (drama) 1918
*Le cahier gris (novel) 1922
*Le pénitencier (novel) 1922
*La belle saison. 2 vols. (novel) 1923
*La consultation (novel) 1928
*La sorellina (novel) 1928
*La mort du père (novel) 1929
Confidence africaine (novella) 1931
  [*Confidence Africaine*, 1983]
Un taciturne (drama) 1932
Vieille France (novel) 1933
  [*The Postman*, 1954]
*L'été 1914. 3 vols. (novel) 1936
*Epilogue (novel) 1940
The World of the Thibaults. 2 vols. (novel cycle) 1941
Notes sur André Gide (biographical memoirs) 1951
  [*Notes on André Gide*, 1953]
Oeuvres complètes. 2 vols. (novels, dramas, essays, memoirs, and novella) 1955
Correspondance générale (letters) 1980
Le lieutenant-colonel de Maumort (unfinished novel) 1983

*These works comprise the eight-part, eleven-volume novel, *Les Thibault*, which was translated into English as *The World of the Thibaults*, listed separately above.

ROGER MARTIN DU GARD (essay date 1937)

[*The following is a translation of Martin du Gard's 1937 Nobel Prize address.*]

The presence of so many illustrious persons assembled under the patronage of His Highness, the Crown Prince, heightens the emotions that I feel at finding myself here and hearing the words of praise that have just been addressed to me. I feel rather like an owl, suddenly roused from its nest and exposed to the daylight, whose eyes, used to the dark, are blinded by dazzling brightness.

I am proud of the exceptional mark of esteem the Swedish Academy has bestowed on me, but I cannot conceal my surprise from you. Ever since I felt your favor lie upon and almost overwhelm me, I have asked myself how to interpret it.

My first thought was of my country. I am happy that in making a *French* author its choice for this year, the distinguished Swedish Academy has thought fit to glorify our French literature in particular. On the other hand, I know some great poets among my compatriots, noble and powerful minds, whom your votes might have chosen with much better reason. Why then am I today in this place of honor?

The demon of vanity, never completely silenced, at first whispered to me some flattering presumptions. I even went so far as to ask myself whether by granting this distinction to the "man without dogma" that I profess to be, the Academy did not wish to emphasize that in this century, when everyone "believes" and "asserts," it is perhaps useful that there should be some who "hestitate," "put in doubt," and "question"— independent minds that escape the fascination of partisan ideologies and whose constant care is to develop their individual consciences in order to maintain a spirit of "inquiry" as objective, liberal, and fair-minded as is humanly possible.

I should also like to think that this sudden honor acknowledges certain principles dear to me. "Principles" is a big word to be used by a man who says that he is always ready to revise his opinions. I must, however, admit that in the practice of my art I have imposed upon myself certain guidelines to which I have tried to be faithful.

I was still very young when I encountered, in a novel by the English writer Thomas Hardy, this reflection on one of his characters: "The true value of life seemed to him to be not so much its beauty, as its tragic quality." It spoke to an intuition deep within me, closely allied to my literary vocation. Ever since that time I have thought that the prime purpose of the novel is to give voice to the tragic element in life. Today I would add: the tragic element in the life of an individual, the tragedy of a "destiny in the course of being fulfilled."

At this point I cannot refrain from referring to the immortal example of Tolstoy, whose books have had a determining influence on my development. The born novelist recognizes himself by his passion to penetrate ever more deeply into the knowledge of man and to lay bare in each of his characters that individual element of life which makes each being unique. It seems to me that any chance of survival which a novelist's work may have rests solely on the quantity and the quality of the individual lives that he has been able to create in his books. But that is not all. The novelist must also have a sense of life in general; his work must reveal a personal vision of the universe. Here again Tolstoy is the great master. Each of his creatures is more or less secretly haunted by a metaphysical obsession, and each of the human experiences that he has recorded implies, beyond an inquiry into man, an anxious question about the meaning of life. I admit that I take pleasure in the thought that, in crowning my work as a novelist, the members of the Swedish Academy wished to pay indirect homage to my devotion to that unapproachable model and to my efforts to profit from the instruction of his genius.

I should like to conclude with a more somber hypothesis, although I am embarrassed to disturb this festive mood by arousing those painful thoughts that haunt all of us. However, perhaps the Swedish Academy did not hesitate to express a special purpose by drawing the attention of the intellectual world to the author of *L'Été 1914 (Summer 1914)*.

That is the title of my last book. It is not for me to judge its value. But at least I know what I set out to do: in the course of these three volumes I tried to revivify the anguished atmosphere of Europe on the eve of the mobilizations of 1914. I tried to show the weakness of the governments of that day, their hesitations, indiscretions, and unavowed desires; I tried above all to give an impression of the stupefaction of the peaceful masses before the approach of that cataclysm whose victims they were going to be, that cataclysm which was to leave nine million men dead and ten million men crippled.

When I see that one of the highest literary juries in the world supports these books with the prestige of its incontestable authority, I ask myself whether the reason may not be that these books through their wide circulation have appeared to defend certain values that are again being threatened and to fight against the evil contagion of the forces of war.

For I am a son of the West, where the noise of arms does not let our minds rest. Since we have come together today on the tenth of December, the anniversary of the death of Alfred Nobel (that man of action, "no mere shadow," who in the last years of his life seems indeed to have put his supreme hope in the brotherhood of nations), permit me to confess how good it would be to think that my work—the work that has just been honored in his name—might serve not only the cause of letters, but even the cause of peace. In these months of anxiety in which we are living, when blood is already being shed in two extreme parts of the globe, when practically everywhere in an atmosphere polluted by misery and fanaticism passions are seething around pointed guns, when too many signs are again heralding the return of that languid defeatism, that general consent which alone makes wars possible: at this exceptionally grave moment through which humanity is passing, I wish, without vanity, but with a gnawing disquietude in my heart, that my books about *Summer 1914* may be read and discussed, and that they may remind all—the old who have forgotten as well as the young who either do not know or do not care—of the sad lesson of the past. (pp. 9-11)

Roger Martin du Gard, in an acceptance speech in Nobel Prize Library: Roger Martin du Gard, Gabriela Mistral, Boris Pasternak, *Alexis Gregory, 1971, pp. 9-11.*

RÉGIS MICHAUD   (essay date 1938)

[*Michaud was a French critic and educator. In the following excerpt, he discusses Martin du Gard's major works and themes.*]

Since he received the Nobel Prize, Roger Martin du Gard has become a familiar figure in many lands, yet the French critics seem to have been puzzled by this award to a man whom they admired, but whom they never took for a star of the first magnitude. Du Gard always shunned publicity and literary honors. He never trod the path that leads to the French Academy and, after the publication of the seventh volume of *Les Thibault,* in 1929, he left the lime-light. It was rumored that he was tired of his serial novel and did not know how to finish it. When three new volumes appeared suddenly in 1936, under the title

L'Été 1914, critics were rather nonplussed to see his psychological and individualistic novel turn into a real epic. Du Gard's obscurity was only comparative. He was known for his affiliation with Gide and the *Nouvelle Revue Française,* and especially for his friendship with Jacques Copeau and the Vieux Colombier, which gave one of his plays, *Le Testament du Père Leleu,* a rustic farce. But who remembered his pre-war novel, *Jean Barois?* There were other French candidates for the much-coveted Nobel Prize and some of them more brilliant and better equipped socially. Among the five French writers already awarded the prize at Stockholm, were Anatole France, Romain Rolland and Bergson, against whom French opinion has become rather antipathetic. It is entirely to the honor of the Swedish Academy to have given recognition, beyond their native frontiers, to those writers acclaimed by the world at large as the best exponents of the great humanitarian tradition in France. It is an honor, too, for Martin du Gard to have been placed among them.

We can well now, at a safe distance, cast a retrospective glance at his works and try to appraise their true significance. We clearly see a link between his post-war and pre-war novels. They all belong to the same cycle and show the same purpose. Viewed between Rolland's *Jean-Christophe* and Romains' *Men of Good Will,* they fit very well with that impressive pageant of French moral and social life. There is perhaps no more accurate and dramatic record of the French crises, from the Dreyfus Affair to 1914, than *Jean Barois.* There Martin du Gard showed himself fully aware of all the intellectual cross-currents that carried France to a critical turn in her destinies. French religious, scientific, moral and social problems were all treated by him as an accurate historian, who was at the same time an artist. Already his talent for harmoniously blending history and fiction was evident, and his exactitude as an historian was such that it made him a prophet. Most of the controversies and conflicts which are tearing France asunder nowadays were foreseen or studied in that first book. Barois and the young intellectuals who fought around him for Captain Dreyfus were life-like portraits and Du Gard saw every episode of that famous trial in its true light as an impartial witness. All the actors in the great drama were there under transparent disguise, Zola and "J'accuse," Charles Péguy and his *Cahiers de la Quinzaine* under the pseudonym *Le Semeur.* That the Dreyfus trial came as a real revolution in French affairs, that it opened a new era, before it finally ended in disillusion for many. Du Gard saw all that clearly in 1913, and he was also well acquainted with the nationalistic reaction on the fateful eve of 1914. The last chapters of *Jean Barois* are indeed a most faithful record of those critical years.

Then the war came and Martin du Gard left his books to serve in the army for four years. When he came back to his desk the world and France were no longer the same. The heroes and the mystics were gone, and the new generation gave the lie to the pre-war and war prophets. Heroism was out of fashion. Heroes had been replaced by esthetes, nationalisms by revolutions, traditions by the "revolt of youth," Péguy was dead and Marcel Proust and André Gide were the men of the hour. Martin du Gard went back to work and, in 1922, appeared the first volume of *Les Thibault.* They took us back to a world now gone, but Du Gard could not ignore the new generation around him and it is natural that we find it in his books. The revolt of youth and its attempts at evasion came to a climax in the nineteen twenties and they fill the first seven volumes of Du Gard's work. There we meet with the Thibaults and the De Fontanins. We see Antoine and Jacques, the two brothers,

fighting against the tyranny of a bigoted and inhibited father. The central theme of the book can well be summed up in André Gide's battle cry: "Familles, je vous hais!" ["Families, I hate you!"] as we find it illustrated in *The Counterfeiters.* The impulsive friendship of Jacques and Daniel, the ambiguous love of Jacques for both Gise and Jenny, his revolt against bourgeois morals, his feud with his brother, his secret writings, his flights, all this showed the influence of André Gide. Jacques acted, to the letter, the part of the Prodigal Son in Gide's "treatise" with that name. His revolt however and his flights did not take him to the battle-field with the disciples of Barrès and Péguy. At the end of the seventh volume (1929), we find Jacques in Geneva among the revolutionists, and there we meet him again in the first volume of *L'Été 1914.*

The first series of *Les Thibault* belonged rather to the so-called "adolescence" and "family-life" novel, but already in it we found Du Gard's scrupulous method of inquiry, his solid sense of reality, his precautions to add nothing to his characters that did not come out of their own logical development. A clever psychologist, he was already an excellent historian. We know now that the interruption of *Les Thibault* in 1929 did not at all mean that Du Gard had exhausted his possibilities. The pressure of the political and social events around 1930 very likely had something to do with the new turn of his stories. After destroying a first sequel to the Thibaults, he went back to work and, after five years, brought forth *L'Été 1914,* three volumes of more than one thousand pages, covering, from June 28 to August 10, 1914, the first fifty days of the war.

No doubt, at first sight, *L'Été 1914* was a new book and a historical rather than a personal novel. What we must most admire this time is how Du Gard succeeded in gathering all the threads of the tragic plot into the hands of his central characters. Not that his success was complete. From the artistic point of view the new book reads too much like a reporter's account. We feel that the author is hampered by the fiction which he built up fifteen years before, and this is evident in the way he drags along the survivors of his love story and abruptly dismisses them at the end. The devices he uses to gather his war records are, to a large extent, arbitrary and we are sorry, at the end of each of those fifty strenuous days, for all the errands poor Jacques Thibault has to run, through Paris and several foreign countries, to bring us "the latest news." Never did a reporter meet with such a hard task. The material itself has not always been fully digested. And yet Jacques and Antoine are not drowned in this mass of facts, and they enact very convincingly their individual part in the drama. We see the birth of the world-war through their consciousness. *LÉté 1914* is a natural continuation of *Les Thibault* and the link between the two parts of the novel is well indicated by Du Gard when, for instance, we hear Jacques declare: "What made a revolutionist of me was the fact that I was born in this house (the Thibault house) and that I am the son of a bourgeois." It took all the pangs and pains told in the first seven volumes to allow Jacques to find at last his true identity, and without his personal rebellion there would have been no social revolt. Conversion to revolutionary socialism was not common in 1914. Youthful insurgents preferred religious conversion, death on the "field of honor" or suicide. Others went to poetry and music (see Jean-Christophe) for freedom. The flight to revolution came later, at about the time Roger Martin du Gard began writing his last volumes.

Readers of *L'Été 1914* hardly need to be reminded of all the literary beauties in the books—portraits, dramatic incidents, street pageants where the mob plays the leading rôle, Jaurès' assassination, mobilization, the first battles, the flight of Jacques over the lines, his death at the hands of a gendarme. Du Gard does not surrender to pathos, he keeps himself detached and objective to the end, but the book is teeming with emotion.

French critics are still discussing the part played by the author in these books. Whom is he for, in the conflict of ideals between the two brothers? Let me refer the reader to the conversations between Antoine and Jacques to solve this problem. Du Gard's sympathies were evidently on the side of Jacques in the first series, and they are still with him in those new volumes, although he is always careful to weigh all the pros and cons of his characters and to qualify what they say or do. This makes him the more convincing.

No historian could give a more accurate account of the beginnings of the world-war than he did in these volumes. To judge his accuracy as a psychologist let me refer the readers to the first chapters in the first volume of the new series where he psycho-analyzes Jacques as a revolutionist. He announces an epilogue to the book and we must wait for his conclusions, but we well know already, from what we have just read, that dishonest or mistaken politicians were largely responsible for the world-war, that Social Democracy was not equal to its task, that the world-war, like all other wars, had all the best moral and social reasons against it, that, before his own conscience and the conscience of mankind, Jacques Thibault was right in doing what he did, although it was useless. Martin du Gard did not say all this, but it is all there in his book. It is true that he did not tell the whole story and that, now and then, he was not quite fair to the revolutionary side, but (for instance in the episode where the revolutionary leader suppresses some evidence that might have prevented the war), he told much more than half the truth.

This is a great book, one of the greatest of our time, without any flourishes of the pen, a huge and solid rock hewn out of the human quarry, a book to be placed beside those of Zola, Romain Rolland, Marcel Proust, and Tolstoy, whom Du Gard admires so much. With Jules Romains, André Malraux, and others following in their footsteps, there is a chance for French fiction to go back to its great realistic, epic and emancipatory tradition. (pp. 149-51)

> *Régis Michaud, "Roger Martin du Gard," in* Books Abroad, *Vol. 12, No. 2, Spring, 1938, pp. 149-51.*

HOWARD C. RICE (essay date 1941)

[*In the following excerpt from a pamphlet issued by the publisher of* The World of the Thibaults *in order to familiarize the American public with Martin du Gard's works, Rice praises the realism and intellectual depth of* Jean Barois *and* The World of the Thibaults.]

Jean Barois is a novel of ideas, but not the novel of a single idea. It traces, in episodic fashion, the religious and intellectual development of the central figure, Jean Barois, an unusually honest man who finds himself torn between his heritage of mystic beliefs and the logical demands of his rational mind. But the novel is more than the story of Barois's ideas; it is the drama of his conscience in relation to the events of his age. The peak of his vitality and influence comes at the time of the Dreyfus Case, in which he is an active participant. Although Barois and his intimates, as well as their publication *Le Semeur*, are imaginary creations, Martin du Gard has ingeniously and naturally brought them into contact with historic events and personages. He has even incorporated into his story actual documents, including fragments of Bernard Lazare's pamphlets and parts of the stenographic reports of the Zola trial. Historian and novelist collaborate to give something which may not be an objective treatment of the Dreyfus Affair, but which is most certainly a moving history of what the Affair meant to those who lived through it. To understand the moral significance of this crisis is to possess one of the important keys to French affairs, for even now, in a "new regime" which Jean Barois would have deplored, the Affair is still an active force. In this respect, *Jean Barois* remains not only an absorbing novel, but an invaluable document.

Jean Barois is a significant type in the history of modern French thought. He does not represent Martin du Gard's own contemporaries, but rather those who came of age between 1880 and 1890, whose intellectual masters had been Taine and Renan. In reviewing *Jean Barois* for *Le Matin*, Gustave Lanson remarked that "nothing perhaps has been written which expresses with greater truth the soul of the generations of 1880-1890." At the time of the novel's publication the intellectual and moral values of Jean Barois's generation were being frequently and loudly questioned. In fact, Martin du Gard has introduced in the final chapters of his novel some of these young critics, representatives of Barrès's traditionalism or the "Catholic revival," who condescendingly treat Jean Barois's dilemmas and his militant battle for free-thinking as something pathetically old-fashioned.

Martin du Gard found the originals for these youngsters among his own contemporaries, such as Henri Massis, who has since gained some reputation as a militant for the literary Right and whose works are, I believe, admired in America by disciples of the late Irving Babbitt. After the award of the Nobel Prize, Massis, in his *Revue Universelle*, berated the Swedish Academy for its consistent crowning of none but "de-nationalized" works and Martin du Gard for the pacifistic implications of his writing. This Massis *vs.* Martin du Gard alignment is something deeper than mere quibbling. It is a familiar pattern in the history of French thought, which leads one to believe that the conflict of generations sketched in *Jean Barois* is, after all, only another example of that permanent duality in French tradition which has produced both the Ancien Régime and the Revolution. It is a duality which explains in part, perhaps, the tragedy of 1940. (pp. 13-15)

The first two parts of *Les Thibault* were written in 1920-1921 and published the following year. The eighth and final installment, or *Epilogue*, appeared in Paris in February 1940. The dates are worth emphasizing, especially in the United States, where our knowledge of foreign literature so frequently depends upon the accidents of translation or publicity. So many novel-cycles and so many novels of adolescence have come out of France since the last war that it is easy to conclude that Martin du Gard has merely followed fashions. The truth of the matter is that he has not followed styles but has had a share in setting them. The first volumes of *Les Thibault* preceded Romains's *Men of Good Will* and Duhamel's *Pasquier Chronicles* by a decade, and also came before Gide's *The Counterfeiters*, which incidentally, is dedicated to Martin du Gard.

The parchment presented to Martin du Gard by the Swedish Academy represents his novel in symbolic fashion by means of a tree growing out of the Parisian landscape. The Swedish artist was right in taking Paris for the background, for, although the action ranges over Europe, Paris is always the center, the soil from which it grows. The choice of the tree, if it is the

Thibault family tree, as it seems to be, is less fortunate, for the novel is not that of a single family, but of several. It is, in fact, as the English translation suggests, "the world of the Thibaults." A critic, who is not unaware of Martin du Gard's admiration for Tolstoy, has suggested that the phrase "War and Peace" accurately describes it. The psychology of *Les Thibault* is distinctly "modern," although the style and the narrative method are "traditional." In this latter respect Martin du Gard's novel is far closer to Galsworthy's *Forsyte Saga* or Thomas Mann's *Buddenbrooks* than to Thomas Wolfe's *Of Time and the River* or Dos Passos's *U.S.A.* (pp. 17-18)

While completing *Les Thibault* Roger Martin du Gard has demonstrated his skill in dramatic writing with *Un Taciturne*, successfully acted in 1932, and his mastery of the *nouvelle* in *Confidence africaine* . . . and *Vieille France*. . . . From these, as well as from his major novel, it is possible to attempt some summary of the general meaning of his work. Martin du Gard imaginatively identifies himself with the ideas of his characters, but he uses no one of them as his personal mouthpiece. In fact it is this very ability to portray different types and points of view with sympathy and with complete plausibility that makes him the artist he is. His characters remain human individuals, and never become mere vehicles for ideas. Under the novelist's apparent indifference there is, however, a thirst for justice, under his detachment there smolders a spark of perpetual revolt. It is what he calls "inactive revolt": revolt against injustice, sham, and hypocrisy; inactive, in so far as it has not found expression in a doctrine or a partisan crusade.

Any definition of Roger Martin du Gard's personality must, then, take into account a variety of figures: the historical investigator patiently reconstructing experience, the understanding and tender confidant of human secrets, the brutally outspoken enemy of false sentimentality. Finally, there is an idealist who believes in mankind. Martin du Gard has not in the past publicly explained himself or his credo except through the indirect channel of his fiction. The award of the Nobel Prize led him to depart from this precedent, and, having created literature "well and for a long time," he consented, for a moment, to talk about it. Attempting to explain the attribution of the prize to his work, he told members of the Swedish Academy that he supposed they had wanted to reward "an independent writer who had escaped the fascination of partisan ideologies, an investigator as objective as is humanly possible, as well as a novelist striving to express the tragic quality of individual lives." (pp. 21-2)

> *Howard C. Rice, in his* Roger Martin du Gard and "The World of the Thibaults," *The Viking Press, 1941, 23 p.*

MALCOLM COWLEY (essay date 1941)

[*Cowley, an American critic, has made several valuable contributions to contemporary letters with his editions of important American authors (Nathaniel Hawthorne, Walt Whitman, Ernest Hemingway, William Faulkner, F. Scott Fitzgerald), his writings as a literary critic for the* New Republic, *and, above all, with his chronicles and criticism of modern American literature. Cowley's literary criticism does not attempt a systematic philosophical view of life and art, nor is it representative of a neatly defined school of critical thought. Rather, Cowley focuses on works that he considers worthy of public appreciation and that he believes personal experience has qualified him to explicate, such as the works of "lost generation" writers he knew. The critical approach Cowley follows is thus undogmatic and is characterized by a willingness to work from whatever perspective—social, historical,*

aesthetic—that the work itself seems to demand for its illumination. In the following excerpt from an essay originally published in the New Republic *in 1941, Cowley considers the merits and shortcomings of* The World of the Thibaults.]

With glazed eyes and swollen lids, I have just finished *The World of the Thibaults* in the complete English translation—both volumes and all the 1,900 pages. It isn't fair to blame Roger Martin du Gard, a kindly man and a conscientious writer, for the dull headache that comes from reading too much. Yet I wonder whether this business of writing oversize novels hasn't been carried much too far since Marcel Proust first set the fashion. Is there any human subject that can't be treated in a hundred or at most two hundred thousand words, instead of spinning the story out to nearly a million? Is there any reason for believing that a novel published in eleven books—as this one was in France—is eleven times or even twice as good as a novel in one reasonably large volume with a beginning, a middle and an end, and not too many extraneous incidents? Isn't it possible that giantism in fiction is quite as unhealthy a symptom as giantism in business or architecture or armies?

The least one can say is that the author who writes an inordinately long novel is like the orator who delivers an inordinately long speech: he is disregarding the capacity for attention of his audience. Either the book must be leisurely sampled over a period of weeks, in which case the reader is likely to have forgotten the beginning before reaching the end; or else it must be read as a reviewer's chore, hour after hour and day after day, in which case it leaves one with aching eyes and perhaps a blurred picture of the author's intentions. And the author, too, is running a risk. Any man who sets out to write a 2,000-page novel is betting against fate and human experience that he can remain unchanged until the book is finished. He is also betting that the world he describes will remain unchanged, instead of being shattered to pieces. After starting a novel of contemporary life, he may end by writing ancient history.

Something like that has happened with Jules Romains, whose *Men of Good Will* is far from being completed, although it is already the longest serious novel of all time. Martin du Gard is more fortunate, since he had finished *The World of the Thibaults* before Paris fell. Yet the book was twenty years in the writing, with the first of its eleven volumes started not long after the Armistice and the last published in the midst of another war. We should not be surprised that the theme of it changed in the middle, or that it can best be approached as two separate novels.

The book started out as what the French call a "river novel," flowing on from volume to volume. Apparently the author intended to make an extended study of family life in the *haute bourgeoise*, choosing as his examples the Thibaults and their neighbors the Fontanins. He would show how Oscar Thibault, a rich and pious Catholic, tyrannized over his two sons without ceasing to love them. He would show how the sons hated their father and rebelled against him—Antoine, the elder, becoming a rather commonplace atheist, while Jacques, the younger, transformed his private emotions toward the family into a revolt against bourgeois society as a whole. At the same time he would make it clear that both Antoine and Jacques were molded in their father's image. He would portray the Fontanins as a Protestant family ruled by the mother, who was a kindlier soul than Oscar Thibault, yet in her own way just as domineering. The novel would be written—quite consciously, it seems—under the influence of André Gide. It would embody a good deal of his philosophy, would present several characters modeled after those in *The Counterfeiters,* and would even repeat some of his characteristic phrases.

Seven books of the novel had been finished by 1929; all of them are included in the first of the two big American volumes. In writing them, Martin du Gard had remained moderately faithful to his plan—but, like a moderately faithful husband, he had found other interests outside the family. Some of the independent episodes—like the love affair between Antoine and the equestrienne—had become almost as important as the main theme. Already one could say that the novel as a whole was not so much a river as a chain of lakes—some deep and clear, others shallow, and with only a rivulet connecting them.

In 1930, the author had finished an eighth book, dealing with the adventures of Jacques Thibault among the international revolutionists. The manuscript was never delivered to his publishers. For Martin du Gard had a moral crisis, during which he decided that his novel was moving in the wrong direction, was failing to treat the real issue of his time. He tore up the book he had called "Under Sail" and started to work on the three volumes of *Summer 1914.* Here, family matters have retreated into the background, even though the author finds room for a desperate love affair between Jacques Thibault and Jenny de Fontanin. Jacques instead of Antoine is now the principal character, and the principal subject is the coming of the war.

Through his Socialist group, which has members in every European capital and a private intelligence service, Jacques is kept almost as well informed of international maneuvers as the diplomats themselves. From Geneva he has an eagle's-eye view of the events that follow the murder at Serajevo. Moreover, he is sent on missions to Berlin, to Brussels, and twice to Paris, where he haunts the meeting places of Socialist politicians and hears the shot that killed Jaurès. His information is almost too complete to be completely credible, as fiction. In one sense, *Summer 1914* might be read as a fair-minded and impressively documented treatise on war guilt. But it is also, in the end, a surprisingly effective novel.

The influence of Gide has practically disappeared from its philosophy and its method. In this section of his work, Martin du Gard's fictional technique is at least as old as Zola's: it consists in the simple and realistic treatment of events, with nothing left to chance, with no experimental or poetic writing, and with the author's personality kept strictly out of the picture. Scrupulously fair, he presents all points of view—those of Cabinet Ministers, of the conservative middle classes, of the fire-eating Royalists, of the international Socialists and Anarchists, of the workingmen in the streets. Sometimes one gets pretty impatient with him for trying to say everything; part of his exposition might have been left to the historians. Yet slowly he rises to the emotional level of his subject, writing with more and more intensity as the story continues. Day by day he notes the changes in the collective mood of Paris—from indifference to alarm, from alarm to gestures of rebellion, from rebellion to surrender in the face of what seems inevitable, from surrender to a mad patriotic fervor. And the tempo of his story grows more clearly marked from page to page, until everything is timed to the tramp of hobnailed boots and the clank of guns through the Paris streets, all moving toward the front.

Then comes an episode that is pure nightmare. Jacques, who has remained faithful to his international ideals when almost everyone else has abandoned them, plans a last suicidal attempt to stop the war. He will fly over the lines in an airplane, scattering leaflets that call upon the soldiers of both sides to lay down their arms. But the plane has hardly left the Swiss border when it crashes in Alsace. Horribly mutilated, unable to speak but still breathing—an object wrapped in bandages and splints from a packing case, so that the soldiers refer to him as "Chinaware"—Jacques is carried along in the vast disorder of the French retreat, until finally a gendarme puts a bullet through his head. That is the real end of the novel. The epilogue, designed to round off the story and unite the two themes of war and family, impressed me as being a somber and rather tedious anticlimax—though by the time I reached it, my eyes were too tired to make me a fair judge.

Summer 1914 is the work for which Martin du Gard will be remembered and for which he deserved to receive the Nobel Prize. . . . Yet it would have been better, I think, if it had been written quite independently, without regard to the family affairs of the Thibaults and the Fontanins. Standing alone, without seven other books as an introduction and without an epilogue, it would be even more impressive. It could be read for itself, and with clearer eyes. (pp. 364-68)

> Malcolm Cowley, "Roger Martin du Gard: The Next-to-Longest Novelist," in his Think Back on Us . . . : A Contemporary Chronicle of the 1930's, *edited by* Henry Dan Piper, Southern Illinois University Press, 1967, pp. 364-68.

P. M. PASINETTI (essay date 1950)

[*In the following excerpt, Pasinetti points out the stylistic flaws of* Jean Barois.]

As work of fiction, it is almost too simple to say that *Jean Barois* is unsatisfactory. In the hero's biography, from the early split with the traditional values (abandonment of his very religious wife, etc.) through the years of struggle and success (editorship of a review called *The Sower,* etc.) to the late doubts (when his daughter, on her firmly religious ground, proves a capable intellectual match for him) to the final conversion (his daughter, in the blissful serenity of conviction, enters a nunnery), all the various episodes and encounters are, we feel, strictly and punctually devised in order to follow and illustrate a certain ideological pattern. In other words it is not as though some sort of pattern developed out of a dramatically "inevitable" vision; it is, alas, the reverse. Most of the characters, rather than count in their own right, seem to act as spokesmen. It is difficult at any rate to present a character intent upon living an "idea"; and here we have a good deal of just flat statement of ideas, even in the most familiar dialogue. Indeed it is quite possibly hopeless to get dramatically very far with characters whose main exploits are lectures, newspaper work, and endless ideological talk. For all these reasons, there is here something "external" and perfunctory in the treatment of character and action. But character and action are the things about which a piece of fiction cannot afford to be vague, so that the impression of vagueness, or of excessive simplification, extends to the work as a whole. A novel cannot help being a unified work of literature, and any distinction between its ideas or themes, and its characters and actions, can only be a rather artificial one. Our dealings as readers, so to speak, are with the characters: we tend not to believe the narrator on his mere word and want it backed by fact. Characters and action are the ways through which the novel can achieve a persuasive complexity. The curious and fatal thing is that any vagueness on that score seems naturally to extend also to the "ideological structure," to the element which, in a novel of this sort, the sympathetic reader may consider as the very backbone. So, for example, in the case of **Jean Barois** some of us may feel a certain irremediable paleness about the character, and soon discover that that is another way of saying that we find a certain shallowness and naïveté in his "ideological" life. Style, in the most comprehensive sense, is again what the question can be reduced to. And this is the way some of these characters talk, lecture, and write:

> "Something we know not is stirring in the world. . . ."

> What is this 'something' that is active beneath the surface? It is the increasing activity of human thought, of progress. You see how that theme could be developed. One might speak of the maturation of a gigantic task, in which each of the emotions we experience, each of our struggles, plays its part. And this movement carries in its womb all the solutions we are groping after, all those truths of tomorrow which still elude us, but which in the fullness of time will fall into our hands like ripe fruit and reveal themselves, one after the other, to the questing mind of man. . . .

In other words those of us who feel that the phase of optimism and of faith in scientific progress illustrated in this story was based on almost unbelievably shallow premises, will find their expectations often confirmed in terms of language and style. So much so that the book becomes interesting in that sense as a period piece. When the material becomes more dramatically tense (the Dreyfus section) that documentary interest, rather than the interest in the novel as such, is increased. And here I would suggest . . . the reading of bare historical accounts, direct documents or, say, epistolaries, can be so much more *interesting;* there are moments when we don't know whether the business of carrying on the thin apparatus of fictitiousness is more of a nuisance to us or to the author. Here I found myself more than once wishing that I had the records of the Dreyfus trial, *straight,* while the narrator in his turn carried on his job as unobtrusively but also as flatly as he could, as though he were simply editing his material. This is, in fact, what constitutes the special narrative manner of this novel: a very considerable percentage of it is written in dramatic form, with the name of the character at the beginning of his line, like the text of a play or a parliamentary report. Much of the narrative is in brief present-tense phrases, like stage instructions. It is naïve to describe this as a daring technical innovation, at whatever time it may have occurred; and I doubt not only its profound originality but also its real literary effectiveness. The book, technically speaking, somehow turns out to be a novel what an oratorio without music would be to an opera. And in conclusion, considering it as literature, it makes us miss the concreteness of vision which distinguishes successful narrative art, without, on the other hand, rewarding us with the more abstract intellectual delight of pure Platonic dialogue. (pp. 551-53)

> P. M. Pasinetti, *"Fiction from Three Languages,"* in The Sewanee Review, *Vol. LVIII, No. 3, Summer, 1950, pp. 547-62.*

ALBERT CAMUS (essay date 1955)

[*An Algerian-born French novelist, essayist, dramatist, and critic, Camus was one of the most important literary figures of the* twentieth century. Throughout his varied writings, he consistently, often passionately, explored his major theme: the belief that people can be happy in a world without meaning. He defended the dignity and decency of the individual and asserted that through purposeful action one can overcome the despair of nihilism. His notion of an "absurd" universe, delineated in his essay "Le mythe de Sisyphe" (1943; "The Myth of Sisyphus") and illustrated in his most renowned novel, L'etranger (1942; The Stranger), is premised on the tension between life in an irrational universe and the human desire for rationality. Although this world view has led critics of his work to link Camus with the Existentialists, Camus himself rejected this classification. In the following excerpt from his introduction to the 1955 edition of Martin du Gard's complete works, he discusses the style and themes of The World of the Thibaults.]

It is already obvious that if art is a religion, it will not be an attractive one. On this point Martin du Gard quickly cut himself off from the theoreticians of art for art's sake. Symbolism, which caused so much exquisite damage among the writers of his generation, never had any effect on him, except in certain stylistic indulgences which he later outgrew, like adolescent acne. He was only twenty-seven when he wrote **Devenir!**, and the writer who is quoted with enthusiasm in this first work is already Tolstoi. From here on, Martin du Gard was to remain faithful all his life to an ascetic vocation, an artistic Jansenism that would make him shun ostentation and effect, in order to sacrifice everything to uninterrupted labor on a work he wanted to make endure. "What is difficult," says this precocious and perspicacious thinker, "is not to have been someone but to stay that way." Genius runs the risk, in fact, of being no more than a fleeting accident. Only character and work can transform it into fame and a livelihood. Hard work, and the organization and humility that go with it, are thus at the very core of free creation and consequently indispensable in a craft where work, but work humbly pursued, is also the rule of life. It is no exaggeration to say that Martin du Gard's very aesthetic principles made it inevitable that his work, in which individual problems have the starring roles, take on historical dimensions. The man who finds his reasons for living and his delights in free work can, in the end, bear any humiliation except the humiliation justly inflicted on his work, just as he can accept every privilege except those that separate him from his liberty, the work to which he is chained. Works like Roger Martin du Gard's sometimes unknowingly restore artistic toil to its rightful place in the city, and can no longer be divorced then from its victories or defeats.

But even before any other discovery, the result is this work, solid as stone, whose main body is **Les Thibault** and whose buttresses are **Devenir!, Jean Barois, Vieille France, Confidence africaine,** and the plays. We can discuss this work, we can try to see its limitations. But we cannot deny that it exists, and does so superbly, with an unbelievable honesty. Commentaries can add to it or detract from it, but the fact remains that we have here one of those works, exceptional in France, around which one can turn, as one walks around a building. The same generation that gave us so many aestheticians, so many subtle, delicate writers, also brought a work rich in people and in passions, constructed according to the plans of a well-tried technique. This nave of men, built solely with the rigor of an art practiced a whole lifetime, testifies that in a time of poets, essayists, and novelists concerned with the soul, a master craftsman, a Pierre de Craon without a religion but not without faith, was born in our land.

Nevertheless, a law exists in art which says that every creator should be buried beneath the weight of his most obvious virtues. The proverbial honesty of his art has sometimes hidden the true Martin du Gard in a time which, for various reasons, put genius and improvisation above everything else, as if genius could do without a work schedule and improvisation without arduous leisure. The critics thought they had done enough by paying homage to virtue, forgetting that in art virtue is only a means placed at the service of risk. There is certainly no lack of audacity in the work that concerns us. It stems nearly always from the obstinate pursuit of psychological truth. It thus serves to emphasize the ambiguity of human beings, without which this truth is meaningless. We are already surprised, reading *Devenir!*, by the cruel modernity of the ending; André, who has just buried his wife in great grief, notices the young servant girl standing at the window. We know that he has desired her, and realize that she will help him digest his sorrow.

Martin du Gard deals frankly with sexuality and with the shadowy zone of darkness it casts over every life. Frankly, but not crudely. He has never given way to the temptation of suggestive licentiousness that makes so many contemporary novels as boring as guides to social etiquette. He has not obligingly described monotonous excesses. He has chosen rather to show the importance of sexual life through its inopportunity. Like a true artist, he has not painted directly what it consists of, but indirectly, what it forces people to become. It is sensuality, throughout her life, for example, that makes Mme de Fontanin vulnerable in the presence of her unfaithful husband. We know this, and yet it is never said, except as Mme de Fontanin watches over her husband on his deathbed. What is also noticeable in *Les Thibault* is a curious intermingling of the themes of desire and death. (Once more, it is the night before the burial of Mother Frubling that Jacques is initiated by Lisbeth.) Certainly we must see this intermingling as one of the obsessions that are an artist's privilege and at the same time as a means of underlining the unusual nature of the sexual life.

But desire is not only mingled with the things of death, it also contaminates morality and makes it ambiguous. The righteous man, the man who observes the outward show of Christianity, the father in *Les Thibault*, writes in his diary: "Do not confuse with the love of our neighbor the emotion we feel at the approach, at the touch, of certain young people, even children." Then he crosses out only the final words, and this omission reconciles him with both modesty and sincerity. Just as Jérôme de Fontanin savors the delight of the repentant libertine when he saves Rinette from the prostitution into which he had cast her. "I am good, I am better than they think," he repeats tenderly to himself. But he cannot resist sleeping with her one last time, adding the pleasures of the flesh to those of virtue. One sentence is all Martin du Gard needs to summarize the mechanical inspiration of the pose: "His fingers were automatically unfastening her skirt, as his lips rested on her forehead in a paternal kiss."

The whole work has this flavor of truth. The admirable *Vieille France* not only offers us Martin du Gard's most sinister character, the postman Joigneau, a sort of Astaroth on bicycle, but it also abounds in pitiless revelations about the provincial heart, and the last page gives an astonishing conclusion. Similarly, in *African Secret*, the very simplicity of an incestuous brother's tone will make his unfortunate adventure seem natural. In 1931, with *Un taciturne*, Martin du Gard dared to put on the stage, without the slightest vulgarity of tone, the drama of a respectable industrialist who discovers he has homosexual leanings. At last, in *Les Thibault*, the brilliant touches multiply. One could quote the scene in which Gise secretly allows the child

that the man she loves has had with another woman to suck her virgin breast; or the meal Antoine and Jacques have, after the father's death, that almost in spite of themselves takes on a slight air of celebration. But there are two such touches I rank higher than the others, for they show the great novelist at work.

The first is Jacques' stubborn silence when, for the first time, Antoine comes to see him at the reform school in Crouy. How could there be a better way to convey humiliation than this silence. The rapidly muttered words, the onsets of reticence in which this silence is clothed, and which serve to underline it even further, are so accurately calculated and proportioned that mystery and pity suddenly erupt into what was until then a straightforward story, opening much wider vistas than those of the middle-class Parisian milieu in which it had begun. Humiliation has never been depicted more objectively or more successfully, except by Dostoevski, whose technique is either frenzied or grating (I am not counting Lawrence, who describes a personal humiliation) and by Malraux, in the epic mode (especially in *La Voie royale*, which I persist in liking whatever its author may say). No one, however, has ever tried to paint it in subdued and even colors, and Martin du Gard has perhaps achieved what is most difficult in art. If there are artistic miracles, they must resemble those that come from grace. I have always thought it would be easier to redeem a man steeped in vice and crime than a greedy, narrow-minded, pitiless merchant. Thus, in art, the more prosaic the reality chosen as one's subject matter, the more difficult it is to transfigure. Even here, however, there is a point beyond which we cannot go, that makes any claim to absolute realism quite untenable. But it is here nonetheless, half way between reality and its stylization, that art from time to time achieves the perfect triumph. The portrait of Jacques in his humiliation remains, in my view, one of these triumphs. (pp. 260-65)

But even more than his art it is Martin du Gard's themes that coincide with our own preoccupations. The path he has followed with so fortunate and deliberate a pace is one the rest of us have had to race along, with history at our heels. I mean, generally, the personal evolution that leads one to a recognition of the history of all men and to an acceptance of their struggles. Even in this, of course, Martin du Gard has his own particular stamp. He stands midway between his predecessors and his peers (who talked of nothing but the individual and never let history play more than a circumstantial role) and his successors (who make only embarrassed allusions to the individual). In *Les Thibault*, and in *Jean Barois*, individuals are intact and the pain of history still quite fresh. They have not yet worn each other out. Martin du Gard has not experienced our situation, in which we inherit at the same time shop-worn people and a history tensed and paralyzed by several wars and the fear of final destruction. We can say without paradox that what is alive in our present-day experience lies behind us, in a work like Roger Martin du Gard's. (pp. 266-67)

The great theme of the individual caught between history and God will be orchestrated symphonically in *Les Thibault*, where all the characters move toward the catastrophe of the summer of 1914. The religious problem, however, is upstaged. It runs through the first volumes, disappears as history gradually swamps individual destinies, reappearing in negative form in the final volume, with the description of Antoine Thibault's solitary death. The reappearance is nonetheless significant. Like any true artist, Martin du Gard cannot get rid of his obsessions. It is significant, therefore, that his great work ends with the constant theme of all his books, the death agony, in which man is, if I may put it this way, finally faced with the ultimate question. But in the *Epilogue* that ends *Les Thibault*, Martin du Gard's two main characters—the priest and the doctor—have disappeared, or come very near to doing so. *Les Thibault* ends with the death of a doctor, alone among other doctors. It seems that for Martin du Gard, as for Antoine, the problem has now ceased to present itself solely on the individual human level. And it is indeed the experience of history, and his enforced involvement in it, which explains this evolution on Antoine's part. Historical passion (in the two senses of the word) is atheistic today, or seems to be. In simple terms, this means that the historical misfortunes of the twentieth century have marked the collapse of bourgeois Christianity. A symbolic illustration of this idea can be seen in the fact that the father, who represents religion to Antoine, dies just after Antoine has proclaimed his atheism. War breaks out at the same time, and a world that thought it could live by trade and still be religious collapses in bloodshed. If it is legitimate to see *Les Thibault* as one of the first committed novels, the point should simply be made that it has better claims to this description than those published today. For Martin du Gard's characters, unlike ours, have something to commit and something to lose in historical conflicts. The pressure of immediate events struggles in their very being against traditional structures, whether religious or cultural. When these structures are destroyed, in a certain way man himself is destroyed. He is simply ready to exist, some day. Thus Antoine Thibault first becomes aware that other people exist, but this first step leads him only to confront death in an attempt to discover, beyond any consolation or illusion, the final secret of his reasons for living. With *Les Thibault*, the man of our half-century is born, the human being we are concerned with, and whom we can choose to commit or to liberate. He is ready for everything, so long as we have not decided what he is. (pp. 270-71)

Since I have concentrated on the relevance of Martin du Gard's work to the present day, I still must show that his very doubts are our own. The birth of an awareness of history in the Thibault brothers is paired with the posing of a problem we can well understand. *Summer 1914*, which reveals along with the impending war the failure of socialism in circumstances decisive to the future of the world, offers a summary of all Martin du Gard's doubts. He was not lacking in lucidity. We know that *Summer 1914*, appearing in 1936, was published long after *The Death of the Father* (1929). During this long interval, Martin du Gard carried out a veritable revolution in the structure of his work. He abandoned his original plan, and decided to give *Les Thibault* an ending different from the one he had originally intended. The first plan involved thirty or so volumes; the second reduces *Les Thibault* to eleven. Martin du Gard had no hesitation next about destroying the manuscript of *L'Appareillage (Setting Sail)*, a volume which was to follow *The Death of the Father* and which had cost him two years' work. Between 1931, the date of this sacrifice, and 1933, the year when armed with a new plan he began to write *Summer 1914*, there were two years of quite natural confusion. This is perceptible in the book's very structure. After a long pause the machine at first had some difficulty getting started again, and really gets going only in the second volume. But it seems to me that we also feel this change in a number of new perspectives. Begun at the moment of Hitler's ascendance to power, when the Second World War could already be sensed on the horizon, this great historical fresco of a conflict men tried to hope would be the last is almost compelled to call itself into question. In *Vieille France*, written during the years when Martin du Gard had

given up *Les Thibault*, the schoolmistress was already asking herself a formidable question: "Why is the world like this? Is it really society's fault? . . . Is it not rather man's own fault?" The same question worries Jacques at the height of his revolutionary fervor, just as it explains most of Antoine's attitudes toward historical events. One can therefore suppose it must have haunted the novelist himself.

None of the contradictions of social action are, in any case, eluded in the long, perhaps overlong, ideological conversations that fill *Summer 1914*. The main problem, the use of violence in the cause of justice, is discussed at great length in the conversations between Jacques and Mithoerg. The famous distinction between the yogi and the commissar has already been made by Martin du Gard: within the revolution, in fact, it brings about the confrontation between the apostle and the technician. Better still, the nihilistic aspect of the revolution is isolated, in order to be treated in depth, in the character of Meynestrel. The latter believes that after having put man in the place of God, atheism ought to go even further and abolish man himself. Meynestrel's reply, when asked what will replace man, is "Nothing." Elsewhere, the Englishman Patterson defines Meynestrel as "the despair of believing in nothing." Finally, like all those who join the revolution from nihilism, Meynestrel believes that the best results are achieved by the worst means. He has no hesitation about burning the secret papers Jacques has brought back from Berlin, which prove the collusion between the Prussian and Austrian general staffs. The publication of these documents would risk altering the attitude of the German social democrats, thus making the war, which Meynestrel considers as the "trump card" for social upheaval, far less likely.

These examples are enough to show that there was nothing naïve in Martin du Gard's socialism. He cannot manage to believe that perfection will one day be embodied in history. If he does not believe this, it is because his doubt is the same as the schoolteacher's in *Vieille France*. This doubt concerns human nature. "His pity for men was infinite; he gave them all the love his heart contained; but whatever he did, however hard he tried, he remained skeptical about man's moral potentialities." To be certain only of men, and to know that men have little worth, is the cry of pain that runs through the whole of this work, for all its strength and richness, and that brings it so close to us. For, after all, this fundamental doubt is the same doubt that is hidden in every love and that gives it its tenderest vibration. This ignorance, acknowledged in such simple terms, moves us because it is the other side of a certainty we also share. The service of man cannot be separated from an ambiguity that must be maintained in order to preserve the movement of history. From this come the two pieces of advice that Antoine bequeaths to Jean-Paul. The first is one of prudent liberty, assumed as a duty. "Don't let yourself be tied down to a party. Feeling your way in the dark is no joke. But it is a lesser evil." The other is to trust oneself in taking risks: to keep going forward, in the midst of others, along the same path that crowds of men have followed for centuries, in the nighttime of the species, marching and stumbling toward a future that they cannot conceive.

Clearly, there are no certainties offered here. And yet this work communicates courage and a strange faith. To wager, as Antoine does, over and above doubts and disasters, on the human adventure, amounts in the end to praising life, which is terrible and irreplaceable. The Thibault family's fierce attachment to life is the very force that inspires the whole work. Father

*Holograph copy of an essay by Martin du Gard. From
Martin du Gard, by Jacques Brenner. Gallimard, 1961.*

Thibault dying takes on an exemplary quality; he refuses to
disappear, comes unexpectedly to life again, lunges at the enemy, struggles physically against death, bringing nurses and
relatives into the fray. Inevitably, we are reminded of the Kar-
amazovs' love of life and pleasure, of Dimitri's despairing
remark, "I love life too much. It's even disgusting." But life
is not polite, as Dimitri is well aware. In this great struggle to
escape by any and every means from annihilation lies the truth
of history and its progress, of the mind and all its works. Here
indeed is one of those works conceived in the refusal to despair.
This refusal, this inconsolable attachment to men and the world,
explains the roughness and the tenderness of Martin du Gard's
books. Squat, heavy with the weight of flesh in ecstasy and
humiliation, they are still sticky with the life that has given
them birth. But, at the same time, a vast indulgence runs
through all their cruelties, transfiguring and alleviating them.
"A human life," writes Antoine, "is always broader than we
realize." However low and evil it may be, a life always holds
in some hidden corner enough qualities for us to understand
and forgive. There is not one of the characters in this great
fresco, not even the hypocritical Christian bourgeois who is
painted for us in the darkest colors, who goes without his
moment of grace. Perhaps, in Martin du Gard's eyes, the only
guilty person is the one who refuses life or condemns people.
The key words, the final secrets, are not in man's possession.

But man nevertheless keeps the power to judge and to absolve.
Here lies the profound secret of art, which always makes it
useless as propaganda or hatred, and which, for example, prevents Martin du Gard from depicting a young follower of Maurras except with sympathy and generosity. Like any authentic
creator, Martin du Gard forgives all his characters. The true
artist, although his life may consist mostly of struggles, has
no enemy.

The final word that can be said about this work thus remains
the one that it has been difficult to use about a writer since the
death of Tolstoi: goodness. Even then I must make it clear that
I am not talking about the screen of goodness that hides false
artists from the eyes of the world while at the same time hiding
the world from them. Martin du Gard himself has defined a
certain type of bourgeois virtue as the absence of the energy
necessary to do evil. What we are concerned with here is a
particularly lucid virtue, which absolves the good man because
of his weaknesses, the evil man because of his generous impulses, and both of them together because of their passionate
membership in a human race that hopes and suffers. Thus
Jacques, returning home after long years of absence, and having
to help lift up his dying father, finds himself overwhelmed by
the contact with this enormous body, which in his eyes had
formerly symbolized oppression: "And suddenly the contact
with this moistness so overwhelmed him that he felt something
totally unexpected—a physical emotion, a raw sentiment which
went far beyond pity or affection: the selfish tenderness of man
for man." Such a passage marks the true measure of an art
that seeks no separation from anything, that overcomes the
contradictions of a man or a historical period through the obscure acceptance of anonymity. The community of suffering,
struggle, and death exists; it alone lays the foundation of the
hope for a community of joy and reconciliation. He who accepts
membership in the first community finds in it a nobility, a
faithfulness, a reason for accepting his doubts; and if he is an
artist he finds the deep wellsprings of his art. Here man learns,
in one confused and unhappy moment, that it is not true he
must die alone. All men die when he dies, and with the same
violence. How, then, can he cut himself off from a single one
of them, how can he ever refuse him that higher life, which
the artist can restore through forgiveness and man can restore
through justice. This is the secret of the relevance to our times
I spoke of earlier. It is the only worthwhile relevance, a timeless
one, and it makes Martin du Gard, a just and forgiving man,
our perpetual contemporary. (pp. 282-87)

> *Albert Camus, "Roger Martin du Gard," in his* Lyr-
> ical and Critical Essays, *edited by Philip Thody,
> translated by Ellen Conroy Kennedy, Alfred A. Knopf,
> 1968, pp. 254-87.*

GERMAINE BRÉE AND MARGARET GUITON   (essay date 1957)

[*Brée is a French-born American critic and translator whose
critical works are devoted to modern French literature. Concerning her work as a critic, Brée has written: "I do not consider
myself a writer and should probably by classed among the 'academic' critics . . . I have no particular critical method and am,
in fact, an eclectic. Each writer seems himself to suggest to me
the method of approach I should use as I attempt to elucidate the
kind of book he has written. . . . I attempt, with a good deal of
difficulty, to communicate what seems to me essential about each,
rather than to prove, attack or praise." Guiton is the author of
a critical study of the works of La Fontaine. In the following
excerpt, they comment on the political and philosophical aspects
of* The World of the Thibaults.]

Although accurately and almost too meticulously documented as it moves to a climax in the three massive volumes of *Eté 1914, Les Thibaults* is not a historical novel. It would seem that for Martin du Gard the significance of a period of social crisis lies not in any fundamental change in man's fate but in a change in man's understanding of his fate. What characterizes the society Martin du Gard evokes is the rapid change in its intellectual horizon. The change was accomplished within the lifetime of two generations and culminated at the time of World War I.

It is their continuing search for values, in itself an act of faith, that makes Martin du Gard's characters so human and endearing. Their search recalls the attitudes of Corneille's characters, though these, to be sure, are less deeply baffled. But the very stubbornness and stoicism with which Antoine and Jacques find their human way in an inhuman situation, drawing their values and their dignity only from themselves, is reminiscent of their seventeenth century predecessors.

Martin du Gard does not sacrifice the fundamental private experiences to which all human beings are subject, and all his characters are strong and convincing. Jacques's love for Jenny, Antoine's career as a doctor, his liaison, Oscar Thibault's battle with death, are especially moving. Behind this objectivity lies a warm imagination, an understanding of life fashioned by long meditation on the history of ideas as it evolves in each generation. Like Duhamel in *La Chronique des Pasquiers,* Martin du Gard has set his characters in the period leading up to the first world war. He goes more deeply into the vital changes of his time, however, and measures their consequences, not, as does Duhamel, in terms of right and wrong, but in terms of bafflement, strife and suffering. Like Jules Romains, he studies the interrelation of individual lives and historical events such as the Dreyfus case and World War I, but he does not inject a personal myth into his understanding of history. He is concerned with the problems the individual finds in his existence at a particular historical period. He is not interested in the collectivity as such.

Strictly objective in its form, meticulously composed according to traditional techniques, *Les Thibaults* is an achievement of stature. And, within its limits, it is a far more probing document on the first years of the twentieth century than the novels of either Duhamel or Romains. (pp. 82-4)

> Germaine Brée and Margaret Guiton, "Roger Martin du Gard: 'The Corneille of the Bourgeois Novel',"· *in their* An Age of Fiction: The French Novel from Gide to Camus, *Rutgers University Press, 1957, pp. 76-84.*

VICTOR BROMBERT   (essay date 1960)

[*Brombert is an American critic who has written extensively on modern French literature, including a major study of the works of Gustave Flaubert. In the following excerpt, he discusses Martin du Gard's portrayal of the intellectual in* Jean Barois.]

Few novelists have been as successful in dramatizing ideas as Roger Martin du Gard. The epigraph to *Jean Barois* . . . announces the main theme of the novel: the struggle between man and ideology. "The sick conscience—there is the battleground of modern fate." The hero of this struggle with ideas may be looked on as a prototype of the modern French intellectual. Son of a professor of medicine, Jean Barois is attracted to the broader field of the philosophy of science, obtains his *licence* and *agrégation*, teaches for a while, but soon prefers

the more dynamic role of lecturer and propagandist. He becomes the director of a militant publication and sets out to "emancipate" his contemporaries. *S'Affranchir* ["Break free"] was the title Roger Martin du Gard had originally planned for the book.

The plot of the novel is deceptively uncomplicated. Reduced to its simplest terms, it is the story of faith lost and faith regained. Equally simple, on first sight, are the style and the technique employed. The form is that of dramatic dialogues supported by terse objective notations that read like stage directions, and which the author uses with great effect to set the scene and to allow the reader brief glimpses into the inner drama of the protagonists. Martin du Gard's lasting achievement is not, however, this technique, which has its limitations, but his ability to orchestrate the moral crisis of an individual with the crisis of an entire generation.

The story of Jean Barois follows a classical pattern. As a young boy, his sensibilities heightened by a latent malady, he experiences religious fervor. Soon, however, his active mind begins to raise questions which eventually turn into theological doubts. He is distressed by the problem of Evil and suffering. Studies at the Sorbonne further corrode his faith. His initiation into the world of science exalts and dizzies him. In these Parisian lecture halls where universal laws are discussed without any reference to God, he succumbs to what his confessor calls "the poison of scientific pride." His contact with modern exegesis creates further anguish; all of modern scholarship seems to be in absolute contradiction with the basic articles of faith. For a while, Barois tries desperately to hold on. He finds a temporary compromise and some respite in symbolic interpretations of the Bible. But this sapping of fundamental beliefs cannot be arrested. Very soon, the total collapse of his faith leaves him with an exhilarating feeling of liberation, but also with a bitterness and belligerence *à rebours* characteristic of all those who have lost their faith, yet still need to believe.

This need is now directed against religion and against his former self. The second phase of Barois' life is a permanent act of rebellion. Unable to tolerate any longer his wife's superstitious religiosity, he separates from her after bitter quarrels, and gives up the security of an irksome teaching position. He now dedicates himself exclusively to research, to working out and propagating a gospel of "free thought." When the time comes, he throws himself and his group into the maelstrom of the Dreyfus case. This period of his life is one of struggle and ideological commitment. Barois becomes a renowned scholar and polemicist, the acknowledged leader of an intellectual movement of which his paper, *Le Semeur,* is both the instrument and the symbol.

After battles have been won and lost, after the excitement of success and failure, comes frustration and loneliness. The third phase of Barois' existence is marked by disenchantment. A nearly fatal accident brings to his lips, at the peak of terror, a long-forgotten prayer to the Virgin. From that point on, despite the stubborn resistance of a still rebellious intellect, his fear of suffering and of death gradually lead him back to the fold. Aware that the religious experience remains untouched by the onslaught of reason, Barois gradually repudiates his life work and becomes an apostate for the second time. Age and sickness make him yearn for appeasement, for the secure world of his childhood. He withdraws to the old family house in Buis, accepts his wife's care, renounces his pride and is finally converted by a priest who, ironically, regains his own lost faith when he witnesses the pathetic happiness of a mind consoled by the Cross.

It is characteristic of Martin du Gard's art that Jean Barois should rediscover his faith at the very moment that the priest who consoles him is on the point of losing his. Such irony is far from gratuitous. It mirrors one of the author's favorite subjects of meditation: the cyclical recurrence of events, the interplay of action and reaction, the ebb and flow of human relationships. The very structure of *Jean Barois* suggests a cyclical movement. Martin du Gard's skillful use of atavism (the hero's father, when weakened by disease and the fear of death, also returns to religion) is only one of many structural devices. Barois' death is the re-enactment of a scene which operates retrospectively as a prefiguration. Martin du Gard makes use of ironic contrasts: the boy believer who should rejoice over his father's deathbed conversion feels the same unvoiced regret as the priest from whom he himself will receive extreme unction, in very similar circumstances. The entire novel is thus carefully built up on a series of parallels and contrasts, of departures and returns. The novel begins in an atmosphere of disease. The opening pages describe the boy's struggle against tuberculosis. From disease to health and back to illness; from death to life and back to death; from faith to atheism and back to faith—the ineluctable nature of the cycle is reinforced by the structural patterns of the book. Martin du Gard seems to play a number of symmetrical variations on the same fundamental theme. From Buis to Paris and back to Buis: Jean Barois not only returns to his wife after a long separation, but he insists on settling in his father's house, and dies in the very room and in the very bed in which his father died. The somewhat formal architecture of the book serves to strengthen the theme of the return. The Abbé Lévys, who confesses Barois at the end of the novel, takes the place of the Abbé Joziers who confesses him at the beginning.

This formal structure may suggest that the central part of the novel stands for health, intelligence and emancipation. But this is only an illusion. Barois actually betrays his rationalism at the moment his rationalistic fervor attains its highest pitch. The structure of the book is thus more involuted than may appear at first glance. Barois falls into hybris at the midpoint of his existence. On the very page that follows the account of his public lecture on "The Future of Irreligion," an accident which nearly kills him forces him to cry out in anguish: *"Je vous salue, Marie, pleine de grâces. . . ."* ["Hail, Mary, full of grace. . . ."] The man who proclaimed the revolutionary role of intelligence and hailed the era of irreligion once more becomes, without warning, the timid and fervently religious boy who constitutes the core of his personality. Ironically, he was closest to prayer at the moment he prided himself on his remoteness from it. The exultation of the intellect is suddenly metamorphosed into defeat. But even this defeat remains ambivalent: it may turn out to be a victory.

Ideologically, of course, the adventure of Barois ends in failure. The figure of Michelangelo's *Slave,* which appears as a frontispiece to the novel, is clearly symbolic: the gesture of liberation, as though petrified by the sculptor's material, remains forever uncompleted, doomed to frustration. The plaster cast standing on Barois' mantelpiece foreshadows his destiny; it functions as an ironic commentary of which Barois himself, in moments of crisis, is unavoidably aware. The struggling figure, exerting all his strength, expends himself in sterile effort. Lonely and naked, he remains eternally frozen in his desperate tenseness. "Look at him!" Barois cries out. "He

cannot even raise one free arm! . . . Perhaps, like him, I have in all these years acted out a sham emancipation. . . ." Martin du Gard obviously looked on the statue as a key symbol. During his own illness, he asked to have a reproduction placed in front of his bed so that the image of Barois' destiny—the pathetic story of a rebellious individual who remains prisoner of his myths—might serve as a warning. Barois' defeat is indeed a nearly total abdication. During the last months of his life, haunted by fear of death and longing for reassurance, he abandons all intellectual effort. On his large desk, now symbolically empty, only two objects remain, a small crucifix and a handkerchief, as though to suggest that faith regained is dependent on disease.

The author's severity toward his character reveals itself in a number of ways. But it is not an unmitigated severity. Martin du Gard never casts discredit on the quest for emancipation and social justice. Moreover, Barois exhibits some truly admirable traits. He is among those happy few who have known the "intoxication of reason and of pure thought." He displays an impressive capacity for work; in fact, his unremitting, selfless dedication to causes is in part responsible for his untimely physical collapse. He is a victim of intellectual labor. As a fighter, he is at his toughest and most inspiring when others begin to lose hope. Despising easy victories, he relishes the struggle against public opinion and overwhelming odds. His comrades—before his final conversion—certainly do not consider his life a fiasco: "You have helped uproot some errors and maintain a few tottering truths."

What his companions have overlooked—even Barois is unaware of it—is the extent to which this ideological life-struggle is based on self-delusion. Temperamentally, he is unfit for the role he assigned himself. Very subtly (Martin du Gard's art here is rich in nuances), the reader is made to suspect that Barois' Jacobinic attitude, his dogmatic anti-dogmatism, his intolerant assertion of the metaphysics of Tolerance, all stem from a deep need to *believe*. In fact, his aggressiveness can be attributed to the intransigence of youth; life will mellow him and teach him that truths and errors may be provisional. Yet even in this youthful ardor there is something excessive. His lyrical hymns to intellectual liberty are no less disquieting than his "proud insolence." Far from freeing his mind, his so-called *"affranchissement"* only leads to an uncompromising attitude. All becomes for him a matter of principle; his relations with his wife, the education of his daughter—everything involves his "dignity," his "self-respect," his "fidelity" to himself and to his ideas. Free thought, paradoxically, turns into a doctrine. The apostate transmutes himself into a proselytizer. Such fanaticism casts doubt on Barois' ability to free himself. And, deep within him, he knows well what a strong hold these spurned beliefs still have on him. His very militancy bears witness to the resilience and elasticity of the Catholic faith. (pp. 94-8)

Barois' destiny is not the supreme message conveyed by the novel. Martin du Gard denies himself and the reader the right to draw conclusions from this private failure. The fate of the individual merges with the fate of his generation, and cannot be evaluated apart. The epigraph thus carries a double meaning: the "sick conscience," the battleground of modern fate, is in large part a collective conscience. In his Trocadéro lecture, Barois asserts with passion that he and his public belong to a privileged generation confronted by the arduous task of bringing about a scientific evolution. "We are one of the tragic moments of the painful agony of the past." Similarly Luce, at the end of the novel, assessing the hero's moral situation: "Barois, like so many others, is a victim of our times. His life has been that of many of my contemporaries:—tragic." Every character in the novel seems to be aware of his immersion in a particularly critical moment of history. They are not merely historical witnesses, but active participants in the political gest. Martin du Gard's studies at the Ecole des Chartes are no doubt largely responsible for the historical perspective. "It became impossible for me," he confides in his **"Souvenirs,"** "to conceive a modern character detached from his time." Claude-Edmonde Magny's contention that the Dreyfus case and the issue of modernism constitute "unhappy screens" between the reader and the inner life of Barois takes into account neither the originality of the author nor his success in binding together a private and a collective fatum.

Martin du Gard's non-religious, deterministic cast of mind goes a long way toward explaining his unwillingness ever to look on tragedy as an absolute. Each drama, for him, is tributary to a broader drama. He is, moreover, permanently fascinated by *groups;* they are, in his fictional world, as much a symbol of solidarity as a dissolvent of individual energies. Mazerelles, the young hero of *Devenir,* is enthused by the discovery of Barrès' *Les Déracinés,* and aspires to become the historian of his own generation. This interest in the life of a group, in its struggle and ultimate failure, owes much, it would seem, to the nineteenth-century novel: *Illusions perdues, L'Education sentimentale, Manette Salomon, L'Œuvre*—all portray successive generations, their dreams and their defeats. But no French novelist before Martin du Gard—not even Flaubert—has situated the human drama as unequivocally in its political and social context. "I will have had three somber dates in my life," Dr. Philip confides to Antoine in *L'Eté 1914.* "The first revolutionized my adolescence, the second unsettled my mature years, the third will probably poison my old age." Characteristically, all three crises, though profoundly personal, evoke the experience of an entire generation. The first is the discovery of the rift between science and faith; the second is the Dreyfus Affair; the third is the mass tragedy of the First World War.

Man—and more particularly the intellectual—is thus for Martin du Gard what Sartre was later to call an *être-en-situation:* a human being condemned to responsibility. First of all, responsibility in the face of inescapable issues. In *Jean Barois* these issues are so clear and so numerous that the editor Bernard Grasset hesitated to publish it, saying that it was less a novel than a "dossier." They are the problems which tormented serious-minded men at the turn of the century: Justice versus national interests; the clash between the temporal powers and the rights of the individual conscience; the prestige of Science (can an ethical system be derived from the scientific method?); the struggle between religion and free thought; the issue of Modernism (traditional Christian apologetics versus symbolist interpretations); popular universities and the duties of the intellectual toward the working class. . . . The clash of ideas, in *Jean Barois,* takes on heroic proportions; thought wrestles with thought. "A nation still capable of such effervescence over ideas," says Jean Barois as the fever of intellectual excitement reaches its highest pitch, "is far from declining."

"Barois découvre les hommes" ["Barois discovers men"], writes Camus—meaning that in the process of personal evolution he is led from his individuality to the awareness of a common history, the experience of human solidarity. This may only be partially true of Barois himself: his discovery of the community of men is soon followed by a withdrawal. But it is certainly true that the general movement of the book, even when it is most deeply rooted in an individual conscience, projects us toward the world of men and ideas. The lesson of Dr. Benassis in Balzac's *Le Médecin de campagne* applies directly: "Our conscience is the point of departure. We always proceed from ourselves to other men, never from other men to ourselves." The moral implications are clear. The intellectual, especially, has a debt to society. The privilege to devote himself to peaceful research and meditation—one of the protagonists explains—implies "inescapable obligations." He does not have the right to remain silent. Twenty-five years ahead of time, Martin du Gard uses the very vocabulary the Existentialists will wear threadbare in their praise of authenticity: *"Il faut que chacun de nous consente à sa vie"* ["Each of us must consent to his life"].

The structure of the novel points to the constant interpenetration of self and others, to the subsumption of the individual in a collective destiny. *Jean Barois* is divided into three parts: Part I ("The Will to Live," "The Symbolist Compromise," "The Ring," "The Chain," "The Rupture") deals with Barois' private problems, his religious doubts, his unhappy marriage, his separation from his wife; Part II (*"Le Semeur,"* "The Wind is Rising," "Storm," "Calm") centers primarily on the ideological war which is rending France; Part III ("The Flaw," "The Child," "The Critical Age," "Twilight") again stresses Barois' personal tragedy, his relation with his daughter, his illness, his religious conversion and his death. The novel seems, structurally, to move from Barois to the world of men and ideologies, and then back to Barois. Yet this is not altogether the case: the inner architecture of each section, and the very titles used, reveal that the author set out deliberately to alternate and intertwine the individual and the collective themes. Part I contains the obviously philosophical chapter "The Symbolist Compromise." Part III deals with such collective issues as the betrayal of the Dreyfus mystique and the rift between successive generations. As for the central portion of the novel, though primarily concerned with the storm into which Barois leads his group, it also suggests personal reasons for Barois' militant behavior and relates his encounter with death and fear in a chapter ironically entitled "Calm."

The collective theme finds its fullest orchestration in the lyrical passages that sing the enthusiasm, ideals and combativeness of the young intelligentsia. Subject and treatment alike are completely original. Only a few years earlier, Romain Rolland's Jean-Christophe remarked to his friend Olivier that the real poet of the Dreyfus case had as yet not appeared on the literary horizon. "The Dreyfus case has lifted your nation to the stars and plunged it into abysses. Where is the poet who has been inspired by the storm? The most beautiful struggle is taking place in religious minds between the authority of the Church and the rights of the individual conscience. Where is the poet who will reflect this sacred anguish?"

Jean Barois seems to answer this call. Certainly, no other work of fiction so movingly recaptures the epic climate of this battle of ideas. Léon Blum, who witnessed this "holy hysteria," considered *Jean Barois* an astonishing artistic re-creation of the *âme dreyfusarde* ["Dreyfusard spirit"]. Martin du Gard was no doubt well served by his objective-historical technique which not only permitted factual authenticity, but lent the occasional lyric outbursts the added intensity of restraint. The organizational meeting for *Le Semeur* is one of the most stirring episodes of the novel. The symbolic title echoes the spirit and aims of such actual publications as Péguy's famous *Cahiers.*

The youthful group discusses its projects with a timid, clumsy idealism. They all wish to give their intellectual life a social and political direction. With a common vibration, they respond to some lines quoted from Lamennais' *Paroles d'un croyant* which appear to sum up their own sense of prophetic mission. "Son of man! Ascend to the mountain top and proclaim what you behold!" Animated by a joyous and virile defiance, their first meeting culminates in a hymn to Progress. But the most solemn moments are to come. The decision to throw their energies into the Dreyfus battle is an apocalypse of commitment which makes all hearts beat in proud unison. "It is the beginning of superhuman exaltations. . . ." In passages such as these, the novel far transcends the problems or exploits of the individual protagonist. A whole generation is involved. "Many of us were heroes."

But this collective heroism also ends in collective frustration. The common *élan* is destined to lose its momentum and degenerate. This process, which parallels Barois' private decadence, is presented in three phases. The first is Luce's speech at the 1900 Exposition, his funeral oration of the Dreyfus case. Surveying the achievement of their group, Luce points to a number of disheartening facts. Agitators have exploited their victory; the flag of justice has been torn out of their hands and is now used by political opportunists to betray their idealism. A handful of pure *dreyfusistes* has been submerged by an army of *dreyfusards*. So many illusions have been lost along the way that it has become difficult, Luce concludes, not to surrender to pessimism. The second phase is the transfer of Zola's remains to the Panthéon—a vulgar, theatrical parade that marks the official exploitation of their victory. A great sadness weighs on the group: the very sadness experienced by a Péguy when he realized that the *mystique* of the crusade had degenerated into a *politique*. *Le Semeur* is losing its most faithful subscribers and mourns a "general bankruptcy." The third phase coincides with Barois' decision to resign as director of *Le Semeur*. With bitterness, he recapitulates the group's disillusions and concludes with the futility of their efforts. "Everywhere I see lies, self-interest, social injustice as before." Nothing has changed; nothing can change. A profound historical pessimism seems to be the answer to the loftiest ideals. "All the injustices, all the errors are reborn with each new generation; it will always be the same struggle, the same victory of the strong over the weak, of the young over the old—eternally." Cresteil's suicide is like an open proclamation of the group's tragic failure.

The futile antagonism between successive generations is given masterful treatment in the long scene that opposes an aging though still resilient Barois and two aggressive university students whose Catholic nationalism and virulent anti-liberalism have a strong Maurrassian flavor. Martin du Gard never dramatized more brilliantly a conflict of ideas. The altercation is presented with such stark economy, with such a concentration on essentials, that ideas no longer seem to require human beings to express them, and the antagonists appear to be there only to incarnate them much as an actor may assume a role which transcends the performance. Martin du Gard's private obsession—his intuition of the loneliness that comes with old age—is unquestionably at the center of this scene. Grenneville and Tillet, the two students, are insolent and unfair. Their deference is only another form of hostility. Their "impertinent smile" wounds Barois. But the personal suffering is less important here than the historico-philosophical implications of this *agon* of ideas.

Irresistibly impelled to view individuals and entire generations in the broader perspective of history and the necessary conjunction of Time and Circumstance, Martin du Gard seems to regard the outcome of collective effort no less pessimistically than he does that of the individual. Michelangelo's struggling *Slave* is also the adequate symbol for the group of *Le Semeur*. No generation can liberate itself. This is so partly because generations also are subject to the laws of atavism, and partly because even the most dynamic movement is only a reaction, and consequently part of the eternal ebb and flow. This is precisely Barois' most telling answer to the juvenile arrogance of his two young visitors: "Don't delude yourselves, gentlemen, as to your role.... You are nothing but a *reaction*. And this reaction is so inevitable that you can't even pride yourselves on having caused it: it's the oscillation of the pendulum...." No conclusion is ever possible because of the very necessity of movement. The pessimism is both philosophical and historical: the deterministic forces of the Universe make even rebellion synonymous with heredity. (pp. 105-11)

> Victor Brombert, "Martin du Gard's 'Jean Barois' and the Challenge of History," in his The Intellectual Hero: Studies in the French Novel, 1880-1955, *1961. Reprint by The University of Chicago Press, 1964, pp. 94-118.*

ROBERT GIBSON (essay date 1961)

[Gibson is an English critic and educator. In the following excerpt, he analyzes the world view presented in Martin du Gard's works.]

In the great bulk of his published work, Martin du Gard strictly observed the Flaubertian rule that the artist must take care to efface himself completely before his subject. But he himself was fully aware that complete impersonality was unattainable in literature, that even though the writer completely eschews personal confession, he still expresses himself through his choice of subjects, characters, and words. When he was invited to discuss his private life by newspaper reporters in Stockholm in 1937 he declined with the comment: "If you want to discover the true nature of an author, all you need do is to take the trouble to search through his writings. His work is the only reliable guide, the one unimpeachable witness, for it is there that even the most secretive of artists removes his mask and, in spite of himself, reveals his secret."

Though Martin du Gard warned critics not to be over-hasty in identifying him with any of his characters, it seems safe to assume that if, from work to work they continue to pursue the same ideals, they are likely to express certain of the essential preoccupations of their creator. It is of considerable significance, therefore, that each of the protagonists in *Devenir! Jean Barois*, and *Les Thibault* should reject any supernatural account of the Universe and seek purely human solutions to the major problems that confront them: it is no less significant that all their efforts should end in humiliating failure. Each of them stresses, or is warned, that self-knowledge is the key to all forms of human achievement: "The difficult thing is to be true to oneself, resolutely enough and long enough to discover how to be really authentic," Bernard Grosdidier says to the hero of *Devenir!*, and he adds with characteristic pessimism, "Nearly everyone fails." . . . Luce, Jean Barois, and Jacques Thibault state this same basic axiom in almost the same terms and with the same gloomy rejoinder. The most important message Antoine Thibault believes he can leave for his nephew, Jean-Paul, is the importance of self-knowledge and the difficulty of acquiring it: he dies confessing that he has never really been able to understand himself or the world about him. Armand, one of the minor characters in *Un Taciturne,* whose sardonic humour has much in common with Martin du Gard's own, reflects: "Your life is played out before your eyes like a charade . . . You spend your time looking for the answer to the riddle . . . Some people even find it, right at the end, when it's too late to be of any use." . . . (pp. 89-91)

Martin du Gard's central characters have even less success in understanding other people than in understanding themselves, and for this reason they are doomed to unhappiness in love. In Martin du Gard's world lasting satisfaction in love seems impossible chiefly because the basic aims of his men and women are utterly opposed. All his heroines are ready to consider the world well lost for love: Ketty Varine *(Devenir!),* Julia *(Jean Barois),* the prostitute who seduces the schoolboy Daniel *(Le Cahier gris),* Lisbeth *Le Pénitencier),* Rachel and Rinette *(La Belle Saison),* Anne de Battaincourt *(La Consultation, L'Eté 1914),* Amalia *(Confidence Africaine),* Isabelle and Wanda *(Un Taciturne)*—all these are powerfully sensual women, each ready to take the initiative, each prepared to sacrifice all moral scruples and conventional self-restraint to gratify their physical appetites once these have been aroused. Thérèse and Jenny de Fontanin have the same passionate natures and are able to dominate them only by the inhibiting power of their no less passionate puritanism. But while love, to Martin du Gard's women characters, is or could easily become their whole existence, to Barois and the Thibault brothers it can never be more than a brief diversion from their life's work. The only occasion when they are as passionately stirred as their partners is when they find themselves together in the presence of death or mortal danger: Barois first embraces Cécile as they stand at the bedside of his dying father, and he and Julia first feel intense physical desire for each other as a violent mob threatens to wreck the *Semeur* office; Jacques is seduced by Lisbeth immediately after the death of her aunt, and finally consummates his love with Jenny soon after the death of her father, when Europe is clearly intent on plunging into war; Antoine's passionate love-affair with Rachel begins immediately after, even in the course of, his dramatic fight to save a child's life, and he first feels violently attracted to Anne de Battaincourt when she pays her respects after the death of his father. For Martin du Gard's heroes, however, these are quite exceptional occasions: sexual indulgence is necessary to them, but it is never allowed to distract them for long from their main quest for integrity and truth.

For this same reason, Martin du Gard's protagonists all show a marked reluctance to take on marital responsibility: in *Devenir!* Mazerelles deserts Ketty Varine because she is so manifestly intent on marrying him, and he is finally persuaded to marry Denise Herzeaux only because of the lure of her attractive dowry; in *Jean Barois* Barois abruptly ends a youthful liaison with Huguette because he feels too domesticated; the section of the novel dealing with his marriage is significantly entitled *The Chain,* has for epigraph a sentence from Herzog, "Marriage is a danger only to the man who has ideas," and contains extracts from Jean's diary, in which he scorns women for what he considers to be their incurable sentimentality and their irremediable intellectual inferiority. None of the major characters in *Les Thibault* finds a happy or lasting love. (pp. 91-3)

Martin du Gard does not view sexual relationships, whether normal or abnormal, legal or illicit, with any of the mingled relish and distaste that characterizes the treatment of such subjects in the works of Zola, Gide, or Mauriac. Sexual passion may, in certain parts of Martin du Gard's work, stimulate over-

lurid flights of imagination, but it is never a subject for prurient gloating or righteous indignation. In his frank *Notes sur André Gide,* he takes a very much more serious view of his friend's continual self-dramatization than of his sexual misadventures: these are censured only because of the probable suffering they inflicted on Madame Gide, not because they are held to be wrong in themselves. "These things seem to happen quite naturally," says Leandro, discussing his incestuous love-affair with his own sister. "It's all perfectly simple really, when you think about it, if you see how one thing leads to another." . . . Armand makes almost the same resigned comment on Thierry's homosexuality as he does on middle-aged men who take to collecting obscene photographs: "These things just happen, you know—they can happen to perfectly respectable people." . . . Like Leandro and Armand, and like Antoine uncovering his patients' sordid secrets in *La Consultation,* Martin du Gard seems to have viewed deviations from the norm with compassion and with complete amorality, accepting them, like the sexual norm itself, as an inescapable part of human experience.

In his treatment of religious or political problems Martin du Gard preserves almost the same equanimity: he makes every conceivable effort to give a full, fair hearing to each side in any dispute, neither priests nor free-thinkers, neither bourgeois nor Marxists are allowed a monopoly of either virtues or vices. Though his Left Wing, humanistic sympathies are occasionally too strong to be disguised in *Jean Barois* and *Les Thibault,* in both these works he fully justifies his own description of himself as "a writer without prejudice . . . an independent who has freed himself from the fascination of any partisan ideology," one of those "whose constant care is to develop their personal conscience, in order to keep their inquiring mind as objective, as emancipated, and as fair as is humanly possible."

On one topic, however, Martin du Gard seems to have been quite unable to remain impartial. One section of the community remained in his view the subject for either coarse humour—the only humour in his work, in fact, apart from the inconsiderable eccentricities of Monsieur Chasles—or savage satire: these were the French peasants.

Martin du Gard's two rural farces, both written as a diversion from the prosperous bourgeois world in which he spent his life and which he chose to portray in each of his major novels, were both composed in authentic Berrichon dialect. Both recall medieval *fabliaux,* with the unequivocal earthiness of their language and situations and the guilt and rapacity of their peasant protagonists. In *Le Testament du Père Leleu,* Alexandre, an old countryman, dies without leaving a will; Torine, who for long has acted as his servant and his concubine, on the tacit understanding that she is to be his sole legatee, decides not to report his death until old Leleu, a neighbour who bears a striking resemblance to Alexandre, has impersonated the dead man in the village notary's presence and drawn up a will in her favour. Leleu agrees to the masquerade, but outwits his accomplice by willing both the chattels and Torine to his real self. *La Gonfle* is rather more indelicate in language and situation, and has never been acted: La Bique, a possessive spinster, is suffering from acute dropsy; her servant girl, La Nioule, a deaf mute, is pregnant either by the local veterinary surgeon, Gustave, who is La Bique's nephew, or by Andoche, her handyman and paramour, who is also the village sacristan. The action is completely dominated by Andoche, who extracts the maximum personal benefit from the situation, and recounts a great number of scabrous stories while his various plots are being hatched: Gustave is persuaded, by fear of scandal and hope of reward, to administer an anaesthetic to both women, to relieve La Bique of her dropsy and to deliver La Nioule of her baby, which is at once transported to the bed of her still unconscious employer: Andoche thus averts the danger of losing his job for having seduced La Nioule and, by claiming to be the father of La Bique's child, ensures that she will marry him and so give him complete charge of her possessions.

In *Vieille France,* which Martin du Gard wrote at Sauveterre in the spring of 1932 after destroying *L'Appareillage,* the humour is no less earthy but very much more sardonic. Like *La Consultation* or *Le Diable Boiteux,* it describes the hidden and, for the most part, sordid lives of the outwardly respectable citizens with whom the central character comes into contact in the course of a single day. Martin du Gard's Astaroth is Joigneau, postman to the imaginary village of Maupeyrou, and by the time his daily round is over, the secrets of every household have been laid bare. There is not a single contented character in the whole community, and scarcely a virtuous one: the younger wives and husbands all lust after their neighbours' bodies and worldly goods, and are all unfaithful and dishonest in thought if not in deed; the young people think only of escaping to the bright lights of the city, the old live in squalor and look to death for merciful release. Everyone is consumed with either envy or lust or malice or physical decay: the postman who dominates the action is different from the others only because he is more cunning, more grasping, and more actively lecherous than the rest. There are only two small centres of comparative enlightenment in this primeval jungle, and they themselves are menaced from within by disillusionment: these are the village church, attended only by prurient old maids and by sex-starved war-widows, where the village curé has long since turned his back on his flock to devote all his attention to his gardening, and the village school, where the frustrated schoolmaster and his sister are saved from total despair only by their Marxist hopes that their fellowmen will be miraculously transformed by social revolution.

In *Vielle France* Martin du Gard has clearly abandoned the principles of impersonality and benign equanimity which play so conspicuous a part in shaping all his other work. His overt satirical intentions are conveyed not only by the relish with which he highlights every ugly defect, or by the care he takes to suppress every possible redeeming virtue of country life, but by a variety of minute details. By what are obviously his own personal interpolations: thus, the clerical Church clock is always *"naturally"* ten minutes slower than the clock on the Republican schoolhouse; the inside window-sills of the *bien-pensant* Madame Massot are strewn with dead flies, "they died," observes the narrator, "of sheer boredom"; Joseph, the young apprentice who lodges with Joigneau, pauses for a moment outside the bedroom door behind which waits Madame Joigneau, only too eager to pay back her husband for his many acts of infidelity; Joseph, however, innocently decides to continue his way upstairs, followed by what can only be the author's comment, "The fool!" Other ways in which Martin du Gard expresses his irony are the figures of speech he occasionally employs, zeugma particularly: thus, "Madame Massot knits away, shut away inside her room and her deafness"; and Tulle, a one-armed war-veteran, is said to be supported by "France and his sister, Madame Bosse." But what most eloquently conveys Martin du Gard's distaste for the characters he is portraying is his use of animal-imagery.

Animal-magery is sometimes applied to characters in *Les Thibault*: thus the eyes of Mademoiselle de Waize, the Thibault

family housekeeper, are said to be like a doe's when she is in repose, but like a hen's when she is startled; Gise's eyes are compared to those of a faithful dog; and Pastor Gregory, to both a spider and a monkey. It is noticeable, however, that these are all minor characters, and that the undistinguished animal similes are employed in the main for mildly comic purposes. In *Vieille France* Martin du Gard's use of animal-imagery to describe the physical or moral deficiencies of his villagers is at once more savage and more systematic. Scarcely a single inhabitant of Maupeyrou is spared: Joigneau, the arch-schemer, is likened to a spider spinning a web; Loutre, the market-gardener, has a neck like a chicken; Mademoiselle Ennberg, the schoolmistress, has the jaws of a pike; . . . Madame Touche, one of three embittered war-widows, has cheeks like cutlets of raw veal; Monsieur des Navières, who in his senile decay keeps a tormented vigil over the worthless pieces of rubbish he imagines to be valuable antiques, "swallows back his saliva with the noise a carp makes as it sucks a piece of moist bread." The whole work, Martin du Gard declared in the brief description he composed for advance publicity purposes, was meant to portray "a swarm of microbes in a drop of stagnant water".

Because of its sustained virulence, *Vieille France* occupies a unique place among Martin du Gard's works. It makes the same scathing indictment of French country life as *Les Paysans* of Balzac, as *La Terre,* as the rural *contes* of Maupassant, but it is not a mere pastiche: it is the deliberate expression of bitter personal antipathy. In a letter to Jean Schlumberger he described *Vieille France* as "a picture gallery filled with ugly faces and cold, cruel, greedy hearts—a world impossible to defend." When he was criticized by Marcel Arland for drawing such a gloomy picture of French country life Martin du Gard felt obliged, for the only time in his long career, to explain his motives in a letter to the Press. "Even though one examines that accursed race [of peasants] with all one's love for one's fellow-men," he wrote in *La Nouvelle Revue Française* in June 1933, "it is rare indeed to find the slightest spark of decency. . . ." "I did not think people would find any cruelty in my book," he said in this same letter, "I thought they would be struck only by its note of despair." (pp. 96-104)

In the letter he wrote in 1933 to defend *Vieille France,* Martin du Gard insisted that he had not intended to satirize the whole of humanity, merely the French peasant; he maintained that he had high hopes of the urban proletariat and that if genuine Socialism were allowed to transform the world, mankind would reveal undreamed-of unselfish, fraternal, and possibly even spiritual qualities. This view is expressed recurrently throughout Martin du Gard's novels, but with significantly less confidence in his later work: in *Jean Barois* Marc-Elie Luce and the *Semeur* group are serene in their conviction that world social revolution will inevitably bring about a moral rejuvenation of the human race; Mademoiselle Ennberg, the Marxist schoolmistress in *Vieille France,* is much less optimistic:

> She broods over her loneliness, over the life of the village, over this bestial humanity still crawling in the lower depths. Why is the world like this? Is it really the fault of society? . . . And the terrifying question she has so often asked herself returns to haunt her once more: 'Is the fault not really in mankind itself?' But she has in her heart such a need for faith and so much innocent fervour, that she cannot bring herself to doubt in human nature. No, no! . . .

Only let a new social order come into being—
better organized, less irrational, less unjust—
and perhaps at last Man will show what he is
really capable of. . . .

                                        (pp. 106-07)

Jacques Thibault clings no less desperately to his Socialist
hopes because they are all that give his life any purpose, but
only intermittently can he feel any confidence in Mankind
itself: "He felt infinite pity for his fellow-men, but he remained
sceptical about their moral possibilities"; . . . and his scepticism is amply justified when the nations of Europe march so
eagerly to war, and when, as he lies dying after his futile leaflet
flight, hostile peasants refuse to give him a drink, and burn
him with lighted cigarette stubs. The war destroys Antoine's
faith in the unbounded powers of Science as it destroys Jacques'
faith in the strength of international Socialism. Antoine dies,
willing himself to believe in Humanity, but like Voltaire at the
end of his *Essai sur les Mœurs*, appalled by the spectacle of
the docility of the common people in the clutches of their rulers,
and all too grimly aware of the thousands of years that must
still elapse before Reason can bring about the reign of universal
brotherhood on earth.

The greatest single cause of both individual and international
suffering in Martin du Gard's world is not the wilful malice
of his characters, but their helplessness against the blind and
omnipotent forces of determinism: Barois is foredoomed to
failure because the lessons of his Catholic upbringing leave as
permanent an imprint on his mind as his grave childhood illness
on his body; Jacques Thibault is driven to become a Socialist
rebel because of his father's tyranny and the insensitivity of
his Catholic schoolteachers; Antoine is shocked to discover,
as he lies dying, that he has unconsciously adopted the laugh
and speech-habits of his father; the Fontanin children inherit
their parents' passionate natures, but because of their mother's
different attitude to them both, Daniel becomes a lecher and
Jenny grows up a prude; Thierry and his father both commit
suicide because they fall hopelessly in love with their secretary;
Michel Luzzato is condemned to a sickly life and an early death
because his parents were brother and sister. The nations are
no less subject to the rigorous rule of determinism than individuals: Jacques and Antoine both conclude that the First World
War was mainly caused neither by the machinations of a few
evil statesmen, nor by overpugnacious General Staffs, nor even
by the effects of international capitalism, but by the inability
of the human race to evolve beyond its tribal past. Propa-
gandists of each State can always make a successful appeal to
the primitive pride and fears of their citizens, because in all
men lurks a powerful atavistic urge to destroy: Philip, the most
outstanding clinician in *Les Thibault,* reflects: "Perhaps the
instinctive urge to destroy, the periodic need to bring crashing
to the ground all that we have so laboriously raised up, is one
of the fundamental laws which impose a limit on the constructive possibilities of our nature. Perhaps this is one of those
mysterious and galling laws which the wise man must recognize
and accept." . . . Philip is as much admired by Antoine as
Marc-Elie Luce by Barois, and it is difficult to avoid the conclusion that, with Luce, he is the character who most directly
expresses the views of Martin du Gard himself.

It was not, however, his belief in universal determinism that
most dominated Martin du Gard's thought and work. He noted
in 1918: "I realize that *all my life*, the whole secret of my life
(and also of my artistic vocation, of my will to survive), the
motive force of all my efforts, the source of all my emotions

is my *fear of death*, my struggle against oblivion, dust and
Time." His lifelong preoccupation with death is apparent from
the remarkable amount of space it occupies in his work: in
Noizemont-les-Vierges he reveals that as a very young child
one of the favourite haunts during his school holidays was the
village cemetery, and that his first awareness of the reality of
death came just after the funeral service for his beloved grandmother; in his discarded youthful novel, *Marise,* he planned
to study the old age and death of his heroine with particular
care; Denise Mazerelles in *Devenir!,* Luce, Jean Barois and
his father, M. Thibault, Jacques, Antoine, Jérôme de Fontanin,
his mistress Noémie, Nicole's baby daughter—the deaths of
each of these are not only described in minute detail but inspire
his most powerful writing.

What most fascinated Martin du Gard was not so much the
physical processes of death, as the emotional responses of the
dying person. Like Montaigne, he considered that "he who
could teach men how to die, would teach them how to live."
His main characters all search for a faith that will enable them
to die with peace and dignity, and it is clearly indicative of
Martin du Gard's own personal views that while his Catholics,
Barois and Monsieur Thibault, die hysterically, his rationalists,
Luce and Antoine, die with unruffled calm. Their quiet acceptance of death was the ideal that Martin du Gard himself
aspired to in life: he was particularly inspired by his former—
Catholic—schoolteacher, l'abbé Hébert, whose serenely So-
cratic approach to death provided the model for the death of
Marc-Elie Luce, and by the last moments of Gide, whose death
he witnessed. "To see such a calm death, does one good,"
he declared at the end of his *Notes sur André Gide.* "This
renunciation and this exemplary acceptance of the natural law
are contagious. We must be infinitely grateful to him for having
been able to die so *well.*" . . . All the evidence that has been
made available since his own death suggests that Martin du
Gard approached it with the same serenity as the most stoical
of his characters and his friends.

Because, throughout his career, Martin du Gard remained convinced of the omnipotence of determinism and the finality of
death, and could find no consolation in any scientific, political,
or religious beliefs, it is scarcely surprising that the most distinctive quality of his thought and of his work should be pessimism. The ambitions of all his characters are for the most
part cruelly thwarted: Mazerelles never becomes a great writer;
the materialist testament of Barois and the pacifist tracts of
Jacques Thibault, the writings they most want to be read, are
destroyed before they reach their public; Antoine is struck down
in the prime of life with his dreams of fame unrealized, and
like Jérôme de Fontanin and Thierry, he takes his own life.
Martin du Gard's personal despair is given distinctive stress,
however, not only by the number of agonizing deaths and
suicides in his works but by the scenes and images which so
often end them: the closing words of *L'Eté 1914, "Fumier!
Fumier! Fumier!"* ["Trash! Trash! Trash!"], which serve as
ordinary mankind's final comment on Jacques' foolhardy bid
to avert war; Armand's bitter cry of *"L'imbècile!"* on which
the final curtain descends on *Un Taciturne,* after Thierry has
just committed suicide; Mademoiselle Ennberg's nightmare at
the end of *Vieille France* when she, the most fervent guardian
of what little human decency there is in the village, dreams
her brother is strangling his wife with a clothes-line. Each of
these is as telling as the last line of a successful sonnet or the
final fade-out shot of a well-made film.

Certain of Martin du Gard's other works, however, end on a
slightly less despairing note: the servant girl watching Mazer-

elles from the window, at the end of **Devenir!** and who, it is subtly implied, will sooner or later console him for the loss of his wife; the scene that concludes **Confidence Africaine,** in which the hero's sister, transformed from a lithe adolescent to an obese matron, is seen suckling a gluttonous infant; Antoine's last message to Jean-Paul, telling him that he must pass on the torch of life to his son in turn, even though its purpose might for ever elude him. These conclusions express the last meagre hope that the humanist still desperately clings to, when confronted with such abundant evidence of man's inhumanity and of God's indifference to man: the irrational faith that though human lives may be destroyed, Life itself goes on, probably imperfectible and, in the pre-nuclear age when Martin du Gard was writing, seemingly indestructible. (pp. 107-13)

Robert Gibson, in his Roger Martin du Gard, *Hillary House Publishers Ltd.*, 1961, 128 p.

DENIS BOAK   (essay date 1963)

[*Boak is an English critic whose area of special interest is modern French fiction. In the following excerpt, he discusses humanism and pessimism in Martin du Gard's work.*]

The question of humanism is cardinal to an understanding of Martin du Gard; indeed, in the last analysis, his work stands or falls with the humanist philosophy. Despite his aim of transparency of style, despite his attempt to remain impartial and objective in his narrative, his entire work rests upon the philosophy of humanism, which we may define as the search for a meaning in life in a world without God. This is indeed one of the fundamental themes of the modern novel, but its implications have rarely been so searchingly examined as by Martin du Gard. For him, death is the primary *donnée* of the human condition, and death inevitably means personal annihilation; man must therefore find a meaning within life, since no escape from death is possible. Man has in fact to act as if there were no death.

This humanism pervades his entire work, but is especially prominent in **Les Thibault.** Its manifestations are to be found in the identification of evil with suffering, so that Antoine in his fight against disease becomes a symbol of Man; or in such details as Martin du Gard's apparently more favourable attitude towards the Fontanins in the first two volumes. This springs from his belief in the value of the individual and in individual responsibility: the Protestant religion approaches closer to this ideal than the Catholic, so he regards Mme de Fontanin's upbringing of her children as superior to M. Thibault's more rigid methods. Yet his treatment, even of morally objectionable characters, is always charitable; their weaknesses are painted as essentially human ones; and if any character, such as Jérôme, is utterly condemned in the novel, it is not on moral principles but because his attitude to life is inadequate to guarantee happiness either to himself or to others.

The theme of vocation is central to this humanism, which accounts for its importance in the novel, together with the related themes of education, adolescence, and ambition. Antoine's strictures to Jean-Paul in **Epilogue** form Martin du Gard's final message: "Accepte-toi, avec tes bornes et tes manques. Et applique-toi à te développer, sainement, normalement, sans tricher, dans ta vraie destination . . ." ["Accept yourself, with your limitations and deficiencies. And apply yourself to developing yourself, sanely, normally, without cheating, toward your true objective"]; and the lives of Daniel, Jacques, and Antoine himself, can only be judged in the light of this theme.

Daniel, prior to the war, seems to have developed a satisfactory attitude towards life, in his life of unbridled egoism and calculated irresponsibility. He embodies the Gidean ideal, and the damage he inflicts on others, such as Rinette, has already been shown in **La Belle Saison.** In *Eté 1914* and **Epilogue** he is no longer able to live divorced from the historical context of the age—"ce merveilleux refuge où il avait eu le privilège de pouvoir installer sa vie" ["This marvellous refuge into which he had had the privilege of being able to install his life"]—after violent contact with that historical context, he finds himself unable to live at all. His art had depended not upon his spiritual resources but upon his sexual capabilities, and once these are destroyed he cannot face life. His attitude is therefore clearly negative, both morally and practically.

In Jacques's case, we are shown another aspect of the relationship of the individual with society, Jacques never attempts, like Daniel, completely to isolate himself from his fellow men; even his *fugues* are primarily motivated by his inability to make adequate contact with his family and those around him, not by any fundamental misanthropy. But in fact he can never adjust himself, even to ordinary social contacts; his egoism is no less thoroughgoing than Daniel's. Not only does he unnecessarily ruin two lives—those of Jenny and Gise—his craving for total ideological independence prevents him from making the best use of his gifts and abilities. His desire for purity largely takes the form, not of spiritual or sexual innocence, but of escape from any type of practical social responsibility—despite his emotional sympathy for the underprivileged. He can never bring himself to abdicate his individuality and submit himself to the will of the collectivity; he is indeed a rebel, not a revolutionary, and his rebellion is caused by his own psychological deficiencies. There is no doubt that Jacques is not intended to be the subject of admiration; his attitude too is inadequate in the face of the more violent aspects of life. When the cataclysm overtakes Europe he cannot accept it, and his death is only another form of escape. Thus pure idealism is not satisfactory; heroism even less so, since it merely leads him to an absurdly undignified end. (Meynestrel offers another illustration of the inadequacy of the revolutionary attitude; although war will, he believes, offer the opportunity for successful revolutionary action, he cannot live without a satisfactory emotional relationship; and when Alfreda leaves him he too takes refuge in virtual suicide.)

This negative conclusion in respect of Daniel and Jacques is, at first sight, reversed in Antoine's case, since his development appears to follow a steadily positive course (with the exception of his worldly attitude immediately prior to the outbreak of war, an episode inserted, no doubt, mainly to serve as an antithesis to Jacques's life in Geneva and to Antoine's own subsequent career). He is, above all, the representative of the humanist philosophy; the keynote is *équilibre* ["equilibrium"] and *sens de la mesure* ["sense of proportion"]. In the original plan, we may well believe that he was intended as the successful counterpart to Jacques, achieving full development, a complete sense of integration in and involvement with society. In **Epilogue** he does so: only to die. It is a strange but deliberate parallel that the lives of so many of the characters end in suicide: Jacques, Jérôme, Daniel (who intends suicide), and Antoine. Yet only in one case does the act of suicide not imply escapism from life: Antoine takes his own life as the supreme method of showing that even in death he has some control over his environment, that only he can decide the exact moment of death. Elsewhere there is no dignity in death. Yet Antoine is destroyed nevertheless. His fate represents Martin du Gard's final conception of life: in the end, whatever man's success within life, death will claim him. In a world without God, no attitude is adequate: the attempt to transcend the self, to find a replacement for religion—and immortality—must always fail. Daniel attempts a life of art and sensuality, Jacques one of revolutionary action, Antoine one of energetic activity and service to the community, Barois a crusade for freedom of thought; in the long run, none succeeds, and the only difference is in the degree of temporary satisfaction. In the privileged conditions of pre-1914 life, Daniel and both Thibaults seem to have found solutions which are adequate in the short run; but once those favourable circumstances have disappeared, only Antoine can adjust his attitude. Finally he too is destroyed, but from outside, not from within. His death is in the stoical tradition; while his diary, intended for Jean-Paul, is a second *Bouteille à la mer* ["bottle in the sea"].

There can be no doubt that Martin du Gard's conclusion is one of black pessimism; and this has earned him a good deal of criticism, on the ground that his work represents an arid materialism, that no ray of light is visible in his conception of man. Mme Magny has, for instance, charged him with creating "un univers sans issue" [a universe without escape], and has claimed that his world is "muré dans son tragique intérieur" ["walled up in its tragic interior"]. Yet this criticism is largely beside the point. His tragic conception of life is not the conclusion, but the premiss of his work; and to disagree with this conception is to pass a moral judgment in his *Weltanschauung*, not an aesthetic judgment upon his artistic achievement. (This would be perfectly legitimate, but it implies assimilating all aesthetic judgments to moral ones, a step which few literary critics are willing to take.) Mme Magny goes on to state that the idea of *la condition humaine* is absent from *Les Thibault*; this again would appear to be misconceived, for it is precisely a vivid perception of the human condition which inspires Martin du Gard's tragic conception of life and therefore his pessimism. The primary themes of his work are metaphysical, as we have seen, and it is this which most clearly differentiates him from writers following more closely in the Naturalist tradition. Pessimism is an integral part of humanism; self-transcendence, *dépasser l'homme* ["to go beyond man"], is by definition impossible. Man must live upon his own moral resources; each individual is both unique and uniquely valuable.

This pessimistic humanism was Martin du Gard's basic attitude throughout his life, since it sprang fundamentally from his lack of religious belief. It was however powerfully reinforced by the effect of the 1914-18 War upon him. Although, when he began *Les Thibault,* he was treating largely the same themes which had interested him before 1914, by the early 1930's he found himself unable to ignore the disaster which had overtaken the Europe of his youth, and, almost alone among modern novelists, he chose to end his major novel with a catastrophe. This is a long way from the naïve belief in progress which some critics have claimed to perceive in his work. He does not believe that the world is bound to improve, but that the only hope for mankind lies in the possibility of its being perfected, in the intelligent employment of man's rational faculties. Antoine's action in spending the last weeks of his life writing advice to Jean-Paul and keeping a record of his own mortal illness for publication, so that it might help future sufferers, illustrates this hope in the future. Ultimately all effort is absurd, but while we are still alive it must be regarded as worth while. Only thus can man attain any final dignity in life. In Martin du Gard we can observe the same search for ethical imperatives in a meaningless world which we later find in

Existentialist writers, the quest for an answer to the question, "A quoi ça rime, la vie?" ["What is the point of it all?"]. He can find no answer, and his pessimism is ultimately absolute; but it would be a bold man who today would prophesy that this pessimism could in no circumstances be justified.

It is difficult to assess Martin du Gard's chances of survival as a novelist. It is certain, however, that since the last war his reputation has been in decline, outshone by younger writers whose works seem to have more relevance to the present generation. One criticism has been that his thought has never progressed beyond 1918, or even 1914. In one sense his is true: he was never able (unless he finally succeeded in *Maumort*) to find an adequate poet-1918 vehicle for his themes and characters. The modern reader tends to demand a modern setting for the novel, and the idea of a leisurely work in ten or more volumes has been running counter to the popularity of the quick-moving narrative of the novel of adventure or violence. Even a studied realism has tended to give way to fantasy and allegory. Yet basically Martin du Gard's themes are very similar to those of Malraux, Sartre, or Camus: one need only compare Jacques's career and his attempt at a heroic suicide with that of Kyo Gisors or Tchen in *La Condition humaine,* or Mathieu in *Les Chemins de la Liberté.* The theme of the relationship of the individual and the collectivity and the search for a satisfactory replacement for religion is common to both Malraux and Martin du Gard; while Antoine's fight against disease and suffering is closely paralleled by that of Rieux in *La Peste* (it is not for nothing that Camus has shown such sympathetic understanding of Martin du Gard's work in his *Préface*). There is even a parallel between *Barois* and *Les Mandarins:* in both novels we find the same rather arid intellectual atmosphere, the same preoccupation with ideas and their propagation, the same involvement with practical politics. The greatest difference between Martin du Gard and these later writers (apart from his greater pessimism) lies in the vehicle chosen, which in their case is more striking and more immediately relevant to the present historical context.

Les Thibault, in particular *Eté 1914* and *Epilogue,* is not adequate to carry the full burden of Martin du Gard's message and his art. Yet it has qualities which may well, in an era possessed of more leisure—or more perseverance—than our own, ensure its survival as a minor classic; above all its moral coherence as an expression of humanism and its absolute refusal to distort the reality of life, however unpalatable that reality may be. Martin du Gard is not a great thinker, despite the appearance of *Barois,* since all his ideas are no more than second-hand (save in the one sphere of literary technique, where he follows in the tradition of Flaubert and Henry James). His work lacks Proust's depth of psychological analysis; but he has nevertheless created an admirable gallery of characters, and in particular of sexuality is vivid and convincing, without ever descending to obscenity or exhibitionism. His attitude to life makes him a *moraliste* in the finer sense: he portrays the world from a definite moral viewpoint; his patient craftsmanship and the ideal of transparent style made his work immune from facile imitation (he has no obvious mannerisms), and it will always yield value to the perceptive reader. His life and achievement will remain a minor monument in the field of human endeavour. (pp. 207-13)

Denis Boak, in his Roger Martin du Gard, *Oxford at the Clarendon Press, 1963, 223 p.*

JUSTIN O'BRIEN   (essay date 1967)

[*O'Brien is an American critic who has written extensively on modern French literature and has translated important works by*

*André Gide, Albert Camus, and Paul Valéry. In the following
excerpt, he explains why he considers* The World of the Thibaults
a masterpiece.]

It is one thing to call a book a masterpiece of irony or its
author's masterpiece and quite another to call it a masterpiece.
The qualifying phrase reduces the value of that fearful and
magic word by at least one-half. A scrupulous reviewer is
inclined to sterilize the word thus every time he uses it, but
twice or thrice in a lifetime he meets a book about which he
feels no hesitation. This is such a case, for [*The World of the
Thibaults*] is a masterpiece.

Perhaps the work's chief distinction lies in the fact that it is a
pure novel—in other words, one which aims to represent life
rather than to reflect upon it. The ascetic régime Martin du
Gard followed for so many years at Bellême, writing a regular
number of hours every day in a room lined with reference
works and filing cases, recalls the arduous life of Flaubert, the
hermit of Croisset, whom he resembles moreover in his willingness to destroy completed manuscripts and rewrite the same
volume four or five times. In his early paleographical and
archeological study at the Ecole des Chartes he acquired a
scholarly method which makes of his work the result of a unique
collaboration between the historian and the novelist. Yet for
all that, he possesses the true artist's faculty for synthesis,
which protects him from being blinded by the individual as
Jules Romains often is, in whose work documentation too frequently substitutes for creation. Roger Martin du Gard differs
from all his contemporaries, besides, in that his style marks
an absence of style. In an age of literary affectation, he has
written with such directness and limpidity that not even the
slightest film, as Gide commented, interposes itself between
the reader and the life whose unfolding he follows with passionate interest.

The reality of that life, throbbing and multiform, strikes one
from the very first page with its sudden projection of the reader
into the drama of Jacques's and Daniel's flight from home.
The gradual revelation of the various personalities within the
Thibault and Fontanin families becomes so absorbing that not
until a second reading does one notice the author's skillful use
of the multiple plot that Gide and Huxley were to borrow in
The Counterfeiters and *Point Counter Point*. Jérôme de Fontanin's many infidelities, his daughter Jenny's illness and the
Christian Science healer's intervention, Antoine Thibault's reactions to his father's pomposity, all in the first chapters, seize
the reader's attention. The rest of the novel contains no disappointment: Antoine's improvised operation on a little girl
(already included in French anthologies) and his passionate
love affair with Rachel, Daniel's philanderings in the manner
of his father, Jacques's tender love for Jenny and his sufferings
in the reformatory, Antoine's daring effort to shorten his father's death agony, are passages which show the author's mastery of situations and emotions. At once the reader establishes
direct contact with the characters.

For over fifteen years Martin du Gard has lived in seclusion
with the same characters, whose number, in view of the extent
of the novel, is remarkably small—only ten or a dozen of major
importance. As Daniel, now a young painter, says in the second
half of the novel: "Everything I have learned I have drawn
from the tenacious study of a single model. Why change? You
do much better work when you force yourself to return constantly to the same starting point, when each time you have to
start all over again and go farther in the same direction. If I
had been a novelist, I think that instead of changing my char-

acters with each book I should have clung indefinitely to the
same ones, in order to dig deeper.'' This passage, the only
one in which a character seems to speak for the author, reveals
Martin du Gard's method. Combining a taste for vast constructions and a lively sense of individual qualities, he still does
not claim to reconstruct all of contemporary life in the manner
of Balzac or Zola. Rather he gives, under the name of one of
them, the history of two families during about a dozen prewar
years. Though these families, one Catholic and the other Protestant, represent a large section of the Parisian *bourgeoisie*,
the author in no way uses them as symbols. In *The Counterfeiters*, André Gide likewise depicts the dissolution of two
families of the same class, one Catholic and the other Protestant, and the dedication of that novel to Roger Martin du
Gard implies a recognition of his debt, fully acknowledged
elsewhere.

The debt is, however, mutual, as is evident from the unforgettable description . . . of Daniel de Fontanin's discovery of
Gide's *Nourritures terrestres*. That breviary of revolt and self-
expression gave Daniel the courage to be himself. It may well
have furnished also the starting point for *The World of the
Thibaults*, for the novel's major theme is that of evasion with
the idea of revolt either expressed or implied. Jacques Thibault
constantly burns with a peculiarly Gidian gemlike flame. After
his first unsuccessful flight with Daniel at fourteen, followed
by a period of calm smouldering, he makes another break for
freedom, this time fully successful, years later; and his last
act, after the outbreak of war, is to attempt to soar above the
horrible reality into the ideological. Rachel's mysterious departure for Africa to join a man she fears provides another
example of evasion. Gide himself has hardly more often illustrated his doctrine of fervor and unrest leading to a salutary
uprooting of body and mind. Nor has he, in *his* chronicle of
the liquidation of two families, more vigorously translated into
action his early statement: "Families, I hate you! Closed circles
around the hearth! Fast shut doors . . . .'' Gide has unquestionably influenced, and in turn been influenced by, Martin du
Gard, thus providing the truth of his contention that literary
influence does not create but rather awakens. Even if Gide had
never existed, Roger Martin du Gard would still be one of the
few truly great modern writers of French prose.

In French the entire novel is simply called *Les Thibault*. But
the English title is quite justified since around old Oscar Thibault and his sons Jacques and Antoine, there move other
characters and there exists a palpable world made up of objects
and places that are as real to us as their analogues in our own
lives. Often they are so real as to usurp a place in the reader's
life: for whoever has been enthralled by the novel—and I doubt
if anyone who has begun has not been—certain squares and
corners of Paris and Geneva belong now to Jacques or Antoine.
Upon meeting a flesh-and-blood Dr. Thibault in Paris not long
ago, I told him that I already knew someone with the same
name and title; "Yes," he replied, "through Martin du Gard,
but my first name is not Antoine.''

In the second volume the canvas broadens perceptibly and the
Thibault microcosm reflects more fully the European macro-
cosm of 1914 and its headlong rush toward war. Jacques, by
then a militant socialist, does his part in Geneva, Paris, and
Brussels to warn of the impending catastrophe and to organize
resistance to a passive acceptance of it. Before the summer of
1939, those chapters might have seemed to some readers too
faithful a reproduction of the anguish felt only by the most
alert in 1914; today they have an added poignancy and truth

because we have all lived through such emotions. Actually, the approach of war, seen from the vantage point of the Second International and contrasted in its last stage with the successful outcome of Jacques's and Jenny's love, forms a stirring narrative. (pp. 246-49)

Until his tragic and futile, yet wholly appropriate, death soon after the outbreak of hostilities, Jacques holds the reader's attention most insistently. In a sense the whole novel could have ended there, for its most obvious subject is the story of an adolescent who never grew up, who refused indeed to grow up. A youth marked by "an innate revulsion from injustice" finds himself at fourteen in a world full of injustice. Quite naturally he revolts, first by fleeing home and school, a second time by fleeing his recent past and a brilliant future career, and finally by spurning the whole war-torn world and dying for an ideal. The Epilogue, however, is essential not only to round out the world of the Thibaults, but also to provide a very human and very real apotheosis of Jacques. For by 1918, when his and Jenny's son is four years old and Antoine, fatally gassed, is slowly dying in a hospital, Jacques's spirit has communicated itself to all the other principal characters. Not only Jenny, who now idolizes his memory, but also Antoine and Daniel and even the diplomat Rumelles have seen the futility of the war and come to share the ideas with which Jacques shocked them in 1914. Antoine's diary, at the end of the whole novel, shows him resembling his brother more and more as he approaches death; in him a maturer Jacques dies a second time. More acutely than ever, the reader recognizes that these characters, with whom he has lived in close communion, remain faithful to themselves through all the changes brought by time, accidents, disease, and world catastrophe.

Although the action of the novel covers only the period from about 1905 to the end of 1918, it also reflects very strongly the last twenty years during which Martin du Gard composed it. As a result, it brings out by implication more strongly than any other novel the close affinity between what we called until lately the prewar and the postwar. Chronicling an era that ended during the First World War, the author constantly has a thought for death—despite the general robustness and health of his work. Part six deals with the father's agony, part seven ends with Jacques's death, and part eight with Antoine's. Even making allowances for the technical utility and brilliance of some of the death scenes, one must admit that this is a pessimistic novel written by an idealist who nevertheless sees life as it is and deliberately remains objective. Upon receiving the Nobel Prize in 1937—one of the very few times that he has consented to speak of himself publicly—Roger Martin du Gard defined himself as "an independent writer who has escaped the fascination of partisan ideologies, an investigator as objective as is humanly possible, as well as a novelist striving to express the tragic quality of human lives." That quality is here in abundance. Yet the disappearance of Jacques and Antoine is also symbolic. And as he wrote the last lines of his novel, the author already knew that he was witnessing the death of another epoch. But he has wisely left these implications for the reader to make.

Though he is anything but reactionary in politics and his general view of life, Roger Martin du Gard remains a conservative in his literary method and habits of mind. His patient system of documentation that filled his house in the French countryside with reference cards for his great work, his love of the exact sciences that caused him to give medicine such an important role, and his general distrust of religion and metaphysics came

to him doubtless during his early studies as a paleographer and archeologist. But they also belong to the nineteenth century. In addition to his faithful and whole reproduction of life, this is another reason why one is so often led to compare him with the giants of the past—Flaubert, Zola, and Tolstoy. (pp. 249-50)

Justin O'Brien, "Martin du Gard: 'The World of the Thibaults'," in his The French Literary Horizon, *Rutgers University Press, 1967, pp. 245-50.*

HENRI PEYRE (essay date 1967)

[*Peyre is a French-born critic who has lived and taught in the United States for most of his career. One of the foremost American critics of French literature, he has written extensively on modern French literature in works that blend superb scholarship with a clear style accessible to the non-specialist reader, most notably in* French Novelists of Today *(rev. ed. 1967). Peyre is a staunch defender of traditional forms of literature that examine the meaning of life in modern society and the role of individual destiny in an indifferent universe; he dislikes experimentalism for its own sake, noting that "many experimenters are the martyrs of a lost cause." Peyre particularly disagrees with critical trends that attempt to subsume literary analysis under the doctrines of restrictive theories, such as those of structuralism. Regarding his critical stance, Peyre has written that "there is no single approach that is infallible or systematically to be preferred when dealing with literature. Pluralism seems to me to be a far more fruitful attitude. . . . Any dogmatism, while it may provide the lover of systems with a cheaply acquired consistency and unity of point of view, soon proves detrimental to the most varied of human pursuits—the pursuit of beauty, truth, and 'greatness' in works of art. Fiction . . . sets everything in motion in us: our senses . . . , our sensibility, our intellect, our religious, philosophical, and social views, our esthetic joys, our desire to know ourselves better and to penetrate other lives. Any approach to the novel, therefore, that is honest and intelligently sustained is valid if it draws us nearer to the work of art or its creator." For these reasons, Peyre has utilized several different approaches in his criticism—aesthetic, biographical, philosophical, political, and social. In the following excerpt, he discusses* Jean Barois *and* The World of the Thibaults.]

Roger Martin du Gard was ten and twelve years younger than Proust and Gide respectively. He was born near Paris in 1881 and lived much of his life in isolation in central France. Neither his technique, nor his preoccupations and implicit philosophy, rank him as a contemporary of the existentialists or of other newcomers in the field of the novel, whose vision of man is more tragic and whose tone is that of bitter individual revolt. But for anyone who disregards the flux of fashions, the author of *Les Thibault* stands as the most faithful imaginative portrayer of the conflicts that tore the French conscience between 1880 and 1930. "The sick conscience is the theatre of modern fatality" is the epigraph from the essayist André Suarès which Martin du Gard selected for *Jean Barois*. No history of the Third Republic has yet succeeded in bringing to life the significance of those French crises, which also became crises for the rest of the Western world, as have the novels of this man trained in history, but who contended in a letter to Claude Roy that "the novelist does nothing good with reality . . . only good reporting."

Martin du Gard has consistently been the most discreet of all French men of letters in his age. Very few private letters by him have been published. He is almost alone among the moderns in never having written or revealed a private diary or memoirs. He has kept to himself whatever opinions he may have entertained on the present and the future of the novel, on his fellow novelists (we do know that Gide heeded his advice), and on his own aims and technique. His acceptance speech of the Nobel Prize was conspicuously reserved on these subjects. Critics who often balk at dissecting a work of fiction and prefer to branch off on the writer's opinions and avowals have been baffled by his exemplary discretion. Very few have written on him. Vercors, Prévost, Ikor, and Camus (in his fine introduction to the Pléiade edition of Martin du Gard's fictional saga) have paid him a moving tribute. Young men have relived the sorrows and yearnings of the teenage hero of *Les Thibault.* Literary craftsmen have respected him. His work has worn less thin than that of Duhamel and Romains, and will probably outlive Gide's *Counterfeiters.*

His early training, like that of Mauriac and Malraux, was in history and in archaeology. He wrote a thesis for the *Ecole des Chartes* on the Norman abbey of Jumièges. He had thus learned how to consult and interpret documents; his subsequent reconstruction of the Dreyfus debate and of the impact of the war in 1914 was supported by an impeccable, almost obtrusive utilization of the most faithful contemporary accounts. He also mastered the more valuable art of submitting to his characters as he had created them and to his narrative as it logically and smoothly unfolded. Hence his equanimity appears almost inhuman to some readers who today prefer the vituperations of Georges Bernanos or Louis-Ferdinand Céline and wax impatient at the serene impartiality of a novelist who refuses to intervene and tell us what he thinks of his heroes. The style itself has a uniform transparency, which reveals events and moods without any willful distortion on the author's part.

Some of the volumes in *Les Thibault* have been linked with the French naturalists, especially when Martin du Gard depicts, with clinical precision, a doctor's workday or the onslaught of disease and death upon old Oscar Thibault, then upon Antoine, the war-wounded doctor. The author's latent view of man cherishing the pursuit of truth, spurning many of the solaces of traditional religion, and stressing clear-headedness and the senseless inhumanity of war and of fanaticism has reminded some of the positivism of the earlier French naturalists. The analogy is superficial. Unlike the naturalists, Martin du Gard derives no joy from exploring the lower side of man or from exposing the selfish meanness of the bourgeois class. His novel or volume of sketches on peasant life, *La Vieille France,* is doubtless somewhat reminiscent of Zola in its satirical onslaught on the agrarian myth. Sentimental idyls are not to the taste of that clear-sighted observer. But if such a great name is not too over-powering, Tolstoi is the writer with whom Martin du Gard has most in common—except for Tolstoi's faith and crusade. *The Death of Ivan Ilyich,* that extraordinary record of a man feeling himself dying of cancer, is the model, unconsciously perhaps, for the death scenes in *Les Thibault* and in many subsequent French novels. A tone of pity and of generosity, only half audible but excluding cynical contempt for man, a creature more stupid than criminal, and sinned against by fate more than sinning, is the tone of Martin du Gard. Camus, in the following generation more fond of displaying its philosophical reading and more vocal in its revolt, will not be remote from the author of *Les Thibault.*

Lucidity, humanity, and sorrowful, but perforce resigned, evocation of the agony of all his men characters and of prewar Europe are the chief virtues of the fine saga-novel, which it is not our purpose here to analyze or to discuss at length. In spite of some overstressed symmetry, especially in the earlier volumes, between the two families delineated, the novel eschews the characterization of social classes as such. It scathes the tyrannical family pride and hypocrisy of the bourgeoisie, but even the self-righteous old Thibault is treated with sympathy. (Indeed, what services the much-maligned bourgeois have rendered modern fiction, not only by purchasing it but by providing it with three-fourths of its best characters and unweariedly absorbing its fiercest blows!) It moves according to a plan that the author nowhere has made too obvious or too rigid, and the reader remains in suspense and shares in the spontaneity the novelist has maintained in his characters. Though less ambitiously comprehensive than his successor Jules Romains, Martin du Gard has avoided the peril of venturing to describe environments and scenes that he did not know through imagination and feeling. He realized how inadequate is knowledge of the intellect alone, even supported by documents. The limitations of the author are real: he is not enough of a poet in the deeper sense of the word, and his most effective scenes lack the visionary *élan,* the mysterious thrill that alone could engrave them unforgettably upon our memories; and his lighting is probably too uniform, his effects of chiaroscuro or of lurid abysses of night illuminated by sparse rays from the author's projector are too few or too weak. The series of volumes is thus prevented, in spite of the not undeserved Nobel Prize, from ranking among the great masterpieces of fiction. His own discretion and overready submission to a traditional form of narrative may well have been a disservice to the author.

These limitations, which will be even more conspicuous in other *romans-fleuves,* are perhaps inseparable from the genre itself. No one, except a feverishly inspired genius like Balzac, can turn out one or two novels a year steadily. The author of a long saga-novel inevitably suffers from lapses of inspiration and phases of sterility. He then lets a few years go by without resuming his convict's forced labor, and the sweep of the work, the inspired unity, are compromised. This was true of the earlier volumes of *Les Thibault,* begun 1922, interrupted after 1928, and resumed only in 1936 with the series about the summer of 1914. The tone then was altered; the gloom weighing over a universe in which little hope was left for man crushed by physical forces had become all-pervading; the freshness of the scenes of adolescence and love had wilted. In spite of the deep pity of the author for his characters, who are all brooding victims of a monstrous game in which the dice are loaded against man's kindness and courage, we fret at his impassive portrayal of their defeats. Other novelists have proved far less intellectually honest in their description of modern man, less coolly objective; but we find them less disconsolate, for they at least imply that sin exists and therefore perhaps redemption also, that some grace may call their characters from the most horrible abysses of vice. Evil to them, even to Mauriac and Genet, Céline and Gide, assumes the appearance of a positive, diabolical force, and it is depicted with such truculence that we may, upon closing the book, imagine that *we* are immune from such a violent condemnation. The author of *Les Thibault* leaves us with no such illusion. Science, progress, knowledge, and good will alone could have turned this into a better world; and man has misused them irretrievably. There is no hell; but we are all sick, and no faith illuminates our dismal hospital abode.

Some critics have consequently dismissed Martin du Gard as a man of the nineteenth century who had accepted the benefit neither of neo-Thomism nor of existentialism. Such labels are absurd, for the faith in the possibilities once offered by science was no less valid than the assertion that man's freedom is all-powerful; the disappointment of those who were forced to

Martin du Gard's country home Le Tertre. From Martin du Gard, *by Jacques Brenner. Gallimard, 1961.*

disbelieve in progress and in ethical behavior severed from religion is no more old-fashioned than the trust of a later generation in a religious, Freudian, or Marxist *mystique*. Physical suffering, stressed by Martin du Gard, is just as revolting and humiliating (perhaps more tragic even if monotonously ancient) as the philosophical anguish of more recent fictional heroes in pondering over the problems of language or of total sincerity. The comparison between our war-ridden twentieth century, with its fanatical clashes of ideas (as we pompously call our propagandized assumptions and our complacently lauded ways of life), and the one that preceded it may well put ours to shame.

Artistically, Martin du Gard had doubtless achieved a greater success with his less ambitious **Jean Barois**. . . . Through its rich content and its symbolical significance, the book may well be one of the most important novels of the years 1900-1918, along with Gide's *La Porte étroite* and Proust's *Swann*. The author experimented with the form of a novel transposed into a dramatic dialogue, which enabled him to avoid some of the smoothness of his later narratives as an omniscient novelist. The conversations between the characters faithfully express the style, the emotions, and the behavior of the interlocutors, without the novelist's having to intrude with comments of his own. High lights can thus be focused sharply, while didactic parts (on the background and details of the Dreyfus case) and especially descriptions, the dead weight in so many novels of

Balzac and Dostoevski, are cut short. A few stage directions conjure up the setting of the main scenes.

Such a technique, however, cannot avoid some artificial devices or some monotony. Martin du Gard, who has written farces for the stage with marked dramatic flair and is not without a bitter comic sense, does not succeed in animating some of his crucial scenes. His women characters in particular are too reserved, closer, even in their scenes of anger and protest, to women as men want them to be in life—composed, outwardly resigned, inwardly sure of their own ultimate victory—than to woman as men like to find her depicted in novels of other nations—hysterical, as in Dostoevski, shrieking with orgiastic laughter, clinging to the man who has scorned her most and following him to Siberia after his inevitable crime. The passions that impel Jean Barois, Luce, and the other characters are mainly intellectual. The love element is restricted. The noble impartiality of the novelist disconcerts readers who like to have the author's position stated unambiguously.

This dramatized novel is likely to remain as the most vivid portrayal of the two crises lived by the author and by France between 1880 and 1910: the struggle waged between Catholicism and science, and the loss of the traditional faith in many minds that has received a historical and exegetic training; and the Dreyfus case, which drove some of the same minds to anticlericalism. These crises go a long way toward elucidating the attitude of France even in 1965 and help explain how, to this day, Frenchmen may, in the face of grave exterior perils, refuse to compromise on such questions as the state support of clerical schools.

The drama of Jean Barois lies in his anxiety to fill the gap left by the breakdown of the Catholic faith of his youth, shattered by the study of natural history and exegesis. The rigidity of Church dogmas and his own uncompromising temperament drive him to an active crusade for new values, which he cherishes and which he opposes to traditional Christianity. He soon clashes with his pious wife, Cécile, whose religion has become narrow and superstitious. They separate. The Dreyfus affair breaks out. Jean Barois plunges into it on the side of the defenders of Dreyfus and, even more, on the side of liberalism and abstract justice. After seven years of trial and retrial, of organized lying by the anti-Semites and by the defenders of the army, prone, as Goethe once confessed he was, to prefer an injustice to disorder, Dreyfus is vindicated. Socialism, tinged with anticlericalism and antimilitarism, triumphs. The noble *mystique* of liberal champions of justice and truth has to give way to a spoils system in which the army is weakened, the Church is persecuted, and the mediocrity of profiteers of politics replaces the lofty dream of elevating the people and of teaching them socialism as an untarnished Messianic faith.

Jean Barois does not moralize on the event. The novel gives us insight into the minds of some of the fighters in that great duel of consciences. Jean himself has had his nerves shattered by the long fight. He sees death close to him in a carriage accident, and his lips voluntarily whisper a prayer memorized in his pious childhood. He admits that he fears death. His own daughter, whom his wife alone has brought up, chooses to be a nun. Her father realizes that any onslaught on dogmas and rites, any historical and philosophical refutation leave the will to believe, the hope of triumphing over death, and the solitude of human beings yearning for charity and love untouched in many a heart. On his death bed he prays and is comforted. Roger Martin du Gard, who had the "irony" of an artist and has never forsaken his intellectual honesty, avoided the naïveté of letting his own unbelief win in the denouement. The overtones of sadness in the final pages, however, half reveal his own sorrow at man's inability to act rationally.

To people who have read about the Dreyfus case only in history books, *Jean Barois,* better than any other novel written on that civil war, offers an accurate and vividly dramatized account of the problems of ethics and of conscience then posed to many Frenchmen. The last sections of *Les Thibault,* which deal with the summer of 1914 when all idealistic pacifist dreams were destroyed, and then with Antoine, the doctor, slowly dying from the gas which had corroded his lungs when he was at the front, are pregnant with restrained emotion and with melancholy anger at men's incurable folly. One thought inevitably recurs when those volumes are reread: the probity of the author is admirable. Nothing is unduly magnified. The novelist's objectivity is never forsaken. He effaces himself and conceals his passion and his pessimistic fear of death and of the future under a clarity lent equally to all scenes. The characters are presented in their relations with other men, horizontally as it were, but seldom vertically in relation to a presence above or in the act of delving into their own deeper and turbid darkness, for to convey an unforgettable impression of the chaos, of the absurdity, and of the greatness of war would have required more familiarity with mystery, perhaps more partiality, and even charlatanry, than Martin du Gard could have stooped to. (pp. 39-45)

Henri Peyre, "Martin du Gard, Duhamel, Romains, and Radiguet," in his *French Novelists of Today,* revised edition, Oxford University Press, 1967, pp. 37-66.

CATHERINE SAVAGE   (essay date 1968)

[*Savage is an American critic and poet who has published studies of several prominent French authors, including André Gide and Martin du Gard. In the following excerpt, she discusses Martin du Gard's place in the development of the modern novel.*]

In his Nobel Prize speech in Stockholm on December 10, 1937, Martin du Gard stated what he considered to be the *raison d'être* of the contemporary novel:

> It was still young when I discovered, in a novel by Thomas Hardy, this reflection in one of his characters: *The real value of life seemed to him to be less in its beauty than in its tragedy.* That corresponded to a profound intuition in me, closely tied to my literary vocation. From that time on, I thought (I still think) that the principal object of the novel is to express the tragic quality of life. I will add today: the tragic quality of an individual life, the tragedy of a destiny *being accomplished* [see excerpt dated 1937].

This understanding, closer to Malraux's excellent formula that the novel is "a privileged means of expression of human tragedy," than to realistic traditions of the nineteenth-century novel, supports Martin du Gard's claim to be our contemporary. That the novelist's point of departure was the realistic novel of Tolstoy and that his philosophical view resembles that late nineteenth century pessimism of which Hardy was the most outstanding example only add to his achievement of adapting an inherited form to contemporary preoccupations. The trajectory of an individual life becomes, in Martin du Gard's major novels, not a case history but an illumination of the tragic quality of all life, against a background of philosophical questioning and political unrest which is the collective tragedy of our times.

Those readers who are interested in formal experiments or those, like Nathalie Sarraute, for whom the nineteenth century novel is an inaccurate, unauthentic form because of its presuppositions, would insist that the modern consciousness of the tragic quality of life should be seized, and molded, in a new form. It is part of André Malraux's achievement that he did this. Martin du Gard's more classical understanding of literary form is not, however, to be scorned. Like his admired predecessors in the novel, he believed that, as Henry James put it, any form which makes the most of its subject is the correct form—any form by which the novelist can express his vision; and he did not reject those nineteenth century narrative prerogatives of omniscience, authorial exposition, and authorial judgment which could help him draw his subject out of the shadows. If we may grant any fictional conventions, even the minimum one of verbalizing and writing on paper, we may certainly grant those others which an author uses to good effect. Changes in points of view, breaks in narrative time, intrusions into characters' minds, and summarizing judgments do not detract from *Les Thibault,* but rather allow the novelist to handle a wide scope of physical action and psychological study which he could not manage with only one of the more rigorous, but more restricted, devices such as scenic presentation, strict point of view, the diary form, and the like.

That Martin du Gard should make this choice to subordinate the pursuit of beauty or rigor of technique to the needs of a subject indicates that his esthetic is essentially utilitarian and that in literature he gives the primary role to discursive expression of insights or characters who have their own value. Though protesting against the polemical literature of the middle decades of the century, he was not adverse to a literature of *ideas,* with a content. His writings are dramatic, historical, and psychological but not poetical. A passage from his Journal expresses his own awareness of this esthetic: "Always the eternal question of form and content. Haedens considers it absurd for one to separate them. And I insist that one can; that I do so; and you wouldn't have to push me hard to make me declare that one should do so. . . . To me, form and content are as distinct as the rabbit and the sauce." . . . If, in a generation of experimentation in literary forms and a pursuit of pure form in the novel as in painting, this view of the novel as a container seems pedestrian, it is more than likely that readers in future generations will return to *Jean Barois* and *Les Thibault* and, tolerating the forms which may no longer be current, read them for their content: the portrait of manners, the psychological analyses, and the historical frescoes.

It remains true, nevertheless, that it is for style that we return to many writers whose perceptions seem unimaginative and that, among the greatest French writers, style and content both draw us back (one thinks, in their different genres, of Racine and Pascal, of Stendhal and Proust). What value one may give to Martin du Gard's fictional style—insofar as it can be separated from the content—is a moot point. He is often accused of flatness—a flatness achieved, perhaps, deliberately in the interests of exactness, but perhaps stultifying. Marcel de Coppet wrote to him in 1920:

> This turn of mind, this tone, this specific flavor, this particularity of thought and expression, this quality that you alone possess, I see it constantly in your conversation, in your correspondence; but never in your works. As soon as you take up your novelist's pen, it seems that the effort of creation, the technical skill, an excessive concern for correct and proper style, smother your original gifts and make what you write banal. . . .

Shortly thereafter, both Gaston Gallimard and Gide told him that he should work less on his style. "It is," said Gallimard, "by naturalness, simplicity, and spontaneity that you will give to your novels their perfect form. Let others pursue. . . . a bold syntax, the rare epithet. . . . Be happy with a clear, correct, unadorned style." . . . (pp. 161-63)

One not familiar with Martin du Gard's conversation and intimate letters has difficulty in seeing what his "other style" may have been; and perhaps he purged his prose too much of its color and flavor. Still, Gallimard's comment would suggest that his simplicity *was* his natural style, and that his matter-of-factness should not be betrayed at the risk of falling into artificiality. In spite of the verve of *Le Père Leleu* and *La Gonfle,* it would seem that for Martin du Gard, character portrayal and analysis and the narration of a serious action belonged in a careful, disciplined prose which would not risk overwhelming the content or falsifying a feeling, a sentiment, a perception. In this view, Martin du Gard is in the best classical French tradition. "La vraie éloquence," wrote Pascal, "se moque de l'éloquence" ["True eloquence laughs at eloquence"]. Not belonging to the category of the greatest writers,

for whom accuracy of expression and great force and beauty of language are twins, Martin du Gard nevertheless deserves consideration as one who made language fit the meaning.

Another classical value which Martin du Gard retains is the emphasis on clarity, not just clarity of style but clarity of vision and understanding. In a century when the novel, like poetry, is increasingly used to explore the shadows of man's psyche, of the phenomenon of language itself, and of the human situation—when the demands *resistance* from a work rather than the yielding up of a secret—Martin du Gard's aims remained the traditional ones of clarity of expression and view. He wanted to look carefully enough at the human enigma to say something toward the elucidation, rather than the mere recognition, of it. This is, if not an idealistic viewpoint, at least a somewhat optimistic one. Rather than calling into question the very act of writing, as Mallarmé had done before him and Samuel Beckett, Valéry, and Alain Robbe-Grillet would variously do later, he accepted the assumptions of the French literary tradition and, in particular, of the nineteenth century. Literature is to show and do something. He expressed in his Nobel Prize speech the hope that his portrait of Europe before 1914 might contribute to building European peace. Those who have called him a thorough-going pessimist might recognize that he retained, in the midst of social upheaval and with his keen observation for the destructive currents in man's mind, an understanding of both man and language as possibility.

Clarity was not simplistic for him, however: in *Les Thibault* one finds continual rectifications and cross-reflections of the truth, and, in an effort to corner the truth and capture some understanding, both Antoine's and Jacques' minds return over and over like restless animals to the problems of self and society and morality which gnaw at them. Finally, the effort of the individual is unsuccessful: Antoine recognizes that the puzzle of life is no smaller as he looks at it from the far end; and Armand, in *Un Taciturne,* reminds us that understanding is rare, and that, if it comes, it comes too late. The effort of the novelist, however, is different: escaping from the solipsistic enigma, he can at least see relationships between men and men, and men and their society and their wars. In his microcosmic society he reveals the force of ideas, the tenacious mystery of the passions, the movement of men in time; and he even throws some light on that experience of death which remained for him the most resistant, as the most terrifying, of human experiences.

Clarity thus has a moral and metaphysical value as well as an esthetic one. For the artist, it is the means by which he sees and expresses the tragic quality which is the subject of his writing. For the individual, it is his own elucidation of man's dilemma. Though Antoine cannot, with all his medical knowledge, slow down significantly his decline toward death, he does not cease postulating the value of understanding. He wants to *see* himself die and thus know himself in that supreme way. Thus, he supposes, he may be able to come to terms with himself in the world which, for Martin du Gard no less than for Camus, is the world of the absurd. For society, clarity is a necessary first step. Jacques' futile gesture was based on correct premises: one must get the truth to the masses before they will be other than willing accomplices in their own destruction. Perhaps man cannot organize society successfully—Antoine thinks it will be thousands of years before it *may* happen—but in any case he cannot do so before he knows himself. A conscious life, and a conscious death—these are the *one* moral principle which Antoine recognizes for himself.

Thus, the literature of the self, in the individualistic tradition to which Martin du Gard belongs—writing of and for himself— meets the literature of the collectivity in the need for knowledge, and Martin du Gard's illumination of the individual drama can take its place against the background of the contemporary tragic sentiment and the awareness of the world drama, of which, like the figures in Greek tragedy, our individual destinies are a paradigm.

The repeated failures at the end of Martin du Gard's works— the inevitable confrontation of anticipations and realities, of construction and destruction—place the author in the naturalistic tradition, with its social and moral pessimism, and also relate him to the novelists of the absurd of the '30s and '40s. The gloominess of destiny, seen in the careers of André Mazarelles, Jean Barois, and the Thibaults and Fontanins, recalls the accusations that Hardy made of determinism, where men appear as flies to the gods. In a later generation, Camus, who spoke in *The Myth of Sisyphus* of the "bloody mathematics of our condition," nevertheless voiced the more modern view that because life has no transcendent meaning, no universal guarantee, does not mean that it is not worth living. The political action of Luce, Barois, and Jacques is not, in the author's eyes, without resonance on the practical plane. Moreover, the conscious death of Luce and the intensity of experience which is characteristic of Jacques, while not justifying their disappointments and Jacques' absurd early death, nevertheless give to their destinies that quality of "revolt without resignation" which is the stance of the existentialist hero. In spite of the robust humor which characterizes his peasant farces, Martin du Gard is most closely attuned not to a literary tradition that reflects a stable society and widely accepted values, but to the contemporary novel which, to use Gide's phrase, is perpetual questioning. From the interrogation, which calls into question all of modern liberalism, emerge nevertheless the value of life and the value of consciousness, limited but fundamental assumptions which are the point of departure for rethinking man and the world. (pp. 163-66)

> *Catherine Savage, in her* Roger Martin du Gard, *Twayne Publishers, Inc., 1968, 184 p.*

IRVING HOWE (essay date 1968)

[*A longtime editor of the leftist magazine* Dissent *and a regular contributor to* The New Republic, *Howe is one of America's most highly respected literary critics and social historians. He has been a socialist since the 1930s, and his criticism is frequently informed by a liberal social viewpoint. Howe is widely praised for what F. R. Dulles has termed his "knowledgeable understanding, critical acumen and forthright candor." Howe has written: "My work has fallen into two fields: social history and literary criticism. I have tried to strike a balance between the social and the literary; to fructify one with the other; yet not to confuse one with the other. Though I believe in the social approach to literature, it seems to me peculiarly open to misuse; it requires particular delicacy and care." In the following excerpt from an essay originally published in* Harper's, November 1968, Howe assesses The World of the Thibaults *and compares Martin du Gard with Leo Tolstoy.*]

I first came across Roger Martin du Gard's *The Thibaults* in 1944 while lying about, idle and depressed, in an army camp waiting to be shipped overseas. A gash upon the western Pennsylvania countryside, this camp seemed an ultimate denial of human life, a way station to those zones of combat and death we kept nervously discussing in the barracks. In this place of

half-spoken fears and emotional sterility, I began to read *The Thibaults,* one of those gigantic family chronicles that had been so popular in Europe at the turn of the century and which up-to-date literary people would dismiss as hopelessly old-fashioned during the postwar years when "everyone" was reading Faulkner and Kafka.

Old-fashioned *The Thibaults* may well seem. In a fine appreciation that recently appeared in the Italian journal *Tempo Presente,* Nicola Chiaramonte has called it "the last great novel in the classical nineteenth-century manner." The book moves with the measured pace of the nineteenth-century novel, as if to register a world at ease with its own norms, rational in its apprehension of time and causality, secure in its expectation that the decades of a man's life will follow and fulfill one another with a stately rightness. I lost myself, with mounting gratitude, in the French bourgeois world of the years between 1890 and World War I, the world of Oscar Thibault, an overpowering Catholic "public man," and his two sons, Jacques and Antoine: Jacques, neurotic, fevered, and destined to become a left-wing socialist who destroys himself in a hopeless pacifist adventure during the war, and Antoine, healthy, balanced, destined to end his life gassed in the war and at the moment of his expiration to keep a remarkable journal of his psychological and physiological reactions.

I say that I felt a mounting gratitude while reading this sequence of novels—in their sum about the length of Proust's *Remembrance of Things Past*—but actually that is a pallid understatement. For Martin du Gard's book brought a sense of life's renewal, regained for me a connection with the immediacies and delights of experience. As never before, I understood what D. H. Lawrence meant when he praised the novel as the greatest of literary genres, the book of life from which we best gain the illusion of transparency and identification.

At the outset, *The Thibaults* seems a little like Thomas Mann's *Buddenbrooks,* the story of a solid, representative family. Jacques Thibault, an inflamed boy who loves and hates his insufferable father, runs away with a Protestant friend (the ghastliness of it, an infidel Protestant!) and wanders off through the streets of Marseilles, only to be caught, chained again into the prison life of the French *bourgeoisie,* and then sent off to a reform school sponsored by his father. Juxtaposed to him is the older brother, Antoine, whose life moves—for a time—as a harmonious development, a gradual slide into manhood and the liberating disciplines he finds in his work as a physician. But as the book proceeds, one comes to see that the comparison to be made is not merely with Mann's *Buddenbrooks* but also with *The Magic Mountain,* a novel that ends with its protagonist, Hans Castorp, caught in World War I.

Reading further and further into *The Thibaults,* one becomes aware that Martin du Gard . . . was not a nineteenth-century writer at all. He was really "one of us," a modern man troubled by our skepticisms and anxieties. Somewhat like Boris Pasternak in *Doctor Zhivago,* Martin du Gard employed a traditional literary form, but not out of a mindless wish to mimic the past; his purpose was to gain an oblique or roundabout perspective on modern life. Traditional in technique, he was radical in sensibility. Martin du Gard was one of those rare twentieth-century novelists alert to the corrosions of bourgeois Europe, such as would lead a few decades later to the crisis literature of Sartre and Camus, yet still able to appropriate, without anachronism or slackness of mind, the Tolstoyan novel. The Tolstoyan novel in all its plenitude of representation, the novel of a seemingly stable world with its rich "gallery of characters'' and interplay of incidents—precisely this ''outmoded'' form became for Martin du Gard a way of registering the death throes of the nineteenth century, the suicide of the traditional culture of Europe.

Why then did *The Thibaults* never win a large American audience? I can only speculate. Written in the years between 1920 and 1940, it must already have come to seem too ordered and rational, too leisurely and dispassionate, for our anguished decades. Every once in a while I would meet a person or read a book that spoke with admiration of Martin du Gard—most recently H. Stuart Hughes's fine study of contemporary French thought, *The Obstructed Path*. But perhaps because he was a writer without fanaticism or ideology, Martin du Gard never became the object of a cult. It was just as well.

Martin du Gard began his novel with the customary expectation—customary for premodernist writers—that he would chart the destinies of linked individuals within the spectrum of roles allowed them by family and society. As he later remarked, he proposed to show

> two beings with temperaments as different, as divergent, as possible, but fundamentally marked by the obscure similarities which are created, between two people of the same blood, by a very powerful common atavism. Such a subject offered me the possibility of simultaneously expressing two contradictory tendencies in my nature: the instinct of independence, of evasion, of revolt, the refusal of all conformity; and that instinct for order, for measure, that refusal of extremes, which I owe to my heredity.

The passage is notable for what it reveals about the making of a novel—and not merely Martin du Gard's novel. He starts with the assumption that a stable social background will permit the etching of fine nuances of character in the foreground. That traditional bourgeois France can be assumed to be ''there,'' solid and unmovable; that the elder Thibault in his own bulky person forms a barrier of will and prejudice, incarnating the conservatism of Catholic France, against which his sons must thrust themselves to achieve a degree of definition; that the fixity of social norms and manners allows the novelist to chart moral formation through seemingly trivial incidents of family life—all these are among the deepest foundations of the nineteenth-century novel. At the start, but only at the start, Martin du Gard turns to them almost instinctively. The revolt of Jacques Thibault begins as a friendship, slightly tinged by eroticism, with a Protestant schoolboy; he then enters the home of his friend's family and finds among the Fontanins a purity of moral life and an openness of feeling—but also a libertinism in the handsome, wandering father—he has not known in his own family. This juxtaposition of family environments and, indirectly, religious styles, creates a strong immediate effect: it helps prepare the way for Jacques's lifelong rebellion. But while Martin du Gard is himself a thorough skeptic, he understands that the novelist must always strengthen those forces within his book which resist his own sentiments and predispositions; so that many pages later the tables are turned and the seeming anti-Catholic bias is complicated. As Antoine Thibault leaves the funeral of his father, he engages in a sustained dialogue with a sensitive Catholic priest in which the latter has the last and perhaps the best word. In the world of the great novelists, no debate is ever done.

The single overriding theme of the European novel has been the conflict between rigid social arrangements and a protagonist straining for personal freedom—a conflict seen not as resolved but as continuous, and thereby open to changes wrought by the will and intelligence of the characters. It is in these terms that *The Thibaults* begins. The older Thibault, barricaded behind his moralism and righteousness, is an unattractive man, but also the most passionate and vigorous in the book; he looms as the archetypal father, an Abraham to be feared and loved as the principle of authority made flesh. Jacques rebels against individual and idea, but his rebellion takes on its fiercely dramatic quality because he remains enthralled by both Oscar Thibault the man and the paternal power he represents. There follows a prolonged struggle of wills, first as an unavoidable encounter of generations, hot blood against cold, and then as a confrontation of two world views, secular denial against religious authority. The conflict becomes internalized within Jacques, as a division between his need for self-assertion and his yearning for parental affection. And it is here that the felt presence of a stable society, even an unjust or authoritarian one, is for the novelist an enormous advantage. If Jacques were able simply to discard the bonds of family life, if he could simply decide that the old man is a tyrant or a bore who need no longer be listened to, the result might be socially pleasing or psychologically enabling; but it would damage the entire structure of relationships and meanings Martin du Gard has created. The incidents multiply: Jacques brought home contrite and sullen; Jacques at the reform school almost, as we would say, brainwashed and unable, in the swamp of his humiliation, to tell his brother how unhappy he is; Jacques later passing his examinations brilliantly but still beyond reconciliation with his father. In all these bits of narrative, what establishes the tension is the fact that the emotional tie Jacques feels to his father is more powerful and enduring than the social or intellectual values the father represents; that life has a dynamism and thrust beyond any beliefs we may have about it. Jacques can declare himself a revolutionary, but when the time comes to return for the old man's death he still trembles like a frightened little boy.

Which other modern novelist, by contrast, has been able to employ the family as a binding and defining unit in his work? Faulkner, I suppose. But he sees the Southern family as a collapsing institution, so that in his greatest novel, *The Sound and the Fury,* there is an extremely poignant sense of how much has been lost through the collapse of the Compsons but little evidence that the family still shapes and disciplines the lives of its members. And in our own moment it is almost impossible to imagine a novel in which youthful rebellion finds a force of resistance among the older generation sufficient to allow for sustained drama.

Martin du Gard's stress upon the settled traits of Jacques and Antoine Thibault creates for the reader the fascinating possibility of ''choosing'' between the two characters—and choosing is here more than a game, it is a kind of moral signature. The two brothers are strongly drawn and highly intelligent men, each with his own claim on our sympathies. Jacques reminds one a little of Stendhal's Fabrice in *The Charterhouse of Parma*, that curious mixture of rebellion against the world and a dreamy abstracted removal from it, almost as if the character were musing away his own existence. Antoine is given a whole book in which a day in his life as a doctor is depicted with enormous detail, and the result is a *tour de force* in the dramatization of commonplace life and the vindication of work as the rationale for our existence.

Albert Camus observes: "In art, the more prosaic the reality chosen as one's subject matter, the more difficult it is to transfigure." And he feels that it is Antoine who emerges as the true protagonist of the novel, for he argues brilliantly that Jacques is a kind of Dostoevskian echo, "the terrorist" as foreshadowed in *The Possessed*, one of those men "who want to change life in order to change themselves," and who "leave life untouched . . . sterile and disturbing witnesses for everything in man that refuses and always will refuse to live." A telling point; yet even as one sees its truth for the novel and its truth for our times, one is inclined to ask: does not the entire momentum of twentieth-century history, which in turn becomes the momentum of Martin du Gard's novel, force a wrenching from private life to a life engulfed by historical consciousness? And does this not provide a justification of sorts for Jacques—the kind of dangerous justification Bertholt Brecht employs in his great poem, "To Posterity," where he asks later generations to understand why twentieth-century men had to become so brutal: "we changed our countries more often than our shoes"? I say, a dangerous justification, because it could be used, as Brecht did, to rationalize the ghastliness of totalitarian society; yet who, turning away in disgust from Brecht, could simply accept the private life of an Antoine Thibault? In any case, that was the dilemma which Martin du Gard dramatized with a sympathetic detachment few modern writers have equaled.

Martin du Gard's stress upon the seemingly fixed differences in character between Jacques and Antoine Thibault is but one instance of the ruling psychology of the book. It is a pre-Freudian psychology, rationalistic and empirical, which assumes that character is marked by contained and knowable traits and that our conduct is explainable through categories of thought. We are inclined, at this moment in the twentieth century, to discount this sort of psychology: it does not make sufficient allowance for the irrational; it blots out the chaos of the unconscious, it overestimates the coherence and accessibility of the psyche. No doubt. But an advance in knowledge, if that is what the various depth psychologies really constitute, is not necessarily an advantage for literature. Even as we recognize the theoretic limitations of Martin du Gard's psychology, we must also acknowledge its creative uses. Because the characters, *as a preliminary step,* can easily be assigned to familiar psychological categories, Martin du Gard is then free to draw upon a superb repertoire of variation and nuance. Just as tradition, for the writer, can yield possibilities for freedom and innovation, so the relatively conventional psychology of *The Thibaults* makes possible novelty and surprise.

I want to develop this point a little further. If character consists in a given potential of traits, as a rationalistic psychology tends to assume, then we are going to see the growth of a character as the realization of fulfillment of that potential. In the abstract this may seem very mechanistic; but in Martin du Gard's novel itself, since we can never really know what the full potentiality of a Jacques or Antoine may be, our gradual discovery of their characters comes, in fact, as a series of small surprises. In the traditional novel, that is, *surprise comes from the fact that the characters act according to their true natures,* which we know in general but never completely.

At first Antoine Thibault seems the essence of the normal. Then, during an emergency operation, he meets a vivid and mysterious woman named Rachel, and in the glowing romance that follows his life is transformed—but transformed through fulfillment, a release of the capacities for sexual pleasure and love we have already sensed him to possess. Here the writing becomes more intense and lyrical, the tone of realism gives way for a time to a tone of romanticism, as if the quickening of life means a quickening of language. Martin du Gard the novelist-healer becomes Martin du Gard the novelist-romancer. And while his psychology may be rationalistic, that does not keep him from recognizing the powers of the sub- and irrational, the thrust of desire, the autonomous demands of the body, the imperiousness of ego.

Martin du Gard offers almost no description of the physical love-making of Antoine and Rachel, yet the pages in which they come together are among the most erotically stimulating I have ever read, infinitely more suggestive—to say nothing of romantic!—than those contemporary novels which chart a full course of sexual calisthenics. Martin du Gard understands, for he is a writer with an enormous sense of *experience*, that sexuality itself can rarely be made interesting in a serious novel; what can be made interesting is the force of desire which leads to sexuality, the complications of feeling that surround it, the aftermath of loss which is perhaps inevitable.

Through his immersion in sensual pleasure, soon brought to an end by Rachel's departure, Antoine suffers and grows. Later, dying from poison gas, he will think back: "It was a sorry adventure, but that sorry adventure is, despite all, the best that there is in my sorry life."

Equally impressive as a depiction of that continuous physical life which commands us even in the most firmly structured of societies, is Martin du Gard's lengthy depiction of the elder Thibault's deathbed agonies. I think Martin du Gard must be the greatest master in fiction of the death struggle, realistic, detailed, yet never sensational in effect: the death struggle as it becomes a kind of impersonal *agon* leaving character and social definition behind it. Toward the end of the whole chronicle there will be another great death scene, the one in which Antoine watches himself dying with the detachment of a physician. Oscar Thibault struggles with animal-like ferocity against death, Antoine Thibault accepts it with that loss of energy which seems inseparable from the stoical imagination.

To read *The Thibaults* is sooner or later to ask oneself, why and in which ways is Martin du Gard inferior as a novelist to Tolstoy? Even to put the question is, of course, to pay Martin du Gard an enormous compliment.

The difference between the two writers is not merely, perhaps not even mainly, a difference in the magnitude of their talents. There are, to be sure, things that Tolstoy can do and Martin du Gard cannot: massive scenes of warfare in which whole groups of characters become the protagonists of the action, intervals of religious elevation in which a saintly figure finds himself in communion with the godhead, excursions into primitivist simplicity which serve Tolstoy as equivalents to his early-Christian faith. Camus develops this contrast beautifully:

> Martin du Gard shares with Tolstoy a liking for human beings, the art of depicting them in the mystery of their flesh, and a knowledge of forgiveness—virtues outdated today. The world Tolstoy described nevertheless formed a whole, a single organism animated by the same faith; his characters meet in the supreme adventure of eternity. One by one, visibly or not, they all, at some point in their stories, end up on their knees.

Martin du Gard lacks the faith—and to go a step beyond Camus, he thereby lacks the *animation*—of Tolstoy's world. Composed in the twentieth century, his work, as Camus says, "is one of doubts, of disappointed and persevering reason, of ignorance acknowledged, and of a wager that man has no other future than his own." *The Thibaults* presents a world in a twilight gray, even if sometimes streaked with a brilliant flare of color. As Jacques and Antoine move into the war, no one knows any longer why their world exists, what it means, or why it kills. And the result finally is not merely a difference in tone between Tolstoy and Martin du Gard, but a loss of creative energy, a greatness in the French writer but a diminished greatness.

A further crucial difference between the two writers: Where Tolstoy integrated, indeed could not even conceive as long separate, the two main strands of his narrative, that dealing with individual lives and that dealing with historical events, Martin du Gard could not manage this. The logic of his narrative leads to an abandonment of personal life, even though in its early parts personal life is treated as self-sufficient, even sacred. One of his French critics, Pierre-Henri Simon, writes that in the early years of the twentieth century Western man "lost the experience and the sense of history. . . . It took, to reawaken him [to history], the tocsin and the cannon of August 1914." This is certainly a description of a major theme in *The Thibaults;* but I think it must also be added that Martin du Gard is one of those writers for whom this "reawakening" had the quality of nightmare: he believes in the absolute value of personal experience, and toward the end of his life remarks in a letter: ". . . you are completely correct in emphasizing how many of my qualities are due to my bourgeois origins. . . . All my life I have *struggled against,* and at the same time, *made my peace with,* these elements.

The shift to historical narrative which occurs in the later parts of *The Thibaults* is one that its author, like his characters, negotiates reluctantly, under the blows of circumstance; and when he comes to the war and the socialist movement in *Summer 1914* (the concluding portion of the whole sequence), his writing becomes a little uncertain and abstract. A lifelong pacifist and man of the left, Martin du Gard is still in his innermost being a private man, the historian of individual fate rather than the individual who chronicles the fate of history.

> The final word that can be said about this work (says Camus), remains the one that it has been difficult to use about a writer since the death of Tolstoy: goodness. . . . What we are concerned with here is a particularly lucid virtue, which absolves the good man because of his weaknesses, the evil man because of his generous impulses, and both of them together because of their passionate membership in a human race that hopes and suffers [see excerpt dated 1955].

I should like to add to "goodness" one other word, "acceptance." Unavoidably the writers of this century have been driven to play the role of visionary or prophet. Much has thereby been gained for literature, but something also lost. The visionary or prophet tends to impose himself on his work, to twist and wrench his characters in behalf of his presuppositions, to stamp his personality on each phrase and word. Martin du Gard is another kind of novelist entirely. We do gain from his work the sense of a man profoundly humane and stoical, at once passionate and withdrawn, though forever sympathetic to all those who risk themselves in the human enterprise. But we

feel that this writer does not want to fix his imagined creatures into the mold of his own theories, he wants instead to give them a full range of freedom to live out their own destinies. He does not wish to tyrannize over his world, but rather to accept human life as it is, with all its faults and weaknesses. He understands Jacques and shares in his aspirations; but in the end it is Antoine's spirit which encloses the book.

Perhaps that is what leads Camus, in his remarkable essay, to place Martin du Gard in the line of Tolstoy "against" the line of Dostoevsky and then to say, a bit more hopefully than we now could:

> There is a strong possibility, in fact, that the real ambition of our authors, after they have assimilated *The Possessed,* will be one day to write *War and Peace.* After tearing through wars and negations, they keep the hope, even if it's unadmitted, of rediscovering the secrets of a universal art that, through humility and mastery, will once again bring characters back to life in their flesh and with intensity.

This possibility does not seem "very strong" at the moment, but I find Camus' wish tremendously stirring. In the long run, it is the only way. (pp. 43-53)

> *Irving Howe, "Martin du Gard: The Novelty of Goodness," in his* Decline of the New, *Harcourt, Brace Jovanovich, 1970, pp. 43-53.*

R. JOUEJATI (essay date 1977)

[In the following excerpt, Jouejati discusses political ideology in The World of the Thibaults.*]*

Martin du Gard belonged to an epoch of turmoil, economic confusion and conflict. He lived through two world wars, conducted on a scale unprecedented in history, and a depression which almost wrecked the foundations of the capitalist system. He also witnessed the spread of revolution, which claimed equality instead of privilege, and freedom instead of oppression. All of these things placed on trial man's destiny and the future of civilization.

The political crisis, the crisis of modern man, challenges the ingenuity of thinking men to find a solution for the problems of humanity. Thus, Martin du Gard, being conscious of "so many innocent victims and endless suffering without remedy," grows impatient to prove his genius, which he does by plunging into "this vast enterprise," the enterprise of writing *Les Thibault.*

From describing the experiences of two brothers, differing in temperament, one seeking evolution, the other revolution, he goes on to portray two families separated by religious beliefs. He then opens a window on a society torn between conventionality and emancipation of ideas, nationalism and international socialism, capital and labor, conservatives and radicals. He aligns himself with no faction, adheres to no specific ideology and refrains from advocating violence in class strife. He calls for an end to injustices and the establishment of equal opportunity. He also demands that the metaphysical element in morality should be eliminated as, in the guise of religious or patriotic faith, it causes fanaticism and intolerance.

He progresses from the tragedy of an individual, to that of society and from there, to the tragedy of mankind as a whole, culminating in war of widespread death and destruction. Thus, he imparts to his readers a deep sense of participation in the unfolding of a drama. At first, the readers are mere spectators of what happens to Antoine and Jacques, but the same readers gradually realize that the boys' tragedy is the universal tragedy of mankind. The chronicle of Les Thibault, as a family, becomes the chronicle of every family, and their catastrophe, a catastrophe which engulfs all humanity. He relates the march of events with every human being in whom there is awakened a sense of responsibility. The most persuasive sermons fail to do what Martin du Gard's novel, with its powerful impact, accomplishes, its eloquence being that of realism. Thus, for a mother, war means the crippling of her son, Daniel; for a bride, the death of her fiance, Jacques, caused by his fervor for truth; for a child, Jean-Paul, deprivation of his father; for hundreds of patients, the loss of their benevolent and tireless doctor, Antoine; for an orphan girl, Giselle, whose only pleasure was anticipation of better things, the frustration of life; for humanity at large, the very evil it contends with, death. This is why du Gard's message is fundamentally human. He does not undertake to elaborate a theory, nor to multiply dogmas. His vision of a world where peace and justice prevail is intuitive. It is of no avail to criticize his failure to understand certain events, to appreciate certain standards and to espouse certain principles. He does not attempt to refute any doctrine, or to replace it by another. What he does do is to analyze principles and idoelogies, attitudes and policies, passions and instincts, so that he may discover whatever they entail that is "inhuman" and worth fighting against.

The student of du Gard's political thought will be disappointed if he seeks a new formulation or political and international organization. He must rather study the new method Martin du Gard employs, to raise men's hearts above human hate and prejudice, above exclusive chauvinism, above submission to injustice, above state or class ambition for self-aggrandizement at the expense of weaker states of groups and, most important of all, above their own base instincts. Martin du Gard's method is one that, figuratively speaking, "consummates the marriage of the political and the psychological, in the temple of History," by means of literary artistry. It is also a method which, while firmly clinging to the principle of "art for art's sake," upholds the ultimate triumph of the literary art over human despair. Martin du Gard does not offer concrete propositions for establishing the international harmony which he advocates. Rather, he emphasizes, for rivals and belligerents, the fact that they are human beings before they are German, French, English or Russian. Although belonging to different nationalities, they share a common humanity, so that their well-being should not be sought exclusively within their own borders, but also in cooperation with others, transcending frontiers and racial differences. Thus, the aim of his philosophy, which is the defense of humanity, coincides with its fundamental principles of peace and harmony.

Furthermore, for a student of du Gard's political thought, the example of his own career is more enlightening than his social theories. Dedicating his life to the cause of humanity, he is motivated by a positive faith, rather than by negative defeatism. As a bourgeois who is yet dedicated to the cause of social equality, his message has special significance, and has not failed to bear fruit. Claude Magny affirms that, "The true originality of certain works is best revealed by their consequences." The same author, however, attributes failure to du Gard, whose message is divorced from "ethics, metaphysics and cohesive reflection." But contemporary events speak more eloquently. The Franco-German reconciliation could not have

Martin du Gard in his library at Le Tertre. From Martin du Gard, *by Jacques Brenner. Gallimard, 1961.*

been brought about by Maurras' and Barras' theories of exclusive nationalism, and Nazi fanaticism could not have been overcome, if it had not been for the passionate appeals of writers like Martin du Gard. The universal concern for peace, which served as a basis for the pact of the League of Nations, and is gradually maturing in the United Nations, would not have existed without a progressive forming of public opinion in favor of internationalism. Although, in du Gard's novel, Jacques is the victim of his temerity (while undertaking an act of inconsequential heroism), his pamphlet will be read, thoughtfully and for a long time. Moreover, Antoine, before dying of poison gas says, "I am condemned to die without having much understanding of myself or of the world." Such is the outcry of a rebel, doomed to die, before seeing the fruition of his "vast enterprise."

The birth and growth of Jacques' son, Jean-Paul, however, form an allegory which symbolizes the continuity of a revolution destined to transform man. Would the improved condition of the "forgotten man" have been attained in relative peace had there not been widespread condemnation of violence, together with a growing sense of responsibility and common interests, binding together all classes of society? Historians may one day realize that among the outstanding achievements of the twentieth century is the transforming of certain ideals into actual practices. Thus, the ideals of political evolution, declared by social reformers and once thought to be mere abstractions, are being converted by mankind into realities. Indeed the lifework of Martin du Gard is one of the contributions of exceptional and continual value to the transformation of social ideals into actual achievements. (pp. 105-08)

R. Jouejati, in his The Quest for Total Peace: The Political Thought of Roger Martin du Gard, *Frank Cass, 1977, 111 p.*

MARY JEAN GREEN   (essay date 1980)

[*In the following excerpt, Green discusses Martin du Gard's portrayal of the doctor in* The World of the Thibaults, *viewing Antoine*

Thibault as a representative of the author's ideas regarding modern science.]

In his fictional chronicle of the Thibault family, written in the troubled period between the two world wars, Roger Martin du Gard examines the different responses to life of two brothers, Jacques and Antoine Thibault. Jacques, the eternal rebel, is a political activist. Antoine, less alienated from his society, is a doctor. Although Jacques dies bravely and selflessly in a futile effort to prevent the outbreak of the First World War, it is the figure of Antoine, as both doctor and dying patient, that embodies Martin du Gard's vision of human moral action in the chaotic and incomprehensible modern world.

Summing up the conclusion of Martin du Gard's Nobel prize-winning novels, Albert Camus wrote: "Of Martin du Gard's two central characters, the priest and the doctor, the former has all but disappeared. The Thibault series ends with the death of a doctor, alone among other doctors. It seems that questions are now asked only within the domain of humanity." Camus's words, and Martin du Gard's novels, point to the modern displacement of the religious by the secular, a replacement of the ideal of sainthood by that of the doctor.

Dr. Antoine Thibault's world is clearly that of the twentieth century, with its advanced technology, its promise of material prosperity, and—as the war suddenly reveals to him—its unprecedented potential for mass destruction. Unlike his perpetually discontented younger brother, Antoine is a man with a healthy appetite for personal happiness and an active sensuality. It is his preference for the concrete over the abstract, a life of action rather than contemplation, that has drawn him to the study of medicine and its daily contact with physical reality. Medical science represents, in his eyes, "the greatest achievement of twenty centuries of efforts in all fields of knowledge, the richest domain open to the genius of man." . . . (p. 98)

Martin du Gard is so convinced of the importance of Antoine's work as a doctor that he devotes an entire volume of his series, *The Consultation,* to describing one afternoon in his character's medical practice. As Louis Aragon has commented, "it has always amazed me that it was necessary to await the modern era and Martin du Gard to find in a novel a doctor who is really practicing medicine and not arranging marriages or setting up industries in mountain villages." Antoine's overriding concern is the alleviation of human suffering, and he gives each of the cases before him an exclusive, sympathetic attention. Although he is not indifferent to the growth of his reputation as a specialist in children's diseases, Antoine does not allow his personal concerns to distract his attention from the welfare of his patients. Always sensitive to beautiful women, he nevertheless refuses to let a seductive mother prevent his careful diagnosis of her stepdaughter's spinal tuberculosis. And he spends more time treating an inflammation on the arm of a neighborhood orphan than attending to his richer clientele.

Since many of his patients are children, Antoine finds himself vaguely troubled by the metaphysical implications of the cases he sees before him. The repeated evidence of the suffering of innocents seems to call into question the very order of the universe. But Antoine's inability to understand the overarching structure of reality cannot threaten his conviction that his own activity within it is of some value.

Indeed, a superabundance of work leaves him little time for adequate meals, let alone metaphysical speculation, and he must develop his ethics in response to the demands of the moment. Without the support of the traditional religious world view, which had died with his father's generation, Antoine, like many other men of his century, must discover values and principles of action through his own experience. His medical duties themselves, as he tells a friend, provide him with a rule of conduct. As a doctor of integrity, he is always careful to make an honest diagnosis, even when such a diagnosis may cost him personal advancement. This actually happens later in the war, when the military medical command refuses to admit the existence of typhoid at the front, despite abundant evidence to the contrary. But Antoine is able to bend his principles when strict honesty would cause needless suffering: in *The Consultation* he lies without remorse to reassure a guilt-ridden father who blames his son's retardation on his own youthful exposure to syphilis.

Antoine's operating principle, that departure from conventional moral principles may be justified in the effort to relieve suffering, is put to a severe test in the case of a friend's dying child, for whom he can do nothing. Yet he refuses the silent supplication of the father, as well as the more articulate exhortation of a young medical assistant, to put the child out of her misery with a merciful overdose. Stammering something about "respect for life" and, more significantly, "a limit to our power," . . . he is bothered by his inability to fully articulate his intuitive rejection of this appeal. Not long afterwards, however, Antoine is confronted with a similar situation, and this time the patient is his own father, who is dying a long and difficult death from renal failure. Martin du Gard's detailed symptomatic description of the father's condition has drawn him the unqualified praise of medical critics, some of whom have devoted entire theses to his works. As the physical degeneration progresses, the old man has time to make his preparations for an imminent death before sinking into a state of delirium broken by periodic crises. After nights of helpless observation of his father's suffering, and unable to bear the strain any longer, Antoine finally administers a calming—and fatal—injection. What he had not been able to do *as a doctor*, who, he believes, must impose severe limitations on his sometimes godlike power, he can now do in good conscience as a son faced with a suffering, terminally ill father.

The provisional morality that Antoine develops through his experience as a general practitioner must soon confront two major challenges: his inheritance of the family fortune and the outbreak of the First World War. Each of these situations, of course, reflects a more general characteristic of the modern world: a preoccupation with material prosperity and the possibility of mass destruction. The inheritance of wealth is by far the less serious challenge; yet it threatens to distract Antoine from his meaningful life of service to patients. He uses his inheritance to pursue his dream of making his name immortal by setting up his own luxurious private research laboratory. Martin du Gard is not criticizing Antoine's desire to participate in medical research, but rather his preoccupation with personal glory, which threatens to turn him away from his original concern for human beings and his contact with patients. Although Antoine plans to take the credit for discoveries, the actual research is to be done by his three young research assistants, whose services he has bought. Progressively cutting himself off from real work and from real human beings, Antoine demonstrates the dangers of an all-consuming commitment to personal glory and material wealth, temptations inherent in the career of a modern doctor.

Antoine is so taken up with his own concerns that he is deaf to the noise of the world around him, and even the urgent warnings of his politically conscious brother Jacques fail to rouse him from the illusion that he exists independently of his social environment. But the year is 1914, and Antoine is soon forced to acknowledge his participation in the common destiny when he is ordered to join his medical unit at the front. On the battlefield he rediscovers the importance of his original vocation of active service to patients, and he sees the worthlessness of his vain ambitions, to which the war has brought a decisive end.

Yet the war, with its involvement of previously inconceivable numbers of troops, its use of modern weaponry, its manipulation of the media for mass propaganda, raises other problems. In this new situation Antoine must seek a model of individual action that can most effectively preserve his basic humanistic values. He is momentarily tempted by his brother Jacques's political action, just as Martin du Gard himself was attracted by political involvement in the troubled years that preceded World War II. But Jacques's suicidal attempt to prevent the war proves futile: badly injured in the crash of a plane from which he had planned to drop pacifist leaflets, he is shot in the panic of the initial French retreat. The nineteenth-century ideal of individual heroism is symbolically overwhelmed by the mass catastrophes of the twentieth. Individual action seems to have little significance in modern history. In Martin du Gard's historical analysis, even great men like Jaurès and Clemenceau fail to dominate events. But, although individuals cannot change history, they can continue to combat its destructive consequences. Here again the model is a doctor, in the person of Antoine's revered teacher, Dr. Philip. Philip has effected one of the major life-saving enterprises of the war by reorganizing a medical service ill-prepared for the massive casualties. Antoine, too, performs a life-saving service, more humble but equally valuable, risking his life under enemy fire in the most primitive of conditions. The wartime doctor thus embodies a moral image of modern man, fighting to preserve human values in the midst of chaos.

At the end of the war, as he lies dying in a clinic for victims of poison gas, Antoine finally has the time to face the ultimate questions always pushed aside by the demands of the moment. In this meditation of a dying doctor, which forms the substance of the last novel in the Thibault series, Martin du Gard comes to a new and more profound understanding of the meaning of the medical profession. Writing in his journal, Antoine realizes that his profession has provided him with the foundations of an entire philosophy of life, which has proven capable of steering him through the menacing and unpredictable world born of the war.

The doctor, with his experience of life and death, is accustomed to facing unpleasant facts without illusion. Antoine must carry this painful lucidity to its logical conclusion when a consultation with Philip forces him to recognize that his own condition has become incurable. As a doctor, he cannot delude himself with hope for a miracle, and he has always known that all his therapeutic successes were only temporary victories in the long battle with death. But, like the doctor who continues his efforts despite this knowledge, the individual must go on with his own struggle in a world that provides little reason for optimism.

The world view he has adopted as a man of science, accustomed to dealing only with the facts before him, leaves Antoine no room for belief in immortality, or even in the comforting historical theories of modern political doctrines. These he dismisses as illusory consolations that interfere with lucid analysis. As he tells his nephew, a "man of value," like a doctor,

must preserve his freshness of vision: "Each disease—like each social crisis—presents itself as a case without identical precedent, as an *exceptional* case, for which a new therapy is always to be invented." . . . Any solution adopted must be regarded as provisional: "we must renounce the notion of a stable truth, we must hold something to be true only with great reservations and only until such time as we have proof to the contrary." . . . Antoine sees life as a continual process of research, like that of a doctor who adopts new treatments and submits them to the test of experience. He offers as an instructive example the early use of antiseptics, when a too thorough application of the new remedy killed living cells as well as bacteria.

Although science cannot be expected to solve all human problems, the progress of medicine, extraordinary in this century, provides a realistic example of what it can do. In the modest hope of contributing to this progress, Antoine refrains from ending his suffering with a fatal injection in order to keep a daily record of his own terminal case. But the First World War has also provided a vivid illustration of the destructive potential of technological progress. As Antoine, himself a victim of this technology, contemplates the vastness of the starry universe, he finds a certain consolation in this evidence of human finitude and realizes that the study of science, if understood properly, can also help man to accept his own limitations. His medical practice, as distinct from its theory, has brought Antoine into daily contact with human beings, and it is the knowledge drawn from this experience that provides him with a modest optimism. Seeing himself and his contemporaries as the most recent links in a chain stretching back into time, he affirms the continuing existence of a human moral consciousness that provides some foundation for a realistic faith in human progress, even if only in a distant future.

Through his close observation of Antoine Thibault's life as a doctor, Martin du Gard has given us a model of individual ethical action in the modern world. In his consultations with patients, his heroic service on the battlefield, and, especially, in his courageous confrontation with his own death, Martin du Gard's Dr. Antoine Thibault has consistently exemplified the highest ideals of the medical profession; and his example becomes, by extension, a model for all human action. Despite his lucid skepticism, he affirms the creative, life-sustaining power of human science in a world dominated by death and destruction; the strength of human fraternity against the inhuman forces of disease and war; and the value of individual ethical endeavors in the context of a modern mass society. (pp. 98-102)

> Mary Jean Green, "A Moral Image of Modern Man: The Doctor in the Work of Martin du Gard," in Medicine and Literature, *edited by Enid Rhodes Peschel, Neale Watson Academic Publications, Inc., 1980, pp. 98-102.*

PETER FAWCETT (essay date 1984)

[*In the following excerpt, Fawcett praises Martin du Gard's later novel* Le lieutenant-colonel de Maumort.]

Two years after the completion of **Les Thibault,** during a sleepless night in 1941, Martin du Gard conceived the project of a diary kept by a septuagenarian colonel confined to a single room in his château by the occupying German forces and remembering his past. It was to be a "livre somme", reflecting all his contemporary preoccupations and displaying some of the qualities Gide and others found in his personal writings but which were so far lacking in his fiction. From the start, however, he ran into difficulties with the form he had chosen. As long as Maumort commented on current events, it was impossible to distinguish between him and his creator. Whence Martin du Gard felt the need to embark on a "gigantesque travail préparatoire" ["gigantic preparatory work"], which suited his gifts as a novelist and involved providing not only his protagonist but each of the major characters in his life with a full biography.

After the war, the perspective having changed, he decided to begin the diary in 1945 instead of 1940 and altered his hero's date of birth from 1866 to 1870. Gradually the diary gave place to memoirs, though the final form imagined for the novel was that of letters. Following his wife's death in 1949, he confessed to Gide: "J'ai passé l'âge des grandes entreprises" ["I have passed the age of great enterprises"], and, with his own health beginning to fail, it became increasingly clear that the work would never be finished.

The largest and most complete section of [*Le lieutenant-colonel de Maumort*] consists of Maumort's memoirs of his first twenty-five years up to the time of his marriage. Particular emphasis is placed on his sexual education, about which he states his intention to "tout dire franchement, crûment" ["tell everything frankly, harshly"]. After listening to the confidences of his friends and reading the reports of sexologists, Martin du Gard wanted to show that masturbation was an inevitable part of adolescence and he dwells at length on the "liberté de moeurs incroyable" ["unbelievable moral liberty"] Maumort finds in the boarding-school to which he is sent at the age of fifteen. He is careful to stress that Maumort is a perfectly normal, healthy individual. Aware that this aspect of the work risked upsetting its balance and shocking some readers, he even thought of publishing these chapters separately in a limited edition. Nowadays such a precaution would appear unnecessary. The one example of genuine homosexuality in the book, drawn from the diary of Maumort's former tutor, Xavier de Balcourt, is a brief romantic idyll which ends in drowning and a suicide.

Maumort's intellectual development is of equal importance. His arrival in Paris at eighteen to live with his uncle and aunt Chambost-Lévadé, while preparing for Saint-Cyr, brings him into contact with a world of exceptional brilliance. His uncle Eric himself, based on the strange and enigmatic character of Paul Desjardins, founder of the famous *décades de Pontigny*, is a member of the Institut de France. Among the regular visitors to his house who appear in the novel are Renan, Taine, Berthelot and Brunetière.

It is for its picture of this outstanding intellectual milieu, at a time when France, we are told, "a vécu sous le régime le plus libre, de beaucoup, qu'elle ait jamais connu, que jamais, je crois, aucun pays n'a connu" ["lived under the most liberal regime by far that she had ever known, that ever, I believe, any country had known"], that the novel may be chiefly read. Little subsists, unfortunately, of Maumort's planned later career, his resignation over the Dreyfus Affair, his campaigns with Lyautey in Morocco, his subsequent work with the Resistance. But there is more to the novel than this. We must be grateful to M Daspre for publishing, alongside the chapters he has successfully constructed out of the various fragments, a selection from the numerous "dossiers" formed in preparation for the novel and which alone give it its proper dimension.

Maumort was conceived originally as "un vieil Erasme libéral revenu de tout" ["an aged, liberal Erasmus remembering ev-

erything"]. Later he was modelled to some extent on Vauvenargues, who combined, like him, the qualities of a man of action and a thinker. But above all it is Montaigne who lurks in the background to the novel. Both Maumort and Martin du Gard felt themselves to be "dépassés" ["surpassed"] by the post-war world of Existentialism and "engagement", which seemed like a return to the fanaticism of the Wars of Religion. The importance of this last novel to Martin du Gard was that, "piètre penseur" ["poor thinker"] though he considered himself to be, he wished to include in it, in the manner of the "grand sceptique", all the notes and observations he had accumulated over forty years and which appear in the "dossiers". Maumort was the *alter ego* who would make this ambition possible.

It is doubtful if Martin du Gard could ever have fully reconciled the conflicting demands of fiction and self-expression, as he saw them, in this instance. But no matter. His stately, classical prose, here at its most expansive, is a joy to read and his belief that "il y a plus de vérité dans le souvenir que dans la notation quotidienne" ["there is more truth in memory than in day to day observation"] lends the work a Proustian flavour, nowhere more so than in a memorable page where Maumort compares his fishing for memories with childhood angling with his sister. It can indeed be seen as a cross between *A la recherche du temps perdu* and the *Essais* of Montaigne. If Martin du Gard's first major novel, **Jean Barois**, invites comparison with Michelangelo's "Rebellious Slave" in the Louvre which was its original frontispiece, his last calls to mind the "Slaves" in the Accademia in Florence, all the more moving for the contrast between their emerging form and the raw material from which they are partly hewn.

Peter Fawcett, *"Fishing for Memories,"* in The Times Literary Supplement, *No. 4234, May 25, 1984, p. 595.*

ADDITIONAL BIBLIOGRAPHY

Barbert, Gene J. "Not in the Reviews." *Books Abroad* 32, No. 4 (Autumn 1958): 379-81.
 Account of the critic's meeting with Martin du Gard in 1957.

——. "Roger Martin du Gard: Recent Criticism." *French Review* XLI, No. 1 (October 1967): 60-9.
 Bibliographical essay in which Barbert lists and discusses the major criticism of Martin du Gard's work.

Blake, Patricia. "The Perpetual Drefusard." *Partisan Review* XVI, No. 9 (Summer 1949): 955-57.
 Examines some political implications of *Jean Barois*.

Boak, C. D[enis]. "An Early Work by Roger Martin du Gard." *AUMLA*, No. 20 (November 1963): 318-30.
 Discusses Martin du Gard's early works and their presentation of themes that would recur throughout his career.

——. "Roger Martin du Gard: The Need to Dramatize." *AUMLA*, No. 45 (May 1976): 69-79.
 Analyzes dramatic elements in *The World of the Thibaults*.

——. "Roger Martin du Gard 1881-1981." *Essays in French Literature*, No. 18 (November 1981): 42-64.
 Biographical and bibliographical essay.

Brosman, Catherine Savage. "André Gide and Roger Martin du Gard: For and Against Commitment." *Rice University Studies* 59, No. 3 (Summer 1973): 1-8.

Discusses the varying degrees of political commitment displayed in Gide's and Martin du Gard's works, maintaining that while Gide harbored stronger political opinions, his art was "less engaged" than that of Martin du Gard.

DeJongh, William F. J. "Unnatural Death in *Les Thibault*." *Romance Notes* IX, No. 2 (Spring 1968): 190-94.
Considers those episodes in *The World of the Thibaults* which might serve as a treatise on ethical suicide and euthanasia.

Field, Trevor. "The Internal Chronology of *Jean Barois*." *Studi Francesi* n. s. XVII, No. 50 (May-August 1973): 300-03.
Examines some discrepancies of chronology in the various parts of *Jean Barois*.

Gide, André. *The Journals of André Gide,* Vols. 2 & 3, pp. 44ff., pp. 11ff. New York: Alfred A. Knopf, 1949.
Numerous brief references to Martin du Gard and his work.

Gilbert, John. "Symbols of Continuity and the Unity of *Les Thibault*." In *Image and Theme: Studies in Modern French Fiction*, edited by W. M. Frohock, pp. 124-48. Cambridge: Harvard University Press, 1969.
Analysis of *The World of the Thibaults* as an example of the roman-fleuve form. Gilbert disagrees with the opinion, held by many critics, that the novel lacks continuity.

Hughes, H. Stuart. "Roger Martin du Gard and the Unattainable Epic." In his *The Obstructed Path*, pp. 107-20. New York: Harper & Row, 1966.
Biographical essay which concentrates upon the role of environmental factors in Martin du Gard's intellectual development.

Kaiser, Grant E. "Roger Martin du Gard's *Jean Barois:* An Experiment in Novelistic Form." *Symposium* XIV, No. 2 (Summer 1960): 135-41.
Discusses stylistic elements in *Jean Barois*.

Keene, Francis. "The Petty Snoopers." *The New York Times Book Review* (6 March 1955): 5, 28.
Review of *The Postman* in which Keene states: "*The Postman* is worth reading. Despite flamboyancies it is a coherent work of art."

Moore-Rinvolucci, Mina J. "*Les Thibault* and Their Creator." *Modern Languages* XXXIII, No. 3 (September 1952): 85-9.
Discusses *The World of the Thibaults,* emphasizing the differences between the first seven volumes and the last four.

O'Nan, Martha. "The Influence of Tolstoy on Martin du Gard." *Kentucky Foreign Language Quarterly* IV, No. 1 (Winter 1957): 7-14.
Maintains that Martin du Gard's reading of both *War and Peace* and *Anna Karenina* strongly influenced his work.

———. "Form in the Novel: André Gide and Martin du Gard." *Symposium* XII, Nos. 1-2 (Spring-Fall 1958): 81-93.
Discusses the friendship between Martin du Gard and Gide and its impact upon their respective literary theories.

Roudiez, Leon S. "The Function of Irony in Martin du Gard." *The Romantic Review* XLVIII, No. 4 (December 1957): 275-86.
Discusses the correlation between the intellectual development of Martin du Gard's characters and that of the author himself.

Roza, Robert. "Roger Martin du Gard, Master-Builder of the Novel." *The American Society Legion of Honor Magazine* 38, No. 2 (1967): 73-88.
Considers Martin du Gard's work as "an alternative to the mainstream of modern fiction."

Schalk, David L. *Roger Martin du Gard: The Novelist and History*. Ithaca, N.Y.: Cornell University Press, 1967, 257 p.
Extensive analysis of the historical context which underlies Martin du Gard's works.

Spurdle, Sonia M. "Roger Martin du Gard's Debt to Ibsen in *L'une de nous* and *Les Thibault*." *The Modern Language Review* 65, No. 1 (January 1970): 54-64.
Study of Martin du Gard's "borrowings" from Ibsen.

———. "Some Sources of Roger Martin du Gard's Inspiration in *Devenir!*" *Neophilologus* LV, No. 3 (July 1971): 261-69.
Traces the influence of Tolstoy, Zola, and Gide in Martin du Gard's early works.

———. "Tolstoy and Martin du Gard's *Les Thibault*." *Comparative Literature* XXIII, No. 4 (Fall 1971): 325-45.
Discusses similarities between *War and Peace* and *The World of the Thibaults*.

Weber, Eugen. "The Secret World of *Jean Barois:* Notes on the Portrait of an Age." In *The Origins of Modern Consciousness*, edited by John Weiss, pp. 79-109. Detroit: Wayne State University Press, 1965.
Discusses the impact of the Dreyfus Affair on French intellectuals of the period.

Wilson, W. D. "The Theme of Abdication in the Novels of Roger Martin du Gard." *Neophilologus* LIX, No. 2 (April 1975): 190-98.
Analyzes the implications of spiritual defeat in Martin du Gard's novels.

Wood, John S. "Roger Martin du Gard." *French Studies* XIV, No. 2 (April 1960): 129-40.
Discusses elements of nihilism in Martin du Gard's novels.

(Benjamin) Frank(lin) Norris (Jr.)

1870-1902

(Also wrote under pseudonym of Justin Sturgis) American novelist, short story writer, essayist, journalist, critic, and poet.

A popular novelist at the turn of the century, Norris is best remembered as a pioneer of American literary Naturalism. Adopting the methods of the French novelist and literary theorist Emile Zola, Norris attempted to represent aspects of life, such as poverty and physical cruelty, which had previously been ignored by writers of the genteel tradition in American literature. Norris's first significant novel, *McTeague*, which one early critic subtitled "A Study in Stinks," shocked much of its original audience with its frank and graphic depictions of violence and degradation. In his later novels *The Octopus* and *The Pit,* Norris followed the example of Zola's novel *Paris* (1898) as he attempted to depict the entire socioeconomic life of a circumscribed locale. Although passages of his works betray a romantic and moralistic sensibility antithetical to the deterministic outlook characteristic of Naturalism, Norris is regarded with Hamlin Garland and Stephen Crane as a primary architect of the American naturalistic novel.

Born and raised in Chicago, Norris was the son of a prosperous wholesale jeweler and a onetime actress. At the age of fourteen he moved with his family to San Francisco, where his father became a real estate developer, renting cheap housing to working class families while retaining his jewelry business in Chicago. Norris was educated in private schools, and his mother shared with him her love for poetry and art. In 1887, entertaining ambitions to become a painter, Norris was enrolled in the Atelier Julien art school in Paris, but his interest in painting soon waned, and he took up writing as a diversion, sending home successive installments of a medieval romance to his brother. Upon finding these and learning that his son was neglecting his artistic studies, Norris's father removed him from the Atelier Julien and enrolled him in the University of California in 1890 to earn a bachelor's degree, in preparation for assuming his father's position in the jewelry business.

Although Norris entered the university against his will and later considered his education practically useless, the experience which he gained during those four years proved to be pivotal to the maturation of his writing. While in his freshman year, he wrote a romantic narrative poem, *Yvernelle,* which was published in book form the following year. During the same period his father divorced his mother, remarried, and moved back to Chicago; Norris never saw him again. By the time *Yvernelle* was published, Norris had lost his youthful interest in purely romantic literature and soon began to use more realistic subject matter in his writing. Although his unconventional topics and writing technique brought him into conflict with the university English faculty concerning proper form and content, his stories and articles were accepted by local journals and student newspapers. By the time he left the University of California—without a degree due to his failure in mathematics—he had begun the novel *McTeague.*

Norris entered Harvard University in 1894 as a special student in English and French, and during his year there he worked on both *McTeague* and another novel, *Vandover and the Brute.*

These two volumes are considered by critics to be the most naturalistic and the most ambitious of his early work. Under the direction of Professor Lewis Gates, Norris cultivated an affinity for the works of Emile Zola and began to base his own fiction on a more realistic foundation than he had previously considered. After a year Norris returned to San Francisco to become an editor, contributor, and journalist for the local periodical the *Wave.* During this time he also finished *McTeague,* for which he could not find a publisher, and subsequently wrote *Moran of the Lady Letty,* a more commercial adventure story that was serialized in 1898 by the *Wave* and by the S. S. McClure syndicate in New York. The novel caught the attention of S. S. McClure himself, who hired Norris as a journalist for *McClure's Magazine* and a reader for the Doubleday and McClure Company, where Norris discovered Theodore Dreiser's novel *Sister Carrie. Moran of the Lady Letty, McTeague,* and Norris's next novel, *Blix,* a semi-autobiographical love story, were all subsequently published in book form by Doubleday.

Early in 1899 Norris conceived of the idea of an "epic of wheat," the first volume of which would be devoted to the production of wheat in California, the second to its distribution in Chicago, and the third to its consumption in Europe. It was, as Norris wrote, "an idea as big as all outdoors," an attempt to portray in a single, massive work the various social milieux of the United States. He published the first volume of the series, *The Octopus,* in 1901, and finished writing the second, *The Pit,* in 1902. Norris never lived to finish the trilogy, however. He died at the age of thirty-two from an attack of appendicitis. Volumes of his short stories and essays were published after his death, and the early novel *Vandover and the Brute,* the manuscript of which was thought to have been lost in the San Francisco Earthquake, was discovered and published in 1914.

Vandover and the Brute, McTeague, The Octopus, and *The Pit* together constitute Norris's major naturalistic novels. Naturalism, as defined by Zola, sought to create "the impersonal novel in which the novelist is nothing but a recorder of facts, who has no right to judge or form conclusions." However, the movement was not wholly impersonal or objective and, under the influence of Charles Darwin and contemporary theories of hereditary determinism, the subject matter for many Naturalist novels concentrated upon the suffering and degradation of the working class. Norris's naturalistic novels attempt to introduce similar themes into American literature, although he never pretended to achieve the clinical objectivity which the French Naturalists held as their ideal. Norris's purpose was to expose what he considered the truth, but he also tried to weave an enthralling story.

Most criticism of Norris's fiction focuses upon two basic tensions which underlie his work, one of which is the struggle between realism and romance, and the other, the conflict between determinism and moralism. Norris himself addressed the question of romance and realism in *The Responsibilities of the Novelist,* in which he defined realism as that which conformed to ordinary life, and romance as that which departed from the pattern of ordinary life. Norris was clearly more interested in the latter mode, deeming realism as characterized by its chief American theorist, William Dean Howells, to be too restricted to the mundane. Nevertheless, in patterning his type of "romance" after the Naturalism of Emile Zola, Norris did attempt to depict life in a realistic manner that emphasized human cruelty and suffering. Norris was highly praised by Howells, who was also one of the first critics to note the incongruity between romance and realism in Norris's fiction. In a review of *McTeague,* he praised the work but noted the melodramatic nature of the romance between two minor characters and of McTeague's death in the desert, chained to the dead body of his mortal enemy, while his half-dead canary sings. Although most critics feel that the final scene mars the novel, Norris protested that it was "correct" and a few critics have defended its inclusion by demonstrating that the desert is a natural culmination of the images of barrenness found throughout the novel. Some critics feel that Norris's writing progressed from romanticism to naturalism while others believe that he held both conceptions concurrently and never completely resolved the conflict between them. His final novels, *The Octopus* and *The Pit,* are considered by some critics notable achievements in the type of large-scale naturalism which Zola attempted in his *Paris,* while others see the "epic of wheat" concept as essentially a romantic one, in which the traditional adventures of warfare are replaced by those of business.

Along with a conflict between realism and romanticism, Norris's work also displays a tension between deterministic and moralistic philosophical perspectives. Generally considered a determinist, holding that free will is largely illusory and that human action is primarily determined by evolutionary and social forces beyond the individual's control, Norris nonetheless

betrayed a moralistic bent, punishing evil characters in ways that reflect a crude sense of poetic justice. The most prominent example of this occurs in *The Octopus.* In this novel, the wheat farmers and the railroad which transports their wheat are both portrayed as the products of economic laws of supply and demand, with individuals serving as incidental functions in the production and distribution of wheat. Thus the conflict between the railroad and the farmers, and the corruption which occurs as a result of their mutual thirst for profit, are considered amoral and possibly necessary elements in the inexorable flow of wheat. Nevertheless, despite this deterministic framework, the corrupt tycoon S. Behrman, who throughout *The Octopus* survives several attempts on his life, implausibly falls into one of the grain holds in a ship and is crushed by his own shipment of wheat, suggesting retribution for acts that were theoretically inevitable. A more believable example of poetic justice occurs in *The Pit,* in which the speculator Curtis Jadwin attempts to corner the wheat market and is financially ruined by the enormous wheat crop, grown in anticipation of the high prices Jadwin himself had created. A number of Marxist critics during the 1930s vigorously attacked such fortuitous conclusions as evasions of social problems which the novel had confronted. Critics consider Norris to be most successful when he avoids romanticism and moralism in his work: his two greatest books, *McTeague* and *The Octopus,* while not free from such defects, are those which most firmly hold to the naturalistic goal of impersonal observation of actual human conditions.

Critics have noted that Norris is more respected for what he attempted than for what he accomplished, and for what it is assumed he could have written had he lived longer than for what he wrote during his lifetime. When divorced from speculation concerning what he could have achieved, critical consensus finds Norris to be a brilliant and eclectic, although flawed, writer. Nevertheless, his vision of a literature which found romance in squalid realities made him one of the most distinctive and important authors of the American naturalist movement.

(See also *Contemporary Authors,* Vol. 110 and *Dictionary of Literary Biography,* Vol. 12: *American Realists and Naturalists.*)

PRINCIPAL WORKS

Yvernelle (poetry) 1892
Moran of the Lady Letty (novel) 1898
Blix (novel) 1899
McTeague (novel) 1899
A Man's Woman (novel) 1900
The Octopus (novel) 1901
A Deal in Wheat (short stories) 1903
The Pit (novel) 1903
The Responsibilities of the Novelist, and Other Literary Essays (essays) 1903
The Joyous Miracle (novel) 1906
The Third Circle (short stories) 1909
*Vandover and the Brute (novel) 1914
The Complete Edition of Frank Norris (novels, short stories, criticisms, essays, and sketches) 1928
Two Poems and "Kim" Reviewed (poetry and criticism) 1930
Frank Norris of "The Wave" (short stories and sketches) 1931
The Letters of Frank Norris (letters) 1956

The Literary Criticism of Frank Norris   (criticism)   1970

*This work was written in the mid-1890s.

JOHN D. BARRY   (essay date 1899)

[*Barry was an American journalist, novelist, essayist, and critic. In the following excerpt, he offers an enthusiastic review of* McTeague.]

The Doubleday & McClure Company has lately brought out in *McTeague: a Story of San Francisco,* a volume which seems to me worthy to rank among the few great novels produced in this country. Before reading the story I had heard it well spoken of; but I was astonished by its profound insight into character; its shrewd humor; its brilliant massing of significant detail, and by its dramatic force. Many readers would consider the subject too unpleasant to be treated in fiction; but for those who do not go to fiction merely to be amused and diverted, and who believe that fiction may profitably be made an expression of life, *McTeague* will be a revelation. An authoritative reviewer recently spoke of it as a study of people who were on the verge of the criminal class. This statement, apparently made as reproach, was hardly fair. But even if it were absolutely true, why should the author be blamed? People on the verge of the criminal classes, as well as the criminal classes themselves, offer excellent material for serious study in fiction. "I can't understand,"said a novelist the other day, "why reviewers are always blaming writers for making their disagreeable characters true, instead of praising them for making the characters express their evil meaning as they do in life." Mr. Frank Norris has been blamed and will unquestionably be blamed again and again for choosing the theme of *McTeague;* but it is only just to him to say that he has handled his material fearlessly, that he has steadfastly followed out his premises to the end. His characters are all common, and they make a picture of the common life in the San Francisco of today that, for clearness and vigor, leaves very little for criticism. Every figure is perfectly realized; every episode has its significance. The main theme, the relations between McTeague and the little German-American girl who becomes his wife, are indicated with extraordinary fidelity, the man's natural brutality, brought out through misfortune, being thrown into play with the woman's instinctive economy, stimulated into wild avarice by the chance that has won for her a five thousand dollar prize in a lottery. The description of the wedding feast of these two people is one of the strongest pieces of writing that I have ever read. It is the kind of writing that, in its vivid presentation of the comic and the pathetic makes the reader feel like laughing and crying at the same time. The subordinate interests are very skillfully woven into the work of the narrative. Perhaps the strange love affair between little Miss Baker, the retired dressmaker, and old Grannis, conducted in silence on either side of the partition that separates their rooms, has a little of the unreality of romance; and the marriage between the drudge, Maria Macapa, and Zerkow, the miser, founded on the story told by Maria of a wonderful gold service of one hundred pieces, contains a curious suggestion of the more extravagant fancies of Dickens. But both these motives are made absorbingly interesting, and many readers will find in the love of the two old people an exquisite poetry and pathos. The book deserves a great success, and it ought to place Mr. Norris in the first rank among our writers, beside Mary Wilkins, and Howells, and Stephen Crane. Indeed, *McTeague* is in treatment not unlike Stephen Crane's work, though without the least suggestion of imitation and without, too, the least suggestion of that striving for effect that Crane's writing shows. The style is wholly free from trickiness, and is simple and virile, evidently the natural expression of the author's thought. It is by no means, however, a mature and finished style, and in this regard Mr. Norris is sure to develop. Now and then the reader sees the author pulling the strings, so to speak, standing off and explaining the characters in a way that suggests superiority . . . Mr. Norris would have gained in power if he had not only projected his characters and allowed them to explain themselves as much as possible, but also used, wherever he spoke in his capacity as author, language wholly in harmony with theirs. (pp. 88-9)

> John D. Barry, "New York Letter," in The Literary World, *Vol. XXX, No. 5, March 18, 1899, pp. 88-9.*

THE LITERARY WORLD   (essay date 1899)

[*In the following review, the critic faults* McTeague *for unnecessary depictions of cruelty and human degradation.*]

It is seldom that we have any opportunity to differ from our New York correspondent, but with his enthusiastic estimate of *McTeague* in the last number of the *Literary World* [see John Barry excerpt dated 1899] we must confess ourselves somewhat out of sympathy. At the time Mr. Barry's letter was received we had seen only the outside of Mr. Norris's book, and as soon as time permitted we turned to it with all our expectations roused in its favor by Mr. Barry's high recommendation. With much that Mr. Barry says we must agree; Mr. Norris is undeniably a powerful writer. He has drawn his characters with rare skill; he has told their stories in most graphic fashion; he has presented the actuality of their life in San Francisco or the wildernesses of California mountains with all its sordidness, its wretchedness, and crime. That huge, stupid animal, McTeague the dentist, his anaemic little wife Trina, the quaint old maid seamstress and the equally quaint old bachelor dog doctor, the repulsive Jew junk dealer, all stand out from the pages with the individuality of life, and the inevitable consequences of misused life follow in their tracks. With relentless truth we are made to follow the decay of McTeague's prosperity, and accompanying it the decay of his own manhood. Stupid he was always, but the one victory he won over his animal nature was the prelude to uninterrupted defeats and a final descent into the very depths of animal brutality. Even more terrible was Trina's wretched life, for she had something to start with in mind and spirit, and the slatternly figure, maimed already through her husband's cruelty—which the story leaves face downward in a pool of blood, battered to death by her husband's fists— was once as neat and trim a little woman as you could find, and the idol of her big husband's heart. One has not the consolation of saying that in real life it could not have happened so. Trina's sordid miserliness, which worked the mischief, was the natural outcome of unnecessary petty economy in a character like hers, and in McTeague's elemental nature hate was quickly stirred and brutally followed. No stronger picture could be given of the evil that lies rooted in the love of money.

That Mr. Norris has written an exceptionally strong and powerful novel we do not wish to deny. Neither do we hold that an author may not choose harsh and brutal subjects. But we do believe that highest art is not merely a question of execution, and that the spirit with which the brutal or the beautiful is treated is the quality that redeems or damns. To our thinking, with all our genuine admiration for its exceptional qualities, *McTeague* cannot be classed among great novels, for the spirit that animates is false to the highest standards. We can pardon, accept even with intellectual pleasure, loathsome details that are necessary to the artistic progress of the story, but grossness for the sake of grossness is unpardonable. Mr. Norris has written pages for which there is absolutely no excuse, and his needless sins against good taste and delicacy are fatal spots upon his work. *McTeague* undoubtedly will be widely read—it is too remarkable to pass speedily into oblivion; but we pray that a kind fate may bring it only to those of vigorous mind and, shall we say it, strong stomach. Mr. Norris has reason to be proud of his work, but the world will not be proud of it in that distant tomorrow which irrevocably sets the true value on books of today.

> *"McTeague," in* The Literary World, *Vol. XXX, No. 7, April 1, 1899, p. 99.*

JACK LONDON   (essay date 1901)

[*One of the most popular Naturalist writers of the early twentieth century, London combined adventure, socialism, mysticism, Darwinian determinism, and Nietzschean theories of race in such classic novels as* Call of the Wild *(1903) and* The Sea-Wolf *(1904). His high regard for the writings of Charles Darwin and Friedrich Nietzsche is demonstrated by the doctrines of rugged individualism and of the amoral ubermensch ("superman") that dominate his early adventure novels and which in his later fiction took the more malignant form of advocating white supremacy. Nevertheless, London also wrote socialist novels and essays in support of labor reform and a united effort by the working class to bring about a better future. In the following excerpt from an essay originally published in the journal* Impressions *in June 1901, London offers a laudatory review of* The Octopus.]

Very long ago, we of the West heard it rumored that Frank Norris had it in mind to write the "Epic of the Wheat". Nor can it be denied that many of us doubted—not the ability of Frank Norris merely, but the ability of the human, of all humans. This great, incoherent, amorphous West! Who could grip the spirit and the essence of it, the luster and the wonder, and bind it all, definitely and sanely, within the covers of a printed book? Surely we of the West, who knew our West, may have been pardoned our lack of faith.

And now Frank Norris has done it; has, in a machine age, achieved what has been peculiarly the privilege of the man who lived in an heroic age; in short, has sung the "Epic of the Wheat". "More power to his elbow," as Charles F. Lummis would say.

On first sight of the Valley of the San Joaquin, one can not help but call it the "new and naked land." There is apparently little to be seen. A few isolated ranches in the midst of the vastness, no timber, a sparse population—that is all. And the men of the ranches, sweating in bitter toil, they must likewise be new and naked. So it would seem; but Norris has given breadth to both, and depth. Not only has he gone into the soil, into the womb of the passionate earth, yearning for motherhood, the sustenance of nations; but he has gone down into the heart of its people, simple, elemental, prone to the ruder amenities of existence, growling and snarling with brute anger under cruel wrong. One needs must feel a sympathy for these men, workers and fighters, and for all of their weakness, a respect. And, after all, as Norris has well shown, their weakness is not inherent. It is the weakness of unorganization, the weakness of the force which they represent and of which they are a part, the agricultural force as opposed to the capitalistic force, the farmer against the financier, the tiller of the soil against the captain of industry.

No man, not large of heart, lacking in spontaneous sympathy, incapable of great enthusiasms, could have written *The Octopus.* Presley, the poet, dreamer and singer, is a composite fellow. So far as mere surface incident goes, he is audaciously Edwin Markham; but down in the heart of him he is Frank Norris. Presley, groping vaguely in the silence of the burning night for the sigh of the land; Presley, with his great Song of the West forever leaping up in his imagination and forever eluding him; Presley, wrestling passionately for the swing of his "thundering progression of hexameters"—who is this Presley but Norris, grappling in keen travail with his problem of *The Octopus,* and doubting often, as we of the West have doubted?

Men obtain knowledge in two ways: by generalizing from experience; by gathering to themselves the generalizations of others. As regards Frank Norris, one can not avoid pausing for speculation. It is patent that in this, his last and greatest effort, he has laid down uncompromisingly the materialistic conception of history, or, more politely, the economic interpretation of history. Now the question arises: Did Frank Norris acquire the economic interpretation of history from the printed records of the thoughts of other men, and thus equipped, approach his problem of *The Octopus?* or, rather, did he approach it, naive and innocent? and from direct contact with the great social forces was he not forced to so generalize for himself? It is a pretty question. Will he some day tell us?

Did Norris undergo the same evolution he has so strongly depicted in Presley? Presley's ultimate sociological concept came somewhat in this fashion: Shelgrim the president and owner of the Pacific and Southwestern, laid "a thick, powerful forefinger on the table to emphasize his words. 'Try to believe this—to begin with—that railroads build themselves. Where there is a demand, sooner or later there will be a supply. Mr. Derrick, does he grow his wheat? The wheat grows itself. What does he count for? Does he supply the force? What do I count for? Do I build the railroad? You are dealing with forces, young man, when you speak of wheat and the railroads, not with men. There is the wheat, the supply. It must be carried to feed the people. There is the demand. The wheat is one force, the railroad another, and there is the law that governs them—supply and demand. Men have only little to do in the whole business. Complications may arise, conditions that bear hard on the individual—crush him, maybe—but the wheat will be carried to feed the people as inevitably as it will grow.'"

One feels disposed to quarrel with Norris for his inordinate realism. What does the world care whether Hooven's meat safe be square or oblong; whether it be lined with wire screen or mosquito netting; whether it be hung to the branches of the oak tree or to the ridge-pole of the barn; whether, in fact, Hooven has a meat safe or not? "Feels disposed" is used advisedly. In truth, we can not quarrel with him. It is confession and capitulation. The facts are against us. He *has* produced results, Titanic results. Never mind the realism, the unimportant detail, minute description, Hooven's meat safe and the rest. Let it be stated flatly that by no other method could Frank Norris or anybody else have handled the vast Valley of the San Joaquin and the no less vast-tentacled *Octopus.* Results? It was the only way to get results, the only way to paint the broad canvas he has painted, with the sunflare in his brush.

But he gives us something more than realism. Listen to this:

> Once more the pendulum of the seasons swung in its mighty arc.

> Then, faint and prolonged, across the levels of the ranch, he heard the engine whistling for Bonneville. Again and again, at rapid intervals in its flying course, it whistled for road crossings, for sharp curves, for trestles; ominous notes, hoarse, bellowing, ringing with the accents of menace and defiance; and abruptly Presley saw again, in his imagination, the galloping monster, the terror of steel and steam, with its single eye, cyclopean, red, shooting from horizon to horizon; but saw it now as the symbol of a vast power, huge, terrible, flinging the echo of its thunder over all the reaches of the valley, leaving blood and destruction in its path; the leviathan, with tentacles of steel clutching into the soil, the soulless Force, the iron-hearted Power, the monster, the Colossus, the Octopus. . . .

> The direct brutality of ten thousand acres of wheat, nothing but wheat as far as the eye could see, stunned her a little. There was something vaguely indecent in the sight, this food of the people, this elemental force, this basic energy, weltering here under the sun in all the unconscious nakedness of a sprawling, primordial Titan. . . .

> Everywhere throughout the great San Joaquin, unseen and unheard, a thousand ploughs upstirred the land, tens of thousands of shears clutched so deep into the warm, moist soil. It was the long, stroking caress, vigorous, male, powerful, for which the Earth seemed panting. The heroic embrace of a multitude of iron hands, gripping down into the brown, warm flesh of the land that quivered responsive and passionate under this rude advance, so robust as to be almost an assault, so violent as to be veritably brutal. There, under the sun and under the speckless sheen of the sky, the wooing of the Titan began, the vast primal passion, the two world-forces, the elemental Male and Female, locked in a colossal embrace, at grapples in the throes of an infinite desire, at once terrible and divine, knowing no law, untamed, savage, natural, sublime.

Many men, and women, too, pass through the pages of *The Octopus,* but one, greatest of all, we can not forbear mentioning in passing—Annixter. Annixter, rough almost to insolence, direct in speech, intolerant in his opinions, relying upon absolutely no one but himself; crusty of temper, bullying of disposition, a ferocious worker, and as widely trusted as he was widely hated; obstinate and contrary, cantankerous, and deliciously afraid of "feemale women"—this is Annixter. He is worth knowing. In such cunning fashion has Norris blown the breath of life into him, that his death comes with a shock which is seldom produced by deaths in fiction. Osterman, laying his head on his arms like a tired man going to rest, and Delaney, crawling instinctively out of the blood-welter to die in the growing wheat; but it is Annixter, instantly killed, failing with-

out movement, for whom we first weep. A living man there died.

Well, the promise of *Moran* and *McTeague* has been realized. Can we ask more? Yet we have only the first of the trilogy. The "Epic of the Wheat" is no little thing. Content with *The Octopus,* we may look forward to *The Pit* and *The Wolf.* We shall not doubt this time. (pp. 67-9)

Jack London, "On Norris' 'The Octopus'," in American Literary Realism 1870-1910, *Vol. 6, No. 1, Winter, 1973, pp. 66-9.*

FRANK NORRIS   (essay date 1901)

[*In the following essay, originally published in* World's Work *in 1901 and reprinted in* The Responsibilities of the Novelist, *Norris expresses his disdain for commercial novelists, his view that romance and realism are compatible, and his conviction that truth should be expressed in the novel.*]

Not that one quarrels with the historical novel as such; not that one does not enjoy good fiction wherever found and in whatever class. It is the method of attack of the latter-day copyists that one deplores—their attitude, the willingness of so very, very many of them to take off the hat to Fashion and then hold the same hat for Fashion to drop pennies in.

Ah, but the man must be above the work or the work is worthless and the man better off at some other work than that of producing fiction. The eye never once should wander to the gallery, but be always with single purpose turned *inward* upon the work, testing it and retesting it that it rings true.

What one quarrels with is the perversion of a profession, the detestable trading upon another man's success. No one can find fault with those few good historical novels that started the fad. There was good workmanship in these, and honesty. But the copyists, the fakirs—they are not novelists at all, though they write novels that sell by the hundreds of thousands. They are business men. They find out—no, they allow *someone else* to find out—what the public wants, and they give it to the public cheap and advertise it as a new soap is advertised. Well, they make money; and, if that is their aim—if they are content to prostitute the good name of American literature for a sliding scale of royalties—let's have done with them. They have their reward. But the lamentable result will be that these copyists will in the end so prejudice the people against an admirable school of fiction—the school of Scott—that for years to come the tale of historic times will be discredited and many a great story remain unwritten, and many a man of actual worth and real power hold back in the ranks for very shame of treading where so many fools have rushed in.

For the one idea of the fakir—the copyist—and of the public which for the moment listens to him, is Clothes, Clothes, Clothes, first, last and always Clothes. Not Clothes only in the sense of doublet and gown, but Clothes of speech, Clothes of manner, Clothes of customs. Hear them expatiate over the fashion of wearing a cuff, over a trick of speech, over the architecture of a house, the archeology of armour, and the like. It is all well enough in its way, but so easily dispensed with if there be flesh and blood underneath. Veronese put the people of his Marriage at Cana into the clothes of his contemporaries. Is the picture any less a masterpiece?

Do these Little People know that Scott's archeology was about one thousand years "out" in *Ivanhoe,* and that to make a parallel we must conceive of a writer describing Richelieu—say—in small clothes and a top hat? But is it not Richelieu we want, and Ivanhoe, not their clothes, their armour? And in spite of his errors Scott gave us a real Ivanhoe. He got beneath the clothes of an epoch and got the heart of it and the spirit of it (different essentially and vitally from ours or from every other, the spirit of feudalism); and he put forth a masterpiece.

The Little People, so very precise in the matter of buttons and "bacinets," do not so. Take the clothes from the people of their romances and one finds only wooden manikins. Take the clothes from the epoch of which they pretend to treat and what is there beneath? It is only the familiar, well-worn, well-thumbed nineteenth or twentieth century after all. As well have written of Michigan Avenue, Chicago, as "La Rue de la Harpe," "The Great North Road" or the "Appian Way."

It is a masquerade, the novel of the copyists; and the people who applaud them—are they not the same who would hold persons in respect because of the finery of their bodies? A poor taste, a cheap one; the taste of serving men, the literature of chambermaids.

To approach the same subject by a different radius: why must the historical novel of the copyist always be conceived of in the terms of Romance? Could not the formula of Realism be applied at least as well, not the Realism of mere externals (the copyists have that), but the Realism of motives and emotions? What would we not give for a picture of the fifteenth century as precise and perfect as one of Mr. James's novels? Even if that be impossible, the attempt, even though halfway successful, would be worth while, would be better than the wooden manikin in the tin-pot helmet and baggy hose. At least we should get somewhere, even if no farther than Mr. Kingsley took us in *Hereward*, or Mr. Blackmore in *Lorna Doone*.

How about the business life and the student life, and the artisan life and the professional life, and above all, the home life of historic periods? Great heavens! There was something else sometimes than the soldier life. They were not always cutting and thrusting, not always night riding, escaping, venturing, posing.

Or suppose that cut-and-thrust must be the order of the day, where is the "man behind," and the heart in the man and the spirit in the heart and the essential vital, elemental, all-important true life within the spirit? We are Anglo-Saxons enough to enjoy the sight of a fight, would go a block or so out of the way to see one, or be a dollar or so out of pocket. But let it not be these jointed manikins worked with a thread. At least let it be Mr. Robert Fitzsimmons or Mr. James Jeffries. Clothes, paraphernalia, panoply, pomp and circumstance, and the copyist's public and the poor bedevilled, ink-corroded hack of an overdriven, underpaid reviewer on an inland paper speak of the "vivid colouring" and "the fine picture of a bygone age"—it is easy to be vivid with a pot of vermilion at the elbow. Anyone can scare a young dog with a false face and a roaring voice, but to be vivid and use grays and browns, to scare the puppy with the lifted finger, that's something to the point.

The difficult thing is to get at the life immediately around you—the very life in which you move. No romance in it? No romance in *you*, poor fool. As much romance on Michigan Avenue as there is realism in King Arthur's court. It is as you choose to see it. The important thing to decide is, which formula is the best to help you grip the Real Life of this or any other age. Contemporaries always imagine that theirs is the prosaic age, and that chivalry and the picturesque died with

their forbears. No doubt Merlin mourned for the old time of romance. Cervantes held that romance was dead. Yet most of the historical romances of the day are laid in Cervantes's time, or even after it.

Romance and realism are constant qualities of every age, day, and hour. They are here to-day. They existed in the time of Job. They will continue to exist till the end of time, not so much in things as in point of view of the people who see things.

The difficulty, then, is to get at the immediate life—immensely difficult, for you are not only close to the canvas, but are yourself part of the picture.

But the historic age is almost done to hand. Let almost anyone shut himself in his closet with a history and Violet LeDuc's *Dictionaire du Mobilier* and, given a few months' time, he can evolve an historical novel of the kind called popular. He need not know men—just clothes and lingo, the "what-ho-without-there" gabble. But if he only chose he could find romance and adventure in Wall Street or Bond Street. But romance there does not wear the gay clothes and the showy accoutrements, and to discover it—the real romance of it—means hard work and close study, not of books, but of people and actualities.

Not only this, but to know the life around you you must live—if not *among* people, then *in* people. You must be something more than a novelist if you can, something more than just a writer. There must be that nameless sixth sense or sensibility in you that great musicians have in common with great inventors and great scientists; the thing that does not enter into the work, but that is back of it; the thing that would make of you a good *man* as well as a good novelist; the thing that differentiates the mere business man from the financier (for it is possessed of the financier and poet alike—so only they be big enough).

It is not genius, for genius is a lax, loose term so flippantly used that its expressiveness is long since lost. It is more akin to sincerity. And there once more we halt upon the great word—sincerity, sincerity, and again sincerity. Let the writer attack his historical novel with sincerity and he cannot then do wrong. He will see then the man beneath the clothes and the heart beneath both, and he will be so amazed at the wonder of that sight that he will forget the clothes. His public will be small, perhaps, but he will have the better reward of the knowledge of a thing well done. Royalties on editions of hundreds of thousands will not pay him more to his satisfaction than that. To make money is not the province of a novelist. If he is the right sort, he has other responsibilities, heavy ones. He of all men cannot think only of himself or for himself. And when the last page is written and the ink crusts on the pen point and the hungry presses go clashing after another writer, the "new man" and the new fashion of the hour, he will think of the grim, long grind of the year of his life that he has put behind him and of his work that he has built up volume by volume, sincere work, telling the truth as he saw it, independent of fashion and the gallery gods, holding to these with gripped hands and shut teeth—he will think of all this then, and he will be able to say: "I never truckled; I never took off the hat to Fashion and held it out for pennies. By God, I told them the truth. They liked it or they didn't like it. What had that to do with me? I told them the truth; I knew it for the truth then, and I know it for the truth now."

And that is his reward—the best that a man may know; the only one really worth the striving for. (pp. 13-18)

Frank Norris, "The True Reward of the Novelists," in his The Responsibilities of the Novelist [and] The Joyous Miracle, Vol. VII, Doubleday, Doran & Company, Inc., 1928, pp. 13-18.

W. D. HOWELLS (essay date 1902)

[*Howells was the chief progenitor of American realism and the most influential American literary critic during the late nineteenth century. Recognized as one of the major literary figures of the nineteenth century, he successfully weaned American literature away from the sentimental romanticism of its infancy, earning the popular sobriquet "the Dean of American Letters." Through realism, a theory central to his fiction and criticism, Howells sought to disperse "the conventional acceptations by which men live on easy terms with themselves" that they might "examine the grounds of their social and moral opinions." To accomplish this, according to Howells, the writer must strive to record detailed impressions of everyday life, endowing characters with true-to-life motives and avoiding authorial comment in the narrative. In the following excerpt from an essay written upon the occasion of Norris's death, Howells offers an appreciative assessment of Norris's novels* McTeague *and* The Octopus.]

Those who know *The Octopus* know how Norris's work justified his faith in himself; but those who had known *McTeague* could not have doubted but he would do what he had undertaken, in the spirit of the undertaking. Norris did give the time and toil to the right documentation of his history. He went to California and renewed his vital knowledge of his scene; he was in California again, studying the course of the fact which was to bring him to Chicago, when death overtook him and ended his high emprise. But in the meantime he had given us *The Octopus,* and before that he had given us *McTeague,* books not all so unlike in their nature as their surfaces might suggest. Both are epical, though the one is pivoted on the common ambition of a coarse human animal, destined to prevail in a half-quackish triumph, and the other revolves about one of the largest interests of modern civilization. The author thought at first of calling *McTeague,* as he told me, "The Golden Tooth," which would have been more significant of the irregular dentist's supremacy in the story, and the ideal which inspired him; but perhaps he felt a final impossibility in the name. Yet, the name is a mere mask; and when one opens the book, the mask falls, and the drama confronts us with as living a physiognomy as I have seen in fiction. There is a bad moment when the author is overcome by his lingering passion for the romantic, and indulges himself in a passage of rank melodrama; but even there he does nothing that denies the reality of his characters, and they are always of a reality so intense that one lives with them in the grotesquely shabby San Francisco street where, but for the final episode, the action passes.

What is good is good, it matters not what other things are better or worse; and I could ask nothing for Norris, in my sense of his admirable achievement, but a mind freed to criticism absolute and not relative. He is of his time, and, as I have said, his school is evident; and yet I think he has a right to make his appeal in *The Octopus* irrespective of the other great canvases beside which that picture must be put. One should dissociate it as far as possible from the work of his masters—we all have masters; the masters themselves had them—not because it is an imitation, and would suffer from the comparison, but because it is so essentially different, so boldly and frankly native, that one is in danger of blaming it for a want of conformity to models, rather than for too close a following. Yet this, again, does not say quite the right thing, and what I feel,

and wish others to feel, in regard to it, is the strong security of its most conscientious and instructed art. Here is nothing of experiment, of protest, of rebellion; the author does not break away from form in any sprawling endeavor for something newly or incomparably American, Californian, Western, but finds scope enough for his powers within the limits where the greatest fiction of our period "orbs about." The time, if there ever was one, for a prose Walt Whitman was past; and he perceived that the indigenous quality was to be imparted to his work by the use of fresh material, freshly felt, but used in the fashion and the form which a world-old art had evolved in its long endeavor.

McTeague was a personal epic, the Odyssey of a simple, semi-savage nature adventuring and experiencing along the low social levels which the story kept, and almost never rose or fell from. As I review it in the light of the first strong impressions, I must own it greater than I have ever yet acknowledged it, and I do this now with the regret which I hope the critic is apt to feel for not praising enough when praise could have helped most. I do not think my strictures of it were mistaken, for they related to the limits which certain facts of it would give it with the public, rather than to the ethical or æsthetic qualities which would establish it with the connoisseur. Yet, lest any reader of mine should be left without due sense of these, I wish now to affirm my strong sense of them, and to testify to the value which this extraordinary book has from its perfectly simple fidelity: from the truthfulness in which there is no self-doubt and no self-excuse.

But, with all its power, *McTeague* is no such book as *The Octopus,* which is the Iliad to its Odyssey.

It will not be suggesting too much for the story to say, that there is a kind of Homeric largeness in the play of the passions moving it. They are not autochthons, these Californians of the great Wheat farms, choking in the folds of the railroad, but Americans of more than one transplantation; yet there is something rankly earthy and elemental in them, which gives them the pathos of tormented Titans. It is hard to choose any of them as the type, as it is hard to chose any scene as the representative moment. If we choose Annixeter, growing out of an absolute, yet not gross, materiality, through the fire of a purifying love, into a kind of final spirituality, we think, with misgiving for our decision, of Magnus Derrick, the high, pure leader of the rebellion against the railroad, falling into ruin, moral and mental, through the use of the enemy's bad means for his good cause. Half a score of other figures, from either camp, crowd upon the fancy to contest the supreme interest, men figures, women figures; and, when it comes to choosing this episode or that as the supreme event, the confusion of the critic is even greater. If one were to instance the fight between the farmers and the sheriff's deputies, with the accompanying evictions, one must recall the tremendous passages of the train-robbery by the crazy victim of the railroad's treachery, taking his revenge in his hopeless extremity. Again, a half score of other scenes, other episodes rise from the remembered pages, and defy selection.

The story is not less but more epical, in being a strongly interwrought group of episodes. The play of an imagination fed by a rich consciousness of the mystical relations of nature and human nature, the body and the soul of earthly life, steeps the whole theme in an odor of common growth. It is as if the Wheat sprang out of the hearts of men, in the conception of the young poet who writes its Iliad, and who shows how it overwhelms their lives, and germinates anew from their deaths.

Cover of McTeague.

His poem, of which the terms are naked prose, is a picture of the civilization, the society, the culture which is the efflorescence of the wheaten prosperity; and the social California, rank, crude, lusty, which he depicts is as convincing as the agricultural California, which is the ground of his work. It will be easily believed that in the handling nothing essential to the strong impression is blinked; but nothing, on the other hand, is forced in. The episode of Venamee and Angèle, with its hideous tragedy, and the long mystical epilogue ending almost in anti-climax, is the only passage which can be accused of irrelevance, and it is easier to bring than to prove this accusation.

As I write, and scarcely touch the living allegory here and there, it rises before me in its large inclusion, and makes me feel once more how little any analysis of a work of art can represent it. After all the critic must ask the reader to take his word for it that the thing is great, and entreat him to go see for himself: see, in this instance, the breadth and the fineness, the beauty and the dread, the baseness and the grandeur, the sensuality and the spirituality, working together for the effect of a novel unequalled for scope and for grasp in our fiction. (pp. 773-76)

> W. D. Howells, "Frank Norris," in The North American Review, *Vol. 175, No. 6, December, 1902, pp. 769-78.*

FREDERIC TABER COOPER　(essay date 1911)

[*An American educator, biographer, and editor, Cooper served for many years as literary critic at the* Bookman, *a popular early twentieth-century literary magazine. In the following excerpt, he discusses Norris's importance, his debt to Emile Zola, and the grandiose vision of his later books.*]

During the closing years of the nineteenth century, or to be more specific, from 1897 to 1902, the period of Norris's activity, there were easily a score of new writers who leaped suddenly into prominence on the strength of a single book. The volumes that come casually to mind and may be regarded as fairly representative are Winston Churchill's *Richard Carvel,* Robert Herrick's *Gospel of Freedom,* Mrs. Wharton's *The Greater Inclination,* Booth Tarkington's *Gentleman from Indiana,* Brand Whitlock's *Thirteenth District,* George Horton's *Long Straight Road,* Theodore Dreiser's *Sister Carrie,* Morgan Robertson's *Spun Yarn,* Harry Leon Wilson's *The Spenders,* Owen Wister's *The Virginian,* Jack London's *Sons of the Wolf,*— the list might be stretched to twice the length. In glancing over this array of names, the various associations and contrasts they offer strike one to-day as exceedingly odd. Certain of these reputations seem now curiously stunted; certain others loom up unexpectedly large; but in spite of the unforeseen readjustments that time has wrought, the significant fact remains that Norris in his lifetime dwarfed them all. At the time of the appearance of **The Octopus** and **The Pit,** there was not a single volume produced by this younger group, with the possible exception of *The Virginian,* that even approached them in breadth of view or bigness of intent. And when we measure the ten years' growth in individual cases, when we compare the promise of *The Gospel of Freedom,* or *The Greater Inclination* with the accomplishment of *Together* or *The House of Mirth,* then the fact is suddenly forced home to us, how much greater growth that same ten years would have shown in the best craftsman and the bravest, biggest soul of them all. One realizes now that even in his last and maturest books, Norris had not fully found himself, that he was still in the transition period, still groping his way tirelessly, undauntedly towards self-knowledge. He had adopted the creed of naturalism ardently, refashioning it to suit the needs of a younger, cleaner civilization, a world of wider expanses, purer air, freer life. And even while he wrought, he witnessed the apparent downfall of that very creed in the land of its birth, saw its disintegration beneath the hands of its chief champion. It is impossible to read Norris's works without perceiving that from first to last there was within him an instinct continually at war with his chosen realistic methods; an unconquerable and exasperating vein of romanticism that led him frequently into palpable absurdities,—not because romanticism in itself is a literary crime, but because it has its own proper place in literature, and that place is assuredly not in a realistic novel. How this inner warfare would eventually have worked out; what compromises, innovations, iconoclasms would have paved the way to full maturity of accomplishment, it is of course impossible now even to guess. But one thing is certain: Norris would have found that way; and when found, it would have proved not merely big, rugged, compelling, but also clean as the open, wind-swept spaces that he loved, and fine as gold that has no dross. (pp. 296-98)

Norris's debt to Zola . . . is too obvious to have need of argument. Everywhere, from his earliest writings to his last, in one form or another, it stares us in the face, compelling recognition. Like Zola, his strength lay in depicting life on a gigantic scale, portraying humanity in the mass: like Zola, he could not work without the big, underlying Idea, the dominant symbol. In *McTeague,* the symbol is Gold, the most fitting emblem he could devise to personify the State of California. The whole book is flooded with a shimmer of yellow light,— we see it in the floating golden disk that the sunlight, through the trees, casts upon the ground; in the huge gilded tooth of the dentist's sign; in the lottery prize which Trina wins; in the Polish Jew, Zerkow, "the Man with the Rake, groping hourly in the muck heap of the city for gold, for gold, for gold"; in the visionary golden dishes of Maria Macapa's diseased fancy, "a yellow blaze like fire, like a sunset"; and again in the hoarded coins on which Trina delighted to stretch her naked limbs at night, in her strange passion for money,—the coins which finally lured McTeague and his enemy to their hideous death in the alkali desert. In the "Epic of the Wheat," as we shall see more specifically when we come to examine *The Octopus* in detail, the central symbol had become an even vaster, more relentlessly dominant element. A single State no longer satisfied him. What he wanted was a symbol which should sum up at once American life and American prosperity. His friends are still fond of telling of the day when he came to his office trembling with excitement, incapacitated for work, his brain seething with a single thought, the "Trilogy of the Wheat." "I have got a big idea, the biggest I ever had," was the burden of all he had to say for many a day thereafter.

Another obvious debt that Norris owed to the creator of *Les Rougon-Macquart* is his style: the swing and march of phrase and sentence; the exuberant wealth of noun and adjective; the insistent iteration with which he develops an idea, expanding and elaborating and dwelling upon it, forcing it upon the reader with accumulated synonym and metaphor, driving it home with the dogged persistence of a trip-hammer. Here is a passage which, brief as it is, admirably illustrates this quality:

> Outside, the unleashed wind yelled incessantly, like a sabbath of witches, and spun about their pitiful shelter and went rioting past, leaping and somersaulting from rock to rock, tossing hand-fuls of dry, dust-like snow into the air; folly-stricken, insensate, an enormous, mad monster gamboling there in some hideous dance of death, capricious, headstrong, pitiless, as a famished wolf.

(pp. 309-11)

Of *McTeague* almost enough has been said already. It is the most frankly brutal thing that Norris ever wrote; its realism is as unsparing as d'Annunzio's, though its theme is cleaner. It is a remorseless study of heredity and environment, symbolizing the greed of gold and dominated throughout by the gigantic figure of the dull and brutish dentist, ox-like, ponderous and slow. Necessarily, it is a repellent book; and yet there is about it that curious attraction which certain forms of ugliness possess when they attain a degree of perfection amounting to a fine art. *McTeague* does not begin to show the breadth of purpose or the technical skill of *The Octopus* or *The Pit;* yet there are times when one is tempted to award it a higher place for all-around excellence. There is a better balance between the central theme and the individual characters,—or to state it differently, between the underlying ethics and the so-called human interest. If Norris had never written another book, he would still have lived in *McTeague,* just as surely as George Douglas Brown still lives in *The House with the Green Shutters.* (p. 320)

It remains now to speak briefly of *The Octopus* and *The Pit,* the opening volumes of the trilogy which Norris was destined never to finish, just as Zola was destined never to finish his tetralogy, *Les Quatre Évangiles.* It is not surprising that, in this "Epic of the Wheat," Norris had undertaken a task for which he was hardly ripe, that he was attempting a feat beyond his years and his stature. The vast canvas, the colossal theme, the multitudinous, thronging incident, the crowded stage,— these, we have seen, are Norris's necessary materials,—not throngs of people but of things, immensities of prairie and ocean and sky. But a man must grow slowly to his full attainment; and Norris showed a feverish impatience to attain at a bound heights that he should have been glad to reach after twenty years of slow and sure toiling. Zola had a lifetime of work and twoscore volumes behind him before attempting to sum up the complex of a whole city in a single volume, *Paris.* Norris, with the experience gained in four volumes and barely eight years of work, wished to sum up the life of a whole continent. *The Octopus* is a vast allegory, an example of symbolism pushed to the extreme limit, rather than a picture of real life. With the two succeeding volumes, it was destined to portray American life as a whole,—not merely the life of some small corner of a single State, but America, in its entirety, with all its hopes and aspirations, from the Canadian to the Mexican border, from the Atlantic to the Pacific. And for the central symbol he chose Wheat, as being quite literally the staff of this life, the ultimate source of American power and prosperity. This first volume, dealing with wheat in the field, shows us a corner of California, the San Joaquin valley, where a handful of ranchmen are engaged in irrigating and plowing, planting, reaping, and harvesting, performing all the slow, arduous toil of cultivation,—and at the same time carrying on a continuous warfare against the persistent encroachment of the railroad, whose steel arms are reaching out, octopus-like, to grasp, encircle and slowly crush, one after another, whoever ventures to oppose it. In a broader sense, it symbolizes the hold that capital has upon labor, the aggression of the corporation and the trust upon the rights of the individual. But back of the individual, stronger than the trusts, is the spirit of the people, the dauntless energy of the nation, typified by the Wheat,—a perennial, exhaustless fruition, a mighty, resistless tide, rising, spreading, gathering force, rolling onward in vast, golden waves throughout the length and breadth of the continent, bearing with it the promise of health and strength and prosperity. Such is the underlying scheme, the nucleus of *The Octopus;* and the manner in which the technical difficulties have been overcome and the intricate structure reared compels wondering approval even from such readers as find the human story in the book somewhat disappointing. Especially admirable is the way in which Norris's double theme, his twofold symbolism, is kept constantly before the reader like two recurrent and interwoven *leitmotive* of a Wagnerian opera. First, there is the *motif* of the railway, visible symbol of corporate greed, insistent, aggressive, refusing to be forgotten, making its presence felt on every page,—through the shrill scream of a distant engine, the heavy rumble of a passing freight train, the substantial presence of S. Behrmann, the local agent, whose name greets us at the outset of the story in huge flaring letters of a painted sign upon a water-tank, "S. Behrmann has something to say to *you,*" and whose corpulent, imperturbable, grasping personality obtrudes itself continually, placid, unyielding, invincible. Now and then we are brought face to face with the road itself, as, for instance, in the grim, gruesome episode of an engine plowing its way through a flock of sheep which have somehow forced an opening in a barbed-wire fence and strayed upon the track:

> The pathos of it was beyond expression. It was a slaughter, a massacre of innocents. The iron monster had charged full into the midst, merciless, inexorable. To the right and left, all the width of the right of way, the little bodies had been flung; backs were snapped against the fence-posts; brains knocked out. Caught in the barbs of the wire, wedged in, the bodies hung suspended. Under foot it was terrible; the black blood, winking in the starlight, seeped down into the clay between the ties with a long sucking murmur.... Abruptly, Presley saw again in his imagination the galloping monster, the terror of steel and steam, with its single eye, cyclopean, red, shooting from horizon to horizon; but saw it now as the symbol of a vast power, huge, terrible, flinging the echo of its thunder over all the reaches of the valley, leaving blood and destruction in its path; the leviathan, with tentacles of steel clutching into the soil, the soulless Force, the iron-hearted Power, the Monster, the Colossus, the Octopus.

And simultaneously we have the second *motif* of the Wheat, underlying that of the railroad and, in a measure, subordinated to it, yet always with an unspoken suggestion of final triumph:

> Men—motes in the sunshine—perished, were shot down in the very noon of life, hearts were broken, little children started in life lamentably handicapped; young girls were brought to a life of shame; old women died in the heart of life for lack of food. In that little isolated group of human insects, misery, death and anguish spun like a wheel of fire.
>
> *But the wheat remained.* Untouched, unassailable, undefiled, that mighty world force, that nourisher of nations, wrapped in Nirvanic calm, indifferent to the human swarm, gigantic, resistless, moved onward in its appointed grooves. Through the welter of blood at the irrigation ditch, through the sham charity and shallow philanthropy of famine relief committees, the great harvest of Los Muertos rolled, like a flood, from the Sierras to the Himalayas to feed thousands of starving scare-crows on the barren plains of India.

Such, in brief, were the plan and purpose of Norris's *Octopus*, a book saturated with the quenchless enthusiasm of youth and conscious strength. One cannot read it without a responsive thrill at the breadth of purpose, the earnestness, the astounding verbal power of its author. But considered as a study of character, a picture of flesh-and-blood humanity, it must be frankly owned that *The Octopus* is as much farther away from actuality than *A Man's Woman* as that book was further away from *McTeague*. A few of the characters are good; they promise at first to win our sympathies,—characters like the slow, tenacious German, Hooven; the tall, commanding figure of Magnus Derrick, the "Governor," to whom life was one huge gamble; the coarse-fibered, combative young farmer, Annixter, with his scorn of "feemales," and his morbid concern over the vagaries of a stomach which would persist in "getting out of

whack." But, taken as a whole, the characters do not wear well; they come and go, love, suffer and die; and their joy and their misery fail equally to reach our heart-strings. And of course the reason is simple enough: it is impossible to magnify any one thing vastly excepting at the expense of something else; it is impossible throughout an entire volume to make a Colossus out of a steam-engine or a wheat-field by the simple expedient of calling men and women "human insects," "motes in the sunshine," without at last making us feel that these men and women are rather small, rather insignificant, rather like the ants that we carelessly tread under foot. I think that Norris came to realize his mistake,—at all events, in *The Pit* he pictured humanity on a relatively bigger scale. It is true that here again that term, "human insects," occasionally recurs; that here again the Wheat is the central symbol, a vast world power, chief source of the nation's growth and wealth. But the reason why *The Pit*, considered as a human story, has a stronger, more direct appeal is that the symbolism is kept further in the background, the interest focused more directly on the central characters. And these characters, especially the women, are simpler, and in a measure truer than those of his earlier volumes; they have less of the primordial and the titanic in their composition and considerably more of the average, every-day foibles and weaknesses. One feels that somehow and somewhere he had gained a deeper insight into the hearts of the men and women about him; and that this was what Owen Wister had in mind when he wrote, "In *The Pit* Norris has risen on stepping-stones to higher things." And yet *The Pit* is just as much a structural part of the whole design of Norris's trilogy as was *The Octopus;* it has that same inherent epic bigness of theme;—a gigantic attempt to corner the entire world's supply of wheat, to force it up, up, up, and hold the price through April, and May, and June,—and then finally the new crop comes pouring in and the daring speculator is overwhelmed by the rising tide, "a human insect, impotently striving to hold back with his puny hand the output of the whole world's granaries."

Such are the books which Norris, with feverish impatience and tireless nervous energy, produced in the few short years that fate allotted him. They stand to-day as the substructure of a temple destined never to be finished, the splendidly rugged torso of a broken statue. That is the way, the best, the truest, the only way, in which to think of Norris's place in American fiction,—as only a partial fulfillment of a rarely brilliant promise. Had he lived to attain his full stature, there is small doubt that he would have given us bigger, stronger, more vital novels than the younger American school has yet produced. (pp. 323-30)

Frederic Taber Cooper, "Frank Norris," in his Some American Story Tellers, *1911. Reprint by Books for Libraries Press, 1968, pp. 295-330.*

JOHN CHAMBERLAIN   (essay date 1933)

[*Chamberlain is an American essayist and critic who has edited several popular American magazines, including* Harper's *and* Life, *and is noted for his writings on social and economic subjects. In the following excerpt from* Farewell to Reform, *Chamberlain discusses issues of economics and morality in Norris's fiction.*]

When he was a student at the University of California in the early nineties, the young Frank Norris contributed a story to the *Wave*, a San Francisco weekly. The tale was so horrifying to the literary taste of the time that a friend of Mr. Norris, senior, stopped him on the street one day and said: "If I had a son who wrote a story like that, I'd have him put out of the world in a lethal chamber." At least that is how Charles G. Norris, Frank's brother, recalls the anecdote. The wording, Charles intimates, may not be exact, but the sentiment at least testifies to the early formulation of purpose of the author of the terrible *McTeague* and the still more terrible *Vandover and the Brute*. Norris may have had his Stevenson side, and even his humorous side, but America's first really conscious naturalist meant to write of life in the raw, and he did write of life in the raw. His was a dedicated career, pursued relentlessly from the time he went East to Harvard to the time he slipped into the rôle of rather silly moralist in the final chapters of *The Pit*.

Unlike Garland, Norris had a brain that could see human beings in the whole perspective of economic law. Like Garland, he had a reverence for the new science of the late nineteenth century. And again like Garland, he was a realist who couldn't hold the pose; ethical values insisted upon intruding into his later fiction. A preternaturally earnest young man when it came to his art, he believed he had a mission to tell the exact truth, to treat of the plain people for the plain people, to see human beings in their relation to the mass, following them into the toils and gins set for them by the inexorable laws of nature. The novelist, he wrote, must "deal with elemental forces, motives that stir whole nations. These cannot be handled as abstractions [but] must be expressed by means of an analysis of the characters of the men and women who compose . . . society, and the two must be combined and manipulated to evolve the purpose—to find the value of *x*." (p. 104)

Thomas Beer, in the most memorable phrases ever written about Norris, has spoken of the "immense common life" that swirls and eddies about the principal figures of *McTeague* and *Vandover*. The youth in love with broad forces, who saw life in terms of the ant-heap, spent the years of 1896 and 1897 practicing a trick which is employed lavishly in *The Octopus* to give the book a cosmic setting. This is the trick of piling detail on rhythmic detail, as in his report on the Santa Cruz carnival end: "And then, in that immense silence, when all the shrill staccato, trivial noises of the day were dumb, you heard again the prolonged low hum that rose from the city, even in its sleep, the voice of something individual, living a huge, strange life apart, raising a diapason of protest against shams and tinsels and things transient in that other strange carnival, that revel of masks and painted faces, the huge grim joke that runs its four-score years and ten. But that was not all.

"There was another voice, that of the sea; mysterious, insistent, and there through the night, under the low, red moon, the two voices of the sea and of the city talked to each other in that unknown language of their own; and the two voices mingling together filled all the night with an immense and prolonged wave of sound, the bourdon of an unseen organ—the vast and minor note of life."

In that passage Norris was practicing a trick that was to become the notable, although thoroughly specious, peroration of *The Octopus*, when he wrote, in terms of similar tonal swell, of how the wheat flowed out from California, in spite of grasping freight rates and the petty connivings of the economic man, to reach ultimately the starving populations of India. He was practising the trick of piling detail on detail that makes his descriptions of the Chicago Board of Trade the saving grace of his cheapest novel, *The Pit*. He was playing with his fictional ground tone—the cosmic tone that sounds below and above and around all the Norris men and women.

The trick is, of course, more than a literary device; it is the key to the Norris philosophy. The broad-scale, collective novel should be, in Norris's own words, a work that "draws conclusions from a whole congeries of forces, social development, race impulses." Single men live by chance—it is only the cosmic that is perdurable. Individual lives are items of a "huge, grim joke"; and when America's first naturalist wrote of McTeague, the giant dentist, and his petite wife, Trina, it was to show how accident, complete and amoral accident, disposed of the pair. The novel is a study in blind determinism from the start, with gold calling the turn. McTeague was never a licensed dentist; he entered the profession by chance. Chance again intervenes when a lottery brings $5,000 into the lives of the couple. Trina holds on to the money with the intensity of a French peasant who has seen his father robbed; her miserliness in turn affects McTeague, who is inclined by nature to be generous, and who resents the stinginess which luck has brought into their married life together. The pair, given their tragic economic setting, help each other along in the process of disintegration—but neither is at fault; it is the universe that is at fault, the vast purposeless universe that gives men tiny brains and great bodies and marries them to women who act as the catalytic agents of human catastrophe.

McTeague represents Norris's sense of one phase of the industrial process that was transforming America—the phase that tossed men into slums, that made them dependent on forces beyond their single control, on laws, for instance, that required a dentist to have a token of his skill in the form of a diploma, even after years of practice had given him an empiric certificate of ability. But Norris not only understood this phase of the process; he had the imagination and the insight to go out from the city which had nourished him and reach an understanding of the theme that preoccupied Hamlin Garland—the theme of the farmer who had gotten out of balance in a national economy which was weighted to favor industry and the rich of the urban centers. It is the ability to encompass a grasp of the totality of the situation which distinguishes Norris from both Garland and the earlier Theodore Dreiser.

In *The Octopus,* an epic of the San Joaquin Valley, Norris became, quite emphatically, a muck-raker, a commentator in fictional form on the acts of the Southern Pacific Railroad which were so to arouse Charles Edward Russell in the next decade. In this vast drama of the growing of the wheat the novelist becomes, definitely, the moralist. In the pages of struggle there is no specific denunciation from the novelist's own mouth of the "octopus," Mr. Huntington's railroad that had raised and lowered rates at will, charging "all the traffic will bear." But Jehovah, as Thomas Beer has said, thunders at the close. He thunders when the villain of the piece, S. Behrman, a fat gentleman whose function in the story is that of foreclosure of the farmers' mortgages, is tumbled, ridiculously, into the hold of a vessel, there to perish under a shower of the very wheat crop which he had hoped to sell in India for a fortune. The death is the crudest possible melodrama—a sudden panicky concession to all that Norris had fought in the fiction of his time. Throughout the book the railroad has been an economic necessity, called into existence by the laws of the unfolding universe, which care not what individuals perish. But Norris goes on from the sudden retribution of Behrman's death to comment on the railroad, and his comment springs from a quick dip into Matthew Arnold; the "wheat remains," and the moral law is upheld. "The larger view always and through all shams, all wickedness, discovers the truth that will, in the end, prevail, and all things, surely, inevitably, resistlessly, work together for good.''

But what and whose ''good'' is another matter; the railroad has killed Vanamee's sheep; it has killed Buck Annixter, the leader of the San Joaquin ranchers who were fighting to hang on to their property; it has destroyed Magnus Derrick's honesty, making of an upright citizen a crude politician who countenances bribery on the theory that is necessary to stoop morally to conquer an immoral monster. It has brought the country of the San Joaquin—which might stand as symbol of rural America from the Georgia cotton acres to the fruit ranches of the Northwest—under the domination of the city money-changers, and has sounded the knell of Jefferson and the triumph of Hamilton. And all this that famine might be prevented in India!

The scene of the nineties is in *The Octopus* in a variety of illuminating ways. Caraher, the anarchist whose ''cure'' for the inquities of the railroad is a piece of lead pipe stuffed with dynamite, is brought West from the city orbit of Johann Most. Presley, the poet, is obviously patterned on the Edwin Markham of ''The Man With the Hoe''; and Presley's poem carries out over the country as ''The Man With the Hoe'' carried over the country, following upon publication in a San Francisco newspaper. The lethargy of the people as a whole in a land of growing ''trusts'' is noted. And the underlying economic philosophy—a philosophy which Norris does not develop in so many cold words of his own—is Populist. Norris's sympathies, made plain by the death of Behrman, the middle-man, are obviously with the ranchers who are the shippers of grain. He was no Marxian novelist—although his novel, as I have said, is our finest *collective* work of fiction.

It is collective where Dos Passos's *1919*, for example, is individualistic. For it shows a *group* of people, and how they make common cause to bear up under economic forces beyond their joint control; it portrays them largely in their group relationship to society. The Marxian Dos Passos, on the other hand, takes his individuals as single symbols of a decaying society, and he follows them as individuals; they nowhere work together, collectively, for a group end. But the question of the collective versus the individualistic novel is, at best, an academic question; the novel is something to be used by social philosophers, not something to be written definitely to support a philosophy. It matters not whether Norris favored one group as against another in his work; what does matter is that Norris, by and large, was an honest novelist and a perceptive one, a novelist who could see America whole. ''I never truckled,'' he wrote, ''I never took off the hat to Fashion, and held it out for pennies. I told them the truth. They liked it or they didn't like it. What had that to do with me? I told them the truth.'' In the light of the close of *The Pit*, where the moralist once more intrudes to spoil a theme which is, ostensibly, that of the marketing of the grain, and its effect on the marketers, these words may seem overbrave, but they have a large measure of truth. That they could have been written with any appositeness at all in the nineties, given the prevalent taste in fiction, is a matter for national congratulation. (pp. 106-10)

> *John Chamberlain, ''Minority Report of the Novelists,'' in his* Farewell to Reform: The Rise, Life and Decay of the Progressive Mind in America, *second edition, The John Day Company, 1933, pp. 86-118.*

GRANVILLE HICKS (essay date 1935)

[*Hicks was an American literary critic whose famous study* The Great Tradition: An Interpretation of American Literature since the Civil War *(1933) established him as the foremost advocate of Marxist critical thought in Depression-era America. Throughout the 1930s, he argued for a more socially engaged brand of literature and severely criticized such writers as Henry James, Mark Twain, and Edith Wharton, who he believed failed to confront the realities of their society and, instead, took refuge in their own work. Hicks was shocked by the effects of the Great Depression and believed that events demanded a new commitment on the part of writers to clearly understand and express their times. In Marxist terms this meant that all American artists should comprehend the growth of capitalism and its negative side effects, such as war, periodic depressions, and the exploitation and alienation of the working class. Thus the question Hicks posed was always the same: to what degree did an artist come to terms with the economic condition of the time and the social consequences of those conditions? He believed that it was the task of American literature to provide an extremely critical examination of the capitalist system itself and of what he considered its inherently repressive nature. After 1939, Hicks sharply denounced communist ideology, which he called a ''hopelessly narrow way of judging literature,'' and in his later years adopted a less ideological posture in critical matters. In the following excerpt, Hicks discusses the conflict between Norris's conservative economic outlook and his sympathy for the common people, and judges Norris's deterministic philosophy to be an inadequate solution to this conflict.*]

Norris is remembered for his contributions to American realism. *McTeague,* which was begun in 1893, was finished in 1899, the year in which Norris published *A Man's Woman,* the last of his purely romantic novels. *McTeague* marked as great an advance over *Maggie* as *Maggie* had marked over *A Modern Instance.* Norris was less direct than Crane, less emancipated from prejudice; he did not drive so surely to his objective. But he built solidly out of intimate knowledge and a not unsympathetic understanding of his people. He said of *Maggie:* ''The author . . . is writing from the outside. Mr. Crane does not seem to *know* his people. He does not seem to have gotten down *into* their life.'' That charge could not be made against *McTeague.* We overlook the book's faults—the moralizing of the scene in which the dentist kisses his unconscious patient, the forced humor of the picnic, the failure to prepare us for Trina's miserliness, the explosive melodrama of the ending; we forgive all that because of the description of McTeague's daily life, the building in which he has his office, Polk Street, the Sieppe family, the dentist's friends. Through a multitude of petty details Norris gives us McTeague and his world. (pp. 169-70)

[Norris argued that the novel] is the characteristic mode of expression of the twentieth century: ''The Pulpit, the Press and the Novel—these indisputably are the greatest molders of public opinion and public morals to-day.'' ''The novelist to-day is the one who reaches the greatest audience. Right or wrong, the People turn to him the moment he speaks, and what he says they believe.'' Therefore, he maintained, the novelist is responsible to the people: ''A literature that cannot be vulgarized is no literature at all.'' ''It is all very well to jeer at the People and at the People's misunderstanding of the arts, but the fact is indisputable that no art that is not in the end understood by the People can live or ever did live a single generation.'' The novelist fulfils his responsibilities, Norris continued, only when he devotes himself to a high purpose: the novel may be ''a great force, that works together with the pulpit and the universities for the good of the people, fearlessly proving that power is abused, that the strong grind the faces of the weak, that an evil tree is still growing in the midst of the garden, that undoing follows hard upon unrighteousness, that the course of Empire is not yet finished, and that the races of men have yet to work out their destiny in those great and terrible movements that crush and grind and rend asunder the pillars of the house of the nations.'' The novel serves this purpose when it portrays life in such a way as to enlighten the reader, when it ''draws conclusions from a whole congeries of forces, social tendencies, race impulses, devotes itself not to a study of men but of man.''

McTeague did not wholly conform to this theory, and certainly it did not satisfy the needs of Norris' temperament. It illustrated his belief that ''no piece of information—mere downright acquisition of fact—need be considered worthless,'' and it showed how much ''a receptivity, an acute sensitivity'' could do for a writer. But he had said that the highest type of novel ''draws conclusions from a whole congeries of forces,'' and he could be content with nothing less. The task required, he felt, an enormous canvass; only an epic would suffice. And so he planned his trilogy. There was to be enough action in it to satisfy his own romanticism; it would grow out of the lives of the plain people and it would appeal to them; it would be honest and exact but never dull; it would reveal the pattern underlying seemingly unrelated events and thus would influence men's thoughts and deeds. All that Norris thought literature should be he proposed to make his ''Epic of the Wheat.''

Though the second volume, *The Pit,* falls far below Norris' conception, the first, *The Octopus,* is not wholly unworthy of the name of epic. Woven out of a dozen strands, it achieves the dimensions necessary for the adequate portrayal of a great economic struggle. It depicts a movement by depicting people, scores of them, all caught up in the battle between the wheat-raisers and the railroad. On page after page, in analyses of character, in descriptions of ranchers' meetings, of wheat fields, of fighting, Norris gives us the substance of a struggle that, in its fundamentals, was nationwide. He had at least one quality of greatness: he could seize upon the central issues of his time and create people in whose lives those issues were reflected.

Yet *The Octopus* can scarcely be called a great book; it is too confused, and in the end too false. Norris' growing sympathy with the people made him sorry for the dispossessed ranchers, and he could even become indignant at their misfortunes. But on the other hand, he admired the romantic boldness of Collis P. Huntington, who appears in the book under the name of Shelgrim. Moreover, he had talked with Huntington, as Presley talks with Shelgrim, and he could see no flaw in the railroad president's argument that the way of the railroad was the way of progress. Somehow he had to reconcile these conflicting sympathies if he was to make his novel an interpretation of life. His reading of Zola had introduced him to determinism, which he had employed as a literary device in both *McTeague* and *Vandover and the Brute,* though he seems never to have understood its philosophic implications. And a deterministic version of the apologies of the captains of industry, as stated in Shelgrim's interview with Presley, provided him with his method of interpretation. One recalls Presley's meditations at the end of the book: ''Men—motes in the sunshine—perished, were shot down in the very noon of life, hearts were broken, little children were started in life lamentably handicapped; young girls were brought to a life of shame; old women died in the heart of life for lack of food. . . . *But the WHEAT remained.* Untouched, unassailable, undefiled, that mighty world-force, that nourisher of nations, wrapped in Nirvanic calm, indifferent to the human swarm, gigantic, resistless, moved onward in its appointed grooves. . . . Falseness dies; injustice and oppression in the end of everything fade away. Greed, cruelty, selfishness,

and inhumanity are short-lived, the individual suffers, but the race goes on. . . . The larger view always and through all shams, all wickedness, discovers the Truth that will, in the end, prevail, and all things, surely, inevitably, resistlessly work together for good.''

This is consoling doctrine, and no doubt it seemed to Norris to answer his purposes. The thoughtful reader, however, finds Presley's rhapsody the most disturbing kind of anti-climax. As a theory it is ridiculous, and it destroys the emotional effect of the book, for it means that the contemptible Behrman has worked as surely for good as the noble Derrick, the impulsive Annixter, or the violent Dyke. Moreover, the consequences of this philosophy are found on page after page. How many problems Norris leaves unsolved: Magnus Derrick's ethical dilemma, the whole question of the use of violence, the place of the poet in such a struggle as that between the railroad and the ranchers! And how far he is from a consistent interpretation of character! For example, in interpreting Magnus' downfall he wavers between the view that his surrender is ignoble and the view that it is inevitable. Presley hovers on the edge of the struggle, now repelled, now drawn in, and at last takes refuge in his mystical optimism. The confusion permeates even the minutiae of the book: we are asked to believe that Vanamee has a sixth sense, that Annixter is capable of a miraculous transformation under the influence of pure love. Norris' old romanticism creeps in again and again, sheltered by the incoherence of his philosophy. Even the method is confused, for austere realism often yields to overt melodrama and careful objectivity to special pleading.

But if in *The Octopus* an impressive novel is marred by such defects, in *The Pit* a fine theme is ruined because of them. In *The Octopus* Norris was at least concerned with the victims, and his sympathy to some extent counteracted the effects of his theories. In *The Pit* it was the exploiter who occupied him, and he was strongly tempted, because of his admiration for the daring exploits of the captains of industry, to make Curtis Jadwin a romantic hero. His theory, however, required him to portray Jadwin as simply an instrument of benevolent natural forces. And his growing concern with the people showed Norris the cost of Jadwin's exploits: while such men were gambling, ''the farmer—he who raised the wheat—was ruined upon one hand; the working man—he who consumed it—was ruined on the other.'' Unable to decide whether to regard Jadwin as hero, automaton, or villain, he avoided the problem by making the corner in wheat a subordinate theme in the story. The novel is principally concerned with the relations between Jadwin and his wife, and this involves Laura's affair with Sheldon Corthell, an artist whose wide range of interests attracts her when she is weary of her husband's preoccupation with business. But Corthell is as weak and aimless as Jadwin is determined and powerful, and it was easy enough to end the book with Laura in the arms of her defeated and penitent husband. For the reader who is chiefly interested in the love story there is this romantic and presumably satisfying ending. For the reader who accepts Norris' philosophy there is a purple passage about the wheat, which ''had passed on, resistless, along its ordered and predetermined courses from West to East, like a vast Titanic flood, had passed, leaving Death and Ruin in its wake, but bearing Life and Prosperity to the crowded cities and centres of Europe.'' But for the reader who wants to understand the mind of the business man, and wants to see how speculative operations actually affect human lives, for the reader who asks that this novel should help him to understand the forces it deals with and to realize their expression in credible characters and events, for such a reader there is little but disappointment—some stirring descriptions of the Pit, some insight into the lust of the gambler, a few pictures of Chicago society, and not much more.

It is easy to see what Norris planned to do with the third volume of the series, and one fears that, neatly as it would have fitted his plan, it must still further have revealed the inadequacies of his philosophy. Whether he would in time have outgrown that philosophy is, of course, an insoluble problem. Other faults he was slowly overcoming: his prudishness, his fondness for melodrama, his reliance on the cliches of the Victorians. When one remembers his youth, one forgives all his faults—even his theories, which may well have been part of his relative immaturity—and thinks only of his virtues: the ambitiousness of his themes, the seriousness of his method, his mastery of a large canvass, the power of his descriptions. If clarity had been added, what might he not have accomplished? (pp. 170-75)

> *Granville Hicks, "The Years of Hope," in his* The Great Tradition: An Interpretation of American Literature since the Civil War, *revised edition, Macmillan Publishing Company, 1935, pp. 164-206.*

ALFRED KAZIN   (essay date 1942)

[*A highly respected American literary critic, Kazin is best known for his essay collections* The Inmost Leaf *(1955) and* Contemporaries *(1962), and particularly for* On Native Grounds *(1942), a study of American prose writing since the era of William Dean Howells. Having studied the works of "the critics who were the best writers—from Sainte-Beuve and Matthew Arnold to Edmund Wilson and Van Wyck Brooks" as an aid to his own critical understanding, Kazin has found that "criticism focussed many—if by no means all—of my own urges as a writer: to show literature as a deed in human history, and to find in each writer the uniqueness of the gift, of the essential vision, through which I hoped to penetrate into the mystery and sacredness of the individual soul." In the following excerpt, Kazin discusses the epic scope of Norris's novels, a quality which he feels sentimentalizes them. He nonetheless judges* McTeague *to be a great novel and an excellent example of literary naturalism.*]

If we think of all the repressed influences that were set loose by the insurgency of the Progressive period, all the exuberant romanticism out of the West that was to find its expression in the adventurousness of the new decade, it is easy enough to see why Frank Norris, who died on the eve of the Progressive period in 1902, must yet seem always so representative of it. For Norris, with his boundless energy and worship of force, his delight in life and willingness to learn from every source, was the perfect child of the Roosevelt era. In fact, if Theodore Roosevelt had had a taste for novels and an admiration for Zola, he might have produced huge transcripts of contemporary life not much different from Norris's. Where Stephen Crane seems so significantly a symbol of the fin de siècle, the last glowing ember of a dying century, Norris, who was his almost exact contemporary, was the counterpart in literature of the tough and muscular new men of the new century—Roosevelt and Big Bill Haywood, Borah and Darrow. (p.97)

Norris became a naturalist by that hatred of "pure literature" which developed in Europe after Flaubert into the social studies of Zola. "Who cares for fine style!" he wrote in 1899. "Tell your yarn and let your style go to the devil. We don't want literature, we want life." With a certain boyish opportunism that was characteristic of him, he selected from the naturalist creed chiefly its delight in violence, and accepted its deter-

minism only as it satisfied his dramatic sense. The philosophy behind naturalism in Europe, with its attempt to imitate the studious objectivity of science, its profound tragic sense, he ignored. Studying Zola as the high priest of naturalism, he may, however, have shown a shrewder understanding of Zola, as Franklin Walker has suggested, than of the naturalist creed itself. While still at college Norris wrote:

> Naturalism, as understood by Zola, is but a form of romanticism after all. . . . The naturalist takes no note of common people, common in so far as their interests, their lives, and the things that occur in them are common, are ordinary. Terrible things must happen to the characters of the naturalistic tale. They must be twisted from the ordinary, wrenched from the quiet, uneventful round of everyday life and flung into the throes of a vast and terrible drama that works itself out in unleashed passions, in blood and in sudden death. The world of M. Zola is a world of big things. The enormous, the formidable, the terrible, is what counts; no teacup tragedies here.

This was hardly what the naturalists had sought in their hope of observing human life under conditions of "clinical objectivity," but it was characteristic of Norris's spirit. He was obsessed by size and violence, and his delight in bigness was a curious blend of his love for the California frontier and an invincible youthfulness that was not exhausted in the thumping romances he wrote as a boy—the autobiographical *Blix* and the red-blooded *Moran of the Lady Letty* so plainly derived from Kipling. Like Roosevelt and Jack London, he had more than his share of the facile Nordicism of his day; yet he believed so passionately in a literature close to the masses that he once wrote that "a literature that cannot be vulgarized is no literature at all." His love of quantity came out most strikingly in the technique of his sprawling novels and particularly in the rhetorical perorations that spoil so many of his books, a trick of piling detail on detail in one grand symphonic swell to suggest the hugeness of Nature. To that overflowing vitality, however, he owed the extraordinary feeling for the common brutality of life that makes his best novel, *McTeague*, one of the great works of the modern American imagination.

For the key to Norris's mind is to be found in a naïve, open-hearted, and essentially unquenchable joy as radiant as the lyricism of Elizabethan poetry, a joy that is like the first discovery of the world, exhilarating in its directness, and eager to absorb every flicker of life. Norris wrote as if men had never seen California before him, or known the joy of growing wheat in those huge fields that could take half a day to cross, or of piling enough flour on trains to feed a European nation. It is out of the surge and greed of that joy that his huge, restless characters grow, men so abundantly alive that the narrow life of cities and the constraints of the factory system can barely touch them. He was the poet of the bonanza, teeming with confidence, reckless in the face of that almost cosmological security that was California to him. Every object in his books was huge, brought up to scale—the wheat fields in *The Octopus* that are like Napoleonic duchies, the eating and drinking in *McTeague*, the fantastic debaucheries in *Vandover and the Brute* (like a Boy Scout's daydreams of ancient Egypt), the Renaissance prodigality in *The Pit*, and even the back-alley slugging and thievery in an adventure yarn like *Moran of the Lady Letty*, whose heroine, characteristically, is a Viking princess in blue jeans.

When Norris planned his trilogy of wheat, inevitably it became "an idea big as all outdoors." It was to span two continents and, as he boasted to Bruce Porter, deal with the primitive, record man's struggle with nature, depict the conquering of the frontier, the growth of business enterprise, and at the last take in Europe. It was to be the last affirmation of nature's promise in an America rapidly veering away from even industrial promise. The conflict between the railroads and the farmers, as he revealed it in *The Octopus,* was unconsciously conceived in terms of the Biblical legend of evil. It is this fact that explains the book's sentimental mysticism and the shambles he made out of its sequel, *The Pit.* The San Joaquin Valley (rather like Steinbeck's Salinas) is Eden; Magnus and Derrick and his fellows Nature's children; and the Southern Pacific the serpent in the garden. *The Octopus* was, in a sense, the first muckraking novel, and it remains the most confused. Norris was still torn between Zola and Kipling, and though he was already a considerable artist, he was still a boy. He knew that in the society of which he wrote, an agricultural community geared to industry, a railroad could do nothing else; but his appreciation of economic necessity yielded to his desire to pay a last—and majestic—tribute to the frontier. Powerful as the book is, its fervor remains sentimental, its heroes and villains stock figures in a conflict Norris could project passionately but did not comprehensively understand. In the end the rascally railroad agent, S. Behrman, falls to his death amid circumstances reminiscent of the cheapest Victorian melodrama, the railroad takes all the land, and Norris is left to the celebration of the wheat that brings the book noisily to a close.

In *The Pit* Norris intended to tell the second phase of the wheat story, its fortunes on the Chicago market; but he succeeded only in completing a mediocre counterpiece to the stock novel of finance that became popular six years later. Like so many of these novels, it inevitably became a sentimental study in marriage, and proved no more than that the hold of the pit over Curtis Jadwin was exactly like the hold of drink over the good but erring father in a temperance novel. Exciting in its detail, *The Pit* was astonishingly uncritical of the very financial framework Norris had sought to expose in *The Octopus.* Norris's characteristic esteem for pure achievement led him to inflate the commonplace figure of Jadwin into an almost romantic type of adventurer, kindly at times and even magnificently generous, but one hardly typical of his world and certainly never a clue to its morality. As the story of Jadwin and his wife occupied Norris's mind, the place of the market in the blueprint of his epic obviously lost all significance for him. No one turning to *The Pit* first would guess its purpose in the projected trilogy. There is not even an echo of the struggles of *The Octopus,* for the novel rapidly dwindles to a romantic story rooted in one place and centered in one theme. Narrow and compact, it does, however, illustrate that mastery of episode which Norris attained beyond most novelists of his day.

Norris's ambition, it is clear, was to make America equal to the cosmic, to find a literary equivalent for his nation's bigness. Yet it is in *McTeague,* that history of degeneration, that he lives. In his wheat novels he tried to expand local scenes, and that local patriotism which has no parallel in the literature of the frontier, into the cosmic view that fascinated him; it was in this early book, much of which was written before he left college, that he exposed the crude foundations of a whole civilization in his bitterly remorseless drama of one soul's failure. There was a certain coarseness in Norris which was the obverse side of his boyish sentimentality, and if it was sadistic and painfully "literary" in *Vandover,* it lifted Norris's

passion for reality to new heights in *McTeague.* "The Dentist," as he referred to the book in letters to his friends, became at once the portrait of a city and the matchless reproduction of its culture. Norris crammed into it the darkness of that world of the poor which always beckoned to him like Nemesis, a world frozen in necessity, merciless to those who lost their foothold, savagely inexorable even in death. It was a melodrama, as all Norris's books were melodramas; but the violence was something more than his usual exhalation of boyish energy; it supported a conception of life. The tragedy of McTeague and Trina was arranged, for once, on a scale of genuine determinism; blindness became the arena and accident the avenging angel; the universe was a wasteland in which men grappled for bread, and life was emptied into the sewers of the city.

Yet perfect an object lesson in naturalism as the book is, despite all its extravagance and crudity, the novel glows in a light that makes it the first great tragic portrait in America of an acquisitive society. McTeague's San Francisco is the underworld of that society, and the darkness of its tragedy, its pitilessness, its grotesque humor, is like the rumbling of hell. Nothing is more remarkable in the book than the detachment with which Norris saw it—a tragedy almost literally classic in the Greek sense of the debasement of a powerful man—and nothing gives it so much power. For McTeague himself, it is safe to say, Norris cared very little; but out of his own instinct for brute force he invested McTeague's own brutality with an imperishable significance. The red-blooded, aggressively tough novelist to the end, he had almost casually improvised a livid modern tragedy out of his own sensitiveness to McTeague's failure; and the tragedy was perhaps more real than he knew. For Norris's gift, to the very end, was a peculiarly indiscriminate one; he was still trying his hand, still the inveterately curious, overgrown boy alternating between Kipling and Zola; still a precocious master of violence whose greatest pride was that he was tough as any in his imperialist generation. "I never truckled," Norris boasted before his death. "I never took off the hat to Fashion and held it out for pennies. I told them the truth. They liked it or they didn't like it. What had that to do with me? I told them the truth." (pp. 98-102)

Alfred Kazin, "Progressivism: The Superman and the Muckrake," in his On Native Grounds: An Interpretation of Modern American Prose Literature, 1942. Reprint by Harcourt Brace Jovanovich, Inc., 1963, pp. 91-126.

GEORGE WILBUR MEYER (essay date 1943)

[*In the following excerpt, Meyer discusses* The Octopus *as a thesis novel in which Norris set out to demonstrate that conflict between the natural order of life and the American socioeconomic system has resulted in social evils which indicate the need for the reform of that system.*]

The Octopus was the first book of a projected three-volume study in economic determinism intended to describe the growing, distribution, and consumption of a crop of wheat. The trilogy was to show how the wheat moved from the fields of California through the elevators and the board of trade in Chicago to millions of hungry mouths in some hypothetical famine-racked nation of southwestern Europe. This the wheat would do, according to Norris, "in spite of the quarrels of the farmers and the railroads, and in spite of the manipulation of the bulls and the bears on the stock market." . . . In *The Octopus,* the subject of which is the struggle between the California farmers and the Pacific and Southwestern Railroad for control of a crop of wheat, Norris' particular purposes seem to have been three: (1) to show by means of the symbol of the wheat the immutability of the natural order; (2) to demonstrate that the American socioeconomic system of the late nineteenth century was maladjusted to nature and was, consequently, the cause of unnecessary social evil; and (3) to suggest to his readers the need for reforming the American system along the naturalistic lines briefly sketched for them in the novel.

The philosophic first premise of *The Octopus* is the notion that the wheat will flow irresistibly from the fields where it is grown to mouths that need to be fed. Since Norris presented this idea not as a mere theory but as a fundamental law of nature, an understanding of its implications is indispensable to any sound interpretation of the novel. According to Norris, the wheat moves from the fields to regions of famine as inevitably as masses of air move from high to lower areas of barometric pressure. Obstacles in its path may retard its progress or alter its course, but the goal is invariably attained. This tendency of the wheat should not, however, be regarded as evidence that the natural order is intelligent, purposive, or benign. Ultimately, it is true, the wheat benefits those masses of the people who use it for food. But it is also true that the natural force represented by the wheat in *The Octopus* injures or destroys many individuals unlucky enough to be standing in its path. Nature thus might appear to be both benign and malevolent, depending upon the point of view. Actually she is neither. She is merely a fact, established and eternal. She can be both creative and destructive. Which she will be depends for the most part upon man's ability first to understand and then to adjust himself to her changeless laws.

Norris appears to have designed the main action of *The Octopus* to illustrate his conviction that Americans wrought unnecessary evil by supporting an economic system that clashed violently with manifest facts of nature. After introducing his main characters and briefly defining the issues of the conflict in which they are engaged, Norris devotes the fourth chapter of the book to presenting his conception of the wheat and to establishing a norm for his criticism of American society.

In a passage that emphasizes the dynamic fertility of nature, Norris begins by describing the land, the unplowed fields of the San Joaquin after the first rain of early spring:

> All about between the horizons, the carpet of the land unrolled itself to infinity. But now it was no longer parched with heat, cracked and warped by a merciless sun, powdered with dust. The rain had done its work; not a clod that was not swollen with fertility, not a fissure that did not exhale the sense of fecundity. One could not take a dozen steps upon the ranches without the brusque sensation that underfoot the land was alive; roused at last from its sleep, palpitating with the desire of reproduction. Deep down there in the recesses of the soil, the great heart throbbed once more, thrilling with passion, vibrating with desire, offering itself to the caress of the plow, insistent, eager, imperious. Dimly one felt the deep-seated trouble of the earth, the uneasy agitation of its members, the hidden tumult of its womb, demanding to be made fruitful, to reproduce, to disengage the eternal renascent germ of Life that stirred and struggled in its loins.

Then, in the overwrought but important conclusion to his account of the plowing, Norris expresses his idea of the fundamental relationship of man to nature:

> It was the long stroking caress, vigorous, male, powerful, for which the Earth seemed panting. The heroic embrace of a multitude of iron hands, gripping deep into the brown, warm flesh of the land that quivered responsive and passionate under this rude advance, so robust as to be almost an assault, so violent as to be veritably brutal. There, under the sun and under the speckless sheen of the sky, the wooing of the Titan began, the vast primal passion, the two world-forces, the elemental Male and Female, locked in a colossal embrace, at grapples in the throes of an infinite desire, at once terrible and divine, knowing no law, untamed, savage, natural, sublime.

Finally, through the character Vanamee, Norris comments explicitly upon the significance of the life led by the hardy ranchers in the vital season when the land is ready to replenish the earth with a crop of wheat:

> Vanamee, simple, uncomplicated, living so close to nature and the rudimentary life, understood its significance.... Work, food, and sleep, all life reduced to its bare essentials, uncomplex, honest, healthy. They were strong, these men, with the strength of the soil they worked, in touch with the essential things, back again to the starting point of civilization, coarse, vital, real, and sane.

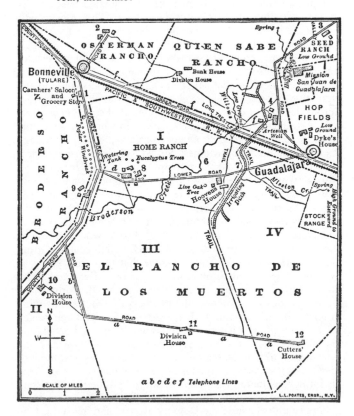

Map of the country in which The Octopus *is set.*

These passages reveal a group of men engaged co-operatively with nature in the act of reproduction. Knowing by experience, and perhaps by instinct, when it is time to plow and plant the seed, the farmers perform the male function of impregnating the fertile soil. While they are thus engaged, they lead unsophisticated lives; they exist, like the legendary noble savage of the eighteenth century, in a happy state of nature. Such an existence represents Norris' idea of a rational adjustment of men to their environment. As long as men live such a life, they are "honest, healthy . . . strong . . . in touch with the essential things, back again to the starting point of civilization, coarse, vital, real, and sane." As long as men maintain this harmonious relationship with the natural order, their actions are good and useful, for, by exploiting successfully her potentialities as an agency of humane and social purpose, they give to nature the appearance of intelligent benignity.

But the farmers of *The Octopus* live double lives. To their misfortune, they do not long remain at "the starting point of civilization." Once they have played their part in the titanic love affair, they return to the chaotic word of late-nineteenth-century America—to the competitive world of the railway trust and the bulls and bears, and to that overwhelming desire for private profit which dwarfs all other values in their society. They do not remain elemental aspects of the male force in nature; instead, they become selfish individualists, social and economic anarchists out to make a fortune at any cost. In so far as they pursue this selfish purpose, they are at odds with nature and their actions are evil and socially injurious. To an account of this perverse portion of their behavior and its tragic social consequences Frank Norris devotes the bulk of his novel.

One cause of the confusion in previous comment upon *The Octopus* seems to have been a general misunderstanding of Norris' estimate of the California farmers. This is especially true of the remarks of those critics whose belligerent sympathy for the defeated in any conflict resembling a class struggle leads them to regard the ranchers as a group of persecuted innocents. If Norris' descriptions of them are valid evidence, however, it is clear that Magnus Derrick and his confederates were not created to represent the old frontier individualism before that individualism was strangled in the iron grip of big business. Despite their superficial resemblance to an earlier type, these late-nineteenth-century farmers are not pathetic relics of Jeffersonian agrarianism forced to live in a society dedicated to Mammon and the principles of Alexander Hamilton. Norris' wheat-growers have little in common with the toil-worn countrymen of the Middle border whom we encounter in the works of Hamlin Garland. They are even less like the itinerant ranch-hands of Steinbeck's *Of Mice and Men* or those desperate creatures of *The Grapes of Wrath,* who, torn by the superior economic dislocations of the twentieth century, struggle to work for a few cents an hour that they may enjoy an evening's meal. Compared to the people of Garland and Steinbeck, Norris' characters are lords of creation: the former lack the necessities of existence; the ranchers of *The Octopus* think in terms of large fortunes. The Joads are like children beaten for reasons of which they are ignorant; Magnus Derrick and his fellow-conspirators are sufficiently endowed with cash and information to plan and launch a counterattack against the railroad trust. It is a serious mistake to believe that Norris regarded his farmers as mere symbols of an abused proletariat. The truth is that he saw them as reckless would-be profiteers, as speculators so unfortunate as to be less powerful and ingenious than their competitors in a ruinous struggle for economic power.

Norris insists that the ranchers of the San Joaquin were ruthless exploiters of the soil who plotted to manipulate freight rates with the single purpose of acquiring fortunes from one gigantic crop of wheat. His emphasis upon this fact is clearly seen in his preliminary sketch of the character of Magnus Derrick, the noblest rancher of them all, according to conventional ethical standards:

> He was always ready to take chances, to hazard everything on the hopes of colossal returns. In the mining days at Placerville there was no more redoubtable poker player in the county. He had been as lucky in his mines as in his gambling, sinking shafts and tunneling in violation of expert theory and finding "pay" in every case. Without knowing it, he allowed himself to work his ranch much as if he was still working his mine. The old-time spirit of '49, haphazard, unscientific, persisted in his mind. Everything was a gamble—who took the greatest chances was most apt to be the greatest winner. The idea of manuring Los Muertos, of husbanding his great resources, he would have scouted as niggardly, Hebraic, ungenerous.

Further on, Norris affirms that these salient features of Magnus' character—his gambling instinct, his willingness to exploit his land to the utmost, his selfishness were not peculiar to Magnus but were typical of the ranchers as a group. Magnus was sure that it would be necessary to "fix" only one rate commission. He did not worry lest a later commission undo the work of the first: "By then," he says, "it will be too late. We will, all of us, have made our fortunes by then."

> That was it precisely [Norris explains]. "After us the deluge.". . . . It was in this frame of mind that Magnus and the multitude of other ranchers of whom he was a type formed their ranches. They had no love for their land. They were not attached to the soil. . . . To get all there was out of the land, to squeeze it dry, to exhaust it, seemed their policy. When, at last, the land, worn out, would refuse to yield, they would invest their money in something else; by then, they would all have made fortunes. They did not care. "After us the deluge."

Probably because he tells the story of *The Octopus* from the point of view of the farmers, Norris provides no detailed appraisal of the men who work for the railroad. It is plain enough, however, that he regards them, like the farmers, as agents of both good and evil and that he conceives of the railroad itself as a part of the dynamic order of nature. Such at least appears to be the meaning of the speech made by Shelgrim, the president of the Pacific and Southwestern, when he tries to give Presley a sound explanation of the unfortunate massacre at Magnus Derrick's irrigation ditch:

> " . . . .*Railroads build themselves.* Where there is a demand sooner or later there will be a supply. Mr. Derrick, does he grow his wheat? The Wheat grows itself. What does he count for? Does he supply the force? What do I count for? Do I build the Railroad? You are dealing with forces . . . when you speak of Wheat and the Railroads, not with men. There is the Wheat, the supply. It must be carried to feed the People.

There is the demand. The Wheat is one force, the Railroad, another, and there is the law that governs them—supply and demand. Men have only little to do in the whole business. Complications may arise, conditions that bear hard on the individual—crush him maybe—*but the Wheat will be carried to feed the people* as inevitably as it will grow. If you want to fasten the blame of the affair at Los Muertos on any one person, you will make a mistake. Blame conditions, not men.''

According to this, as long as the railroad men work to fulfil the manifest purpose of the railroad—as long, that is, as they strive to make the railroad an efficient carrier of food to the people—they are well adjusted to their environment, and their actions are of indisputable benefit to society. But when, like the ranchers, they interfere with the growth and transportation of the wheat; when they plot and conspire, break contracts and bribe, tamper with the law of supply and demand for personal gain; then they become the authors of evil which their leader, Shelgrim, erroneously attributes to the natural order.

Shelgrim's conclusion that "conditions, not men" were to blame for the massacre at the irrigation ditch is fallacious, for it is obvious that the faulty "conditions" were produced by men who meddled with the wheat and the railroad—forces which in themselves are quite innocuous. One of Norris' main purposes in *The Octopus* was to criticize the unnatural society of late-nineteenth-century America. This he did by describing pointedly those conditions—actually created by men motivated by a lust for profit for which Shelgrim fatalistically holds the natural order of things responsible. These conditions include, among others, the unjust discharge and blacklisting by employers of faithful employees; the flagrant violation of verbal contracts, the corruption by bribery of public officials and the custodians of the agencies of written communication, blackmail, starvation in the midst of plenty, the ruthless exploitation of natural resources, and a tragic waste of men, work, and material. But the outstanding and most reprehensible condition produced by men in this socioeconomic system is the appearance of senselessness that characterizes virtually all human endeavor. The chief characteristic of the society described in *The Octopus* is the abject submission of its members to the irrational force of chance.

The fact that chance governs the fate of the majority of the characters in *The Octopus* is established by the two most sensational incidents in the book. It is chance, after all—chance set free by misdirected human action—that kills the ranchers at the irrigation ditch. And it is chance that destroys S. Behrman in the hold of the ''Swanhilda.'' Such an accident as Behrman's cannot of course by prevented by any socioeconomic system, but situations like that at the irrigation ditch need not occur. At Los Muertos the opportunity to murder the farmers and the agents of the railroad was given to chance by the peculiar economic interests of the men involved. For months these men had been working at cross-purposes, distrusting, hating, and fearing one another, forgetful of the manifest facts of nature, mindful only of the first principle of late-nineteenth-century economics—''Dog eat dog and the devil take the hindmost.'' When at last they faced one another armed, the individuals on both sides were predisposed to fire on their competitors at the slightest provocation. Chance then intervened to provide the overwrought ranchers with what appeared to be an unmistakable sign of active belligerence in the ranks of their opponents.

The real tragedy of the irrigation ditch is that men should have given chance such a favorable opportunity to express itself. It is this tragedy—the decisive interference of chance in human affairs—that is chiefly responsible for the senselessness which Theodore Dreiser and other pessimists discover in their studies of the universe. Unlike the pessimists, who are content to describe mere appearances, Norris suggests that chance, and the disorder caused by its pervasive influence in society, may be for the most part eliminated if men will co-operate with one another and adjust themselves to nature. Until men do so co-operate and gear their socioeconomic system to the inflexible cogs of nature's vast machine, they must expect to suffer a thousand unnatural shocks that human flesh is not necessarily heir to.

With this understanding of the first two of Norris' three chief purposes in *The Octopus,* it is not difficult to discover his final purpose—that of persuading his readers to reform their society. Neither is it impossible now to reconcile those elements of the novel which most critics have thus far found irreconcilable: the philosophy of determinism, the description of a tragic action in an ugly society, and the optimistic doctrines, voiced by Vanamee and Presley, with which Norris chose to end his novel.

According to the philosophy of determinism, it is plain that none of the characters in *The Octopus* may be blamed for his contribution to the general socioeconomic disorder in which he exists. It is true that the perverse actions of Magnus Derrick and S. Behrman give to the forces of nature—the wheat and the railroad—the false appearance of deliberate malevolence. But this is not to say that Derrick and Behrman are guilty of deliberate misbehavior. They cannot be held morally responsible for their unnatural endeavors, because their characters have been determined by environmental factors beyond their control. They participate willingly in an unnatural system of economics because they have been taught to believe that such a system is natural and inevitable. They tamper with natural forces in the hope of personal gain, not because they are essentially vicious, but because they fail to understand nature and her laws. They err through ignorance, and in their ignorance lies their innocence. Shelgrim alone among them approaches knowledge of the truth; but even he, reasoning—or rather rationalizing—from sound premises, reaches conclusions that are false.

The fact that the tragedy of *The Octopus* was determined by forces which the characters of the novel could not control, and that it was therefore inevitable, does not mean that the tragedy must inevitably be repeated. Neither does the fact that Magnus Derrick and S. Behrman must be absolved of moral responsibility for their actions mean that all men forever shall be guiltless for similar behavior. Unlike many of his critics, Frank Norris did not confuse determinism with fatalism. He did not believe that what had happened once must necessarily happen again. Specifically, he did not believe that the socioeconomic confusion of the world he lived in—the world described in *The Octopus*—was predestined to continue throughout eternity. Norris was confident that the people were capable of correcting old errors and of reforming a society that was unsatisfactory. His belief that the people waited only for information and for some external force to rouse them to constructive action is expressed near the beginning of the second book of *The Octopus* by Cedarquist, the shipbuilder, when he observes that the greatest evil in American life is ''the indifference of the better people to public affairs.'' Economic injustice and despotism, according to Cedarquist, exist only by permission of the people: they "have but to say 'No,' and not the strongest tyranny, political, religious, or financial, that was ever organized, could survive one week."

Norris, like his master, Émile Zola, thought that the novel could and should be made to educate the people in the determinism of social evil and to stimulate in them the determination to say "No" to all forms of injustice and despotism. In his essay **"The Novel with a 'Purpose,'"** Norris insists that the novel

> may be a great force, that works together with the pulpit and the universities for the good of the people, fearlessly proving that power is abused, that the strong grind the faces of the weak, that an evil tree is still growing in the midst of the garden. . . .

In **The Octopus,** Norris attempted to make the novel such a force. By emphasizing the immutability of nature, by describing the human suffering and waste that result from laissez faire economics, and by outlining his conception of a healthy adjustment of men to those parts of their environment which cannot be changed, Norris hoped to move his readers to intelligent reformatory action. Whether or not his readers were so moved, this much at least should be certain: although Magnus Derrick and S. Behrman, because of their ignorance, are not to blame for their misguided endeavors, the readers of **The Octopus** will be to blame if, having been instructed in the determinism of the social evils wrought by laissez faire economics, they continue to support a system whose outstanding feature is its tendency to bring unnecessary evil out of nature. (pp. 352-58)

George Wilbur Meyer, "A New Interpretation of 'The Octopus'," in College English, Vol. 4, No. 6, March, 1943, pp. 351-59.

LARS ÅHNEBRINK (essay date 1950)

[Åhnebrink is a Swedish educator and critic specializing in American literature. In the following excerpt, he illustrates Norris's debt to Émile Zola by comparing McTeague to two of Zola's novels.]

We know that Norris was well acquainted with many of Zola's novels, and that he looked upon the French writer as his avowed master. In an article entitled **"Why Women Should Write the Best Novels"** he wrote in a manner which suggests he himself had faced the problem he was describing:

> But the fascination of a great story-writer— especially upon the young, untried little story- writer—is strong, and before the latter is well aware he is taking from the big man that which he has no right to take. He is taking his code of ethics, his view of life, his personality, even to the very incidents and episodes of his story. He is studying literature and not life.

Norris's debt to Zola may be traced, at least to some extent, in all his novels, but it is fully apparent in four novels: **McTeague, Vandover and the Brute, The Octopus,** and **The Pit.** These novels have one feature in common: all depict the slow but inevitable course of man toward destruction—a common naturalistic pattern. Different elements contributed to the disintegration of the characters, but, as in Crane's works, usu-

ally social conditions, heredity, and circumstances were the principal factors conducive to their ruin. Norris had probably learnt this by reading Zola's novels, a source which he used extensively but almost always with judiciousness and moderation. (p. 277)

Like Zola, [Norris] did not want to portray characters, but to study temperaments. Both authors chose to depict two different temperaments and to record the influence which they exerted on each other. The parts played by Thérèse and Laurent [in *Thérèse Raquin*] correspond in many ways to those of Trina and McTeague, with the important and significant difference, however, that Zola described a case of adultery and a subsequent ill-fated marriage, whereas Norris only depicted an unhappy marriage. In both cases, the influence which the one temperament exerted on the other became fatal, and led to the characters' slow but inevitable destruction.

Besides the fact that the fundamental ideas of the two books are similar, a close analysis reveals other resemblances. The exterior portraits of Thérèse and Trina exhibit points of similarity: each of them had an attractive, lithe figure, big, expressive eyes, a face of striking paleness contrasted by a mass of black hair. Mentally they were also alike; both were of a nervous disposition, hysterical, unbalanced, and abnormal. Beneath the quiet surface Thérèse was extremely passionate. Her sexual urge uas her predominant characteristic, whereas Trina's chief idiosyncrasy, despite her temporary passionate outbursts, was greed. The two women's emotions, resulting from their nervous temperaments, oscillated from one extreme to another. Moments of calmness and placid quietude alternated with spells of violent outbursts of passion. The women's passions and nervous crises frightened the men. This is Laurent's attitude:

> Tous ses instincts de femme nerveuse éclatèrent avec une violence inouïe; le sang de sa mère, ce sang africain qui brûlait ses veines, se mit à couler, à battre furieusement dans son corps maigre, presque vierge encore. Elle s'étalait, elle s'offrait avec une impudeur souveraine. Et, de la tête aux pieds, de longs frissons l'agitaient.
>
> Jamais Laurent n'avait connu une pareille femme. Il resta surpris, mal à l'aise. . . . Les sanglots, les crises de Thérèse l'epouvantèrent presque . . .

And this is McTeague's reaction:

> During the first months of their married life these nervous relapses of hers had alternated with brusque outbursts of affection when her only fear was that her husband's love did not equal her own. Without an instant's warning, she would clasp him about the neck, rubbing her cheek against his . . . Those sudden outbursts of affection on the part of his little woman, outbursts that only increased in vehemence the longer they lived together, puzzled rather than pleased him.

Against these small, nervous, and easily roused women both writers set huge and indolent men: Zola the sanguine and somewhat sluggish Laurent, and Norris the phlegmatic McTeague. Both Laurent and McTeague belonged to a primitive type of man, in whom the lower, animal instincts predominated; both were young giants, angular, with enormous hands, heavy muscles, and bull-like necks; both were of great strength and their movements and mentalities were slow. (pp. 278-80)

To illustrate the strength of their heroes, Zola said that Laurent could have killed a bull with his fist, whereas Norris asserted that McTeague had once "knocked down a half-grown heifer with a blow of his fist between the eyes." . . . Moreover, Laurent loved to sit in a warm room, slowly digesting his meal, smoking his pipe and drinking his "gloria à trois sous." And "Il aurait voulu bien manger, bien dormir, contenter largement ses passions." . . . McTeague's only pleasures were "to eat, to smoke, to sleep, and to play upon his concertina," and he loved to sit in his "Dental Parlours" drinking his beer and smoking his huge porcelain pipe while his food digested. Whereas Laurent was depicted as a sluggard possessing a craving appetite for women, McTeague was portrayed as a hard-working though immensely stupid dentist who had nothing erotic about him.

Circumstances willed that these men of strong physique and slow temperaments come under the influence of nervous women. Laurent was drawn to Thérèse with the same deterministic necessity as McTeague was drawn to Trina. . . . In the beginning, both women, owing to their nervous and alert tempers, succeeded in rousing the sluggish mentalities of their husbands. Later, the influence of the women became destructive, for both men, from having been dull and slow but fairly harmless, developed into brutal murderers. Actually, it was Thérèse's passion for Laurent that drove him to murder Camille, her husband. Similarly, it was chiefly Trina's greed which made McTeague murder her. Of course, the characters influenced each other mutually. The stages of the married life of each couple went from irresistible passion to satiety, hatred, and violent death. They destroyed each other's lives. Laurent was in part responsible for Thérèse's tragedy. Likewise, McTeague was partly the cause of Trina's ruin.

Prior to the violent death of the two couples, the husbands displayed their viciousness and brutality by beating their wives, who took abnormal pleasure in having pain inflicted upon them. (pp. 280-82)

Apart from the leading idea, two different temperaments which clashed with each other, and apart from certain character traits no doubt suggested by *Thérèse Raquin*, **McTeague** resembles *L'Assommoir* as regards plot and episodes. The opening scenes of the two novels resemble each other, although the atmosphere is different—in Norris's novel it is one of comfort and peace, whereas in Zola's it is mingled with anguish. In *L'Assommoir* Gervaise sat by her window looking down into the street, noticing the stores and shops, and observing various groups of workers on their way to their jobs. It was early morning and the town was waking up. This is "le boulevard de la Chapelle":

> . . . elle [Gervaise] retourna s'accouder à la fenêtre . . . Il y avait là . . . un défilé sans fin d'ouvriers allant au travail, leurs outils sur le dos, leur pain sous le bras. . . . On reconnaissait les serruriers à leurs bourgerons bleus, les maçons à leurs cottes blanches, les peintres à leurs paletots . . . à la porte des deux marchands de vin qui enlevaient leurs volets, des hommes ralentissaient le pas. . . .
>
> Gervaise s'entêta encore à la fenêtre pendant deux mortelles heures, jusqu'à huit heures. Les boutiques s'étaient ouvertes. Le flot de blouses descendant des hauteurs avait cessé. . . . Aux ouvriers avaient succédé les ouvrières, les brunisseuses, les modistes, les fleuristes, se serrant dans leurs minces vêtements, trottant le long des boulevards extérieurs; elles allaient par bandes de trois ou quatre, causaient vivement, avec de légers rires et des regards luisants jetés autour d'elles. . . . Puis, les employés étaient passés . . . des jeunes gens efflanqués . . . de petits vieux . . . Et les boulevards avaient pris leur paix du matin; les rentiers du voisinage se promenaient au soleil; les mères, en cheveux, jupes sales, berçaient dans leurs bras des enfants en maillots, qu'elles changeaient sur les bancs; toute une marmaille mal mouchée, débraillée, se bousculait, se traînait par terre, au milieu de piaulements, de rires et de pleurs.

Norris introduced Polk Street in the same manner, by letting McTeague walk up to the window, observing the street with its corner drug stores, barber shops, cheap restaurants, and its procession of workers. This is the awakening of Polk Street:

> Bull-like, he heaved himself laboriously up, and, going to the window, stood looking down into the street. . . .
>
> On week days the street was very lively. It woke to its work about seven o'clock, at the time when the newsboys made their appearance together with the day labourers. The labourers went trudging past in a straggling file— plumbers' apprentices, their pockets stuffed with sections of lead pipe, tweezers, and pliers; carpenters, carrying nothing but their little pasteboard lunch baskets painted to imitate leather; gangs of street workers, their overalls soiled with yellow clay, their picks and long-handled shovels over their shoulders; plasterers, spotted with lime from head to foot. This little army of workers, tramping steadily in one direction, met and mingled with other toilers of a different description . . . all along the street could be seen the shop keepers taking down their shutters.
>
> Between seven and eight the street breakfasted. . . . A little later, following in the path of the day labourers, came the clerks and shop girls, dressed with a certain cheap smartness, always in a hurry, glancing apprehensively at the power-house clock. Their employers followed an hour or so later—on the cable cars for the most part—whiskered gentlemen with huge stomachs, reading the morning papers with great gravity; bank cashiers and insurance clerks with flowers in their buttonholes.
>
> At the same time the school children invaded the street, filling the air with a clamour of shrill voices, stopping at the stationers' shops . . .
>
> Towards eleven o'clock the ladies from the great avenue a block above Polk Street made their appearance, promenading the sidewalks leisurely, deliberately. They were at their morning's marketing. They were handsome women, beautifully dressed.

There seems to be no reason to doubt that Norris had *L'As-sommoir* in mind when composing the first chapter of *Mc-Teague*. Norris, like Zola, described the laborers coming in a line, and then followed a detailed enumeration of different categories of workers, and then employers, wealthy gentlemen, ladies, and children. One category was added to the file by Norris, namely the newsboys, who appeared at the same time as the workers. Zola's description of the street is perhaps more graphic and artistic than Norris's, because the former depicted the street and its people by letting Gervaise, in agony, from her window try to catch sight of her belated husband on the boulevard. There is no such motivation in Norris's scene.

Zola appears to have been an inspiration also for other episodes. The description of the marriage ceremony in *L'Assommoir* resembles in many ways the marriage scene in *McTeague*. The atmosphere during the wedding in both novels was rather unecclesiastical. The ceremony was performed at lightning speed "pendant une absence du bon Dieu." Irritating noises heightened the impression of secularity. Zola gave the following picture of the ceremony:

> ... l'église s'emplissait du piétinement des sacristains, du vacarme des chaises remises en place. On devait préparer le maître-autel pour quelque fête, car on entendait le marteau des tapissiers clouant des tentures. Et, au fond de la chapelle perdue, dans la poussière d'un coup de balai donné par le bedeau, le prêtre à l'air maussade promenait vivement ses mains sèches sur les têtes inclinées de Gervaise et de Coupeau, et semblait les unir au milieu d'un déménagement, pendant une absence du bon Dieu, entre deux messes sérieuses.

And Norris described the attendant noises as follows: "Outside the noises of the street rose to the windows in muffled undertones, a cable car rumbled past, a newsboy went by chanting the evening papers; from somewhere in the building itself came a persistent noise of sawing."

Moreover, in *L'Assommoir* the haphazard ceremony was over quite abruptly, leaving behind a sense of disappointment:

> Et les formalités, la lecture du Code, les questions posées, la signature des pièces, furent expédiées si rondement, qu'ils se regardèrent, se croyant volés d'une bonne moitié de la cérémonie. . . . Quand la noce eut de nouveau signé sur un registre, à la sacristie, et qu'elle se retrouva en plein soleil, sous le porche, elle resta un instant là, ahurie, essoufflée d'avoir été menée au galop.
>
> —Voilà! dit Coupeau, avec un rire gêné.
>
> Il se dandinait, il ne trouvait rien là de rigolo. Pourtant, il ajouta:
>
> —Ah bien! ça ne traîne pas. Ils vous envoient ça en quatre mouvements . . . C'est comme chez les dentistes: on n'a pas le temps de crier ouf! ils marient sans douleur.
>
> —Oui, oui, de la belle ouvrage, murmura Lorilleux en ricanant. Ça se bâcle en cinq minutes et ça tient bon toute la vie . . .

Norris followed the same procedure:

All at once the ceremony was over before anyone expected it. . . . She [Trina]—perhaps McTeague as well—felt that there was a certain inadequateness about the ceremony. Was that all there was to it? Did just those few muttered phrases make them man and wife? It had been over in a few moments, but it had bound them for life. Had not something been left out? Was not the whole affair cursory, superficial? It was disappointing.

By depicting the wedding in such a hasty and worldly fashion, the writers, at all events Zola, intended to give a satirical picture of the servants of the church. Moreover, in both novels the ceremonies became symbolic of coming evil. (pp. 283-87)

[The] picture given by Norris of the [wedding] supper is strongly reminiscent of the wedding feast in *L'Assommoir,* as well as of the famous goose dinner in the same novel. The goose appeared also in Norris's novel. The goose dinner in *L'Assommoir* ended with singing, and Mme Lerat sang "L'enfant du bon Dieu" in a melancholy way; similarly, in *McTeague* the guests intoned "Nearer, My God, to Thee," but "They sang in very slow time. The song became a dirge, a lamentable, prolonged wail of distress." It should, however, be pointed out that Norris, in contradistinction to Zola, carefully avoided all indecencies and obscene allusions.

In addition to similarities of characterization, plot, and episodes between *McTeague* and Zola's two novels, there are also affinities between the subplot of *McTeague* and an incident in *La Bête humaine*. The general motive underlying the subplot was avarice. Zerkow married Maria Macapa only to be able to listen again and again to her story of a set of gold plates, hoping to find it some day, for Maria had told Zerkow that she had hidden it somewhere. He believed that the treasure was to be found in his junk shop, and he searched for it everywhere, night and day, but in vain. Finally he murdered his wife. The handling of this subplot may have been suggested by an episode in *La Bête humaine,* where a signalman, named Misard, lived with his wife, Phasie, to whom a legacy of a thousand francs had been given by her father. She had hidden it and refused to hand it over to her husband. Slowly he poisoned her to death. Although he searched everywhere, he was not able to find the treasure. After the death of his wife, Misard employed an old woman of the neighborhood, La Ducloux, to help him, and in the end she induced him to marry her by pretending that she had discovered the secret hoard. The motive underlying both episodes was greed. The hidden treasure, real or not, was never found, despite frantic searching. The description of the maniacal seeking for the lost treasure is similar in both books. This is Misard's pursuit: "Je [Flore] l'ai entendu, la nuit, qui tapait dans tous les murs." And again: ". . . il [Misard] se mit à quatre pattes . . . Plusieurs carreaux étaient descellés, il les arracha. Rien, toujours rien!" "Et un bruit inaccoutumé lui ayant fait prêter l'oreille, elle comprit que Misard, avec une pioche, était en train de fouiller le sol battu de la cuisine." Zerkow was as maniacal as Misard in his seeking:

And at night Maria would sometimes wake to find Zerkow gone from the bed, and would see him burrowing into some corner by the light of his dark lantern . . . "I'll find it. It's here somewheres, hid somewheres in this house." . . . "I woke up about an hour ago," Maria explained, "and Zerkow wasn't in bed; maybe he hadn't come to bed at all. He was down on his knees by the sink, and he's pried up some boards off the floor and was digging there.''

These quotations seem to confirm the assumption that Norris may in part have been inspired by *La Bête humaine* for his subplot. As to the half-mad greaser's obsession with the set of a hundred golden plates, Norris may have heard such a story and found it suitable for his novel. Then he linked it with the Zola episode, but gave the story a more dramatic ending through the cruel murder of Maria and the suicide of Zerkow.

The influence of Zola is predominant in *McTeague* and shows that Norris consciously aimed at adapting Zola's naturalistic method to native American material. (pp. 289-90)

> Lars Åhnebrink, "The Influence of Zola," in his The Beginnings of Naturalism in American Fiction: 1891-1903, Vol. IX, Cambridge, Mass.: Harvard University Press, 1950, pp. 233-308.

FREDERICK J. HOFFMAN   (essay date 1951)

[*Hoffman was an American educator and critic who wrote extensively on twentieth-century American literature. In the following excerpt, he discusses Norris's narrative technique in* McTeague.]

One of the most skillful portrayals of tension through the description of physical action is to be found in Frank Norris's *McTeague*. The nature of the two characters locked in deadly combat (Trina and McTeague) determines the nature of that tension and of its issue in action; Norris's description requires skillful shifting of vantage point, a reserve and caution of exposition. McTeague has come to the school where Trina works; he is drunk but "alert, unnaturally intelligent, vicious, perfectly steady, deadly wicked." Trina, instantly aware of the crisis, fights back, briefly with words, then with fists. These two deadly enemies cannot delay action by means of saving dialogue; the dialogue is merely a sparring before action begins:

> "For the last time, will you give me that money?"
>
> "No."
>
> "You won't huh? You won't give me it? For the last time."
>
> "No, *no.*"

Norris is obviously not interested in the dialogue, except to restrict it to the limits of his characters' minds. It is not hastily done; it is simply not done at all, save as a brief exchange between persons whose bodies and not their minds demonstrate their wills. The flaws in the description of the action are not serious; they argue occasionally a slight failure of pace.

> Beside herself with terror, Trina turned and fought him back; fought for her miserable life with the exasperation and strength of a harassed cat; and with such energy and such wild, unnatural force, that even McTeague for the moment drew back from her. But her resistance was the one thing to drive him to the top of his fury. He came back at her again, his eyes drawn to two fine twinkling points, and his enormous fists, clenched till the knuckles whitened, raised in the air.

In this brief description of powerful action the tensions become almost explicitly real; they are far better explained than are those of many other passages in the same novel, in which Norris's disposition toward McTeague *as type* forces him to interfere with the characterization. It is not the action itself in this scene, but rather the restraint in the description of it that makes the passage so effective. After this brief passage Norris shifts his point of vantage and withdraws from the principals, the cat, hidden behind the coal scuttle, is allowed to hear out the struggle to its conclusion:

> In the schoolroom outside, behind the coal scuttle, the cat listened to the sounds of stamping and struggling and the muffled noise of blows, wildly terrified, his eyes bulging like brass knobs. At last the sounds stopped on a sudden; he heard nothing more. Then McTeague came out, closing the door. The cat followed him with distended eyes as he crossed the room and disappeared through the street door.

Crude as this is ("like brass knobs," "distended eyes," "on a sudden"), it approaches a point of almost perfect effectiveness of tone, consistent within the limits of space, character, and action. A mastery of fact (not merely *knowing* fact but possessing skill in seeing it) is one of the best of naturalist attainments. It is fundamentally a realist's skill, involved as it is in a nonsymbolic maneuvering of fact, controlled only by a sense of balance and discretion. But the naturalist's extension of this skill, or his use of it, often involves its subordination to an ideational purpose, almost always amateurish, at best imperfectly understood. It leads to what are all but unpardonable errors of judgment—to forced, ideologically determined coincidences and parallels through which the "world view" is expressed. It leads also to crude symbols, to out-of-character dialogue and gestures, which are remote from any simple realization of realistic truth. McTeague and Fleming suffer less from this fault of maneuvering than do most characters in naturalist fiction. It is, in fact, of a piece with the unfortunate consequence of the "scientific view" which Henry James so shrewdly discerns as one of Zola's obsessive concerns:

> Science accepts surely *all* our consciousness of life; even, rather, the latter closes maternally round it—so that, becoming thus a force within us, not a force outside, it exists, it illuminates only as we apply it. We do emphatically apply it in art. But Zola would apparently hold that it much more applies us.

(pp. 34-7)

> Frederick J. Hoffman, "Prewar Naturalism, 1900-1915," in his The Modern Novel in America: 1900-1950, Henry Regnery Company, 1951, pp. 28-51.

CHARLES CHILD WALCUTT   (essay date 1956)

[*Walcutt is an American educator and critic who has written extensively on American literature. In the following excerpt, Walcutt compares* The Octopus *to Emile Zola's novel* Germinal *(1885).*]

The Octopus is in the naturalistic tradition in its delineation of the broad sweep of economic forces. It is naturalistic in the Zola tradition, and its qualities may be further elucidated by comparison with those of Zola's novel which it most closely resembles, *Germinal*.

The most striking quality that the two works have in common is the epic sweep. Zola is famous for his ability to handle great movements, for the tremendous canvas which he is able to paint before his readers' eyes. In this, Norris's first attempt to deal comprehensively with a social and economic movement, he reproduced much of Zola's magnitude. *The Octopus* seems to picture the heart of the California social body: the reader senses that his eye is directed toward that point where the maximum number of social forces converge; he is constantly made to feel that all the activity of city and ranch is going forward while his attention is confined to a particular sequence of events. The richness of Norris's conception is illustrated by this magnificent description of the spring plowing:

> The ploughing, now in full swing, enveloped him in a vague, slow-moving whirl of things. Underneath him was the jarring, jolting, trembling machine; not a clod was turned, not an obstacle encountered, that he did not receive the swift impression of it through all his body, the very friction of the damp soil, sliding incessantly from the shiny surface of the shears, seemed to reproduce itself in his finger-tips and along the back of his head. He heard the horse-hoofs by the myriads crushing down easily, deeply, into the loam, the prolonged clinking of trace-chains, the working of the smooth brown flanks in the harness, the clatter of wooden hames, the champing of bits . . . the sonorous, steady breaths wrenched from the deep, laboring chests, strap-bound, shining with sweat, and all along the line the voices of the men talking to the horses . . .

Such a passage is reminiscent of the celebration of the earth's fecundity in *La Terre,* and it is comparable to many of the descriptions in *Germinal*. Its tone and quality are probably not conscious and specific imitations of Zola, for it is characteristic of Norris whether he is writing romance or "naturalism" to reach out for the epic sweep. But this tendency to create pictures of gigantic movement and force is more and more frequently to be observed in his last two novels. It satisfies, perhaps, the epic conception of his trilogy and the symbol underlying it; it reflects an increasing indebtedness to the style and method— the literary qualities—of Zola; it has little relation to the intellectual conception upon which the work rests.

Another Zolaesque element in *The Octopus* is the use of symbols to give emotional weight to the forces which play so large a part in its movement. In *Germinal* the black buildings and tower of the Voreux, the coal mine, are pictured again and again as symbols of the alien force which crushes the miners. Early in *The Octopus* a flying locomotive cuts through a herd of sheep:

> The pathos of it was beyond expression. It was a slaughter, a massacre of innocents. The iron monster had charged full into the midst, merciless, inexorable. To the right and left, all the width of the right of way, the little bodies had been flung; backs were snapped against fence posts; brains knocked out. Caught in the barbs of the wire, wedged in, the bodies hung suspended. Under foot it was terrible. The black blood, winking in the starlight, seeped down into the clinkers between the ties with a prolonged sucking murmur. . . .

Again, the inexorable malignancy of the Railroad is symbolized by a map of its lines:

> It was as though the state had been sucked white and colorless, and against this pallid background the red arteries of the monster stood out, swollen with life-blood reaching out to infinity, gorged to bursting; an excrescence, a gigantic parasite fattening upon the life-blood of an entire commonwealth. . . .

A further similarity, and a basic one, between *The Octopus* and *Germinal* is that both depend for their structure on the operation of an economic institution upon the lives of a social group who struggle for existence under or within it. To ruminate upon and digest the intellectual implications of this great struggle, both authors provide a number of commentators who interpret conditions from their particular points of view. Zola has three: a socialist, an anarchist, and the hero, Lantier, an average thinking man who is turned into a reformer by the evils he sees. In *The Octopus* Caraher is an anarchist—a saloon keeper—who, like Zola's anarchist, has been converted into a passionate hater of monied power by his wife's death at the hands of Pinkerton strike-breakers. Again it must be observed that if these similarities represent an influence of Zola upon Norris it is a literary influence, a matter of method, of storytelling, that has no necessary relation to the philosophy of naturalism.

More interesting and fruitful are the dissimilarities between these novels, for it is through them that Norris's position in the naturalistic movement may be explained. The most important problem in the consideration of any panoramic naturalistic novel is the relation between the characters and the external forces that oppress or control them, the amount of will displayed, and the extent to which such "will" is explained in terms of the forces which the novel presents. In *Germinal*, it will be recalled, the mine has made the miners what they are, has determined their economic situation and physical characteristics from generation to generation. During the action of the novel it pervades and directs their thoughts. It is the object against which they struggle even while it is responsible for having made them what they are. No two characters can affect each other without the mine's having some part in their activity. Physically and spiritually ubiquitous, it is a force with amazing power and scope of operation.

In *The Octopus* conditions are otherwise. The characters begin their struggle with the Trust as free, ethical, and independent men who have achieved a high degree of prosperity upon the frontier. They have struggled with nature and triumphed. And the struggle of such titans with the Octopus is Homeric in conception rather than a pathetic illustration of determining forces controlling helpless and insignificant automata. Annixter is the most striking example of an heroic frontiersman. He is a despiser of "feemale girls," a distruster of marriage, hot-tempered, contentious, gruffly generous. He calls his enemy a *pip*, eats quantities of dried prunes, and re-reads *David Copperfield* constantly. He is college educated, and his ranch is a model of efficiency and modern brightness. Considerable attention is given to his romance with Hilma Tree, who works for him: "Annixter turned into the dairy-house . . . Hilma stood bathed from head to foot in the torrent of sunlight that poured in upon her from the three wide-open windows. She was charming, delicious, radiant of youth, of health, of well-being." He intrudes upon her innocence by a clumsy attempt to kiss her, is properly mortified at his own gaucherie, and stamps off in

Frank Norris at the time he was composing his trilogy of the "Epic of the Wheat."

a rage. But the seed is planted, the hater of women is trapped. It is some time before he can accept the idea of love, and, above all, marriage. Finally he drives her from him, but an all-night vigil under the stars shows him the way:

> By a supreme effort, not of the will, but of the emotion, he fought his way across that vast gulf that for a time had gaped between Hilma and the idea of his marriage. Instantly, like the swift blending of beautiful colours, like the harmony of beautiful chords of music, the two ideas melted into one, and in that moment into his harsh, unlovely world a new idea was born. Annixter stood suddenly upright, a mighty tenderness, a gentleness of spirit, such as he had never conceived of, in his heart strained, swelled, and in a moment seemed to burst. Out of the dark furrows of his soul, up from the deep rugged recesses of his being, something rose, expanding . . .

> "Why . . . I *love* her," he cried.

These activities enhance Annixter's personal independence. They add "spiritual" elements to his character that defy explanation in terms of heredity and environment. His stature is further increased by a duel which he has with a discharged farm hand who dashes on horseback into the dance that Annixter is giving in honor of his new barn. Firing blindly through the smoke, Annixter is astonished to discover that he has hit his opponent in the hand:

> "Well, where did *you* learn to shoot *that* way?" someone in the crowd demanded. Annixter

moved his shoulders with a gesture of vast unconcern.

> "Oh," he observed carelessly, "it's not my *shooting* that ever worries *me*, m'son."

> The crowd gaped with delight. There was a great wagging of heads.

Such offhanded, humorous bravado takes us out of the feeling of a confined, determined life. This same freedom becomes headstrong defiance when the Railroad serves, an hour later, its notice of the new land prices. The ranchers' league is formed in an explosion of defiance. Knowing the power of the Railroad, the reader will regard this event as tragic irony rather than as an illustration of economic determinism. Annixter's death at the climax is tragically wasteful but also heroic. It is almost a glorious death.

A further instance of what I have termed the heroic character of the struggle is to be found in the presentation of Magnus Derrick, chief of the ranchers and president of the league. Talking to his son—the one who is expected to aid the league by reducing rates on wheat—he reveals a tragic flaw:

> "I know you will be fair to the Railroad. That is all we want. Fairness to the corporation is fairness to the farmer, and we won't expect you to readjust the whole matter out of hand. Take your time. We can afford to wait."

> "And suppose the next commission is a railroad board, and reverses all our figures?"

> The one-time mining king, the most redoubtable poker player of Calaveras County, permitted himself a momentary twinkle of his eyes.

> "By then it will be too late. We will, all of us, have made our fortunes by then."

> Magnus was by nature a public man, judicious, deliberate, standing firm for principle, yet upon rare occasions, by some such remark as this, he would betray the presence of a sub-nature of recklessness, inconsistent, all at variance with his creeds and tenets.

Such an analysis raises the conflict to Homeric levels. Frontier heroics we see, battles waged with lives and fortunes at stake—and on one side at least the actors are responsible for their deeds even though they are faced with a fairly impossible choice. On the other side—the villainous side of the Octopus—the supposed economic forces receive such concrete embodiment in characters of inhuman viciousness that all idea of economic determinism is forgotten in the reader's moral indignation at their brutal deeds. S. Behrman, symbol of the Railroad's greed, "was a large, fat man, with a great stomach; his cheek and the upper part of his thick neck ran together to form a great tremulous jowl, shaven and blue-grey in colour; a roll of fat, sprinkled with sparse hair, moist with perspiration, protruded over the back of his collar." Throughout the story he is motivated, apparently, by an unchanging resolve to crush the farmers by fair means or foul. His actions could be explained only by a deep-seated hatred which he is not shown to harbor. In *Germinal* the mine owners are almost as helpless as the miners. Economic forces are clearly portrayed. In *The Octopus* Behrman's villainy is a thing apart from economic forces. It makes excellent material for the story, it adds to the passion of the conflict, but it also obscures whatever forces

Behrman is meant to represent. Lyman Derrick's betrayal of the ranchers, similarly, is presented as a piece of personal baseness, motivated doubtless by the lure of railroad gold, but possible only in a man devoid of loyalty and decency.

The same difference of conception between the *Octopus* and *Germinal* extends to the very symbols which the two authors employ. The Octopus, as we have seen, is an actively evil and malignant force. Adjectives like "inexorable," "iron-hearted," and "pitiless" are constantly applied to it. It is cruel and villainous—a thing to be hated. Compare with this the mine buildings and the black tower of the Voreux in *Germinal*. Gloomy, black, immobile, they stand as a symbol of oppression. But no false attempt is made to have them reach out and devour the miners. Instead they squat there as gaunt and horrible symbols of the forces which the miners cannot evade. Their immobility makes them ideally representative of the economic forces which dominate the book. No moral values can be attached to them; they do not indulge in active evil for which they can be hated. They represent the nature of deterministic forces—inescapable, unchanging, destroyed only by the earth-shaking catastrophe of revolution or the destructive anarchy of Souverine who lets in the water that floods the mine and swallows up the buildings. Zola's symbol carries philosophical as well as dramatic significance. Norris's is almost solely dramatic.

A Homeric conflict between free agents and a fatal but malign institution raises more questions than it answers about the workings of the cosmic mechanism which it is presented as illustrating. What natural laws are demonstrated? What processes are explained? What scientific insights are achieved? And what do we discover about man's relation to nature? The answer takes us into a new set of symbols and related ideas, which I should designate generally by the label natural dynamism. Under this concept nature is presented as a conscious, living, benign force—as in the description of the plowing, where rows of horse-drawn plows, as far as the eye can reach, turn the rich earth:

> It was the long stroking caress, vigorous, male, powerful, for which the Earth seemed panting. The heroic embrace of a multitude of iron hands, gripping deep into the brown, warm flesh of the land that quivered responsive and passionate under this rude advance, so robust as to be almost an assault, so violent as to be veritably brutal. There, under the sky, the wooing of the Titan began, the vast primal passion, the two world-forces, the elemental Male and Female, locked in a colossal embrace, at grapples in the throes of an infinite desire . . .

A second expression of this theme is the story of Vanamee. He became a solitary when his fiancée, having been mysteriously assaulted in the night, died in childbirth. During the course of the novel he frequently appears, experiencing a mystical call that reaches to him out of the night in answer to his conscious willing for his dead love. The experience grows sharper with each repetition, until finally She comes to him—the daughter of his dead Angele—and with the morning he finds that the wheat has appeared above the ground; stretching as far as the eye can see: thus the Vanamee motif is related to the wheat, symbol of fruitfulness and benign natural force. Vanamee achieves the same affirmation of life which the reader is expected to recognize in the nourishing grain:

There it was. The Wheat! The Wheat! In the night it had come up. It was there, everywhere, from margin to margin of the horizon. The earth, long empty, teemed with green life. Once more the pendulum of the seasons swung in its mighty arc, from death back to life. Life out of death, eternity rising from out dissolution. There was the lesson. Angele was not the symbol, but the *proof* of immortality. The seed dying, rotting and corrupting in the earth; rising again in life unconquerable, and in immaculate purity—Angele dying as she gave birth to her little daughter, life springing from her death, the pure, unconquerable, coming forth from the defiled. . . . So Angele, so life, so also the resurrection of the dead. . . . It is sown in weakness. It is raised in power. Death was swallowed up in Victory.

Annixter, too, relates his newborn love to the benign natural compulsion which produces the first shoots of wheat on the morning of his long vigil:

> There it was, the Wheat! The Wheat! The little seed long planted, germinating in the deep, dark furrows of the soil, straining, swelling, suddenly in one night had burst upward to the light. . . . The earth, the loyal mother, who never failed, who never disappointed, was keeping her faith again. Once more the strength of nations was renewed. Once more the Titan, benignant, calm, stirred and woke, and the morning abruptly blazed into glory upon the spectacle of a man whose heart leaped exuberant with the love of a woman, and an exulting earth gleaming transcendent with the radiant magnificence of an inviolable pledge.

The most striking and adventitious illustration of this natural dynamism is the famous scene in which S. Behrman, gloating over a ship that is being filled with wheat, falls into the hold and is smothered under the rushing stream of grain. One feels that this is the very wheat that was stolen from the ranchers, when their lands were taken just at the time of harvest, and that the wheat is taking revenge upon the villain who presumed to interfere with its growth and distribution.

Such invocations of the wheat abound in *The Octopus*. Presley goes out to look at it after the painful scene in which Lyman Derrick's perfidy is revealed, and his thoughts provide a convenient transition to the economic ideology underlying the action:

> Ah, yes, the Wheat—it was over this that the Railroad, the ranchers, the traitor false to his trust, all the members of an obscure conspiracy, were wrangling. As if human agency could affect this colossal power! What were these heated, tiny squabbles, this feverish, small bustle of mankind, this minute swarming of the human insect, to the great majestic, silent ocean of the Wheat itself! Indifferent, gigantic, resistless, it moved in its appointed grooves. Men. Lilliputians, gnats in the sunshine, buzzed impudently in their tiny battles, were born, lived through their little day, died, and were forgotten; while the Wheat, wrapped in Nirvanic calm,

grew steadily under the night, alone with the stars and with God.

Here are forces intelligent, benign, purposeful, leading the world and its people into the felicity of God's love. Economic determinism is a mere incident in the cosmic enterprise. Zola, to continue our comparison, makes it clear that both his miners and the mine owners are caught up in the strangling grip of the capitalistic system: they are destined to clash, but neither can profit by winning the battle within the framework of capitalism, for if the miners' wages are raised the owners will be ruined. The only answer is world revolution. Zola's theory is explicit and coherent without being unduly obtruded upon the story. It emerges as the only possible meaning of the action.

Norris presents his situation in various ways. At one point the economic struggle results from the moral laxness of the public: "Every State has its own grievance. If it is not a railroad trust, it is a sugar trust, or an oil trust, or an industrial trust, that exploits the People, *because the People allow it*. The indifference of the People is the opportunity of the despot." Elsewhere the Railroad is said to be operated by the blackest of villains. As Presley shouts: "They swindle a nation of a hundred million and call it Financiering; they levy a blackmail and call it Commerce; they corrupt a legislature and call it Politics . . . they prostitute the honor of a State and call it Competition." The Railroad is cursed and the people are exhorted to action, always against a *responsible* evil force which moral rightness demands should be curbed. But when Norris thinks of the wheat his love of great forces and resounding phrases impels him to body it forth, again and again, as a positive, God-sent, benign force which will triumph in spite of temporary conflicts waged over the enjoyment of wealth to be derived from its control. In Presley's thought, already quoted, it is a "colossal power" containing apparently within itself the ability to bring about its own distribution and consumption. It wills to be the feeder of nations. Nothing can stop its movement. Stated in less rhapsodic language this conviction comes forth as a blind and outmoded form of utilitarianism—which Shelgrim, head of the Railroad—expounds with the author's approval:

> "Believe this, young man . . . try to believe this—to begin with—*that railroads build themselves*. Where there is a demand sooner or later there will be a supply. Dr. Derrick, does he grow his wheat? The Wheat grows itself. What does he count for? Do I build the Railroad? You are dealing with forces, young man, when you speak of Wheat and the Railroads, not with men. There is the Wheat, the supply. It must be carried to feed the People. There is the demand. The Wheat is one force, the Railroad another, and there is the law that governs them—supply and demand. Men have only little to do in the whole business. Complications may arise, conditions that bear hard on the individual—crush him maybe—*but the Wheat will be carried to feed the people* as inevitably as it will grow."

Such language condones the evils of competition because through it the wheat reaches the people. The fact that it is finally eaten, we are told, makes it a symbol of truth, a concrete proof that good triumphs in the end, that nature works for human betterment through the economic system:

> Greed, cruelty, selfishness, and inhumanity are short-lived; the individual suffers, but the race

goes on. Annixter dies, but in a far distant corner of the world a thousand lives are saved. The larger view always and through all shams, all wickedness, discovers the Truth that will, in the end, prevail, and all things, surely inevitably, resistlessly work together for good.

Here, then, is where the fabric of reason is thinnest in *The Octopus*. The wheat as an incarnation of natural dynamism, of an inherent desire in nature to be bountiful, is equated with the prevailing social arrangements for buying and selling. Laissez-faire economics is treated as if it were an aspect of nature's dynamic urge to reproduce herself and feed her children. We are told that *how* the wheat is distributed does not matter; we are almost persuaded that the manner of its distribution is a part of nature's larger plan. One does not of course question a novelist's right to accept laissez-faire economics. But we must note that these conclusions do not satisfactorily answer the *problem as posed* in the novel. That problem is not whether the wheat will finally be eaten (it always was in those days) but whether the railroads must and will continue to swindle and oppress the less powerful American citizens whom, if the will of our democracy is to find expression, it is supposed to serve in a free market. The question is whether the people must or should stand for such criminal injustice, whether our social order must countenance a condition in which a corporation controls the press, the banks, and the courts and so becomes a law unto itself in defiance of democratic process. This problem is not solved. It is simply evaded, while a vaguely religious affirmation of ultimate good is offered to appease the emotions aroused by the action.

When Behrman, the immediate individual object of the reader's dislike, is smothered in the hold of the wheat ship, pent-up emotions are released. The reader is made to feel, by this poetic fusion of disparate elements, that the wheat as a force has answered the social and economic problem of the novel, the problem of monopoly and coercion. Of course it has not, and the thoughtful reader is bound after a time to feel that it is he who has been swindled of a solution. Conditions in the American West differed essentially from those in the coal mines of *Germinal* where there was no answer for either miner or owner. Zola was true to his materials and wove a consistently dark tragic pattern—leaving at the end a single bright thread in the suggestion that revolution must inevitably come. Norris copies this tragic pattern for a conflict that did not have to end tragically. The democratic process could still work in America, where there were natural resources in abundance and relatively few people. Not revolution but a safer legal basis for trade was indicated. The tragedy of the story speaks magnificently for itself. It is the attempt to explain it that does irreparable harm to the novel. Only once is there a strong expression of the new naturalistic philosophy, when Presley ponders the idea of a mechanistic universe, indifferent and unchangeable, which pursues its way not toward the utilitarian goal of prosperity but toward no goal at all, operating merely because motion is the law of the cosmic mechanism:

> Nature was, then, a gigantic engine, a vast Cyclopean power, huge, terrible, a leviathan with a heart of steel, knowing no compunction, no forgiveness, no tolerance; crushing out the human atom standing in its way with nirvanic calm, the agony of destruction sending never a jar, never the faintest tremor through all that prodigious mechanism of wheels and cogs.

One is tempted to perceive a close relationship between the incoherence of Norris's philosophy and the steadily growing orotundity of his style. In *The Octopus* there is an endless accumulation of sonorous adjectives. The rolling periods throb and rumble. Sometimes they produce superb effects; at other times they seem rather to be giving voice to a love of power and size which, an end in itself, sweeps careful ratiocination aside. Norris's development thus far shows a steady movement toward this love of high-sounding words. As the style inflates, the conviction of his books diminishes. *McTeague,* though better built, carries less final conviction than *Vandover. The Octopus,* still better constructed, has less than *McTeague.*

But in the last analysis *The Octopus* is one of the finest American novels written before 1910. It towers immeasurably far above the sickly sentiment of Norris's contemporaries. Its chief weakness can be traced to a certain feebleness of intellectual grip, and this feebleness is reflected in the inadequacy of his grasp on the ideology—naturalism—through which he chose to work. It must be emphasized that he does not fall short merely because he was not a perfect naturalist, but because of the intellectual softness which prevented him from completely mastering the set of ideas he adopted. We may assume that he would have similarly failed in the comprehension of another philosophy that required the same sharpness of perception. We may, further, conclude that the naturalistic philosophy provided a much-needed discipline for Norris's creative exuberance—a discipline which aided him wonderfully in directing his genius toward expression in significant form. (pp. 141-51)

Charles Child Walcutt, "Frank Norris and the Search for Form," in his American Literary Naturalism: A Divided Stream, *University of Minnesota Press, 1956, pp. 114-56.*

ROBERT W. SCHNEIDER (essay date 1962)

[*Schneider is an American educator, critic, and historian. In the following excerpt, he discusses Victorian attitudes and values in Norris's work that were antithetical to the principles of Naturalism.*]

The literature of the progressive period still needs to be subjected to . . . an analysis of basic, underlying assumptions. There has been some excellent work done on the writers of the period, but in reading most of the general and monographic studies, one gets the impression that, in the field of literature, the "watershed" period of the 1890's was peopled with a totally new breed of writers called naturalists—men who rejected the traditional assumptions and values of the past for the new cult of science.

What were the basic tenets of this American creed which the naturalists are supposed to have overthrown? First, and perhaps most important, was the philosophic side of the code, centering around the doctrine of the free individual. Americans had been the inheritors of the dual concept of man postulated by the seventeenth century English political theorists. This concept, found in its most familiar form in the writings of John Locke, held that the natural man was essentially good, rational and unselfish, but in his social relations gave expression to the evil, selfish, irrational side of his nature. This essentially benevolent individual was free and creative and could construct or reform society in the light of human reason. During the nineteenth century the scope of man's freedom and creativity was so emphasized that the complexity of the earlier concepts was obscured. The idea of man as good, rational, free and creative

came to be looked upon as *the* American concept. The qualifying factor was that man was basically good only so long as he remained the natural man apart from the corrupting influence of institutions and traditions. This philosophy found its most extravagant expression in the lais-sez-faire creed of the Gospel of Wealth.

Man's freedom to will and act, however, placed a grave responsibility on his shoulders. He lived his life in a universe that operated on a system of moral law and he could understand this moral law through the exercise of his reason. Because he had the freedom and rationality to direct his own life, he was held totally responsible for his own actions. Both his material success and his eternal salvation were his own responsibility.

This was one side of the traditional creed that is supposed to have been overthrown by the naturalistic code that was being formulated in the 1890's. Under the pressure of the new, chaotic industrialism and guided by the evolutionary philosophy of Darwin and Spencer, the writers of this "watershed" period supposedly rejected the traditional notion that man was the free and creative center of a moral universe for an amoral philosophy of biological determinism. Critics and literary historians have disagreed rather violently as to the exact nature of this new philosophy of naturalism, but Ernest Marchand has given a good working description of the naturalistic view of man which indicates some of the basic ideas.

> Man was seen to be a complex of instincts, desires, hungers, toward the satisfaction of which all his energies were bent. All the elaborate machinery of law and custom developed by civilization is scarcely sufficient to hold in check the self-assertive impulses, the hard-driving force of the ego. Hence the continual aggressions, unscrupulous acts, crimes of all sorts, which trouble society. It was readily imagined that man in his primitive state would admit no restraints to the fulfillment of his desires but superior force, whether of things, of beasts, or of other men. . . . Concentration on the animal in man and on instinct tended to diminish the importance of reason and of ethics in human life and to magnify brute strength and energy.

Here then is a philosophy which not only rejected the traditional assumptions about morals, ethics and human nature, but which also was in complete revolt against the Victorianism of the so-called Genteel Tradition. The young writers of the 1890's could not tolerate what they considered to be the overfastidious, prudish character of contemporary writing. The notion that sex was evil and a subject to be avoided at all cost was supposedly foreign to them. The grip of the Genteel Tradition, where all was sweetness and light, where all love was platonic, and sexual intercourse was a degradation of noble womanhood, had to be broken.

In the field of literature, as in many other fields, the picture of the 1890's has been distorted by overemphasis on change. Were these writers actually in rebellion against the intellectual and moral world of their own day? If so, to what extent did they manage to free themselves from traditional assumptions and value judgments? This essay will be concerned with answering these questions in the instance of a man who is considered by most literary historians to be a prime example of pre-War American Naturalism but who was, in many ways, typical of the Victorian Age—Frank Norris. (pp. 13-15)

Although it was not published until 1914, *Vandover and the Brute* was the first novel Frank Norris completed, and the theme—the degeneration of an upper-middle class youth—would seem to be a perfect one for a naturalistic novel. In the beginning Vandover was a complete innocent; when he learned about sex he could not believe that people were so "vile." Yet, even as he was shocked "the innate vice stirred in him, the brute began to make itself felt." Norris suggested that this side of Vandover's nature might have corrupted the boy in his early teens, had it not been that the other side of his nature—the artistic side—began to develop at the same time. Here, as later, Norris, like a good Victorian, seemed to see evil epitomized in the sex act.

At college Van spent most of his time studying art and trying to be collegiate. When he returned to San Francisco he established a studio and entered into the life around him. In the social whirl, Van again found that his purity and clean habits made him an exception, and again his pliable character gave way as he entered into the night life of the city.

Finding that his respect for women stood in the way of desired sensual pleasures, Van set out to destroy that respect, knowing as he did so that "it was the wilful and deliberate corruption of part of that which was best in him." He permitted the beast to satisfy its demands, "feeding its abominable hunger from that part of him which he knew to be the purest, the cleanest, and the best." Norris continually emphasized that this was an act of will on Van's part—a wilful action taken with knowledge of the consequences.

Three years passed during which Van engaged in occasional debauches and, at the same time, carried on a courtship of the pure and lovely Turner Ravis who, Norris wrote, "influenced him upon his best side, calling out in him all that was cleanest, finest and most delicate." Meanwhile Van struck up an acquaintance with a "gay" girl named Ida Wade, who committed suicide when she discovered she was pregnant with Van's child. This was the beginning, and a causal factor, in a series of disasters that resulted in the death of Van's father and his own exile from the social circle of his friends. Van was upset by the exile, "yet he took his punishment in the right spirit. He did not blame anyone but himself; it was only a just retribution for the things he had done."

Now, beyond the restraining bonds of society, Van entered upon a year-long period of dissipation during which he lost contact with all his old friends. Then one night he found himself at the opera where, for the moment, his love of beauty saved him and he came to understand himself. In this rather extended passage Norris reveals many of the ethical and moral presuppositions upon which the novel is based.

> There came over him a vague sense of those things which are too beautiful to be comprehended. . . . To be better, to be true and right and pure, these were the only things that were worth while, these were the things that he seemed to feel in the music. . . . The appeal had been made directly to what was best and strongest in Vandover, and the answer was quick and overpowering. . . . He had not yet destroyed all that was good in him; now it had turned in one more revolt, crying out against him, protesting for the last time against its own perversion and destruction. . . . He had been lured into a mood where he was himself at his very best, where

the other Vandover, the better Vandover, drew apart with eyes turned askance, looking inward and downward into the depths of his own character, shuddering, terrified. Far down there in the darkest, lowest places he had seen the brute, squat, deformed, hideous. . . . And with the eye of his better self he saw again, little by little, the course of his whole life, and witnessed again the eternal struggle between good and evil that had been going on within him since his earliest years. He was sure that at the first the good had been the strongest. Little by little the brute had grown, and he, pleasure-loving, adapting himself to every change of environment, luxurious, self-indulgent, shrinking with the shrinking of a sensuous artist-nature from all that was irksome and disagreeable, had shut his ears to the voices that shouted warnings of the danger, and had allowed the brute to thrive and grow.

Norris makes it quite evident that Vandover's problem was his own dual nature and his failure to curb the evil, sensual side of that nature. It was his surrender to the animal in him that was the basic cause of Van's decline. One by one he had separated himself from, or caused to be separated from him, all of the influences that had cultivated the better part of him—his father, Turner Ravis and society itself. Even his ability as an artist had slipped away through neglect. "It was gone—his art was gone, the one thing that could save him. That, too, like all the other good things of his life, he had destroyed." (pp. 16-17)

Norris' other early novel displays many of the same ethical and moral judgments that linked *Vandover* to the Victorian intellectual climate. In *McTeague,* however, the connection is not presented so blatantly. Most of the literary historians seem to be in agreement that Trina and McTeague were not free individuals in charge of their own destiny, as was Vandover, but prisoners of hereditary and environmental forces. Carvel Collins, in an introduction to *McTeague,* has written, "The novel records the destruction of an innocent." But does it?

Has not the critic's emphasis upon heredity and environment been rather misplaced? In the case of McTeague himself, the inherited tendency toward viciousness when drunk was undoubtedly a factor, but that appears to have been the only inherited characteristic which Norris stressed. Environment was not important at all. It is true that Norris gave some rather detailed descriptions of Polk Street, but he did not show that these conditions were causal factors in the lives of his principals. The story could have been set in another place and another social stratum without injury to the plot or the logic of the events.

What then were the controlling factors in the fall of Mac and Trina? Mac was a fairly good dentist and was happy in his little world. Then the snake entered the Garden of Eden as Trina awakened his sexual instincts. So long as the affair continued on a rather platonic plane Norris treated it with quiet amusement. But when McTeague's sexual instinct rose to the flood as Trina was helpless under the ether, Norris' tone changed accordingly. He wrote, "Suddenly the animal in the man stirred and woke; the evil instincts that in him were so close to the surface leaped to life." If McTeague had been solely an animal he would simply have followed his instinct, but here a crisis arose because man for Norris is not simply a predatory animal—he has a dual nature.

> Blindly, and without knowing why, McTeague fought against it, moved by an unreasoned instinct of resistance. Within him, a certain second self, another better McTeague rose with the brute; both were strong, with the huge crude strength of the man himself. . . . There in that cheap and shabby "Dental Parlor" a dreaded struggle began. It was the old battle, old as the world, wide as the world—the sudden panther leap of the animal . . . and the simultaneous arousing of the other man, the better self.

McTeague wondered why it was that this perverse urge arose to defile a love that was pure and clean. Then occurs this famous passage.

> Below the fine fabric of all that was good in him ran the foul stream of hereditary evil, like a sewer. The vices and sins of his father and of his father's father, to the third and fourth and five hundredth generation, tainted him. The evil of an entire race flowed in his veins. Why should it? He did not desire it. Was he to blame?
>
> But McTeague could not understand this thing. It had faced him, as sooner or later it faces every child of man.

Most of the critics apparently have not read beyond the first sentence of this quotation, for almost invariably they have stressed the fact that this evil was inherited by McTeague. But the rest of the quotation makes it obvious that this evil is part of the nature of man. McTeague inherited it as a man, not as the son of a particular family.

In these two passages Norris' close connection with traditional ideas again becomes clear. His Victorian attitude toward the sexual relationship was clearly shown in McTeague's thoughts and actions. As much as the huge dentist desired Trina, he realized that if he took her she would never be the same to him. "Under the shadow of her royal hair, he would surely see the smudge of a foul ordure." Indeed, this was what happened when she did surrender to him—a kiss only—at the railroad station. Immediately she became less desirable; he thought less of her. (pp. 18-19)

In *The Octopus,* Norris' main emphasis with regard to the efficacy of human moral action was that man is insignificant in comparison with the fecundity of the wheat and the force of the railroad. All of the ranchers of the San Joaquin valley had united to defeat the railroad, but they had failed. Why? Because man is an insignificant gnat in the totality of things.

> What were these heated, tiny squabbles, this feverish, small bustle of mankind, this minute swarming of the human insect, to the great, majestic, silent ocean of the Wheat itself! Indifferent, gigantic, resistless, it moved in its appointed grooves. Men. Lilliputians, gnats in the sunshine, buzzed impudently in their tiny battles, were born, lived through their little day, died, and were forgotten; while the Wheat, wrapped in Nirvanic calm, grew steadily under the night, alone with the stars and with God.

In this and dozens of similar passages throughout the novel, Norris presented man as an insignificant insect in an amoral universe. The railroads built themselves and the wheat grew itself; everything operated automatically through natural laws. By sheer weight and bulk this was the predominant picture which Norris presented in *The Octopus.*

But, on the other hand, the most carefully presented character study in the novel was that of Magnus Derrick, whose destruction, Norris implied, lay on his own head. Magnus was a man about sixty, tall, broad and erect, a man of great dignity. People looked up to him as their natural leader and he was proud that they did so. He had abandoned politics because he refused to lower his principles, but it looked as though any victory over the railroad required the securing of a friendly railroad commission, and to do this he would have to acquiesce in some crooked political dealings. But what about his honor? His wife reminded him of this, and "again Magnus wavered, about to yield to his better instincts and to the entreaties of his wife." In this and similar passages, Norris indicated that Magnus had a free moral choice about whether or not to enter the League against the railroad. But at other times he presented the old rancher as a prisoner of circumstances.

> But now it was too late. He was pledged. He had joined the League. He was its chief, and his defection might mean its disintegration at the very time when it needed all its strength to fight the land cases. More than a mere deal in bad politics was involved. There was the land grab. His withdrawal from an unholy cause would mean the weakening, perhaps the collapse, of another cause that he believed to be righteous as truth itself. He was helplessly caught in the mesh. Wrong seemed indissolubly knitted into the fabric of Right.

At still other times Norris speaks of Magnus as a great gambler, risking all on one cast of the dice. One wonders if Magnus was actually the free man capable of choice, the moral man caught in a dilemma where his freedom of action was limited to a choice between two evils, or "the gambler, willing to play for colossal stakes, to hazard a fortune on the chance of winning a million."

Norris' solution was presented in the events of the story. Magnus, as president of the League in its fight against the railroad, achieved the position he had so long sought—to be honored, well-known and respected. But it brought him no pleasure. He had suddenly aged and his old erect carriage slumped. He could not forget that he was a briber. All his life he had been honest, but now he had succumbed to the harrassment of the railroads; he had fallen from virtue. Consequently, he lost his old assurance and with it his old mastery. Norris' conclusion was presented when it became known that the man whom the League had elected by bribery, Magnus' own son, was really in the pay of the railroad. The author wrote, "Gambler that he was, he had at last chanced his highest stake, his personal honor, in the greatest game of his life, and had lost." There seems to be no question that Norris held Magnus morally responsible for his own destruction.

Here, then, is moral and ethical confusion—a confusion in the view of man itself, man held responsible for his actions in a universe that takes no account of those actions. But there is yet a third view presented in *The Octopus,* a view in which good will triumph and the forces of evil be confounded, not by human action but by the forces of benevolent nature.

This view was presented in the sub-plot dealing with the young ascetic, Vanamee, who had the power to call people to him by intense concentration. It would not be particularly important were it not for the fact that in the end Presley, through whom Norris pulled together all the various strands of his complex story, came to accept Vanamee's position. According to this view, the ranchers of the San Joaquin were defeated in this battle not by S. Behrman and Mr. Shelgrim, but by the force of the railroad itself. This, however, was an individual instance, unimportant in the totality of things, and in the end the forces of good would prevail. Men, individuals, would be shot down; misery and death were their lot. But the wheat remained and it would go in its appointed grooves to feed the world despite the evil forces of the railroad. Presley's analysis, and the novel, end with this paragraph.

> Falseness dies; injustice and oppression in the end of everything fade and vanish away. Greed, cruelty, selfishness, and inhumanity are short-lived; the individual suffers, but the race goes on. Annixter dies, but in a far-distant corner of the world a thousand lives are saved. The larger view always and through all shams, all wickednesses, discovers the Truth that will, in the end, prevail, and all things, surely, inevitably, resistlessly work together for good.

In this novel Norris tackled, for what is really the first and only time, the problem of man and the cosmos. Is there any clear view of man's ethical position presented here? Are human affairs directed by moral decisions or by amoral forces? Did Norris himself have a clear understanding of his own ideas? None of these questions can be answered completely, yet it is possible to reconcile, at least partially, the contradictions which have been pointed out. Through Magnus Derrick one sees that man can bring about his own destruction, and through another sub-plot one sees that man can achieve his own moral salvation. Buck Annixter did so before he was shot down by the railroad men. Man can bring about his own personal salvation or destruction, and to that degree he is free; the efficacy of the moral decision is upheld. But in his fight with the forces of evil, as here represented by the railroad, he can be defeated. Over and above this, however, is the great life force, the spirit of the universe, which, in the end, will bring about the greatest good for the greatest number. It is not a very clear view and it is clouded with confusions and contradictions, but it appears to be what Norris was trying to demonstrate in his most ambitious novel. (pp. 21-4)

Those who have tried to present Frank Norris as a complete rebel against the Victorian code of his own day have insisted upon separating his essays about fiction, which they admit are traditionalist, from his fiction itself. But it is the contention of the present writer that such a separation should not be made. The same Victorian sexual code is as prominent in the novels as in the essays. The same belief in the efficacy of human freedom in the face of naturalistic forces can be seen in both. The same insistence that personal salvation or destruction is dependent upon the moral actions of the individual forms as integral part of nearly all his writings.

This is not to say that there are no deterministic, amoral elements in Norris' writings—certainly there are. The story of the destruction of Vandover because of his surrender to the beast must be balanced by the rise of the amoral Charlie Geary and the innocent suffering of Dolliver Haight. But it is very seldom that evil doing is not punished in a Norris novel, and where he is deterministic, as he tries to be in the Wheat Series, that determinism is of the progressive, Spencerian variety and not strictly evolutionary and amoral.

Norris himself was probably not aware of the many cross currents of his mind. Like most men, he was largely a product of the intellectual and moral climate in which he was nourished. He tried to break out of that climate of opinion toward a new way of thinking in which he consciously believed, and it is this unassimilated combination of strong moral and ethical assumptions with conflicting intellectual ideas that brings philosophical confusion to his novels.

It is the contention of the present writer that in the case of Frank Norris, as in that of so many of his contemporaries, the traditional cluster of ideas had more force in directing his thinking than the new concepts. Here again intellectual and literary historians have distorted the climate of opinion and missed the drama of transition in their honest attempts to solve the problem of periodization and dramatize the changes in the intellectual climate of America in the dynamic years between 1890-1917. An examination of individual beliefs, like those of Frank Norris, and those of the Progressive social scientists, would seem to indicate that those changes were not so great as has sometimes been suggested. (pp. 26-7)

Robert W. Schneider, "Frank Norris: The Naturalist as Victorian," in Midcontinent American Studies Journal, Vol. 3, No. 1, Spring, 1962, pp. 13-27.

WARREN FRENCH (essay date 1962)

[*French is an American author, editor, and essayist who has written several important studies of twentieth-century American writers and literary movements. In addition to his works on celebrated American authors, French also served as an editor of the influential* Twayne Theatrical *series and the* Twayne United States Authors *series, to which he contributed a study of Frank Norris. In the following excerpt from that study, French disputes the categorization of Norris as a Naturalist, placing him instead in the tradition of the American Transcendentalists as exemplified by Ralph Waldo Emerson and Walt Whitman.*]

Posterity has served Frank Norris well. Few American authors have had their remains handled with such loving care as the exuberant Californian who died at thirty-two, his most ambitious project uncompleted.

His works have been enthusiastically if uncritically preserved in a collected edition. He is the subject of an able biography and an exhaustive analysis of the influences upon his writing. His letters have been tastefully edited, and his literary remains made the subject of a nation-wide search by the University of California library. His most memorable works are in print in reasonably priced editions, while many of his contemporaries languish. He is almost always mentioned respectfully—occasionally affectionately—by historians of American literature as a drum major of the native naturalistic movement.

Despite all this attention—including a recent revival of interest that has produced intelligent revaluations that enable us to see his work in new perspectives—Norris has not been recognized for what he principally is. The very stressing of his relationship to the naturalistic movement has been an understandable misfortune—not only because it led to his temporary eclipse after

World War II when naturalism went out of fashion, but also because it has obscured the most distinctive characteristic of his works.

Norris is actually best described not by one of the many writers about his works, but by John Berryman's offhand remark in *Stephen Crane* that Norris was "a romantic moralist, with a style like a great wet dog." Many critics—especially those influenced by Granville Hicks's *The Great Tradition* (1933)—have pounced upon inconsistencies in Norris' thinking and allegedly naturalistic writing that they have supposed adequate to deny his claim to fame. What such critics fail to realize is that rigorous scientific consistency would be utterly alien to Norris' dramatic, dynamic personality, and that his closest link is not with the imported naturalistic tradition but with the transcendentalist tradition of those native writers who most vigorously denounced consistency—Emerson and Whitman.

The most useful clue to understanding Norris' work is provided by Alfred Kazin's passing remark in *On Native Grounds* (1942) that *The Pit* "proved no more than that the hold of the pit over Curtis Jadwin was exactly like the hold of drink over the good but erring father in a temperance novel" [see excerpt dated 1942]. Kazin does not go on to observe, however, that the similarity he notes is by no means limited in Norris' work to the portrayal of Jadwin. All of the author's novels resemble temperance tracts.

Richard Chase comments in *The American Novel and Its Tradition* (1957) that Norris employs "the conspiracy theory of history"—the idea that man's ills can all be traced back to some single specific evil (not just the "money power" that Chase cites, but alcohol, slavery, bleached flour, bathing, etc.) that has always been the mainstay of the panacea-seeking tractarian. Like most romantic thinkers, Norris is essentially one who seeks to reform not specific institutions, but human nature; and the vehicle of moral reform is the tract, one of the bulkiest if least admired pillars of the American literary tradition.

The reasons for the original classification of Norris as a naturalist are apparent. Early readers and critics, distressed by the violence of Norris' best received books, *McTeague* and *The Octopus,* had to seek a theoretical justification for works they found literally distasteful. As late as 1915 such a conservative spokesman as Fred Lewis Pattee was writing in *American Literature since 1870* that Norris was "an ardent disciple of Zola," who swung to the extreme of the French author's theories, as if "to tell the truth was to tell with microscopic details the repulsive things of physical life" [see Additional Bibliography].

Although the attitude Pattee represents persists at least as late as 1951 when Arthur Hobson Quinn's *The Literature of the American People* appeared, few today need to call upon experimental naturalism to excuse Norris. We have become calloused against far grosser events and language than he employed. Since those who have maintained that Norris is not a consistent naturalist are quite right . . . , we must find another justification for considering his work worth attention.

My argument is that this justification is found in Norris' preserving almost unadulterated in an age characterized by the pessimism and cynicism of Mark Twain, Stephen Crane, and Ambrose Bierce, a transcendentalist romantic faith in the grand design of a benevolent "Nature" epitomized in the story of the shepherd Vanamee in *The Octopus.* There is defeat and tragedy in Norris' work; but his characters suffer not because—like Stephen Crane's—they are victims of an indifferent universe but because of their selfish efforts to thwart Nature's benevolent intentions.

Norris was unquestionably profoundly influenced by the naturalists, especially Zola. How much he owes to the French author—perhaps even in the way of incidents as well as techniques—has been established by Lars Åhnebrink's exhaustive monographs [see excerpt 1950]. Yet Norris himself did little to advance the efforts of the naturalists. He nowhere gives evidence of being much interested in naturalistic devices except as a means to tractarian ends. Far from being a "literary scientist," he probably found much of Zola's theorizing incomprehensible. What Norris realized was that naturalism had provided him with a tool for refurbishing the nearly moribund tractarian tradition. The endless repetition of nineteenth-century tracts and the squeamishness of genteel "parlor reformers" had driven bored readers to continental fiction or to the despised dime novels for literary excitement. Imitating the naturalists might, however, make tracts as thrilling as dime novels. Charles Walcutt calls Norris' naturalism a "mannerism," but it was more that that—like the ingenious devices advertisers resort to today when sales languish, it was a technique to revive dwindling interest. Norris owes more to naturalism than it does to him. This scientific and objective literary doctrine provided techniques to give new vigor to what is best described as Norris' "romantic anarchism," the intuitive and subjective belief that

A page of the manuscript of McTeague.

a beneficent "Nature" will prevail despite the organized efforts of selfish men.

Norris' work remains valuable because the kind of "romantic anarchism" which his thinking illustrates still persists—as is indicated by the incessant cries today for "natural rights" without "civilized responsibilities." . . . [Norris is not] a historical landmark or a museum piece, but . . . one manifestation of a persisting American state of mind—not . . . an American convert to a foreign literary tradition, but . . . a scion of the transcendentalists who, with proverbial Yankee ingenuity, borrowed the latest techniques to give new impetus to the irrepressible tradition of American romanticism. (pp. 7-10)

> Warren French, in his Frank Norris, *Twayne Publishers, Inc., 1962, 160 p.*

JOSEPH R. McELRATH, JR.   (essay date 1975)

[*McElrath is an American educator and critic. In the following essay, he points out the largely neglected humorous aspect of* McTeague.]

One of the problems attending the definition of any novel as Naturalistic is that the mere use of the term activates a set of axioms which form the character of one's critical response. No one, of course, fully accepts Vernon L. Parrington's helpful but too broadly phrased six-point definition of Naturalism; but it seems that many commentators approach *McTeague* still thinking along roughly the same lines. Because *McTeague* is a novel of degeneration depicting an individual as a victim of forces, hereditary and environmental, beyond his control and even his comprehension, readers look for related Naturalistic traits in Norris's vision and technique in that work. And those readers usually manage to find them, more or less. Thus we read in critical literature on Norris that he is somewhat amoral, objective, pessimistic, and coldly serious in tone—though not purely so, as the classic Naturalists are. That Norris's *impure* Naturalism was the result of lack of restraint in style and an apparently compulsive need to moralize is the qualification that commentators offer when defining his place in American literary history.

I would like to examine here one of those impure traits that mars the Naturalistic shape of *McTeague* and suggest that that impurity is actually one of the better features of the novel. I would also like to point out how the strict application of traditional critical tenets concerning Naturalistic fiction can, in its effects, ruin *McTeague* for the modern reader. *McTeague* is Naturalistic, but it is many other fine things as well. I propose that it is also a comic book—deliberately conceived and executed as such—and that the major critics have overlooked or distorted this characteristic because in their approach to the work they do not allow for the simultaneous presence of comedic and pathetic authorial intentions. Ridiculous, grotesque, laughable events transpire in *McTeague* (as they do in *Maggie* also), and they are not the lamentable results of Norris's ineptitude, lack of taste, or stupidity.

An appreciation of the humor of *McTeague* hinges upon one's perception of Norris's attitude toward his hero. McTeague, clearly, does not immediately resemble Henry Fleming, Martin Eden, Hurstwood, or Nick Adams. In fact, as we read the first half of *McTeague,* it proves difficult to make use of the work *hero* at all. For McTeague is a colorful oddity, a bumpkin, a clod, a fool—"a clown with ass's ears" as Norris terms him. . . . As we become familiar with our principal character, the al-

lusion to Shakespeare's comedy rings true: the dentist is kin to Bottom, inhabiting the stage of comedy and, for a good while, quite remote from the stage of Macbeth and Hamlet. In no other novel that I know has an author directly termed his main character "stupid" and employed the adverb "stupidly" so many times as Norris does, to make clear just what his attitude toward him is and to prompt the reader as to what attitude he should assume. As Norris sits back and repeatedly roars at the behavior of the dentist, we too are to enjoy the show that McTeague and his equally grotesque comrades put on. Mad Maria Macapa, insanely avaricious Zerkow, loudmouthed and empty-headed Marcus, and the geriatric lovers Old Grannis and Miss Baker join in to create the broad farce of a strange but true *comédie humaine*. I simply cannot understand why no one has yet written in earnest about the antics of these characters as comedic.

An apparent reason for the repeatedly mirthless reading of *McTeague* is that observers seem to approach the work with a strong preconception as to what a Naturalistic work *should* be like. It seems presumed that Mac should be viewed as though he were a Hurstwood. Consequently, these readers see Norris, from the first page on, as exclusively interested in seriously constructing a pathetic hero who, through a series of unfortunate incidents, suffers a terrible fall and is worthy of our unreserved sympathy. When it turns out that the narrative tone of *McTeague* does not quite correspond to such an alleged authorial intention, and when Norris thus seems to be violating the alleged purpose of the novel, these readers are quite naturally disconcerted and disappointed. One reading *McTeague* as straight Naturalism throughout may be especially alarmed when the tragic situation being developed is suddenly counterpointed by what sounds like a faint, somewhat sinister, authorial snicker. And the cacophony that that reader hears gives cause for outrage and amazement. Who is this Norris to be laughing at the plight of poor McTeague? Who is this Norris who, like a Naturalistic fiend, is self-complacently pulling off the wings of his specimens, chuckling at their unlikely gaits?

Norris thus becomes a writer with unfeeling, aristocratic airs, offensively expressing his ironic disdain for the lowly proles. And we thereby encounter a critical response similar to what might result if a reader had decided to respond to Falstaff as though he were King Lear. As that Shakespeare critic might, the Norris commentator gets huffy about Norris's inappropriate levity, and he ultimately chides Norris for a nigh incredible degree of smugness.

One may speak of a kind of derision to which Norris subjects his characters. One may. But if derision it is, it is phrased in the broadly humourous tones of burlesque, and there is no more serious "derision" than is to be found in Spenser's attitude toward the clownish Braggadochio or in Wilde's attitude toward his outrageous characters in *The Importance of Being Earnest*. Consider the scene in which Marcus—egomaniacal buffoon that he is, who never has thought seriously of Trina Sieppe in terms of love—steps aside for Mac to plight his troth. Marcus is clearly becoming vicariously involved in the romantic bathos that any 1890s American might have enjoyed, and learned, when viewing staged melodrama like Hope's *The Prisoner of Zenda* or when reading popular romances like Davis's *The King's Jackal.*

> "Well, say, Mac," he cried, striking the table with his fist, "go ahead. I guess you—you want her pretty bad. I'll pull out; yes, I will. I'll give her up to you, old man."

The sense of his own magnanimity all at once overcame Marcus. He saw himself as another man, very noble, self-sacrificing; he stood apart and watched this second self with boundless admiration and with infinite pity. He was so good, so magnificent, so heroic, that he almost sobbed. Marcus made a sweeping gesture of resignation, throwing out both his arms, crying:

"Mack, I'll give her up to you. I won't stand between you." There were actually tears in Marcus's eyes as he spoke. There was no doubt he thought himself sincere....

The scene continues and what ensues is clearly mock heroic. Norris employs the time-tested comic device of placing the ignoble in the context of nobility, dressng two dunces in the garb of heroic personages. And in the first of the following sentences Norris asks the reader to recall that it is *Mac*—stupid, ox-like Mac—who partakes in the melodrama that Marcus has initiated: "It was a great moment; even McTeague felt the drama of it'." ... That lead, "even McTeague," bears consideration in light of the sombre response usually afforded a work that is supposed to be monolithically Naturalistic. We may recall what Marcus and McTeague are actually like before proceeding. For Norris pulls out all stops and develops the comic inflation in earnest.

What a fine thing was this friendship between men! The dentist treats his friend for an ulcerated tooth and refuses payment; the friend reciprocates by giving up his girl. This was nobility. Their mutual affection and esteem suddenly increased enormously. It was Damon and Pythias; it was David and Jonathan; nothing could ever estrange them. Now it was for life or death.

McTeague then holds forth in this heroical context:

"I'm much obliged," murmured McTeague. He could think of nothing better to say. "I'm much obliged," he repeated; "much obliged, Mark."

"That's all right, that's all right," returned Marcus Schouler, bravely, and it occurred to him to add, "You'll be happy together. Tell her for me—tell her—tell her—" Marcus could not go on. He wrung the dentist's hand silently....

(pp. 88-91)

What could be more conscious, deliberate, and obvious than the humor generated here? Norris is not snickering up his sleeve or malevolently barking dark laughter; he openly invites us to share in the absurdity of the moment as two jackdaws are made to strut in peacock feathers.

Moreover, who is the object of these heroic sentiments? What damsel of Petrarchan sublimity is it our Damon and Pythias worship in courtly fashion? Trina enters the story as a young lady who "had fallen out of a swing the afternoon of the preceding day; one of her teeth had knocked loose and the other altogether broken out." ... She is the loved one who happens to vomit during the scene in which McTeague unexpectedly blurts a proposal of marriage as she shakes off the effects of anesthesia. Consider her portrait as she refuses the proposal—screaming "No, no" through a rubber dam in her mouth,

cringing in the dental chair as the Neanderthal beau leans toward her.... (p. 91)

McTeague abounds in such silly moments. It is low comedy, but it is there and should be recognized as such. Auguste wets his pants at the vaudeville show to the embarassment of our polite heroine; Papa Sieppe marches a family party to the picnic grounds in military fashion, blows up Auguste's toy boat, and initiates his daughter's wedding procession with a command of "Vorwarrts!" Zerkow marries Maria to feed his crazed imagination with the story of her family's gold plate, only to have her become sane and declare, "I don't know what you're talking about, Zerkow.... There never was no gold plate, no gold service. I guess you must have dreamed it." ... Grannis and Baker step from a Mary E. Wilkins Freeman tale into *McTeague* to flutter timidly through an unlikely courtship. McTeague drinks champagne at his wedding supper and pronounces it the best beer he has ever had, to the merriment of all—all, that is, except literary critics who suppose that Naturalism precludes the possibility of such elements being present in a book like *McTeague*.

Ironic inflation is the major comic device that Norris employs. Enjoying his rise in fortune and status, McTeague envisions himself as someday becoming a venerable patriarch, the head of a dynasty with a son named Daniel "who would go to High School, and perhaps turn out to be a prosperous plumber or house painter." ... The technique is simple: create a context and then drop the inappropriate, the unexpected into it. Making even more obvious the humorous intent are Norris's tongue-in-cheek direct comments, like the one concerning his hero's taste in music as revealed at the vaudeville theater. "'That's what you call musicians,' [McTeague] announced gravely." Norris then intrudes: "'Home, Sweet Home,' played upon a trombone. Think of that! Art could go no farther." ... A third comic device is that of the *non sequitur*, one of which introduced this essay. Another, involving Mac and Trina, merits full quotation to indicate the way Norris plays his characters for good fun. It is an uneasy moment, early in their courtship, when hero and heroine seek to make a favorable impression upon each other. McTeague has just disclosed to Trina that he has never attended a picnic.

"Never went on a picnic?" she cried, astonished. "Oh, you'll see what fun we'll have. In the morning father and the children dig clams in the mud by the shore, an' we bake them, and—oh, there's thousands of things to do."

"Once I went sailing on the bay," said McTeague. "It was in a tugboat; we fished off the heads. I caught three codfishes."

"I'm afraid to go out on the bay," answered Trina, shaking her head, "sailboats tip over so easy. A cousin of mine, Selina's brother, was drowned one Decoration Day. They never found his body. Can you swim, Doctor McTeague?"

"I used to at the mine."

"At the mine? Oh, yes, I remember, Marcus told me you were a miner once."

"I was a car-boy; all the car-boys used to swim in the reservoir by the ditch every Thursday evening. One of them was bit by a rattlesnake once while he was dressing. he was a French-

man, named Andrew. He swelled up and began
to twitch.''

"Oh, how I hate snakes! They're so crawly and
graceful—but, just the same, I like to watch
them. You know that drug store over in town
that has a showcase full of live ones?''

"We killed the rattler with a cart whip.''

"How far do you think you could swim? Did
you ever try? D'you think you could swim a
mile?''

"A mile? I don't know. I never tried. I guess
I could.''

"I can swim a little. Sometimes we all go out
to the Crystal Baths.''

"The Crystal Baths, huh? Can you swim across
the tank?''

"Oh, I can swim all right as long as papa holds
my chin up. Soon as he takes his hand away,
down I go. Don't you hate to get water in your
ears?''

"Bathing's good for you.''. . .

(pp.91-3)

Should this be read seriously? It can be. There is nothing
necessarily hilarious about Mac associating "sailing" with fishing
for cod from a tugboat, and no one need fall off his chair with
laughter as slow-witted McTeague fails to keep up with the
pace of Trina's comments on picnics, drowning, "crawly and
graceful" snakes, and swimming. But I think that we would
miss something that Norris intended should we pass over the
rambling, loosely connected dialogue as little more than filler,
the main value of which would be the incrementation of background on Mac's early life at the Big Dipper Mine. Surely
Mac's preoccupation with a Frenchman-named-Andrew's
twitching, in the context of a courting scene, merits some
response.

The response need not be that Norris's laughter is sardonic and
that his laughter is chillingly condescending. It is not the mirth
of Nathanael West or Joseph Heller. The laughter is hearty,
as much as McTeague's is at the vaudeville show, when he
goes on until his eyes fill with tears. For vaudevillean in spirit
is just what *McTeague* is for at least half its length: it is a
quick-moving panoramic display of the colorful, the quirky,
the lively, and the entertaining.

Norris's pre-*McTeague* writings reveal a sensibility in awe of
the incredible variety of life: its dynamism, its oddities, and
its naturally spontaneous sensationality. Surprise and delight
are not uncommon tones in the pieces published in *The Wave;*
and comical sketches such as **"Fantaisie Printaniere"** and
"Judy's Service of Gold Plate" are not chance deviations from
the norm. *McTeague* begins with an expressed fascination for
the life of Polk Street and the strange, interesting collection of
characters who live and work near McTeague's dental parlor.
It's a *Story of San Francisco*—to Norris a place where anything
can happen, a "story city" where fact is often stranger than
fiction. And for near two-hundred pages Norris romps on with
one of the most bizarre, humorously eccentric groups one might
imagine. It is not until after the midpoint that things turn dark,
when Trina becomes deranged, Maria is murdered, Zerkow

drowned, and McTeague clutched by the horrible working out
of unfortunate circumstances.

It is these later events, occurring after Norris has switched
from a humorous tone to one of darkening seriousness, that
commentators seem to remember most when writing about
McTeague. That is, critics may not be simply applying preconceptions concerning Naturalistic fiction when distorting the
characer of the first half of the novel. The real force of the
dark second half may be coloring the first in the commentators'
memories, and the conclusion may shape the critics' responses
to the first half upon a subsequent reading. 1890s reviewers
of *McTeague* expressed the same reaction as modern critics,
describing the novel as a tale of unrelieved suffering. But there
were some reviewers who did not blur the halves and who
praised the light, comic moments, declaring that Norris was
clearly capable of good humor in scenes like the wedding
supper.

Now, Trina hiccoughing in a pool of blood is no laughing
matter, nor is McTeague's truly pathetic state during his decline. But what we should note is that by the time Norris begins
straightforwardly developing McTeague's pathos—by the time
that McTeague begins to solicit credibility as a suffering human
being in the manner of Hurstwood and Martin Eden—Norris
has stopped calling him "stupid," a 'gigantic, good-natured
Saint Bernard," and an elephant wagging his head from side
to side. When the novel ends with McTeague chained to Marcus, "stupidly looking around him". . . , the connotation of
the adverb is totally other from that in the first half. The extended joke was good, but Norris ended it when life began to
close in upon the McTeagues.

Reading *McTeague,* then, should involve recognition of the
active presence of two authorial tones, the one eventually being
replaced by the other. The latter tone, the Naturalistic, has
been emphasized too much at the expense of the first. To view
the novel in terms of both tones will, at least, explain the
function of the Grannis-Baker episodes which have troubled
commentators from William Dean Howells on. The comical-
sentimental episodes do not belong in a consistently developed,
monistically pure example of Naturalism (if there is, indeed,
such a creature). But they do belong in *McTeague* which is
more than merely Naturalistic. The recognition of the gradual
transition from comic, to serio-comic, to pathetic in the authorial perspective and narrative tone of *McTeague* seems a
necessary first step in revising our critical view of that work.
It may be the means by which we can appreciate *all* that Norris
offers us, the tart and the sweet. (pp. 93-5)

> *Joseph R. McElrath, Jr., 'The Comedy of Frank
> Norris's 'McTeague',''* in Studies in American Hu-
> mor, *Vol. II, No. 2, October, 1975, pp. 88-95.*

DON GRAHAM (essay date 1978)

[*Graham is an American educator and critic whose work concentrates on the literature and popular culture of Texas and the
American West. In the following excerpt from his study* The Fiction
of Frank Norris: The Aesthetic Context, *he discusses references
to art in Norris's fiction.*]

No matter how useful Norris is for defining naturalism as a
fictional enterprise or for displaying classic nineteenth-century
assumptions about man and reality, most critics who like him
for these reasons dislike him when it comes down to the real
question of his art. As an artist, Norris is barely on the literary

map. Thus one critic says of a Norris novel that he thinks major: "As art *McTeague* leaves much to be desired. The novel is not likely to excite much enthusiasm among critics who cherish formal perfection." And another critic, who believes that Norris's reputation is largely an "accident of publicity," provides a summary indictment of his formal crudities: "All in all, composition in Norris' novels seems to be reckoned exclusively in calculations of decibels and gross tonnage." These are severe condemnations, and these critics are not alone. For a complete rundown of charges against Norris, Crisler and McElrath's study [see Additional Bibliography] supplies a useful compendium.

In the face of such disapproval, one can scarcely hope to overturn anti-Norris sentiment. Nothing that I say is going to persuade readers who think *The Ambassadors* the highest form of art that *McTeague* is its equal. (Besides, I don't think that Norris's novel is as great as James's.) But it is my opinion that Norris deserves more credit as an artist than he has received. (p. 3)

In order to accomplish these ends, a new perspective on Norris's fiction is required. Aesthetic documentation gives us that perspective. By the phrase *aesthetic documentation,* I am referring to the extensive references to all manner of art in Norris's fiction, including paintings, interior decor, drama, literature, sculpture, music, landscapes. For a novelist thought to be preoccupied with the seamier aspects of life—Zelda Sayre thought she had never read a smellier book than *McTeague*—Norris's works contain an extraordinary amount of highbrow aesthetic material. This dimension of his fiction has been noted in passing but has never been subjected to sustained discussion. It is, I believe, one of the keys to Norris's mind and craft.

All his adult life, Norris was keenly involved in the aesthetic atmosphere of the nineties. In 1891, for example, when he petitioned the university authorities at Berkeley for a change of status from student-at-large to special student—he wanted to be exempt from mathematics and Latin—Norris emphasized his adolescent dedication to the arts. He explained, with pardonable exaggeration: "Previous to entering the University I spent upwards of five years in Paris and in various parts of Italy and Germany studying, [*sic*] painting, gothic architecture and medieval archeology." In portraying himself as an aesthete-in-training, Norris was not overstating the case too much, however. He had studied painting seriously at the Académie Julian in Paris, as William Dillingham has shown conclusively in his study of Norris's Paris years; he had visited museums and acquired a fairly technical understanding of medieval armor; he had developed an appreciation of opera; and judging from later evidence, he had gained some knowledge of architectural styles. This youthful interest in the fine arts was to form a constant part of his personal and creative life.

Norris's journalism reflects his aesthetic breadth. His contributions to the *Wave* include reviews of art exhibits, architecture, and plays; interviews with artists, dramatists, and actresses; and of course book reviews and critical essays on literature. In addition, aesthetic commentary is apt to occur in surprising contexts in his journalism. A description of a visit to the Swiss Colony vineyards in the Napa Valley, for example, contains one of his best formulations of the opposition between vital "Life" and stultifying "Art."

Beyond these tangible expressions of aesthetic interest in diverse arts, there is the impressive group of artists and dilettantes whom Norris knew, in some cases as close friends, in the colorful San Francisco of the 1890s. This circle included the chief figures in the publication of the *Lark*, the little magazine that from 1895 to 1897 enjoyed a national reputation. The talents of this group were quite varied: Ernest Piexotto was a painter, illustrator, and author; Bruce Porter, a stained-glass artisan, painter, and author; Willis Polk, an architect and author; Porter Garnett, an artist and author; and Gelett Burgess, an editor, humorist, and author. In addition, Norris knew painters such as William Keith and Charles Rollo Peters, and the photographer Arnold Genthe; and he knew, by reputation at least, a host of San Francisco literary figures, including Joaquin Miller, Bailey Millard, Edwin Markham, Ambrose Bierce, Charles Warren Stoddard, Will Irwin, and Yone Noguchi. During the years 1891-1902 Norris was, with one exception, cognizant of every aesthetic tremor in San Francisco. The exception was the rise to prominence of Jack London, which occurred in the years 1899-1902, when Norris was mostly in the East.

Norris possessed what I would call the aesthetic habit of mind. He tended to approach experience from a perspective of taste and to be absorbed in presenting characters that reflected either consciously or unconsciously their cultural ambience. This is true even of McTeague, the most lowbrow hero in American literature up to 1899. Norris's preoccupation with questions of taste and with the aesthetic milieu of his time will be relentlessly before us in the pages to follow, but I should here like to demonstrate two instances of this preoccupation that reveal how completely characteristic this habit of mind is in Norris's work. The first example is from Norris's worst novel, *A Man's Woman*. The passage in question is, as it were, a second thought. In the first edition Norris described an amputation so graphically that he was asked, as he had been with the famous pants-wetting episode in *McTeague,* to write an inoffensive version. The first edition (1900) reads:

> Dr. Street nodded to her, signifying that he was ready, and Lloyd, exerting her strength, pulled down upon the leg, at the same time turning it outward. The hip-joint dislocated easily, the head of the bone protruding. While Lloyd held the leg in place Farnham put a towel under this protruding head, and the surgeon, with a chainsaw, cut it away in a few strokes. And that was all—the joint was exsected.

The revised passage (1902) replaces the disturbing clinical details with material as characteristic of Norris as anything he ever wrote:

> He [the Enemy, Death] had arrived there in that commonplace little room, with its commonplace accessories, its ornaments, that suddenly seemed so trivial, so impertinent—the stopped French clock, with its simpering, gilded cupids, on the mantelpiece; the photograph of a number of picknickers "grouped" on a hotel piazza gazing with monolithic cheerfulness at this grim business, this struggle of the two world forces, this crisis in a life.
>
> Then abruptly the operation was over.

Surely Norris must have delighted in this revision, for it mocks the very taste that the first version offended, the tame conventionality of drawing-room art. The inadequacy of such art is exposed through the allegorical figure of the Enemy, which is really as much romance as death. The revised passage fictionalizes some of the principal concerns of Norris's literary criticism. In essay after essay he championed the power of romance to enliven the surface dullness of realism. The repetition of *commonplace,* also an echo from the essays, is Norris's attempt to add a new dimension to Howells's devotion to the average range of experience as realism's true sphere.

The second example is perhaps even more revealing. In a late short story, "**A Lost Story**" (1903), Norris brought together Howells and conventional aesthetic representation. The story deals with a young woman novelist who reads manuscripts for a publishing firm (as Norris did when he first came to New York) and who appropriates the ideas of a manuscript that comes across her desk. But the most interesting part of the story is the character of Trevor, who is clearly a fictionalization of Howells. Trevor is described as "This old gentleman, this elderly man of letters, who had seen the rise and fall of a dozen schools, was above the influence of fads, and he whose books were among the classics even before his death was infallible in his judgments of the work of the younger writers." Clearly this writer and critic is a titan, yet Trevor has another dimension as well; he is human, down-to-earth, and as bourgeois as a Balzac novel. The presentation is quintessential Norris:

> And Trevor himself was a short, rotund man, rubicund as to face, bourgeois as to clothes and surroundings (the bisque statuette of a fisher boy obtruded the vulgarity of its gilding and tinting from the mantelpiece), jovial in manner, indulging even in slang. . . .

The bisque fisherboy is Norris's shorthand transcription of the accoutrements of Gilded Age culture and the concerns of realism. The figure appears in similarly parenthetical syntax in the 1901 essay "**A Plea For Romantic Fiction,**" where its function is to depict realism's tameness and limitations. In *Blix* (1899) it is a source of mirth for the two young lovers. But no matter how much Norris derided the bisque object for its gilded and tinted effects, he needed the fisherboy, the objet d'art, as completely as did the tradition that he felt paid too much homage to such surface detail.

When we consider Norris's complaints against realism and recall his own novels, we realize that adding another dimension to realism did not mean abandoning the commitment to cultural and aesthetic documentation. Thus he writes,

> Let Realism do the entertaining with its meticulous presentation of teacups, rag carpets, wall paper and haircloth sofas, stopping with these, going no deeper than it sees, choosing the ordinary, the untroubled, the commonplace.

The meticulous presentation of rag carpets and wallpaper is a self-characterization of Norris's own novels; although Norris wanted to go beyond objective decor, he nevertheless depended on it for a base, for a specificity and density without which novels like *A Man's Woman* drifted into abstract, simpleminded, and above all, unrealized polarities. Norris saw himself, in short, challenging American realism on its home ground, the drawing room; his fiction is a kind of dialectical engagement with the furniture of American homes and American minds. Dialectic involves synthesis, not displacement; and Norris's novels are a true effort to synthesize warring elements, to combine explorations into the "black, unsearched penetralia of the soul of man" with commonplace detail, bisque statuettes, and the like. (pp. 3-8)

Don Graham, in his The Fiction of Frank Norris: The Aesthetic Context, *University of Missouri Press, 1978, 172 p.*

RICHARD ALLAN DAVISON (essay date 1979)

[*In the following excerpt, Davison offers an examination of characterization in* The Pit.]

Although I have discovered no direct evidence that Frank Norris read Marcus Aurelius or the stoic philosophers, much that is urged in their philosophy is evident in many of Norris's writings, particularly in his last novel, *The Pit.* When describing the Roman emperor's stoic philosophy, one finds oneself using words and phrases such as "duty," "patience," "obligation," "courage," "fortitude," "practical goodness," and "divine reason." Norris extols all these virtues in his writings, placing them in a more clearly Christian context. When his characters violate these rules of conduct, they are out of the rhythm of an ordered universe and suffer accordingly. The only characters that seem to survive or die with dignity are those who have learned the lessons preached by the stoic Marcus Aurelius and his Christian predecessor St. Paul. These characters function in the context of a moral reality. Furthermore, attunement to this moral order is ameliorative. (p. 77)

While St. Paul is quoted extensively and used centrally in *The Octopus,* overt references to religion in *The Pit* are not as evident, often confined to Curtis Jadwin's adherence to D. L. Moody's Sunday School morality. But religion in the sense of a transcendental moral law is every bit as evident, albeit muted, in Norris's last novel. Both novels reveal the dangers of sophistry. Both Shelgrim and Jadwin rationalize and excuse their abuses of power, their toying with the laws of nature. Norris nowhere condones Jadwin's attempt to corner the wheat market any more than he condones the manipulations of Magnus Derrick or Shelgrim. Page Dearborn (functioning as a lesser Vanamee) is a barometer reflecting the moral impulses in *The Pit.* Through her (and eventually through Laura Dearborn) Norris points to a muted optimism that smacks of humanistic stoicism, made mutedly optimistic by Pauline Christianity, and affirms the principle of moral order in the universe. The dramatic exploration of his characters's involvement in this universe is handled with a clear sense of structure and artistic control.

In a letter to Issac Marcosson, Norris demonstrates the awareness of a purpose, if one not always followed. It contains his only extant comments on the structure of *The Pit*:

> The story is told through Laura Dearborn. She occupies the center of the stage all the time, and I shall try to interest the reader more in the problems of her character and career than in any other human element in the book. The two main themes, consequently, are the story of Jadwin's corner of the May wheat and the story of his wife's 'affair' with Corthell. I shall try to show that all these are American issues, modern, typical and important. The 'big scenes' will be the scene between Laura and Corthell in her apartment the evening that Jadwin fails to appear, and the scene on the floor of the Chicago Board of Trade when the Jadwin corner breaks.

Norris, then, planned to make Laura's character development the central element in the novel. However, although he did succeed in interesting the reader more in Laura than "in any other human element in the book," the fascination of the giddy price fluctuations of the wheat in the huge monolithic Board of Trade Building threatens to overshadow all else. It is Jadwin's attempt to corner the nation's wheat and the wheat's inevitable cornering of him that are the most dynamic elements in a novel that draws its very title from the scene of his most enthralling battles. It is the scene of Jadwin's crushing defeat in the Pit that is the bigger of the two "big scenes." And, although Jadwin's character lacks the depth and complexity of Laura's in Norris's portrayal, his character is both the more magnetic and the more sympathetic. In fact, Jadwin, as memorable as Silas Lapham or Frank Cowperwood, is potentially one of the great figures in American literature. Why does she fall short? How important to the limitations of Jadwin's characterization is the effect of Norris's major emphasis on Laura?

An examination of the aesthetic unity of *The Pit* reveals Norris's growing awareness of the potential tragedy involved in lack of communication among individuals and the problems that transpire when one is out of tune with the tenets of stoicism and the moral forces of the universe.

By narrowing his canvas to one city in one locale of America, Norris again follows his dicta in **"An American School of Fiction."** In fact most of the action, with the exception of the first scene, occurs in two buildings—the Chicago Board of Trade and the Jadwin mansion. Having spent his childhood in Chicago and months of research on the market there, Norris once more drew upon personal experiences to flesh out a skeleton plot. However autobiographical and locally American much of the action may be, his probings of the human condition in an affluent society have enough universal implications to make *The Pit* a worthy successor to *The Octopus*. It is a sturdy middle link in what was to be a world-spanning wheat trilogy.

Perhaps because of this happy blend of universals with particulars, Norris achieved his deepest penetration into the psychology of his characters in *The Pit*. Jadwin is a more sympathetic character to us than is Magnus Derrick, and Laura becomes more alive than Hilma Tree. Even the other, minor, characters are more complex than their counterparts in *The Octopus*. Just as the entire novel is dichotomized into two major conflicting centres of interest from the initial counterpoint of business and art in chapter I, so there is a contrast in each of the main characters.

The Pit contains considerable evaluation of various fields of art. Much of this commentary Norris puts into the mouth of the aesthete, Sheldon Corthell, but it becomes apparent that, even though Corthell demonstrates a refined taste for art, his pontifications are pretentious. If his snobbishness, delicately trimmed beard, and preference for cigarettes over cigars do not suggest that he is as overbalanced on the artistic side as Jadwin is overbalanced in his commercial drive to corner the wheat, then Landry Court's astute criticism and the artist's own almost psuedo-Le Contean speeches on aesthetics should. Through Landry's comments Norris reveals in Corthell's otherwise appealing character a falseness that is reminiscent of the bohemian dilettantes Norris lambastes in his critical writings, and of such ignoble types as Mrs. Cedargist's leeching "artistic" protégés in *The Octopus*.

Corthell does point out some palatable artistic truths, such as the superiority of Liszt's "Mephisto Waltz" over the "Anvil Chorus." However, his lengthy disquisition on the categories of art and the passion of musical creativity (dramatically in-terrupted by Jadwin's announcement of his "killing" on the market) seems too precious for Norris to be offering in earnest. Corthell, having just demonstrated his musical abilities on the organ in the Jadwin library, speaks to an enraptured audience of one—Laura:

> "Of all the arts, music, to my notion, is the most intimate. At the other end of the scale you have architecture, which is an expression of and appeal to the common multitude, a whole people, the mass. Fiction and painting, and even poetry, are affairs of the classes, reaching the groups of the educated. But music—ah, that is different, it is one soul speaking to another soul. The composer meant it for you and himself. No one else has anything to do with it. Because his soul was heavy and broken with grief, or bursting with passion, or tortured with doubt, or searching for some unnamed ideal, he has come to you—you of all the people in the world—with his message, and he tells you of his yearnings and his sadness, knowing that you will sympathize, knowing that your soul has, like his, been acquainted with grief, or with gladness; and in the music his soul speaks to yours, beats with it, blends with it, yes, is even, spiritually, married to it."

> And as he spoke the electrics all over the gallery flashed out in a sudden blaze, and Curtis Jadwin entered the room, crying out:

> "Are you here, Laura? By George, my girl, we pulled it off, and I've cleaned up five—hundred—thousand—dollars." . . .

In this scene Norris is deftly undercutting both the pseudo-romantic, unrealistic verbal claptrap of an aesthete trying to impress a sensitive, but critically naive, young woman with his fine sensibility, and the hard-headed, rather boorish, tunnel-visioned concern of a market speculator who has momentarily shut out all else from his life but business. At the same time Norris's dramatic, rather comical juxtaposition of the two most extreme points of view in the novel suggests a need for some communication between these disparate worlds, each with its own peculiar weaknesses and strengths.

Norris here, as in *The Octopus,* is attempting to demonstrate the efficacy of the surging power in the continuum of nature on man, and the dynamics of love on human relationships. Only for this novel his camera shifts from the railroad agents and wheatfields of California to the stockbrokers and the Pit of the Chicago Board of Trade; from characters whose stage is ten thousand broad acres of prairie to those whose dramas are enacted in the tight enclosure of city rooms. Instead of depicting the maturation of several characters, he focuses on one. I do not agree with Charles Kaplan's statement: "*The Pit* could, with equal (or greater) appropriateness have been called *The Rise of Curtis Jadwin*" [see Additional Bibliography]. For it is Jadwin's lack of growth that leads to his destruction. His only spiritual movement is away from his wife and their early marital happiness. The morality in his Sunday school projects and his abhorrence of gambling are easily brushed aside by the temptations of the Pit. Unlike Silas Lapham, Jadwin hardly takes the time to rationalize his inconsistencies; at no time does he make a choice against his speculative impulse for moral or ethical bettermennt. *The Rise of Laura Dearborn Jadwin* would be a far more appropriate title than Kaplan's.

Not enough has been said about the effect of the experience of love and suffering on Laura's maturation—a maturation that Norris develops from the slow-paced early pages of exposition to the stirring pages of the climax.

The structure of *The Pit,* embodying and reinforcing Norris's most mature observations, is more complex than most critics have noted. Reinforcing the broader structural elements are more subtle strands and threads that give the novel a greater toughness. The business-art dichotomy that permeates the entire work warrants closer examination. Critics have mentioned Corthell as artist and Jadwin as businessman, between whom Laura is torn, but they have neglected the structurally important antitheses in each one of the other characters, many of whom bridge this gap between the uncompromising business world and the world of art so often associated with Laura's romantic reveries. Most of the major and minor characters alike are mirrors or sounding-boards for either Laura or Jadwin.

Page Dearborn, impressionable, serious, naive about her own life through much of the novel, demonstrates a growing, penetrating influence on her older sister's character. She serves as a kind of philosophical instructress. Relatively unimportant in her own right, she is one of many strong links between the love plot and the business plot. It is Page who first attempts to draw her sister's attention towards the business world. . . . It is Page who continually hammers at Laura's proud, selfish exterior, sees the blindness in Laura's attempt to live up to the affected *hauteur* of her grand manner.'' . . . Page rapidly outgrows her own morbid attachment to the deceptive allurement of romantic novels and offers her older sister practical advice about human relationships. This advice is crucial to Laura's maturing love for Jadwin. Yet, human and fallible, Page also retains much of the naivety of inexperienced youth. Although she strives to understand Landry's business affairs, by the time of her marriage she has achieved only a general awareness of the complex workings of the market. It is Norris's allowance of her semi-comprehension that makes Page such a perfect witness to the ''Jadwin failure'' from the gallery overlooking the Pit. Much of the scene, climaxing in Jadwin's Bull charge into the Pit, after which he is jeered at by the victorious Bears and led dumbly off the floor by Landry, is viewed through Page's eyes. Page brings to Laura the report of a great man whom some cheered on appearance, but who seemed to have suffered a severe defeat. She admonishes Laura to take a greater interest in Jadwin's affairs. Only later do these words make their impression. But it is largely because of Page's constant demand for practical goodness and adherence to moral obligations that Laura shifts her intellectual allegiance and emotional sympathy to her husband when he appears in the doorway, haggard and exhausted, obliterating her impulsive decision to run away with Sheldon Corthell.

Landry Court, clerk in ''the great brokerage firm of Gretry, Converse and Co.,'' erstwhile suitor of Laura, later husband of Page, is also an effective link between the two major plots. It is Landry who buys and sells Jadwin's wheat from the first scene in the Pit to the very last. His admiration for Jadwin as a financial genius and magnetic father-figure carries over from the Pit into the love plot. Jadwin's personality has affected Landry so deeply that he harbours no jealousy when the older man wins Laura, even though Page is a soothing consolation prize. Landry's praise of Jadwin and his refusal to desert him during the devastating moments of the crash succeed in un-

derlining the more sympathetic qualities of the financier as well as his own sense of loyalty. Landry embodies the qualities that Norris admired in many of his bright fraternity brothers at Berkeley. Successful in business, receptive to culture, Landry, in his marriage to Page, represents a merging of two worlds that are so long to remain apart in the Jadwin-Laura marriage. Landry and Page's marriage prefigures the subsequent harmony of the Jadwins's.

But Landry, too, is a mixture of contradictions, only some of which are resolved. He is also a dual personality. He is little Landry Court, the callow suitor of Laura, who forgets appointments and makes social *faux pas*. In the Pit he is Landry Court the businessman, a fighter with a level head, fortitude, and a keen financial sense. In the same dual manner Norris draws the other characters, all of whom participate in or comment upon the main action.

Cressler is the calm, steady, kindly feeder of pigeons who admonishes Jadwin of the evils of speculation; he is also a reckless speculator. Mrs Cressler is a good friend of Jadwin and quick to praise his virtues to Laura; she is also a gossip. Crookes is a double-dealing, cold-blooded tycoon who can give tribute to a better man even if he thinks the man a partial fool. The closest candidate for villain in the novel, Crookes, does not embody the evil, the nearly motiveless malignancy, of S. Behrman of *The Octopus*. Like all those struggling in the Pit, Crookes is concerned with his private fortune. Although he lacks the propensity for joy and excitement of battle that is Jadwin's chief reason for fanatical involvement in the Pit, Crookes does have a respect for the wheat that Jadwin does not learn until he has experienced what is his first and final defeat. Crookes acknowledges a force in the universe that is more powerful than he. Unlike Behrman, he will not allow himself to be crushed by the wheat. He knows that Jadwin's failure is due to no lack of greatness or genius, but to the overwhelming power of millions of bushels of wheat, pouring from thousands of farms all over the world in a torrent that sweeps out of its path all who attempt to block it in its rush to the sea and the open mouths of Europe and Asia. Crookes also knows that Jadwin's failure is partly due to the rebellion of other speculators. With all this insight Crookes embraces many of the opportunistic attitudes of a Behrman or a Shelgrim, unmixed with either the magnetism of one or the stature of the other. Norris dared not make Crookes too powerful because he did not want a human to be Jadwin's main adversary, but rather Jadwin's own pride and wilful humanity. He wanted the wheat, both material and symbolic, to be Jadwin's nemesis.

Even Hargus, the bankrupt, half-crazed old man who once had a corner on the market, has his complexities. Obviously he is an ever-present reminder of the fool-hardiness of excessive speculation and he foreshadows Jadwin's imminent defeat. He is in the background of all Jadwin's victories. Just before his first big speculative venture with Gretry, Jadwin notices the tattered old man ''mumbling a sandwich'' and does not recognize him. When Gretry assures him it is Hargus, the revelation turns Jadwin cold: ''I don't want to think of it, Sam!'' . . . It is fitting that the old man later refuses to lend Jadwin the very money that Jadwin has given to him with compulsive magnanimity. At the price of his sanity Hargus has learned a cruel lesson about speculation that Jadwin cannot learn second-hand. The old man still has a tinge of the gambling urge; he may still beg another for a market ''tip'' and try to make a living as an ''eighth grabber,'' but Jadwin's gift of ''about'' half a million dollars will accumulate its 4 per cent interest.

Hargus's niece will be provided for. Thus Hargus guards his niece's future while Jadwin recklessly sacrifices his own wife's spiritual and material comfort. It is only pride that prevents Jadwin from also sacrificing Laura's small personal fortune. Gretry represents the happiest combination of these extremes of reckless Bull speculation and conservative Bear patience and self-control. His brokerage house does not collapse as Jadwin's did.

Finally, Sheldon Corthell also embraces conflicting qualities. He is both the calm, cool, aloof, prejudiced critic of art and the passionate would-be lover of Laura. Although Corthell courageously removes himself to Europe after Laura's first rejection, his restraint fails him before her final rebuff.

Norris neatly divides the novel into ten chapters with a brief conclusion whose iterative function is similar to that of the conclusion of *The Octopus.* There is a three-year break, almost exactly in the middle, between chapters 5 and 6. Kaplan's insistence that Laura's story (which dominates the first five chapters) slips into the background as Jadwin's business career takes the spotlight is only partially valid. Laura's deepest complexities are explored in the second half of the novel. Although much of the space is taken up with Jadwin's turbulent affairs, Laura remains equally conspicuous. Fascinating in its own right, the business plot serves primarily both to counterpoint and to complicate the love plot. Norris uses the wheat as a catalyst for his examination of the nature of human love and connubial happiness seen against the backdrop of an ordered universe. The parallels that exist between the Jadwins and Norris's own eventually divorced parents suggest a possible explanation for his preoccupation with marital problems. *The Pit,* however, transcends a compulsive attempt to expiate the divorce of the elder Mr and Mrs Norris. Norris's use of the workings of the market along with some details from Joseph Leiter's life (on which he based Jadwin's cornering of the wheat) further suggests that he was a creative artist, and not merely a writer of thinly veiled autobiography. (pp. 78-84)

> Richard Allan Davison, "A Reading of Frank Norris's 'The Pit'," in The Stoic Strain in American Literature: Essays in Honour of Marston LaFrance, edited by Duane J. MacMillan, University of Toronto Press, 1979, pp. 77-94.

ADDITIONAL BIBLIOGRAPHY

Astro, Richard. "*Vandover and the Brute* and *The Beautiful and Damned:* A Search for Thematic and Stylistic Reinterpretations." *Modern Fiction Studies* XIV, No. 4 (Winter 1968-69): 397-413.
  Maintains that *Vandover and the Brute* was used as a model by F. Scott Fitzgerald for his novel *The Beautiful and Damned.*

Beer, Thomas. *The Mauve Decade: American Life at the End of the Nineteenth Century,* pp. 12 ff. New York: Garden City Publishing Co., 1926.
  Mentions Norris a number of times in connection with other literary figures of the 1890s.

Brooks, Van Wyck. "Frank Norris and Jack London." In his *The Confident Years: 1885-1915,* pp. 217-37. New York: E. P. Dutton & Co., 1941.
  A discussion of Norris's life and career.

Cargill, Oscar. "The Naturalists." In his *Intellectual America: Ideas on the March,* pp. 48-175. New York: Macmillan Co., 1941.
  Contains an overview of Norris's career, emphasizing his contribution to the Naturalist school of literature.

Conder, John J. "Norris and Hard Determinism: *McTeague.*" In his *Naturalism in American Fiction: The Classic Phase,* pp. 69-85. Lexington: University Press of Kentucky, 1984.
  Discusses the conflict between sexual and social determinism in *McTeague.*

Crisler, Jesse S., and McElrath, Joseph R., Jr. *Frank Norris: A Reference Guide.* Boston: G. K. Hall & Co., 1974, 131 p.
  An annotated bibliography of criticism of Norris's works.

Review of *The Octopus. The Dial* XXXI, No. 365 (1 September 1901): 136.
  An early review comparing Norris to Emile Zola and faulting Norris for unduly favoring the farmers in *The Octopus.*

Dillingham, William B. *Frank Norris: Instinct and Art.* Lincoln: University of Nebraska Press, 1969, 179 p.
  A biographical study of Norris's work.

Dondore, Dorothy Anne. "The Realism of the Mississippi Valley." In her *The Prairie and the Making of Middle America: Four Centuries of Description,* pp. 288-344. Cedar Rapids, Iowa: Torch Press, 1926.
  Contains a plot summary of *The Pit,* noting the extraordinary power of natural forces which Norris presents as thwarting human efforts to control it.

Dreiser, Theodore. "The Great American Novel." *The American Spectator* I, No. 2 (December 1932): 1-2.
  Discusses the progress of American realistic fiction. Dreiser writes of *McTeague:* "Here we have as fine an illustration of what American realism might be as America offers."

Folsom, James K. "Social Darwinism or Social Protest? The 'Philosophy' of *The Octopus.*" *Modern Fiction Studies* VIII, No. 4 (Winter 1962-63): 393-400.
  Presents the possibility that the ending of *The Octopus* is ironic, and that the summation of the meaning of the events of the novel offered by the character of Presley is intentionally fallacious.

Garland, Hamlin. "Aisles of Gold and Streams of Silver." In his *Companions on the Trail: A Literary Chronicle,* pp. 159-71. New York: Macmillan Co., 1931.
  An assessment of Norris's novels *McTeague, The Octopus,* and *The Pit* by a contemporary Naturalist writer.

Goldman, Suzy Bernstein. "*McTeague:* The Imagistic Network." *Western American Literature* VII, No. 2 (Summer 1972): 83-99.
  Discusses imagery in *McTeague* and asserts that the ending in the desert is the logical culmination of the imagery of the whole work.

Graham, D. B. "Art in *McTeague.*" *Studies in American Fiction* III, No. 2 (Autumn 1975): 144-55.
  Discusses McTeague's artistic appreciation, arguing that "with McTeague, aesthetic perception is a constant and fundamental part of his being. It expresses a need and loyalty beyond Trina's capacity for feeling."

"The Last Work of Frank Norris." *Harper's Weekly* XLVII, No. 2412 (14 March 1903): 433.
  An early review of *The Pit,* comparing it unfavorably to *The Octopus.*

Hoffman, Charles G. "Norris and the Responsibility of the Novelist." *The South Atlantic Quarterly* LIV (1955): 508-15.
  Discusses naturalistic, moralistic, and romantic approaches to the plots of Norris's various novels.

Horowitz, Howard. "'To Find the Value of *X*': *The Pit* as a Renunciation of Romance." In *American Realism: New Essays,* edited by Eric J. Sundquist. Baltimore: Johns Hopkins University Press, 1982.
  Discusses relationships between the two plots of *The Pit:* the affair of Laura Jadwin and the speculation on the commodities market of her husband.

Howells, W. D. "Frank Norris." In his *Criticism and Fiction and Other Essays,* pp. 276-82. New York: New York University Press, 1959.

Contains a reprint of an early review by Howells, originally published in 1899, of *McTeague*.

Johnson, George W. "Frank Norris and Romance." *American Literature* XXXIII, No. 1 (March 1961): 52-63.
Discusses conventions of romance, as opposed to realism, in Norris's novels.

Kaplan, Charles. "Norris's Use of Sources in *The Pit*." *American Literature* XXV (March 1953): 75-84.
Compares the plot of *The Pit* to a historical incident involving an attempt to corner the wheat market.

Kwiat, Joseph J. "Frank Norris: The Novelist as Social Critic and Literary Theorist" *The Arizona Quarterly* XVIII, No. 4 (Winter 1962): 319-28.
Discusses Norris's fiction in relation to his essays collected in *The Responsibilities of the Novelist*.

Lewis, Oscar. Introduction to *Frank Norris of "The Wave"*, edited by Oscar Lewis, pp. 1-15. San Francisco: Westgate Press, 1931.
Provides biographical information concerning Norris during the time he wrote for *The Wave*.

Marchand, Ernest. *Frank Norris: A Study*. Stanford: Stanford University Press, 1942, 258 p.
A laudatory assessment of Norris as a pioneer of American Naturalism.

Martin, Ronald E. "Frank Norris: Naive Omniscience and the Universe of Force." In his *American Literature and the Universe of Force*, pp. 146-83. Durham, N.C.: Duke University Press, 1981.
Discusses the relationship between Norris's determinism and his fiction. Martin explains that "despite all his aggressive naturalism, there is a wide streak of conventional moralism in Norris's writings."

"*The Pit*: A Dispassionate Examination of Frank Norris's Posthumous Novel." *The New York Times Saturday Review of Books* (31 January 1903): 66.
An early review of *The Pit*.

Pattee, Fred Lewis. "Shifting Currents of Fiction." In his *A History of American Literature Since 1870*, pp. 385-415. 1915. Reprint. New York: Cooper Square Publishers, 1968.
States that "In the higher sense of the word [*The Octopus* and *The Pit*] are not literature; they are remarkably well done newspaper 'stories'." This evaluation was subsequently repudiated by Pattee.

———. "Frank Norris." in his *The New American Literature: 1890-1930*, pp. 36-48. New York: D. Appleton-Century Co., 1935.
Praises *McTeague* and *The Octopus*, reassessing his earlier opinion of Norris's works. Pattee writes, "What novel written in America before 1900 comes nearer being the 'great American novel' than *The Octopus* by the young Frank Norris?"

Pizer, Donald. *The Novels of Frank Norris*. Bloomington: Indiana University Press, 1966, 209 p.
A discussion of Norris's work as an attempt to resolve conflicts posed by the development of scientific and political thought during the late nineteenth century.

Snell, George. "Crane and Norris." In his *The Shapers of American Fiction: 1798-1947*, pp. 223-33. New York: E. P. Dutton & Co., 1947.

An overview of Norris's work, noting its affinities with Realism as defined by William Dean Howells, Naturalism as defined by Emile Zola, and popular romance.

Spiller, Robert. "Toward Naturalism in Fiction." In his *Literary History of the United States*. New York: Macmillan Publishing Co., 1974.
Praises *The Octopus* for its great ambition, while noting its faults.

Stronks, James B. "John Kendrick Bangs Criticizes Norris's Borrowings in *Blix*." *American Literature* XLII, No. 3 (November 1970): 380-86.
Discusses an early review of *Blix* which pointed out direct sources to episodes in the story.

Taylor, Walter Fuller. "Frank Norris." In his *The Economic Novel in America*, pp. 282-306. Chapel Hill: University of North Carolina Press, 1942.
A discussion of Norris's political orientation and his use of the competitive business world as a milieu for modern adventure, as war had been traditionally used as the milieu for historical adventure.

Thompson, Francis. Review of *The Responsibilities of the Novelist, and Other Literary Essays*. *The Academy and Literature*, No. 1644 (7 November 1903): 491.
An early review of *The Responsibilities of the Novelist*, noting its inadequacies as a comprehensive theory of literature but praising it as an interesting source of insight into Norris's own work.

Vance, William L. "Romance in *The Octopus*." *Genre* III, No. 2 (June 1970): 111-36.
Demonstrates that five fictional modes—Allegorical Melodrama, Naturalism, Tragedy, Realism, and Romance—coexist in *The Octopus*, and that while the first four remain compatible, the subgenre of Romance conflicts with the others, disallowing a coherent philosophical viewpoint to be maintained throughout the novel.

Wagenknecht, Edward. "Frank Norris in Retrospect." *The Virginia Quarterly Review* VI, No. 2 (April 1930): 313-20.
A favorable assessment of Norris's work.

Walker, Don D. "The Western Naturalism of Frank Norris." *Western American Literature* II, No. 1 (Spring 1967): 14-29.
Discusses the American West in relation to Norris's work.

Walker, Franklin. *Frank Norris: A Biography*. New York: Russell & Russell, 1963, 317 p.
The first book-length biography of Norris.

Walker, Philip. "*The Octopus* and Zola: A New Look." *Symposium* XXI, No. 2 (Summer 1967): 155-65.
Compares and contrasts Norris's *The Octopus* with the works of Emile Zola.

Wyatt, Edith. "*Vandover and the Brute*." In her *Great Companions*, pp. 48-58. New York and London: D. Appleton and Co., 1917.
An assessment of *Vandover and the Brute*. Wyatt states that the novel "is strengthened, I believe, in some respects in being written so freshly and obviously from the author's own native endowment, and in ending with his own natural completion like *McTeague* and *Blix*, uninfluenced by the tendency to standardization which makes *The Octopus* and *The Pit* more like manufactured articles."

Ziff, Larzer. "Life Without Style: Frank Norris." In his *American 1890s: Life and Times of a Lost Generation*, pp. 250-74. New York: Viking Press, 1966.
A biographical study of Norris with short discussions of each of his books.

Su Man-shu

1884-1918

(Pseudonym of Su Chin; also wrote under pseudonyms of Su Hsüan-ying, Su Yüan-ying, and Reverend Mandju) Chinese poet, translator, novelist, short story writer, and painter.

While he is remembered in China primarily for his poetry and for his translations of English Romantic literature, Su is known in the West as the author of the autobiographical novel *Tuanhung ling-yen chi (The Lone Swan)*. A political progressive and cultural cosmopolite, Su hoped to aid in the modernization of Chinese society by introducing European revolutionary ideals, and to enrich his country's literature by creating a greater awareness of Western verse. As a result of his great success in achieving the latter aim, Su is recognized as a central figure in the development of modern Chinese poetry.

Born in Yokohama, Japan, Su was the son of a Chinese tea trader and his Japanese concubine. At the age of five he was sent to live in his father's ancestral village in Southern China, and it was there that he received his early education. Returning to Yokohama in 1898, Su attended a secondary school run by Chinese royalists; he later attended Waseda University in Tokyo for one year. Although no record of Su's studies remains, biographers believe that his early education focused on traditional Chinese culture, while his secondary studies were of a more modern nature and included English language and literature. In Tokyo, Su became involved with the many expatriate Chinese who advocated the overthrow of the Manchu dynasty, and by late 1903 he was contributing adamantly revolutionary prose and verse to leftist journals. In one such essay Su applauded the activities of the American anarchist Emma Goldman, while in others he launched vitriolic attacks on the Chinese people for submitting to dynastic oppression. During this period he also began a free translation of Victor Hugo's *Les Misérables*, calling it "The Miserable Society," but this project was never completed.

In the spring of 1904, Su disappeared for several weeks; when next seen, he had adopted the dress and demeanor of a Buddhist monk. He offered no explanation for his sudden transformation and continued to lead the life of a political activist for several years thereafter. Gradually, however, he became less interested in political affairs and more preoccupied with art and metaphysics. After the publication of his translations of Lord Byron's poetry in 1909, Su's reputation as a man of letters far surpassed his political renown, and he devoted the final years of his life exclusively to writing and painting. He died in 1918.

Written in a traditional Chinese form of four seven-word lines, Su's poetry exhibits many characteristic features of classical Buddhist verse, including frequent use of nature imagery, linguistic simplicity, and metaphysical speculation. His interest in Romantic literature, however, led him to introduce into his work an emotionalism that is antithetical to the Buddhist ideal of dispassionate consciousness. This disparity reflects a basic conflict in Su's life, for although he wished to devote himself entirely to the pursuit of spiritual enlightenment, an endeavor which in Buddhist tradition necessitates the relinquishing of all material attachments and pleasures, he was also acutely aware of the many compelling aspects of carnal existence. In

The Lone Swan, Su most directly revealed this inner conflict. Saburo, the protagonist of the novel, is a young Japanese man who becomes a monk in order to escape the pain of his existence. Yet Saburo, like Su, has great difficulty in severing his ties to material existence, and particularly in eschewing the company of women. This theme of romantic love in conflict with religious and social duty appears throughout Su's stories and novels.

Immensely popular in China during the early decades of this century, Su's works are still widely read. While his prose works are often criticized for their slow pace and incomplete characterizations, his poetry is highly regarded, and his best poems are considered a major achievement in Chinese literature. Perhaps more importantly, his sensitive portrayal of his struggle to live according to his spiritual ideals has made him a revered figure in Chinese society.

PRINCIPAL WORKS

Ch'ao-yin chi (translations) 1911
Tuan-hung ling-yen chi (novel) 1912
 [*The Lone Swan,* 1924]
Yen-tzu-han sui-pi (essays) 1913
Man-shu ta-shih ch'üan-chi (poetry, short stories, translations, essays, and novel) 1934

LIU WU-CHI (essay date 1972)

[In the following excerpt, Liu discusses formal and ideological elements of Su's works.]

Although Su Man-shu died prematurely half a century ago, his works have survived the wreckage of the times and will long remain a part of the Chinese cultural heritage. We can now state with some assurance that he will be remembered as a major literary figure of the first two decades of the twentieth century. Posterity has come to revere him for his writings, which are substantial, considering his short span of life, and for a personality that endeared him to friends and readers alike. (p. 122)

From both the literary and artistic works, insights into the character and thought of the poet-painter can be gained. Like his poetry, his pictures present an image of a creative artist richly endowed with imagination and sensitivity. But, while the poetry shows him to be a man of sentiment who, despite otherworldly yearnings, often yielded to the attractions of physical love and patriotic urgings, the paintings are even more ethereal and possess a magic touch of serene beauty that transforms the grubby commonness of life. On the other hand, the prose writings, both polemic essays and short stories, reveal the turbulent mind of a young idealist passionately concerned with social problems. Nonetheless, in all his creative works there is nothing incongruous in conception or feeling. These seeming contradictions merely point to the many-faceted nature of the man, in whom idealistic, romantic, and revolutionary sentiments came together. In moments of despair due to sickness and loneliness, his idealism sometimes degenerated into a profound pessimism or an obstinate disdain for human values. Although he critically favored Byron over Shelley, he seems to have been more like Shelley than Byron—an ineffectual angel, flapping his wings in vain.

Like Shelley he was ardently dedicated to revolutionary causes in early youth, yet he lacked lasting convictions and any understanding of the true nature of revolution, either in its nationalistic or ideological aspects. Typical of Chinese intellectuals in the pre-Republican period, he was hostile to the Manchu regime and was overjoyed at its overthrow, but he failed to adhere resolutely to his revolutionary faith once he became disillusioned with the course of political events after the revolution. Thus, youthful zeal quickly evaporated, giving way to political apathy and a growing disenchantment with life. The fiery young author who had once praised the patriotic deeds of brave officials and virtuous women in their resistance to the Manchu conquest, who had excoriated his fellow Cantonese for fawning servility towards westerners, who had deplored the Dutch oppression of Chinese communities in Java, who had re-echoed the woeful cries of the Indian people after the British conquest, who had sung passionately of Byron's "Isles of Greece," and who had glorified the American anarchist Emma Goldman, later became contrariwise an aimless wanderer who confined himself to making pretty but frivolous remarks on life and to discussing the affairs of "the flowers and the moon." So well did Man-shu camouflage his true feelings that even Liu Ya-tzu was deceived when he once remarked: "Man-shu refused absolutely to talk about politics."

There were also perceptible changes in his attitude toward religion. Persistent in his hostility toward Christianity and Christian missionaries, only the Reverend Lopez (possibly the Reverend George Candlin?) was an exception. Even his fervor for Buddhism, like that for revolution, seems to have cooled considerably in the last years of his life. Apparently, he did not find it inconsistent to preach revolution and to espouse Buddhism at the same time. His dedication to the Buddhist faith reached its fullest development in 1908, when, after having issued with Chang Ping-lin **"An Admonishment to All Buddhist Disciples"** and **"A Manifesto to Both Officials and Commoners,"** he went to Nanking to teach at the Jetavana School founded by Yang Wen-hui, the venerable Buddhist scholar. Soon afterward for reasons that have not yet been ascertained, his commitment to Buddhism seems to have subsided, and what might have made him the "Martin Luther of the Chinese Buddhist Reform Movement" never developed—this appelation was no more than an idealization by his panegyrists. To be sure, in speech and published writings he continued to keep alive the image of a Buddhist monk, but this appears to have been more a deliberate posture or façade than a true devotion to religion.

On matters pertaining to love and the opposite sex, his ideas are not only incongruous but also strangely paradoxical. The romantic lover in poetry and the sympathetic narrator of tragic love in fiction, he impresses one on the other hand as a follower of Schopenhauer in his denunciation of the female sex as "the source of calamity." The translation of *An Account of My Refugee Life on the Seashores of Sala* contains a series of slanderous attacks on womanhood, where woman are compared to poisonous serpents and hungry ghosts sent by hell to destroy man's spiritual body. Possibly an original work rather than a translation, these ideas may provisionally be credited to Su Man-shu. In certain instances, he was not only pessimistic but almost misanthropic, as when he wrote angrily to Liu Ya-tzu: "I say, one more Chinese student abroad will produce one more traitor to the country. . . . As for girls studying abroad, they would be better off if they learned how to act in an all-female vaudeville." Although utterances of this kind are rare in his collected writings, they are, nevertheless, what one may regard as manifestations of psychological abnormalities in a once fervent and open-minded young man who reacted violently in moments of bitter resentment against social evils. (pp. 123-25)

Intellectually, Man-shu was only a country bumpkin when he first entered Ta-t'ung School in Yokohama, and his senior schoolmates like Feng Tzu-yu had little regard for his scholarly abilities. Nor did he distinguish himself later as a student at Waseda University in Tokyo, notwithstanding a certain industry and perseverance. When he returned to Shanghai at the age of twenty as a newspaper hack, his Chinese prose style was so poor that his colleagues had to polish it for him. It was not until 1907 when, inspired by Chang Ping-lin and others, he first made a serious attempt to write poetry. Already twenty-four at the time, he was still a novice in a country where precociousness in versification was relatively common. But, in the short span of seven years from 1907 to 1914, he managed to produce some of the best Chinese poetry of the period. To be sure, when compared with the vast quantities of poetry composed by his friends of the Southern Society during a comparable period, his poetic output was small, totaling only some ninety verses. Nonetheless, while most of these poets have been forgotten by posterity, Su Man-shu alone continues to enjoy both popularity and critical acclaim.

Critics generally attribute his success as a poet to genius, that illusive and unfathomable natural capacity for creative expression possessed more by some than others. That he was endowed with a certain genius is true, but one still has to delve deeper into his poetry to discover those qualities which distinguish his verse. First of all, it must be observed that he was by no means a great poet in the sense that Li Po, Tu Fu, and Su Shih were. His work is limited mainly to one form of Chinese poetry, the *ch'i-chüeh* or seven-word four-line stanza. In this particular poetic form, however, his achievement was outstanding. Comprising a total of only twenty-eight words, the *ch'i-chüeh* is in one sense the easiest form to employ, but also the most difficult to use well. Very few poets excelled in this form, which attained its highest development at the hands of the T'ang dynasty masters. Even the Sung poets, who branched out into other domains of Chinese poetry, failed to match the T'ang poets in this respect. Therefore, one risks the criticism of partiality in asserting that some of Man-shu's best *ch'i-chüeh* rank with the best T'ang poems in the same form, but this is nonetheless a critical assessment arrived at after due consideration and held with conviction.

Not all Man-shu's poems are of the highest quality. Quite a few are professedly imitations of late T'ang poetry and are often marred by clichés, conceits, artificiality, and excessive elaboration in description and overuse of image and metaphor. At times, he was not averse to borrowing from the earlier poets. This practice has of course long been commonly accepted; for anyone who falls under the magic spell of great poetry—there is such a considerable amount of it in the Chinese tradition—will consciously or unconsciously retain or adopt fine expressions and beautiful images as a part of his own poetic vocabulary. Finally, to a strict prosodist, Man-shu's versification may seem faulty in a number of instances, but then the T'ang poets themselves took liberties with the rules of prosody whenever it suited their individual purposes.

What one can do, therefore, is to discover and identify the lyrical elements in his verse. Briefly, these can be listed as naturalness, a sensitivity to beauty, and a spontaneous flow of emotion. Naturalness as an element of his style is sometimes deceptive, as his poems also reveal a subtlety that is scarcely noticeable in a superficial reading. The Chinese fondness for erudite words and obscure references can sometimes be construed as a façade to hide a paucity of emotions and ideas. Man-shu's limited scholarship and his disinclination to employ literary devices should not however be considered as a weakness. In contrast to the works of the expert versifiers of the Southern Society, his poems are remarkably devoid of literary allusions, and the few that intrude into his lines appear delightfully amateurish in tone. One gains, on the other hand, a clear impression of natural ease in the expression of personal feelings, though this does not preclude an ingenious use of poetic devices. Compare, for instance, the following two poems:

(1)

Ask me not whether our parting is for life or death!
A lonely monk, I wander like clouds floating and
    waters flowing.
For no reason at all, I madly laugh and then loudly
    wail.
Although a warm and glad heart I had, it is as cold as
    ice.
          —**"To Ch'en Tu-hsiu as I Pass by Wakamatsu-cho in a
                  State of Emotion"**

(2)

Spring rain pattering on an upper chamber—the sound
    of a "foot-and-eight flute."

How I yearn to go to watch the tide at Ch'ien-t'ang!
With straw sandals and a broken alms-bowl, all
    unknown I roamed.
I wonder how many bridges I've crossed, where the
    cherry blossoms bloom.
                         —"Occasional Poem, No. 1"

Alike in their expression of a prevailing mood of sadness, the poems differ greatly in the way the emotional state is revealed. The first poem is a plain statement of the poet's melancholy that arises from a lonely and wandering life, whereas in the second the same mood is conjured up in a subtle, artistic manner through the use of associations and intimations. "Spring Rain on an Upper Chamber" is the title of a popular melody for the long flute which, introduced from China, can still be heard in Japan. Its melancholy sound arouses in the poet, as he passes by the house of an unseen flute player in a drizzling rain, a sense of loneliness and desolation. In turn it gives rise to a nostalgic feeling for his home country, especially at a time when the tide at Ch'ien-t'ang near the scenic city of Hangchow presents a spectacular view and an occasion for joy when watching it in the company of friends. But here on foreign soil, his plight as a mendicant monk, unknown as the flute player is unseen, contrasts vividly with the cheerful view of the cherry blossoms.

While his poetry reveals a sensitivity to the beauties of nature, it is also enlivened with a human touch. Just as the scenery he describes is always delightfully charming and exquisite, rather than grand and majestic, so the feelings he expresses are tranquil and serene, in keeping with the landscape and often blending with it. The following poems . . . are worth citing . . . as examples of his achievement in this respect:

Amidst the dense white clouds which embrace Thunder
    Peak,
Stand a few wintry plum trees, their red blooms clothed
    with snow.
After a vegetable repast I sink slowly, completely into a
    deep meditation,
As the sound of a distant bell falls on shadows in the
    monastery pool.
   **—"Written during My Stay at White Clouds Monastery at
                       West Lake"**

Deep under the willow's canopying shadows the horse
    treads proudly,
Where a vast expanse of silvery sand pursues the ebbing
    tide.
The ice-flag atop a thatched store signals the nearby
    market;
The red leaves on the mountain top the lasses gather for
    firewood.
                         —"Passing by Kamata"

In both poems, the scenery is unspoiled but enlivened by human presence as man and nature learn to live in harmony with each other. The same kind of happy interaction and affinity between the two is shown in the following highly imaginative lines:

Riding a lean horse, I need not worry about the long
    road ahead—
The peach blossoms, so lovely red, yearn to come up to
    my singing whip.
                 —"Singing on My Way to Yodoe"

In all these instances, the charms of nature gently strike a responsive chord in the heart of the poet.

Likewise, one finds a soft rippling of the emotions in a number of his poems. To be sure, he did sometimes abandon himself to violent passions, as when he chanted and wailed over Byron's poems when boating in the moonlight; nevertheless, in his own verse, he speaks in a calm and restrained voice even while giving vent to strong personal emotion:

> At this moment, even if I am full of emotion and tears,
> I'll talk randomly on topics that range from the sea of
>   men to men in heaven.
> > —**"Poems without Titles, No. 6"**

> I can only give back to you, dear maiden, an alms-bowl
>   of unfeeling tears,
> Regretting that I did not meet you before my head was
>   shaved.
> > —**"Occasional Poems, No. 4"**

> Please do not ask me, when we meet, about affairs in
>   this mortal world.
> The old country so grieves my heart that only tears
>   flow.
> > —**"Nineteen Miscellaneous Poems Written during My Sojourn in Japan, No. 2"**

In these three selections, be it fond memories of a childhood sweetheart, internal conflict between love and religion, or sorrow for the grievous situation in his own country, the outpouring of emotion is kept under control, so that there is tranquility and placidness on the surface, notwithstanding currents of agitated feelings underneath. It is only by reading between the lines that one comes to realize what a passionately sentimental individual he must have been.

A large number of Man-shu's poems are about friendship, love, and feminine charms, themes that have been explored repeatedly by Chinese poets throughout the ages. Man-shu seems to have been especially captivated by seductive feminine traits. There is nothing lascivious in his poetry, yet he took nonetheless a keen interest in the toilet, hairdo, gestures, and movements of beautiful women. An expert on feminine coiffure—he once collected and sketched a hundred styles of the ancient period—he was particularly keen on the description of hair styles:

> Dabbing lightly her moth eyebrows, she comes to pay
>   her respects to the master painter,
> Her elegant hairknot, shaped like a twin-heart, bound
>   together by black silk.
> > —**"On Painting the Portrait of a Harpsichord Player, Poem 2"**

> A lotus hairdo aslant her head, with lovely looks and
>   lustrous hair,
> She imprinted her powdered fingers on a green bamboo
>   book.
> > —Title Lost

Examples of other lines on the attractions of lovely women are "Her slender, willowy waist, most lovely to behold"; "Her cheeks blooming and her lips enticing, she sits, playing the mouth organ"; "On her arms linger faintly a trace of beancurd fragrance"; "As she fondles her silken girdle, putting to shame the pale maiden in the moon." The following poem is a good example of his portrayal of a blooming, vivacious, but bashful girl:

> Having changed into a silken shirt, she descends from
>   the western chamber,
> Like the warm fragrance of a tender bloom, and keeps
>   on talking.
> But when one inquires about her age, she becomes even
>   more bashful.
> Behind the crystal screen she goes to practice on the
>   lute.
> > —**"Nineteen Miscellaneous Poems Written during My Sojourn in Japan, No. 3"**

In addition to their lyrical qualities, these poems have a charm of their own derived from the poet's experiences in Japan and his Buddhist background, which, in turn, lends these verses an exotic coloration. The figures of the ice-flag on the thatched store, the cherry-blossom bridges, the foot-and-eight flute have been mentioned previously as typical of the Japanese scene. Also numerous are references to Buddhism, in which Man-shu found consolation, a contemplative peace of mind, and a source of exhilaration in this fleeting life. Religion triumphed over love in his life and poetry, and a total surrender to the Buddhist faith is indicated in the following stanza:

> A mind in meditation cares not for the envy of the
>   moth-eyebrowed.
> In Buddha's precept a common origin have anger and
>   affection.
> Wearing a rain-hat and a cloak of mist, I shall return
>   whence I came,
> Without a trace of love or hate for my fellow man.

Religion also inspires the following **"Note to Fan-jen,"** a fellow monk:

> Let's get drunk with the dew on a golden stem,
> And paint with rouge the peony blossoms.
> Here, fallen petals pile up a foot deep;
> There is no need to bring along a prayer mat.

The clever blending of natural setting with art and religion in the poem produces a delightful effect, making this poem something of a perfect little gem. Thus, one gets tipsy on his poetry, on the "dew on a golden stem"; it exhilarates but does not intoxicate.

In my opinion, his contributions lie more in the realm of poetry than prose, although the latter looms much larger in bulk. His prose writings can be divided into three categories: (1) miscellaneous notes and essays, (2) letters, and (3) stories. Except for the general knowledge they impart and the information they provide about his personal feelings and thoughts, the random notes and prefaces are not particularly noteworthy as works of literature, while the early political essays are immature in content and crude in language. On the other hand, his letters are among the best of his writings and rank high in epistolary style in a literature long noted for this genre. . . . [These] letters bear the distinct stamp of his genius with their exquisite style and fine phraseology, humor and warmth of feeling, delicate touches of sentimentality, and intimate revelations of personality. In the preface to the *Poetic Remains of the Swallow's Mausoleum*, Liu Ya-tzu tells us: "Man-Shu was fond of writing in a fine calligraphy on pink stationery, his characters as small as the head of a fly. His letters have grace and elegance, but they are often colored by melancholy and sentimentality. Like the poet of yore, he had a bellyful of grievances against the times." . . . (pp. 129-35)

The Lone Swan and other stories ... excel with respect to literary style, the expression of personal sentiment, and the presentation of conflict, either internal or external. However, the weaknesses of these stories are also obvious and many. Some of them are cluttered with long series of episodes that weaken the plot and dilute the characterization, both of which cannot be said to have been his strong points. Digressions and lengthy discourses hamper the movement of the plot and create a sense of artificiality. *The Lone Swan,* for instance, could gain in intensity and unity if pruned of extraneous matters. The same view is expressed by Yü Ta-fu in his "Miscellaneous Criticism of Man-shu's Writings" (1927). While several inaccuracies in Yü's summary of the plot indicate the casual manner of his criticism, as a whole the general arguments advanced are well taken and valid. Apparently unaware of the fact that the novel was left unfinished and that the last sentence is a later addition, Yü Ta-fu takes Man-shu to task for the poor ending of the novel. He also criticizes **"Tale of a Broken Hairpin"** for its inferior narrative technique and inadequate character delineation: "Man-shu uses a semi-realistic form of narration, which constantly reminds the reader of the fictitious nature of his plot. In this story, especially weak is the connection between the hero's character and the plot development; something is amiss in the sequence of cause and effect. Sometimes, to arouse the reader's expectations and curiosity, he employs a form of suspense which, however, is not in keeping with techniques adopted by talented modern writers familiar with Western fiction; rather, it is a method used by the popularizers of vulgar and tawdry stories." Similarly, Henry McAleavy comments that **"Tale of a Broken Hairpin"** makes strange reading today [see Additional Bibliography].

If we view Man-shu's stories from a historical perspective, we shall be able to appreciate them better and to understand that their limitations and failings are typical of the fiction of the times. It is true that Man-shu, who must have dipped widely into Western novels, failed to take advantage of more sophisticated methods of narration and character delineation developed by English and European writers of the nineteenth century; but he was essentially a poet, a romancer, who was interested primarily in presenting the emotions of love in a language both expressive and eloquent. Granted that there are certain absurdities in situation and morbidity of sentiment in his fiction, these are but minor flaws when compared to the "cheap, tawdry materials" commonly found in the so-called Mandarin Duck and Butterfly School of Fiction that was in vogue at that time. It is also true that he failed to learn from the best traditions of native storytelling, which are to be found in the *Dream of the Red Chamber*.... (pp. 135-36)

While we have already surveyed Man-shu's contributions to creative writing, it seems proper in this connection to define his role as a translator. As we know, he was the first Chinese writer to translate Byron and Shelley, whose names were only vaguely known in China in the first decade of the present century. Man-shu wrote enthusiastically of them and called both poets of love and liberty, ideals which also inspired him in his own writings. A decade later, members of the Creation Society like Kuo Mo-jo and others came once again under the influence of Byron and Shelley, but even at the height of the New Literature Movement, no Chinese translator appeared to rival Man-shu's dedication to Byron. His *Selected Poems of Byron* is still the only important volume of Chinese translations from the English poet. Man-shu was also attracted to the great novels of the West, particularly Victor Hugo's *Les Misérables* and Dumas fils's *La Dame aux camélias*. Though he failed to

translate the latter and did poorly with respect to the former, he nevertheless extended the horizon of Chinese knowledge of Western literature by his writings, just as he brought to the general reader's attention Western efforts in translating Chinese poetry. His chief contribution in this vein was as a promoter of cultural exchange between East and West. With four published works (*Affinities in Literature*..., *Selected Poems of Byron*..., *Voices of the Tide*..., *Esoteric Essences of Chinese-English Poetry*...) to his credit, he was both a pioneer translator of English poetry and an outstanding anthologist of Chinese poetry in English translation. As such, he contributed to the furtherance of East-West literary relationships long before his countrymen were aware of foreign literature and its merits and significance. (p. 141)

[In] the last fifty years Su Man-shu has influenced two generations of the Chinese people, by whom he will be remembered not as "a figure of legend" but as an early revolutionary and a talented writer of unfulfilled renown. The product of a transitional age that was listless in mood, turbulent in thought, throbbing with adventures, and yet filled with great expectations, he was a literary figure whose writings created more than a ripple in the mainstream of early twentieth-century Chinese literature. He personifies a happy union of the age-old literary traditions of China with the fresh invigorating romanticism of the West. His greatest asset, however, is his genial and genuine personality, which gives to all that he wrote, sang, and painted a touch of the beautiful, compounded of sensitivity, spontaneity, and childlike simplicity. A poet-monk, he subscribed to a faith that does not deny to its followers the enjoyment of secular life but recognizes also its concomitant sorrows and miseries. (pp. 142-43)

> *Liu Wu-chi in his* Su Man-shu, *Twayne Publishers, Inc., 1972, 173 p.*

LEO OU-FAN LEE (essay date 1973)

[*In the following excerpt, Lee considers Su's works as a key to understanding the more obscure aspects of the poet's life.*]

No scholar can claim full knowledge of the inside story of Su Man-shu.

We learn that he is immensely versatile. "He is versed in the arts, especially painting." He writes old-style poetry. He is a translator and knows at least five languages: Chinese, Japanese, English, French, and Sanskrit. We are then told by his friend Ch'en Tu-hsiu that Su never studied Chinese carefully in childhood and Ch'en taught him how to write classical poetry. According to another friend, Chang Shih-chao, he became an established master in no more than two to three years. Ch'en Tu-hsiu therefore considered him "truly a genius."

Then, there is his self-perpetuated reputation for gourmandism.... His death was caused, according to one account, by his having eaten sixty meat dumplings in order to win a bet. When he finished about fifty, his friends were alarmed, but he insisted and finished the last ten with a cup of coffee.

He gave himself a great number of names (32 altogether; his English name, Pev Mandju) some identifiable, some not. He loved to send his friends photographs of himself, when he was not making surprise visits and begging them for loans. Once, a friend saw him in Canton with his beard "as long as a full inch"; some time later, Su sent him a photo from Shanghai in which he appeared as a clean-shaven, dashing dandy. Another admirer one day saw a young man wearing a cassock, with his

Su Man-Shu in his monk's robe.

woolen underwear sticking out, and sitting at the edge of a cliff. Then, the young hero would be transformed, according to another account, into a disheveled monk sitting with his face toward the wall and wearing a shabby, dust-laden cassock, in a shattered wooden house hidden under the trees behind a monastery, as if he had not set foot outside for a whole year. The poor monk turned out to be the same person who only three days ago had lived in comfort and luxury in Shanghai. Sometimes he would simply disappear for months, leaving no traces for his anxious friends.

Was he indeed a man of such profound sorrow that from time to time he had to seek temporary solutions in solitary meditation? To an outside observer, his many poses impart an air of narcissistic affectation, as if the adulations of his friends—especially females—were not enough. The many anecdotes supplied by his friends and admirers only lead us to suspect that he was craving a lofty style of life. To be both a monk and a poet conjures many glamorous images in the Chinese tradition. But Su did not seem satisfied with emulating one model. He experimented and, with his ingenuity, invented. The result was, of course, the picture of a melancholy genius whose thoughts were too unique and whose sensitivities were too acute to be wholly understood by his age—a posture that many self-styled men of letters were later to adopt eagerly. Su Man-shu was among the first men to exemplify the idea that

the style of a man is, both to himself and his public, as important as the man himself. The fact that Su Man-shu could gain popularity from his personality and life style as much as from his literary accomplishments reflects an even larger phenomenon—the gradual erosion of the established norms and customs of behavior, which made it necessary for men like Su to create new ones. (pp. 62-5)

Styles, appearances, and idiosyncrasies are the stuff of legends. Su Man-shu, however, has added another component: his fictional writings. Since most of them are imaginary reconstructions of many actual events in his life, they are of the utmost importance for a historian. The most popular and the most closely autobiographical of his fictional works is undoubtedly *The Lone Swan*. Thus it serves as a logical beginning for . . . probings into the Su Man-shu legend.

The story begins with the hero, Saburo, a Sinified Japanese (described in the first person) already completing his training as a monk, in a secluded monastery on the coast of southern Kwangtung. A chance encounter with a boy leads him to find his former nurse, who recalls how she came to be employed by a cultured Japanese lady, Saburo's mother. She also tells him that his father was a well-respected Japanese from Tokyo who died a few months after Saburo was born. She then describes how his mother was ill treated by his stepfather's Chinese concubines. Filled with emotion, he decides to travel to Japan in search of his mother. Saburo also meets, quite accidentally, his childhood fiancée, Hsüeh-mei (Snow plum), whose father has retracted their marriage contract after the death of his stepfather. In order to have Hsüeh-mei enjoy the happiness of another marriage, Saburo has decided to become a monk. But he finds his former fiancée still very devoted to him. (p. 65)

Saburo's trip to Japan is financed by Hsüeh-mei and Reverend Lopez of Madrid. The reunion of mother and son is one of the most lachrymose parts of the novel. Saburo visits his aunt and meets Shizuko, his cousin. Shizuko falls madly in love with him, but being a monk he cannot repay the intensity of her feelings. Nor can he accept the offer of marriage to Shizuko from the two kind ladies. Accordingly, after much mental self-torture, he finally resolves to leave surreptitiously for Shanghai. In a farewell letter to Shizuko, he reveals the secret of his monkhood:

> Alas! You and I shall never meet again! A Buddhist monk ordained in the grand precepts of the law, I can never have the life-long companionship of any woman. But, being neither wood nor stone, how could I not be grateful for your gracious and generous sentiments, your lofty virtue that reaches high to the skies? Born under the ill-omened Waterstar, I have encountered in this life unutterable sorrows. . . . With a monk's staff in my hand, I shall now roam afar as a mendicant. In this dusty world, chances are slim of our seeing each other again. I beg you, elder sister, to let me drag out alone my lingering existence. What else could I do?

Upon returning to China, Saburo immediately changes into his monk's attire and goes back to his monastic life. During a service at which he officiates, he meets a brother and sister named Mai who happen to be his former classmates. From them he learns that Hsüeh-mei has committed suicide. He goes to the village burial ground but fails to find her grave. The story ends with our hero wailing among a heap of desolate mounds. "Readers, please consider, how could my sorrows at this moment be matched anywhere in this human world? Now my tears have been exhausted. I feel my heart is like wood and stone. I have made up my mind to return to the monastery of my original teacher. I do not know how much more sorrow is in store for me."

Three themes clearly present themselves: the hero's monastic bent, his search for his mother, and the triangular relationship of the hero with two women devoted to him—themes which give a clue to an understanding not only of Su's works but also of his life, or the legend of his life.

Although we are unable to ascertain the reasons for Su's monkhood, we can still accept it as a fact of his life and attempt to gauge its role in the structure of the novel and the legend of his life. Many critics have noticed the similarity in the pattern of characterization between *The Lone Swan* and *Dream of the Red Chamber (Hung-lou meng)*. Both portray a fragile, sensitive hero wavering between two heroines. It is almost certain that Su, like most writers of the so-called "talent-beauty" stories *(ts'ai-tzu chia-jen)*, owed a great debt to this greatest novel in China. Not merely in the superficial pattern of characters but also in the basic ethos, the two novels are very much alike.

In one sense, *Dream of the Red Chamber* could be regarded as a microcosm of the conflict between Confucianism and Buddhism. Preordained, in the popular Buddhist sense, in his previous karma, the hero Chia Pao-yü descends into this mundane realm to suffer the trials and temptations of the "red dust," the setting of which is a large family imbedded in long-established Confucian norms. Love—both aggressive and tender as represented by Hsüeh Pao-ch'ai and Lin Tai-yü—is treated in this dual context. Its flow has to be curbed by the rigors of Confucian ethics, but it is also, in the Buddhist framework, merely an ephemeral, kaleidoscopic bubble or gleaming grain of sand in the red dust that evaporates into nothingness.

Su Man-shu seems to belong thoroughly to the *Dream of the Red Chamber* tradition. But unlike the *Dream* . . . the Confucian elements are much more diluted. The "curse" that the hero Saburo carries is almost the same as Pao-yü's, but he is not subject to the torture of that grand matrix of Confucian relations—the big gentry-official family. The problem of filial piety . . . is symbolized in Su's novel by Saburo's somewhat nostalgic attachment to his Japanese mother, a well-respected woman, of course, but from a different cultural tradition. If one compares Su's fictional portrait of his mother with his real life experience with his mother, the implications that could be drawn would seem more vaguely Freudian than strictly Confucian.

Su Man-shu was very detached from his father. He even refused to go home for his father's funeral. Was it due to his distaste for the comprador class? No serious scholar is in a position to give a convincing interpretation of Su's relationship with his father because he himself has written almost nothing about his father. His mother, however, presents an entirely different case. If Liu Wu-chi's chronology of Man-shu is to be trusted, Su left Kawai, whom he always thought of as his mother, in 1889 at the age of six, and did not see her until 1907 when he was twenty-four. This indicates clearly that during his entire adolescent period he was without a mother. The lack of a normal family milieu, especially the loving care of a mother, perhaps underlies his self-image as a lone traveler stricken with "unutterable sorrows." The sorrows could be compounded if,

indeed, Su had been torn by his quandaries about the identity of his real mother. It is in this context that Man-shu's nostalgic attachment to and loving idealization of his mother has to be viewed. Not only in *The Lone Swan* but elsewhere the image of a cultured Japanese lady has been perpetuated. She has allegedly written in Japanese a preface to a collection of her son's paintings, but some of Su's biographers and friends strongly suspected that the real author was Su Man-shu himself.

The central role of his mother in Man-shu's life leads us naturally to the baffling question of women in his life, always a major component of his legend. Every reader of Man-shu's fiction would be immediately struck by a recurring phenomenon: the hero is always the object of single-hearted devotion of two women—one tender and docile, the other more passionate and aggressive, both loyal and self-sacrificing. Does Su Man-shu crave certain psychological compensations for the lack of female attention in his real life?

Even given the possible existence in real life of Man-shu's two or three early loves, the traces of their idealization in the stories are clearly discernible. This can be seen in Su's last story, **"Sui-tsan chi"** (**"Tale of a Broken Hairpin"**). Set in two coastal cities—Shanghai and Hangchow—where foreign merchandise and foreign fashions were becoming the vogue, the story presents, as usual, two lovely girls clinging to a fragile, vacillating, often bedridden young man. One of them, rich and more aggressive, wears chic Western dresses and carries opera binoculars to attend Western-style plays. One wonders why she should be modern and fashionable in appearance but traditional in her devotional virtues. Such heroines might have indeed existed, but it is more likely that his heroines are composite figures combining what Su himself considered as reigning ideals. Thus the dual personality of his heroines represent Su's own feeling of ambivalence toward women in general. On the one hand, he cannot totally break away from the Chinese tradition. Born outside China and not adequately educated in Chinese culture, he may have harbored more intense yearnings for the best in Chinese culture. Hence, . . . Su gives a highly emotional coloration to the traditional womanly virtue of devotion. . . . Su also looks with distaste at the erosion of traditional virtues and the invasion of Western manners. The cynicism exhibited in some of his critical essays about "modern women" is the cynicism of a man who finds his idealized images increasingly shattered by the reality around him. "Let this humble monk respectfully admonish our fellow female countrymen. Henceforward you should not follow the fashion of high breasts and slender waists. Rather, the motto at your dressing mirror should be: a gentle woman should marry for virtue and not appearance. . . . The virtues of women are fidelity and chastity." Yet, on the other hand, having been exposed to foreign influences through his reading and traveling, Su may not have been content with the uneducated and parochial types of traditional women. Hence the femmes fatales in his novels, who combine the still Chinese virtues of devotion with somewhat foreign attributes of passion, aggressiveness, and sensual abandon. (Shizuko, the more passionate heroine in *The Lone Swan*, is a Japanese.)

But Su seems not equipped to cope with such women. In **"A Broken Hairpin,"** he wrote, "All women under heaven are the sources of calamity." In another work one finds the following slanderous words: "There is nothing more fearful than women, tender and charming in appearance but viciously evil at heart. Women are the harbingers of hell; when they utter beautiful speech, they are in fact pouring poison." Such utterances reflect more than the cynicism of a man "who reacted violently in moments of bitter resentment against the evil forces of society"; they verge on the pathological. Are we to suppose, with McAleavy [see Additional Bibliography], that Su was born with a sexual incapacity? Further conjectures could be made with regard to Su's attitude and behavior toward prostitutes.

Sing-song girls—refined prostitutes—had been an established part of the glitter and sophistication of Shanghai society. Su Man-shu, a frequenter of this city, was known for his patronage of the sing-song girls. Many anecdotes have been told by his friends. It is said that he often lavished large sums of money on them and attended dinner parties in their company. After calling the girls to the party, he would attempt to practice meditation to the chagrin of his female companions. In one revealing account, Su fell deeply in love with a prostitute and practically lived at her place, but he never attempted sexual intercourse. When the women asked him for an explanation, he reportedly said with solemnity:

> Love is air for the soul. The soul can live forever when nourished by love, just as the body relies on air in order to live. In our daily humdrum lives, we have all the time been swimming in the sea of sentiment. It is said that the sea of sentiment is the sea of calamity; a few steps into it and you will be drowned. This statement mistakenly confuses the sea of desire with the sea of sentiment. But things, when pushed to the extreme, often have opposite effects. . . . Sexual desire is the extremity of love. We love each other but do not reach for abandon, so as to preserve this sentiment forever. . . . After reaching abandon, the fervor of passion will recede. . . . I do not intend to seek pleasures of the flesh at the expense of love of the spirit.

This reported statement might serve to confirm McAleavy's conjecture. For our purposes, however, it rather provides the best perspective to summarize Su's ambivalent attitudes toward women.

The treatment of women in Su's fiction is but one aspect of the basic outlook that Su shares in common with Lin Shu. The themes of Buddhism, mother, and women all revolve around one leitmotif, that of sentiment. Su Man-shu . . . is a man of strong emotions. Whether imaginary or real, the basic story line in Su's fiction and some of his poetry is the odyssey of a sensitive soul in the sea of sentiment. One of his own remarks profoundly summarizes the fundamental concerns of his life: "I am sad because I seek the way [implying perhaps the Buddhist path] through sentiments" *(wei-ch'ing ch'iu-tao).*

In the imaginary world of his fiction—the world of his dreams—he aspires toward that quintessence of sentiments, love. But he is overpowered by the physical aspects of love—the sea of desire—as personified by women who commit their whole beings to the seduction of the gentle weak hero. Therefore the hero either escapes from the mundane web of entanglements into the serene sanctity of the monastery or opts for the gentler and more traditional woman, thereby causing the suicide of the seductress but too late to save the gentle heroine from sacrificing herself also. But to lead a life without love is tantamount to death of the soul, and to enter the gate of Buddhism means the rejection of mundane life, hence death of the body. Thus

the tragedies in his fiction are invariably the tragedies of love and death, of love consummated in death. At its best, Su's treatment of this theme is reminiscent of Wilde, as some of his more learned friends hastened to point out. In his short story, **"Chiang sha chi"** (**"Tale of Crimson Silk"**), Hsüeh Meng-chu (quasi-homophonous with Su Man-shu) was once in love with Hsüeh Ch'iu-yün but later became a Buddhist monk. The narrator accompanied Ch'iu-yün to a Soochow monastery to seek him:

> When we got there, the pine shadows covered the front gate, it being the night of the full moon. I noticed that the door was ajar; so I asked Ch'iu-yün to wait outside as I entered the temple. Inside, the courtyard was empty, the night still, and only the light of Buddha's lamp flickered on the four walls. I continued forward to a side room, which was also quiet and vacant. Thinking that Meng-chu had not yet returned, I retraced my steps until I caught a glimpse of a white-faced idol at a corner of the courtyard corridor. As I approached, I saw that it was Meng-chu himself, sitting there lifeless with his eyes closed and grass growing between his knees. I called him but got no reply. I pulled at his hand and it was as stiff as iron. Only then did I realize that Meng-chu had met a Buddhist death.

> I hurried out to tell Ch'iu-yün. She entered and stood silently in front of him, without uttering one word. All of a sudden, she saw a corner of a crimson silk kerchief protruding from the lapel of his cassock. She pulled it out with her hand, looked around, and turned it over. Then she nestled herself in Meng-chu's lap as she embraced and kissed him with streaming tears. All this time I stood still. Suddenly, I heard the rustling of the wind as Meng-chu's corpse dissolved into ashes, only the piece of crimson silk remaining in Ch'iu-yün's hand.

Here is the nirvana of Man-shu's ideal sentiment, the intensity of his passion—the kind of passion which arises not so much from the exertions of the flesh as from the depth of the spirit, of emotion condensed and sublimated in tranquility. This ideal points toward many ramifications, embracing many elements from both Chinese and foreign traditions.

The literary fame of Su Man-shu rests, in addition to his poetry and fiction, also on his translations; he was the first to introduce Byron into China. (pp. 66-72)

It is apparent that from the very beginning Su was attracted to Byron on account of the affinities between them. Both are wandering free spirits; both spent a portion of their lives in a foreign land (Su chose to translate among Byron's longer poems, "The Ocean," "The Isles of Greece," and "My Native Land, Good Night"); and both are emotional poets with a host of female admirers. One admirer wrote: "He has introduced Byron to us because he loves Byron, loves the similarities between Byron and himself, loves the Byron in Greece like himself in Japan. In letting China know of Byron, Man-shu inwardly also wants to make us understand himself."

What are we to understand of Man-shu through Byron? In his preface to the *Selected Poems of Byron*, he praised his hero in the following words: "As a poet who conveyed in his songs the sorrows of departure from his own country and who would not claim any credit for helping the people of another country, Byron vied for glory with the sun and the moon.'' Man-shu could easily reciprocate the ''sorrows of departure'' from his own country. But unlike Byron, a dandy poet turned self-styled revolutionist, Su was a frustrated revolutionist who became a self-styled wandering poet. Thus Byron, like the heroes and heroines in Su's fiction, represents a composite image of what Su could identify with and for which he could only yearn. Byron's later experience may remind Su of his early years. But he could only admire Byron as a heroic fighter. This kind of heroic pose represented by Byron, introduced by Su Man-shu but perpetuated by Hsü Chih-mo and others, was but another of his favourite imaginary poses, like that cassock-clad youth sitting at the edge of a cliff. Moreover, the problem of the Su Man-shu legend is also in a sense reminiscent of that of Byron. Through the popular accounts of his time and his own works we have inherited a legacy of Byroniana, a hero with many masks. Was Su aware that the headstrong, impetuous, and pretentious dandy might have his weaker and more sober side, that the Byron in *Childe Harold* might be quite different from the Byron in *Don Juan?* Did he notice that Byron's physical defect might have reinforced his heroic pretensions? Most likely, Byron's Chinese translator was more fascinated by the legend of Byron than by the real Byron himself, and the legacy of Chinese Byroniana, begun by Su Man-shu, has perpetuated this English poet in the glittering image of the Byronic hero.

In the preface to *Ch'ao-yin chi* (*Voices of the Tide*), written originally in English, Man-shu attempted to compare Byron with Shelley, another favorite Western poet:

> Byron and Shelley are two of the greatest British poets. Both had the lofty sentiment of creation, love, as the theme of their poetic expressions. Yes, although both wrote principally on love, lovers, and their fortunes, their modes of expression differ as widely as the poles.
>
> Byron was born and brought up in luxury, wealth, and liberty. He was an ardent and sincere devotee of liberty—yes, he dared to claim liberty in every thing—great and small, social or political. He knew not how or where he was extreme.
>
> Byron's poems are like a stimulating liquor— the more one drinks, the more one feels the sweet fascination. They are full of charm, full of beauty, full of sincerity throughout.
>
> In sentimentality, enthusiasm and straightforwardness of diction, they have no equal. He was a free and noble hearted man. His end came while he was engaged in a noble pursuit. He went to Greece, where he sided with the patriots who were fighting for their liberty. His whole life, career and production are intertwined in Love and Liberty.
>
> Shelley, though a devotee of love, is judicious and pensive. His enthusiasm for love never ap-

pears in any strong outburst of expression. He is a ''Philosopher-lover.'' He loves not only the beauty of love, or love for love, but ''love in philosophy'' or ''philosophy in love.'' He had depth, but not continuance: energy without youthful devotion. His poems are as the moonshine, placidly beautiful, solemnly still, reflected on the waters of silence and contemplation.

> Shelley sought Nirvana in love; but Byron sought Action for love, and in love. Shelley was self-contained and quite engrossed in his devotion to the Muses. His premature and violent death will be lamented so long as English literature exists.
>
> Both Shelley and Byron's works are worth studying by every lover of learning, for enjoyment of poetic beauty, and to appreciate the lofty ideas of Love and Liberty.

This preface summarizes perfectly Su Man-shu's reactions to Byron. His juxtaposition of Byron and Shelley presents, in fact, two sides of his image of love which in turn reflects, like the heroines in his fiction, two sides of his temper. He admires and may indeed have imaginatively longed for the tempestuous outbursts of Byron. But Byron's volcanic dynamism is much too overpowering, like ''stimulating liquor,'' for his gentle soul. He has to seek the more contemplative Shelley in whose serenity and depth he finds the ''nirvana of love.'' (pp. 73-5)

Leo Ou-fan Lee, ''Su Man-shu,'' in his The Romantic Generation of Modern Chinese Writers, *Cambridge, Mass.: Harvard University Press, 1973, pp. 58-78.*

ADDITIONAL BIBLIOGRAPHY

Leung, George Kin. Introduction and Appendix to *The Lone Swan*, by Su Man-shu, pp. ix-xii; pp. 141-43. Shanghai: The Commercial Press, 1924.
  Gives biographical and textual background for *The Lone Swan*.

McAleavy, Henry. *Su Man-shu (1884-1918): A Sino-Japanese Genius*. London: China Society, 1960, 51 p.
  Biographical speculations based primarily on information drawn from *The Lone Swan*. McAleavy also includes some translated excerpts from that work.

Woon, Ramon L. Y. and Lo, Irving Y. ''Poets and the Poetry of China's Last Empire.'' *Literature: East and West* IX, No. 4 (December 1965): 331-61.
  Discusses Su in the context of early twentieth-century Chinese literary movements. Woon and Lo maintain that Su's ''admiration for Byron and Shelley was probably motivated by the circumstances of their lives: their revolutionary zeal and their ebullient personalities. Su's own career might also be said to have been guided by the same desire to combine patriotism with literature. He believed that translations of *Childe Harold's Pilgrimage* and Shelley's *A New World* could make the Chinese people recognize the innate dignity and enthusiasm of the youth of other nations.''

Mary (Gladys Meredith) Webb

1881-1927

English novelist, essayist, poet, critic, and short story writer.

Webb was an early twentieth-century regional novelist whose works explored human relationships against the eloquently depicted background of her native Shropshire. Writing in an era when novels of rural life were very popular, Webb produced works infused with her personal vision of nature, an unusual frankness regarding sexuality, and a wide knowledge of the history, topography, and folklore of the rural area where she spent most of her life. Although she forged no new paths in literature, Webb's novels are considered preeminent examples of local color fiction, and she has been praised in recent years for the serious consideration that she gave to everyday life in her work.

Webb was the oldest of six children born to a Leighton, Shropshire, schoolmaster and his wife. Except for two years spent at a private girls' school, she was educated at home. In 1895, when a debilitating accident left her mother a semi-invalid, the fourteen-year-old girl assumed many of the household's responsibilities until she was herself incapacitated by illness at twenty. Diagnosed as having Grave's disease, a thyroid condition characterized by physical weakness, protruding eyes, and goiter, Webb was bedridden intermittently for several years, and during her convalescence began writing the essays that were later published as *The Spring of Joy*. Never entirely free of the effects of her disease, Webb became acutely self-conscious about her altered appearance—obsessively so, according to some biographers. Critics maintain that the spiritually beautiful but physically disfigured heroines of her novels reflect Webb's self-image, which may have been unnecessarily harsh: contemporaries have written that during her healthiest periods the external signs of her hyperthyroidism were barely noticeable.

After recuperating from her first major bout of illness, Webb remained somewhat retiring, and spent much of her time writing essays and poetry. Her reclusive nature was reinforced by her family's move to a remote house in Stanton, described by one family member as "five miles from anywhere." As Webb's health gradually improved she became involved in church activities and began publishing poems in the Stanton parish magazine. However, she remained devoted to her home and family, and in particular to her father, who was the model for the "visionary mystic" John Arden of her first novel, *The Golden Arrow*. Biographers agree that Webb was helped in overcoming severe depression at her father's death by her growing involvment with the schoolmaster Henry Bertram Law Webb, whom she met in 1910 and married in 1912. Following her marriage Webb began to write fiction, publishing five novels between 1916 and 1924. After her death from pernicious anemia, brought on by her thyroid condition, a novel fragment, poetry, and some short stories were found and published.

Webb's novels share a number of characteristics, in particular the use of her native Shropshire as a setting, a tendency toward didacticism and authorial intrusiveness, and the repetition of several themes regarding individual spirituality. Critics disagree, however, on whether these similarities from novel to

novel indicate artistic consistency of vision or a lack of development on Webb's part. Webb's vivid evocation of the Shropshire countryside is most often singled out for praise. She interwove details about the distinctive topography, customs, legends, folklore, and dialect of this English-Welsh border region into all her works. This skilled use of local color is often cited as lending an air of realism to works that, noticeably lacking in social awareness and contemporary detail, often seem vaguely mythic or founded in fable. Webb's earliest novels are generally assessed as fairly conventional explorations of themes common to fiction of the time, remarkable chiefly for her adept portrayals of locale, her surprisingly frank treatment of sex, and the touches of nature mysticism that inform them. In *The Golden Arrow*, Webb told parallel stories of the courtships and marriages of three couples, contrasting the characters' personalities to illustrate her conviction that only a certain kind of person—one closely attuned to nature—could find true happiness in relationships with others. In *Gone to Earth* and *Seven for a Secret*, Webb portrayed a heroine unable to decide between two men who love her: one who embodies primarily physical passion and the other whose purely spiritual love has little of fleshly desire in it. Webb's forthright discussion of sexuality led many early commentators to hastily explain that she was not writing *about* sex, but only acknowledging its importance in human relationships. Webb's third novel, *The House in Dormer Forest*, has been described as a standard Gothic tale, with a heroine rescued from the stifling confines of her gloomy, mystery-haunted ancestral home by a dashing hero. This novel has been commended, however, for its theme of the importance of individual consciousness in opposition to what Webb referred to as the "herd mind."

Webb's last completed novel, *Precious Bane*, is generally considered her best work. It was the only one of her novels to attract much notice during her lifetime and was awarded the Femina Vie Heureuse prize by the Institut Français as "the best imaginative work in prose or verse descriptive of English life by an author who has not gained sufficient recognition." The novel is comprised of both a love story and a tragedy. Prudence Sarn's "precious bane" is the harelip that causes others to shun her. She longs to have the deformity corrected, but does not regret having experienced an affliction that led her, through enforced solitude, to develop an introspective and spiritual temperament. Prudence's brother Gideon suffers the bane of lust for money. He sacrifices normal human relationships to his overwhelming desire to amass wealth, destroying the lives of his lover and child and ultimately killing his mother and himself. Superstitious neighbors accuse the deformed Prudence of causing the deaths through witchcraft and nearly kill her before she is rescued by the weaver Kester Woodseaves, whom Prudence has loved secretly without knowing that he has come to love her for the beauty of her soul. Although melodramatic in plot, as are all of Webb's novels, *Precious Bane* avoided many of the faults common to the earlier works. For example, Webb employed a first-person narrator for the first time. In the earlier novels, her tendency to comment editorially on her characters' actions disrupted the flow of narrative. However, *Precious Bane* is related by Prudence Sarn as an old woman near the end of her life, and the editorializing is more appropriately attributed to a central figure in the action. Critics have found, too, that in this novel Webb employed local color with a lighter hand, introducing just enough particulars of locale and custom to enhance the story and facilitate the plot, without overburdening the novel with meticulous detail. In her evident desire to tell the most effective story possible, she even took some liberties with local superstitions. For example, she portrayed the Welsh custom of "sin-eating" at a funeral bier, even though this practice no longer occurred in the novel's time period, in order to provide a vivid and compelling symbol of Gideon's willingness to imperil his soul in his quest for wealth.

Webb's career has undergone two posthumous revivals of interest: the first shortly after her death when Britain's prime minister, Stanley Baldwin, praised her work in a public address; and the second in the late 1970s and early 1980s, when feminist critics began reexamining the careers of many neglected women writers. Neither of these revivals, however, was predicated on literary concerns. Baldwin's favorable response reflected the pleasure of a Shropshire native encountering descriptions of "that part of the world which I know and love so well," while the feminist studies focus primarily on her portrayals of women's lives or on her own accomplishments as a working woman. While these extraliterary aspects of Webb's novels are of sociological and biographical interest, they do not bear directly on the artistic value of the novels. According to Patricia Beer, Webb's novels "are not very good, and no amount of drawing attention to them or talking of neglected talent will make them so." Most commentators have not been so negative in final assessment. It has been suggested that the attention Baldwin drew to Webb had a deleterious

effect on her standing as a novelist. Although his praise brought her name to wider public attention, some commentators maintain that the literary establishment resented a politician's encroachment upon their territory and tended therefore to deride the author who was favored by the prime minister. Nevertheless, when the rural novel enjoyed a period of popularity during the Georgian era, Webb's works sold widely. However, Stella Gibbon's satire of the genre, *Cold Comfort Farm*, published in 1932, signaled a decline in its popularity and the preference for novels with urban themes and settings during World War II eclipsed the vogue of the rural novel, and for nearly fifty years after her death, Webb's works retained primarily historical significance. In recent years, however, renewed interest in the genre of rural fiction, together with widespread research into the careers of women writers, has led to the republication of many of her works and positive reappraisals of her accomplishments in literature.

(See also *Dictionary of Literary Biography*, Vol. 34: *British Novelists, 1890-1929: Traditionalists*.)

PRINCIPAL WORKS

The Golden Arrow   (novel)   1916
Gone to Earth   (novel)   1917
The Spring of Joy   (essays)   1917
The House in Dormer Forest   (novel)   1920
Seven for a Secret   (novel)   1922
Precious Bane   (novel)   1924
Poems, and the Spring of Joy   (poetry and essays)   1928
The Collected Works of Mary Webb. 7 vols.   (novels,
    poetry, essays, and short stories)   1928-29
Armour Wherein He Trusted   (unfinished novel)   1929
Fifty-One Poems   (poetry)   1946
Mary Webb: Collected Prose and Poems   (short stories,
    essays, reviews, and poetry)   1977

THE NEW YORK TIMES BOOK REVIEW   (essay date 1917)

[*In the following excerpt, the reviewer notes some praiseworthy qualities of* The Golden Arrow.]

The novel [*The Golden Arrow*] is at its best in the beginning, for it is one of those books which seem never quite to get anywhere. Several of the characters, especially Deborah, her father and her matter-of-fact mother, are well drawn; the vivid, selfish Stephen of the opening chapters is real, but the reader finds his later development difficult to credit. There are some interesting pictures of life in the remote Welsh countryside which is the scene of the entire narrative, quite a number of unusually well-written passages, and altogether the book is a thoughtful one, possessed of many commendable qualities.

> A review of "The Golden Arrow," in The New York Times Book Review, *May 6, 1917, p. 183.*

THE DIAL   (essay date 1917)

[*In the following excerpt, an American critic regrets the sentimentality in* Gone to Earth, *noting that this flaw was absent from Webb's first novel*.]

Strange that the English, steeped in ancestry and civilization, should write so far more poignantly of the hold upon man of the primitive and the things of earth, than we, the pioneers. Mary Webb is one of these more sympathetic English. In *Gone to Earth* . . . she writes of her corner of the Welsh mountains with a very real understanding of the country folk, and also, alas, with unmistakable sentimentality. This is the more regrettable in that her earlier novel [*The Golden Arrow*] was free from false emotionalism and exaggerated pathos. *Gone to Earth* suffers from both these faults.

> *A review of "Gone to Earth," in* The Dial, *Vol. LXIII, No. 749, September 13, 1917, p. 220.*

THE NATION   (essay date 1917)

[*In the following excerpt, the critic emphasizes the pessimism of* Gone to Earth.]

The Hazel Woodus of *Gone to Earth* is [a] victim of childish simplicity and passion. As in her earlier novel, *The Golden Arrow,* the author has employed a rustic English scene suggestive of Mr. Phillpotts's Dartmoor, but narrower and more gloomy, its very sunlight a treacherous and ironical force. "Small, feckless clouds were hurried across the vast untroubled sky—shepherdless, futile, imponderable—and were torn to fragments on the fangs of the mountains, so ending their ephemeral adventures with nothing of their fugitive existence left but a few tears." Thus, in the opening sentence, the sad note of the chronicle is struck. Beautiful Hazel, with her gypsy inheritance, is doomed from the outset. Her capacity for joy and kindness is to win her nothing better than marriage with a pure-hearted and futile young parson, later enslavement to a strong and brutal male, and a ruthless quietus at the moment when life begins to have some sort of meaning for her. On the whole, the "localism" of this writer is hardly more than a garb for her bitter distrust of human nature and society. More than once she gives vent to this bitterness in passages like this: "For civilization as it now stands is based solely on this one thing—vicarious suffering. From the central doctrine of its chief creed to the system of its trade; from the vivisection table to the consumptive genius dying so that crowds of fat folk may get his soul in a cheap form, it is all built up on sacrifice of other creatures." Poor Hazel's death is itself a sort of protest against the established cruelty of life. (p. 317)

> *"Among the 'Localists'," in* The Nation, New York, *Vol. CV, No. 2725, September 20, 1917, pp. 316-17.*

EDWIN PUGH   (essay date 1923)

[*In the following excerpt, Pugh, who was a friend of Webb, offers an enthusiastic appreciation of her work.*]

To pass from the work of the average modern novelist to the work of Mary Webb is like stepping out of a stuffy room into the fresh air. Behind us is the hectic glare and sticky heat of artificial light and fire; before us, the golden glory and still beauty of the dayspring.

There never was an author in closer kinship with nature. The palpable hills and streams, fields and forests, flowers and fruit, the impalpable skies and winds, mists and clouds, sun and shade, all alike are real and living in her eyes as sentient creatures. From the beginning of consciousness Nature must have become for her, as for Amber Darke in *The House in Dormer Forest,* "not a fortuitous assemblage of pretty things,

but a harmony, a poem solemn and austere. It was for her no longer a flat painting on the wall of life. Beauty breathed there, light shone there that was not of the flower or the star. A tremor, mysterious and thrilling, seemed to run with the light through all matter." . . . "The understanding of beauty is a priesthood," says our author in another place, and surely she is vowed to that high calling. She speaks of hills that "lay under the sun like ripe plums in a huge basket"; of "sheep that looked up in a contemplative, ancient way, like old ladies at a concert with their knitting"; . . . of a plain that was "rimmed with sorrowful blue—the blue of swallows that flash and are gone; the blue of drowned forget-me-nots; the faded blue of old men's eyes; the blue, lucent and pure, of a child's veins; all mingled, running into one another beyond the cloud shadows, all gathered into one sad, perfect circle"; . . . of "tormented trees, where ran the furious electric wind, like a hunting leopard."

These are but a few of the daring images, mournful, gay, bodeful, menacing, whimsically humorous, sombrely profound, but always apposite, that scintillate with the sudden brilliance of lightning at a touch from the magic of Mary Webb's genius. And I have, as it were, flung them down haphazard on the threshold of this temple I would raise in her honour in the faint hope that these scattered gems may serve as samples of her boundless store of like treasures.

But she is no mere artificer in words. That her greatness is not yet acclaimed is because, as it seems to me (to quote her words), "in the world of art and letters . . . the artist must elbow and push. . . . If he did not often stop his honeyed utterance to shout his wares he would not be heard at all." Unfortunately for Mary Webb, but more unfortunately still for those who as yet know nothing of her work, no one—not even her bitterest enemy—if it were barely possible to think of Mary Webb as having enemies—would gainsay that she is as incapable of the methods of the hustler as one of her own violets. Indeed her modesty is almost maddening (to me, anyhow), and would be embarrassing if it were not so essentially a part of her strong shy personality, the grace and charm of her gentle ways and simple manners. . . .

Doubtless her native talents are largely the heritage of her race that is bred of the soil; for she was born of an ancient yeoman line, and has lived for the most part of her life, for certainly that most vital part of her life, her childhood, on Wenlock Edge and in other country homes in one of the Welsh marches. (p. 7)

Mary Webb, by thought and study and labour, by the exercise of her every faculty of mind and heart, by the quickening of her spirit and the nurture of her soul, has cultivated her God-given gifts to the highest pitch of excellence. She has the full dower of the poet and seer: wit and wisdom, humour and fancy, the twin senses of tragedy and comedy, and those attributes of human sympathy and divine compassion which are born only of a full understanding and great love. She has not yet taken her place in the hierarchy of literature. Says she: "Material conquest usually means spiritual defeat." She has her reward in that knowledge which is power, a power mightier than the sword, mightier even than the money-bags.

Mrs. Webb has written four novels, including *Seven for a Secret,* and one nature-book, besides poems and a few short stories and essays. I read her first novel, *The Golden Arrow,* quite by chance. It is part of my daily work to read novels, and consequently I read so many of them that I remember very, very few. But no one, having read it, could forget *The Golden*

Arrow. I forgot its title. I forgot the name of the author. The only thing I did not forget was the book itself, the story, the people, the atmosphere, the power and the charm. After nearly five years of vain seeking I did at last get hold of that book once more. And I have read it again—and again. I have now read nearly all that Mrs. Webb has written; and before I proceed further I would say at once that my only aim and purpose in writing this appreciation is to declare that if my judgment counts for anything, Mary Webb is one of the greatest of English novelists in this genre.

This is not to depreciate her contemporaries, especially those other women novelists who seem to me to be doing far better work than the men novelists nowadays. But most of them, women and men alike, are too preoccupied with that sentimentalised form of concupiscence which they miscall Love to see things in their true proportions. They lack the clearsightedness and poise of Mary Webb. She is far from blind to the urgent facts of passion and its immense influence in the scheme of sex relationship. She deals with it in plain downright fashion. "It inna talking straight that's indecent," says the noble Deborah to the ignoble Lily in *The Golden Arrow.* "It's smiling and sniggering and colouring up over things." . . .

I want to tell you how Mary Webb's stories hold and grip you from the first word to the last by sheer dint of their humanism. There is hardly a false touch, a blundering step, in all their progress from their felicitous beginning to their inevitable end. It is as if you followed an inspired guide over such difficult territory that only genius could reveal its manifold new aspects.

And as Mary Webb goes with you through these mazy wildernesses of poignant beauty her words ring out like peals of bells illuminating the silence. . . .

I would have liked to add a few words about Mary Webb's poetry. My love of poetry is like the love of a dog for its master: instinctive rather than intelligent, but wholly sincere and sometimes even passionate. So there is just one poem I must cite: **"An Old Woman."** She lies dead, and they bring her flowers—"more flowers than she in all her life possessed," and "now she sleeps in them, and cannot see or smell or touch. . . . They give her tears—affection's frailest flowers." . . .

Mary Webb, who wrote these lines, is still young and in the sweet of life. And the days of the bourgeoning spring are upon us, and summer's crown of roses, and the golden aftermath of harvest-home. (p. 8)

> Edwin Pugh, "Mary Webb," in The Bookman, London, Vol. LXIV, No. 379, April, 1923, pp. 7-8.

L. P. HARTLEY   (essay date 1924)

[*Author of the acclaimed novel trilogy* Eustace and Hilda *(1944-47), Hartley was an English novelist and short story writer whose fiction is unified by the theme of the search for individuality and meaning in the post-Christian era. In his examination of moral dilemmas he is often compared to Nathaniel Hawthorne, while his effective use of symbolism and close attention to craft and plot unity evoke frequent comparisons to the works of Henry James. A literary critic as well, Hartley contributed reviews for many years to the* Saturday Review, Time and Tide, *the* Spectator, *and other periodicals. In the following excerpt, he praises the biblical style, lyrical mood, and regional colloquialisms of* Precious Bane.]

Precious Bane has many qualities which, though not pernicious in themselves, require careful handling, and when present in

the work of the inexpert are very tiresome indeed. It is Biblical in style, lyrical in mood, and is written in an archaic dialect and in a tone of voice—the intonation of someone who, though brought up in it all his life, is for ever finding out fresh facts about the countryside. Unassimilated fragments of folklore; curious customs culled from diverse centuries; proverbs and wise saws made unfamiliar by local words; attractive tit-bits from the antiquary's store—these are some of the features usually found in novels of this class. They are to be found in *Precious Bane;* but how transfigured, how reanimated, how refreshed! Mrs. Webb makes them an aid, not a bar, to the development of her theme. We do not ask ourselves whether the people of Shropshire about 1815 believed in wizards; we only feel how awkward it was for Mr. Beguildy that his wife scouted his pretensions to occult power. The office of sin-eater was a terrible one, but our chief concern is how it will affect the life of Gideon Sarn, who thus piously took upon himself the burden of his father's misdeeds. In fact the story and the costume fit each other perfectly.

The excellence of its love scenes alone would make *Precious Bane* a memorable book. They have a Meredithian quality in that they kindle anticipation and recollection: they are a secret thought, a secret longing, seldom indulged because the mere knowledge that they are there to be called upon is pleasure enough. The language of love is at the command of most novelists; but in how few do we feel, as we feel here, the quickening of being, the expectation of delight, the minutes flying, the whole unanalyzable process by which the various currents of consciousness lose their wearisome independence, unite, and flow to one object. "His voice made its own summer": how evocative the phrase is, how it recaptures the breath of halcyon days, proclaiming at once the variety and the unmistakableness of love, setting it apart, the accompaniment of nothing, the end of everything. "Love is the peace to which all hearts do strive." *Precious Bane* is an amplification and an exposition of this fine saying.

> L. P. Hartley, "Sacred and Profane Love," in The Spectator, Vol. 133, No. 5014, August 2, 1924, p. 168.

JOSEPH COLLINS   (essay date 1924)

[*Collins is an American physician and essayist who has written the literary studies* The Doctor Looks at Literature *(1923),* Taking the Literary Pulse *(1924), and* The Doctor Looks at Biography *(1925). In the following excerpt, Collins criticizes Webb for what he considers her lack of development as a novelist.*]

It is always fascinating to attempt to explain why a deserving writer is not read. It has the same lure as riddle-guessing, puzzle-solving and prophesying. Mrs. Mary Webb has small acquaintance here, and it, I fear, is merely a bowing one; perhaps it is because the promise of her first book has not been redeemed and perhaps it is because she has not been able to put heroic notes in them that novels of the kind she writes should have. If British women novelists had to be counted on the fingers, she would have to be given a finger, but the digit allotted her may soon be appropriated by some one else unless she does something equal to *The Golden Arrow* and *Gone to Earth.*

Were it not that we are wax in the hands of maxims, as many believe we are in the hands of taboos, we would not profess astonishment on finding that a writer's last books are not so good as the first. Practice does not always make perfect. It has done nothing for Mrs. Webb save to make her more ecstatic, to increase her sensibility to the charm of nature and make her more determined to put it in words. As her prose was from the beginning too ecstatic and her description of nature suggestive of obsession one is forced to admit she has involuted as a novelist rather than developed.

Gone to Earth lends itself best to the display of her particular talent. The story gives free play to her nature-rapture—not only in mere descriptions but in the wealth of folk-lore and superstition which she has woven into it and in the temperament and the life of the heroine. Hazel, half-gipsy, and innocent of education and civilisation, is a sort of modern wood-nymph with all the fascination of a romantic, imaginative child's soul in the body of a beautiful young animal. Looked at as a prose idyl rather than as a possible story, it is full of charm for the person who likes that kind of reading. As a human Hazel is about as probable in this age, even in the most primitive part of rustic England, as Little Red Riding-Hood.

The author has a romantic and almost archaic love of villains and super-good men of the innocuous, spiritless kind. Edward Marston, the young minister, represents the maximum of her art in this line. He marries the artless Hazel with the promise and intention of making a "sister" of her until she herself elects to change her status. Instead, he makes a goddess of her, going after her and taking her back into her high place after the villain Reddin, who is a hunting, sporting squire of forty, has magnetised her into going with him, and even receiving her back a second time after she has returned to Reddin of her own accord. . . . (pp. 208-09)

Taken as a bit of fancy, as a vehicle for the expression of a poetic imagination associated with the love of nature and of the folk-lore of the country people she describes, *Gone to Earth* has great charm. The plot shows lack of imagination and of experience, and the characterisation does not invite serious consideration.

The Golden Arrow, Mrs. Webb's first book, . . . is a simple study of character development presented through sharply defined contrasts. The four young people whose courtship and early married life form the theme of the story represent four distinct and not rare types. In real life, of course, such clearcut types of any class are seldom found, but the infinite complexities and gradations of reality spoil fiction, and these four form convincing representatives of fairly common classes. (pp. 209-10)

In *The House in Dormer Forest* Mrs. Webb made an obvious effort to make her menu at once more appetizing and more nourishing. Doubtless she had read psychology and had been impressed, perhaps one might say awed, by some of its pronouncements. (p. 212)

The scenes, the settings, the characters vary little in Mrs. Webb's books. They are like plays given by the same company in theatres of a country town. The subject also is invariable, but in *The House in Dormer Forest* it is handled as if Mrs. Webb knew more about it than when she wrote *The Golden Arrow.* (p. 213)

Mrs. Webb's last book, *Seven for a Secret,* does not reveal the development which one was entitled to expect from the writer of five novels. Indeed, comparison of it with *The Golden Arrow* is unfavourable to it. It might almost be said that steady retrogression marks the course of her five novels, all published within seven years. The same care as to detail and background

that marked the first book are to be noted, but one feels that, even more than in that book, the interminable descriptions of scenery have no essential, in fact little vital connection with the theme of the story. Scenery is still an obsession, but it is more of a habit, and less of an inspiration, than in her early work.

The Golden Arrow left the reader with a certain impatience due to the feeling that the emotional tension which the author had set herself to produce was only sustained by a studied effort to wring out of the given setting and characters more violent reactions than one was justified in expecting from them. This same straining for effort is multiplied many times in *Seven for a Secret.* The result is that instead of heightening the reader's suspense by reserving the why and wherefore of the story until the very last pages, the thread of interest is drawn out very thin, so thin at times as all but to snap with the query as to whether or not the story is worth finishing at all.

Scenery and manners form the strong features of the book. . . . (pp. 215-16)

One hesitates giving up going to a hotel where he has often been because once or twice he got an uncomfortable room and an unwholesome meal. But no one will keep up his patronage if bed and board are always poor, unless there is assurance of fresh furnishings and a new chef.

Mrs. Webb should refurnish, perhaps remodel, her literary house; and her servants have outlived their usefulness. (p. 218)

> Joseph Collins, "Reading Matter for Invalids and the Novels of Mrs. Mary Webb," in his Taking the Literary Pulse: Psychological Studies of Life and Letters, George H. Doran Company, 1924, pp. 207-18.

STANLEY BALDWIN   (essay date 1928)

[*Baldwin was a British statesman and writer chiefly remembered for his settlement of war debts with the United States following World War I. A Conservative member of Parliament from 1908, he became prime minister in 1923 and, though succeeded for one term by Ramsay MacDonald, was again prime minister from 1924 to 1929, and from 1935 to 1937. After Webb's death, Baldwin's enthusiastic public mention of her work is credited with instigating widespread interest in her writing. In the following excerpt from his introduction to* Precious Bane, *Baldwin praises the local color aspects of Webb's fiction.*]

The stupid urban view of the countryside as dull receives a fresh and crushing answer in the books of Mary Webb. All the novels except *Precious Bane* are set in the hill country of southwest Shropshire, between the Clee Hills and the Breiddens, and between Shrewsbury and Ludlow. The scene of *Precious Bane* is the country of north Shropshire meres—the Ellesmere district, but the dialect is that of south Shropshire. It is the country of the Severn lowlands and of isolated upland ridges where Celt and Saxon have met and mingled for centuries. For the passing traveller it is inhabited by an uncommunicative population dwelling among places with names like Stedment and Squilver and Stiperstone, Nipstone and Nind. There are of course the old castles and timbered black and white houses for the motoring visitors. But to the imaginative child brought up among the ploughlands and pools and dragonflies there is "a richness on the world, so it looked what our parson used to call sumptuous." It is this richness which Mary Webb saw and felt as a girl and remembered with lyrical intensity as a woman.

She has interlaced with this natural beauty the tragic drama of a youth whose whole being is bent on toil and thrift and worldly success only to find himself defeated. . . . (pp. x-xi)

One reviewer compared *Precious Bane* to a sampler stitched through long summer evenings in the bay window of a remote farmhouse. And sometimes writers of Welsh and Border origin, like William Morris, have had their work compared to old tapestries. But while these comparisons suggest something of the harmonies of colour they fail to convey the emotional force which glows in these pages. Nature to Mary Webb was not a pattern on a screen. Her sensibility is so acute and her power over words so sure and swift that one who reads some passages in Whitehall has almost the physical sense of being in Shropshire cornfields.

Precious Bane is a revelation not of unearthly but of earthly beauty in one bit of the England of Waterloo, the Western edge, haunted with the shadows of superstition, the legendary lore and phantasy of neighbours on the Border, differing in blood and tongue. This mingling of peoples and traditions and turns of speech and proverbial wisdom is what Mary Webb saw with the eye of the mind as she stood at her stall in Shrewsbury market, fastened in her memory, and fashioned for us in the little parcel of novels which is her legacy to literature. (pp. xi-xii)

> Stanley Baldwin, in an introduction to Precious Bane by Mary Webb, E. P. Dutton & Company, Inc., 1929, pp. ix-xii.

ROBERT LYND   (essay date 1929)

[*Lynd, an Irish journalist and author, served as literary editor of the* London News Chronicle *and contributed regularly to the* New Statesman and Nation *under the pseudonym "Y. Y." Primarily an essayist, Lynd cultivated the conversational style of Charles Lamb; his work is imaginative and gently whimsical. His many miscellaneous essay collections, among them* The Pleasures of Ignorance *(1921) and* In Defense of Pink *(1937), indicate his eclectic interests. His literary criticism has been called by J. B. Priestley "acute, witty, yet tolerant." In the following excerpt, Lynd discusses Webb's abilities as a novelist.*]

Mary Webb had that always fascinating quality of genius—imaginative energy. It is a quality so precious that, when an author possesses it, the waves of criticism beat against his work in vain. . . . There are other qualities as enchanting in literature—wisdom, humour, and observation without fear or favour—but there is no other quality that, by itself, exercises such power over us.

I do not suppose that many of the admirers of the work of Mary Webb—and they were a larger multitude during her lifetime than is generally realized—if asked to express an opinion as to which is the best of her books, would name *Seven for a Secret*. Yet in its pages what a tempestuous energy storms through that landscape "between the dimpled lands of England and the gaunt purple steeps of Wales—half in Faery and half out of it!" Gillian Lovekin, the farmer's daughter, may be a fool from the beginning—a greater fool, indeed, than Mary Webb supposed her to be—but at least she is a fool to whom we can no more be indifferent than we can be indifferent to a gale that blows a house down. Not that Gillian is magnificently ruinous: she is no Helen of Troy. She is petty even in the magnitude of her ambition—as petty as a parish Hedda Gabler. She has, when we meet her first, no real ambition, except to be a greater Gillian Lovekin and to escape from the farm that

is too small a stage for her. . . . "She wanted," we are told, "to make men and women hear her, love her, rue her." It is probably a common enough daydream of egotists of both sexes, and with most of them it remains a daydream. But Gillian put her egotism into practice, and began by causing the death of the elderly gentleman who wooed her aunt with readings from Crabbe and by the end of the story had caused a murder.

The story would have been a sordid one if Mary Webb, with her imaginative and fantastic gifts, had not exalted it into a tale of the conflict between light and the powers of darkness in a setting in which Gillian's lover's house is like a refuge of the sun, and the house to which her husband takes her is a predestined habitation of evil spirits. Mr. W. B. Yeats once declared, when defending Synge's *Playboy*, that art is "exaggeration à propos," and *Seven for a Secret* is written in a vein of noble and appropriate exaggeration. . . . Mary Webb has in this book created her characters in a high fervour of the romantic spirit.

This in a novelist is possibly more important than psychology. At least, when it is present, we are less likely to be critical of an author's psychology. We may wonder whether Gillian, at an hour when she was deep in love with Robert Rideout, would have yielded so easily to Elmer on the night of the fair at Weeping Cross, but our doubts are lost in the romance of her subsequent sufferings and salvation. . . . We may not quite believe that Gillian, the egotist, when she finally found safety in Robert Rideout's arms, whispered to him: "Oh, Robert! Robert! The powers of darkness have lost their hold, and I'm not a child of sin any more"; but because of the vehement good faith with which the fable has been told, we do not quarrel with the author for putting into Gillian's mouth a sentence that rounds it off like a moral.

If it is necessary to classify novelists—and we all attempt to do it—Mary Webb must be put in a class that contains writers so different as Emily Brontë and Thomas Hardy, for whom the earth is predominantly a mystery-haunted landscape inhabited by mortals who suffer. To class her with these writers is not to claim that she is their equal: all that we need claim is that her work is alive with the fiery genius of sympathy, pity and awe. There is scarcely a scene in *Seven for a Secret* that some touch of poetic observation does not keep alive in the memory. The characters, as I have suggested, may seem at times a little fabulous, but with what a poetic intensity of emotion she compels us to believe in the scenes in which they take part! It is not too much, indeed, to say that in her writings fiction became a branch of poetry—a flowering branch that will still give pleasure for many years to come. (pp. 11-13)

> Robert Lynd, in an introduction to Seven for a Secret: A Love Story by Mary Webb, Jonathan Cape, 1929, pp. 11-13.

HILDA ADDISON   (essay date 1931)

[*Addison is the author of the first critical biography of Webb. In this study she devotes separate chapters to Webb's life and character, her novel* Precious Bane, *her poetry, her quality of humor, the religious development evident in her works, and her portrayals of relationships between men and women. In the following excerpt, Addison examines Webb's forthright treatment of sexual themes.*]

From *The Golden Arrow* to *Armour Wherein He Trusted* [Mary Webb's] work is fraught with the significance of "the world-old conflict between sex and altruism."

She shares a tendency common to most contemporary writers of fiction in treating of sex with extreme frankness, though a beauty of touch and depth of understanding—by no means common characteristics—lend an added richness to an interpretation peculiarly her own. There are those who, while admiring her genius, are constantly repulsed by what they conceive to be too obvious an emphasis laid upon physical passion. Clearly it was a subject which interested her, just as the idea of marriage interested Charlotte Brontë. The novels, short stories, and even the poems are witnesses to this very obvious fact, and also to one of her finest characteristics, namely, an unflinching candour. In her humour and pathos, in the dramatic situations with which the stories abound, as well as in the lively dialogue, she was drawing from actual experience and from a wealth of knowledge accumulated by shrewd untiring observation. It was scarcely to be expected that in these days when reserve has—at any rate, temporarily—been thrown overboard, a woman remarkable for her honesty of spirit should modify her realism when she handled sex. She writes of it as she had observed it in nature and without reticence or squeamishness, conscious of man's affinity to the brute, but consistently revealing herself as the champion of "the small company of men who hold the world back from the beast—the self-givers, the lovers, in whom the flesh and spirit burn together with a steadfast flame and light the earth."

Nevertheless, though this is at the centre of her thought, odd sentences, hints and references as well as special incidents, will occur to the minds of those familiar with the novels, which—on the surface—appear to show an extraordinary absorption in physical passion. The theme of *Gone To Earth* is largely based upon it, viewed from one standpoint. The novel is a study of "over virility" in Jack Reddin, who had "the insensitive nature that could enjoy the physical side of sex without the spiritual," and of misguided, overspiritualized love in Edward Marston. In *Seven For A Secret* Ralph Elmer typifies the sensualist and Robert Rideout the true lover. Again in this novel Mary Webb spares no detail in showing Elmer's passion for Gillian Lovekin. . . . There is the amorous night at "The Drover's Arms" and Gillian's candid reflection in the bitterness of morning that "this was all that lay behind the locked and guarded door that the matrons kept so carefully!" *Armour Wherein He Trusted* contains at least one scene so predominantly sensual in emphasis as to be sheer animalism. The reference is to the incident after Gilbert's marriage to Nesta when he hurries her away to the wood. . . . *The House in Dormer Forest,* too, gains nothing in beauty or literary merit, and little in psychological unfolding, by the inclusion of the absurd scene in the corridor on Ruby Darke's wedding night. There is about it a flippant, ridiculous air, utterly alien to the spirit of Mary Webb, although it is plain that she wishes to expose the horror of a loveless marriage, and contrasts it later in the book with Amber's happy union with Michael.

But those well-bred blue stockings who have, as one has heard, peremptorily dismissed *Gone To Earth* and other of the novels as "too fleshy, my dear, I would never recommend them," must look a little closer if they would understand Mary Webb's outlook on life and in particular her attitude to a very vital element in it. (pp. 139-43)

At the very core of her belief, and affecting her religion, her understanding of nature, her lofty conception of love and marriage, was the conviction that body and spirit are inseparably bound together. For her the flesh was the garment of spirit, the spirit—the life, light, and *raison d'être* of the body. She

believed that they were so fused and intermingled that the sanction of the spirit was a guide, a law, for the flesh, but that the triumph of flesh over spirit inevitably brought its own tragic nemesis. Often she arranges pairs of lovers in juxtaposition so that her ideas shall be thrown up with the clarity of a silhouette. In *The Golden Arrow* Lily Huntbatch is compared with Deborah Arden. This snatch of conversation between the two recently wedded girls reveals the idealism worked out in the story:

> "Stephen's not 'a man.' He's my man. And he's my lad, and my friend." . . . She searched for a way of making Lily understand. "And the lover of my soul," she concluded.
>
> (pp. 143-44)
>
> "I'm thinking it's only then ('when a man's the lover of your soul') as you've a right to be called his wife and sleep along of him."
>
> "You talk very indecent, Deborah, to my thinking."
>
> "It inna talking straight that's indecent; it's smiling and sniggering and colouring up over things."

Thus for common sense, frankness, and no mincing of words. Mary had to be definite because she was proclaiming the faith that was in her, and she desired to make it clear that when "the body and not the soul awoke first," Stephen Southernwood—and anyone else for that matter—"was like a drunkard." And if a reason be necessary for giving the honest details of Gillian's fatal night at "The Drover's Arms," it must be traced back to her unshakable belief in the oneness of body and spirit. Gillian had sacrificed herself "on an altar older than mythology." She had worshipped one who "has lust in her treasury as well as love." Because her relation with Elmer had "no love in it—it was a lamp unlit," and she "found out that she had awakened by the side of the wrong man." All of which is Mary Webb's method of proving (through her narrative) that love means the union of spirit as much as of body, and that physical passion apart from this large interpretation is bitter and unbeautiful.

A little careful thought would dispel the notion that she has over-emphasized sex; rather it is not difficult to imagine cynics sneering at her spiritualization of it. At the beginning of *The House In Dormer Forest* she inscribes the sentence: "Let the sleeping soul awake." This might be taken as an interpretive guide to all her work, in which, though sex may play an important part, it can never truthfully be claimed that undue emphasis marks its physical aspect. Always, whether we like them or not, the references, incidents, and general themes—as for example the greater part of *Gone To Earth*—will be found to show either the littleness of physical union apart from love, or its mystic sacramental beauty when given the full scope of a rich comradely marriage. The freedom of the experimentalists is once more pitted against the conservatism of the apostles of restraint, and undoubtedly Mary Webb's novels prove that she is on the side of the latter.

The House In Dormer Forest is as pensive and slow-moving as *Gone To Earth* is brimful of action, but throughout its leisurely movement there is much self-revealing writing for which those who love the author are grateful. Here we find the most attractive pair of lovers she ever depicted, excepting of course her masterpiece, in which Kester Woodseaves and Prudence Sarn gain the love which is "the peace to which all hearts do strive.'' As Kester saw beyond the poor disfigured face of Prue, so Michael's courtship of Amber Darke was a wooing of the spirit as much as the body. (pp. 144-47)

Mrs. Webb constitutes in herself a clear proof of the truth that ''the mystic understands sex better than the sensualist.'' Therefore at the outset a just estimate of the novels is impossible for those who are not prepared to take at least a few steps along the Mystic Way. To say this, however, affords no explanation of the reason why sex occupies so large a portion of her canvas. One might say in facile and obvious argument that any half-dozen novels from a given author would, if they mirrored life at all faithfully, be found to have some reference to this dominating fact in the study of human personality. But sex in Mary Webb's work cannot be dismissed in this superficial way. Mysticism apart, the least critical of readers will have felt that there is a fundamental difference between her conception of the physical and spiritual relationships of men and women and that of most modern novelists.

It is worth noting that if she allows these matters to play an important part in her work it is because they have grown, as her humour did, from the reality of the characterization. The universality of physical passion makes for its unfailingly wide appeal, but leads only halfway to the appreciation of Mary Webb's skilful manipulation. She knew how intrinsic, how vital a part sex plays in the life of country people. She knew the crude level of existence in the dilapidated homes of the Hazel Wooduses; how downright the talk of the Patty Ardens; how sensual the imagination of the Jack Reddins; and—less stressed perhaps, but full of subtle emphasis—the lofty attitude to be found in the minds of the Prue Sarns, the Deborahs, the Kester Woodseaves. Those unfamiliar with village life little realize the fidelity with which these various types are depicted, and, never having met them, are slow in grasping that only the unspoiled country life can produce either Prudence Sarns, or tragic lovers like Tess of the D'Urbervilles and Hazel Woodus. The great bulk of novel readers are town dwellers who live so far from the soil that it is almost impossible for them to understand the particular kind of allurement sex has for the purely rustic character. The factory hand will comprehend the fact that Gideon loved Jancis out of wedlock, that he took Tivvy in the attic, as Peter did Marigold in Dormer Woods, that Jack Reddin lay in wait for Hazel and threw her in the bracken, that Ralph Elmer planned the night at ''The Drover's Arms,'' but to the full understanding of those wild matings, blessed by love or sordid with lust, must be brought a mind familiar with the painful sweetness of country sights and sounds, the rough uneven lanes, alive with the joyous marriage of pollen and pistil in a thousand flowered cups, with the fragrant silence pulsating vitally, drawing—nay, almost driving—lovers into each others' arms. Mary Webb was as much a naturalist as a mystic, and her nearness to, and innate sympathy with, the soil has to be borne in mind when seeking to grasp her understanding of marriage, mating, and offspring. She loved the sonorous hum of the bees in a great ''tossy ball,'' the ''blackbird at his golden weaving,'' the willow wren coquetting with her small head on one side, the riot of colour and perfume, and every beautiful device by which Nature allures her wild children into mating.

But if Mary observed the life of the countryside minutely, she watched the ways of the Shropshire villagers with no less interest. Here she found sex almost as plainly at work as in the meadows and farm-yards. Those qualities in her which encouraged simple ungarnished confidence brought the reward of an astonishingly accurate knowledge of the peasant mind.

Few, if any, genuinely country women would not join in hearty affirmation of Patty Arden's concise summary of—to them—a long accepted philosophy of life:

> there's only three things as matters to a good 'ooman—the bride-bed, the child-bed and the death-bed.

(pp. 148-51)

The Bible is put to many strange uses; it is comparatively rare, however, to find a novelist who is indebted to it in her treatment of sex. To those least familiar with the Bible it will be known that the warmth of Eastern passion is there retold with unabashed Elizabethan candour. Now, when books, places or people influenced Mary Webb they did so in countless unexpected ways, and her nook and corner knowledge of the Bible, besides affecting her thought and style, profoundly affected her here. She, like Edward Marston in *Gone To Earth,* read into Biblical stories their full quota of human longing. . . . [Mary Webb] both knew and loved ''the sweet frank love-stories'' of the Bible. Being honest she loved them for their lack of humbug, being an artist she loved them for their tender beauty. (pp. 152-54)

Finally Mary Webb owes something in her treatment of sex to the Middle Ages. She had not the full equipment of a competent mediaevalist, but her intuitive understanding leapt to the core of what she read, and what she read she mused upon until it became part of her own mind. Thus not only her thought but her style reflects the impression Chaucer, Malory, Richard Rolle, and Julian of Norwich made upon her. From them she drank in the colour, simplicity, candour and homeliness, of those earlier centuries. She could enjoy the wife of Bath as well as the prim little nun.

The mystic is the antithesis of the sentimentalist and can therefore digest stronger meat. So that far from being incongruous it was natural that a mind which fed upon reality should grasp the full flavour of *The Canterbury Tales,* and seeing their vivid counterparts in the life stories of the living pilgrims around her, follow the example of that old historian of human nature, who in telling of man's loves spares no one's blushes. *Armour Wherein He Trusted* bears in its style as well as its theme signs of Mrs. Webb's indebtedness to the past. Here physical passion is shown at its crudest, but as part of the gay, coarse life of those distant half-civilized days, when the very hardness of living brought out the traits of a man's character like bright contrasting colours. Gilbert Polrebec's capacity for self-sacrifice is as vivid as his physical desire. This clarity of outline in character-drawing is mediaeval rather than modern, romantic rather than psychologically accurate.

Mary Webb's attitude to sex, then, was that of a mystic for whom flesh and spirit burn together in a steady flame, and her delineation is reinforced by those books (few but great) from the distant past which had been her spiritual nourishment on the way to mental and moral maturity. These influences fell upon the fertile soil of a perceptive, fearless mind, which not only understood its fellow-creatures, but placed them in the teeming world of nature where sex works its way with continuous though unconscious beauty. (pp. 154-56)

> *Hilda Addison, in her* Mary Webb: A Short Story of Her Life and Work, *Cecil Palmer, 1931, 189 p.*

G. K. CHESTERTON (essay date 1932)

[*Regarded as one of England's premier men of letters during the first half of the twentieth century, Chesterton is best known today*

470

as a colorful bon vivant, a witty essayist, and creator of the Father Brown mysteries and the fantasy The Man Who Was Thursday *(1908). Much of Chesterton's work reveals his childlike joie de vivre and reflects his pronounced Anglican and, later, Roman Catholic beliefs. His essays are characterized by their humor, frequent use of paradox, and chatty, rambling style. In the following excerpt, Chesterton notes the local color aspects of Webb's novel* The Golden Arrow.]

Many of us can remember the revelation of poetical power given to the world with the songs of a Shropshire Lad. Much of the noble, though more neglected, work of Mary Webb might be called the prose poems of a Shropshire Lass. Most of them spoke in the spirit, and many through the mouth, of some young peasant woman in or near that western county which lies, romantic and rather mysterious, upon the Marches of Wales. Such a Shropshire Lass was the narrator of *Precious Bane;* such a one is the heroine, and a very heroic heroine, of *The Golden Arrow.* But the comparison suggested above involves something more than the coincidence of a county and a social type. Those two writers of genius, devoted to the spirit of Shropshire and the western shires, do really stand for two principles in all living literature to-day; and especially in all literature concerned with the very ancient but very modern subject of the peasantry. I do not put them side by side here for comparison in the paltry sense of competition. I have the strongest admiration for both literary styles and both literary achievements. But the comparison is perhaps the clearest and most rapid way of representing what is really peculiar to writers like Mary Webb and to books like *The Golden Arrow.*

There are two ways of dealing with the dignity, the pain, the prejudice or the rooted humour of the poor; especially of the rural poor. One of them is to see in their tragedy only a stark simplicity, like the outline of a rock; the other is to see in it an unfathomable though a savage complexity, like the labyrinthine complexity of a living forest. The Shropshire Lad threw on all objects of the landscape a hard light like that of morning, in which all things are angular and solid; but most of all the gravestone and the gallows. The light in the stories of the Shropshire Lass is a light not shining on things, but through them. It is that mysterious light in which solid things become semi-transparent; a diffused light which some call the twilight of superstition and some the ultimate violet ray of the sixth sense of man; but which the strictest rationalist will hardly deny to have been the luminous atmosphere of a great part of literature and legend. In one sense it is the light that never was on sea or land, and in another sense the light without which sea and land are invisible; but at least it is certain that without that dark ray of mystery and superstition, there might never have been any love of the land or any songs of the sea. Nobody doubts that peasantries have in the past, as a matter of fact, been rooted in all sorts of strange tales and traditions, like the legend of *The Golden Arrow.* The only difference is between two ways of treating this fact in the two schools of rural romance or poetry. For the pessimist of the school of Housman or of Hardy, the grandeur of poverty is altogether in the pathos of it. He is only softened by hard facts; by the hard facts of life and death. The beliefs of the peasant are a mere tangle of weeds at the feet of the pessimist; it is only the unbelief of the peasant, the disillusion and despair of the peasant, which remind the pessimist of dignity and warm him with respect. There is nobility in the benighted darkness of the hero; but there is no light or enlightenment, except from the atheism of the author. The poor man is great in his sufferings; but not in anything for which he suffered. His traditions are a tangle of weeds; but his sorrows are a crown of thorns. Only there is no nimbus round the crown of thorns. There is no nimbus round anything. The pessimist sees nothing but nakedness and a certain grandeur in nakedness; and he sees the poor man as a man naked in the winter wind.

But the poor man does not see himself like that. He has always wrapped himself up in shreds and patches which, while they were as wild as rags, were as emblematic as vestments; rags of all colours that were worn even more for decoration than for comfort. In other words, he has had a mass of beliefs and half-beliefs, of ancestral ceremonies, of preternatural cures and preternatural consolations. It is amid this tangle of traditions that he has groped and not merely in a bleak vacuum of negation; it is in this enchanted forest that he has been lost so long, and not merely on the open moor; and it is in this rich confusion of mystical and material ideas that the rural characters of Mary Webb walk from the first page to the last. (pp. 7-9)

The legend of The Golden Arrow, which lovers went wandering to find, . . . is a myth bearing witness, as do all myths and mythologies, to the ancient beauty for which man was made, and which men are always unmaking. But this mystical or mythological sense would not be genuine, if it did not admit the presence of an evil as well as a good that is beyond the measure of man. One of the things that makes a myth so true is that it is always in black and white. And so its mysticism is always in black magic as well as white magic. It is never merely optimistic, like a new religion made to order. And just as in *Precious Bane,* the old necromancer was driven by an almost demoniac rage to raise up the ghost of the Pagan Goddess, so in *The Golden Arrow* a man is lured into the ancient and mazy dance of madness by that heathen spirit of fear which inhabits the high places of the earth and the peaks where the brain grows dizzy. These things in themselves might be as tragic as anything in the realistic tragedies; but the point to seize is the presence of something positive and sacramental on the other side; a heroism that is not negative but affirmative; a saintship with the power to cast out demons; expressed in that immemorial popular notion of an antidote to a poison and a counter-charm against a witch.

The characterization in *The Golden Arrow,* if rather less in scope than that in *Precious Bane,* is sometimes even more vivid within its limits. The difference between the two girls, brought up under the same limitations, observing the same strict rural conventions, feeling the same natural instincts in two ways which are ten thousand miles apart, is very skilfully achieved within the unities of a single dialect and a single scene. And through one of them there passes, once or twice, like the noise and rushing of the Golden Arrow, that indescribable exaltation and breathing of the very air of better things; which, coming now and again in human books, can make literature more living than life. (pp. 9-10)

> *G. K. Chesterton, in an introduction to* The Golden Arrow *by Mary Webb, Jonathan Cape, 1932, pp. 7-10.*

CORNELIUS WEYGANDT (essay date 1937)

[*Weygandt was an American critic and historian whose* Irish Plays and Playwrights *(1913) has been credited with introducing the new Irish drama of the early twentieth century to the United States. In the following excerpt, he examines Webb's poetry and maintains that she made notable accomplishments in both verse and prose.*]

An enthusiast could make out a plausible case for the priority of Mary Webb . . . among the women who have written verse in English. Beside the one-poem women, like Lady Caroline Nairn, of whom there are perhaps a score, the women poets are surprisingly few. There are Elizabeth Barrett Browning, Emily Brontë, Christina Rossetti, Emily Dickinson, Alice Meynell—but hardly a sixth that one could, in real seriousness, call major. There have been women whose verse bulked big to a day or generation . . . , but they have all shrunk away, or they are fast shrinking away, into mere historical importance. . . . Even the best of the women poets are of a lesser stature entirely than Jane Austen and Charlotte Brontë and George Eliot. . . . Of all the women who have essayed verse and the prose story, Mary Webb alone might be claimed to have an unchallenged place in both fields.

Full of verbal felicities, fresh in imagery, rich in imagination as is the verse of Mary Webb, it shows in nearly every set of verses the absence of a revising hand. *Poems* was published posthumously in 1929. . . . Had she herself gathered her verses together for a volume, she would have noted certain repetitions, the weak insistence on "elphin" things, on intangible presences, on a something discerned in nature beyond the good thing seen by the eyes. There is hardly a set of verses in the eighty-three of *Poems* without the stuff of poetry in them, but the effects of a good many are too closely allied. Had she had a chance to select from her store of them, or to work them over when they came to too like conclusions, there would have been fewer included that progressed after the fashion of a formula.

Mary Webb, is, therefore, better to recall than to reread. She is good to reread, for there is always new phrasing and the catching of some beauty of out-of-doors uncaught before she caught it that had slipped your memory. Rereading though, you come on thinness of matter, the result of an impatience on her part to imprison aspects of landscape and personal moods before they had swum into her ken often enough or returned to her enough times to body themselves into the proportions of a poem. There are poems, of course, which are visitations, but most poems are records of recurrences of sights or emotions or moods that grow with each recurrence until they finally almost say themselves aloud and compel the poet to write them down.

So it is dangerous to send friends who care for poetry, but who have missed this particular poet, to the verse of Mary Webb. She is a poet to read first by accident, with no expectation of a find. If you so come upon her you may escape the sense that there is not enough root in her poetry to bear so much blossom. Beauty of a new kind she has unquestionably, a new ecstasy over out-of-doors and over the wonder of life, but not the perfection in poem after poem that comes with disciplined and mature art. You feel similar imperfections in her prose, particularly in the studies of nature, beautiful here, overwritten there. Even the novels, in whose art she was more practised than in the art of the nature essay or of verse, have a like way of falling below the great and thrilling moments they attain to and lead you to expect they will consistently maintain. *Precious Bane* ∴ . . is the most uniformly of high level of all the stories. *Gone to Earth* . . . hardly makes credible its strange story, and *Seven for a Secret* . . . is an in-and-out sort of book. If it all were of the caliber of that early chapter in which Gillian Lovekin, unawakened, comes with her conies, strung on a wire, through the twilight to Robert, what a book it would be!

In both verse and prose, though, Mary Webb has extended the limits of the art in which she worked; in both she did things that had not been done before; in both she created a new romance. She is sure of a hearing as long as there shall be lovers of beauty in the world.

There are several notes dominant in her verse, none more dominant than that old lament of poetry for the transitoriness of all good things. Perhaps she was aware when she wrote certain of her verses that her days were numbered. Perhaps she wrote in pain. Yet there is no faltering of the spirit or any disloyalty to life.

> June droops to winter, and the sun droops west.
> Flight is our life. We build our crumbling nest
> Beneath the dark eaves of the infinite.

That is her most notable declaration of the sort. (pp. 414-16)

Next oftenest, perhaps, sounds in her verse the intimation of something beyond the thing seen. . . . If there is not this something beyond the thing seen, that thing, good though it is in itself, lacks perfection. In **"To the World"** she cries out against the world that it has taken away her "small ecstasies." Yet Mary Webb can delight greatly in the tangible sweet things of earth. She and her husband were market-gardeners for a while, taking the stuff they raised themselves to Shrewsbury and selling it from a stall in the market there. **"Market Day"** is an idyll in little, charming all the way from onset to finale. (pp. 416-17)

Grove Cottage, where Webb wrote Precious Bane, *sketched by Gladys Mary Coles. From* The Flower of Light: A Biography of Mary Webb, *by Gladys Mary Coles. Duckworth, 1978. Reproduced by permission of Gladys Mary Coles.*

One wonders how many of these country poems, with the hunger for Shropshire in them, were written after their author went, in 1921, to live in London. It was in London that that other poet from the Welsh Marches wrote his *Shropshire Lad* (1896), and it may well be that Mary Webb remembered the blush rose, and the "red fruits of the orchard," and all the hundred and one other country things that so throng all her verse, after they were gone from the sight of her eyes. "**The Happy Life**" and "**You Are Very Brown**" are two of the friendliest of these poems.

There is picture after picture clear in the seeing and equally clear in the rendering in her poetry. Sometimes she flashes one before you in a line, as in "A lone green valley, good for sheep." More often it takes a four-liner to limn it.

There are human dramas in little, too, one of them "**Going for the Milk.**" In this poem of seventeen lines are recounted four chapters of the life story of an old woman in a workhouse who recalls going for the milk as a toddling child, as a girl of seventeen, as a young mother with her first baby sleeping on her arm. Now in her age she is drinking "the pauper's skim." Companion pieces to this are "**An Old Woman,**" and "**The Neighbour's Children,**" studies in pathos both.

There are poems of otherworldliness, too, "**The Land Within,**" "**The Ancient Gods,**" and "**Colomen,**" the last the best of the three. In "**Colomen**" we are with the Pre-Raphaelites again. There are affinities between the work of Mary Webb and that of many poets her elders and betters, Coleridge, Rossetti, Christina Rossetti, William Morris, Emily Brontë, Emily Dickinson, Yeats, and Housman, but she is here nearest to the Pre-Raphaelites. There is something of the color of "The Goblin Market" in "**Colomen,**" if less of magic. There is more of Miss Rossetti's brother here, though, than of Miss Rossetti, and of the Coleridge who was his master. "**Colomen**" is a tale of a sorrow and of a death so remote and so long ago it affects you no more personally than do the old airs haunted with Celtic melancholy. It is pleasantly sad, gently sad, sad in a far-off fashion. . . . Fresher, though, more wholly her own, discovered for herself, are the Shropshire poems, poems all compound of long hours out-of-doors in the southern part of the county. Shropshire has been fortunate indeed in its most recent poets, and it is only just to say that the last of them, Mary Webb, measures up well in comparison with A. E. Housman and John Masefield. (pp. 417-18)

Cornelius Weygandt, "The Latest Phases of English Poetry," in his The Time of Yeats: English Poetry of To-Day Against an American Background, *1937. Reprint by Russell & Russell, 1969, pp. 386-428.*

GLEN CAVALIERO (essay date 1977)

[*An English poet, critic, and former Anglican cleric, Cavaliero is a member of the Faculty of English at Cambridge. A well-read critic, he is the author of acclaimed studies of the works of E. M. Forster, John Cowper Powys, and of the rural tradition in the early twentieth-century English novel. In the following excerpt, Cavaliero examines Webb's five novels and discusses the reasons for the popularity they once enjoyed.*]

Mary Webb . . . is the most well known rural novelist of her time. Her work was popularly supposed to be the chief model for *Cold Comfort Farm,* and she has on occasion been derided for the praise showered upon her by Stanley Baldwin at a Royal Literary Fund dinner. The fame resulting from the latter came seven months after her death, and led to a collected edition of her works, the five novels being installed as classics of the rural school. But, although part of literary legend (as a romantically neglected author—to the pseudo-sophisticated a "primitive" one) and an easy target for ignorant satirists, she had established herself as a rural novelist of repute without the aid of any non-literary publicity. She had won a steady body of admirers long before her death, and was awarded the Femina Vie Heureuse Prize for *Precious Bane* . . . three years before Baldwin was recommended to read it by his secretary.

She was a native of Shropshire, the setting of all her novels and of many of her attractive, highly personal poems. . . . Her last two novels were written while she and her husband were living in Hampstead, but Shropshire remained her inspiration.

Her novels, poems and essays are all propelled by the belief that the world of nature holds a secret not to be found in cities or communities. The opening chapter of her book of essays, *The Spring of Joy* . . . , has as epigraph the words of Sir Thomas Browne: "We live the life of plants, the life of animals, the life of men, and at last the life of spirits." Mary Webb took these words very literally: her belief in the presence of that life informs her poetry and novels alike. In *The Spring of Joy* she writes of it meticulously, in extreme and occasionally obfuscating detail; but this pedantry of the senses is the result of a seriously held belief, one she shares with Richard Jefferies and Llewelyn Powys.

> Life—the unknown quantity, the guarded secret—circles from an infinite ocean through all created things, and turns again to the ocean. This miracle that we eternally question and desire and adore dwells in the comet, in the heart of a bird, and the flying dust of pollen. It glows upon us from the blazing sun and from a little bush of broom, unveiled and yet mysterious, guarded only by its own light—more impenetrable than darkness.

For Mary Webb this inner life is realised in the blossoming of individual consciousness. . . . For the herd is the arch-enemy of individual fulfilment: the novels are insistent on the mindless cruelty of men and women in the mass. . . . The most explicit condemnation of the herd mind comes in *The House in Dormer Forest.* . . . (pp. 133-34)

Mary Webb is rather more than a nature-mystic; she takes her mysticism (so to call this hypersensitiveness to physical shapes and currents) as the basis of a fuller understanding of human life, and all her novels have a strong didactic quality. . . . Her gift lies not so much in simple perceptiveness as in a feeling for the correlation between perceiver and perceived. (p. 135)

The Golden Arrow, Mary Webb's first novel, is the story of Stephen Underwood, a man of intense sensitivity who has no corresponding power of self-expression. Having lived all his life at second-hand until his meeting with the country girl Deborah Arden, he finds himself unable to love her with a strength sufficient to meet and overcome the pressures of uncongenial work and of a landscape which terrifies him. There is an absolute division between what he sees and what he feels; he is too immature in love for the kind of trust and self-forgetfulness of which his wife is capable. But *The Golden Arrow* is memorable less for the story of Stephen and Deborah than for that of the shallow Lily Huntbatch and Deborah's brother Joe, whom she marries; for the descriptions of the landscape of the Shropshire highlands; and for a certain terseness and vigour in the writing which Mary Webb was never to recapture.

This shows itself not only in a command of rapid narrative, but also in a dry humour, as when she observes of Deborah's father that "He was very sensitive about his business faculty, not having any." . . . Had Mary Webb been content to make her points by such strokes of observation and subtle humour, her novels would have been more persuasive than they are.

All of them have elements of the parabolic, *The Golden Arrow* especially. The two girls are sharply, at times crudely, contrasted in character, and so are their fathers, Eli and John. The latter, modelled on the author's own father, is rather sentimentally drawn. . . . Her obsession with the cruelty of life is balanced by a poignant awareness of its beauty. . . . Superficially this passage resembles the work of Hardy; but the whole tone is softer, the rhythms more relaxed; the human element predominates, even to the "climbing" shadows and the "troubled" sky. The scene interprets an interior state.

To say this is to indicate the difference between Hardy and Mary Webb. She is not simply a lesser writer in the same genre, but a novelist who is doing something altogether different. Mary Webb's Shropshire is a land of romance, a region in which her characters act out fantasies of her contriving which can embody more effectively than her highly personal poems her passionate conviction of the kinship between man and nature. In some respects she is closer to Lawrence than to Hardy, for, like Lawrence, she saw in sexual wholeness the proof of a man's capacity to live and to experience.

The point is further developed in *Gone to Earth*. Hazel Woodus, an attractively outspoken gipsy girl, is doomed from the outset, a victim of the insufficient humanity of man. Her seduction by the dissolute Squire Reddin is followed by her unconsummated marriage to the simple preacher, Edward Marston; and the book recounts his tragedy as well as Hazel's. His self-denying consideration is helpless in a world dominated by the ethos of the pack; indeed, his very goodness determines Hazel's unhappy fate. But, as is usual in Mary Webb's work, the male characters are only partially realised, and both Reddin and Marston seem to have stepped out of the pages of some twopenny romance. More successful are the lesser figures, most notably Edward's mother, "who was one of nature's opiates, and . . . administered herself unconsciously to everyone who saw much of her".

> No one ever saw her hurried or busy, yet the proofs of her industry were here. She worked like the coral insect, in the dark, as it were, of instinct unlit by intellect, and, like the coral insect, she raised a monumental structure that hemmed her in.

The wit of this passage is marred by that intrusive attempt at explication, which is a feature of this and the succeeding novel: the point could have been better made without the reference to intellect and instinct. The book's message is hammered home with such insistence that even its comedy is infected with didacticism. (pp. 135-38)

The central weakness of *Gone to Earth* is that Hazel's story is too remote from ordinary human concerns, and is forced to bear a burden of cosmic significance which it cannot really sustain: in this it epitomises the limitations of the rural genre. Moreover, the anthropomorphising of natural forces recoils upon the human protagonists, and all alike are rendered unbelievable. Even in the relatively simple *Golden Arrow* Mary Webb can liken a honeysuckle petal to "the tongue of a faery hound in age-long chase of a deathless quarry"; in *Gone to*

Earth such similitudes are legion, all harnessed with misguided consistency to the central theme of pursuit and chase. A genuine and original sensitivity is being worked to death. (p. 138)

However, there is more to *Gone to Earth* than this. It is swift and vivid, with at times a ballad-like quality. Hazel and her father, the bee-keeper, are not mild and simple creatures in the way that, for example, so many of T. F. Powys's "innocent birds" are: they are tough, lacking in affection for each other, often violent, and only half-aware of their relationship with nature. Hazel's devotion to animals is more questionably handled: the taming of the wild hardly matches her own wildness, and her death, while protecting her pet cub Foxy from the hounds, is too obviously symbolic for entire conviction. There is an element of false picturesqueness about it, betrayed by the careful elaboration of the writing: however passionate the feeling that informs the passage, the catastrophe has been led up to so insistently throughout the book that its final incidence appears contrived.

Still more contrived is *The House in Dormer Forest,* which develops the conflict between the individual and the herd. Dormer Old House, with its hide-bound customs and rigid exclusion of the unorthodox and unexpected, is the symbol of a civilisation ossified. But, whereas the Darke family, conceived deliberately as grotesques (in the manner of the inhabitants of Mervyn Peake's Gormenghast), might have been successful as an image of the herd mentality, as presented realistically they are clearly the chief inspiration for the Starkadder family in *Cold Comfort Farm.* Their vitality is that of brightly painted marionettes. (p. 139)

Although *Seven for a Secret* . . . is more free from didacticism than its two predecessors, there are signs that the author is beginning to repeat herself. Gillian, torn between Rideout and Elmer, is a variation on Hazel torn between Marston and Reddin; Farmer Lovekin has features in common with Solomon Darke. Even Rideout brooding on the moor recalls Enoch Gale, the hired man at Dormer Old House. . . . *Seven for a Secret* would be a more satisfactory book had it attempted less. In essence a straightforward tale of abduction, murder and intrigue, it is invested with a spurious "significance" through Robert's kinship with the moor. The final climax is oddly half-hearted, and out of keeping with the portentous references to it in the earlier part of the novel. As in *The House in Dormer Forest* one is aware of a disintegrated imagination.

Indeed, all four of these novels suffer from the same shortcomings of a sensibility divided against itself. On the one hand they reflect a brisk and humorous vision of human character and behaviour; on the other an ardent and almost anguished susceptibility to the forces of nature. But this susceptibility is essentially a psychological affair. Except in *The Golden Arrow,* Mary Webb's Shropshire, although she was a native of the county, bears little resemblance to the Shropshire landscape as it actually is: it is an interior landscape, a projection of emotions, terrors, above all of a feeling of pity. Hazel's predicament with Foxy is a mirror of her creator's predicament with her own sensitivity. Mary Webb might have been a novelist of rural life and manners, for her knowledge of rural life was first-hand, her acquaintance with ancient customs and intuitive sympathy with them comparable to Hardy's; but alongside this straightforward human responsiveness there existed a fervent romanticism that knew man and nature as parts of a reality greater than either. Her rejection of orthodox religion did not, however, issue in pantheism, but rather in a clothing of the landscape with human attributes, and the belief in a spiritual presence within nature less akin to Pan than to Jesus Christ. And the tension between these two elements in her work, the realistic and the mystical, resulted in the uneasy see-saw between narrative economy and rhetorical didacticism which has been already noted. In part the problem was technical, and the two voices, those of the characters and of the author-commentator, were to be fused by the simple expedient of using a first-person narrative. In *Precious Bane* Prudence Sarn embodies both the homely wisdom of the countrywoman and the fervid romanticism of her creator.

The success of *Precious Bane* is also linked to another problem. In all the earlier books the element of fable had been predominant; but this had been weakened by the awareness that we were also in a contemporary world—or, more strictly, by a failure to imply that we were not. In *Precious Bane,* however, by setting her tale in the time of the Napoleonic wars and after, Mary Webb succeeds in distancing it sufficiently for it to exist in a world that is at once physically real and yet psychologically abstracted. To say that the book attains to the full grandeur of myth would be to praise it beyond its deserts or its intention; but the charm that it still has the power to exert is the charm of a tale which at once establishes its own imaginative world and which, both in the manner and the matter of its telling, illuminates that world's significance.

As a story *Precious Bane* is simple. Gideon Sarn, the young farmer brother of the narrator, Prue, sacrifices his youth, his sweetheart and his family in order to better himself in the world by getting rich—gold is the precious bane; but on the eve of his final achievement his ricks are destroyed by the father of the girl whom he has seduced. The girl's suicide and his own failure cause him to drown himself; and Prudence, with her hare-shotten lip, is nearly drowned also, by the neighbours as a witch. She is saved by the weaver, Kester Woodseaves, whom she loves. The novel is thus as much of an old-fashioned melodrama as is its predecessor; but the conventional plot is here an advantage. It reads like some country ballad, some story told by Hardy; and in its style of narration it evokes the kind of world in which its telling would be natural. Style is indeed the governing element in *Precious Bane.* Everything depends on Prue Sarn and how she tells her story.

Through the use of a deliberately mannered and artificial diction Mary Webb succeeds in combining the two elements in her imaginative world. Prue's speech is lulling and rhythmic, full of old-world turns of phrase, swelling up to periodic intensities, sinking down to quietness. It has the flow of monologue with the fluidity of free association; and the descriptive passages are mediated through the corporate consciousness by the use of local names, quotations of local proverbs, references to local beliefs. Thus even the more implausible people and events are presented with a leaven of worldly wisdom, of matter-of-fact physical detail. The world of the novel is self-contained and self-consistent; it is both factually and imaginatively persuasive. (pp. 141-43)

The attractiveness of *Precious Bane* is bound up with the attractiveness of Prue herself. She might easily have been sentimentalised, being of the breed of the heroically long-suffering who are notoriously a trap for the romantic novelist. But Prue is spirited and stoical, with a vein of humour and no self-pity: her hare-lip is a source of wonder to her as much as heartbreak. Her love-on-sight for Kester is more convincing than that of Amber Darke for Michael Hallowes. Kester, however, remains the most shadowy of the characters in the book: he is seen with the nimbus of Prue's adoration. He is given Christ-like nota-

tions, as when he takes the place of the bull at the baiting, or, more specifically, when Prue refers to him as "the very marrow of Him that loved the world so dear." . . . Kester is a less sombre figure than Michael, and his final appearance when he rescues Prue from the villagers is more like that of St George than of the Jesus of the New Testament. But it is he, and Prue's love for him and his for her, which is the informing spirit of nature in *Precious Bane.* At one point near the end of the book Prue remarks that it seemed as though "Sarn, all the live part of it, us and our beasts, the trees full of birds, and the wood ways with the wild creatures in them, had sunk to the bottom of the mere," and it is when Prue is about to be drowned in the mere that Kester rides up to save her. She undergoes a kind of resurrection.

Precious Bane is the epitome of the rural romance as enjoyed by the early twentieth-century public. It is easy to account for its popularity. Apart from its compelling readability, it told of a vanished past, setting a high value on what was being destroyed. There is no social awareness in Mary Webb's novels, no knowledge shown of agricultural problems, no attempts at social criticism. Whether she would have developed further as a writer is doubtful. Her surviving fragment, *Armour Wherein He Trusted,* is set in the time of the First Crusade, but the voice of the narrator, Gilbert de Polrebec, is the voice of Prudence Sarn. This tale of a young knight's love for a witch maiden carries little imaginative vitality, and the author was disenchanted with it before she died.

The popularity of Mary Webb's novels in the 1930s and 1940s is understandable. She was a genuine original and her work, for all its extravagance, carries imaginative conviction: this is a world believed in, felt with, inhabited. She is an excellent story-teller and treats her characters with respect; and she is free from whimsy. But the rural world that she describes is remote not only in location but also in presentation. There is no real sense of an England existing outside her fictional Shropshire, no sense of that Shropshire being a part of something greater than itself. The world of the novels is entirely self-contained. Hence perhaps their appeal: they are a part, and a not inconsiderable part, of the literature of fantasy and dream. (pp. 144-46)

> *Glen Cavaliero, "Romantic Landscapes: Mary Webb,*
> *E. H. Young," in his* The Rural Tradition in the
> English Novel: 1900-1939, *Rowman and Littlefield,*
> *1977, pp. 133-56.*

GLADYS MARY COLES (essay date 1978)

[*Coles is an English biographer and critic. In her* The Flower of Light: A Biography of Mary Webb, *Coles made use of documentary sources not found by earlier biographers of Webb, including family diaries and letters, and correspondence between Webb and her publishers, finding that "to study her life is to study her work, and conversely, for to an extraordinary degree in Mary Webb life and work are an inseparable whole." In the following excerpt from her biography of Webb, Coles examines* Seven for a Secret, *which she considers an inferior example of Webb's talents, and* Precious Bane, *which she assesses as Webb's finest work.*]

In *Seven for a Secret* we find another variation on a major theme that recurs throughout Mary Webb's work from first novel to last: the antithesis between sacred and profane love. Again in a story of human passion, sacrifice and redemption, this obsessional theme is embedded and her concept of love illustrated—a deeply held conviction intrinsic to her vision of life. The love that ennobles and enriches human relationships is again shown to be primarily, fundamentally, of spiritual quality: without this spiritual union with the other's soul or essential inner being, physical passion (merely the satisfying of sexual urge) is not love, cannot bring lasting harmony, and tragic experience often ensues. For Mary, as we have seen, her view of the nature of human love and passion was an *idée fixe* central to both her life and art.

Gillian Lovekin, the central character of *Seven for a Secret,* is demonstrating the author's concept of love when she is involved in a struggle . . . between the higher and lower in her nature, a struggle that brings suffering to herself and others. . . . Gillian is magnetic, strong-willed, utterly selfish, determined to get everything out of life rather than give to it: insensitive to the steadfast but silent spiritual love of Robert Rideout, her father's cowman-shepherd, she is lured by the sexual attraction of wealthy Ralph Elmer, who seduces her. . . . Gillian emerges from the tangle of lust and sin to higher being and new life in union with Robert. The relationships of Gillian, on the one hand with Ralph Elmer and on the other with Robert Rideout, form the hub of the book's meaning. [In a footnote, the critic adds: "Looked at another way *Seven for a Secret* is something of a *bildungsroman,* the unheroic heroine being educated by experience, her adventures transforming her from a selfish adventuress into a chastened lover eager to make the most of her second chance with Rideout."]

Seven for a Secret is as much the story of the passionate poet Rideout (loved by the dumb, doomed Rwth) as it is of the self-centred Gillian. Rideout endures anguish, Rwth dies and Gillian, redeemed by love, does not escape unscathed. As in all Mary Webb's novels, suffering is the index of inner development, of the progression of her characters to fuller vision and deeper insight.

Together with the major theme of the nature of love, this associated theme of the significance of suffering is . . . of central importance in Mary Webb's reading of human experience: as leading preoccupations of her fictional art such themes have binding, cohesive power. In *Seven for a Secret,* however, in contrast to the other novels, they are themes pursued on one level only. This novel in fact marks a departure or a falling away from Mary Webb's usually finely wrought work: again in the tradition of moral fable, it is slight, lacking the density and fullness of implication hitherto so characteristic of her writing; unlike its three predecessors, each richly meaningful novel written in highly charged prose, *Seven for a Secret* does not extend in the symbolic level. However, it was not Mary Webb's intention on this occasion to write another work such as *Gone to Earth* or *The House in Dormer Forest,* poetic, allusive, resonant with multiple suggestiveness, requiring sustained vigour of imagination. To this type of novel she was to return splendidly and successfully in *Precious Bane.*

Seven for a Secret, though thematically linked, stands separately in the body of Mary Webb's work and can be regarded as an attempt on her part to write a different kind of novel, blending satire, fantasy and fable. But this book was prepared and written at a difficult period for her—during exhaustion and illness following publication of *The House in Dormer Forest,* the move to London, the effort of adjustment to new surroundings. A literary friend, who had personal knowledge of Mary and her circumstances during the composition of *Seven for a Secret,* emphasised that it was written during a period of "lowered creative vitality." At this stage of her literary career she had not yet recovered from the blow to her hopes that the

critical reception of *The House in Dormer Forest* constituted. Dismayed at the general lack of understanding of this work, she had deliberately written *Seven for a Secret* in a lighter vein, had set out to tell a fabulous tale (although still embedding central concerns) creating her characters as Robert Lynd noted, "in a high fervour of the romantic spirit" [see excerpt dated 1929]. And such a novel with its vivid surface presentation and interwoven elements of love, mystery and murder would perhaps have wider popular appeal. Subtitled "A Love Story," it seems to be almost a parody of her own previous work. (pp. 227-29)

[Using] the omniscient mode of narration, Mary Webb views her characters with mild affection, gentle amusement—no doubt her conscious artistic intention, but the characters are over-distanced and this creates cumulatively a sense of unreality. The world of the novel loses solidity and human depth, lacks a sense of the vitality of life. One feels a detachment in the narration (at times even a tiredness). We do not experience intimate involvement with her characters, their lives and affairs never seem part of a complex pattern of life—as one reviewer said, they "seem too far away to make us grieve or shiver." This novel, half-fantasy, half-parable, has a somewhat abstract, remote quality. Occasionally an authorial comment takes us too far out of her fictional scene. The total effect of the book is unconvincing—the elements of fantasy and realism do not cohere; the "uncommon" and the "ordinary" (to use Hardy's terms) are harnessed uneasily and unsatisfactorily in this, the least aesthetically satisfying of the Mary Webb novels. If by her imaginative energy she still compels us to "suspend disbelief," there are parts of *Seven for a Secret* (especially the last third of the book) where she only just succeeds in this.

Yet we feel, nevertheless, that, as one reviewer commented, "the author loves her art": this novel does not entirely lack (particularly in the early chapters) that feeling of joy in composition, an inspirational zest usually so sustained in her work. Although *Seven for a Secret* contains some of her worst writing, it also contains some of her finest and most arresting: while the closing chapter, for example, is clumsy and makeshift (as several reviewers were to point out), the opening chapter is one of her best. And even in its least successful parts there are flashes of poetry, brilliant nature drawing, an abundance of sharp sense-impressions. (pp. 230-31)

A shared feature of Mary Webb's novels is, of course, the always superb evocation of the Shropshire countryside in all its contrasting aspects and the way in which the characters are revealed in relation to this environment. In this book the relationships of the characters are developed in the vast wild landscape of high moors where the seasons roll on magnificently indifferent to human passions and aspirations. . . . There is a pervading sense of the onward sweep of the natural cycle, its beauty, terror and mystery; of dark elemental forces both within man and without in the ancient untamed places. . . . Here we find a synthesis of Mary Webb's preoccupations with folklore, superstition and the problem of evil. She understood, and demonstrated in her novels, how a combination of these, their interaction in the human mind, can weave invisible cross-threads of fate to create a tragic nemesis.

But in her novels . . . Mary Webb also reveals as strong a sense of comedy as of tragedy, and in *Seven for a Secret . . .* she creates with humorous relish a group of secondary characters—accident-prone, garrulous Jonathan Makepeace, grim Aunt Fanteague, insipid faded Emily, the strange toothless Fringal—these joining Sarah Jowell, Andrew Vessons, Mrs Marston,

Patty Arden and other successfully realised minor characters who contribute so much to the vivid actuality of life in her novels. It is primarily by means of these lesser figures that she gives the sense of contact with a real world.

The major figures of *Seven for a Secret* (apart from Robert Rideout) are more stereotyped. . . . (pp. 231-32)

It would, of course, be easy to interpret the central characters of *Seven for a Secret* as a fourfold projection of aspects of Mary's personality. . . .

However, such a line of exploration in this particular novel with its overtones of fantasy and deliberately "larger than life" flavour could be a misleading exercise, for while Mary undoubtedly did draw on self-knowledge in creating these characters, it would be presumption to regard them as anything more than either conscious (perhaps ironic) inflations of parts of her own immensely complex nature. . . . It is, however, generally accepted that in creating heroines who in one way or another lack physical beauty—Gillian with her facial blemish ("the scar which seamed one side of her forehead and gave that profile an intent, relentless look"), Amber Darke plain and sallow, Prudence Sarn marred by a hare-lip—Mary is symbolising her own disfigurement, her sense of physical inferiority. (p. 233)

Seven for a Secret . . . gained wider, more lengthy critical attention than any of her previous novels. The reviews, while containing the usual mixed comments, were on the whole far more favourable than those of *The House in Dormer Forest*. (p. 234)

[Mary] took three months to write *Precious Bane*, and according to her family she made a draft of the last chapter first—an indication of how thoroughly she had worked out the whole book, if not on paper, certainly in her mind. And we feel from the novel's opening sentence—"It was at a love-spinning that I saw Kester first"—that the entire story has been held within her, awaiting only the onrush of creative energy. (pp. 250-51)

Set in nineteenth-century Shropshire in the decade of Waterloo, *Precious Bane* is narrated by Prudence Sarn who, as a "very old woman and a tired woman, with a task to do before she says good night to this world," looks back, telling her own story woven with the tragic story of her brother Gideon. The title—taken from Milton's *Paradise Lost* (I. 690-2: "Let none admire / That riches grow in Hell; that soyle may best / Deserve the pretious bane")—held a personal sigificance for Mary Webb, and is appropriate to the stories of both Prudence and Gideon Sarn. Prudence's bane is her disfigurement—a "hare-shotten lip"—the affliction which brings her to a mystical "blessedness she might otherwise never have found" (this clearly a reflection of her creator's own experience); Gideon's bane is gold—his lust for wealth and ruthless determination to acquire it by means of the potential (and actual) gold of corn. (pp. 251-52)

Gideon spares neither himself nor anyone else in his drive for wealth. After a few years of hard work and thrift, his rick yards are filled with corn; he falls in love with his childhood friend, the blonde Jancis, daughter of Beguildy. . . . Prue meets, and loves at once, "a man to die for"—the Weaver, Kester Woodseaves, who discerns her beauty of spirit. (pp. 252-53)

Gideon . . . agrees to marry [Jancis] a week after the harvest if it is a good one. It seems as though his fortune is made as the rich golden grain is gathered in: contented at last, he awaits the valuer. But not waiting for the wedding, he takes Jancis to bed—and all is lost in a single night when the ricks are fired by her enraged father, Beguildy. The harvest is consumed in the flames and with it "the very stuff of Gideon's soul." After this, his nature hardens beyond reach—hating Jancis ("'Like father like child'") he totally rejects her, and in the dark winter months that follow, he poisons his ageing mother because she can no longer work for her keep. Finally, when Jancis returns with their baby, Gideon spurns them both, wanting "neither the one nor the other." Jancis drowns herself and the baby in the mere. From then on, Gideon is haunted by the ghost of his mother and even more by the ghosts of Jancis and her child until he commits suicide. . . . The superstitious local people, led by Prue's enemies, blame her for the deaths at Sarn, accusing her of evil eye and witchcraft. . . . The crowd seizes Prue and ties her in a ducking stool—half-drowned, she is rescued at the last moment by Kester who carries her away on his saddle and kisses her "full on the mouth."

A summary brings out only the sensational, melodramatic lines of the plot, but cannot convey the densely wrought texture of this novel or the power and poetry of the vision which informs it. *Precious Bane* is a strange blend of romantic allegory and personal testament; and it is remarkable not so much for what Mary Webb says, but for the way in which she says it.

Again merging reality and unreality, she creates a half-real, half-fantasy world uniquely her own, peopled by figures as like as they are unlike those of the world we know. Her narrative power is as unflagging as in her first two novels, but this—her last completed work—is richer, more complex. Once again she presents those themes, variously embodied in her novels, which give coherence to her imaginative world—universal themes, the significance of suffering, the struggle between spiritual and material values, love and lust, the givers and the takers. Of all her works, *Precious Bane* is most readily comprehensible as a poetic parable. Looked at from another standpoint it is a rather bizarre, historical novel, but certainly far more than just a "Georgian brew" or period piece. Mary Webb had learned much from Thomas Hardy in her use of a regional past: she took great care in the preparatory research, aiming to incorporate accurate historical detail yet achieve a sense of rural timelessness.

Written when she was reaching her artistic maturity, *Precious Bane* is Mary Webb's most technically perfect novel. She was well suited by the first person narrative form and employed it with unerring sureness of touch, surmounting the considerable technical difficulties of this method. The story unfolds at the same time as the mind of an individual is revealed—a country mind, highly susceptible to superstition, augury, sign and symbol. There is one centre of consciousness controlling, ordering, unifying the whole: the informing consciousness, the innately poetic sensibility of the narrator Prudence Sarn—that of Mary herself. So Mary's personality and spirit, mirrored in Prudence, permeate the book: the unity of the work radiates from the central figure and from the richly evoked sense of the Shropshire world in which she moves. The filtering of everything through this single, ardent consciousness gives the novel a curious, sustained intensity.

The plot is linear, but Mary Webb makes subtle use of the independence of consciousness from chronological sequence as in telling her story the mind of Prudence Sarn moves back and forth in time, merging past and present experience. Her technique has remarkable fluidity. She achieves depth and penetration by the stylistic device of "telescoping" from carefully chosen contact points of association and recollection. This gives us some of the most memorable parts of the novel. . . . (pp. 253-55)

In *Precious Bane* Mary Webb is less overtly didactic than in her previous novels, as her opinions are presented as those of the narrator who indulges in homely moralising and philosophising now and then. Thoughts expressed by Prue are clearly Mary's own. . . .

Further illumination of Mary's attitude to life at this time is given by the yearning undertone in the narration and a sense of the joys and troubles of life intermingled, the tragic note relieved by flashes of humour (usually in descriptions lit by effective similes, such as that depicting the rooks "sitting each in his tree like Parson in pulpit"). It is essentially a romantic and emotional vision which colours all. . . . And this (offputting to some readers) is true of the entire work of Mary Webb. . . . (p. 255)

In *Precious Bane,* the interaction between human and landscape is handled more subtly than in the earlier books. The fusion of the inner world of the individual sensibility and the outer physical world, is now almost imperceptible, giving a greater unity to the novel. Sarn Mere is the essence of Gideon's character as well as the stage for his tragedy. Mary Webb here has mastered her tendency to overdo the use of suggestive atmosphere, to manipulate details of the natural scene as chorus to the action. We have a sense of the shifting seasons moving on beyond the world of the protagonists, passive as well as active in the events. And nowhere in her work does she surpass the descriptive passages threaded throughout this novel which, it is generally agreed, are peculiarly, hauntingly evocative. . . .

Her symbolism is now more delicate and covert. . . . Throughout the novels, her artistic portrayal of her countryside is the product of her spiritual experience. And in *Precious Bane,* the development in her treatment of nature corresponds to a development in her mysticism—this already discernible in *The House in Dormer Forest.* (p. 256)

In *Precious Bane* [a] deepening and extension of her mysticism is clearly reflected in the inward experience of Prudence Sarn who has a vibrant affinity with her surroundings but not the ecstatic communing with nature, the "mystical exaltation" of Hazel Woodus and Amber Darke. In her last completed novel Mary has gone beyond the pantheistic mysticism which permeates the earlier works and is no longer striving to express her mysticism through descriptions of nature: these are the more effective because her perceptions and similes are as arresting as ever but she is not now straining after her effects. Such is the unique spiritual quality of her art that her own experience of illumination is mirrored in her writing like moonlight on water.

In *Precious Bane* she shows us not only the latest phase of her own spiritual development but also her early bruising: the shock of realising physical inferiority and rejection when eager for life and reaching out to it. So the withdrawal into herself of the young, keenly sensitive Prue who, hurt by the realisation that because of her marred appearance she is cruelly set apart, retreats to the attic "close under the thatch" where apples and pears are stored and where she first experiences pure mystical intuition. . . . (p. 257)

Precious Bane is projected more fully and directly than any of the preceding novels from the centre of Mary Webb's experience. Prudence Sarn, possessed of her creator's mysticism and intense emotionalism, has also her deep need for unitive experience in human relationship. With a desire grounded in humility, Prudence longs for a lover, a "Master" to whom she will surrender her total being—and she finds such a man in the Weaver, Kester Woodseaves. In her mystical unitive state, Prue's spiritual love has no religious focus; but in her love relationship with Kester, she unconsciously blends her image of a lover with Christ's image. Kester, seen through Prue's eyes, is a Christ-like figure—"the very marrow of Him that loved the world so dear!" At the bull-baiting he fulfils Prue's vision of him when he takes the place of the bull which is to be set on, prepared to sacrifice himself in his solitary crusade against cruelty. . . . There are several parallels and allusions to the crucifixion in this central episode in which Kester sheds his blood. (p. 258)

Mary Webb's own passionate archetypal projection, still possessing her mind and imagination, is clearly reflected here—her obsessive love, first for her father and then for [her husband] Henry. Kester (as the Meredith family have affirmed) is based on Henry, and the novel is dedicated "to my dear H.B.L.W." . . .

In the character of Kester, Mary Webb was attempting—as with Michael Hallowes—to embody a higher reality and, in so doing, to demonstrate the human potentiality of inner wholeness. Both Kester and Michael are integrated personalities, balanced in their totality, having, as a result, considerable vitality and charisma; both are keenly perceptive (Kester sees Prue's loveliness of inner self, as Michael has the shining soul of Amber Darke); and both transcend their environment. These characters lack, however, the human complexity and substance of their early counterparts, John Arden and Stephen Southernwood, and in considering this we arrive at a central problem in Mary Webb's literary art: at this stage of her artistic development, she was striving to create characters representative of a higher, extended consciousness, expressive of her vision of wholeness, but she had not yet succeeded in investing these with true human presence—they do not seem to act out of a complete existence. Hence the criticism that these figures are not convincing portrayals, do not 'develop', are little more than abstractions or stereotype. Yet Mary Webb had considerable ability in character creation, manifest in her acutely observed and vivified lesser characters. Had she lived longer, she may well have surmounted this difficulty (as her unfinished novel indicates), and successfully combined in her central figures both the embodiment of a valid higher reality and full, vivid presence as real people. (p. 259)

In this novel, Mary Webb perfected her unique literary style— a poetic style, of "exceptional flexibility," as Frank Swinnerton said; in fact the critics are in agreement that in this respect at least, *Precious Bane* is a remarkable book. The fusion of Shropshire dialect and natural speech with evocative descriptive prose is perfect for the expression of Prudence Sarn's (and Mary's) reflective mind and emotional sensibility, innately disposed to see allegorical meaning.

The language, lyrical but artificial, has echoes of various moulding influences—the Bible, works of seventeenth-century prose writers and the medieval mystics, especially Dame Julian of Norwich. Prudence Sarn's quaint phrases, the spice of humour in her observations, the simplicity of her wisdom, are strongly reminiscent of Dame Julian: but on the whole this is due less to direct imitation than to affinity of personality, as that particular blend of warm homeliness and mysticism, simplicity and depth, gravity and joy is as characteristic of Mary (and her "mommet" Prudence) as it is of the anchoress.

Again and again there are passages imbued with a peculiarly Biblical atmosphere—Prudence's description of Sarn fields under corn is typical:

> There would be warmship that wrapped you round, and the queenly gift of the scent of corn. What other scent is like it? There is so much in it, beyond other sweets. There is summer in it, and frost. There is water in it, and the heart of the flint which the corn has taken up into its hollow stalks. There is bread in it, and life for man and beast.
>
> (pp. 260-61)

While in each of the novels this tone, an echo of the rhythms of the Bible (and the use of aptly chosen texts usually for humorous or ironic effect) recur more or less, it is most apparent in *Precious Bane.*

An important feature of Mary Webb's style is her lyrical handling of dialect. Fascinated from an early age by the talk of Shropshire country folk, Mary had . . . lived among her people and grown to know intimately at their hearthsides how they lived, thought and spoke. With so keen an ear for the substance, rhythms and intrinsic beauty of country speech, she was able skilfully and with innate poetry to blend the local idiom with her own prose. . . . Hers was an expert's knowledge of the Shropshire dialect through which she came in direct touch with the peasant mind and spirit—and to a continuity with the past. (p. 261)

But the artist in Mary Webb was uppermost—though she loved the rich, apple-like quality of the words in dialect she was aware, like Thomas Hardy, of the danger of excessive localism, and only occasionally employed purely dialect words, achieving her effect more subtly by idiomatic suggestion, the use here and there of a well-placed local word or turn of phrase giving widespread flavour. And the meaning of these vivid words or expressions can always be "caught" through the context. When Hazel Woodus tells us "the sun's undering" and Prue Sarn . . . describes how under the elms "it was all dimmery with summer leaves," we know what they mean. Many of the local words and turns of phrase which she incorporated are not exclusive to Shropshire and the Welsh border but are modifications of those in use elsewhere: in *Precious Bane* such country speech is particularly appropriate, adding to the authenticity of a narrative told by a countrywoman, helping to create the feeling that this story really has come out of Prudence Sarn. With sureness of touch, Mary Webb sustains from beginning to end the natural flow and rich country flavour of her narrator's speech, yet this is charged through and through with poetry. Prue's descriptions have a rare lucidity and simplicity—before the close of the first chapter, in which she sets the scene at Sarn, we are captured; her words are as arresting as birdsong. . . . (pp. 261-62)

In the dialogue as well, Mary Webb carefully conventionalises dialect speech, again using purely dialect words sparingly, but conveying the spirit of peasant talk by employing pronunciation spellings, elided or modified common words and local expressions ("in good sadness," "comic-struck," "in very poor case"). This rustic speech, mainly of the lesser characters, is found throughout the novels, but most extensively in *Precious Bane.* And it is primarily by means of dialogue that the minor characters are so effectively realised, the ease, naturalness and differentiation in their speech adding to the sense of vital and varied human presence.

In *Precious Bane,* as in each of the preceding novels, there is a group of memorable secondary figures, again lively portrayals given considerable individual variation, but not obtrusive. . . . The host of rustic figures in *Precious Bane* adds richly to Mary Webb's gallery of country characters—while some, such as Sexton's Sammy, Grimble, Moll and Sukey, or Huglet are little more than sharp caricatures, others such as Tivvy, Missis Beguildy and Felena are deftly touched in. (pp. 262-63)

[Mary Webb] knew from a life lived in the West Shropshire border hills and valleys, the extent to which folklore and superstition penetrated the everyday existence of countrydwellers, influencing the unconscious as well as the conscious mind—and this even more so in the days to which she reached back in *Precious Bane,* a time when superstition was rife and often closely interknit with religion in such isolated rural areas.

Drawing on her great fund of knowledge, she wove almost two hundred instances of lore, legend, custom and superstition into the fabric of *Precious Bane,* some obscure, others well-known—not only traditional Shropshire folklore but also universal motifs. Among the most important are the superstitions about a hare-lip and witchcraft, the custom of sin-eating, the telling of the bees and the telling of the rooks (after a death), the night burial with mourners carrying sprigs of rosemary, the love-spinning, and the legends of the Seven Whistlers (a death warning by mysterious birds), the drowned village, Wild Edric, the bogeys of the mere, "the roaring bull o' Bagbury" and the ghostly chariots. Mary Webb used folklore and superstition partly to heighten the local flavour and authenticity (together with traditional farming customs such as the Love Carriage and Harvest Home), but mainly to establish and support the mood of impending tragedy which permeates the entire book. Portents of disaster are introduced from the first chapter onwards. . . . (pp. 263-64)

Too many customs and superstitions are brought in; and though most of them are incorporated with skill so that they are never meaningless embellishments, occasionally their inclusion is rather contrived. Folk beliefs and practices, and mythological motifs are assimilated more finely and successfully in *Gone to Earth.* But two of the superstitions integrated in *Precious Bane*—namely those associated with a harelip and the custom of sin-eating—are of fundamental importance to almost every aspect of the novel. And again, as in *Gone to Earth,* these dominant mythic forms taken by Mary's imagination give us insight into the darker crevasses of her mind, revealing her deepest preoccupations and anxieties.

Throughout the novel the oblique references to Prudence Sarn's bane—her harelip—are particularly well done. As Prue grows to young womanhood, she becomes aware of the suspicion in which she is regarded by others, of the tales spreading "in the lonely farms" that she is cursed and has the devil's mark, that she assumes the form of a hare at midnight and is a witch. In Prudence's bewildered sensitivity, in her increasing hurt at being set apart by her fellow creatures and thought of as odd, evil, a witch, we see Mary's own extreme vulnerability, especially as her thyroid condition was now worsening, her goitre growing: even in Shropshire she was shunned, viewed with suspicion, and remembered years later for her "peculiarities" (untidy clothes, "odd eyes," solitary ways) rather than for her achievements. The hurts and slights felt keenly by Prue are Mary's own experience. . . . (pp. 264-65)

While much of the strength of *Precious Bane* lies in how intimately and effectively Mary has embodied her own person-

Webb's husband, Henry Bertram Law Webb, 1924. From
The Flower of Light: A Biography of Mary Webb, *by Gladys
Mary Coles. Duckworth, 1978. Reproduced by permission
of Gladys Mary Coles.*

ality and thoughts in Prudence Sarn, one of the main weaknesses of the novel is that ultimately it fails to convince and satisfy because of the weak, almost fairy-tale "happy ending." Mary's need to provide such an ending . . . evidently overcame her finer artistic sense. In her imagination Mary was reshaping the world close to her heart's yearning. (p. 265)

Precious Bane, with its strange story, its compelling tone, its unusual and poetic literary style, undoubtedly will remain the favourite Mary Webb book for many readers. . . . (p. 267)

> Gladys Mary Coles, in her *"The Flower of Light":
> A Biography of Mary Webb,* Duckworth, 1978, 352 p.

MICHÈLE BARALE   (essay date 1981)

[*In the following excerpt, Barale discusses* Seven for a Secret *as
an unusual example of a Bildungsroman in that it traces the growth
and development to maturity of a fairly ordinary young woman.*]

The *Bildungsroman,* a tale of the growth and development of a young person, has almost exclusively told the story of a boy: David Copperfield, Ernest Pontifex, Stephen Dedalus, young Werther, Tom Sawyer. Those novels which describe the ma-

turation of a young girl are few, and most frequently detail the life of a woman in some way exceptional: Moll Flanders, for instance, or Emma Bovary, or Becky Sharp. Mary Webb's *Seven for a Secret* can most certainly be read as a *Bildungsroman,* as a novel which tells the story of Gillian Lovekin's growth and maturity. It is a novel which shows how a callow and selfish young girl, a girl who could use everything and everyone to satisfy her curiosity and vanity, becomes a woman able to love selflessly. And it is a novel which, in detailing Gillian's history, does not omit the part which the erotic plays in all maturation. In this presentation of adolescent female sexuality, Webb is unusually honest and admirably realistic. It is a frank, overwhelming sexual curiosity which impels Gillian's early behaviour. But it is a wiser Gillian, a Gillian no longer physically or emotionally virginal, who has come to understand nature's great mystery of regeneration and life, a Gillian who can, therefore, love without selfishness. For Mary Webb, this mature knowledge redeems Gillian, bringing her from darkness to light, healing completely the scar which was her mark.

But Mary Webb was unwilling to create a young Gillian whose narcissism makes her despicable to the reader. Instead, we cannot help but enjoy Gillian's vitality, her desire for independence, her flirtatious attempts to wield power. She seeks escape from the farmhouse of her father, despite her love of the Welsh moorlands and her pleasure in the "incipient splendour" of the common things of her life, because she would have a larger world to experience and because she would herself be larger: wiser in the ways of the world. Robert Lynd, in the introduction to the 1929 edition of the novel, characterises Gillian's quest as being of little worth: "She has, when we meet her first, no real ambition, except to be a greater Gillian Lovekin and to escape from the farm that is too small a stage for her." But Lynd's claim of—"no real ambition" is far from correct; Gillian Lovekin, despite the crassness of her yearnings or the confined terms of her desires—confined and crass they well might be since she has never been but twelve miles from the farm—wants all that is to be had. She wants the power of self-definition and the power, as well, that comes from others' acceptance of this definition. Gillian Lovekin wants to shape herself rather than be shaped by the dictates of her father, a man who is loud rather than wise, or by the proprieties of her aunt, a woman who defines a lady as distinguished by her lack of any presence whatsoever: "You can tell a lady, because nobody ever knows she's there."

Mary Webb certainly had sympathy for Gillian's longings for "a sparkling band round my head, and sparkling slippers on my feet, and a gown that goes 'hush! hush!'", shallow though such longings are. Webb understood in her creation of Gillian that her character's adolescent desire for a multitude of admiring young men, for the adulation of the crowd was a childish desire for just another sort of glitter and sparkle. But she also understood that the roots of such a desire were not to be dismissed. Gillian's vision of herself is far from infantile; rather, it is "the vision desired by all humanity—the vision of a secure small nest of immortality built upon the crumbling walls of time. She wants to go on being herself even when she is dissolved in nothingness." Gillian, like all of us, would cheat death. She wants to use her "art"—her as yet unlearned music—to achieve fame and power and thus attain a sort of immortality. Mary Webb, in other words, created in the character of Gillian Lovekin one whose maturation reflects the deepest levels of human maturation. We do not only see a country girl marry in haste, repent in leisure and finally discover who it is that she has loved all along. We see, too, something that is larger; in Gillian's quest for self-definition, autonomy, power and, ultimately, immortality, we see something mythic.

It is, of course, not at all expected to find the mythical in the story of a young country girl. Although we have a literary tradition which allows for the intrusion of the mythical in the story of the young boy—Stephen Dedalus—not even so compelling a figure as Maggie Tulliver of George Eliot's *Mill on the Floss* has led the reader into the strange literary grove wherein the life of one small girl suggests those tales that chart the growth of human consciousness and culture. I do not wish to lay too heavy a burden upon Webb's novel; it is not the undiscovered masterpiece of twentieth-century literature. But neither is it merely a piece of once-popular fiction, interesting only from an historical perspective. *Seven for a Secret* is an intriguing novel, tightly written, ambiguously resolved, and purposely didactic: the author wishes to make a point. And her point is that the young girl is prompted to dream and act by those same human impulses which spur a young boy. (pp. ix-xi)

Mary Webb demonstrates [that] power and love cannot coexist. Ultimately, if love is to be experienced, the power of self-determination must be willingly forsaken. Thus, in what was doubtlessly read by her contemporaries as a pleasantly passionate novel about life and love and the relationships between the sexes, Webb reflects Sigmund Freud's revolutionary presentation of the dualism of love and the will to power, Freud's belief in the warring forces of love and death. In what most of her contemporary reviewers considered a gentle, pantheistic mysticism, Mary Webb presents, in fact, a facet of mystical apprehension which is at equal ease with beauty and terror—with the Dionysian. Regeneration and motherhood, murder and brutality are presented at the novel's end as having equal value in life's terms; nature makes no moral distinctions in the world of this novel. (pp. xi-xii)

[*Seven for a Secret*] is Webb's fourth novel and has been criticised as tired and even melodramatic in plot, as reflecting yet again a theme common to Webb: the contrast of sacred and profane love. To view the novel as merely reflective of a contrast is, however, to ignore the novel as the story of growth, as *Bildungsroman,* and is to see Gillian Lovekin as a puppet created to enact a rather thin melodrama. If, instead, the novel is understood in terms of the mythic references and images which are woven through it, the novel then seems an example of authorial craft, and more, of authorial courage. Webb took the life of a not terribly unusual moorland girl and through mythic imagery made that life—filled with all the details of farm and middle-class existence—comment upon the meaning of human love, sexuality, culture, art and death.

Despite Mary Webb's reputation, both contemporary and posthumous, as the sweet apostle of nature, the lyrical poet of joy, *Seven for a Secret* gives evidence of Webb as a writer who did far more than trip lightly through the tulips. She contemplated, instead, with a total lack of squeamishness, the meaning of human value in amoral nature. She had no apparent difficulty maintaining love—passionate, sexual, and spiritual—as the supreme value even while admitting that only reproduction has value in nature's larger scheme. She could accept the notion that human understanding is filled with ellipses, accept the possibility that even our most noble, most beautiful gestures are without ultimate meaning—and still not appear cynical, not appear despairing, not appear to value the human gesture´ any less. While Mary Webb was certainly not Thomas Hardy's

literary equal in terms of style or complexity, like him she did not flinch from portraying the world as she perceived it to be, both beautiful and terrible at once. (pp. xii-xiii)

Michèle Barale, in an introduction to Seven for a Secret *by Mary Webb, Virago, 1982, pp. ix-xiv.*

JOHN H. PATERSON AND EVANGELINE PATERSON   (essay date 1981)

[*In the following excerpt, the Patersons examine some reasons for Webb's utilization of an actual geographical region as the setting of her fictional works.*]

Why should a novelist—any novelist—choose a real place, in a known area, and then use it as a setting, under the thinnest of disguises, for an imaginary cast of characters? If the imagination can stretch to the casting, why can it not cover the topography as well? Why allow oneself to be constrained from the outset by a geography dictated not by the fiction but by the reality? What advantage, if any, does this give to the novelist?

These are obvious questions, but they do not seem previously to have been asked, let alone answered. (p. 209)

The first reason why the novelist may set the story in a real landscape is because there—and perhaps only there—does he or she feel confident of presenting a familiar and ordered life. The characters in any story engage our interest and sympathy, not so much by the extraordinary as by the ordinary circumstances of their living: not by murder or mayhem but by the intrusion of these things, if intrude they must, upon a stable and credible lifestyle. On one side, then, the topographic setting acts as a *stabilising* factor if, as novelists sometimes find, their characters take on a life of their own and get out of hand. On the other, it imposes upon the writer a necessary *discipline* against his wilder flights of fancy.

In any case, the novelist writes out of his or her own experience, and that experience has, for many writers, been acquired within a geographically restricted area. This may be the *only* ordered life known to the novelist, but the corollary of that is that he or she can write of it with confidence. A part of the imaginative effort involved in the writing can be transferred away from the setting, which in this sense is a known quantity, and concentrated upon the actors.

This first reason for choosing a regional setting we might characterise as *authenticity.* It is possible, although not necessary, then, to take the argument further, and to claim that the region imparts not only realism to the story but a necessary inspiration to the writer. It was W. B. Yeats who wrote that he and his friends in the Irish renaissance thought

> All that we did, all that we said or sang
> Must come from contact with the soil, from that
> Contact everything Antaeus-like grew strong.

As it happens, the Irish writers, whether considered individually or as a group, afford this belief little support, but it was a belief which Mary Webb certainly held, as her essay "Vis Medicatrix Naturae" shows, and therefore has a certain relevance to our present study. Away from Shropshire, it seems clear, she was less than herself.

The second reason for using a regional setting we might call *identity.* Familiar with a region and its inhabitants, the writer sets out deliberately to display it to the outside world, perhaps as an example to be shunned or followed; perhaps as a museum piece to be preserved or understood. And displayed not to the outside world only, but to its own people also, to make them more aware of what surrounds them and of the way of life they have inherited. (p. 210)

The third reason for choosing real landscape as the setting for a novel may be *symbolism*. This requires some explanation. Studies in perceptual geography have, in recent years, carried us some way towards an understanding of the mental maps which we all carry in our minds, and of the principle that what we *think* is there is more important to our decision-making than what actually *is*. But there are other perceptions of great antiquity and ancient understanding, whereby the real world is symbolising something—is conveying a series of messages. Nature is a book to be read; spatial features can be, and are to be, *interpreted*. This introduces us to the mythical-magical conception of space, in which the disposition and shape of things take on a significance beyond themselves, and particular places become symbols of events which have, or are believed to have, taken place there. The problem then becomes one of reading this book of nature, this *paysage moralisé*, as Mary Webb's own biographer [Gladys M. Coles] calls it.

This third use of regional landscape is not common among regional novelists, and for very obvious reasons. The danger of appearing to support an antiquated determinism is evident. Credibility on the part of the modern reader is hard to achieve, and those who do believe are unlikely to be the same people as those who read the novel. (p. 211)

Most of the better-known landscapes of symbolism are to be found in pure works of the imagination where, following the lead of medieval painters of heaven and hell (with appropriate topographic detail), they have been deliberately created to fit the story, whether it is Bunyan's *Pilgrim's Progress* or C. S. Lewis's *Narnia* tales. But Mary Webb's first novel, as we shall see, is built upon a symbolic landscape, and all her books abound in references to the superstitions of country folk about people, places and things. (pp. 211-12)

Of the three explanations for the choice of a real regional setting for an account of fictitious events—authenticity, identity and symbolism—the first can be immediately applied to our author. Born in Shropshire, Mary Webb lived successively in Leighton, Much Wenlock, Stanton-upon-Hine Heath, Meole Brace, Pontesbury and Lyth Hill, and was desperately unhappy whenever marriage or family demands removed her elsewhere. If she was ever going to write of a world she knew, then it had to be Shropshire: there was no other.

That world, however, she knew intimately, with an intimacy recognised by her friends and neighbours, and which comes through to the reader of both her prose and her poetry. (p. 212)

Most of Mary Webb's place-specific allusions express . . . [the] consciousness that she lived in a border zone . . . between the wild hills of Wales and the fertile lowlands of England, with ''her'' country—the hills between Shrewsbury and Bishops Castle—marking a sort of divide. . . .

To begin with, to be sure, she was inclined to overdo the landscape description. It was the error of inexperience, and was largely confined to her first novel, *The Golden Arrow*. . . . (p. 213)

But it was an error which she swiftly corrected; the second of her novels, *Gone To Earth,* and the subsequent books have all the atmosphere, and the carefully reconstructed country speech,

yet almost none of the descriptive passages, of the first. The players in the drama have, very properly, become more important than the stage.

We come now to the second justification for the regionally based novel, that of establishing a regional identity. That Mary Webb saw Shropshire as a region intermediate between England and Wales, and sharing some of the characteristics of each, both in landscape and people, has already been recognised. Its distinctiveness lay in the mixture. That Mary Webb's intentions were in part didactic can also be readily established from the novels, and even more clearly from her non-fiction. She wished to teach others to see with her eyes, to recognise the character of things around them, to pause and consider nature in its immense variety. That there were lessons to be learned she had no doubt:

> We need no great gifts—the most ignorant of us can draw deep breaths of inspiration from the soil. . . . The primal instincts can seldom be so dead that no pleasure or kinship wakens at the thronging of these vivid colours and mysterious sounds. Here is a kingdom of wonder and of secrecy into which we can step at will.

That her didactic impulse drove her further than this (and it did so) is, perhaps, unfortunate. She seems at times to have been trying to convert her readers into nature-lovers against their will. And she fell, in the beginning, into the habit of commenting editorially on the actions of her characters in a way which, by the time *The Golden Arrow* appeared in 1916, was distinctly out of fashion in the English novel, and which is liable to vex the modern reader. This is the more curious and regrettable when we consider that, in her comments on sexual matters and on relations between the sexes she was, if anything, *ahead* of her time—frank and open for the period and especially frank and open for a lady novelist of the period.

So she established a regional identity for her Shropshire homeland and its people, and she strove to teach her readers to observe and appreciate landscape. How successful was she? There can, of course, be no objective criteria by which to judge, but there can be comparisons. Compared with Hardy (whom she read and admired) she was surely no less successful in the creation of regional atmosphere: reading her novels, one is no less aware than with Hardy's of the background of land and sky—at least when, from *Gone To Earth* onwards, she had indeed placed them in the background, where they belong. Her novels have survived and attracted new readers and new editions, without (perhaps in spite of) the efforts of Stanley Baldwin to draw attention to them. We speak today of the Mary Webb country, and we know precisely where it is to be found. By these criteria, at least, she succeeded.

But we must now turn to our third topic: landscape as symbol in Mary Webb's work. . . . In her first and last novels, *The Golden Arrow* and the unfinished *Armour Wherein He Trusted*, Mary Webb attempted the formidable task of using the topography of her settings as a symbol of the characters and their actions. . . . [This] has not often been successfully attempted in English-language fiction. . . . (pp. 214-15)

Obviously, the major obstacles to the whole operation are, first, the commitment to a particular kind of what a geographer might call environmental determinism, and the need to sustain the naturalistic parallel through thick and thin; secondly, the difficulty of finding a landscape amenable to this type of interpretation. It is a commonplace to find deities located by popular consent on the highest and most inaccessible mountain top, or spirits speaking to untutored minds from volcanoes or caves or waterfalls, but none of this is particularly appropriate to the English Midlands.

To have a *paysage moralisé* one must above all have *contrast;* otherwise the story built upon it is hardly likely to generate momentum. With Hawthorne, it was the contrast between the wilderness and the sown—the same contrast which Scott exploited across the Highland Boundary Fault in Scotland. And Mary Webb was fortunate—is there any other word one can use?—to be born into, and live her life in, an area which offered contrast at two levels, local and regional. Such skill as she showed in exploiting this fact was hers alone but, compared with other novelists, she was in this respect off to a flying start before she realised it.

The local landscape contrast which first caught her imagination, and which underlies **The Golden Arrow,** is that between the two ridges of mountain to the west of Church Stretton: the Long Mynd (which she called the Wilderhope Range) and the Stiperstones ridge (her Diafol Mountain). Topographically, the contrast between them is clear: the first, or easterly, ridge rises above the Church Stretton Fault in a series of rounded hills, concordant in summit, in places plateau-like, and covered by grass and heather moor. The westerly ridge, by contrast, is narrow and topped by a line of rocky outcrops, the most impressive of which is known as the Devil's Chair. The geological distinction between the two ridges accounts for these outlines: the Long Mynd is composed of Pre-Cambrian grits while the Stiperstones ridge (from which it is separated by a valley cut in Cambrian shales) represents the outcrop of Ordovician quartzites which form the upthrust eastern extremity of a wide area of Ordovician formations known as the Shelve district.

Around the Devil's Chair, generations of country people had woven a web of legend and the novelist, to begin with, was doing no more than record a widely felt sensation when she wrote:

> On the highest point of the bare, opposite ridge, now curtained in driving storm-cloud, towered in gigantic aloofness a mass of quartzite. . . . It was understood that only when vacant could the throne be seen. Whenever rain or driving sleet or mist made a grey shechinah there people said, "There's harm brewing. He's in his chair."

The novelist with a Devil's Chair in his or her region is clearly possessed of a valuable property. The problem then becomes one of using that property to advantage. In her first novel, Mary Webb decided to extend or enlarge her *paysage moralisé* to embrace the whole of the two ridges, and to create parallels to the landscape in the lives of her characters. So the Long Mynd became a place of security, order and comfort, where the Flockmaster tended his stock with skill and devotion; a placid land where there was nothing to threaten—at least, not so long as the shepherd was on hand. It came to symbolise peace and virtue.

The Stiperstones ridge stood in complete contrast: "The sheep that inhabited these hills would, so the shepherds said, cluster suddenly and stampede for no reason, if they had grazed too near it (the Devil's Chair) in the night." Its inhabitants were for the most part miners—dark, underground creatures—and its landscape symbolised the wild and wayward streak in Mary Webb's characters. Here took place events in the story which tremble on the brink of the Gothic: the daughter of the Flock-

master went to live there with the mine foreman, out of wedlock, and ended by burning down her own cottage and possessions, while the young man, tormented by passions which he could neither understand nor control, tried eventually to blow up the Devil's Chair with explosives from the mine. . . . (pp. 215-17)

He failed, of course, and abandoned home and family for America, only to return at the end of the book for a reconciliation scene into which Mary Webb tries again to introduce a symbolic note. This time,

> It seemed to her that there was no hostility now between the two ranges, between the towering throne and the small white cross (a signpost on the Long Mynd). Always before, she had superstitiously regarded the Chair as wholly evil, the Flockmaster's signpost as wholly good. Now she saw good and evil mingled. . . .

But this is the trouble with symbolic landscapes: you cannot alter the symbols half way through to suit the story—the symbolism must be consistent. . . . As it happens, and despite this difficulty, however, Mary Webb came remarkably close to consistency in **The Golden Arrow**—to the detriment of the story, most readers would feel. The packaging into two contrasting landscapes and groups of characters is a little too neat.

The second novel, **Gone To Earth,** continues the packaging of characters, but not of landscapes. The principal action takes place, however, on the Stiperstones ridge, and the climax on its northern end, Lords Hill (easily recognisable in the story as God's Little Mountain). This forewarns us, perhaps, that the ending will be tragic, as indeed it is, but the landscape symbolism is on this occasion not pressed. Of the two men who pursue the heroine, Coles says, in the introduction to the 1978 reprint of the novel, "they are representative of the opposing physical and spiritual values between which Hazel swings (this gives the flavour of a Morality): the well-defined contrast between them is fundamental to plot and theme." In other words, the search for contrast goes on, in the sphere of character, but without pressing further the landscape symbolism.

This being the case, it is remarkable that, in her last, unfinished novel, Mary Webb returned to her topographic symbolism, this time on the larger, regional scale. *Armour Wherein He Trusted* . . . is set in the eleventh century and represents an exceedingly bold venture for an authoress whose most daring (and largely successful) previous exploration of the past had been the reconstruction (in **Precious Bane**) of the life of nineteenth-century Shropshire, depicted through the eyes of a countrywoman of the period. But a gap of eight centuries or so is an imaginative obstacle of an altogether different order of magnitude; yet Mary Webb tackled it, by general critical consent, with a real measure of success.

It is not, however, the quality of this first draft of half a novel which concerns us here, but its setting. For the author has turned back in her last work to those regional contrasts in which Shropshire stands midway between two worlds, Wales and England. Here on the Marches the two were for centuries in conflict, and the novel is full of castles and crusading. And these two worlds symbolised for her a personal conflict. (pp. 217-18)

[She] seems to have been fascinated by those distant glimpses of the Welsh mountains which one obtains from "her" hill country—by the distant presence of Cader Idris and the mystery of the unknown and (so far as we can tell) unvisited region between. Imagination must have filled the world to the west with both mystery and wonder. For her, there was a regional distinctiveness here which transcended even topography and language.

Mary Webb could probably be described as a mystic; perhaps as a pantheist; certainly as a woman with a passion for nature and its preservation. (p. 219)

> *John H. Paterson and Evangeline Paterson, "Shropshire: Reality and Symbol in the Work of Mary Webb,"* in Humanistic Geography and Literature: Essays on the Experience of Place, *edited by Douglas C. D. Pocock, Barnes & Noble Books, 1981, pp. 209-20.*

GAIL POOL   (essay date 1982)

[*In the following excerpt, Pool places* Gone to Earth *next to* Precious Bane *as the works on which Webb's lasting reputation may be founded.*]

It is easy to be critical of Mary Webb's novels, their faults are so apparent—contrived plots, didactic tone, romantically idealized heroes and overly emotional prose. It is understandable that she has been reduced to a historical footnote, her five novels, hundreds of poems, essays and reviews all but forgotten. And yet, her best work is surprisingly powerful. The word "primitive," so often and justly applied to her lack of sophistication, applies as well to her major strength: the use of nature and myth, which gives her best novels the force of legend or fairy tale.

Webb's ability to integrate nature and myth into her fiction derives from her attachment to Shropshire, where she was born and grew up, and which she never emotionally left. . . .

Webb's relationship with [her husband] Henry offers insight into her work's limitations. Although she wrote poems and essays throughout her 20s, she did not begin writing novels until after her marriage, and the idealized heroes of her fiction were based on her husband. This was true of Michael Hallowes in *The House in Dormer Forest,* and of Robert Rideout in *Seven For a Secret,* but it was particularly true of Kester Woodseaves in *Precious Bane.* Both Kester's idealization and his dashing rescue of the harelipped Prue Sarn in the book's strainedly happy conclusion mar what is otherwise a rich and unsettling work.

Of Webb's five novels, only *Gone to Earth* has neither an idealized hero nor a happy ending, and it is that tragic ending, its inevitability and the author's ability to confront it, that gives the book its power. . . . *Gone to Earth* was Webb's second novel. it was well received upon publication . . . and it is on this work, along with *Precious Bane,* that her reputation may at length be built.

Gone to Earth is the story of young Hazel Woodus and the two men who want her: Jack Reddin, the rough farmer-squire who awakens her to physical passion; and Edward Marston, the minister who marries her and seeks to awaken her to spiritual passion. Hazel—the daughter of a mute Welsh gypsy woman, dead for some years, and of a harpist-beekeeper-coffinmaker—is a wild, innocent spirit who wants to be owned by nobody. But Hazel is pursued by her fate with the same urgency with which the Black Huntsman and the phantom death pack—the central mythical figures of the book—stalk their prey.

Hunting, with all it represents, is the theme of *Gone to Earth;* the book's main opposition is that of the hunter and the hunted. Hazel, who is completely at one with nature, finds her friends among the wildlife; her closest companion is her pet fox, Foxy. For Hazel, "hounds symbolized everything she hated. . . . She identified herself with Foxy, and so with all things hunted and snared and destroyed." (p. 279)

Hazel's relationship with Foxy eventually emerges as the most satisfactory friendship in the book. Hazel alone accepts Foxy as she is. . . .

Reddin and Marston, by contrast, do not even see Hazel for what she is. Each falls in love with, and seeks to attain, what he wants. Reddin, who lusts after her and lures her away from her husband, cannot see that he has destroyed not only her sexual innocence but also her spiritual innocence. Marston, who worships Hazel's innocence and refuses to defile it by consummating their marriage, cannot see that Hazel is not all spirit, that she craves physical love. As Reddin and Marston each lives out his image of himself, Hazel is split in two and ultimately destroyed.

Webb has drawn a powerful portrait here of two men's relationships to a woman, but it would be a mistake to interpret that portrait as feminist. For Webb, women are fulfilled through their relationships with men: "A woman who has not supremely given herself is not supremely herself," she wrote in *Seven For a Secret.* Although the failure of love in *Gone to Earth* is central to the novel, Hazel is not a symbol of downtrodden womanhood. She symbolizes something larger: downtrodden life, anyone or any living thing hunted, trapped, caught, used. (p. 280)

Gone to Earth is a compelling book, carried along by sheer energy. Its faults are plain to see: Hazel is innocent beyond belief, Reddin physical beyond belief, Marston spiritual beyond belief, the plot itself beyond belief in every way. And yet, at its core is something all too believable: a vision of the relentlessness of human cruelty. . . .

In Webb's philosophy, which sustains the best of her work, the individual's relationship with nature parallels his or her relationship with fellow human beings: if kindness, cruelty or sensitivity characterizes one set of relationships, it will characterize the other set as well. In her weaker novels, philosophy overwhelms fiction—with excessive romanticism in *The Golden Arrow* and *Seven For a Secret,* with didacticism in *The House in Dormer Forest.* But in *Gone to Earth* and *Precious Bane,* ideas give dimension to the narrative.

Although Webb may never be viewed as a major writer, she is certainly worth reading. . . . Perhaps in time, critics will acknowledge Webb's novels without the obligatory reference to their many flaws, and readers will enjoy them without apology. (p. 281)

> *Gail Pool, "The Hunters and the Hunted," in* The Nation, New York, *Vol. 235, No. 9, September 25, 1982, pp. 279-81.*

ADDITIONAL BIBLIOGRAPHY

Adcock, St. John. "Mary Webb." In his *The Glory That Was Grub Street: Impressions of Contemporary Authors,* pp. 321-29. Toronto: Musson Book Co., 1928.

Critical survey. Adcock expresses regret that Webb's novels were largely neglected by the reading public until after her death.

Beer, Patricia. "The Crudities of the Soul." *The Times Literary Supplement*, No. 3990 (22 September 1978): 1049.
Review of Gladys Mary Coles's biography of Webb and Webb's *Collected Prose and Poems*. Beer concludes that "the reason Mary Webb's novels are little regarded today is that they are not very good, and no amount of drawing attention to them or talking of neglected talent will make them so."

Buchan, John. Introduction to *Gone to Earth*, by Mary Webb, pp. 7-10. London: Jonathan Cape, 1929.
Praises the "rare beauty and simplicity" of Webb's literary style, as well as the plotting, characterization, and descriptive passages in *Gone to Earth*.

Chapman, Grace. "Mary Webb." *The London Mercury* XXIII, No. 1 (February 1931): 365-71.
Briefly comments on Webb's life and works, noting especially her use of nature and regional elements.

Collard, Lorna. "Mary Webb." *The Contemporary Review* CXLIII (April 1933): 455-64.
Appreciative essay focusing on Webb's poetry.

Higgs, Laquita. "Conquer? or Green Gravel? The Use of Games in *Precious Bane*." *Kentucky Folklore Record* 22, No. 4 (October-December 1976): 104-10.
Considers Webb's use of Shropshire folklore in *Precious Bane* a deliberate artistic device essential to her delineation of character and theme.

Kees, Weldon. "Moons, Nestled Like Tawny Birds." *The New York Times Book Review* (9 November 1947): 6.
Disparaging review of Webb's posthumously published volume of poetry, criticizing in particular her dated Victorian romanticism.

Lewis, Janet. "Postscripts: *Fifty-One Poems*, by Mary Webb." *Poetry* 73, No. 1 (October 1948): 49-52.
Highly favorable review of Webb's posthumously published volume of poetry, suggesting that a familiarity with Webb's prose enhances the enjoyment of reading her verse.

McNeil, W. K. "The Function of Legend, Belief, and Custom in *Precious Bane*." *Folklore* 82 (Summer 1971): 132-46.
Studies Webb's use of traditional songs, speech patterns, proverbs, legends, beliefs, customs, and local folklore in *Precious Bane* to establish mood, supply realistic local color, and provide comic relief.

Moult, Thomas. *Mary Webb: Her Life and Work*. London: Jonathan Cape, 1932, 287 p.
Noncritical biography in which the critic quotes extensively from Webb's poetry to illustrate incidents in her life or to illuminate her state of mind on various occasions.

Pugh, Edwin. "Mary Webb." *The Bookman*, London LXXIV, No. 442 (July 1928): 193-95.
Reminiscence by a friend proclaiming Webb's "genius" as a novelist.

Sanders, Charles. "Webb's *Precious Bane*, Book III, Chapter 2." *The Explicator* XXV, No. 2 (October 1966): 1, 3.
Consideration of the bearbaiting scene from *Precious Bane* as a "re-enactment" of the Crucifixion that reinforces the author's identification of Kester Woodseaves as a Christ figure.

————. "*The Golden Arrow:* Mary Webb's 'Apocalypse of Love'." *English Literature in Transition* 10, No. 1 (1967): 1-8.
Analysis of character, setting, and incident in *The Golden Arrow*.

Swinnerton, Frank. "The Younger Novelists." In his *The Georgian Scene: A Literary Panorama*, pp. 279-315. New York: Farrar & Rinehart, 1934.
Briefly summarizes the local color aspects and realistic characterization of Webb's novels.

Sykes, Marjorie. "The Anglo-Welsh Genius: Mary Webb." *Anglo-Welsh Review*, No. 68 (1981): 74-81.
Biographically-oriented analysis of the English and Welsh local-color elements in Webb's fiction.

Wrenn, Dorothy R. H. *Goodbye to Morning: A Biographical Study of Mary Webb*. Shrewsbury: Wilding and Son, 1964, 111 p.
Noncritical biography.

Appendix

The following is a listing of all sources used in Volume 24 of *Twentieth-Century Literary Criticism*. Included in this list are all copyright and reprint rights and acknowledgments for those essays for which permission was obtained. Every effort has been made to trace copyright, but if omissions have been made, please let us know.

THE EXCERPTS IN TCLC, VOLUME 24, WERE REPRINTED FROM THE FOLLOWING PERIODICALS:

The Academy, v. XVIII, July 31, 1880; v. XLVII, January 5, 1895; v. LXXV, November 7, 1908.

American Anthropologist, n.s. v. 46, 1944.

American Literary Realism 1870-1910, v. 4, Fall, 1971; v. 6, Winter, 1973. Copyright © 1971, 1973 by the Department of English, The University of Texas at Arlington. Both reprinted by permission of the publisher.

American Literature, v. XLVIII, January, 1977. Copyright © 1977 Duke University Press, Durham, NC. Reprinted by permission of the publisher.

Ariel, (The University of Calgary), v. 17, July, 1986 for "Betrayal and Theft: Beerbohm, Parody, and Modernism" by Terry Caesar. Copyright © 1986 The Board of Governors, The University of Calgary. Reprinted by permission of the publisher and the author.

The Arts, v. VI, November, 1924.

The Athenaeum, n. 3071, September 4, 1886; n. 3376, July 9, 1892; n. 3502, December 8, 1894; n. 4677, December 19, 1919; n. 4727, December 3, 1920.

The Atlantic Monthly, v. LXXV, May, 1895.

Author, v. II, June 1, 1891.

The Book Buyer, v. VIII, May, 1891.

The Bookman, London, v. XV, November, 1898; v. XXXVII, February, 1910; v. LXIV, April, 1923.

The Bookman, New York, v. I, April, 1895; v. XVI, October, 1902, v. XXIX, January, 1906; v. XLIX, August, 1919.

Books Abroad, v. 12, Spring, 1938.

Books from Finland, v. XII, 1978. Reprinted by permission of the publisher.

The Cambridge Journal, v. V, May, 1952.

The Chap-Book, v. 1, August 15, 1894.

College English, v. 4, March, 1943.

Daily Chronicle, December 13, 1901.

The Dial, v. LXIII, September 13, 1917; v. LXXXIII, December, 1927.

The Dublin Magazine, v. XIV, January-March, 1939.

English, v. VI, Spring, 1947.

Essays in Criticism, v. XII, January, 1962 for " 'The Turn of the Screw': Jamesian Gothic" by Manfred Mackenzie. Reprinted by permission of the Editors of *Essays in Criticism* and the author.

The Fortnightly Review, n.s. v. CXXXI, January 1, 1932.

Harper's New Monthly Magazine, v. LXXXIII, September, 1891.

The Hudson Review, v. XI, Spring, 1958. Copyright © 1958 by The Hudson Review, Inc. Reprinted by permission of the publisher.

The Independent, v. LI, January 5, 1899.

The Journal of English and Germanic Philology, v. XIX, January, 1920.

Journal of Modern Literature, v. 3, February, 1973. © Temple University 1973. Reprinted by permission of the publisher.

The Liberator, New York, v. 2, September, 1919.

Life and Letters and the London Mercury, v. 52, January, 1947.

The Literary Half-Yearly, v. III, July, 1962. © *The Literary Half-Yearly.*

The Literary World, v. XXX, March 18, 1899; v. XXX, April 1, 1899.

The Little Review, v. II, September, 1915.

Midcontinent American Studies Journal, v. 3, Spring, 1962 for "Frank Norris: The Naturalist as Victorian" by Robert W. Schneider. Copyright, Mid-America American Studies Association, 1962. Reprinted by permission of *American Studies,* formerly *Midcontinent American Studies Journal,* and the author.

The Midwest Quarterly, v. XXVII, Summer, 1986. Copyright, 1986, by *The Midwest Quarterly,* Pittsburg State University. Reprinted by permission of the publisher.

MLN, v. LVI, March, 1941; v. LXII, November, 1947.

Modern Fiction Studies, v. V, Summer, 1959; v. IX, Winter, 1963-64. Copyright © 1959, 1963-64 by Purdue Research Foundation, West Lafayette, IN 47907. All rights reserved. Both reprinted with permission.

Modern Language Quarterly, v. 45, March, 1984. © 1984 University of Washington. Reprinted by permission of the publisher.

The Nation, New York, v. LX, January 10, 1895; v. LXIII, September 10, 1896; v. LXXXIV, January 17, 1907; v. CV, September 20, 1917; v. CIX, September 6, 1919; v. CXXV, November 2, 1927./ v. 235, September 25, 1982. Copyright 1982 *The Nation* magazine, The Nation Company, Inc. Reprinted by permission of the publisher.

The Nation, London, v. 86, June 25, 1908.

The New Mexico Quarterly Review, v. XII, February, 1942.

THE EXCERPTS IN TCLC, VOLUME 24, WERE REPRINTED FROM THE FOLLOWING BOOKS:

Addison, Hilda. From *Mary Webb: A Short Story of Her Life and Work*. Cecil Palmer, 1931.

Ahnebrink, Lars. From *The Beginnings of Naturalism in American Fiction: 1891-1903, Vol. IX*. Cambridge, Mass.: Harvard University Press, 1950.

Ahokas, Jaakko. From *A History of Finnish Literature*. Indiana University, 1973. Copyright © 1973 by Indiana University. All rights reserved. Reprinted by permission of the publisher.

Alba, Pedro de. From "Eugenio Maria de Hostos and His Ideas of Social Morality," in *Eugenio Maria de Hostos: Promoter of Pan Americanism*. Edited by Eugenio Carlos de Hostos. Juan Bravo, 1954?

Anderson, Sherwood. From *Sherwood Anderson: Selected Letters*. Edited by Charles E. Modlin. The University of Tennessee Press, Knoxville, 1984. Copyright © 1984 by Eleanor C. Anderson. All rights reserved. Reprinted by permission of the publisher.

Archer, William. From *Poets of the Younger Generation*. John Lane, 1902.

Asselineau, Roger. From *The Transcendentalist Constant in American Literature*. New York University Press, 1980. Copyright © 1980 by New York University. Reprinted by permission of the publisher.

Bălan, Ion Dodu. From *A Concise History of Romanian Literature*. Translated by Andrei Bantaş. Editura Ştiinţifică şi Enciclopedică, 1981.

Baldwin, Stanley. From an introduction to *Precious Bane*. By Mary Webb. E. P. Dutton & Company, Inc., 1929.

Barale, Michèle. From an introduction to *Seven for a Secret*. By Mary Webb. Virago, 1982. Introduction copyright © Michèle Barale 1982. All rights reserved. Reprinted by permission of the publisher.

Barbellion, W. N. P. From *A Last Diary*. George H. Doran Company, 1920.

Bluefarb, Sam. From *The Escape Motif in the American Novel: Mark Twain to Richard Wright*. Ohio State University Press, 1972. Copyright © 1972 by the Ohio State University Press. All rights reserved. Reprinted by permission of the publisher.

Boak, Denis. From *Roger Martin du Gard*. Oxford at the Clarendon Press, Oxford, 1963. © Oxford University Press, 1963. Reprinted by permission of the publisher.

Branch, Michael. From an introduction to *Whitsongs*. By Eino Leino, translated by Keith Bosley. The Menard Press, 1978. Introduction © 1978 Michael Branch. All rights reserved. Reprinted by permission of Michael Branch.

Brée, Germaine and Margaret Guiton. From *An Age of Fiction: The French Novel from Gide to Camus*. Rutgers University Press, 1957. Copyright © 1957 by Rutgers, The State University. Renewed 1985 by Germaine Brée and Margaret Guiton. Reprinted by permission of the publisher.

Brightman, Edgar Sheffield. From "Eugenio Maria de Hostos: Philosopher of Personality," in *Eugenio Maria de Hostos: Promoter of Pan Americanism*. Edited by Eugenio Carlos de Hostos. Juan Bravo, 1954?

Brombert, Victor. From *The Intellectual Hero: Studies in the French Novel, 1880-1955*. J. B. Lippincott Company, 1961. Copyright © 1960, 1961 by Victor Brombert. Reprinted by permission of Harper & Row, Publishers, Inc.

Brome, Vincent. From *Frank Harris*. Cassell and Company Limited, 1959. © 1959 by Vincent Brome. Reprinted by permission of the author.

Burbank, Rex. From *Sherwood Anderson*. Twayne, 1964. Copyright 1964 by Twayne Publishers. All rights reserved. Reprinted with the permission of Twayne Publishers, a division of G. K. Hall & Co., Boston.

Burdett, Osbert. From *Critical Essays*. Henry Holt and Company, 1926.

Camus, Albert. From *Lyrical and Critical Essays*. Edited by Philip Thody, translated by Ellen Conroy Kennedy. Alfred A. Knopf, 1968. Copyright © 1968 by Alfred A. Knopf, Inc. Copyright © 1967 by Hamish Hamilton Ltd. and Alfred A. Knopf, Inc. All rights reserved. Reprinted by permission of the publisher.

Cargill, Oscar. From *Intellectual America: Ideas on the March*. Macmillan, 1941. Copyright 1941 by Macmillan Publishing Company. Renewed 1969 by Oscar Cargill. All rights reserved. Reprinted with permission of Macmillan Publishing Company.

Cavaliero, Glen. From *The Rural Tradition in the English Novel: 1900-1939*. Rowman and Littlefield, 1977. © Glen Cavaliero 1977. All rights reserved. Reprinted by permission of the publisher.

Chamberlain, John. From *Farewell to Reform: The Rise, Life and Decay of the Progressive Mind in America*. Second edition. The John Day Company, 1933. Copyright 1932, renewed 1960, by John Chamberlain. Reprinted by permission of the author.

Chesterton, G. K. From an introduction to *The Golden Arrow*. By Mary Webb. Jonathan Cape, 1932.

Cockshut, A. O. J. From *Man and Woman: A Study of Love and the Novel, 1740-1940*. Collins, 1977, Oxford University Press, 1978. Copyright © 1977 by A. O. J. Cockshut. Reprinted by permission of Oxford University Press, Inc. In Canada by William Collins Sons & Co., Ltd.

Coles, Gladys Mary. From *"The Flower of Light": A Biography of Mary Webb*. Duckworth, 1978. © 1978 by Gladys Mary Coles. All rights reserved. Reprinted by permission of Gerald Duckworth and Co. Ltd.

Collie, Michael. From *The Alien Art: A Critical Study of George Gissing's Novels*. William Dawson & Sons Ltd., 1979. © Michael Collie 1978. All rights reserved. Reprinted by permission of the author.

Collins, Joseph. From *Taking the Literary Pulse: Psychological Studies of Life and Letters*. Doran, 1924. Copyright, 1924, by George H. Doran Company. Renewed 1951 by L. Beverly Chaney and Richard B. Duane. Reprinted by permission of the Literary Estate of Joseph Collins.

Cooper, Frederic Taber. From *Some American Story Tellers*. Henry Holt and Company, 1911.

Cowley, Malcolm. From an introduction to *Winesburg, Ohio*. By Sherwood Anderson. Revised edition. The Viking Press, 1960. Copyright © 1960 by The Viking Press, Inc. Reprinted by permission of Viking Penguin Inc.

Cranfill, Thomas Mabry and Robert Lanier Clark, Jr. From *An Anatomy of "The Turn of the Screw."* University of Texas Press, 1965. Copyright © 1965 by Thomas M. Cranfill and Robert L. Clark, Jr. All rights reserved. Reprinted by permission of the publisher and authors.

Crawford, William Rex. From *A Century of Latin-American Thought*. Cambridge, Mass.: Harvard University Press, 1944. Copyright 1944 by the President and Fellows of Harvard College. Renewed 1980 by William Rex Crawford. Excerpted by permission of the publishers.

Cummings, Arthur J. From "The Life and Character of Barbellion," in *A Last Diary*. By W. N. P. Barbellion. George H. Doran Company, 1920.

Cunha, Euclides da. From *Rebellion in the Backlands*. Translated by Samuel Putnam. The University of Chicago Press, 1944. Copyright 1944 by The University of Chicago. Renewed 1972 by Samuel Putnam. All rights reserved. Reprinted by permission of the publisher.

Dathorne, O. R. From *The Black Mind: A History of African Literature*. University of Minnesota Press, 1974. © copyright 1974 by the University of Minnesota. All rights reserved. Reprinted by permission of the publisher.

Davison, Richard Allan. From "A Reading of Frank Norris's 'The Pit'," in *The Stoic Strain in American Literature: Essays in Honour of Marston LaFrance*. Edited by Duane J. MacMillan. University of Toronto Press, 1979. © University of Toronto Press 1979. Reprinted by permission of the publisher.

Dukes, Ashley. From *Modern Dramatists*. Frank Palmer, 1911.

Eliot, T. S. From a preface to *John Davidson: A Selection of His Poems*. By John Davidson. Edited by Maurice Lindsay. Hutchinson of London, 1961. © Hutchinson & Co. (Publishers) Ltd. 1961. Reprinted by permission of the publisher.

Felstiner, John. From *The Lies of Art: Max Beerbohm's Parody and Caricature*. Alfred A. Knopf, 1972. Copyright © 1972 by John Felstiner. All rights reserved. Reprinted by permission of the author.

Fineman, Hayim. From *John Davidson: A Study of the Relation of His Ideas to His Poetry*. University of Pennsylvania, 1916.

Flaxman, Seymour L. From *Herman Heijermans and His Dramas*. Martinus Nijhoff, 1954.

French, Warren. From *Frank Norris*. Twayne, 1962. Copyright 1962 by Twayne Publishers. Reprinted with the permission of Twayne Publishers, a division of G. K. Hall & Co., Boston.

Gertz, Elmer. From ''Afterword: The Legend of Frank Harris,'' in *The Short Stories of Frank Harris: A Selection*. By Frank Harris, edited by Elmer Gertz. Southern Illinois University Press, 1975. Copyright © 1975 by Southern Illinois University Press and Arthur Leonard Ross as executor of the Frank Harris Estate. All rights reserved. Reprinted by permission of the publisher.

Gibson, Robert. From *Roger Martin du Gard*. Bowes & Bowes, 1961. © Robert Gibson 1961. Reprinted by permission of The Bodley Head Ltd.

Gissing, George. From *Selections Autobiographical and Imaginative from the Works of George Gissing*. Jonathan Cape & Harrison Smith, 1929.

Goldberg, Isaac. From *Brazilian Literature*. Alfred A. Knopf, 1922.

Graham, Don. From *The Fiction of Frank Norris: The Aesthetic Context*. University of Missouri Press, 1978. Copyright © 1978 by The Curators of the University of Missouri. All rights reserved. Reprinted by permission of the publisher.

Green, Mary Jean. From ''A Moral Image of Modern Man: The Doctor in the Work of Martin du Gard,'' in *Medicine and Literature*. Edited by Enid Rhodes Peschel. Neale Watson Academic Publications, 1980. © Neale Watson Academic Publications, Inc. 1980. All rights reserved. Reprinted by permission of the publisher.

Hardwick, Elizabeth. From "Sad Brazil," in *Bartleby in Manhattan and Other Essays*. Random House, 1983. Copyright © 1974 by Elizabeth Hardwick. All rights reserved. Reprinted by permission of Random House, Inc.

Harris, Frank. From a letter in *The Playwright and the Pirate: Bernard Shaw and Frank Harris, A Correspondence*. Edited by Stanley Weintraub. The Pennsylvania State University Press, University Park, 1982. Copyright © 1982 Edgar M. and Ralph G. Ross. All rights reserved. Reprinted by permission of the Literary Estate of Frank Harris.

Hellyar, Richmond H. From *W. N. P. Barbellion*. George H. Doran Company, 1926.

Henríquez-Ureña, Pedro. From *Literary Currents in Hispanic America*. Cambridge, Mass.: Harvard University Press, 1945. Copyright 1945, renewed 1972, by the President and Fellows of Harvard College. Excerpted by permission of the publishers.

Hicks, Granville. From *The Great Tradition: An Interpretation of American Literature Since the Civil War*. Revised edition. Macmillan Publishing Company, 1935.

Hind, Charles Lewis. From *Authors and I*. John Lane Company, 1921.

Hoffman, Frederick J. From *The Modern Novel in America: 1900-1950*. Henry Regnery Company, 1951.

Howe, Irving. From *Decline of the New*. Harcourt Brace Jovanovich, 1970. Copyright © 1970 by Irving Howe. Reprinted by permission of Harcourt Brace Jovanovich, Inc.

Hynes, Samuel. From *Edwardian Occasions: Essays on English Writing in the Early Twentieth Century*. Oxford University Press, 1972, Routledge & Kegan Paul, 1972. Copyright © 1972 by Samuel Hynes. Reprinted by permission of Oxford University Press, Inc. In Canada by Routledge & Kegan Paul PLC.

Ingram, Forrest L. From *Representative Short Story Cycles of the Twentieth Century: Studies in a Literary Genre*. Mouton, 1971. © copyright 1971 Mouton & Co., Publishers. Reprinted by permission of Mouton de Gruyter, a Division of Walter de Gruyter & Co.

Jackson, Holbrook. From *The Eighteen Nineties: A Review of Art and Ideas at the Close of the Nineteenth Century*. Grant Richards, 1913.

James Henry. From *The Novels and Tales of Henry James: The Aspern Papers, The Turn of the Screw, The Liar, The Two Faces, Vol. 12*. Charles Scribner's Sons, 1908.

Jouejati, R. From *The Quest for Total Peace: The Political Thought of Roger Martin du Gard*. Frank Cass, 1977. Copyright © 1977 R. Jouejati. All rights reserved. Reprinted by permission of Frank Cass & Co. Ltd.

July, Robert W. From *The Origins of Modern African Thought: Its Development in West Africa during the Nineteenth and Twentieth Centuries*. Frederick A. Praeger, 1967. © Robert W. July 1967. All rights reserved. Reprinted by permission of the author.

Kazin, Alfred. From *On Native Grounds: An Interpretation of Modern American Prose Literature*. Reynal & Hitchcock, 1942. Copyright 1942, 1970, by Alfred Kazin. Reprinted by permission of Harcourt Brace Jovanovich, Inc.

Keating, P. J. From *George Gissing: New Grub Street*. Edward Arnold (Publishers) Ltd., 1968. © P. J. Keating, 1968. Reprinted by permission of the author.

Weygandt, Cornelius. From *The Time of Yeats: English Poetry of To-Day Against an American Background*. Appleton-Century, 1937. Copyright, 1937 by D. Appleton-Century Company, Inc. Renewed 1964 by Cornelius N. Weygandt. Reprinted by permission of the Literary Estate of Cornelius Weygandt.

Wilson, Edmund. From *The Triple Thinkers: Twelve Essays on Literary Subjects*. Revised edition. Oxford University Press, 1948. Copyright 1938, 1948 by Edmund Wilson. Copyright renewed © 1956, 1971 by Edmund Wilson, and 1976 by Elena Wilson, Executrix of the Estate of Edmund Wilson. Reprinted by permission of Farrar, Straus and Giroux, Inc.

Woolf, Virginia. From *The Common Reader*. Harcourt Brace Jovanovich, 1925, L. & V. Woolf, 1925. Copyright 1925 by Harcourt Brace Jovanovich, Inc. Renewed 1953 by Leonard Woolf. Reprinted by permission of Harcourt Brace Jovanovich, Inc. In Canada by the Literary Estate of Virginia Woolf and The Hogarth Press.

Yoder, Hilda Van Neck. From *Dramatizations of Social Change: Herman Heijermans' Plays as Compared with Selected Dramas by Ibsen, Hauptmann, and Chekhov*. Nijhoff, 1978. © 1978 by Martinus Nijhoff Publishers, bv. All rights reserved. Reprinted by permission of the publisher.

Ziff, Larzer. From *American 1890's: Life and Times of a Lost Generation*. The Viking Press, 1966. Copyright © 1966 by Larzer Ziff. All rights reserved. Reprinted by permission of Viking Penguin Inc.

Literary Criticism Series
Cumulative Author Index

This index lists all author entries in the Gale Literary Criticism Series and includes cross-references to other Gale sources. For the convenience of the reader, references to the *Yearbook* in the *Contemporary Literary Criticism* series include the page number (in parentheses) after the volume number. References in the index are identified as follows:

AITN: *Authors in the News*, Volumes 1-2
CAAS: *Contemporary Authors Autobiography Series*, Volumes 1-4
CA: *Contemporary Authors* (original series), Volumes 1-118
CABS: *Contemporary Authors Bibliographical Series*, Volumes 1-2
CANR: *Contemporary Authors New Revision Series*, Volumes 1-18
CAP: *Contemporary Authors Permanent Series*, Volumes 1-2
CA-R: *Contemporary Authors* (revised editions), Volumes 1-44
CDALB: *Concise Dictionary of American Literary Biography*
CLC: *Contemporary Literary Criticism*, Volumes 1-43
CLR: *Children's Literature Review*, Volumes 1-12
DLB: *Dictionary of Literary Biography*, Volumes 1-53
DLB-DS: *Dictionary of Literary Biography Documentary Series*, Volumes 1-4
DLB-Y: *Dictionary of Literary Biography Yearbook*, Volumes 1980-1985
LC: *Literature Criticism from 1400 to 1800*, Volumes 1-5
NCLC: *Nineteenth-Century Literature Criticism*, Volumes 1-15
SAAS: *Something about the Author Autobiography Series*, Volumes 1-2
SATA: *Something about the Author*, Volumes 1-44
TCLC: *Twentieth-Century Literary Criticism*, Volumes 1-24
YABC: *Yesterday's Authors of Books for Children*, Volumes 1-2

Anderson, Roberta Joan 1943-
 See Mitchell, Joni

Anderson, Sherwood
 1876-1941............TCLC **1, 10, 24**
 See also CAAS 3
 See also CA 104
 See also DLB 4, 9
 See also DLB-DS 1

Andrade, Carlos Drummond de
 1902-......................CLC **18**

Andrewes, Lancelot 1555-1626 ...... LC **5**

Andrews, Cicily Fairfield 1892-1983
 See West, Rebecca

Andreyev, Leonid (Nikolaevich)
 1871-1919.................. TCLC **3**
 See also CA 104

Andrézel, Pierre 1885-1962
 See Dinesen, Isak
 See also Blixen, Karen (Christentze
   Dinesen)

Andrić, Ivo 1892-1975 ....CLC **8**
 See also CA 81-84
 See also obituary CA 57-60

Angelique, Pierre 1897-1962
 See Bataille, Georges

Angell, Roger 1920-...............CLC **26**
 See also CANR 13
 See also CA 57-60

Angelou, Maya 1928- .... CLC **12, 35**
 See also CA 65-68
 See also DLB 38

Annensky, Innokenty
 1856-1909.................. TCLC **14**
 See also CA 110

Anouilh, Jean (Marie Lucien Pierre)
 1910-............. CLC **1, 3, 8, 13, 40**
 See also CA 17-20R

Anthony, Florence 1947-
 See Ai

Anthony (Jacob), Piers 1934-.......CLC **35**
 See also Jacob, Piers A(nthony)
   D(illingham)
 See also DLB 8

Antoninus, Brother 1912-
 See Everson, William (Oliver)

Antonioni, Michelangelo 1912- .....CLC **20**
 See also CA 73-76

Antschel, Paul 1920-1970
 See Celan, Paul
 See also CA 85-88

Anwar, Chairil 1922-1949 .... TCLC **22**

Apollinaire, Guillaume
 1880-1918................. TCLC **3, 8**
 See also Kostrowitzki, Wilhelm Apollinaris
   de

Appelfeld, Aharon 1932- ....CLC **23**
 See also CA 112

Apple, Max (Isaac) 1941-....... CLC **9, 33**
 See also CA 81-84

Aquin, Hubert 1929-1977.........CLC **15**
 See also CA 105
 See also DLB 53

Aragon, Louis 1897-1982....... CLC **3, 22**
 See also CA 69-72
 See also obituary CA 108

Arbuthnot, John 1667-1735..........LC **1**

Archer, Jeffrey (Howard)
 1940-........................CLC **28**
 See also CA 77-80

Archer, Jules 1915-...............CLC **12**
 See also CANR 6
 See also CA 9-12R
 See also SATA 4

Arden, John 1930-......... CLC **6, 13, 15**
 See also CAAS 4
 See also CA 13-16R
 See also DLB 13

Arenas, Reinaldo 1943-............CLC **41**

Arguedas, José María
 1911-1969................ CLC **10, 18**
 See also CA 89-92

Argueta, Manlio 1936- ....CLC **31**

Armah, Ayi Kwei 1939- .... CLC **5, 33**
 See also CA 61-64

Armatrading, Joan 1950-..........CLC **17**
 See also CA 114

Arnim, Achim von 1781-1831 ..... NCLC **5**

Arnold, Matthew 1822-1888 ...... NCLC **6**
 See also DLB 32

Arnow, Harriette (Louisa Simpson)
 1908-1986............... CLC **2, 7, 18**
 See also CANR 14
 See also CA 9-12R
 See also obituary CA 118
 See also DLB 6
 See also SATA 42

Arp, Jean 1887-1966...............CLC **5**
 See also CA 81-84
 See also obituary CA 25-28R

Arquette, Lois S(teinmetz)
 See Duncan (Steinmetz Arquette), Lois
 See also SATA 1

Arrabal, Fernando 1932- ..... CLC **2, 9, 18**
 See also CANR 15
 See also CA 9-12R

Arrick, Fran 19??-.................CLC **30**

Artaud, Antonin 1896-1948 .... TCLC **3**
 See also CA 104

Arthur, Ruth M(abel)
 1905-1979....................CLC **12**
 See also CANR 4
 See also CA 9-12R
 See also obituary CA 85-88
 See also SATA 7
 See also obituary SATA 26

Arundel, Honor (Morfydd)
 1919-1973....................CLC **17**
 See also CAP 2
 See also CA 21-22
 See also obituary CA 41-44R
 See also SATA 4
 See also obituary SATA 24

Asch, Sholem 1880-1957......... TCLC **3**
 See also CA 105

Ashbery, John (Lawrence)
 1927-.....CLC **2, 3, 4, 6, 9, 13, 15, 25,
                                        41**
 See also CANR 9
 See also CA 5-8R
 See also DLB 5
 See also DLB-Y 81

Ashton-Warner, Sylvia (Constance)
 1908-1984....................CLC **19**
 See also CA 69-72
 See also obituary CA 112

Asimov, Isaac
 1920-............. CLC **1, 3, 9, 19, 26**
 See also CLR 12
 See also CANR 2
 See also CA 1-4R
 See also SATA 1, 26
 See also DLB 8

Astley, Thea (Beatrice May)
 1925-........................CLC **41**
 See also CANR 11
 See also CA 65-68

Aston, James 1906-1964
 See White, T(erence) H(anbury)

Asturias, Miguel Ángel
 1899-1974............... CLC **3, 8, 13**
 See also CAP 2
 See also CA 25-28
 See also obituary CA 49-52

Atheling, William, Jr. 1921-1975
 See Blish, James (Benjamin)

Atherton, Gertrude (Franklin Horn)
 1857-1948.................. TCLC **2**
 See also CA 104
 See also DLB 9

Atwood, Margaret (Eleanor)
 1939-........CLC **2, 3, 4, 8, 13, 15, 25**
 See also CANR 3
 See also CA 49-52
 See also DLB 53

Auchincloss, Louis (Stanton)
 1917-....................CLC **4, 6, 9, 18**
 See also CANR 6
 See also CA 1-4R
 See also DLB 2
 See also DLB-Y 80

Auden, W(ystan) H(ugh)
 1907-1973..... CLC **1, 2, 3, 4, 6, 9, 11,
                                   14, 43**
 See also CANR 5
 See also CA 9-12R
 See also obituary CA 45-48
 See also DLB 10, 20

Audiberti, Jacques 1899-1965......CLC **38**
 See also obituary CA 25-28R

Auel, Jean M(arie) 1936- ....CLC **31**
 See also CA 103

Austen, Jane 1775-1817 .... NCLC **1, 13**

Avison, Margaret 1918- .... CLC **2, 4**
 See also CA 17-20R
 See also DLB 53

Ayckbourn, Alan
 1939-...................CLC **5, 8, 18, 33**
 See also CA 21-24R
 See also DLB 13

Aymé, Marcel (Andre)
 1902-1967....................CLC **11**
 See also CA 89-92

Ayrton, Michael 1921-1975 ....CLC **7**
 See also CANR 9
 See also CA 5-8R
 See also obituary CA 61-64

Azorín 1874-1967.................CLC **11**
 See also Martínez Ruiz, José

Böll, Heinrich (Theodor)
   1917-1985...... CLC 2, 3, 6, 9, 11, 15,
                            27, 39 (291)
   See also DLB-Y 85
   See also Boell, Heinrich (Theodor)

Bolt, Robert (Oxton) 1924- ....CLC 14
   See also CA 17-20R
   See also DLB 13

Bond, Edward 1934-......CLC 4, 6, 13, 23
   See also CA 25-28R
   See also DLB 13

Bonham, Frank 1914-.............CLC 12
   See also CANR 4
   See also CA 9-12R
   See also SATA 1

Bonnefoy, Yves 1923- .... CLC 9, 15
   See also CA 85-88

Bontemps, Arna (Wendell)
   1902-1973................. CLC 1, 18
   See also CLR 6
   See also CANR 4
   See also CA 1-4R
   See also obituary CA 41-44R
   See also SATA 2, 44
   See also obituary SATA 24
   See also DLB 48

Booth, Martin 1944-.............CLC 13
   See also CAAS 2
   See also CA 93-96

Booth, Philip 1925- ....CLC 23
   See also CANR 5
   See also CA 5-8R
   See also DLB-Y 82

Booth, Wayne C(layson) 1921- .....CLC 24
   See also CANR 3
   See also CA 1-4R

Borchert, Wolfgang 1921-1947 .... TCLC 5
   See also CA 104

Borges, Jorge Luis
   1899-.......CLC 1, 2, 3, 4, 6, 8, 9, 10,
                            13, 19
   See also CA 21-24R

Borowski, Tadeusz 1922-1951 ..... TCLC 9
   See also CA 106

Borrow, George (Henry)
   1803-1881................... NCLC 9
   See also DLB 21

Bosschère, Jean de
   1878-1953................. TCLC 19

Boswell, James 1740-1795 .... LC 4

Bourget, Paul (Charles Joseph)
   1852-1935................. TCLC 12
   See also CA 107

Bourjaily, Vance (Nye) 1922-........CLC 8
   See also CAAS 1
   See also CANR 2
   See also CA 1-4R
   See also DLB 2

Bourne, Randolph S(illiman)
   1886-1918................. TCLC 16

Bowen, Elizabeth (Dorothea Cole)
   1899-1973...... CLC 1, 3, 6, 11, 15, 22
   See also CAP 2
   See also CA 17-18
   See also obituary CA 41-44R
   See also DLB 15

Bowering, George 1935-...........CLC 15
   See also CANR 10
   See also CA 21-24R
   See also DLB 53

Bowering, Marilyn R(uthe)
   1949-........................CLC 32
   See also CA 101

Bowers, Edgar 1924-...............CLC 9
   See also CA 5-8R
   See also DLB 5

Bowie, David 1947-...............CLC 17
   See also Jones, David Robert

Bowles, Jane (Sydney)
   1917-1973....................CLC 3
   See also CAP 2
   See also CA 19-20
   See also obituary CA 41-44R

Bowles, Paul (Frederick)
   1910-............. CLC 1, 2, 19
   See also CAAS 1
   See also CANR 1
   See also CA 1-4R
   See also DLB 5, 6

Box, Edgar 1925-
   See Vidal, Gore

Boyd, William 1952-..............CLC 28
   See also CA 114

Boyle, Kay 1903-............ CLC 1, 5, 19
   See also CAAS 1
   See also CA 13-16R
   See also DLB 4, 9, 48

Boyle, Patrick 19??- ....CLC 19

Boyle, T. Coraghessan 1948-.......CLC 36

Brackenridge, Hugh Henry
   1748-1816.................. NCLC 7
   See also DLB 11, 37

Bradbury, Edward P. 1939-
   See Moorcock, Michael

Bradbury, Malcolm (Stanley)
   1932-........................CLC 32
   See also CANR 1
   See also CA 1-4R
   See also DLB 14

Bradbury, Ray(mond Douglas)
   1920-............ CLC 1, 3, 10, 15, 42
   See also CANR 2
   See also CA 1-4R
   See also SATA 11
   See also DLB 2, 8
   See also AITN 1, 2

Bradley, David (Henry), Jr.
   1950-........................CLC 23
   See also CA 104
   See also DLB 33

Bradley, Marion Zimmer
   1930-........................CLC 30
   See also CANR 7
   See also CA 57-60
   See also DLB 8

Bradstreet, Anne 1612-1672 .... LC 4
   See also DLB 24

Bragg, Melvyn 1939-..............CLC 10
   See also CANR 10
   See also CA 57-60
   See also DLB 14

Braine, John (Gerard)
   1922-1986...............CLC 1, 3, 41
   See also CANR 1
   See also CA 1-4R
   See also DLB 15

Brammer, Billy Lee 1930?-1978
   See Brammer, William

Brammer, William 1930?-1978.....CLC 31
   See also obituary CA 77-80

Brancati, Vitaliano
   1907-1954.................. TCLC 12
   See also CA 109

Brancato, Robin F(idler) 1936-.....CLC 35
   See also CANR 11
   See also CA 69-72
   See also SATA 23

Brand, Millen 1906-1980 ....CLC 7
   See also CA 21-24R
   See also obituary CA 97-100

Brandes, Georg (Morris Cohen)
   1842-1927.................. TCLC 10
   See also CA 105

Branley, Franklyn M(ansfield)
   1915-........................CLC 21
   See also CANR 14
   See also CA 33-36R
   See also SATA 4

Brathwaite, Edward 1930-.........CLC 11
   See also CANR 11
   See also CA 25-28R
   See also DLB 53

Brautigan, Richard (Gary)
   1935-1984..........CLC 1, 3, 5, 9, 12,
                            34 (314), 42
   See also CA 53-56
   See also obituary CA 113
   See also DLB 2, 5
   See also DLB-Y 80, 84

Brecht, (Eugen) Bertolt (Friedrich)
   1898-1956..............TCLC 1, 6, 13
   See also CA 104

Bremer, Fredrika 1801-1865 ..... NCLC 11

Brennan, Christopher John
   1870-1932.................. TCLC 17

Brennan, Maeve 1917- ....CLC 5
   See also CA 81-84

Brentano, Clemens (Maria)
   1778-1842.................. NCLC 1

Brenton, Howard 1942- ....CLC 31
   See also CA 69-72
   See also DLB 13

Breslin, James 1930-
   See Breslin, Jimmy
   See also CA 73-76

Breslin, Jimmy 1930- .... CLC 4, 43
   See also Breslin, James
   See also AITN 1

Bresson, Robert 1907-............CLC 16
   See also CA 110

Breton, André 1896-1966..... CLC 2, 9, 15
   See also CAP 2
   See also CA 19-20
   See also obituary CA 25-28R

Breytenbach, Breyten
   1939-.................... CLC 23, 37
   See also CA 113

Crichton, (John) Michael
1942- . . . . CLC **2, 6**
See also CANR 13
See also CA 25-28R
See also SATA 9
See also DLB-Y 81
See also AITN 2

Crispin, Edmund 1921-1978 . . . . . . .CLC **22**
See also Montgomery, Robert Bruce

Cristofer, Michael 1946- . . . . .CLC **28**
See also CA 110
See also DLB 7

Crockett, David (Davy)
1786-1836 . . . . NCLC **8**
See also DLB 3, 11

Croker, John Wilson
1780-1857 . . . . NCLC **10**

Cronin, A(rchibald) J(oseph)
1896-1981 . . . . .CLC **32**
See also CANR 5
See also CA 1-4R
See also obituary CA 102
See also obituary SATA 25

Cross, Amanda 1926-
See Heilbrun, Carolyn G(old)

Crothers, Rachel 1878-1953 . . . . . . TCLC **19**
See also CA 113
See also DLB 7

Crowley, Aleister 1875-1947 . . . . . . TCLC **7**
See also CA 104

Crumb, Robert 1943- . . . . .CLC **17**
See also CA 106

Cryer, Gretchen 1936?- . . . . .CLC **21**
See also CA 114

Csáth, Géza 1887-1919 . . . . TCLC **13**
See also CA 111

Cudlip, David 1933- . . . . CLC **34** (38)

Cullen, Countee 1903-1946 . . . . TCLC **4**
See also CA 108
See also SATA 18
See also DLB 4, 48

Cummings, E(dward) E(stlin)
1894-1962 . . . . CLC **1, 3, 8, 12, 15**
See also CA 73-76
See also DLB 4, 48

Cunha, Euclides (Rodrigues) da
1866-1909 . . . . TCLC **24**

Cunningham, J(ames) V(incent)
1911-1985 . . . . CLC **3, 31**
See also CANR 1
See also CA 1-4R
See also obituary CA 115
See also DLB 5

Cunningham, Julia (Woolfolk)
1916- . . . . .CLC **12**
See also CANR 4
See also CA 9-12R
See also SAAS 2
See also SATA 1, 26

Cunningham, Michael
1952- . . . . CLC **34** (40)

Dąbrowska, Maria (Szumska)
1889-1965 . . . . .CLC **15**
See also CA 106

Dabydeen, David 1956?- . . . . . CLC **34** (147)

Dagerman, Stig (Halvard)
1923-1954 . . . . TCLC **17**

Dahl, Roald 1916- . . . . CLC **1, 6, 18**
See also CLR 1, 7
See also CANR 6
See also CA 1-4R
See also SATA 1, 26

Dahlberg, Edward
1900-1977 . . . . CLC **1, 7, 14**
See also CA 9-12R
See also obituary CA 69-72
See also DLB 48

Daly, Maureen 1921- . . . . .CLC **17**
See also McGivern, Maureen Daly
See also SAAS 1
See also SATA 2

Däniken, Erich von 1935-
See Von Däniken, Erich

Dannay, Frederic 1905-1982
See Queen, Ellery
See also CANR 1
See also CA 1-4R
See also obituary CA 107

D'Annunzio, Gabriele
1863-1938 . . . . TCLC **6**
See also CA 104

Danziger, Paula 1944- . . . . .CLC **21**
See also CA 112, 115
See also SATA 30, 36

Darío, Rubén 1867-1916 . . . . TCLC **4**
See also Sarmiento, Felix Ruben Garcia
See also CA 104

Darley, George 1795-1846 . . . . NCLC **2**

Daryush, Elizabeth
1887-1977 . . . . CLC **6, 19**
See also CANR 3
See also CA 49-52
See also DLB 20

Daudet, (Louis Marie) Alphonse
1840-1897 . . . . NCLC **1**

Daumal, René 1908-1944 . . . . TCLC **14**
See also CA 114

Davenport, Guy (Mattison, Jr.)
1927- . . . . CLC **6, 14, 38**
See also CA 33-36R

Davidson, Donald (Grady)
1893-1968 . . . . CLC **2, 13, 19**
See also CANR 4
See also CA 5-8R
See also obituary CA 25-28R
See also DLB 45

Davidson, John 1857-1909 . . . . TCLC **24**
See also CA 118
See also DLB 19

Davidson, Sara 1943- . . . . .CLC **9**
See also CA 81-84

Davie, Donald (Alfred)
1922- . . . . .CLC **5, 8, 10, 31**
See also CAAS 3
See also CANR 1
See also CA 1-4R
See also DLB 27

Davies, Ray(mond Douglas)
1944- . . . . .CLC **21**
See also CA 116

Davies, Rhys 1903-1978 . . . . .CLC **23**
See also CANR 4
See also CA 9-12R
See also obituary CA 81-84

Davies, (William) Robertson
1913- . . . . CLC **2, 7, 13, 25, 42**
See also CANR 17
See also CA 33-36R

Davies, W(illiam) H(enry)
1871-1940 . . . . TCLC **5**
See also CA 104
See also DLB 19

Davis, Rebecca (Blaine) Harding
1831-1910 . . . . TCLC **6**
See also CA 104

Davis, Richard Harding
1864-1916 . . . . TCLC **24**
See also CA 114
See also DLB 12, 23

Davison, Frank Dalby
1893-1970 . . . . .CLC **15**
See also obituary CA 116

Davison, Peter 1928- . . . . .CLC **28**
See also CAAS 4
See also CANR 3
See also CA 9-12R
See also DLB 5

Davys, Mary 1674-1732 . . . . LC **1**
See also DLB 39

Dawson, Fielding 1930- . . . . .CLC **6**
See also CA 85-88

Day Lewis, C(ecil)
1904-1972 . . . . CLC **1, 6, 10**
See also CAP 1
See also CA 15-16
See also obituary CA 33-36R
See also DLB 15, 20

Day, Thomas 1748-1789 . . . . LC **1**
See also YABC 1
See also DLB 39

Dazai Osamu 1909-1948 . . . . TCLC **11**
See also Tsushima Shūji

De Crayencour, Marguerite 1903-
See Yourcenar, Marguerite

Defoe, Daniel 1660?-1731 . . . . LC **1**
See also SATA 22
See also DLB 39

De Hartog, Jan 1914- . . . . .CLC **19**
See also CANR 1
See also CA 1-4R

Deighton, Len 1929- . . . . CLC **4, 7, 22**
See also CA 9-12R

De la Mare, Walter (John)
1873-1956 . . . . TCLC **4**
See also CA 110
See also SATA 16
See also DLB 19

Delaney, Shelagh 1939- . . . . .CLC **29**
See also CA 17-20R
See also DLB 13

Delany, Samuel R(ay, Jr.)
1942- . . . . CLC **8, 14, 38**
See also CA 81-84
See also DLB 8, 33

De la Roche, Mazo 1885-1961 . . . . . .CLC **14**
See also CA 85-88

Author Index

Author Index

Goytisolo, Juan 1931- .... CLC **5, 10, 23**
  See also CA 85-88
Grabbe, Christian Dietrich
  1801-1836 .... NCLC **2**
Gracq, Julien 1910- .... CLC **11**
Grade, Chaim 1910-1982 .... CLC **10**
  See also CA 93-96
  See also obituary CA 107
Graham, R(obert) B(ontine) Cunninghame
  1852-1936 .... TCLC **19**
Graham, W(illiam) S(ydney)
  1918- .... CLC **29**
  See also CA 73-76
  See also DLB 20
Graham, Winston (Mawdsley)
  1910- .... CLC **23**
  See also CANR 2
  See also CA 49-52
Granville-Barker, Harley
  1877-1946 .... TCLC **2**
  See also CA 104
Grass, Günter (Wilhelm)
  1927- .... CLC **1, 2, 4, 6, 11, 15, 22, 32**
  See also CA 13-16R
Grau, Shirley Ann 1929- .... CLC **4, 9**
  See also CA 89-92
  See also DLB 2
  See also AITN 2
Graves, Robert (von Ranke)
  1895-1985 .... CLC **1, 2, 6, 11, 39 (320)**
  See also CANR 5
  See also CA 5-8R
  See also DLB 20
  See also DLB-Y 85
Gray, Alasdair 1934- .... CLC **41**
Gray, Amlin 1946- .... CLC **29**
Gray, Francine du Plessix
  1930- .... CLC **22**
  See also CAAS 2
  See also CANR 11
  See also CA 61-64
Gray, John (Henry)
  1866-1934 .... TCLC **19**
Gray, Simon (James Holliday)
  1936- .... CLC **9, 14, 36**
  See also CAAS 3
  See also CA 21-24R
  See also DLB 13
  See also AITN 1
Gray, Thomas 1716-1771 .... LC **4**
Grayson, Richard (A.) 1951- .... CLC **38**
  See also CANR 14
  See also CA 85-88
Greeley, Andrew M(oran)
  1928- .... CLC **28**
  See also CANR 7
  See also CA 5-8R
Green, Hannah 1932- .... CLC **3, 7, 30**
  See also Greenberg, Joanne
  See also CA 73-76
Green, Henry 1905-1974 .... CLC **2, 13**
  See also Yorke, Henry Vincent
  See also DLB 15

Green, Julien (Hartridge)
  1900- .... CLC **3, 11**
  See also CA 21-24R
  See also DLB 4
Green, Paul (Eliot) 1894-1981 ...... CLC **25**
  See also CANR 3
  See also CA 5-8R
  See also obituary CA 103
  See also DLB 7, 9
  See also DLB-Y 81
Greenberg, Ivan 1908-1973
  See Rahv, Philip
  See also CA 85-88
Greenberg, Joanne (Goldenberg)
  1932- .... CLC **3, 7, 30**
  See also Green, Hannah
  See also CANR 14
  See also CA 5-8R
  See also SATA 25
Greene, Bette 1934- .... CLC **30**
  See also CLR 2
  See also CANR 4
  See also CA 53-56
  See also SATA 8
Greene, Gael 19??- .... CLC **8**
  See also CANR 10
  See also CA 13-16R
Greene, Graham (Henry)
  1904- .... CLC **1, 3, 6, 9, 14, 18, 27, 37**
  See also CA 13-16R
  See also SATA 20
  See also DLB 13, 15
  See also DLB-Y 85
  See also AITN 2
Gregor, Arthur 1923- .... CLC **9**
  See also CANR 11
  See also CA 25-28R
  See also SATA 36
Gregory, Lady (Isabella Augusta Persse)
  1852-1932 .... TCLC **1**
  See also CA 104
  See also DLB 10
Grendon, Stephen 1909-1971
  See Derleth, August (William)
Greve, Felix Paul Berthold Friedrich
  1879-1948
Grey, (Pearl) Zane
  1872?-1939 .... TCLC **6**
  See also CA 104
  See also DLB 9
Grieg, (Johan) Nordahl (Brun)
  1902-1943 .... TCLC **10**
  See also CA 107
Grieve, C(hristopher) M(urray) 1892-1978
  See MacDiarmid, Hugh
  See also CA 5-8R
  See also obituary CA 85-88
Griffin, Gerald 1803-1840 .... NCLC **7**
Griffin, Peter 1942- .... CLC **39 (398)**
Griffiths, Trevor 1935- .... CLC **13**
  See also CA 97-100
  See also DLB 13
Grigson, Geoffrey (Edward Harvey)
  1905-1985 .... CLC **7, 39 (330)**
  See also CA 25-28R
  See also obituary CA 118
  See also DLB 27

Grillparzer, Franz 1791-1872 ..... NCLC **1**
Grimm, Jakob (Ludwig) Karl 1785-1863
  See Grimm, Jakob (Ludwig) Karl and
  Grimm, Wilhelm Karl
Grimm, Jakob (Ludwig) Karl 1785-1863
  and **Grimm, Wilhelm Karl**
  1786-1859 .... NCLC **3**
  See also SATA 22
Grimm, Wilhelm Karl 1786-1859
  See Grimm, Jakob (Ludwig) Karl and
  Grimm, Wilhelm Karl
Grimm, Wilhelm Karl 1786-1859 and
  Grimm, Jakob (Ludwig) Karl
  1785-1863
  See Grimm, Jakob (Ludwig) Karl and
  Grimm, Wilhelm Karl
Grindel, Eugene 1895-1952
  See also CA 104
Grossman, Vasily (Semënovich)
  1905-1964 .... CLC **41**
Grove, Frederick Philip
  1879-1948 .... TCLC **4**
  See also Greve, Felix Paul Berthold
  Friedrich
Grumbach, Doris (Isaac)
  1918- .... CLC **13, 22**
  See also CAAS 2
  See also CANR 9
  See also CA 5-8R
Grundtvig, Nicolai Frederik Severin
  1783-1872 .... NCLC **1**
Guare, John 1938- .... CLC **8, 14, 29**
  See also CA 73-76
  See also DLB 7
Gudjonsson, Halldór Kiljan 1902-
  See Laxness, Halldór (Kiljan)
  See also CA 103
Guest, Barbara 1920- .... CLC **34 (441)**
  See also CANR 11
  See also CA 25-28R
  See also DLB 5
Guest, Judith (Ann) 1936- ...... CLC **8, 30**
  See also CANR 15
  See also CA 77-80
Guild, Nicholas M. 1944- .... CLC **33**
  See also CA 93-96
Guillén, Jorge 1893-1984 .... CLC **11**
  See also CA 89-92
  See also obituary CA 112
Guillevic, (Eugène) 1907- .... CLC **33**
  See also CA 93-96
Gunn, Bill 1934- .... CLC **5**
  See also Gunn, William Harrison
  See also DLB 38
Gunn, Thom(son William)
  1929- .... CLC **3, 6, 18, 32**
  See also CANR 9
  See also CA 17-20R
  See also DLB 27
Gunn, William Harrison 1934-
  See Gunn, Bill
  See also CANR 12
  See also CA 13-16R
  See also AITN 1
Gurney, A(lbert) R(amsdell), Jr.
  1930- .... CLC **32**
  See also CA 77-80

Harrison, Tony 1937- ....CLC 43
See also CA 65-68
See also DLB 40

Harriss, Will(ard Irvin)
1922- .... CLC 34 (192)
See also CA 111

Harte, (Francis) Bret(t)
1836?-1902................. TCLC 1
See also CA 104
See also SATA 26
See also DLB 12

Hartley, L(eslie) P(oles)
1895-1972................ CLC 2, 22
See also CA 45-48
See also obituary CA 37-40R
See also DLB 15

Hartman, Geoffrey H. 1929- ....CLC 27

Haruf, Kent 19??- .... CLC 34 (57)

Harwood, Ronald 1934- ....CLC 32
See also CANR 4
See also CA 1-4R
See also DLB 13

Hašek, Jaroslav (Matej Frantisek)
1883-1923.................... TCLC 4
See also CA 104

Hass, Robert 1941- ...... CLC 18, 39 (145)
See also CA 111

Hauptmann, Gerhart (Johann Robert)
1862-1946.................. TCLC 4
See also CA 104

Havel, Václav 1936- ....CLC 25
See also CA 104

Haviaras, Stratis 1935-...........CLC 33
See also CA 105

Hawkes, John (Clendennin Burne, Jr.)
1925-......CLC 1, 2, 3, 4, 7, 9, 14, 15,
                                                    27
See also CANR 2
See also CA 1-4R
See also DLB 2, 7
See also DLB-Y 80

Hawthorne, Nathaniel
1804-1864................NCLC 2, 10
See also YABC 2
See also DLB 1

Haycraft, Anna 19??-
See Ellis, Alice Thomas

Hayden, Robert (Earl)
1913-1980...........CLC 5, 9, 14, 37
See also CA 69-72
See also obituary CA 97-100
See also CABS 2
See also SATA 19
See also obituary SATA 26
See also DLB 5
See also CDALB 1941-1968

Haywood, Eliza (Fowler)
1693?-1756..................... LC 1
See also DLB 39

Hazzard, Shirley 1931-............CLC 18
See also CANR 4
See also CA 9-12R
See also DLB-Y 82

H(ilda) D(oolittle)
1886-1961.......... CLC 3, 8, 14, 31,
                                                34 (441)
See also Doolittle, Hilda

Head, Bessie 1937-.................CLC 25
See also CA 29-32R

Headon, (Nicky) Topper 1956?-
See The Clash

Heaney, Seamus (Justin)
1939-........... CLC 5, 7, 14, 25, 37
See also CA 85-88
See also DLB 40

Hearn, (Patricio) Lafcadio (Tessima Carlos)
1850-1904................... TCLC 9
See also CA 105
See also DLB 12

Heat Moon, William Least
1939-......................CLC 29

Hébert, Anne 1916-........ CLC 4, 13, 29
See also CA 85-88

Hecht, Anthony (Evan)
1923-.................. CLC 8, 13, 19
See also CANR 6
See also CA 9-12R
See also DLB 5

Hecht, Ben 1894-1964..............CLC 8
See also CA 85-88
See also DLB 7, 9, 25, 26, 28

Hedayat, Sadeq 1903-1951....... TCLC 21

Heidegger, Martin 1889-1976 ......CLC 24
See also CA 81-84
See also obituary CA 65-68

Heidenstam, (Karl Gustaf) Verner von
1859-1940................... TCLC 5
See also CA 104

Heifner, Jack 1946-...............CLC 11
See also CA 105

Heijermans, Herman
1864-1924.................. TCLC 24

Heilbrun, Carolyn G(old)
1926-.......................CLC 25
See also CANR 1
See also CA 45-48

Heine, Harry 1797-1856
See Heine, Heinrich

Heine, Heinrich 1797-1856........ NCLC 4

Heiney, Donald (William) 1921-
See Harris, MacDonald
See also CANR 3
See also CA 1-4R

Heinlein, Robert A(nson)
1907-............. CLC 1, 3, 8, 14, 26
See also CANR 1
See also CA 1-4R
See also SATA 9
See also DLB 8

Heller, Joseph
1923-.......... CLC 1, 3, 5, 8, 11, 36
See also CANR 8
See also CA 5-8R
See also DLB 2, 28
See also DLB-Y 80
See also AITN 1

Hellman, Lillian (Florence)
1905?-1984.......CLC 2, 4, 8, 14, 18,
                                                34 (347)
See also CA 13-16R
See also obituary CA 112
See also DLB 7
See also DLB-Y 84
See also AITN 1, 2

Helprin, Mark 1947-.....CLC 7, 10, 22, 32
See also CA 81-84
See also DLB-Y 85

Hemingway, Ernest (Miller)
1899-1961...... CLC 1, 3, 6, 8, 10, 13,
         19, 30, 34 (477), 39 (398; 427), 41
See also CA 77-80
See also DLB 4, 9
See also DLB-Y 81
See also DLB-DS 1
See also AITN 2

Hempel, Amy 1951-.......... CLC 39 (67)
See also CA 118

Henley, Beth 1952- ....CLC 23
See also Henley, Elizabeth Becker

Henley, Elizabeth Becker 1952-
See Henley, Beth
See also CA 107

Henley, William Ernest
1849-1903................... TCLC 8
See also CA 105
See also DLB 19

Hennissart, Martha
See Lathen, Emma
See also CA 85-88

Henry, O. 1862-1910 ....TCLC 1, 19
See also Porter, William Sydney

Hentoff, Nat(han Irving) 1925- .....CLC 26
See also CLR 1
See also CANR 5
See also CA 1-4R
See also SATA 27, 42

Heppenstall, (John) Rayner
1911-1981....................CLC 10
See also CA 1-4R
See also obituary CA 103

Herbert, Frank (Patrick)
1920-1986.............CLC 12, 23, 35
See also CANR 5
See also CA 53-56
See also obituary CA 118
See also SATA 9, 37
See also DLB 8

Herbert, Zbigniew 1924- .... CLC 9, 43
See also CA 89-92

Herbst, Josephine
1897-1969.............. CLC 34 (448)
See also CA 5-8R
See also obituary CA 25-28R
See also DLB 9

Herder, Johann Gottfried von
1744-1803................... NCLC 8

Hergesheimer, Joseph
1880-1954................. TCLC 11
See also CA 109
See also DLB 9

Herlagñez, Pablo de 1844-1896
See Verlaine, Paul (Marie)

Herlihy, James Leo 1927-..........CLC 6
See also CANR 2
See also CA 1-4R

Herriot, James 1916-..............CLC 12
See also Wight, James Alfred

Hersey, John (Richard)
1914-........... CLC 1, 2, 7, 9, 40
See also CA 17-20R
See also SATA 25
See also DLB 6

Kherdian, David 1931- .... CLC 6, 9
  See also CAAS 2
  See also CA 21-24R
  See also SATA 16

Khlebnikov, Velimir (Vladimirovich)
  1885-1922.................. TCLC 20
  See also CA 117

Khodasevich, Vladislav (Felitsianovich)
  1886-1939.................. TCLC 15
  See also CA 115

Kielland, Alexander (Lange)
  1849-1906.................. TCLC 5
  See also CA 104

Kiely, Benedict 1919- .... CLC 23, 43
  See also CANR 2
  See also CA 1-4R
  See also DLB 15

Kienzle, William X(avier)
  1928-......................CLC 25
  See also CAAS 1
  See also CANR 9
  See also CA 93-96

Killens, John Oliver 1916- ....CLC 10
  See also CAAS 2
  See also CA 77-80
  See also DLB 33

Killigrew, Anne 1660-1685........... LC 4

Kincaid, Jamaica 1949?- ....CLC 43

King, Francis (Henry) 1923- ....CLC 8
  See also CANR 1
  See also CA 1-4R
  See also DLB 15

King, Stephen (Edwin)
  1947-.................CLC 12, 26, 37
  See also CANR 1
  See also CA 61-64
  See also SATA 9
  See also DLB-Y 80

Kingman, (Mary) Lee 1919- ....CLC 17
  See also Natti, (Mary) Lee
  See also CA 5-8R
  See also SATA 1

Kingston, Maxine Hong
  1940-................... CLC 12, 19
  See also CANR 13
  See also CA 69-72
  See also DLB-Y 80

Kinnell, Galway
  1927-........... CLC 1, 2, 3, 5, 13, 29
  See also CANR 10
  See also CA 9-12R
  See also DLB 5

Kinsella, Thomas 1928- .... CLC 4, 19
  See also CA 17-20R
  See also DLB 27

Kinsella, W(illiam) P(atrick)
  1935-................... CLC 27, 43
  See also CA 97-100

Kipling, (Joseph) Rudyard
  1865-1936............... TCLC 8, 17
  See also CA 105
  See also YABC 2
  See also DLB 19, 34

Kirkup, James 1927-...............CLC 1
  See also CAAS 4
  See also CANR 2
  See also CA 1-4R
  See also SATA 12
  See also DLB 27

Kirkwood, James 1930- ....CLC 9
  See also CANR 6
  See also CA 1-4R
  See also AITN 2

Kizer, Carolyn (Ashley)
  1925-............... CLC 15, 39 (168)
  See also CA 65-68
  See also DLB 5

Klausner, Amos 1939-
  See Oz, Amos

Klein, A(braham) M(oses)
  1909-1972....................CLC 19
  See also CA 101
  See also obituary CA 37-40R

Klein, Norma 1938-...............CLC 30
  See also CLR 2
  See also CANR 15
  See also CA 41-44R
  See also SAAS 1
  See also SATA 7

Klein, T.E.D. 19??- .... CLC 34 (70)

Kleist, Heinrich von
  1777-1811................... NCLC 2

Klimentev, Andrei Platonovich 1899-1951
  See Platonov, Andrei (Platonovich)
  See also CA 108

Klinger, Friedrich Maximilian von
  1752-1831................... NCLC 1

Klopstock, Friedrich Gottlieb
  1724-1803.................. NCLC 11

Knebel, Fletcher 1911-............CLC 14
  See also CAAS 3
  See also CANR 1
  See also CA 1-4R
  See also SATA 36
  See also AITN 1

Knight, Etheridge 1931-............CLC 40
  See also CA 21-24R
  See also DLB 41

Knowles, John 1926-......CLC 1, 4, 10, 26
  See also CA 17-20R
  See also SATA 8
  See also DLB 6

Koch, C(hristopher) J(ohn)
  1932-........................CLC 42

Koch, Kenneth 1925- .... CLC 5, 8
  See also CANR 6
  See also CA 1-4R
  See also DLB 5

Koestler, Arthur
  1905-1983....... CLC 1, 3, 6, 8, 15, 33
  See also CANR 1
  See also CA 1-4R
  See also obituary CA 109
  See also DLB-Y 83

Kohout, Pavel 1928- ....CLC 13
  See also CANR 3
  See also CA 45-48

Konrád, György 1933- .... CLC 4, 10
  See also CA 85-88

Konwicki, Tadeusz 1926-....... CLC 8, 28
  See also CA 101

Kopit, Arthur (Lee)
  1937-.................. CLC 1, 18, 33
  See also CA 81-84
  See also DLB 7
  See also AITN 1

Kops, Bernard 1926-.................CLC 4
  See also CA 5-8R
  See also DLB 13

Kornbluth, C(yril) M.
  1923-1958................... TCLC 8
  See also CA 105
  See also DLB 8

Korolenko, Vladimir (Galaktionovich)
  1853-1921................. TCLC 22

Kosinski, Jerzy (Nikodem)
  1933-........... CLC 1, 2, 3, 6, 10, 15
  See also CANR 9
  See also CA 17-20R
  See also DLB 2
  See also DLB-Y 82

Kostelanetz, Richard (Cory)
  1940-........................CLC 28
  See also CA 13-16R

Kostrowitzki, Wilhelm Apollinaris de
  1880-1918
  See Apollinaire, Guillaume
  See also CA 104

Kotlowitz, Robert 1924-............CLC 4
  See also CA 33-36R

Kotzwinkle, William
  1938-................ CLC 5, 14, 35
  See also CLR 6
  See also CANR 3
  See also CA 45-48
  See also SATA 24

Kozol, Jonathan 1936- ....CLC 17
  See also CANR 16
  See also CA 61-64

Kozoll, Michael 1940?-
  See Bochco, Steven and Kozoll, Michael

Kramer, Kathryn 19??- ...... CLC 34 (74)

Kramer, Larry 1935- ....CLC 42

Krasicki, Ignacy 1735-1801 .... NCLC 8

Krasiński, Zygmunt
  1812-1859................... NCLC 4

Kraus, Karl 1874-1936........... TCLC 5
  See also CA 104

Kristofferson, Kris 1936- ....CLC 26
  See also CA 104

Krleža, Miroslav 1893-1981.........CLC 8
  See also CA 97-100
  See also obituary CA 105

Kroetsch, Robert 1927-......... CLC 5, 23
  See also CANR 8
  See also CA 17-20R
  See also DLB 53

Kroetz, Franz Xaver 1946- ....CLC 41

Krotkov, Yuri 1917- ....CLC 19
  See also CA 102

Krumgold, Joseph (Quincy)
  1908-1980....................CLC 12
  See also CANR 7
  See also CA 9-12R
  See also obituary CA 101
  See also SATA 1
  See also obituary SATA 23

Krutch, Joseph Wood
  1893-1970....................CLC 24
  See also CANR 4
  See also CA 1-4R
  See also obituary CA 25-28R

Lee, (Nelle) Harper 1926-..........CLC 12
  See also CA 13-16R
  See also SATA 11
  See also DLB 6
  See also CDALB 1941-1968

Lee, Lawrence 1903-........ CLC 34 (457)
  See also CA 25-28R

Lee, Manfred B(ennington) 1905-1971
  See Queen, Ellery
  See also CANR 2
  See also CA 1-4R
  See also obituary CA 29-32R

Lee, Stan 1922- ....CLC 17
  See also CA 108, 111

Lee, Vernon 1856-1935........... TCLC 5
  See also Paget, Violet

Lee-Hamilton, Eugene (Jacob)
  1845-1907.................. TCLC 22

Leet, Judith 1935-.................CLC 11

Le Fanu, Joseph Sheridan
  1814-1873.................. NCLC 9
  See also DLB 21

Leffland, Ella 1931-...............CLC 19
  See also CA 29-32R
  See also DLB-Y 84

Léger, (Marie-Rene) Alexis Saint-Léger
  1887-1975
  See Perse, St.-John
  See also CA 13-16R
  See also obituary CA 61-64

Le Guin, Ursula K(roeber)
  1929-.................. CLC 8, 13, 22
  See also CLR 3
  See also CANR 9
  See also CA 21-24R
  See also SATA 4
  See also DLB 8
  See also AITN 1

Lehmann, Rosamond (Nina)
  1901-........................CLC 5
  See also CANR 8
  See also CA 77-80
  See also DLB 15

Leiber, Fritz (Reuter, Jr.)
  1910-.......................CLC 25
  See also CANR 2
  See also CA 45-48
  See also DLB 8

Leino, Eino 1878-1926 .... TCLC 24

Leithauser, Brad 1953-.............CLC 27
  See also CA 107

Lelchuk, Alan 1938- ....CLC 5
  See also CANR 1
  See also CA 45-48

Lem, Stanislaw 1921- .... CLC 8, 15, 40
  See also CAAS 1
  See also CA 105

Lemann, Nancy 1956-....... CLC 39 (75)
  See also CA 118

Lemonnier, (Antoine Louis) Camille
  1844-1913.................. TCLC 22

L'Engle, Madeleine 1918-..........CLC 12
  See also CLR 1
  See also CANR 3
  See also CA 1-4R
  See also SATA 1, 27
  See also AITN 2

Lengyel, József 1896-1975 ....CLC 7
  See also CA 85-88
  See also obituary CA 57-60

Lennon, John (Ono)
  1940-1980....................CLC 35
  See also Lennon, John (Ono) and
    McCartney, Paul
  See also CA 102

Lennon, John (Ono) 1940-1980 and
  McCartney, Paul 1942- ....CLC 12

Lennon, John Winston 1940-1980
  See Lennon, John (Ono)

Lentricchia, Frank (Jr.)
  1940-.................. CLC 34 (571)
  See also CA 25-28R

Lenz, Siegfried 1926- ....CLC 27
  See also CA 89-92

Leonard, Elmore
  1925-.............. CLC 28, 34 (212)
  See also CANR 12
  See also CA 81-84
  See also AITN 1

Leonard, Hugh 1926- ....CLC 19
  See also Byrne, John Keyes
  See also DLB 13

Lerman, Eleanor 1952-.............CLC 9
  See also CA 85-88

Lermontov, Mikhail Yuryevich
  1814-1841.................. NCLC 5

Lesage, Alain-René 1668-1747........ LC 2

Lessing, Doris (May)
  1919-....... CLC 1, 2, 3, 6, 10, 15, 22,
                      40
  See also CA 9-12R
  See also DLB 15
  See also DLB-Y 85

Lester, Richard 1932-.............CLC 20

Leverson, Ada 1865-1936........ TCLC 18

Levertov, Denise
  1923-.........CLC 1, 2, 3, 5, 8, 15, 28
  See also CANR 3
  See also CA 1-4R
  See also DLB 5

Levi, Peter (Chad Tiger) 1931-.....CLC 41
  See also CA 5-8R
  See also DLB 40

Levi, Primo 1919- ....CLC 37
  See also CANR 12
  See also CA 13-16R

Levin, Ira 1929-................ CLC 3, 6
  See also CANR 17
  See also CA 21-24R

Levin, Meyer 1905-1981............CLC 7
  See also CANR 15
  See also CA 9-12R
  See also obituary CA 104
  See also SATA 21
  See also obituary SATA 27
  See also DLB 9, 28
  See also DLB-Y 81
  See also AITN 1

Levine, Philip
  1928-.......... CLC 2, 4, 5, 9, 14, 33
  See also CANR 9
  See also CA 9-12R
  See also DLB 5

Lévi-Strauss, Claude 1908- ....CLC 38
  See also CANR 6
  See also CA 1-4R

Levitin, Sonia 1934- ....CLC 17
  See also CA 29-32R
  See also SAAS 2
  See also SATA 4

Lewis, Alun 1915-1944 .... TCLC 3
  See also CA 104
  See also DLB 20

Lewis, C(ecil) Day 1904-1972
  See Day Lewis, C(ecil)

Lewis, C(live) S(taples)
  1898-1963........ CLC 1, 3, 6, 14, 27
  See also CLR 3
  See also CA 81-84
  See also SATA 13
  See also DLB 15

Lewis, (Harry) Sinclair
  1885-1951.............TCLC 4, 13, 23
  See also CA 104
  See also DLB 9
  See also DLB-DS 1

Lewis (Winters), Janet 1899-.......CLC 41
  See also Winters, Janet Lewis

Lewis, Matthew Gregory
  1775-1818.................. NCLC 11
  See also DLB 39

Lewis, (Percy) Wyndham
  1882?-1957................TCLC 2, 9
  See also CA 104
  See also DLB 15

Lewisohn, Ludwig 1883-1955 .... TCLC 19
  See also CA 107
  See also DLB 4, 9, 28

Lezama Lima, José
  1910-1976.................. CLC 4, 10
  See also CA 77-80

Li Fei-kan 1904-
  See Pa Chin
  See also CA 105

Lie, Jonas (Lauritz Idemil)
  1833-1908.................. TCLC 5

Lieber, Joel 1936-1971 ....CLC 6
  See also CA 73-76
  See also obituary CA 29-32R

Lieber, Stanley Martin 1922-
  See Lee, Stan

Lieberman, Laurence (James)
  1935-.................... CLC 4, 36
  See also CANR 8
  See also CA 17-20R

Lightfoot, Gordon (Meredith)
  1938-........................CLC 26
  See also CA 109

Liliencron, Detlev von
  1844-1909................. TCLC 18

Lima, José Lezama 1910-1976
  See Lezama Lima, José

Lima Barreto, (Alfonso Henriques de)
  1881-1922................. TCLC 23
  See also CA 117

Lind, Jakov 1927-.........CLC 1, 2, 4, 27
  See also Landwirth, Heinz
  See also CAAS 4
  See also CA 9-12R

Niven, Laurence Van Cott 1938-
See Niven, Larry
See also CANR 14
See also CA 21-24R

Nixon, Agnes Eckhardt 1927- ......CLC 21
See also CA 110

Nordhoff, Charles 1887-1947..... TCLC 23
See also CA 108
See also SATA 23
See also DLB 9

Norman, Marsha 1947-............CLC 28
See also CA 105
See also DLB-Y 84

Norris, (Benjamin) Frank(lin)
1870-1902.................. TCLC 24
See also CA 110
See also DLB 12

Norris, Leslie 1921-...............CLC 14
See also CANR 14
See also CAP 1
See also CA 11-12
See also DLB 27

North, Andrew 1912-
See Norton, Andre

North, Christopher 1785-1854
See Wilson, John

Norton, Alice Mary 1912-
See Norton, Andre
See also CANR 2
See also CA 1-4R
See also SATA 1, 43

Norton, Andre 1912-..............CLC 12
See also Norton, Mary Alice
See also DLB 8

Norway, Nevil Shute 1899-1960
See Shute (Norway), Nevil
See also CA 102
See also obituary CA 93-96

Nossack, Hans Erich 1901-1978 .....CLC 6
See also CA 93-96
See also obituary CA 85-88

Nova, Craig 1945-............. CLC 7, 31
See also CANR 2
See also CA 45-48

Novalis 1772-1801 .... NCLC 13

Nowlan, Alden (Albert) 1933-......CLC 15
See also CANR 5
See also CA 9-12R
See also DLB 53

Noyes, Alfred 1880-1958 .... TCLC 7
See also CA 104
See also DLB 20

Nunn, Kem 19??-............ CLC 34 (94)

Nye, Robert 1939-............ CLC 13, 42
See also CA 33-36R
See also SATA 6
See also DLB 14

Nyro, Laura 1947-................CLC 17

Oates, Joyce Carol
1938-.....CLC 1, 2, 3, 6, 9, 11, 15, 19,
33
See also CA 5-8R
See also DLB 2, 5
See also DLB-Y 81
See also AITN 1

O'Brien, Darcy 1939-.............CLC 11
See also CANR 8
See also CA 21-24R

O'Brien, Edna
1932-............. CLC 3, 5, 8, 13, 36
See also CANR 6
See also CA 1-4R
See also DLB 14

O'Brien, Flann
1911-1966.......... CLC 1, 4, 5, 7, 10
See also O Nuallain, Brian

O'Brien, Richard 19??-............CLC 17

O'Brien, (William) Tim(othy)
1946-.................. CLC 7, 19, 40
See also CA 85-88
See also DLB-Y 80

Obstfelder, Sigbjørn
1866-1900.................. TCLC 23

O'Casey, Sean
1880-1964......... CLC 1, 5, 9, 11, 15
See also CA 89-92
See also DLB 10

Ochs, Phil 1940-1976 ....CLC 17
See also obituary CA 65-68

O'Connor, Edwin (Greene)
1918-1968....................CLC 14
See also CA 93-96
See also obituary CA 25-28R

O'Connor, (Mary) Flannery
1925-1964...... CLC 1, 2, 3, 6, 10, 13,
15, 21
See also CANR 3
See also CA 1-4R
See also DLB 2
See also DLB-Y 80
See also CDALB 1941-1968

O'Connor, Frank
1903-1966............... CLC 14, 23
See also O'Donovan, Michael (John)

O'Dell, Scott 1903- ....CLC 30
See also CLR 1
See also CANR 12
See also CA 61-64
See also SATA 12

Odets, Clifford 1906-1963 ...... CLC 2, 28
See also CA 85-88
See also DLB 7, 26

O'Donovan, Michael (John) 1903-1966
See O'Connor, Frank
See also CA 93-96

Ōe, Kenzaburō 1935- .... CLC 10, 36
See also CA 97-100

O'Faolain, Julia 1932- .... CLC 6, 19
See also CAAS 2
See also CANR 12
See also CA 81-84
See also DLB 14

O'Faoláin, Seán
1900-................CLC 1, 7, 14, 32
See also CANR 12
See also CA 61-64
See also DLB 15

O'Flaherty, Liam
1896-1984........... CLC 5, 34 (355)
See also CA 101
See also obituary CA 113
See also DLB 36
See also DLB-Y 84

O'Grady, Standish (James)
1846-1928.................. TCLC 5
See also CA 104

O'Hara Family
See Banim, John and Banim, Michael

O'Hara, Frank
1926-1966............... CLC 2, 5, 13
See also CA 9-12R
See also obituary CA 25-28R
See also DLB 5, 16

O'Hara, John (Henry)
1905-1970...... CLC 1, 2, 3, 6, 11, 42
See also CA 5-8R
See also obituary CA 25-28R
See also DLB 9
See also DLB-DS 2

O'Hehir, Diana 1922-.............CLC 41
See also CA 93-96

Okigbo, Christopher (Ifenayichukwu)
1932-1967....................CLC 25
See also CA 77-80

Olds, Sharon 1942- ...... CLC 32, 39 (186)
See also CANR 18
See also CA 101

Olesha, Yuri (Karlovich)
1899-1960....................CLC 8
See also CA 85-88

Oliphant, Margaret (Oliphant Wilson)
1828-1897.................. NCLC 11
See also DLB 18

Oliver, Mary 1935- ...... CLC 19, 34 (246)
See also CANR 9
See also CA 21-24R
See also DLB 5

Olivier, (Baron) Laurence (Kerr)
1907-.......................CLC 20
See also CA 111

Olsen, Tillie 1913-.............. CLC 4, 13
See also CANR 1
See also CA 1-4R
See also DLB 28
See also DLB-Y 80

Olson, Charles (John)
1910-1970...... CLC 1, 2, 5, 6, 9, 11,
29
See also CAP 1
See also CA 15-16
See also obituary CA 25-28R
See also CABS 2
See also DLB 5, 16

Olson, Theodore 1937-
See Olson, Toby

Olson, Toby 1937-................CLC 28
See also CANR 9
See also CA 65-68

Ondaatje, (Philip) Michael
1943-................... CLC 14, 29
See also CA 77-80

Oneal, Elizabeth 1934-
See Oneal, Zibby
See also CA 106
See also SATA 30

Oneal, Zibby 1934-................CLC 30
See also Oneal, Elizabeth

Rio, Michel 19?? ....CLC 43

Ritsos, Yannis 1909- .... CLC 6, 13, 31
See also CA 77-80

Rivers, Conrad Kent 1933-1968 .....CLC 1
See also CA 85-88
See also DLB 41

Robbe-Grillet, Alain
1922- ..... CLC 1, 2, 4, 6, 8, 10, 14, 43
See also CA 9-12R

Robbins, Harold 1916- ....CLC 5
See also CA 73-76

Robbins, Thomas Eugene 1936-
See Robbins, Tom
See also CA 81-84

Robbins, Tom 1936- .... CLC 9, 32
See also Robbins, Thomas Eugene
See also DLB-Y 80

Robbins, Trina 1938- ....CLC 21

Roberts, (Sir) Charles G(eorge) D(ouglas)
1860-1943.................. TCLC 8
See also CA 105
See also SATA 29

Roberts, Kate 1891-1985 ....CLC 15
See also CA 107
See also obituary CA 116

Roberts, Keith (John Kingston)
1935-.........................CLC 14
See also CA 25-28R

Roberts, Kenneth 1885-1957 ..... TCLC 23
See also CA 109
See also DLB 9

Robinson, Edwin Arlington
1869-1935.................. TCLC 5
See also CA 104

Robinson, Henry Crabb
1775-1867.................. NCLC 15

Robinson, Jill 1936-...............CLC 10
See also CA 102

Robinson, Kim Stanley
19??- .... CLC 34 (105)

Robinson, Marilynne 1944- ....CLC 25
See also CA 116

Robinson, Smokey 1940- ....CLC 21

Robinson, William 1940-
See Robinson, Smokey
See also CA 116

Robison, Mary 1949-..............CLC 42
See also CA 113, 116

Roddenberry, Gene 1921- ....CLC 17

Rodgers, Mary 1931- ....CLC 12
See also CANR 8
See also CA 49-52
See also SATA 8

Rodgers, W(illiam) R(obert)
1909-1969....................CLC 7
See also CA 85-88
See also DLB 20

Rodríguez, Claudio 1934-..........CLC 10

Roethke, Theodore (Huebner)
1908-1963......... CLC 1, 3, 8, 11, 19
See also CA 81-84
See also CABS 2
See also DLB 5
See also CDALB 1941-1968

Rogers, Sam 1943-
See Shepard, Sam

Rogers, Will(iam Penn Adair)
1879-1935.................. TCLC 8
See also CA 105
See also DLB 11

Rogin, Gilbert 1929-..............CLC 18
See also CANR 15
See also CA 65-68

Rohan, Kōda 1867-1947........ TCLC 22

Rohmer, Eric 1920-...............CLC 16
See also Scherer, Jean-Marie Maurice

Roiphe, Anne (Richardson)
1935-..................... CLC 3, 9
See also CA 89-92
See also DLB-Y 80

Rolfe, Frederick (William Serafino Austin
Lewis Mary) 1860-1913..... TCLC 12
See also CA 107
See also DLB 34

Rolland, Romain 1866-1944...... TCLC 23
See also CA 118

Rölvaag, O(le) E(dvart)
1876-1931.................. TCLC 17
See also DLB 9

Romains, Jules 1885-1972 ....CLC 7
See also CA 85-88

Romero, José Rubén
1890-1952.................. TCLC 14
See also CA 114

Rooke, Leon 1934-....... CLC 25, 34 (250)
See also CA 25-28R

Rosa, João Guimarães
1908-1967....................CLC 23
See also obituary CA 89-92

Rosen, Richard (Dean)
1949-.................. CLC 39 (194)

Rosenberg, Isaac 1890-1918...... TCLC 12
See also CA 107
See also DLB 20

Rosenblatt, Joe 1933- ....CLC 15
See also Rosenblatt, Joseph
See also AITN 2

Rosenblatt, Joseph 1933-
See Rosenblatt, Joe
See also CA 89-92

Rosenthal, M(acha) L(ouis)
1917-.......................CLC 28
See also CANR 4
See also CA 1-4R
See also DLB 5

Ross, (James) Sinclair 1908- ....CLC 13
See also CA 73-76

Rossetti, Christina Georgina
1830-1894................... NCLC 2
See also SATA 20
See also DLB 35

Rossetti, Dante Gabriel
1828-1882.................. NCLC 4
See also DLB 35

Rossetti, Gabriel Charles Dante 1828-1882
See Rossetti, Dante Gabriel

Rossner, Judith (Perelman)
1935-...................CLC 6, 9, 29
See also CANR 18
See also CA 17-20R
See also DLB 6
See also AITN 2

Rostand, Edmond (Eugène Alexis)
1868-1918.................. TCLC 6
See also CA 104

Roth, Henry 1906-...........CLC 2, 6, 11
See also CAP 1
See also CA 11-12
See also DLB 28

Roth, Philip (Milton)
1933-......CLC 1, 2, 3, 4, 6, 9, 15, 22,
31
See also CANR 1
See also CA 1-4R
See also DLB 2, 28
See also DLB-Y 82

Rothenberg, Jerome 1931-..........CLC 6
See also CANR 1
See also CA 45-48
See also DLB 5

Roumain, Jacques 1907-1944 .... TCLC 19

Rourke, Constance (Mayfield)
1885-1941.................. TCLC 12
See also CA 107
See also YABC 1

Roussel, Raymond 1877-1933 .... TCLC 20
See also CA 117

Rovit, Earl (Herbert) 1927-.........CLC 7
See also CA 5-8R

Rowson, Susanna Haswell
1762-1824................... NCLC 5
See also DLB 37

Roy, Gabrielle 1909-1983...... CLC 10, 14
See also CANR 5
See also CA 53-56
See also obituary CA 110

Różewicz, Tadeusz 1921- .... CLC 9, 23
See also CA 108

Ruark, Gibbons 1941-..............CLC 3
See also CANR 14
See also CA 33-36R

Rubens, Bernice 192?- .... CLC 19, 31
See also CA 25-28R
See also DLB 14

Rudkin, (James) David 1936- ......CLC 14
See also CA 89-92
See also DLB 13

Rudnik, Raphael 1933-.............CLC 7
See also CA 29-32R

Ruiz, José Martínez 1874-1967
See Azorín

Rukeyser, Muriel
1913-1980..........CLC 6, 10, 15, 27
See also CA 5-8R
See also obituary CA 93-96
See also obituary SATA 22
See also DLB 48

Rule, Jane (Vance) 1931- ....CLC 27
See also CANR 12
See also CA 25-28R

Rulfo, Juan 1918-1986 ....CLC 8
See also CA 85-88
See also obituary CA 118

Runyon, (Alfred) Damon
  1880-1946.................. TCLC 10
  See also CA 107
  See also DLB 11

Rushdie, (Ahmed) Salman
  1947-.................... CLC 23, 31
  See also CA 108, 111

Rushforth, Peter (Scott) 1945-......CLC 19
  See also CA 101

Ruskin, John 1819-1900......... TCLC 20
  See also CA 114
  See also SATA 24

Russ, Joanna 1937-...............CLC 15
  See also CANR 11
  See also CA 25-28R
  See also DLB 8

Russell, George William 1867-1935
  See A. E.
  See also CA 104

Russell, (Henry) Ken(neth Alfred)
  1927-........................CLC 16
  See also CA 105

Ruyslinck, Ward 1929-............CLC 14

Ryan, Cornelius (John)
  1920-1974....................CLC 7
  See also CA 69-72
  See also obituary CA 53-56

Rybakov, Anatoli 1911?- ....CLC 23

Ryder, Jonathan 1927-
  See Ludlum, Robert

Ryga, George 1932-...............CLC 14
  See also CA 101

Sabato, Ernesto 1911-......... CLC 10, 23
  See also CA 97-100

Sachs, Marilyn (Stickle) 1927-......CLC 35
  See also CLR 2
  See also CANR 13
  See also CA 17-20R
  See also SAAS 2
  See also SATA 3

Sachs, Nelly 1891-1970............CLC 14
  See also CAP 2
  See also CA 17-18
  See also obituary CA 25-28R

Sackler, Howard (Oliver)
  1929-1982....................CLC 14
  See also CA 61-64
  See also obituary CA 108
  See also DLB 7

Sade, Donatien Alphonse François, Comte de
  1740-1814.................. NCLC 3

Sadoff, Ira 1945-.................CLC 9
  See also CANR 5
  See also CA 53-56

Safire, William 1929- ....CLC 10
  See also CA 17-20R

Sagan, Carl (Edward) 1934- ....CLC 30
  See also CANR 11
  See also CA 25-28R

Sagan, Françoise
  1935-............ CLC 3, 6, 9, 17, 36
  See also Quoirez, Françoise
  See also CANR 11
  See also CA 9-12R

Sainte-Beuve, Charles Augustin
  1804-1869.................. NCLC 5

Sainte-Marie, Beverly 1941-
  See Sainte-Marie, Buffy
  See also CA 107

Sainte-Marie, Buffy 1941- ....CLC 17
  See also Sainte-Marie, Beverly

Saint-Exupéry, Antoine (Jean Baptiste Marie Roger) de 1900-1944 .... TCLC 2
  See also CA 108
  See also SATA 20

Sait Faik (Abasıyanık)
  1906-1954.................. TCLC 23

Saki 1870-1916.................. TCLC 3
  See also Munro, H(ector) H(ugh)

Salama, Hannu 1936-.............CLC 18

Salamanca, J(ack) R(ichard)
  1922-.................... CLC 4, 15
  See also CA 25-28R

Salinas, Pedro 1891-1951....... TCLC 17

Salinger, J(erome) D(avid)
  1919-.................CLC 1, 3, 8, 12
  See also CA 5-8R
  See also DLB 2
  See also CDALB 1941-1968

Salter, James 1925-.................CLC 7
  See also CA 73-76

Saltus, Edgar (Everston)
  1855-1921.................. TCLC 8
  See also CA 105

Samarakis, Antonis 1919-...........CLC 5
  See also CA 25-28R

Sánchez, Luis Rafael 1936- ....CLC 23

Sanchez, Sonia 1934-...............CLC 5
  See also CA 33-36R
  See also SATA 22
  See also DLB 41

Sand, George 1804-1876.......... NCLC 2

Sandburg, Carl (August)
  1878-1967........ CLC 1, 4, 10, 15, 35
  See also CA 5-8R
  See also obituary CA 25-28R
  See also SATA 8
  See also DLB 17

Sandburg, Charles August 1878-1967
  See Sandburg, Carl (August)

Sanders, Lawrence 1920-..........CLC 41
  See also CA 81-84

Sandoz, Mari (Susette)
  1896-1966....................CLC 28
  See also CANR 17
  See also CA 1-4R
  See also obituary CA 25-28R
  See also SATA 5
  See also DLB 9

Saner, Reg(inald Anthony)
  1931-.......................CLC 9
  See also CA 65-68

Sansom, William 1912-1976...... CLC 2, 6
  See also CA 5-8R
  See also obituary CA 65-68

Santiago, Danny 1911- ....CLC 33

Santmyer, Helen Hooven 1895-.....CLC 33
  See also CANR 15
  See also CA 1-4R
  See also DLB-Y 84

Santos, Bienvenido N(uqui)
  1911-........................CLC 22
  See also CA 101

Sarduy, Severo 1937- ....CLC 6
  See also CA 89-92

Sargeson, Frank 1903-1982........CLC 31
  See also CA 25-28R
  See also CA 106

Sarmiento, Felix Ruben Garcia 1867-1916
  See also CA 104

Saroyan, William
  1908-1981.......... CLC 1, 8, 10, 29,
                                      34 (457)
  See also CA 5-8R
  See also obituary CA 103
  See also SATA 23
  See also obituary SATA 24
  See also DLB 7, 9
  See also DLB-Y 81

Sarraute, Nathalie
  1902-........... CLC 1, 2, 4, 8, 10, 31
  See also CA 9-12R

Sarton, (Eleanor) May
  1912-.................... CLC 4, 14
  See also CANR 1
  See also CA 1-4R
  See also SATA 36
  See also DLB 48
  See also DLB-Y 81

Sartre, Jean-Paul
  1905-1980...... CLC 1, 4, 7, 9, 13, 18,
                                      24
  See also CA 9-12R
  See also obituary CA 97-100

Sassoon, Siegfried (Lorraine)
  1886-1967....................CLC 36
  See also CA 104
  See also Obituary CA 25-28R
  See also DLB 20

Saura, Carlos 1932-...............CLC 20
  See also CA 114

Sauser-Hall, Frédéric-Louis 1887-1961
  See Cendrars, Blaise
  See also CA 102
  See also obituary CA 93-96

Savage, Thomas 1915- ....CLC 40

Sayers, Dorothy L(eigh)
  1893-1957................ TCLC 2, 15
  See also CA 104
  See also DLB 10, 36

Sayles, John (Thomas)
  1950-.................. CLC 7, 10, 14
  See also CA 57-60
  See also DLB 44

Scammell, Michael 19??- .... CLC 34 (480)

Schaeffer, Susan Fromberg
  1941-.................. CLC 6, 11, 22
  See also CANR 18
  See also CA 49-52
  See also SATA 22
  See also DLB 28

Schell, Jonathan 1943- ....CLC 35
  See also CANR 12
  See also CA 73-76

Scherer, Jean-Marie Maurice 1920-
  See Rohmer, Eric
  See also CA 110

Sagan, Françoise Sahgal, Nayantara
  (Pandit) 1927- ....CLC 41
  See also CANR 11
  See also CA 9-12R

Schevill, James (Erwin) 1920- .... CLC 7
See also CA 5-8R

Schisgal, Murray (Joseph)
1926- .... CLC 6
See also CA 21-24R

Schlee, Ann 1934- .... CLC 35
See also CA 101
See also SATA 36

Schlegel, August Wilhelm von
1767-1845 .... NCLC 15

Schlegel, Johann Elias (von)
1719?-1749 .... LC 5

Schmitz, Ettore 1861-1928
See Svevo, Italo
See also CA 104

Schnackenberg, Gjertrud
1953- .... CLC 40
See also CA 116

Schneider, Leonard Alfred 1925-1966
See Bruce, Lenny
See also CA 89-92

Schnitzler, Arthur 1862-1931 ..... TCLC 4
See also CA 104

Schorer, Mark 1908-1977 .... CLC 9
See also CANR 7
See also CA 5-8R
See also obituary CA 73-76

Schrader, Paul (Joseph) 1946- ...... CLC 26
See also CA 37-40R
See also DLB 44

Schreiner (Cronwright), Olive (Emilie
Albertina) 1855-1920 .... TCLC 9
See also CA 105
See also DLB 18

Schulberg, Budd (Wilson) 1914- ..... CLC 7
See also CA 25-28R
See also DLB 6, 26, 28
See also DLB-Y 81

Schulz, Bruno 1892-1942 .... TCLC 5
See also CA 115

Schulz, Charles M(onroe)
1922- .... CLC 12
See also CANR 6
See also CA 9-12R
See also SATA 10

Schuyler, James (Marcus)
1923- .... CLC 5, 23
See also CA 101
See also DLB 5

Schwartz, Delmore
1913-1966 .... CLC 2, 4, 10
See also CAP 2
See also CA 17-18
See also obituary CA 25-28R
See also DLB 28, 48

Schwartz, Lynne Sharon 1939- ..... CLC 31
See also CA 103

Schwarz-Bart, André 1928- ...... CLC 2, 4
See also CA 89-92

Schwarz-Bart, Simone 1938- .... CLC 7
See also CA 97-100

Schwob, (Mayer Andre) Marcel
1867-1905 .... TCLC 20
See also CA 117

Sciascia, Leonardo 1921- ..... CLC 8, 9, 41
See also CA 85-88

Scoppettone, Sandra 1936- .... CLC 26
See also CA 5-8R
See also SATA 9

Scorsese, Martin 1942- .... CLC 20
See also CA 110, 114

Scotland, Jay 1932-
See Jakes, John (William)

Scott, Duncan Campbell
1862-1947 .... TCLC 6
See also CA 104

Scott, Evelyn 1893-1963 .... CLC 43
See also CA 104
See also obituary CA 112
See also DLB 9, 48

Scott, F(rancis) R(eginald)
1899-1985 .... CLC 22
See also CA 101
See also obituary CA 114

Scott, Paul (Mark) 1920-1978 ...... CLC 9
See also CA 81-84
See also obituary CA 77-80
See also DLB 14

Scott, Sir Walter 1771-1832 ...... NCLC 15
See also YABC 2

Scudéry, Madeleine de 1607-1701 ..... LC 2

Seare, Nicholas 1925-
See Trevanian
See also Whitaker, Rodney

Sebestyen, Igen 1924-
See Sebestyen, Ouida

Sebestyen, Ouida 1924- .... CLC 30
See also CA 107
See also SATA 39

Seelye, John 1931- .... CLC 7
See also CA 97-100

Seferiades, Giorgos Stylianou 1900-1971
See Seferis, George
See also CANR 5
See also CA 5-8R
See also obituary CA 33-36R

Seferis, George 1900-1971 ...... CLC 5, 11
See also Seferiades, Giorgos Stylianou

Segal, Erich (Wolf) 1937- .... CLC 3, 10
See also CA 25-28R

Seger, Bob 1945- .... CLC 35

Seger, Robert Clark 1945-
See Seger, Bob

Seghers, Anna 1900- .... CLC 7
See Radvanyi, Netty

Seidel, Frederick (Lewis) 1936- ..... CLC 18
See also CANR 8
See also CA 13-16R
See also DLB-Y 84

Seifert, Jaroslav 1901- ...... CLC 34 (255)

Selby, Hubert, Jr.
1928- .... CLC 1, 2, 4, 8
See also CA 13-16R
See also DLB 2

Sender, Ramón (José)
1902-1982 .... CLC 8
See also CANR 8
See also CA 5-8R
See also obituary CA 105

Serling, (Edward) Rod(man)
1924-1975 .... CLC 30
See also CA 65-68
See also obituary CA 57-60
See also DLB 26
See also AITN 1

Serpières 1907-
See Guillevic, (Eugène)

Service, Robert W(illiam)
1874-1958 .... TCLC 15
See also CA 115
See also SATA 20

Seth, Vikram 1952- .... CLC 43

Seton, Cynthia Propper
1926-1982 .... CLC 27
See also CANR-7
See also CA 5-8R
See also obituary CA 108

Settle, Mary Lee 1918- .... CLC 19
See also CAAS 1
See also CA 89-92
See also DLB 6

Sexton, Anne (Harvey)
1928-1974 ...... CLC 2, 4, 6, 8, 10, 15
See also CANR 3
See also CA 1-4R
See also obituary CA 53-56
See also CABS 2
See also SATA 10
See also DLB 5
See also CDALB 1941-1968

Shaara, Michael (Joseph)
1929- .... CLC 15
See also CA 102
See also DLB-Y 83
See also AITN 1

Shackleton, C. C. 1925-
See Aldiss, Brian W(ilson)

Shacochis, Bob 1951- .... CLC 39 (198)

Shaffer, Anthony 1926- .... CLC 19
See also CA 110
See also CA 116
See also DLB 13

Shaffer, Peter (Levin)
1926- .... CLC 5, 14, 18, 37
See also CA 25-28R
See also DLB 13

Shalamov, Varlam (Tikhonovich)
1907?-1982 .... CLC 18
See also obituary CA 105

Shamlu, Ahmad 1925- .... CLC 10

Shange, Ntozake 1948- ...... CLC 8, 25, 38
See also CA 85-88
See also DLB 38

Shapcott, Thomas W(illiam)
1935- .... CLC 38
See also CA 69-72

Shapiro, Karl (Jay) 1913- ..... CLC 4, 8, 15
See also CANR 1
See also CA 1-4R
See also DLB 48

Sharpe, Tom 1928- .... CLC 36
See also CA 114
See also DLB 14

Shaw, (George) Bernard
1856-1950 .... TCLC 3, 9, 21
See also CA 104, 109
See also DLB 10

Singer, Isaac Bashevis
1904-...... CLC 1, 3, 6, 9, 11, 15, 23, 38
See also CLR 1
See also CANR 1
See also CA 1-4R
See also SATA 3, 27
See also DLB 6, 28
See also CDALB 1941-1968
See also AITN 1, 2

Singh, Khushwant 1915-..........CLC 11
See also CANR 6
See also CA 9-12R

Sinyavsky, Andrei (Donatevich)
1925-.........................CLC 8
See also CA 85-88

Sissman, L(ouis) E(dward)
1928-1976................. CLC 9, 18
See also CA 21-24R
See also obituary CA 65-68
See also DLB 5

Sisson, C(harles) H(ubert) 1914-.....CLC 8
See also CAAS 3
See also CANR 3
See also CA 1-4R
See also DLB 27

Sitwell, (Dame) Edith
1887-1964................. CLC 2, 9
See also CA 9-12R
See also DLB 20

Sjoewall, Maj 1935-
See Wahlöö, Per
See also CA 65-68

Sjöwall, Maj 1935-
See Wahlöö, Per

Skelton, Robin 1925-..............CLC 13
See also CA 5-8R
See also AITN 2
See also DLB 27, 53

Skolimowski, Jerzy 1938-..........CLC 20

Skolimowski, Yurek 1938-
See Skolimowski, Jerzy

Skrine, Mary Nesta 1904-
See Keane, Molly

Škvorecký, Josef (Václav)
1924-............... CLC 15, 39 (220)
See also CAAS 1
See also CANR 10
See also CA 61-64

Slade, Bernard 1930- ....CLC 11
See also Newbound, Bernard Slade
See also DLB 53

Slaughter, Frank G(ill) 1908- ......CLC 29
See also CANR 5
See also CA 5-8R
See also AITN 2

Slavitt, David (R.) 1935-........ CLC 5, 14
See also CAAS 3
See also CA 21-24R
See also DLB 5, 6

Slesinger, Tess 1905-1945........ TCLC 10
See also CA 107

Slessor, Kenneth 1901-1971........CLC 14
See also CA 102
See also obituary CA 89-92

Słowacki, Juliusz 1809-1849 ..... NCLC 15

Smart, Christopher 1722-1771 ...... LC 3

Smith, A(rthur) J(ames) M(arshall)
1902-1980...................CLC 15
See also CANR 4
See also CA 1-4R
See also obituary CA 102

Smith, Betty (Wehner)
1896-1972...................CLC 19
See also CA 5-8R
See also obituary CA 33-36R
See also SATA 6
See also DLB-Y 82

Smith, Cecil Lewis Troughton 1899-1966
See Forester, C(ecil) S(cott)

Smith, Clark Ashton
1893-1961...................CLC 43

Smith, Dave 1942-............ CLC 22, 42
See also Smith, David (Jeddie)
See also DLB 5

Smith, David (Jeddie) 1942-
See Smith, Dave
See also CANR 1
See also CA 49-52

Smith, Florence Margaret 1902-1971
See Smith, Stevie
See also CAP 2
See also CA 17-18
See also obituary CA 29-32R

Smith, Lee 1944-.................CLC 25
See also CA 114
See also DLB-Y 83

Smith, Martin Cruz 1942-.........CLC 25
See also CANR 6
See also CA 85-88

Smith, Martin William 1942-
See Smith, Martin Cruz

Smith, Mary-Ann Tirone
1944-.................. CLC 39 (97)
See also CA 118

Smith, Patti 1946-.................CLC 12
See also CA 93-96

Smith, Sara Mahala Redway 1900-1972
See Benson, Sally

Smith, Stevie 1902-1971...... CLC 3, 8, 25
See also Smith, Florence Margaret
See also DLB 20

Smith, Wilbur (Addison) 1933-.....CLC 33
See also CANR 7
See also CA 13-16R

Smith, William Jay 1918-...........CLC 6
See also CA 5-8R
See also SATA 2
See also DLB 5

Smollett, Tobias (George)
1721-1771..................... LC 2
See also DLB 39

Snodgrass, W(illiam) D(e Witt)
1926-.................CLC 2, 6, 10, 18
See also CANR 6
See also CA 1-4R
See also DLB 5

Snow, C(harles) P(ercy)
1905-1980....... CLC 1, 4, 6, 9, 13, 19
See also CA 5-8R
See also obituary CA 101
See also DLB 15

Snyder, Gary (Sherman)
1930-.............. CLC 1, 2, 5, 9, 32
See also CA 17-20R
See also DLB 5, 16

Snyder, Zilpha Keatley 1927- ......CLC 17
See also CA 9-12R
See also SAAS 2
See also SATA 1, 28

Sokolov, Raymond 1941-...........CLC 7
See also CA 85-88

Sologub, Fyodor 1863-1927....... TCLC 9
See also Teternikov, Fyodor Kuzmich

Solomos, Dionysios
1798-1857................. NCLC 15

Solwoska, Mara 1929-
See French, Marilyn

Solzhenitsyn, Aleksandr I(sayevich)
1918-.....CLC 1, 2, 4, 7, 9, 10, 18, 26, 34 (480)
See also CA 69-72
See also AITN 1

Somers, Jane 1919-
See Lessing, Doris (May)

Sommer, Scott 1951-..............CLC 25
See also CA 106

Sondheim, Stephen (Joshua)
1930-............... CLC 30, 39 (172)
See also CA 103

Sontag, Susan
1933-............ CLC 1, 2, 10, 13, 31
See also CA 17-20R
See also DLB 2

Sorrentino, Gilbert
1929-............ CLC 3, 7, 14, 22, 40
See also CANR 14
See also CA 77-80
See also DLB 5
See also DLB-Y 80

Soto, Gary 1952- ....CLC 32

Souster, (Holmes) Raymond
1921-.................... CLC 5, 14
See also CANR 13
See also CA 13-16R

Southern, Terry 1926- ....CLC 7
See also CANR 1
See also CA 1-4R
See also DLB 2

Southey, Robert 1774-1843 .... NCLC 8

Soyinka, Akin-wande Oluwole 1934-
See Soyinka, Wole

Soyinka, Wole 1934-......CLC 3, 5, 14, 36
See also CA 13-16R

Spacks, Barry 1931- ....CLC 14
See also CA 29-32R

Spark, Muriel (Sarah)
1918-.....CLC 2, 3, 5, 8, 13, 18, 40
See also CANR 12
See also CA 5-8R
See also DLB 15

Spencer, Elizabeth 1921- ....CLC 22
See also CA 13-16R
See also SATA 14
See also DLB 6

Spencer, Scott 1945-..............CLC 30
See also CA 113

Spender, Stephen (Harold)
1909-............. CLC 1, 2, 5, 10, 41
See also CA 9-12R
See also DLB 20

Spenser, Edmund 1552?-1599 .... LC 5

Spicer, Jack 1925-1965......... CLC 8, 18
See also CA 85-88
See also DLB 5, 16

Spielberg, Peter 1929-.............CLC 6
See also CANR 4
See also CA 5-8R
See also DLB-Y 81

Spielberg, Steven 1947-............CLC 20
See also CA 77-80
See also SATA 32

Spillane, Frank Morrison 1918-
See Spillane, Mickey
See also CA 25-28R

Spillane, Mickey 1918- .... CLC 3, 13
See also Spillane, Frank Morrison

Spitteler, Carl (Friedrich Georg)
1845-1924.................. TCLC 12
See also CA 109

Spivack, Kathleen (Romola Drucker)
1938-..........................CLC 6
See also CA 49-52

Spoto, Donald 1941- .... CLC 39 (444)
See also CANR 11
See also CA 65-68

Springsteen, Bruce 1949- ....CLC 17
See also CA 111

Spurling, Hilary 1940- ...... CLC 34 (494)
See also CA 104

**Staël-Holstein, Anne Louise Germaine
Necker, Baronne de**
1766-1817.................. NCLC 3

Stafford, Jean 1915-1979 ..... CLC 4, 7, 19
See also CANR 3
See also CA 1-4R
See also obituary CA 85-88
See also obituary SATA 22
See also DLB 2

Stafford, William (Edgar)
1914-.................. CLC 4, 7, 29
See also CAAS 3
See also CANR 5
See also CA 5-8R
See also DLB 5

Stanton, Maura 1946-.............CLC 9
See also CANR 15
See also CA 89-92

Stapledon, (William) Olaf
1886-1950................. TCLC 22
See also CA 111
See also DLB 15

Stark, Richard 1933-
See Westlake, Donald E(dwin)

Stead, Christina (Ellen)
1902-1983.............CLC 2, 5, 8, 32
See also CA 13-16R
See also obituary CA 109

Steffens, (Joseph) Lincoln
1866-1936................. TCLC 20
See also CA 117
See also SAAS 1

Stegner, Wallace (Earle) 1909- ......CLC 9
See also CANR 1
See also CA 1-4R
See also DLB 9
See also AITN 1

Stein, Gertrude 1874-1946...... TCLC 1, 6
See also CA 104
See also DLB 4

Steinbeck, John (Ernst)
1902-1968........CLC 1, 5, 9, 13, 21,
34 (404)
See also CANR 1
See also CA 1-4R
See also obituary CA 25-28R
See also SATA 9
See also DLB 7, 9
See also DLB-DS 2

Steiner, George 1929-.............CLC 24
See also CA 73-76

Steiner, Rudolf(us Josephus Laurentius)
1861-1925.................. TCLC 13
See also CA 107

Stephen, Leslie 1832-1904 ...... TCLC 23
See also CANR 9
See also CA 21-24R

Stephens, James 1882?-1950 ...... TCLC 4
See also CA 104
See also DLB 19

Steptoe, Lydia 1892-1982
See Barnes, Djuna

Sterling, George 1869-1926 ...... TCLC 20
See also CA 117

Stern, Gerald 1925-.............CLC 40
See also CA 81-84

Stern, Richard G(ustave)
1928-............... CLC 4, 39 (234)
See also CANR 1
See also CA 1-4R

Sternberg, Jonas 1894-1969
See Sternberg, Josef von

Sternberg, Josef von
1894-1969...................CLC 20
See also CA 81-84

Sterne, Laurence 1713-1768 .... LC 2
See also DLB 39

Sternheim, (William Adolf) Carl
1878-1942.................. TCLC 8
See also CA 105

Stevens, Mark 19??- .... CLC 34 (111)

Stevens, Wallace
1879-1955................ TCLC 3, 12
See also CA 104

Stevenson, Anne (Katharine)
1933-.................... CLC 7, 33
See also Elvin, Anne Katharine Stevenson
See also CANR 9
See also DLB 40

Stevenson, Robert Louis
1850-1894................NCLC 5, 14
See also CLR 10, 11
See also YABC 2
See also DLB 18

Stewart, J(ohn) I(nnes) M(ackintosh)
1906-.................. CLC 7, 14, 32
See also CAAS 3
See also CA 85-88

Stewart, Mary (Florence Elinor)
1916-.................... CLC 7, 35
See also CANR 1
See also CA 1-4R
See also SATA 12

Stewart, Will 1908-
See Williamson, Jack

Sting 1951-
See The Police

Stitt, Milan 1941-.................CLC 29
See also CA 69-72

Stoker, Bram (Abraham)
1847-1912................... TCLC 8
See also CA 105
See also SATA 29
See also DLB 36

Stolz, Mary (Slattery) 1920-........CLC 12
See also CANR 13
See also CA 5-8R
See also SATA 10
See also AITN 1

Stone, Irving 1903- ....CLC 7
See also CAAS 3
See also CANR 1
See also CA 1-4R
See also SATA 3
See also AITN 1

Stone, Robert (Anthony)
1937?-................. CLC 5, 23, 42
See also CA 85-88

Stoppard, Tom
1937-........ CLC 1, 3, 4, 5, 8, 15, 29,
34 (272)
See also CA 81-84
See also DLB 13
See also DLB-Y 85

Storey, David (Malcolm)
1933-..................CLC 2, 4, 5, 8
See also CA 81-84
See also DLB 13, 14

Storm, Hyemeyohsts 1935-..........CLC 3
See also CA 81-84

Storm, (Hans) Theodor (Woldsen)
1817-1888.................. NCLC 1

Storni, Alfonsina 1892-1938...... TCLC 5
See also CA 104

Stout, Rex (Todhunter)
1886-1975....................CLC 3
See also CA 61-64
See also AITN 2

Stow, (Julian) Randolph 1935- .....CLC 23
See also CA 13-16R

Stowe, Harriet (Elizabeth) Beecher
1811-1896.................. NCLC 3
See also YABC 1
See also DLB 1, 12, 42

Strachey, (Giles) Lytton
1880-1932................. TCLC 12
See also CA 110

Strand, Mark 1934-........ CLC 6, 18, 41
See also CA 21-24R
See also SATA 41
See also DLB 5

Straub, Peter (Francis) 1943- ......CLC 28
See also CA 85-88
See also DLB-Y 84

Author Index

Author Index

Watkins, Vernon (Phillips)
 1906-1967....................CLC 43
 See also CAP 1
 See also obituary CA 25-28R
 See also CA 9-10
 See also DLB 20

Waugh, Auberon (Alexander)
 1939-......................CLC 7
 See also CANR 6
 See also CA 45-48
 See also DLB 14

Waugh, Evelyn (Arthur St. John)
 1903-1966......CLC 1, 3, 8, 13, 19, 27
 See also CA 85-88
 See also obituary CA 25-28R
 See also DLB 15

Waugh, Harriet 1944-..............CLC 6
 See also CA 85-88

Webb, Beatrice (Potter) 1858-1943
 See Webb, Beatrice (Potter) and Webb,
   Sidney (James)
 See also CA 117

Webb, Beatrice (Potter) 1858-1943 and
   Webb, Sidney (James)
 1859-1947.................. TCLC 22

Webb, Charles (Richard) 1939-......CLC 7
 See also CA 25-28R

Webb, James H(enry), Jr.
 1946-......................CLC 22
 See also CA 81-84

Webb, Mary (Gladys Meredith)
 1881-1927.................. TCLC 24
 See also DLB 34

Webb, Phyllis 1927- ....CLC 18
 See also CA 104
 See also DLB 53

Webb, Sidney (James) 1859-1947
 See Webb, Beatrice (Potter) and Webb,
   Sidney (James)
 See also CA 117

Webb, Sidney (James) 1859-1947 and
   Webb, Beatrice (Potter) 1858-1943
 See Webb, Beatrice (Potter) and Webb,
   Sidney (James)

Webber, Andrew Lloyd 1948-
 See Rice, Tim and Webber, Andrew Lloyd

Weber, Lenora Mattingly
 1895-1971....................CLC 12
 See also CAP 1
 See also CA 19-20
 See also obituary CA 29-32R
 See also SATA 2
 See also obituary SATA 26

Wedekind, (Benjamin) Frank(lin)
 1864-1918.................. TCLC 7
 See also CA 104

Weidman, Jerome 1913-............CLC 7
 See also CANR 1
 See also CA 1-4R
 See also DLB 28
 See also AITN 2

Weil, Simone 1909-1943........ TCLC 23
 See also CA 117

Weinstein, Nathan Wallenstein 1903?-1940
 See West, Nathanael
 See also CA 104

Weir, Peter 1944- ....CLC 20
 See also CA 113

Weiss, Peter (Ulrich)
 1916-1982................. CLC 3, 15
 See also CANR 3
 See also CA 45-48
 See also obituary CA 106

Weiss, Theodore (Russell)
 1916-................... CLC 3, 8, 14
 See also CAAS 2
 See also CA 9-12R
 See also DLB 5

Welch, James 1940-........... CLC 6, 14
 See also CA 85-88

Welch, (Maurice) Denton
 1915-1948................. TCLC 22

Weldon, Fay
 1933-......... CLC 6, 9, 11, 19, 36
 See also CANR 16
 See also CA 21-24R
 See also DLB 14

Wellek, René 1903- ....CLC 28
 See also CANR 8
 See also CA 5-8R

Weller, Michael 1942-............CLC 10
 See also CA 85-88

Weller, Paul 1958-................CLC 26

Welles, (George) Orson
 1915-1985....................CLC 20
 See also CA 93-96

Wells, H(erbert) G(eorge)
 1866-1946............TCLC 6, 12, 19
 See also CA 110
 See also SATA 20
 See also DLB 34

Wells, Rosemary 19??-............CLC 12
 See also CA 85-88
 See also SAAS 1
 See also SATA 18

Welty, Eudora (Alice)
 1909-..........CLC 1, 2, 5, 14, 22, 33
 See also CA 9-12R
 See also DLB 2
 See also CDALB 1941-1968

Werfel, Franz (V.) 1890-1945 ..... TCLC 8
 See also CA 104

Wergeland, Henrik Arnold
 1808-1845.................. NCLC 5

Wersba, Barbara 1932- ....CLC 30
 See also CLR 3
 See also CA 29-32R
 See also SAAS 2
 See also SATA 1

Wertmüller, Lina 1928- ....CLC 16
 See also CA 97-100

Wescott, Glenway 1901-...........CLC 13
 See also CA 13-16R
 See also DLB 4, 9

Wesker, Arnold 1932-........ CLC 3, 5, 42
 See also CANR 1
 See also CA 1-4R
 See also DLB 13

Wesley, Richard (Errol) 1945-.......CLC 7
 See also CA 57-60
 See also DLB 38

West, Jessamyn 1907-1984...... CLC 7, 17
 See also CA 9-12R
 See also obituary SATA 37
 See also DLB 6
 See also DLB-Y 84

West, Morris L(anglo)
 1916-..................... CLC 6, 33
 See also CA 5-8R

West, Nathanael
 1903?-1940...............TCLC 1, 14
 See Weinstein, Nathan Wallenstein
 See also DLB 4, 9, 28

West, Paul 1930-.............. CLC 7, 14
 See also CA 13-16R
 See also DLB 14

West, Rebecca 1892-1983..... CLC 7, 9, 31
 See also CA 5-8R
 See also obituary CA 109
 See also DLB 36
 See also DLB-Y 83

Westall, Robert (Atkinson)
 1929-......................CLC 17
 See also CANR 18
 See also CA 69-72
 See also SAAS 2
 See also SATA 23

Westlake, Donald E(dwin)
 1933-..................... CLC 7, 33
 See also CANR 16
 See also CA 17-20R

Whalen, Philip 1923-........... CLC 6, 29
 See also CANR 5
 See also CA 9-12R
 See also DLB 16

Wharton, Edith (Newbold Jones)
 1862-1937................. TCLC 3, 9
 See also CA 104
 See also DLB 4, 9, 12

Wharton, William 1925-....... CLC 18, 37
 See also CA 93-96
 See also DLB-Y 80

Wheatley (Peters), Phillis
 1753?-1784....................LC 3
 See also DLB 31, 50

Wheelock, John Hall
 1886-1978....................CLC 14
 See also CANR 14
 See also CA 13-16R
 See also obituary CA 77-80
 See also DLB 45

Whelan, John 1900-
 See O'Faoláin, Seán

Whitaker, Rodney 1925-
 See Trevanian
 See also CA 29-32R

White, E(lwyn) B(rooks)
 1899-1985......... CLC 10, 34 (425),
                        39 (369)
 See also CLR 1
 See also CANR 16
 See also CA 13-16R
 See also obituary CA 116
 See also SATA 2, 29
 See also obituary SATA 44
 See also DLB 11, 22
 See also AITN 2

White, Edmund III 1940-..........CLC 27
 See also CANR 3
 See also CA 45-48

White, Patrick (Victor Martindale)
1912-............**CLC 3, 4, 5, 7, 9, 18**
See also CA 81-84

White, T(erence) H(anbury)
1906-1964...................**CLC 30**
See also CA 73-76
See also SATA 12

White, Walter (Francis)
1893-1955.................**TCLC 15**
See also CA 115

Whitehead, E(dward) A(nthony)
1933-..........................**CLC 5**
See also CA 65-68

Whitemore, Hugh 1936-...........**CLC 37**

Whitman, Walt 1819-1892....... **NCLC 4**
See also SATA 20
See also DLB 3

Whitney, Phyllis A(yame)
1903-........................**CLC 42**
See also CANR 3
See also CA 1-4R
See also SATA 1, 30
See also AITN 2

Whittemore, (Edward) Reed (Jr.)
1919-..........................**CLC 4**
See also CANR 4
See also CA 9-12R
See also DLB 5

Whittier, John Greenleaf
1807-1892.................. **NCLC 8**
See also DLB 1

Wicker, Thomas Grey 1926-
See Wicker, Tom
See also CA 65-68

Wicker, Tom 1926-...............**CLC 7**
See also Wicker, Thomas Grey

Wideman, John Edgar
1941-............**CLC 5, 34** (297), **36**
See also CANR 14
See also CA 85-88
See also DLB 33

Wiebe, Rudy (H.) 1934-..... **CLC 6, 11, 14**
See also CA 37-40R

Wieners, John 1934-..............**CLC 7**
See also CA 13-16R
See also DLB 16

Wiesel, Elie(zer)
1928-...............**CLC 3, 5, 11, 37**
See also CAAS 4
See also CANR 8
See also CA 5-8R
See also AITN 1

Wight, James Alfred 1916-
See Herriot, James
See also CA 77-80
See also SATA 44

Wilbur, Richard (Purdy)
1921-.................**CLC 3, 6, 9, 14**
See also CANR 2
See also CA 1-4R
See also CABS 2
See also SATA 9
See also DLB 5

Wild, Peter 1940-.................**CLC 14**
See also CA 37-40R
See also DLB 5

Wilde, Oscar (Fingal O'Flahertie Wills)
1854-1900..............**TCLC 1, 8, 23**
See also CA 104
See also SATA 24
See also DLB 10, 19, 34

Wilder, Billy 1906- ....**CLC 20**
See also Wilder, Samuel
See also DLB 26

Wilder, Samuel 1906-
See Wilder, Billy
See also CA 89-92

Wilder, Thornton (Niven)
1897-1975......**CLC 1, 5, 6, 10, 15, 35**
See also CA 13-16R
See also obituary CA 61-64
See also DLB 4, 7, 9
See also AITN 2

Wilhelm, Kate 1928-...............**CLC 7**
See also CANR 17
See also CA 37-40R
See also DLB 8

Willard, Nancy 1936- ....**CLC 7, 37**
See also CLR 5
See also CANR 10
See also CA 89-92
See also SATA 30, 37
See also DLB 5

Williams, C(harles) K(enneth)
1936-........................**CLC 33**
See also CA 37-40R
See also DLB 5

Williams, Charles (Walter Stansby)
1886-1945................**TCLC 1, 11**
See also CA 104

Williams, (George) Emlyn
1905-........................**CLC 15**
See also CA 104
See also DLB 10

Williams, Hugo 1942-..............**CLC 42**
See also CA 17-20R
See also DLB 40

Williams, John A(lfred)
1925-......................**CLC 5, 13**
See also CAAS 3
See also CANR 6
See also CA 53-56
See also DLB 2, 33

Williams, Jonathan (Chamberlain)
1929-.......................**CLC 13**
See also CANR 8
See also CA 9-12R
See also DLB 5

Williams, Joy 1944-...............**CLC 31**
See also CA 41-44R

Williams, Norman 1952-..... **CLC 39** (100)

Williams, Paulette 1948-
See Shange, Ntozake

Williams, Tennessee
1911-1983....... **CLC 1, 2, 5, 7, 8, 11,**
15, 19, 30, 39 (444)
See also CA 5-8R
See also obituary CA 108
See also DLB 7
See also DLB-Y 83
See also DLB-DS 4
See also CDALB 1941-1968
See also AITN 1, 2

Williams, Thomas (Alonzo)
1926-........................**CLC 14**
See also CANR 2
See also CA 1-4R

Williams, Thomas Lanier 1911-1983
See Williams, Tennessee

Williams, William Carlos
1883-1963...... **CLC 1, 2, 5, 9, 13, 22,**
42
See also CA 89-92
See also DLB 4, 16, 54

Williamson, Jack 1908-............**CLC 29**
See also Williamson, John Stewart
See also DLB 8

Williamson, John Stewart 1908-
See Williamson, Jack
See also CA 17-20R

Willingham, Calder (Baynard, Jr.)
1922-........................**CLC 5**
See also CANR 3
See also CA 5-8R
See also DLB 2, 44

Wilson, A(ndrew) N(orman)
1950-........................**CLC 33**
See also CA 112
See also DLB 14

Wilson, Andrew 1948-
See Wilson, Snoo

Wilson, Angus (Frank Johnstone)
1913-........ **CLC 2, 3, 5, 25, 34** (579)
See also CA 5-8R
See also DLB 15

Wilson, August 1945- .... **CLC 39** (275)
See also CA 115

Wilson, Brian 1942- ....**CLC 12**

Wilson, Colin 1931-............. **CLC 3, 14**
See also CANR 1
See also CA 1-4R
See also DLB 14

Wilson, Edmund
1895-1972.......... **CLC 1, 2, 3, 8, 24**
See also CANR 1
See also CA 1-4R
See also obituary CA 37-40R

Wilson, Ethel Davis (Bryant)
1888-1980..................**CLC 13**
See also CA 102

Wilson, John 1785-1854.......... **NCLC 5**

Wilson, John (Anthony) Burgess 1917-
See Burgess, Anthony
See also CANR 2
See also CA 1-4R

Wilson, Lanford 1937- ...... **CLC 7, 14, 36**
See also CA 17-20R
See also DLB 7

Wilson, Robert (M.) 1944-....... **CLC 7, 9**
See also CANR 2
See also CA 49-52

Wilson, Sloan 1920-...............**CLC 32**
See also CANR 1
See also CA 1-4R

Wilson, Snoo 1948- ....**CLC 33**
See also CA 69-72

Author Index

TCLC Cumulative Nationality Index

NICARAGUAN
Darío, Rubén 4

NORWEGIAN
Bjørnson, Bjørnstjerne 7
Grieg, Nordhal 10
Hamsun, Knut 2, 14
Ibsen, Henrik 2, 8, 16
Kielland, Alexander 5
Lie, Jonas 5
Obstfelder, Sigbjørn 23
Undset, Sigrid 3

PERUVIAN
Vallejo, César 3

POLISH
Borowski, Tadeusz 9
Reymont, Wladyslaw
   Stanislaw 5
Schulz, Bruno 5
Sienkiewitz, Henryk 3
Witkiewicz, Stanislaw
   Ignacy 8

PUERTO RICAN
Hostos, Eugenio María de 24

RUMANIAN
Bacovia, George 24

RUSSIAN
Aldanov, Mark 23
Andreyev, Leonid 3

Annensky, Innokenty 14
Babel, Isaak 2, 13
Balmont, Konstantin
   Dmitriyevich 11
Bely, Andrey 7
Blok, Aleksandr 5
Bryusov, Valery 10
Bulgakov, Mikhail 2, 16
Bunin, Ivan 6
Chekhov, Anton 3, 10
Esenin, Sergei 4
Gorky, Maxim 8
Hippius, Zinaida 9
Ilf, Ilya 21
Khlebnikov, Velimir 20
Khodasevich, Vladislav 15
Korolenko, Vladimir 22
Kuprin, Aleksandr 5
Mandelstam, Osip 2, 6
Mayakovsky, Vladimir 4, 18
Petrov, Evgeny 21
Pilnyak, Boris 23
Platonov, Andrei 14
Sologub, Fyodor 9
Tolstoy, Alexey
   Nikolayevich 18
Tolstoy, Leo 4, 11, 17
Trotsky, Leon 22
Tsvetaeva, Marina 7
Zamyatin, Yevgeny
   Ivanovich 8
Zhdanov, Andrei 18
Zoshchenko, Mikhail 15

SCOTTISH
Barrie, J. M. 2
Bridie, James 3
Davidson, John 24
Gibbon, Lewis Grassic 4
Graham, R. B.
   Cunninghame 19
Lang, Andrew 16
MacDonald, George 9
Muir, Edwin 2
Tey, Josephine 14

SOUTH AFRICAN
Campbell, Roy 5
Schreiner, Olive 9

SPANISH
Barea, Arturo 14
Baroja, Pío 8
Benavente, Jacinto 3
Blasco Ibáñez, Vicente 12
Echegaray, José 4
García Lorca, Federico 1, 7
Jiménez, Juan Ramón 4
Machado, Antonio 3
Martínez Sierra, Gregorio 6
Miró, Gabriel 5
Ortega y Gasset, José 9
Pereda, José María de 16
Salinas, Pedro 17
Unamuno, Miguel de 2, 9
Valera, Juan 10
Valle-Inclán, Ramón del 5

SWEDISH
Dagerman, Stig 17
Heidenstam, Verner von 5
Lagerlöf, Selma 4
Strindberg, August 1, 8, 21

SWISS
Spitteler, Carl 12
Walser, Robert 18

TURKISH
Sait Faik 23

URUGUAYAN
Quiroga, Horacio 20

WELSH
Davies, W. H. 5
Lewis, Alun 3
Machen, Arthur 4
Thomas, Dylan 1, 8

YIDDISH
Aleichem, Sholom 1
Asch, Sholem 3
Peretz, Isaac Leib 16

Nationality Index

TCLC Cumulative Title Index

Title Index

Title Index

Title Index

Title Index

Title Index

"Fekete virágot lattál" (Black Was the
Blossom You Sighted) **11**:18, 20
*Der Feldzug nach Sizilien (The Sicily
Campaign)* **9**:145-46
"La felicidad imminente" **17**:368
Felicitá dell'infelice **22**:287
"Félise" **8**:437
Fell the Tree-Trunks **22**:164
"The Fellowship of Caiaphas" **7**:448
"Female Emancipation"
See "Frauenemancipation"
"The Female God" **12**:299-300, 307, 309
Femeninas **5**:485
"The Feminine"
See "Zhenskoe"
Feminism, Feminity, and the Spanish Spirit
6:274
Feminism in Spain **6**:277
"Feminismus" **3**:112
La femme assise **3**:42; **8**:12, 16
La femme cachée **5**:169
*Une femme è sa fenêtre (A Woman in the
Window)* **21**:33
*La femme pauvre (The Woman Who Was
Poor)* **22**:30-3, 38-9, 45-6, 50-1, 53
"Une femme qui passe" **20**:83
"Les femmes" (The Women) **3**:37-8
"Femte natten" **8**:419, 420
"Fen River" **22**:213
"Les fenêtres" **3**:44
"Fenimore Cooper's Literary Offenses"
6:477
"Un fenómeno inexplicable" **15**:293
"Die Fensterrose" **1**:410
"Feodaly a rezidentsiya" **22**:182
"Fergus and the Druid" **11**:512; **18**:461
Feria d'agosto **3**:336
*La feria de los discretos (The City of the
Discreet)* **8**:61
Ferments
See *Fermenty*
Fermenty (Ferments) **5**:393, 395
Fermina Márquez **9**:196, 198, 202, 204,
206-07
"Fern Hill" **1**:470-71, 473, 475; **8**:460-61
"Fernando and Elvira" **3**:213
"The Fernery" **2**:119
"The Ferry of Unfulfilment" **19**:173
"Festal Slaughter" **13**:148-49, 155
"Festina lente" **14**:240, 242
"The Festival" **22**:219
"Festnacht und Frühgang" **18**:206, 215
"The Fête" **8**:294, 298, 301
*Le feu follet (The Fire Within; Will o' the
Wisp)* **21**:19, 21-4, 33, 40
Feu la mère de madame **22**:79, 91, 95
Le feu (Under Fire) **5**:11-14, 17-20
"Feudal" **18**:209
Feuer aus den Kesseln (Draw the Fires)
10:480, 485, 489, 492
Die Fever-Kantate (The Fire-Cantata)
10:489, 490
A Few Figs from Thistles **4**:306-10,
313-17
"Fey Joan" **7**:515
La fiaccola sotto it moggio **6**:137, 142
"Les fiançailles" (The Betrothal) **3**:36,
39, 43-4
*Les fiançailles (The Betrothal: A Sequel to
The Blue Bird)* **3**:323
Les fiancés de Loches **22**:77
Die Fibel: Auswahl erste Verse **14**:204
"The Fiddle and the Slipper" **22**:192

Fidessa **15**:46
"Das Fieber" **21**:227
"Das Fieberspital" **9**:142
"The Field of Kulikovo" **5**:85
"The Field of Mustard" **5**:180
The Field of Mustard **5**:181
"Fielding" **8**:103
Fields of Castile
See *Campos de Castilla*
The Fierce and Beautiful World
14:410-12, 414, 421, 424
The Fiery Angel
See *Ognennyi angel*
"Fièvre" **13**:195
"The Fifteenth of April" **6**:393
"Fifth Eclogue" **16**:420
"Fifth Elegy" **1**:412, 420
"The Fifth International" **4**:292; **18**:270
"The Fifth of October"
See "Der Fünfte Oktober"
*The Fifth Queen: And How She Came to
Court* **1**:282-83, 288, 291; **15**:85-86, 92,
94
"The Fifth Wheel" **19**:172
"Fifty Faggots" **10**:463
"Fifty Grand" **2**:329
Fifty-One Tales **2**:136-37, 140-41
"Fifty Years" **3**:239
"Fifty Years After" **5**:255
Fifty Years, and Other Poems **3**:239, 241,
243, 245; **19**:209-11
"The Fight" **8**:456, 463
"The Fight between Jappe and Do
Escobar" **8**:261
"The Fight for the Crowd" **12**:216
"A Fight with the Great Lord"
See "Harc a nagyúrral"
"Fight with the Great One"
See "Harc a nagyúrral"
The Fighting Littles **9**:469
The Fighting Man of Mars **2**:82
La figlia di jorio (The Daughter of Jorio)
6:131, 141
*Figuras de la pasion del Señor (Figures of
the Passion of Our Lord)* **5**:335-37
"The Figure in the Carpet" **2**:262
"The Figure of Arthur" **1**:519
The Figure of Beatrice: A Study in Dante
1:512, 519; **11**:496, 502
"The Figure of the Youth as Virile Poet"
12:362
"Figures" **11**:294
Figures et choses qui passaient **11**:356
Figures of Earth **6**:64-5, 69, 71, 75
Figures of the Passion of Our Lord
See *Figuras de la pasion del Señor*
Un fil à la patte **22**:77, 86, 93
"Filboid Studge" **3**:365
Filibuth **6**:191
"Le fille de Lilith" **9**:40, 57
La fille du policeman **8**:438-41, 443
"Film"
See "Mozgófénykép"
Il filo (The Thread) **7**:310
"Filomania" **22**:281
Filosofia e letterature **22**:287
Fimiamy (Incense) **9**:444
La fin de Antonia **13**:189, 190-91
La fin de Chéri (The Last of Chéri) **5**:163,
168-69; **16**:117, 120, 133, 137
"Fin de fête" **8**:297-98
"La fin de la jalousie" **7**:538-39
"Fin de race" **19**:116

El fin de una raza **16**:364-65
La fin des bourgeois **22**:198, 202-03
"La fin d'une guerre" **21**:27-9
"Final Soliloquy of the Interior Paramour"
12:364, 387
"Final Song" **14**:215
"The Finances of the Gods" **8**:185, 204
The Financier **10**:164-65, 167-69, 173,
175-80, 182-87; **18**:53-5, 57, 60-1, 63-6,
68-72
Financiers
See *Pankkiherroja*
"Financing Finnegan" **6**:172
"The Finding of Zach" **12**:108, 120
"The Fine" **18**:41
"Fine Feathers" **5**:180
"Fine Fiddle" **5**:145
"Fine Furniture" **10**:193
A Fine Gentleman **3**:505
"A Fine Summer Evening" **22**:164
The Finer Grain **2**:246, 258
"Finger Man" **7**:172
"The Finish of Patsy Barnes" **12**:120
Finished **11**:246, 254-55
Finn and His Companions **5**:348, 352,
355-56
Finnegans Wake **3**:259-63, 268-77,
280-82; **8**:160-62, 167, 169-70, 172;
16:208, 227-28, 233, 237, 241
Fiorenza **14**:341, 350, 354
Fir-Flower Tablets **8**:226, 229, 237
"The Fir Woods" **8**:314
"Fire!" **22**:160
"Fire and Sleet and Candlelight" **8**:521
"A Fire at Tranter Sweattey's" **4**:152
The Fire Bird **21**:267
"Fire by Night" **11**:209, 212-13
The Fire-Cantata
See *Die Fever-Kantate*
The Fire in the Flint **15**:473-75, 480-81,
483-86
"Fire in the Heavens" **17**:43
Fire in the Opera House
See *Der Brand im Opernhaus*
"The Fire in the Wood" **22**:446, 456
The Fire of Egliswyl
See *Der Brand von Egliswyl*
The Fire Within
See *Le feu follet*
The Firebird
See *Zhar-ptitsa*
"The Firemen's Ball" **17**:222, 224-25,
227
"Firenze" **20**:85
The Fires of Saint Dominic
See *Ogni svyatogo Dominika*
"Fireworks" **8**:230
The Fireworks
See *Ilotulitus*
The Firm Desire to Endure **7**:260-61
*First and Last Things: A Confession of
Faith and Rule of Life* **6**:529; **12**:490;
19:436, 436
"The First Day of an Immigrant" **4**:142
"First Elegy" **1**:412, 419-20
The First Encounter
See *Pervoe svidanie*
"First Fruit" **12**:299
"The First Game" **14**:300-01
The First Gentleman of America **6**:76-7
"The First Idea Is Not Our Own" **3**:448
The First Lady Chatterley **9**:228
"First Love" (Babel) **2**:28; **13**:22-3, 34

Title Index

Title Index

Title Index

Title Index

Title Index

Title Index

Title Index

Title Index

Title Index

Title Index

Title Index

Title Index

Title Index

Title Index

Title Index

Title Index

Title Index

Title Index

Title Index

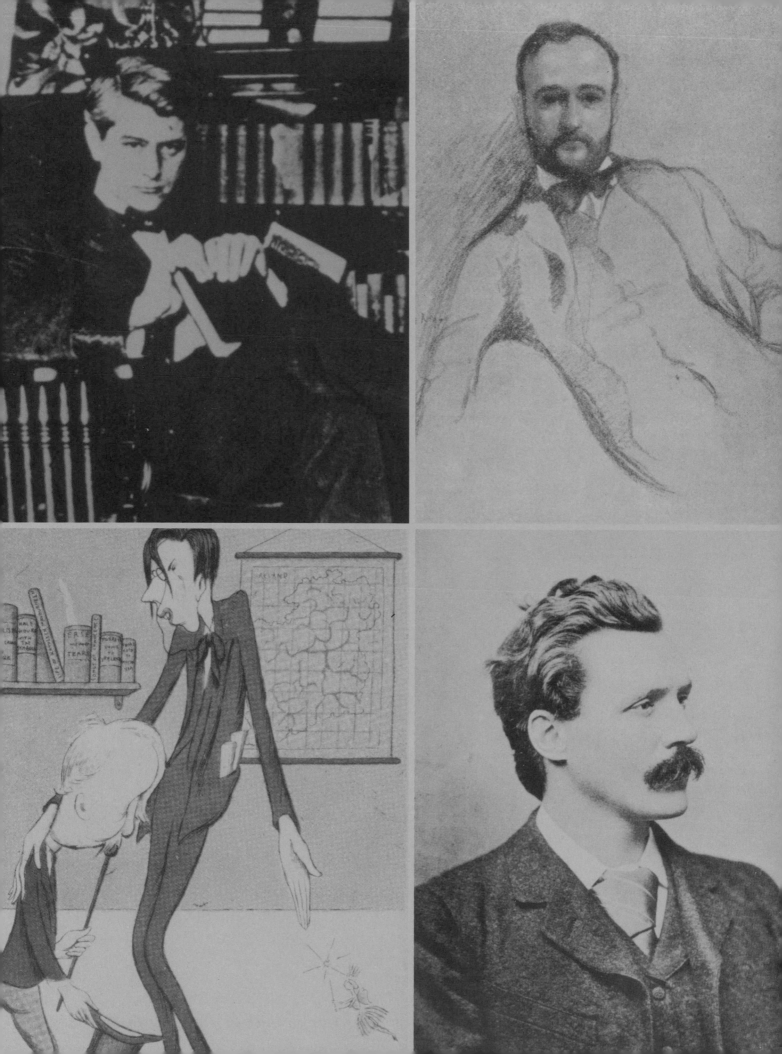